T0189181

Lecture Notes in Computer Science 13792

More information about this series at https://link.springer.com/bookseries/558

Shweta Agrawal · Dongdai Lin (Eds.)

Advances in Cryptology – ASIACRYPT 2022

28th International Conference on the Theory
and Application of Cryptology and Information Security
Taipei, Taiwan, December 5–9, 2022
Proceedings, Part II

Editors
Shweta Agrawal
Indian Institute of Technology Madras
Chennai, India

Dongdai Lin
Chinese Academy of Sciences
Beijing, China

ISSN 0302-9743 ISSN 1611-3349 (electronic)
Lecture Notes in Computer Science
ISBN 978-3-031-22965-7 ISBN 978-3-031-22966-4 (eBook)
https://doi.org/10.1007/978-3-031-22966-4

This Springer imprint is published by the registered company Springer Nature Switzerland AG
The registered company address is: Gewerbestrasse 11, 6330 Cham, Switzerland

Preface

The 28th Annual International Conference on Theory and Application of Cryptology and Information Security (ASIACRYPT 2022) was held in Taiwan during December 5–9, 2022.

The conference covered all technical aspects of cryptology, and was sponsored by the International Association for Cryptologic Research (IACR).

We received a total of 364 submissions from all over the world, and the Program Committee (PC) selected 98 papers for publication in the proceedings of the conference. The two program chairs were supported by a PC consisting of 79 leading experts in aspects of cryptology. Each submission was reviewed by at least three PC members (or their sub-reviewers). The strong conflict of interest rules imposed by IACR ensure that papers are not handled by PC members with a close working relationship with the authors. The two program chairs were not allowed to submit a paper, and PC members were limited to two submissions each. There were approximately 331 external reviewers, whose input was critical to the selection of papers.

The review process was conducted using double-blind peer review. The conference operated a two-round review system with a rebuttal phase. After the reviews and first-round discussions the PC selected 224 submissions to proceed to the second round and the authors were then invited to participate in an interactive rebuttal phase with the reviewers to clarify questions and concerns. The second round involved extensive discussions by the PC members.

Alongside the presentations of the accepted papers, the program of ASIACRYPT 2022 featured two invited talks by Jian Guo and Damien Stehlé. The conference also featured a rump session which contained short presentations on the latest research results of the field.

The four volumes of the conference proceedings contain the revised versions of the 98 papers that were selected. The final revised versions of papers were not reviewed again and the authors are responsible for their contents.

Using a voting-based process that took into account conflicts of interest, the PC selected the three top papers of the conference: "Full Quantum Equivalence of Group Action DLog and CDH, and More" by Hart Montgomery and Mark Zhandry, "Cryptographic Primitives with Hinting Property" by Navid Alamati and Sikhar Patranabis, and "SwiftEC: Shallue–van de Woestijne Indifferentiable Function to Elliptic Curves" by Jorge Chavez-Saab, Francisco Rodriguez-Henriquez, and Mehdi Tibouchi. The authors of all three papers were invited to submit extended versions of their manuscripts to the Journal of Cryptology.

Many people have contributed to the success of ASIACRYPT 2022. We would like to thank the authors for submitting their research results to the conference. We are very grateful to the PC members and external reviewers for contributing their knowledge and expertise, and for the tremendous amount of work that was done with reading papers and contributing to the discussions. We are greatly indebted to Kai-Min Chung and Bo-Yin Yang, the General Chairs, for their efforts and overall organization. We thank

Bart Preneel, Ron Steinfeld, Mehdi Tibouchi, Jian Guo, and Huaxiong Wang for their valuable suggestions and help. We are extremely grateful to Shuaishuai Li for checking all the LaTeX files and for assembling the files for submission to Springer. We also thank the team at Springer for handling the publication of these conference proceedings.

December 2022

Shweta Agrawal
Dongdai Lin

Organization

General Chairs

Kai-Min Chung	Academia Sinica, Taiwan
Bo-Yin Yang	Academia Sinica, Taiwan

Program Committee Chairs

Shweta Agrawal	Indian Institute of Technology, Madras, India
Dongdai Lin	Institute of Information Engineering, Chinese Academy of Sciences, China

Program Committee

Divesh Aggarwal	National University of Singapore, Singapore
Adi Akavia	University of Haifa, Israel
Martin Albrecht	Royal Holloway, University of London, UK
Ghada Almashaqbeh	University of Connecticut, USA
Benny Applebaum	Tel Aviv University, Israel
Lejla Batina	Radboud University, Netherlands
Carsten Baum	Aarhus University, Denmark
Sonia Belaïd	CryptoExperts, France
Mihir Bellare	University of California, San Diego, USA
Andrej Bogdanov	Chinese University of Hong Kong, China
Christina Boura	Université de Versailles, France
Ran Canetti	Boston University, USA
Jie Chen	East China Normal University, China
Yilei Chen	Tsinghua University, China
Jung Hee Cheon	Seoul National University, South Korea
Ilaria Chillotti	Zama, France
Michele Ciampi	The University of Edinburgh, UK
Craig Costello	Microsoft Research, USA
Itai Dinur	Ben-Gurion University, Israel
Nico Döttling	Helmholtz Center for Information Security (CISPA), Germany
Maria Eichlseder	Graz University of Technology, Austria
Saba Eskandarian	University of North Carolina at Chapel Hill, USA
Marc Fischlin	TU Darmstadt, Germany

Yu Sasaki	NTT Corporation, Japan
Tobias Schneider	NXP Semiconductors, Austria
Dominique Schröder	Friedrich-Alexander-Universität Erlangen-Nürnberg, Germany
abhi shelat	Northeastern University, USA
Mark Simkin	Ethereum Foundation, USA
Ling Song	Jinan University, Guangzhou, China
Fang Song	Portland State University, USA
Pratik Soni	Carnegie Mellon University, USA
Akshayaram Srinivasan	Tata Institute of Fundamental Research, India
Damien Stehlé	ENS de Lyon, France
Ron Steinfeld	Monash University, Australia
Qiang Tang	University of Sydney, Australia
Yiannis Tselekounis	Carnegie Mellon University, USA
Meiqin Wang	Shandong University, China
Xiaoyun Wang	Tsinghua University, China
David Wu	University of Texas at Austin, USA
Wenling Wu	Institute of Software, Chinese Academy of Sciences, China
Shota Yamada	AIST, Japan
Takashi Yamakawa	NTT Corporation, Japan
Jiang Zhang	State Key Laboratory of Cryptology, China

Additional Reviewers

Behzad Abdolmaleki
Calvin Abou Haidar
Damiano Abram
Bar Alon
Pedro Alves
Ravi Anand
Anurag Anshu
Victor Arribas
Thomas Attema
Christian Badertscher
Anubhab Baksi
Zhenzhen Bao
James Bartusek
Christof Beierle
Ritam Bhaumik
Alexander Bienstock
Olivier Blazy
Alex Block
Maxime Bombar
Charlotte Bonte
Carl Bootland
Katharina Boudgoust
Lennart Braun
Marek Broll
Chris Brzuska
BinBin Cai
Matteo Campanelli
Federico Canale
Avik Chakraborti
Suvradip Chakraborty
John Chan
Rohit Chatterjee
Long Chen
Yu Long Chen
Hongyin Chen
Shan Chen
Shiyao Chen
Rongmao Chen
Nai-Hui Chia
Arka Rai Choudhuri
Jiali Choy
Qiaohan Chu
Hien Chu
Eldon Chung
Sandro Coretti-Drayton
Arjan Cornelissen
Maria Corte-Real Santos
Anamaria Costache
Alain Couvreur
Nan Cui
Benjamin R. Curtis
Jan-Pieter D'Anvers
Joan Daemen
Wangchen Dai
Hannah Davis
Luca De Feo
Gabrielle De Micheli

Thomas Debris-Alazard
Amit Deo
Patrick Derbez
Julien Devevey
Siemen Dhooghe
Benjamin Dowling
Leo Ducas
Yen Ling Ee
Jonathan Eriksen
Daniel Escudero
Muhammed F. Esgin
Thomas Espitau
Andre Esser
Hulya Evkan
Jaiden Fairoze
Joël Felderhoff
Hanwen Feng
Joe Fitzsimons
Antonio Flórez-Gutiérrez
Pouyan Forghani
Cody Freitag
Georg Fuchsbauer
Pierre Galissant
Tommaso Gagliardoni
Daniel Gardham
Pierrick Gaudry
Romain Gay
Chunpeng Ge
Rosario Gennaro
Paul Gerhart
Satrajit Ghosh
Ashrujit Ghoshal
Niv Gilboa
Aarushi Goel
Aron Gohr
Jesse Goodman
Mike Graf
Milos Grujic
Aurore Guillevic
Aldo Gunsing
Chun Guo
Hosein Hadipour
Mathias Hall-Andersen
Shuai Han
Helena Handschuh
Lucjan Hanzlik
Yonglin Hao
Keisuke Hara
Patrick Harasser
Jingnan He
Rachelle Heim-Boissier
Minki Hhan
Shoichi Hirose
Seungwan Hong
Akinori Hosoyamada
James Hsin-Yu Chiang
Zhicong Huang
Senyang Huang
Chloé Hébant
Ilia Iliashenko
Laurent Imbert
Joseph Jaeger
Palak Jain
Ashwin Jha
Mingming Jiang
Zhengzhong Jin
Antoine Joux
Eliran Kachlon
Bhavana Kanukurthi
Alexander Karenin
Shuichi Katsumata
Mojtaba Khalili
Hamidreza Khorasgani
Dongwoo Kim
Duhyeong Kim
Young-Sik Kim
Fuyuki Kitagawa
Kamil Kluczniak
Yashvanth Kondi
Rajendra Kumar
Noboru Kunihiro
Fukang Liu
Russell W. F. Lai
Jason LeGrow
Jooyoung Lee
Hyung Tae Lee
Byeonghak Lee
Charlotte Lefevre
Zeyong Li
Yiming Li
Hanjun Li
Shun Li
Xingjian Li
Xiao Liang
Benoît Libert
Damien Ligier
Chao Lin
Chengjun Lin
Yunhao Ling
Eik List
Jiahui Liu
Feng-Hao Liu
Guozhen Liu
Xiangyu Liu
Meicheng Liu
Alex Lombardi
Patrick Longa
Wen-jie Lu
Yuan Lu
Donghang Lu
You Lyu
Reinhard Lüftenegger
Bernardo Magri
Monosij Maitra
Mary Maller
Lenka Mareková
Mark Marson
Takahiro Matsuda
Alireza Mehrdad
Simon-Philipp Merz
Pierre Meyer
Michael Meyer
Peihan Miao
Tarik Moataz
Hart Montgomery
Tomoyuki Morimae
Fabrice Mouhartem
Tamer Mour
Marta Mularczyk
Michael Naehrig
Marcel Nageler
Yusuke Naito
Mridul Nandi
Patrick Neumann
Ruth Ng

Ky Nguyen
Khoa Nguyen
Ngoc Khanh Nguyen
Jianting Ning
Oded Nir
Ryo Nishimaki
Olga Nissenbaum
Semyon Novoselov
Julian Nowakowski
Tabitha Ogilvie
Eran Omri
Hiroshi Onuki
Jean-Baptiste Orfila
Mahak Pancholi
Omer Paneth
Lorenz Panny
Roberto Parisella
Jeongeun Park
Rutvik Patel
Sikhar Patranabis
Alice Pellet-Mary
Hilder Vitor Lima Pereira
Ludovic Perret
Thomas Peyrin
Phuong Pham
Guru Vamsi Policharla
Sihang Pu
Luowen Qian
Chen Qian
Kexin Qiao
Willy Quach
Rahul Rachuri
Srinivasan Raghuraman
Adrian Ranea
Shahram Rasoolzadeh
Christian Rechberger
Krijn Reijnders
Maxime Remaud
Ling Ren
Mahshid Riahinia
Peter Rindal
Mike Rosulek
Adeline Roux-Langlois
Paul Rösler
Yusuke Sakai
Kosei Sakamoto
Amin Sakzad
Simona Samardjiska
Olga Sanina
Roozbeh Sarenche
Santanu Sarker
Tobias Schmalz
Markus Schofnegger
Jacob Schuldt
Sruthi Sekar
Nicolas Sendrier
Akash Shah
Yaobin Shen
Yixin Shen
Yu Shen
Danping Shi
Rentaro Shiba
Kazumasa Shinagawa
Omri Shmueli
Ferdinand Sibleyras
Janno Siim
Siang Meng Sim
Luisa Siniscalchi
Yongsoo Song
Douglas Stebila
Lukas Stennes
Igors Stepanovs
Christoph Striecks
Ling Sun
Siwei Sun
Bing Sun
Shi-Feng Sun
Akira Takahashi
Abdul Rahman Taleb
Chik How Tan
Adrian Thillard
Sri Aravinda Krishnan Thyagarajan
Yan Bo Ti
Elmar Tischhauser
Yosuke Todo
Junichi Tomida
Ni Trieu
Monika Trimoska
Yi Tu
Aleksei Udovenko
Rei Ueno
Mayank Varia
Daniele Venturi
Riad Wahby
Roman Walch
Mingyuan Wang
Haoyang Wang
Luping Wang
Xiao Wang
Yuejun Wang
Yuyu Wang
Weiqiang Wen
Chenkai Weng
Benjamin Wesolowski
Yusai Wu
Yu Xia
Zhiye Xie
Shengmin Xu
Guangwu Xu
Sophia Yakoubov
Hailun Yan
Rupeng Yang
Kang Yang
Qianqian Yang
Shao-Jun Yang
Li Yao
Hui Hui Yap
Kan Yasuda
Weijing You
Thomas Zacharias
Yupeng Zhang
Kai Zhang
Lei Zhang
Yunlei Zhao
Yu Zhou
Chenzhi Zhu
Paul Zimmermann
Lukas Zobernig
matthieu rambaud
Hendrik Waldner
Yafei Zheng

Sponsoring Institutions

- Platinum Sponsor: ZAMA
- Gold Sponsor: BTQ, Hackers in Taiwan, Technology Innovation Institute
- Silver Sponsor: Meta (Facebook), Casper Networks, PQShield, NTT Research, WiSECURE
- Bronze Sponsor: Mitsubishi Electric, Algorand Foundation, LatticeX Foundation, Intel, QSancus, IOG (Input/Output Global), IBM

Contents – Part II

Isogeny Based Cryptography

A New Isogeny Representation and Applications to Cryptography

Antonin Leroux[1,2,3](✉)

[1] DGA, Paris, France
[2] LIX, CNRS, Ecole Polytechnique, Institut Polytechnique de Paris, Palaiseau, France
antonin.leroux@polytechnique.org
[3] INRIA, Le Chesnay, France

Abstract. This paper focuses on isogeny representations, defined as ways to evaluate isogenies and verify membership to the language of isogenous supersingular curves (the set of triples D, E_1, E_2 with a cyclic isogeny of degree D between E_1 and E_2). The tasks of evaluating and verifying isogenies are fundamental for isogeny-based cryptography.

Our main contribution is the design of the suborder representation, a new isogeny representation targetted at the case of (big) prime degree. The core of our new method is the revelation of endomorphisms of smooth norm inside a well-chosen suborder of the codomain's endomorphism ring. This new representation appears to be opening interesting prospects for isogeny-based cryptography under the hardness of a new computational problem: the SubOrder to Ideal Problem (SOIP). As an application, we introduce pSIDH, a new NIKE based on the suborder representation. Studying new assumption appears to be particularly crucial in the light of the recent attacks against isogeny-based cryptography.

In order to manipulate efficiently the suborder representation, we develop several heuristic algorithmic tools to solve norm equations inside a new family of quaternion orders. These new algorithms may be of independent interest.

1 Introduction

Isogeny-based cryptography has been receiving an increasing amount of interest over the last few years due to its presumed resistance to quantum computers. As the variety of primitives achievable from isogenies is expanding, new problems are arising. The problem of proving the knowledge of an isogeny between two elliptic curves is one that appears more and more central in isogeny-based cryptography. It has applications in validation of SIDH public keys [JDF11, GPST16, FP22, UXT+22], digital signatures [YAJ+17, DFG19, BKV19, JS14], VDFs [DFMPS19, CSRHT22], delay encryption [BDF21] and oblivious PRF [BKW20].

Intuitively, proving a statement requires an efficient way to represent and manipulate the objects involved in that statement. In the case of isogenies, the standard representation is obtained from the Vélu formulas [Vél71] that give

S. Agrawal and D. Lin (Eds.): ASIACRYPT 2022, LNCS 13792, pp. 3–35, 2022.
https://doi.org/10.1007/978-3-031-22966-4_1

a way to compute and evaluate an isogeny from its kernel. The best generic algorithm to compute these formulas requires $\tilde{O}(\sqrt{D'})$ operations over the field of definition of the isogeny's kernel where D' is the biggest factor of the degree (see [BdFLS20]). Thus, the computation is only efficient when the degree is smooth and the kernel points are defined over a small field extension. In full generality, this only happens when the degree is powersmooth but there are ways to make it work for smooth degrees as well. All the schemes we mentioned above are subject to these computational limitations and use smooth degrees. However, the recent trend of works studying the Deuring correspondence and its applications to isogeny-based cryptography has provided us the means to represent and manipulate efficiently isogenies of arbitrary degrees.

This story begins with the KLPT algorithm from Kohel, Lauter, Petit and Tignol [KLPT14] to solve the quaternion analog of the isogeny path problem. In [EHL+18], Eisentrager et al. heuristically showed that quaternion ideals can be used as an *efficient representation* of isogenies, with the *"effiency"* stemming from KLPT and other heuristic polynomial-time algorithms. Wesolowski presented provable variants of these algorithms in his recent article [Wes22].

The original motivation behind the study of the Deuring correspondence in [KLPT14, EHL+18] is cryptanalysis. The tools developped toward that end have only recently started to be used constructively. The main building blocks of the signature scheme from Galbraith, Petit and Silva [GPS17] and the later generalization of SQISign by De Feo, Kohel, Leroux, Petit and Wesolowski [DFKL+20] are variants of the KLPT algorithm from Kohel et al. The key generation of the encryption scheme Séta [DFFdSG+21] is also based on the same techniques. The first complete implementation of all these algorithmic blocks was another contribution of the authors of SQISign. Additionally, this protocol is the first example of a scheme that is explicitly making use of isogenies of big prime degree that are manipulated as ideals. In [DFKL+20], the authors argue that using a secret key of prime degree provides better efficiency for the same level of security. The motivation of our paper is to provide a new way of representing isogenies of prime degree that can open up some interesting cryptographic applications. This appears particularly interesting in light of the recent attacks [CD22, MM22, Rob22] that break SIDH and Séta. These attacks are targetting smooth degree secret isogenies and we will see how these attacks fail to break the assumption based on the new representation we introduce.

A first small contribution of this work is to introduce a new terminology of *isogeny representation*, hoping that it can help formalizing some results about isogenies by providing a common framework on the different methods of isogeny computations.

Our main contribution is a new generic isogeny representation that we call a *suborder representation*. This representation is constituted of the endomorphism ring of the domain and several endomorphisms of the isogeny's codomain. We present heuristic polynomial-time algorithms to compute and verify the suborder representation when the degree D is prime. The case of composite D is more complicated and does not seem to be more interesting for cryptography, so it is treated in the full version. The *suborder representation* is not equivalent to the *ideal representation* under the hardness of a new computational problem: the Suborder to Ideal Problem (SOIP), or its equivalent reformulation: the Suborder to Endomorphism Ring Problem (SOERP). The assumed hardness of the SOERP implies that the knowledge of a suborder of rank 4 is not always enough to derive the full endomorphism ring of a supersingular curve. We include in Sect. 4.5, a discussion about the hardness of those new problems where we also prove that the SOIP is equivalent to some instances of the Torsion to Ideal Problem (TIP), a new problem that can be seen as a generalization of the CSSI, the key recovery problem of SIDH [JDF11]. Because we consider an instance of this problem where the degree of the secret isogeny is prime, the recent attacks on SIDH does not seem to apply directly.

Our new isogeny representation requires to solve norm equations inside a new family of quaternion orders and ideals and we develop the necessary heuristic tools for that task. This contribution may be of independent interest as solving norm equations inside different types of order have proven to be useful in various situations such as [DFKL+20, DFFdSG+21].

Finally, we illustrate the cryptographic interest of our new isogeny representation by building pSIDH, a NIKE based on a generalization of SIDH to the prime degree setting. The key recovery problem is the SOIP and the key exchange is secure under the hardness of a decisional variant of the SOIP. The efficiency of pSIDH is not likely to be competitive and it needs to be considered as a first step toward more involved applications.

The rest of this paper is organized as follows: Sect. 2 is dedicated to the background materials. In Sect. 3, we give the definition for $\mathcal{L}_{\mathsf{isog}}$, the language of isogenous curves, and show that it is in NP using the *ideal representation* of isogenies. In Sect. 4, we introduce our new *suborder representation*. We provide some algorithms to compute and verify these representations, and analyze how they differ from *ideal representations*. The algorithmic gaps left in Sect. 4 are filled in Sect. 5 where we introduce new algorithms to solve norm equations inside a new family of quaternion orders. Finally, in Sect. 6, we introduce a new isogeny-based NIKE scheme based on the suborder representation.

2 Background Material

The set of prime numbers is denoted $\mathbb{P}$. For a prime $\ell \in \mathbb{P}$, we define $\ell^\bullet = \{\ell^k | k \in \mathbb{N}\}$.

We call *negligible* a function $f : \mathbb{Z}_{>0} \to \mathbb{R}_{>0}$ if it is asymptotically dominated by $O(x^{-n})$ for all $n > 0$. In the analysis of a probabilistic algorithm, we say that an event happens with *overwhelming probability* if its probability of failure is a negligible function of the length of the input.

2.1 Notations and Simplifications

Throughout this work, $p > 3$ is a prime number and $B_{p,\infty}$ is the unique quaternion algebra ramified at p and ∞. For ease of exposition, we use a simplified terminology and conventions that we will keep during the entire paper. We introduce them below.

When talking about elliptic curves and isogenies, we always consider isomorphism classes of curves and isogenies respectively. This means that when needed (in an algorithm for instance) we represent curves by their j-invariant that we write $j(E)$ for a curve E (implicitly deriving a full equation of a canonical representative of the isomorphism class if needed). For an isogeny φ, we implicitly adapt whatever isogeny representation we use to this convention, so we pre and post-compose with the relevant isomorphisms to have an isogeny defined on the canonical representatives of the domain and codomain. For an isogeny of domain E and kernel G, we note the codomain class as E/G.

Any four dimensional lattice Λ of $B_{p,\infty}$ is given by 16 coefficients in $\mathbb{Q}$ corresponding to the decomposition over a basis of $B_{p,\infty}$ of a basis of Λ. This is what we call the *representation* of an order or an ideal and is what is used when a computation is required. For an order $\mathcal{O} \in B_{p,\infty}$, an $\mathcal{O}$-ideal of $B_{p,\infty}$ will always be a left integral $\mathcal{O}$-ideal of norm coprime with p unless said otherwise. An isogeny will always be a cyclic separable isogeny.

Quaternion Notations. We list below a few notations that are used throughout the paper. We refer the reader to the full version for more details. The *left and right orders* of an ideal are written $\mathcal{O}_L(\cdot), \mathcal{O}_R(\cdot)$. Two ideals are *equivalent* if $J = I\beta$ for $\beta \neq 0$ and we say that I, J are equivalent. The *norm* of an ideal I is denoted by $n(I)$.

2.2 The Deuring Correspondence

The Deuring correspondence is an equivalence of categories between isogenies of supersingular elliptic curves and the left ideals over maximal order $\mathcal{O}$ of $\mathcal{B}_{p,\infty}$, inducing a bijection between conjugacy classes of supersingular j-invariants and maximal orders (up to equivalence) [Koh96]. This bijection is explicitly constructed as $E \to \mathrm{End}(E)$. Hence, given a supersingular curve E_0 with endomorphism ring $\mathcal{O}_0$, the pair (E_1, φ), where E_1 is another supersingular elliptic curve and $\varphi : E_0 \to E_1$ is an isogeny, is sent to a left integral $\mathcal{O}_0$-ideal (obtained by considering kernel ideals [Wat69]) with $\mathcal{O}_R(I) \cong \mathrm{End}(E_1)$ (Table 1).

Definition 1. *Let $I \subset \mathrm{End}(E_0)$ be an integral ideal, we define $E_0[I] = \{P \in E_0(\overline{\mathbb{F}}_{p^2}) : \alpha(P) = 0$ for all $\alpha \in I\}$ and the isogeny corresponding to I is $\varphi_I : E_0 \to E_0/E_0[I]$. Conversely, given an isogeny φ with domain E_0, the corresponding ideal is $I_\varphi = \{\alpha \in \mathcal{O}_0 : \alpha(P) = 0$ for all $P \in \ker(\varphi)\}$.*

Quaternion orders admit what we call a *Gorenstein decomposition.* Any quaternion order $\mathcal{O}$ can be expressed as $\mathbb{Z} + f\mathcal{O}'$, where f is the *Brandt Invariant* and $\mathcal{O}'$ is the *Gorenstein closure.* We will try to understand the *Brandt Invariant* through the Deuring correspondence in Sect. 4.1.

Table 1. The Deuring correspondence, a summary from [DFKL+20].

Supersingular j-invariants over $\mathbb{F}_{p^2}$ $j(E)$ (up to Galois conjugacy)	Maximal orders in $B_{p,\infty}$ $\mathcal{O} \cong \mathrm{End}(E)$ (up to isomorpshim)
(E_1, φ) with $\varphi : E \to E_1$	I_φ integral left $\mathcal{O}$-ideal and right $\mathcal{O}_1$-ideal
$\theta \in \mathrm{End}(E_0)$	Principal ideal $\mathcal{O}\theta$
$\deg(\varphi)$	$n(I_\varphi)$
$\hat{\varphi}$	$\overline{I_\varphi}$
Supersingular j-invariants over $\mathbb{F}_{p^2}$	Ideal class set of a maximal order $\mathcal{O}$

3 The Language of Isogenous Curves and the Ideal Representation

Let us fix a prime p. We will study $\mathcal{L}_{\mathsf{isog}}$, the language of isogenous supersingular curves in characteristic p.

We write $\mathcal{S}_p$ as the set of isomorphism classes of supersingular elliptic curves in characteristic p, and Isog_D the set of cyclic D-isogenies between curves of $\mathcal{S}_p$.

Definition 2. *The language of isogenous supersingular curves is*

$$\mathcal{L}_{\mathsf{isog}} = \{(D, E_1, E_2) \in \mathbb{N} \times \mathcal{S}_p^2 \mid \exists\ \varphi : E_1 \to E_2 \in \mathsf{Isog}_D\}.$$

An isogeny representation is a string s_φ associated to an isogeny $\varphi : E_1 \to E_2$ of degree D. This string can be used as input to two algorithms: one that can verify that the element D, E_1, E_2 is in $\mathcal{L}_{\mathsf{isog}}$ and one that can compute $\varphi(P)$ for some point $P \in E_1$.

We call the former a *verification algorithm* and the latter an *evaluation algorithm.* We can regroup isogeny representations in *families of representations* by looking at the associated verification and evaluation algorithms. Thus, to a family XX of representations we associate two algorithms XXVerification and XXEvaluation.

Standard Isogeny Representation. The *default isogeny representation* of $\varphi \in \mathsf{Isog}_D$ is made of the rational maps $f_1, f_2 \in \mathbb{F}_{p^m}(x, y)$ such that the image under φ of any point (x, y) of the domain is $(f_1(x, y), f_2(x, y))$ and $\mathbb{F}_{p^m}$ is the field of definition of $\ker\varphi$. The degree of the polynomials used in f_1, f_2 are in $O(\mathsf{poly}(D))$. Since any isogeny of degree D_1D_2 is the composition of a D_1-isogeny and a D_2-isogeny, decomposing φ in smaller isogenies allows us to get a default representation of size $O(\mathsf{poly}(\log(pD)))$ when D has smoothness bound in $O(\mathsf{poly}(\log(pD)))$. When not said otherwise, this default representation is used for the computation of isogenies of smooth degree. It is also standard in the literature to use a generator of $\ker\varphi$ as a representation, we call that the *kernel representation.* This representation can be used to compute the default isogeny representation with the Vélu Formulae [Vél71]. The computational cost is also $O(\mathsf{poly}(\log(pD)))$ when D has smoothness bound in $O(\mathsf{poly}(\log(pD)))$.

3.1 Polynomial-Time Algorithms of the Deuring Correspondence

We give below a list of algorithms taken from the literature. Throughout this paper, we are going to use the provable version of these algorithms, most of which were introduced by Wesolowski in [Wes22]. For a concrete instantiation of any of them, one will rather want to use the efficient heuristic version (see [DFKL+20] for instance). The KLPT algorithms depend on some special extremal order $\mathcal{O}_0$ that we consider as a fixed parameter. We use the default representation of isogenies.

- ConnectingIdeal: takes two maximal orders $\mathcal{O}_1, \mathcal{O}_2 \subset B_{p,\infty}$ and outputs an ideal I with $\mathcal{O}_L(I) = \mathcal{O}_1$ and $\mathcal{O}_R(I) = \mathcal{O}_2$.
- $\mathsf{KLPT}_{\ell^\bullet}$: takes a left $\mathcal{O}$-ideal I and outputs $J \sim I$ of norm ℓ^e.
- $\mathsf{KLPT}_{\mathsf{PS}}$: takes a left $\mathcal{O}$-ideal I and outputs $J \sim I$ of powersmooth norm.
- $\mathsf{IdealToIsogeny}_T$: takes a left $\mathcal{O}$-ideal I of norm T and computes φ_I.
- $\mathsf{IsogenyToIdeal}_T$: takes an isogeny $\varphi : E \to E'$ of degree T, a maximal order $\mathcal{O} \cong \mathrm{End}(E)$ and computes I_φ.

We reformulate below in Proposition 1 to Proposition 5, some of the results proven in [Wes22].

Proposition 1. *ConnectingIdeal terminates in $O(\mathsf{poly}(\log(p) + C)))$ where C is the size of the representation of $\mathcal{O}_1, \mathcal{O}_2$.*

Proposition 2. *Assuming GRH, $\mathsf{KLPT}_{\ell^\bullet}$ terminates in expected $O(\mathsf{poly}(\log(pD) + C))$ where D is the norm of the input and outputs an ideal of norm e where $e = O(\mathsf{poly}(\log(p))$ and the representation of $\mathcal{O}$ has C bits.*

Proposition 3. *Assuming GRH, $\mathsf{KLPT}_{\mathsf{PS}}$ terminates in expected $O(\mathsf{poly}(\log(pD) + C)$ where D is the norm of the input and outputs an ideal of norm in $O(\mathsf{poly}(p))$ with smoothness bound in $O(\mathsf{poly}(\log(p)))$ and the representation of $\mathcal{O}$ has C bits.*

Proposition 4. *For any number $T = O(\mathsf{poly}(p))$ with smoothness bound in $O(\mathsf{poly}(\log(p)))$, $\mathsf{IsogenyToIdeal}_T$ terminates in expected $O(\mathsf{poly}(\log(p)))$ and the output has size $O(\mathsf{poly}(\log(p)))$.*

Proposition 5. *For any number $T = O(\mathsf{poly}(p))$ with smoothness bound in $O(\mathsf{poly}(\log(p)))$, $\mathsf{IdealToIsogeny}_T$ terminates in expected $O(\mathsf{poly}(\log(p) + C))$ and the output has size $O(\mathsf{poly}(\log(p)))$ and the representation of $\mathcal{O}$ has C bits.*

3.2 Ideal Witnesses: Membership Proofs to $\mathcal{L}_{\mathsf{isog}}$ from the Deuring Correspondence

We define the *ideal representation* for the isogeny φ as a representation of the associated kernel ideal I_φ. Note that this implies the knowledge of the endomorphism rings of both E_1 and E_2. With Lemma 1 below, we prove that the ideal representation can be compact.

Lemma 1. *Any ideal I of norm D is isomorphic to an ideal J with a representation of size $O(\log(pD))$.*

Proof. It was shown in [EHL+18] that any maximal order is isomorphic to an order with a representation of size $O(\log(p))$. Let us write $\mathcal{O}$ for the maximal order with the small representation isomorphic to $\mathcal{O}_L(I)$. We can write J for the image of I under the isomorphism between $\mathcal{O}_L(I)$ and $\mathcal{O}$. Since $D\mathcal{O} \subset J$ (this is true for any cyclic $\mathcal{O}$-ideal of norm D), we see that we can choose a basis of J inside the basis of $\mathcal{O}$ with coefficients of size $O(\log(D))$. Thus, there exists a representation of J of size $O(\log(p) + \log(D))$.

For simplicity, we assume in the rest of this work, that ideals and orders are given with a compact representation as in Lemma 1.

We now present IdealVerification as Algorithm 1. It is a verification algorithm that takes a triple $x = (D, E_1, E_2)$ and an ideal I and decides if $x \in \mathcal{L}_{\mathsf{isog}}$. The idea is to compute the curves whose endomorphism ring are isomorphic to the left and right order of I. If the curves obtained in this way are isomorphic to E_1, E_2, the verification passes. To do that, we will use the following procedure on ideals connecting a special order $\mathcal{O}_0$ with $\mathcal{O}_L(I)$ and $\mathcal{O}_R(I)$: use KLPT to get an equivalent ideal of smooth norm and compute the codomain of the corresponding isogeny with IdealToIsogeny. Since these isogenies have smooth norm, they can be efficiently computed.

Algorithm 1. IdealVerification(x, I)

Input: $x \in \mathbb{N} \times \mathcal{S}_p^2$ and I an ideal of $B_{p,\infty}$.
Output: A bit indicating if $x \in \mathcal{L}_{\mathsf{isog}}$.
1: Parse x as D, E_1, E_2 and take ℓ a small prime.
2: Compute $n(I)$ and $\mathcal{O}_L(I), \mathcal{O}_R(I)$.
3: **if** $n(I) \neq D$ or $I \not\subset \mathcal{O}_L(I)$ **then**
4: Return 0.
5: **end if**
6: Take a curve E_0 defined over $\mathbb{F}_p$ with $\mathrm{End}(E_0) \cong \mathcal{O}_0$ and compute $I_1 =$ ConnectingIdeal$(\mathcal{O}_0, \mathcal{O}_L(I))$, $I_2 = I_1 \cdot I$.
7: **for** $i \in [1, 2]$ **do**
8: Compute $J_i = \mathsf{KLPT}_{\ell^\bullet}(I_i)$ and $\varphi_i : E_0 \to E_i' = \mathsf{IdealToIsogeny}_{\ell^\bullet}(E_0, J_i)$.
9: **end for**
10: **if** $(j(E_1'), j(E_2')) \notin \{(j(E_1), j(E_2)), (j(E_1)^p, j(E_2)^p)\}$ **then**
11: Return 0.
12: **end if**
13: **return** 1.

Lemma 2. *Let D be any integer in $\mathbb{N}$ coprime with p. If $\varphi : E_1 \to E_2$ has degree D, then IdealVerification$((D, E_1, E_2), I_\varphi) = 1$.*

Conversely, for $(D, E_1, E_2) \in \mathbb{N} \times \mathcal{S}_p^2$, if there exists an ideal I such that IdealVerification$((D, E_1, E_2), I) = 1$ *then $(D, E_1, E_2) \in \mathcal{L}_{\mathsf{isog}}$.*

Proof. Let us take $\varphi : E_1 \to E_2$ of degree D. By definition of I_φ, we have $n(I_\varphi) = D$ and $I_\varphi \subset \mathcal{O}_L(I_\varphi)$ so the first check passes. Then, the codomain of the two φ_{I_i} have endomorphism ring isomorphic to $\mathcal{O}_R(I_i)$ so they might be either both E_i or both E_i^p (since $I_2 = I_1 I_\varphi$, it cannot be E_1, E_2^p or E_1^p, E_2). In both cases, the final output is 1.

If there exists an ideal I such that IdealVerification$((D, E_1, E_2), I) = 1$, then $n(I) = D$ and I is integral (this is from the first verification). Since $I = \overline{I_1} \cdot I_2/n(I_1) \sim \overline{J_1} \cdot J_2$ is an integral ideal of degree D, there exists an isogeny of degree D between E_1', E_2'. Since the final output is 1, the two curves E_1', E_2' are equal to either E_1, E_2 or E_1^p, E_2^p. Since $\varphi : E_1^p \to E_2^p$ of degree D imply the existence of $\varphi^p : E_1 \to E_2$ of degree D, in both cases we have that $(D, E_1, E_2) \in \mathcal{L}_{\mathsf{isog}}$.

Proposition 6. *Under GRH,* IdealVerification *terminates in expected* $O(\mathsf{poly}(\log(pD) + C)$ *where* C *is the bit size of the representation of* I.

Proposition 6 follows directly from Propositions 1, 2 and 5.

Isogeny Evaluation from Ideals. It is also possible to evaluate an isogeny from its ideal representation. In the full version of the paper, we present an algorithm IdealEvaluation solving that task. The main idea is to apply KLPT and IdealToIsogeny to find an equivalent isogeny of powersmooth degree and making use of it to perform the computation. Note that an algorithm very similar to IdealEvaluation can be found in [FKMT22].

4 A New Isogeny Representation

In this section, we propose a new way to prove the existence of a D-isogeny between two curves when D is a prime number. We call it the *suborder representation/witness.* Composite degrees require more care and we will argue in the full version that they do not appear more interesting. We will briefly explain how to extend the suborder representation to composite degrees in the full version as well. From now on, unless stated otherwise, D can be assumed to be prime. The suborder representation has also another small limitation: the proof only shows that either E_1, E_2 or E_1, E_2^p are D-isogenous and works only when $\mathrm{End}(E_1) \not\cong \mathrm{End}(E_2)$. Thus, we consider the alternate language $\mathcal{L}_{\mathsf{p-isog}}$ defined as follows:

$$\mathcal{L}_{\mathsf{p-isog}} = \{(D, E_1, E_2) \in \mathbb{P} \times S_p^2 | E_1 \not\cong E_2, E_2^p \text{ and } (D, E_1, E_2) \in \mathcal{L}_{\mathsf{isog}} \text{ or } (D, E_1, E_2^p) \in \mathcal{L}_{\mathsf{isog}}\}$$

In Sect. 4.1, we introduce the mathematical results underlying our new method. The method to extract the new representation from the ideal representation is the goal of Sect. 4.2. Then, in Sect. 4.3, we explain how to perform a heuristic polynomial-time verification of this new witness.

4.1 Brandt Invariant and Relation with Isogenies

The goal of this section is to prove Proposition 7 that links the *Brandt invariant* of some orders with isogenies through the Deuring correspondence.

Proposition 7. *Let $D \neq p$ be a prime number and E_1, E_2 be two supersingular curves over $\mathbb{F}_{p^2}$, $\mathcal{O}_1 \subset B_{p,\infty}$ is a maximal order isomorphic to* $\mathrm{End}(E_1)$. *The order $\mathbb{Z} + D\mathcal{O}_1$ is embedded inside* $\mathrm{End}(E_2)$ *if and only if either $j(E_2) \in \{j(E_1), j(E_1)^p\}$ or $(D, E_1, E_2) \in \mathcal{L}_{\mathsf{p-isog}}$.*

We will prove the backward direction of Proposition 7 with a simple argument using orders and ideals, but it is worth noting that the concrete embedding can be obtained with the map $\alpha_0 \mapsto [d] + \varphi \circ \alpha_0 \circ \hat{\varphi}$ between $\mathrm{End}(E_1)$ and $\mathrm{End}(E_2)$ when there exists $\varphi : E_1 \to E_2$ of degree D. This is not the first appearance of this map that was introduced by Waterhouse [Wat69, Section 3.1]. It is also at the heart of the attacks [Pet17,KMP+20] on the SIDH key exchange and underlies the decryption process of the Séta encryption scheme [DFFdSG+21]. In the proof of Proposition 7. The forward direction is more subtle and we use the preliminary Lemma 3.

Lemma 3. *Let Let D be prime number different from p and $\mathfrak{O} \subset B_{p,\infty}$ be a quaternion order such that $\mathfrak{O} = \mathbb{Z} + D\mathfrak{O}_0$ for another order $\mathfrak{O}_0 \subset B_{p,\infty}$. When $\mathfrak{O}$ is embedded in a maximal order $\mathcal{O}$, either $\mathcal{O}$ contains $\mathfrak{O}_0$ or there exists a left-$\mathcal{O}$ integral primitive ideal I of norm D whose right order $\mathcal{O}_0$ contains $\mathfrak{O}_0$.*

Proof. Let us assume that $\mathfrak{O}_0$ is not contained in $\mathcal{O}$. We set $I = \{x \in \mathcal{O}, x\mathfrak{O}_0 \subset \mathcal{O}\}$. First, it is easy to verify that I is an integral left $\mathcal{O}$-ideal since it is contained in $\mathcal{O}$. Then, we are going to see that it has norm D. It suffices to show that $D\mathcal{O} \subsetneq I \subsetneq \mathcal{O}$. To see that $I \neq \mathcal{O}$, it suffices to note that $1 \notin I$ since $\mathfrak{O}_0 \not\subset \mathcal{O}$. Then, with $D\mathfrak{O}_0 \subset \mathcal{O}$ we have $Dx\mathfrak{O}_0 = xD\mathfrak{O}_0 \subset \mathcal{O}$ for every $x \in \mathcal{O}$, which proves that $D\mathcal{O} \subset I$. Finally, to prove that $D\mathcal{O} \neq I$, we take $x_0 \in \mathfrak{O}_0$ and not contained in $\mathcal{O}$. It is clear that $Dx_0 \in I$, but $Dx_0 \notin D\mathcal{O}$. Finally, from the definition of I it is quite clear that $\mathfrak{O}_0$ is contained in $O_R(I)$. This concludes the proof.

Proof (Proposition 7). For the forward direction, let us take a maximal order $\mathcal{O}_2 \cong \mathrm{End}(E_2)$ such that $\mathbb{Z} + D\mathcal{O}_1 \subset \mathcal{O}_2$ (which is possible since $\mathbb{Z} + D\mathcal{O}_1$ is embedded inside $\mathrm{End}(E_2)$). Then, we apply Lemma 3 to $\mathfrak{O}_0 = \mathcal{O}_1$, and $\mathcal{O} = \mathcal{O}_2$, we obtain that either $\mathcal{O}_2$ contains $\mathcal{O}_1$ (in which case $\mathcal{O}_2 = \mathcal{O}_1$ since $\mathcal{O}_1$ is maximal) and so we have $\mathrm{End}(E_1) \cong \mathrm{End}(E_2) \Rightarrow j(E_2) \in \{j(E_1), j(E_1)^p\}$, or there must be an $\mathcal{O}_2$-integral ideal of norm D whose right order contains $\mathcal{O}_1$. Once again, since $\mathcal{O}_1$ is maximal, we have in fact equality and so we have an ideal of norm D whose right order is $\mathcal{O}_2$ and left order is $\mathcal{O}_1$. By the Deuring correspondence, this means that $(D, E_1, E_2) \in \mathcal{L}_{\mathsf{p-isog}}$.

For the backward direction, let us consider the ideal I corresponding to the D-isogeny $\varphi : E_1 \to E_2$ (w.l.o.g, we can assume that $D, E_1, E_2 \in \mathcal{L}_{\mathsf{isog}}$). This ideal has norm D. Since $\mathcal{O}_L(I)$ is maximal, the local order $\mathcal{O}_L(I) \otimes \mathbb{Z}_D$ is a principal ideal domain (see [Voi18, Chapter 23]) and so the ideal I is locally principal. This proves that we can write $I = \mathcal{O}_L(I)\alpha + \mathcal{O}_L(I)D$ for some element $\alpha \in \mathcal{O}_L(I)$ and so $D\mathcal{O}_L(I) \subset I \subset \mathcal{O}_R(I)$. Thus, we obtain that $\mathbb{Z} + D\mathcal{O}_L(I) \subset \mathcal{O}_R(I)$, and the proof is concluded by $\mathcal{O}_L(I) \cong \mathrm{End}(E_1)$ and $\mathcal{O}_R(I) \cong \mathrm{End}(E_2)$.

4.2 Deriving the Suborder Representation from the Ideal Representation

Proposition 7 suggests that the embedding $\mathbb{Z} + D\mathrm{End}(E_1) \hookrightarrow \mathrm{End}(E_2)$ can be used to prove the existence of an isogeny of degree D between E_1 and E_2. The goal of this section is to introduce an algorithm $\mathsf{IdealToSuborder}$ that takes a maximal order $\mathcal{O} \cong \mathrm{End}(E_1)$ and an $\mathcal{O}$-ideal I of norm D and outputs a suborder representation for φ made of $\mathcal{O}$ and the embedding $\mathbb{Z}+D\mathcal{O} \hookrightarrow \mathrm{End}(E_2)$. By a representation of the embedding, we actually mean the embeddings of a *generating family* for $\mathbb{Z}+D\mathcal{O}$ (see Definition 3 below). We give the full definition for a suborder representation as Definition 4.

Definition 3. *A generating family $\theta_1, \cdots, \theta_n$ for an order $\mathcal{O}$ is a set of elements in $\mathcal{O}$ such that any element $\rho \in \mathcal{O}$ can be written as a linear combination of* 1 *and $\prod_{j\in\mathcal{I}} \theta_j$ for all $\mathcal{I} \subset \{1, \cdots, n\}$. In that case, we write $\mathcal{O} = \mathsf{Order}(\theta_1, \ldots, \theta_n)$.*

Definition 4. *Let $\varphi : E_1 \to E_2$ be an isogeny of degree D. A suborder representation π_φ for φ is made of an order $\mathcal{O} \cong \mathrm{End}(E_1)$ and of the default representations $s_1, \ldots, s_n$ of n endomorphisms of E_2 corresponding to a generating family of $\mathbb{Z} + D\mathcal{O}$.*

Our algorithm $\mathsf{IdealToSuborder}$ (Algorithm 2) is built upon a $\mathsf{SmoothGen}_{\mathcal{N}}$ sub-algorithm that we will present in Sect. 5.3. This algorithm computes a generating family $\theta_1, \ldots, \theta_n \in B_{p,\infty}$ for the order $\mathbb{Z} + D\mathcal{O}$ on input $D, \mathcal{O}$ where each θ_i has norm in $\mathcal{N}$. For Proposition 8 and Proposition 10, we are going to assume several things about this $\mathsf{SmoothGen}$ algorithm. We summarize them in Assumption 1.

Assumption 1. *Let $\mathcal{N} \subset \mathbb{N}$ be either $\ell^\bullet$ for some prime $\ell = O(\mathsf{poly}(\log(pD)))$, or the set of divisors of T for some integer $T > p^{7/2}D^6$ of size $O(\mathsf{poly}(pD))$ and smoothness bound $O(\mathsf{poly}(\log(pD)))$. On input $\mathcal{O}, D$, the algorithm $\mathsf{SmoothGen}_{\mathcal{N}}$ is deterministic, correct and terminates in $O(\mathsf{poly}(\log(pD) + C))$ where $\mathcal{O}$ is represented by C bits. It outputs $n = O(1)$ quaternion elements whose norms are contained in $\mathcal{N}$ for all $1 \leq i \leq n$.*

Remark 1. We hide several heuristics and a conjecture under Assumption 1. We discuss these heuristics in Sect. 5.3.

$\mathsf{IdealToSuborder}$ can be divided in two main parts: $\mathsf{SmoothGen}$ to obtain quaternion elements $\theta_1, \ldots, \theta_n$ and an $\mathsf{IdealToIsogeny}$ step to convert the ideals $\mathcal{O}_R(I)\theta_i$ to isogenies $\varphi_i : E_2 \to E_2$. For all the algorithms of this section, we are going to assume that a small constant prime ℓ has been fixed and we write $\ell^\bullet$ for the set $\{\ell^e, e \in \mathbb{N}\}$.

Algorithm 2. $\mathsf{IdealToSuborder}(I)$

Input: I an integral ideal of maximal orders inside $B_{p,\infty}$ of norm D.
Output: Endomorphisms $\varphi_i : E_2 \to E_2$ such that $\iota : \mathrm{End}(E_2) \xrightarrow{\sim} \mathcal{O}_R(I)$ sends $\varphi_1, \ldots, \varphi_n$ to a generating family $\theta_1, \ldots, \theta_n$ for $\mathbb{Z} + D\mathcal{O}_L(I)$.
1: Compute $D = n(I)$ and $\mathcal{O} = \mathcal{O}_L(I), \mathcal{O}' = \mathcal{O}_R(I)$.
2: Compute $\theta_1, \ldots, \theta_n = \mathsf{SmoothGen}_{\ell^\bullet}(\mathcal{O}, D)$.
3: **for** $i \in [1, n]$ **do**
4: Compute $\varphi_i : E_2 \to E_2 = \mathsf{IdealToIsogeny}_{\ell^\bullet}(\mathcal{O}'\theta_i)$.
5: Compute the default representation s_i of φ_i.
6: **end for**
7: Choose $\mathcal{O}_c$, a maximal order isomorphic to $\mathcal{O}$ of small representation.
8: **return** $\pi = \mathcal{O}_c, (s_i)_{1 \le i \le n}$.

Proposition 8. *Under Assumption 1 and GRH, IdealToSuborder is correct and terminates in $O(\mathsf{poly}(\log(pD) + C))$ where C is the bitsize of I and the output has size $O(\mathsf{poly}(\log(pD)))$.*

Proof. Correctness follows from the correctness of IdealToIsogeny and SmoothGen. The left and right orders of I have representation of size smaller than C, and so termination follows from GRH, Assumption 1 and Proposition 5 (with $n = O(1)$). The degree and smoothness bound of all the $\deg \varphi_i$ is given by Assumption 1 and this implies that the default isogeny representation has size $O(\mathsf{poly}(\log(pD)))$ as we explained in the beginning of Sect. 3. An $\mathcal{O}_c$ with representation of size $O(\log(p))$ can be found and this concludes the proof.

4.3 Verification of the Suborder Representation

This section focuses on the verification of the representation computed with IdealToSuborder. From Proposition 7, we know that it suffices to convince the verifier that $\mathbb{Z} + D\mathrm{End}(E_1)$ is embedded inside $\mathrm{End}(E_2)$ and $\mathrm{End}(E_1) \not\cong \mathrm{End}(E_2)$. The second part is easy to verify, it suffices to compute the j-invariants and verify that neither $j(E_1) = j(E_2)$ nor $j(E_1) = j(E_2)^p$. The first part of the verification is achieved with the endomorphisms $\varphi_1, \ldots \varphi_n$. With Lemma 4, we show that it suffices to check some traces and norms of endomorphisms computed from the $(\varphi_i)_{1 \le i \le n}$. Due to the lack of space, the proof of Lemma 4 can be found in the full version.

Lemma 4. *Two orders $\mathcal{O}_1 = \mathsf{Order}(\theta_1, \ldots, \theta_n)$ and $\mathcal{O}_2 = \mathsf{Order}(\omega_1, \ldots, \omega_n)$ of rank 4 in a quaternion algebra are isomorphic if $n(\theta_i) = n(\omega_i)$ for all $i \in [1, n]$ and $\mathrm{tr}(\prod_{j \in \mathcal{I}} \theta_j) = \mathrm{tr}(\prod_{j \in \mathcal{I}} \omega_j)$ for all $\mathcal{I} \subset [1, n]$.*

As Lemma 4 indicates, we need to compute some traces for the verification. This will be done by an algorithm $\mathsf{CheckTrace}_M$ (whose description we postpone until Sect. 5.4) that will verify the validity of the traces modulo the parameter M (see Proposition 19).

Lemma 5 below gives a bound above which equality will hold over $\mathbb{Z}$ if it holds mod M. In the full version of the paper, we also explore the option of choosing a value of M below the bound of Lemma 5, producing a tradeoff between efficiency and soundness.

Lemma 5. *Given any* $\theta \in \mathrm{End}(E_1)$, *if* $\mathrm{tr}(\theta) = t \mod M$ *for* $M > 4\sqrt{n(\theta)}$ *and* $|t| \leq M/2$, *then* $\mathrm{tr}(\theta) = t$.

Proof. Over $B_{p,\infty}$, the norm form is $n : (x, y, z, w) \mapsto x^2 + qy^2 + pz^2 + qpw^2$ where $q > 0, p > 0$. Since $\mathrm{tr} : (x, y, z, w) \mapsto 2x$, we can easily verify that $\mathrm{tr}(\theta)^2 < 4n(\theta)$. This gives a bound of $2\sqrt{n(\theta)}$ on the absolute value of $\mathrm{tr}(\theta)$. The result follows.

Algorithm 3. $\mathsf{SuborderVerification}_M(x, \pi)$

Input: $M \in \mathbb{N}$, $x \in \mathbb{P} \times \mathcal{S}_p^2$ and π a suborder representation.
Output: A bit indicating if $x \in \mathcal{L}_{\mathsf{p-isog}}$.
1: Parse x as D, E_1, E_2 and $\pi = \mathcal{O}, (s_i)_{1 \leq i \leq n}$.
2: **if** If disc $\mathcal{O} \neq p$ **then**
3: Return 0.
4: **end if**
5: Compute $\theta_1, \ldots, \theta_n = \mathsf{SmoothGen}_{\ell^\bullet}(\mathcal{O}, D)$.
6: Compute $J = \mathsf{ConnectingIdeal}(\mathcal{O}_0, \mathcal{O})$ and $L = \mathsf{KLPT}_{\ell^\bullet}(J)$.
7: Compute $\psi : E_0 \to E_1' = \mathsf{IdealToIsogeny}_{\ell^\bullet}(L)$.
8: **if** $j(E_1) \neq j(E_1')$ **or** $j(E_1) \neq j(E_1')^p$ **then**
9: Return 0.
10: **end if**
11: **for** $i \in [1, n]$ **do**
12: Parse s_i as the default representation of an isogeny of degree $n(\theta_i) \in \ell^\bullet$ and compute it as $\varphi_i : E_2 \to F_i$.
13: **if** $j(F_i) \neq j(E_2)$ **then**
14: Return 0.
15: **end if**
16: **end for**
17: **return** $\mathsf{CheckTrace}_M(\varphi_1, \ldots, \varphi_n, \theta_1, \ldots, \theta_n, E_2)$.

Proposition 9. *If* $M > \max_{1 \leq j \leq n} 2\sqrt{n(\theta_j)^n}$, *then for* $x \in \mathbb{P} \times \mathcal{S}_p^2$, *there exists a suborder representation* π *such that* $\mathsf{VerifSuborderIProof}_M(x, \pi) = 1$ *if and only if* $x \in \mathcal{L}_{\mathsf{p-isog}}$.

Proof. Assume that there exists a representation π passing the verification for a given $x = (D, E_1, E_2)$. The check in Step 2 proves that $\mathcal{O}$ is a maximal order of $B_{p,\infty}$. The second verification in Step 8 proves that $\mathrm{End}(E_1) \cong \mathcal{O}$. Finally, the verification is Step 13 proves that the φ_i are endomorphisms of E_2. Then, if $\mathsf{CheckTrace}_M(\varphi_1, \ldots, \varphi_n, \theta_1, \ldots, \theta_n, E_2) = 1$, the correctness of SmoothGen, CheckTrace, Lemmas 4 and 5 imply that $\mathbb{Z} + D\mathcal{O}$ is embedded inside $\mathrm{End}(E_2)$ and Proposition 7 proves that $x \in \mathcal{L}_{\mathsf{p-isog}}$.

Now let us take $(D, E_1, E_2) \in \mathcal{L}_{\mathsf{p-isog}}$. By definition there exists an ideal I of norm D and $\mathcal{O}_L(I) \cong \mathrm{End}(E_1)$, $\mathcal{O}_R(I) \cong \mathrm{End}(E_2)$. We are going to show that if $\pi = \mathsf{IdealToSuborder}(I)$, then we have $\mathsf{SuborderVerification}_M(x, \pi) = 1$. First, since $\mathcal{O}_L(I)$ is a maximal order, the verification of Step 2 passes succesfully. This is also the case for the verification of Step 8 since $\mathcal{O}_L(I) \cong \mathrm{End}(E_1)$. Then, by the correctness of IdealToSuborder showed in Proposition 8, we have that s_i can be parsed as isogenies $\varphi_i : E_2 \to E_2$ that corresponds to the $\mathcal{O}_R(I)\theta_i$ through the Deuring correspondence (since SmoothGen is deterministic). Thus, it is clear that CheckTrace will output 1 and this concludes the proof.

With Assumption 1 and Proposition 9, we see that we can take $M = \#E(\mathbb{F}_{p^m})$ for the smallest $m \in \mathbb{N}$ such that M is bigger than the bound in Proposition 9. We refer to Proposition 19 for correctness and complexity of the CheckTrace algorithm.

Proposition 10. *Let m, M be as defined above. Under GRH and Assumption 1,* $\mathsf{SuborderVerification}_M$ *terminates in probabilistic $O(\mathsf{poly}(\log(p) + \log(D)))$.*

Proof. Since $m = O(\mathsf{poly}(\log(pD)))$ by Proposition 9 and Assumption 1, the result follows from Assumption 1, Propositions 1, 2, 5 and 19.

4.4 Evaluating with the Suborder Representation

In this section, we show that we can evaluate an isogeny from the suborder representation. By Proposition 7, any suborder representation π defines a unique isogeny that we write φ_π. The algorithm SuborderEvaluation that we introduce below shows how to use π to evaluate φ_π. This algorithm is going to be one of the major building blocks behind the NIKE scheme of Sect. 6. For this application of our algorithm, we only need to compute the image of cyclic subgroups of the form $E_1[J]$ for some ideal J. Thus, SuborderEvaluation take a suborder representation for φ and an ideal J as input and outputs $\varphi(E_1[J])$.

The SuborderEvaluation algorithm is built on a subprotocol IdealSuborderNormEquation that we will introduce in Sect. 5.2. This algorithm is only heuristic and we summarize in Assumption 2, what we expect of this algorithm.

Assumption 2. *Let $\mathcal{N} \subset \mathbb{N}$ be either $\ell^\bullet$ for some prime $\ell = O(\mathsf{poly}(\log(pD)))$, or the set of divisors of T for some integer $T > B$ of size $O(\mathsf{poly}(pD))$ and smoothness bound $O(\mathsf{poly}(\log(pD)))$ and where $B = p^2D^6n(I)^3n(J)^2$. The algorithm* $\mathsf{IdealSuborderNormEquation}_{\mathcal{N}}$ *takes in input an integer D, two ideals I, J and outputs an element $\beta \in (\mathbb{Z} + DI) \cap J$ with $n(\beta)/n(J) \in \mathcal{N}$, it terminates in expected $O(\mathsf{poly}(\log(pDn(I)n(J))))$ with overwhelming probability.*

The principle of SuborderEvaluation is different from the one of IdealEvaluation we sketched in Sect. 3.2. Indeed, as we will argue in Sect. 4.5, solving the alternate path problem (which is the key step in IdealEvaluation) appears hard from the suborder representation. Instead, we propose to use the fact that the embedding of $\mathbb{Z} + D\mathrm{End}(E_1)$ inside $\mathrm{End}(E_2)$ is obtained by push-forwards through φ_π.

More precisely, this means that $\ker \iota(\beta) = \varphi_\pi(\ker \beta)$ for any $\beta \in \mathbb{Z} + D\mathrm{End}(E_1)$ where $\iota : \mathbb{Z} + D\mathrm{End}(E_1) \hookrightarrow \mathrm{End}(E_2)$. Thus, to find $\varphi_\pi(E_1[J])$, we want to find an endomorphism $\beta \in \mathbb{Z} + D\mathrm{End}(E_1)$ such that $\ker \beta \cap E_1[n(J)] = E_1[J]$. By definition of $E_1[J]$, and Assumption 2, such a β is exactly found by IdealSuborderNormEquation. After that, it suffices to compute $\ker \iota(\beta) \cap E_2[n(J)]$ and we are done. The integer m is taken as in Proposition 10.

Algorithm 4. $\mathsf{SuborderEvaluation}(E_1, E_2, \pi, D, J)$

Input: two curves E_1, E_2, a prime D, π a suborder representation for $(D, E_1, E_2) \in \mathcal{L}_{\mathsf{p-isog}}$ and an ideal J of norm coprime with D and ℓ.
Output: $\perp$ or $\varphi_\pi(E_1[J])$.
1: Parse π as $\mathcal{O}, s_1, \ldots, s_n$.
2: **if** $\mathcal{O}_L(J) \not\supseteq \mathcal{O}$ **then**
3: Return $\perp$.
4: **end if**
5: **if** $\mathsf{SuborderVerification}_{\#E_1(\mathbb{F}_{p^m})}((D, E_1, E_2), \pi) = 0.$ **then**
6: Return $\perp$.
7: **end if**
8: **for** $i \in [1, n]$ **do**
9: Parse s_i as the default representation of an isogeny of degree $n(\theta_i) \in \ell^\bullet$ and compute it as $\varphi_i : E_2 \to E_2$.
10: **end for**
11: Compute $\theta_1, \ldots, \theta_n = \mathsf{SmoothGen}_{\ell^\bullet}(\mathcal{O}, D)$.
12: Compute $L = \mathsf{ConnnectingIdeal}(\mathcal{O}_0, \mathcal{O})$ and $I = \mathsf{RandomEquivalentPrimeIdeal(L)}$ with $I = L\alpha$.
13: Compute $\beta = \mathsf{IdealSuborderNormEquation}_{\ell^\bullet}(D, I, \alpha^{-1}J\alpha)$.
14: Express $\alpha\beta\alpha^{-1} = \sum_{\mathcal{I} \subset \{1,\ldots,n\}} c_{i,\mathcal{I}}(\prod_{j \in \mathcal{I}} \theta_j)$.
15: Compute P, Q, a basis of $E_2[n(J)]$.
16: Compute $R, S = \sum_{\mathcal{I} \subset \{1,\ldots,n\}} c_{i,\mathcal{I}}(\prod_{j \in \mathcal{I}} \varphi_j)(P, Q)$.
17: **if** $S = 0$ **then**
18: **return** $\langle Q \rangle$.
19: **end if**
20: Compute $a = \mathsf{DLP}(R, S)$.
21: **return** $\langle P - [a]Q \rangle$.

Proposition 11. *Under GRH and Assumptions 1 and 2,* SuborderEvaluation *is correct when the output is not $\perp$ and terminates in probabilistic $O(\mathsf{poly}(\log(pD)) + C_{\mathsf{DLP}}(n(J))$ operations over the $n(J)$ torsion where $C_{\mathsf{DLP}}(n(J))$ is the complexity of the discrete logarithms in groups of order $n(J)$.*

Proof. First, we will prove correctness. The verification at the beginning proves that if the output is not $\perp$, π is a valid suborder representation. When $L = \mathsf{ConnectingIdeal}(\mathcal{O}_0, \mathcal{O})$ and $I = \mathsf{RandomEquivalentPrimeIdeal(L)}$ with $I = L\alpha$, then if $\beta \in (\mathbb{Z} + DI) \cap \alpha^{-1}J\alpha$, then $\alpha\beta\alpha^{-1} \in (\mathbb{Z} + DL) \cap J \subset (\mathbb{Z} + D\mathcal{O}) \cap J$. This explains that we can decompose $\alpha\beta\alpha^{-1}$ on the generating family $\theta_1, \ldots, \theta_n$.

Since π gives a correct embedding of $\mathbb{Z} + D\mathcal{O}$ inside $\text{End}(E_1)$ and so $\sigma = \sum_{\mathcal{I} \subset \{1,\dots,n\}} c_{i,\mathcal{I}} \prod_{j \in \mathcal{I}} \varphi_j$ is an endomorphism of E_2 whose degree is a multiple of $n(J)$. To conclude the proof of correctness, it suffices to show that $\ker \sigma \cap E_2[n(J)] = \varphi_\pi(E_1[J])$. If $\alpha\beta\alpha^{-1} = [d] + [D]\gamma$ for some $\gamma \in \text{End}(E_1)$, we have that $\sigma = [d] + \varphi_\pi \circ \gamma \circ \hat{\varphi}_\pi$. Now let us take $P_0 \in E_1[J]$. Since $\alpha\beta\alpha^{-1} \in J$, we have $([d] + [D]\gamma)P_0 = 0$ and $\sigma(\varphi_\pi(P_0)) = [d]\varphi_\pi(P_0) + \varphi_\pi(\gamma \circ \hat{\varphi}_\pi \circ \varphi_\pi(P_0)) = \varphi_\pi(([d] + [D]\gamma)P_0 = 0$. This proves that $\varphi_\pi(E[j]) \subset \ker \sigma \cap E_2[n(J)]$. And we obtain equality since the two subgroups have the same order. Thus, we have showed that our protocol is correct. In $\ell^\bullet$, we can always select an element $\ell^e = O(\mathsf{poly}(\log(pDn(I)n(J))))$ of norm bigger than the bound B from Assumption 2 so the complexity follows from Assumptions 1 and 2, Propositions 1 and 10 and the fact that $n(I) = O(\mathsf{poly}(p))$ by Proposition 14.

4.5 Deducing the Ideal Representation from the Suborder Representation

We saw with Proposition 8 that our new suborder representation can be computed from the ideal representation in polynomial time. The goal of this section is to study the reverse problem of extracting an ideal representation from a suborder representation. We are going to try to argue that this problem is hard in general and describe some cases where it is easy. We also introduce several other problems and prove that they are equivalent.

Problem 1 (SubOrder to Ideal Problem, SOIP). Let $x = (D, E_1, E_2) \in \mathcal{L}_{\mathsf{p-isog}}$, and π be a suborder representation such that $\mathsf{SuborderVerification}(x, \pi) = 1$. Compute I, an ideal such that $\mathsf{IdealVerification}(x, I) = 1$ or $\mathsf{IdealVerification}((D, E_1, E_2^p), I) = 1$.

We will show in Proposition 12 the equivalence of Problem 1 with the problem of computing the endomorphism ring of the codomain from the suborder representation (Problem 2).

Problem 2 (SubOrder to Endormophism Ring Problem (SOERP)). Let $x = (D, E_1, E_2) \in \mathcal{L}_{\mathsf{p-isog}}$, and π be a suborder representation such that $\mathsf{SuborderVerification}(x, \pi) = 1$. Compute $\mathcal{O}_2 \subset B_{p,\infty}$ with $\mathcal{O}_2 \cong \text{End}(E_2)$.

Proposition 12. *Under Assumption 1 and GRH, The SOIP and SOERP are equivalent.*

Due to lack of space, the full proof is given in the full version of the paper but we summarize the important elements below. One of the two reductions is trivial since the right order of a solution to the SOIP is exactly a solution to the SOERP. The other reduction is more complex, the idea is that with the knowledge of the endomorphism ring of E_2, the endomorphisms of the suborder representation can be translated into principal ideals over the quaternions and with that, it is possible to compute a generator of the desired ideal.

Interestingly, we can show that the SOIP is also equivalent to another problem, the Torsion to Ideal Problem (TIP) that can be seen as a generalization of the CSSI problem introduced by De Feo and Jao for SIDH [JDF11]. Due to lack of space, the proof of Proposition 13 is given in the full version.

Problem 3 (T-Torsion to Ideal (T-TI)). Let T be an integer. Let $x = (D, E_1, E_2) \in \mathcal{L}_{\mathsf{isog}}$ where D is coprime with T and let $\varphi : E_1 \to E_2$ be an element of Isog_D. Let P, Q be a basis of $E_1[T]$. Given $\mathrm{End}(E_1)$ and $\varphi(P), \varphi(Q) \in E_2[T]$, Compute I, an ideal such that $\mathsf{IdealVerification}(x, I) = 1$.

Proposition 13. *For every D, p, there exists a value of T, such that the SOIP is equivalent to the T-TIP.*

A Sub-exponential Quantum Attack Against the SOIP. To the best of our knowledge, the attack we describe below is the most efficient against the generic SOIP. We use a result from [KMPW21] that a one-way function $f : \mathcal{E} \to \mathcal{F}$ can be inverted at $f(e)$ by solving an instance of the hidden shift problem when there exists a group action $\star : G \times \mathcal{E} \to \mathcal{E}$ for which there is a malleability oracle: i.e., an efficient way to evaluate the function $g \mapsto f(g \star e)$ on any $g \in G$. The hidden shift problem can be solved in quantum sub-exponential time. In our context, we consider the group action of $(\mathrm{End}(E_1)/D\mathrm{End}(E_1))^*$ on the set of cyclic subgroups of order D. This set is in correspondence with cyclic ideals of norm D inside $\mathrm{End}(E_1)$ and so we can invert the function $I \mapsto E/E[I]$ in sub-exponential time if we have a malleability oracle. In [KMPW21], it was shown that this malleability oracle could be obtained as soon as the image of a big enough torsion-group through the secret isogeny was given. This is can done with our algorithm $\mathsf{SuborderEvaluation}$. As a consequence, we can evaluate φ_I on any subgroup of powersmooth order and this is more than enough to obtain a malleability oracle with the ideas of [KMPW21]. Thus, we can apply the reduction from [KMPW21] and get a sub-exponential quantum method to solve Problem 1.

Remark 2. The existence of a sub-exponential attack is inevitable as soon as one non-trivial endomorphism $\sigma : E_2 \to E_2$ is revealed. The attack stems from the existence of a group action of $\mathrm{Cl}(\mathbb{Z}[\sigma])$ on the set of $\mathbb{Z}[\sigma]$-orientations (i.e pairs E, ι where $\iota : \mathbb{Z}[\sigma] \hookrightarrow \mathrm{End}(E_1)$, see [CK19, DFFdSG+21] for more on orientations). With the knowledge of σ, one can apply the idea (first introduced by Biasse, Jao and Sankar [BJS14] in the special case where $\mathbb{Z}[\sigma] = \mathbb{Z}[\sqrt{-p}]$) that the algorithm from Childs et al. [CJS14] can be adapted to find a path of powersmooth degree between two $\mathbb{Z}[\sigma]$-oriented curves. When this algorithm is applied between E_2 and E_1, a curve of known endomorphism ring, the path obtained in output allows the attacker to compute the endomorphism ring of E_2. This algorithm has sub-exponential complexity in $\log h(\mathbb{Z}[\sigma])$ as it reduces to an instance of the hidden shift problem. The attack we just outlined is similar to the ones exposed in [Wes22, ACL+22].

In the remaining of this section, we will describe other attacks, analyze the cases in which they prove to be efficient and explain why they fail to solve the generic SOIP.

Torsion Point Attacks. With the terminology torsion point attack, we designate any attack that aims at recovering an isogeny representation of a secret isogeny $\varphi : E \to F$ from the knowledge of $\varphi(P), \varphi(Q)$ where P, Q is a basis of $E[T]$ for some integer T. This definition covers attacks against the T-TIP and the CSSI problem of SIDH, including the recent attacks by Castryck and Decru [CD22], Maino and Martindale [MM22] and Robert [Rob22]. These new attacks against SIDH can be seen as a generalization to higher dimension of the original torsion point attack due to Petit [Pet17]. Here is how we can explain their common generic principle: use the torsion points $\varphi(P), \varphi(Q)$ to compute θ, a T-endomorphism/isogeny of abelian varieties in dimension g (for some constant g) whose expression depends on φ. When T is big enough with respect to $\deg \varphi$, the computation of θ can be made solely from $\varphi(P), \varphi(Q)$. Then, θ can be evaluated on the $\deg \varphi$-torsion to recover $\ker \varphi$. The real advantage of the new attacks against the initial idea of Petit is that they reduce the constraint to $T > \deg \varphi$ which mean they can be applied to SIDH. With our algorithm SuborderEvaluation, it is possible to get the image of any subgroup under the isogeny φ of degree D from a suborder representation π_φ. Thus, it is always possible to apply a torsion point attack to the setting of the SOIP. However, the complexity of this attack will not always be polynomial. The main obstacle seems to be the field of definition of the D-torsion. In general, for a random integer D, we can expect the D-torsion to be defined over $\mathbb{F}_{p^k}$ where $k = O(D)$. This is true in particular when D is prime. When the field of definition of the torsion point is too big, there does not seem to be any way to express the kernel of φ in a compact manner and thus the attack does not have a polynomial complexity.

On the other hand, when the degree k of the field extension is polynomial in D, there is a quantum polynomial attack against the SOIP. Indeed, in this case, the torsion point attacks allow us to compute the kernel of φ in polynomial time and this kernel admits a representation of polynomial size. Then, the only remaining task to solve the SOIP is to compute the ideal I corresponding to φ. Since the endomorphism ring of the domain E_1 is known, this can be done in quantum polynomial time using the algorithm from Galbraith, Petit and Silva [GPS17, Algorithm 3]. It is only quantum polynomial time because the algorithm requires to solve some DLPs over the D-torsion, every other aspect of the algorithm can be executed in classical polynomial time.

To conclude, we need that the D-torsion is not defined over a small field extension to ensure hardness of the SOIP. Fortunately, this should happen with overwhelming probability when D is chosen at random, and it can be verified by computing the order of p mod D (the degree k is equal to this order up to a factor 2).

Other Attacks. We start by analyzing the complexity of the brute-force algorithm. In full generality, for a given D, the brute force will take $O(\min(p, D))$.

The idea is that since $\text{End}(E_1)$ is part of the suborder representation, it suffices to enumerate through all $\text{End}(E_1)$ ideals of norm D until $\mathsf{IdealVerification}$ passes. There are $O(D)$ such ideals, but since there are only $O(p)$ curves, we need to test at most $O(p)$ of them. Thus, the generic complexity of the brute force is $O(\min(D, p))$. Note that when D is prime, there does not seem to be an adaptation of the meet-in-the-middle attack which provides a quadratic speed-up over a brute-force search, and is considered to be the most efficient method to find an isogeny of smooth degree between two random supersingular curves.

Another way to solve the problem in a generic manner is by computing $\text{End}(E_2)$ (see Proposition 12). Without using the proof π as a hint, the complexity is believed to be $\tilde{\Theta}(p^{1/2})$ for classical computers and $\tilde{\Theta}(p^{1/4})$ for quantum computers (see [EHL+20]).

Even after seeing the above analysis, the hardness of the SOERP may still come as a surprise to a reader familiar with isogeny-based cryptography. In particular, the fact that we reveal several endomorphisms of E_2 might seem like a very troublesome thing to do. This concern is legitimate: the algorithm from [EHL+20] to compute the endomorphism ring of any supersingular curve is based on the principle that knowing two distinct non-trivial endomorphisms is enough to recover the full endomorphism ring in polynomial-time. The idea behind this algorithm is that Bass orders are contained in a small number of maximal orders. Thus, when the two non-trivial endomorphisms generate a Bass order, it suffices to enumerate all the maximal orders containing that same Bass order to find the solution. The authors from [EHL+20] prove their result under the conjecture that two random cycles will form a Bass order with good probability. However, the endomorphisms that we reveal in the suborder representation are not random cycles. By design, the suborder they generate is not Bass and we know that it is contained in an exponential number of maximal orders (this number is equal to the number of D-isogenies by Lemma 3). As such, when using the endomorphisms of the suborder representation, the algorithm described in [EHL+20] is essentially the brute force attack where each ideal of norm D is tested.

Readers might also be concerned with the quaternion alternate path problem. A way to break the SOERP would be to use the embedding of $\mathbb{Z} + D\text{End}(E_1)$ inside $\text{End}(E_2)$ to compute a path from E_2 to a curve E_0 of known endomorphism ring. Following the (now standard) blueprint that underlies most of the algorithm in this work, such an attack would be divided in two steps: first a computation over the quaternions (analog to KLPT) and then a conversion through the Deuring correspondence to obtain an isogeny connecting E_2 to E_0 (analog to $\mathsf{IdealToIsogeny}$). This supposed attack would have to work over orders of non-trivial Brandt invariant rather than maximal orders to exploit the suborder representation. It appears that the first part of this method can be made to work over non-Gorenstein orders. In fact, the $\mathsf{IdealSuborderNormEquation}$ that we describe in Algorithm 6 is exactly the analog of KLPT for orders of the form $\mathbb{Z} + D\mathcal{O}$. However, the fact that the Brandt invariant is non-trivial appears like a serious obstacle to the second part of the proposed attack. Indeed, as the number of curves admitting an embedding of $\mathbb{Z} + D\mathcal{O}$ inside their endomorphism ring is big, it becomes hard to tell which pair of curves are connected by any ideal of the form $(\mathbb{Z} + D\mathcal{O}) \cap J$ (which was not the case for maximal orders because we have almost a $1 - to - 1$ correspondence between curves and maximal orders). Thus, it seems implausible to be able to find a path between E_2 and a given curve E_0 in that manner. Another way of seeing this is that since $\mathbb{Z} + D\mathcal{O}$ is a generic suborder shared by a lot of curves, we cannot compute anything that will be specific to a given curve from the knowledge of $\mathbb{Z} + D\mathcal{O}$ only.

5 Sub-algorithms over the Quaternion Algebra

In this section, we fill the blanks left in the Sect. 4. We provide precise descriptions of the algorithms IdealSuborderNormEquation,SmoothGen, and $\mathsf{CheckTrace}_M$ in Sects. 5.2 to 5.4 respectively. We recall that the first algorithm is used to evaluate isogenies from the suborder representation in SuborderEvaluation (Algorithm 4 of Sect. 4.4) and the last two are building blocks for SuborderVerification (Algorithm 3 of Sect. 4.3) for the verification of our new suborder representation. Note that IdealSuborderNormEquation and SmoothGen are only heuristic as for the algorithms from [KLPT14, DFKL+20]. We expand on this matter in Remark 3.

We use the basis $1, i, j, k$ for $B_{p,\infty}$ where $i^2 = -q$, $j^2 = -p$ and $k = ij = -ji$ for some small integer $q > 0$ (see [KLPT14] for values of q for all p, when $p = 3 \mod 4$ we can take $q = 1$). Following the classical approach in the literature ([KLPT14, DFKL+20]), we take $\mathcal{O}_0 \subset B_{p,\infty}$ as a special extremal order as defined in [KLPT14], i.e., a maximal order containing a suborder with orthogonal basis $\langle 1, \omega, j, \omega j \rangle$ where $\mathbb{Z}[\omega] \subset \mathbb{Q}[i]$ is a quadratic order of small discriminant.

5.1 Algorithms from Previous Works

In the next sections, we rely upon several algorithms existing in the literature. The full version of [DFKL+20] is a good reference for all these algorithms. We briefly recall their purpose.

- RandomEquivalentPrimeIdeal(I), given a left $\mathcal{O}_0$-ideal I, finds an equivalent left $\mathcal{O}_0$-ideal of prime norm.
- IdealModConstraint(I, γ), given an ideal I of norm N, and $\gamma \in \mathcal{O}_0$ of norm n coprime with N, finds $(C_0 : D_0) \in \mathbb{P}^1(\mathbb{Z}/N\mathbb{Z})$ such that $\mu_0 = j(C_0 + \omega D_0)$ satisfies $\gamma\mu_0 \in I$.
- EichlerModConstraint(I, γ), given an ideal I of norm N, and $\gamma \in \mathcal{O}_0$ of norm n coprime with N, finds $(C_0 : D_0) \in \mathbb{P}^1(\mathbb{Z}/N\mathbb{Z})$ such that $\mu_0 = j(C_0 + \omega D_0)$ satisfies $\gamma\mu_0 \in \mathbb{Z} + I$.
- $\mathsf{StrongApproximation}_{\mathcal{N}}(N, C_0, D_0)$, given a prime N and $C_0, D_0 \in \mathbb{Z}$, finds $\mu = \lambda\mu_0 + N\mu' \in \mathcal{O}_0$ of norm in $\mathcal{N}$, with $\mu_0 = j(C_0 + \omega D_0)$ and $\mu' \in \mathcal{O}_0$.

The following result on the size of the output of RandomEquivalentPrimeIdeal will prove useful.

Proposition 14. *Let I be an integral ideal of maximal orders. The output* $J = \mathsf{RandomEquivalentPrimeIdeal}(I)$ *has norm* $n(J) = O(\mathsf{poly}(p))$.

Remark 3. The algorithms that we have introduced above are all expected to terminate in polynomial-time under various plausible heuristic assumptions introduced in [KLPT14, DFKL+20]. By plausible, we mean that these assumptions were verified experimentally. These assumptions mostly concern the probability that some integers represented by specific quadratic forms are prime and satisfy some quadratic reduosity condition (as in Remark 4 for instance, see also [Wes22] for more details). Our new algorithms are based on the sub-algorithms from [KLPT14] and this is why our results will be subject to the same assumptions. However, these assumptions are only used to justify the termination and expected running time of the sub-algorithms, and so they do not appear directly in our proofs, and this is also why we do not state them clearly.

Remark 4. The $\mathsf{StrongApproximation}_{\mathcal{N}}(N, \cdot)$ algorithm was originally introduced for a prime number N in [KLPT14]. The probability of success depends on some quadratic reduosity condition mod N. We can easily extend StrongApproximation to the case of composite N (and this is the version that we use in the algorithms below) if we allow the success probability to decrease. In general, under the heuristic assumption that the integers we consider mod N behave like random integers of the same size, we can see that the success probability should be $1/2^k$ where k is the number of distinct prime divisors of N. Below, we are going to use the algorithm with N having at most three large prime divisors.

5.2 Solving Norm Equations Inside Non-Gorenstein Orders

In this section, we extend the range of 4-dimensional lattices $\Lambda \subset B_{p,\infty}$ inside which we know how to solve norm equations. Each of our norm equation algorithm is parameterized by a set $\mathcal{N} \subset \mathbb{N}$ that defines the possible norm of the outputs. This set $\mathcal{N}$ can be either $\ell^\bullet$ for some prime ℓ or $\mathcal{M}(T)$, the divisors of T for some $T \in \mathbb{N}$.

The first algorithms targetting that task were introduced in [KLPT14] where Λ was either a special extremal maximal order like $\mathcal{O}_0$ or an ideal of left (and right) maximal order. In [DFKL+20], new methods were introduced to work inside Eichler orders and their ideals, thus covering lattices of the form $\mathbb{Z} + I$ and $(\mathbb{Z} + I) \cap J$ where I, J are cyclic integral ideals with $\gcd(n(I), n(J)) = 1$. We continue this trend of work by exploring the case of non-Gorenstein orders with Gorenstein closure equal to Eichler orders and their ideals. Concretely, this means lattices of the form $\mathbb{Z} + DI$ and $(\mathbb{Z} + DI) \cap J$ where I, J are cyclic integral ideals and $\gcd(n(I), n(J), D) = 1$.

Our motivation is the resolution of norm equations inside $\mathbb{Z} + D\mathcal{O}$ for any maximal order $\mathcal{O} \subset B_{p,\infty}$. In the particular case where $\mathcal{O}$ is a maximal extremal order as $\mathcal{O}_0$, an algorithm to find elements of given norm inside $\mathbb{Z} + D\mathcal{O}$ was introduced in [Pet17]. Unfortunately, the generic case requires a different treatment. We apply the idea from De Feo et al. in [DFKL+20] that consists in restricting the resolution to the suborder $(\mathbb{Z} + D\mathcal{O}) \cap \mathcal{O}_0$. Since $\mathcal{O} \cap \mathcal{O}_0 = \mathbb{Z} + I$ where $I = \mathsf{ConnectingIdeal}(\mathcal{O}_0, \mathcal{O})$, our main tool is an algorithm EichlerSuborderNormEquation to solve norm equations inside $\mathbb{Z} + DI = (\mathbb{Z} + D\mathcal{O}) \cap (\mathbb{Z} + I)$. This algorithm is going to be the main building block of SmoothGen (whose description we give in Sect. 5.3). In the end of this section, we show with IdealSuborderNormEquation how to extend EichlerSuborderNormEquation to solve norm equations inside $(\mathbb{Z} + DI) \cap J$ where $\gcd(n(J), n(I)) = 1$.

To clarify the explanations, we try to extract a pattern in the formulations of the algorithms from [KLPT14, DFKL+20] and ours. We will explain how the ideas from [KLPT14, DFKL+20] fit into a common framework before introducing our approach. We hope that it might provide some insights on these algorithms and help the reader understand how they work and how they were designed.

Each algorithm is parameterized by two integers N_1, N_2. We look for elements of norm contained in some set $\mathcal{N} \subset \mathbb{N}$. In practice $\mathcal{N}$ is going to be either $\ell^\bullet$ or the divisors of some powersmooth integer T. The algorithms can be decomposed as follows:

1. Find γ satisfying a set of conditions and having a norm dividing $N_1 n'$ where $n' \in \mathcal{N}$.
2. Find $C, D \in \mathbb{Z}$ such that $\gamma j(C + D\omega) \in \Lambda$.
3. Compute $\mu = \mathsf{StrongApproximation}_{\mathcal{N}}(N_2, C, D)$.
4. Output $\gamma\mu$.

The goal of these "conditions" on γ in the first step is to ensure that the second step will always have a solution. As we are going to see, the only real difference between the several algorithms are the values of N_1, N_2 and these conditions on γ. The second step is always solved using linear algebra mod N_2. When N_2 is composite, we will decompose it in sub-operations modulo the different factors before using a CRT to put everything together.

In the rest of this section, we may assume for simplicity that ideals have prime norm. When not, the algorithm EquivalentRandomPrimeIdeal can be used to reduce the computation to the prime case. The first algorithm fitting the framework above was introduced in [KLPT14] and targetted the case where Λ is an $\mathcal{O}_0$-ideal of norm N. The condition on γ is summarized by Lemma 6 that is a reformulation of some of the results from [KLPT14]. We have $N_1 = N$ and $N_2 = N$.

Lemma 6 *[KLPT14]. Let I be an $\mathcal{O}_0$ ideal of norm N and $\gamma \in \mathcal{O}_0$. When $\gcd(n(\gamma), N^2) = N$, there exists $C, D \in \mathbb{Z}$ such that $\gamma j(C + D\omega) \in I$ with overwhelming probability.*

The goal of the authors of [DFKL+20]. was to obtain a generalization of the algorithm of [KLPT14] when Λ is an $\mathcal{O}$-ideal K for any maximal order $\mathcal{O}$ (and not just the special case $\mathcal{O}_0$). To do that, they proposed to solve the norm equation inside $K \cap \mathcal{O}_0$ which can be written as $(\mathbb{Z} + I) \cap J$ for two $\mathcal{O}_0$-ideals I, J. To achieve that goal they started by implicitly introducing a method to solve the norm equation inside $\mathbb{Z}+I$ before combining that with the ideas from [KLPT14] to get the full method.

For the case $\Lambda = \mathbb{Z} + I$ where I has norm N, the condition on γ can be summarized with Lemma 7. In that case, $N_1 = 1$ and $N_2 = N$.

Lemma 7 *[DFKL+20]. Let I be an $\mathcal{O}_0$ ideal. When* $\gcd(\gamma, N) = 1$, *there exists $C, D \in \mathbb{Z}$ such that $\gamma j(C + D\omega) \in \mathbb{Z} + I$ with overwhelming probability.*

When $\Lambda = (\mathbb{Z}+I) \cap J$ with $n(I) = N$ and $n(J) = N'$, the solution presented in [DFKL+20, Section 5] is simply obtained by combining Lemmas 6 and 7 with $N_1 = N'$, $N_2 = NN'$.

Norm equations inside $\mathbb{Z} + DI$. Next, we explain our method for the case $\Lambda = \mathbb{Z}+DI$. This time, we need γ to satisfy more conditions than a simple constraint on its norm. We will introduce the necessary condition in Proposition 15. The constraint proves to be slightly inconvenient, and will impact the size of the final solution, but we managed to find a way to keep some control on the norm of γ while ensuring that the linear algebra step always has a solution.

Proposition 15. *Let I be an integral left $\mathcal{O}_0$-ideal of norm N and let D be a prime number distinct from N. If $\gamma \in \mathcal{O}_0$ can be written as $j(C_2 + \omega D_2) + D\mu_2$ with $\mu_2 \in \mathcal{O}_0$ and γ has norm coprime with N, then there exists $C_1, D_1 \in \mathbb{Z}$ such that $\gamma j(C_1 + \omega D_1) \in \mathbb{Z} + DI$.*

Proof. If γ has norm coprime with N, we know from [DFKL+20] that there exists C_0, D_0 such that $\gamma j(C_0 + \omega D_0) \in \mathbb{Z} + I$ (this is Lemma 7). Then, if we set $C_2' = -D_2' C_2 (D_2)^{-1} \mod D$ for any D_2', it is easy to verify that $\gamma j(C_2' + \omega D_2') \in \mathbb{Z}+D\mathcal{O}_0$. Hence, if C_1, D_1 satisfies $C_1 = C_0 \mod N, D_1 = D_0 \mod N$, $C_1 = C_2', D_1 = D_2' \mod D$ and $\gcd(N, D) = 1$, we have that $\gamma j(C_1 + \omega D_1) \in \mathbb{Z} + D\mathcal{O}_0 \cap (\mathbb{Z} + I) = \mathbb{Z} + DI$. By the CRT, we know we can find such C_1, D_1.

With Proposition 15, we see that we must take $N_1 = 1$ and $N_2 = ND$ and that we must also apply a strong approximation $\mod D$ to compute exactly γ. When we apply these ideas to the framework described above, we obtain EichlerSuborderNormEquation.

We remind the reader that the heuristics in Proposition 16 are the same as the ones from [KLPT14] (see Remark 3). This goes for Propositions 17 and 18 as well.

Proposition 16 *(Heuristic). When N, D are distinct primes, Algorithm 5 terminates in expected $O(\mathsf{poly}(\log(DN)))$ and outputs an element of $\mathbb{Z}+DI$ of norm in $\mathcal{N}$ when $\mathcal{N}$ contains an elements bigger than $p^{7/2}D^6$. The expected norm is in $O(\mathsf{poly}(p, D, N))$.*

Proof As mentioned in Remark 4, because D is prime, under plausible heuristics, the algorithm $\mathsf{StrongApproximation}_{\mathcal{N}}(D, \cdot)$ finds a solution of norm in $\mathcal{N}$ with probability at least $1/2$ in polynomial time when $\mathcal{N}$ contain a big enough element (we will look at the required size at the end of the proof). As a result

Algorithm 5. $\mathsf{EichlerSuborderNormEquation}_{\mathcal{N}}(D, I)$

Input: I a left $\mathcal{O}_0$-ideal of norm N coprime with D.
Output: $\beta \in \mathbb{Z} + DI$ of norm dividing F.
1: Select a random class $(C_2 : D_2) \in \mathbb{P}^1(\mathbb{Z}/D\mathbb{Z})$.
2: Compute $\mu_2 = \mathsf{StrongApproximation}_{\mathcal{N}}(D, C_2, D_2))$. If the computation fails, go back to Step 1.
3: Compute $(C_0 : D_0) = \mathsf{EichlerModConstraint}(\mu_2, I)$.
4: Sample a random D'_2 in $\mathbb{Z}/D\mathbb{Z}$, compute $C'_2 = -D'_2 C_2 (D_2)^{-1} \mod D$.
5: Compute $C_1 = \mathsf{CRT}_{N,D}(C_0, C'_2)$, $D_1 = \mathsf{CRT}_{N,D}(D_0, D'_2)$.
6: Compute $\mu_1 = \mathsf{StrongApproximation}_{\mathcal{N}}(ND, C_1, D_1)$. If it fails, go back to step 1.
7: **return** $\beta = \mu_2\mu_1$.

of Proposition 15, EichlerModConstraint always succeeds in finding a solution $(C_0 : D_0)$. Then, the second StrongApproximation has a 1/4 success probability when N, D are prime. Assuming that a new choice of $(C_2 : D_2)$ randomizes $(C_1 : D_1)$ sufficiently we can show that a solution can be found with overwhelming probability after a constant number of repetitions. This proves the algorithm's termination.

For correctness, we can verify easily that $j(C_2 + D_2\omega)j(C'_2 + \omega D'_2) \in \mathbb{Z} + D\mathcal{O}_0$. Since $\beta - j(C_2 + D_2\omega)j(C'_2 + \omega D'_2) \in D\mathcal{O}_0$ this proves that $\beta \in \mathbb{Z} + D\mathcal{O}_0$. By the correctness of EichlerModConstraint and the fact that $N\mathcal{O}_0$ is contained in I we can also show that $\beta \in \mathbb{Z} + I$. Hence, $\beta \in (\mathbb{Z} + D\mathcal{O}_0) \cap (\mathbb{Z} + I) = \mathbb{Z} + DI$.

The estimates provided in [DFKL+20] allow us to predict that we can find a solution β of norm in $\mathcal{N}$ if $\mathcal{N}$ contains elements of size $\approx 2\log_\ell(p) + 6\log_\ell(D) + 3\log_\ell(N)$. This comes from the fact that a strong approximation mod N' can find solutions of norm approximately equal to pN'^3. Other estimates provided in [DFKL+20] prove that we will have $N \approx \sqrt{p}$ and this yields the final bound $p^{7/2}D^6$.

Norm Equations Inside $(\mathbb{Z} + DI) \cap J$. We set $N = n(I)$ and $N' = n(J)$. For this final case, it suffices to combine Lemmas 6 and 7 and Proposition 15 and take $N_1 = N'$, $N_2 = NN'D$. This yields Algorithm 6.

Proposition 17 *(Heuristic). Assumption 2 holds.*

Proof. Due to Lemmas 6 and 7 and Proposition 15, we know that we can find $(C_0 : D_0), (C_3 : D_3)$ and $(C'_2 : D'_2)$ with overwhelming probability and that the result will be correct. The computation takes $O(\mathsf{poly}(\log(DNN')))$ since it consists of linear algebra mod D, N, N'. The executions of Strong Approximations terminates in probabilistic polynomial time and output a value with constant probability. So the global computations terminates in probabilistic $O(\mathsf{poly}(\log(DNN')))$. It is correct because StrongApproximation is correct. The computation succeeds as soon as the target set $\mathcal{N}$ contains elements that have size bigger than $2\log_\ell(p) + 6\log_\ell(D) + 3\log_\ell(N) + 2\log_\ell(N')$ and this is the value we can take for the bound B (the first execution of StrongApproximation gives an element of size $\sim pD^3/N'$ and the second $p(DNN')^3$).

Algorithm 6. $\mathsf{IdealSuborderNormEquation}_{\mathcal{N}}(D, I, J)$

Input: An integer D, and I, J two left $\mathcal{O}_0$-ideals of norm N, N' with $\gcd(N, N', D) = 1$.

Output: $\beta \in (\mathbb{Z} + DI) \cap J$ of norm $N'N''$ where $N'' \in \mathcal{N}$.

1: Select a random class $(C_2 : D_2) \in \mathbb{P}^1(\mathbb{Z}/D\mathbb{Z})$.
2: Compute $\mu_2 = \mathsf{StrongApproximation}_{\mathcal{N}}(D, C_2, D_2))$. If the computation fails or if $\gcd(n(\mu_2), N') = 1$, go back to Step 1.
3: Compute $(C_0 : D_0) = \mathsf{EichlerModConstraint}(\mu_2, I)$.
4: Compute $(C_3 : D_3) = \mathsf{IdealModConstraint}(\mu_2, J)$.
5: Sample a random D_2' in $\mathbb{Z}/D\mathbb{Z}$, compute $C_2' = -D_2' C_2 (D_2)^{-1} \mod D$.
6: Compute $C_1 = \mathsf{CRT}_{N,D,N'}(C_0, C_2', C_3)$, $D_1 = \mathsf{CRT}_{N,D,N'}(D_0, D_2', D_3)$.
7: Compute $\mu_1 = \mathsf{StrongApproximation}_{\mathcal{N}}(NDN', C_1, D_1)$. If it fails, go back to step 1.

8: **return** $\beta = \mu_2 \mu_1$.

5.3 Computing a Smooth Generating Family

In this section, we describe the $\mathsf{SmoothGen}$ algorithm that takes in input a maximal order $\mathcal{O}$ and a prime D, outputs a generating family of $\mathbb{Z} + D\mathcal{O}$ of elements whose norms are in $\mathcal{N}$. The idea behind this algorithm is quite straightforward: apply $\mathsf{EichlerSuborderNormEquation}$ on I, for various ideals I connecting $\mathcal{O}_0$ and orders isomorphic to $\mathcal{O}$. This gives a way to sample elements in $\mathbb{Z} + D\mathcal{O}$, and we iterate this method until we obtain a generating family from this set. Experimental results show that after taking a few elements in that manner (for instance, no more than ten for parameters of cryptographic sizes, i.e., of a few hundred bits), we can extract a generating family of size three. We formulate this more precisely as Conjecture 1.

Conjecture 1. Let $\mathcal{O}_1$ be a maximal order in $B_{p,\infty}$. Let I_1, I_2, I_3 be random $\mathcal{O}_0$-ideals of prime norms with $\alpha_i \mathcal{O}_R(I_i) \alpha_i^{-1} = \mathcal{O}$ for some $\alpha_i \in B_{p,\infty}^*$. If $\theta_1, \theta_2, \theta_3$ are random outputs of $\mathsf{EichlerSuborderNormEquation(D, I_i)}$ for $i = 1, 2, 3$, then $\mathbb{Z} + D\mathcal{O} = \mathsf{Order}(\alpha_1 \theta_1 \alpha_1^{-1}, \alpha_2 \theta_2 \alpha_2^{-1}, \alpha_3 \theta_3 \alpha_3^{-1})$ with probability $1/c$ where $c = O(\mathsf{poly}(\log(pD)))$.

Proposition 18 *(Heuristic). Assuming Conjecture 1, Assumption 1 holds.*

Proof. Proposition 1 proves the desired running time for $\mathsf{ConnectingIdeal}$. The same holds for $\mathsf{RandomEquivalentPrimeIdeal}$ and the outputs of this algorithm have norms in $O(\mathsf{poly}(p))$ by Proposition 14. By Conjecture 1, $n = 3$ and we need only to repeat a polynomial number of times the algorithm $\mathsf{EichlerSuborderNormEquation}$ which terminates in polynomial time by Proposition 16 and the outputs have norm in $O(\mathsf{poly}(pD))$. By the termination condition, the output is a generating family of $\mathbb{Z} + D\mathcal{O}$.

Algorithm 7. $\mathsf{SmoothGen}_{\mathcal{N}}(\mathcal{O}, D)$

Input: A maximal order $\mathcal{O}$ and a prime D.
Output: A generating family $\theta_1, \theta_2, \theta_3$ for $\mathbb{Z} + D\mathcal{O}$ where each θ_j has norm in $\mathcal{N}$.
1: Set $L = \emptyset$ and $I_0 = \mathsf{ConnectingIdeal}(\mathcal{O}_0, \mathcal{O})$.
2: **while** There does not exist $\theta_1, \theta_2, \theta_3 \in L$ s.t $\mathbb{Z} + D\mathcal{O} = \mathsf{Order}(\theta_1, \theta_2, \theta_3)$ **do**
3: $I = \mathsf{RandomEquivalentPrimeIdeal}(I_0)$ and $I = I_0\alpha$.
4: Compute $\theta = \mathsf{EichlerSuborderNormEquation}_{\mathcal{N}}(D, J)$.
5: $L = L \cup \{\alpha\theta\alpha^{-1}\}$.
6: **end while**
7: **return** $\theta_1, \theta_2, \theta_3$.

5.4 Checking Traces

In this section, we present an algorithm $\mathsf{CheckTrace}_M$ to perform the verification of the suborder representation.

Computing the trace of an endomorphism is a well-studied problem, as it is the primary tool of the point counting algorithms such as SEA [Sch95]. For our application the task is even simpler as we merely have to verify the correctness of the alleged trace value and not compute it. With the formula $\mathrm{tr}(\theta) = \theta + \hat{\theta}$, it suffices to evaluate θ and $\hat{\theta}$ on a basis of the M-torsion, and then verify the relation. In particular, we do not need M to be smooth since we just want to check equality.

Algorithm 8. $\mathsf{CheckTrace}_M(E, \varphi_1, \dots, \varphi_n, \theta_1, \dots, \theta_n)$

Input: $\theta_1, \dots, \theta_n$, n endomorphisms of E and n elements of $B_{p,\infty}$ $\omega_1, \dots, \omega_n$.
Output: A bit b equal to 1 if and only if $\mathrm{tr}(\theta_i) = \mathrm{tr}(\omega_i) \mod M$ for all $i \in [1, n]$.
1: Compute P, Q a basis of $E[M]$ over the appropriate field extension. Set $b = 1$.
2: **for** All $\mathcal{I} \subset [1, n]$ **do**
3: Set $\theta_{\mathcal{I}} = \prod_{j \in I} \theta_j$ and $\varphi_{\mathcal{I}} = \prod_{j \in I} \varphi_j$.
4: Verify $\varphi_{\mathcal{I}}(R) + \hat{\varphi}_{\mathcal{I}}(R) = [\mathrm{tr}(\theta_{\mathcal{I}})]R$ for $R \in \{P, Q\}$. If not, set $b = 0$.
5: **end for**
6: **return** b.

Proposition 19. *When* $M = \#E(\mathbb{F}_{p^m})$, $n = O(1)$ *and* $\deg \varphi_i = O(\mathsf{poly}(p))$ *and have smoothness bound in* $O(\mathsf{poly}(\log(p)))$ *for all* $1 \leq i \leq n$, $\mathsf{CheckTrace}_M$ *terminates in* $O(\mathsf{poly}(m \log(p))$

Proof. By choice of M, P, Q are defined over $\mathbb{F}_{p^m}$ and so operations over the M-torsions have $O(\mathsf{poly}(m \log(p))$ complexity. By the assumption on the degree of the φ_i, computing all the $\varphi_{\mathcal{I}}(P, Q)$ can be done in $O(\mathsf{poly}(\log(p)))$ since $n = O(1)$ and this concludes the proof.

6 A New NIKE Based on a Generalization of SIDH for Big Prime Degrees

We present here pSIDH (prime-SIDH) a new NIKE scheme. It is based on a SIDH-style isogeny diagram (see Fig. 1) but with prime degrees. For secret keys we propose to use ideal representations and then take suborder representations as public keys. The key exchange will be made possible with SuborderEvaluation (Algorithm 4 of Sect. 4.4). The full description can be found in In terms of security, the pSIDH key recovery problem is exactly the SOIP and our NIKE is secure under the hardness of a decisional variant of the SOIP (Problem 1) in a similar manner to SIDH with the CSSI and SSDDH problems introduced in [JDF11].

As pSIDH is a NIKE and the best attack is quantum-subexponential (see Sect. 4.5), pSIDH has an application profile similar to CSIDH (there is even a group action involved). The SOIP in itself is closer to the key recovery problem of CSIDH than it is to the one of SIDH (in the sense that they can be both seen as isogeny problems with partial endomorphism ring information which is not really the case for SIDH). However, despite some similarities, the protocols relies on different assumptions. Moreover, the underlying structure in pSIDH is not the same as in CSIDH so it might open new possibilities.

We discuss a concrete instantiation and the efficiency of pSIDH in Sect. 6.2, where we also compare with the efficiency of CSIDH.

6.1 The Description of pSIDH

The idea of SIDH is the following: the two participants Alice and Bob generate isogenies φ_A, φ_B of degree $\gcd(N_A, N_B) = 1$. Their public keys are the curves E_A, E_B, together with additional pieces of information to make possible the computation of the two push-forward isogenies $[\varphi_A]_*\varphi_B$ and $[\varphi_B]_*\varphi_A$ depicted in Fig. 1. It is possible to show that the codomains of these push-forward isogenies are isomorphic (thus providing a way to derive the common key from $j(E)$). We have $\ker[\varphi_A]_*\varphi_B = \varphi_A(\ker \varphi_B)$ and this is why Alice's SIDH-public key is the curve E_A together with $\varphi_A(P_B), \varphi_A(Q_B)$ where $\langle P_B, Q_B\rangle = E_0[N_B]$ (and the reverse for Bob's). For efficiency, the degrees N_A, N_B need to be smooth.

To do the same thing for two prime degrees D_A, D_B, we need a new method to compute the codomain of the push-forward isogenies. We propose to use the ideal representations as secret keys and the suborder representations as public keys. The computation of the common key $j(E)$ can be done as follows. Given an ideal I of norm D_A and the suborder $\mathbb{Z} + D_B\mathcal{O}_0$, it is possible to find an element $\theta \in (\mathbb{Z} + D_B\mathcal{O}_0) \cap I$ of norm $D_A S$ where S is a powersmooth integer with the algorithm IdealSuborderNormEquation (Algorithm 6 in Sect. 5.2). The embedding $\iota_B : \mathbb{Z} + D_B\mathcal{O}_0 \hookrightarrow \mathrm{End}(E_B)$, is obtained by pushing forward the embedding of $\mathbb{Z} + D_B\mathcal{O}_0$ inside $\mathrm{End}(E_0)$ through φ_B and so we have $\iota_B(\theta) = \psi_A \circ [\varphi_B]_*\varphi_A$ where ψ_A has degree S. Thus, using π_B, the suborder representation of φ_B, we can use SuborderEvaluation to compute $\ker \hat{\psi}_A$ and $\hat{\psi}_A$. The codomain of $\hat{\psi}_A$ is isomorphic to E and so the common secret $j(E)$ can be derived from that.

These ideas are summarized in Fig. 1 and the full description of the key exchange mechanism is given as Algorithm 10. The key generation algorithm is also described in Algorithm 9. To be able to run this algorithm in polynomial-time, we need to be able to compute efficiently isogenies of degree ψ_A and to be able to manipulate the full deg ψ_A torsion. This is why we take the degree of ψ_A as a divisor of a powersmooth integer T. To be able to apply SuborderEvaluation, we also need that T is coprime with the degree of the endomorphisms of the suborder representation (so we take T coprime with ℓ). We write $\mathcal{M}(T)$ for the set of divisors of T. The integer m is taken to be as in Proposition 10.

The public parameters of pSIDH should include a prime p and a starting curve E_0 together with a description of $\text{End}(E_0)$. For simplicity, we may assume that $\text{End}(E_0) \cong \mathcal{O}_0$, where $\mathcal{O}_0$ is the special extremal order introduced in the beginning of Sect. 5.

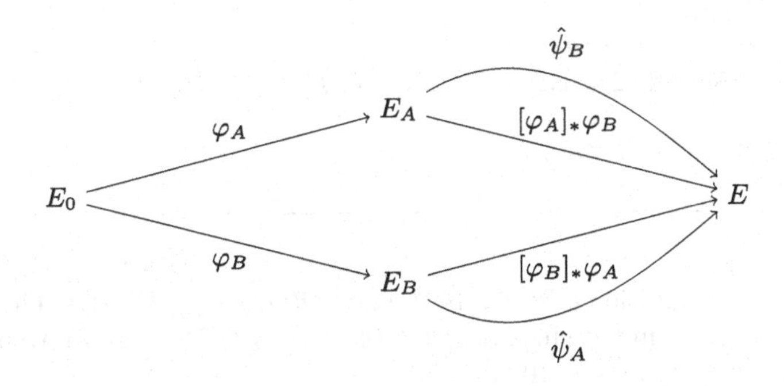

Fig. 1. SIDH/pSIDH-isogeny diagram.

Algorithm 9. KeyGeneration(D)

Input: A prime number $D \neq p$.
Output: The pSIDH public key $\mathsf{pk} = E, \pi$ and the pSIDH secret key $\mathsf{sk} = I$ where π is a suborder representation and I an ideal representation for $(D, E_0, E) \in \mathcal{L}_{\mathsf{p-isog}}$.

1: Sample I as a random $\mathcal{O}_0$-ideal of norm D.
2: Compute $\pi =$ IdealToSuborder(I) and set E as the domain of the endomorphisms in π.
3: **return** $\mathsf{pk}, \mathsf{sk} = (E, \pi), I$.

Proposition 20. *Under GRH, Assumption 1, Assumption 2,* KeyExchange *terminates in expected* $\mathsf{poly}(\log(pD'D)$.

Proof. Since $B = O(\mathsf{poly}(\log(pDD')))$, we can choose a value of T with a smoothness bound equal in $O(\mathsf{poly}(\log(pDD')))$. Thus, all operations over the T-torsion

Algorithm 10. $\mathsf{KeyExchange}(I, D', E', \pi)$

Input: I an ideal of degree D and a prime $D' \neq D, p$. A curve E' and a suborder representation π.
Output: A j-invariant or $\bot$.
1: Parse $\pi = (\mathcal{O}_0, \varphi_1, \dots, \varphi_n)$.
2: Compute $\theta_1, \cdots, \theta_n = \mathsf{SmoothGen}_{\ell^\bullet}(\mathcal{O}_0, D')$.
3: **if** $!\mathsf{SuborderVerification}_{\#E'(\mathbb{F}_{p^m})}((D', E_0, E'), \pi)$ **then**
4: Return $\bot$.
5: **end if**
6: Take a powersmooth integer T coprime with ℓ with $B < T < 2B$ where B is the bound in Assumption 2 and T has the smallest possible smoothness bound.
7: Set $J = \mathcal{O}_0 1$.
8: Compute $\theta = \mathsf{IdealSuborderNormEquation}_{\mathcal{M}(T)}(D', J, I)$.
9: Factorize $T = \prod_{i=1}^r \ell_i^{e_i}$.
10: Set $G = \langle 0_{E'} \rangle$.
11: **for** $i \in [1, r]$ **do**
12: Compute $J_i = \mathcal{O}_0 \overline{\alpha^{-1}\theta\alpha} + \mathcal{O}_0 \ell_i^{e_i}$.
13: $G = G + \mathsf{SuborderEvaluation}(E_0, E', \pi, D', J_i)$.
14: **end for**
15: Compute $\psi : E' \to E'/G$.
16: **return** $j(E'/G)$.

and the final computation of ψ can be done in $O(\mathsf{poly}(\log(pD'D)))$. The remaining computations terminate in expected $O(\mathsf{poly}(\log(pD'D)))$ due to Assumptions 1 and 2 and Propositions 1, 10, 11 and 14.

Proposition 21. *Let $D_A, D_B \neq p$ be two distinct prime numbers. If $E_A, \pi_A, I_A = \mathsf{KeyGen}(D_A)$ and $E_B, \pi_B, I_B = \mathsf{KeyGen}(\mathsf{D_B})$, then*

$$\mathsf{KeyExchange}(I_A, D_B, E_B, \pi_B) = \mathsf{KeyExchange}(I_B, D_A, E_A, \pi_A).$$

Proof. Let us write φ_A, φ_B the isogenies corresponding to the two ideals I_A, I_B. Let us write θ_A the quaternion element defined in Step 8 of $\mathsf{KeyExchange}(I_A, D_B, E_B, \pi_B)$. Then, the quaternion element $\overline{\alpha_A^{-1}\theta_A\alpha_A} \in (\mathbb{Z} + D_B\mathcal{O}_0) \cap I_A$ corresponds to an endomorphism $\psi_{A,0} \circ \varphi_A \in \mathrm{End}(E_0)$ for some isogeny $\psi_{A,0} : E_A \to E_0$. Since it is contained in $(\mathbb{Z} + D_B\mathcal{O}_0) \cap I_A$, we can embed it inside the endomorphism ring of E_B by Proposition 7 and we obtain in that manner the endomorphism $\psi_A \circ [\varphi_B]_* \varphi_A$ where $\hat{\psi}_A = [\varphi_B]_* \hat{\psi}_{A,0}$. In particular, the codomain of $\hat{\psi}_A$ is isomorphic to the codomain of $[\varphi_B]_* \varphi_A$. We can make the same reasoning by swapping A and B and by definition of push-forward isogenies and Proposition 11, the two j-invariants obtained at the end of the two executions of $\mathsf{KeyExchange}$ are equal.

Remark 5. The purpose of Algorithm 10 is to present a simple version of the protocol for the key exchange. However, as it is written, our solution is not very optimized. For instance, a lot of redundant computations are made through the call to $\mathsf{SuborderEvaluation}$. In an optimized implementation of this key exchange, one would want to skip all the first steps which are already executed in KeyExchange to focus on the important steps.

We analyze the security of pSIDH in the full version of the paper, it is very similar to the security proof of SIDH.

6.2 About Efficiency and Concrete Instantiations

Efficiency. We have proven (at least heuristically) that all our new algorithms can be executed in polynomial time. However, this does not prove anything on the concrete efficiency. We did not make a full implementation but we can obtain a good idea of the efficiency by comparison with the SQISign signature [DFKL+20]. This comparison is relevant for two reasons: we can take the same size of prime p (and measure relative efficiency by counting the number of operations over $\mathbb{F}_{p^2}$) and the bottlenecks should be the same. We elaborate on that below.

Our analysis in Sect. 4.5 indicates that the only security constraint on the prime p is that it needs to be big enough to prevent the exponential attacks against the endomorphism ring problem (which is the SQISign key recovery problem). Once p has been fixed, the hardness of our new SOIP depends on the value of D. The main attack against the SOIP that we introduce in Sect. 4.5 has quantum sub-exponential complexity in D. It is unclear what should be the size of D but we can expect it to be bigger than p. This gap between p and D will also induce a gap between the performances of SQISign and the performances of pSIDH. Based on empirical observations, we can predict that the bottleneck in our algorithms is going to be the same as the bottleneck in SQISign's signature: executions of the IdealToIsogeny sub-algorithm. The method introduced in [DFKL+20] and the improvement in [DFLW22] for IdealToIsogeny both requires to perform a number of arithmetic operations over $\mathbb{F}_{p^2}$ that is linear in the length of the isogeny to be translated. For SQISign the degree 2^e where e is linear in the security parameter. For pSIDH, the size estimates from Sect. 5.2 show that we may expect element of degree whose logarithm is in $6\log(D)$ (and some linear dependency on $\log(p)$).

On a Concrete Instantiation. We believe that finding a parameter D to reach a NIST-1 level of security for pSIDH is a problem on its own. However, we can easily find parameters that reaches the same security level as CSIDH-512. For that, we can take p of at least 256-bits (one of the SQISign primes should be good) and we can take E_0 to be any starting curve of known endomorphism ring. For instance, if $p = 3 \mod 4$, we can take the curve of j-invariant 1728 with endomorphism ring isomorphic to $\langle 1, i, \frac{1+k}{2}, \frac{i+j}{2} \rangle$ where $1, i, j, k$ is the canonical basis of the quaternion algebra ramified at p and ∞.

We need D of at least 256-bits as well (so that the set of subgroups of order D has the same size as the class number inf CSIDH-512). We remind the reader that, for the hardness of the SOIP, the D-torsion of supersingular curves in characteristic p needs to be defined over an extension of big degree (roughly equal to 2^{256} to have the best possible security). This condition can be checked by computing the order of p mod D. If $(D-1)/2$ is prime, then the computation of the order will have polynomial time (because $D-1$ is easy to factor) and the order of p mod D is going to be bigger than $(D-1)/2$ with overwhelming probability. Such a prime D can be found after trying roughly $\log D$ primes. Apart from that, there is no constraint on the choice of D.

Even though we did not make an implementation, it is clear, looking at the latest performances of SQISign [DFLW22], that an implementation of pSIDH with the parameters we propose, is going to be a lot slower than CSIDH-512.

However, we want to stress that the asymptotic behaviour is rather on the side of pSIDH. Indeed, as we said, the complexity of pSIDH is linear in $\log(D)$ whereas the complexity of CSIDH is worst than linear in $\log(p)$ (and the quantum attack is sub-exponential in $\log(p)$ for CSIDH).

Acknowledgements. We are very grateful to Steven Galbraith for a very thorough review of the paper and numerous comments to help improve the current write-up. We would also like to thank anonymous reviewers for their insight on our work. Finally, we thank Luca De Feo for useful remarks regarding the best way to define an isogeny representation.

References

[ACL+22] Arpin, S., Chen, M., Lauter, K.E., Scheidler, R., Stange, K.E., Tran, H.T.: Orienteering with one endomorphism. arXiv preprint arXiv:2201.11079 (2022)

[BDF21] Burdges, J., De Feo, L.: Delay encryption. In: Canteaut, A., Standaert, F.-X. (eds.) EUROCRYPT 2021. LNCS, vol. 12696, pp. 302–326. Springer, Cham (2021). https://doi.org/10.1007/978-3-030-77870-5_11

[BdFLS20] Bernstein, D. J., De Feo, L., Leroux, A., Smith, B.: Faster computation of isogenies of large prime degree. In: Galbraith, S., editor, ANTS-XIV - 14th Algorithmic Number Theory Symposium, pp. 39–55, Auckland, New Zealand (2020)

[BJS14] Biasse, J.-F., Jao, D., Sankar, A.: A quantum algorithm for computing isogenies between supersingular elliptic curves. In: Meier, W., Mukhopadhyay, D. (eds.) INDOCRYPT 2014. LNCS, vol. 8885, pp. 428–442. Springer, Cham (2014). https://doi.org/10.1007/978-3-319-13039-2_25

[BKV19] Beullens, W., Kleinjung, T., Vercauteren, F.: CSI-FiSh: efficient isogeny based signatures through class group computations. In: Galbraith, S.D., Moriai, S. (eds.) ASIACRYPT 2019. LNCS, vol. 11921, pp. 227–247. Springer, Cham (2019). https://doi.org/10.1007/978-3-030-34578-5_9

[BKW20] Boneh, D., Kogan, D., Woo, K.: Oblivious pseudorandom functions from isogenies. In: Moriai, S., Wang, H. (eds.) ASIACRYPT 2020. LNCS, vol. 12492, pp. 520–550. Springer, Cham (2020). https://doi.org/10.1007/978-3-030-64834-3_18

[CD22] Castryck, W., Decru, T.: An efficient key recovery attack on SIDH (preliminary version). Cryptology ePrint Archive (2022)

[CJS14] Childs, A., Jao, D., Soukharev, V.: Constructing elliptic curve isogenies in quantum subexponential time. J. Math. Cryptol. **8**(1), 1–29 (2014)

[CK19] Colò, L., Kohel, D.: Orienting supersingular isogeny graphs. Number-Theoretic Methods in Cryptology (2019)

[CSRHT22] Chavez-Saab, J., Rodríguez-Henríquez, F., Tibouchi, M.: Verifiable isogeny walks: towards an isogeny-based postquantum VDF. In: AlTawy, R., Hülsing, A. (eds.) SAC 2021. LNCS, vol. 13203, pp. 441–460. Springer, Cham (2022). https://doi.org/10.1007/978-3-030-99277-4_21

[DFFdSG+21] De Feo, L., et al.: Séta: supersingular encryption from torsion attacks. In: Tibouchi, M., Wang, H. (eds.) ASIACRYPT 2021. LNCS, vol. 13093, pp. 249–278. Springer, Cham (2021). https://doi.org/10.1007/978-3-030-92068-5_9

[DFG19] De Feo, L., Galbraith, S.D.: SeaSign: compact isogeny signatures from class group actions. In: Ishai, Y., Rijmen, V. (eds.) EUROCRYPT 2019. LNCS, vol. 11478, pp. 759–789. Springer, Cham (2019). https://doi.org/10.1007/978-3-030-17659-4_26

[DFKL+20] De Feo, L., Kohel, D., Leroux, A., Petit, C., Wesolowski, B.: SQISign: compact post-quantum signatures from quaternions and isogenies. In: Moriai, S., Wang, H. (eds.) ASIACRYPT 2020. LNCS, vol. 12491, pp. 64–93. Springer, Cham (2020). https://doi.org/10.1007/978-3-030-64837-4_3

[DFLW22] De Feo, L., Leroux, A., Wesolowski, B.: SQISign twice as fast. Cryptology ePrint Archive, New algorithms for the deuring correspondence (2022)

[DFMPS19] De Feo, L., Masson, S., Petit, C., Sanso, A.: Verifiable delay functions from supersingular isogenies and pairings. In: Galbraith, S.D., Moriai, S. (eds.) ASIACRYPT 2019. LNCS, vol. 11921, pp. 248–277. Springer, Cham (2019). https://doi.org/10.1007/978-3-030-34578-5_10

[EHL+18] Eisenträger, K., Hallgren, S., Lauter, K., Morrison, T., Petit, C.: Supersingular isogeny graphs and endomorphism rings: reductions and solutions. In: Nielsen, J.B., Rijmen, V. (eds.) EUROCRYPT 2018. LNCS, vol. 10822, pp. 329–368. Springer, Cham (2018). https://doi.org/10.1007/978-3-319-78372-7_11

[EHL+20] Eisenträger, K., Hallgren, S., Leonardi, C., Morrison, T., Park, J.: Computing endomorphism rings of supersingular elliptic curves and connections to path-finding in isogeny graphs. Open Book Ser. **4**(1), 215–232 (2020)

[FKMT22] Fouotsa, T.B., Kutas, P., Merz, S.P., Ti, Y.B.: On the isogeny problem with torsion point information. In: Hanaoka, G., Shikata, J., Watanabe, Y. (eds.) Public-Key Cryptography PKC 2022. Lecture Notes in Computer Science, vol. 13177, pp. 142–161. Springer, Cham (2022)

[FP22] Fouotsa, T.B., Petit, C.: A new adaptive attack on SIDH. In: Galbraith, S.D. (ed.) CT-RSA 2022. LNCS, vol. 13161, pp. 322–344. Springer, Cham (2022). https://doi.org/10.1007/978-3-030-95312-6_14

[GPS17] Galbraith, S.D., Petit, C., Silva, J.: Identification protocols and signature schemes based on supersingular isogeny problems. In: Takagi, T., Peyrin, T. (eds.) ASIACRYPT 2017. LNCS, vol. 10624, pp. 3–33. Springer, Cham (2017). https://doi.org/10.1007/978-3-319-70694-8_1

[GPST16] Galbraith, S.D., Petit, C., Shani, B., Ti, Y.B.: On the security of supersingular isogeny cryptosystems. In: Cheon, J.H., Takagi, T. (eds.) ASIACRYPT 2016. LNCS, vol. 10031, pp. 63–91. Springer, Heidelberg (2016). https://doi.org/10.1007/978-3-662-53887-6_3

[JDF11] Jao, D., De Feo, L.: Towards quantum-resistant cryptosystems from supersingular elliptic curve isogenies. In: Yang, B.-Y. (ed.) PQCrypto 2011. LNCS, vol. 7071, pp. 19–34. Springer, Heidelberg (2011). https://doi.org/10.1007/978-3-642-25405-5_2

[JS14] Jao, D., Soukharev, V.: Isogeny-based quantum-resistant undeniable signatures. In: Mosca, M. (ed.) PQCrypto 2014. LNCS, vol. 8772, pp. 160–179. Springer, Cham (2014). https://doi.org/10.1007/978-3-319-11659-4_10

[KLPT14] Kohel, D., Lauter, K., Petit, C., Tignol, J.P.: On the quaternion-isogeny path problem. LMS J. Comput. Math. **17**(A), 418–432 (2014)

[KMP+20] Kutas, P., Martindale, C., Panny, L., Petit, C., Stange, K.E. : Weak instances of SIDH variants under improved torsion-point attacks. Cryptology ePrint Archive, Report 2020/633 (2020). https://eprint.iacr.org/2020/633

[KMPW21] Kutas, P., Merz, S.-P., Petit, C., Weitkämper, C.: One-way functions and malleability oracles: hidden shift attacks on isogeny-based protocols. In: Canteaut, A., Standaert, F.-X. (eds.) EUROCRYPT 2021. LNCS, vol. 12696, pp. 242–271. Springer, Cham (2021). https://doi.org/10.1007/978-3-030-77870-5_9

[Koh96] Kohel, D.: Endomorphism rings of elliptic curves over finite fields. PhD thesis, University of California at Berkeley (1996)

[MM22] Maino, L., Martindale, C.: An attack on SIDH with arbitrary starting curve. Cryptology ePrint Archive (2022)

[Pet17] Petit, C.: Faster algorithms for isogeny problems using torsion point images. In: Takagi, T., Peyrin, T. (eds.) ASIACRYPT 2017. LNCS, vol. 10625, pp. 330–353. Springer, Cham (2017). https://doi.org/10.1007/978-3-319-70697-9_12

[Rob22] Robert, D.: Breaking SIDH in polynomial time. Cryptology ePrint Archive (2022)

[Sch95] Schoof, R.: Counting points on elliptic curves over finite fields. J. de théorie des nombres de Bordeaux **7**(1), 219–254 (1995)

[UXT+22] Ueno, R., Xagawa, K., Tanaka, Y., Ito, A., Takahashi, J., Homma, N.: Curse of re-encryption: a generic power/em analysis on post-quantum kems. IACR Trans. Cryptographic Hardw. Embed. Syst., 296–322 (2022)

[Vél71] Vélu, J.: Isogénies entre courbes elliptiques. Comptes-Rendus de l'Académie des Sciences, Série I, 273:238–241, juillet (1971)

[Voi18] Voight, J.: Quaternion Algebras. Springer Cham (2018)

[Wat69] Waterhouse, W.C.: Abelian varieties over finite fields. Annales Scientifiques de l'E.N.S, (1969)

[Wes22] Wesolowski, B.: The supersingular isogeny path and endomorphism ring problems are equivalent. In: FOCS 2021–62nd Annual IEEE Symposium on Foundations of Computer Science (2022)

[YAJ+17] Yoo, Y., Azarderakhsh, R., Jalali, A., Jao, D., Soukharev, V.: A post-quantum digital signature scheme based on supersingular isogenies. In: Kiayias, A. (ed.) FC 2017. LNCS, vol. 10322, pp. 163–181. Springer, Cham (2017). https://doi.org/10.1007/978-3-319-70972-7_9

Group Action Key Encapsulation and Non-Interactive Key Exchange in the QROM

Julien Duman, Dominik Hartmann, Eike Kiltz, Sabrina Kunzweiler, Jonas Lehmann, and Doreen Riepel(✉)

Ruhr-Universität Bochum, Bochum, Germany
{julien.duman,dominik.hartmann,eike.kiltz,sabrina.kunzweiler, jonas.lehmann-c6j,doreen.riepel}@rub.de

Abstract. In the context of quantum-resistant cryptography, cryptographic group actions offer an abstraction of isogeny-based cryptography in the Commutative Supersingular Isogeny Diffie-Hellman (CSIDH) setting. In this work, we revisit the security of two previously proposed natural protocols: the Group Action Hashed ElGamal key encapsulation mechanism (GA-HEG KEM) and the Group Action Hashed Diffie-Hellman non-interactive key-exchange (GA-HDH NIKE) protocol. The latter protocol has already been considered to be used in practical protocols such as Post-Quantum WireGuard (S&P '21) and OPTLS (CCS '20).

We prove that *active* security of the two protocols in the Quantum Random Oracle Model (QROM) inherently relies on very strong variants of the Group Action Strong CDH problem, where the adversary is given arbitrary *quantum access* to a DDH oracle. That is, quantum accessible Strong CDH assumptions are not only sufficient but also necessary to prove active security of the GA-HEG KEM and the GA-HDH NIKE protocols.

Furthermore, we propose variants of the protocols with QROM security from the classical Strong CDH assumption, i.e., CDH with classical access to the DDH oracle. Our first variant uses key confirmation and can therefore only be applied in the KEM setting. Our second but considerably less efficient variant is based on the twinning technique by Cash et al. (EUROCRYPT '08) and in particular yields the first actively secure isogeny-based NIKE with QROM security from the standard CDH assumption.

Keywords: Group actions · CSIDH · Hashed ElGamal · NIKE · QROM · Twinning

1 Introduction

A non-interactive key exchange (NIKE) is a protocol that allows two parties to establish a common secret key in a non-interactive way. The first and most famous NIKE is the Diffie-Hellman key exchange [16] which forms the basis for a

S. Agrawal and D. Lin (Eds.): ASIACRYPT 2022, LNCS 13792, pp. 36–66, 2022.
https://doi.org/10.1007/978-3-031-22966-4_2

lot of other cryptographic protocols like ElGamal [19]. Most notably however, the existence of a secure NIKE implies secure key encapsulation mechanisms (KEM) (and hence public-key encryption) and authenticated key exchange (AKE) [21]. A NIKE can therefore be seen as one of the most basic and important primitives in cryptography.

The emergence of quantum computing however continues to have an unprecedented impact on public key cryptography. When scaled to a suitable size, quantum computers pose a threat to almost all classical public-key primitives, including Diffie-Hellman and ElGamal [36]. To mitigate this threat, researchers started building quantum resisting public-key cryptography based on certain quantum-hard problems on codes, lattices and isogenies. Even though quantum-resistant public-key encryption from lattices seems to offer the favorable trade-off over codes and isogenies in terms of speed, ciphertext expansion, and security, building an efficient (even passively secure) NIKE from codes or lattices remains an unsolved research problem.

Isogeny-Based Cryptography. A promising alternative approach to post-quantum security is based on isogenies. An isogeny is a non-constant homomorphism between elliptic curves. In an algebraic context, isogenies can be used to build a commutative group action that behaves similarly to exponentiation in finite fields. This was first observed by Couveignes [14] and independently by Rostovtsev and Stolbunov [34]. The first practical instantiation was obtained by Castryck et al. [12] which in contrast to previous work uses the group action on the set of *supersingular* elliptic curves. Throughout this paper, we will use the abstract framework of cryptographic group actions introduced by Alamati et al. [2] to model isogeny-based constructions. (See Sect. 2.3 for formal definitions.) At a syntactical level, cryptographic group actions allow for a simple Group Action Diffie-Hellman (GA-DH) key exchange and Group Action ElGamal (GA-EG) public-key encryption scheme. With this abstraction in mind, the famous Commutative Supersingular Isogeny Diffie-Hellman (CSIDH) key exchange protocol of [12] can be seen as a specific instantiation of GA-DH.

For cryptographic group actions, the analog of the traditional Computational Diffie-Hellman assumption (over prime-order groups) is the *Group Action Computational Diffie-Hellman assumption* (GA-CDH) [2,12,14,34], see also Definition 5. GA-CDH is sufficient to prove passive security of "hashed versions" of GA-DH and GA-EG in the random oracle model. In analogy to the prime-order group setting, for active security one requires a "strong" type of Computational Diffie-Hellman assumption [1]. Providing the adversary additional access to a Group Action Decisional Diffie-Hellman oracle GA-DDH$(\cdot, \cdot)$, i.e. an oracle which tells us whether a pair of elements forms a Diffie-Hellman tuple, defines the *Group Action Strong Computational Diffie-Hellman assumption* (GA-StCDH). The prefix *strong* refers to the fact that the first input to this oracle is fixed (as opposed to the stronger and non-falsifiable *gap* assumptions). This assumption is well-known in the standard prime-order group setting and has already been used in proving active security of several protocols [15,28,38] in the group action setting as well.[1]

QUANTUM RANDOM ORACLE MODEL. The random-oracle model (ROM) [7] is commonly used in modern cryptography to argue *practical security* of cryptographic schemes. Adversaries with access to quantum computers will be able to implement the hash function on those, and therefore can evaluate the hash function on arbitrary quantum superpositions. To account for this gain in capabilities, the *quantum(-accessible)* random-oracle model (QROM) has been introduced [9]. The QROM has become the accepted model for proving post-quantum security and it is generally believed that proofs in the classical ROM are not sufficient to claim post-quantum security.

ACTIVELY SECURE KEMS AND NIKE PROTOCOLS. In this work we are interested in constructing actively (i.e. IND-CCA) secure KEMs and actively secure NIKE protocols over cryptographic group actions.

Let us first look at the simpler case of KEMs. Generally speaking, we know of two natural approaches to build efficient IND-CCA secure KEMs. The first approach is generic and applies the Fujisaki-Okamoto (FO) transform [22,24] to an IND-CPA secure PKE scheme (such as GA-EG) to obtain an IND-CCA secure KEM, with provable security in the QROM. The second, non-generic approach is to adapt the well-known (prime-order group) Hashed ElGamal encryption framework of [1] to group actions by "hashing the raw KEM key" to obtain the *Group Action Hashed ElGamal KEM* (GA-HEG). Indeed, [38] proved the security of GA-HEG (called CSIDH-ECIES in [38]) under the GA-StCDH assumption in the ROM.[2] GA-HEG was implicitly and explicitly used in [15,28,38] and its active (IND-CCA) security in the QROM was left as an open problem in [38].[3]

For building an actively secure NIKE, one cannot apply the FO transformation and hence has to resort to adapting the (prime-order group) Hashed Diffie-Hellman NIKE [21] to obtain the *Group Action Hashed Diffie-Hellman* NIKE protocol (GA-HDH). To the best of our knowledge, the active security of the GA-HDH NIKE has not been formally analyzed yet, not even in the ROM. This is in particular unsatisfactory since GA-HDH has already been considered to be used in practical protocols such as Post-Quantum WireGuard [26] and OPTLS [35].

---

[1] We stress that GA-StCDH over standard cryptographic group actions is well defined (and falsifiable), even though it is an interactive assumption. Furthermore, for some groups actions (i.e., ones implied by cryptographic pairings over prime-order groups) the Decisional Diffie-Hellman oracle is publicly computable and hence GA-StCDH becomes non-interactive.

[2] The QROM proof of a variant called CSIDH-PSEC in [38] is severely flawed (see the full version [18] for details).

[3] There also exist IND-CCA secure PKE schemes constructed directly from CSIDH, using additional structure of the elliptic curves. [31] proposed the SimS scheme which is an extension of SiGamal [20] and relies on a non-standard knowledge-of-exponent assumption to achieve IND-CCA security in the standard model. These protocols and assumptions cannot be modeled in the abstract group action framework.

In conclusion, while the IND-CCA security of GA-HEG in the ROM is known to be implied by the GA-StCDH assumption, it remains an open problem to prove its IND-CCA security in the QROM (under any assumption). Similarly, studying the active security of the GA-HDH NIKE in the QROM also remains an open problem.

1.1 Our Contributions

In this paper we study the active security of the Group Action Hashed Diffie-Hellman NIKE GA-HDH and the Group Action Hashed ElGamal KEM GA-HEG in the QROM, and derive variants thereof with improved security guarantees. We now discuss our results in detail. For an overview of our results obtained for KEMs we refer to Fig. 1.

GA-HEG KEM AND GA-HDH NIKE. It is easy to see that in the (non-quantum) ROM the active security of GA-HEG is implied by the GA-StCDH assumption. The first main contribution of this paper is to notice that in the QROM one requires a considerably stronger assumptions to prove security of GA-HEG. To this end we define the following two stronger variants of GA-StCDH which differ only in the access to the decision oracle (for implications see Fig. 1):

- Partial Quantum access Strong Diffie-Hellman (GA-PQ-StCDH): the first input to the GA-DDH$(\cdot,\cdot)$ oracle is classical and the second is in quantum superposition.
- Full Quantum access Strong Diffie-Hellman (GA-FQ-StCDH): both inputs to the GA-DDH$(\cdot,\cdot)$ oracle are in quantum superposition.

Similar to the QROM, the answer of a quantum superposition query to the two quantum-accessible GA-DDH oracles is also in quantum superposition.

Our first main theorem states that under the GA-FQ-StCDH assumption (full quantum access to the DDH oracle), GA-HEG is IND-CCA secure in the QROM. Furthermore, IND-CCA security in the QROM of GA-HEG implies the GA-PQ-StCDH assumption (partial quantum access to the DDH oracle), hence GA-PQ-StCDH is necessary for GA-HEG's IND-CCA security. The situation for the GA-HDH NIKE is similar, with the difference that "double base" strong assumptions (called GA-DPQ-StCDH and GA-DFQ-StCDH) are required.

This leaves us in the alarming situation that active security of GA-HEG and GA-HDH inherently require a group action CDH assumption with quantum access to the DDH oracle. Due to the quantum access, the latter assumptions cannot be considered as standard assumptions and require further cryptanalysis before we can recommend using GA-HEG KEM and GA-HDH NIKE in practice.

We will now propose two modifications to get security without quantum access to the decision oracles. The first and more efficient modification is using "key confirmation" and only works for KEMs. The second and less efficient modification relies on the "twinning technique" and can be applied to NIKEs and KEMs.

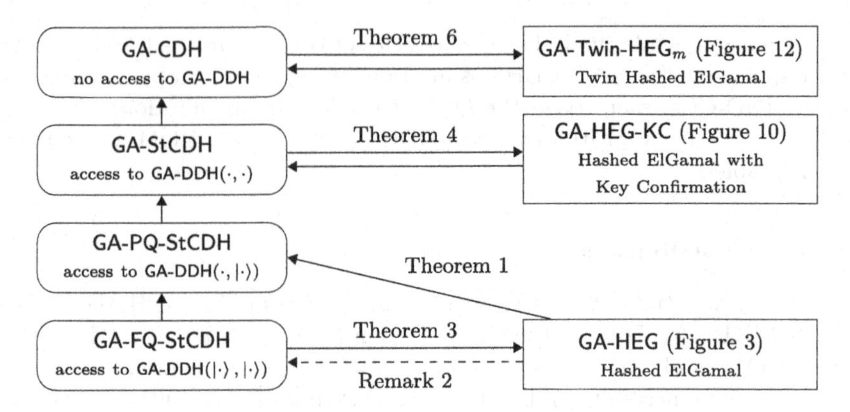

Fig. 1. Overview of our assumptions and results for different variants of hashed ElGamal. The assumptions (elements with rounded corners) are given in Definitions 5 and 6. Solid arrows without indication of a theorem correspond to trivial implications. For the assumptions the only difference is a more limited access to the decision oracle GA-DDH, where $|\cdot\rangle$ denotes quantum access. The dashed arrow holds for *quantum* security, where the adversary is allowed to issue decapsulation queries in superposition.

GA-HEG-KC KEM: Key Confirmation. Our first method is to update GA-HEG the KEM with a key confirmation hash, i.e., every ciphertext additionally contains a hash of the "raw KEM key". This only increases the ciphertext size by one hash, but allows for a different IND-CCA proof technique in the QROM. To be more precise, in the classical ROM, one can use the additional hash to extract the secret information from a ciphertext. In the QROM, this is more involved, but we can use the extractable oracle simulator from [17] to use similar techniques and give a security proof only relying on the more standard GA-StCDH assumption. Specifically, we rely on the fact that decapsulation queries are classical, which allows us to partially measure the simulated random oracle and extract its queries without noticeably disturbing its quantum state.

Unfortunately, it is not possible to use key confirmation in a NIKE setting.

GA-Twin-HEG$_m$ KEM and GA-Twin-HDH$_m$ NIKE: Twinning. We show how to use the twinning technique [11] in the context of group actions to build an actively secure KEM and NIKE from the standard GA-CDH assumption (no DDH oracle access) in the QROM. Since group actions only have limited structure compared to prime-order groups, it seems unavoidable to pursue a bitwise approach for the twinning technique. Our main leverage is a trapdoor test which allows us to check if several adversarial inputs form a Diffie-Hellman tuple with the challenge elements. The failure probability of this trapdoor test can be reduced to the generic quantum search problem, for which the quantum hardness is optimally bounded by the Grover algorithm. Although this approach does not achieve practical efficiency, it is interesting from a theoretical viewpoint. We specify the twinning parameter m for 128-bit security to instantiate the twinned versions of our GA-Twin-HEG$_m$ KEM and GA-Twin-HDH$_m$ NIKE. At this point we want to highlight that our $\mathsf{GA\text{-}Twin\text{-}HDH}_m$ protocol is the only known NIKE with active security from a standard assumption (without quantum accessible DDH oracles).

EFFICIENCY COMPARISON. In Table 1 in Sect. 6, we give an overview of the schemes analyzed in this work and compare them to the FO variant GA-EG-FO of Group Action ElGamal. The KEM variants GA-HEG and $\mathsf{GA\text{-}Twin\text{-}HEG}_m$ share the same minimal ciphertext size but we cannot recommend using them since GA-HEG's security inherently relies on the GA-FQ-StCDH assumption (with quantum accessible DDH oracle) and $\mathsf{GA\text{-}Twin\text{-}HEG}_m$ is computationally very expensive. In comparison, the KEM variants GA-HEG-KC and GA-EG-FO only add one additional hash to the ciphertext but offer security from standard assumptions. Here GA-HEG-KC is preferable since decapsulation is about twice as efficient as in GA-EG-FO (due to FO's re-encryption).

As for the more important case of NIKEs, one either has to use the efficient GA-HDH variant with security under the GA-DFQ-StCDH assumption (with quantum accessible DDH oracles) or use the inefficient $\mathsf{GA\text{-}Twin\text{-}HDH}_m$ NIKE. We leave it as an important open problem to construct a practically efficient actively secure NIKE under a standard hardness assumption.

QROM PROOF DETAILS. One of the standard tools to prove security in the QROM is the O2H [37] lemma, which unfortunately leads to quite loose bounds. Recently, there has been a lot of progress in developing new variants which give tighter bounds, such as the measure-rewind-measure O2H (MRM-O2H) [30] lemma. While these variants give usually tighter bounds, they can often only be applied in more limited scenarios due to additional constraints. In our work we show how to apply MRM to GA-HEG and $\mathsf{GA\text{-}Twin\text{-}HEG}_m$ to obtain tighter bounds than the by applying the original O2H lemma. For proving GA-HEG-KC we need to extract the preimages of the key-confirmation hash. We use the extractable random-oracle simulator of [17], which allows use to prove it from the GA-StCDH assumption.

For $\mathsf{GA\text{-}Twin\text{-}HEG}_m$ and $\mathsf{GA\text{-}Twin\text{-}HDH}_m$, the main tool to remove the need for the GA-StCDH is the trapdoor test. While it is easy to show its indistinguishability for regular groups in the standard model, it is unclear whether or not a quantum adversary has a significant advantage against the trapdoor test compared to a classical adversary. We solve the second problem by showing that the indistinguishability of the trapdoor test can be (tightly) reduced to the Generic Distinguishing Problem (GDP). This allows us to use well-known results on the hardness of quantum search to bound the advantage of such adversaries and apply the trapdoor test as a substitute for the decision oracle of the GA-StCDH assumption.

1.2 Further Applications

We believe our QROM analysis carries over to the following primitives and constructions.

AUTHENTICATED KEY EXCHANGE. Kawashima et al. as well as de Kock et al. [15,28] translated the Diffie-Hellman based AKE protocol of [13] to the CSIDH setting and proved security in the ROM assuming the GA-StCDH assumption. However, both works left it as an open question to prove security in the QROM. Our analysis demonstrates that this proof will only work assuming (at least partial) quantum access to the decision oracle. In this case, our proof techniques carry over directly. Alternatively, we can also extend the AKE protocol by an additional round to include key confirmation. Using the same technique as in our result on hashed ElGamal with key confirmation will allow to prove security of this extended AKE protocol in the QROM based on the GA-StCDH assumption without quantum access to the decision oracle. However, the additional benefit here is that key confirmation enables explicit authentication, whereas the protocol without key confirmation only achieves implicit authentication.

SIGNCRYPTION AND AUTHENTICATED KEMS. The DH-AKEM which was analyzed in the context of the HPKE standard [3] can easily be translated to the group action setting. The scheme is syntactically a signcryption KEM and will be combined with a symmetric encryption scheme. This construction, also named the authenticated mode of HPKE, was proposed to be used in the Message Layer Security (MLS) secure group messaging protocol [6] and the Encrypted Server Name Indication (ESNI) extension for TLS 1.3 [32]. So far, a post-quantum secure instantiation was not proposed, but our results show how to prove security of a group action based construction in the QROM under GA-FQ-StCDH (full quantum access to the decision oracle). Alternatively, we can also extend the scheme by key confirmation and prove security under GA-StCDH.

POST-QUANTUM SECURE TLS. Currently, there is a great effort in replacing the Diffie-Hellman based approach in the TLS handshake by a post-quantum secure alternative. In order to avoid signature schemes which are rather inefficient, a generic KEM-based approach was considered to allow for an easy instantiation [35], however at the cost of efficiency since it requires an additional round. Instead of signatures, it is also possible to use a NIKE directly, as considered for the case of long-term Diffie-Hellman keys in the OPTLS protocol by Krawczyk and Wee in [29] and in a subsequent IETF draft [33]. In this case, a security analysis of the group-action NIKE in the QROM is crucial and our work provides the first results in this direction, namely that a security proof for group action OPTLS will need to rely at least on the GA-PQ-StCDH assumption (partial quantum access to the decision oracles) and is implied by the GA-FQ-StCDH assumption (full quantum access).

MORE APPLICATIONS. In the group setting, Hashed ElGamal can be used to build multi-recipient multi-message PKE (mmPKE) by using the same randomness for multiple messages. This reduces sender bandwidth and computation substantially and can be used in Continuous Group Key Agreement (CGKA), which underlies modern and scalable Secure Group Messaging (SGM) such as MLS [6] to significantly improve performance [4]. Since GA-HEG has an identical structure, reusing randomness can yield a similar construction with post-quantum security. This is a first step towards efficient, post-quantum secure SGM.

Game IND-CCA($\mathcal{A}$)	Oracle DECAPS(ct)
00 $(\mathsf{pk}, \mathsf{sk}) \leftarrow \mathsf{Gen}$	06 **if** $\mathsf{ct} = \mathsf{ct}^*$
01 $b \xleftarrow{\$} \{0,1\}$	07 **return** $\bot$
02 $(\mathsf{ct}^*, K_0) \leftarrow \mathsf{Encaps}(\mathsf{pk})$	08 **return** $\mathsf{Dec}(\mathsf{sk}, \mathsf{ct})$
03 $K_1 \xleftarrow{\$} \mathcal{K}$	
04 $b' \leftarrow \mathcal{A}^{\text{DECAPS}}(\mathsf{pk}, \mathsf{ct}^*, K_b)$	
05 **return** $[\![b = b']\!]$	

Fig. 2. The IND-CCA game for a key encapsulation mechanism KEM.

2 Preliminaries

For integers m, n where $m < n$, $[m, n]$ denotes the set $\{m, m+1, ..., n\}$. For $m = 1$, we simply write $[n]$. By $\log(x)$ we denote the logarithm over the reals with base 2. For a (finite) set S, $s \xleftarrow{\$} S$ denotes that s is sampled uniformly and independently at random from S. $y \leftarrow \mathcal{A}(x_1, x_2, ...)$ denotes that on input $x_1, x_2, ...$ the probabilistic algorithm $\mathcal{A}$ returns y. $\mathcal{A}^{\text{O}}$ denotes that algorithm $\mathcal{A}$ has access to oracle O. An adversary is a probabilistic algorithm. We will use code-based games, where $\Pr[\text{G} \Rightarrow 1]$ denotes the probability that the final output of game G is 1. The notation $[\![B]\!]$, where B is a boolean statement, refers to a bit that is 1 if the statement is true and 0 otherwise. For all algorithms and oracles, we implicitly require that they check whether (adversarial) inputs are from the expected input space. If this is not the case, the algorithm (oracle) will simply return a failure symbol $\bot$.

2.1 Key Encapsulation Mechanisms

SYNTAX. Let $\mathcal{PK}$, $\mathcal{SK}$, $\mathcal{C}$, $\mathcal{K}$ be sets. A *key encapsulation mechanism* $\mathsf{KEM} = (\mathsf{Gen}, \mathsf{Encaps}, \mathsf{Decaps})$ consists of the following three algorithms

- Gen: The key generation algorithm outputs a public key $\mathsf{pk} \in \mathcal{PK}$ and a secret key $\mathsf{sk} \in \mathcal{SK}$.
- Encaps(pk): On input a public key pk, the encapsulation algorithm returns a ciphertext $\mathsf{ct} \in \mathcal{C}$ and a key $K \in \mathcal{K}$, where ct is an encapsulation of K.
- Decaps(sk, ct): On input a secret key sk and a ciphertext ct, the decapsulation algorithm returns a key $K \in \mathcal{K}$ or a special failure symbol $\bot$.

We require perfect correctness, i.e. for all $(\mathsf{pk}, \mathsf{sk}) \leftarrow \mathsf{Gen}$, $(\mathsf{ct}, K) \leftarrow \mathsf{Encaps}(\mathsf{pk})$, we have $\mathsf{Decaps}(\mathsf{sk}, \mathsf{ct}) = K$.

Definition 1 (Security against Chosen Ciphertext Attacks (IND-CCA)). *Consider the* IND-CCA *security game in Fig. 2. For a key encapsulation mechanism* KEM *we define the advantage of $\mathcal{A}$ winning the game as*

$$\mathsf{Adv}^{\mathsf{IND\text{-}CCA}}_{\mathsf{KEM}}(\mathcal{A}) := \left|\Pr[\mathsf{IND\text{-}CCA}(\mathcal{A}) \Rightarrow 1] - 1/2\right|.$$

2.2 Non-Interactive Key Exchange

We recall syntax and the CKS security model of a Non-Interactive Key Exchange (NIKE) scheme, as defined in [11,21].

SYNTAX. A non-interactive key exchange scheme NIKE consists of three algorithms $\mathsf{NIKE.Setup}$, $\mathsf{NIKE.Gen}$ and $\mathsf{NIKE.SharedKey}$ together with an identity space $\mathcal{ID}$ and a shared key space $\mathcal{SHK}$, where identities in the scheme are only used to track which public key is associated to which user.

- $\mathsf{NIKE.Setup}$: The setup algorithm outputs a set of public parameters pp.
- $\mathsf{NIKE.Gen}(\mathsf{pp}, \mathsf{ID})$: On input pp and $\mathsf{ID} \in \mathcal{ID}$, the key generation algorithm outputs a public key pk and a secret key sk.
- $\mathsf{NIKE.SharedKey}(\mathsf{ID}_1, \mathsf{pk}_1, \mathsf{ID}_2, \mathsf{sk}_2)$: On input $\mathsf{ID}_1 \in \mathcal{ID}$ together with a public key pk_1 and $\mathsf{ID}_2 \in \mathcal{ID}$ together with a secret key sk_2, the shared key algorithm outputs a shared key K. In case $\mathsf{ID}_1 = \mathsf{ID}_2$, the algorithm outputs a failure symbol $\perp$.

CORRECTNESS. We require that for any pair of identities $\mathsf{ID}_1, \mathsf{ID}_2 \in \mathcal{ID}$ and any corresponding key pairs $(\mathsf{pk}_1, \mathsf{sk}_1)$ and $(\mathsf{pk}_2, \mathsf{sk}_2)$, it holds that

$$\mathsf{NIKE.SharedKey}(\mathsf{ID}_1, \mathsf{pk}_1, \mathsf{ID}_2, \mathsf{sk}_2) = \mathsf{NIKE.SharedKey}(\mathsf{ID}_2, \mathsf{pk}_2, \mathsf{ID}_1, \mathsf{sk}_1).$$

CKS SECURITY MODEL. The security of a NIKE protocol is modeled as a game between a challenger and an adversary $\mathcal{A}$. First, the challenger runs $\mathsf{NIKE.Setup}$ to generate the public parameter pp which it outputs to $\mathcal{A}$. The challenger also draws a random bit b and gives $\mathcal{A}$ access to the following oracles.

- REGISTERHONEST: $\mathcal{A}$ supplies an identity $\mathsf{ID} \in \mathcal{ID}$ and the challenger runs $\mathsf{NIKE.Gen}(\mathsf{pp}, \mathsf{ID})$ to generate a key pair $(\mathsf{pk}, \mathsf{sk})$. It records $(\mathit{honest}, \mathsf{ID}, \mathsf{pk}, \mathsf{sk})$ and returns the public key pk to $\mathcal{A}$.
- REGISTERCORRUPT: $\mathcal{A}$ supplies an identity $\mathsf{ID} \in \mathcal{ID}$ and a public key pk and the challenger records $(\mathit{corrupt}, \mathsf{ID}, \mathsf{pk}, \perp)$. If $\mathcal{A}$ issues a query with the same ID again later, only the most recent entry is kept. Note here that we do not require that $\mathcal{A}$ knows the corresponding secret key.
- CORRUPTREVEAL: $\mathcal{A}$ supplies two identities ID_1 and ID_2 with the restriction that one identity was registered as *honest* and the other one as *corrupt*, otherwise the oracle returns $\perp$. The challenger looks in its record to fetch the secret key of the honest party and the public key of the corrupted party. If ID_1 was honest, it computes and returns $\mathsf{NIKE.SharedKey}(\mathsf{ID}_2, \mathsf{pk}_2, \mathsf{ID}_1, \mathsf{sk}_1)$ and otherwise $\mathsf{NIKE.SharedKey}(\mathsf{ID}_1, \mathsf{pk}_1, \mathsf{ID}_2, \mathsf{sk}_2)$.
- TEST: $\mathcal{A}$ supplies two identities ID_1 and ID_2 with the restriction that both were registered as *honest* and $\mathsf{ID}_1 \neq \mathsf{ID}_2$, otherwise the oracle returns $\perp$. The challenger fetches the public key of ID_1 and the secret key of ID_2 from its records and computes $K_0 = \mathsf{NIKE.SharedKey}(\mathsf{ID}_1, \mathsf{pk}_1, \mathsf{ID}_2, \mathsf{sk}_2)$. It also chooses a random key $K_1 \xleftarrow{\$} \mathcal{SHK}$ and records it for later. It outputs K_b, depending on the bit b chosen at the beginning. If $b = 1$ and $\mathcal{A}$ queries the same identities again, in either order, the recorded key is output again.

The oracles can be queried adaptively and an arbitrary number of times. We require that no identity that was registered as corrupt can be later registered as honest, and vice versa. Finally, the adversary outputs a bit b'.

Definition 2 (Security of NIKE). *Consider the* CKS *security game as described above. Then the advantage of adversary $\mathcal{A}$ against a non-interactive key exchange scheme* NIKE *is defined as*

$$\mathsf{Adv}^{\mathsf{CKS}}_{\mathsf{NIKE}}(\mathcal{A}) := |\Pr[b = b'] - 1/2| .$$

2.3 (Restricted) Effective Group Actions

We recall the definition of (restricted) effective group actions from [2], which provides an abstract framework to build cryptographic primitives relying on isogeny-based assumptions such as CSIDH.

Definition 3 (Group Action). *Let $(\mathcal{G}, \cdot)$ be a group with identity element $e \in \mathcal{G}$, and $\mathcal{X}$ a set. A map*

$$\star : \mathcal{G} \times \mathcal{X} \to \mathcal{X}$$

is a group action if it satisfies the following properties:

1. *Identity: $e \star x = x$ for all $x \in \mathcal{X}$.*
2. *Compatibility: $(g \cdot h) \star x = g \star (h \star x)$ for all $g, h \in \mathcal{G}$ and $x \in \mathcal{X}$.*

Remark 1. Throughout this paper, we only consider group actions, where $\mathcal{G}$ is commutative. Moreover we assume that the group action is regular. This means that for any $x, y \in \mathcal{X}$ there exists precisely one $g \in \mathcal{G}$ satisfying $y = g \star x$.

Definition 4 (Effective Group Action). *Let $(\mathcal{G}, \mathcal{X}, \star)$ be a group action satisfying the following properties:*

1. *$\mathcal{G}$ is finite and there exist efficient (PPT) algorithms for membership testing, equality testing, (random) sampling, group operation and inversion.*
2. *The set $\mathcal{X}$ is finite and there exist efficient algorithms for membership testing and to compute a unique representation.*
3. *There exists a distinguished element $\tilde{x} \in \mathcal{X}$ with known representation.*
4. *There exists an efficient algorithm to evaluate the group action, i.e. to compute $g \star x$ given g and x.*

Then we call $\tilde{x} \in \mathcal{X}$ the origin and $(\mathcal{G}, \mathcal{X}, \star, \tilde{x})$ an effective group action (EGA).

In practice, the requirements from the definition of EGA are often to strong. Therefore we will consider the weaker notion of restricted effective group actions which is defined in the full version [18].
Alamati et al. [2] introduced the definition of a weak unpredictable group action. We will use a different notation for that property which is syntactically closer to the prime-order group setting. Note that both definitions are equivalent. In particular, we will use the following assumption.

Definition 5 (Group Action Computational Diffie-Hellman Problem). *On input* $(g \star \tilde{x}, h \star \tilde{x})$, *the group action computational Diffie-Hellman problem* (GA-CDH) *requires to compute the set element* $gh \star \tilde{x}$. *To an effective group action* EGA, *we associate the advantage function of an adversary* $\mathcal{A}$ *as*

$$\mathsf{Adv}_{\mathsf{EGA}}^{\mathsf{GA\text{-}CDH}}(\mathcal{A}) := \Pr[\mathcal{A}(g \star \tilde{x}, h \star \tilde{x}) \Rightarrow gh \star \tilde{x}] \ ,$$

where $g, h \xleftarrow{\$} \mathcal{G}$.

The most promising post-quantum secure instantiation of REGAs is provided by CSIDH. We recall its properties in the full version [18].

2.4 QROM Preliminaries

We use different well-known results from post-quantum cryptography. Specifically, our proofs use the oneway-to-hiding [37] (O2H) lemma from [5] and its measure-rewind-measure (MRM) variant from [30] as well as the online extractable quantum random oracle framework from [17]. We recall the MRM O2H lemma below. Further definitions as well as some basic techniques such as random oracle simulation can be found in the full version [18].

Lemma 1 (Measure-Rewind-Measure O2H. Lemma 3.3 in [30]). *Let* $\mathsf{G}, \mathsf{H}\colon \mathcal{X} \to \mathcal{Y}$ *be random functions,* z *be a random value, and* $\mathcal{S} \subseteq \mathcal{X}$ *be a random set such that* $\mathsf{G}(x) = \mathsf{H}(x)$ *for every* $x \notin \mathcal{S}$. *The tuple* $(\mathsf{G}, \mathsf{H}, \mathcal{S}, z)$ *may have arbitrary joint distribution. Furthermore, let* $\mathcal{A}^{\mathsf{O}}$ *be a unitary/reversible quantum oracle algorithm which queries oracle* O *with query depth* d. *Then we can construct an algorithm* $\mathsf{Ext}^{\mathsf{G},\mathsf{H}}(z)$ *such that the running time of* Ext *is about at most three times the one of* $\mathcal{A}^{\mathsf{O}}$ *and*

$$\left| \Pr_{\mathsf{H},z}[\mathcal{A}^{\mathsf{H}}(z) \Rightarrow 1] - \Pr_{\mathsf{G},z}[\mathcal{A}^{\mathsf{G}}(z) \Rightarrow 1] \right| \leq 4d \Pr_{\mathsf{G},\mathsf{H},\mathcal{S},z}[\mathcal{S} \cap \mathcal{T} \neq \emptyset \colon \mathcal{T} \leftarrow \mathsf{Ext}^{\mathsf{G},\mathsf{H}}(z)].$$

Some of our proofs rely on the hardness of the Generic Distinguishing Problem (GDP), a decisional variant of the Generic Search Problem (GSP) [25,27,39]. Intuitively, an adversary gets oracle access to a function from some domain $\mathcal{D}$ into $\{0,1\}$, which is either the all-zero function or a function where the probability that any given point maps to 1 is small (i.e. bounded by some $\lambda \in (0,1)$), and has to decide which is the case. While the complexity of this problem is clear in the classical case, it is somewhat more difficult in the quantum case. We recall and adapt the well-known bounds to the GDP problem in this section.

Lemma 2 (Generic Distinguishing Problem, decision version of Lemma 2 in [5], Lemma 2.9 from [25]). *Let* $\mathsf{F}\colon \mathcal{X} \to \{0,1\}$ *be a random function drawn from a distribution such that* $\Pr[\mathsf{F}(x) = 1] \leq \lambda$ *for all* x *and* $\mathsf{K}\colon \mathcal{X} \to \{0\}$ *be the zero-function. Let* $\mathcal{A}$ *be a* q*-query algorithm with query depth* d *with quantum-access to its oracle. Then*

$$\mathsf{Adv}_{\mathsf{F},q,d}^{\mathsf{GDP}}(\mathcal{A}) := \left| \Pr[\mathsf{GDP}_{\mathsf{F},0}^{\mathcal{A}} \Rightarrow 1] - \Pr[\mathsf{GDP}_{\mathsf{F},1}^{\mathcal{A}} \Rightarrow 1] \right| \leq 4\sqrt{(d+1)q\lambda}, \quad (1)$$

Gen	Encaps(pk)	Decaps(sk, ct)
00 $\mathsf{sk} := g \xleftarrow{\$} \mathcal{G}$	03 $r \xleftarrow{\$} \mathcal{G}$	07 $z := \mathsf{sk} \star \mathsf{ct}$
01 $\mathsf{pk} := g \star \tilde{x}$	04 $\mathsf{ct} := r \star \tilde{x}$	08 $K := \mathsf{H}(\mathsf{ct}, z)$
02 **return** $(\mathsf{pk}, \mathsf{sk})$	05 $K := \mathsf{H}(\mathsf{ct}, r \star \mathsf{pk})$	09 **return** K
	06 **return** (ct, K)	

Fig. 3. Key encapsulation mechanism GA-HEG for an effective group action $\mathsf{EGA} = (\mathcal{G}, \mathcal{X}, \star, \tilde{x})$, where $\mathsf{H} : \mathcal{X} \times \mathcal{X} \to \{0,1\}^\kappa$ is a hash function.

where $\mathsf{GDP}^{\mathcal{A}}_{\mathsf{F},0} := \mathcal{A}^{\mathsf{K}}()$ *and* $\mathsf{GDP}^{\mathcal{A}}_{\mathsf{F},1} := \mathcal{A}^{\mathsf{F}}()$. *Moreover, if the outputs of* F *are independent we have*

$$\mathsf{Adv}^{\mathsf{GDP}}_{\mathsf{F},q,d}(\mathcal{A}) \leq 8(q+1)^2\lambda. \quad (2)$$

We prove Eq. (1) in the full version [18]. The bound in Eq. (2) is a reformulation from Lemma 2.9 from [25].

3 Necessary Assumptions for Group Action KEM and NIKE in the QROM

In this section we will first recall the two schemes we are looking at: Group Action Hashed ElGamal and the Group Action Hashed Diffie-Hellman NIKE scheme. We denote the schemes by GA-HEG and GA-HDH, respectively.

Group Action Hashed ElGamal. The scheme is given in Fig. 3. Note that this is the same scheme as the CSIDH-ECIES-KEM considered in [38]. The public parameters consist of an effective group action $\mathsf{EGA} = (\mathcal{G}, \mathcal{X}, \star, \tilde{x})$ and a hash function $\mathsf{H} : \mathcal{X}^2 \to \{0,1\}^\kappa$. Further we set $\mathcal{PK} = \mathcal{X}$, $\mathcal{SK} = \mathcal{G}$ and $\mathcal{K} = \{0,1\}^\kappa$. The key generation algorithm samples a random group element $g \xleftarrow{\$} \mathcal{G}$ as secret key. In order to compute the public key, g is applied to the origin element $\tilde{x}$ using the group action operation. The set element $\mathsf{pk} = g \star \tilde{x}$ is the public key. The encapsulation algorithm also first samples a random group element $r \xleftarrow{\$} \mathcal{G}$ and then calculates the ciphertext $\mathsf{ct} = r \star \tilde{x}$. The key is derived by first computing $r \star \mathsf{pk}$ (the shared DH value) and subsequently hashing $r \star \mathsf{pk}$ together with the ciphertext ct. Decapsulation first recomputes the shared DH value $g \star \mathsf{ct} = r \star \mathsf{pk}$ and then applies the hash function H. Correctness of the scheme holds due to the commutativity of the group action.

Group Action Hashed Diffie-Hellman. A schematic overview of the hashed Diffie-Hellman NIKE scheme GA-HDH is given in Fig. 4. As in the hashed ElGamal scheme, the public parameters pp include the description of EGA together with a hash function $\mathsf{H} : \{0,1\}^* \to \{0,1\}^\kappa$ such that $\mathcal{PK} = \mathcal{X}$, $\mathcal{SK} = \mathcal{G}$ and $\mathcal{SHK} = \{0,1\}^\kappa$. We assume that $\mathcal{ID} = \{0,1\}^\mu$, which means that each identity is represented by a bitstring of length μ and there is a natural ordering $<$ on the space of identities. On input an $\mathsf{ID} \in \mathcal{ID}$, the key generation algorithm chooses a group element $g \xleftarrow{\$} \mathcal{G}$ which will be the secret key $\mathsf{sk}_{\mathsf{ID}}$. The public key is

Alice A	**Bob B**
$\mathsf{sk_A} = a \xleftarrow{\$} \mathcal{G}$	$\mathsf{sk_B} = b \xleftarrow{\$} \mathcal{G}$
$\mathsf{pk_A} = a \star \tilde{x}$	$\mathsf{pk_B} = b \star \tilde{x}$
$z := a \star \mathsf{pk_B}$	$z := b \star \mathsf{pk_A}$
$K := \mathsf{H}(\mathsf{A}, \mathsf{B}, \mathsf{pk_A}, \mathsf{pk_B}, z)$	

Fig. 4. Group action Non-Interactive Key Exchange scheme GA-HDH for an effective group action $\mathsf{EGA} = (\mathcal{G}, \mathcal{X}, \star, \tilde{x})$, where $\mathsf{H} : \{0,1\}^* \to \{0,1\}^\kappa$ is a hash function.

computed as $\mathsf{pk_{ID}} = g \star \tilde{x} \in \mathcal{X}$. The shared key of an identity ID_1 with public key $\mathsf{pk}_{\mathsf{ID}_1} = x$ and an identity $\mathsf{ID}_2 \neq \mathsf{ID}_1$ with secret key $\mathsf{sk}_{\mathsf{ID}_2} = g$ is defined as

$$K = \begin{cases} \mathsf{H}(\mathsf{ID}_1, \mathsf{ID}_2, \mathsf{pk}_{\mathsf{ID}_1}, \mathsf{pk}_{\mathsf{ID}_2}, g \star x) & \textbf{if } \mathsf{ID}_1 < \mathsf{ID}_2 \\ \mathsf{H}(\mathsf{ID}_2, \mathsf{ID}_1, \mathsf{pk}_{\mathsf{ID}_2}, \mathsf{pk}_{\mathsf{ID}_1}, g \star x) & \textbf{if } \mathsf{ID}_2 < \mathsf{ID}_1 \end{cases} .$$

Correctness again holds because of the commutativity of the group action itself and the ordering of IDs.

One of the goals of this work is to prove these schemes secure in the QROM (cf. Sect. 4). However, as it turns out, we will need stronger assumptions for the proofs than those defined in the literature. In the next section we introduce the corresponding assumptions. Furthermore, we show that a (somewhat) stronger assumption is indeed necessary by showing that it is implied by the security of the schemes themselves.

3.1 Computational Group Action Diffie-Hellman with Quantum Oracle Access

Our new assumptions are all variants of the group action strong computational Diffie-Hellman problem (GA-StCDH). The GA-StCDH assumption is basically the translation of the strong CDH problem to group actions (cf. also [15,28]), where the adversary is given access to a (fixed-base) decision oracle. What we need for our proofs is actually *quantum* access to the decision oracle, which is a considerably stronger assumption that was never considered before. For the NIKE proofs, we will also need a double-sided oracle definition, where the adversary gets access to two decision oracles, one for each of the challenge set elements, and its quantum variants. All variants are captured by Definition 6.

Definition 6 (Variants of GA-StCDH). *On input* $(g \star \tilde{x}, h \star \tilde{x})$, *the* GA-XXX-StCDH *requires to compute the set element* $gh \star \tilde{x}$ *with access to a decision oracle which is specified below. To an effective group action* EGA *and an adversary* $\mathcal{A}$, *we associate the advantage function*

$$\mathsf{Adv}^{\mathsf{GA\text{-}XXX\text{-}StCDH}}_{\mathsf{EGA}}(\mathcal{A}) := \Pr[\mathcal{A}^{\mathsf{O}}(g \star \tilde{x}, h \star \tilde{x}) \Rightarrow gh \star \tilde{x}] ,$$

where $g, h \xleftarrow{\$} \mathcal{G}$ *and*

$$\mathrm{O} := \begin{cases} \mathsf{GA\text{-}DDH}_g(\cdot,\cdot), & \mathsf{XXX} = \{\} \quad \textit{(classical)} \\ \mathsf{GA\text{-}DDH}_g(\cdot,|\cdot\rangle), & \mathsf{XXX} = \mathsf{PQ} \quad \textit{(partially quantum)} \\ \mathsf{GA\text{-}DDH}_g(|\cdot\rangle,|\cdot\rangle), & \mathsf{XXX} = \mathsf{FQ} \quad \textit{(fully quantum)} \\ \{\mathsf{GA\text{-}DDH}_g(\cdot,\cdot), \mathsf{GA\text{-}DDH}_h(\cdot,\cdot)\}, & \mathsf{XXX} = \mathsf{D} \quad \textit{(double-sided classical)} \\ \{\mathsf{GA\text{-}DDH}_g(\cdot,|\cdot\rangle), \mathsf{GA\text{-}DDH}_h(\cdot,|\cdot\rangle)\}, & \mathsf{XXX} = \mathsf{DPQ} \quad \textit{(double-sided partially quantum)} \\ \{\mathsf{GA\text{-}DDH}_g(|\cdot\rangle,|\cdot\rangle), \mathsf{GA\text{-}DDH}_h(|\cdot\rangle,|\cdot\rangle)\}, & \mathsf{XXX} = \mathsf{DFQ} \quad \textit{(double-sided fully quantum)} \end{cases}$$

On basis-state inputs (y, z), $\mathsf{GA\text{-}DDH}_g$ *returns 1 if* $g \star y = z$ *and 0 otherwise.* $\mathsf{GA\text{-}DDH}_h$ *is defined equivalently. Note that superposition queries are implicitly then defined by linearity (i.e.,* $\mathrm{O}(\sum_x \alpha_x x) = \sum_x \alpha_x \mathrm{O}(x)$*). We emphasize that the partially quantum variants of the oracle measure their corresponding first input implicitly.*

3.2 Necessity of the GA-(D)PQ-StCDH Assumption

We now show that partial quantum access to the decision oracle is indeed a *necessary* assumption to prove IND-CCA security of GA-HEG and CKS security of GA-HDH. We do that by showing the opposite direction, namely that the assumption is implied by the security of the corresponding scheme. This is captured by the following two theorems.

Theorem 1. *Let* $\mathsf{H}\colon \mathcal{X} \times \mathcal{X} \to \{0,1\}^\kappa$ *be a random oracle. For any quantum adversary* $\mathcal{A}$ *against* GA-PQ-StCDH *making at most* q *queries to its decision oracle, there exists a quantum adversary* $\mathcal{B}$ *against* IND-CCA *security of* GA-HEG *making at most* q *decapsulation queries and* $q+1$ *quantum random oracle queries with*

$$\mathsf{Adv}_{\mathsf{EGA}}^{\mathsf{GA\text{-}PQ\text{-}StCDH}}(\mathcal{A}) \le 2 \cdot \mathsf{Adv}_{\mathsf{GA\text{-}HEG}}^{\mathsf{IND\text{-}CCA}}(\mathcal{B}) + \frac{8(q+1)^2+1}{2^\kappa},$$

and the running time of $\mathcal{B}$ *is about that of* $\mathcal{A}$.

Theorem 2. *Let* $\mathsf{H}\colon \{0,1\}^* \to \{0,1\}^\kappa$ *be a random oracle. For any quantum adversary* $\mathcal{A}$ *against* GA-DPQ-StCDH *making at most* q *queries to its decision oracles, there exists a quantum adversary* $\mathcal{B}$ *against the* CKS *security of* GA-HDH *making* 2 *queries to the* RegisterHonest *oracle, at most* q *queries to the* RegisterCorrupt *oracle and* $q+1$ *quantum random oracle queries with*

$$\mathsf{Adv}_{\mathsf{EGA}}^{\mathsf{GA\text{-}DPQ\text{-}StCDH}}(\mathcal{A}) \le 2 \cdot \mathsf{Adv}_{\mathsf{GA\text{-}HDH}}^{\mathsf{CKS}}(\mathcal{B}) + \frac{8(q+1)^2+1}{2^\kappa},$$

and the running time of $\mathcal{B}$ *is about that of* $\mathcal{A}$.

We will prove Theorem 1 below. The proof of Theorem 2 is very similar and we refer to the full version [18] for more details.

Proof (of Theorem 1). The idea of the proof is to construct a reduction which implements the decision oracle using the decapsulation oracle by testing whether $\mathsf{Decaps}(x_1) = \mathsf{H}(x_1, x_2)$ on a decision oracle query $\mathrm{O}(x_1, x_2)$. Whenever $\mathrm{O}(x_1, x_2)$ returns 1, so will $\mathsf{Decaps}(x_1) = \mathsf{H}(x_1, x_2)$, except when x_1 is

Games G_1-G_5		**Oracle $O(x_1, x_2)$**	
00 $g \xleftarrow{\$} \mathcal{G}$		05 Let $a := e$	$\backslash\backslash G_2$-G_5
01 $h \xleftarrow{\$} \mathcal{G}$		06 **if** $x_1 = h \star \tilde{x}$: Let $a := \hat{g}$	$\backslash\backslash G_3$-G_5
02 $\hat{g} \xleftarrow{\$} \mathcal{G} \setminus \{e\}$	$\backslash\backslash G_3$-G_5	07 **return** $[\![\mathsf{Decaps}(g, a \star x_1) = \mathsf{H}(a \star x_1, a \star x_2)]\!]$	$\backslash\backslash G_5$
03 $z \leftarrow \mathcal{A}^{O(\cdot, \vert \cdot \rangle)}(g \star \tilde{x}, h \star \tilde{x})$		08 **return** $[\![\mathsf{H}(a \star x_1, (a \cdot g) \star x_1) = \mathsf{H}(a \star x_1, a \star x_2)]\!]$	$\backslash\backslash G_4$
04 **return** $[\![z = gh \star \tilde{x}]\!]$		09 **return** $[\![(a \star x_1, (a \cdot g) \star x_1) = (a \star x_1, a \star x_2)]\!]$	$\backslash\backslash G_2$-G_3
		10 **return** $[\![g \star x_1 = x_2]\!]$	$\backslash\backslash G_1$

Fig. 5. Games G_1–G_5 for the proof of Theorem 1.

Distinguisher $\mathcal{D}^{\mathsf{F}}$	**Oracle $O(x_1, x_2)$**
00 $g \xleftarrow{\$} \mathcal{G}$	05 **if** $g \star x_1 = x_2$ **return** 1
01 $h \xleftarrow{\$} \mathcal{G}$	06 **if** $x_1 = h \star \tilde{x}$
02 $\hat{g} \xleftarrow{\$} \mathcal{G} \setminus \{e\}$	07 **return** $\mathsf{F}(\hat{g} \star x_1, \hat{g} \star x_2)$
03 $z \leftarrow \mathcal{A}^{O(\cdot, \vert \cdot \rangle)}(g \star \tilde{x}, h \star \tilde{x})$	08 **else**
04 **return** $[\![z = gh \star \tilde{x}]\!]$	09 **return** $\mathsf{F}(x_1, x_2)$

Fig. 6. Distinguisher $\mathcal{D}$ for the Generic Distinguishing Problem to bound G_4–G_5.

the challenge ciphertext. Therefore, whenever x_1 is the challenge ciphertext, the reduction is going to do the same test, except that it first "shifts" x_1 and x_2 by some other group element $\hat{g}$. After simulating all decision oracle queries, the reduction returns whether the challenge KEM key K does not equal $\mathsf{H}(c^*, z)$ where z is the group action CDH solution obtained by $\mathcal{A}$. We now proceed with the formal proof.

Let $\mathcal{A}$ be a quantum adversary as described in Theorem 1. Consider the sequence of games given in Fig. 5.

GAME G_1. This is the GA-PQ-StCDH game, where $O = \mathsf{GA\text{-}DDH}_g$. By definition,

$$\Pr[G_1^{\mathcal{A}} \Rightarrow 1] = \mathsf{Adv}_{\mathsf{EGA}}^{\mathsf{GA\text{-}PQ\text{-}StCDH}}(\mathcal{A}).$$

GAME G_2. In this game, instead of returning whether $g \star x_1 = x_2$, the decision oracle returns whether $(x_1, g \star x_1) = (x_1, x_2)$. In order to prepare for the next game hop, we additionally introduce a new variable a which denotes a group element. In G_2, a is always the neutral element e of $\mathcal{G}$, thus applying a on any set element does not have any effect. Since we always have $x_1 = x_1$, the check in line 09 is the same as in line 10. Hence we have $\Pr[G_1^{\mathcal{A}} \Rightarrow 1] = \Pr[G_2^{\mathcal{A}} \Rightarrow 1]$.

GAME G_3. In this game we sample a group element $\hat{g} \xleftarrow{\$} \mathcal{G} \setminus \{e\}$ uniformly at random in line 02. For all queries (x_1, x_2) to O, where $x_1 = h \star \tilde{x}$, we now set a to $\hat{g}$. In this case, this will change the boolean test in line 09. However, since the group action operation is a bijection, this change is only conceptual. The reason for doing this, is that in the final reduction we are going to set $h \star \tilde{x}$ to be the challenge ciphertext c^* which we cannot query to the decapsulation oracle. Shifting by $\hat{g}$ in the case that $x_1 = h \star \tilde{x}$ will allow us to still simulate O. We get $\Pr[G_2^{\mathcal{A}} \Rightarrow 1] = \Pr[G_3^{\mathcal{A}} \Rightarrow 1]$.

Adversary $\mathcal{B}^{\text{DECAPS},\mathsf{H}}(\mathsf{pk}, c^*, K)$	**Oracle** $\mathsf{O}(x_1, x_2)$
00 $\hat{g} \xleftarrow{\$} \mathcal{G} \setminus \{e\}$	03 **if** $x_1 = c^*$
01 $z \leftarrow \mathcal{A}^{\mathsf{O}(\cdot,|\cdot\rangle)}(\mathsf{pk}, c^*)$	04 **return** $[\![\text{DECAPS}(\hat{g}\star x_1) = \mathsf{H}(\hat{g}\star x_1, \hat{g}\star x_2)]\!]$
02 **return** $[\![K \neq \mathsf{H}(c^*, z)]\!]$	05 **return** $[\![\text{DECAPS}(x_1) = \mathsf{H}(x_1, x_2)]\!]$

Fig. 7. Adversary $\mathcal{B}$ against IND-CCA security for bounding G_6.

GAME G_4. In this game we perform the boolean test by first hashing both sides using a random oracle. In particular, we check if $\mathsf{H}(a \star x_1, (a \star g) \star x_1) = \mathsf{H}(a \star x_1, a \star x_2)$ in line 08. This introduces false positives into the decision oracle, when for any $\hat{x}_1 \in \mathcal{X}$ we have that $\mathsf{H}(\hat{x}_1, g \star \hat{x}_1)$ has preimages of the form $(\hat{x}_1, \hat{x}_2)$ with $\hat{x}_2 \neq g \star \hat{x}_1$. We can bound this change by reducing to the GDP problem, which we do in Fig. 6. In particular, for every $(\hat{x}_1, \hat{x}_2)$ we have $\mathsf{F}(\hat{x}_1, \hat{x}_2)$ returns 1 with probability $\lambda := 1/2^\kappa$, which is the probability to find a second preimage for $\mathsf{H}(\hat{x}_1, g \star \hat{x}_1)$. If F is the zero function, the distinguisher $\mathcal{D}$ simulates G_3 and otherwise it simulates G_4. Thus by Eq. (2) of Lemma 2 where we have set $\lambda := 1/2^\kappa$ we have

$$\begin{aligned} &\left|\Pr[G_3^{\mathcal{A}} \Rightarrow 1] - \Pr[G_4^{\mathcal{A}} \Rightarrow 1]\right| \\ &= \left|\Pr[\mathsf{GDP}_{\mathsf{F},0}^{\mathcal{D}} \Rightarrow 1] - \Pr[\mathsf{GDP}_{\mathsf{F},1}^{\mathcal{D}} \Rightarrow 1]\right| \leq 8(q+1)^2/2^\kappa. \end{aligned}$$

GAME G_5. In this game we change the boolean test again and check whether $\mathsf{Decaps}(g, a \star x_1) = \mathsf{H}(a \star x_1, a \star x_2)$ in line 07. By definition of decapsulation, this change is again only conceptual. We have $\Pr[G_4^{\mathcal{A}} \Rightarrow 1] = \Pr[G_5^{\mathcal{A}} \Rightarrow 1]$.

It remains to bound G_5. We claim

$$\Pr[G_5^{\mathcal{A}} \Rightarrow 1] \leq 2 \cdot \mathsf{Adv}_{\mathsf{GA\text{-}HEG}}^{\mathsf{IND\text{-}CCA}}(\mathcal{B}) + 1/2^\kappa. \tag{3}$$

The adversary $\mathcal{B}$ in Fig. 7 simulates G_5 as follows: it runs $\mathcal{A}$ on its own inputs (pk, c^*), thus defining $g \star \tilde{x} := \mathsf{pk}$ and $h \star \tilde{x} := c^*$. Note that it can simulate oracle O as in G_5 using its own DECAPS oracle and random oracle H provided by the IND-CCA challenger. If $\mathcal{A}$ queries O on the challenge ciphertext c^*, we make use of the additional element $\hat{g}$, thus $\mathcal{B}$ never queries DECAPS on the challenge ciphertext. Finally $\mathcal{A}$ outputs z. If $\mathsf{H}(c^*, z) = K^*$, where K^* is the challenge key $\mathcal{B}$ received at the beginning, it returns 0 (real), otherwise it returns $b' := 1$ (random). Clearly, if $\mathcal{A}$ computes z as $gh \star \tilde{x}$, $\mathcal{B}$ always wins the IND-CCA game when it is in the real world. In the random world, it will win only with probability $1 - 1/2^\kappa$ since the challenge key might be the same as the real key with probability $1/2^\kappa$. When z is not the correct solution and K is the real key, then $\mathcal{B}$ will only win if the output of H still coincides with K, i.e. with probability $1/2^\kappa$. However, if K is a random key, $\mathcal{B}$ will win again with probability $1 - 1/2^\kappa$. Collecting the conditional probabilities yields the bound claimed in Eq. (3).

It remains to analyze the running time of $\mathcal{B}$ and its additional oracle calls. $\mathcal{B}$ runs $\mathcal{A}$ once and for every query to O, $\mathcal{B}$ makes one call to the decapsulation oracle and random oracle. After running $\mathcal{A}$ it makes one additional call to the random oracle, which yields the claimed number of additional oracle calls, which concludes our proof. □

Remark 2. Quantum-secure signatures and public-key encryption schemes have been studied in [10], where the adversary gets quantum access to the signing and decryption oracle, respectively. One can show that the *Quantum* IND-CCA (IND-qCCA) security of GA-HEG is equivalent to the GA-FQ-StCDH assumption, that is the assumption is necessary and sufficient. The proof that IND-qCCA implies the GA-FQ-StCDH assumption is the same as the proof of Theorem 1. Therefore, observe that since the first input of the decision oracle is not measured, the reduction needs a quantum-accessible decapsulation oracle, which is provided by the IND-qCCA game. The sufficiency follows by observing that the reduction in the proof of Theorem 3 can actually simulate quantum decapsulation queries. We leave it as an open problem whether the GA-PQ-StCDH assumption is sufficient for IND-CCA security GA-HEG.

4 Security of Group Action Hashed ElGamal and NIKE

We now prove security of the two schemes in the quantum random oracle model. In particular, we prove IND-CCA security of GA-HEG under the GA-FQ-StCDH assumption and CKS security of GA-HDH under the GA-DFQ-StCDH assumption, i.e., with full quantum access to the decision oracle.

Due to our results in Sect. 3.2, we cannot hope to prove security of the (un-modified) schemes based on assumptions without quantum access. However, adding key confirmation to GA-HEG allows us to do so. We elaborate in more detail in Sect. 4.2. Unfortunately, key confirmation cannot be applied in the context of non-interactive schemes such as GA-HDH.

4.1 Security of GA-HEG

The following theorem states security of GA-HEG based on the GA-FQ-StCDH assumption. For the proof we will use the MRM O2H lemma (Lemma 1).

Remark 3. Alternatively, we could use the O2H variant of [8] (also for proving $\mathsf{GA\text{-}Twin\text{-}HEG}_m$) by using its extractor in the proof, yielding a bound of $\sqrt{\mathsf{Adv}}$. Since both versions are applicable, one can essentially choose between a quadratic loss independent of the adversary's query depth or a linear loss in the query depth. To keep proofs and theorems simple, we only prove the bound using MRM.

Theorem 3. *For any quantum adversary $\mathcal{A}$ against* IND-CCA *security of* GA-HEG *that issues at most q queries to the quantum-accessible random oracle* H *of query depth d with query parallelism $p := q/d$, there exists an adversary $\mathcal{B}$ against* GA-FQ-StCDH *such that*

$$\mathsf{Adv}^{\mathsf{IND\text{-}CCA}}_{\mathsf{GA\text{-}HEG}}(\mathcal{A}) \leq 4d\mathsf{Adv}^{\mathsf{GA\text{-}FQ\text{-}StCDH}}_{\mathsf{EGA}}(\mathcal{B}),$$

```
Games G1-G5                                   Oracle Decaps(sk, c)
00 sk := g <-$ G                              10 if c = c* return ⊥
01 pk := x := g ⋆ x̃                           11 return H1(c)                  \\ G4-G5
02 b <-$ {0,1}                                12 return H(c, sk ⋆ c)
03 r <-$ G
04 c* := r ⋆ x̃                                Oracle H(x1, x2)                 \\ G2-G5
05 K0 := H(c*, r ⋆ pk)                        13 if (x1, x2) = (x1, g ⋆ x1)
06 H[(c*, r ⋆ pk)] <-$ {0,1}^κ      \\ G5     14    return H1(x1)              \\ G3-G5
07 K1 <-$ {0,1}^κ                             15    return H1(x1, x2)
08 b' <- A^{H,Dec}(pk, c*, Kb)                16 return H2(x1, x2)
09 return [[b = b']]
```

Fig. 8. Games G_1–G_5 for the proof of Theorem 3, where H_1 and H_2 are internal random oracles.

and the running time of $\mathcal{B}$ is about three times that of $\mathcal{A}$ plus at most $\mathcal{O}(q+p)$ queries to the decision oracle and the time to simulate up to $\mathcal{O}(\max\{q_D, q\})$ random oracle queries, where q_D is the number of decapsulation queries.

Proof. Let $\mathcal{A}$ be a quantum adversary as described in Theorem 3. Consider the games given in Fig. 8. We proceed by analyzing the different games.

GAME G_1. This is the IND-CCA game where we unfolded the definition of GA-HEG. By definition,

$$\left|\Pr[G_1^{\mathcal{A}} \Rightarrow 1] - 1/2\right| = \mathsf{Adv}^{\mathsf{IND\text{-}CCA}}_{\mathsf{GA\text{-}HEG}}(\mathcal{A}).$$

GAME G_2. Here we introduce the following conceptual change: the random oracle H is simulated using two *internal* random oracles H_1 and H_2, where the first one is used on valid DH tuples, and the second on invalid ones. For this change to be meaningful (i.e., simulatable) later on, we need a quantum-accessible decision oracle, which is provided by the GA-FQ-StCDH assumption. Clearly, the change is only conceptual and we have $\Pr[G_1^{\mathcal{A}} \Rightarrow 1] = \Pr[G_2^{\mathcal{A}} \Rightarrow 1]$.

GAME G_3. Next, we drop the input x_2 in the case where the random oracle H_1 is used, that is we return $\mathsf{H}_1(x_1)$ instead of $\mathsf{H}_1(x_1, x_2)$. Since relative to pk and x_1 there exists a *unique* x_2 s.t. $(x_1, x_2) = (x_1, g \star x_1)$, due to the regularity property of EGA, this change is again only conceptual and we have $\Pr[G_2^{\mathcal{A}} \Rightarrow 1] = \Pr[G_3^{\mathcal{A}} \Rightarrow 1]$.

GAME G_4. In this game we remove the usage of the secret key in the random oracle calls of the decapsulation oracle by returning $\mathsf{H}_1(c)$ instead of $\mathsf{H}(c, g \star c)$. Note that the secret key is only used to check for the DDH condition, which can be simulated with access to $\mathsf{GA\text{-}DDH}_g(|\cdot\rangle, |\cdot\rangle)$. Due to the previous conceptual change $\mathsf{H}_1(c) = \mathsf{H}(c, g \star c)$ holds by definition and therefore this change is again only conceptual, thus $\Pr[G_3^{\mathcal{A}} \Rightarrow 1] = \Pr[G_4^{\mathcal{A}} \Rightarrow 1]$.

GAME G_5. In this game we reprogram the random oracle on the challenge input $(c^*, r \star \mathsf{pk})$, after querying $\mathsf{H}(c^*, r \star \mathsf{pk})$ in line 06. Now K_0 is identically distributed as K_1, therefore the key is now independent of the challenge bit b and we have $\Pr[G_5^{\mathcal{A}} \Rightarrow 1] = 1/2$. Due to Lemma 1 (MRM-O2H) we have

```
Adversary B^{|O⟩}(g ⋆ x̃, h ⋆ x̃)                     Oracle Decaps(sk, c)
00 pk := g ⋆ x̃, c* := h ⋆ x̃                          07 if c = c* return ⊥
01 K_0, K_1 ←$ {0,1}^κ, b ←$ {0,1}                   08 return H_1(c)
02 T ← Ext^{H,H',Dec}(pk, c*, K_b)                   Oracle H/H'(x_1, x_2)
03 for (a, z) ∈ T                      \\ |T| = p    09 if O(x_1, x_2) = 1
04   if a = h ⋆ x̃ ∧ O(a, z) = 1                      10   if x_1 = c* return K_0   \\ H only
05     return z                        \\ = gh ⋆ x̃   11   return H_1(x_1)
06 return ⊥                                          12 return H_2(x_1, x_2)
```

Fig. 9. Adversary $\mathcal{B}$ for the game-hop G_4–G_5 for the proof of Theorem 3. H_1 and H_2 are internal random oracles. The oracle O is the GA-DDH$_g$ oracle.

```
Gen                      Encaps(pk)                    Decaps(sk, ct)
00 sk := g ←$ G          03 r ←$ G                     08 z := sk ⋆ c
01 pk := x := g ⋆ x̃      04 c := r ⋆ x̃                 09 if G(c, z) ≠ d
02 return (pk, sk)       05 d := G(c, r ⋆ pk)          10   return ⊥
                         06 K := H(c, r ⋆ pk)          11 K := H(c, z)
                         07 return (ct := (c, d), K)   12 return K
```

Fig. 10. Key encapsulation mechanism GA-HEG-KC for an effective group action EGA $= (\mathcal{G}, \mathcal{X}, \star, \tilde{x})$, where $\mathsf{G} : \mathcal{X} \times \mathcal{X} \to \{0,1\}^n$ and $\mathsf{H} : \mathcal{X} \times \mathcal{X} \to \{0,1\}^\kappa$ are hash functions.

$$\left|\Pr[G_4^{\mathcal{A}} \Rightarrow 1] - \Pr[G_5^{\mathcal{A}} \Rightarrow 1]\right| \leq 4d \Pr[G_6^{\mathsf{Ext}} \Rightarrow 1],$$

where G_6^{Ext} is like $G_4^{\mathcal{A}}$, except that instead of running $\mathcal{A}$, it runs the extraction algorithm $\mathsf{Ext}^{\mathsf{Decaps},\mathsf{H},\mathsf{H}'}$ from the MRM-O2H lemma to obtain a set $\mathcal{T}$ and the winning condition is changed to $[\![\mathcal{S} \cap \mathcal{T} \neq \emptyset]\!]$, where $\mathcal{S} := \{(c^*, r \star \mathsf{pk})\}$ and H' is the reprogrammed random oracle.

We bound the right-hand probability by the adversary $\mathcal{B}$ given in Fig. 9, which runs the extraction algorithm simulating Decaps and H as in G_4 and H' (the reprogrammed H) as in G_5. Observe that $\mathcal{B}$ can simulate quantum decapsulation queries, since it has quantum access to H_1, which is why we can apply the MRM-O2H lemma. Since $\mathcal{B}$ wins if $\mathcal{S} \cap \mathcal{T} \neq \emptyset$, we have

$$\Pr[G_6^{\mathsf{Ext}} \Rightarrow 1] \leq \mathsf{Adv}_{\mathsf{EGA}}^{\mathsf{GA\text{-}FQ\text{-}StCDH}}(\mathcal{B}).$$

Combining all inequalities yields the claimed bound. We conclude our proof by analyzing the running time of $\mathcal{B}$. $\mathcal{B}$ runs the extraction algorithm Ext, whose running time is at most three times that of $\mathcal{A}$. For every run of $\mathcal{A}$, it has to simulate at most $\max\{q_D, q\}$ calls to H_1 and q calls to H_2 (through H, H'), where it calls O on every query. Then, after obtaining $\mathcal{T}$, it makes at most p queries to O, thus $q + p$ total queries to O. Multiplying the parts of simulating $\mathcal{A}$ by 3, adding up and applying $\mathcal{O}$ notation yields the claimed running time and additional oracle calls, which concludes our proof. □

4.2 Security of GA-HEG via Key Confirmation

We recall the Hashed ElGamal scheme with key confirmation in Fig. 10. We denote this scheme by GA-HEG-KC. Compared to the original scheme in Fig. 3, we now have a second hash function $\mathsf{G}\colon \mathcal{X} \times \mathcal{X} \to \{0,1\}^n$ which is used to compute an additional ciphertext element d. The input to this hash function is the same as for the final key. The decapsulation algorithm now first checks if d is valid by recomputing it. If this check passes, the actual key is computed and returned, otherwise the algorithm outputs a failure symbol $\perp$.

Theorem 4 establishes security of GA-HEG-KC based on the GA-StCDH assumption, that is without quantum access to the decision oracle. One reason for the looser bound is that the classical decision oracle does not enable us to apply the more recent O2H lemmata. The other is that we have to first apply O2H, before applying the extractable RO simulator.

Theorem 4. *Let $\mathsf{G}\colon \mathcal{X} \times \mathcal{X} \to \{0,1\}^n$ be a random oracle. For any quantum adversary $\mathcal{A}$ against* IND-CCA *security of* GA-HEG-KC *that issues at most d parallel queries each of size p (in total $q := dp$ queries) to the quantum-accessible random oracles* H *and* G *and q_D decapsulation queries, there exists an adversary $\mathcal{B}$ against the* GA-StCDH *such that*

$$\mathsf{Adv}^{\mathsf{IND\text{-}CCA}}_{\mathsf{GA\text{-}HEG\text{-}KC}}(\mathcal{A}) \leq 2d\sqrt{\mathsf{Adv}^{\mathsf{GA\text{-}StCDH}}_{\mathsf{EGA}}(\mathcal{B})} + \frac{8(q+1)^2}{2^n} + \sqrt{\frac{32q_D(q_D+q)}{\sqrt{2^n}}} + \sqrt{\frac{4q_D}{2^n}} + \sqrt{\frac{40e^2(q+2q_D+2)^3}{2^n}},$$

and the running time of $\mathcal{B}$ is about that of $\mathcal{A}$ plus the running time for using extractable random-oracle simulator for q_D extraction queries and q hash queries, which is about $\mathcal{O}(q\cdot q_D+q^2)$ and simulating H *for q queries, additionally $\mathcal{B}$ makes at most q_D+p queries to its decision oracle.*

Note that n depends on the desired security level. Due to the fourth root term, n needs to be around four times the security parameter in bits. We discuss this in more detail in Sect. 6. We will now sketch the proof of Theorem 4. The full proof can be found in the full version [18].

Proof (Sketch). After some simple changes we first reprogram the random oracle H and G on the challenge inputs using O2H. Then the main idea of the proof is to simulate the random oracle G using the extractable random-oracle simulator. The reduction can then simulate decapsulation queries by extracting the inputs from the key-confirmation hash and verify the validity using the decision oracle $\mathsf{GA\text{-}DDH}(g \star \tilde{x},\cdot,\cdot)$. Note that since the decapsulation oracle is classical, the extracted values are also classical and we only need classical access to $\mathsf{GA\text{-}DDH}(g \star \tilde{x},\cdot,\cdot)$. Once we can simulate decapsulation without the secret key using the classical decision oracle, we can reduce the game to the GA-StCDH problem. □

4.3 Security of GA-HDH

The following theorem establishes security of GA-HDH based on the GA-DFQ-StCDH assumption. As opposed to the proof of GA-HEG, we have to use the semi-classical variant of the O2H lemma which yields a worse bound. We explain the reason in the full version [18].

Theorem 5. *For any quantum adversary $\mathcal{A}$ against the* CKS *security of* GA-HDH *that issues at most d parallel queries, each of size p, to the quantum-accessible random oracle* H*, there exists an adversary $\mathcal{B}$ against* GA-DFQ-StCDH *such that*

$$\mathsf{Adv}^{\mathsf{CKS}}_{\mathsf{GA\text{-}HDH}}(\mathcal{A}) \leq \sqrt{8(d+1)\mathsf{Adv}^{\mathsf{GA\text{-}DFQ\text{-}StCDH}}_{\mathsf{EGA}}(\mathcal{B})},$$

and the running time of $\mathcal{B}$ is about three times that of $\mathcal{A}$ plus $\mathcal{O}(q+p)$ queries to the decision oracle and the running time for simulating $\mathcal{O}(\max\{d \cdot p, q_R, q_T\})$ queries to the random oracle and $\mathcal{O}(q_O)$ rerandomizations on the set elements, where q_O, q_R and q_T are the number of register-honest, reveal and test queries.

We will only sketch the proof here. The full proof can be found in the full version [18].

Proof (Sketch). As in the proof of Theorem 3, our goal is to use a variant of the O2H lemma in order to randomize all challenge keys and bound the advantage of the O2H extractor using the GA-DFQ-StCDH assumption. However, instead of just a decapsulation oracle, we have to simulate the CorruptReveal oracle and the Test oracle. Although the adversary is allowed to choose identities for honest keys, we can compute all honest keys before the adversary can make any queries, so we can vary the behavior of the random oracle when it interacts with honest or corrupted keys. Note that this technique is not generally possible as the key generation could depend on the provided ID in other schemes. This allows to only hash $(\mathsf{ID}_1, \mathsf{ID}_1, \mathsf{pk}_1, \mathsf{pk}_2)$ without the shared DH value between pk_1 and pk_2, when at least one key is honest. Additionally, we can use a different internal random oracle, when both keys are honest. In the final reduction on GA-DFQ-StCDH, we embed the challenge set elements into the public keys using rerandomization. For each public key, we randomly choose which challenge element we use such that the adversary will issue a test query at least for one pair of identities containing both challenge elements. We can check whether quantum random oracle queries contain valid DH tuples using quantum access to the decision oracles. Then we can use the O2H lemma in its semi-classical variant and bound the success probability of its extractor with the GA-DFQ-StCDH assumption. □

5 Twinning for Group Actions

In this section, we adapt the twinning technique from [11] to the group actions setting. Due to the limited structure that group actions offer, we need a novel approach to develop and analyze the underlying trapdoor test. The trapdoor test will allow us to effectively simulate a decision oracle, apart from a small error probability. In contrast to the original twinning approach, the analysis of the error term is more involved and depends on an additional parameter m, which affects the "twinning factor". To illustrate this in an example: whereas in the traditional prime-order group setting, twinning doubles the size of public keys, the group action twinning technique will result in a public key of length m.

Using this technique we get two new schemes $\mathsf{GA\text{-}Twin\text{-}HEG}_m$ and $\mathsf{GA\text{-}Twin\text{-}HDH}_m$, the twinned versions of GA-HEG and GA-HDH, which will be presented and analyzed in Sects. 5.2 and 5.3. It allows us to remove the strong variants of GA-CDH including quantum access to decision oracles in the security proofs. Consequently we obtain a proof based on the standard GA-CDH assumption, albeit in exchange for larger keys and overall increased computation cost. Nevertheless, using our new twinning technique is thus far the only known method that allows for a security proof of a NIKE scheme from standard assumptions in the QROM. In Sect. 6 we discuss different parameter choices for m.

5.1 A Trapdoor Test

In order to replace the GA-(FQ-)StCDH assumption, an algorithm must be able to simulate the decision oracle $\mathsf{GA\text{-}DDH}_g$ without knowing g explicitly. The following trapdoor test will be our basic tool to achieve this task.

Lemma 3 (Trapdoor Test). *Let* $\mathsf{EGA} = (\mathcal{G}, \mathcal{X}, \star, \tilde{x})$, $\ell, m \in \mathbb{N}$ *such that* $1 < \ell < m/2$. *Suppose* $x_0, x_1, ..., x_{\ell-1}$, $s_\ell, ..., s_m$, $h_\ell, ..., h_m$ *are mutually independent random variables, where* $x_0, x_1, ..., x_{\ell-1}$ *take values in* $\mathcal{X}$, *and for all* $i \in [\ell, m]$ s_i *are uniformly distributed over* $[0, \ell-1]$ *with the additional condition that each value in* $[0, \ell-1]$ *is taken at least once. Further, for all* $i \in [\ell, m]$ h_i *are uniformly distributed over* $\mathcal{G}$. *Define random variables* $x_\ell, ..., x_m$, *where* $x_i = h_i \star x_{s_i}$ *for* $i \in [\ell, m]$. *Further, let* $g_i \in \mathcal{G}$ *such that* $x_i = g_i \star \tilde{x}$ *for every* $i \in [m]$. *In addition, suppose that* $\bar{z}_0, \bar{z}_1, ..., \bar{z}_m$ *are random variables taking values in* $\mathcal{X}$.

We define

$$F_0(\bar{z}_0, \ldots, \bar{z}_m) := \begin{cases} 1 & \text{if } \bar{z}_i = h_i \star \bar{z}_{s_i} \quad \forall i \in [\ell, m] \\ 0 & \text{else} \end{cases} \tag{4}$$

and

$$F_1(\bar{z}_0, \ldots, \bar{z}_m) := \begin{cases} 1 & \text{if } \bar{z}_i = g_i \star \bar{z}_0 \quad \forall i \in [m] \\ 0 & \text{else} \end{cases} \tag{5}$$

and the advantage of an adversary $\mathcal{A}$ *in distinguishing* F_0 *from* F_1 *with oracle access to one of the two functions and making at most* q *queries of depth* d *as*

$$\mathsf{Adv}^{\mathsf{TDT}}_{\mathsf{EGA},q,d,\ell,m}(\mathcal{A}) := \left|\Pr[\mathcal{A}^{F_0} \Rightarrow 1] - \Pr[\mathcal{A}^{F_1} \Rightarrow 1]\right|$$

We call Eq. (4) *the* Trapdoor Test. *The following properties hold:*

1. $x_\ell, ..., x_m$ *are uniformly distributed over* $\mathcal{X}$;

```
Adversary B^T                 Oracle F(z̄0,...,z̄m)              Function Convert(z0,...,zm)
00 x0 := x̃                    06 if z̄i = hi ⋆ z̄0 for i ∈ [m]   10 for i ∈ [ℓ, m]
01 for i ∈ [m]                07    return 1                    11   for j ∈ [0, ℓ−1]
02   hi ←$ G                  08 t := Convert(z̄0,...,z̄m)       12     if zi = (hi · hj) ⋆ z0
03   xi := hi ⋆ x̃             09 return T(t)                    13       si := j
04 b ← A^F(x0,...,xm)                                           14 return map(sℓ,...,sm)
05 return b
```

Fig. 11. Adversary $\mathcal{B}^{|T\rangle}$ against the GDP problem for the function T. The function "map" is the selected bijection from the set of possible s_i into $\mathcal{Y}$.

2. x_i *and* x_j *are independent for all* $i \in [0, \ell-1], j \in [\ell, m]$*;*
3. if $F_1(z) = 1$*, then also* $F_0(z) = 1$ *for any input vector* z*;*
4. for any classical (quantum) adversary $\mathcal{A}$ *with oracle access to* F_b *for* $b \in \{0,1\}$*, the probability that* $\mathcal{A}$ *outputs 1 after at most* q *queries to* F_b *with query depth* d *is upper-bounded by the advantage of a classical (quantum) adversary* $\mathcal{B}$ *against the* GDP *problem for a function* $T : \mathcal{Y} \to \{0,1\}$ *with* $\Pr[T(x) = 1 : x \xleftarrow{\$} \mathcal{Y}] \leq \frac{1}{|\mathcal{Y}|}$ *and* $|\mathcal{Y}| = \ell!\ell^{m-2\ell+1}$ *(see Remark 4). Specifically,*

$$\mathsf{Adv}^{\mathsf{TDT}}_{\mathsf{EGA},q,d,\ell,m}(\mathcal{A}) \leq \mathsf{Adv}^{\mathsf{GDP}}_{T,q,d}(\mathcal{B}) \leq \begin{cases} \frac{2q}{|\mathcal{Y}|} & \textit{(classical)} \\ 4\sqrt{\frac{(d+1)q}{|\mathcal{Y}|}} & \textit{(quantum).} \end{cases}$$

Proof. Properties 1. to 3. hold by inspection. For property 4., we build an adversary $\mathcal{B}$ on the GDP problem from a successful distinguisher $\mathcal{A}$ of the trapdoor test. The proofs are identical for the classical and quantum case as the oracles that $\mathcal{B}$ has to implement can all be defined as classical functions which make classical queries to other oracles, so by making all oracles quantum, the proof does not change.

First note that if $\mathcal{A}$ only queries tuples $z_0, \ldots, z_m$ to its function F_b for which x_i, z_0, z_i form a DH tuple, then both oracles always behave identically, so we assume that it will not make such queries. Since the s_i take all values in $[0, \ell-1]$, for non-DH queries, the oracles differ only if $\mathcal{A}$ guesses *all* s_i used to generate the x_i correctly. In that case it could choose the first ℓ elements at random and set the last $m - \ell + 1$ elements to $g_i \star x_{s_i}$, where the g_i are the discrete logarithms of the i-th randomly chosen element. If the s_i do not cover all values in $[0, \ell-1]$, this argument does not hold (see Remark 5).

We will construct an adversary $\mathcal{B}$ on the GDP problem for a function T, which will simulate the function F_1 if T is the all-zero function and F_0, i.e. the trapdoor test, if not. Specifically, let $T : \mathcal{Y} \to \{0,1\}$ such that there is a bijective mapping from $\mathcal{Y}$ into the set of all possible combinations of s_i.

We describe $\mathcal{B}$ in Fig. 11. First, $\mathcal{B}$ sets x_0 to the origin element $\tilde{x}$ and chooses m random elements $x_1, \ldots x_m$ and runs $\mathcal{A}$ on them as input. When $\mathcal{A}$ makes a query to F, $\mathcal{B}$ first checks if $\mathcal{A}$ provided a valid DH tuple and if so, returns 1. Otherwise, it computes which s_i were (implicitly) chosen to generate the query and maps them to the unique element they correspond to in $\mathcal{Y}$. Then it queries this element to its own function T and returns the result.

If T is the all-zero function, then F only returns 1 if the first check succeeds, i.e., F is equal to F_1 from Eq. (5). Otherwise, there is exactly one entry in T for which it returns 1. Therefore, by returning the result of the query to T, $\mathcal{B}$ implicitly chooses its s_i as the ones corresponding to said entry in T and therefore simulates F_0 from Eq. (4). So by outputting the same result as $\mathcal{A}$, $\mathcal{B}$ wins if and only if $\mathcal{A}$ wins and the claim follows. The quantum bound then follows directly from Lemma 2. □

Remark 4 (Sampling s_i). Let $\ell, m \in \mathbb{N}$ as in Lemma 3 and $k = m - \ell + 1$. Define

$$\mathcal{Y}^* = \{(s_\ell, \ldots, s_m) \in [0, \ell-1]^k \mid \forall i \in [0, \ell-1]\ \exists j : s_j = i\}.$$

In principal this is the set of possible values for the $(s_\ell, \ldots, s_m)$ from the lemma. The cardinality of $\mathcal{Y}^*$ may be described by the *Stirling partition number* multiplied by $\ell!$, more precisely

$$|\mathcal{Y}^*| = \ell! \cdot \left\{ {k \atop \ell} \right\} = \sum_{i=0}^{d} (-1)^i \binom{\ell}{i} (\ell - i)^k.$$

One possibility to sample randomly from the entire set $\mathcal{Y}^*$ is rejection sampling from $[0, \ell-1]^k$. Since this is not very practical, we suggest the following sampling method which samples from the strictly smaller subset $\mathcal{Y}$ of size $\ell! \ell^{k-\ell}$.

In order to ensure that the s_i take each value in $[0, \ell - 1]$, we first sample exactly these ℓ elements and then sample the remaining $k - \ell$ elements uniformly at random from $[0, \ell - 1]$.

Remark 5 (Necessity of the condition on s_i). The assumption that each value in $[0, \ell - 1]$ is taken at least once by the s_i is a necessary assumption. Otherwise, an adversary can simply guess a value $\alpha \in [0, \ell - 1]$ that is not taken by the s_i and subsequently choose $\bar{z}_\alpha$ randomly while computing all other $\bar{z}_i$ honestly. This would lead to

$$1 = F_0(\bar{z}_0, ..., \bar{z}_\alpha, ..., \bar{z}_m) \neq F_1(\bar{z}_0, ..., \bar{z}_\alpha, ..., \bar{z}_m) = 0$$

because $\bar{z}_\alpha$ is never used on the right side of $\bar{z}_i = h_i \star \bar{z}_{s_i}$ during the trapdoor test in (4). Therefore, the adversary is able to distinguish both functions without guessing all s_i which prevents the aforementioned reduction.

In order to use the trapdoor test in security proofs, we need to choose m and ℓ such that the advantage defined above becomes a small statistical factor. In Sect. 6, we compute these values for a security level of 128 bits.

5.2 Twin Hashed ElGamal

Applying the twinning technique to Hashed ElGamal yields the Twin Hashed ElGamal encryption scheme $\mathsf{GA\text{-}Twin\text{-}HEG}_m$ for an integer $m \in \mathbb{N}$, which is formally described in Fig. 12. While twinning significantly increases the public key size and computation for both encapsulation and decapsulation, it allows us to prove its IND-CCA security without the use of strong variants of the GA-CDH problem. Furthermore, the ciphertext still consists of only one element.

Gen	Encaps(pk)	Decaps(sk, ct)
00 $\mathsf{sk} := (h_1, ..., h_m) \xleftarrow{\$} \mathcal{G}^m$	03 $r \xleftarrow{\$} \mathcal{G}$	07 $K := \mathsf{H}(\mathsf{ct}, h_1 \star \mathsf{ct}, ..., h_m \star \mathsf{ct})$
01 $\mathsf{pk} := (y_1, ..., y_m) := (h_1 \star \tilde{x}, ... h_m \star \tilde{x})$	04 $\mathsf{ct} := r \star \tilde{x}$	08 **return** K
02 **return** (pk, sk)	05 $K := \mathsf{H}(\mathsf{ct}, r \star y_1, ..., r \star y_m)$	
	06 **return** (ct, K)	

Fig. 12. Twin Hashed ElGamal KEM $\mathsf{GA\text{-}Twin\text{-}HEG}_m$ with twinning parameter m. $\mathsf{H} : \mathcal{X}^{m+1} \to \{0,1\}^\kappa$ is a hash function.

Theorem 6. *Let $\ell, m \in \mathbb{N}$ such that $1 < \ell < m/2$. For any quantum adversary $\mathcal{A}$ against* IND-CCA *security of* $\mathsf{GA\text{-}Twin\text{-}HEG}_m$ *that issues at most q queries to the quantum-accessible random oracle* H *with query depth d, there exists a quantum adversary $\mathcal{B}$ against* GA-CDH *such that*

$$\mathsf{Adv}^{\mathsf{IND\text{-}CCA}}_{\mathsf{GA\text{-}Twin\text{-}HEG}_m}(\mathcal{A}) \leq 4d\mathsf{Adv}^{\mathsf{GA\text{-}CDH}}_{\mathsf{EGA}}(\mathcal{B}) + 4\sqrt{\frac{(d+1)q}{\ell!\ell^{m-2\ell+1}}},$$

and the running time of $\mathcal{B}$ is about three times that of $\mathcal{A}$ plus the time to simulate $\mathcal{O}(\max\{q, q_D\})$ queries to H, *where q_D is the number of decapsulation queries.*

We will only sketch the proof here and refer to the full version [18] for the full proof. In fact, it is similar to the one of Theorem 3, only that we use the trapdoor test whenever the other proof uses the decision oracle.

Proof (Sketch). Let $\mathcal{A}$ be a quantum adversary in the IND-CCA game. Our goal is to construct an adversary $\mathcal{B}$ against GA-CDH. The main question is how $\mathcal{B}$ simulates decapsulation queries. Therefore, let H_1 and H_2 be *internal* random oracles, the first is used for valid DH tuples and the second for invalid ones. Since for every ciphertext element x_1 there exists a unique vector of m set elements s.t. these form a DH tuple with the public key set elements, the output of H_1 only depends on x_1. We can check if a query consists of valid DH tuples using the trapdoor test. After this change, $\mathcal{B}$ can simulate decapsulation queries by just returning $\mathsf{H}_1(x_1)$. Next, we can apply the MRM-O2H lemma to reprogram H on the challenge ciphertext c^* and the corresponding DH tuples $(\mathsf{sk}[i] \star c^*)_{i \in [m]}$. For this the adversary $\mathcal{B}$ needs to be able to simulate H and H′ (the reprogrammed H), which it can do using the trapdoor test. Note that since we applied the variant which considers parallel random oracle queries, the measured inputs are a set of size p. Due to the trapdoor test $\mathcal{B}$ can find the correct solution. In the final game, since the key K^* is now independent of the bit b, the adversary wins the game with probability 1/2 and the claimed bound follows. □

5.3 Twin NIKE

We construct a NIKE scheme $\mathsf{GA\text{-}Twin\text{-}HDH}_m$ from an effective group action $\mathsf{EGA} = (\mathcal{G}, \mathcal{X}, \star, \tilde{x})$, which defines the public parameters pp together with an integer $m \in \mathbb{N}$ and a hash function $\mathsf{H} : \{0,1\}^* \to \{0,1\}^\kappa$, thus defining $\mathcal{SHK} = \{0,1\}^\kappa$. As in Sect. 3, we assume that the identities can be represented

Alice A	**Bob B**
$\mathsf{sk_A} = (a_1, ..., a_m) \xleftarrow{\$} \mathcal{G}^m$	$\mathsf{sk_B} = (b_1, ..., b_m) \xleftarrow{\$} \mathcal{G}^m$
$\mathsf{pk_A} = (x_1^{\mathsf{A}}, ..., x_m^{\mathsf{A}}) = (a_1 \star \tilde{x}, ..., a_m \star \tilde{x})$	$\mathsf{pk_B} = (x_1^{\mathsf{B}}, ..., x_m^{\mathsf{B}}) = (b_1 \star \tilde{x}, ..., b_m \star \tilde{x})$
for $i \in [m], j \in [m]$	**for** $i \in [m], j \in [m]$
$z_{i,j} := a_i \star x_j^{\mathsf{B}}$	$z_{i,j} := b_j \star x_i^{\mathsf{A}}$

$$K := \mathsf{H}(\mathsf{A}, \mathsf{B}, \mathsf{pk_A}, \mathsf{pk_B}, z_{1,1}, ..., z_{1,m}, ..., z_{m,1}, ..., z_{m,m})$$

Fig. 13. Our NIKE protocol $\mathsf{GA\text{-}Twin\text{-}HDH}_m$.

by bitstrings of fixed length μ. On input an ID, the key generation algorithm chooses m group elements $(g_1, ..., g_m) \xleftarrow{\$} \mathcal{G}^m$ which form the secret key $\mathsf{sk_{ID}}$. The public key is computed as $\mathsf{pk_{ID}} = (g_1 \star \tilde{x}, ..., g_m \star \tilde{x}) \in \mathcal{X}^m$. The shared key of an identity ID_1 with public key $\mathsf{pk}_{\mathsf{ID}_1} = (x_1, ..., x_m)$ and an identity ID_2 with secret key $\mathsf{sk}_{\mathsf{ID}_2} = (g_1, ..., g_m)$ is defined as

$$K = \begin{cases} \mathsf{H}(\mathsf{ID}_1, \mathsf{ID}_2, \mathsf{pk}_{\mathsf{ID}_1}, \mathsf{pk}_{\mathsf{ID}_2}, g_1 \star x_1, ..., g_1 \star x_m, ..., g_m \star x_1, ..., g_m \star x_m) & \textbf{if } \mathsf{ID}_1 < \mathsf{ID}_2 \\ \mathsf{H}(\mathsf{ID}_2, \mathsf{ID}_1, \mathsf{pk}_{\mathsf{ID}_2}, \mathsf{pk}_{\mathsf{ID}_1}, g_1 \star x_1, ..., g_m \star x_1, ..., g_1 \star x_m, ..., g_m \star x_m) & \textbf{if } \mathsf{ID}_2 < \mathsf{ID}_1 \end{cases}$$

See Fig. 13 for a schematic overview of our construction.

Again, twinning significantly increases the public key size and computation of $\mathsf{GA\text{-}Twin\text{-}HDH}_m$ compared to $\mathsf{GA\text{-}HDH}$, but allows us to use the same techniques as in Theorem 6 to prove security without relying on strong assumptions. This is formalized in Theorem 7.

Theorem 7. *Let $\ell, m \in \mathbb{N}$ such that $1 < \ell < m/2$. For any quantum adversary $\mathcal{A}$ against the* CKS *security of* $\mathsf{GA\text{-}Twin\text{-}HDH}_m$ *that issues at most q queries to the quantum-accessible random oracle* H *of query depth d, there exists a quantum adversary $\mathcal{B}$ against* GA-CDH *such that*

$$\mathsf{Adv}^{\mathsf{CKS}}_{\mathsf{GA\text{-}Twin\text{-}HDH}_m}(\mathcal{A}) \leq \sqrt{8d\mathsf{Adv}^{\mathsf{GA\text{-}CDH}}_{\mathsf{EGA}}(\mathcal{B})} + 4\sqrt{\frac{(d+1)q}{\ell!\ell^{m-2\ell+1}}},$$

and the running time of $\mathcal{B}$ is about three times that of $\mathcal{A}$ plus the time needed to simulate $\mathcal{O}(\max\{q, q_R, q_T\})$ queries to the random oracle, to perform $\mathcal{O}(q_O)$ rerandomizations on set elements and to run the trapdoor test $\mathcal{O}(q)$ times, where q_O, q_R and q_T are the number of register-honest, reveal and test queries.

The proof is similar to the proof of Theorem 5 with the main difference that we use the trapdoor test whenever the other proof used the decision oracles. We defer the complete proof to the full version [18].

Proof (Sketch). As in the KEM proof, our goal is to use a variant of the O2H lemma in order to randomize all challenge keys and bound the advantage of the O2H extractor using the GA-CDH assumption. However, instead of just a decapsulation oracle, we have to simulate the CORRUPTREVEAL and TEST oracles.

Table 1. Overview of our different protocols and comparison to FO variants. By $|\mathcal{X}|$ we denote the length of a set element in bits. The columns "Gen", "Encaps" and "Decaps" state the number of group action evaluations that are needed in order to perform the corresponding algorithm. For NIKE schemes this refers to the SharedKey algorithm. Bounds are stated without statistical terms and q, d denote the number of random oracle queries and the query-depth. The security parameter is denoted by λ. For $\lambda = 128$ bit security, we need $m = 85$. For FO-EG we assume the implicit rejection variants.

Scheme	$\|\mathsf{pk}\|$	$\|\mathsf{ct}\|$	Gen	Encaps	Decaps	Assumption	Bound
GA-HEG (Fig. 3)	$\|\mathcal{X}\|$	$\|\mathcal{X}\|$	1	2	1	GA-FQ-StCDH	$d\,\mathsf{Adv}$
GA-HEG-KC (Fig. 10)	$\|\mathcal{X}\|$	$\|\mathcal{X}\| + 4\lambda$	1	2	1	GA-StCDH	$d\sqrt{\mathsf{Adv}}$
GA-Twin-HEG$_m$ (Fig. 12)	$m \cdot \|\mathcal{X}\|$	$\|\mathcal{X}\|$	m	$m+1$	m	GA-CDH	$d\,\mathsf{Adv}$
GA-EG-FO [12,17]	$\|\mathcal{X}\|$	$\|\mathcal{X}\| + 2\lambda$	1	2	2	GA-CDH	$q\sqrt{\mathsf{Adv}}$
GA-EG-FO [12,30]	$\|\mathcal{X}\|$	$\|\mathcal{X}\| + 3\lambda$	1	2	2	GA-DDH	$d^2\,\mathsf{Adv}$
GA-HDH (Fig. 4)	$\|\mathcal{X}\|$	-	1	1 (SharedKey)		GA-DFQ-StCDH	$\sqrt{d\,\mathsf{Adv}}$
GA-Twin-HDH$_m$ (Fig. 13)	m	-	m	m^2 (SharedKey)		GA-CDH	$\sqrt{d\,\mathsf{Adv}}$

Although the adversary is allowed to choose identities for honest keys, we can compute the public keys before it makes any queries, so we can vary the behavior of the random oracle when it interacts with honest or corrupted keys. Note that this technique is not generally possible as the key generation could depend on the provided ID in other schemes. This allows us to make similar conceptual changes as in the KEM proof, where we only hash $(\mathsf{ID}_1, \mathsf{ID}_1, \mathsf{pk}_1, \mathsf{pk}_2)$ without the $z_{i,j}$, when at least one key is honest. Additionally, we can use a different internal random oracle, when both keys are honest. By using the trapdoor test, we can remove the need for the secret keys completely. Finally, we can use the O2H lemma in its semi-classical variant and bound the success probability of its extractor with the GA-CDH assumption. □

6 Parameter Choices and Comparison

In order to compare the different schemes we need to elaborate on the parameter n, which is the bit length of the output of hash function G in the hashed ElGamal scheme with key confirmation, and the twinning parameter m. Both depend on the desired security level which is usually stated in bits. Taking the corresponding terms in the bounds of Theorems 4 and 6 into account, we determine the success ratio of an adversary $\mathcal{A}$. The success ratio of $\mathcal{A}$ is computed as its advantage $\epsilon_{\mathcal{A}}$ divided by its running time $t_{\mathcal{A}}$ [23]. For λ-bit security, we then require $\epsilon_{\mathcal{A}}/t_{\mathcal{A}} \leq 2^{-\lambda}$.

Key Confirmation. The output of the hash function G determines the length of the second ciphertext element. In order to determine the length, we analyze the statistical terms in Theorem 4. Note the one with the fourth root is the most dominating one. Thus, for λ-bit security, we need to set $n \approx 4\lambda$, where we assume $q_D \leq q \lessapprox t_{\mathcal{A}}$ and ignore additive constants.

Twinning. The efficiency of the Twin ElGamal encryption scheme GA-Twin-HEG$_m$ and the Twin NIKE scheme GA-Twin-HDH$_m$ depends on the twinning parameter m which directly translates to the length of the public key. The security level is determined by the value of $\ell!\ell^{m-2\ell+1}$, where $\ell \in [1, m/2]$ may be chosen arbitrarily. Note that ℓ only appears in the proofs of Theorem 6 and Theorem 7, hence it has no direct effect on the corresponding protocols.

Again, we only analyze the statistical term in the bound. For λ-bit security, we need

$$\frac{4}{t_{\mathcal{A}}} \cdot \sqrt{\frac{(d+1)q}{\ell!\ell^{m-2\ell+1}}} \leq 2^{-\lambda}.$$

Similar as before, we may assume that $d \leq q \lessapprox t_{\mathcal{A}}$, hence for an optimal success ratio an adversary would choose $d = q$. This means that we need to choose m large enough so that $\ell!\ell^{m-2\ell+1} \geq 2^{2\lambda+4}$ for some $\ell \in [1, m/2]$. As an example, for $\lambda = 128$, optimality is achieved by $m = 85$ (with $\ell = 17$).

Instantiation of the Group Action. Every set element $x \in \mathcal{X}$ is represented by a bitstring. In CSIDH the length of this bitstring is $\log(p)$, where the size of $\mathcal{X}$ is in $O(\sqrt{p})$. Choosing the correct parameter size for CSIDH is an actively discussed topic in the community. Castryck et al. [12] propose a 1792-bit prime p to achieve $\lambda = 128$ bit quantum security.

Comparison. Table 1 provides an overview of the schemes analyzed in this paper and a comparison to the ElGamal KEMs that can be obtained by the FO transform. The base scheme is the most efficient one, with one ciphertext element and two group action evaluations for Encaps. It also achieves the best QROM bound without any square root terms, but it relies on the strongest non-standard assumption. Hashed ElGamal with key confirmation has a slightly larger ciphertext and comes with a worse bound, however, it relies only on the GA-StCDH assumption. Since twinning cannot be done efficiently in the group action setting, the twinned version of hashed ElGamal is the least efficient in terms of public key size and group action computation. Nevertheless, the ciphertext still consists of only one set element and we get security based on the standard GA-CDH assumption. At this point we want to stress again that this seems the only way to construct an actively-secure NIKE based on a standard assumption. Otherwise, one has to rely on the assumption with a quantum-accessible decision oracle.

Acknowledgments. The work of Julien Duman was supported by the German Federal Ministry of Education and Research (BMBF) in the course of the 6GEM Research Hub under Grant 16KISK037. Dominik Hartmann was supported by the BMBF iBlockchain project. Eike Kiltz was supported by the BMBF iBlockchain project, the Deutsche Forschungsgemeinschaft (DFG, German research Foundation) as part of the Excellence Strategy of the German Federal and State Governments - EXC 2092 CASA - 390781972, and by the European Union (ERC AdG REWORC - 101054911). Sabrina Kunzweiler, Jonas Lehmann and Doreen Riepel were funded by the Deutsche Forschungsgemeinschaft (DFG, German Research Foundation) under Germany's Excellence Strategy - EXC 2092 CASA - 390781972.

References

1. Abdalla, M., Bellare, M., Rogaway, P.: The oracle Diffie-Hellman assumptions and an analysis of DHIES. In: Naccache, D. (ed.) CT-RSA 2001. LNCS, vol. 2020, pp. 143–158. Springer, Heidelberg (2001). https://doi.org/10.1007/3-540-45353-9_12
2. Alamati, N., De Feo, L., Montgomery, H., Patranabis, S.: Cryptographic group actions and applications. In: Moriai, S., Wang, H. (eds.) ASIACRYPT 2020. LNCS, vol. 12492, pp. 411–439. Springer, Cham (2020). https://doi.org/10.1007/978-3-030-64834-3_14
3. Alwen, J., Blanchet, B., Hauck, E., Kiltz, E., Lipp, B., Riepel, D.: Analysing the HPKE standard. In: Canteaut, A., Standaert, F.-X. (eds.) EUROCRYPT 2021. LNCS, vol. 12696, pp. 87–116. Springer, Cham (2021). https://doi.org/10.1007/978-3-030-77870-5_4
4. Alwen, J., Hartmann, D., Kiltz, E., Mularczyk, M.: Server-aided continuous group key agreement. Cryptology ePrint Archive, Report 2021/1456 (2021)
5. Ambainis, A., Hamburg, M., Unruh, D.: Quantum security proofs using semi-classical oracles. In: Boldyreva, A., Micciancio, D. (eds.) CRYPTO 2019. LNCS, vol. 11693, pp. 269–295. Springer, Cham (2019). https://doi.org/10.1007/978-3-030-26951-7_10
6. Barnes, R., Millican, J., Omara, E., Cohn-Gordon, K., Robert, R.: Message layer security (MLS) WG. https://datatracker.ietf.org/wg/mls/about/
7. Bellare, M., Rogaway, P.: Random oracles are practical: a paradigm for designing efficient protocols. ACM CCS **93**, 62–73 (1993)
8. Bindel, N., Hamburg, M., Hövelmanns, K., Hülsing, A., Persichetti, E.: Tighter proofs of CCA security in the quantum random oracle model. In: Hofheinz, D., Rosen, A. (eds.) TCC 2019. LNCS, vol. 11892, pp. 61–90. Springer, Cham (2019). https://doi.org/10.1007/978-3-030-36033-7_3
9. Boneh, D., Dagdelen, Ö., Fischlin, M., Lehmann, A., Schaffner, C., Zhandry, M.: Random oracles in a quantum world. In: Lee, D.H., Wang, X. (eds.) ASIACRYPT 2011. LNCS, vol. 7073, pp. 41–69. Springer, Heidelberg (2011). https://doi.org/10.1007/978-3-642-25385-0_3
10. Boneh, D., Zhandry, M.: Secure signatures and chosen ciphertext security in a quantum computing world. In: Canetti, R., Garay, J.A. (eds.) CRYPTO 2013. LNCS, vol. 8043, pp. 361–379. Springer, Heidelberg (2013). https://doi.org/10.1007/978-3-642-40084-1_21
11. Cash, D., Kiltz, E., Shoup, V.: The twin Diffie-Hellman problem and applications. In: Smart, N. (ed.) EUROCRYPT 2008. LNCS, vol. 4965, pp. 127–145. Springer, Heidelberg (2008). https://doi.org/10.1007/978-3-540-78967-3_8
12. Castryck, W., Lange, T., Martindale, C., Panny, L., Renes, J.: CSIDH: an efficient post-quantum commutative group action. In: Peyrin, T., Galbraith, S. (eds.) ASIACRYPT 2018. LNCS, vol. 11274, pp. 395–427. Springer, Cham (2018). https://doi.org/10.1007/978-3-030-03332-3_15
13. Cohn-Gordon, K., Cremers, C., Gjøsteen, K., Jacobsen, H., Jager, T.: Highly efficient key exchange protocols with optimal tightness. In: Boldyreva, A., Micciancio, D. (eds.) CRYPTO 2019. LNCS, vol. 11694, pp. 767–797. Springer, Cham (2019). https://doi.org/10.1007/978-3-030-26954-8_25
14. Couveignes, J.-M.: Hard homogeneous spaces. Cryptology ePrint Archive, Report 2006/291 (2006)

15. de Kock, B., Gjøsteen, K., Veroni, M.: Practical isogeny-based key-exchange with optimal tightness. In: Dunkelman, O., Jacobson, Jr., M.J., O'Flynn, C. (eds.) SAC 2020. LNCS, vol. 12804, pp. 451–479. Springer, Cham (2021). https://doi.org/10.1007/978-3-030-81652-0_18
16. Diffie, W., Hellman, M.E.: New directions in cryptography. IEEE Trans. Inf. Theory **22**(6), 644–654 (1976)
17. Don, J., Fehr, S., Majenz, C., Schaffner, C.: Online-extractability in the quantum random-oracle model. In: Dunkelman, O., Dziembowski, S. (eds.) EUROCRYPT 2022. LNCS, vol. 13277, pp. 677–706. Springer, Cham (2022). https://doi.org/10.1007/978-3-031-07082-2_24
18. Duman, J., Hartmann, D., Kiltz, E., Kunzweiler, S., Lehmann, J., Riepel, D.: Group action key encapsulation and non-interactive key exchange in the QROM. Cryptology ePrint Archive, Report 2022/1230 (2022)
19. ElGamal, T.: A public key cryptosystem and a signature scheme based on discrete logarithms. IEEE Trans. Inf. Theory **31**, 469–472 (1985)
20. Fouotsa, T.B., Petit, C.: SimS: a simplification of SiGamal. In: Cheon, J.H., Tillich, J.-P. (eds.) PQCrypto 2021 2021. LNCS, vol. 12841, pp. 277–295. Springer, Cham (2021). https://doi.org/10.1007/978-3-030-81293-5_15
21. Freire, E.S.V., Hofheinz, D., Kiltz, E., Paterson, K.G.: Non-interactive key exchange. In: Kurosawa, K., Hanaoka, G. (eds.) PKC 2013. LNCS, vol. 7778, pp. 254–271. Springer, Heidelberg (2013). https://doi.org/10.1007/978-3-642-36362-7_17
22. Fujisaki, E., Okamoto, T.: Secure integration of asymmetric and symmetric encryption schemes. In: Wiener, M. (ed.) CRYPTO 1999. LNCS, vol. 1666, pp. 537–554. Springer, Heidelberg (1999). https://doi.org/10.1007/3-540-48405-1_34
23. Håstad, J., Impagliazzo, R., Levin, L.A., Luby, M.: A pseudorandom generator from any one-way function. SIAM J. Comput. **28**(4), 1364–1396 (1999)
24. Hofheinz, D., Hövelmanns, K., Kiltz, E.: A modular analysis of the Fujisaki-Okamoto transformation. In: Kalai, Y., Reyzin, L. (eds.) TCC 2017. LNCS, vol. 10677, pp. 341–371. Springer, Cham (2017). https://doi.org/10.1007/978-3-319-70500-2_12
25. Hövelmanns, K., Kiltz, E., Schäge, S., Unruh, D.: Generic authenticated key exchange in the quantum random oracle model. In: Kiayias, A., Kohlweiss, M., Wallden, P., Zikas, V. (eds.) PKC 2020. LNCS, vol. 12111, pp. 389–422. Springer, Cham (2020). https://doi.org/10.1007/978-3-030-45388-6_14
26. Hülsing, A., Ning, K.-C., Schwabe, P., Weber, F., Zimmermann, P.R.: Post-quantum WireGuard. In: 2021 IEEE Symposium on Security and Privacy (SP), pp. 304–321 (2021)
27. Hülsing, A., Rijneveld, J., Song, F.: Mitigating multi-target attacks in hash-based signatures. In: Cheng, C.-M., Chung, K.-M., Persiano, G., Yang, B.-Y. (eds.) PKC 2016. LNCS, vol. 9614, pp. 387–416. Springer, Heidelberg (2016). https://doi.org/10.1007/978-3-662-49384-7_15
28. Kawashima, T., Takashima, K., Aikawa, Y., Takagi, T.: An efficient authenticated key exchange from random self-reducibility on CSIDH. In: Hong, D. (ed.) ICISC 2020. LNCS, vol. 12593, pp. 58–84. Springer, Cham (2021). https://doi.org/10.1007/978-3-030-68890-5_4
29. Krawczyk, H., Wee, H.: The OPTLS protocol and TLS 1.3. In: 2016 IEEE European Symposium on Security and Privacy (EuroSP), pp. 81–96 (2016)

30. Kuchta, V., Sakzad, A., Stehlé, D., Steinfeld, R., Sun, S.-F.: Measure-rewind-measure: tighter quantum random oracle model proofs for one-way to hiding and CCA security. In: Canteaut, A., Ishai, Y. (eds.) EUROCRYPT 2020. LNCS, vol. 12107, pp. 703–728. Springer, Cham (2020). https://doi.org/10.1007/978-3-030-45727-3_24
31. Moriya, T., Onuki, H., Takagi, T.: SiGamal: a supersingular isogeny-based PKE and its application to a PRF. In: Moriai, S., Wang, H. (eds.) ASIACRYPT 2020. LNCS, vol. 12492, pp. 551–580. Springer, Cham (2020). https://doi.org/10.1007/978-3-030-64834-3_19
32. Rescorla, E., Oku, K., Sullivan, N., Wood, C.A.: TLS encrypted client hello. Internet-Draft draft-ietf-tls-esni-13, Internet Engineering Task Force (2021)
33. Rescorla, E., Sullivan, N., Wood, C.A.: Semi-static Diffie-Hellman key establishment for TLS 1.3. Internet-Draft draft-rescorla-tls-semistatic-dh-02, Internet Engineering Task Force (2019)
34. Rostovtsev, A., Stolbunov, A.: Public-key cryptosystem based on isogenies. Cryptology ePrint Archive, Report 2006/145 (2006)
35. Schwabe, P., Stebila, D., Wiggers, T.: Post-quantum TLS without handshake signatures. ACM CCS **2020**, 1461–1480 (2020)
36. Shor, P.W.: Algorithms for quantum computation: discrete logarithms and factoring. In: 35th FOCS, pp. 124–134 (1994)
37. Unruh, D.: Revocable quantum timed-release encryption. In: Nguyen, P.Q., Oswald, E. (eds.) EUROCRYPT 2014. LNCS, vol. 8441, pp. 129–146. Springer, Heidelberg (2014). https://doi.org/10.1007/978-3-642-55220-5_8
38. Yoneyama, K.: Post-quantum variants of ISO/IEC standards: compact chosen ciphertext secure key encapsulation mechanism from isogeny. In: Proceedings of the 5th ACM Workshop on Security Standardisation Research Workshop, SSR 2019, pp. 13–21 (2019)
39. Zhandry, M.: How to construct quantum random functions. In: 53rd FOCS, pp. 679–687 (2012)

Horizontal Racewalking Using Radical Isogenies

Wouter Castryck[1,4], Thomas Decru[1], Marc Houben[1,2,3(✉)], and Frederik Vercauteren[1]

[1] imec-COSIC, KU Leuven, Leuven, Belgium
[2] Departement Wiskunde, KU Leuven, Leuven, Belgium
{wouter.castryck,thomas.decru,marc.houben, frederik.vercauteren}@kuleuven.be
[3] Mathematisch Instituut, Universiteit Leiden, Leiden, The Netherlands
[4] Vakgroep Wiskunde: Algebra en Meetkunde, Universiteit Gent, Ghent, Belgium

Abstract. We address three main open problems concerning the use of radical isogenies, as presented by Castryck, Decru and Vercauteren at Asiacrypt 2020, in the computation of long chains of isogenies of fixed, small degree between elliptic curves over finite fields. Firstly, we present an interpolation method for finding radical isogeny formulae in a given degree N, which by-passes the need for factoring division polynomials over large function fields. Using this method, we are able to push the range for which we have formulae at our disposal from $N \leq 13$ to $N \leq 37$ (where in the range $18 \leq N \leq 37$ we have restricted our attention to prime powers). Secondly, using a combination of known techniques and ad-hoc manipulations, we derive optimized versions of these formulae for $N \leq 19$, with some instances performing more than twice as fast as their counterparts from 2020. Thirdly, we solve the problem of understanding the correct choice of radical when walking along the surface between supersingular elliptic curves over $\mathbb{F}_p$ with $p \equiv 7 \bmod 8$; this is non-trivial for even N and was settled for $N = 2$ and $N = 4$ only, in the latter case by Onuki and Moriya at PKC 2022. We give a conjectural statement for all even N and prove it for $N \leq 14$. The speed-ups obtained from these techniques are substantial: using 16-isogenies, the computation of long chains of 2-isogenies over 512-bit prime fields can be accelerated by a factor 3, and the previous implementation of CSIDH using radical isogenies can be sped up by about 12%.

Keywords: Post-quantum cryptography · Isogenies · Modular curves · CSIDH

This work was supported in part by the European Research Council (ERC) under the European Union's Horizon 2020 research and innovation programme (grant agreement ISOCRYPT - No. 101020788) and by CyberSecurity Research Flanders with reference number VR20192203. The third-listed author is supported by the Research Foundation – Flanders (FWO) under a PhD Fellowship Fundamental Research.

S. Agrawal and D. Lin (Eds.): ASIACRYPT 2022, LNCS 13792, pp. 67–96, 2022.
https://doi.org/10.1007/978-3-031-22966-4_3

1 Introduction

One of the core operations in isogeny-based cryptography is the fast computation of the codomain curve of a cyclic chain of horizontal $\mathbb{F}_q$-isogenies of some fixed small-to-moderate degree $N \geq 2$ between elliptic curves over a finite field $\mathbb{F}_q$. Here, let us recall that an $\mathbb{F}_q$-isogeny between two elliptic curves over $\mathbb{F}_q$ is called horizontal if their $\mathbb{F}_q$-rational endomorphism rings are isomorphic imaginary quadratic orders. The primary use cases are CRS [10,22] and CSIDH [7], which are proposals for post-quantum key exchange. However fast horizontal isogenies are also key to various other recent constructions, including digital signatures [2], oblivious transfer constructions [15], verifiable delay functions [12], and schemes for delay encryption [11].

This paper presents a speed-up of such computations. More concretely, we upgrade the radical isogeny approach from [6], where for any given N one produces an iterable formula for computing the elliptic curves in a cyclic chain of N-isogenies, with each step involving the extraction of an Nth root of some radicand $\rho_N \in \mathbb{F}_q$; whence the name "radical". Asymptotically, for fixed N and growing q, the cost of evaluating this formula is dominated by one exponentiation in $\mathbb{F}_q$. This should be compared to one scalar multiplication on an elliptic curve over $\mathbb{F}_q$, which is the dominant cost of the standard approach using Vélu's formulae [26]. In practice however, radical isogenies are useful for small N only, because they come with a large overhead; part of the goal of the current paper is to reduce this overhead.

A first problem is simply *finding* radical isogeny formulae. Indeed, while their existence was argued in [6, §3] by means of the Tate pairing, producing concrete instances is a non-trivial task. The method proposed in [6, §4] relies on finding a zero of the reduced N-division polynomial of a Vélu-type codomain curve over a certain modular function field over $\mathbb{Q}$. As N grows, not only the division polynomial but also this codomain curve and the function field become increasingly complicated, and one quickly reaches the point where this method becomes infeasible. Consequently, the GitHub repository accompanying [6] contains no radical isogeny formulae beyond $N = 13$.

A second problem is that radical isogeny formulae are highly non-unique, with freedom coming from the choice of curve-point model (e.g., the Tate normal form), from the choice of the radicand ρ_N, and from relations in the modular function field. Different radical isogeny formulae for the same value of N can have very different practical performances, and in view of the large overhead it is crucial to try and produce the most efficient version. Here we should mention recent work by Onuki and Moriya [17], who use Montgomery curves to find faster formulae in degrees $N = 3, 4$. Chi-Dominguez and Reijnders [9] have presented projective (= inversion-free) radical isogeny formulae in degrees $2 \leq N \leq 5$ and $N = 7, 9$, but these are constructed directly from the corresponding formulae from [6].

A third problem is that it is not always clear *which* Nth root of ρ_N needs to be chosen in order to walk horizontally. In the CSIDH setting of supersingular elliptic curves over a finite prime field $\mathbb{F}_p$, horizontality comes for free if N is odd; in this case ρ_N has exactly one Nth root in $\mathbb{F}_p$. But even-degree $\mathbb{F}_p$-isogenies, of which non-trivial cyclic chains exist when $p \equiv 7 \bmod 8$ only, are a concern.

In this case ρ_N will admit two Nth roots in $\mathbb{F}_p$, and selecting the wrong option will lead to a change of endomorphism ring and, as a result, in a breakdown of the iteration. This can be circumvented by an additional quadratic residuosity check at each step, but this is an annoying extra cost. In [4, Lem. 4] it was shown that this cost can be avoided when $N = 2$, because for the concrete radical isogeny formula presented there, the correct choice always turns out to be the principal square root, i.e. the unique square root which is again a square. This observation was extended to $N = 4$, now in terms of a principal fourth root, first as a conjecture [6, Conj. 2] and recently proved by Onuki and Moriya [17]. As mentioned in [6, §7], the correct generalization to arbitrary even N is not immediately apparent.

Contributions

We contribute significantly to each of the above open problems, which are listed explicitly in [6, §7]. Concretely, we address:

1. *Formula generation.* We develop an entirely different method for finding radical isogeny formulae in any given degree N, which avoids the need for factoring division polynomials over large function fields. The method uses interpolation over the modular curve $X_1(N)$ and is inspired by an alternative, Galois-theoretic proof of the existence of radical isogeny formulae along the lines of [5]. Using this method, we managed to generate radical isogeny formulae in degree as large as $N = 37$.
2. *Formula optimization.* The optimization and/or simplification of rational expressions modulo relations is an old and complicated problem, see for example [16]. In our case however, ad-hoc manipulations seem to yield the best results. We now believe to have found reasonably optimized formulae up to $N = 19$, with e.g. formulae for $N = 11, 13$ that can compete with our (optimized) version of $N = 7$. To highlight one example, for $N = 8$ we present the iteration
$$A \leftarrow \frac{-2A(A-2)\alpha^2 - A(A-2)}{(A-2)^2\alpha^4 - A(A-2)\alpha^2 - A(A-2)\alpha + A} \text{ with } \alpha = \sqrt[8]{\frac{-A^2(A-1)}{(A-2)^4}}$$
whose counterpart from [6] spanned nearly a quarter of a page.
3. *Ensuring horizontality.* We believe to have found the correct generalization, at least conjecturally, of the observations from [4, Lem. 4], [6, Conj. 2] and [17, §5] for $N = 2, 4$ to arbitrary even N. The surprising new ingredient beyond $N = 4$ is that the principal Nth root needs to be tweaked by the Legendre symbol of a certain coefficient appearing in Tate's normal form; for $N = 4$ this Legendre symbol is always -1 so it goes unnoticed. With the aid of Magma we managed to prove this generalization up to $N = 14$.

One illustrative example where the three contributions resonate is the case $N = 16$. When computing long chains of 2-isogenies, e.g. as in the set-up phase of the delay function from [11], we can use radical 16-isogenies to take 4 horizontal steps "at once", resulting in an asymptotic speed-up by a factor of 4. Experimentally, we observed a speed-up by a factor of about 3 over a 512-bit prime field.

As for CSIDH, we have generated a new prime CRAD-513 capable of handling radical 8- and 9-isogenies, and using our new and optimized formulae we obtained a speed-up of about 12% when compared to the implementation of CSURF-512 from [6]. Furthermore, comparing this to the pre-radical isogenies implementation of CSIDH-512, one sees that the overall speed-up caused by radical isogenies at the 512-bit prime level is about 35%. We expect that there remains room for pushing this quite a bit further, for example by optimizing formulae for $N > 19$.

2 Background

Throughout, we let K denote a field, unless otherwise specified. The base point (= neutral element) of an elliptic curve E/K is denoted by $\mathcal{O}_E$, or just $\mathcal{O}$ if E is clear from the context.

2.1 Division Polynomials

For an elliptic curve $E: y^2 + a_1xy + a_3y = x^3 + a_2x^2 + a_4x + a_6$, $a_i \in K$ in long Weierstrass form we set $b_2 = a_1^2 + 4a_2$, $b_4 = 2a_4 + a_1a_3$, $b_6 = a_3^2 + 4a_6$, $b_8 = a_1^2a_6 + 4a_2a_6 - a_1a_3a_4 + a_2a_3^2 - a_4^2$. For each integer $N \geq 0$ we define the *N-division polynomial* as

$$\Psi_{E,0} = 0, \quad \Psi_{E,1} = 1, \quad \Psi_{E,2} = 2y + a_1x + a_3, \quad \Psi_{E,N} = t \cdot \prod_{Q \in (E[N] \setminus E[2])/\pm} (x - x(Q)),$$

where $t = N$ if N is odd and $t = \frac{N}{2} \cdot \Psi_{E,2}$ if N is even. Note that $\Psi_{E,2}^2 = 4x^3 + b_2x^2 + 2b_4x + b_6$ is a univariate polynomial in x. These division polynomials can be computed efficiently, thanks to the following recurrence relations:

$$\begin{aligned}
\Psi_{E,3} &= 3x^4 + b_2x^3 + 3b_4x^2 + 3b_6x + b_8, \\
\frac{\Psi_{E,4}}{\Psi_{E,2}} &= 2x^6 + b_2x^5 + 5b_4x^4 + 10b_6x^3 + 10b_8x^2 + (b_2b_8 - b_4b_6)x + b_4b_8 - b_6^2, \\
\Psi_{E,2N+1} &= \Psi_{E,N+2}\Psi_{E,N}^3 - \Psi_{E,N-1}\Psi_{E,N+1}^3 \text{ if } N \geq 2, \\
\Psi_{E,2N} &= \frac{\Psi_{E,N}}{\Psi_{E,2}}(\Psi_{E,N+2}\Psi_{E,N-1}^2 - \Psi_{E,N-2}\Psi_{E,N+1}^2) \text{ if } N \geq 3.
\end{aligned}$$

By definition, we have that $\Psi_{E,N}(P) = 0$ for any non-trivial $P \in E[N]$. If one is interested in the points of exact order N, then one can use the *reduced N-division polynomial* $\psi_{E,N}$ defined as $\Psi_{E,N}/\mathrm{lcm}_{d|N, d \neq N}\{\Psi_{E,d}\}$. For all primes ℓ, we simply have $\Psi_{E,\ell} = \psi_{E,\ell}$. Observe that for $N > 2$, the reduced N-division polynomial of E is a univariate polynomial in x.

Scalar multiplication by N on E can be expressed explicitly using division polynomials [20, Ex. 3.6]:

$$[N]P = \left(\frac{\phi_{E,N}(P)}{\Psi_{E,N}(P)^2}, \frac{\omega_{E,N}(P)}{\Psi_{E,N}(P)^3} \right), \tag{1}$$

with $\phi_{E,N} = x\Psi_{E,N}^2 - \Psi_{E,N+1}\Psi_{E,N-1}$ and $\omega_{E,N} = \frac{1}{2\Psi_{E,N}}(\Psi_{E,2N} - \Psi_{E,N}(a_1\phi_{E,N} + a_3\Psi_{E,N}^2))$.

2.2 Tate's Normal Form

We study elliptic curves E/K that are equipped with a distinguished K-rational point P of finite order N. For $N \geq 4$ such a curve-point pair (E, P) is isomorphic to a unique pair of the form

$$E_{b,c} : y^2 + (1-c)xy - by = x^3 - bx^2, \qquad P = (0,0), \tag{2}$$

for some $b, c \in K$. This distinguished model is called the *Tate normal form.* It is worth mentioning that the first few scalar multiples of $(0,0) \in E_{b,c}$ are easy expressions in terms of b and c, e.g.,

$$-(0,0) = (0,b),\ 2(0,0) = (b,bc),\ -2(0,0) = (b,0),$$
$$3(0,0) = (c, b-c),\ -3(0,0) = (c, c^2).$$

Expressions for higher multiples can be found using (1).

Furthermore, for every $N \geq 4$ one can write down a polynomial $F_N \in \mathbb{Z}[b,c]$ whose vanishing, along with the non-vanishing of the discriminant

$$\Delta(E_{b,c}) = b^3(16b^2 - 8bc^2 - 20bc + b + c(c-1)^3),$$

characterizes in any characteristic that the point $(0,0) \in E_{b,c}$ has exact order N. This polynomial can be found as a factor of the constant term of $\psi_{E_{b,c},N}(x) \in \mathbb{Z}[b,c][x]$, or by analyzing $N(0,0)$. It is uniquely determined up to sign. The first few instances are $F_4 = c$, $F_5 = c - b$, $F_6 = c^2 - b + c$, $F_7 = c^3 - b^2 + bc$, $F_8 = bc^2 - 2b^2 + 3bc - c^2$, see again [23, §2]. Thus, when viewing $E_{b,c}$ over the fraction field of $K[b,c]/(F_N)$, one can think of it as a "universal" curve-point pair from which all elliptic curves $E/\overline{K}$ equipped with a point $P \in E$ of order N are obtained through specialization at (unique) concrete values in $\overline{K}$ for b, c.

2.3 Radical Isogenies

Vélu's formulae from [26] must be fed with the explicit coordinates of the points in $G = \ker \varphi$. In many applications, this kernel is a priori described in a more implicit form. For instance, in CSIDH it typically concerns the "unique subgroup of $E(\mathbb{F}_p)$ of order ℓ" for some odd prime number ℓ. An explicit generator of this subgroup can be found by repeatedly sampling $Q \leftarrow E(\mathbb{F}_p)$ and computing

$\frac{p+1}{\ell}Q$ until its order is ℓ, but this scalar multiplication comes at a major cost which can dominate the application of Vélu's formulae itself. Radical isogenies, as introduced in [6], are an attempt at mitigating this.

The key observation behind radical isogenies is that if $\ker\varphi$ is cyclic, say generated by a point $P \in E(K)$ of order $N \geq 2$ coprime to $\operatorname{char} K$, then Vélu's formulae for producing a defining equation of $E' = E/\langle P\rangle$ can be augmented with formulae yielding the coordinates of a point $P' \in E'$ such that

$$E \xrightarrow{\varphi} E' = E/\langle P\rangle \to E'/\langle P'\rangle$$

is cyclic of degree N^2. Consequently, when computing a non-backtracking chain of N-isogenies, from the second step onwards the formulae allow to bypass the scalar multiplication. The formulae depend on N and can be chosen to

- be *radical*, in that they are algebraic expressions in the coefficients of E, the coordinates of P and a radical $\sqrt[N]{\rho_N}$, where the radicand ρ_N is itself an algebraic expression in the coefficients of E and the coordinates of P,
- be *complete*, in that changing the choice of $\sqrt[N]{\rho_N}$, i.e., scaling it with Nth roots of unity, produces generators for the kernel of each N-isogeny that cyclically extends φ,
- have *good reduction*, in the sense that they have coefficients in $\mathbb{Z}[1/N]$ and they can be applied to any elliptic curve E, over any field K with $\operatorname{char} K \nmid N$, equipped with a point $P \in E(K)$ of order N.

In [6] the existence of such formulae is argued using properties of the Tate pairing. The good reduction property is in fact stated as a conjecture [6, Conj. 1].

Remark 1. When working over $K = \mathbb{F}_q$ for some prime power q satisfying $\gcd(q-1, N) = 1$, one usually wants to choose the unique instance of $\sqrt[N]{\rho_N}$ belonging to $\mathbb{F}_q$; see [6, §5.1]. This instance can be computed as ρ_N^μ with $\mu \in \mathbb{Z}$ a multiplicative inverse of N modulo $q-1$. So the cost of evaluating the formulae is asymptotically dominated by one field exponentiation. Unfortunately, the formulae come with a large overhead and, for fixed q, they outperform plain Vélu for small values of N only. The main goal of this paper is to push this crossover point to larger values of N.

Example 2 (taken from [6, §4]*).* Consider an elliptic curve E with a point P of order $N = 5$. The Tate normal form of this curve-point pair is $E_{b,b} = y^2 + (1-b)xy - by = x^3 - bx^2$, $P = (0,0)$ for some $b \neq 0, (11 \pm 5\sqrt{5})/2$. Vélu's formulae produce the following equation for $E' = E/\langle P\rangle$:

$$y^2 + (1-b)xy - by = x^3 - bx^2 - 5b(b^2 + 2b - 1)x - b(b^4 + 10b^3 - 5b^2 + 15b - 1).$$

Analyzing the roots of $\psi_{E',5}(x)$ shows that for $\alpha = \sqrt[5]{\rho_5}$ with $\rho_5 = b$ the point

$$P' = \big(5\alpha^4 + (b-3)\alpha^3 + (b+2)\alpha^2 + (2b-1)\alpha - 2b,$$
$$5\alpha^4 + (b-3)\alpha^3 + (b^2 - 10b + 1)\alpha^2 + (13b - b^2)\alpha - b^2 - 11b\big)$$

on E' has order 5 and generates the kernel of a cyclic extension of φ (it is such that $\hat{\varphi}(P') = P$). There are five such cyclic extensions, corresponding to the five possible choices for α. Rewriting the curve-point pair (E', P') into Tate normal form produces the curve $E_{b',b'}$ where b' is given by the iterable formula

$$\rho_5' = b' = \alpha \frac{\alpha^4 + 3\alpha^3 + 4\alpha^2 + 2\alpha + 1}{\alpha^4 - 2\alpha^3 + 4\alpha^2 - 3\alpha + 1}. \tag{3}$$

The above example illustrates the strategy from [6] for *finding* radical isogeny formulae. The cases $N = 2, 3$ are easy to handle [6, §4] so we assume that $N \geq 4$. One starts from the "universal" curve-point pair $E = E_{b,c}$, $P = (0, 0)$ over

$$\mathbb{Q}_N(b, c) := \operatorname{Frac} \frac{\mathbb{Q}[b, c]}{(F_N)}$$

and one computes a defining equation for $E' = E/\langle P \rangle$ using Vélu's formulae. One then computes the division polynomial $\psi_{E',N}(x)$ and, for a suitable radicand $\rho_N \in \mathbb{Q}_N(b, c)$, one finds the root $x_0' \in \mathbb{Q}_N(b, c)(\sqrt[N]{\rho_N})$ that is the x-coordinate of a point $P' \in E'$ such that $\hat{\varphi}(P') = P$, using a root-finding algorithm; this step is a severe bottleneck. If successful, then the corresponding y-coordinate $y_0' = y(P')$ can be found by solving a quadratic equation over $\mathbb{Q}_N(b, c)(\sqrt[N]{\rho_N})$. The coordinates x_0', y_0' are the radical isogeny formulae we are after; one hopes, and observes in practice, that the good reduction property comes for free. By writing the curve-point pair (E', P') back in Tate normal form $(E_{b',c'}, (0, 0))$ one obtains formulae for b', c' that can be applied iteratively, as in the case of (3).

Concerning the radicand ρ_N, it was argued in [6, §3] that $\rho_N = f_{N,P}(-P)$ works, where $f_{N,P}$ is the function on $E_{b,c}$ with divisor $N(P) - N(\mathcal{O})$ and having leading coefficient 1 when expanded in terms of the uniformizer x/y at $\mathcal{O}$, so that ρ_N is a representative of the Tate pairing $t_N(P, -P)$; see [14, Lem. 1].

3 Modular Curves and Galois Theory

This section recalls some of the theory of Galois coverings of modular curves. We mainly refer to [18, 19]. Along the way we present an alternative proof of the existence of radical isogeny formulae [6, Thm. 5]. This closely resembles the discussion in [5, §3].

3.1 Congruence Subgroups

Classically, as Riemann surfaces, modular curves are quotients $X = X_\Gamma = \mathbb{H}^*/\Gamma$ of the extended complex upper half plane $\mathbb{H}^* = \mathbb{H} \cup \mathbb{P}^1(\mathbb{Q})$ by a *congruence subgroup* $\Gamma \subset \mathrm{SL}_2(\mathbb{Z})$, i.e. a subgroup containing $\Gamma(N) \subset \mathrm{SL}_2(\mathbb{Z})$, the kernel of reduction modulo N, for some $N \in \mathbb{Z}_{>0}$. The minimal N for which this last property holds is called the *level* of X. The modular curve X admits a natural Zariski-open subset $Y = \mathbb{H}/\Gamma$, and the (finite collection of) points $X \setminus Y$ are called the *cusps* of X. Modular curves can be seen as irreducible smooth complex projective curves, and they always have a “moduli interpretation”, in the sense that they (specifically, the non-cuspidal points) parametrize complex elliptic curves together with some additional structure on the N-torsion subgroup.

To make this latter viewpoint more precise, we will consider a different, slightly more general, method to construct “modular” curves. These modular curves will be more general in the sense that they may be reducible as complex projective curves; but they will be irreducible over $\mathbb{Q}$, and their geometrically irreducible components shall be modular curves in the classical sense. Let $N \geq 1$ be an integer and consider the “universal” elliptic curve

$$E_j : y^2 = 4x^3 - \frac{27j}{j-1728}x - \frac{27j}{j-1728}$$

over $\mathbb{Q}(j)$, whose j-invariant equals the indeterminate j. Let $\mathbb{Q}(j, E_j[N]) \subset \overline{\mathbb{Q}(j)}$ be the field obtained by adjoining the coordinates of all N-torsion points of E_j. Then this is a Galois extension, whose Galois automorphisms are completely determined by their action on $E[N]$. In particular, we have that the Galois group is isomorphic to the automorphism group $\mathrm{GL}_2(\mathbb{Z}/N\mathbb{Z})$ of the N-torsion.

For each subgroup $H \subset \mathrm{GL}_2(\mathbb{Z}/N\mathbb{Z})$, the fixed field $\mathbb{Q}(j, E_j[N])^H$ is the function field of a smooth projective curve over $\mathbb{Q}$, which we will denote by X_H. This curve has a natural moduli interpretation, in the sense that away from a finite set its geometric points parametrize elliptic curves over $\overline{\mathbb{Q}}$ together with a certain structure on the N-torsion. More explicitly, it parametrizes pairs (E, α) up to H-isomorphism, where $\alpha : E[N] \to (\mathbb{Z}/N\mathbb{Z})^2$ is an isomorphism of abelian groups and two pairs (E_1, α_1) and (E_2, α_2) are called H-isomorphic if there exists an isomorphism $\varphi : E_1 \to E_2$ and an element $h \in H$ such that $\alpha_1 = h \circ \alpha_2 \circ \varphi$; see [19, §3] for more details. E.g. if we take for H the subgroup of $\mathrm{GL}_2(\mathbb{Z}/N\mathbb{Z})$ of upper-diagonal matrices then X_H is the classical modular curve $X_0(N)$, which parametrizes elliptic curves together with a cyclic subgroup of order N.

The connection to modular curves in the classical sense is quite straightforward. If we denote by $\Gamma_H = \pi^{-1}(\mathrm{GL}_2(\mathbb{Z}/N\mathbb{Z})) \subset \mathrm{SL}_2(\mathbb{Z})$ the congruence subgroup that is the inverse image of H under the reduction modulo N map $\pi : \mathrm{SL}_2(\mathbb{Z}) \to \mathrm{GL}_2(\mathbb{Z}/N\mathbb{Z})$, then we have that $X_H \cong X_{\Gamma_H}$ as complex projective curves if and only if $\det(H) = (\mathbb{Z}/N\mathbb{Z})^\times$; in general X_H will be geometrically isomorphic to the disjoint union of $[(\mathbb{Z}/N\mathbb{Z})^\times : \det(H)]$ copies of X_{Γ_H}.

3.2 The Main Suspects

Let $N \geq 3$. The subgroups $H \supset H'$ of $\mathrm{GL}_2(\mathbb{Z}/N^2\mathbb{Z})$ consisting of matrices having respective forms

$$\begin{pmatrix} \pm 1 \bmod N & * \\ 0 \bmod N & * \end{pmatrix}, \quad \text{and} \quad \begin{pmatrix} \pm 1 \bmod N & * \\ 0 & * \end{pmatrix}$$

correspond to the modular curves which we denote $X_1(N) = X_H$ and $X_1'(N) = X_{H'}$ respectively. The curve $X_1(N)$ is the classical modular curve parametrizing pairs (E, P) where E is an elliptic curve and $P \in E$ is an N-torsion point. The curve $X_1'(N)$ parametrizes triples (E, P, P') where P' is a *P-distinguished point*, i.e. a point $P' \in E/\langle P\rangle$ that maps to P under the dual isogeny $E/\langle P\rangle \to E$. Alternatively, it parametrizes pairs (E, C), where $C = \{Q, Q+P, \ldots, Q+(N-1)P\}$ is a coset on E modulo the order-N point P, where $NQ = P$.

Let us denote by $K \subset L$ the respective function fields over $\mathbb{Q}$ of these curves:

$$K := \mathbb{Q}(X_1(N)) = \mathrm{GL}_2(\mathbb{Z}/N^2\mathbb{Z})^H, \quad L := \mathbb{Q}(X_1'(N)) = \mathrm{GL}_2(\mathbb{Z}/N^2\mathbb{Z})^{H'}.$$

Then K, L are the fields $\mathbb{Q}_N(b,c)$ and $\mathbb{Q}_N(b,c,\sqrt[N]{\rho_N})$ from Sect. 2.3. The canonical inclusion $K \hookrightarrow L$ corresponds to the degree-N forgetful map $X_1'(N) \to X_1(N) : (E,P,P') \mapsto (E,P)$. As we will see in the next section, it is possible to deduce from a purely Galois-theoretic argument that the extension L/K is radical.

3.3 The Galois Structure

Lemma 3. *Let $N \in \mathbb{Z}_{>0}$ and let $K \subset L$ be a degree N extension of fields whose characteristic does not divide N. Let $\zeta_N \in \overline{L}$ be a primitive Nth root of unity and assume that $L(\zeta_N)$ is Galois over K with Galois group*

$$\mathrm{Gal}(L(\zeta_N)/K) = \mathrm{Gal}(L(\zeta_N)/K(\zeta_N)) \rtimes \mathrm{Gal}(L(\zeta_N)/L),$$

where the first factor is cyclic of order N, say generated by σ, and where the semidirect product is according to the rule

$$\tau_j \circ \sigma^i \circ \tau_j^{-1} = \sigma^{ij} \tag{4}$$

for all $i = 0, 1, \ldots, N-1$ and all $\tau_j : \zeta_N \mapsto \zeta_N^j \in \mathrm{Gal}(L(\zeta_N)/L)$. Then there exists an $\alpha \in L$ such that $L = K(\alpha)$ and $\alpha^N \in K$.

Proof. The restricted maps $\sigma^i|_L : L \to L(\zeta_N)$ are pairwise distinct. Indeed, if $i, i' \in \{0, 1, \ldots, N-1\}$ are such that $\sigma^i|_L = \sigma^{i'}|_L$, then

$$\sigma^{i-i'} \in \mathrm{Gal}(L(\zeta_N)/K(\zeta_N)) \cap \mathrm{Gal}(L(\zeta_N)/L) = \{\mathrm{id}\},$$

which can only be true if $i = i'$. From [21, Lem. 0CKL] we get that these restricted maps are linearly independent over $L(\zeta_N)$. Thus there exists $\beta \in L$ such that $\alpha := \sum_{i=0}^{N-1} \zeta_N^i \sigma^i(\beta)$ is non-zero. From

$$\tau_j(\alpha) = \sum_i \zeta_N^{ij}(\tau_j \circ \sigma^i)(\beta) = \sum_i \zeta_N^{ij}(\sigma^{ij} \circ \tau_j)(\beta) = \sum_i \zeta_N^{ij}\sigma^{ij}(\beta) = \alpha$$

it follows that $\alpha \in L$ as well. Now observe that α was constructed in such a way that $\sigma^i(\alpha) = \zeta_N^{-i}\alpha$ for $i = 0, 1, \ldots, N-1$, which has two crucial consequences. On the one hand, it implies that $\mathrm{Gal}(L(\zeta_N)/L)$ is the exact group of automorphisms fixing $K(\alpha)$, or in other words $L = K(\alpha)$. On the other hand, it implies that $\sigma(\alpha^N) = \sigma(\alpha)^N = (\zeta_N\alpha)^N = \alpha^N$, so that α^N is fixed by the entire Galois group, i.e. $\alpha^N \in K$ as wanted. □

Now let K, L as in Sect. 3.2. Below we give an alternative proof of the fact that L/K is a radical extension. Our strategy is to apply Lemma 3, so we will first prove that $L(\zeta_N)/K$ is Galois, and then find explicitly elements $\sigma, \tau_j \in \mathrm{Gal}(L(\zeta_N)/K)$ satisfying (5).

Theorem 4. *The morphism $X_1'(N) \to X_1(N)$ is a simple radical extension, i.e. the degree N extension of function fields*

$$\mathbb{Q}(j, E_j[N^2])^H \subseteq \mathbb{Q}(j, E_j[N^2])^{H'}$$

can be realized by adjoining $\sqrt[N]{\rho}$ for some function ρ on $X_1(N)$.

Proof. Let $\mathcal{H} \subset H'$ be the subgroup consisting of matrices whose determinant is $\equiv 1 \pmod{N}$. Then the corresponding fixed field $\mathbb{Q}(j, E_j[N^2])^{\mathcal{H}}$ is $L(\zeta_N)$. One can verify that $\mathcal{H}$ is a normal subgroup of H, which implies that $L(\zeta_N)/K$ is Galois of degree $N\varphi(N)$ with Galois group $H/\mathcal{H}$.

In order to understand its structure, we first consider the intermediate extension $L \subsetneq L(\zeta_N)$, which is just a cyclotomic extension with Galois group $\{\tau_j : \zeta_N \mapsto \zeta_N^j \mid 0 \leq j < N, \gcd(j, N) = 1\} \cong (\mathbb{Z}/N)^*$. When viewed as elements of $H/\mathcal{H}$, these maps can be identified with

$$\tau_j = \begin{pmatrix} 1 & 0 \\ 0 & j \end{pmatrix} \bmod \mathcal{H}.$$

Next, we concentrate on the intermediate extension $K(\zeta_N) \subset L(\zeta_N)$ which is of degree N, and its Galois group can be identified with the cyclic group

$$\left\langle \sigma := \begin{pmatrix} 1 & 0 \\ N & 1 \end{pmatrix} \right\rangle = \left\{ \sigma^i = \begin{pmatrix} 1 & 0 \\ iN & 1 \end{pmatrix} \,\middle|\, i = 0, 1, \ldots, N-1 \right\},$$

which, as before, we consider modulo $\mathcal{H}$. It is easy to see that the elements $\tau_j \circ \sigma^i$ are pairwise distinct (e.g. because j is fully determined by the action of $\tau_j \circ \sigma^i$ on ζ_N, and then the uniqueness of i follows at once). Therefore these $N\varphi(N)$ elements must constitute the whole Galois group.

The structure of the Galois group is then determined by the rules $\sigma^N = 1$, $\tau_j^{\varphi(N)} = 1$ and

$$\sigma^i \circ \tau_j = \begin{pmatrix} 1 & 0 \\ iN & j \end{pmatrix} = \tau_j \circ \sigma^{ij^{-1}}, \tag{5}$$

which matches with (4), so this indeed allows for a successful application of Lemma 3. □

Remark 5. The subgroup $\mathcal{H} \subset \mathrm{GL}_2(\mathbb{Z}/N^2\mathbb{Z})$ introduced in the proof of the Theorem corresponds to a modular curve $\mathcal{X}_1'(N)$ over $\mathbb{Q}$ with function field $L(\zeta_N)$. Since $[(\mathbb{Z}/N^2\mathbb{Z})^\times : \det(\mathcal{H})] = \varphi(N)$ it consists geometrically of $\varphi(N)$ copies of $X_1'(N)$, labeled by the different primitive Nth roots of unity ζ_N.

The level structure induced by $\mathcal{H}$ yields the following moduli interpretation of $\mathcal{X}_1'(N)$: it parametrizes triples (E, C, R), where $(E, C) \in X_1'(N)$ is as in Sect. 3.2

and $R \in E[N]$ is an N-torsion point independent of P (i.e. such that $E[N] = \langle P, R \rangle$), where we identify two such points R_1 and R_2 if their Weil pairing with P yields the same (primitive) Nth root of unity, i.e. if $e_N(P, R_1) = e_N(P, R_2)$. Forgetting R leads to a covering $\mathcal{X}_1'(N) \to X_1'(N)$ of degree $\varphi(N)$.

One can make sense of the Galois action of $L(\zeta_N)/K$ in terms of this moduli interpretation. Given a triple $\mathcal{P} = (E, \{Q, Q+P, \ldots, Q+(N-1)P\}, R)$, the images under σ and τ_j are

$$\sigma(\mathcal{P}) = (E, \{Q+R, Q+R+P, \ldots, Q+R+(N-1)P\}, R),$$
$$\tau_j(\mathcal{P}) = (E, \{jQ, jQ+P, \ldots, jQ+(N-1)P, R).$$

4 Radical Isogeny Formulae Through Interpolation

We now describe the method we used to compute the radical isogeny formulae. Explicitly, starting from the universal Tate normal curve $E = E_{b,c}$ over $K = \mathbb{Q}_N(b, c)$ together with the point $P = (0, 0) \in E$ of order $N \geq 4$, we would like to find an expression for the coordinates of a P-distinguished point P' on the quotient curve $E' = E/\langle P \rangle$ (whose Weierstrass model, let us assume, is given by Vélu's formulae). These coordinates live over some radical field extension L of K. For simplicity, we will mostly focus on computing the x-coordinate of P', as the computation of the y-coordinate is more or less analogous.

4.1 A Linear System

Let us denote by $\overline{K}$ an algebraic closure of K, and let $Q \in E(\overline{K})$ be such that $NQ = P$. We would like to find an expression for

$$\beta_0 := \sum_{i=0}^{N-1} x(Q + iP),$$

since by Vélu's formulae this is equivalent to finding the x-coordinate of P'. If we define

$$\gamma_d := \sum_{S \in E[N]} e_N(P, S)^d x(Q + S),$$

then $\gamma_d^N \in K$ for all $d \in \mathbb{Z}$: indeed, let $R \in E(\overline{K})$ be an N-torsion point so that $E[N] = \langle P, R \rangle$ and denote by $e_N : E[N] \times E[N] \to \overline{K}$ the Weil pairing. Then $\zeta_N := e_N(P, R)$ is a primitive Nth root of unity. By Remark 5, it follows that

$$\gamma_d = \sum_{j=0}^{N-1} e_N(P, jR)^d \sum_{i=0}^{N-1} x(Q + jR + iP) = \sum_{j=0}^{N-1} \zeta_N^{jd} \sigma^j(\beta_0),$$

for some generator $\sigma \in \mathrm{Gal}(L(\zeta_N)/K)$ of $\mathrm{Gal}(L(\zeta_N)/K(\zeta_N))$. Following the last paragraph of the proof of Lemma 3 now shows that $\gamma_d^N \in K$.

Note that $\gamma_d \in L(\zeta_N)$ depends on the choice of Q. However all of them are related as follows:

Lemma 6. *Let $Q, Q' \in E[N^2]$ be such that $NQ = NQ' = P$. Then there exists an Nth root of unity $\zeta \in \overline{K}$ such that $\gamma_d(Q) = \zeta^d \gamma_d(Q')$ for all $d \in \mathbb{Z}$. Moreover, for all $d \in \mathbb{Z}$ we have that γ_d/γ_1^d is an element of K that is independent of the choice of Q.*

Proof. We have that Q' differs from Q by an N-torsion point. Note that adding multiples of P to Q clearly does not affect the value of γ_d while adding a multiple kR of R scales it by ζ_N^{-kd}. This shows the first statement with $\zeta = \zeta_N^{-k}$. For the second part, note that the independence on Q already follows from the first part. Now let σ be as above and let τ_j be a generator for the cyclotomic extension $L(\zeta_N)/K(\gamma_1)$. Then $\tau_j(\gamma_d) = \gamma_d$, whereas $\sigma(\gamma_d) = \zeta_N^{-d}\gamma_d$. Since σ, τ_j together generate $\mathrm{Gal}(L(\zeta_N)/K)$ we see that γ_d/γ_1^d is invariant under all Galois automorphisms of $L(\zeta_N)/K$ and we conclude that it is an element of K. □

Defining

$$\beta_j := \sigma^j(\beta_0) = \sum_{i=0}^{N-1} x(Q + jR + iP),$$

we now have the following linear system.

$$\begin{pmatrix} 1 & 1 & 1 & \cdots & 1 \\ 1 & \zeta_N & \zeta_N^2 & \cdots & \zeta_N^{N-1} \\ \vdots & \vdots & \vdots & \ddots & \vdots \\ 1 & \zeta_N^{N-1} & \zeta_N^{2(N-1)} & \cdots & \zeta_N^{(N-1)^2} \end{pmatrix} \begin{pmatrix} \beta_0 \\ \beta_1 \\ \vdots \\ \beta_{N-1} \end{pmatrix} = \begin{pmatrix} \gamma_0 \\ \gamma_1 \\ \vdots \\ \gamma_{N-1} \end{pmatrix}.$$

In particular, if we set $\alpha := \gamma_1$ then we see that

$$\beta_0 = \frac{1}{N}\sum_{d=0}^{N-1} \gamma_d = \frac{1}{N}\sum_{d=0}^{N-1} \left(\frac{\gamma_d}{\gamma_1^d}\right) \alpha^d \in K(\alpha) = L. \tag{6}$$

We have now reduced the problem of finding radical isogeny formulae (at least the determination of the x-coordinate of P') to finding expressions for the elements $\gamma_d/\gamma_1^d \in K$ for all $d \in \{0, \ldots, N-1\}$. In the next subsection we will describe the method we used to do this. Before that we should point out one subtlety. To ensure that (6) is well defined we must have $\alpha \neq 0$; in fact, to be able to use the formula in practice, we should know exactly the value of $\alpha^N \in K$. Though, given N, this is not so difficult to establish (or even guess) in practice; a proof of a closed expression for α^N that works for all N can be found in the appendix (from which it also follows that α is never zero), see Theorem 14.

4.2 Finding the Formulae

Expressions for $c_d := \gamma_d/\gamma_1^d$ will of course depend heavily on how one represents the field $K = \mathbb{Q}(X_1(N))$. It turns out that the representation $K = \mathbb{Q}_N(b, c)$ as presented in Sect. 2.3 is not always optimal. In order to minimize the complexity of the resulting formulae, as well as the running time complexity of the algorithm used to find them, we will instead employ Sutherland's optimized models of $X_1(N)$ [24]. These models are optimal in the sense that they write K as the fraction field, which we will denote $\mathbb{Q}_N(A,B)$, of $\mathbb{Q}[A,B]/G_N(A,B)$ for some modular polynomial $G_N(A,B)$ whose degree in B matches the gonality of $X_1(N)$ over $\mathbb{Q}$ (at least for $N \leq 40$). In particular, we can theoretically write every element of K, specifically the c_d we are after, as a polynomial in $\mathbb{Q}(A)[B]$, where the degree in B is as small as one could hope for. It is also possible, and relatively easy in fact, to find an explicit expression for $b, c \in K$ in terms of Sutherland's functions A, B, so one can also express the universal Tate normal curve $E_{b,c}$ as a curve $E_{A,B}$ over $\mathbb{Q}_N(A,B)$.

The idea is now to determine the reduction $\overline{c_d} \in \mathbb{F}_p(A)[B]$ of the coefficients c_d modulo several primes p, and then to lift the results to $\mathbb{Q}(A)[B]$ using the Chinese Remainder Theorem. To find the $\overline{c_d}$, we sample many curves $E_{A,B}$ over $\mathbb{F}_p$ for which Q, R, and ζ_N of the previous section are all defined over $\mathbb{F}_p$. For each of these curves, we explicitly compute the coefficients c_d as elements of $\mathbb{F}_p$. Then, as long as the number of samples is sufficiently large, we can determine an expression for $\overline{c_d} \in \mathbb{F}_p(A)[B]$ by means of rational interpolation (this last step can be achieved purely by linear algebra over $\mathbb{F}_p$).

The main problem that arises is how to efficiently generate suitable samples $(A,B) \in X_1(N)(\mathbb{F}_p)$. The requirement that ζ_N be defined over $\mathbb{F}_p$ is rather trivially met by demanding that $p \equiv 1 \pmod{N}$. The condition that $Q, R \in E_{A,B}(\mathbb{F}_p)$, however, is more intricate, and simply generating random curves turns out to be far too inefficient for large N. Instead, we rely on an approach based on the theory of complex multiplication.

The CM Method. The endomorphism ring of an elliptic curve $E/\mathbb{C}$ is isomorphic to either $\mathbb{Z}$ or an order $\mathcal{O}$ in an imaginary quadratic number field. In the latter case we say that E has complex multiplication (CM) by $\mathcal{O}$. The j-invariants of such elliptic curves are algebraic integers. The *Hilbert class polynomial* $H_D(X) \in \mathbb{Z}[X]$ is the minimal polynomial over $\mathbb{Q}$ of the j-invariant of an elliptic curve $E/\mathbb{C}$ with CM by the quadratic order of discriminant D.

Ordinary elliptic curves over a finite field always have CM. An elliptic curve $E/\mathbb{F}_q$ with CM by the imaginary quadratic order $\mathcal{O}$ of discriminant D exists if and only if there exist $t, u \in \mathbb{Z}$ such that $u^2 D = t^2 - 4q$. In this case H_D splits completely over $\mathbb{F}_q$ and its roots are precisely the j-invariants of elliptic curves with CM by $\mathcal{O}$. The trace of Frobenius of such curves is $\pm t$, so they will have $q + 1 \pm t$ points. One can use this to find curves over $\mathbb{F}_q$ with a desired number of points; this is known as the *CM Method.*

Sampling Curves with Torsion. We now describe how to use the CM method to construct curves $E_{A,B}$ with full N^2-torsion over $\mathbb{F}_p$; this will certainly ensure that the desired points Q, R be defined over $\mathbb{F}_p$. We thus want to find curves with number of points divisible by N^4. One approach is to strengthen the requirement that $p \equiv 1 \pmod{N}$ to $p \equiv 1 \pmod{N^4}$ and construct curves of trace 2 using the CM method, i.e. with CM by an order of discriminant D dividing $2^2 - 4p$.

The structure of the $\mathbb{F}_p$-rational N^∞-torsion also be controlled by D; if we choose D a divisor of $(2^2 - 4p)/N^4$ then $E[N^2](\mathbb{F}_p) \cong (\mathbb{Z}/N^2\mathbb{Z})^2$, see e.g. [8, Thm. 7].

Algorithm. We summarize the above discussion in the following pseudo algorithm generating radical isogeny formulae for $N \geq 4$. The SageMath code we used can be found in the GitHub repository accompanying this paper.

(i) Find all prime numbers $p \equiv 1 \pmod{N^4}$ up to a certain bound.
(ii) For each prime number p, determine the roots j_i of the Hilbert class polynomials H_D modulo p for every $D \mid 4(p-1)/N^4$.
(iii) For each root j_i, determine the $(A, B) \in X_1(N)(\mathbb{F}_p)$ for which $j(E_{A,B}) = j_i$.
(iv) For each pair (A, B), if $E_{A,B}$ has trace $+2$, determine $c_d \in \mathbb{F}_p$ for all $d \in \{0, \ldots, N-1\}$.
(v) For each d, find a formula for $c_d \in \mathbb{F}_p(A)[B]$ by rational interpolation.
(vi) Lift the formulae to $\mathbb{Q}(A)[B]$ by the Chinese Remainder Theorem.

4.3 Iterative Formulae

The above describes how to find an expression for the x-coordinate of P' as an element of $L = K(\alpha)$. An analogous method can be used to find an expression for the y-coordinate. By transforming the pair (E', P') to Tate normal form one can then also determine explicit formulae for Sutherland's parameters $A', B' \in L$ corresponding to the point $(E', P') \in X_1(N)(L)$. In this way, we obtain radical isogeny formulae that can be applied iteratively. We list formulae for prime powers $16 < N \leq 37$ in our GitHub repository.

5 Optimizing the Formulae

When optimizing radical isogeny formulae, one needs to take into account all of the following choices.

- The radicand ρ_N is not unique: it can be scaled with Nth powers in $\mathbb{Q}_N(b, c)$, and it can be raised to exponents that are coprime with N. Switching from one radicand to another results in different radical isogeny formulae with different performances.
- It is not self-evident that the optimized representations of $X_1(N)$ by Sutherland from [24] will result in optimized radical isogeny formulae.
- Elements in $\mathbb{Q}_N(b, c, \alpha)$ can be expressed in several ways since we work modulo the two relations $F_N(b, c) = 0$ and $\alpha^N = \rho_N(b, c)$.
- It is a priori not clear what formulae we are trying to optimize; e.g. for $E' = E/\langle P \rangle$ we can try to find optimal expressions for a P-distinguished point P' on E', or we can try to write E' in Tate normal form immediately.

We will focus on finding efficient enough formulae in this setting, where it seems nigh impossible to prove that they are indeed the most optimal (especially for $N \geq 10$ as we will see further up ahead). Hence we do not claim they are optimal, but they should not be far off and at the very least in certain cases a big improvement compared to the work in [6].

For $N \in \{4, 5, \ldots, 10\} \cup \{12\}$, the Tate normal form can be parametrized by a single parameter, say A. This means that the codomain curve of a radical N-isogeny can be put into a (new) Tate normal form with a single parameter, say A', where we translated the P-distinguished point P' to $(0, 0)$. In practice, this new parameter seems a good candidate to try to optimize, as can be seen from the case of $N = 4, 5$ from [6]. The raw equation for A' can be easily obtained by any algebraic software package for these small N.

To find an efficient representation of A', consider the curve $X_1'(N)$ defined by $\alpha^N - \rho_N, F_N = 0$. Then A' can be seen as a function on this curve and we can compute its divisor. For $N < 10$, an algebraic software package has no issues checking which linear combinations of places in its support constitute principal divisors, and we can use this to peel off (easy) factors from A'. For every $N \in \{4, \ldots, 9\}$, there are clear contenders for which factorization is most efficient. We list them all, skipping the case $N = 5$ which can be found in (3). Note that for $N \geq 6$, our "factorization" merely amounts to writing A' as the quotient of two easyish expressions in A and α.

N = 4. In this case we have $b = A$, $c = 0$ and for $\alpha^4 = A$ we have that

$$A' = \alpha \frac{4\alpha^2 + 1}{(2\alpha + 1)^4}. \tag{7}$$

N = 6. In this case we have $b = A(A-1)$, $c = A-1$ and for $\alpha^6 = -A^2(A-1)$ we have that

$$A' = \frac{(-3A + 2)\alpha^4 + 3A^2\alpha^2 + 2A\alpha - 3A^3 + 4A^2}{\alpha^4 + 2A\alpha^2 + 3A\alpha + A^2}. \tag{8}$$

N = 7. In this case we have $b = A^2(A - 1)$, $c = A(A - 1)$ and for $\alpha^7 = A^4(A - 1)$ we have that

$$A' = \frac{\alpha^6 + A\alpha^5 + 2A^3\alpha^2 - A^3\alpha + A^4}{-\alpha^6 + A\alpha^4 + A^3\alpha^2 - 2A^3\alpha + A^4}.$$

N = 8. In this case we have that $b = \frac{A(A-1)}{(A-2)^2}$, $c = \frac{-A(A-1)}{A-2}$ and for $\alpha^8 = \frac{-A^2(A-1)}{(A-2)^4}$ we have that

$$A' = \frac{-2A(A - 2)\alpha^2 - A(A - 2)}{(A - 2)^2\alpha^4 - A(A - 2)\alpha^2 - A(A - 2)\alpha + A}.$$

N = 9. In this case we have that $b = A^2(A - 1)(A^2 - A + 1)$, $c = A^2(A - 1)$ and for $\alpha^9 = A^4(A - 1)(A^2 - A + 1)^3$ we have that

$$A' = \frac{A(A^2 - A + 1)(\alpha^5 + A(A^2 - A + 1)\alpha^2 + A^2(A^2 - A + 1)^2)}{\alpha^7 - A(A^2 - A + 1)(A - 1)\alpha^4 - A^3(A^2 - A + 1)^2\alpha + (A(A^2 - A + 1))^3}.$$

For $N \geq 10$, Magma struggles to efficiently verify whether a given divisor is principal, and those that do get found are less clean than the above factors, so we will optimize these two cases with the more general method for larger N.[1]

If we compute E' as $E/\langle P \rangle$ by means of Vélu's formulae, then E' is in (long) Weierstrass form and we still need to compute an isomorphism to put E' back in Tate normal form E'_t for certain $b', c' \in \mathbb{Q}_N(b, c, \alpha)$. By [20, Prop. 1.3(d)], the isomorphism $\iota : E'_t \to E'$ is determined by a 4-tuple (u, r, s, t), where $P' = (r, t)$ is the P-distinguished point and u is a unit. This u, when seen as a polynomial of degree $N-1$ in $\mathbb{Q}_N(b, c)[\alpha]$, seems to always be efficient to write down and evaluate. Furthermore, the expressions uc' and ub'/c' also enjoy this feature. In particular, a factor that arises in the coefficient of α^i has a high chance of also being there in the coefficient of α^j for $j > i$, which makes this efficient to evaluate in a Horner scheme with rising powers of α. We provide the concrete expressions for $N = 10$ and refer the reader to our GitHub repository for larger N. Remark that for $N = 10$ we still work with a one-parameter family of curves and the expression uA' is just as efficient as uc' or ub'/c'. The operation counts for all formulae $N \in \{4, 5, \ldots, 17\} \cup \{19\}$ can be found in Table 1.

N = 10. In this case we have

$$b = \frac{A^3(A-1)(2A-1)}{(A^2-3A+1)^2}, \quad c = \frac{-A(A-1)(2A-1)}{(A^2-3A+1)}, \quad \alpha^{10} = \frac{A^9(A-1)(2A-1)^2}{(A^2-3A+1)^5},$$

and then $A' = v_{A'}/u$ with

$$\begin{aligned} u = {} & 1 + 3\alpha + \frac{4A-1}{A}\alpha^2 + \frac{2c}{b}\alpha^3 - \frac{c(A-4)}{bA}\alpha^4 + \frac{(A-1)(4A-1)}{bA}\alpha^5 + \\ & \frac{(A+1)(A-1)}{bA^2}\alpha^6 + \frac{4c(A-1)}{b^2A}\alpha^7 + \frac{c(A-1)(4A-1)}{b^2A^2}\alpha^8 - \frac{c^2(A-1)}{b^3A}\alpha^9, \\ v_{A'} = {} & A + 2\alpha + \frac{A+1}{A}\alpha^2 + \frac{3c}{b}\alpha^3 + \frac{c(A+1)}{bA}\alpha^4 + \frac{(A-1)(A+1)}{bA}\alpha^5 + \\ & \frac{(A+1)(4A-1)}{bA^2}\alpha^6 + \frac{c(A-1)}{b^2A}\alpha^7 + \frac{c(A+1)(A-1)}{b^2A^2}\alpha^8 + \frac{c^2(A-1)}{b^3A}\alpha^9. \end{aligned}$$

6 Ensuring Horizontality

If both E and P are defined over a finite field $\mathbb{F}_q$ with $\gcd(q-1, N) = 1$ then, as discussed in [6, §5.1], the isogeny $\varphi : E \to E' = E/\langle P \rangle$ is necessarily horizontal. The radicand $\rho_N \in \mathbb{F}_q$ admits a unique Nth root $\alpha \in \mathbb{F}_q$, and for this choice of α the resulting point $P' \in E'$ is again defined over $\mathbb{F}_q$, so the argument repeats. Thus, if N and $q-1$ are coprime, then walking horizontally using radical isogenies is natural and easy. As explained in Remark 1, for any fixed N the cost of an iteration is dominated by this Nth root extraction, which amounts to one

[1] We remark that for the smaller N it can be extremely fast to let a computer algebra software package verify that a given divisor is *not* principal, but to prove it is principal is harder in the majority of cases.

Table 1. The computational cost of radical N-isogenies for $N \in \{2, 3, \ldots, 17\} \cup \{19\}$ compared to previous work [6, Tbl. 3]. The letters $\mathbf{E}, \mathbf{M}, \mathbf{A}$ and $\mathbf{I}$ denote exponentiation, (full) multiplication (including squaring), addition and inversion respectively. The letter $\mathbf{m}$ denotes multiplication with a small constant. The last column expresses the cost of an N-isogeny relative to a 2-isogeny, based on the evaluation of a chain of 100 000 horizontal N-isogenies over $\mathbb{F}_p$, where p is the CRAD-513 prime from Sect. 7. Remark that the cost of $\mathbf{E}$ is approximately $(1.5 \log p)\mathbf{M}$ with the square-and-multiply algorithm. In particular, the last column would converge to 1 for larger values of p since the cost of a radical isogeny will be dominated by $\mathbf{E}$.

	Previous work [6]	This work	Cost relative to 2-isogeny
2-isogeny	-	E + M + 3m + 2A	1
3-isogeny	E + 6M + 3A	E + 2M + 3m + 3A	1.023
4-isogeny	E + 4M + 3A + I	E + 3M + m + 3A + I	1.008
5-isogeny	E + 7M + 6A + I	E + 6M + m + 6A + I	1.034
6-isogeny	-	E + 9M + 6m + 9A + I	1.090
7-isogeny	E + 24M + 20A + I	E + 12M + 2m + 9A + I	1.043
8-isogeny	-	E + 11M + m + 9A + 2I	1.151
9-isogeny	E + 69M + 58A + I	E + 17M + 9A + I	1.062
10-isogeny	-	E + 57M + 5m + 31A + 3I	1.196
11-isogeny	E + 599M + 610A + I	E + 50M + 21m + 71A + 2I	1.293
12-isogeny	-	E + 90M + 8m + 35A + 3I	1.296
13-isogeny	E + 783M + 776A + I	E + 89M + 33m + 120A + 2I	1.448
14-isogeny	-	E + 159M + 16m + 131A + 4I	1.613
15-isogeny	-	E + 149M + 32m + 125A + 2I	1.599
16-isogeny	-	E + 120M + 4m + 40A + 3I	1.388
17-isogeny	-	E + 217M + 55m + 332A + 3I	1.921
19-isogeny	-	E + 329M + 125m + 437A + 3I	2.532

exponentiation in $\mathbb{F}_q$. But if $\gcd(q - 1, N) > 1$ then maintaining horizontality is more subtle.

In the remainder of this section we focus on the CSIDH case of supersingular elliptic curves over a finite prime field $\mathbb{F}_p$, where this issue arises (only) if $p \equiv 7 \bmod 8$ and one navigates with cyclic isogenies of even degree N, see [13, Thm. 2.7]. In this case $\gcd(p - 1, N) = 2$ because $N \mid \#E(\mathbb{F}_p) = p + 1$. Let us recall that if $p \equiv 7 \bmod 8$ then supersingular elliptic curves over $\mathbb{F}_p$ come in two kinds: curves on the surface of their 2-isogeny volcano, and curves on the floor. The surface is characterized by the existence of three $\mathbb{F}_p$-rational points of order 2; more precisely, the group of $\mathbb{F}_p$-rational points is isomorphic to $\mathbb{Z}_2 \times \mathbb{Z}_{(p+1)/2}$. The points of order 2 can be classified as follows (see Fig. 1):

- a point $P_{\rightarrow}$, whose halves are $\mathbb{F}_p$-rational,
- a point $P_{\leftarrow}$, whose halves are not $\mathbb{F}_p$-rational, but their x-coordinates are,
- a point $P_{\downarrow}$, the x-coordinates of whose halves are not $\mathbb{F}_p$-rational.

Each of these points spans the kernel of a 2-isogeny. The point $P_\downarrow$ takes us to the floor, while the other two isogenies are horizontal. It can be checked that the dual of an isogeny in the $P_\rightarrow$-direction is in the $P_\leftarrow$-direction, and vice versa. Therefore, non-backtracking chains of horizontal 2-isogenies necessarily happen on the surface and consistently walk in either of these two directions.

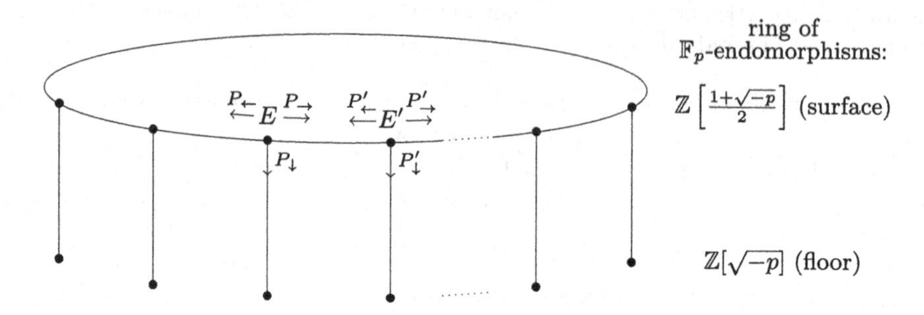

Fig. 1. *Component of the 2-isogeny graph over $\mathbb{F}_p$ when $p \equiv 7 \bmod 8$. The top layer belongs to the surface; the bottom layer belongs to the floor; and $\sqrt{-p}$ is identified with the Frobenius endomorphism.*

6.1 Horizontal vs. Non-horizontal N-isogenies

Fix $N \geq 2$ even and assume that $p \equiv -1 \bmod \operatorname{lcm}(2N, 8)$, so that every curve E on the surface satisfies

$$E(\mathbb{F}_p)[N] \cong \mathbb{Z}_2 \times \mathbb{Z}_N. \tag{9}$$

Then $E(\mathbb{F}_p)$ has 2 or 3 cyclic subgroups of order N, depending on whether $t = \operatorname{ord}_2(N) > 1$ or $t = 1$ (see Lemma 7 below). Every corresponding isogeny $\varphi : E \rightarrow E/\langle P \rangle$ can be decomposed as $\varphi = \theta \circ \psi$, where ψ is the $N/2$-isogeny with kernel $\langle 2P \rangle$ and θ is the 2-isogeny with kernel $\langle \psi(P) \rangle$. The isogeny ψ is necessarily horizontal: indeed, if it would involve a vertical step, then composing with θ would necessarily involve backtracking, rendering φ non-cyclic. However, θ may take us to the floor.

Lemma 7. *Write $r = \operatorname{ord}_2(p+1) \geq \operatorname{ord}_2(2N) = t + 1$.*

(i) If $t = 1$ then there are 3 options for $\langle P \rangle$, corresponding to θ being in the $P_\rightarrow$-direction, the $P_\leftarrow$-direction or the $P_\downarrow$-direction.
(ii) If $t \geq 2$ then there are 2 options for $\langle P \rangle$, corresponding to θ being in the $P_\rightarrow$-direction or the $P_\downarrow$-direction.
(iii) If $r \geq t+2$ (automatic if $t = 1$) then the group corresponding to θ being in the $P_\rightarrow$-direction can be characterized as follows: it is the unique group all of whose elements admit halves in $E(\mathbb{F}_p)$.

Proof. (i) Under the isomorphism (9), the cyclic subgroups of order N are generated by $(0,1)$, $(1,1)$ or $(1,2)$. Note that the group $\langle 2P \rangle$ does not depend on this choice, hence neither does ψ. Necessarily, the three groups must then correspond to the three stated options for θ.

(ii) If $t \geq 2$ then only the groups generated by $(0,1)$ or $(1,1)$ remain. Also note that we can further decompose $\psi = \theta' \circ \psi'$, where θ' is a 2-isogeny with kernel $\langle \psi'(2P) \rangle$. Since $\psi'(2P)$ is halvable over $\mathbb{F}_p$, this isogeny is necessarily in the $P_{\rightarrow}$-direction. But then θ cannot be in the $P_{\leftarrow}$-direction, otherwise φ would be non-cyclic.

(iii) If $r \geq t+2$ then $E(\mathbb{F}_p)[2N] \cong \mathbb{Z}_2 \times \mathbb{Z}_{2N}$ from which we see that the group generated by $(0,1)$ under the isomorphism (9) is uniquely characterized by its elements being halvable over $\mathbb{F}_p$. But then $\psi(P)$ is also halvable over $\mathbb{F}_p$, from which the claim follows. □

The central question of Sect. 6 is: how do we avoid that $\ker \theta = \langle P_{\downarrow} \rangle$, within the framework of radical isogenies?

6.2 Square vs Non-square Radicands

As explained in [6, §5.3], there is a simple algebraic criterion for determining whether quotienting out an order-N point $P \in E$ keeps us on the surface or takes us to the floor. Namely, we stay on the surface if and only if $\rho_N = f_{N,P}(-P)$ is a non-zero square in $\mathbb{F}_p$. In this case ρ_N admits two different Nth roots $\alpha \in \mathbb{F}_p$, which are each other's negatives. The challenge is to select the sign in such a way that the next radicand ρ'_N is again a square. Indeed, for this choice of Nth root the argument repeats and one keeps walking horizontally. Of course, one fallback is to make an arbitrary choice for α, at the cost of an exponentiation in $\mathbb{F}_q$ as before. One then computes the resulting ρ'_N and checks if it is a square. If it is not, then one switches to $-\alpha$.

It was observed in [4, Lem. 4] that for $N = 2$ the extra quadratic residuosity check can be avoided, because the correct choice of α admits an explicit description in terms of the "principal" square root of ρ_2, by which we mean the unique square root which is itself a square.

Remark 8. More generally, for any non-zero square $\rho \in \mathbb{F}_p$ we will refer to the unique Nth root of ρ that is a square as the principal Nth root. Note that when computing the Nth root through exponentiation, i.e., as $\rho^{(p+1)/2N}$, then it is automatically principal.

Then, in more detail, the observation from [4, Lem. 4] was as follows: the radical isogeny iteration

$$E : y^2 = x^3 + Ax^2 + Bx \quad \rightarrow \quad E' : y^2 = x^3 + (A + 6\alpha)x^2 + 4\alpha(A + 2\alpha)x,$$

with $\alpha = \sqrt{B}$, repeatedly quotients out $(0,0)$. If $(0,0) \in E$ is the point $P_{\rightarrow}$, then $(0,0) \in E'$ is the point $P'_{\rightarrow}$ if and only if α is the principal square root. This changes if $(0,0) \in E$ is the point $P_{\leftarrow}$, in which case $(0,0) \in E'$ is the point $P'_{\leftarrow}$ if and only if α is the non-principal square root.

This convenient fact was adapted to $N = 4$, first as a conjecture [6, Conj. 2] but recently this got proved by Onuki and Moriya [17, §5]. We will recall the precise statement of this adaptation in Sect. 6.4, where it will arise as an easy consequence to our generalization to arbitrary even N. But let us first highlight two takeaways that are already apparent from the case $N = 2$:

(i) When considering radical isogeny formulae for even N, then substituting $-\alpha$ for α produces formulae that are equally legitimate, e.g., because -1 is an Nth root of unity. Consequently, one cannot hope for a general rule saying that the $P_{\rightarrow}$-direction always corresponds to the principal Nth root.

(ii) Even worse, imagine that the rule does apply to some concrete choice of formulae, and now scale the radicand ρ_N with g^N for some arbitrary modular unit $g \in \mathbb{Q}_N(b,c)$, i.e. a function whose zeroes and poles are supported on the cuspidal part of $X_1(N)$; see [23]. The radical isogeny formulae transform into a version in which each occurrence of $\sqrt[N]{\rho_N}$ gets replaced by $\sqrt[N]{\rho_N}\,/g$. For these new formulae, the correct Nth root will depend on the Legendre symbol of the evaluation of g at the point $(E,P) \in X_1(N)$ under consideration.

6.3 Conjectural Shape of ρ'_N Modulo Squares (proved for $N \leq 14$)

We ran into the following property of ρ'_N, which unfortunately we could not prove beyond $N = 14$, but which implies a generalization of the aforementioned observations for $N = 2, 4$ to arbitrary even N. Concretely, for every even $N \geq 4$ we can consider

$$\phi_{E,2}(x) = x^4 + b(1-c)x^2 - 2b^2x + b^3, \tag{10}$$

whose roots are the x-coordinates of the four halves of $P = (0,0)$ on $E = E_{b,c}$. Over $\mathbb{Q}_N(b,c)(\alpha^{N/2})$ this polynomial splits in two quadratic factors, with one quadratic factor corresponding to a pair of points

$$\frac{N}{2}Q, \; \frac{N}{2}Q + \frac{N}{2}P,$$

mapping to $\frac{N}{2}P'$ under φ. The discriminant of said quadratic factor is a modular unit of $X_1'(N)$ that we denote by Δ.

Example 9. Over $\mathbb{Q}_4(b,c)(\alpha^2)$ the polynomial (10) splits as $(x^2 - \alpha^2 x - \alpha^6)(x^2 + \alpha^2 x + \alpha^6)$. The roots of the first factor are the x-coordinates of two preimages of $2P'$. The discriminant of that factor is $\Delta = \alpha^4(1 + 4\alpha^2)$.

Our conjecture is as follows:

Conjecture 10. If the radicand $\rho_N = f_{N,P}(-P)$ was chosen, then one has

$$\rho'_N \equiv \sigma\alpha b\Delta \tag{11}$$

modulo multiplication with a non-zero square in $\mathbb{Q}_N(b,c)(\alpha)$, for some $\sigma \in \{\pm 1\}$.

Here, we note:

- The sign σ should be viewed against our first takeaway message *(i)* above: substituting $-\alpha$ for α produces equally valid radical isogeny formulae but flips the sign.
- The congruence sign absorbs squares, so the conjecture is insensitive to replacing ρ'_N with any other representative of $t_N(P', -P')$, or even $t_N(P', \lambda P')$ for whatever odd λ. However, as discussed in our second takeaway *(ii)* above, in the case of ρ_N the precise representative does matter. Interestingly, scaling with b^N would make the statement somewhat cleaner, as it would remove the mysterious factor b. This suggests that the radicand from Theorem 14 in the appendix is in fact a more natural choice than $f_{N,P}(-P)$.

It is exactly the presence of this factor b that made it difficult to guess how to go beyond the case $N = 4$; in the case $N = 4$ we have $b = -\alpha^4$ so that modulo squares this factor just appeared as a sign.

Theorem 11. *Conjecture 10 is true for $N \leq 14$.*

Proof (sketch). From (7) and Example 9 we see that $\rho'_4 \equiv \alpha\Delta$ modulo squares, which matches with Conjecture 10 with $\sigma = -1$ because $-b = \alpha^4$ is a square. So the case $N = 4$ is immediate.

The case $N = 6$ is more illustrative. Take A', α, b as in (8) and let

$$\Delta = 4(1 - A)\alpha^3 + 3A^3 - 7A^2 + 4A$$

be the discriminant of the relevant quadratic factor of (10). One verifies, aided by the Magma command `IsPrincipal`, that for $\rho'_6 = f_{6,P'}(-P') = -A'^2(A'-1)$ the function $-b\rho'_6/\alpha\Delta$ is a square in the function field of $X'_1(6) : \alpha^6 + A^2(A-1) = 0$. So this again matches with Conjecture 10 (now with a minus sign).

In a similar way we have managed to deal with all even N up to 14, with further help coming from the observation that $\rho'_N = f_{N,-P'}(-P') \equiv f_{2,\frac{N}{2}P'}(P')$ modulo squares, see [3, Thm. IX.9(2)]. The right-hand side is a simpler function and therefore easier to handle by Magma. □

As mentioned, beyond $N = 14$ we were no longer able to verify Conjecture 10, although for $N = 16$ we gathered evidence by experimentally verifying Proposition 12 below for various concrete horizontal supersingular isogeny walks over finite prime fields.

6.4 Horizontal Isogenies and Principal Nth Roots

Proposition 12. *Let $N \geq 4$ be even and consider radical isogeny formulae for computing chains of N-isogenies in terms of the radicand $\rho_N = f_{N,P}(-P)$. Assume that Conjecture 10 applies to these formulae and let $\sigma = \pm 1$ be the sign involved in its statement.*

Let $p \equiv -1 \bmod \operatorname{lcm}(2N, 8)$ and consider a supersingular elliptic curve $E/\mathbb{F}_p$ on the surface, along with a point $P \in E(\mathbb{F}_p)[N]$ such that the resulting isogeny

$\varphi : E \to E' = E/\langle P \rangle$ is horizontal; let θ be the corresponding degree-2 component as in Sect. 6.1 and let $b, c \in \mathbb{F}_p$ be the corresponding Tate normal form coefficients. Let $P' \in E'$ be the point produced by our radical isogeny formulae, where $\alpha = \sqrt[N]{\rho_N(b,c)}$ was computed as

$$\sigma \cdot s \cdot b^{(p-1)/2} \rho_N(b,c)^{(p+1)/2N}.$$

Here the sign s is determined as follows:

(i) if θ walks in the $P_{\rightarrow}$-direction and $r > t+1$ then $s = 1$,
(ii) if θ walks in the $P_{\rightarrow}$-direction and $r = t+1$ then $s = -1$,
(iii) if θ walks in the $P_{\leftarrow}$-direction (only possible if $t = 1$) then $s = -1$.

Then the isogeny $E' \to E'/\langle P' \rangle$ is horizontal.

Proof. Recall that the goal is to choose the instance of α that renders ρ'_N a square. Assuming Conjecture 10, this happens if and only if $\sigma\alpha b \Delta$ is a square.

In case *(i)* the point P is fully halvable over $\mathbb{F}_p$ thanks to Lemma 7(iii), so that Δ always evaluates to a square, regardless of the choice of α. So in order for ρ'_N to be a square, it is necessary and sufficient to choose α such that $\sigma\alpha b$ is a square: the claim follows.

If we are in cases *(ii)* or *(iii)* then none of the halves of P belong to $E(\mathbb{F}_p)$. Even stronger: none of these halves can have an $\mathbb{F}_p$-rational x-coordinate, because otherwise such a half H would satisfy $\pi_p(H) = -H$ and therefore $P = \pi_p(P) = -P$; a contradiction. This means that Δ is a non-square, regardless of the choice of α, and we can conclude as before. □

Example 13. For $N = 4$ we recover [6, Conj. 2], proved in [17]. Indeed, recall that $\sigma = -1$ and that b is always non-square in view of $\rho_4 = -b = \alpha^4$. Thus we have to compute $\alpha = s\rho_4^{(p+1)/8}$ with $s = -1$ if $p \equiv 7 \bmod 16$ and $s = 1$ if $p \equiv 15 \bmod 16$.

We conclude by noting that $b^{(p-1)/2}\rho^{(p+1)/2N} = b^{-1}(b^N \rho_N)^{(p+1)/2N}$, effectively showing that the cost of root computation remains a single exponentiation.

7 Implementation

In this section we focus on N-isogenies between supersingular elliptic curves over prime fields $\mathbb{F}_p$ such that computing the required radical can be done deterministically by a single exponentiation. All tests were done in Magma v2.32-2 on an Intel(R) Xeon(R) CPU E5-2630 v2 @ 2.60GHz with 128 GB memory.

7.1 Isogeny Chains

The main application of these radical isogeny formulae is that they can be used to efficiently compute a cyclic N^k-isogeny for small N and large k. This is similar to the work in [6], but we can now use larger N, have more efficient formulae for smaller N and are not restricted to odd N.

Remark that the radical 5-isogeny formulae from [6] were already optimized. Table 1 however shows a modest to strong speed up for radical N-isogenies for $N = 7, 9, 11, 13$. Over the field $\mathbb{F}_p$ with p the 513-bit CRAD-513 prime from Sect. 7.2, they provide a speed-up of respectively 4%, 13%, 55% and 57% compared to the work of [6].

The best known method to compute a chain of 17- or 19-isogenies so far was by sampling 17- or 19-torsion points and then applying Vélu-style formulae to compute the codomain. The cost of this is dominated by the computation of an appropriate torsion point. With the new radical formulae from Sect. 5, we only need to initialize the chain by computing such a torsion point once, and then can iteratively apply the radical isogeny formulae. Working over a prime field of roughly 512 bits, this results in an asymptotic speed-up of chaining 17-isogenies by a factor of 14, and a factor of 10 for chaining 19-isogenies. There is somewhat of a jump in complexity when going to optimized equations from $X_1(19)$ to $X_1(23)$ due to a jump in gonality. In particular, we do not expect radical 23-isogenies to be much of a speed-up over prime fields of characteristic roughly 512 bits,[2] so we did not try to optimize these. Nonetheless, for asymptotically large p the computational cost of a radical isogeny is expected to be dominated by a full exponentiation over $\mathbb{F}_p$.

For composite N, one can make a similar argument with regards to speed-up but the comparison is more subtle. For instance, the cost of computing a 15-isogeny is dominated by one exponentiation and 149 full multiplications according to Table 1. Alternatively, a 15-isogeny can also be computed by means of the concatenation of a 3- and 5-isogeny, the cost of which is dominated by two exponentiations and 8 full multiplications. Assuming we work over a prime field of cryptographic size - say at least 128 bits - the 15-isogeny will be the fastest method. However, assuming we have rational 9-torsion available, we have access to highly efficient radical 9-isogeny formulae, so asymptotically a 3-isogeny can be seen as half the cost of a 9-isogeny.

In general, composite N seem to yield more efficient formulae compared to prime N as can be seen in Table 1. This stems from the fact that optimized equations for $X_1(N)$ typically have lower degree when N is composite, but also from the radical isogeny formulae themselves which appear to have parameterless integer coefficients (including zero) noticeably more often for composite N. These zero coefficients are even more frequently present in the radical isogeny formulae for prime-power N. In Table 2 one can see a comparison for computing low-degree prime-power chains of isogenies for three levels of prime bitsizes.

As can be seen, computing a chain of prime-power degree isogenies can be done more efficiently than a chain of prime degree isogenies for at least these values. The effect is more prominent for larger prime fields, since the exponentiation in those cases is more dominating in the overall cost of the radical isogeny formulae. We did not optimize the formulae for $N = 25$, since an optimal parametrization of $X_1(25)$ is already more complex than $X_1(19)$, and from

[2] Especially in the CSIDH setting from Sect. 7.2 where the initializing overhead is less negligible.

Table 2. Comparison in speed with regards to computing a chain of radical ℓ-isogenies over a prime field $\mathbb{F}_p$ for $\ell \in \{2,3\}$ by means of different prime powers. The bit levels correspond to the size of p.

	512 bits	1024 bits	1536 bits
$2^{60,000}$-isogeny	23.38 s	97.42 s	264.59 s
$4^{30,000}$-isogeny	11.93 s	49.51 s	133.12 s
$8^{20,000}$-isogeny	8.77 s	34.58 s	91.33 s
$16^{15,000}$-isogeny	7.92 s	29.23 s	75.01 s
$3^{60,000}$-isogeny	23.39 s	98.08 s	266.31 s
$9^{30,000}$-isogeny	12.77 s	49.88 s	134.61 s

Table 1 it is clear that computing chains of 5-isogenies would most likely be just as fast or faster (at least on the 512-bit level). Assuming the arithmetic for a radical ℓ^{k+1}-isogeny is always more complex than the arithmetic for a radical ℓ^k-isogeny, the asymptotic speed-up that can be gained from going to the next prime power is always bounded by $(k+1)/k$. For this reason, we expect that optimized radical 27- and 32-isogenies would be less efficient than radical 9- and 16-isogenies for all bitsizes in Table 2, though from a certain threshold onwards they would be the most efficient option again.

7.2 Impact on CSIDH

An application where chains of isogenies can be used is CSIDH [7]. We proceed just as in [6, §6], with the following differences:

- We make use of radical 17- and 19-isogenies.
- The optimzed formulae allow us to sample higher exponents of N-isogenies for $N = 7, 9, 11, 13$.
- We no longer use radical 4-isogenies, instead switching to radical 8-isogenies.

This last point may seem counterintuitive considering that chains of 16-isogenies are faster on the 512-bit prime level, as illustrated in Table 2. In CSIDH however, p is chosen such that $p+1$ is divisible by as many small primes as possible. If we want to make use of radical 16-isogenies, we would need to have that $32 \mid p+1$ (instead of $16 \mid p+1$ for radical 8-isogenies). This means that p would need to be roughly one bit larger, making all the other arithmetic more expensive. The trade-off in practice seems to be not worth it, considering the relative small gain from switching from chains of radical 8-isogenies to chains of radical 16-isogenies. The gap in efficiency between radical 4-isogenies and radical 8-isogenies does make a noticeable difference so we will use those. Nonetheless, we still need an extra factor of 2 that divides $p+1$ compared to the suggested prime in [6], so we choose CRAD-513 as the prime

$$p = 2^4 \cdot 3 \cdot \underbrace{(3 \cdot 5 \cdot \ldots 367)}_{\text{72 consecutive primes}} \cdot 379 \cdot 409 - 1.$$

The following sampling interval for the private key was determined heuristically, but can be considered (near) optimal:

$$[-303;303] \times [-198;198] \times [-103;103] \times [-101;101] \times [-91;91]$$
$$\times [-68;68] \times [-51;51] \times [-41;41] \times [-6;6]^{13} \times [-5;5]^{13}$$
$$\times [-4;4]^{11} \times [-3;3]^{10} \times [-2;2]^{10} \times [-1;1]^{10}.$$

Using these parameters, the class group action of the maximal private key can be computed 12% more efficiently than in the case of [6]. For an average private key, this speed-up will be roughly halved but from a constant-time implementation angle, the maximal private key is a more apt benchmark. This implementation in Magma is meant as a comparison to the work of [6], and can not be translated directly to other (constant-time) implementations such as CTIDH [1].

Appendix: An Explicit Radicand

The goal of the appendix is to prove the following result.

Theorem 14. *Let $N \in \mathbb{Z}_{>2}$. Let $K = \mathbb{Q}_N(b,c)$ as in Sect. 2.3. Let E/K be the elliptic curve given by $y^2 + (1-c)xy - by = x^3 - bx^2$. Let $P = (0,0) \in E$. Denote by Ψ_j the j-th division polynomial on E. Set $k = \lceil N/2 \rceil$. Then*

$$\left(\sum_{S \in E[N]} e_N(P,S) x(Q+S) \right)^N = N^{2N} \cdot \begin{cases} \frac{\Psi_k^2}{\Psi_{k-1}^2}(P) & \text{if } N \text{ is odd;} \\ \frac{\Psi_{k+1}}{\Psi_{k-1}}(P) & \text{if } N \text{ is even.} \end{cases}$$

Pairings and Division Polynomials

Let K be a field and let E/K be an elliptic curve. Suppose $P \in E(K)$ is of order N, such that $\operatorname{char} K \nmid N$. Let $Q \in E(\overline{K})$ satisfying $NQ = P$. Let $f \in K(E)$, $g \in \overline{K}(E)$ with respective divisors

$$\operatorname{div} f = N(P) - N(\mathcal{O}), \qquad \operatorname{div} g = \sum_{S \in E[N]} ((Q+S) - (S)).$$

Assume that g is such that $g^N = f \circ [N]$. Denote by $e_N : E[N] \times E[N] \to \mu_N$ the Weil pairing and by $t_N : E(K)[N] \times E(K)/NE(K) \to K^\times/(K^\times)^N$ the Tate pairing. For $\mathcal{P} \in E$, denote by $\tau_{\mathcal{P}} : E \to E$ the translation-by-$\mathcal{P}$ map. Let $\omega \in \Omega_E$ be an invariant differential and denote by $\operatorname{res}_{\mathcal{P}}(-) : \Omega_E \to \overline{K}$ the residue at $\mathcal{P}$ as defined in [25].

Lemma 15. *For every $Q \in E(K)$ we have*

$$t_N(P,Q) = \frac{\text{“Leading coefficient of } f \text{ at } Q\text{”}}{\text{“Leading coefficient of } f \text{ at } \mathcal{O}\text{”}} \in K^\times/(K^\times)^N.$$

Remark 16. Note that the leading coefficient of f (meaning the leading coefficient of the expansion of f with respect to a uniformizer) is everywhere well defined up to Nth powers, since the order of vanishing of f is at every point divisible by N (hence a different choice of uniformizer scales the leading coefficient by an Nth power). Also, the quotient in Lemma 15 is invariant under scaling f by an element of K, hence well-defines an element of $K^\times/(K^\times)^N$ given only the divisor of f.

Proof. If $P = \mathcal{O}$ or $Q = \mathcal{O}$ then both sides are equal to 1, so assume $P \neq \mathcal{O} \neq Q$. We distinguish two cases.

Case $P = Q$. Let $h \in K(E)$ be any function such that $\mathrm{ord}_P(h) = -1$ and $\mathrm{ord}_\mathcal{O}(h) = 1$. Then $t_N(P, P) = f(\mathrm{div}(h) + (P) - (\mathcal{O}))$. By Weil reciprocity

$$\prod_R (-1)^{\mathrm{ord}_R(f)\,\mathrm{ord}_R(h)} \frac{f^{\mathrm{ord}_R(h)}}{g^{\mathrm{ord}_R(f)}}(R) = (-1)^{-2N} \frac{f^{-1}}{h^N} \frac{f^1}{h^{-N}}(P) \prod_{R \neq P, \mathcal{O}} f^{\mathrm{ord}_R(h)}(R).$$

equals 1. Hence

$$t_N(P, P) = \prod_{R \neq P, \mathcal{O}} f^{\mathrm{ord}_R(h)}(R) = \frac{h^N f(P)}{h^N f(\mathcal{O})} \in K^\times/(K^\times)^N.$$

Case $P \neq Q$. Let $h \in K(E)$ be any function such that $\mathrm{ord}_P(h) = 0$, $\mathrm{ord}_Q(h) = -1$, $\mathrm{ord}_\mathcal{O}(h) = 1$. Then $t_N(P, Q) = f(\mathrm{div}(h) + (Q) - (\mathcal{O}))$. By Weil reciprocity

$$1 = \prod_R (-1)^{\mathrm{ord}_R(f)\,\mathrm{ord}_R(h)} \frac{f^{\mathrm{ord}_R(h)}}{g^{\mathrm{ord}_R(f)}}(R) = (-1)^{-N} \frac{f}{h^{-N}}(\mathcal{O}) \frac{\prod_{R \neq \mathcal{O}} f^{\mathrm{ord}_R(h)}(R)}{h^N(P)}$$

Hence $t_N(P, Q)$ can be rewritten as

$$f(Q) \prod_{R \neq \mathcal{O}} f^{\mathrm{ord}_R(h)}(R) = (-1)^N \frac{h^N(P)}{(h^N f)(\mathcal{O})} f(Q) = \frac{f(Q)}{(h^N f)(\mathcal{O})} \in K^\times/(K^\times)^N.$$

□

Lemma 17. *Let $R \in E[N]$ such that P, R generate $E[N]$. We have*

$$t_N(P, P) = \left(\sum_{i,j=0}^{N-1} e_N(P, R)^i x(Q + iR + jP) \right)^N \quad \text{in } K^\times/(K^\times)^N.$$

Proof. We rely on the residue theorem [25, Thm. 3], whose use was suggested to us by Alexander Lemmens. This theorem implies that $\sum_{\mathcal{P} \in E} \mathrm{res}_\mathcal{P}(xg^{-1}\omega) = 0$, therefore

$$\begin{aligned} -\mathrm{res}_\mathcal{O}(xg^{-1}\omega) &= \sum_{S \in E[N]} \mathrm{res}_{Q+S}(xg^{-1}\omega) \\ &= \sum_{S \in E[N]} x(Q + S) \frac{g}{g \circ \tau_S}(Q) \mathrm{res}_Q(g^{-1}\omega) \\ &= \mathrm{res}_Q(g^{-1}\omega) \sum_{S \in E[N]} e_N(P, S) x(Q + S). \end{aligned}$$

It follows that (the last equivalence is due to Lemma 15)

$$\begin{aligned}\left(\sum_{S\in E[N]} e_N(P,S)x(Q+S)\right)^N &= (-1)^N \frac{x^N(g^N\circ\tau_Q)}{g^N}(\mathcal{O})\\ &= (-1)^N \frac{x^N}{x^N\circ[N]}\frac{(x^N\circ[N])(f\circ[N]\circ\tau_Q)}{f\circ[N]}(\mathcal{O})\\ &= (-1)^N N^{2N}\frac{x^N(f\circ\tau_P)}{f}(\mathcal{O})\end{aligned}$$

which equals $t_N(P,P)$ in $K^\times/(K^\times)^N$. □

Now let $K = \mathbb{Q}(b,c)$, where b and c are both transcendental over $\mathbb{Q}$, though possibly algebraically dependent. Let E/K be the elliptic curve given by $y^2 + (1-c)xy - by = x^3 - bx^2$ and set $P := (0,0) \in E$.

For $Q \in E(K)$, we denote by $h_{P,Q} \in K(E)^\times$ any function with divisor $(P)+(Q)-(P+Q)-(\mathcal{O})$. For $j \in \mathbb{Z}$, we define

$$L_j := \left(\left(\frac{x}{y}\right)^{\mathrm{ord}_{\mathcal{O}}(h_{P,jP})-\mathrm{ord}_P(h_{P,jP})}\cdot\frac{h_{P,jP}\circ\tau_P}{h_{P,jP}}\right)(\mathcal{O}).$$

In other words, L_j is the leading coefficient at $\mathcal{O}$ of the Laurent expansion of the function $(h_{P,jP}\circ\tau_P)/h_{P,jP}$ with respect to the uniformizer x/y. Note that, whereas $h_{P,Q}$ is only well-defined up to scalar multiplication, we have that L_j is a well-defined element of $K^\times$.

Lemma 18. *We have*

$$L_j = \begin{cases} b & \textit{if } jP = -2P \textit{ or } jP = -P;\\ 1 & \textit{if } jP = \mathcal{O};\\ -b & \textit{if } jP = P;\\ b\cdot\dfrac{y_{jP}}{x_{jP}\cdot x_{(j+1)P}} & \textit{else.}\end{cases}$$

Proof. Using (note that $h_{P,Q}$ as given by the formula below indeed has the desired divisor)

$$h_{P,Q} = \begin{cases} x & \text{if } Q = -P;\\ 1 & \text{if } Q = \mathcal{O};\\ \dfrac{y}{x - x_{2P}} & \text{if } Q = P;\\ \dfrac{y-(y_Q/x_Q)x}{x-x_{P+Q}} & \text{else,}\end{cases}$$

this is a straightforward check for $Q \in \{-2P,-P,\mathcal{O},P\}$. If $Q \notin \{-2P,-P,\mathcal{O},P\}$ then in particular $x_{P+Q} \neq 0$. Let $u = x/y$. Then $x\circ\tau_P = bu + O(u^2)$ and

$y \circ \tau_P = O(u^2)$, while $x = u^{-2} + O(u^{-1})$ and $y = u^{-3} + O(u^{-2})$. Thus the leading term at $\mathcal{O}$ of $(h_{P,Q} \circ \tau_P)/h_{P,Q}$ becomes

$$\frac{-y_Q/x_Q \cdot b}{-x_{P+Q}} = b \cdot \frac{y_Q}{x_Q \cdot x_{Q+P}}$$

as claimed. □

In what follows, $N > 2$ will always denote an integer and $k = \lceil N/2 \rceil$. We will assume that b, c are such that P has order at least $k+1$. Let $f \in K(E)$ be any function with divisor $N(P) - N(\mathcal{O}) + ((k-N)P) - (kP)$.

Lemma 19. *We have*

$$\left(x^N \cdot \frac{f \circ \tau_P}{f}\right)(\mathcal{O}) = \prod_{j=-\lfloor N/2 \rfloor}^{\lfloor (N-1)/2 \rfloor} L_j.$$

Proof. This follows by noting that

$$\left(\left(\frac{x}{y}\right)^{2N} \cdot x^N\right)(\mathcal{O}) = 1.$$

and that $f = \prod_{j=-\lfloor N/2 \rfloor}^{\lfloor (N-1)/2 \rfloor} h_{P,jP}$ has the desired divisor. □

Define

$$\rho_N := \begin{cases} \dfrac{\Psi_k^2}{\Psi_{k-1}^2}(P) & \text{if } N \text{ is odd;} \\ \\ \dfrac{\Psi_{k+1}}{\Psi_{k-1}}(P) & \text{if } N \text{ is even,} \end{cases} \quad \text{and} \quad \pi(N) := \prod_{j=-\lfloor N/2 \rfloor}^{\lfloor (N-1)/2 \rfloor} L_j.$$

Lemma 20. *For all $N \in \mathbb{Z}_{>2}$, we have $\pi(N) = (-1)^N \rho_N$.*

Proof. We use induction on N. One easily verifies the claim for $N = 3, 4, 5$. Suppose $N = 2k \geq 6$ is even. Then

$$\pi(N)/\pi(N-1) = b \cdot \frac{y_{-kP}}{x_{-kP} \cdot x_{(-k+1)P}}, \quad \text{and} \quad \pi(N+1)/\pi(N) = b \cdot \frac{y_{kP}}{x_{kP} \cdot x_{(k+1)P}},$$

whereas $-\rho_N/\rho_{N-1} = -(\Psi_{k+1}\Psi_{k-1}/\Psi_k^2)(P) = -\rho_{N+1}/\rho_N$. But the middle term $-(\Psi_{k+1}\Psi_{k-1}/\Psi_k^2)(P)$ can be rewritten as $x_{kP} = x_{-kP}$ (from the multiplication-by-k formula using division polynomials; e.g. [20, Ex. 3.7]), so we can conclude using Lemma 21. □

Lemma 21. *For all $k \in \mathbb{Z} \setminus \{-1, -2\}$, we have $x_{kP}^2 x_{(k+1)P} = b \cdot y_{kP}$.*

Proof. Using the coordinate-wise addition formula for Weierstrass elliptic curves (e.g. [20, III.2.3]), we find $x_{kP}^2 x_{(k+1)P} = y_{kP}^2 + (1-c)x_{kP}y_{kP} + bx_{kP}^2 - x_{kP}^3 = by_{kP}$.

Proof of Theorem 14. In the proof of Lemma 17, we already saw that the left hand side equals $(-1)^N N^{2N} \left(x^N \cdot \frac{f \circ \tau_P}{f}\right)(\mathcal{O})$. The desired result now follows by combining Lemmas 19 and 20. □

References

1. Banegas, G., et al.: CTIDH: faster constant-time CSIDH. IACR Trans. Cryptogr. Hardw. Embed. Syst. **2021**(4), 351–387 (2021)
2. Beullens, W., Kleinjung, T., Vercauteren, F.: CSI-FiSh: efficient isogeny based signatures through class group computations. In: Galbraith, S.D., Moriai, S. (eds.) ASIACRYPT 2019. LNCS, vol. 11921, pp. 227–247. Springer, Cham (2019). https://doi.org/10.1007/978-3-030-34578-5_9
3. Blake, I., Seroussi, G., Smart, N.: Elliptic Curves in Cryptography. Cambridge University Press, London (1999)
4. Castryck, W., Decru, T.: CSIDH on the surface. In: Ding, J., Tillich, J.-P. (eds.) PQCrypto 2020. LNCS, vol. 12100, pp. 111–129. Springer, Cham (2020). https://doi.org/10.1007/978-3-030-44223-1_7
5. Castryck, W., Decru, T.: Multiradical isogenies. In: Arithmetic, Geometry, Cryptography, and Coding Theory 2021, volume 779 of Contemporary Mathematics, pp. 57–89. American Mathematical Society, Washington, D.C (2022)
6. Castryck, W., Decru, T., Vercauteren, F.: Radical isogenies. In: Moriai, S., Wang, H. (eds.) ASIACRYPT 2020. LNCS, vol. 12492, pp. 493–519. Springer, Cham (2020). https://doi.org/10.1007/978-3-030-64834-3_17
7. Castryck, W., Lange, T., Martindale, C., Panny, L., Renes, J.: CSIDH: an efficient post-quantum commutative group action. In: Peyrin, T., Galbraith, S. (eds.) ASIACRYPT 2018. LNCS, vol. 11274, pp. 395–427. Springer, Cham (2018). https://doi.org/10.1007/978-3-030-03332-3_15
8. Castryck, W., Sotáková, J., Vercauteren, F.: Breaking the decisional Diffie-Hellman problem for class group actions using genus theory. In: Micciancio, D., Ristenpart, T. (eds.) CRYPTO 2020. LNCS, vol. 12171, pp. 92–120. Springer, Cham (2020). https://doi.org/10.1007/978-3-030-56880-1_4
9. Chi-Dominguez, J.-J., Reijnders, K.: Fully projective radical isogenies in constant-time. In: Galbraith, S.D. (ed.) CT-RSA 2022. LNCS, vol. 13161, pp. 73–95. Springer, Cham (2022). https://doi.org/10.1007/978-3-030-95312-6_4
10. Couveignes. J.-M.: Hard homogeneous spaces. Cryptology ePrint Archive (2006). https://eprint.iacr.org/2006/291
11. Burdges, J., De Feo, L.: Delay encryption. In: Canteaut, A., Standaert, F.-X. (eds.) EUROCRYPT 2021. LNCS, vol. 12696, pp. 302–326. Springer, Cham (2021). https://doi.org/10.1007/978-3-030-77870-5_11
12. De Feo, L., Masson, S., Petit, C., Sanso, A.: Verifiable delay functions from supersingular isogenies and pairings. In: Galbraith, S.D., Moriai, S. (eds.) ASIACRYPT 2019. LNCS, vol. 11921, pp. 248–277. Springer, Cham (2019). https://doi.org/10.1007/978-3-030-34578-5_10
13. Delfs, C., Galbraith, S.D.: Computing isogenies between supersingular elliptic curves over $\mathbb{F}_p$. Des. Codes Cryptogr. **78**(2), 425–440 (2016). https://arxiv.org/abs/1310.7789
14. Granger, R., Hess, F., Oyono, R., Thériault, N., Vercauteren, F.: Ate pairing on hyperelliptic curves. In: Naor, M. (ed.) EUROCRYPT 2007. LNCS, vol. 4515, pp. 430–447. Springer, Heidelberg (2007). https://doi.org/10.1007/978-3-540-72540-4_25
15. Lai, Y.-F., Galbraith, S.D., Delpech de Saint Guilhem, C.: Compact, Efficient and UC-secure isogeny-based oblivious transfer. In: Canteaut, A., Standaert, F.-X. (eds.) EUROCRYPT 2021. LNCS, vol. 12696, pp. 213–241. Springer, Cham (2021). https://doi.org/10.1007/978-3-030-77870-5_8

16. Monagan, M., Pearce, R.: Rational simplification modulo a polynomial ideal. In: ISSAC 2006, pp. 239–245. ACM (2006)
17. Onuki, H., Moriya, T.: Radical isogenies on Montgomery curves. In: Hanaoka, G., Shikata, J., Watanabe, Y. (eds.) Public-Key Cryptography –PKC 2022. PKC 2022. LNCS, vol. 13177, pp. 473–497. Springer, Cham (2022). https://doi.org/10.1007/978-3-030-97121-2_17
18. Rohrlich, D.E., Rohrlich, G.F.: Modular curves, Hecke correspondences, and L-functions. In: Cornell, G., Silverman, J.H., Stevens, G. (eds.) Modular Forms and Fermat's Last Theorem, pp. 41–100. Springer, New York (1997). https://doi.org/10.1007/978-1-4612-1974-3_3
19. Siksek, S.: Explicit arithmetic of modular curves. Summer school notes (2019) https://homepages.warwick.ac.uk/staff/S.Siksek/teaching/modcurves/lecturenotes.pdf
20. Silverman, J.H.: The Arithmetic of Elliptic Curves, volume 106 of Graduate Texts in Mathematics, 2nd edn. Springer, New York (2009). https://doi.org/10.1007/978-0-387-09494-6
21. The Stacks project authors. The Stacks project (2021). https://stacks.math.columbia.edu
22. Stolbunov, A.: Public-key encryption based on cycles of isogenous elliptic curves. Master's thesis, Saint-Petersburg State Polytechnical University (2004). (In Russian)
23. Streng, M.: Generators of the group of modular units for $\Gamma_1(N)$ over the rationals. Cornell University arXiv, https://arxiv.org/abs/1503.08127v2, (2015)
24. Sutherland, A.V.: Constructing elliptic curves over finite fields with prescribed torsion. Math. Comput. **81**, 1131–1147 (2012)
25. Tate, J.: Residues of differentials on curves. Ann. Sci. École Norm. Sup. **4**(1), 149–159 (1968)
26. Vélu, J.: Isogénies entre courbes elliptiques. Comptes-Rendus de l'Académie des Sciences, Série **I**(273), 238–241 (1971)

Homomorphic Encryption

Threshold Linearly Homomorphic Encryption on $\mathbf{Z}/2^k\mathbf{Z}$

Guilhem Castagnos[1(✉)], Fabien Laguillaumie[2], and Ida Tucker[3,4]

[1] Université de Bordeaux, CNRS, INRIA, IMB, UMR 5251, 33400 Talence, France
guilhem.castagnos@math.u-bordeaux.fr
[2] LIRMM, Université de Montpellier, CNRS, Montpellier, France
[3] IMDEA Software Institute, Madrid, Spain
[4] Zondax AG, Zug, Switzerland

Abstract. A threshold public key encryption protocol is a public key system where the private key is distributed among n different servers. It offers high security since no single server is entrusted to perform the decryption in its entirety. It is the core component of many multiparty computation protocols which involves mutually distrusting parties with common goals. It is even more useful when it is homomorphic, which means that public operations on ciphertexts translate to operations on the underlying plaintexts. In particular, Cramer, Damgård and Nielsen at Eurocrypt 2001 provided a new approach to multiparty computation from linearly homomorphic threshold encryption schemes. On the other hand, there has been recent interest in developing multiparty computations modulo 2^k for a certain integer k, that closely match data manipulated by a CPU. Multiparty computation would therefore benefit from an encryption scheme with such a message space that would support a distributed decryption.

In this work, we provide the first threshold linearly homomorphic encryption whose message space is $\mathbf{Z}/2^k\mathbf{Z}$ for any k. It is inspired by Castagnos and Laguillaumie's encryption scheme from RSA 2015, but works with a class group of discriminant whose factorisation is unknown.

Its natural structure *à la* Elgamal makes it possible to distribute the decryption among servers using linear integer secret sharing, allowing any access structure for the decryption policy. Furthermore its efficiency and its flexibility on the choice of the message space make it a good candidate for applications to multiparty computation.

Keywords: Class groups of quadratic fields · Linearly homomorphic encryption · Threshold cryptography

1 Introduction

Encryption protocols are the core of any communication architecture. They provide confidentiality, defined in terms of semantic security or indistinguishability of encryptions by Goldwasser and Micali [37]. On top of this security property,

S. Agrawal and D. Lin (Eds.): ASIACRYPT 2022, LNCS 13792, pp. 99–129, 2022.
https://doi.org/10.1007/978-3-031-22966-4_4

many applications require an "algebraic" property of the encryption scheme, in the sense that an operation on the ciphertexts translates into an operation on the underlying plaintexts. An encryption protocol possessing this property is said to be *homomorphic*. While *fully* homomorphic encryption schemes allow any operation to be evaluated on ciphertexts, protocols that only allow linear transformations are also very useful and significantly more efficient.

The first linearly homomorphic encryption appears in Goldwasser and Micali's seminal work [37]. Then a line of factoring based schemes was developed, culminating with Paillier's scheme [49] which was then generalized by Damgård and Jurik [26], allowing to encrypt larger messages.

An alternative was proposed by Castagnos and Laguillaumie using class groups of quadratic fields in [17]. This allows to work with the additive group $\mathbf{Z}/q\mathbf{Z}$ as a message space where q is an odd prime, whereas Paillier and Damgård and Jurik' schemes work modulo N^s where N is an RSA integer. The case of message space $\mathbf{Z}/q^s\mathbf{Z}$ for an odd prime q, and more generally that of $\mathbf{Z}/N\mathbf{Z}$ with $N = \prod q_i^{s_i}$ for odd primes q_i, were sketched in the conclusion of [17]. This was further analyzed in [28] which gives a detailed construction and implementation. As a consequence, the Castagnos-Laguillaumie scheme allows to construct message spaces of any odd order N (with known factorization). There is a restriction however: many cryptographic applications and proofs require that this order N be relatively prime to the order of the underlying class group. This can only be ensured with high probability if each prime q_i dividing N is large enough to make $1/q_i$ negligible. Hence only relatively large values of odd integers N are possible in practice. The case of message spaces defined modulo 2^k were left open in these works.

Another elegant work, by Benhamouda, Herranz, Joye, Libert [3] (refining a scheme by Joye and Libert [41]), generalizes the Goldwasser-Micali cryptosystem using 2^k–th power residue symbols, and produces efficient protocols in terms of bandwidth and speed (for both encryption and decryption). It is proven secure under the quadratic residuosity assumption for RSA moduli $N = pq$, where the primes p and q have a special form. The message space of their scheme is the additive group $\mathbf{Z}/2^k\mathbf{Z}$, which is a very interesting feature, especially for the purpose of multi-party computation. Indeed, it has been used by Catalano, Di Raimondo, Fiore and Giacomelli [19] to design a new 2–party protocol for secure computation over the ring $\mathbf{Z}/2^k\mathbf{Z}$. Their work follows a new line of secure computation modulo 2^k, initiated by Cramer, Damgård, Escudero, Scholl, and Xing in [23] who introduced a new information theoretic MAC that allows to authenticate messages in the ring $\mathbf{Z}/2^k\mathbf{Z}$ to achieve security against malicious adversaries. This choice is driven by the fact that modern CPU computations are performed in such a ring, and it allows protocol designers to directly apply optimizations that are often expensive to emulate modulo p or N.

On the other hand, several multi-party computation protocols, starting with the pioneering work of Cramer, Damgård and Nielsen [24], rely on threshold linearly homomorphic encryption. A (t, n)–threshold public key encryption (TPKE) scheme allows n parties to share the decryption key so that if t of them collaborate, they can decrypt ciphertexts, whereas $t-1$ users learn nothing about the underlying plaintext. Katz and Yung proposed a threshold variant of Goldwasser-Micali in [42], but this does not extend to a message space of order 2^k. Furthermore, it is an open problem to devise an efficient threshold variant of Benhamouda, Herranz, Joye, Libert's scheme. In a nutshell, This scheme uses an RSA integer $N = pq$ where $p \equiv 1 \pmod{2^k}$. A ciphertext for $m \in \mathbf{Z}/2^k\mathbf{Z}$ is $c = y^m x^{2^k} \in \mathbf{Z}/N\mathbf{Z}$ for a random x, and a public y, which is a fixed non quadratic residue, with Jacobi Symbol 1. Decryption is done modulo p, by removing the 2^k-th power using an exponentiation to the power $(p-1)/2^k$ and then finding m thanks to an easy discrete logarithm computation using Pohlig-Hellman's algorithm in the subgroup of $(\mathbf{Z}/p\mathbf{Z})^\times$ of order 2^k. As a result, lots of operations are done modulo the secret prime p, which prevents an efficient adaptation in a multiparty setting.

A solution would be to design an Elgamal version of this scheme, that fits the CL framework [17] of a DDH group with an easy DL subgroup. In this framework, one works with a cyclic group G isomorphic to $H \times F$ where H and F are subgroups of G of respective unknown order s and known order q, with q and s co-prime. The group H consists of q–th powers, and in F discrete logarithms are easy to compute. This makes it possible to encode messages $m \in \mathbf{Z}/q\mathbf{Z}$ in f^m where f is a generator of F. Then f^m is hidden by a random q–th power.

To make Benhamouda et al's scheme fit the CL framework, the idea would be to use two primes $p, q \equiv 1 \pmod{2^k}$ and encode the message in the exponent of an element $f \in (\mathbf{Z}/N\mathbf{Z})^\times$ of order 2^k both modulo p and q. A ciphertext for m could then be of the form $(g^r, f^m \mathsf{pk}^r)$, with $\mathsf{pk} = g^{\mathsf{sk}}$. During decryption, after recovering f^m, the discrete logarithm computation could then be done modulo the public N, and only one exponentiation would have to be distributed among the parties. However, this simple solution has some drawbacks due to the fact that this element f must be public and seems hard to generate without knowing the factorization. As a consequence, such a variant would rely on *ad hoc* security assumptions that include this element f. Moreover, it would be less efficient than the scheme that we propose in this work, at least in terms of bandwidth. Devising a variant without a trusted dealer would also be very complicated. So this question remains open:

Is it possible to design an efficient threshold linearly homomorphic encryption with message space $\mathbf{Z}/2^k\mathbf{Z}$?

Our Contributions. In this work, we first propose a new linearly homomorphic encryption (LHE) scheme with message space of order 2^k that solves the aforementioned issues (Sect. 4). This LHE has an Elgamal structure as it follows the CL framework, with an element f of order 2^k that is used to encrypt the messages in the exponent. We emphasize that this element can be generated from public parameters. Thanks to its Elgamal shape, it can be converted into the first threshold linearly homomorphic encryption with message space $\mathbf{Z}/2^k\mathbf{Z}$.

The part of the decryption which involves the secret key uses an exponentiation to that secret key in a group of unknown order. We use linear integer secret sharing schemes (LISS), introduced in [27], to share the secret key over the integers. This allows to set up a scheme allowing any access structure for the decryption policy and in particular a threshold decryption (Sect. 5).

Furthermore, we suggest how to add robustness and a distributed setup to our scheme. We also sketch several application domains: multiparty computation, homomorphic secret sharing and lossy trapdoor functions (Sect. 6).

The security of our schemes relies on a hard subgroup membership (HSM) assumption, which is a natural adaptation of the assumption used in the CL framework. One could also design a variant based on the DDH assumption.

The setup of our schemes is flexible and allows to encrypt messages modulo 2^k for any integer k, and in particular natural choices such as $k = 1, 32, 64, 128$ or even larger values. We show that our schemes are efficient by reporting timings from an implementation in SageMath.

Technical Overview and Challenges. Our construction uses class groups of imaginary quadratic fields like the encryption schemes modulo an odd prime q of [17,55]. One of the challenges is to stay within the CL framework, while working modulo a power of 2. As we will see, plugging $q = 2^k$ does not work.

In the original framework, a class group with a cyclic subgroup of order q is generated. This is done by considering two class groups, $Cl(\Delta_K)$ with discriminant $\Delta_K = -pq$ and $Cl(\Delta)$ with discriminant $-pq^3$. In this case, there is a surjection from $Cl(\Delta)$ to $Cl(\Delta_K)$, and the kernel of which is precisely the required subgroup of order q.

However, as usual in number theory, moving from an odd prime q to 2 or 2^k is not an easy task. Firstly, setting $q = 2^k$ in the construction above does not always give a cyclic subgroup of order 2^k. Further difficulties arise from the fact that in class groups, knowing the factorization of the discriminant allows to compute square roots, and decide if elements are squares. And as we will see, this allows to completely break a scheme which uses an Elgamal in the exponent with a subgroup of order 2^k.

We solve this issue by constructing a discriminant from an RSA integer N of unknown factorization. But other technical reasons make the choice of this discriminant tricky, and lead to arithmetic conditions on the primes composing N (which have no negative impact in practice). We thus have to delve into the genus theory associated to class groups of quadratic fields, introduced by Gauss, to select discriminants that make it possible to securely work with the group of squares of cardinality $2^k s$ where s is odd (Sect. 3). Indeed, we need to carefully handle the fact that some genera can leak information on discrete logarithms. Controlling the 2-Sylow subgroup of $Cl(\Delta_K)$ and expliciting the shape of the kernel of the surjection from $Cl(\Delta)$ to $Cl(\Delta_K)$ when the conductor is equal to 2^k allows to find a element f of the group of squares of order 2^k which does not depend on the factorization of N.

Relying on the factorization assumption implies slightly larger elements (compared to the original CL scheme), but the timings that we provide in Table 2 of Sect. 4.3 from a non-optimized implementation of our protocol with SageMath, show that the scheme is actually very efficient.

2 Background

2.1 Threshold Public Key Encryption

In a threshold PKE (TPKE) scheme, the decryption key is divided into a number of key shares which are distributed to multiple decryption servers, according to a certain access structure. To decrypt a message, each server creates its own decryption share, and these shares can be publicly combined to result in a full decryption.

Definition 1. *A monotone access structure on $\{1,\ldots,n\}$ is a non-empty collection $\mathbb{A} \subseteq \{1,\ldots,n\}$ such that $\emptyset \notin \mathbb{A}$, and such that for all $A \in \mathbb{A}$, and all sets B such that $A \subseteq B \subseteq \{1,\ldots,n\}$ it holds that $B \in \mathbb{A}$.*

For a positive integer $t < n$, the threshold-t access structure $T_{t,n}$ is the collection of sets $A \subseteq [n]$ for which $|A| > t$. The sets in $\mathbb{A}$ are called qualified, *whereas the sets outside A which should not be able to obtain any information about the secret are called* forbidden.

Definition 2 (Threshold PKE). *Let $P = \{P_1,\ldots,P_n\}$ be a set of parties and let $\mathbb{A}$ be an access structure. A threshold PKE scheme for a message space $\mathcal{M}$ and access structure $\mathbb{A}$ is a tuple of PPT algorithms* $\mathsf{TPKE} = (\mathsf{Setup}, \mathsf{Encrypt}, \mathsf{PartDec}, \mathsf{FinalDec})$ *with the following syntax.*

$\mathsf{Setup}(1^\lambda, \mathbb{A}) \to (\mathsf{pp}, \mathsf{ek}, \mathbf{sk})$ *Takes as input a security parameter 1^λ and an access structure $\mathbb{A}$. It outputs public parameters* pp, *an encryption key* ek, *and a vector of n secret-key shares* $\mathbf{sk} = (\mathsf{sk}_1,\ldots,\mathsf{sk}_n)$.
Party P_i is given the share sk_i *that allows deriving decryption shares for any ciphertext.*

$\mathsf{Encrypt}(\mathsf{ek}, m) \to c$ *On input the encryption key* ek *and a plaintext $m \in \mathcal{M}$, outputs a ciphertext* ct.

$\mathsf{PartDec}(\mathsf{pp}, \mathsf{sk}_i, \mathsf{ct}) \to \mu_i \cup \bot$ *Takes as input the public parameters* pp, *a secret-key share* sk_i, *and a ciphertext* ct. *It outputs a partial decryption share μ_i.*

$\mathsf{FinalDec}(\mathsf{pp}, \{\mu_i\}_{i\in S}) \to m \cup \bot$ *Given* pp *and a subset $S \subset \{1,\ldots,n\}$ with decryption shares $\{\mu_i\}_{i\in S}$, this algorithm outputs either a plaintext m or $\bot$.*

We require a TPKE *scheme to satisfy the following correctness, and security requirements.*

Definition 3 (Decryption correctness). *We say that a* TPKE *scheme for an access structure $\mathbb{A}$ satisfies decryption correctness if for all λ, and all qualified sets S, the following holds. For* $(\mathsf{pp}, \mathsf{ek}, \mathbf{sk}) \leftarrow \mathsf{Setup}(1^\lambda, \mathbb{A})$, $\mathsf{ct} \leftarrow \mathsf{Encrypt}(\mathsf{ek}, m)$, $\mu_i \leftarrow \mathsf{PartDec}(\mathsf{pp}, \mathsf{sk}_i, \mathsf{ct})$ *for $i \in S$*, $\Pr[\mathsf{FinalDec}(\mathsf{pp}, \{\mu_i\}_{i\in S}) = m] = 1 - \mathsf{negl}(\lambda)$.

Definition 4 (following [34]) is a classical extension of semantic security for an encryption scheme to the threshold case. The attacker actively (but non-adaptively) corrupts a set S of servers outside $\mathbb{A}$, gets their secret keys, and can ask for partial decryptions of ciphertexts for which he already knows the corresponding plaintext. The idea is that partial decryptions give no information about the private keys of non-corrupted users.

Definition 4 (T-ind-cpa-security). *We say a* TPKE *scheme for an access structure* $\mathbb{A}$ *is adaptive chosen plaintext (*T-ind-cpa*) secure if for any large enough* $\lambda \in \mathbf{N}$*, and any PPT adversary* $\mathcal{A}$ *the experiments* $\mathsf{Expt}_{\mathcal{A},\mathsf{TPKE},0}$ *and* $\mathsf{Expt}_{\mathcal{A},\mathsf{TPKE},1}$ *of Fig. 1 are computationally indistinguishable.*

Choose structure: On input 1^λ, the adversary $\mathcal{A}$ chooses an access structure $\mathbb{A}$.
Set up: The challenger $\mathcal{C}$ runs $(\mathsf{pp}, \mathsf{ek}, \mathbf{sk}) \leftarrow \mathsf{Setup}(1^\lambda, \mathbb{A})$ and sends pp, ek to $\mathcal{A}$.
Choose set: $\mathcal{A}$ outputs a set S such that $S \notin \mathbb{A}$, and $\mathcal{C}$ sends the set of secret keys $\{\mathsf{sk}_i\}_{i \in S}$ to $\mathcal{A}$.
Partial decryption queries: $\mathcal{A}$ queries partial decryption on encryptions of plaintexts m_j of his choice. For $\mathsf{ct}_j = \mathsf{Encrypt}(\mathsf{pp}, \mathsf{ek}, m_j)$, it then gets $\mathsf{PartDec}(\mathsf{pp}, \mathsf{sk}_i, \mathsf{ct}_j)$ for $i \notin S$
Choose challenge: $\mathcal{A}$ outputs a pair of challenge messages $m_0, m_1 \in \mathcal{M}$.
Challenge: $\mathcal{C}$ computes $\mathsf{ct}_b \leftarrow \mathsf{Encrypt}(\mathsf{ek}, m_b)$ and sends ct_b to $\mathcal{A}$.
Partial decryption queries: Again, $\mathcal{A}$ queries partial decryption on encryptions of plaintexts m_j of his choice : it gets $\mathsf{ct}_j = \mathsf{Encrypt}(\mathsf{pp}, \mathsf{ek}, m_j)$ and $\mathsf{PartDec}(\mathsf{pp}, \mathsf{sk}_i, \mathsf{ct}_j)$ for $i \notin S$
Guess: $\mathcal{A}$ outputs a bit b', which is the output of the experiment.

Fig. 1. Experiment $\mathsf{Expt}_{\mathcal{A},\mathsf{TPKE},\mathsf{b}}$

Linearly Homomorphic Threshold Encryption. This primitive is particularly useful for applications to multi-party computation.

Definition 5. *Consider a* TPKE *with message space* $(\mathcal{M}, +)$*. A linearly homomorphic* TPKE *scheme additionally has the following* evaluation *algorithms:*

$\mathsf{EvalAdd}(\mathsf{pp}, c_1, c_2) \to c^*$ *Takes as input* pp *and two ciphertexts* c_1 *and* c_2*, and outputs a new ciphertext* c^* *which decrypts to* $m_1 + m_2$ *where each* c_i, $i \in \{1, 2\}$ *decrypts to* m_i.

$\mathsf{EvalScal}(\mathsf{pp}, c, \alpha) \to c^*$ *Takes as input* pp*, a ciphertexts* c *which decrypts to* m*, and a scalar* α*, and outputs a new ciphertext* c^* *which decrypts to* $\alpha \cdot m$.

Informally, evaluations should be correct, meaning that decryption should lead to the correct plaintext message $m_1 + m_2$ *(resp.* αm*).*

2.2 Linear Integer Secret Sharing

In the threshold setting for groups of unknown orders, key generation schemes share the secret decryption key using the linear integer secret sharing (LISS) primitive of Damgård and Thorbek [27], which is similar to linear secret sharing schemes except that it works over $\mathbf{Z}$.

They show that any integer span program (ISP) as defined in [25] can be used to build a secure LISS scheme. Roughly speaking, an ISP is specified by a matrix with integer entries, and these entries are used as coefficients in the linear combinations that produce the shares from secret and randomness. They also show that any LISS scheme can be used to build a distributed exponentiation protocol, which is what we will use in our threshold decryption.

Goal. Let $P = \{1, \ldots, n\}$ denote the n shareholders and D the dealer. Let $\mathbb{A}$ be a monotone access structure on P. The dealer D wants to share a secret s in a publicly known interval $[-2^l, 2^l]$ with the shareholders, such that any set $A \in \mathbb{A}$ can reconstruct s, but any set $A \notin \mathbb{A}$ gets no (or negligible) information on s.

Distributing the Secret. To this end, D uses a distribution matrix $\mathbf{M} \in \mathbf{Z}^{d \times e}$ and a distribution vector $\boldsymbol{\rho} = (s, \rho_2, \ldots, \rho_e)^\top$, where s is the secret, and the ρ_i's are integers sampled uniformly at random in $[-2^{l_0+\lambda}, 2^{l_0+\lambda}]$ for $2 \leq i \leq e$, where l_0 is a constant that is part of the description of the scheme.

The dealer D computes a vector $\mathbf{s} \in \mathbf{Z}^d$ of share units as:

$$\mathbf{s} = (s_1, \ldots, s_d)^\top = \mathbf{M} \cdot \boldsymbol{\rho}.$$

Let $\psi : \{1, \ldots, d\} \mapsto P$ be a surjective function. Shareholder $\psi(i)$ is given the i-th share unit, and is said to *own* the i-th row in $\mathbf{M}$. For a set of shareholders $A \subset P$, $\mathbf{M}_A \in \mathbf{Z}^{d_a \times e}$ denotes the restriction of $\mathbf{M}$ to the rows jointly owned by A, while d_A denotes the number of these rows.

Likewise, $s_A \in \mathbf{Z}^{d_A}$ denotes the restriction of $\mathbf{s} \in \mathbf{Z}^d$ to the coordinates jointly owned by the parties in A. Shareholder j's share consists of $s_{\psi^{-1}(j)} \in \mathbf{Z}^{d_j}$, so that it receives $d_j = |\psi^{-1}(j)|$ out of the $d = \sum_{j=1}^{n} d_j$ share units. The *expansion rate* $\mu = d/n$ is the average number of share units per player.

To construct LISS schemes, Damgård and Thorbek [27] used integer span programs [25], which were originally used to construct black-box secret sharing which does not extend shares in the ring of integers.

Definition 6 (Integer Span Program (ISP) [25]). *The tuple $\mathcal{M} = (\mathbf{M}, \psi, \epsilon)$ is called an* integer span program *(ISP), if $\mathbf{M} \in \mathbf{Z}^{d \times e}$ and the d rows of $\mathbf{M}$ are labeled by a surjective function $\psi : \{1, \ldots, d\} \mapsto \{1, \ldots, n\}$. Finally, $\boldsymbol{\epsilon} = (1, 0, \ldots, 0)^\top \in \mathbf{Z}^e$ is called the target vector. The size of $\mathcal{M}$ is the number of rows d of $\mathbf{M}$.*

Definition 7. *Let $\mathbb{A}$ be a monotone access structure and let $\mathcal{M} = (\mathbf{M}, \psi, \epsilon)$ be an ISP. Then $\mathcal{M}$ is an ISP for $\mathbb{A}$ if for all $A \subset \{1, \ldots, n\}$ the following conditions hold:*

- *If $A \in \mathbb{A}$, there is a reconstruction vector $\boldsymbol{\lambda} \in \mathbf{Z}^{d_A}$ such that $\boldsymbol{\lambda}^\top \cdot \mathbf{M} = \boldsymbol{\epsilon}^\top$.*
- *If $A \notin \mathbb{A}$, there exists $\boldsymbol{\kappa} = (\kappa_1, \ldots, \kappa_e)^\top \in \mathbf{Z}^e$ such that $\mathbf{M}_A \cdot \boldsymbol{\kappa} = \mathbf{0} \in \mathbf{Z}^d$, and $\boldsymbol{\kappa}^\top \cdot \boldsymbol{\epsilon} = 1$. The vector $\boldsymbol{\kappa}$ is called a* sweeping vector *for A.*
  We also define $\kappa_{\max} = \max_{A \notin \mathbb{A}}(\|\kappa\|_\infty)$.

In other words, the rows owned by a qualified set must include the target vector in their span, while for a forbidden set, there must exist a sweeping vector which is orthogonal to all rows of the set, but has inner product 1 with the target vector. We also say that $\mathcal{M}$ *computes* $\mathbb{A}$.

Damgård and Thorbek [27] showed that from an ISP $\mathcal{M} = (\mathbf{M}, \psi, \epsilon)$ which computes the access structure $\mathbb{A}$, a statistically private LISS scheme for $\mathbb{A}$ can be obtained with $\mathbf{M}$ as the share generating matrix and $l_0 = l + \lceil \log_2(\kappa_{max}(e-1)) \rceil + 1$, where l is the length of the secret.

Then LISS can be obtained from Cramer-Fehr [25] or Benaloh-Leichter [2]. Although this later case was designed to work over finite groups, Damgård and Thorbek generalized it to share integers using access structures consisting of any monotone Boolean formula. Thanks to results of Valiant [56], LISS schemes can therefore be constructed for any threshold access structure. From a monotone Boolean function f, Damgård and Thorbek's technique from Benaloh-Leichter results allows binary share distribution matrices in $\{0,1\}^{d \times e}$ such that $d, e = O(\mathsf{size}(f))$ and which have at most $\mathsf{depth}(f) + 1$ non-zero entries, so that each share unit has magnitude $O(2^{l_0+\lambda}\mathsf{depth}(f))$. Valiant's results, improved by [38] gives a monotone formula of size $O(n^{1+\sqrt{2}})$ and depth $O(\log n)$ for the majority function (from which any threshold-t function can be built). This reduces the average share size to $O(n^{\sqrt{2}}(l_0 + \lambda + \log\log(n)))$ bits.

Lemma 1 (**[53, Lemma 3.1]**). *Let $l_0 = l + \lceil \log_2(\kappa_{max}(e-1)) \rceil + 1$. Consider a secret to be shared, $s \in [-2^l, 2^l]$, and $\boldsymbol{\rho}$ randomly sampled from $[-2^{l_0+\lambda}, 2^{l_0+\lambda}]^e$ conditionally on $\langle \boldsymbol{\rho}, \boldsymbol{\epsilon} \rangle = s$, then the LISS scheme derived from $\mathcal{M}$ is private. For any arbitrary $s, s' \in [-2^l, 2^l]$ and any forbidden set of shareholders $A \in [n]$, the two distributions $\{s_A = \mathbf{M}_A \cdot \boldsymbol{\rho} \mid \boldsymbol{\rho} \leftarrow U([-2^{l_0+\lambda}, 2^{l_0+\lambda}]^e)$ s.t. $\langle \boldsymbol{\rho}, \boldsymbol{\epsilon} \rangle = s\}$, and $\{s'_A = \mathbf{M}_A \cdot \boldsymbol{\rho} \mid \boldsymbol{\rho} \leftarrow U([-2^{l_0+\lambda}, 2^{l_0+\lambda}]^e)$ s.t. $\langle \boldsymbol{\rho}, \boldsymbol{\epsilon} \rangle = s'\}$ are $2^{-\lambda}$ close.*

2.3 Class Groups

Class Groups. Given a non square integer $\Delta < 0$, $\Delta \equiv 0, 1 \pmod 4$, called discriminant, the imaginary quadratic order of discriminant Δ, denoted $\mathcal{O}_\Delta$ is the ring $\mathbf{Z}[(\Delta + \sqrt{\Delta})/2]$. The associated class group $Cl(\Delta)$ is defined as the quotient of the group of invertible fractional ideals of $\mathcal{O}_\Delta$ by the subgroup of principal ideals. Precise definitions of these objects can be found in e.g., [11].

In a nutshell, the class group $Cl(\Delta)$ is a finite Abelian group, with an efficiently computable group law and a compact representation of elements. Elements are classes of ideals, with a unique reduced representative. The order of $Cl(\Delta)$, the class number, denoted $h(\Delta)$ is close to $\sqrt{|\Delta|}$.

Historically, with the works of Lagrange and Gauss, the class group $Cl(\Delta)$ was defined using the language of positive definite binary quadratic forms of discriminant Δ. Let $a, b, c \in \mathbf{Z}$ such that $a > 0$ and $\Delta = b^2 - 4ac$, we will denote for short $f := (a, b, c)$ the positive definite binary quadratic form over the integers, $f(X, Y) = aX^2 + bXY + cY^2$. Such a form is said to be primitive if a, b and c are relatively prime. In the following, we will just call "forms" the primitive positive definite binary quadratic forms over the integers. Two forms f and g are said to equivalent if $g(X, Y) = f(AX + BY, CX + DY)$ for integers A, B, C, D such that $AD - BC = 1$.

The class group $Cl(\Delta)$ is isomorphic to the set of forms modulo this equivalence relation. In fact, it is more natural to work with forms for algorithmic purposes: the class of the form (a, b, c) corresponds to the class of the $\mathcal{O}_\Delta$–ideal $a\mathbf{Z} + \frac{-b+\sqrt{\Delta}}{2}\mathbf{Z}$. Moreover, the definition of the unique representative of the class is more natural when working with forms: it is the reduced form (a, b, c), which satisfies $-a < b \leqslant a$, $a \leqslant c$ and if $a = c$ then $b \geqslant 0$. A reduced form satisfies $a \leqslant \sqrt{|\Delta|/3}$. As a result, elements of $Cl(\Delta)$ can be represented by (a, b) using $\log_2(|\Delta|)$ bits. Dobson *et al.* recently proposed in [32] an elegant method to reduce this representation to $3/4 \log_2(|\Delta|)$ bits.

Computations in $Cl(\Delta)$ can be performed with a reduction algorithm for forms, devised by Lagrange (which corresponds to lattice reduction in dimension 2), and Gauss' composition of forms (which corresponds to product of ideals). More recently, efficient algorithms have been proposed for practical implementation by Shanks (cf. [40]). The neutral element of $Cl(\Delta)$ is the class of the (reduced) principal form: $(1, b, (b - \Delta)/4)$ where $b = \Delta \mod 2$.

Class Group-Based Cryptography. Class group cryptography dates back to the late 80s with the first key exchange in the class group of ideals of maximal orders of imaginary quadratic fields, and related protocols that can be found in Buchmann and Williams' work [12] or McCurley's [46]. After several years, a family of class group based cryptosystems, NICE, was designed using class groups of non-maximal orders [51]. The area remained dormant for another decade until a serious cryptanalysis of this whole family of NICE cryptosystems was proposed [16]. Since then, there has actually been a high regain of interest in class groups to design new advanced cryptosystems, especially for secure multi-party computation. Built upon Castagnos and Laguillaumie's linearly homomorphic encryption scheme (CL) [17], projective hash functions relying on class groups allowed to design efficient inner product functional encryption [18], 2-party and fully-threshold ECDSA signatures [14,15,29,58].

The main advantage of class-group cryptography is that it is well-suited when multi-party protocols require a one-time transparent (or public-coin) setup with minimal interaction among parties. For instance, [54] presented a scalable distributed randomness generator with enhanced security and transparent setup that relies on a variant of the CL encryption scheme. The verifiable random functions from [57] take advantage of an exponentiation in a group of unknown order without trusted setup, as well as accumulators in [45], and succinct non-interactive arguments of knowledge in [13,44].

Another advantage is that the underlying algorithmic problems are harder that equivalent problems in $(\mathbf{Z}/N\mathbf{Z})^\times$ or $(\mathbf{Z}/p\mathbf{Z})^\times$. Indeed, the current best known algorithms to solve the discrete logarithm problem in the class group of ideals of order of imaginary quadratic fields, or to compute the class number have a sub-exponential complexity of complexity $L_{|\Delta|}(1/2, o(1))$ (cf. [4]). This means that elements in the class group are asymptotically *smaller*, and this actually matters in practice for a given security parameter. For example, a 112-bit (resp. 256-bit) security determinant will be of size 1348 bits (resp. 5971 bits), while an RSA modulus will be of size 2048 bits (resp. 15360 bits).

Genus Theory, Squares and Square Roots. We now give a quick introduction on genus theory and properties of squares of the class group. A comprehensive exposition of the subject with a historical perspective can be found in [22]. The theory of quadratic forms was originally motivated by the representation problem: given $m \in \mathbf{Z}$ and a quadratic form f, are there integers $(x, y) \in \mathbf{Z}^2$ such that $f(x, y) = m$? A first remark is that all the forms in an equivalent class represent the same numbers. Genus theory aims at characterizing primes represented by quadratic forms of a fixed discriminant Δ. A genus consists of classes of forms that represent the same classes of numbers in $(\mathbf{Z}/\Delta\mathbf{Z})^\times$. Genera are related to squares of the class group: Gauss proved that the genus of the principal form, the principal genus, corresponds to the subgroup of squares in the class group $Cl(\Delta)$. Moreover, genera can be identified by values of some characters.

Before going into more details, let us make a parallel with the well-known properties of squares in $(\mathbf{Z}/N\mathbf{Z})^\times$ where $N = pq$ is an RSA integer. Given $x \in (\mathbf{Z}/N\mathbf{Z})^\times$, there are 4 possible values for the Legendre symbols $((x/p), (x/q))$ which gives a partition in 4 sets of $(\mathbf{Z}/N\mathbf{Z})^\times$. One could speak of 4 "genera". The value $(1, 1)$ corresponds to squares of $(\mathbf{Z}/N\mathbf{Z})$ which is the "genus" of 1. Given the factorization of N, one can thus identify the "genus" of an element x. But without it, one can only compute the Jacobi symbol of x. Given an element x of Jacobi symbol 1, the quadratic residuosity problem asks to decide if x is in the principal genus with symbol $(1, 1)$ or in the genus with symbol $(-1, -1)$ without knowing the factorization of N.

For a class group $Cl(\Delta)$, the situation is similar: there are $2^{\mu-1}$ genera, where μ is related to the number of odd primes factor of the discriminant. One can define μ "assigned characters", whose joint values determine the genus (the product of all characters is always one, so we indeed have $2^{\mu-1}$ genera). The characters are for the majority Legendre symbols with respect to the odd prime factors of the discriminant. Let us describe in more details the setting that we will use to define our cryptosystem, where $\Delta = -8N$ and $N = pq$ is an RSA integer. In this case, where $\Delta = 0 \mod 4$ and $2N = 2 \mod 4$ (see [22, Prop. 3.11, Th. 3.15]), it holds that $\mu = 3$, and there are 4 genera. If f is a quadratic form, the first two assigned characters are respectively

$$\chi_p(f) := \left(\frac{a}{p}\right) \text{ and } \chi_q(f) := \left(\frac{a}{q}\right)$$

where a is any integer represented by f, respectively prime to p, prime to q. The third one, is

$$\chi_8(f) := (-1)^{(a^2-1)/8} \text{ or } \chi_{-8} := \chi_{-4} \cdot \chi_8(f) := (-1)^{(a-1)/2} \cdot (-1)^{(a^2-1)/8},$$

depending if $N \equiv 3 \mod 4$ or $N \equiv 1 \mod 4$, where a is any odd integer represented by f. The genus of the class of a form f is thus identified by $(\chi_p(f), \chi_q(f), \chi_8(f))$ or $(\chi_p(f), \chi_q(f), \chi_{-8}(f))$ depending on N modulo 4. The subgroup of squares of $Cl(\Delta)$ is the subgroup of forms of genus with symbol $(1, 1, 1)$, the three other genera have symbols $(-1, -1, 1)$, $(-1, 1, -1)$, $(1, -1, -1)$. Given the complete factorization of Δ (thus of N), one can identify in polynomial time the genus of an element of the class group (see also [43, Theorem 6.3]).

Without it, only χ_8 or χ_{-8} and the Jacobi symbol relative to N, *i.e.*, the product $\chi_p \cdot \chi_q$ can be computed.

The situation of elements of order $\leqslant 2$ of the class group is similar. In the general case, there are also $2^{\mu-1}$ such elements and there are classes of forms $(a, 0, c)$, (a, a, c) and (a, b, a) [22, Lemma 3.10, Prop. 3.11]). As a result, finding these elements is equivalent to factoring the discriminant. For example, the discriminant of the form $(a, 0, c)$ is $-4ac$.

Computing square roots can also be done efficiently given the factorization of the discriminant [43, Theorem 6.10]. The algorithm, due to Gauss, uses reduction of ternary forms, and the factorization of Δ is needed to extract square roots modulo Δ.

Two Classgroups. Starting with the NICE family of cryptosystems, the idea of using the relationship between two class groups has enabled many developments. Let us first consider Δ_K a fundamental negative discriminant: this means that either $\Delta_K \equiv 1 \pmod 4$ and Δ_K is square-free or $\Delta_K = 4m$ where m is square-free and $m \equiv 2, 3 \pmod 4$. This discriminant defines the maximal order $\mathcal{O}_{\Delta_K}$ of the quadratic field $Q(\sqrt{\Delta_K})$. Now let us consider a non fundamental discriminant $\Delta_\ell := \Delta_K \ell^2$ where ℓ is called a conductor. Then, there exists a surjective map $\varphi_\ell : Cl(\Delta_\ell) \to Cl(\Delta_K)$, moreover, for $\Delta_K < -4$, the kernel of this surjection is isomorphic to

$$\left(\mathcal{O}_{\Delta_K}/\ell\mathcal{O}_{\Delta_K}\right)^\times / \left(\mathbf{Z}/\ell\mathbf{Z}\right)^\times .$$

This isomorphism is used in [22, Theorem 7.24] to establish that for $\Delta_K < -4$,

$$h(\mathcal{O}_{\Delta_\ell}) = h(\mathcal{O}_{\Delta_K}) \cdot \ell \cdot \prod_{p|\ell} \left(1 - \left(\frac{\Delta_K}{p}\right)\frac{1}{p}\right). \tag{1}$$

3 A Class Group with a Cyclic Subgroup of Order 2^k

In this section, we show how to generate a class group $Cl(\Delta)$ that contains a cyclic subgroup of order 2^k, inspired by the CL cryptosystem of [17], that builds a subgroup of order a prime q by using Eq. 1 with a conductor $\ell = q$, and a fundamental discriminant Δ_K divisible by q. Unfortunately, the situation is not as simple as setting $\ell = 2^k$: as usual, working with 2 instead of an odd prime induces a lot of technicalities.

3.1 Choice for Δ_K

Let us begin with the generation of the fundamental discriminant Δ_K. Firstly, as we shall see in Subsect. 3.4, we cannot reach any security in our applications if computing square roots in the class group is easy. As mentioned in Subsect. 2.3 this means Δ_K must be hard to factor. As a consequence we will construct a discriminant Δ_K from an RSA integer, $N = pq$, which is a first difference with the CL encryption.

Secondly, we will need to work with a subgroup of $Cl(\Delta)$ of odd order. This subgroup will be isomorphic to the subgroup of squares of $Cl(\Delta_K)$. The subgroup of squares has cardinality $\hat{s} := h(\Delta)/2^{\mu-1}$ where $2^{\mu-1}$ is the number of elements of order $\leqslant 2$. If we ensure that the 2–Sylow of $Cl(\Delta)$ is restricted to the elements of order $\leqslant 2$, then the subgroup of squares will correspond to the odd-part and $\hat{s}$ will be odd as required. This is done by ensuring that elements of order 2 are not squares, thereby imposing conditions on the prime factors of Δ_K.

Several choices are possible to construct Δ_K from N. In order for the conditions on the prime p and q to be the less restrictive possible, we choose to work with a fundamental discriminant $\Delta_K := -8N$. The next lemma gives the conditions that ensures that the 2–Sylow is restricted to elements of order 2.

Lemma 2. *Consider two distinct odd primes p and q of same bit-size, with values modulo 8 and Legendre symbols chosen according to Table 1. Let $N = pq$, and consider the fundamental discriminant $\Delta_k = -8N$. Then the 2–Sylow subgroup of $Cl(\Delta_K)$ is isomorphic to $\mathbf{Z}/2\mathbf{Z} \times \mathbf{Z}/2\mathbf{Z}$.*

Table 1. Choices of (p, q) such that the 2–Sylow of $Cl(-8pq)$ is isomorphic to $\mathbf{Z}/2\mathbf{Z} \times \mathbf{Z}/2\mathbf{Z}$. The star $*$ means that there is no restriction on the values (p/q) and (p/q).

p mod 8	q mod 8	(p/q)	(q/p)
1	3	−1	−1
1	5	−1	−1
3	1	−1	−1
3	5	*	
3	7	−1	1
5	1	−1	−1
5	3	*	
5	5	*	
5	7	−1	−1
7	3	1	−1
7	5	−1	−1

Proof. If $N = pq$, and $\Delta_k = -8N$, as seen in Subsect. 2.3, $\mu = 3$, so there are $2^{3-1} - 1 = 3$ elements of order 2 in $Cl(\Delta_K)$. Looking at forms of the type $(a, 0, c)$ of discriminant $-4ac = -8N$, we find the following ones:

$$f_2 := (2, 0, N); f_p := (p, 0, 2q); f_q := (q, 0, 2p).$$

By hypothesis, $N > 2$, $2q > p$ and $2p > q$ so these three distinct forms are reduced, and their classes gives the 3 elements of order 2 of $Cl(\Delta_k)$.

We now compute the genus of f_2, f_p and f_q. For this, we need the value of χ_p, χ_q and χ_8 or χ_{-8} depending of the value of $N \mod 4$. Let us see in details the case of f_2. We have $\chi_p(f_2) = \left(\frac{a}{p}\right)$ where a is an integer represented by f_2 prime to p. One can choose $a = 2 = f_2(1,0)$. As a result

$$\chi_p(f_2) = \left(\frac{2}{p}\right) = (-1)^{\frac{p^2-1}{8}},$$

which gives 1 if $p \equiv 1, 7 \pmod 8$, and -1 if $p \equiv 3, 5 \pmod 8$.

Likewise, $\chi_q(f_2) = (2/q)$, whose value is determined by $q \pmod 8$.

If $N \equiv 3 \pmod 4$, to compute $\chi_8(f_2)$ we need an odd integer represented by f_2. We can choose $f_2(0,1) = N$. We then have

$$\chi_8(f_2) = (-1)^{\frac{N^2-1}{8}},$$

and again this value depends only on $N \mod 8$. If $N \equiv 1 \pmod 4$, we can also take N to evaluate $\chi_{-8}(f_2)$, which also depends only on $N \mod 8$.

For f_p, we use $f_p(0,1) = 2q$ to evaluate $\chi_p(f_p) = \left(\frac{2}{p}\right) \cdot \left(\frac{q}{p}\right)$. We also have $\chi_q(f_p) = \left(\frac{p}{q}\right)$ using $f_p(1,0) = p$, and the value of χ_8 and χ_{-8} are also determined using p. The genus of f_p can thus be determined by the values of $p \mod 8$ and the Legendre symbols $\left(\frac{p}{q}\right)$ and $\left(\frac{q}{p}\right)$. Note that by the law of quadratic reciprocity, these Legendre symbols are equal if $p \equiv 1 \pmod 4$ or $q \equiv 1 \pmod 4$ and $\left(\frac{p}{q}\right) = -\left(\frac{q}{p}\right)$ if $p \equiv q \equiv 3 \pmod 4$. The determination of the genus of f_q is similar to the one of f_p by exchanging the roles of q and p.

Now in order to have a 2–Sylow subgroup isomorphic to $\mathbf{Z}/2\mathbf{Z} \times \mathbf{Z}/2\mathbf{Z}$, f_p, f_q and f_2 must all not be squares, which means that their genus must not have symbols $(1,1,1)$. As shown above, this only depends on the values of $p, q \pmod 8$ and of the relative Legendre symbols of p and q. By inspection of these values, we fill the Table 1 which gives all possibilities ensuring that f_p, f_q and f_2 are all not squares. □

3.2 Choice for Δ

We now want to construct a non fundamental discriminant such that $Cl(\Delta)$ contains a cyclic subgroup of order 2^k by using Eq. 1. We will therefore consider as conductor ℓ a power of 2. As $\Delta_K = -8N$, we get $\left(\frac{\Delta_K}{2}\right) = 0$, and denoting, $\Delta = \ell^2 \Delta_K$, the class number $h(\Delta) = \ell h(\Delta_K)$, *i.e*, the kernel of the surjection φ_ℓ has order ℓ.

If we set $\ell = 2^k$, we thus get a subgroup of $Cl(\Delta)$ of order 2^k, and one can prove that this subgroup is cyclic, in our case where $\Delta_K = -8N$. Unfortunately, a similar computation to that of the proof of the next theorem shows that generators of this subgroup are not squares: the character χ_{-4} is equal to -1. This would break all our security assumptions, as the value of this character would leak the parity of discrete logarithms.

We thus set $\ell = 2^{k+1}$, and as a consequence, the kernel of φ_ℓ has order 2^{k+1}, and we can work in its cyclic subgroup of squares, of order 2^k. Note that other choices of Δ_K depending on N lead to similar constructions.

Theorem 1. *Let $\Delta_K = -8N$ with $N = pq$ as in Lemma 2. Let $\Delta = 2^{2k+2} \cdot \Delta_K$, then the class of $f := (2^{2k}, 2^{k+1}, 1 + 8N)$ is a square of order 2^k in $Cl(\Delta)$.*

Proof. Let $\ell = 2^{k+1}$ be the conductor. The strategy of the proof is as follows: we use the fact that $\ker \varphi_\ell$ is isomorphic to

$$G_\ell := \left(\mathcal{O}_{\Delta_K}/\ell\mathcal{O}_{\Delta_K}\right)^\times / \left(\mathbf{Z}/\ell\mathbf{Z}\right)^\times .$$

We will exhibit a system of representatives of this quotient group, and an element of order 2^k. As the isomorphism to $\ker \varphi_\ell$ is explicit, we will apply it to this element to get f of the same order 2^k in $Cl(\Delta)$. Then a computation of the assigned characters will show that f is a square.

The first step is to establish a system of representatives of the group G_ℓ. As $\Delta_K = 4m$, with $m := -2N$, $\mathcal{O}_{\Delta_K} = \mathbf{Z} + \mathbf{Z}\sqrt{m} \equiv \mathbf{Z}[X]/(X^2 - m)$ and $\mathcal{O}_{\Delta_K}/\ell\mathcal{O}_{\Delta_K} \equiv \mathbf{Z}/\ell\mathbf{Z}[X]/(X^2 - m)$. First observe that when $\ell = 2$, we have $m \equiv 0 \mod \ell$ and the invertible elements of $\mathcal{O}_{\Delta_K}/2\mathcal{O}_{\Delta_K}$ are therefore 1 and $1 + X$. For $k \geqslant 0$, we will then have

$$\left(\mathcal{O}_{\Delta_K}/\ell\mathcal{O}_{\Delta_K}\right)^\times = \left\{a + bX, (a, b) \in (\mathbf{Z}/\ell\mathbf{Z})^\times \times \mathbf{Z}/\ell\mathbf{Z}\right\}$$

To get the group G_ℓ, we identify $a + bX$ with $ac + bcX$ for $c \in (\mathbf{Z}/\ell\mathbf{Z})^\times$. We then have the system of representatives:

$$\{1 + bX, b \in \mathbf{Z}/\ell\mathbf{Z}\}.$$

Now we show that $1 + 2X$ is of order 2^k in this group (one could prove that $1+X$ is of order 2^{k+1} and this group is cyclic, but considering $1+2X$ is sufficient for our applications). For this we first prove that for $k \geqslant 2$,

$$(1 + 2X)^{2^{k-1}} = 1 + 2^k X + 2^k X^2 \in \mathbf{Z}/2^{k+1}\mathbf{Z}[X]. \tag{2}$$

This can been shown by induction: the equality is clear for $k = 2$. Now suppose, that there exists a polynomial Q, s.t. $(1 + 2X)^{2^{k-2}} = 1 + 2^{k-1}X + 2^{k-1}X^2 + 2^k Q(X)$. Squaring both sides, we indeed get that $(1+2X)^{2^{k-1}} = 1+2^k X+2^k X^2$ modulo 2^{k+1}, which proves Eq. 2.

As a result we get that for $k \geqslant 2$, $(1 + 2X)^{2^{k-1}} \equiv 1 + 2^k m + 2^k X$ which is equivalent to $1+(1+2^k)^{-1}2^k X = 1+2^k X \neq 1$ in the group G_ℓ. But $(1+2^k X)^2 = 1$ which proves that $1+2X$ is of order 2^k for $k \geqslant 2$. It is straightforward to verify that $1 + 2X$ is also of order 2^k for $k = 0, 1$.

The next step is to map $1 + 2X$ in $\ker \varphi_\ell$ using the explicit isomorphism. This isomorphism consists in taking a representative α of the class of $1 + 2X$ in $\mathcal{O}_{\Delta_K}$, to compute a basis of the ideal $\alpha\mathcal{O}_{\Delta_K}$ and then to move it to $Cl(\Delta)$ by considering the class of the ideal $\alpha\mathcal{O}_{\Delta_K} \cap \mathcal{O}_\Delta$. The element $1 + 2X$ corresponds to the quadratic integer $\alpha := 1 + 2\sqrt{m} = 1 + \sqrt{\Delta_K}$. Following [10, Prop. 2.9], one writes $\alpha = \frac{x+y\sqrt{\Delta_K}}{2}$ with $x = y = 2$. Then applying the Extended Euclidean algorithm on $y = 2$ and $(x + y\Delta_K)/2 = 1 + \Delta_K$ one gets $\kappa = 1 - 4N$, $\lambda = -1$, $\mu = 1$ s.t. $\kappa y + \lambda(x + y\Delta_K)/2 = \mu$. The ideal $\alpha\mathcal{O}_{\Delta_K}$ then corresponds to the form (a, b, c) where $a = N(\alpha)/\mu = 1 - \Delta = 1 + 8N$; and $b \equiv -\kappa x - \lambda(x+y)\Delta_K/2 \pmod{2a}$. One gets $b \equiv -2 - 8N \equiv 8N \pmod{2a}$, and $c = 2N$.

We then move this form to $Cl(\Delta)$ following [39, Algorithm 2] as a is odd so prime to the conductor 2^{k+1}. We get the form $(1 + 8N, 2^{k+4}N, 2^{2k+3}N)$. We then reduce this form, first by normalizing the b coefficient modulo $2a$: $2^{k+4}N - 2^{k+1}a = -2^{k+1}$, and computing the new value of c, we get 2^{2k}. As a result, this normalization gives the form $(1+8N, -2^{k+1}, 2^{2k})$ which is equivalent to the form $f = (2^{2k}, 2^{k+1}, 1+8N)$. Note that this form is reduced if $2^{2k} < 1+8N$ which will be the case in our applications.

The final step of the proof is to prove that f is a square. In $Cl(\Delta)$, the assigned characters are $\chi_8, \chi_{-4}, \chi_p, \chi_q$. Using $f(1,0) = 2^{2k}$ which is a square, one gets that $\chi_p(f) = \chi_q(f) = 1$. Using the odd integer $f(0,1) = 1 + 8N$, $\chi_{-4}(f) = (-1)^{4N} = 1$ and $\chi_8(f) = 1$ as $1 + 8N \equiv 1 \pmod 8$. □

3.3 The Gen_{2^k} Algorithm

We depict our group generator in Algorithm 1. We first select a fundamental discriminant $\Delta_K := -8N$ as in Lemma 2. This ensures that the 2–Sylow subgroup of $Cl(\Delta_K)$ has order 4 and $h(\Delta_K) = 4\hat{s}$ where $\hat{s}$ is odd, and $\hat{s}$ is the cardinality of the subgroup of squares of $Cl(\Delta_K)$.

Algorithm 1: Gen_{2^k}

Input: 1^λ
Result: pp

—

sample two random distinct $\eta(\lambda)$-bit primes p, q according to Table 1
$N := pq$
$\Delta_K := -8N$
$\Delta := 2^{2k+2} \cdot \Delta_K$
$f := (2^{2k}, 2^{k+1}, 1 + 8N) \in Cl(\Delta)$
sample r a random square of $Cl(\Delta)$
$h := r^{2^k} \in Cl(\Delta)$
compute $\tilde{s}$ an upper bound $h(\Delta_K)$
return $\mathsf{pp} := (f, h, \tilde{s})$

We then consider the class group $Cl(\Delta)$ of the non maximal order of discriminant $\Delta := 2^{2k+2} \cdot \Delta_K$ as in Lemma 1. This setting ensures that the class of the form $f := (2^{2k}, 2^{k+1}, 1 + 8N)$ generates a subgroup F of order 2^k of the group of squares of $Cl(\Delta)$.

For the discriminant Δ, the parameter μ equals 4 and there are $h(\Delta)/2^{\mu-1} = 2^{k+1} \cdot h(\Delta_K)/8 = 2^k \cdot \hat{s}$ squares in $Cl(\Delta)$ (cf. [22, Prop. 3.11]). We then consider h a random 2^k–power of a square of $Cl(\Delta)$. By construction, the order of h, denoted s, is odd as it divides $\hat{s}$. We denote H the subgroup generated by h. Denoting G the cycling subgroup of the squares of $Cl(\Delta)$ of order $2^k s$, we have the isomorphism $G \simeq F \times H$ and F (resp. H) is the subgroup of 2^k–roots of unity of G (resp. the 2^k–th powers of G). Finally, we denote $\tilde{s}$ a known upper bound for s: the order s is *unknown* in our generator, but $\tilde{s}$ can be computed from an upper bound on the class number of $Cl(\Delta_K)$: $h(\Delta_K) < \frac{1}{\pi} \log|\Delta_K|\sqrt{|\Delta_K|}$, or obtain a slightly better bound using the analytic class number formula (cf. [46]).

Size of p and q. The bitsize $\eta(\lambda)$ of the primes p and q is chosen such that the best algorithms for factoring $N := pq$ take 2^λ time. This ensures that computing s via the class number of $Cl(\Delta_K)$ takes more that 2^λ time as known algorithms for computing class numbers have worse complexities. In practice, for 112 bits (resp. 128 bits) of security, we take N of 2048 bits (resp. 3072 bits).

3.4 Assumptions

The semantic security of our linearly homomorphic encryption (and its threshold variant) relies on the following hard subgroup membership assumption, which is a natural extension of the HSM assumption underlying CL encryption [18]. In a nutshell, in the group G, we assume that it is hard to distinguish elements of the subgroup H, the 2^k–th powers, from random elements. As we shall see, in our particular context, this assumption implies the factorization assumption.

Definition 8 (HSM_{2^k} assumption). *Let $\mathcal{A}$ be an adversary for the HSM_{2^k} problem, its advantage is defined as:*

$$\mathsf{Adv}_{\mathcal{A}}^{\mathsf{HSM}_{2^k}}(\lambda) := \Big| 2 \cdot \Pr[b = b^* \ : \ \mathsf{pp} := (f, h, \tilde{s}) \stackrel{\$}{\leftarrow} \mathsf{Gen}_{2^k}(1^\lambda), x \hookleftarrow \mathcal{D}_{\mathcal{H}},$$
$$u \stackrel{\$}{\leftarrow} U((\mathbf{Z}/2^k\mathbf{Z})^\times), b \stackrel{\$}{\leftarrow} \{0,1\}, z_0 := h^x f^u, z_1 := h^x, b^* \leftarrow \mathcal{A}(\mathsf{pp}, z_b)] - 1 \Big|$$

where $\mathcal{D}_H$ is a distribution over the integers such that the distribution $\{h^x,\ x \hookleftarrow \mathcal{D}_H\}$ is at distance less than $2^{-\lambda}$ from the uniform distribution in H. The HSM_{2^k} assumption holds if for any probabilistic polynomial-time adversary $\mathcal{A}$, its advantage is negligible.

Relations with Factoring and Computing the Class Number. Let $\Delta_K = -8N$, as defined in Algorithm 1. The class number $n := h(\Delta_K)$ is an integer multiple of s, the unknown order of h. So computing n allows to break the HSM_{2^k} assumption by checking if $z_b^n = 1$ or not.

The knowledge of n also allows to find the elements of order 2 of $Cl(\Delta_K)$, and, as shown in the background section, these elements gives the factorisation of Δ_K and thus of N. So computing n allows to factor N.

Conversely, there is no known method of computing $h(\Delta_K)$ given the factorisation of N, and best algorithms for computing $h(\Delta_K)$ have worse complexities than algorithms to factor N. However, the factorization of N allows to break HSM_{2^k}. As already mentioned in Subsect. 2.3, computing square roots and deciding if an element is a square in $Cl(\Delta)$ is feasible in polynomial-time if the factorisation of the discriminant is available. The HSM_{2^k} problem asks to distinguish between an element of the form $z_0 = h^x f^u$ for a random odd integer u and an element of the form $z_1 = h^x$, for a random x. As h is a 2^k-th power of a square, it is a square, and at least one of its square roots is a square itself, even if $k = 1$. This is not the case for $h^x f^u$. By construction, f is a square whose square roots are *not* squares: if there exists a square a such that $f = a^2$ then a would be a square of order 2^{k+1}, and we get a contradiction with the fact that the group of squares of $Cl(\Delta)$ has order $2^k \cdot \hat{s}$ where $\hat{s}$ is odd. So to distinguish the two cases, one has to compute a square root of the challenge element, and by inspection, compute the genera of the forms, check whether there exists a square root that is a square (and in this case the attacker outputs $b^\star = 1$) or not (and in this case the attacker outputs $b^\star = 0$). These relations between algorithmic assumptions are summarize in Fig. 2.

It can be shown that the factorization allows in fact to compute a *partial discrete logarithm* of any $y = g^x$ in the class group, *i.e.*, the value $x \mod 2^k$ (and gives therefore a trapdoor to decrypt a ciphertext).

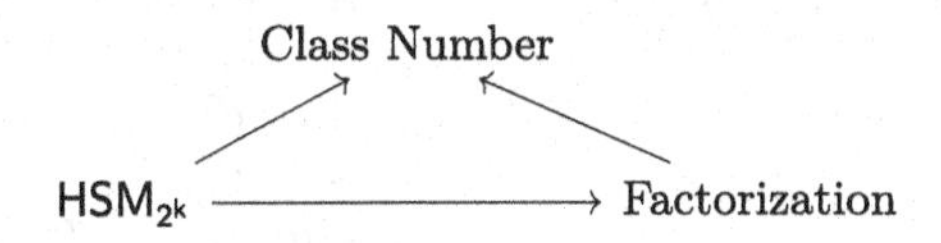

Fig. 2. Relations between the algorithmic assumptions underlying our protocols

4 Linearly Homomorphic Encryption Scheme on $\mathbf{Z}/2^k\mathbf{Z}$

4.1 Description of the New Encryption Scheme

Let $\mathcal{D}_H$ (resp. $\mathcal{D}_G$) be a distribution over the integers, such that $\{x \bmod s : x \xleftarrow{\$} \mathcal{D}_H\}$ (resp. $\{x \bmod 2^k s : x \xleftarrow{\$} \mathcal{D}_G\}$) is δ-close to the uniform distribution in $\{1, \ldots, s\}$ (resp. $\{1, \ldots, 2^k s\}$), where $\delta \leq 2^{-\lambda}$.

The distribution $\mathcal{D}_G$ is only used in the security proof and the distribution $\mathcal{D}_H$ can be instantiated by sampling x uniformly in $\{1, \ldots \tilde{s} \cdot 2^{\lambda+2}\}$ using the upper bound $\tilde{s}$ on s (cf. [17, Appendix C]).

Our linearly homomorphic encryption scheme on $\mathbf{Z}/2^k\mathbf{Z}$ is described in Fig. 3, where the key generation algorithm takes as input the public parameters $\mathsf{pp} := (f, h, \tilde{s})$ that come from the Gen_{2^k} algorithm. There is no condition on the value of k, typical values are 32, 64 or 128.

Algorithm 2: KeyGen

Input: pp
Result: (pk, sk)
—
sample $\mathsf{sk} \xleftarrow{\$} \mathcal{D}_H$
$\mathsf{pk} := h^{\mathsf{sk}}$
return (pk, sk)

Algorithm 3: Encrypt

Input: pp, pk, $m \in \mathbf{Z}/2^k\mathbf{Z}$
Result: ciphertext (c_1, c_2)
—
sample $r \xleftarrow{\$} \mathcal{D}_H$
$c_1 := h^r$
$c_2 := f^m \mathsf{pk}^r$
return (c_1, c_2)

Algorithm 4: Decrypt

Input: pp, sk, (c_1, c_2)
Result: $m \in \mathbf{Z}/2^k\mathbf{Z} \cup \{\perp\}$
—
$M := c_2 \cdot c_1^{-\mathsf{sk}}$
if $M \notin F$ **then**
  return $\perp$
end
return $\log_f(M)$

Algorithm 5: EvalAdd

Input: pp, pk, $(c_1, c_2), (c_1', c_2')$
Result: ciphertext (c_1'', c_2'')
—
$c_1'' := c_1 \cdot c_1'$
$c_2'' := c_2 \cdot c_2'$
sample $r \xleftarrow{\$} \mathcal{D}_H$
return $(c_1'' \cdot h^r, c_2'' \cdot \mathsf{pk}^r)$

Algorithm 6: EvalScal

Input: pp, pk, $(c_1, c_2), \alpha$
Result: ciphertext (c_1', c_2')
—
$c_1' := c_1^\alpha$
$c_2' := c_2^\alpha$
sample $r \xleftarrow{\$} \mathcal{D}_H$
return $(c_1' \cdot h^r, c_2' \cdot \mathsf{pk}^r)$

Fig. 3. Linearly homomorphic encryption scheme with message space $\mathbf{Z}/2^k\mathbf{Z}$

Correctness and Decryption. The correctness of the protocol comes from the fact $c_2 \cdot c_1^{-\mathsf{sk}} = f^m \cdot \mathsf{pk}^r \cdot (h^r)^{-sk} = f^m \cdot (h^{\mathsf{sk}})^r \cdot (h^r)^{-\mathsf{sk}} = f^m$. To recover m from f^m, one has to compute a discrete logarithm. In this case, this discrete logarithm computation is trivial since f generates a subgroup of order 2^k. Pohlig-Hellman algorithm makes it possible to recover m by extracting m bit by bit. The algorithm to retrieve the discrete logarithm is described in Fig. 4. It consists mainly of $O(k^2)$ squaring in the class group.

4.2 Security of the Encryption Scheme

Semantic Security

Theorem 2. *The scheme described in Fig. 3 is semantically secure under chosen plaintext attacks* (ind − cpa) *if the* HSM_{2^k} *assumption holds.*

Proof. The proof proceeds as a sequence of games, starting with the real ind−cpa experiment and ending in a game where the ciphertext statistically hides the

Algorithm 7: Pohlig-Hellman

Input: $\mathsf{pp}, M \in F$
Result: m such that $M = f^m$
—
$m := 0$;
$\tilde{f} := f^{2^{k-1}}$;
for $i = 0$ *to* $k - 1$ **do**
  if $(f^{-m}M)^{2^{k-1-i}} = \tilde{f}$ **then**
    $m := m + 2^i$;
  end
end
return m

Fig. 4. Pohlig-Hellman algorithm to compute $\log_f(M)$

random bit b chosen by the challenger. We denote S_i the event 'adversary $\mathcal{A}$ outputs $b = b^*$ in Game i'.

In Game 1, instead of sampling sk from $\mathcal{D}_H$, it is sampled from $\mathcal{D}_G$. The rest of the experiment is unchanged, so the only difference from $\mathcal{A}$'s view is the distribution of $\mathsf{pk} := h^{\mathsf{sk}}$. The distribution $\mathcal{D}_H$ is chosen such that $\{h^x : x \xleftarrow{\$} \mathcal{D}_H\}$ is δ-close to the uniform distribution in H. Furthermore, since s divides $2^k s$, sampling x in the previous expression also yields a distribution δ-close to the uniform distribution in H, so $|\Pr[S_1] - \Pr[S_0]| \leq 2\delta$.

In Game 2, the challenge ciphertext is computed as $c_1 := h^r$ and $c_2 := f^{m_b} c_1^{\mathsf{sk}}$, where $r \xleftarrow{\$} \mathcal{D}_H$. As $\mathsf{pk}^r = c_1^{\mathsf{sk}}$ this game is identical to the previous one, *i.e*,

$$\Pr[S_1] = \Pr[S_2].$$

In Game 3, the challenger additionally samples $u \xleftarrow{\$} (\mathbf{Z}/2^k\mathbf{Z})^\star$ uniformly at random. It sets $c_1 := h^r f^u$, and $c_2 := f^{m_b} c_1^{\mathsf{sk}}$. Now if $\mathcal{A}$ could distinguish game 2 from game 3, one could use $\mathcal{A}$ to solve the HSM_{2^k} problem, by setting c_1 to be the HSM_{2^k} challenge. Hence, denoting $\epsilon_{\mathsf{HSM}_{2^k}}$ the maximum advantage of any polynomial time adversary for the HSM_{2^k} problem, $\mathcal{A}$'s success probability in Game 2 and Game 3 can not differ by more than $\epsilon_{\mathsf{HSM}_{2^k}}$. This implies that

$$|\Pr[S_3] - \Pr[S_2]| \leq \epsilon_{\mathsf{HSM}_{2^k}}.$$

We now demonstrate that in game 3, the challenge bit b is perfectly hidden from $\mathcal{A}$'s view. Since $G \simeq H \times F$, the element $c_1 = h^r f^u$ information theoretically fixes the value of $(u \bmod 2^k)$ and of $(r \bmod s)$ from $\mathcal{A}$'s view. Furthermore $\mathcal{A}$ receives $c_2 = f^{m_b + u \cdot \mathsf{sk}} \mathsf{pk}^r$. Given c_1 and pk, the value of pk^r is information theoretically fixed, hence an unbounded adversary could infer $(m_b + u \cdot \mathsf{sk} \bmod 2^k)$.

Since sk is sampled from $\mathcal{D}_G$, the distribution followed by $(\mathsf{sk} \bmod 2^k s)$ is at negligible distance $\delta \leq 2^{-\lambda}$ of the uniform modulo $2^k s$. Furthermore, since s and 2^k are co-prime, $(\mathsf{sk} \bmod 2^k)$ is δ-close to the uniform modulo 2^k and is independent of ($\mathsf{sk} \bmod s$). So even if $\mathsf{pk} = h^{\mathsf{sk}}$ fixes the value of ($\mathsf{sk} \bmod s$), that of ($\mathsf{sk} \bmod 2^k$) remains δ-close to $U(\mathbf{Z}/2^k\mathbf{Z})$ from $\mathcal{A}$'s view. Finally since u is invertible modulo 2^k, ($u \cdot \mathsf{sk} \bmod 2^k$) is also δ-close to $U(\mathbf{Z}/2^k\mathbf{Z})$, and perfectly masks m_b. Therefore $|\Pr[S_2] - 1/2| \leq \delta$. Combining the probability equations, we conclude the proof with the following inequality:

$$\mathsf{Adv}_{\mathcal{A}}^{\mathsf{ind\text{-}cpa}}(\lambda) \leq \epsilon_{\mathsf{HSM}_{2k}} + 3\delta.$$

□

We note that a DDH assumption can also be used in the group G similarly to [17], which would lead to slightly different encryption scheme (using $g = hf$ instead of h).

Circuit Privacy for Linear Functions. The ciphertexts of our encryption protocol guarantees circuit privacy, in the sense that ciphertexts obtained through the homomorphic evaluation process are indistinguishable from fresh encryptions of the resulting message. This property is very useful in multi-party computation (see [19,20] for instance). More precisely, the definition is as follows.

Definition 9 (Circuit privacy for linear functions). *We say that a linearly homomorphic encryption* LHE *is private if there exists a probabilistic polynomial-time simulator* Sim *such that for any $\lambda \in \mathbf{N}$, for any $(\mathsf{pk}, \mathsf{sk}) \leftarrow \mathsf{KeyGen}(\lambda, \mathsf{pp})$, any pair of messages m_1, m_2 in the message space, and two ciphertexts c_1 and c_2 of m_1 and m_2 respectively, and any scalar α, the statistical distances between $\mathsf{LHE.EvalAdd}(\mathsf{pp}, \mathsf{pk}, c_1, c_2)$ and $\mathsf{Sim}(1^\lambda, \mathsf{pp}, \mathsf{pk}, m_1 + m_2)$ and between $\mathsf{LHE.EvalScal}(\mathsf{pp}, \mathsf{pk}, c_1, \alpha)$ and $\mathsf{Sim}(1^\lambda, \mathsf{pp}, \mathsf{pk}, \alpha m_1)$ are negligible.*

Theorem 3. *The scheme of Fig. 3 is circuit private for linear functions.*

Proof. For both pair of distributions, the simulator just encrypts the message it has as input ($m_1 + m_2$ or αm_1). The randomization applied during homomorphic evaluations (LHE.EvalAdd and LHE.EvalScal) ensures that the distributions are statistically close. □

4.3 Experiments

We have implemented our encryption protocol using Sagemath with calls to the PARI native C Library [50] for the operations in class groups. All benchmarks were done on a standard laptop (Intel Core i5-6267U @ 2.90 GHz). Our experiments have been run for security levels of $\lambda = 112$ and 128 bits. The RSA modulus N has therefore respective sizes of 2048 bits and 3072 bits. The bit size of the ciphertexts is $2 \times \frac{3}{4}(5 + 2k + \ell_N)$ where ℓ_N is the bit size of N. The crucial part of KeyGen, Encrypt and Decrypt are exponentiations in class groups where the exponent is upper bounded by $\tilde{s} \approx \sqrt{N}$.

These timings show that even a straightforward implementation is practical, and an optimized C implementation of our system would drastically improve the running times.

Table 2. Bit size and running time of our homomorphic encryption in seconds.

k	λ (bits)	Ciphertext (bits)	Setup	KeyGen	Encrypt	Decrypt
32	112	3176	0.037	0.101	0.096	0.101
	128	4712	0.231	0.212	0.214	0.222
64	112	3272	0.086	0.098	0.098	0.118
	128	4808	0.201	0.217	0.219	0.243
128	112	3464	0.076	0.103	0.105	0.178
	128	5000	0.398	0.230	0.230	0.309

5 Threshold Encryption on $\mathbf{Z}/2^k\mathbf{Z}$ with Trusted Setup

5.1 A TPKE Scheme from Class Groups

In this subsection we adapt the PKE scheme from the previous section to the threshold setting. The threshold decryption relies on the LISS construction from Damgård and Thorbek [27] based on [2]. Let n be the number of servers, from the threshold access structure $\mathbb{A}$, the dealer generates a share-generating matrix $\mathbf{M} \in \{0,1\}^e$, where $e \in O(n^{1+\sqrt{2}})$ which computes the Boolean formula associated to $\mathbb{A}$ as well as a surjective function $\psi : \{1,\ldots,d\} \mapsto P$ as defined in Subsect. 2.2.

Our new threshold encryption protocol with message space of order 2^k is described in Fig. 5. We omit the EvalAdd and EvalScal algorithm that are exactly the same as the ones for our linearly homomorphic encryption scheme (Algorithms 5 and 6 of Fig. 3).

Theorem 4. *The scheme described in Fig. 5 achieves* T-ind-cpa-*security under the* ind − cpa *security of the non-threshold scheme of Fig. 3.*

Proof. This theorem is a direct corollary of the privacy of the LISS and the ind-cpa of the non-threshold encryption scheme.

From an attacker against the T-ind-cpa-security $\mathcal{A}$, we construct an attacker against the ind-cpa security of the basic scheme, which receives public parameters pp and a public key $\mathsf{pk} = h^x$ for an unknown x.

After $\mathcal{A}$ chooses an access structure $\mathbb{A}$, he is fed with pp and pk as ek. He chooses a set S outside $\mathbb{A}$, and waits for the corresponding secret keys. They are simulated after the computation of a sharing of 0, *i.e.*, the distribution vector is $\boldsymbol{\rho} = (0, \rho_1, \ldots, \rho_d)^T$ and the shares are $\mathbf{s} = (s_1, \ldots, s_d)^\top = \mathbf{M} \cdot \boldsymbol{\rho}$, where $\mathbf{M}$ is the matrix corresponding to the access structure $\mathbb{A}$. $\mathcal{A}$ receives the shares belonging to the servers in S.

Now, $\mathcal{A}$ can query partial decryptions: he queries the oracle on plaintext m and server i. The message m is encrypted as $\mathsf{ct} = \mathsf{Encrypt}(\mathsf{pp}, \mathsf{ek}, m) = (\mathsf{ct}_1, \mathsf{ct}_2)$. We must simulate the contributions that this honest party i computes, namely $\mathbf{d}_i := (c_1^{s_j})_{j \in \psi^{-1}(i)}$, from $\mathsf{pk}^r = \mathsf{ct}_1^x$. This is done as in [27] for the distribution of an exponentiation. Let $\boldsymbol{\kappa}_S$ be the sweeping vector of Definition 7 for S. Now, let R be a row in the distribution matrix $\mathbf{M}$ belonging to the honest server P_i

Algorithm 8: Setup

Input: $1^\lambda, \mathbb{A}$
Result: pp, ek, **sk**
—
generate $pp := (f, h, \tilde{s}) \xleftarrow{\$} \mathsf{Gen}_{2^k}(1^\lambda)$
sample $\mathsf{sk} \xleftarrow{\$} \{1, \ldots, 2^{\lambda+2}\tilde{s}\}$
$\mathsf{ek} := h^{\mathsf{sk}}$
Set $e, d \in O(n^{1+\sqrt{2}})$
Compute the matrix $\mathbf{M} \in \{0,1\}^{d \times e}$ that computes $\mathbb{A}$ // Benaloh-Leichter
sample $(\rho_2, \ldots, \rho_e) \xleftarrow{\$} [2^{l_0+\lambda}, 2^{l_0+\lambda}]^{e-1}$
$\boldsymbol{\rho} := (\mathsf{sk}, \rho_2, \ldots, \rho_e)^\top$
for $i \in \{1, \ldots, n\}$ **do**
  $\mathsf{sk}_i := (\mathbf{M}_j \cdot \boldsymbol{\rho})_{j \in \psi^{-1}(i)} \in \mathbf{Z}^{d_i}$
end
$\mathbf{sk} := (\mathsf{sk}_i)_{1 \leqslant i \leqslant n}$
return pp, ek, **sk**

Algorithm 9: Encrypt

Input: ek, $m \in \mathbf{Z}/2^k\mathbf{Z}$
Result: ciphertext
  $\mathsf{ct} := (c_1, c_2)$
—
sample $r \xleftarrow{\$} \mathcal{D}_H$
$c_1 := h^r$
$c_2 := f^m \mathsf{ek}^r$
return (c_1, c_2)

Algorithm 10: PartDec

Input: pp, sk_i, ct
Result: $\mathbf{d}_i \in G \cup \{\perp\}$
—
parse ct as (c_1, c_2)
parse sk_i as $(s_j)_{j \in \psi^{-1}(i)}$
$\mathbf{d}_i := (c_1^{s_j})_{j \in \psi^{-1}(i)}$
return $\mathbf{d}_i$

Algorithm 11: FinalDec

Input: pp, $\{\mathbf{d}_i\}_{i \in S}$ for $S \in \mathbb{A}$
Result: $m \in \mathbf{Z}/2^k\mathbf{Z} \cup \{\perp\}$
—
parse S as $(j_1, \ldots, j_t)$
compute $\boldsymbol{\lambda}_S := (\boldsymbol{\lambda}_{j_1}^\top, \ldots, \boldsymbol{\lambda}_{j_t}^\top)^\top \in \{-1, 0, 1\}^{d_S}$ such that

$$\boldsymbol{\lambda}_S \cdot \mathbf{M}_{\psi^{-1}(S)} = (1, 0, \ldots, 0)^\top$$

where $d_S := \sum_{i \in S} d_i$ and $\boldsymbol{\lambda}_{j_i} := (\lambda_{j_1,1}, \ldots, \lambda_{j_1,d_{j_i}})^\top$ for all $i = 1, \ldots, t$.
compute $d := \prod_{i \in [t]} \prod_{k \in [d_{j_i}]} d_i^{\lambda_{j_i,k}}$
$M := c_2 \cdot d^{-1}$
if $M \notin F$ **then**
  return $\perp$
end
return $\log_f(M)$ using Algo. 7

Fig. 5. TPKE scheme with message space 2^k

and let s_j be one component of the server's share we computed from this row. Had we used $\boldsymbol{\rho}' = \boldsymbol{\rho} + x\boldsymbol{\kappa_S}$ instead of $\boldsymbol{\rho}$, then the share component coming from R would have been $s'_j = (\boldsymbol{\rho} + x\boldsymbol{\kappa_S})R = s_j + x\boldsymbol{\kappa_S}R$ instead. The observation is now that because we know ct_1^x and s, we can compute $\mathsf{ct}_1^{s'_j}$ even though we do not know x. Concretely, we simulate the contribution from P by

$$\mathsf{ct}_1^{s_j}(\mathsf{ct}_1^x)^{\boldsymbol{\kappa_S}R} = \mathsf{ct}_1^{s_j + x\boldsymbol{\kappa_S}R} = \mathsf{ct}_1^{s'_j}.$$

After this partial decryption phase, $\mathcal{A}$ outputs his messages m_0 and m_1 which are forwarded to the ind-cpa challenger which answers with a challenge ciphertext $c^\star$ of one of this two messages $m_{b^\star}$, which is given to $\mathcal{A}$. After another series of queries for partial decryptions, answered in the same way, $\mathcal{A}$ outputs a bit b, which is set as the output of the ind-cpa adversary.

To see that the simulation is correct, we see that the simulated shares are statistically indistinguishable from the real shares by the privacy of the LISS scheme. Second, honest parties always output the correct value ct_1^x, by correctness of the LISS scheme. Finally, given ct_1, ct_1^x, the simulated contributions from honest parties are statistically indistinguishable, since the vector we use for the simulated sharing is $\boldsymbol{\rho}' = \boldsymbol{\rho} + x\boldsymbol{\kappa_S}$ which is statistically close to a uniformly chosen sharing vector for x. The advantage of the ind-cpa attacker will therefore be that of the T-ind-cpa attacker. □

In terms of efficiency, the only difference between the thresold scheme and the encryption scheme of Sect. 4 is in the decryption algorithms (encryption is exactly the same). Therefore, the additional costs come from the LISS, and translate in an additional number of exponentiations in the class group. Exact numbers depend on the considered access structure. For a concrete example, taking the access structure construction for a 2-out-of-3 policy (cf. [53, Example 3.4 p. 26]), the shares have roughly the same bitsize as the secret key and we get 2 exponentiations (in total) for PartDec and a negligible extra cost in FinalDec consisting of multiplication and inversion since the reconstruction vector has components in $\{-1, 0, 1\}$. As a result, PartDec takes twice the classical decryption time (or the same with parallelisation).

5.2 Extensions

Some extensions and improvements (in terms of security or functionality) are possible for our threshold encryption scheme: we suggest few of them.

- *Robustness:* It informally captures that no malicious adversary can prevent a honest majority from decrypting a valid ciphertext. It can be achieved in our context by using Σ-protocols proving equality of discrete logarithms in groups of unknown orders to prove the validity of decryption shares.
- *Removing the trusted dealer:* It is one of the most interesting feature that can be achieved, especially compared to a potential Elgamal version of Benhamouda *et al.*'s scheme. It first requires to generate in a distributed manner

an RSA modulus satisfying the needed congruences. Many efficient techniques can be employed, such as [21], secure against any subset of maliciously colluding parties. The class group can then be computed publicly and the factorization ignored. To share the secret key without trusted dealer, it is possible to use verifiable linear integer secret sharing [53] and techniques from [35] to distribute key generation for discrete-log based cryptosystems.
In addition, zero-knowledge arguments for several relations (well-formdness of a key or equality of discrete logarithms) in group of unknown orders will be needed and can be found in the literature [5,15,29,58].

- *CCA security:* Using techniques of [30] for their chosen ciphertext secure threshold cryptosystems from the Decision Composite Residuosity (DCR) assumption, it should be possible to make our threshold encryption scheme CCA secure (even though we would be loosing the crucial homomorphic encryption), as well as adaptively secure (i.e., secure against an adversary who dynamically corrupts servers throughout the protocol), and non-interactive (i.e., decryption servers do not interact amongst themselves but rather contribute, each, a single message). Note that several building blocks need to be adapted: for example, a Trapdoor Σ-protocol showing that an element is a 2^k-th power. As shown at the end of Subsect. 3.4, the factorization of the discriminant could be the trapdoor of such a protocol.

6 Applications

We here discuss future work, and provide intuition for some of the many applications we see to our scheme.

6.1 Secure Multi-party Computation

The goal here is to devise an MPC protocol (for dishonest majority) that works over $\mathbf{Z}/2^k\mathbf{Z}$, and provides better (bandwidth) efficiency than current solutions.

The topic of malicious MPC for $\mathbf{Z}/2^k\mathbf{Z}$ has drawn significant attention since 2018, when Cramer et al. revelled their $\mathsf{SPD}\mathbf{Z}_{2^k}$ protocol [23] which aims at solving this issue.

Computations modulo 2^k, closely match what happens in a CPU, thereby allowing protocol designers to take advantage of tricks already known there. Typical examples being comparison operations and bitwise operations which seem to be easier modulo 2^k (and harder to emulate modulo p).

The solution from [23] follows a blueprint that is by now standard for many fast (maliciously) secure MPC protocols. The protocol phase is divided in two stages. An offline (slow) phase where some precomputation is done without knowing the actual inputs of the computation; and a very fast, information theoretic, phase which requires knowing the inputs and takes advantage of the data computed offline.

The offline stage consists, mainly, in creating sharings of many triplets of the form $[a], [b], [ab]$, where a and b are random in $\mathbf{Z}/2^k\mathbf{Z}$. These triplets are used to speed up the online phase.

The computations on the input data executed in the online phase require performing additions and multiplications. To add two shared secrets $[x]$, $[y]$, players simply add their shares non interactively. Multiplication is less straightforward. In order to compute $[xy]$ *quickly*, given a (yet unused) triplet $[a]$, $[b]$, $[ab]$, players proceed as follows. First jointly open $[x]-[a]=c$ and $[y]-[b]=d$. Then, without further interaction, each player can compute: $[xy]=cd+[a]d+[b]c+[ab]$. Since the online phase is very fast (essentially the same for all protocols following this blueprint) the question is *how to improve efficiency of the offline stage?*

In SPDZ_{2^k} they use oblivious transfer, which is fast but expensive in terms of bandwidth consumption. One way of reducing bandwidth would be to rely on homomorphic encryption (and indeed the original SPDZ protocol uses somewhat homomorphic encryption for degree two polynomials to compute triplets). The issue is how to do this in the $\mathbf{Z}/2^k\mathbf{Z}$ setting, since we don't know many homomorphic encryption schemes that cope well with this setting.

To our knowledge, two solutions exist to this problem, and both have issues. The first is a protocol due to Orsini et al. [48], which presents significant efficiency gains with respect to [23], but remains very complex. The second, much simpler, is due to Catalano et al. [19]. Their protocol relies on the Joye-Libert encryption scheme, but has lower bandwidth gain and only works in the two party case. Indeed, though the Joye-Libert protocol allows for a message space of order 2^k, it is unclear how to enhance it with threshold decryption. Hence each player in the [19] protocol has their own public and secret key pair, and computing multiplications is performed via a protocol *à la* Gilboa [36] which entails a number of zero-knowledge proofs – hence the small gain in bandwidth consumption.

How Does Our Scheme Help? Our encryption scheme both allows for a message space of order 2^k, and for threshold decryption. Given both these properties, one can easily generate triplets as follows. Each player P_i chooses a random a_i, a random b_i, encrypts them $\mathsf{Encrypt}_{\mathsf{pk}}(a_i)$, $\mathsf{Encrypt}_{\mathsf{pk}}(b_i)$ and broadcasts these values. Every player homomorphically adds the shares it sent and received to obtain encryptions $\mathsf{Encrypt}_{\mathsf{pk}}(a)$, $\mathsf{Encrypt}_{\mathsf{pk}}(b)$, where $a=\sum_i a_i$, and $b=\sum_i b_i$. Then, using a trick from Catalano et al. [20], every player can multiply the underlying plaintexts to obtain $\mathsf{Encrypt}_{\mathsf{pk}}(ab)$. Finally each player P_i uses the partial decryption algorithm with its secret key sk_i to obtain an additive share c_i of ab.

6.2 Homomorphic Secret Sharing (HSS)

Homomorphic secret sharing is a form of secret sharing that allows parties to non-interactively perform computations on shared private inputs. HSS can be viewed as a distributed variant of homomorphic encryption: in HSS multiple parties are given a share of the inputs, and, without further interaction, they each perform (non interactively) homomorphic evaluations over these inputs to obtain a share of the desired output. HSS can be used instead of fully/somewhat homomorphic encryption in many scenarios, including low-communication MPC (e.g. [9]), private querying to remote databases (e.g. [7]), methods of succinctly generating correlated randomness (e.g. [6]), and more. Using our TPKE scheme, combined with recent techniques introduced by Orlandi et al. [47], one should be able to devise the first HSS protocol that efficiently performs computations modulo 2^k, without requiring a correctness/efficiency trade-off, and without the need to restrict the size of the shared inputs.

Details. Based on the breakthrough work by Boyle et al. [8], Fazio et al. [33] provided a blueprint to build an HSS scheme for an expressive class of programs[1]. Precisely, from the [8] protocol, which was based on (circular secure) Elgamal encryption, [33] abstract the key ingredients required of an encryption scheme to build an HSS.

1. The encryption scheme must be both message and key (linearly) homomorphic over a finite quotient.
2. Given an encryption of a small integer w, and substractive secret sharings $\langle x \rangle$ and $\langle \mathsf{sk} x \rangle$ (where sk is the decryption key), there must be a non-interactive method for parties to compute multiplicative shares of the group element g^{xw}, which lives in the ciphertext space of the encryption scheme.
3. A non-interactive technique to convert the multiplicative sharing of g^{xw} into an additive sharing of xw which lives in the plaintext space of the encryption scheme.

Our TPKE scheme naturally satisfies item 1, as it is linearly homomorphic, and threshold decryption can provide us the aforementioned key homomorphic property.

Regarding item 2, we leverage the Elgamal-like structure of our TPKE. Consider a ciphertext $(h^r, f^w \mathsf{pk}^r)$ encrypting w, where $\mathsf{pk} = h^{\mathsf{msk}}$. For each memory value x in the RMS program, the value of x and of $\mathsf{sk}x$ are each held as an additive secret sharing across parties (let us denote P_i's shares $\langle x \rangle_i$ and $\langle \mathsf{sk}x \rangle_i$). P_i's computes its' multiplicative share of f^{wx} as $g_i := (h^r)^{-\langle \mathsf{sk}x \rangle_i} (f^w \mathsf{pk})^{\langle x \rangle_i}$.

Item 3 has for long been the tricky part of the protocol. An ingenious distributed discrete logarithm (DDLog) protocol was first suggested by [8]. In their protocol, to obtain substractive shares of $z := xw$, parties P_0 and P_1, respectively owning shares g_0, g_1 such that $g_0 = g_1 g^{xw}$, agree upon some distinguished element $\tilde{g}$ that is not too far away from g_0, g_1 in terms of multiplications by g. If they find such a $\tilde{g}$, then party i can compute the distance of g_i from $\tilde{g}$ by brute force: by multiplying $\tilde{g}$ by g repeatedly, and seeing how many multiplications it takes to get to g_i. If $\tilde{g}$ isn't too far away, this should not be too inefficient. The primary challenge is agreeing upon a common point $\tilde{g}$. [8] had the parties first fix a set of random, distinguished points in the group; party i then finds the closest point in this set to g_i. As long as both parties find the same point, this will lead to a correct share conversion. To make this process efficient, the distance d

[1] Restricted Multiplication Straight-line Programs. This class captures polynomial-size branching programs, which includes arbitrary logspace computations and NC1 circuits.

between successive points can't be too large, as running time will be $O(d)$. But this induces an inherent $\approx 1/d$ probability of failure, in case a point lies between the original two shares and parties fail to agree. Furthermore, Dinur et al. [31] showed that if one could do better than $1/d$ error probability in $O(\sqrt{d})$ steps, the algorithm could be used to improve the cost of finding discrete logarithms in an interval, a well-studied problem which is believed to be hard.

In recent work, Orlandi et al. [47] overcame this barrier by leveraging the easy discrete logarithm subgroup present in the Paillier framework. As we also have such a setup, we benefit from their technique, and parties can both agree on a distinguished point and efficiently find the distance of a multiplicative share from that point, without requiring a correctness/efficiency trade-off. The high level idea (applied to our group elements), is that both g_0 and g_1 can be seen as elements of the coset $X_{g_0} := \{g_0, g_0 f, \ldots, g_0 f^{2^k-1}\}$. If both parties agree on a point $\tilde{h}$ in this set, then there exists z such that $\tilde{h} = g_0 f^z$, and so P_0 can efficiently compute $\log_F(\tilde{h} \cdot g_0^{-1}) = z$. Furthermore, since $g_0 = g_1 f^{xw}$, P_1 can efficiently compute $\log_F(\tilde{h} \cdot g_1^{-1}) = z + xw$. And it holds that $z + xw - z = xw$ as desired.

Now to agree on the point $\tilde{h}$ the parties compute the smallest element from X_{g_0}. This may be done using the surjection φ_{2^k} from $Cl(\Delta)$ to the class group of the maximal order $Cl(\Delta_K)$. Finally, we note that in prior work, the size of the shared inputs had to be bounded, either for efficiency, as in [8], or for correctness of computations in [47]. The upper bound in Orlandi et al's protocol ensures that no wrap around occurs modulo N. On the other hand, using our TPKE scheme with message space 2^k, we can set the order of the message space to be the modulus desired for practical computations, and potentially avoid such constraints.

6.3 Lossy Trapdoor Functions (LTDFs)

Lossy trapdoor functions, introduced by Peikert and Waters [52], are families of functions where injective functions are computationally indistinguishable from lossy functions, which lose many bits of information about their input. Among many interesting applications, LTDFs are known to imply chosen-ciphertext-secure PKE [52] or deterministic encryption [1] for instance.

Huge efficiency gains were obtained by Joye and Libert [41] over previous constructions from linearly homomorphic scheme, by leveraging the 2^k order of their message space in order to batch evaluation and process k-bit blocks of the input at once.

Applying both techniques to our linearly homomorphic PKE of Fig. 3 would yield an efficient LTDF which supports evaluation over k-bit blocks at once. This allows for compact outputs of the functions. We note however that, due to the Elgamal-like structure of our underlying PKE, trapdoors and function descriptions would be larger than in the Joye-Libert LTDF: for inputs of size n, our trapdoors would require an extra n/k integers, while our function descriptions would require an extra n/k elements in H.

Acknowledgements. We thank Dario Catalano for helpful early discussions about these results and the anonymous reviewers for their comments in improving the work. This work was partially supported by the French ANR SANGRIA project (ANR-21-CE39-0006) and the French PEPR Cybersecurité SecureCompute project (ANR-22-PECY-0003). This work also recieved funding from the European Research Council (ERC) under the European Union's Horizon 2020 research and innovation program under projects PICOCRYPT (grant agreement No. 101001283), and TERMINET (grant agreement No. 957406), by the Spanish Government under projects SCUM (ref. RTI2018-102043-B-I00), by the Madrid Regional Government under project BLOQUES (ref. S2018/TCS-4339), and by a grant from Nomadic Labs and the Tezos foundation.

References

1. Bellare, M., Boldyreva, A., O'Neill, A.: Deterministic and efficiently searchable encryption. In: Menezes, A. (ed.) CRYPTO 2007. LNCS, vol. 4622, pp. 535–552. Springer, Heidelberg (2007). https://doi.org/10.1007/978-3-540-74143-5_30
2. Benaloh, J., Leichter, J.: Generalized secret sharing and monotone functions. In: Goldwasser, S. (ed.) CRYPTO 1988. LNCS, vol. 403, pp. 27–35. Springer, New York (1990). https://doi.org/10.1007/0-387-34799-2_3
3. Benhamouda, F., Herranz, J., Joye, M., Libert, B.: Efficient cryptosystems from 2^k-th power residue symbols. J. Cryptol. **30**(2), 519–549 (2017)
4. Biasse, J.-F., Jacobson, M.J., Silvester, A.K.: Security estimates for quadratic field based cryptosystems. In: Steinfeld, R., Hawkes, P. (eds.) ACISP 2010. LNCS, vol. 6168, pp. 233–247. Springer, Heidelberg (2010). https://doi.org/10.1007/978-3-642-14081-5_15
5. Block, A.R., Holmgren, J., Rosen, A., Rothblum, R.D., Soni, P.: Time- and space-efficient arguments from groups of unknown order. In: Malkin, T., Peikert, C. (eds.) CRYPTO 2021. LNCS, vol. 12828, pp. 123–152. Springer, Cham (2021). https://doi.org/10.1007/978-3-030-84259-8_5
6. Boyle, E., Couteau, G., Gilboa, N., Ishai, Y., Kohl, L., Scholl, P.: Efficient pseudorandom correlation generators: silent OT extension and more. In: Boldyreva, A., Micciancio, D. (eds.) CRYPTO 2019. LNCS, vol. 11694, pp. 489–518. Springer, Cham (2019). https://doi.org/10.1007/978-3-030-26954-8_16
7. Boyle, E., Gilboa, N., Ishai, Y.: Function secret sharing. In: Oswald, E., Fischlin, M. (eds.) EUROCRYPT 2015. LNCS, vol. 9057, pp. 337–367. Springer, Heidelberg (2015). https://doi.org/10.1007/978-3-662-46803-6_12
8. Boyle, E., Gilboa, N., Ishai, Y.: Breaking the circuit size barrier for secure computation under DDH. In: Robshaw, M., Katz, J. (eds.) CRYPTO 2016. LNCS, vol. 9814, pp. 509–539. Springer, Heidelberg (2016). https://doi.org/10.1007/978-3-662-53018-4_19
9. Boyle, E., Gilboa, N., Ishai, Y.: Group-based secure computation: optimizing rounds, communication, and computation. In: Coron, J.-S., Nielsen, J.B. (eds.) EUROCRYPT 2017. LNCS, vol. 10211, pp. 163–193. Springer, Cham (2017). https://doi.org/10.1007/978-3-319-56614-6_6
10. Buchmann, J., Thiel, C., Williams, H.: Short representation of quadratic integers. In: Bosma, W., van der Poorten, A. (eds.) Computational Algebra and Number Theory. MAIA, vol. 325, pp. 159–185. Springer, Dordrecht (1995). https://doi.org/10.1007/978-94-017-1108-1_12

11. Buchmann, J., Vollmer, U.: Binary Quadratic Forms: An Algorithmic Approach. Algorithms and Computation in Mathematics, Springer, Berlin (2007). https://doi.org/10.1007/978-3-540-46368-9
12. Buchmann, J., Williams, H.C.: A key-exchange system based on imaginary quadratic fields. J. Cryptol. **1**(2), 107–118 (1988). https://doi.org/10.1007/BF02351719
13. Bünz, B., Fisch, B., Szepieniec, A.: Transparent SNARKs from DARK compilers. In: Canteaut, A., Ishai, Y. (eds.) EUROCRYPT 2020. LNCS, vol. 12105, pp. 677–706. Springer, Cham (2020). https://doi.org/10.1007/978-3-030-45721-1_24
14. Castagnos, G., Catalano, D., Laguillaumie, F., Savasta, F., Tucker, I.: Two-party ECDSA from hash proof systems and efficient instantiations. In: Boldyreva, A., Micciancio, D. (eds.) CRYPTO 2019. LNCS, vol. 11694, pp. 191–221. Springer, Cham (2019). https://doi.org/10.1007/978-3-030-26954-8_7
15. Castagnos, G., Catalano, D., Laguillaumie, F., Savasta, F., Tucker, I.: Bandwidth-efficient threshold EC-DSA. In: Kiayias, A., Kohlweiss, M., Wallden, P., Zikas, V. (eds.) PKC 2020. LNCS, vol. 12111, pp. 266–296. Springer, Cham (2020). https://doi.org/10.1007/978-3-030-45388-6_10
16. Castagnos, G., Laguillaumie, F.: On the security of cryptosystems with quadratic decryption: the nicest cryptanalysis. In: Joux, A. (ed.) EUROCRYPT 2009. LNCS, vol. 5479, pp. 260–277. Springer, Heidelberg (2009). https://doi.org/10.1007/978-3-642-01001-9_15
17. Castagnos, G., Laguillaumie, F.: Linearly homomorphic encryption from DDH. In: Nyberg, K. (ed.) CT-RSA 2015. LNCS, vol. 9048, pp. 487–505. Springer, Cham (2015). https://doi.org/10.1007/978-3-319-16715-2_26
18. Castagnos, G., Laguillaumie, F., Tucker, I.: Practical fully secure unrestricted inner product functional encryption modulo p. In: Peyrin, T., Galbraith, S. (eds.) ASIACRYPT 2018. LNCS, vol. 11273, pp. 733–764. Springer, Cham (2018). https://doi.org/10.1007/978-3-030-03329-3_25
19. Catalano, D., Di Raimondo, M., Fiore, D., Giacomelli, I.: Mon$\mathbb{Z}_{2^k}$a: fast maliciously secure two party computation on $\mathbb{Z}_{2^k}$. In: Kiayias, A., Kohlweiss, M., Wallden, P., Zikas, V. (eds.) PKC 2020. LNCS, vol. 12111, pp. 357–386. Springer, Cham (2020). https://doi.org/10.1007/978-3-030-45388-6_13
20. Catalano, D., Fiore, D.: Using linearly-homomorphic encryption to evaluate degree-2 functions on encrypted data. In: CCS 2015, pp. 1518–1529. ACM (2015)
21. Chen, M., et al.: Diogenes: lightweight scalable RSA modulus generation with a dishonest majority. In: 2021 IEEE Symposium on Security and Privacy (SP), pp. 590–607 (2021)
22. Cox, D.: Primes of the Form $x^2 + ny^2$: Fermat, Class Field Theory, and Complex Multiplication. Pure and Applied Mathematics. Wiley, Hoboken (2014)
23. Cramer, R., Damgård, I., Escudero, D., Scholl, P., Xing, C.: SPD$\mathbb{Z}_{2^k}$: efficient MPC mod 2^k for dishonest majority. In: Shacham, H., Boldyreva, A. (eds.) CRYPTO 2018. LNCS, vol. 10992, pp. 769–798. Springer, Cham (2018). https://doi.org/10.1007/978-3-319-96881-0_26
24. Cramer, R., Damgård, I., Nielsen, J.B.: Multiparty computation from threshold homomorphic encryption. In: Pfitzmann, B. (ed.) EUROCRYPT 2001. LNCS, vol. 2045, pp. 280–300. Springer, Heidelberg (2001). https://doi.org/10.1007/3-540-44987-6_18
25. Cramer, R., Fehr, S.: Optimal black-box secret sharing over arbitrary abelian groups. In: Yung, M. (ed.) CRYPTO 2002. LNCS, vol. 2442, pp. 272–287. Springer, Heidelberg (2002). https://doi.org/10.1007/3-540-45708-9_18

26. Damgård, I., Jurik, M.: A generalisation, a simplification and some applications of Paillier's probabilistic public-key system. In: Kim, K. (ed.) PKC 2001. LNCS, vol. 1992, pp. 119–136. Springer, Heidelberg (2001). https://doi.org/10.1007/3-540-44586-2_9
27. Damgård, I., Thorbek, R.: Linear integer secret sharing and distributed exponentiation. In: Yung, M., Dodis, Y., Kiayias, A., Malkin, T. (eds.) PKC 2006. LNCS, vol. 3958, pp. 75–90. Springer, Heidelberg (2006). https://doi.org/10.1007/11745853_6
28. Das, P., Jacobson, M.J., Scheidler, R.: Improved efficiency of a linearly homomorphic cryptosystem. In: Carlet, C., Guilley, S., Nitaj, A., Souidi, E.M. (eds.) C2SI 2019. LNCS, vol. 11445, pp. 349–368. Springer, Cham (2019). https://doi.org/10.1007/978-3-030-16458-4_20
29. Deng, Y., Ma, S., Zhang, X., Wang, H., Song, X., Xie, X.: Promise Σ-protocol: how to construct efficient threshold ECDSA from encryptions based on class groups. In: Tibouchi, M., Wang, H. (eds.) ASIACRYPT 2021. LNCS, vol. 13093, pp. 557–586. Springer, Cham (2021). https://doi.org/10.1007/978-3-030-92068-5_19
30. Devevey, J., Libert, B., Nguyen, K., Peters, T., Yung, M.: Non-interactive CCA2-secure threshold cryptosystems: achieving adaptive security in the standard model without pairings. In: Garay, J.A. (ed.) PKC 2021. LNCS, vol. 12710, pp. 659–690. Springer, Cham (2021). https://doi.org/10.1007/978-3-030-75245-3_24
31. Dinur, I., Keller, N., Klein, O.: An optimal distributed discrete log protocol with applications to homomorphic secret sharing. In: Shacham, H., Boldyreva, A. (eds.) CRYPTO 2018. LNCS, vol. 10993, pp. 213–242. Springer, Cham (2018). https://doi.org/10.1007/978-3-319-96878-0_8
32. Dobson, S., Galbraith, S., Smith, B.: Trustless unknown-order groups. Math. Cryptol. **1**(1), 1–15 (2021)
33. Fazio, N., Gennaro, R., Jafarikhah, T., Skeith, W.E.: Homomorphic secret sharing from Paillier encryption. In: Okamoto, T., Yu, Y., Au, M.H., Li, Y. (eds.) ProvSec 2017. LNCS, vol. 10592, pp. 381–399. Springer, Cham (2017). https://doi.org/10.1007/978-3-319-68637-0_23
34. Fouque, P.-A., Poupard, G., Stern, J.: Sharing decryption in the context of voting or lotteries. In: Frankel, Y. (ed.) FC 2000. LNCS, vol. 1962, pp. 90–104. Springer, Heidelberg (2001). https://doi.org/10.1007/3-540-45472-1_7
35. Gennaro, R., Jarecki, S., Krawczyk, H., Rabin, T.: Secure distributed key generation for discrete-log based cryptosystems. J. Crypto. **20**(1), 51–83 (2007). https://doi.org/10.1007/s00145-006-0347-3
36. Gilboa, N.: Two party RSA key generation. In: Wiener, M. (ed.) CRYPTO 1999. LNCS, vol. 1666, pp. 116–129. Springer, Heidelberg (1999). https://doi.org/10.1007/3-540-48405-1_8
37. Goldwasser, S., Micali, S.: Probabilistic encryption. J. Comput. Syst. Sci. **28**(2), 270–299 (1984)
38. Hoory, S., Magen, A., Pitassi, T.: Monotone circuits for the majority function. In: Díaz, J., Jansen, K., Rolim, J.D.P., Zwick, U. (eds.) APPROX/RANDOM -2006. LNCS, vol. 4110, pp. 410–425. Springer, Heidelberg (2006). https://doi.org/10.1007/11830924_38
39. Hühnlein, D., Jacobson, M.J., Paulus, S., Takagi, T.: A cryptosystem based on non-maximal imaginary quadratic orders with fast decryption. In: Nyberg, K. (ed.) EUROCRYPT 1998. LNCS, vol. 1403, pp. 294–307. Springer, Heidelberg (1998). https://doi.org/10.1007/BFb0054134
40. Jacobson, M.J., van der Poorten, A.J.: Computational aspects of NUCOMP. In: Fieker, C., Kohel, D.R. (eds.) ANTS 2002. LNCS, vol. 2369, pp. 120–133. Springer, Heidelberg (2002). https://doi.org/10.1007/3-540-45455-1_10

41. Joye, M., Libert, B.: Efficient cryptosystems from 2^k-th power residue symbols. In: Johansson, T., Nguyen, P.Q. (eds.) EUROCRYPT 2013. LNCS, vol. 7881, pp. 76–92. Springer, Heidelberg (2013). https://doi.org/10.1007/978-3-642-38348-9_5
42. Katz, J., Yung, M.: Threshold cryptosystems based on factoring. In: Zheng, Y. (ed.) ASIACRYPT 2002. LNCS, vol. 2501, pp. 192–205. Springer, Heidelberg (2002). https://doi.org/10.1007/3-540-36178-2_12
43. Lagarias, J.: Worst-case complexity bounds for algorithms in the theory of integral quadratic forms. J. Algorithms **1**(2), 142–186 (1980)
44. Lai, R.W.F., Malavolta, G.: Subvector commitments with application to succinct arguments. In: Boldyreva, A., Micciancio, D. (eds.) CRYPTO 2019. LNCS, vol. 11692, pp. 530–560. Springer, Cham (2019). https://doi.org/10.1007/978-3-030-26948-7_19
45. Lipmaa, H.: Secure accumulators from Euclidean rings without trusted setup. In: Bao, F., Samarati, P., Zhou, J. (eds.) ACNS 2012. LNCS, vol. 7341, pp. 224–240. Springer, Heidelberg (2012). https://doi.org/10.1007/978-3-642-31284-7_14
46. McCurley, K.S.: Cryptographic key distribution and computation in class groups. In: NATO Advanced Study Institutes on Number Theory and Applications. Kluwer (1989)
47. Orlandi, C., Scholl, P., Yakoubov, S.: The rise of Paillier: homomorphic secret sharing and public-key silent OT. In: Canteaut, A., Standaert, F.-X. (eds.) EUROCRYPT 2021. LNCS, vol. 12696, pp. 678–708. Springer, Cham (2021). https://doi.org/10.1007/978-3-030-77870-5_24
48. Orsini, E., Smart, N.P., Vercauteren, F.: Overdrive2k: efficient secure MPC over $\mathbb{Z}_{2^k}$ from somewhat homomorphic encryption. In: Jarecki, S. (ed.) CT-RSA 2020. LNCS, vol. 12006, pp. 254–283. Springer, Cham (2020). https://doi.org/10.1007/978-3-030-40186-3_12
49. Paillier, P.: Public-key cryptosystems based on composite degree residuosity classes. In: Stern, J. (ed.) EUROCRYPT 1999. LNCS, vol. 1592, pp. 223–238. Springer, Heidelberg (1999). https://doi.org/10.1007/3-540-48910-X_16
50. PARI Group, Univ. Bordeaux. PARI/GP version 2.11.4 (2020)
51. Paulus, S., Takagi, T.: A new public-key cryptosystem over a quadratic order with quadratic decryption time. J. Cryptol. **13**(2), 263–272 (2000). https://doi.org/10.1007/s001459910010
52. Peikert, C., Waters, B.: Lossy trapdoor functions and their applications. In: 40th ACM STOC, pp. 187–196. ACM Press (2008)
53. Thorbek, R.: Linear integer secret sharing. Ph.D. thesis, Department of Computer Science, University of Aarhus (2009)
54. Thyagarajan, S.A.K., Castagnos, G., Laguillaumie, F., Malavolta, G.: Efficient CCA timed commitments in class groups. In: ACM CCS 2021, pp. 2663–2684 (2021)
55. Tucker, I.: Functional encryption and distributed signatures based on projective hash functions, the benefit of class groups. Ph.D. thesis, Université de Lyon (2020)
56. Valiant, L.: Short monotone formulae for the majority function. J. Algorithms **5**(3), 363–366 (1984)
57. Wesolowski, B.: Efficient verifiable delay functions. J. Cryptol. **33**(4), 2113–2147 (2020). https://doi.org/10.1007/s00145-020-09364-x
58. Yuen, T.H., Cui, H., Xie, X.: Compact zero-knowledge proofs for threshold ECDSA with trustless setup. In: Garay, J.A. (ed.) PKC 2021. LNCS, vol. 12710, pp. 481–511. Springer, Cham (2021). https://doi.org/10.1007/978-3-030-75245-3_18

Large-Precision Homomorphic Sign Evaluation Using FHEW/TFHE Bootstrapping

Zeyu Liu, Daniele Micciancio, and Yuriy Polyakov(✉)

Duality Technologies, Hoboken, NJ, USA
ypolyakov@dualitytech.com

Abstract. A comparison of two encrypted numbers is an important operation needed in many machine learning applications, for example, decision tree or neural network inference/training. An efficient instantiation of this operation in the context of fully homomorphic encryption (FHE) can be challenging, especially when a relatively high precision is sought. The conventional FHE way of evaluating the comparison operation, which is based on the sign function evaluation using FHEW/TFHE bootstrapping (often referred in literature as *programmable bootstrapping*), can only support very small precision (practically limited to 4–5 bits or so). For higher precision, the runtime complexity scales linearly with the ciphertext (plaintext) modulus (i.e., exponentially with the modulus bit size). We propose sign function evaluation algorithms that scale logarithmically with the ciphertext (plaintext) modulus, enabling the support of large-precision comparison in practice. Our sign evaluation algorithms are based on an iterative use of homomorphic floor function algorithms, which are also derived in our work. Further, we generalize our procedures for floor function evaluation to arbitrary function evaluation, which can be used to support both small plaintext moduli (directly) and larger plaintext moduli (by using a homomorphic digit decomposition algorithm, also suggested in our work). We implement all these algorithms using the PALISADE lattice cryptography library, introducing several implementation-specific optimizations along the way, and discuss our experimental results.

1 Introduction

The ability to compare two encrypted numbers is required in many real-world applications, and often these applications need to combine comparisons with arithmetic operations, such as additions or multiplications (e.g., neural network or decision tree inference/training [3,28]). The main non-interactive method for

This work was funded primarily by Duality Technologies. This material is partially based upon work supported by the Defense Advanced Research Projects Agency (DARPA) under Agreement No. HR00112090102.

S. Agrawal and D. Lin (Eds.): ASIACRYPT 2022, LNCS 13792, pp. 130–160, 2022.
https://doi.org/10.1007/978-3-031-22966-4_5

performing these computations in a privacy-preserving manner is fully homomorphic encryption (FHE), a powerful cryptographic primitive that enables performing computations over encrypted data without having access to the secret key.

The FHE schemes are generally broken down into three classes: the FHEW/TFHE schemes for evaluating boolean circuits, which are best suited for comparisons and decision diagram computations [16,19,29]; Brakerski-Gentry-Vaikuntanathan (BGV) and Brakerski/Fan-Vercauten (BFV) schemes for evaluating modular arithmetic over finite fields, which are also often applied for small-integer computations [9,10,20]; and Cheon-Kim-Kim-Song (CKKS) scheme for approximate computations over real and complex numbers [14].

One of the open challenges is that although the CKKS scheme can efficiently support additions, multiplications, and more generally, polynomial function evaluation, with relatively high precision, the current FHE capabilities of evaluating the encrypted comparison is limited. One method to resolve this problem is to use scheme switching between CKKS and FHEW/TFHE, first introduced in the CHIMERA paper by Boura et al. [8], and later improved in the PEGASUS paper by Lu et al. [3]. However, after switching to FHEW/TFHE the comparison capability for these "high-precision" numbers is very limited. For instance, we show in Sect. 7 that a single FHEW/TFHE bootstrapping, a typical way to perform an encrypted comparison in FHE, can efficiently support at most 4 bits of precision for encrypted comparison using typical parameters as in [29], which is also close to the precision used in [3]. Any further precision improvement for this method makes the encrypted comparison highly inefficient. Therefore, there is a significant interest in developing methods for large-precision comparison of encrypted numbers that would scale significantly better (both asymptotically and practically) with input precision.

The comparison of two encrypted numbers is equivalent to computing the difference of these numbers followed by the evaluation of the sign function. As evaluating the difference is trivial for any additively homomorphic encryption scheme, the difficulty lies in the sign function computation. In the rest of the paper, we will focus on the sign function, assuming that all our results for the sign function readily apply to encrypted comparison.

The sign function evaluation is closely related to the main idea of FHEW/TFHE bootstrapping, where we need to find the most significant bit (MSB) of an encrypted number. Hence, one could directly apply the FHEW/TFHE bootstrapping to find the sign. However, this approach only works for a very limited precision (up to 4 bits, as pointed out above) for the parameters currently used for efficient Boolean circuit evaluation [1,29]. The complexity of the FHEW/TFHE bootstrapping procedures scales linearly with the ciphertext modulus Q, i.e., exponentially with the bit-size of Q. This implies that already for 10 bits of precision, one would need to increase the runtime by a factor of $2^6 = 64$, as compared to the current results for Boolean arithmetic. Clearly, this approach is not viable for practical applications that require 10 or even more bits of precision.

A major goal of our work is to develop a sign function evaluation procedure that scales logarithmically with Q. We also use the central idea of our sign evaluation algorithm to derive efficient general functional bootstrapping procedures, which support the evaluation of arbitrary functions. Note that functional bootsrapping is often also called *programmable bootstrapping* [18].

Our Contributions. More concretely, the contributions of our work can be summarized as follows:

- We propose a novel procedure for large-precision homomorphic sign evaluation using FHEW/ TFHE bootstrapping: a large-precision ciphertext is broken down into digits, and then the homomorphic floor function is executed sequentially to clear each digit, starting from the least significant one. After each digit is cleared, the ciphertext is scaled down to work with a smaller ciphertext modulus Q, until at the last iteration the current modulus becomes small enough to evaluate the fast FHEW/TFHE bootstrapping procedure (with the same parameters as used for Boolean arithmetic).
- We develop two algorithms for the homomorphic floor function. The first algorithm requires two invocations of FHEW/TFHE bootstrapping and has a specific constraint for the input noise. The second algorithm requires three invocations of FHEW/TFHE bootstrapping, but has no constraint on the input noise.
- We use the central idea of the homomorphic floor function algorithms to develop a general functional bootstrapping procedure, which supports arbitrary functions for small plaintext spaces (up to 4 bits in practical settings). Our general functional bootstrapping procedure has asymptotically smaller noise than other recent works.
- We derive a homomorphic digit decomposition algorithm based on the sign-evaluation algorithm to extend the general functional bootstrapping procedure to larger plaintext spaces.
- We implement all these capabilities using the PALISADE lattice cryptography library, introducing several implementation–specific optimizations. Our comparison of the two algorithms for floor function evaluation implies that the method based on two invocations of bootstrapping is always more efficient in practice. We also demonstrate an application of our method in the context of a CKKS-based computation.

Techniques. We describe a method to compute the sign of an encrypted value using bootstrapping techniques. The input is the encryption of a numerical value $m \in \mathbb{Z}$, usually a signed integer, or a fractional number in fixed-point, binary, two's complement representation. We assume the input is presented as an LWE ciphertext, i.e., a vector of elements in $\mathbb{Z}_Q$. The message m is an integer modulo Q/α. We assume that $\alpha = 2^l$ and $Q = 2^h$ are powers of 2, so that the message m can also be interpreted as a $(h-l)$-bit integer. The problem is to compute an encryption of the most significant bit of m, i.e., $\lfloor m/2^{h-l-1} \rfloor$. If $m \in \mathbb{Z}_{2^{h-l}}$ is the standard (two's complement) representation of a signed integer, this bit is the sign of m, i.e., it equals 1 if and only if m represents a negative number.

We treat FHEW/TFHE bootstrapping as a black box, implying that any of the bootstrapping functions described in [16,19,29] can be used interchangeably. For conciseness, we refer to this function as FHEW bootstrapping in the rest of the paper.

FHEW supports functional/programmable bootstrapping for negacyclic functions, i.e., functions $f\colon \mathbb{Z}_Q \to \mathbb{Z}$ satisfying $f(x+Q/2) = -f(x)$. If we add $\alpha/2$ to the LWE ciphertext, yielding a modified message $m' = \alpha m + e + \alpha/2$, where e is the noise, and define a sign function $\gamma\colon \mathbb{Z}_Q \to \{-1,+1\}$, mapping $\gamma(x) = +1$ for $x \in \{0,\ldots,Q/2-1\}$ and $\gamma(x) = -1$ for $x \in \{-Q/2,\ldots,-1\}$, we can directly apply the FHEW bootstrapping procedure for the evaluation function γ (it is easy to observe that γ is already negacyclic). The problem is that the complexity of the FHEW bootstrapping procedure (in particular, the size of the FHEW accumulators) is linear in the ciphertext modulus Q. So, while conceptually the sign computation can be performed directly using the FHEW procedure, the resulting algorithm would be terribly inefficient, both in theory (exponential in the bit size of the input) and in practice.

To circumvent this problem, we "break down" the ciphertext modulo Q into multiple digits, each working internally with a much smaller modulus q, which enables the use of efficient FHEW bootstrapping. For each digit, we evaluate a homomorphic floor function that can be used to clear the least significant digit from the ciphertext. As soon as the current least significant digit is cleared, the ciphertext is scaled down using modulus switching from Q to $\alpha Q/q$. This iterative procedure is repeated until Q becomes less than or equal to q. At that point, efficient FHEW bootstrapping for $\gamma(x)$ can be used directly to evaluate the sign function. Conceptually, this algorithm corresponds to the "schoolbook" long division algorithm. The main challenge in this long division algorithm is associated with evaluating the floor function, which is not negacyclic and hence cannot be directly evaluated using FHEW bootstrapping.

The idea of our first floor function algorithm is to first evaluate the sign function $\gamma(x)$ to clear the MSB of each digit (first bootstrapping) and then subtract the remaining bits in the digit using the second invocation of FHEW bootstrapping. Both of these evaluation functions are negacyclic, enabling us to use FHEW bootstrapping. If we had a perfect (noiseless) bootstrapping procedure, this would take care of clearing all the bits of the digit. But FHEW bootstrapping (just like any lattice-based bootstrapping procedure) is noisy. In order to accommodate for the bootstrapping noise, this method requires the introduction of a constraint on the noise of the input ciphertext: $\beta \leq \alpha/4$, where $|e| < \beta$. This floor function algorithm can clear up to q/α bits.

We also propose an alternative floor function, which does not have the input noise constraint, but requires an extra invocation of FHEW bootstrapping. The first invocation of FHEW bootstrapping is used to clear the second-most significant bit in the digit. Intuitively, this first invocation has the effect of enforcing the $\beta \leq \alpha/4$ constraint of the first floor computation algorithm. So, we can proceed with another invocation of FHEW bootstrapping that clears the MSB, and, finally, the remaining bits in the digit are cleared using the third invocation of FHEW bootstrapping. In other words, the main difference between the two floor function algorithms is in the first bootstrapping operation, which clears the second-most significant bit. In practice, the alternative floor function evaluation algorithm gains one extra bit of precision compared to the first algorithm, but has a cost of an additional invocation of FHEW bootstrapping.

Then, we generalize the algorithms for homomorphic floor function to arbitrary function evaluation for small plaintext moduli, i.e., restricting the ciphertext modulus to q that supports efficient FHEW bootstrapping. Consider the generalization of our first floor function algorithm as an example. We first extend the ciphertext from modulus q to $2q$. This introduces, as a byproduct, a random MSB modulo $2q$. Then we evaluate the $\gamma(x)$ function modulo $2q$ to clear this MSB. Finally, we invoke the desired function for the remaining bits unaffected by noise. Compared to the homomorphic floor function, we loose just one bit of precision.

Finally, we derive a homomorphic digit decomposition algorithm that can be combined with the general functional bootstrapping for small-precision ciphertexts to achieve the evaluation of arbitrary functions over large-precision ciphertexts, i.e., evaluate large lookup tables. The digit decomposition algorithm is closely related to the homomorphic sign evaluation algorithm: it basically performs the same sequence of applications of the homomorphic floor function evaluation, while keeping track of the (encrypted) digits produced by each invocation.

Note that most of the homomorphic encryption schemes support the efficient extraction of LWE ciphertexts. So the methods described here can be applied to those schemes by first extracting an LWE representation of the input, and then applying the main algorithm. For details on the algorithms for efficient extraction of LWE ciphertexts, we refer the reader to [12,28].

1.1 Related Works

Related Concurrent Works. Two concurrent and independent works [18,26] propose algorithms for homomorphic evaluation of arbitrary functions for small plaintext moduli. Table 1 summarizes the results of the comparison between our main algorithm for arbitrary function evaluation with their algorithms. An expanded comparison with concrete parameters is presented in Sect. 8.

Table 1. Comparison of noise growth and complexity of our method for arbitrary function evaluation with other recent works; here, β is the FHEW functional bootstrapping noise (see details in Sect. 6.5), N is the ring dimension used for functional bootstrapping, p is the plaintext modulus, Q' is the underlying RLWE ciphertext modulus, q is the output LWE ciphertext modulus, and $d'_g \geq 2$ is the number of digits for gadget decomposition specific to functional bootstrapping in [26].

	Noise growth	# of bootstrappings
[18]	$\beta \cdot O(Np)$	2
[26]	$\beta \cdot O(\sqrt{Nd'_g}Q'^{1/d'_g})$	$d'_g + 1$
Our work	β	2

The main idea of both works is to use the fact that $-1 \cdot (-m) = m$ and extract the MSB as part of their procedures by invoking FHEW/TFHE bootstrapping. Both approaches hence require one multiplication operation, which increases the noise requirements. This also implies that the main homomorphic encryption scheme should support both additions and multiplications. Our approach does not require any multiplications, and can be applied to any additively homomorphic encryption scheme, similar to the Boolean circuit construction in the original FHEW paper [19].

The approach in [18] executes two bootstrapping operations (one to extract the MSB and another to evaluate the desired function), and then multiplies the results using a multiplication operation similar to the one in Brakerski's and BFV schemes [9,20]. As a result, the noise increases by $O(Np)$, which implies that the cost of the bootstrapping operations in this method is higher than in ours. Our analysis in Sect. 8 predicts that the runtime complexity will be at least two times higher for practical parameters.

The method in [26] applies the same blueprint, but instead of performing a BFV-like multiplication, initially uses a multiplication by a GSW ciphertext, and then further optimizes it to replace it with a cheaper multiplication by an LWE′ ciphertext (i.e., a vector of LWE ciphertexts, see details in [29]). This approach requires at least $d'_g + 1$ bootstrapping operations, where d'_g is a design parameter. Note that the value of d'_g also affects the noise growth. If the noise cost is minimized (a larger d'_g is chosen), then the number of bootstrapping invocations increases. It is clear that the method in [26] is always at least 1.5x slower than ours as $d'_g \geq 2$, and it also substantially increases the noise unless d'_g is much larger than 2.

Both methods [18,26] can be extended to support large-precision sign evaluation (though this was not done in these works), but will have the same drawbacks (compared to our approach) as for arbitrary function evaluation: asymptotically higher noise growth (both methods) and (for [26]) increased number of bootstrapping operations.

A recent paper [32] independently developed an arbitrary function evaluation method similar to ours. This work was published after our results became available and hence we do not examine it here.

Other Approaches for Evaluating Sign Function. Although we focus on the approaches to evaluating the comparison/sign functions based on FHEW/TFHE bootstrapping, other methods have also been considered in literature.

We note that all of the methods described below have their own merits and method selection is application-dependent. For instance, the FHEW/TFHE-based method is preferred when only a small number of comparisons are needed or a small number of levels are available for the comparisons. The CKKS-based method may work better when a large number of comparisons are needed in parallel and a sufficient multiplicative depth or CKKS bootstrapping are available (see Sect. 8.2 for details). The desired precision of comparison is also an important factor. A comprehensive comparison of these methods is outside the scope of this paper and is suggested as a topic for future work.

One approach is based on evaluating special interpolation polynomials over finite fields using the BGV or BFV scheme (see [24] for an extensive review of these techniques). This approach does not typically require bootstrapping but involves a complicated encoding of interpolation polynomials into the native polynomial space of BGV and BFV. Although high efficiency can be achieved (this method may even have a smaller complexity than the techniques considered in our work), this approach is somewhat special-purpose and becomes challenging when the comparison operations need to be combined with multiplications and additions. The main advantage of our approach is the ability to combine comparisons with regular arithmetic operations, resulting in a more general functionality.

Another approach is based on minimax or other polynomial approximations using the CKKS scheme (see [15,27] for recent results). This approach can be very efficient for relatively small precision, and takes full advantage of CKKS packing. However, the input numbers typically have to be within a specific known range, and the runtime complexity may sharply increase with precision or minimum difference allowed between two numbers. In contrast, the computational complexity of our approach is guaranteed to scale linearly with the number of precision bits, and does not depend on how close two numbers are to each other, i.e., how close the value of the sign function input is to zero. We provide a high-level comparison between the CKKS method and our approach in Sect. 8.2.

A leveled bit-wise version of TFHE (without bootstrapping) was also previously considered. For example, Chillotti et al. showed that two $(\log p)$-bit numbers can be compared by evaluating a deterministic automaton made of $5 \log p$ CMux gates [17]. Though this comparison complexity is much smaller than for the approach considered in our paper, it has the drawback of requiring the input to be encrypted in a bit-wise fashion. So, their approach will quickly become inefficient in scenarios where comparisons need to be combined with additions and multiplications, as these operations are very expensive in bit-wise representation. Note that our main motivation for developing the general comparison capability based on FHEW/TFHE bootstrapping was to support mixed computations involving additions, multiplications, or, more generally, polynomial evaluation, as well as comparisons.

Another potentially promising approach is based on a limited form of functional bootstrapping supported by BFV/BGV. Chen at al. show how BFV bootstrapping can be used to compute the sign function [13]. It is not clear whether the BFV/BGV approach can be extended to arbitrary functions (look-up tables), but it is certainly an interesting research problem.

1.2 Organization

The rest of the paper is organized as follows. In Sect. 2 we provide the necessary background on FHEW bootstrapping. Section 3 describes our algorithms for homomorphic sign and floor evaluation. Section 4 shows how our homomorphic floor algorithms can be generalized to arbitrary function evaluation. Section 5 introduces homomorphic digit decomposition algorithms based on our sign evaluation algorithms. Section 6 discusses how parameters should be selected, and introduces some optimizations. Section 7 describes our implementation and presents experimental results, and Sect. 8 compares our algorithms with other concurrent works. Section 9 discusses an application of large-precision comparison. Section 10 concludes the paper.

2 Background

All logarithms are expressed in base 2 if not indicated otherwise. Vectors are indicated in bold, e.g., $\mathbf{a}$. We choose the ring dimension N as a power of two for efficiency reasons.

2.1 FHEW Functional/Programmable Bootstrapping

In this section we recall the definition of LWE ciphertexts [30], and the properties of the FHEW [19] "functional" bootstrapping procedure needed by our algorithms.

The LWE cryptosystem [30] is parametrized by a plaintext modulus p, ciphertext modulus q, and secret dimension n. The LWE encryption of a message $m \in \mathbb{Z}_p$ under (secret) key $\mathbf{s} \in \mathbb{Z}^n$ is a vector $(\mathbf{a}, b) \in \mathbb{Z}_q^{n+1}$ such that

$$b = \langle \mathbf{a}, \mathbf{s} \rangle + (q/p) \cdot m + e \pmod q$$

where e is a small error term, $|e| < q/(2p)$. The message m is recovered by first computing the approximate LWE decryption function

$$\mathsf{Dec}_{\mathbf{s}}(\mathbf{a}, b) = b - \langle \mathbf{a}, \mathbf{s} \rangle \pmod q = (q/p) \cdot m + e$$

and then rounding the result to the closest multiple of (q/p).

The ciphertext modulus of LWE ciphertexts can be changed (at the cost of a small additional noise proportional to the secret key size) simply by scaling and rounding its entries, as described in the following lemma.

Lemma 1 (Modulus Switching). *Let $(\mathbf{a}, b) \in \mathbb{Z}_q^{n+1}$ be an LWE encryption of a message $m \in \mathbb{Z}_p$ under secret key $\mathbf{s} \in \mathbb{Z}^n$ with ciphertext modulus q and noise bound $|\mathsf{Dec}_{\mathbf{s}}(\mathbf{a}, b) - (q/p)m| < \beta$. Then, for any modulus q', the rounded ciphertext $(\mathbf{a}', b') = \lceil (q'/q) \cdot (\mathbf{a}, b) \rfloor$ is an encryption of the same message m under $\mathbf{s}$ with ciphertext modulus q' and noise bound $|\mathsf{Dec}_{\mathbf{s}}(\mathbf{a}', b') - (q'/p)m| < (q'/q)\beta + \beta''$, where $\beta'' = \frac{1}{2}(\|\mathbf{s}\|_1 + 1)$.*

In practice, when the input ciphertext is sufficiently random, or when modulus switching is performed by *randomized* rounding, it is possible to replace the additive term β'' with a smaller probabilistic bound $O(\|\mathbf{s}\|_2)$. For uniformly random ternary keys $\mathbf{s} \in \{0, 1, -1\}^n$, this is $\beta'' \approx O(\sqrt{n})$.

A key feature of FHEW is that it allows to perform certain homomorphic computations (described by an "extraction" function) on ciphertexts during bootstrapping at no additional cost. We will use (a slight generalization of) the FHEW [19] bootstrapping procedure, and its optimized variants for binary [16] and ternary secrets [29], as implemented in PALISADE. The bootstrapping algorithm is parametrized by

- a dimension n and (input ciphertext) modulus q, where q is a power of 2,
- a secret key $\mathbf{s} \in \mathbb{Z}^n$, which must be a short vector. Here we assume $\mathbf{s} \in \{0, 1, -1\}^n$,
- a large ciphertext modulus Q' used internally to the bootstrapping procedure, and which is not required to be a power of 2,
- an output ciphertext modulus Q, which we set to a power of 2 possibly different from q, and
- an extraction function $f\colon \mathbb{Z}_q \to \mathbb{Z}$ which must satisfy the negacyclic constraint

$$f(x + q/2) = -f(x). \tag{1}$$

The bootstrapping procedure also uses a bootstrapping key, which is computed from $\mathbf{s}$, but can be made public. Since this bootstrapping key is only used internally by the bootstrapping procedure, we omit it from the notation.

We remark that, since $\mathbf{s}$ is a small vector (e.g., with ternary entries $\{0, 1, -1\}$), it can be used as a key both modulo q, and modulo Q' or Q. On input an LWE ciphertext $(\mathbf{a}, b) \in \mathbb{Z}_q^{n+1}$, the FHEW bootstrapping procedure first computes an LWE ciphertext $(\mathbf{c}', d') \in \mathbb{Z}_{Q'}^{n+1}$ such that

$$\mathsf{Dec}_{\mathbf{s}}(\mathbf{c}', d') = f'(\mathsf{Dec}_{\mathbf{s}}(\mathbf{a}, b)) + e' \pmod{Q'},$$

where the noise bound $|e'| \leq \beta'$ depends only on the computation performed during bootstrapping (and not the input ciphertext), and

$$f'(x) = \left\lceil \frac{Q'}{Q} \cdot f(x) \right\rfloor$$

is a scaled version of f still satisfying the negacyclic condition (1). Then, modulus switching is applied to $(\mathbf{c}', d')$ to obtain a ciphertext $(\mathbf{c}, d) = \left\lceil \frac{Q}{Q'}(\mathbf{c}', d') \right\rfloor \in \mathbb{Z}_Q^{n+1}$ modulo Q such that

$$\mathsf{Dec}_{\mathbf{s}}(\mathbf{c}, d) = f(\mathsf{Dec}_{\mathbf{s}}(\mathbf{a}, b)) + e \pmod{Q}$$

where $|e| < \beta = (Q/Q')\beta + \beta''$ is the noise bound from Lemma 1.

For the sake of comparison, we recall that in the original FHEW bootstrapping procedure:

- the input LWE ciphertext $(\mathbf{a}, b)$ uses plaintext modulus $p = 4$, so that messages $m \in \{0, 1, 2, 3\}$ are encoded as multiples of $\alpha = q/4$, i.e., $\mathsf{Dec}_{\mathbf{s}}(\mathbf{a}, b) = (q/4) \cdot m + e$ for some error $|e| < q/8$;
- the output modulus $Q = q$ is the same as the input modulus, so that bootstrapping operations can be composed into arbitrary circuits;

- the extraction function f maps the interval $[-q/8, 3q/8) \subset \mathbb{Z}_q$ to $q/8$ and (necessarily, to satisfy (1)) the interval $[3q/8, 7q/8)$ to $-q/8$. Moreover, the output ciphertext is modified to $(\mathbf{c}, d+q/8)$, so that the final output is either an encryption of $q/8+q/8 = q/4 = 1 \cdot \alpha$ (i.e., an encoding 1) when $m \in \{0,1\}$, or an encryption of $-q/8+q/8 = 0 \cdot \alpha$ (i.e., an encoding of 0) when $m \in \{2,3\}$. This allows to evaluate the NAND of two input bits $m_0, m_1 \in \{0,1\}$ as $f(m_0 + m_1 \bmod 4)$.

In this paper, we make extensive use of the FHEW bootstrapping procedure, but for a larger output modulus Q, where $q \leq Q < Q'$, and a number of different (but still negacyclic) extraction functions f.

We write

$$\mathsf{Boot}[f](\mathbf{a}, b)$$

for the result of invoking this bootstrapping procedure for a given function f. We will make blackbox use of Boot, so that the internal workings of the bootstrapping procedure are not important for the rest of the paper, and Boot can be implemented either using the original FHEW bootstrapping procedure [19] or the optimized versions proposed in [16,29]. The properties of the Boot function described in this section and needed in the rest of the paper are summarized in the following theorem.

Theorem 1. *For any LWE ciphertext* $(\mathbf{a}, b) \in \mathbb{Z}_q^{n+1}$ *and function* $f \colon \mathbb{Z}_q \to \mathbb{Z}_Q$ *such that* $f(x+q/2) = -f(x) \pmod{Q}$*, the bootstrapping procedure* $\mathsf{Boot}[f](\mathbf{a}, b)$ *outputs a ciphertext* $(\mathbf{c}, d) \in \mathbb{Z}_Q^{n+1}$ *such that*

$$\mathsf{Dec}_{\mathbf{s}}(\mathbf{c}, d) = f(\mathsf{Dec}(\mathbf{a}, b)) + e \pmod{Q}$$

for some $|e| < \beta$*, where* β *is a noise bound that depends only on the operations performed by* Boot*, but not on the input ciphertext* $(\mathbf{a}, b)$.

For simplicity of presentation, we round β up to a power of 2.

3 Large-Precision Homomorphic Sign Evaluation

In this section we describe our main algorithms to homomorphically compute the sign of an encrypted value.

Let $(\mathbf{c}, d) \in \mathbb{Z}_Q^{n+1}$ be an LWE ciphertext with (large) ciphertext modulus Q and plaintext modulus Q/α. Specifically, assume $\mathsf{Dec}(\mathbf{c}, d) = \alpha m + e$, for some plaintext message $m \in \mathbb{Z}_{Q/\alpha}$ and noise bound $|e| < \beta \leq \alpha/2$. (Later we may set β to a bound strictly smaller than $\alpha/2$.) We assume that Q and α are powers of 2, so that the message m and the decryption $\mathsf{Dec}(\mathbf{c}, d)$ can both be interpreted as signed integers, in two's complement notation, and the sign of m is given by the MSB of m's binary representation. The goal is to homomorphically compute this sign bit.

By adding β to the ciphertext, the error $e + \beta$ becomes a positive value in the range $(0, 2\beta) \subseteq (0, \alpha)$. Hence the sign bit is also the same as the MSB of

$$m' = \mathsf{Dec}(\mathbf{c}, d + \beta) = \alpha m + (e + \beta).$$

At this point, since we only care about the MSB of m', it does not matter which bits of m' are considered "message" bits and which are "noise" bits, and one may think of m' simply as an arbitrary integer modulo Q.

We compute the MSB of m' following the approach outlined in the introduction, using FHEW's functional bootstrapping algorithm Boot with a relatively small modulus q to *clear* the least significant bits of m' in small chunks, until only the MSB is left. We present two algorithms: the first algorithm requiring only two invocations of Boot per chunk, but under the assumption that $|e|$ is smaller than $\alpha/4$ and the second algorithm that works for ciphertexts with an arbitrary error e, but requires three invocations of Boot for each chunk. Although the approach based on two invocations of Boot is more efficient in practice for the large-precision sign evaluation, the approach with three invocations is more general and is of independent interest for evaluating the homomorphic floor function on arbitrary ciphertexts, e.g., noisy ciphertexts in the CKKS scheme.

In both algorithms, we instantiate the bootstrapping procedure as follows:

- We fix the modulus q to an appropriate value that can be efficiently supported by FHEW.
- We set the output modulus to Q by picking an internal modulus Q' larger than Q. (Usually, Q' is not a power of two, in order to support NTT.) We recall that the complexity of FHEW is linear in $\log Q'$, and exponential only in $\log q$. Hence one can use a relatively large Q'.
- We use Boot with one of three possible extraction functions f_0, f_1, f_2 shown in Fig. 1. It can be easily checked that all three functions satisfy the negacyclic requirement (1).

$$f_0(x) = \begin{cases} -q/4 \text{ if } 0 \le x < q/2 \\ +q/4 \text{ otherwise} \end{cases}$$

$$f_1(x) = \begin{cases} x & \text{if } x < q/2 \\ q/2 - x & \text{otherwise} \end{cases}$$

$$f_2(x) = \begin{cases} -q/4 \text{ if } 0 \le x < q/4 \\ +q/4 \text{ if } q/2 \le x < 3q/4 \\ 0 \quad\quad \text{otherwise} \end{cases}$$

Fig. 1. Negacyclic functions used by our homomorphic sign computation algorithms. The value of $f_1(x) = q/2 - x$ for $x \ge q/2$ is not relevant for our algorithms, and added here only to satisfy the negacylic constraint.

3.1 Homomorphic Floor Function Using Two Invocations of Boot

The core of the algorithm is a procedure HomFloor that on input a ciphertext $(\mathbf{c}, d) \in \mathbb{Z}_Q^{n+1}$ encrypting a message $m \in \mathbb{Z}_{Q/\alpha}$ with noise bounded by

$$|\mathsf{Dec}(\mathbf{c}, d) - \alpha \cdot m| < \beta \le \alpha/4$$

outputs another ciphertext $(\mathbf{c}', d') \in \mathbb{Z}_Q^{n+1}$ encrypting the floored message

$$r(m) = \left\lfloor \frac{\alpha}{q} \cdot m \right\rfloor \cdot \frac{q}{\alpha} \tag{2}$$

subject to the same noise bound β, i.e., such that $|\mathsf{Dec}(\mathbf{c}', d') - \alpha \cdot r(m)| < \beta$. Notice that this has precisely the same effect as zeroing the $\log_2(q/\alpha) = \log_2 q - \log_2 \alpha$ least significant bits of m. In particular, the MSB of m is the same as the MSB of $r(m)$.

The main algorithm HomSign uses the HomFloor subroutine to clear the least significant bits of the message until only the sign bit is left, as we describe next. Notice that after the application of HomFloor, the resulting ciphertext

$$\mathsf{Dec}(\mathbf{c}', d') = \alpha \cdot r(m) + e = q \cdot \tilde{m} + e \pmod{Q}$$

can be interpreted as an encryption of the message

$$\tilde{m} = \frac{\alpha}{q} \cdot r(m) = \left\lfloor \frac{\alpha}{q} \cdot m \right\rceil \in \mathbb{Z}_{Q/q}$$

with noise $|e| < \beta$ much smaller than q. Since $r(m)$ is a multiple of q/α, the MSB of $\tilde{m}$ is the same as the MSB of $r(m)$ and m. So, we can switch to a smaller modulus $(\alpha/q) \cdot Q$ using Lemma 1 to obtain an encryption of $\tilde{m}$ with a scaling factor α, and repeat. After $\lceil (\log Q - \log q)/\log(q/\alpha) \rceil$ iterations, the modulus Q will be at most q, and the sign of the message can be computed directly using Boot.

The pseudocode of HomFloor and HomSign is given in Algorithm 1. In the rest of this subsection we analyze the correctness of the algorithm. We first analyze the correctness of HomFloor.

Algorithm 1. Algorithm for Homomorphic Sign Computation

```
1: procedure HomFloor(Q, (c, d))
2:     d ← d + β
3:     (a, b) ← (c, d) mod q
4:     (c, d) ← (c, d) − Boot[f_0](a, b) (mod Q)
5:     d ← d + β − q/4
6:     (a, b) ← (c, d) mod q
7:     (c, d) ← (c, d) − Boot[f_1](a, b) (mod Q)
8:     return (c, d)
9: end procedure
10: procedure HomSign(Q, (c, d))
11:     while Q > q do
12:         (c, d) ← HomFloor(Q, (c, d))
13:         (c, d) ← ⌊(α/q) · (c, d)⌉
14:         Q ← αQ/q
15:     end while
16:     d ← d + β
17:     (a, b) ← (q/Q) · (c, d)
18:     (c, d) ← (−Boot[f_0](a, b)) (mod Q)
19:     return (c, d)
20: end procedure
```

Lemma 2. *For any Q, q, m and $\beta \leq \alpha/4$, the procedure* HomFloor *in Algorithm 1, on input a ciphertext $(\mathbf{c}, d) \in \mathbb{Z}_Q^{n+1}$ such that $|\mathsf{Dec}(\mathbf{c}, d) - \alpha \cdot m| < \beta$ outputs a ciphertext $(\mathbf{c}', d') \in \mathbb{Z}_Q^{n+1}$ such that $|\mathsf{Dec}(\mathbf{c}', d') - \alpha \cdot r(m)| < \beta$, where $r(x)$ is the rounding function defined in (2).*

Proof. Let $\mu = \mathsf{Dec}(\mathbf{c}, d) \in \mathbb{Z}_Q$ be the value encrypted by the input ciphertext $(\mathbf{c}, d)$. By assumption, $\mu = \alpha m + e$ for some $|e| < \beta$. We trace the value of μ and e through the execution of the algorithm. Adding β on line 2 makes the error positive $e \in (0, 2\beta)$. Line 3 computes an LWE ciphertext $(\mathbf{a}, b)$ that decrypts to $\mu' = \mathsf{Dec}(\mathbf{a}, b) = \mu \pmod q \in \mathbb{Z}_q$, that is, the $(\log_2 q)$ least significant bits of μ. Let $\tilde{m} = \lfloor \mu/q \rfloor = \lfloor (\alpha/q)m \rfloor$ be the remaining (most significant) bits, so that $\mu = \tilde{m} \cdot q + \mu'$.

Next, in order to analyze lines 4 and 5, we consider two cases, depending on the most significant bit of μ'. If the most significant bit of μ' is zero, then $\mathsf{Dec}(\mathsf{Boot}[f_0](\mathbf{a}, b)) = -q/4 + e_\beta$, where $|e_\beta| < \beta$. Subtracting $\mathsf{Boot}[f_0](\mathbf{a}, b)$ from $(\mathbf{c}, d)$ in line 4, and adjusting d in line 5, modifies μ by an additive term

$$-(-q/4 + e_\beta) + \beta - q/4 \in (0, 2\beta).$$

On the other hand, if the most significant bit of μ' is 1, then $\mathsf{Dec}(\mathsf{Boot}[f_0](\mathbf{a}, b)) = +q/4 + e_\beta$, and lines 4 and 5 modify μ by the additive term

$$-(q/4 + e_\beta) + \beta - q/4 = -q/2 + (0, 2\beta).$$

In either case, this clears the $(\log_2 q)th$ least significant bit of μ (corresponding to the most significant bit of μ') while increasing the error by at most 2β. Since the initial error is in $(0, 2\beta)$, the final error is in $(0, 4\beta) \subseteq (0, \alpha)$, and does not overflow into the most significant bits.

This shows that, even when accounting for the bootstrapping error, the value of $\mu = \mathsf{Dec}(\mathbf{c}, d)$ at line 6 has its $(\log_2 q)th$ least significant bit set to 0. In formulas, $\mu = q \cdot \tilde{m} + x$ for some $x = (\mu \bmod q) \in [0, q/2)$. The ciphertext $(\mathbf{a}, b)$ computed in line 6 encrypts this value x modulo q. Since $f_1(x) = x$ is the identity function for all $x \in [0, q/2)$, $\mathsf{Boot}[f_1]$ in line 7 returns an encryption of $x + e_\beta$. Subtracting this ciphertext from $(\mathbf{c}, d)$ on line 7, gives an encryption of

$$(q \cdot \tilde{m} + x) - (x + e_\beta) = q \cdot \tilde{m}x - e_\beta = \alpha \cdot r(m) - e_\beta$$

and hence

$$|\alpha \cdot r(m) - e_\beta - \alpha \cdot r(m)| < \beta,$$

as claimed in the lemma. □

The correctness of the main function HomSign easily follows, by repeatedly applying Lemma 2.

Theorem 2. *Let $\beta > 2$ be an upper bound on both the bootstrapping noise (from Theorem 1) and the size of the secret key*[1] *$\|\mathbf{s}\|_1 \leq \beta$. Let $\alpha \geq 4\beta$ be a power of*

[1] The weaker bound $\beta \geq O(\|\mathbf{s}\|_2) = O(\sqrt{n})$ suffices when using randomized modulus switching, or heuristically when assuming the input ciphertext is random. We use this weaker estimate for concrete parameters later in the paper.

2. *The procedure* HomSign *in Algorithm 1, on input an LWE ciphertext* $(\mathbf{c}, d) \in \mathbb{Z}_Q^{n+1}$ *encrypting a message* $m \in \mathbb{Z}_{Q/\alpha}$ *with error bounded by* $|\mathsf{Dec}(\mathbf{c}, d) - \alpha \cdot m| < \beta$*, computes an LWE encryption of the most significant bit of* m*, making at most* $2\left\lfloor \frac{\log Q}{\log(q/\alpha)} \right\rfloor + 1$ *calls to* Boot.

Proof. We need to show that the loop at lines 11–14 preserves the invariant that $(\mathbf{c}, d)$ encrypts a message with the correct MSB, and noise bounded by β. By Lemma 2, at each iteration, at line 12, HomFloor computes an encryption of a value of the form $\tilde{m}q + e$ with $|e| < \beta$, where $\tilde{m}$ has the correct MSB. Then, lines 13–14 switch the ciphertext modulus from Q to $(\alpha/q)Q$. By Lemma 1, the error of the resulting ciphertext is at most

$$(\alpha/q)\beta + (\beta + 1)/2 \leq \beta/4 + \beta/2 + 1/2 < \beta,$$

taking into account the constraint $\beta > 2$. This proves the loop invariant. Upon exiting the loop, in line 15, the modulus has been reduced below $Q \leq q$, and the most significant bit of the message can be directly computed using Boot, using the fact that the sign function (f_0) is negacyclic. The multiplication by q/Q at line 17 is there only to ensure that Boot is always called with the same ciphertext modulus q. Alternatively, one may use a potentially smaller modulus $Q \leq q$ in the last call, which could be slightly faster. □

The final output of HomSign satisfies $\mathsf{Dec}(\mathbf{c}, d) = q/4 \pm \beta$ when the initial input encrypts a nonnegative number, and $\mathsf{Dec}(\mathbf{c}, d) = -q/4 \pm \beta$ when it encrypts a negative number. Sign computation algorithms with different output encodings are easily obtained by simply changing the function f_0 used in line 18. Likewise, the ciphertext modulus of the final output of HomSign can be set arbitrarily by simply changing the output modulus of the last invocation of Boot at line 18.

Remark 1. Since the running time of HomSign is proportional to $\log Q$ / $\log(q/\alpha)$, it is always best to set α to the smallest possible value $\alpha = 4\beta$. So, given values for Q (from the input specification) and q, β from Theorem 1 (typically based on security and efficiency considerations), the running time of HomSign is essentially that of $2\left\lfloor \frac{\log Q}{\log q - \log \beta - 2} \right\rfloor + 1$ invocations of Boot or, equivalently, $\left\lfloor \frac{\log Q}{\log q - \log \beta - 2} \right\rfloor$ invocations of HomFloor + 1 invocation of Boot.

3.2 Homomorphic Floor Function for Arbitrary Ciphertexts Using Three Invocations of Boot

We also propose an alternative floor function evaluation algorithm that works for arbitrary ciphertexts. This algorithm requires three invocations of Boot but makes no assumption on the size of the input error. Although this approach is typically less efficient than HomFloor when used as a subroutine in HomSign (as shown later in Sect. 6.1), it has some advantages when applied directly to an arbitrary ciphertext. For instance, when the message and noise are not separable, as in the CKKS scheme, the use of this procedure avoids calling a prior modulus switching operation, which may accidentally change the sign of encrypted values close to zero. When used as a subroutine for HomSign, the alternative floor function procedure allows us to replace $\alpha = 4\beta$ with $\alpha = 2\beta$, hence gaining one extra bit of precision in each floor function iteration at the expense of one extra invocation of Boot.

Algorithm 2. Alternative Algorithm for Homomorphic Sign Computation

```
1: procedure HomFloorAlt(Q, (c, d))
2:     (a, b) ← (c, d) mod q
3:     (c, d) ← (c, d) − Boot[f_2](a, b) (mod Q)
4:     d ← d + β − q/4
5:     (a, b) ← (c, d) mod q
6:     (c, d) ← (c, d) − Boot[f_0](a, b) (mod Q)
7:     d ← d + β − q/4
8:     (a, b) ← (c, d) mod q
9:     (c, d) ← (c, d) − Boot[f_1](a, b) (mod Q)
10:    return (c, d)
11: end procedure
```

Lemma 3. *Let β be the bootstrapping noise from Theorem 1, and assume $q \geq 16\beta$. The procedure* HomFloorAlt *in Algorithm 2, on input a ciphertext $(\mathbf{c}, d) \in \mathbb{Z}_Q^{n+1}$ with $\mathsf{Dec}(\mathbf{c}, d) = m \in \mathbb{Z}_Q$, outputs a ciphertext $(\mathbf{c}', d') \in \mathbb{Z}_Q^{n+1}$ with $\mathsf{Dec}(\mathbf{c}, d) = \tilde{m}q + e \in \mathbb{Z}_Q$ for $\tilde{m} = \lfloor m/q \rfloor$ and some $|e| < \beta$.*

Proof. The ciphertext $(\mathbf{a}, b)$ computed in line 2 decrypts to $m' = \mathsf{Dec}(\mathbf{a}, b) = m \bmod q$, the $\log_2 q$ least significant digits of m. Let x be the two most significant bits of m'. Function f_2 only works on these two bits, mapping $00 \mapsto 11$, $10 \mapsto 01$, and $01, 11 \mapsto 00$. When $f_2(m')$ is subtracted from $(\mathbf{c}, d)$ in line 3, the corresponding bits of m are mapped either to 11 (when $x = 11$) or to 01 (otherwise). In particular, the second bit is always one. Subtracting $q/4$ from d on line 4 makes this bit always zero. Adding β in line 4 also ensures that the bootstrapping error added by Boot is positive, in the range $(0, 2\beta)$. At this point (line 5) we have a ciphertext such that $\mathsf{Dec}(\mathbf{c}, d) = \tilde{m} \cdot q + b \cdot (q/2) + x + e$ for some (unknown) bit $\tilde{b} \in \{0, 1\}$, positive integer $x \in [0, q/4)$ and positive bootstrapping error $e \in (0, 2\beta)$. Similarly, we have $\mathsf{Dec}(\mathbf{a}, b) = \tilde{b}(q/2) + x + e$. Assuming $q \geq 8\beta$, adding e to $\tilde{b}(q/2)$ does not change the bit $\tilde{b}$. So, $f_0(\tilde{b}(q/2) + x + e) = -q/4$ when $\tilde{b} = 0$ and $+q/4$ when $b = 1$. Similarly to Lemma 2, subtracting $\mathsf{Boot}[f_0](\mathbf{a}, b)$ from $(\mathbf{c}, d)$ in line 6 and adjusting the value of d in line 7 has the effect of clearing the bit $\tilde{b}$, while adding a positive bootstrapping error $e \in (0, 2\beta)$.

This shows that, at line 8, we have $\mathsf{Dec}(\mathbf{c}, d) = \tilde{m}q + x + e + e'$ where $\mathsf{Dec}(\mathbf{a}, b) = x + e + e' \in (0, q/4 + 4\beta)$. Assuming $q \geq 16\beta$, we have $x + e + e' < q/4 + 4\beta \leq q/2$. So, $f_1(x + e + e') = x + e + e'$, and subtracting $\mathsf{Boot}[f_1](\mathbf{a}, b)$ from $(\mathbf{c}, d)$ in line 9, gives a ciphertext such that $\mathsf{Dec}(\mathbf{c}, d) = \tilde{m}q \pm \beta$. □

The HomFloorAlt algorithm can be used to homomorphically compute the sign of a ciphertext using essentially the same process as HomSign. We only need to choose an approximate value of α, and replace the call to $\mathsf{HomFloor}(Q, (\mathbf{c}, d))$ with the call to $\mathsf{HomFloorAlt}(Q, (\mathbf{c}, d+\alpha/2))$ to ensure that the noise is positive, so it does not alter the most significant bit of the message.

By Lemma 3, the ciphertext computed by HomFloorAlt has noise at most β. So, by Lemma 1, switching the modulus to $(\alpha/q)Q$ increases the error to $(\alpha/q)\beta + \beta''$, where β'' is the modulus switching noise. For correctness, we need this error to be bounded by $\alpha/2$. This condition holds when

$$\frac{\beta}{q} + \frac{\beta''}{\alpha} \leq \frac{1}{2}.$$

Setting $q = 16\beta$, this is equivalent to $\alpha \geq (16/7)\beta''$.

In summary, the HomSign algorithm based on the HomFloorAlt procedure proposed in this section makes a total of

$$1 + 3\left\lfloor\frac{\log Q}{\log q + \log_2 7 - 4 - \log\beta''}\right\rfloor \approx 3\frac{\log Q}{\log q - \log\beta''}$$

calls to Boot.

4 From Floor Function to Arbitrary Function Evaluation

As discussed, the FHEW functional bootstrapping requires the evaluated functions to be negacyclic. However, this greatly restricts the power of functional bootstrapping. In this section, we show how to extend our main idea of HomFloor to functional bootstrapping of arbitrary functions.

Let us first formally define the problem. Given a ciphertext $(\mathbf{c}, d)$ with modulus q encrypting a digit $m \in \mathbb{Z}_{q/\alpha}$, and an arbitrary function $f : \mathbb{Z}_{q/\alpha} \to \mathbb{Z}_{Q/\alpha}$, we want to obtain a ciphertext $(\mathbf{c}', d') \in \mathbb{Z}_Q^{n+1}$ such that $\lceil \mathsf{Dec}(\mathbf{c}', d')/\alpha \rfloor = f(m)$.

At a high level, we proceed as follows: first, we use modulus switching to raise the ciphertext modulus from q to $2q$. This process (randomly) maps an encrypted value $m \in \mathbb{Z}_{q/\alpha}$ to either $m \in \mathbb{Z}_{2q/\alpha}$ or $m + q/\alpha \in \mathbb{Z}_{2q/\alpha}$. The main purpose of this step is to double the size of the message space by introducing an extra (most significant) bit.

Next, similar to HomFloor, we first use an extraction function $f_0'(x)$ (similar to f_0 in Fig. 1) to remove the MSB of the (modulus-raised) encrypted plaintext $m \in \mathbb{Z}_{2q/\alpha}$, i.e., for plaintext $m \in \mathbb{Z}_{2q/\alpha}$ we homomorphically evaluate f_0' to obtain an encrypted value $m' = m \pmod{q/\alpha} \in \mathbb{Z}_{2q/\alpha}$. This is the same as the original message m, but as an element of a larger message space.

Then, we create a new function $f_1' : \mathbb{Z}_{2q} \to \mathbb{Z}_Q$ by setting

- $f_1'(x) = \alpha \cdot f(\lceil x/\alpha \rfloor)$ to the function we want to compute for $x < q$, and
- $f_1'(x) = -\alpha \cdot f(\lceil (2q - x)/\alpha \rfloor)$ for $x \geq q$ to satisfy the negacyclic requirement.

We evaluate this function via functional bootstrapping to obtain a ciphertext $(\mathbf{c}', d')$ such that $\lceil \mathsf{Dec}(\mathbf{c}', d')/\alpha \rfloor = f(m')$.

The resulting procedure for arbitrary function evaluation is listed in Algorithm 3.

Algorithm 3. Algorithm for Arbitrary Function Evaluation

Auxiliary math functions $f_0 \colon \mathbb{Z}_{2q} \to \mathbb{Z}_{2q}$

$$f_0'(x) = \left(q \left\lfloor \frac{x}{q} \right\rfloor - \frac{q}{2}\right) \bmod 2q$$

1: **procedure** EvalFunc($f : \mathbb{Z}_{q/\alpha} \to \mathbb{Z}_{Q/\alpha}, q, Q, \alpha, (\mathbf{c}, d)$)
2: Let
$$f_1'(x) = \begin{cases} \alpha f(\lceil x/\alpha \rfloor) & \text{if } x < q \\ -\alpha f(\lceil (2q - x)/\alpha \rfloor) & \text{otherwise} \end{cases} \bmod Q$$
3: $d \leftarrow d + \beta$
4: $(\mathbf{c}, d) \leftarrow (\mathbf{c}, d) \pmod{2q}$
5: $(\mathbf{c}, d) \leftarrow (\mathbf{c}, d) - \mathsf{Boot}[f_0'](\mathbf{c}, d) \pmod{2q}$
6: $d \leftarrow d + \beta - \frac{q}{2}$
7: $(\mathbf{c}, d) \leftarrow \mathsf{Boot}[f_1'](\mathbf{c}, d) \pmod{Q}$
8: **return** $(\mathbf{c}, d)$
9: **end procedure**

Note that if the function $f(x)$ is periodic (i.e., $f(x) = f(x + q/2 \pmod q)$ for all $x \in \mathbb{Z}_q$), the extension to $\mathbb{Z}_{2q}$ is not needed and we can replace all instances of q with $q/2$ in Algorithm 3. This gains one extra bit of precision for periodic functions, as compared to arbitrary functions.

For Algorithm 3, we can formulate the following theorem.

Theorem 3. *For any Q, q, m and $\beta \leq \alpha/4$, the procedure* EvalFunc *in Algorithm 3, on input a ciphertext $(\mathbf{c}, d) \in \mathbb{Z}_q^{n+1}$ such that $|\mathsf{Dec}(\mathbf{c}, d) - \alpha \cdot m| < \beta$ and an arbitrary function $f : \mathbb{Z}_{q/\alpha} \to \mathbb{Z}_{Q/\alpha}$, outputs a ciphertext $(\mathbf{c}', d') \in \mathbb{Z}_Q^{n+1}$ such that $|\mathsf{Dec}(\mathbf{c}', d') - \alpha \cdot f(m)| < \beta$.*

Proof. We prove the theorem by tracing the value encrypted by the input ciphertexts $(\mathbf{c}, d)$. By assumption, $\mathsf{Dec}(\mathbf{c}, d) = \alpha m + e$ for some $|e| < \beta$. Adding β on line 3 makes the error positive $e \in (0, 2\beta)$. Line 4 raises the ciphertext's modulus to $2q$ and thus we (randomly) obtain one of the following: $\mu = \mathsf{Dec}(\mathbf{c}, d) = \alpha m + e \in \mathbb{Z}_{2q}$ or $\mu = \mathsf{Dec}(\mathbf{c}, d) = \alpha m + e + q \in \mathbb{Z}_{2q}$. Then, line 5 executes $\mathsf{Boot}[f_0']$, and line 6 shifts the result by subtracting $q/2$. Based on a similar argument as in the proof of Lemma 2, these two lines together clear the MSB of μ (i.e., now $\mathsf{Dec}(\mathbf{c}, d) = \alpha m + e \in \mathbb{Z}_{2q}$) while increasing the error by at most β, and hence the updated encrypted value is $\mu = \mathsf{Dec}(\mathbf{c}, d) \in [0, q)$. Finally, line 7 executes $\mathsf{Boot}[f_1']$ and we obtain $\mathsf{Dec}(\mathbf{c}, d) = \alpha f(m) + e \in \mathbb{Z}_Q$ with $|e| < \beta$, and therefore, the resulted $(\mathbf{c}, d)$ encrypts a plaintext $m' = \lceil \mathsf{Dec}(\mathbf{c}, d)/\alpha \rfloor = f(m)$ where m is the input plaintext as we required. □

An alternative arbitrary function evaluation can be trivially derived based on HomFloorAlt using the same steps as described here. As the efficiency of this alternative algorithm is worse, we do not discuss it in the paper.

Note that our general bootstrapping algorithm works efficiently in practice only for small plaintext moduli p because the FHEW bootstrapping becomes prohibitively expensive as the plaintext modulus is increased (more than doubles for each extra bit of precision). However, we can extend it to larger plaintext moduli using the procedure for homomorphic digit decomposition described in the next section.

5 Homomorphic Digit Decomposition

The high-level idea of homomorphic digit decomposition is to decompose an LWE ciphertext with a large plaintext (ciphertext) modulus into a vector of LWE ciphertexts with small plaintext (ciphertext) moduli, corresponding to the digit sizes. In this section we extend our sign evaluation algorithm in Sect. 3 to achieve homomorphic digit decomposition.

As pointed out in Sect. 4, one useful application of such digit decomposition is the evaluation of functions over large-precision ciphertexts using lookup tables, i.e., the evaluation of arbitrary functions for large plaintext moduli. Two methods for evaluating a Look-Up Table (LUT) using (a vector of) LWE ciphertexts for each digit are presented in [22]. The first (more general) approach uses tree evaluation while the second (more special-purpose) approach is based on chaining. These methods allow breaking down a large LUT into small LUTs, each of which corresponds to a decomposed digit of the original ciphertext encrypting a large number. These small LUTs can be completely different from each other. In summary, the evaluation of an arbitrary function over a large plaintext space gets expressed as LUT evaluations over encrypted digits.

The LWE ciphertexts for each digit can be "extracted" from a large-precision LWE ciphertext using the homomorphic digit decomposition algorithm presented in this section, and then the general bootstrapping procedure from Sect. 4 can be used to evaluate for each digit arbitrary functions/lookup tables over small plaintext moduli. In other words, the digit decomposition procedure presented in this section and small-LUT evaluation procedure presented in Sect. 4 are two core subroutines in arbitrary function evaluation for larger plaintext spaces.

5.1 Digit Decomposition into Fixed-Size Digits

We first assume for simplicity that all output ciphertexts have the same modulus q and $\log(Q/\alpha)$ divides $\log(q/\alpha)$. Let us formally define the problem. Given an input LWE $(\mathbf{c}, d) \in \mathbb{Z}_Q^{n+1}$ encrypting a message $m \in \mathbb{Z}_{Q/\alpha}$, our goal is to obtain a vector of ciphertexts $((\mathbf{c}_i, d_i) \in \mathbb{Z}_q^{n+1})_{i\in[k]}$, where $k = \frac{\log(Q/\alpha)}{\log(q/\alpha)}$, such that each ciphertext $(\mathbf{c}_i, d_i)$ encrypts a digit $m_i \in \mathbb{Z}_{q/\alpha}$ and $m = \sum_{i=1}^{k} m_i \cdot (q/\alpha)^{i-1}$.

Let $\alpha = 4\beta$ and the input ciphertext $(\mathbf{c}, d) \in \mathbb{Z}_Q^{n+1}$ have noise $< \beta$. Then we can perform digit decomposition using Algorithm 4. The high-level idea is to extract each least significant digit, remove it using HomFloor, and then use the modulus switching procedure to reduce the modulus from Q to $\alpha Q/q$, hence moving to the next least significant digit.

Theorem 4. *Let $\beta > 2$ be an upper bound on both the bootstrapping noise (from Theorem 1) and the size of the secret key*[2] $\|\mathbf{s}\|_1 \leq \beta$. *Let $\alpha \geq 4\beta$ be a power of 2. The procedure* DigitDecomp *in Algorithm 4, on input an LWE ciphertext $(\mathbf{c}, d) \in \mathbb{Z}_Q^{n+1}$ encrypting a message $m \in \mathbb{Z}_{Q/\alpha}$ with error bounded by $|\mathsf{Dec}(\mathbf{c}, d) - \alpha \cdot m| < \beta$, outputs ciphertexts $((\mathbf{c}_i, d_i))_{i \in [k]}$ such that $m = \sum_{i=1}^{k} m_i \cdot (q/\alpha)^i$, where $m_i = \lceil \mathsf{Dec}(\mathbf{c}_i, d_i)/\alpha \rfloor$, $k = \frac{\log(Q/\alpha)}{\log(q/\alpha)}$, and $|\mathsf{Dec}(\mathbf{c}_i, d_i) - \alpha \cdot m_i| < \beta$.*

Proof. By the correctness of HomFloor shown in Lemma 2, we directly see that $m = \sum_{i=0}^{k} m_i \cdot (q/\alpha)^i$, where $m_i = \lceil \mathsf{Dec}(\mathbf{c}_i, d_i)/\alpha \rfloor$. The first ciphertext $(\mathbf{c}_1, d_1)$ in the vector has the same noise as the input ciphertext, i.e., at most β. Then, for $(\mathbf{c}_i, d_i)$, where $i \in [2, k]$, we have the same noise as for input ciphertexts of HomFloor, again at most β, which follows from the proof of Theorem 2. □

Alternatively, we can formulate a digit decomposition algorithm based on HomFloorAlt by trivially replacing HomFloor with HomFloorAlt and changing α from 4β to 2β.

Algorithm 4. Algorithm for Homomorphic Digit Decomposition based on HomFloor

```
1: procedure DIGITDECOMP(Q, q, (c, d))
2:     k ← 1
3:     while Q > q do
4:         (c_k, d_k) ← (c, d) (mod q)
5:         (c, d) ← HomFloor(Q, q, (c, d))
6:         (c, d) ← ⌈(α/q) · (c, d)⌋
7:         Q ← αQ/q
8:         k ← k + 1
9:     end while
10:    (c_k, d_k) ← (c, d)
11:    return {(c_i, d_i)}_{i∈[k]}
12: end procedure
```

5.2 Digit Decomposition into Varying-Size Digits

In some scenarios, it is desired to decompose a large-message LWE ciphertext into a vector of LWE ciphertexts with different digit sizes, where each digit size is a power of two. Our algorithm can also be extended to this more general case.

[2] The weaker bound $\beta \geq O(\|\mathbf{s}\|_2) = O(\sqrt{n})$ suffices when using randomized modulus switching, or heuristically when assuming the input ciphertext is random.

Let us first formally define the problem. Given an input LWE ciphertext $(\mathbf{c}, d) \in \mathbb{Z}_Q^{n+1}$, encrypting a message $m \in \mathbb{Z}_{Q/\alpha}$, our goal is to output a vector of ciphertexts $((\mathbf{c}_i, d_i) \in \mathbb{Z}_{q_i}^{n+1})_{i\in[k]}$, where k denotes the vector size and $(\prod_{i=1}^{k} \frac{q_i}{\alpha}) = \frac{Q}{\alpha}$, such that each ciphertext encrypts a digit $m_i \in \mathbb{Z}_{q_i/\alpha}$ and $m = m_1 + \sum_{i=2}^{k} m_i \cdot (\prod_{j=1}^{i-1} \frac{q_j}{\alpha})$.

This can be achieved by making small modifications in Algorithm 4. Instead of evaluating DigitDecomp with modulus q in every iteration, we use q_i in the ith iteration, and replace $\left\lceil \frac{\alpha}{q} \cdot (\mathbf{c}, d) \right\rfloor$ with $\left\lceil \frac{\alpha}{q_i} \cdot (\mathbf{c}, d) \right\rfloor$.

Note that the computational complexity of varying-size digit decomposition depends on the value of each q_i as different values of N and potentially other parameters may be needed for a given value of q_i.

6 Parameter Selection and Optimizations

The proposed algorithms work with the following parameters:

- q, small (power-of-two) (LWE) modulus;
- n, lattice parameter for the LWE scheme;
- Q', RLWE/RGSW modulus (used for NTTs);
- Q, input (power-of-two) modulus;
- Q_{ks}, LWE/RLWE modulus used for key switching;
- N, ring dimension for RLWE/RGSW;
- B_g, gadget base for digit decomposition in each accumulator update, which breaks integers mod$Q$ into d_g digits;
- B_{ks}, gadget base for key switching, which breaks integers mod Q into d_{ks} digits;

6.1 Selecting the Floor Function Evaluation Method

There are two options for evaluating the floor function: HomFloor and HomFloorAlt. Given a ciphertext modulus q, noise bound β, and small plaintext modulus p, HomFloor can support $p \leq q/\alpha$ where $\alpha \geq 4\beta$ with two bootstrapping operations while HomFloorAlt can support the plaintext modulus of $2p$ with three bootstrapping operations. Hence HomFloorAlt is about 1.5x slower but can process 1 extra bit. If we denote as P the desired (large) plaintext space for sign evaluation (i.e., $P = Q/\alpha$, where Q is the (large) modulus of the input ciphertext), then evaluating HomSign using HomFloor requires $1+2\lfloor \frac{\log P}{\log p} \rfloor$ bootstrapping operations and evaluating HomSign using HomFloorAlt requires $1+3\lfloor \frac{\log P}{\log p+1} \rfloor$ bootstrapping operations.

It is easy to see that for $p = 2$, using HomFloorAlt is faster by a factor of about 4/3. For $p = 2^2 = 4$, the number of bootstrapping operations is roughly the same, and for higher values of p using HomFloor is faster. In practice, the value of p is at least $2^3 = 8$ (or actually $2^4 = 16$ for the optimized setting described in Sect. 6.3), and, therefore, HomFloor is always the preferred floor function evaluation algorithm in practice.

6.2 Module-LWE Vs RLWE

As an alternative to RLWE in the bootstrapping procedure described in Theorem 1, we consider a module-LWE accumulator instead of the RLWE one. In this case, we can replace one ring element of dimension N with w ring elements, each with dimension N/w for some $w \in \mathbb{Z}^+$. Therefore, we use w NTT operations for the ring dimension N/w to replace one NTT operation for the ring dimension N. This can give a speed-up of roughly $\log N/(\log N - \log w)$. However, since $q = 2N$, we would lose one bit as w is doubled, i.e., $\log w$ bits in total. If we have $1 + 2\lfloor \frac{\log P}{\log p} \rfloor$ bootstrapping operations for RLWE, then we will have $\frac{\log N}{\log N - \log w}\left(1 + 2\lfloor \frac{\log P}{\log p - \log w} \rfloor\right)$ as a complexity for Module-LWE in terms of equivalent bootstrapping operations.

For the practical values of N (at least 1024) and p (8 or 16), it can be easily shown that RLWE is always faster than Module-LWE for any $w > 1$. Therefore, RLWE is always preferred in practice.

6.3 Optimizations

Throughout the paper, so far, we have used the worst-case error bound of 4β. This was done primarily for simplicity so we could work with a power-of-two β. In the actual implementation, we can use an average-case error estimate. We consider this as an implementation-level optimization.

If each ciphertext has an error bound β, adding two ciphertexts with errors sampled independently from each other will result in an error bound of $2\sqrt{2}\beta$, which can be easily shown using subgaussian analysis/Central Limit Theorem arguments, and was confirmed experimentally.

Such optimization can end up in an even tighter noise bound in practice (essentially going from $2\sqrt{2}\beta$ to 2β). Our experimental results (based on 1,000 runs) suggest that a single ciphertext after bootstrapping has a standard deviation $\sigma \approx 11.5$. If we set the probability of error to less than 2^{-32}, then the estimated β is 73, which rounds up to 128. When two independent ciphertexts are added together, we get a noise with standard deviation $\sigma \approx 16.3$, and for the same probability the estimated bound β is 103, which also rounds up to 128.

Therefore, in practice, we can remove the second addition of β in HomFloor (at line 5 of Algorithm 1). The same optimization can be applied to HomFloorAlt, DigitDecomp, and EvalFunc.

6.4 Setting the Parameters

For HomSign and DigitDecomp, the main input parameter is Q. Typically $\log Q$ should be set to $\log P + \log(\tilde{\beta} + \beta) + 1$, where $\log P$ is precision in bits of the input plaintext, $\tilde{\beta}$ is the error in the input ciphertext, and β is the FHEW bootstrapping error bound defined in Theorem 1. It is recommended to perform modulus switching to obtain the smallest acceptable value of Q before running the procedures.

After Q is fixed, one needs to find a prime number $Q' > Q$ to support the NTT operations during bootstrapping. Based on the desired security level, we can fix the ring dimension N using the HE standard [4] or LWE estimator [5]. For example, for a ring of dimension $N = 2048$, for 128-bit security against classical computer attacks, we can set $\log Q'$ to at most 54 bits; for 256-bit security, we can support at most 29 bits. With N fixed, we choose $q = 2N$ for maximum performance.

Together with Q', we need to choose B_g, which is the gadget base to decompose Q'. For best performance, we generally set B_g to the smallest power-of-two $> \sqrt{Q'}$, i.e., $d_g = 2$. B_g is the main parameter that determines the noise growth. Roughly speaking, we need $\frac{Q \cdot B_g}{Q'} \ll 1$. For best runtime performance, $B_g = \lceil \sqrt{Q'} \rceil$, we need $\frac{Q}{\sqrt{Q'}} \ll 1$. If we have $B_g = \lceil Q'^{1/3} \rceil$ ($d_g = 3$), we get a slowdown of 3/4, but then we can support larger Q as the requirement is then $\frac{Q}{Q'^{2/3}} \ll 1$. According to our experiments, roughly $\frac{Q \cdot B_g}{Q'} \approx 2^{-11}$ should be sufficient to achieve the noise standard deviation of ≈ 11.5 after one bootstrapping (which is enough to maintain a failure probability $< 2^{-32}$ with error bound 128, because adding two bootstrapped ciphertexts would result in a noise standard deviation ≈ 16.3).

The last remaining parameter is p, which is the small plaintext modulus for each digit in HomSign and Decomp, i.e., the internal plaintext modulus in HomFloor. We have $p = q/(4\beta)$ as the worst-case bound in our algorithms. However, the optimizations in Sect. 6.3 allow us to use $p = q/(2\beta)$ in the implementation.

6.5 Noise Estimates

Bootstrapping results in a ciphertext with an error from a Gaussian distribution of standard deviation $\sigma = \sqrt{\frac{q^2}{Q_{ks}^2}(\frac{Q_{ks}^2}{Q'^2}\sigma_{ACC}^2 + \sigma_{MS_1}^2 + \sigma_{KS}^2) + \sigma_{MS_2}^2}$, where $\sigma_{MS_1}^2 = \frac{|s_N|^2+1}{3}$, $\sigma_{MS_2}^2 = \frac{|s_n|^2+1}{3}$, $\sigma_{ACC}^2 = 4 d_g n N \frac{B_g^2}{6} \sigma_{BK}^2$, and $\sigma_{KS}^2 = \sigma_{BK} N d_{ks}$ for a uniform ternary secret keys s_N with dimension N and s_n with dimension n, as estimated in [29]. Note that here we use a heuristic (average-case) estimate for σ_{MS}^2.

To guarantee that we can have a failure probability $< 2^{-32}$ as proposed in [16,19,29], we set $\beta \approx 6.37\sigma$, and we then round β to the smallest power-of-two greater than 6.37σ. However, sometimes $\sqrt{2} \cdot 6.37\sigma$ is also smaller than the rounded β. Therefore, we can use the same β even if we have a $\sqrt{2}$ loss in Algorithms 1 and 4.

6.6 Computational Complexity

For our experiments, we used the TFHE/GINX bootstrapping method with ternary secret keys [29]. Each bootstrapping takes roughly $2n(d_g + 1)$ NTT operations (we employed the ternary CMUX optimization recently proposed by Bonte et al. [6]) and each NTT operation is $O(N \log N)$.

7 Implementation and Performance Evaluation

7.1 Parameters Used for Our Implementation

In our implementation, we limited Q to at most 2^{29}, which supports up to 21 bits of precision. This precision is sufficient for most applications. One common use of FHEW-based comparisons is in applications that use the CKKS scheme for all polynomial computations, and then switch to FHEW for comparison-based computations [28]. The precision typically achieved in these applications is not higher than 20 bits (as it is limited primarily by the precision of CKKS bootstrapping [7]).

Once Q is fixed, we need to find Q' such that $Q/Q'^{\frac{d_g-1}{d_g}} \ll 1$, as explained in Sect. 6.4. We set $\log Q'$ to 54, which is the largest modulus size that supports 128-bit security for $N = 2048$ [4].

Next, we need to choose B_g. For $Q' < 2^{54}$, there are three main practical options: $B_g = 2^{27}$ (two digits in RGSW gadget decomposition, i.e., $d_g = 2$), $B_g = 2^{18}$ ($d_g = 3$), and $B_g = 2^{14}$ ($d_g = 4$). For $Q \leq 2^{16}$, we can use $B_g = 2^{27}$ (fastest bootstrapping). For $2^{16} < Q \leq 2^{25}$, we use $B_g = 2^{18}$. For $2^{25} < Q \leq 2^{29}$, we use $B_g = 2^{14}$.

Note that we can dynamically change from $B_g = 2^{14}$ to $B_g = 2^{18}$ and then to $B_g = 2^{27}$ as the value of Q gets progressively reduced via HomFloor iterations in HomSign and DigitDecomp, resulting in a speed-up of later bootstrapping operations. When using this dynamic mode, a bootstrapping key for each value of B_g should be generated and loaded in computer memory. Hence, there is a tradeoff between runtime and storage. One can either use the smallest B_g for all bootstrapping operations and the smallest storage for the bootstrapping key or use multiple values of B_g, improving the runtime of later bootstrapping operations at the expense of increased storage requirements.

We use $n = 1305$, $\sigma_{BK} = 3.19$, $Q_{ks} = 2^{35}$, and $B_{ks} = 32$, where σ_{BK} is the standard deviation of the noise to encrypt the bootstrapping keys. All other parameters are set to the same values as in [29].

For the parameters above, the estimated standard deviation σ of a bootstrapped ciphertext is about 11.5 (based on 1,000 bootstrapping runs). For a sum of two bootstrapped ciphertexts, the standard deviation σ_{sum} is about 16.3. We can use this value of σ_{sum} to select the value of plaintext modulus p. The failure probability is given by $1 - \mathsf{erf}(\frac{q/p}{2\sqrt{2}\sigma_{sum}})$. To guarantee the probability of success for HomSign to be at least $1 - 2^{32}$, similar to [16,19,29], we set $p = 16 = 2^4$. For this value of p, the error upper bound β is 128. This implies we can achieve 4 bits of precision in the HomFloor function, i.e., we can work with digits of up to 4 bits per iteration when dealing with large-precision LWE ciphertexts.

Remark 2. Although we restricted Q to 2^{29} and $\log Q'$ to 54 bits, higher values of both Q and Q' can be supported. For Q' larger than 64 bits, the machine word size for many modern computing environments, a Residue Number System (RNS) variant of RLWE and the corresponding RNS digit decomposition can be instantiated using the lattice gadget techniques presented in [21].

7.2 Software Implementation

We implemented HomSign, DigitDecomp, and EvalFunc in PALISADE v1.11.6 [1]. The evaluation environment was a commodity desktop computer system with an Intel(R) Core(TM) i7-9700 CPU @ 3.00 GHz and 64 GB of RAM, running Ubuntu 18.04 LTS. The C++ compiler was g++ 10.1.0. We compiled PALISADE with the following CMake flag: WITH_NATIVEOPT=ON (machine-specific optimizations were applied by the compiler).

7.3 Experimental Results

For Q bounded to 2^{29} and the parameter values discussed in Sect. 7.1, the runtime of HomSign and DigitDecomp can be described in terms of bootstrapping times for $d_g = 2$, $d_g = 3$, and $d_g = 4$. For $Q \leq 2^{16}$ we use $d_g = 2$, for $2^{16} < Q \leq 2^{25}$ we use $d_g = 3$, and for $2^{25} < Q \leq 2^{29}$ we use $d_g = 4$.

The single-threaded runtimes for $d_g = 2$, $d_g = 3$, and $d_g = 4$ in our evaluation environment were 442, 600, and 785 ms, respectively. The runtimes for HomSign, DigitDecomp, and EvalFunc are listed in Table 2. When $\log P = 4$, only one bootstrapping invocation is needed. Then for each next 4 bits (each digit), two more bootstrapping invocations are needed, as explained in Sect. 6.1. Note that although for $Q = 2^{25}$ and $Q = 2^{26}$, the number of bootstrapping operations is the same (four calls to HomFloor, each with two bootstrapping invocations, plus one extra bootstrapping), the runtimes are different because for $Q = 2^{25}$ we have three bootstrapping operations at $d_g = 2$ and six bootstrapping operations at $d_g = 2$, while for $Q = 2^{26}$ we have three bootstrapping operations at $d_g = 2$, four bootstrapping operations at $d_g = 3$, and two more bootstrapping operations at $d_g = 4$. Moreover, note that for $Q = 2^{28}$ and $Q = 2^{29}$, there is a relatively large runtime gap. This is because we need one more call to HomFloor for $Q = 2^{29}$ and therefore two additional bootstrapping invocations. In general, the runtime is roughly linear in $\log Q$. For arbitrary function evaluation, we can process one bit less compared to the HomFloor function in HomSign.

For EvalFunc, we used the function $y = x^3$, but any other function over modulus P could be used instead, and we verified this experimentally. As explained, EvalFunc with $P = 2^3$ can be used as a subroutine to support arbitrary function (LUT) evaluation for larger plaintext moduli; this LUT evaluation is achieved using a combination of either tree or chain method introduced in [22] together with the digit decomposition method proposed in Sect. 5. One can also increase P for a single "digit" by increasing the ring dimension (each extra bit of P requires doubling the ring dimension, i.e., roughly doubling the runtime). We chose specifically $\log P = 3$ for EvalFunc to illustrate the runtime for arbitrary functions as this setting corresponds to the ring dimension $N = 2048$, which was used for all proposed capabilities in our implementation for simplicity.

It is possible to use a smaller ring dimension $N = 1024$ and $\log Q' \leq 27$ for $Q = 2^{12}$ (but not for higher Q) at the cost of reducing $\log P$ by one bit, i.e., use the same bootstrapping parameters as for Boolean circuit evaluation in [29], but we have chosen to run all experiments at $N = 2048$ for simplicity/uniformity

Table 2. Single-threaded timing results of HomSign, DigitDecomp, and EvalFunc for ($\log P$)-bit encrypted numbers at $N = 2048, q = 2N = 4096$. Recall that in HomSign/DigitDecomp, as we proceed, $\log P$ becomes smaller and B_g is dynamically increased to improve the runtime performance, as suggested in Sect. 7.1.

Function	Q	$\log P$ [bits]	runtime [ms]	Initial B_g
HomSign/DigitDecomp	2^{12}	4	442	2^{27}
HomSign/DigitDecomp	2^{16}	8	1,322	2^{27}
HomSign/DigitDecomp	2^{20}	12	2,515	2^{18}
HomSign/DigitDecomp	2^{24}	16	3,709	2^{18}
HomSign/DigitDecomp	2^{25}	17	4,589	2^{18}
HomSign/DigitDecomp	2^{26}	18	5,216	2^{14}
HomSign/DigitDecomp	2^{28}	20	5,222	2^{14}
HomSign/DigitDecomp	2^{29}	21	6,096	2^{14}
EvalFunc	2^{12}	3	884	2^{27}

and best precision. Similarly, we can reduce n and Q_{ks} if $Q < 2^{29}$ is desired, hence reducing the runtime by a factor proportional to n. But we did not include this optimization to provide a general functionality up to 21 bits of precision and illustrate the linear dependence of runtime on $\log Q$ and $\log P$.

For comparison, the TFHE/GINX bootstrapping runtime for $N = 1024$ using the same parameters as in [29] with the CMake flag NATIVE_SIZE=32 for the clang++ 9.0.0 compiler was 74 ms (we observed that clang++ 9.0.0 is faster than g++ 10.1.0 when 32-bit integers are used for modular arithmetic in PALISADE). This implies that the bootstrapping operations in our implementation are 6.0x (for $d_g = 2$), 8.1x (for $d_g = 3$), and 10.6x (for $d_g = 4$) slower than the bootstrapping time for a single Boolean gate evaluation [29] when using our computing environment. This slowdown is primarily caused by increased values of n from 502 to 1305 and N from 1024 to 2048 (both parameters proportionally increase the runtime). If a smaller precision (below 21 bits) is desired, this slowdown can be reduced by using smaller values of n (also, a smaller value of N can be used if the precision of 4 bits is sufficient for a given application).

8 Comparison with Other Recent Works

8.1 Comparison with Algorithms Based on FHEW/TFHE Bootstrapping

There is a recent work proposing algorithms for homomorphic digit decomposition and arbitrary function evaluation [18]. The high-level idea of their approach is to use the fact that $-1 \cdot (-m) = m$ and extract the most significant bit as part of their procedures. They run two bootstrapping operations (one to extract the MSB and another to evaluate the desired function) and then multiply the results using a homomorphic multiplication, similar to the multiplication in Brakerski's and Brakerski/Fan-Vercauteren (BFV) schemes [9,20]. The work [18] does not provide any implementation; hence we focus here on the theoretical comparison of approaches.

The most significant difference is the extra noise added in [18] due to the BFV-like homomorphic multiplication. This adds a multiplicative factor $O(N \cdot p)$ to the prior noise, and hence increases Q' by the same factor. In our method, no additional noise beyond the sum of the noises due to bootstrapping operations is needed. The other difference is that each iteration of their HomFloor-like operation in digit decomposition supports one bit less precision than our method. This bit is lost for the same reason that one extra bit is needed in our arbitrary function evaluation, where we have to extend from $\mathbb{Z}_q$ to $\mathbb{Z}_{2q}$.

We can estimate the concrete noise increase in [18] by using the heuristic BFV multiplication noise estimate, $4Np$, from [23,25]. For the parameters used in our implementation (also accounting for a smaller p, by one bit), the extra factor is $4 \cdot 2^{11} \cdot 2^4 = 2^{17}$. This implies that $\log Q'$ has to be increased by 17 bits. According to [4] and our noise estimates, this will require increasing the ring dimension N from 2048 to 4096 to achieve the same security level and roughly the same precision (i.e., same $\log P$). The reduced precision per iteration of their HomFloor-like function may further increase the computational complexity. In summary, our estimates suggest that the method proposed in [18] will be at least two times slower for digit decomposition for the parameters used in our implementation. We expect a similar improvement for arbitrary function evaluation (except that our algorithm supports the same largest plaintext modulus as their algorithm, i.e., there is no 1-bit advantage as in the case of HomFloor).

Another potential drawback of the approach in [18] is the need for a BFV-like relinearization key and related extra implementation complexity. In this sense, our approach is simpler as it requires only regular FHEW/TFHE keys.

There is another recent work proposing an algorithm for arbitrary function evaluation [26]. The high-level idea is similar to [18], i.e., use the fact that $-1 \cdot (-m) = m$. The difference is that [26] performs multiplication using a GSW ciphertext (which encrypts the sign bit). They also propose a method to use an LWE′ ciphertext (a vector of LWE ciphertexts, see details in [29]) for multiplication instead of using a GSW ciphertext, as only plaintext multiplications are needed in their algorithm, instead of ciphertext multiplications. This makes the extraction of the sign bit two times faster than the GSW-based method. Their algorithm requires $d'_g + 1 \geq 3$ bootstrappings to perform an arbitrary function evaluation whereas our method requires only 2 bootstrappings and is independent of d'_g. Here, d'_g refers to the number of digits for gadget decomposition specific to their LWE′ multiplication. Their algorithm also increases the noise by a multiplicative factor of $O(\sqrt{N d'_g} Q'^{1/d'_g})$, which is the cost of GSW-like multiplication, as compared to our approach.

Both methods [18,26] can be extended to support large-precision sign evaluation (though this was not done in these works), but will have the same drawbacks as for arbitrary function evaluation: asymptotically higher noise growth (both methods) and increased number of bootstrapping operations (applies to [26] only). Another advantage of our method is that no multiplication support is needed for the homomorphic encryption scheme that invokes the FHEW bootstrapping, i.e., an additively homomorphic LWE scheme can be used. In methods [18,26], a homomorphic encryption scheme supporting both additions and multiplications is needed.

8.2 Comparison with CKKS Sign Evaluation

We compare our sign-evaluation method with the state-of-the-art CKKS sign-evaluation method [27] (i.e., CKKS-based comparison between two numbers) and summarize the advantages of our approach below.

- As shown in Table VII of [27], with 20 bits of accuracy, their approach takes $\sim$ 30 seconds (for 64K slots), while ours takes about 6 s (for 1 slot). Therefore, if the number of comparisons needed is small (e.g., 5 comparisons), our method is faster.
- Our method is easily parallelizable while the CKKS method supports limited parallelization (only over RNS residues). Therefore, on a server-grade multi-core machine, our performance can be better even for a larger number of comparisons.
- When combined with CKKS for other applications (as shown in Sect. 9), our method does not require the ring dimension to be very large (2^{15} is already enough), while the CKKS method requires the ring dimension to be 2^{17} or higher, which may not be desired for the original application and therefore can greatly impact the performance, e.g., memory requirements and runtime.
- Higher precision for the CKKS method (e.g., 50 bits) can be harder to support as $\log Q$ can easily exceed 3000 (and the ring dimension will increase accordingly). The scaling factor will also need to be adjusted accordingly, increasing the underlying machine word size from 64-bit to 128-bit, which further reduces the performance (as high as 8x slower, judging by the PALISADE CKKS implementation). On the other hand, our method simply needs to use the RNS variant of RLWE as mentioned in Remark 2 of our paper (there is only an increase in the ring dimension). Hence, the decrease in runtime for higher precision is much smaller for our method.
- Our method is much simpler to implement/use (no special composite polynomials are needed).
- When multiple invocations of CKKS sign evaluation are needed, CKKS bootstrapping should be called in between, which significantly increases the runtime of the CKKS-based approach. Our method does not have any additional requirements for multiple invocations of the sign function as it inherently includes FHEW/TFHE bootstrapping.

9 Application

In this section, we consider an application of our large-precision comparison method where CKKS and FHEW/TFHE are used together. We combine CKKS and FHEW/TFHE using the scheme switching methods described in [28] based on the ideas proposed in [8].

The large-precision comparison is used to evaluate the Heaviside activation function arising in some machine learning applications [2,11,31], which is defined as

$$H(x) = \begin{cases} 1 \text{ if } x > 0, \\ 0 \text{ otherwise.} \end{cases}$$

In the case of artificial neural network networks, e.g., in a deep learning model for functions with jump discontinuities, the input x is often computed as an inner product of (encrypted) inputs and (encrypted) weights, which can be performed using CKKS (along with other linear/polynomial computations needed for the model). In our example, we evaluate an inner product with CKKS and then evaluate the Heaviside function by negating the CKKS ciphertext containing 256 valid slots and switching it to 256 FHEW/TFHE ciphertexts. We perform our large-precision sign evaluation on these 256 ciphertexts using Algorithm 1. Lastly, we switch the comparison results back to a CKKS ciphertext.

In our experiment, the input precision was about 21 bits (by setting $\log Q = 29$ and other parameters as in Sect. 7) and the observed output precision was larger than 30 bits, which are both much higher than the results from [28] (input precision of 5–6 bits and output precision not higher than 13 bits). Similar to [28], the runtime for our experiment with 256 slots was dominated by large-precision comparisons, and the contribution of CKKS-FHEW and FHEW-CKKS scheme switching was not higher than 10%. Hence, the runtime can be estimated by multiplying the runtimes from Table 2 by the number of slots (and dividing them by the number of threads if multi-threading is available).

More generally, one can use large-precision comparison to perform an encrypted branch evaluation by checking the values against a threshold (i.e., if the input is above some threshold T, evaluate circuit B; otherwise, evaluate circuit C). This may require high precision as the behavior of B and C can be greatly different.

10 Concluding Remarks

Our experimental results for homomorphic sign evaluation suggest that increasing the precision from 4 bits to 21 incurs a slow-down of only about 14x. If FHEW/TFHE bootstrapping would be used directly, a slow-down of more than 100,000x would be observed. This implies that our large-precision homomorphic sign evaluation implementation can be used for applications that work with 20-bit-precision numbers (and can be extended to a larger precision, as discussed in Remark 2 in Sect. 7.1). For instance, it can be plugged into the decision tree inference implementation [28] to increase the precision of comparison.

It was also shown that our method for arbitrary function evaluation, which we call general functional bootstrapping (often referred to as programmable bootstrapping in literature), has a lower complexity than two other recently proposed methods [18,26]. Both of these methods require one multiplication operation while our method can be built on top of an additively homomorphic encryption scheme, similar to the original FHEW construction for Boolean gate evaluation [19].

References

1. PALISADE Lattice Cryptography Library (release 1.11.6), January 2022. https://palisade-crypto.org/
2. Spline adaptive filtering algorithm based on heaviside step function. Signal, Image and Video Processing (2022)
3. Akavia, A., Leibovich, M., Resheff, Y.S., Ron, R., Shahar, M., Vald, M.: Privacy-preserving decision tree training and prediction against malicious server. Cryptology ePrint Archive, Report 2019/1282 (2019). https://ia.cr/2019/1282
4. Albrecht, M., Chase, M., Chen, H., et al.: Homomorphic encryption security standard. Technical report, HomomorphicEncryption.org, Toronto, Canada, November 2018
5. Albrecht, M.R., Player, R., Scott, S.: On the concrete hardness of learning with errors. J. Math. Cryptol. **9**(3), 169–203 (2015)
6. Bonte, C., Iliashenko, I., Park, J., Pereira, H.V.L., Smart, N.P.: FINAL: Faster FHE instantiated with NTRU and LWE. Cryptology ePrint Archive, Report 2022/074 (2022). https://ia.cr/2022/074
7. Bossuat, J.P., Mouchet, C., Troncoso-Pastoriza, J., Hubaux, J.P.: Efficient bootstrapping for approximate homomorphic encryption with non-sparse keys. Cryptology ePrint Archive, Report 2020/1203 (2020). https://eprint.iacr.org/2020/1203
8. Boura, C., Gama, N., Georgieva, M., Jetchev, D.: Chimera: combining ring-lwe-based fully homomorphic encryption schemes. J. Math. Cryptol. **14**(1), 316–338 (2020). https://doi.org/10.1515/jmc-2019-0026
9. Brakerski, Z.: Fully homomorphic encryption without modulus switching from classical GapSVP. In: Annual Cryptology Conference, pp. 868–886. Springer (2012). https://doi.org/10.1007/978-3-642-32009-5_50
10. Brakerski, Z., Gentry, C., Vaikuntanathan, V.: (leveled) fully homomorphic encryption without bootstrapping. ACM Trans. Comput. Theory (TOCT) **6**(3), 1–36 (2014)
11. Burlakov, E., Zhukovskiy, E., Verkhlyutov, V.: Neural field equations with neuron-dependent heaviside-type activation function and spatial-dependent delay. Math. Methods Appl. Sci. **44**(15), 11895–11903 (2021). https://onlinelibrary.wiley.com/doi/abs/10.1002/mma.6661
12. Chen, H., Dai, W., Kim, M., Song, Y.: Efficient homomorphic conversion between (ring) LWE ciphertexts. In: Sako, K., Tippenhauer, N.O. (eds.) Applied Cryptography and Network Security, pp. 460–479. Springer, Cham (2021). https://doi.org/10.1007/978-3-030-78372-3_18
13. Chen, H., et al.: Logistic regression over encrypted data from fully homomorphic encryption. Cryptology ePrint Archive, Report 2018/462 (2018). https://ia.cr/2018/462
14. Cheon, J.H., Kim, A., Kim, M., Song, Y.: Homomorphic encryption for arithmetic of approximate numbers. In: International Conference on the Theory and Application of Cryptology and Information Security, pp. 409–437. Springer (2017). https://doi.org/10.1007/978-3-319-70694-8_15

15. Cheon, J.H., Kim, D., Kim, D.: Efficient homomorphic comparison methods with optimal complexity. In: Moriai, S., Wang, H. (eds.) ASIACRYPT 2020. LNCS, vol. 12492, pp. 221–256. Springer, Cham (2020). https://doi.org/10.1007/978-3-030-64834-3_8
16. Chillotti, I., Gama, N., Georgieva, M., Izabachène, M.: Faster fully homomorphic encryption: bootstrapping in less than 0.1 seconds. In: Cheon, J.H., Takagi, T. (eds.) Advances in Cryptology - ASIACRYPT 2016, pp. 3–33. Springer, Berlin, Heidelberg (2016). https://doi.org/10.1007/978-3-662-53887-6_1
17. Chillotti, I., Gama, N., Georgieva, M., Izabachène, M.: Faster packed homomorphic operations and efficient circuit bootstrapping for TFHE. In: Takagi, T., Peyrin, T. (eds.) ASIACRYPT 2017. LNCS, vol. 10624, pp. 377–408. Springer, Cham (2017). https://doi.org/10.1007/978-3-319-70694-8_14
18. Chillotti, I., Ligier, D., Orfila, J.B., Tap, S.: Improved programmable bootstrapping with larger precision and efficient arithmetic circuits for TFHE. Cryptology ePrint Archive, Report 2021/729 (2021). https://eprint.iacr.org/2021/729
19. Ducas, L., Micciancio, D.: FHEW: bootstrapping Homomorphic Encryption in Less Than a Second. In: Oswald, E., Fischlin, M. (eds.) EUROCRYPT 2015. LNCS, vol. 9056, pp. 617–640. Springer, Heidelberg (2015). https://doi.org/10.1007/978-3-662-46800-5_24
20. Fan, J., Vercauteren, F.: Somewhat practical fully homomorphic encryption. IACR Cryptol. ePrint Arch. **2012**, 144 (2012)
21. Genise, N., Micciancio, D., Polyakov, Y.: Building an efficient lattice gadget toolkit: Subgaussian sampling and more. In: Ishai, Y., Rijmen, V. (eds.) EUROCRYPT 2019. LNCS, vol. 11477, pp. 655–684. Springer, Cham (2019). https://doi.org/10.1007/978-3-030-17656-3_23
22. Guimarães, A., Borin, E., Aranha, D.F.: Revisiting the functional bootstrap in TFHE. IACR Transactions on Cryptographic Hardware and Embedded Systems 2021, pp. 229–253, February 2021. https://tches.iacr.org/index.php/TCHES/article/view/8793
23. Halevi, S., Polyakov, Y., Shoup, V.: An improved RNS variant of the BFV homomorphic encryption scheme. In: Matsui, M. (ed.) CT-RSA 2019. LNCS, vol. 11405, pp. 83–105. Springer, Cham (2019). https://doi.org/10.1007/978-3-030-12612-4_5
24. Iliashenko, I., Zucca, V.: Faster homomorphic comparison operations for BGV and BFV. Proc. Privacy Enhancing Technol. **2021**(3), 246–264 (2021). https://doi.org/10.2478/popets-2021-0046
25. Kim, A., Polyakov, Y., Zucca, V.: Revisiting homomorphic encryption schemes for finite fields. In: ASIACRYPT 2021, p. 608–639. Springer, Berlin, Heidelberg (2021). https://doi.org/10.1007/978-3-030-92078-4_21
26. Kluczniak, K., Schild, L.: FDFB: full domain functional bootstrapping towards practical fully homomorphic encryption. Cryptology ePrint Archive, Report 2021/1135 (2021). https://ia.cr/2021/1135
27. Lee, E., Lee, J.W., Kim, Y.S., No, J.S.: Optimization of homomorphic comparison algorithm on RNS-CKKS scheme. Cryptology ePrint Archive, Report 2021/1215 (2021). https://ia.cr/2021/1215
28. Lu, W.J, Huang, Z., Hong, C., Ma, Y., Qu, H.: Pegasus: Bridging polynomial and non-polynomial evaluations in homomorphic encryption. SP 2021 (2020). https://eprint.iacr.org/2020/1606
29. Micciancio, D., Polyakov, Y.: Bootstrapping in FHEW-like Cryptosystems, pp. 17–28. Association for Computing Machinery, New York, NY, USA (2021). https://doi.org/10.1145/3474366.3486924

30. Regev, O.: On lattices, learning with errors, random linear codes, and cryptography. J. ACM (JACM) **56**(6), 1–40 (2009)
31. Siegel, J.W., Xu, J.: Optimal convergence rates for the orthogonal greedy algorithm. IEEE Trans. Inf. Theory, p. 1 (2022)
32. Yang, Z., Xie, X., Shen, H., Chen, S., Zhou, J.: TOTA: fully homomorphic encryption with smaller parameters and stronger security. Cryptology ePrint Archive, Paper 2021/1347 (2021). https://eprint.iacr.org/2021/1347

EvalRound Algorithm in CKKS Bootstrapping

Seonghak Kim[1], Minji Park[2], Jaehyung Kim[1], Taekyung Kim[1], and Chohong Min[2](✉)

[1] Crypto Lab Inc., 1 Gwanak-ro, Gwanak-gu, Seoul 08826, Korea
ksh@cryptolab.co.kr
[2] Ewha Womans University, 52 Ewhayeodae-gil, Seodaemun-gu, Seoul 03760, Korea
qkralswl150@ewhain.net
https://cryptolab.co.kr, http://math.ewha.ac.kr/

Abstract. Homomorphic encryption (HE) has opened an entirely new world up in the privacy-preserving use of sensitive data by conducting computations on encrypted data. Amongst many HE schemes targeting computation in various contexts, Cheon–Kim–Kim–Song (CKKS) scheme [8] is distinguished since it allows computations for encrypted real number data, which have greater impact in real-world applications.

CKKS scheme is a levelled homomorphic encryption scheme, consuming one level for each homomorphic multiplication. When the level runs out, a special computational circuit called bootstrapping is required in order to conduct further multiplications. The algorithm proposed by Cheon et al. [7] has been regarded as a standard way to do bootstrapping in the CKKS scheme, and it consists of the following four steps: ModRaise, CoeffToSlot, EvalMod and SlotToCoeff. However, the steps consume a number of levels themselves, and thus optimizing this extra consumption has been a major focus of the series of recent research.

Among the total levels consumed in the bootstrapping steps, about a half of them is spent in CoeffToSlot and SlotToCoeff steps to scale up the real number components of DFTmatrices and round them to the nearest integers. Each scale-up factor is very large so that it takes up one level to rescale it down. Scale-up factors can be taken smaller to save levels, but the error of rounding would be transmitted to EvalMod and eventually corrupt the accuracy of bootstrapping.

EvalMod aims to get rid of the superfluous qI term from a plaintext $\mathsf{pt} + qI$ resulting from ModRaise, where q is the bottom modulus and I is a polynomial with small integer coefficients. EvalRound is referred to as its opposite, obtaining qI. We introduce a novel bootstrapping algorithm consisting of ModRaise, CoeffToSlot, EvalRound and SlotToCoeff, which yields taking smaller scale-up factors without the damage of rounding errors.

Keywords: Homomorphic encryption · CKKS scheme · Bootstrapping

S. Agrawal and D. Lin (Eds.): ASIACRYPT 2022, LNCS 13792, pp. 161–187, 2022.
https://doi.org/10.1007/978-3-031-22966-4_6

1 Introduction

Homomorphic encryption (HE) refers to a class of encryption schemes which enables computation over encrypted data. The Cheon–Kim–Kim–Song (CKKS) [8] scheme is recognized as one of the most efficient fully homomorphic encryption (FHE) scheme that supports computation on real/complex data. Unlike other FHE schemes that are designed for integer [2–4,14] or binary [10,11,13] messages, the CKKS scheme is designed for real/complex messages, as it supports efficient scaling down operation. Since real numbers are the usual data type for many applications including deep learning, there have been various studies and applications using the CKKS scheme.

In the CKKS scheme, each multiplication consumes certain amount of ciphertext modulus due to rescaling process. As computation including homomorphic multiplications progresses, the total ciphertext modulus in turn decreases, and eventually becomes too small to afford further multiplications. A homomorphic re-encryption of a ciphertext, so called bootstrapping, is required to recover the ciphertext modulus. In this way the levelled CKKS scheme becomes a fully homomorphic encryption (FHE) scheme [15].

The first step towards the conventional bootstrapping algorithm as presented in [7] is called ModRaise, which increases the ciphertext modulus from the bottom to the top modulus. Once the modulus has been raised, an integer polynomial multiple of the base modulus is added to the encrypted plaintext, and an appropriate modular reduction modulo the base modulus should be performed in order to recover the original data. Since it has no simple representation for the modular reduction by the basic algebraic manipulations (addition, multiplication or rotation), the modular reduction must be approximated by a polynomial evaluation with large degree, which is called EvalMod.

The step of CoeffToSlot and SlotToCoeff comes before and after the polynomial evaluation. After ModRaise, the multiples of the base modulus are added on the coefficients of the encrypted plaintext (the 'coefficient side'). However, the homomorphic polynomial evaluation should be performed to the slots of the encrypted message (the 'slot side'). Therefore, to map the value of coefficient side to slot side and vice versa, homomorphic evaluation of DFT/iDFTmatrix multiplication named CoeffToSlot and SlotToCoeff should be performed. As DFT/iDFTmatrices are complex matrices rather than integer ones, we should scale-up them and perform integer matrix multiplication. After multiplying such scaled-up matrices, we should scale-down to get the result which approximates the result of the complex matrix multiplication. Note that the scaling-down consumes modulus bits of the ciphertext.

These linear transformations (CoeffToSlot and SlotToCoeff), together with a polynomial approximation of the modular reduction function (EvalMod), consume a large ciphertext modulus and require a relatively high amount of running time. In particular, in most practical CKKS-FHE parameters, the remaining ciphertext modulus after bootstrapping is far less than the total ciphertext modulus available [1]. Hence, only a limited amount of homomorphic multiplication can be performed after bootstrapping, which degrades the overall performance of the scheme, especially for deeper circuits. Furthermore, the amount of ciphertext modulus consumed in the bootstrapping process is a major factor keeping us from forming an FHE parameter with small ciphertext dimension under a fixed security level, for the total amount of ciphertext modulus needed to keep the security level is bounded once the ciphertext dimension has been fixed.

How much is the ciphertext modulus consumed during the homomorphic evaluation of the linear transformations in CoeffToSlot and SlotToCoeff steps? Since the evaluation of a linear transformation, or equivalently the product of a plaintext dense square matrix M and an encrypted vector $\mathbf{v}$ of dimension n, can be computed homomorphically by

$$M \cdot \mathbf{v} = \sum_{i=0}^{n-1} \text{diag}_i(M) \odot \mathsf{rot}_i(\mathbf{v}) \qquad (\text{matrix} - \text{vectormultiplication}) \tag{1}$$

where $\text{diag}_i(M)$ is the i-th diagonal of the matrix M, $\mathsf{rot}_i(\mathbf{v})$ is the rotation of $\mathbf{v}$ by index i and $\odot$ denotes the Hadamard multiplication, i.e. componentwise vector multiplication. This means that only one multiplicative depth is needed for each CoeffToSlot or SlotToCoeff step. However, this naïve method also requires n multiplications and n rotations, and it becomes quickly computationally infeasible as n grows exponentially in practical parameters.

As a remedy, in [17], the authors focused on the rich mathematical structure of the linear transformations in CoeffToSlot and SlotToCoeff, and proposed to decompose the linear transformations into the products of several sparse block diagonal matrices. In this way one can reduce the number of multiplications and rotations needed for the homomorphic evaluation of the linear transformations at the cost of using certain amount of multiplicative depths (cf. Subsect. 2.4 and [17]). In practice, the depth consumption is equal to the number of decomposed matrices and usually taken to be 3 or 4, and it still requires a large amount of ciphertext modulus.

In this paper, we propose a new bootstrapping algorithm, replacing EvalMod by a new step called EvalRound, which addresses this modulus consuming problem on the evaluation of linear transformations and reduce the amount of ciphertext modulus consumed during bootstrapping.

1.1 Our Contribution

In this work, we propose a novel bootstrap circuit, that yields a reduction of modulus consumed, compared to the conventional circuit [7]. The reduction of modulus amounts to lessening levels. Table 1 shows the reduction of modulus consumption on one of the practical parameters. Here N denotes the ciphertext dimension, $\log(QP)$ denotes the bit lengths of the largest RLWE modulus, and $\widetilde{\Delta}$ denotes the scaling factor of the CoeffToSlot matrix. The proposed method enables us to maintain the bootstrapping precision while using 32 bit smaller scaling factor in CoeffToSlot. The proposed method obtains better bootstrapping precision, while reducing the modulus consumption by 84 bits, which is equivalent to preserving approximately two multiplicative depths. The details of this example is in Example 5.

Table 1. Comparison between conventional and proposed bootstrapping

	N	$\log(QP)$	$\widetilde{\Delta}$	Bootstrap bit precision	Modulus consumption
Conventional	2^{17}	2900	2^{60}	–12.53	1160
Proposed			2^{29}	–14.80	1076 = 1160 – 84

We also constructed an improved parameter set based on the parameter set II proposed in [1], namely II'. New parameter set II' saves 1 depth while losing at most 1 bit of precision. Table 2 describes the comparison between set II and set II'. Here depth denotes the multiplicative level after bootstrapping, Δ denotes the size of the encoding scaling factor, and q_0 denotes the size of the base modulus. The detail of this example is in Example 6.

Table 2. Comparison between the set II in [1] and the proposed set II'.

Set	N	$\log(QP)$	depth	Δ	q_0	Bootstrap precision	$\widetilde{\Delta}$
II	2^{16}	1547	5	2^{45}	2^{60}	-31.5	2^{58}
II'		1543	6			-30.5	2^{34}

It should be emphasized that only a negligible effort is needed to upgrade the conventional circuit to the proposed one. One may directly add one naive subtraction to the existing circuit to compute $\mathsf{EvalRound}(x) = x - \mathsf{EvalMod}(x)$, where $\mathsf{EvalMod}$ is the existing procedure of homomorphic modular reduction and $\mathsf{EvalRound}$ is the proposed homomorphic modular rounding.

1.2 Our Proposal

Our main proposal is the use of $\mathsf{EvalRound}$ rather than $\mathsf{EvalMod}$, which is defined as $\mathsf{EvalRound} : x \mapsto x - \mathsf{EvalMod}(x)$. Below is the bird-eye view of the algorithm.

$$\mathsf{pt} \xrightarrow{\mathsf{ModRaise}} \mathsf{pt} + qI \xrightarrow{\mathsf{CoeffToSlot}^{\#}} (\mathsf{pt} + qI + e)^* \xrightarrow{\mathsf{EvalRound}} (qI)^* \xrightarrow{\mathsf{SlotToCoeff}} qI \xrightarrow{\mathsf{Subtract}} \mathsf{pt}.$$

In comparison, the conventional bootstrap algorithm, which is first presented on [7], would be viewed as below.

$$\mathsf{pt} \xrightarrow{\mathsf{ModRaise}} \mathsf{pt} + qI \xrightarrow{\mathsf{CoeffToSlot}} (\mathsf{pt} + qI)^* \xrightarrow{\mathsf{EvalMod}} (\mathsf{pt})^* \xrightarrow{\mathsf{SlotToCoeff}} \mathsf{pt}.$$

The conventional circuit consists of ModRaise, CoeffToSlot, EvalMod and SlotToCoeff. CoeffToSlot is a sequence of DFTmatrix multiplications. As the matrix elements are scaled up to integers with full scale factor Δ (e.g. 2^{60} or 2^{50}), each matrix multiplication consumes modulus bits. When d number of matrices are multiplied, CoeffToSlot consumes Δ^d modulus. The multiplication results modraised plaintext on slot-side, which is often denoted as pt+ qI. EvalMod refers to the modular reduction $\mathsf{pt} + qI \equiv \mathsf{pt} (\bmod q)$, so that $\mathsf{EvalMod}(\mathsf{pt} + qI) = \mathsf{pt}$. The following step, SlotToCoeff, computes the desired result of plaintext on coefficent-side.

The proposed circuit performs CoeffToSlot$^{\#}$ instead of CoeffToSlot, which utilizes small scale factor $\widetilde{\Delta} \ll \Delta$, which reduces modulus consumption to $\widetilde{\Delta}^d$. In exchange for the modulus reduction, a non-negligible error e is appended to $pt + qI$.

The following step of the proposed algorithm is EvalRound, which refers to the rounding operation, so that $\mathsf{EvalRound}(\mathsf{pt}+qI) = qI$ under assumption $\|\mathsf{pt}\| \ll q$. As EvalRound is piecewise constant, $\mathsf{EvalRound}(\mathsf{pt} + qI + e) = \mathsf{EvalRound}(\mathsf{pt} + qI) = qI$ when $\|\mathsf{pt} + e\|$ remains to be much smaller than q. In other words, the error from the small scale factor is annihilated by EvalRound, allowing the use of the small scale factor while keeping the accuracy. This is the reason why we use EvalRound instead of EvalMod, which propagates error as $\mathsf{EvalMod}(\mathsf{pt}+qI+e) = \mathsf{pt} + e$ and corrupts the overall accuracy.

The output ciphertext of EvalRound then goes into SlotToCoeff, resulting a ciphertext encrypting qI in the coefficient side. So the extra Subtract step is needed for subtracting it from the ciphertext originally resulting from the ModRaise step, encrypting $\mathsf{pt} + qI$, to get the final ciphertext encrypting pt.

To sum up, our proposed circuit consists of ModRaise, CoeffToSlot, EvalRound, SlotToCoeff and Subtract. Since the subtraction is ignorable compared to the overall cost, our proposal is equivalent to the conventional circuit in computational cost, while taking the reduced scale factor $\widetilde{\Delta}$ on CoeffToSlot$^{\#}$ that saves modulus and levels.

1.3 Related Works

Bootstrapping of the CKKS scheme was first introduced in [7]. The notions of evaluating DFT/iDFTmatrix homomorphically and evaluating modular reduction via polynomial approximation of trigonometric function were proposed here. In order to improve the time complexity of the linear transformations, FFT-like decomposition was adopted in [5] and [17]. Since then, numerous studies [5,17–19,21,23] have been conducted to improve the approximation of a modular reduction function. Recently, the use of sine series to reduce the error caused by approximating a trigonometric function was presented in [20] and the method of directly approximating a modular reduction function while minimizing error variance was presented in [22]. Independently, using double hoisting technique to reduce the computation time of homomorphic linear transformation was proposed in [1].

2 Preliminaries

2.1 Encoding and Decoding

In this subsection and what follows, we review the basic CKKS scheme([8]); it will provide us a bird's-eye view of the entire scheme, and it also serves us to fix notations used in our discussions hereafter. For a power-of-two N, denote by $R = \mathbb{Z}[x]/(x^N + 1)$, the ring of integers of the $2N$-th cyclotomic field, which is a fundamental ring for the CKKS scheme and the RLWE problem the CKKS scheme is based on. For a positive q, let $R_q = R/qR = \mathbb{Z}_q[x]/(x^N + 1)$. Here N is determined at the parameter selection step of the CKKS scheme. A CKKS ciphertext can encrypt a complex vector of a power-of-two length which is maximally $N/2$. This vector is called a *(complex) message*, and its encryption is called a ciphertext. Here for the ease of description, we assume every message has an exact length of $N/2$.

Let ζ be a primitive $2N$-th root of unity contained in $\mathbb{C}$, e.g., $\zeta = \exp(\pi\sqrt{-1}/N)$, where $\sqrt{-1}$ is a complex imaginary unit. For integers i, write $\zeta_i := \zeta^{5^i}$. The map

$$\mathsf{DFT}_N : \mathbb{R}[x]/(x^N + 1) \to \mathbb{C}^{N/2}, \quad m(x) \mapsto (m(\zeta_0), m(\zeta_1), \cdots, m(\zeta_{N/2-1})) \quad (2)$$

is known to be an isomorphism by [5], with inverse iDFT_N. When the dimension N is understood, we also omit the subscript N so we write $\mathsf{DFT} = \mathsf{DFT}_N$ and $\mathsf{iDFT} = \mathsf{iDFT}_N$. With these algebraic maps, we can encode a complex message $\mathbf{z} \in \mathbb{C}^{N/2}$ to a *plaintext* $\mathsf{pt} \in R$ and in reverse decode from pt to $\mathbf{z}$.

- $\mathsf{Encode}(\mathbf{z}; \Delta)$. For an $N/2$-dimensional vector $\mathbf{z}$ of complex numbers and a scale factor Δ, the encoding process first transforms $\mathbf{z}$ to a polynomial in $\mathbb{R}[x]/(x^N + 1)$ and quantize it into an element of R. It returns

$$\mathsf{pt} = \mathsf{Encode}(\mathbf{z}; \Delta) = \lfloor \Delta \cdot \mathsf{iDFT}(\mathbf{z}) \rceil, \quad (3)$$

  where $\lfloor \cdot \rceil$ is the coefficient-wise rounding to the nearest integers.
- $\mathsf{Decode}(\mathsf{pt}; \Delta)$. For a plaintext pt and its scale factor Δ, the decoding process returns

$$\mathbf{z} = \mathsf{Decode}(\mathsf{pt}; \Delta) = \mathsf{DFT}(\mathsf{pt}/\Delta). \quad (4)$$

  Here the polynomial pt/Δ is computed in $\mathbb{R}[x]/(x^N + 1)$.

2.2 Basic Operations of the CKKS Scheme

Let χ_{key} be the distribution that outputs polynomials in R with coefficients in $\{-1, 0, 1\}$ with a fixed Hamming weight (the number of nonzero coefficients). By χ_{err} and χ_{enc} denote discrete Gaussian distribution with mean 0 and with some fixed standard deviation.

- **SetUp**. $\mathsf{Params} \leftarrow \mathsf{SetUp}(1^\lambda)$. Take a security level λ as an input and return the public parameters Params such as the ciphertext dimension N and the chain of moduli $Q_0 < Q_1 < \cdots < Q_L$ with maximal level L.

- **Key Generation**. $(\mathsf{sk}, \mathsf{pk}) \leftarrow \mathsf{KeyGen}(\mathsf{Params})$. Take Params and output a pair of a secret key $\mathsf{sk} = (1, s) \in R \times R$ and an encryption key $\mathsf{pk} = (\mathsf{pk}_0, \mathsf{pk}_1) \in R_{Q_L} \times R_{Q_L}$. More precisely,
  - Sample $s \leftarrow \chi_{\text{key}}$, and set $\mathsf{sk} = (1, s) \in R \times R$. For convenience, denote by h the Hamming weight of the polynomial s. This is fixed once Params has been set.
  - Sample $\mathsf{pk}_1 \leftarrow R_{Q_L}$ and $e \leftarrow \chi_{\text{err}}$. Output $\mathsf{pk} = (\mathsf{pk}_0 := [-\mathsf{pk}_1 \cdot s + e]_{Q_L}, \mathsf{pk}_1)$.
- **Switching Key Generation**. $\mathsf{swk}_{\mathsf{sk}' \to \mathsf{sk}} \leftarrow \mathsf{KSGen}_{\mathsf{sk}}(\mathsf{sk}')$. Given two secret keys $\mathsf{sk} = (1, s)$ and $\mathsf{sk}' = (1, s')$, sample $a \leftarrow R_{PQ_L}$ with auxiliary modulus P and $e \leftarrow \chi_{\text{err}}$ and output $\mathsf{swk}_{\mathsf{sk}' \to \mathsf{sk}} := (\mathsf{swk}_0, \mathsf{swk}_1)$ with $\mathsf{swk}_1 = a$ and $\mathsf{swk}_0 = -a \cdot s + e + P \cdot s' \pmod{PQ_L}$.
  - Set the relinearization key as $\mathsf{rlk} := \mathsf{KSGen}_{\mathsf{sk}}(s^2)$.
  - Set the rotation keys for j-step rotation as $\mathsf{rk}_j := \mathsf{KSGen}_{\mathsf{sk}}(s(x^{5^j}))$ for $1 \leq j < N/2$.
- **Encryption**. $\mathsf{ct} \leftarrow \mathsf{Enc}_{\mathsf{pk}}(\mathsf{pt})$. Given a plaintext pt given by a polynomial $m(x) \in R$, sample $v \leftarrow \chi_{\text{enc}}$ and $e_0, e_1 \leftarrow \chi_{\text{err}}$, output the ciphertext $\mathsf{ct} = v \cdot \mathsf{pk} + (m(x) + e_0, e_1) \pmod{Q_L}$.
- **Decryption**. $\mathsf{pt} \leftarrow \mathsf{Dec}_{\mathsf{sk}}(\mathsf{ct})$. Given a ciphertext $\mathsf{ct} = (\mathsf{ct}_0, \mathsf{ct}_1)$, output the plaintext $\mathsf{pt} = [\langle \mathsf{ct}, \mathsf{sk} \rangle]_{Q_0} = [\mathsf{ct}_0 + \mathsf{ct}_1 \cdot s]_{Q_0}$, where Q_0 is the modulus for level zero.
- **Addition and Subtraction**. $\mathsf{ct}_{\text{add}}, \mathsf{ct}_{\text{sub}} \leftarrow \mathsf{Add}(\mathsf{ct}, \mathsf{ct}'), \mathsf{Sub}(\mathsf{ct}, \mathsf{ct}')$, respectively. Given two ciphertexts ct and ct' in $R_{Q_\ell}^2$, output the ciphertext $\mathsf{ct}_{\text{add}} = [\mathsf{ct} + \mathsf{ct}']_{Q_\ell}$ and $\mathsf{ct}_{\text{sub}} = [\mathsf{ct} - \mathsf{ct}']_{Q_\ell}$. The resulting ciphertext ct_{add} and ct_{sub} are encrypting message vectors $\mathbf{z} + \mathbf{z}'$ and $\mathbf{z} - \mathbf{z}'$, respectively, where $\mathbf{z}$ (resp. $\mathbf{z}'$) is the message for ct (resp. ct').
- **Multiplication**. $\mathsf{ct}_{\text{mult}} \leftarrow \mathsf{Mult}(\mathsf{ct}, \mathsf{ct}')$. Given two ciphertexts $\mathsf{ct} = (c_0, c_1)$ and $\mathsf{ct}' = (c_0', c_1')$ in $R_{Q_\ell}^2$, output the ciphertext $\mathsf{ct}_{\text{mult}} := (c_0 c_0', c_1 c_0' + c_0 c_1', c_1 c_1')$. This seemingly unconventional ciphertext can be decrypted by taking the inner product with $(1, s, s^2)$, where $\mathsf{sk} = (1, s)$ is the secret key. One can get rid of the additional component $c_1 c_1'$ which is multiplied by the component s^2 of the secret key by applying the key switching algorithm with the relinearization key rlk.
- **Rotation**. $\mathsf{ct}_{\text{rot},\, j} \leftarrow \mathsf{Rot}_j(\mathsf{ct})$. Given a ciphertext $\mathsf{ct} = (c_0, c_1) \in R_{Q_\ell}^2$, output $\mathsf{ct}_{\text{rot},\, j} := (c_0(x^{5^j}), c_1(x^{5^j}))$. The resulting ciphertext $\mathsf{ct}_{\text{rot},\, j}$ can be decrypted with the secret key $(1, s(x^{5^j}))$ where $(1, s)$ is the secret key for the original ciphertext ct. This discrepancy can also be resolved by key switching algorithm and one can transform $\mathsf{ct}_{\text{rot},\, j}$ to another ciphertext with secret key $(1, s)$.
- **Key Switching**. $\mathsf{ct} \leftarrow \mathsf{KS}_{\mathsf{swk}}(\mathsf{ct}')$. Given a ciphertext ct' which decrypts to a message with a secret key sk' and given a switching key $\mathsf{swk} = \mathsf{swk}_{\mathsf{sk}' \to \mathsf{sk}}$ for another secret key sk, output another ciphertext ct which decrypts to the same message as ct' but with secret key sk. This process is used for eliminating the s^2 term after the multiplication process and also for transforming the result of the rotation process.

- **Rescaling.** $\mathsf{ct}_{\mathsf{rs}} \leftarrow \mathsf{RS}(\ell, \mathsf{ct})$. For a given ciphertext $\mathsf{ct} \in R^2_{Q_\ell}$, output $\mathsf{ct}_{\mathsf{rs}} = \lfloor q_\ell^{-1}\mathsf{ct} \rceil \pmod{Q_{\ell-1}}$, where $Q_\ell = q_\ell \cdot Q_{\ell-1}$. Rescaling process is used for reducing the error by throwing off the LSB of the ciphertext, and at the same time it makes the ciphertext to keep its scaling factor Δ in the similar scale as computation progresses.

2.3 Full CKKS Homomorphic Encryption Scheme and Bootstrapping

For a homomorphic encryption scheme to be used in practice, it must support the computation of complicated circuits. It is only possible if it can conduct homomorphic operations with sufficient efficiency, and if it can compute arbitrarily deep circuits. A major problem for homomorphic encryption schemes is that certain amount of noise must have been accumulated when homomorphic operations proceed. As a result, after certain number of homomorphic operations has been done, HE ciphertexts are "deteriorated" so that it is impossible to conduct further homomorphic multiplications on the ciphertexts. In practice, this phenomenon of deterioration reveals itself as the modulus of the ciphertexts being decreased. For example, in the CKKS scheme, any multiplication requires a rescaling operation to keep the noise under control, and each rescaling consumes certain amount of ciphertext modulus.

The notion of *fully homomorphic encryption*, or in short FHE, indicates homomorphic encryption schemes for which the deterioration problem is resolved, and thus FHE allows their users to do multiplication on their ciphertexts indefinitely. Craig Gentry, in [15], proposed an algorithm for a FHE scheme. His method to renew the deteriorated ciphertexts is called *recryption*, and it is conducted by evaluating the decryption circuits homomorphically. He called HE schemes equipped with such a recryption algorithm *bootstrappable*, and we use the terminology *bootstrapping* to indicate an algorithm to transform such deteriorated ciphertexts to refreshed ciphertexts so one can continue to apply homomorphic operations to them. After [15], an enormous amount of contributions was made to improve Gentry's original idea and to apply bootstrapping to existing HE schemes: [2–4,6,8–14,16].

Bootstrapping in the CKKS Scheme. As decryption circuit of the CKKS scheme involves modular reduction, the bootstrapping in the CKKS scheme is reduced to the problem of performing modular reduction: see [7]. A typical way to achieve bootstrapping in the CKKS homomorphic encryption scheme consists of two steps: we first raise the modulus of the ciphertext to the maximal one, and take a modular reduction modulo the modulus the ciphertext begins with. Suppose that a CKKS ciphertext ct is given with modulus q, encrypting a plaintext $\mathsf{pt} \in R_q$. Mathematically, raising the modulus of ct is equivalent to just treating the same ciphertext ct having a bigger modulus Q. In the perspective of its encrypted plaintext, however, ct with modulus Q now decrypts to $\mathsf{pt} + qI$, where $I \in R$ is a polynomial with sufficiently small size of coefficients. In order to retain the original plaintext, one needs to do modular reduction modulo q at the plaintext side of ct, and this needs to be done in "homomorphic" way, because the decryption is needed to see the plaintext ct has encrypted, and it is not accessible unless the secret key is known.

One problem is the inconsistency at which such two operations take places: the "raising modulus" or ModRaise operation takes place at the plaintext side (or *coefficient side*) so it transforms ct from encrypting pt to a ciphertext encrypting $\mathsf{pt}+qI$, and the "evaluating modular reduction" or EvalMod step takes places at the message side (or *slot side*), because it consists of homomorphic operations like addition/subtraction, multiplication and rotation. So one needs to move coefficients of the plaintext to slot side and *vice versa*, and these can be achieved using two additional steps CoeffToSlot and SlotToCoeff.

Let ct be a ciphertext encrypting a plaintext pt that is so deteriorated that one cannot proceed further multiplication on ct, i.e. ct has ground level, of level 0 with ground modulus q_0. The ciphertext ct is an input of the bootstrapping process.

- ModRaise. Raise the ciphertext modulus from q_0 to the maximal modulus Q_L, which is determined at SetUp step. We can see that the resulting ciphertext now encrypts $\mathsf{pt} + q_0 I$ where $I \in R$ is a polynomial with small integer coefficients.
- CoeffToSlot. Apply iDFThomomorphically to transfer the additional $q_0 I$ part of the plaintext to the slot side. Being linear map, one can do this with cost of couples of homomorphic multiplications and rotations.
- EvalMod. In this step, conduct the modular reduction $[\cdot]_{q_0}$ at the encrypted message of the ciphertext. Since only algebraic operations (addition/subtraction, multiplication and rotation) are provided in the CKKS scheme, one can do this by approximating the modular reduction function with some polynomial function. After the first feasible algorithmic breakthrough [7], this has been a major topic in homomorphic encryption to improve the quality of such approximation: see [1,5,17,18,21–23].
- SlotToCoeff. Final step of bootstrapping is to restore message by transferring the message of EvalMod'd ciphertext to its original space, the coefficient side. Naturally this is the inverse process of CoeffToSlot, and thus this can be done with applying DFThomomorphically.

2.4 On Decomposition of DFT/iDFT Matrices

In CoeffToSlot and SlotToCoeff steps of the bootstrapping algorithm, one computes linear transformations homomorphically on the input ciphertexts, and the linear transformations are represented by the iDFTand DFTmatrices, respectively. Although mathematically they are just matrix-vector multiplications, their homomorphic computations involve homomorphic rotations of various indices and become infeasible while the ciphertext dimension grows exponentially.

In [17], the authors made some clever use of the rich structures of DFTand iDFTto decompose DFTand iDFTinto the products of several sparse block diagonal matrices; it turns out that the homomorphic evaluation of these sequences of matrix-vector multiplications reduces their homomorphic constant multiplication complexity from $O(n)$ to $O(r \log_r n)$ and their homomorphic rotation complexity from $O(\sqrt{n})$ to $O(\sqrt{r} \log_r n)$ (see §5 in [17]), where n is the number of slots encrypted in the ciphertext and r is the radix of the decomposition. Of course, it does not come for free; the multiplicative depth taken in the CoeffToSlot and SlotToCoeff steps gets larger from 1 to $O(\log_r n)$.

In a nutshell, our new bootstrapping algorithm actually reduces this additional multiplicative depth by degrading CoeffToSlot, in such a way that the precision of the final output of the bootstrapping is on par with the original method (Table 1).

3 Error Analysis of CoeffToSlot

CoeffToSlot is basically a procedure to take a matrix multiplication on the message. To do so in integer arithmetic, the real numbers of the matrix is multiplied by a large number Δ, so called scaling factor, and rounded to integers. This section is devoted to a thorough analysis on the error of the rounding.

There are three types of errors in CoeffToSlot, the rounding error, the key switching error, and the rescaling error. One of the very common technique in CoeffToSlot is lazy rescaling, which delays all the rescalings and rescale once only at the end of CoeffToSlot. This technique enables us to remove the effect of the key switching error. In this sense, we only have to consider the remaining two types of errors. Hence, in this section, we analyze the CoeffToSlot error in the plaintext side, instead of in the ciphertext side.

3.1 Rounding Error in Matrix Multiplication

In this section, we estimate the rounding error which occurs when we homomorphically compute matrix multiplication. Encoding a message m into a plaintext pt involves rounding. To focus on the rounding error, we can think of a plaintext without rounding pt^{raw}.

$$\mathsf{pt} = \lfloor \mathsf{iDFT}(z) \cdot \Delta \rceil, \quad \mathsf{pt}^{raw} = \mathsf{iDFT}(z) \cdot \Delta,$$

Let the rounding error $e = \mathsf{pt}^{raw} - \mathsf{pt}$. Note that each entry of the error $[e]_i$ belongs to $[-\frac{1}{2}, \frac{1}{2})$ and distributed uniformly through the range.

When homomorphically computing a matrix multiplication $z \mapsto Az$, we compute

$$Az = V_1 \odot z_1 + V_2 \odot z_2 + \cdots + V_k \odot z_k$$

where V_i are the diagonals of the matrix A ($k < N$ if A is sparse), and z_i are the rotated copies of z, to match V_i. This computation corresponds to the plaintext computation

$$\mathsf{pt}_{Az} = \mathsf{pt}_{V_1} * \mathsf{pt}_{z_1} + \cdots + \mathsf{pt}_{V_k} * \mathsf{pt}_{z_k}$$

where pt_{V_i} are encoded with same scale factor Δ_A, so that the scale factor of pt_{A_z} becomes $\Delta_A \Delta_z$.

Here each V_i is being rounded during the encoding of pt_{V_i}. Using the notations above, we can split the rounding error of matrix multiplication into parts as below. To focus on only the rounding error that occurs when multiplying A, we ignore the rounding error of z which has been occurred before the multiplication. The rounding error e_{Az} can be described as

$$
\begin{aligned}
e_{Az} = \mathsf{pt}_{Az}^{raw} - \mathsf{pt}_{Az} &= \sum_{i=1}^{k} \mathsf{pt}_{V_i}^{raw} * \mathsf{pt}_{z_i} - \sum_{i=1}^{k} \mathsf{pt}_{V_i} * \mathsf{pt}_{z_i} \\
&= \sum_{i=1}^{k} (pt_{V_i}^{raw} - \mathsf{pt}_{V_i}) * \mathsf{pt}_{z_i} = \sum_{i=1}^{k} e_{V_i} * \mathsf{pt}_{z_i}.
\end{aligned}
$$

To take a deeper look into each entry of the sum, we introduce Lemma 1 and Lemma 2 as stated below.

Lemma 1 (convolution of pt and its error). *Let $X_0, \cdots, X_{N-1}$ be independent and identically distributed (i.i.d.) random variables following the uniform distribution $U\left(-\frac{1}{2}, \frac{1}{2}\right)$ on range $\left(-\frac{1}{2}, \frac{1}{2}\right)$ and $X \in \mathbb{R}[x] / \left(x^N + 1\right)$ be a random polynomial with its i-th coefficient being X_i, for all i. Suppose $\mathsf{pt} \in \mathbb{R}[x]/(x^N + 1)$ is given. Then $Y = \mathsf{pt} * X \in \mathbb{R}[x]/x^N + 1$ satisfies*

$$
\mathbb{E}\left(\|Y\|^2\right) = \frac{N}{12} \|\mathsf{pt}\|^2.
$$

Proof. The negative-wrapped convolution is defined as

$$
Y_i = \sum_{j=0}^{i} \mathsf{pt}_j X_{i-j} - \sum_{j=i+1}^{N-1} \mathsf{pt}_j \mathsf{X}_{i-j+N}
$$

or shortly

$$
Y_i = \sum_{j=0}^{N-1} \mathsf{sgn}_{i-j} \mathsf{pt}_j \mathsf{X}_{[i-j]_N}.
$$

where $\mathsf{sgn}_x = \begin{cases} 1, & \text{if } x \geq 0 \\ -1, & \text{otherwise} \end{cases}$

Using the additivity of expectation, we have the following.

$$
\begin{aligned}
\mathbb{E}\left(\|Y\|^2\right) &= \mathbb{E}\left(\sum_{i=0}^{N-1} Y_i^2\right) = \mathbb{E}\left(\sum_{i=0}^{N-1} \left(\sum_{j=0}^{N-1} \mathsf{sgn}_{i-j} \cdot \mathsf{pt}_j \mathsf{X}_{[i-j]_N}\right)^2\right) \\
&= \mathbb{E}\left(\sum_{i=0}^{N-1} \left(\sum_{j=0}^{N-1} \mathsf{pt}_j^2 \mathsf{X}_{[i-j]_N}^2 + \sum_{j=0}^{N-1} \sum_{k \neq j} \mathsf{sgn}_{i-j} \cdot \mathsf{sgn}_{i-k} \cdot \mathsf{pt}_j \mathsf{pt}_k X_{[i-j]_N} X_{[i-k]_N}\right)\right) \\
&= \sum_{i=0}^{N-1} \sum_{j=0}^{N-1} \mathsf{pt}_j^2 \cdot \mathbb{E}\left(X_{[i-j]_N}^2\right) + \sum_{i=0}^{N-1} \sum_{j=0}^{N-1} \sum_{k \neq j} \mathsf{sgn}_{i-j} \cdot \mathsf{sgn}_{i-k} \cdot \mathsf{pt}_j \mathsf{pt}_k \cdot \mathbb{E}\left(X_{[i-j]_N}\right) \mathbb{E}\left(X_{[i-k]_N}\right)
\end{aligned}
$$

Since X_j, X_k are independent and pt_j are fixed,

$$= \sum_{i=0}^{N-1}\sum_{j=0}^{N-1} \mathsf{pt}_j^2 \mathbb{E}(X_{[i-j]_N}^2) = \sum_{i=0}^{N-1} ||\mathsf{pt}||_2^2 \cdot \frac{1}{12} = \frac{N}{12} \cdot ||\mathsf{pt}||_2^2$$

The above result with single plaintext can be generalized to the following with multiple plaintexts.

Lemma 2 (Sum of convolutions of $\mathsf{pt}_1, \cdots, \mathsf{pt}_k$ and error). *Suppose $\mathsf{pt}_1, \cdots, \mathsf{pt}_k \in \mathbb{R}[x]/(x^N+1)$ are given with $\|\mathsf{pt}_1\| = \cdots = \|\mathsf{pt}_k\|$. Let X_{ij} be i.i.d. following $U\left(-\frac{1}{2}, \frac{1}{2}\right)$, $X_i = [X_{i,0}, \cdots, X_{i,N-1}] \in \mathbb{R}[x]/(x^N+1)$ and $Y_i = X_i * \mathsf{pt}_i$ for $i = 1, \cdots, k$ and $j = 0, \cdots, N-1$. Then we have*

$$\mathbb{E}\left(\|Y_1 + \cdots + Y_k\|^2\right) = \frac{kN}{12}\|\mathsf{pt}_1\|^2.$$

Proof. Note that

$$\begin{aligned}
\|Y_1 + \cdots + Y_k\|^2 &= \sum_{j=0}^{N-1}\left(\sum_{i=1}^{k} Y_{ij}\right)^2 \\
&= \sum_{j=0}^{N-1}\left(\sum_{i=1}^{k} Y_{ij}^2 + \sum_{i=1}^{k}\sum_{l\neq i} Y_{ij}Y_{lj}\right) \\
&= \sum_{i=1}^{k}\|Y_i\|^2 + \sum_{j=0}^{N-1}\sum_{i=1}^{k}\sum_{l\neq i} Y_{ij}Y_{lj}.
\end{aligned}$$

For the single entry of $Y_{ij}Y_{lj}$, the following holds.

$$\begin{aligned}
\mathbb{E}(Y_{ij}Y_{lj}) &= \mathbb{E}\left(\left(\sum_{m=0}^{N-1} \mathsf{sgn}_{j-m} \cdot \mathsf{pt}_{im}\mathsf{X}_{i[j-m]_N}\right)\left(\sum_{o=0}^{N-1} \mathsf{sgn}_{j-o} \cdot \mathsf{pt}_{lo}\mathsf{X}_{l[j-o]_N}\right)\right) \\
&= \mathbb{E}\left(\sum_{m=0}^{N-1}\sum_{o=0}^{N-1} \mathsf{sgn}_{j-m}\mathsf{sgn}_{j-o} \cdot \mathsf{pt}_{im}\mathsf{pt}_{lo}\mathsf{X}_{i[j-m]_N}\mathsf{X}_{l[j-o]_N}\right) \\
&= \sum_{m=0}^{N-1}\sum_{o=0}^{N-1} \mathsf{sgn}_{j-m}\mathsf{sgn}_{j-o} \cdot \mathsf{pt}_{im}\mathsf{pt}_{lo}\mathbb{E}\left(\mathsf{X}_{i[j-m]_N}\mathsf{X}_{l[j-o]_N}\right) = 0.
\end{aligned}$$

Therefore,

$$\begin{aligned}
\mathbb{E}\left(\|Y_1 + \cdots + Y_k\|^2\right) &= \mathbb{E}\left(\sum_{i=1}^{k}\|Y_i\|^2 + \sum_{j=0}^{N-1}\sum_{i=1}^{k}\sum_{l\neq i} Y_{ij}Y_{lj}\right) \\
&= \sum_{i=1}^{k}\mathbb{E}\left(\|Y_i\|^2\right) + \sum_{j=0}^{N-1}\sum_{i=1}^{k}\sum_{l\neq i}\mathbb{E}(Y_{ij}Y_{lj}) \\
&= \sum_{i=1}^{k}\mathbb{E}\left(\|Y_i\|^2\right) = \sum_{i=1}^{k}\frac{N}{12}\|\mathsf{pt}_i\|^2 = \frac{kN}{12}\|\mathsf{pt}_1\|^2.
\end{aligned}$$

Example 1. We verify Lemma 2 by experiment in cases of $N = 2^{15}$ and 2^{16}. k and $[\mathsf{pt}_i]_{i=1,\cdots,k}$ is set to 16 and the ith rotated plaintexts of the plaintext pt, which is the encoding of $z \in \mathbb{C}^{N/2}$ given by $z_i = \frac{\cos(i)}{\sqrt{2}} + \frac{\sin(i)}{\sqrt{-2}}$. The empirical mean of 100 trials and the expectation are quite similar and their relative differences are less than 10^{-3}, as stated in the following table. Figure 1 depicts the trials and show that the deviations of the empirical observation to the estimation of Lemma 2 are less than 2.5% and 1.5%, when $N = 2^{15}$ and 2^{16}, respectively.

N	$\mathbb{E}\left(\|Y_1 + \cdots + Y_k\|^2\right)$	$\mathbb{E}^{\text{empirical}}\left(\|Y_1 + \cdots + Y_k\|^2\right)$	$\left\lvert\frac{\mathbb{E}\left(\|Y_1+\cdots+Y_k\|^2\right)-\mathbb{E}^{\text{empirical}}\left(\|Y_1+\cdots+Y_k\|^2\right)}{\mathbb{E}\left(\left\|Y_1+\cdots+Y_k^2\right\|\right)}\right\rvert$
2^{15}	2.7692×10^{34}	2.7718×10^{34}	9.2777×10^{-4}
2^{16}	5.5384×10^{34}	5.5430×10^{34}	8.1469×10^{-4}

Remark 1.

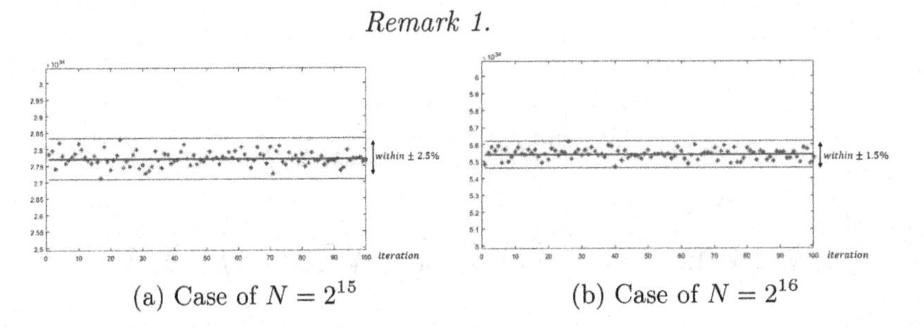

(a) Case of $N = 2^{15}$ (b) Case of $N = 2^{16}$

Fig. 1. 100 trials of $\|Y_1 + \cdots + Y_k\|^2$ in Example 1 that are fairly close to the expectation $\frac{kN}{12}\|\mathsf{pt}_1\|^2$ stated in Lemma 2. The deviation of the trials to the expectation decreases as N increases.

In this section, to estimate the magnitude of error, we eagerly utilize this approximation on $\|Y_1 + \cdots + Y_k\|$ as below.

$$\|Y_1 + \cdots + Y_k\| = \sqrt{\|Y_1 + \cdots + Y_k\|^2} \approx \sqrt{\mathbb{E}\left(\|Y_1 + \cdots + Y_k\|^2\right)} = \sqrt{\frac{kn}{12}}\|\mathsf{pt}\|.$$

Recall that the following equality on the matrix multiplication error holds :

$$e_{Az} = \sum_{i=1}^{k} e_{V_i} * \mathsf{pt}_{z_i}.$$

Applying Lemma 2 on e_{Az}, we prove the following Theorem 1.

Theorem 1. *Let $A \in \mathbb{C}^{\frac{N}{2}\times\frac{N}{2}}$ be a matrix with diagonals $V_1, \cdots, V_k$, so that $Az = V_1 \odot z_1 + V_2 \odot z_2 + \cdots + V_k \odot z_k$ where each z_i is a rotation of $z \in \mathbb{C}^{N/2}$. Assume that A and z are encoded into plaintexts by scale factor Δ_A and Δ_z respectively. Then*

$$\left\|Az - \widetilde{Az}\right\| \approx \sqrt{\frac{kN}{12}\frac{1}{\Delta_A}}\|z\|$$

Proof. Let pt_zbe the plaintext encoding z and $\mathsf{pt}_{V_1}, \cdots, \mathsf{pt}_{V_k}$ be the plaintext encoding $V_1, \cdots, V_k$, respectively.

Recall that the rounding error of matrix multiplication $e_{Az} = \mathsf{pt}_{Az}^{raw} - \mathsf{pt}_{Az} = \sum_{i=1}^{k} e_{V_i} * \mathsf{pt}_{z_i}$. Since we can assume that each entry of e_{V_i} follows $U(-\frac{1}{2}, \frac{1}{2})$ and $\|\mathsf{pt}_{z_1}\| = \cdots = \|\mathsf{pt}_{z_k}\|$, we can apply Lemma 2 on $\sum_{i=1}^{k} e_{V_i} * \mathsf{pt}_{z_i}$.

$$\left\| \sum_{i=1}^{k} e_{V_i} * \mathsf{pt}_{z_i} \right\| \approx \sqrt{\frac{kN}{12}} \|\mathsf{pt}_z\|$$

Note that the following holds for any $z \in \mathbb{C}^{N/2}$ and $\mathsf{pt} = \mathsf{Encode}(\mathbf{z}; \Delta_z)$.

$$\|z\| \approx \left\| \frac{\mathsf{DFT}(\mathsf{pt})}{\Delta_z} \right\| = \frac{1}{\Delta_z} \|\mathsf{DFT}(\mathsf{pt})\| = \frac{1}{\Delta_z} \sqrt{\frac{N}{2}} \|\mathsf{pt}\|$$

Therefore,

$$\left\| Az - \widetilde{Az} \right\| = \frac{1}{\Delta_{Az}} \sqrt{\frac{N}{2}} \left\| \mathsf{pt}_{Az-\widetilde{Az}} \right\| = \frac{1}{\Delta_A \Delta_z} \sqrt{\frac{N}{2}} \|\mathsf{pt}_{Az}^{raw} - \mathsf{pt}_{Az}\|$$

$$\approx \frac{1}{\Delta_A \Delta_z} \sqrt{\frac{N}{2}} \sqrt{\frac{kN}{12}} \|\mathsf{pt}_z\| = \frac{1}{\Delta_A} \sqrt{\frac{kN}{12}} \left(\frac{1}{\Delta_z} \sqrt{\frac{N}{2}} \|\mathsf{pt}_z\| \right) \approx \frac{1}{\Delta_A} \sqrt{\frac{kN}{12}} \|z\|$$

For convenience, we denote $\frac{1}{\Delta_A} \sqrt{\frac{kN}{12}}$ as p_A so that the following holds :

$$\left\| Az - \widetilde{Az} \right\| \approx p_A \|z\| .$$

Theorem 1, which is the error analysis of single matrix multiplication, can be applied to the case of homomorphically multiplying the two matrices A and B successively, i.e. $z \mapsto Az \mapsto BAz$. The first type of rounding error will occur during the multiplication of z by A. Let $\widetilde{Az}$ be the actual result of such computation, which contains the rounding error. The second type of rounding error occurs during the multiplication of $\widetilde{Az}$ by B. Let $\widetilde{B\widetilde{Az}}$ be the result of such computation, which contains the rounding error with respect to the matrix multiplication by B. The total error generalized to a series of matrix multiplications in a straightforward manner as follows.

Theorem 2 (Rounding error in serial matrix multiplication). *Let $A_1, \cdots, A_d \in \mathbb{C}^{N/2 \times N/2}$ and let $\mathbf{z} \in \mathbb{C}^{N/2}$. Let p_i be the multiplier in Theorem 1, i.e. $p_i = \frac{1}{\Delta_{A_i}} \sqrt{\frac{k_i \cdot N}{12}}$. Then we have*

$$\left\| A_d \cdots A_1 \mathbf{z} - (\widetilde{A_d \cdots \widetilde{A_1 \mathbf{z}}}) \right\| \lesssim \left(\sum_{i=1}^{d} p_i \|A_i\|^{-1} \right) \cdot \prod_{i=1}^{d} \|A_i\| \cdot \|\mathbf{z}\|$$

Proof. We use an induction on d. The base case with $d = 1$ is just Theorem 1. Now suppose the theorem holds up to $d-1$. Write $B := A_d \cdots A_2$. Then we have

$$\left\| A_d \cdots A_1 \mathbf{z} - \left(A_d \cdots \widetilde{\widetilde{A_1 \mathbf{z}}} \right) \right\| \leq \left\| B A_1 \mathbf{z} - B \widetilde{A_1 \mathbf{z}} \right\| + \left\| B \widetilde{A_1 \mathbf{z}} - \left(A_d \cdots \widetilde{\widetilde{A_1 \mathbf{z}}} \right) \right\|,$$

by the triangular inequality. Then

$$\left\| B A_1 \mathbf{z} - B \widetilde{A_1 \mathbf{z}} \right\| \lesssim \|B\| \cdot p_1 \cdot \|\mathbf{z}\|$$

by Theorem 1 and

$$\left\| B \widetilde{A_1 \mathbf{z}} - \left(A_d \cdots \widetilde{\widetilde{A_1 \mathbf{z}}} \right) \right\| \lesssim \left(\sum_{i=2}^{d} p_i \|A_i\|^{-1} \right) \prod_{i=2}^{d} \|A_i\| \cdot \left\| \widetilde{A_1 \mathbf{z}} \right\|$$

by the induction hypothesis. Since $p_1 \ll 1$, we get $\left\| \widetilde{A_1 \mathbf{z}} \right\| \leq \|A_1 \mathbf{z}\| + \left\| A_1 \mathbf{z} - \widetilde{A_1 \mathbf{z}} \right\| \leq \|A_1\| \|\mathbf{z}\| + p_1 \|\mathbf{z}\| \approx \|A_1\| \|\mathbf{z}\|$, and hence

$$\left\| A_d \cdots A_1 \mathbf{z} - \left(A_d \cdots \widetilde{\widetilde{A_1 \mathbf{z}}} \right) \right\| \lesssim \left(\sum_{i=1}^{d} p_i \|A_i\|^{-1} \right) \cdot \prod_{i=1}^{d} \|A_i\| \cdot \|\mathbf{z}\|,$$

as expected.

Example 2. We empirically verify Theorem 2 in cases of $N = 2^{15}, 2^{16}$. Again, $z \in \mathbb{C}^{N/2}$ is given by $z_i = \frac{\cos(i)}{\sqrt{2}} + \frac{\sin(i)}{\sqrt{-2}}$. To demonstrate the case of CoeffToSlot, we use A the decomposed iDFTmatrices. [17] introduces the decomposition, so that the iDFTmatrix $\frac{1}{N}\overline{U_0^{NR}}^T$ is decomposed into $A_1 \cdot A_2 \cdots A_{\log N - 1}$ and a permutation matrix, where each of A_is have at most 3 diagonals and has norm of $\|A_i\| = \frac{1}{\sqrt{2}}$. z and A are encoded with the scale factor of $\Delta_z = \Delta_A = 2^{50}$ during the homomorphic computation. The following table shows that the observed error of the matrix multiplication is close to and less than the estimate of Theorem 2.

N	$\|A_d \cdots A_1 \mathbf{z} - (A_d \cdots (A_1 \mathbf{z})^\sim)^\sim\|$	$\left(\sum_{i=1}^{d} p_i \|A_i\|^{-1}\right) \cdot \prod_{i=1}^{d} \|A_i\| \cdot \|\mathbf{z}\|$
2^{15}	7.5697×10^{-10}	9.2196×10^{-9}
2^{16}	2.1414×10^{-9}	2.7939×10^{-8}

3.2 CoeffToSlot

As explained in preliminaries, the linear transform of DFTmatrix maps $\frac{\mathsf{pt}}{\Delta}$ to z, so it holds that $z = [U_0 : U_0\sqrt{-1}](\mathsf{pt}/\Delta)$, where $\sqrt{-1}$ is a complex imaginary

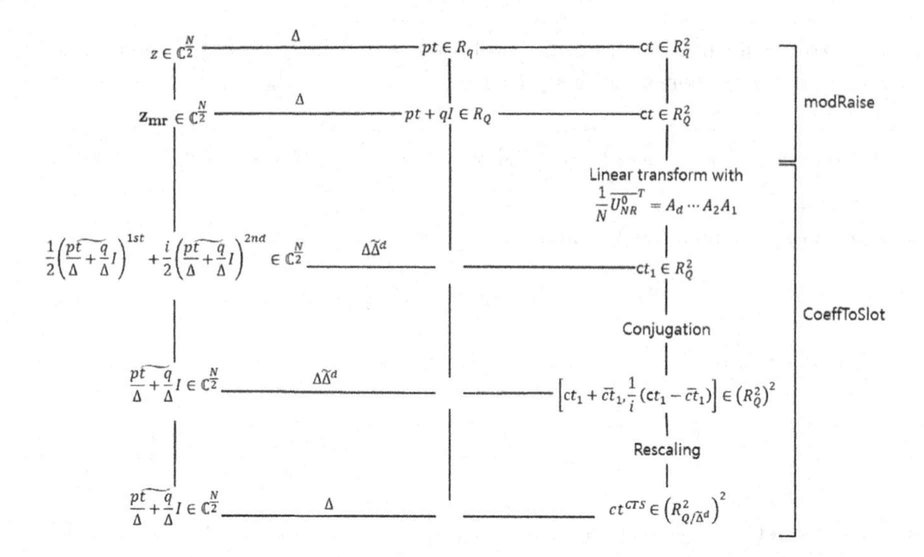

Fig. 2. The diagram illustrates the details of CoeffToSlot procedure. $\widetilde{\Delta}$ is the scale factor to round the real numbers of each matrix $A_i (i = 1, \cdots, d)$ into integers. Because of the rounding errors, the homomorphically calculated message $\widetilde{\frac{\mathsf{pt}}{\Delta} + \frac{q}{\Delta} I}$ does not equal $\frac{\mathsf{pt}}{\Delta} + \frac{q}{\Delta} I$, but approximates it. The error of the approximation is estimated in theorem 3 as $O\left(\frac{1}{\widetilde{\Delta}} N^{1+\frac{1}{2d}} \frac{q}{\Delta}\right)$.

unit and U_0 is the DFTmatrix of size $N/2 \times N/2$. Refer to Sect. 5.1 of [7] for the details. CoeffToSlot is the inversion of the encoding. It calculates the two parts of the plaintext from the message by taking a matrix multiplication and conjugated sums as follows (Fig. 2).

$$z_1 = \frac{1}{N} \overline{U}_0^T z = \frac{1}{2} \left(\frac{\mathsf{pt}^{1st}}{\Delta} + \frac{\mathsf{pt}^{2nd}}{\Delta} \sqrt{-1} \right)$$

$$z_{CTS}^{1st} = z_1 + \overline{z_1} = \frac{\mathsf{pt}^{1st}}{\Delta}$$

$$z_{CTS}^{2nd} = \frac{1}{\sqrt{-1}} (z_1 - \overline{z_1}) = \frac{\mathsf{pt}^{2nd}}{\Delta}$$

In the process of bootstrapping, CoeffToSlot is applied on the ModRaise'd plaintext, which is known to have form of pt+ qI. The result of CoeffToSlot becomes two plaintexts encoding $z_{cts}^{1st} = (\frac{\mathsf{pt}}{\Delta} + \frac{q}{\Delta} I)^{1st}$ and $z_{cts}^{2nd} = (\frac{\mathsf{pt}}{\Delta} + \frac{q}{\Delta} I)^{2nd}$.

On the computation of CoeffToSlot, $\frac{1}{N} \overline{U_0}^T$ is a full matrix of size $N/2 \times N/2$ which is a huge burden to compute naively. In [17], the authors utilized its FFT decomposition

$$\frac{1}{N}\overline{U}_0^{NR^T} = \frac{1}{N}V_{logN-1}\cdots V_2V_1,$$

where each V_i is the matrix of butterfly action having matrix norm $\|V_i\| = \sqrt{2}$ and has up to three diagonal vectors. Each matrix multiplication requires a spending of modulus to scale and round its real numbers into integers. It is customary to group logN-1number of matrix multiplications into fewer number, let us say d(e.g3or4).

$$\frac{1}{N}\overline{U}_0^{NR^T} = A_d\cdots A_2A_1$$

Let $\widetilde{\Delta}$ be the scale factor to round the real numbers of each matrix A_i into integers. Figure 3 illustrates CoeffToSlot that consists of d number of matrix multiplications and two conjugated sums. The following theorem estimates the size of error in CoeffToSlot.

Theorem 3 (Error of *CoeffToSlot*). *Let $\widetilde{\frac{\mathsf{pt}}{\Delta} + \frac{q}{\Delta}I}$ be the approximation of $\frac{\mathsf{pt}}{\Delta} + \frac{q}{\Delta}I$ calculated by the CoeffToSlot in figure (2). Then the error $e = (\widetilde{\frac{\mathsf{pt}}{\Delta} + \frac{q}{\Delta}I}) - (\frac{\mathsf{pt}}{\Delta} + \frac{q}{\Delta}I)$ satisfies*[1]

$$\|e\| \lesssim \frac{C_1}{\widetilde{\Delta}}N^{1+\frac{1}{2d}}\frac{q}{\Delta},$$

where $C_1 = \frac{d\sqrt{(h+1)3^{\lceil\frac{\log N-1}{d}\rceil}}}{12}\cdot 2^{\frac{1}{2d}}$.

Proof. The random integer coefficient polynomial I in $\mathsf{pt}+qI$ is known to follow the Irwin-Hall distribution, and each coefficient of $\mathsf{pt}+qI$ follows a normal distribution $N\left(0, \frac{h+1}{12}q^2\right)$ very accurately when the hamming weight h is large enough (e.g. 64 or 128). Then we have $\|\mathsf{pt}+qI\| \simeq \sqrt{\frac{(h+1)N}{12}}q$ and

$$\|z_{mr}\| = \sqrt{\frac{N}{2}}\frac{1}{\Delta}\|\mathsf{pt}+qI\| \simeq \sqrt{\frac{h+1}{24}}N\frac{q}{\Delta},$$

where z_{mr} is the message being encoded into $\mathsf{pt}+qI$ after the step of ModRaise.

The iDFTmatrix $\frac{1}{N}\overline{U}_0^{NR^T}$ splits into $V_{\log N-1}\cdots V_2V_1$, where each V_i has matrix norm of $\sqrt{2}$ and consists of upto 3 diagonal vectors. Merging the matrices into d number of matrices and scaling by $\frac{1}{N}$, we can assume that

$$\|A_d\| = \cdots = \|A_1\| = \left(\frac{\sqrt{2}^{\log N-1}}{N}\right)^{\frac{1}{d}} = 2^{-\frac{1}{2d}}N^{-\frac{1}{2d}},$$

[1] Provided that $\widetilde{\Delta}$ is sufficiently small, we can assume that the rescale error is negligible. Since we are focusing on the case when $\widetilde{\Delta}$ is as small as possible, such assumption is valid.

and each A_i consists of up to k diagonal vectors, where

$$k = 3^{\lceil \frac{\log N - 1}{d} \rceil}.$$

Utilizing the error analysis in Theorem 2 for the matrix multiplication $A_d \cdots A_2 A_1$ on z_{mr}, we obtain the estimation on $z_1 = A_d \cdots A_2 A_1 z = \frac{1}{2}\left(\left(\frac{\mathsf{pt}}{\Delta} + \frac{q}{\Delta} I\right)^{1st} + \left(\frac{\mathsf{pt}}{\Delta} + \frac{q}{\Delta} I\right)^{2nd} \sqrt{-1}\right)$.

$$\begin{aligned}
\|\widetilde{z_1} - z_1\| &\lesssim \|z_{mr}\| \sqrt{\frac{kN}{12}} \frac{1}{\widetilde{\Delta}} \|A_1\| \cdots \|A_d\| \left(\frac{1}{\|A_1\|} + \cdots + \frac{1}{\|A_d\|} \right) \\
&\simeq \sqrt{\frac{h+1}{24}} N \frac{q}{\Delta} \sqrt{\frac{kN}{12}} \frac{1}{\widetilde{\Delta}} \left(2^{-\frac{1}{2d}} N^{-\frac{1}{2d}}\right)^{d-1} d \\
&= \frac{d\sqrt{(h+1)\, 3^{\lceil \frac{\log N - 1}{d} \rceil}}}{24} 2^{\frac{1}{2d}} \frac{1}{\widetilde{\Delta}} N^{1+\frac{1}{2d}} \frac{q}{\Delta}
\end{aligned}$$

$$\begin{aligned}
\|e\| &= \left\| \widetilde{\left(\frac{\mathsf{pt}}{\Delta} + \frac{q}{\Delta} I\right)} - \left(\frac{\mathsf{pt}}{\Delta} + \frac{q}{\Delta} I\right) \right\| \\
&= \sqrt{ \left\| \widetilde{\left(\frac{\mathsf{pt}}{\Delta} + \frac{q}{\Delta} I\right)}^{1st} - \left(\frac{\mathsf{pt}}{\Delta} + \frac{q}{\Delta} I\right)^{1st} \right\|^2 + \left\| \widetilde{\left(\frac{\mathsf{pt}}{\Delta} + \frac{q}{\Delta} I\right)}^{2nd} - \left(\frac{\mathsf{pt}}{\Delta} + \frac{q}{\Delta} I\right)^{2nd} \right\|^2 } \\
&= \left\| \widetilde{\left(\left(\frac{\mathsf{pt}}{\Delta} + \frac{q}{\Delta} I\right)^{1st} + \left(\frac{\mathsf{pt}}{\Delta} + \frac{q}{\Delta} I\right)^{2nd} \sqrt{-1} \right)} - \left(\left(\frac{\mathsf{pt}}{\Delta} + \frac{q}{\Delta} I\right)^{1st} + \left(\frac{\mathsf{pt}}{\Delta} + \frac{q}{\Delta} I\right)^{2nd} \sqrt{-1} \right) \right\| \\
&= \|2(\widetilde{z_1} - z_1)\| = 2\|\widetilde{z_1} - z_1\| \\
&\lesssim \frac{d\sqrt{(h+1)\, 3^{\lceil \frac{\log N - 1}{d} \rceil}}}{12} 2^{\frac{1}{2d}} \frac{1}{\widetilde{\Delta}} N^{1+\frac{1}{2d}} \frac{q}{\Delta} = C_1 \frac{1}{\widetilde{\Delta}} N^{1+\frac{1}{2d}} \frac{q}{\Delta}.
\end{aligned}$$

Example 3. We provide a proof-of-concept implementation of Theorem 3, at https://github.com/CryptoLabInc/EvalRound. We developed our own source code in C++, which implements the binary version of CKKS bootstrapping. Table 3 describes the parameters used in this example. N denotes the ciphertext dimension, $\log(QP)$ denotes the bit lengths of the largest RLWE modulus, h denotes the hamming weight, λ denotes the security bits, Δ denotes the encoding scale factor, q denotes the base modulus, and d denotes the decomposition number for CoeffToSlot matrix.

Table 3. Parameters for Example 3

Parameter	N	$\log(QP)$	h	λ	Δ	q	d
P1	2^9	2900	128	–	2^{50}	2^{60}	4
P2	2^{13}	2900	128	–	2^{50}	2^{60}	4
P3	2^{17}	2900	128	128	2^{50}	2^{60}	4

C_1 could be computed directly from the statement of Theorem 3, and so are the estimate of $\|z_{mr}\|$ and the bound of $\|e\|$. We checked that $\|z_{mr}\|$ is close to $\|z_{mr}\|^{est}$ and $\|e\|$ is bounded to $\|e\|^{bound}$, as shown in Table 4.

Table 4. Implementation result for Example 3

Parameter	C_1	$\|z_{mr}\|$	$\|z_{mr}\|^{est}$	$\|e\|$	$\|e\|^{bound}$
P1	12.3858	1.2543×10^6	1.1723×10^6	1.93821×10^{-9}	1.25792×10^{-8}
P2	28.6846	1.9509×10^7	1.87575×10^7	1.50875×10^{-7}	9.59557×10^{-7}
P3	37.1574	3.1176×10^8	3.0012×10^8	1.6208×10^{-6}	1.9321×10^{-5}

4 EvalRound instead of EvalMod

Let $[\cdot]_{\frac{q}{\Delta}} : \mathbb{R} \to \mathbb{R}$ be the modular reduction by integer multiple of $\frac{q}{\Delta}$. EvalMod subsequent to CoeffToSlot is a homomorphic evaluation of $[\cdot]_{\frac{q}{\Delta}}$, which removes the ambiguity $\frac{q}{\Delta}I$ from $\frac{\mathsf{pt}}{\Delta} + \frac{q}{\Delta}I$. Let $\mathsf{Mod}_{\frac{q}{\Delta}} : \mathbb{R}^N \to \mathbb{R}^N$ be an element-wise evaluation of $[\cdot]_{\frac{q}{\Delta}}$. We first take a look at $\mathsf{Mod}_{\frac{q}{\Delta}}$, focusing on its role during EvalMod.

We pointed out in the previous section that the homomorphically calculated message $\widetilde{\frac{\mathsf{pt}}{\Delta} + \frac{q}{\Delta}I}$ does not equal $\frac{\mathsf{pt}}{\Delta} + \frac{q}{\Delta}I$ mainly because of the rounding error. Let e be the error of the approximation, then we get

$$\widetilde{\frac{\mathsf{pt}}{\Delta} + \frac{q}{\Delta}I} = \frac{\mathsf{pt}}{\Delta} + \frac{q}{\Delta}I + e \text{ and}$$

$$\mathsf{Mod}_{\frac{q}{\Delta}}\left(\widetilde{\frac{\mathsf{pt}}{\Delta} + \frac{q}{\Delta}I}\right) = \frac{\mathsf{pt}}{\Delta} + e.$$

Note that the rounding error is added to the output of EvalMod and deteriorates the overall accuracy of bootstrapping. Thus the scale factor $\widetilde{\Delta}$ should be taken as large as Δ to keep the rounding error small, in spite of its consumption of d number of levels. Let $\mathsf{Round}_{\frac{q}{\Delta}} : \mathbb{R}^N \to \mathbb{R}^N$ denote the counterpart of $\mathsf{Mod}_{\frac{q}{\Delta}}$, so that

$$\mathsf{Round}_{\frac{q}{\Delta}}(x) := x - \mathsf{Mod}_{\frac{q}{\Delta}}(x).$$

A standard assumption is $\|z\|_\infty \leq 1$, from which $\|\frac{\mathsf{pt}}{\Delta}\|_\infty \leq 1$ is derived, and $\frac{q}{\Delta}$ is much larger than $\frac{\mathsf{pt}}{\Delta}$ (e.g. 2^{10}). When the magnitude of e is also negligible compared to $\frac{q}{\Delta}$, the sum $\frac{\mathsf{pt}}{\Delta} + e$ does not change the qI component in $\frac{\mathsf{pt}}{\Delta} + e + \frac{q}{\Delta}I$. In other words,

$$\mathsf{Round}_{\frac{q}{\Delta}}\left(\widetilde{\frac{\mathsf{pt}}{\Delta}+\frac{q}{\Delta}I}\right)=\frac{q}{\Delta}I=\mathsf{Round}_{\frac{q}{\Delta}}\left(\frac{\mathsf{pt}}{\Delta}+\frac{q}{\Delta}I\right)\text{ but}$$

$$\mathsf{Mod}_{\frac{q}{\Delta}}\left(\widetilde{\frac{\mathsf{pt}}{\Delta}+\frac{q}{\Delta}I}\right)=\frac{\mathsf{pt}}{\Delta}+e\neq\frac{\mathsf{pt}}{\Delta}=\mathsf{Mod}_{\frac{q}{\Delta}}\left(\frac{\mathsf{pt}}{\Delta}+\frac{q}{\Delta}I\right).$$

Let $\mathsf{EvalRound}(\mathsf{ct}) := \mathsf{ct} - \mathsf{EvalMod}(\mathsf{ct})$. The equality of $\mathsf{Round}_{\frac{q}{\Delta}}$ allows us to ignore the rounding error, and the scale factor $\widetilde{\Delta}$ can be taken much smaller than the canonical choice Δ while maintaining the same accuracy. Figure 3 shows the details of our proposed bootstrapping utilizing EvalRound. Our main aim is to take smaller scale factor $\widetilde{\Delta}$ while maintaining the same accuracy as the conventional bootstrapping using EvalMod, and reduce the consumption of modulus bit from Δ^{l+2d} to $\Delta^{l+d}\widetilde{\Delta}^d$, where d is the number of matrix multiplications in DFTand iDFTand l is the number of levels consumed in EvalMod/EvalRound.

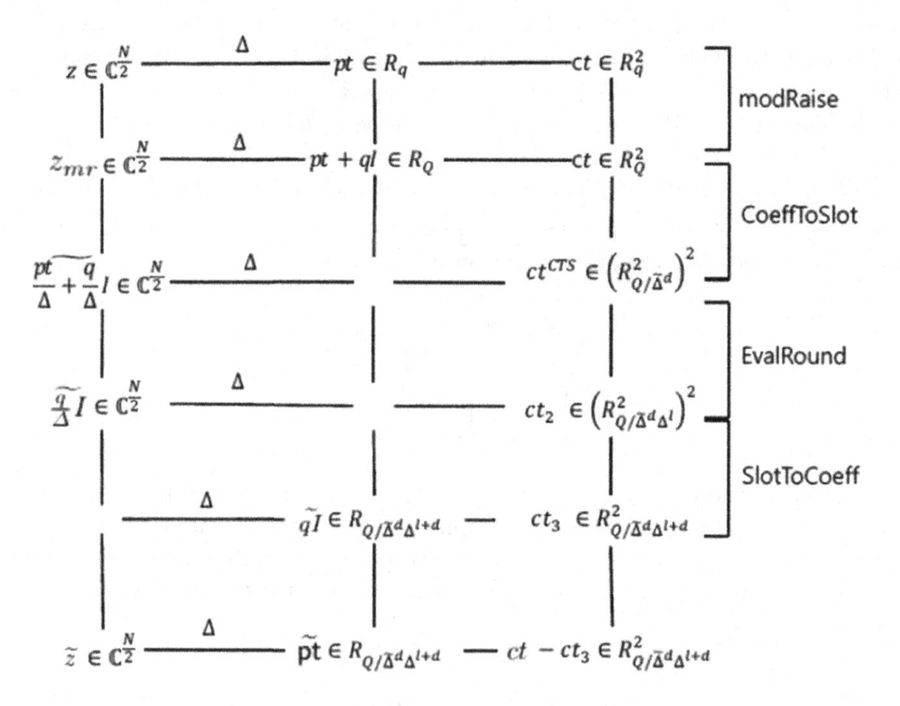

Fig. 3. The proposed bootstrapping utilizing EvalRound : d is the number of matrix multiplications in DFTand iDFT. l is the number of levels consumed in EvalRound, which equals that of EvalMod. The overall modulus bit spent is $\widetilde{\Delta}^d\Delta^{l+d}$. Our main aim is to reduce $\widetilde{\Delta}$, while maintaining the accuracy.

From the identity $\mathsf{Round}_{\frac{q}{\Delta}}(x) = x - \mathsf{Mod}_{\frac{q}{\Delta}}(x)$, EvalRound can be readily implemented just using one of the successful implementations [5,18,21–23] of EvalMod. Referencing one of them, let $\mathsf{EvalMod} : \mathsf{ct} \mapsto \mathsf{ct}_{em}$ be a homomorphic approximation of $\mathsf{Mod}_{\frac{q}{\Delta}}$. Consider the map of end-to-end evaluation of EvalMod, $\mathsf{EvalMod}_z : z \mapsto z_{em}$, or $\mathsf{EvalMod}_z = \psi^{-1} \circ \mathsf{EvalMod} \circ \psi$ where $\psi : z \mapsto \mathsf{ct} = \mathsf{Encrypt} \circ \mathsf{Encode}$. Then $\mathsf{EvalMod}_z$ approximates $\mathsf{Mod}_{\frac{q}{\Delta}}$ with an error bound B^{EvalMod} (e.g. 2^{-20} or 2^{-30}) for each $x \in \mathbb{C}^N$ close to lattice points $\{0, \pm\frac{q}{\Delta}, \pm\frac{2q}{\Delta}, \cdots\}$ within distance ϵ (e.g. 1), so that

$$\mathsf{dist}\left(x, \left\{0, \pm\frac{q}{\Delta}, \pm\frac{2q}{\Delta}, \cdots\right\}\right) \le \epsilon \\ \implies \left\|\mathsf{Mod}_{\frac{q}{\Delta}}(x) - \mathsf{EvalMod}_z(x)\right\|_\infty < B^{\mathsf{EvalMod}}, \quad (5)$$

where dist denotes the maximum distance among its elements.

For $x = \frac{\mathsf{pt}}{\Delta} + \frac{q}{\Delta}I = \frac{\mathsf{pt}}{\Delta} + e + \frac{q}{\Delta}I$, its distance to the lattice points is $\frac{\mathsf{pt}}{\Delta} + e$, and we have

$$\left\|\frac{\mathsf{pt}}{\Delta} + e\right\|_\infty \le \epsilon \implies \left\|\frac{q}{\Delta}I - \mathsf{EvalRound}_z(x)\right\|_\infty < B^{\mathsf{EvalMod}}. \quad (6)$$

From a standard assumption $\|z\|_\infty \le 1$ and theorem 3, we have the following L^2 estimates.

$$\left\|\frac{\mathsf{pt}}{\Delta}\right\| \le 1 \\ \|e\| \le \frac{C_1 N^{1+\frac{1}{2d}} q}{\tilde{\Delta}\Delta} \quad (7)$$

For any x, it holds that $\frac{1}{\sqrt{N}}\|x\| \le \|x\|_\infty \le \|x\|$. The equivalent condition for $\|x\|_\infty = \|x\|$ is that x is a discrete delta function, which is extremely concentrated at one point. When x is not that extreme, we observed in practice that there exists a constant C_2 of moderate size (< 10) that satisfies

$$\left\|\frac{\mathsf{pt}}{\Delta}\right\|_\infty \le \frac{C_2}{\sqrt{N}}\left\|\frac{\mathsf{pt}}{\Delta}\right\| \text{ and} \\ \|e\|_\infty \le \frac{C_2}{\sqrt{N}}\|e\|. \quad (8)$$

Example 4. Let the parameters be determined as in Example 3. We checked that the approximations in inequality 8 are valid, as shown in Table 5. $\|\frac{\mathsf{pt}}{\Delta}\|_\infty^{bound}$ and $\|e\|_\infty^{bound}$ denote the estimates of the actual values under the choice of $C_2 = 5$.

Now we analyze the proposed bootstrapping in Fig. 3 and show the proper range of $\tilde{\Delta}$ that enables the bootstrapping to maintain the same accuracy as EvalMod.

Table 5. Checking the inequality 8

Parameter	$\|\frac{\mathsf{pt}}{\Delta}\|_\infty$	$\|\frac{\mathsf{pt}}{\Delta}\|_\infty^{bound}$	$\|e\|_\infty$	$\|e\|_\infty^{bound}$
P1	8.5345×10^{-2}	1.2273×10^{-1}	4.46107×10^{-10}	2.7796×10^{-9}
P2	2.4474×10^{-2}	3.1755×10^{-2}	3.5204×10^{-9}	2.7234×10^{-8}
P3	7.0179×10^{-3}	7.9874×10^{-3}	2.8059×10^{-8}	2.6684×10^{-7}

Theorem 4 (Proper range of $\widetilde{\Delta}$). *In the bootstrapping proposed in Fig. 3, we have*

$$\left\|\frac{\mathsf{pt}}{\Delta} - \widetilde{\frac{\mathsf{pt}}{\Delta}}\right\|_\infty < B^{\mathsf{EvalMod}}$$

if $\widetilde{\Delta} \geq \widetilde{\Delta}_{min} = \frac{1}{\frac{\epsilon\sqrt{N}}{C_2}-1}\frac{C_1 N^{1+\frac{1}{2d}} q}{\Delta}$. *Here C_1 and C_2 are the constants in theorem 3 and the inequality* (8)*, respectively.*

Proof. If $\widetilde{\Delta} \geq \widetilde{\Delta}_{min}$, the inequalities (8) and (7) lead to

$$\begin{aligned}
\left\|\frac{\mathsf{pt}}{\Delta} + e\right\|_\infty &\leq \frac{C_2}{\sqrt{N}}\left(\left\|\frac{\mathsf{pt}}{\Delta}\right\| + \|e\|\right) \\
&\leq \frac{C_2}{\sqrt{N}}\left(1 + \frac{C_1 N^{1+\frac{1}{2d}} q}{\widetilde{\Delta}\Delta}\right) \\
&\leq \frac{C_2}{\sqrt{N}}\left(1 + \left(\frac{\epsilon\sqrt{N}}{C_2} - 1\right)\right) \\
&= \epsilon.
\end{aligned}$$

From (6), we have

$$\left\|\frac{q}{\Delta}I - \widetilde{\frac{q}{\Delta}I}\right\|_\infty < B^{\mathsf{EvalMod}}.$$

Since $\widetilde{\frac{\mathsf{pt}}{\Delta}} = \frac{\mathsf{pt}}{\Delta} + \frac{q}{\Delta}I - \widetilde{\frac{q}{\Delta}I}^2$, we have the desired result,

$$\left\|\frac{\mathsf{pt}}{\Delta} - \widetilde{\frac{\mathsf{pt}}{\Delta}}\right\|_\infty = \left\|\frac{q}{\Delta}I - \widetilde{\frac{q}{\Delta}I}\right\|_\infty < B^{\mathsf{EvalMod}}.$$

Example 5. We validate our main argument, Theorem 4 on the two parameter sets in Example 3. A standard EvalMod is employed. The minimax polynomial approximation of degree 31 is sought for $\frac{q}{2\pi\Delta}\sin\left(\frac{2\pi\Delta x}{q}\right)$ on $\left[-3\frac{q}{\Delta}, 3\frac{q}{\Delta}\right]$. Repeatedly applying half-angle identity, the domain is extended to $\left[-24\frac{q}{\Delta}, 24\frac{q}{\Delta}\right]$. EvalMod is then the composition of the arcsine polynomial of degree three and the polynomial approximation on the extended domain. The following Table 6 reports the constants in Theorem 4.

[2] Here we assumed that SlotToCoeff error is negligible.

Table 6. Constants in Theorem 4

Parameter	C_2	ϵ	B^{EvalMod}	$\widetilde{\Delta}_{min}$
P1	5	1	1.8696×10^{-8}	2^{22}
P2	5	1	1.5208×10^{-6}	2^{25}
P3	5	1	4.3320×10^{-5}	2^{29}

Table 7. Results of the conventional and proposed bootstrappings

	Parameter	$\widetilde{\Delta} = \widetilde{\Delta}_{min}$		$\widetilde{\Delta} = \widetilde{\Delta}_{can}$	
		Conventional	Proposed	Conventional	Proposed
$\left\lVert \frac{\mathsf{pt}}{\Delta} - \frac{\widetilde{\mathsf{pt}}}{\Delta} \right\rVert_\infty$	P1	1.0778×10^{-1}	8.0376×10^{-9}	6.6876×10^{-9}	6.7038×10^{-9}
	P2	9.9619×10^{-2}	4.9083×10^{-7}	1.2809×10^{-7}	1.2781×10^{-7}
	P3	6.6230×10^{-2}	2.8095×10^{-5}	1.0923×10^{-5}	1.0927×10^{-5}

A conventional bootstrapping takes $\widetilde{\Delta} = \widetilde{\Delta}_{can} = 2^{60}$ and utilizes EvalMod. Our proposed bootstrapping allows for taking any $\widetilde{\Delta} \geq \widetilde{\Delta}_{min}$.

As stated in Theorem 4, the proposed bootstrapping satisfies $\left\lVert \frac{\mathsf{pt}}{\Delta} - \frac{\widetilde{\mathsf{pt}}}{\Delta} \right\rVert_\infty < B^{\mathsf{EvalMod}}$ in all the cases, while the conventional one does not in the case of $\widetilde{\Delta} = \widetilde{\Delta}_{min}$. Let $\tilde{z}$ be the final output of the proposed bootstrapping in Fig. 3. $\lVert z - \tilde{z} \rVert_\infty$ represents the precision of bootstrapping. The following Table 8 reinterprets the result in Table 7 in terms of bootstrapping precision.

Table 8. Precision of bootstrapping obtained from conventional and proposed methods

	Parameter	$\widetilde{\Delta} = \widetilde{\Delta}_{min}$		$\widetilde{\Delta} = \widetilde{\Delta}_{can}$	
		Conventional	Proposed	Conventional	Proposed
$\lVert z - \tilde{z} \rVert_\infty$	P1	1.11	-25.51	-25.45	-25.45
	P2	2.81	-19.24	-19.52	-19.52
	P3	4.25	-12.72	-13.30	-13.30

Finally, we compute the amount of preserved modulus in Parameter II, as in Table 1. In CoeffToSlot, we use $\widetilde{\Delta} = 2^{29}$ instead of 2^{60}, preserving $(60 - 29) \cdot 4 = 124$ bits of modulus. Meanwhile, since the input of SlotToCoeff becomes larger from the size of pt to the size of $\mathsf{pt} + qI$, we should increase the SlotToCoeff scaling factor by $\frac{q}{\Delta} = 2^{10}$, losing a total of $10 \cdot 4 = 40$ bits of modulus. In sum, we save $124 - 40 = 84$ bits of ciphertext modulus. Since $\Delta = 2^{50}$, it is equivalent to preserving approximately two multiplicative depths.

In the state of the art implementations, we multiply a constant $c > 1$ before bootstrapping and divide by c after bootstrapping. This technique increases the bootstrapping precision by $\log_2(c)$ bits. In particular, we use as large c and possible. Let $c-$bootstrapping be a bootstrapping circuit with such constant c.

Corollary 1. *Let* $\mathsf{BTS}_c = (\times c^{-1}) \circ \mathsf{BTS} \circ (\times c)$ *be a c-bootstrapping circuit with* $\mathsf{EvalMod}$ *input bound* ϵ *and* $\mathsf{EvalMod}$ *error bound* B^{EvalMod}*, so that* $\|\frac{c \cdot \mathsf{pt}}{\Delta}\|_\infty \leq \epsilon$*. This bootstrapping satisfies*

$$\left\|\frac{\mathsf{pt}}{\Delta} - \frac{\widetilde{\mathsf{pt}}}{\Delta}\right\|_\infty < \frac{1}{c}B^{\mathsf{EvalMod}}.$$

where $\widetilde{\mathsf{pt}}$ *is defined to be a final output of* BTS_c*. Let* $\mathsf{BTS}^\#$ *be an* $\mathsf{EvalRound}$ *version of* BTS*. We define* $\mathsf{BTS}^\#_{c/2} := (\times 2/c) \circ \mathsf{BTS}^\# \circ (\times c/2)$*. For* $\mathsf{BTS}^\#_{c/2}$*, we have*

$$\left\|\frac{\mathsf{pt}}{\Delta} - \frac{\widetilde{\mathsf{pt}}}{\Delta}\right\|_\infty < \frac{2}{c}B^{\mathsf{EvalMod}}.$$

if $\widetilde{\Delta} \geq \widetilde{\Delta}_{min} = \frac{2C_2}{\epsilon\sqrt{N}} \cdot \frac{C_1 N^{1+\frac{1}{2d}} q}{\Delta}$*. Here* C_1 *and* C_2 *are the constants in theorem 3 and the inequality* (8)*, respectively.*

Proof. If $\widetilde{\Delta} \geq \widetilde{\Delta}_{min}$, the inequalities (8) and (7) lead to

$$\begin{aligned}\left\|\frac{c}{2} \cdot \frac{\mathsf{pt}}{\Delta} + e\right\|_\infty &\leq \frac{\epsilon}{2} + \frac{C_2}{\sqrt{N}}\|e\| \\ &\leq \frac{\epsilon}{2} + \frac{C_2}{\sqrt{N}} \cdot \frac{C_1 N^{1+\frac{1}{2d}} q}{\widetilde{\Delta}\Delta} \\ &\leq \frac{\epsilon}{2} + \frac{\epsilon}{2} = \epsilon \\ &= \epsilon.\end{aligned}$$

From (6), we have

$$\left\|\frac{q}{\Delta}I - \widetilde{\frac{q}{\Delta}I}\right\|_\infty < B^{\mathsf{EvalMod}}.$$

Since $\frac{c}{2} \cdot \frac{\widetilde{\mathsf{pt}}}{\Delta} = \frac{c}{2} \cdot \frac{\mathsf{pt}}{\Delta} + \frac{q}{\Delta}I - \widetilde{\frac{q}{\Delta}I}$, we have the desired result,

$$\left\|\frac{\mathsf{pt}}{\Delta} - \frac{\widetilde{\mathsf{pt}}}{\Delta}\right\|_\infty = \frac{2}{c}\left\|\frac{q}{\Delta}I - \widetilde{\frac{q}{\Delta}I}\right\|_\infty < \frac{2}{c}B^{\mathsf{EvalMod}}.$$

Example 6 (Parameter Construction based on a set in [1]*).* Table 9 describes the overview of the parameter set II proposed in [1]. Here N denotes the ciphertext dimension, $\log(QP)$ denotes the bit length of the largest RLWE modulus, h denotes the hamming weight, depth denotes the number of available multiplication after bootstrapping, Δ denotes the scaling factor for encoding, and q_0 denotes the size of the base modulus.

Using Corollary 1, $\widetilde{\Delta}_{min}$ is computed as 2^{34}. Based on Set II, by applying $\mathsf{EvalRound}$ technique, we can construct a parameter with $\mathsf{depth} = 6$, while losing at most 1 bit of precision. Table 10 describes the new parameter, namely Set II'. Here L denotes the maximum ciphertext level. $\log(q_i)$ and $\log(p_j)$ denote

Table 9. Overview of Set II in [1].

Set	N	$\log(QP)$	h	depth	Δ	q_0	Bootstrap Precision
II	2^{16}	1547	192	5	2^{45}	2^{60}	-31.5

the bit lengths of individual RNS primes and temporary primes for Modulus switching, respectively. Base, Mult, StC, EvalRound, CtS denote the base prime, the multiplication primes, the SlotToCoeff primes, the EvalRound primes, and the CoeffToSlot primes, respectively. The left operand of the dot product denotes the number of primes, and the right operand denotes the bit lengths of primes.

Table 10. Proposed parameter Set II'

II'				
h	N	Δ	$\log(QP)$	L
192	2^{16}	2^{45}	1543	23
$\log(q_i)$				$\log(p_j)$
Base + Mult	StC	EvalRound	CtS	
$60 + 6 \cdot 45$	$3 \cdot 57$	$11 \cdot 60$	$3 \cdot 46$	$4 \cdot 61$

5 Conclusion

In this article, we proposed a method called EvalRound, which is a modification of the EvalMod step in the CKKS bootstrapping. One can reduce the amount of ciphertext modulus consumed in the bootstrapping by modifying the original algorithm with EvalRound. The modulus spent in CoeffToSlot are for the scale factors, each of which has been chosen large enough to take up one level to rescale it down. Smaller scale factors lead to non-negligible rounding errors that are transmitted to EvalMod and eventually corrupt the overall accuracy of the bootstrapping. We introduce a scrutinized analysis that estimates the size of the rounding error with respect to the new scale factors.

Although the rounding error at this step is stuck to the input of the next step EvalMod, it does not pass through EvalRound if it is of a similar size to $\epsilon = \Delta/q$. Thus, when using EvalRound, we can use smaller scale factors for CoeffToSlot compared to the conventional method. In particular, we observed that we can preserve almost half of the modulus consumption in CoeffToSlot. The utilization of the error analysis of CoeffToSlot, reduced scale factors, and EvalRound yielded a saving of approximately two multiplicative levels, in one of practical settings.

Acknowledgements. The research was supported by Basic Science Research Program through the National Research Foundation of Korea(NRF) funded by the Ministry of Education (Grant No. 2019R1A6A1A11051177 and 2021R1A2C1095703) and Institute of Information & Communications Technology Planning & Evaluation (IITP) grant funded by the Korea government (MSIT) [NO.2022-0-01047, Development of statistical analysis algorithm and module using homomorphic encryption based on real number operation].

References

1. Bossuat, J.-P., Mouchet, C., Troncoso-Pastoriza, J., Hubaux, J.-P.: Efficient bootstrapping for approximate homomorphic encryption with non-sparse keys. In: Canteaut, A., Standaert, F.-X. (eds.) EUROCRYPT 2021. LNCS, vol. 12696, pp. 587–617. Springer, Cham (2021). https://doi.org/10.1007/978-3-030-77870-5_21
2. Brakerski, Z., Gentry, C., Vaikuntanathan, V.: (leveled) fully homomorphic encryption without bootstrapping. In: Proceedings of the 3rd Innovations in Theoretical Computer Science Conference, ITCS 2012, pp. 309–325. Association for Computing Machinery, New York (2012). https://doi.org/10.1145/2090236.2090262
3. Brakerski, Z., Vaikuntanathan, V.: Fully homomorphic encryption from ring-LWE and security for key dependent messages. In: Rogaway, P. (ed.) CRYPTO 2011. LNCS, vol. 6841, pp. 505–524. Springer, Heidelberg (2011). https://doi.org/10.1007/978-3-642-22792-9_29
4. Brakerski, Z., Vaikuntanathan, V.: Efficient fully homomorphic encryption from (standard) lwe. SIAM J. Comput. **43**(2), 831–871 (2014). https://doi.org/10.1137/120868669
5. Chen, H., Chillotti, I., Song, Y.: Improved bootstrapping for approximate homomorphic encryption. In: Ishai, Y., Rijmen, V. (eds.) EUROCRYPT 2019. LNCS, vol. 11477, pp. 34–54. Springer, Cham (2019). https://doi.org/10.1007/978-3-030-17656-3_2
6. Cheon, J.H., et al.: Batch fully homomorphic encryption over the integers. In: Johansson, T., Nguyen, P.Q. (eds.) EUROCRYPT 2013. LNCS, vol. 7881, pp. 315–335. Springer, Heidelberg (2013). https://doi.org/10.1007/978-3-642-38348-9_20
7. Cheon, J.H., Han, K., Kim, A., Kim, M., Song, Y.: Bootstrapping for approximate homomorphic encryption. In: Nielsen, J.B., Rijmen, V. (eds.) EUROCRYPT 2018. LNCS, vol. 10820, pp. 360–384. Springer, Cham (2018). https://doi.org/10.1007/978-3-319-78381-9_14
8. Cheon, J.H., Kim, A., Kim, M., Song, Y.: Homomorphic encryption for arithmetic of approximate numbers. In: Takagi, T., Peyrin, T. (eds.) ASIACRYPT 2017. LNCS, vol. 10624, pp. 409–437. Springer, Cham (2017). https://doi.org/10.1007/978-3-319-70694-8_15
9. Cheon, J.H., Stehlé, D.: Fully homomophic encryption over the integers revisited. In: Oswald, E., Fischlin, M. (eds.) EUROCRYPT 2015. LNCS, vol. 9056, pp. 513–536. Springer, Heidelberg (2015). https://doi.org/10.1007/978-3-662-46800-5_20
10. Chillotti, I., Gama, N., Georgieva, M., Izabachène, M.: Faster packed homomorphic operations and efficient circuit bootstrapping for TFHE. In: Takagi, T., Peyrin, T. (eds.) ASIACRYPT 2017. LNCS, vol. 10624, pp. 377–408. Springer, Cham (2017). https://doi.org/10.1007/978-3-319-70694-8_14

11. Chillotti, I., Gama, N., Georgieva, M., Izabachène, M.: TFHE: fast fully homomorphic encryption over the torus. J. Cryptol. **33**(1), 34–91 (2019). https://doi.org/10.1007/s00145-019-09319-x
12. van Dijk, M., Gentry, C., Halevi, S., Vaikuntanathan, V.: Fully homomorphic encryption over the integers. In: Gilbert, H. (ed.) EUROCRYPT 2010. LNCS, vol. 6110, pp. 24–43. Springer, Heidelberg (2010). https://doi.org/10.1007/978-3-642-13190-5_2
13. Ducas, L., Micciancio, D.: FHEW: bootstrapping homomorphic encryption in less than a second. In: Oswald, E., Fischlin, M. (eds.) EUROCRYPT 2015. LNCS, vol. 9056, pp. 617–640. Springer, Heidelberg (2015). https://doi.org/10.1007/978-3-662-46800-5_24
14. Fan, J., Vercauteren, F.: Somewhat practical fully homomorphic encryption. Cryptology ePrint Archive, Report 2012/144 (2012). https://ia.cr/2012/144
15. Gentry, C.: Fully homomorphic encryption using ideal lattices. In: Proceedings of the Forty-First Annual ACM Symposium on Theory of Computing, STOC 2009, p. 169–178. Association for Computing Machinery, New York (2009). https://doi.org/10.1145/1536414.1536440
16. Gentry, C., Sahai, A., Waters, B.: Homomorphic Encryption from Learning with Errors: Conceptually-Simpler, Asymptotically-Faster, Attribute-Based. In: Canetti, R., Garay, J.A. (eds.) CRYPTO 2013. LNCS, vol. 8042, pp. 75–92. Springer, Heidelberg (2013). https://doi.org/10.1007/978-3-642-40041-4_5
17. Han, K., Hhan, M., Cheon, J.H.: Homomorphic encryption from learning with errors: conceptually-simpler, asymptotically-faster, attribute-based. IEEE Access **7**, 57361–57370 (2019). https://doi.org/10.1109/ACCESS.2019.2913850
18. Han, K., Ki, D.: Better bootstrapping for approximate homomorphic encryption. In: Jarecki, S. (ed.) CT-RSA 2020. LNCS, vol. 12006, pp. 364–390. Springer, Cham (2020). https://doi.org/10.1007/978-3-030-40186-3_16
19. Jutla, C.S., Manohar, N.: Modular lagrange interpolation of the mod function for bootstrapping of approximate he. Cryptology ePrint Archive, Report 2020/1355 (2020). https://ia.cr/2020/1355
20. Jutla, C.S., Manohar, N.: Sine series approximation of the mod function for bootstrapping of approximate he. In: Dunkelman, O., Dziembowski, S. (eds.) Advances in Cryptology - EUROCRYPT 2022, vol. 13275, pp. 491–520 (2022). Springer, Heidelberg. https://doi.org/10.1007/978-3-031-06944-4_17
21. Lee, J.-W., Lee, E., Lee, Y., Kim, Y.-S., No, J.-S.: High-precision bootstrapping of RNS-CKKS homomorphic encryption using optimal minimax polynomial approximation and inverse sine function. In: Canteaut, A., Standaert, F.-X. (eds.) EUROCRYPT 2021. LNCS, vol. 12696, pp. 618–647. Springer, Cham (2021). https://doi.org/10.1007/978-3-030-77870-5_22
22. Lee, J.W., Lee, Y., Kim, Y.S., Kim, Y., No, J.S., Kang, H.: High-precision bootstrapping for approximate homomorphic encryption by error variance minimization. In: Dunkelman, O., Dziembowski, S. (eds.) Advances in Cryptology - EUROCRYPT 2022, vol. 13275, pp. 551–580 (2022). Springer, Heidelberg. https://doi.org/10.1007/978-3-031-06944-4_19
23. Lee, Y., Lee, J.W., Kim, Y.S., No, J.S.: Near-optimal polynomial for modulus reduction using l2-norm for approximate homomorphic encryption. IEEE Access (2020). https://doi.org/10.1109/ACCESS.2020.3014369.

FINAL: Faster FHE Instantiated with NTRU and LWE

Charlotte Bonte[1(✉)], Ilia Iliashenko[2], Jeongeun Park[2], Hilder V. L. Pereira[2], and Nigel P. Smart[2,3]

[1] Intel Corporation, Emerging Security Lab, Mountain View, USA
charlotte.bonte@intel.com
[2] imec-COSIC, KU Leuven, Leuven, Belgium
{ilia,Jeongeun.Park,HilderVitor.LimaPereira}@esat.kuleuven.be
[3] Zama Inc., Franklin, USA
nigel.smart@kuleuven.be

Abstract. The NTRU problem is a promising candidate to build efficient Fully Homomorphic Encryption (FHE). However, all the existing proposals (e.g. LTV, YASHE) need so-called 'overstretched' parameters of NTRU to enable homomorphic operations. It was shown by Albrecht et al. (CRYPTO 2016) that these parameters are vulnerable against subfield lattice attacks.

Based on a recent, more detailed analysis of the overstretched NTRU assumption by Ducas and van Woerden (ASIACRYPT 2021), we construct two FHE schemes whose NTRU parameters lie outside the overstretched range. The first scheme is based solely on NTRU and demonstrates competitive performance against the state-of-the-art FHE schemes including TFHE. Our second scheme, which is based on both the NTRU and LWE assumptions, outperforms TFHE with a 28% faster bootstrapping and 45% smaller bootstrapping and key-switching keys.

Keywords: NTRU · FHE · LWE · Bootstrapping

1 Introduction

In the last ten years fully homomorphic encryption based on lattice problems has been a vibrant field of research, with schemes being proposed, sometimes broken and sometimes improved. The initial work of Gentry [18] was truly groundbreaking in that it established not only (what we now call) a compact somewhat homomorphic encryption (SHE) scheme based on lattices, but it also presented a method to bootstrap the compact SHE scheme into a fully homomorphic encryption (FHE) scheme. Gentry's original scheme was based on properties of lattices of ideals of algebraic number fields, which are now considered insecure, but in the

C. Bonte—Work done while at imec-COSIC, KU Leuven.

S. Agrawal and D. Lin (Eds.): ASIACRYPT 2022, LNCS 13792, pp. 188–215, 2022.
https://doi.org/10.1007/978-3-031-22966-4_7

intervening years numerous authors have presented FHE schemes based on LWE [6], Ring-LWE [7], NTRU [27] and the approximate integer GCD problem [31].

NTRU-based schemes seem the most efficient as their ciphertexts can be represented by a single polynomial in comparison to a pair of polynomials in RLWE-based schemes. Hence, these schemes have the potential of halving both the memory requirements and the running time.

In particular, an early FHE scheme based on the NTRU problem, called YASHE [4], was very efficient when compared to similar schemes. However, it was subsequently shown to be insecure due to the parameters being chosen in the so-called 'overstretched' NTRU regime [1]. More specifically, YASHE required the integer modulus q to be exponentially large in n, the degree of the polynomial used as the modulus of the polynomial ring. Howerver, it was discovered [1] that as we "stretch" the parameters by increasing q for a fixed n, the NTRU problem becomes easier, because it becomes possible to exploit a dense sublattice of the NTRU lattice to mount an attack. Therefore, constructing FHE schemes based on the NTRU problem is challenging.

In the initial version of the attack, the subfields of the NTRU field were exploited in order to reduce the dimension of the lattice in which one searches for the secret key. Latter analysis [24] showed that the attack is enabled simply by the existence of a dense sublattice within the NTRU lattice. Thus, this attack stems from the structure of the NTRU lattice and, therefore, cannot be addressed by switching to another polynomial ring. However, it was still difficult to estimate the impact of these sublattice attacks on the security of NTRU and, therefore, it was hard to obtain correct estimates of the security level of NTRU-based schemes. For example, the recent leveled homomorphic encryption scheme for automata [16], which is based in the matrix NTRU problem, used q polynomial in n. Nevertheless, it was quickly shown [26] that this scheme is vulnerable to sublattice attacks.

However, we now have a much better understanding about how the security of the NTRU problem degrades as we increase q. In particular, the recent work of Ducas and van Woerden [13] allows us to estimate the concrete cost of breaking the NTRU problem for any given q. Thus, we now have much more solid ground to try to construct NTRU-based FHE schemes.

Ducas and van Woerden showed that to avoid the aforementioned sublattice attacks one should set $q \in O(n^{2.484})$. This already seems to rule out NTRU-based schemes which follow the blueprint BGV [5] or FV [14]. Therefore, as a starting point, we take the bootstrapping of [3], which is the basis of the FHEW scheme [12] and its extension, TFHE [10].

These schemes have a base homomorphic encryption scheme, in both cases based on LWE, and an accumulator, which is a variant of the GSW scheme [19], instantiate with the RLWE problem. We use the base scheme to evaluate binary gates and the accumulator to refresh the LWE ciphertexts of the base scheme.

The advantage of GSW-like schemes is that noise growth is quasi additive when evaluating long chains of multiplications, thus, the final noise in the refreshed ciphertext can be as small as $\tilde{O}(n)$, which fits the above bound of Ducas and van Woerden.

In this paper, we investigate the construction of FHE schemes based on the NTRU. We show that it is possible to adapt the framework of FHEW [12] to the NTRU setting, by using a matrix version of the NTRU problem to construct the base scheme and the standard NTRU problem to construct a GSW-like scheme. The resulting scheme has a fast bootstrapping algorithm with running times similar to those of the most efficient scheme of this type – TFHE [10]. As the encryption parameters of our scheme can be selected outside of the overstretched regime of NTRU, this allows us to construct competitive FHE based solely on the NTRU assumption. In other words, our result is a positive answer to the open problem of whether it is possible to construct FHE based on NTRU.

In addition, we show that by combining an LWE-based scheme and our NTRU-based GSW-like scheme, called NGS in this paper, we obtain a bootstrapping algorithm that is faster than TFHE's and requires much less key material, which improves the state-of-the-art in FHE constructions.

Concurrently to our own work Kluczniak [25] presented a version of NTRU called NTRU-ν-um which also claims to provide a secure fully homomorphic version of NTRU with small modulus. The scheme is presented to be instantiated over a ring defined by X^N+1 and X^N-1. In [22] Joye shows that the variant defined over X^N-1 is not secure.

1.1 Our Techniques and Results

Homomorphic Scheme Based on the Matrix NTRU Problem. The bootstrapping framework of [12] assumes that the input encryption of the bootstrapping is an LWE ciphertext which means the main step of the decryption is a simple inner product between the ciphertext and the secret key. However, if we want to replace the underlying LWE-based base scheme with one based on NTRU then complications arise. The NTRU decryption involves a polynomial multiplication, which is much more complicated than the inner product.

One way of simplifying the decryption function is by assuming that each NTRU ciphertext encrypts an integer m_0 instead of a polynomial of degree $N-1$. Let R_q be a polynomial ring. We can encrypt m_0 as $c = g/f + \Delta \cdot m_0 \in R_q$ where g is a random element of R_q, f is the secret key and $\Delta \simeq q/4$. Note that we don't add any additional noise other than g in a ciphertext unlike other NTRU based schemes [4,27] in order to keep noise growth small as discussed in Sect. 3. To decrypt, we compute the inner product of the coefficient vector of c, denoted by $\phi(c)$, and the first column of the anti-circulant matrix of f which we will denote as $\boldsymbol{\Phi}(f)$. Given that the secret key of the NTRU scheme will be defined as $f = 1 + 4 \cdot f'$, one can notice that in R_q $c \cdot f = g + 4 \cdot f' \cdot \epsilon + \Delta \cdot m_0$, for some small ϵ, which implies that

$$\phi(c) \cdot \boldsymbol{\Phi}(f) = \phi(g) + 4 \cdot \epsilon \cdot \phi(f') + \Delta \cdot (m_0, 0, \ldots, 0).$$

Hence, $\phi(c) \cdot \mathsf{col}_0(\boldsymbol{\Phi}(f)) = g_0 + 4 \cdot \epsilon \cdot f_0' + \Delta \cdot m_0$, which is enough to recover m_0.

Similarly to [12], one can use NTRU defined over power-of-two cyclotomic rings. However, these rings provide little flexibility in terms of choosing parameters to achieve a certain security level. For example, even if the ring dimension $N = 600$ already satisfies the desired security level, one has to choose $N = 2^{10}$ as this is the smallest power of 2 larger than 600. This problem can be solved by using cyclotomic rings of other orders instead of power-of-two, but in this case, the matrix $\boldsymbol{\Phi}(f)$ loses its anti-circulant property, which, as we will see in Sect. 5, helps to significantly speed up the bootstrapping and reduce encryption parameters.

Driven by the above limitations, we resort to the matrix NTRU problem (MNTRU) instead of its ring-based version. Our MNTRU base scheme is described as follows. We replace the polynomial ratio g/f by the matrix product $\mathbf{G} \cdot \mathbf{F}^{-1}$, where both $\mathbf{G}$ and $\mathbf{F}$ are unstructured random matrices. Hence, a ciphertext of some plaintext matrix $\mathbf{M}$ has the form $\mathbf{C} = \mathbf{G} \cdot \mathbf{F}^{-1} + \Delta \cdot \mathbf{M} \in \mathbb{Z}_q^{n \times n}$ or $\mathbf{C} = (\mathbf{G} + \Delta \cdot \mathbf{M}) \cdot \mathbf{F}^{-1} \in \mathbb{Z}_q^{n \times n}$. A single integer $m \in \{0, 1\}$ is encrypted by a ciphertext of the form

$$\mathbf{c} := (\mathbf{g} + \Delta \cdot \mathbf{m}) \cdot \mathbf{F}^{-1} \in \mathbb{Z}_q^n$$

where $\mathbf{g}$ is a random vector from $\mathbb{Z}_q^n$ and $\mathbf{m} := (m, 0, \ldots, 0) \in \mathbb{Z}^n$. This guarantees that the decryption can be done by the inner product of $\mathbf{c}$ and the first column of the secret matrix $\mathbf{F}$. Therefore, it is simple enough for the bootstrapping algorithm to handle it efficiently. Furthermore, it is easy to adapt the homomorphic NAND gate from [12] to our scheme.

Notice that we are dividing both the noise term ($\mathbf{g}$) and the message ($\Delta \cdot m$) by $\mathbf{F}$, because this reduces the impact of the noise growth due to the multiplication by $\mathbf{F}$ during the decryption, as explained in Sect. 3.

GSW-like Scheme Based on the NTRU Problem. The bootstrapping framework of FHEW [12] uses a GSW-like scheme based on the RLWE problem to evaluate the decryption function of the base scheme efficiently and with low noise growth. Thus, to follow this blueprint, we propose an NTRU-based GSW-like scheme, which we call NGS. As the GSW-like scheme of [30], NGS can encrypt a polynomial $m \in R := \mathbb{Z}[X]/\langle X^N + 1\rangle$ in two ciphertext formats:

- *Scalar*: it is a standard NTRU ciphertext encrypting m as $g/f + \Delta m \in R_Q$.
- *Vector*: we encrypt m as $\mathbf{c} = \mathbf{g}/f + \mathfrak{g} \cdot m \in R_Q^{\ell}$, where $\mathfrak{g}$ is a gadget vector and $\ell \approx \log(Q)$.

As in TFHE [10], we define an external product between these two ciphertexts types, which outputs another scalar ciphertext. Notice that we need only ℓ ring elements per vector ciphertext. Thus, our external product is computed with ℓ products in R_Q, while the ciphertexts of the GSW scheme used in TFHE are composed by $4 \cdot \ell'$ ring elements. Therefore, they need $4 \cdot \ell'$ multiplications per external product. Thus, NGS external product can achieve better running times and memory usage for similar parameters.

Here, we focus on using the NGS scheme as an accumulator to homomorphically evaluate the decrytpion function of a base scheme and compare the performance with TFHE bootstrapping. But it is worth to notice that several other applications that use the GSW scheme could take advantage of the faster homomorphic operations of NGS. For example, by simply replacing GSW by NGS, one could speed up the transciphering for TFHE [20], or the homomorphic evaluation of maximum and minimum functions from [11], or the tree-based private information retrieval from [29].

Fast Bootstrapping with Non-overstretched Parameters. Given our NGS-based external product, we show that MNTRU ciphertexts can be homomorphically decrypted, or bootstrapped, using the NGS scheme with a similar running time as in TFHE. Hence we are able to construct FHE based solely on the NTRU assumption, with similar performance as TFHE.

Given a ciphertext $\mathbf{c} \in \mathbb{Z}_q^n$ of the base scheme, we use the NGS based external product to multiply it with the vector $\mathbf{f}_0 := \mathsf{col}_0(\mathbf{F}) \in \mathbb{Z}^n$, i.e., the first column of the MNTRU secret key. This generates a scalar ciphertext which is then transformed back to an MNTRU ciphertext.

In TFHE's bootstrapping, the LWE secret $\mathbf{s}$ is binary, since this allows one to compute an encryption of $X^{a_i s_i}$ using the fact that $X^{a_i \cdot s_i} = 1 + (X^{a_i} - 1) \cdot s_i$ when $s_i \in \{0, 1\}$. This operation is called a `CMux` gate. Since NTRU has ternary secret keys, adapting the `CMux` would require two consecutive external products, as it was noticed in [28]. Thus, we propose a *ternary* `CMux` gate, which can be executed with a single external product. We notice that this ternary `CMux` is of independent interest, as it can also be applied to other bootstrapping procedures, e.g., if one instantiates TFHE with ternary secrets. Bootstrapping TFHE with ternary keys was also considered in the paper [23].

We also prove that the final noise accumulated by the bootstrapping is $\tilde{O}(n)$, which allows us to choose q as a very low degree polynomial in n, e.g., $q = \tilde{O}(n)$, thus, below the 'fatigue' point that characterizes the overstretched regime of NTRU. Namely, it was shown [13,24] that the dense sublattice attacks against NTRU start to be more efficient than the classic key-recovering attacks when $q = n^{2.484+o(1)}$.

Faster Bootstrapping by Combining LWE and NTRU. Comparing the external product of TFHE with ours, we see that we need less multiplications in R_Q, thus, less fast Fourier transforms (FFT), which is the most expensive building block in the entire bootstrapping. Hence, we would expect our bootstrapping to be faster than theirs by a constant factor. However, the total number of external products is n, the dimension of the base scheme, which is defined by the hardness of the MNTRU problem. Thus, we have to choose n larger than in TFHE and we end up with a bootstrapping that requires essentially the same number of FFTs as in TFHE.

To obtain a smaller value of n, we propose to replace our MNTRU-based scheme by an LWE-based and use the NGS scheme to bootstrap it. Thus, the decryption function of an LWE-based scheme is evaluated by the NGS scheme, which returns an NGS scalar ciphertext. We show that it is possible to adapt existing key-switching procedures to transform this NTRU ciphertext back to an LWE ciphertext, thus completing the bootstrapping.

Therewith, we need essentially the same number of external products as in TFHE, but each external product requires less FFTs, thus leading to a smaller total number of FFTs in our bootstrapping. In addition, our scheme requires much less key material.

Practical Results and C++ Implementation: We implemented our bootstrapping algorithms and compared them with that of TFHE. As a result, the bootstrapping of MNTRU ciphertexts is about 40% slower than TFHE's bootstrapping and it requires 9% more key material. However, when the LWE problem is used to construct the base scheme, our running time is about 28% faster than TFHE. As a concrete example, running on a single core of a 3.1 GHz processor, TFHE takes 66 ms while ours takes 48 ms. Furthermore, our LWE/NGS scheme almost halves the total size of bootstrapping and key-switching keys: from 71 MB in TFHE to 39.3 MB. It is important to notice that one bootstrapping allows us to evaluate any binary gate homomorphically, thus, the homomorphic evaluation of any circuit consists of essentially running one bootstrapping for each gate, therefore, the speedup we obtained in the bootstrapping procedure translates directly as the same speedup for any binary circuit.

Our code is publicly available. More details can be found in Sect. 7.

2 Preliminaries

2.1 Vectors, Polynomials, and Norms

We use lower-case bold letters for vectors and upper-case bold letters for matrices. A zero vector is denoted by $\mathbf{0}$. We denote the $i+1$-th column (resp. row) of a matrix $\mathbf{A}$ by $\mathsf{col}_i(\mathbf{A})$ (resp. $\mathsf{row}_i(\mathbf{A})$). The inner product of two vectors $\mathbf{a}$ and $\mathbf{b}$ is denoted by $\mathbf{a} \cdot \mathbf{b}$. For any vector $\mathbf{u}$, $\|\mathbf{u}\|$ denotes the infinity norm. Let $[B]$ denote a set $\{1, \dots, B\}$ for an integer B.

Throughout the paper, N is always a power of two and $R := \mathbb{Z}[X]/\langle X^N + 1\rangle$ is the $(2N)$-th cyclotomic ring. Any element f of R can be always seen as the unique polynomial of degree smaller than N belonging to the coset $f + \langle X^N + 1\rangle$. Hence, writing $f = \sum_{i=0}^{N-1} f_i \cdot X^i$ is unambiguous and we can then define the coefficient vector of f as $\phi(f) := (f_0, \dots, f_{N-1}) \in \mathbb{Z}^N$. Therefore, we can define the infinity norm of f as $\|f\| := \|\phi(f)\|$. We also define the anti-circulant matrix of f as $\boldsymbol{\Phi}(f) \in \mathbb{Z}^{N\times N}$ such that $\mathsf{row}_i(\boldsymbol{\Phi}(f)) = \phi(f \cdot X^i)$ for $0 \le i \le N-1$. Notice that $\forall (k, f, g) \in \mathbb{Z} \times R \times R$, $\phi(k \cdot f \cdot g) = k \cdot \phi(f) \cdot \boldsymbol{\Phi}(g)$. For any $Q \in \mathbb{Z}$, let $R_Q := R/QR = \mathbb{Z}_Q[X]/\langle X^N + 1\rangle$.

Finally, we define $\mathbb{M} := \{\pm b \cdot X^k : b \in \{0, 1\} \text{ and } k \in \mathbb{N}\}$, which will be used as the plaintext space of the vector ciphertexts defined in Sect. 4.

2.2 Distributions

Discrete Gaussian Distribution. We first describe the discrete Gaussian distribution where our secret elements are sampled from. Typically, a discrete Gaussian distribution is defined as a distribution over $\mathbb{Z}$, where every element in $\mathbb{Z}$ is sampled with probability proportional to its probability mass function value under a Gaussian distribution over $\mathbb{R}$. We first define the Gaussian function as $\rho_{\sigma,c}(x) = \exp(-\frac{|x-c|^2}{2\cdot\sigma^2})$ for $\sigma, c \in \mathbb{R} > 0$. Hence, $\rho_{\sigma,c}(\mathbb{Z}) = \sum_{i=-\infty}^{\infty} \rho_{\sigma,c}(i)$. The discrete Gaussian distribution with standard deviation σ and mean c is a distribution on $\mathbb{Z}$ with the probability of $x \in \mathbb{Z}$ given by $\rho_{\sigma,c}(x)/\rho_{\sigma,c}(\mathbb{Z})$. If $c = 0$, we denote this distribution by χ_σ.

Subgaussian Distribution. For the analysis of encryption parameters, we need subgaussian random variables over $\mathbb{R}$.

Definition 1. *A random variable V over $\mathbb{R}$ is α-subgaussian if its moment generating function satisfies*

$$\mathbb{E}[\exp(t \cdot V)] \leq \frac{1}{2}\exp(\alpha^2 \cdot t^2)$$

for all $t \in \mathbb{R}$.

From the definition, we can prove that the variance of V, denoted by $\mathsf{Var}(V)$ is bounded by α^2, i.e. $\mathsf{Var}(V) \leq \alpha^2$. Informally, the tails of V are dominated by a Gaussian function with standard deviation α. The following lemma is adapted from [17] to our definition.

Lemma 1. *If $\mathbf{x}$ is a discrete random vector over $\mathbb{R}^n$ such that each component x_i of $\mathbf{x}$ is α_i-subgaussian, then the vector $\mathbf{x}$ is a β-subgaussian vector where $\beta = \max_{i\in[n]} \alpha_i$.*

Subgaussian random variables have an important property called Pythagorean additivity. Given two random variables, α-subgaussian X and β-subgaussian Y, and $a, b \in \mathbb{Z}$, the random variable $a \cdot X + b \cdot Y$ is $\sqrt{a^2 \cdot \alpha^2 + b^2 \cdot \beta^2}$-subgaussian. It implies that

$$\mathsf{Var}(a \cdot X) + \mathsf{Var}(b \cdot Y) \leq a^2 \cdot \mathsf{Var}(X) + b^2 \cdot \mathsf{Var}(Y) \leq a^2 \cdot \alpha^2 + b^2 \cdot \beta^2.$$

For $a \in R$ (resp. $\mathbf{x} \in \mathbb{Z}^n$), we denote by $\mathsf{Var}(a)$ (resp. $\mathsf{Var}(\mathbf{x})$) the maximum variance of each coefficient (resp. component) of a (resp. $\mathbf{x}$). The variance of the product of two polynomials $a, b \in R$ is $\mathsf{Var}(a \cdot b) = n \cdot \mathsf{Var}(a) \cdot \mathsf{Var}(b)$. Similarly, we denote by $\mathsf{Var}(\mathbf{X})$ the maximum variance of each column of a matrix $\mathbf{X}$.

2.3 Decompositions

For fixed integers q and B, we set $\ell := \lceil \log_B q \rceil$ and define $\mathfrak{g}_{q,B} := (B^0, \ldots, B^{\ell-1})$. When q and B are clear from the context, we write $\mathfrak{g}$. Then, for any $k \in \mathbb{Z}_q$, we represent k by an integer in $[-q/2, q/2)$ and define its signed decomposition in base B as $\mathfrak{g}^{-1}(k) = (k_0, \ldots, k_{\ell-1})$ for each integer $|k_i| \leq B/2$ for $i \in [\ell]$. It is easy to see that $\mathfrak{g}^{-1}(k) \cdot \mathfrak{g} = k$. For any $f \in R_Q$, we define $\mathfrak{g}^{-1}(f) := \sum_{i=0}^{N-1} \mathfrak{g}^{-1}(f_i) X^i$. It is clear that

$$\mathfrak{g}^{-1}(f) \cdot \mathfrak{g} = \sum_{i=0}^{N-1} \mathfrak{g}^{-1}(f_i) \cdot \mathfrak{g} \cdot X^i = \sum_{i=0}^{N-1} f_i \cdot X^i = f.$$

The digit decomposition $\mathfrak{g}^{-1}$ can be deterministic or randomized [17,21].

2.4 NTRU Problems

It is usual to instantiate the NTRU problem with ternary secrets. In our constructions, we generate the secrets from a distribution on $\{-1, 0, 1\}$ such that zero occurs with probability $1/2$, and 1 and -1 occur with probability $1/4$. This approximates a discrete Gaussian with standard deviation $\sigma = 1/\sqrt{2}$.

Following [13], we can define the *anti-circulant* and the *matrix* versions of the NTRU problem. Each version has a computational and a decisional variant.

Definition 2 (NTRU). *Let $N > 0, Q > 1$ be integers and $R := \mathbb{Z}[X]/\langle X^N + 1\rangle$. Let $\sigma > 0$ be a real number, $g, f \leftarrow \chi_\sigma^N$ and f be invertible in R_Q.*

The (computational) (N, Q, σ)-NTRU problem is to recover f and g given $h := g \cdot f^{-1} \bmod Q$. The (N, Q, σ)-decisional-NTRU problem is to distinguish between h and a uniformly random polynomial sampled from R_Q.

Definition 3 (Matrix NTRU). *Let $n > 0, q > 1$ be integers and $\sigma > 0$ is a real number. Let $\mathbf{G}, \mathbf{F} \leftarrow \chi_\sigma^{n\times n}$ and $\mathbf{F}$ be invertible modulo q.*

The (computational) (n, q, σ)-matrix-NTRU problem is to recover $\mathbf{F}$ and $\mathbf{G}$ given $\mathbf{H} := \mathbf{G} \cdot \mathbf{F}^{-1} \bmod q$. The (n, q, σ)-decisional-matrix-NTRU problem is to distinguish between $\mathbf{H}$ and a uniformly random matrix from $\mathbb{Z}_q^{n\times n}$.

3 Matrix-NTRU Base Encryption Scheme

Our base encryption scheme is based on the matrix NTRU (MNTRU) problem. It encrypts a bit $m \in \{0, 1\}$ as if it were an element of $\mathbb{Z}_4$; i.e. we multiply m by $\Delta := \lfloor q/4 \rceil$.

As such we can evaluate a NAND gate by adding two ciphertexts encrypting a bit and considering the result modulo 4. The result is $m = 2$ if $\mathsf{NAND}(m_0, m_1) = 0$ and $m \in \{0, 1\}$ if $\mathsf{NAND}(m_0, m_1) = 1$. We can transform this ciphertext with the result modulo 4 back to an encryption of $\mathsf{NAND}(m_0, m_1)$ with a simple affine transformation, as shown below. This ensures that after one homomorphic NAND gate, we obtain a message defined in $\mathbb{Z}_2$, i.e. multiplied by $\lfloor q/2 \rceil$. Since the message is only one bit, we can define its ciphertext as a vector in $\mathbb{Z}_q^n$ as shown in Introduction.

A standard MNTRU ciphertext would have the form $\mathbf{g} \cdot \mathbf{F}^{-1} + \Delta \cdot \mathbf{m}$, i.e., with only the noise term being divided by secret key $\mathbf{F}$, however, this would introduce a new noise term in the decrypting, when we multiply the ciphertext by $\mathsf{col}_0(\mathbf{F})$. In more detail, the key switching procedure presented in Sect. 4.5, which transforms a ciphertext from NGS to MNTRU, would output a ciphertext of the form $\mathbf{c}' = \mathbf{g} \cdot \mathbf{F}^{-1} + \mathbf{e} + \Delta \cdot \mathbf{m}$, where $\|\mathbf{e}\| = \Omega(n)$. Then, the decryption would produce $\mathbf{e} \cdot \mathsf{col}_0(\mathbf{F})$, whose norm would be $\Omega(n^2)$. Thus, to avoid such large noise, we define a MNTRU ciphertext with the form $(\mathbf{g} + \Delta \cdot \mathbf{m}) \cdot \mathbf{F}^{-1}$.

Hence, the MNTRU scheme is defined by the following four algorithms. Note that the decryption procedure below is valid for the ciphertexts produced by a NAND gate.

- $\mathsf{MNTRU.ParamGen}(1^\lambda)$: Receives the security parameter and outputs (n, q, σ).
- $\mathsf{MNTRU.KeyGen}$: Sample $\mathbf{F} \leftarrow \chi_\sigma^{n \times n}$ until $\mathbf{F}^{-1}$ exists in $\mathbb{Z}_q^{n \times n}$. Define $\mathsf{sk} := \mathbf{F}$. Create a public evaluation key as $\mathsf{evk} := (\mathbf{g} + \lfloor 5 \cdot q/8 \rceil \cdot (1, \mathbf{0})) \cdot \mathbf{F}^{-1} \in \mathbb{Z}_q^n$, where $\mathbf{g} \leftarrow \chi_\sigma^n$. Output $(\mathsf{evk}, \mathsf{sk})$.
- $\mathsf{MNTRU.Enc}(m, \mathsf{sk})$: Given $m \in \{0, 1\}$, sample $\mathbf{g} \leftarrow \chi_\sigma^n$. Let $\Delta := \lfloor q/4 \rceil$ and output
$$c = (\mathbf{g} + \Delta \cdot (m, \mathbf{0})) \cdot \mathbf{F}^{-1} \in \mathbb{Z}_q^n.$$
We call it a fresh MNTRU ciphertext.
- $\mathsf{MNTRU.Dec}(\mathbf{c}, \mathsf{sk})$: Given the secret key $\mathsf{sk} = \mathbf{F}$ and a ciphertext $\mathbf{c} \in \mathbb{Z}_q^n$, which is of the form $(\mathbf{g} + \lfloor q/2 \rceil \cdot (m, \mathbf{0})) \cdot \mathbf{F}^{-1} \in \mathbb{Z}_q^n$, this algorithm computes $r = \mathbf{c} \cdot \mathsf{col}_0(\mathbf{F}) \bmod q$ and outputs
$$\left\lfloor \frac{2 \cdot r}{q} \right\rceil \bmod 2.$$
- $\mathsf{MNTRU.Nand}(\mathbf{c}_0, \mathbf{c}_1, \mathsf{evk})$: Given the evaluation key evk and two ciphertexts of the form $(\mathbf{g}_i + \lfloor q/4 \rceil \cdot (m_i, \mathbf{0})) \cdot \mathbf{F}^{-1} \in \mathbb{Z}_q^n$, where $m_i \in \{0, 1\}$ output
$$\mathbf{c}_{\mathsf{NAND}} := \mathsf{evk} - \mathbf{c}_0 - \mathbf{c}_1.$$

This homomorphic NAND gate is basically the same as the one presented in [12]. Thus, its output is $\mathbf{c}_{\mathsf{NAND}} = \Big(\mathbf{g} - \mathbf{g}_0 - \mathbf{g}_1 + (e \pm q/8) \cdot (1, \mathbf{0}) + \frac{q}{2} \cdot (m, \mathbf{0})\Big) \cdot \mathbf{F}^{-1}$ where $|e| \le \frac{3}{2}$ and $m = \mathsf{NAND}(m_0, m_1) = 1 - m_0 \cdot m_1$. One can see this through the following computation.

Let $\mathbf{f} := \mathsf{col}_0(\mathbf{F})$, g_0 be the first element of $\mathbf{g}$, $g_{0,0}$ be the first element of $\mathbf{g}_0$ and $g_{1,0}$ be the first element of $\mathbf{g}_1$ then

$$\begin{aligned}
\mathbf{c}_{\mathsf{NAND}} \cdot \mathbf{f} - (1 - m_0 \cdot m_1)\frac{q}{2} &= (\mathsf{evk} - \mathbf{c}_0 - \mathbf{c}_1) \cdot \mathbf{f} - (1 - m_0 \cdot m_1)\frac{q}{2} \\
&= g_0 - g_{0,0} - g_{1,0} + \left\lfloor \frac{5q}{8} \right\rceil - \left\lfloor \frac{q}{4} \right\rceil m_0 - \left\lfloor \frac{q}{4} \right\rceil m_1 \\
&\quad - \frac{q}{2} + \frac{q}{2} m_0 \cdot m_1 \\
&= g_0 - g_{0,0} - g_{1,0} + \frac{q}{8} + \epsilon - \frac{q}{4}(m_0 + m_1 - 2m_0 \cdot m_1) \\
&\quad + \epsilon_0 \cdot m_0 + \epsilon_1 \cdot m_1 \\
&= g_0 - g_{0,0} - g_{1,0} + \frac{q}{8} + \epsilon - \frac{q}{4}(m_0 - m_1)^2 \\
&\quad + \epsilon_0 \cdot m_0 + \epsilon_1 \cdot m_1,
\end{aligned}$$

where $\epsilon, \epsilon_0, \epsilon_1$ are round-off errors whose absolute value is less or equal to 1/2. If we set $e = \epsilon + \epsilon_0 \cdot m_0 + \epsilon_1 \cdot m_1$, we have $|e| \le \frac{3}{2}$.

We now show that decrypting the output of a NAND gate gives the correct answer, as long as the sum of three input noises $\mathbf{g} - \mathbf{g}_0 - \mathbf{g}_1$ is not too large. For simplicity, we consider the ternary noise for the following lemma since we instantiate our scheme with ternary secrets as we mentioned above. Therefore, the noise of evaluation key always satisfies that $\|\mathbf{g}\| = 1$. The noise contained in a fresh ciphertext or an evaluation key is called *fresh.*

Lemma 2 (Correctness of decryption). *For* $0 \le i \le 1$, *let* $\mathbf{c}_i := (\mathbf{g}_i + \lfloor q/4 \rceil \cdot (m_i, \mathbf{0})) \cdot \mathbf{F}^{-1} \in \mathbb{Z}_q^n$ *be an encryption of* $m_i \in \{0,1\}$. *Consider that* evk *is generated with a ternary* $\mathbf{g}$ *and let* $\mathbf{c} := \mathsf{MNTRU.Nand}(\mathbf{c}_0, \mathbf{c}_1, \mathsf{evk})$. *If* $\|\mathbf{g}_0 + \mathbf{g}_1\| < (q-20)/8$, *then* $\mathsf{MNTRU.Dec}(\mathbf{c}, \mathsf{sk})$ *outputs* $\mathsf{NAND}(m_0, m_1)$.

Proof. From the above analysis, we know that

$$\mathbf{c} = \Big(\mathbf{g} - \mathbf{g}_0 - \mathbf{g}_1 + e(1, \mathbf{0}) \pm q/8 \cdot (1, \mathbf{0}) + (q/2) \cdot (m, \mathbf{0})\Big) \cdot \mathbf{F}^{-1} \in \mathbb{Z}_q^n$$

where $m := \mathsf{NAND}(m_0, m_1)$.

Let $\mathbf{f} := \mathsf{col}_0(\mathbf{F})$. To decrypt $\mathbf{c}$, we compute $r := \mathbf{c} \cdot \mathbf{f} \bmod q$. Notice that for some $u \in \mathbb{Z}$, we have

$$r = g - g_0 - g_1 + e \pm q/8 + (q/2) \cdot m - u \cdot q,$$

where g, g_0 and g_1 are the first components of $\mathbf{g}, \mathbf{g}_0$ and $\mathbf{g}_1$, respectively. Thus, the second step of the decryption operation gives us

$$\left\lfloor \frac{2 \cdot r}{q} \right\rceil = \left\lfloor \frac{2 \cdot (g - g_0 - g_1)}{q} + \frac{2 \cdot e}{q} \pm \frac{1}{4} \right\rceil + m - 2 \cdot u$$

which is equal to m modulo 2 as long as $|2 \cdot (g - g_0 - g_1)/q + 3/q \pm 1/4| < 1/2$. Thus, the inequality simply implies that

$$\|\mathbf{g} - \mathbf{g}_0 - \mathbf{g}_1\| < \left(\frac{1}{2} - \frac{1}{4} - \frac{3}{q}\right) \cdot \frac{q}{2} = \frac{q-12}{8}.$$

Since the noise of evaluation key is always fresh and sampled from ternary elements, $\|\mathbf{g}\| = 1$. It implies that if $\|\mathbf{g}_0 + \mathbf{g}_1\| < (q-12)/8 - 1 = (q-20)/8$, then the result holds.

□

4 NGS: NTRU-based GSW-like Scheme

In this section, we present a (ring-based) NTRU-based scheme that has two encryption functions. The first one encrypts a plaintext m which is a ternary polynomial as an element of R_Q, whilst the second one encrypts it as a vector over R_Q using "gadget vectors". To simplify the noise analysis, we assume that all the messages encrypted by the vector ciphertexts belong to the following set of monomials: $\mathbb{M} = \{\pm b \cdot X^k : b \in \{0,1\} \text{ and } k \in \mathbb{N}\}$. We notice that this assumption holds for our bootstrapping procedures.

Our scheme has quasi-additive noise-growth as the GSW scheme [19]. In fact, it is inspired by the simplified variant of GSW proposed in [12]. We call this scheme NGS, which stands for NTRU-GSW-like encryption Scheme. In Sect. 5, the NGS scheme is used as the accumulator to homomorphically evaluate the decryption of another, much simpler scheme based on the matrix NTRU problem. Following the idea of [10] to speed up the bootstrapping, we define an *external product* that multiplies scalar NTRU ciphertexts, i.e. elements of R_Q, and vector NTRU ciphertexts, i.e. vectors over R_Q. This is the framework used to obtain a fast bootstrapping in FHEW [12] and TFHE [10].

Usually NTRU schemes are defined as asymmetric ciphers by publishing a public key $h := g/f \bmod Q$. Since such public keys are not involved in bootstrapping, we present a symmetric version of this scheme. Notice that any encryption of zero could be used as a public key. Moreover, since the NGS ciphertexts are never decrypted in the bootstrapping pipeline, we omit the decryption procedure.

4.1 Basic Procedures

The NTRU-based encryption scheme is defined as follows.

- $\mathsf{NGS.ParamGen}(1^\lambda)$: Receives the security parameter and outputs the tuple $(N, Q, \varsigma, B, \ell)$, where B is a base used to decompose the ciphertexts and $\ell := \lceil \log_B(Q) \rceil$.
- $\mathsf{NGS.KeyGen}$: Sample $f' \leftarrow \chi_\varsigma^N$ and set $f := 1 + 4 \cdot f'$ until f^{-1} exists in R_Q. Output $\mathsf{sk} := f$.
- $\mathsf{NGS.EncS}(\mathsf{sk}, m)$: Given a ternary polynomial m, sample $g \leftarrow \chi_\varsigma^N$, define $\Delta := \lfloor Q/4 \rceil$, and output $c = g/f + \Delta \cdot m \in R_Q$. We call c a *scalar encryption* of m.
- $\mathsf{NGS.EncVec}(\mathsf{sk}, m)$: Given $m \in \mathbb{M}$, sample $g_i \leftarrow \chi_\varsigma^N$ for $0 \le i \le \ell - 1$. Define $\mathbf{g} := (g_0, \ldots, g_{\ell-1})$ and $\mathfrak{g} = (B^0, B^1, \ldots, B^{\ell-1})$. Output $\mathbf{c} = \mathbf{g}/f + \mathfrak{g} \cdot m \in R_Q^\ell$. We call $\mathbf{c}$ a *vector encryption* of m.

4.2 External Product

Having defined two types of encryptions, scalar and vector ciphertexts, we can define the "external product" between them as proposed in TFHE [10]. The external product is cheaper than the NGS homomorphic multiplication (i.e. the convolution of two vector ciphertexts).

Suppose we have a scalar encryption $c := g/f + \Delta \cdot u \in R_Q$ of a ternary polynomial u and a vector encryption $\mathbf{c} := \mathbf{g}/f + \mathfrak{g} \cdot v \in R_Q^\ell$ of a message $v \in \mathbb{M}$. Then, the external product of c and $\mathbf{c}$ is defined as follows

$$c \boxdot \mathbf{c} := \mathfrak{g}^{-1}(c) \cdot \mathbf{c} \in R_Q.$$

Since $\mathbf{g}^{-1}(c) \cdot \mathbf{g} = c$, it is clear that $c_{mult} = c \boxdot \mathbf{c}$ is equal to

$$c_{mult} := (\mathbf{g}^{-1}(c) \cdot \mathbf{g})/f + (\mathbf{g}^{-1}(c) \cdot \mathbf{g} \cdot v) = \underbrace{(\mathbf{g}^{-1}(c) \cdot \mathbf{g} + g \cdot v)}_{g_{mult}}/f + \Delta \cdot u \cdot v.$$

Hence, c_{mult} is a valid scalar encryption of the product $u \cdot v$ as long as the noise term g_{mult} is small enough. We formalize this notion in the next section. Notice that it is important that $\|u \cdot v\| < 4$, otherwise, multiplying it by Δ introduces a round-off error and produces an ill-formed ciphertext. Since we are assuming that $v \in \mathbb{M}$, we have $\|u \cdot v\| \leq \|u\| < 2$.

4.3 Noise Analysis

Instead of performing a worst-case analysis of the noise growth, which boils down to bounding every element by its infinity norm, we provide a more realistic average-case noise analysis. To do so, we can instantiate $\mathbf{g}^{-1}$ with a randomized gadget decomposition algorithm [17,21], or we can use a deterministic decomposition and heuristically assume that all the coefficients of the errors of MNTRU and NGS samples are independent and concentrated; thus, they are subgaussian random variables. The first approach is used in FHEW [12], while the latter is present in TFHE [8,10]. Both methods return a subgaussian random variable. Therefore, our analysis assumes that for all $a \in R_Q$, $\mathbf{g}_{q,B_{\mathsf{ksk}}}^{-1}(a)$ is a γ-subgaussian for some $\gamma = O(B)$.

Definition 4 (Noise of a scalar ciphertext). *Let $c = g/f + \Delta \cdot m \in R_Q$. We define the noise of c as $\mathsf{err}(c) := c \cdot f - \Delta \cdot m \in R_Q$ and interpret it as a polynomial over $\mathbb{Z}[X]$ with coefficients in $[-Q/2, Q/2]$.*

We also define the noise of a vector ciphertext below for our noise analysis.

Definition 5 (Noise of a vector ciphertext). *Let $\mathbf{c} = \mathbf{g}/f + \mathbf{g} \cdot m \in R_Q^{\ell}$. We define the noise of $\mathbf{c}$ as $\mathsf{err}(\mathbf{c}) := \mathbf{c} \cdot f - \mathbf{g} \cdot m \cdot f \in R_Q$ and interpret it as a vector of polynomials over $\mathbb{Z}[X]$ with coefficients in $[-Q/2, Q/2]$.*

We first bound the noise of ciphertexts of a special form, namely fresh ones that encrypt monomials. This includes the important special case of $m \in \{0, 1\}$.

Lemma 3 (Bound on the noise of a (fresh) scalar ciphertext). *Let $c = g/f + \Delta \cdot m \in R_Q$ be a ciphertext of m. If m is a monomial of the form $\pm b \cdot X^k$ for some $b \in \{0, 1\}$, then*

$$\mathsf{Var}(\mathsf{err}(c)) \leq \mathsf{Var}(g) + 4 \cdot \varsigma^2.$$

If m is a ternary polynomial with degree at most $N - 1$, then

$$\mathsf{Var}(\mathsf{err}(c)) \leq \mathsf{Var}(g) + 4 \cdot N \cdot \varsigma^2.$$

Moreover, if c is a fresh ciphertext, then $\mathsf{Var}(\mathsf{err}(c)) \leq 5 \cdot \varsigma^2$ for a monomial m and the variance is bounded by $(4 \cdot N + 1) \cdot \varsigma^2$ for a ternary polynomial m.

Proof. Let $\Delta = Q/4 + \epsilon$ for some $\epsilon \in \mathbb{R}$ such that $|\epsilon| \leq 1/2$. Since in R_Q it holds that

$$c \cdot f = g + (1 + 4 \cdot f') \cdot (Q/4 + \epsilon) \cdot m = g + 4 \cdot f' \cdot \epsilon \cdot m + \Delta \cdot m,$$

we have $\mathsf{err}(c) := c \cdot f - \Delta \cdot m = g + 4 \cdot f' \cdot \epsilon \cdot m$. Notice that, if $m \in \{0, \pm 1, \pm X, \ldots, \pm X^{N-1}\}$, we have $\mathsf{Var}(f' \cdot m) \leq \mathsf{Var}(f')$, thus

$$\mathsf{Var}(\mathsf{err}(c)) \leq \mathsf{Var}(g) + (4 \cdot \epsilon)^2 \cdot \mathsf{Var}(f') \leq \mathsf{Var}(g) + 4 \cdot \varsigma^2.$$

If m is a ternary polynomial of degree at most $N - 1$,

$$\mathsf{Var}(\mathsf{err}(c)) \leq \mathsf{Var}(g) + (4 \cdot \epsilon)^2 \cdot \|m\|_2^2 \cdot \mathsf{Var}(f') \leq \mathsf{Var}(g) + 4 \cdot N \cdot \varsigma^2.$$

If c is a fresh ciphertext, then $\mathsf{Var}(g) = \varsigma^2$ and the rest of the lemma follows. □

We now analyze how the external product increases the noise.

Lemma 4 (Noise growth of external product). *Let* $c := g/f + \Delta \cdot u \in R_Q$ *and* $\mathbf{c} := \mathbf{g}/f + \mathfrak{g} \cdot v \in R_Q^\ell$. *Define* $c_{mult} := c \boxdot \mathbf{c}$ *as above. Then*

$$\mathsf{Var}(\mathsf{err}(c_{mult})) \leq N \cdot \ell \cdot \gamma^2 \cdot \mathsf{Var}(\mathbf{g}) + \|v\|_2^2 \cdot \mathsf{Var}(g) + 4 \cdot \varsigma^2.$$

If $v \in \mathbb{M} := \{\pm b \cdot X^k : b \in \{0, 1\}$ *and* $k \in \mathbb{N}\}$, *then*

$$\mathsf{Var}(\mathsf{err}(c_{mult})) \leq N \cdot \ell \cdot \gamma^2 \cdot \mathsf{Var}(\mathsf{err}(\mathbf{c})) + \mathsf{Var}(\mathsf{err}(c))$$

Proof. From the analysis in Sect. 4.2, we know that $c_{mult} = g_{mult}/f + \Delta \cdot m$, where $g_{mult} := \mathfrak{g}^{-1}(c) \cdot \mathbf{g} + g \cdot v$ and $m := v \cdot u$. Thus, by Lemma 3, we have $\mathsf{Var}(\mathsf{err}(c_{mult})) \leq \mathsf{Var}(g_{mult}) + 4 \cdot \varsigma^2$. Since

$$\mathsf{Var}(g_{mult}) \leq \mathsf{Var}(\langle \mathfrak{g}^{-1}(c), \mathbf{g} \rangle) + \mathsf{Var}(g \cdot v) \leq N \cdot \ell \cdot \gamma^2 \cdot \mathsf{Var}(\mathbf{g}) + \|v\|_2^2 \cdot \mathsf{Var}(g),$$

the result follows. If $v \in \mathbb{M}$, then $\|v\|_2^2 \leq 1$, and the value $\mathsf{Var}(g_{mult}) + 4 \cdot \varsigma^2$ is bounded by $N \cdot \ell \cdot \gamma^2 \cdot \mathsf{Var}(\mathbf{g}) + \mathsf{Var}(g) + 4 \cdot \varsigma^2$, which is $N \cdot \ell \cdot \gamma^2 \cdot \mathsf{Var}(\mathsf{err}(\mathbf{c})) + \mathsf{Var}(\mathsf{err}(c))$ by Definition 5 and Lemma 3. □

Our goal now is to analyze the noise growth caused by a sequence of k such external products, i.e., $c' = c \boxdot_{i=1}^k \mathbf{c}_i = (\ldots((c \boxdot \mathbf{c}_1) \boxdot \mathbf{c}_2) \ldots \boxdot \mathbf{c}_k)$. Since in our bootstrapping the messages encrypted by vector ciphertexts are of the form $\pm b \cdot X^m$ for some bit b, we simplify the analysis by supposing that the messages encrypted by $\mathbf{c}_1, \ldots, \mathbf{c}_k$ belong to $\mathbb{M}$. This allows us to ignore the term $\|v\|_2^2$ in Lemma 4 as it is bounded by 1.

Lemma 5 (Noise of a sequence of external products). *For* $1 \leq i \leq k$, *let* $\mathbf{c}_i := \mathbf{g}_i/f + \mathfrak{g} \cdot m_i \in R_Q^\ell$ *with* $m_i \in \mathbb{M}$. *Let* $c_0 = g_0/f + \Delta \cdot m_0 \in R_Q$ *with a ternary polynomial* m_0. *If* $c' := c \boxdot_{i=1}^k \mathbf{c}_i$, *then*

$$\mathsf{Var}(\mathsf{err}(c')) \leq N \cdot \ell \cdot \gamma^2 \cdot \sum_{i=1}^{k} \mathsf{Var}(\mathbf{g}_i) + \mathsf{Var}(g_0) + 4 \cdot \varsigma^2.$$

Proof. Let $c_i := c_{i-1} \boxdot \mathbf{c}_i = g_i/f + \Delta \cdot m'_i$ for $1 \leq i \leq k$. It is clear that $c' = c_k$. Using the fact that $v_1, \ldots, v_k \in \mathbb{M}$, we apply Lemma 4 k times and obtain

$$\begin{aligned}
\mathsf{Var}(\mathsf{err}(c_k)) &\leq N \cdot \ell \cdot \gamma^2 \cdot \mathsf{Var}(\mathsf{err}(\mathbf{c}_k)) + \mathsf{Var}(\mathsf{err}(c_{k-1})) \\
&\leq N \cdot \ell \cdot \gamma^2 \cdot \mathsf{Var}(\mathsf{err}(\mathbf{c}_k)) + N \cdot \ell \cdot \gamma^2 \cdot \mathsf{Var}(\mathsf{err}(\mathbf{c}_{k-1})) + \mathsf{Var}(\mathsf{err}(c_{k-2})) \\
&\vdots \\
&\leq N \cdot \ell \cdot \gamma^2 \cdot \sum_{i=1}^{k} \mathsf{Var}(\mathsf{err}(\mathbf{c}_i)) + \mathsf{Var}(\mathsf{err}(c_0)) \\
&= N \cdot \ell \cdot \gamma^2 \cdot \sum_{i=1}^{k} \mathsf{Var}(\mathbf{g}_i) + \mathsf{Var}(g_0) + 4 \cdot \varsigma^2.
\end{aligned}$$

□

Corollary 1. *Using the notation of Lemma 5, if all the ciphertexts are fresh, then*

$$\mathsf{Var}(\mathsf{err}(c')) \leq (4 + (k+1) \cdot N \cdot \ell \cdot \gamma^2) \cdot \varsigma^2.$$

4.4 Modulus-switching

In this section, we show that the modulus-switching technique for (R)LWE-based schemes can be adapted to NTRU-based schemes. Given a ciphertext $c = g/f + \Delta \cdot \mu \in R_Q$ for some message μ which is a ternary polynomial, we can multiply c by q/Q and round it to obtain a ciphertext defined modulo q. Since $\lfloor y \rceil = y + \epsilon$, the modulus switching essentially scales the ciphertext and adds a small rounding error, which is then multiplied by the secret key f during decryption. As in the analysis of [12], we define the following randomized rounding function.

Definition 6. *Let $Q, q \in \mathbb{Z}$ and $1 < q < Q$. The randomized rounding function $[\cdot]_{Q:q} : \mathbb{Z}_Q \to \mathbb{Z}_q$ is defined as $[z]_{Q:q} := \lfloor q \cdot z/Q \rfloor + B$ where $B \in \{0, 1\}$ is a Bernoulli random variable with* $\Pr[B = 1] = (q \cdot z/Q) - \lfloor q \cdot z/Q \rfloor \in [0, 1]$.

Notice that the the rounding error $\epsilon := [z]_{Q:q} - (q \cdot z/Q)$ is 1-subgaussian. We extend the definition to polynomials, vectors, and matrices by applying the rounding entry-wise. Thus, the modulus switching is defined as

$$\mathsf{ModSwitch}(c) = \sum_{i=0}^{N-1} [c_i]_{Q:q} \cdot X^i \in R_q.$$

Lemma 6. *Let $c = g/f + \lfloor Q/4 \rceil \cdot \mu \in R_Q$. Then,* $\mathsf{ModSwitch}(c)$ *is a scalar encryption of μ in R_q. Moreover,*

$$\mathsf{Var}(\mathsf{err}(\mathsf{ModSwitch}(c))) \leq (q/Q)^2 \cdot \mathsf{Var}(\mathsf{err}(c)) + 1 + 16 \cdot N \cdot \varsigma^2.$$

Proof. Just notice that $\mathsf{ModSwitch}(c) = (q \cdot g/Q)/f + \epsilon + \Delta \cdot \mu \in R_q$, where $\Delta = \lfloor q/4 \rceil$ and ϵ is a polynomial with infinite norm bounded by 1, therefore, $\mathsf{err}(\mathsf{ModSwitch}(c)) = q \cdot \mathsf{err}(c)/Q + \epsilon \cdot f = q \cdot \mathsf{err}(c)/Q + \epsilon \cdot (1 + 4f')$. Then the variance of the noise is as follows:

$$\begin{aligned} \mathsf{Var}(\mathsf{err}(\mathsf{ModSwitch}(c))) &= \mathsf{Var}(q \cdot \mathsf{err}(c)/Q + \epsilon + 4 \cdot \epsilon \cdot f') \\ &= \mathsf{Var}(q \cdot \mathsf{err}(c)/Q) + \mathsf{Var}(\epsilon) + 16 \cdot \mathsf{Var}(\epsilon \cdot f') \\ &\leq (q/Q)^2 \cdot \mathsf{Var}(\mathsf{err}(c)) + \mathsf{Var}(\epsilon) + 16 \cdot N \cdot \mathsf{Var}(\epsilon) \cdot \mathsf{Var}(f') \\ &\leq (q/Q)^2 \cdot \mathsf{Var}(\mathsf{err}(c)) + 1 + 16 \cdot N \cdot \mathsf{Var}(f'). \end{aligned}$$

The last inequality holds since ϵ is 1-subgaussian.

4.5 Key-switching from NGS to the Base Scheme

As we will see in Sect. 5, our bootstrapping procedure starts with a ciphertext $(\mathbf{g} + \Delta \cdot (m, \mathbf{0})) \cdot \mathbf{F}^{-1} \in \mathbb{Z}_q^n$ of the base scheme. After modulus-switching, it produces an NTRU encryption $c = g/f + \epsilon + \Delta \cdot \mu \in R_q$, where μ is a polynomial whose constant term is equal to $m \in \{0, 1\}$ and $\Delta := \lfloor q/4 \rceil$. To finish the bootstrapping, we want to obtain again a base scheme ciphertext of the form $\mathbf{c}' = (\mathbf{g}' + \Delta \cdot (m, \mathbf{0})) \cdot \mathbf{F}^{-1} \in \mathbb{Z}_q^n$. To achieve this, we define the following key-switching operation.

- Key-switching key generation: The input of this procedure is composed by the secret keys $f \in R$ and $\mathbf{F} \in \mathbb{Z}^{n \times n}$, and the parameters $\sigma_{\mathtt{ksk}}$, q, and $B_{\mathtt{ksk}}$. Let $L = \lceil \log_{B_{\mathtt{ksk}}}(q) \rceil$. Define $\mathbf{P} \in \mathbb{Z}^{(N \cdot L) \times N}$ as the gadget matrix $\mathbf{I}_N \otimes \mathfrak{g}_{q, B_{\mathtt{ksk}}}$, i.e. each "diagonal element" of $\mathbf{P}$ is equal to $\mathfrak{g}_{q, B_{\mathtt{ksk}}} \in \mathbb{Z}^L$. Also, let $\mathbf{E} \in \mathbb{Z}^{N \times n}$ be the matrix whose entries are zeros except for $\mathbf{E}_{0,0} = 1$.
  Then, sample $\mathbf{G} \leftarrow \chi_{\sigma_{\mathtt{ksk}}}^{(N \cdot L) \times n}$ and output
  $$\mathtt{ksk} := (\mathbf{G} + \mathbf{P} \cdot \boldsymbol{\Phi}(f) \cdot \mathbf{E}) \cdot \mathbf{F}^{-1} \in \mathbb{Z}_q^{(N \cdot L) \times n},$$
  where $\boldsymbol{\Phi}(f)$ is the anti-circulant matrix of f.
- Key-Switching algorithm: Given an output of modulus-switching, $c = g/f + \epsilon + \Delta \cdot \mu \in R_q$, and a key-switching key $\mathtt{ksk}$, let
  $$\mathsf{KeySwitch}(c, \mathtt{ksk}) := \mathbf{y} \cdot \mathtt{ksk} \in \mathbb{Z}_q^n$$
  where $\mathbf{y} := (\mathfrak{g}_{q, B_{\mathtt{ksk}}}^{-1}(c_0), \ldots, \mathfrak{g}_{q, B_{\mathtt{ksk}}}^{-1}(c_{N-1})) \in \mathbb{Z}^{N \cdot L}$.

Lemma 7 (Correctness of key-switching). *Let $c = g/f + \epsilon + \Delta \cdot \mu \in R_q$ be a scalar encryption of a ternary polynomial μ, with $\Delta = \lfloor q/4 \rceil$, and $\mathtt{ksk}$ a key-switching key from $f = 1 + 4 \cdot f'$ to $\mathbf{F} \in \mathbb{Z}^{n \times n}$. Then, $\mathsf{KeySwitch}(c, \mathtt{ksk})$ outputs a base scheme ciphertext $\mathbf{c}' = (\mathbf{g} + \Delta \cdot (\mu_0, \mathbf{0})) \cdot \mathbf{F}^{-1} \in \mathbb{Z}_q^{n \times n}$, where μ_0 is the constant term of μ. Moreover, its time complexity is $O(N \cdot n \cdot \log q)$ operations on $\mathbb{Z}_q$.*

Proof. Let $|\epsilon'| \leq 1/2$ such that $\Delta = q/4 + \epsilon'$. Since

$$\mathbf{y} \cdot \mathbf{P} = \phi(c) = \phi(g) \cdot \boldsymbol{\Phi}(f)^{-1} + \phi(\epsilon) + \Delta \cdot \phi(\mu),$$

it is clear that

$$\mathbf{y} \cdot \mathbf{P} \cdot \boldsymbol{\Phi}(f) = \phi(g) + \phi(\epsilon) \cdot \boldsymbol{\Phi}(f) + \epsilon' \cdot \phi(\mu) \cdot 4 \cdot \boldsymbol{\Phi}(f') + \Delta \cdot \phi(\mu) \in \mathbb{Z}_q^N.$$

Therefore, by defining $\mathbf{g}' := \phi(\epsilon) \cdot \boldsymbol{\Phi}(f) + \epsilon' \cdot \phi(\mu) \cdot 4 \cdot \boldsymbol{\Phi}(f')$, the following equality holds modulo q:

$$\mathbf{c}' = \left(\mathbf{y} \cdot \mathbf{G} + \left(\phi(g) + \mathbf{g}' + \Delta \cdot \phi(\mu)\right) \cdot \mathbf{E}\right) \cdot \mathbf{F}^{-1}.$$

And because $\mathbf{v} \cdot \mathbf{E} = (v_0, \mathbf{0}) \in \mathbb{Z}^n$ for any $\mathbf{v} \in \mathbb{Z}^N$, we finally obtain

$$\mathbf{c}' = (\mathbf{y} \cdot \mathbf{G} + (g_0, \mathbf{0}) + (g_0', \mathbf{0}) + \Delta \cdot (\mu_0, \mathbf{0})) \cdot \mathbf{F}^{-1} \in \mathbb{Z}_q^n.$$

If we set $\mathbf{g} = \mathbf{y} \cdot \mathbf{G} + (g_0, \mathbf{0}) + (g_0', \mathbf{0})$, the result holds. Moreover, since the procedure consists in multiplying $\mathbf{y} \in \mathbb{Z}^{N \cdot L}$ by each of the n columns of $\mathtt{ksk}$, it is clear that it costs $O(N \cdot n \cdot \log q)$ operations on $\mathbb{Z}_q$. □

Noise Analysis on the Matrix Key Switching Procedure. We first see that the noise of c which is an output of modulus-switching equals to $g + \epsilon + 4 \cdot \epsilon \cdot f' + 4 \cdot f' \cdot \epsilon' \cdot \mu$ by Definition 4. Then the variance of the noise is following by Lemma 3:

$$\begin{aligned}\mathsf{Var}(\mathsf{err}(c)) &\leq \mathsf{Var}(g) + \mathsf{Var}(\epsilon) + 16 \cdot N \cdot \mathsf{Var}(\epsilon) \cdot \mathsf{Var}(f') + 4 \cdot \|\mu\|_2^2 \cdot \mathsf{Var}(f') \\ &\leq \mathsf{Var}(g) + 1 + 16 \cdot N \cdot \mathsf{Var}(f') + 4 \cdot N \cdot \mathsf{Var}(f') \\ &= \mathsf{Var}(g) + 1 + 20 \cdot N \cdot \varsigma^2\end{aligned}$$

The noise contained in $\mathbf{c}'$ is $\mathbf{y} \cdot \mathbf{G} + (g_0, \mathbf{0}) + (g_0', \mathbf{0})$. In fact, $\mathbf{G}$ is the noise of the key switching key $\mathtt{ksk}$, and $g_0 + g_0'$ is very close to the noise originally contained in c, before key-switching. Notice that

$$\begin{aligned}\mathsf{Var}(g_0') &\leq \mathsf{Var}(\phi(\epsilon) \cdot \boldsymbol{\Phi}(f)) + (4\epsilon')^2 \cdot \mathsf{Var}(\phi(\mu) \cdot \boldsymbol{\Phi}(f')) \\ &\leq \mathsf{Var}(\epsilon) + 16 \cdot N \cdot \mathsf{Var}(\epsilon) \cdot \mathsf{Var}(\boldsymbol{\Phi}(f')) + 4 \cdot \|\phi(\mu)\|_2^2 \cdot \mathsf{Var}(\boldsymbol{\Phi}(f')) \\ &\leq 1 + 16 \cdot N \cdot \mathsf{Var}(\boldsymbol{\Phi}(f')) + 4 \cdot N \cdot \mathsf{Var}(\boldsymbol{\Phi}(f')) \\ &\leq 1 + 20 \cdot N \cdot \varsigma^2.\end{aligned}$$

Thus, assuming the outputs of decomposition $\mathbf{g}^{-1}(\cdot)$ is γ-subgaussian, the variance of $\mathsf{err}(\mathbf{c}')$ is following:

$$\begin{aligned}\mathsf{Var}(\mathsf{err}(\mathbf{c}')) &= \mathsf{Var}(\mathbf{y} \cdot \mathbf{G}) + \mathsf{Var}(g_0, \mathbf{0})) + \mathsf{Var}((g_0', \mathbf{0})) \\ &\leq N \cdot L \cdot \mathsf{Var}(\mathbf{g}^{-1}(\phi(c))) \cdot \mathsf{Var}(\mathbf{G}) + \mathsf{Var}(\phi(g)) + 1 + 20 \cdot N \cdot \varsigma^2 \\ &\leq N \cdot L \cdot \gamma^2 \cdot \mathsf{Var}(\mathsf{err}(\mathtt{ksk})) + \mathsf{Var}(g) + 1 + 20 \cdot N \cdot \varsigma^2 \\ &= N \cdot L \cdot \gamma^2 \cdot \mathsf{Var}(\mathsf{err}(\mathtt{ksk})) + \mathsf{Var}(\mathsf{err}(c)).\end{aligned}$$

5 Bootstrapping

As explained in the introduction, to cope with the ternary secrets inherent in NTRU we utilize a ternary CMux gate. Our *ternary* CMux gate is defined as follows: For a given $f_i \in \{-1, 0, 1\}$, we define two keys $\mathtt{bsk}_{i,0}$ and $\mathtt{bsk}_{i,1}$:

$$\begin{cases} f_i = -1 & \implies \mathtt{bsk}_{i,0} := \mathsf{NGS.EncVec}(0) \wedge \mathtt{bsk}_{i,1} := \mathsf{NGS.EncVec}(1) \\ f_i = 0 & \implies \mathtt{bsk}_{i,0} := \mathsf{NGS.EncVec}(0) \wedge \mathtt{bsk}_{i,1} := \mathsf{NGS.EncVec}(0) \\ f_i = 1 & \implies \mathtt{bsk}_{i,0} := \mathsf{NGS.EncVec}(1) \wedge \mathtt{bsk}_{i,1} := \mathsf{NGS.EncVec}(0) \end{cases} \tag{1}$$

Then, our CMux gate is defined as

$$\mathtt{CMux}_i(c_i) := \mathbf{1} + (X^{c_i} - 1) \cdot \mathtt{bsk}_{i,0} + (X^{-c_i} - 1) \cdot \mathtt{bsk}_{i,1},$$

where $\mathbf{1}$ is a trivial, noiseless, encryption of one, i.e. simply $\mathfrak{g}$. It is easy to see that $\mathtt{CMux}_i(c_i) = \mathsf{NGS.EncVec}(X^{c_i \cdot f_i})$. In particular, the message encrypted by $\mathtt{CMux}_i(c_i)$ belongs to $\mathbb{M}$ as required by our external product from Sect. 4.2.

Algorithm 1: Bootstrapping key generation.

Input: $\mathbf{F} \in \mathbb{Z}_q^{n \times n}$ – the secret key of the base scheme.
Output: $\mathtt{bsk}$ – the bootstrapping key.

1 $(f_0, \ldots f_{n-1}) \leftarrow \mathsf{col}_0(\mathbf{F})$
2 **for** $i \leftarrow 0$ **to** $n - 1$ **do**
3 | Compute $\mathtt{bsk}_{i,0}$ and $\mathtt{bsk}_{i,1}$ accordingly to Equation 1.
4 **Return** $\mathtt{bsk} := \{(\mathtt{bsk}_{i,0}, \mathtt{bsk}_{i,1}) : 0 \leq i \leq n - 1\}$.

Algorithm 2: Bootstrapping algorithm.

Input:
$\mathtt{ct} \in \mathbb{Z}_q^n$ – a base scheme ciphertext encrypting $m \in \{0, 1\}$
$\{\mathtt{bsk}_{i,j}\}_{0 \leq i \leq n-1, 0 \leq j \leq 1}$ – bootstrapping keys, where each $\mathtt{bsk}_{i,j} \in R_{Q,N}^{\ell}$
$\mathtt{ksk}$ – a key-switching key from the NGS secret key $f \in R$ to the base scheme secret key $\mathbf{F} \in \mathbb{Z}^{n \times n}$.
Output: $\mathtt{ct}' \in \mathbb{Z}_q^n$ – a base-scheme ciphertext encrypting the same m.

1 $(c_0, \ldots, c_{n-1}) \leftarrow \left\lfloor \frac{2 \cdot N \cdot \mathtt{ct}}{q} \right\rceil$
2 $\mathtt{ACC} \leftarrow \left\lfloor \frac{Q}{8} \right\rceil \cdot X^{N/2} \cdot \sum_{i=0}^{N-1} X^i$
3 **for** $i \leftarrow 0$ **to** $n - 1$ **do**
4 | $\mathbf{c}_{\mathtt{Mux}} \leftarrow \mathtt{CMux}_i(c_i)$
5 | $\mathtt{ACC} \leftarrow \mathtt{ACC} \boxdot \mathbf{c}_{\mathtt{Mux}}$
6 $\mathtt{ACC} \leftarrow \mathtt{ACC} + \left\lfloor \frac{Q}{8} \right\rceil \cdot \sum_{i=0}^{N-1} X^i$
7 $\mathtt{ACC} \leftarrow \mathsf{ModSwitch}(\mathtt{ACC})$
8 $\mathtt{ct}' \leftarrow \mathsf{KeySwitch}(\mathtt{ACC}, \mathtt{ksk})$
9 **Return** $\mathtt{ct}'$.

Recall that our base-scheme ciphertext $\mathbf{c} = (\mathbf{g} + \Delta \cdot (m, \mathbf{0})) \cdot \mathbf{F}^{-1} \in \mathbb{Z}_q^n$ can be decrypted by multiplying it by the first column of $\mathbf{F}$, Thus, our bootstrapping keys are generated using Eq. 1 for each entry f_i from the first column of $\mathbf{F}$, see Algorithm 1.

By using the $\mathtt{CMux}$ gate n times and multiplying all the resulting ciphertexts, we obtain an encryption of $X^{\mathbf{c}\cdot\mathsf{col}_0(\mathbf{F})} = X^{g+(N/2)\cdot m}$. We can then multiply this by the (plaintext) "test vector" $T(X) := X^{N/2} \cdot \sum_{i=0}^{N-1} X^i \pmod{X^N + 1}$ to produce a scalar encryption of m. Note, we actually put the test vector in the left most position of the product so that each multiplication is an external product instead of a regular "vector-vector" homomorphic multiplication, i.e. we compute $\lfloor Q/8 \rceil \cdot T(X) \cdot \boxdot_{i=0}^{n-1} \mathtt{CMux}_i(c_i)$, which produces $\mathsf{NGS.EncS}(2 \cdot m - 1)$, but with $\Delta = \lfloor Q/8 \rceil$. Then we add $\mathsf{NGS.EncS}(1)$ to obtain $\mathsf{NGS.EncS}(2 \cdot m)$. The factor two is multiplied by $\lfloor Q/8 \rceil$ and so we obtain $\mathsf{NGS.EncS}(m)$ with $\Delta = \lfloor Q/4 \rceil$, as desired. Finally, we use the key-switching procedure defined in Sect. 4 to transform this NTRU ciphertext into a matrix NTRU ciphertext of the base scheme. Our bootstrapping is shown in detail in Algorithm 2.

5.1 Bootstrapping Noise

Firstly, we analyze the noise growth of our $\mathtt{CMux}$ gate. Let $c_{\mathtt{Mux}} := \mathtt{CMux}_i(c_i)$ for any $0 \leq i \leq n-1$. Then, the following holds:

$$\begin{aligned}\mathsf{Var}(\mathsf{err}(c_{\mathtt{Mux}})) &\leq \|X^{c_i} - 1\|_2^2 \cdot \mathsf{Var}(\mathsf{err}(\mathtt{bsk}_{i,0})) + \|X^{-c_i} - 1\|_2^2 \cdot \mathsf{Var}(\mathsf{err}(\mathtt{bsk}_{i,1})) \\ &\leq 4 \cdot \mathsf{Var}(\mathsf{err}(\mathtt{bsk})),\end{aligned}$$

where $\mathtt{bsk}_{i,0}$ and $\mathtt{bsk}_{i,1}$ are the corresponding bootstrapping keys, which are NGS ciphertexts with noise variance $\mathsf{Var}(\mathsf{err}(\mathtt{bsk}))$.

Now we consider the whole bootstrapping algorithm. In the first line, we scale down the input ciphertext to modulus $2 \cdot N$. We denote the resulting vector by $\mathtt{ct}_{2\cdot N}$. Then we have

$$\left| \mathtt{ct} \cdot \mathsf{col}_0(\mathbf{F}) - \frac{q}{2 \cdot N} \cdot \mathtt{ct}_{2\cdot N} \cdot \mathsf{col}_0(\mathbf{F}) \right| \leq \frac{q}{4 \cdot N} \cdot |\mathtt{ct} \cdot \mathsf{col}_0(\mathbf{F})|, \tag{2}$$

where $\mathsf{col}_0(\mathbf{F})$ is the first column of the secret key of $\mathtt{ct}$.

From the line 3 to 5 of Algorithm 2, the output $\mathtt{ACC}$ is obtained by utilizing n external products with $\mathbf{c}_{\mathtt{Mux}}$ whose noise variance is $\mathsf{Var}(\mathsf{err}(c_{\mathtt{Mux}}))$. The variance of the final $\mathsf{err}(\mathtt{ACC})$ based on Lemma 5 is the following:

$$\mathsf{Var}(\mathsf{err}(\mathtt{ACC})) \leq n \cdot N \cdot \ell \cdot \gamma^2 \cdot \mathsf{Var}(\mathsf{err}(\mathbf{c}_{\mathtt{Mux}})) + 4 \cdot \|\mathsf{msg}(\mathtt{ACC})\|_2^2 \cdot \varsigma^2,$$

where $\mathsf{msg}(\mathtt{ACC})$ is $X^{N/2} \cdot \sum_{i=0}^{N-1} X^i$. After line 6, the accumulator $\mathtt{ACC}$ contains a message as a ternary polynomial (say $M(X)$) whose constant term is m. The error term will be changed into

$$\begin{aligned}\mathsf{Var}(\mathsf{err}(\mathtt{ACC})) &\leq n \cdot N \cdot \ell \cdot \gamma^2 \cdot \mathsf{Var}(\mathsf{err}(\mathbf{c}_{\mathtt{Mux}})) + 4 \cdot \|M(X)\|_2^2 \cdot \varsigma^2 \\ &\leq n \cdot N \cdot \ell \cdot \gamma^2 \cdot \mathsf{Var}(\mathsf{err}(\mathbf{c}_{\mathtt{Mux}})) + 4 \cdot N \cdot \varsigma^2\end{aligned}$$

After this step, modulus switching is performed, which results in the noise, by Lemma 6, being

$$\mathsf{Var}(\mathsf{err}(\mathtt{ACC})) \leq (q/Q)^2 \cdot n \cdot N \cdot \ell \cdot \gamma^2 \cdot \mathsf{Var}(\mathsf{err}(\mathbf{c}_{\mathtt{Mux}})) + (q/Q)^2 \cdot 4 \cdot N \cdot \varsigma + 1 + 16 \cdot N \cdot \varsigma$$

After the external product with a key switching key $\mathtt{ksk}$ in line 8, the noise in the resulting $\mathtt{ct}'$ has a variance

$$\begin{aligned}\mathsf{Var}(\mathsf{err}(\mathtt{ct}')) &\leq N \cdot L \cdot \gamma^2 \cdot \mathsf{Var}(\mathsf{err}(\mathtt{ksk})) + \mathsf{Var}(\mathsf{err}(\mathtt{ACC})) \\ &\leq N \cdot L \cdot \gamma^2 \cdot \mathsf{Var}(\mathsf{err}(\mathtt{ksk})) + (q/Q)^2 \cdot n \cdot N \cdot \ell \cdot \gamma^2 \cdot \mathsf{Var}(\mathsf{err}(\mathbf{c}_{\mathtt{Mux}})) \\ &\quad + (q/Q)^2 \cdot 4 \cdot N \cdot \varsigma^2 + 1 + 16 \cdot N \cdot \varsigma^2\end{aligned}$$

where L is the dimension of the key switching key.

After the $\mathtt{for}$ loop from line 3 to 5, the message of the resulting $\mathtt{ACC}$, $\mathsf{msg}(\mathtt{ACC})$, is $\left\lfloor \frac{Q}{8} \right\rceil \cdot X^{\mathtt{ct}_{2\cdot N} \cdot \mathsf{col}_0(\mathbf{F})} \cdot X^{N/2} \cdot \sum_{i=0}^{N-1} X^i$. If we have $|\mathtt{ct} \cdot \mathsf{col}_0(\mathbf{F})| < q/4$, then the ciphertext $\mathtt{ct}$ is encrypting the value zero. This follows from the fact that then $-N/2 < |\mathtt{ct}_{2\cdot N} \cdot \mathsf{col}_0(\mathbf{F})| \leq N/2$ and thus the constant term of the $\mathsf{msg}(\mathtt{ACC})$ is $-\lfloor Q/8 \rceil$, i.e. the constant term of $\mathsf{msg}(\mathtt{ACC})$ in line 6 is zero. If, however, $|\mathtt{ct} \cdot \mathsf{col}_0(\mathbf{F})| < 3 \cdot q/4$ then the ciphertext $\mathtt{ct}$ is encrypting the value one. In this case $N/2 < |\mathtt{ct}_{2\cdot N} \cdot \mathsf{col}_0(\mathbf{F})| \leq 3N/2$, hence the $\mathsf{msg}(\mathtt{ACC})$ is $\lfloor Q/8 \rceil$. Therefore, the constant term of $\mathsf{msg}(\mathtt{ACC})$ in line 6 is $\lfloor Q/4 \rceil$.

We now have the following heuristic for the output noise in average case.

Heuristic. Given $\mathtt{ct}$ encrypting a bit m, Algorithm 2 outputs an MNTRU ciphertext $\mathtt{ct}'$ encrypting the same bit. In addition, under the central limit heuristic, the noise contained in the output behaves as a Gaussian distribution, hence, with overwhelming probability, it satisfies the following bound

$$\|\mathsf{err}(\mathtt{ct}')\| \leq 6 \cdot \begin{pmatrix} N \cdot L \cdot \gamma^2 \cdot \mathcal{E}_{\mathtt{ksk}} + 4 \cdot (q/Q)^2 \cdot n \cdot N \cdot \ell \cdot \gamma^2 \cdot \mathcal{E}_{\mathtt{bsk}} \\ +(q/Q)^2 \cdot 4 \cdot N \cdot \varsigma^2 + 1 + 16 \cdot N \cdot \varsigma^2 \end{pmatrix}^{1/2} \tag{3}$$

where $\mathcal{E}_{\mathtt{ksk}} = O(\mathsf{Var}(\mathsf{err}(\mathtt{ksk})))$ and $\mathcal{E}_{\mathtt{bsk}} = O(\mathsf{Var}(\mathsf{err}(\mathtt{bsk})))$.

The following theorem states that our scheme requires a modulus q that is asymptotically less than the fatigue point as stated in [13].

Theorem 1. *If the output of Algorithm 2 satisfies (3) except with negligible probability and $q = \tilde{O}(n)$, the output of Algorithm 2 can be correctly decrypted except with negligible probability.*

Proof. Since $N \in \Theta(n)$, $q/Q, \mathcal{E}_{\mathtt{bsk}}, \mathcal{E}_{\mathtt{ksk}} \in O(1)$, and $\ell, L \in O(\log Q) = O(\log N)$ and (3) is satisfied, the final noise after bootstrapping is $\tilde{O}(n)$ except with negligible probability. For correctness, Lemma 2 imposes that the sum of two input fresh/refreshed ciphertexts noises should be smaller than $(q-20)/8$. Thus the bound of each refreshed noise needs to be less than $(q-20)/16$, which implies we need $\|\mathsf{err}(\mathtt{ct}')\| < (q-20)/16 = q/16 - 5/4$ to recover the correct message. Therefore, it is sufficient to choose $q \in \tilde{O}(n)$.

We will discuss the concrete value q based on the above heuristic and theorem in Sect. 6.

5.2 Bootstrapping an LWE-based Scheme

As mentioned our external product costs only ℓ multiplications on R_Q versus $4 \cdot \ell'$ in TFHE. In general, our base scheme constructed on top of the matrix NTRU problem requires a larger dimension n than in an LWE-based scheme to achieve the same security level. Since the bootstrapping procedure uses n external products, we can obtain a faster FHE scheme by replacing our base scheme by the LWE-based one used in FHEW and TFHE, and using NGS to bootstrap it. This minimizes the number of external products and also makes each one of them cheaper.

Hence, we propose to use our NGS scheme as the accumulator to refresh LWE ciphertexts as opposed to MNTRU ciphertexts. The decryption function is essentially the same, i.e. the inner product between the ciphertext and the secret key. Since the LWE secret key can be binary, we can use binary homomorphic `CMux` gates instead of the ternary ones. However, at the end of the main loop of the refreshing procedure, we obtain an NTRU ciphertext of the form $c = g/f+\epsilon+\Delta\cdot m \in R_Q$, where ϵ is the rounding error after modulus switching. Then we need to transform it again into an LWE ciphertext. So, we adapt our key-switching from Sect. 4 to also switch the underlying hard problem from NTRU to LWE.

NTRU to LWE Key-Switching: The goal of the following algorithm is to switch the form of a ciphertext from an NGS ciphertext to an LWE ciphertext encrypting the same message. Let $(\mathbf{A}, \mathbf{b})$ be an LWE sample with a secret key $\mathbf{s}$. Let $c = g/f+\epsilon+\Delta\cdot m$ be a scalar NGS ciphertext with a secret key f, where ϵ is the rounding error after modulus swtiching. Define the key-switching key as the following vector of LWE samples:

$$\mathtt{ksk}_{\mathsf{NTRU}\to\mathsf{LWE}} := (\mathbf{A}, \mathbf{b} := \mathbf{A}\cdot\mathbf{s}+\mathbf{e}+\mathbf{P}\cdot\mathbf{f}_0)$$

with $\mathbf{A} \in \mathbb{Z}_q^{(N\cdot L)\times n}$, $\mathbf{e} \leftarrow \chi_{\sigma_e}^{N\cdot L}$, $\mathbf{f}_0 := \mathsf{col}_0(\boldsymbol{\Phi}(f)) \in \mathbb{Z}^N$, and $\mathbf{P} = \mathbf{I}_N \otimes \mathbf{g}_{q,B_{\mathtt{ksk}}}$. Then, given a ciphertext $c = g/f+\epsilon+\Delta\cdot m \in R_q$, the key-switching from NTRU to LWE is defined as follows:

- $\mathsf{KeySwitch}_{\mathsf{NTRU}\to\mathsf{LWE}}(c, \mathtt{ksk}_{\mathsf{NTRU}\to\mathsf{LWE}})$:
  1. Parse $\mathtt{ksk}_{\mathsf{NTRU}\to\mathsf{LWE}}$ as $(\mathbf{A}, \mathbf{b})$
  2. $\mathbf{a} \leftarrow \mathsf{KeySwitch}(c, \mathbf{A})$
  3. $b \leftarrow \mathsf{KeySwitch}(c, \mathbf{b})$
  4. Output $\mathbf{c}' := (\mathbf{a}, b)$

That is, we decompose the coefficient vector of c and multiply by both components of $\mathtt{ksk}_{\mathsf{NTRU}\to\mathsf{LWE}}$. Thus, we define $\mathbf{y} := \mathbf{g}^{-1}(\phi(c)) \in \mathbb{Z}^{N\cdot L}$ and compute

$$\mathbf{c}' := (\mathbf{a}, b) = (\mathbf{y}\cdot\mathbf{A},\ \mathbf{y}\cdot\mathbf{b}) \in \mathbb{Z}_q^{n+1}.$$

Then, we can see that

$$b = \mathbf{a}\cdot\mathbf{s}+\mathbf{y}\cdot\mathbf{e}+\phi(c)\cdot\mathbf{f}_0 = \mathbf{a}\cdot\mathbf{s}+\mathbf{y}\cdot\mathbf{e}+g_0+\epsilon\cdot((1,\mathbf{0})+4\cdot\phi(f'))+4\cdot\epsilon'\cdot\phi(m)\cdot\phi(f')+\Delta\cdot m_0$$

where $\epsilon \in (-1/2, 1/2]$ and m_0 is the constant term of m. In other words, $(\mathbf{a}, b)$ is a valid LWE ciphertext of m_0.

Noise Analysis. We see that the noise of the resulting LWE encryption equals to $\mathbf{y} \cdot \mathbf{e} + g_0 + \epsilon + \epsilon \cdot 4 \cdot \phi(f') + 4 \cdot \epsilon' \cdot \phi(m) \cdot \phi(f')$ as defined in [10], with the variance of the noise satisfying:

$$\begin{aligned}\mathsf{Var}(\mathsf{err}(\mathbf{c}')) &= \mathsf{Var}(\mathbf{y} \cdot \mathbf{e}) + \mathsf{Var}(g_0) + \mathsf{Var}(\epsilon_0) + 16 \cdot \mathsf{Var}(\epsilon \cdot \phi(f')) + 4 \cdot \mathsf{Var}(\phi(m) \cdot \phi(f')) \\ &\le N \cdot L \cdot \mathsf{Var}(\mathbf{y}) \cdot \mathsf{Var}(\mathbf{e}) + \mathsf{Var}(g) + 1 + 16 \cdot N \cdot \mathsf{Var}(\epsilon) \cdot \mathsf{Var}(f') + 4 \cdot \|m\|_2^2 \cdot \varsigma^2 \\ &\le N \cdot L \cdot \mathsf{Var}(\mathbf{y}) \cdot \mathsf{Var}(\mathbf{e}) + \mathsf{Var}(g) + 1 + 16 \cdot N \cdot \varsigma^2 + 4 \cdot \|m\|_2^2 \cdot \varsigma^2 \\ &\le N \cdot L \cdot \mathsf{Var}(\mathbf{y}) \cdot \mathsf{Var}(\mathbf{e}) + \mathsf{Var}(g) + 1 + 20 \cdot N \cdot \varsigma^2 \\ &\le N \cdot L \cdot \gamma^2 \cdot \sigma_e^2 + \mathsf{Var}(\mathsf{err}(c))\end{aligned}$$

6 Security Analysis and Parameter Selection

The CPA-security of our NGS scheme follows directly from the decisional NTRU problem via a standard hybrid argument. Firstly, notice that $\mathbf{G}/\mathbf{F}+\mathbf{M}$ is a secure encryption as the MNTRU assumption states that $\mathbf{G}/\mathbf{F}$ is uniform mod q, then, using the circular security assumption, it is safe to encrypt $\mathbf{M}/\mathbf{F}$ instead of $\mathbf{M}$, i.e., a message that depends on the secret key $\mathbf{F}$, under the matrix NTRU problem. From this, we obtain the format $(\mathbf{G} + \mathbf{M})/\mathbf{F}$ used in our base scheme. Finally, the security of the bootstrapping follows from the (weak) circular security assumption that the NGS scheme can be used to encrypt the key of the base scheme, which in turn, encrypts the key of the NGS scheme. All these circular security assumptions are standard and are used extensively, e.g., [16,30]. In particular, it is not known how to construct FHE without the weak circular security used here.

Concrete Security: Research on the security of the NTRU problem revealed a significant improvement of the performance of lattice reduction attacks on NTRU lattices with large moduli q, which are now known as the overstretched NTRU regime. Several works [1,9,24] showed the susceptibility of the overstretched regimes to attacks. The work of Kirchner and Fouque shows however that the attack is possible due to the choice of parameters and not due to the structure of the fields underlying the NTRU problem. The observation that the choice of parameters causes the attack, started a quest to determine the value of the ciphertext modulus q for which the overstretched regime of NTRU begins and hence the security issue occurs. This turning point is called the fatigue point. Kirchner and Fouque make a first attempt to estimate the fatigue point and their efforts result in an asymptotic upper bound, but it is only the recent work of Ducas and van Woerden [13] that achieves at finding a concrete value for the fatigue point for ternary NTRU.

To determine the fatigue point Ducas and van Woerden identified two events that distinguish the standard regime from the overstretched regime:

- Secret Key Recovery (SKR): The event in which a vector as short as a secret key vector is inserted in the basis of the lattice.

- Dense Sublattice Discovery (DSD): The event in which a vector of the dense sublattice generated by the secret key is inserted in the basis of the lattice. This vector is strictly longer than the secret key, but nevertheless this event leads to a successful attack as either the SKR event follows quickly after the DSD event, the DSD events cascade and generate the dense sublattice from which the secret key can be recovered or the discovered dense sublattice vector is in itself sufficient to decrypt fresh ciphertexts.

Based on an exploration of the occurrence of one of these events, Ducas and van Woerden present an analysis that discovers the fatigue point, which is determined by the value for q for which the DSD attack starts to be more efficient than the SKR attack. To get then an idea of how secure the NTRU problem with this q value still is, they also determine the precise cost of the attacks in the overstretched regime. Their analysis uses the BKZ lattice reduction algorithm and does not focus on a single position but predicts the most relevant positions in which the vector of the SKR or DSD event can occur and takes all these positions into account. This refined analysis leads to the following asymptotic result; the fatigue point of NTRU with ternary secrets happens at $q = n^{2.484+o(1)}$. As well as the determination of this asymptotic result, they perform an average case analysis based on the volume of the relevant lattices and sublattices to arrive at a concrete prediction of the fatigue point instead of a worst-case bound. This concrete prediction puts the fatigue point at $q \approx 0.004 \cdot n^{2.484+o(1)}$ for $n > 100$. This average case analysis differentiates the circulant version of NTRU from its matrix version, as there are minor deviations in the volumes of the relevant sublattices. Our work uses the anti-circulant and matrix versions of NTRU as defined in Sect. 2.4. We argue that the change from the circulant to the anti-circulant version of NTRU does not reduce the security of our NTRU instance, since by using $X^N + 1$ instead of $X^N - 1$, we avoid any weaknesses caused by evaluation at one, which the circulant variant could suffer from. In addition, it does not invalidate the analysis made by Ducas and van Woerden, as that is based on the expected volume of the dense sublattice, which remains the same when $X^N - 1$ is replaced by $X^N + 1$.

Parameter Selection: Using the analysis by Ducas and van Woerden [13] and the scripts that they provided to estimate the concrete hardness of NTRU[1], given the dimension, the modulus q, the variance σ^2, and taking into account the distribution of the secret key, we are able to find the block size β needed by BKZ to break the (matrix) NTRU problem. To convert β to the security level, we used the same (classical) cost model used by TFHE, namely, the number of operations of BKZ-β in dimension d was estimated as $T(d, \beta) := 2^{0.292 \cdot \beta + 16.4 + \log_2(8 \cdot d)}$, where $d = 2 \cdot n$ for the NTRU in dimension n. Thus, a security level of λ bits means that $T(d, \beta) \geq 2^{\lambda}$.

Hence, to choose the parameters of the NGS scheme, we fixed $N = 1024$ and ternary secrets, then found the maximum value of $\log Q$ that gives us $\lambda = 128$.

[1] https://github.com/WvanWoerden/NTRUFatigue.

For the scheme based on the matrix NTRU problem, we fixed $n = 800$ and also used ternary secrets. We chose the parameters for the LWE problem using the LWE estimator [2]. The decomposition bases used in the external product and in the key-switching were then chosen to guarantee correctness. We remark that instead of using a single basis B for all external products, we used B_1 for the first n_1 products and B_2 for the last n_2 (thus, $n = n_1 + n_2$), as this allowed us to reduce the total number of polynomial products computed during the bootstrapping.

The average-case noise bounds determined in the previous section then allows us to compute concrete parameters for our scheme. All the parameters are shown in Table 1.

Table 1. The parameters used in both bootstrappings, depending on whether the underlying problem of the base scheme is the matrix NTRU or the LWE. The columns N and Q refer to the NGS scheme. For each basis B_i we have a different dimension $\ell_i := \lceil \log_{B_i}(Q) \rceil$ for n_i bootstrapping keys.

Base scheme	n	q	N	Q	(B_1, n_1)	(B_2, n_2)	B_{ksk}	ℓ_1	ℓ_2
MNTRU	800	$131071 \approx 2^{17}$	2^{10}	$912829 \approx 2^{19.8}$	$(8, 750)$	$(16, 50)$	3	7	5
LWE	610	$92683 \approx 2^{16.5}$	2^{10}	$912829 \approx 2^{19.8}$	$(8, 140)$	$(16, 470)$	3	7	5

7 Practical Results

Among the three schemes that use the framework of fast bootstrapping with a base scheme and an accumulator [11,12,30], the most efficient one is TFHE. Therefore, we compare our practical results only with TFHE. Similar to the gate bootstrapping in TFHE, we are able to compute a binary gate through a bootstrapping. Therefore we use the bootstrapping as benchmark, as any speedup on the bootstrapping translates directly to the same speedup on any binary circuit. Like for TFHE, the encryption parameters of our schemes stay fixed for any binary circuit. We implemented a proof-of-concept of our bootstrapping procedures in C++. For a fair comparison, we chose the TFHE library as it is written in C++ and is up-to-date. Our code is publicly available[2].

We compiled TFHE with the same FFT library we used in our implementation, namely, FFTW [15]. Moreover, we also compiled our code with the same optimization flags already used by the 'optimal' mode of TFHE. Both TFHE and our implementation use a deterministic decomposition for the external product and also a deterministic rounding for the modulus switching, relying thus on the heuristic assumption that the noise terms obtained during the homomorphic evaluations follow independent subgaussian distributions. All the experiments

[2] https://github.com/KULeuven-COSIC/FINAL.

were conducted on a single core of a machine with 8 GB of RAM and a 3.1 GHz Dual-Core Intel Core i5.

As the fast Fourier transforms (FFT) and element-wise Hadamard vector products dominate the running time of bootstrapping, we used the following formulas to compute $\mathtt{ACC}\boxdot\mathtt{CMux}(c_i)$ in the bootstrapping algorithm (Algorithm 2)

$$((X^{c_i} - 1) \cdot \mathtt{ACC}) \boxdot (\mathbf{bsk}_{i,0} - \mathbf{bsk}_{i,1} \cdot X^{-c_i}) + \mathtt{ACC} \qquad \text{(MNTRU)},$$

$$((X^{c_i} - 1) \cdot \mathtt{ACC}) \boxdot \mathbf{bsk}_i + \mathtt{ACC} \qquad \text{(LWE)}.$$

The LWE formula is actually used in the TFHE library. Notice that no polynomial multiplication is needed to compute $(X^{c_i} - 1) \cdot \mathtt{ACC}$; it can be done by one negacyclic shift of the coefficients of ACC and N subtractions in $\mathbb{Z}_Q$. Assuming that the bootstrapping keys are FFT transformed in advance, the external product requires $\ell_i + 1$ FFTs and ℓ_i Hadamard vector products where ℓ_j is the length of $\mathbf{bsk}_i$, $\mathbf{bsk}_{i,0}$ or $\mathbf{bsk}_{i,1}$. In addition, MNTRU requires extra ℓ_j Hadamard vector products to compute $(\mathbf{bsk}_{i,0} - \mathbf{bsk}_{i,1} \cdot X^{-c_i})$.

In TFHE, the bootstrapping key is composed of $n' := 630$ GSW ciphertexts, where n' is the dimension of the LWE problem used in their base scheme. Moreover, for the GSW ciphertext, they used the ring $R_{q'} := \mathbb{Z}_{q'}[X]/\langle X^{N'} + 1\rangle$, where $q' := 2^{32}$ and $N' = 1024$, but they could set a larger decomposition base than the ones we could use, and they can also ignore the least significant bits during the decomposition, since in the RLWE problem, these bits are noisy, thus, they obtain $\ell' := 3$. However, each GSW ciphertext is composed of $4 \cdot \ell'$ elements of $R_{q'}$, on the other hand our NGS ciphertexts only have ℓ ring elements. Thus, the size of the bootstrapping key in TFHE is $4 \cdot n' \cdot \ell' \cdot N' \cdot \log(q') = 31$ MB.

Since each external product costs $4 \cdot \ell'$ products in $R_{q'}$ for TFHE, their total cost is $4 \cdot n' \cdot \ell' = 7560$ ring multiplications. However, the slowest operations of the bootstrapping are forward and backward FFTs. Since the FFTs of the bootstrapping key are precomputed, the 'for' loop of the bootstrapping has to decompose only the RLWE sample that is accumulating the result, obtaining thus $2 \cdot \ell'$ ring elements. Then, it computes the FFT of these elements, performs the external product to obtain a new RLWE sample in the FFT domain and finally apply two inverse FFTs. Hence, TFHE needs $2 \cdot n' \cdot (\ell' + 2) = 6300$ FFTs per bootstrapping.

In our case, the bootstrapping key is composed by $2 \cdot n$ NGS ciphertexts when the base scheme is based on the MNTRU problem and n when the LWE is used. Our ℓ is a little bigger than the $\ell' = 3$ used in TFHE, but we do not have the factor four in the dimension of the NGS ciphertexts.

The size of each ciphertext, the number of ring multiplications, and the amount of FFTs we have to perform when the LWE problem is used in the base scheme ends up being smaller than what is needed by TFHE. In particular, considering the parameters presented in Table 1, the number of FFTs per bootstrapping is $n_1 \cdot (\ell_1 + 1) + n_2 \cdot (\ell_2 + 1)$, where $\ell_i := \lceil \log_{B_i}(Q) \rceil$. A detailed comparison is presented in Table 2. Since every integer in our implementation is represented by the `int` type, we assume every coordinate or coefficient of our keys occupies 32 bits of memory.

We ran our bootstrapping procedures one thousand times and estimated the standard deviation of the noise of refreshed ciphertexts as $\sigma_{\mathsf{LWE}} = 2^{9.46}$ and $\sigma_{\mathsf{NTRU}} = 2^{9.85}$, which gives us the following decryption failure probabilities: $p_{\mathsf{LWE}} = 1 - \mathrm{erf}(92683/(16 \cdot \sigma_{\mathsf{LWE}} \cdot \sqrt{2})) < 2^{-52}$ and $p_{\mathsf{NTRU}} = 1 - \mathrm{erf}(131071/(16 \cdot \sigma_{\mathsf{NTRU}} \cdot \sqrt{2})) < 2^{-60}$.

The number of FFTs and multiplications shown in Table 2 are computed using the parameters of each scheme as described in the abovementioned explanation. For the running times, we measured the average time of the NAND gate plus bootstrapping over 1000 runs.

Table 2. Practical results of TFHE and of our bootstrapping procedures considering the two base schemes. The last collum shows the average bootstrapping running time over 1000 executions.

	Key switching key	Bootstrapping key	Mult. on R_Q	FFTs	Run. time
TFHE [11]	40 MB	31 MB	7560	6300	66 ms
MNTRU	34.4 MB	43 MB	11000	6300	92 ms
LWE	26.3 MB	13 MB	3330	3940	48 ms

As shown in Table 2, our bootstrapping algorithm for LWE ciphertexts is 28% faster than TFHE. Furthermore, our method nearly halves the total size of key-switching and bootstrapping keys. Namely, TFHE needs 71 MB of key material whereas our approach generates less than 39.3 MB.

Our bootstrapping algorithm for MNTRU ciphertexts is less efficient than TFHE. The first reason is that MNTRU requires a bigger dimension n than LWE to achieve the same security level given that the ciphertext modulus is fixed. In our experiments (see Table 1), $n = 800$ for MNTRU whereas $n' = 630$ in TFHE. The second reason is that the secret key of the MNTRU scheme is ternary. To handle ternary coefficients of the secret key, the `CMux` operation performs more multiplications in the FFT domain, namely $2 \cdot (\ell_1 \cdot n_1 + \ell_2 \cdot n_2)$.

However, the efficiency downgrade of our bootstrapping method for MNTRU ciphertexts is not critical in practice. The bootstrapping takes less than 0.1 s on an average commodity laptop with only 9% increase of the key material size. Hence, if one needs an FHE scheme based solely on NTRU, our scheme is a practical candidate for that.

8 Conclusion and Future Work

We showed that it is possible to construct an efficient FHE scheme based on the NTRU assumption and to instantiate it by setting parameters that are below the "fatigue point" where the sublattice attacks start to apply. This shows that with the current knowledge on the security of NTRU, it seems possible to construct competitive FHE based solely on the NTRU assumption, which motivates further research on NTRU-based FHE schemes. Moreover, we showed that by combining the LWE and the NTRU problems, we can construct an FHE scheme that runs faster and requires less key material than TFHE, which currently has the fastest bootstrapping procedure.

We notice that it would be possible to use better parameters for our scheme, and thus, increase the difference between our running time and TFHE's if we sampled the NTRU secrets f and g with different variances. Namely, the final noise introduced by the bootstrapping depends more on the norm of g than on the norm of f, thus, we could increase the variance of f without having too much impact on the final noise. Intuitively, the NTRU problem should only become harder as the variance of one of its secret increases, thus, this would allow us to increase q. Finally, having a larger value of q for (almost) the same final noise means that we can choose larger decomposition bases, hence, reduce the number of FFTs and Hadamard vector products per external product. However, since there is no formal analysis of the concrete hardness of NTRU with different variances of the secrets, we prefer to leave this as an interesting future work.

As another possible line of work, one could consider the circuit bootstrapping from TFHE, which takes an LWE ciphertext $\mathbf{c} \in \mathbb{Z}_q^{n'+1}$ encrypting a message m and outputs a GSW ciphertext $\mathbf{C} \in R_q^{2\ell' \times \ell'}$ encrypting m with noise independent of the noise of $\mathbf{c}$. In other words, the circuit bootstrapping refreshes $\mathbf{c}$ and transforms it into a GSW ciphertext. This is done by executing ℓ' bootstrappings and $2\ell'$ key switchings, and requires two key-switching keys. However, in our case we would produce an NGS ciphertext $\mathbf{c} \in R_q^{\ell}$, so just ℓ key switchings are needed instead of $2\ell'$, and also only one key-switching key instead of two. Thus, both the running time and the memory usage can be reduced if we are able to use $\ell < 2\ell'$ in our scheme.

Acknowledgements. We would like to thank Leo Ducas for helpful discussions about the security of the NTRU problem.

This work has been supported in part by ERC Advanced Grant ERC-2015-AdG-IMPaCT, by the Research Foundation - Flanders (FWO) under an Odysseus project GOH9718N and a Junior Postdoctoral Fellowship, by CyberSecurity Research Flanders with reference number VR20192203, and by the Defence Advanced Research Projects Agency (DARPA) under contract No. HR0011-21-C-0034 DARPA DPRIVE BASALISC.

Any opinions, findings and conclusions or recommendations expressed in this material are those of the author(s) and do not necessarily reflect the views of the ERC, DARPA, the US Government, Cyber Security Research Flanders or the FWO. The U.S. Government is authorized to reproduce and distribute reprints for governmental purposes notwithstanding any copyright annotation therein.

References

1. Albrecht, M., Bai, S., Ducas, L.: A subfield lattice attack on overstretched NTRU assumptions. In: Robshaw, M., Katz, J. (eds.) CRYPTO 2016. LNCS, vol. 9814, pp. 153–178. Springer, Heidelberg (2016). https://doi.org/10.1007/978-3-662-53018-4_6

2. Albrecht, M.R., Player, R., Scott, S.: On the concrete hardness of learning with errors. J. Math. Cryptol. **9**(3), 169–203 (2015). https://doi.org/10.1515/jmc-2015-0016
3. Alperin-Sheriff, J., Peikert, C.: Faster bootstrapping with polynomial error. In: Garay, J.A., Gennaro, R. (eds.) CRYPTO 2014. LNCS, vol. 8616, pp. 297–314. Springer, Heidelberg (2014). https://doi.org/10.1007/978-3-662-44371-2_17
4. Bos, J.W., Lauter, K., Loftus, J., Naehrig, M.: Improved security for a ring-based fully homomorphic encryption scheme. In: Stam, M. (ed.) IMACC 2013. LNCS, vol. 8308, pp. 45–64. Springer, Heidelberg (2013). https://doi.org/10.1007/978-3-642-45239-0_4
5. Brakerski, Z., Gentry, C., Vaikuntanathan, V.: (Leveled) fully homomorphic encryption without bootstrapping. In: Goldwasser, S. (ed.) ITCS 2012, pp. 309–325. ACM, January 2012
6. Brakerski, Z., Vaikuntanathan, V.: Efficient fully homomorphic encryption from (standard) LWE. In: Ostrovsky, R. (ed.) 52nd FOCS, pp. 97–106. IEEE Computer Society Press, October 2011
7. Brakerski, Z., Vaikuntanathan, V.: Fully homomorphic encryption from Ring-LWE and security for key dependent messages. In: Rogaway, P. (ed.) CRYPTO 2011. LNCS, vol. 6841, pp. 505–524. Springer, Heidelberg (2011). https://doi.org/10.1007/978-3-642-22792-9_29
8. Chen, H., Dai, W., Kim, M., Song, Y.: Efficient multi-key homomorphic encryption with packed ciphertexts with application to oblivious neural network inference. In: Cavallaro, L., Kinder, J., Wang, X., Katz, J. (eds.) ACM CCS 2019. pp. 395–412. ACM Press, November 2019
9. Cheon, J.H., Jeong, J., Lee, C.: An algorithm for NTRU problems and cryptanalysis of the GGH multilinear map without a low-level encoding of zero. LMS J. Comput. Math. **19**(A), 255–266 (2016)
10. Chillotti, I., Gama, N., Georgieva, M., Izabachène, M.: Faster fully homomorphic encryption: bootstrapping in less than 0.1 seconds. In: Cheon, J.H., Takagi, T. (eds.) ASIACRYPT 2016. LNCS, vol. 10031, pp. 3–33. Springer, Heidelberg (2016). https://doi.org/10.1007/978-3-662-53887-6_1
11. Chillotti, I., Gama, N., Georgieva, M., Izabachène, M.: TFHE: fast fully homomorphic encryption over the torus. J. Cryptol. **33**(1), 34–91 (2020)
12. Ducas, L., Micciancio, D.: FHEW: bootstrapping homomorphic encryption in less than a second. In: Oswald, E., Fischlin, M. (eds.) EUROCRYPT 2015. LNCS, vol. 9056, pp. 617–640. Springer, Heidelberg (2015). https://doi.org/10.1007/978-3-662-46800-5_24
13. Ducas, L., van Woerden, W.: NTRU fatigue: how stretched is overstretched? In: Tibouchi, M., Wang, H. (eds.) ASIACRYPT 2021. LNCS, vol. 13093, pp. 3–32. Springer, Cham (2021). https://doi.org/10.1007/978-3-030-92068-5_1
14. Fan, J., Vercauteren, F.: Somewhat practical fully homomorphic encryption. Cryptology ePrint Archive, Report 2012/144 (2012). https://eprint.iacr.org/2012/144
15. Frigo, M., Johnson, S.G.: The design and implementation of FFTW3. Proc. IEEE **93**(2), 216–231 (2005)
16. Genise, N., Gentry, C., Halevi, S., Li, B., Micciancio, D.: Homomorphic encryption for finite automata. In: Galbraith, S.D., Moriai, S. (eds.) ASIACRYPT 2019. LNCS, vol. 11922, pp. 473–502. Springer, Cham (2019). https://doi.org/10.1007/978-3-030-34621-8_17
17. Genise, N., Micciancio, D., Polyakov, Y.: Building an efficient lattice gadget toolkit: subGaussian sampling and more. In: Ishai, Y., Rijmen, V. (eds.) EUROCRYPT

2019. LNCS, vol. 11477, pp. 655–684. Springer, Cham (2019). https://doi.org/10.1007/978-3-030-17656-3_23
18. Gentry, C.: A fully homomorphic encryption scheme. Ph.D. thesis, Stanford University (2009). https://crypto.stanford.edu/craig/
19. Gentry, C., Sahai, A., Waters, B.: Homomorphic encryption from learning with errors: conceptually-simpler, asymptotically-faster, attribute-based. In: Canetti, R., Garay, J.A. (eds.) CRYPTO 2013. LNCS, vol. 8042, pp. 75–92. Springer, Heidelberg (2013). https://doi.org/10.1007/978-3-642-40041-4_5
20. Hoffmann, C., Méaux, P., Ricosset, T.: Transciphering, using FiLIP and TFHE for an efficient delegation of computation. In: Bhargavan, K., Oswald, E., Prabhakaran, M. (eds.) INDOCRYPT 2020. LNCS, vol. 12578, pp. 39–61. Springer, Cham (2020). https://doi.org/10.1007/978-3-030-65277-7_3
21. Jeon, S., Lee, H.S., Park, J.: Efficient lattice gadget decomposition algorithm with bounded uniform distribution. IEEE Access **9**, 17429–17437 (2021)
22. Joye, M.: On NTRU-ν-um modulo $X^N - 1$. Cryptology ePrint Archive, Paper 2022/1092 (2022). https://eprint.iacr.org/2022/1092
23. Joye, M., Paillier, P.: Blind rotation in fully homomorphic encryption with extended keys. In: Dolev, S., Katz, J., Meisels, A. (eds.) Cyber Security, Cryptology, and Machine Learning - 6th International Symposium, CSCML 2022, Be'er Sheva, Israel, June 30–July 1, 2022, Proceedings. LNCS, vol. 13301, pp. 1–18. Springer (2022). https://doi.org/10.1007/978-3-031-07689-3_1
24. Kirchner, P., Fouque, P.-A.: Revisiting lattice attacks on overstretched NTRU parameters. In: Coron, J.-S., Nielsen, J.B. (eds.) EUROCRYPT 2017. LNCS, vol. 10210, pp. 3–26. Springer, Cham (2017). https://doi.org/10.1007/978-3-319-56620-7_1
25. Kluczniak, K.: Ntru-ν-um: Secure fully homomorphic encryption from NTRU with small modulus. Cryptology ePrint Archive, Paper 2022/089 (2022). https://eprint.iacr.org/2022/089
26. Lee, C., Wallet, A.: Lattice analysis on MiNTRU problem. Cryptology ePrint Archive, Report 2020/230 (2020). https://eprint.iacr.org/2020/230
27. López-Alt, A., Tromer, E., Vaikuntanathan, V.: On-the-fly multiparty computation on the cloud via multikey fully homomorphic encryption. In: Karloff, H.J., Pitassi, T. (eds.) 44th ACM STOC, pp. 1219–1234. ACM Press, May 2012
28. Micciancio, D., Polyakov, Y.: Bootstrapping in fhew-like cryptosystems (2021). https://doi.org/10.1145/3474366.3486924
29. Park, J., Tibouchi, M.: SHECS-PIR: somewhat homomorphic encryption-based compact and scalable private information retrieval. In: Chen, L., Li, N., Liang, K., Schneider, S. (eds.) ESORICS 2020. LNCS, vol. 12309, pp. 86–106. Springer, Cham (2020). https://doi.org/10.1007/978-3-030-59013-0_5
30. Pereira, H.V.L.: Bootstrapping fully homomorphic encryption over the integers in less than one second. In: Garay, J.A. (ed.) PKC 2021. LNCS, vol. 12710, pp. 331–359. Springer, Cham (2021). https://doi.org/10.1007/978-3-030-75245-3_13
31. van Dijk, M., Gentry, C., Halevi, S., Vaikuntanathan, V.: Fully homomorphic encryption over the integers. In: Gilbert, H. (ed.) EUROCRYPT 2010. LNCS, vol. 6110, pp. 24–43. Springer, Heidelberg (2010). https://doi.org/10.1007/978-3-642-13190-5_2

NIZK and SNARKs

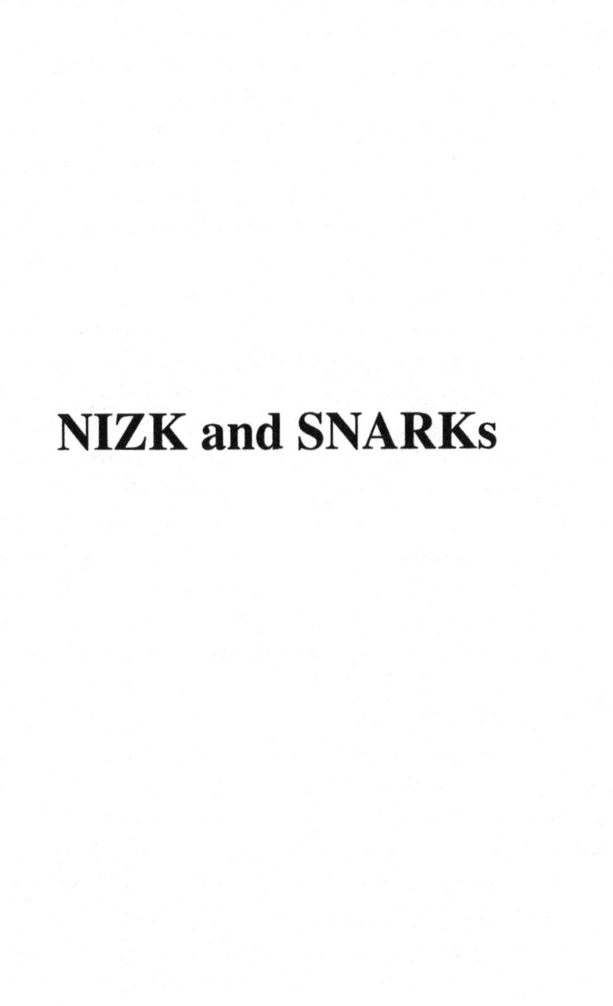

Flashproofs: Efficient Zero-Knowledge Arguments of Range and Polynomial Evaluation with Transparent Setup

Nan Wang(✉) and Sid Chi-Kin Chau

Australian National University, Canberra, Australia
{vincent.wang,sid.chau}@anu.edu.au

Abstract. We propose Flashproofs, a new type of efficient special honest verifier zero-knowledge arguments with a transparent setup in the discrete logarithm (DL) setting. First, we put forth gas-efficient range arguments that achieve $O(N^{\frac{2}{3}})$ communication cost, and involve $O(N^{\frac{2}{3}})$ group exponentiations for verification and a slightly sub-linear number of group exponentiations for proving with respect to the range $[0, 2^N - 1]$, where N is the bit length of the range. For typical confidential transactions on blockchain platforms supporting smart contracts, verifying our range arguments consumes only 237K and 318K gas for 32-bit and 64-bit ranges, which are comparable to 220K gas incurred by verifying the most efficient zkSNARK with a trusted setup (EUROCRYPT ' 16) at present. Besides, the aggregation of multiple arguments can yield further efficiency improvement. Second, we present polynomial evaluation arguments based on the techniques of Bayer & Groth (EUROCRYPT ' 13). We provide two zero-knowledge arguments, which are optimised for lower-degree ($D \in [3, 2^9]$) and higher-degree ($D > 2^9$) polynomials, where D is the polynomial degree. Our arguments yield a non-trivial improvement in the overall efficiency. Notably, the number of group exponentiations for proving drops from $8 \log D$ to $3(\log D + \sqrt{\log D})$. The communication cost and the number of group exponentiations for verification decrease from $7 \log D$ to $(\log D + 3\sqrt{\log D})$. To the best of our knowledge, our arguments instantiate the most communication-efficient arguments of membership and non-membership in the DL setting among those not requiring trusted setups. More importantly, our techniques enable a significantly asymptotic improvement in the efficiency of communication and verification (group exponentiations) from $O(\log D)$ to $O(\sqrt{\log D})$ when multiple arguments satisfying different polynomials with the same degree and inputs are aggregated.

Keywords: Zero-knowledge arguments · Range arguments · Polynomial evaluation arguments · Confidential transactions · Smart contracts

S. C.-K. Chau—This research was supported by ARC Discovery Project No: GA69027/DP200101985.

The original version of this chapter was revised: this paper contains errors in table 2. This has been updated. The correction to this chapter is available at https://doi.org/10.1007/978-3-031-22966-4_24

S. Agrawal and D. Lin (Eds.): ASIACRYPT 2022, LNCS 13792, pp. 219–248, 2022.
https://doi.org/10.1007/978-3-031-22966-4_8

1 Introduction

Zero-knowledge proofs play a critical role in modern secure applications and systems, e.g., confidential transactions, signature schemes, federated learning and multi-party computation. A zero-knowledge proof allows a prover to convince a verifier of the truth of a statement without revealing any secret information. More formally, given an NP-language $\mathcal{L}$, a prover aims to convince a verifier of knowing a witness ω for a statement $u \in \mathcal{L}$ with high probability by a zero-knowledge proof that satisfies three properties:

- *Completeness.* A prover can convince a verifier of $u \in \mathcal{L}$, if $u \in \mathcal{L}$.
- *Soundness.* A prover cannot convince a verifier of $u \in \mathcal{L}$, if $u \notin \mathcal{L}$.
- *Zero-knowledge.* The proof should reveal nothing except the truth that $u \in \mathcal{L}$.

There are varieties of zero-knowledge proofs [2,5–7,13,14,17,28,37,41,46] for general NP-complete languages, e.g., arithmetic circuits satisfiability. However, generic constructions used by these proofs tend to be sub-optimal and may not achieve the best efficiency as in specialised constructions for particular languages. This paper focuses on the zero-knowledge proofs for two particular languages in the discrete logarithm (DL) setting: range arguments and polynomial evaluation arguments. An argument is a computationally sound proof that no probabilistic polynomial-time provers are able to deceive a verifier into falsely accepting it.

Range proofs are designed to prove a committed value is within a specific range. Several zero-knowledge range proofs have been applied to confidential transactions (CT) [26] on blockchain platforms. Blockchain has enabled a significant revolution towards decentralised peer-to-peer transactions. By default, blockchain does not ensure privacy but rather its transparency and immutability properties. However, with growing privacy concerns, confidential transactions have received increasing attention as they protect privacy by hiding transaction information. A plenty of confidential transaction protocols, e.g., AZTEC [45], TornadoCash [40], have been developed on blockchain platforms, e.g., Ethereum. As one of the most emerging blockchain technologies, smart contracts are playing an increasingly important role in promoting confidential transactions. They are publicly verifiable computer programs running on blockchain platforms to automate the execution of agreements without the intervention of intermediaries when some pre-determined conditions are met. To prevent inconsistent transactions, zero-knowledge range proofs are used to demonstrate sufficient funds in accounts for non-negative transfer values. However, many existing proposals for CT zero-knowledge proofs suffer from three drawbacks:

- *Trusted Setup*: Prior zero-knowledge proofs (e.g., zkSNARK [28]) require a "trusted setup", where a group of trusted parties use some secret information to generate public parameters and destroy the secret information without revealing it. However, introducing a trusted setup will compromise the security and notion of decentralisation, which leaves a backdoor for misbehaving provers to exploit and create false proofs.

- *Imbalanced Overhead*: Recent zero-knowledge proofs have replaced trusted setups with transparent setups. However, achieving transparent setups may give rise to imbalanced overhead with either expensive computation costs or large communication costs, which would undermine the scalability of blockchain applications, where scalability refers to the capability of handling transactions in a short period. For example, Bulletproofs [13] achieve a logarithmic proof size but require a linear number of group exponentiations for both proving and verification. The zkSTARK [5] has poly-logarithmic verification efficiency but entails a large proof size about 45 KB [31].
- *Trade-off With Soundness.* There is a new class of range proofs (e.g. CKLR21 [20]) based on bounded integer commitments in the DL setting, which can attain efficient computational and communication costs. However, one has to make a trade-off between the range size and the soundness error for a given group, which undermines the applicability of these range proofs. Note that using RSA or class groups [20] could address this trade-off limitation by removing bounds on the size of integers, which, however, would either require a trusted setup or a different security assumption with considerably large groups[1].

On the other hand, polynomial evaluation proofs are designed to prove a public polynomial relation $y = P(x; D)$ between two committed values x and y, where D is the polynomial degree. Notably, polynomial evaluation proofs are a basic building block for constructing the zero-knowledge proofs of membership and non-membership. For example, a polynomial function $y = P(x; D) = 0$ can be built for membership proofs to prove that a committed value x belongs to a public set X, where the roots are the elements of X. For non-membership proofs, $y \neq 0$ needs to be proved. A prover can commit to a value $z = y^{-1}$ and demonstrate $z \cdot y = 1$ with a multiplication proof. Proofs of membership and non-membership have extensive applications, e.g., anonymous credentials, group signatures, whitelist, and blacklist. Bayer & Groth [3] (BG13) presented polynomial evaluation arguments that achieve $O(\log D)$ efficiency in verification (group exponentiations) and communication based on the DL assumption. Nevertheless, the computational and communication costs for higher-degree polynomials are still high.

1.1 Contributions

In this paper, we propose Flashproofs, efficient special honest verifier zero-knowledge arguments of range and polynomial evaluation with a transparent setup. Flashproofs are 3-round public coin interactive protocols between a prover and a verifier. The prover sends an initial message to the verifier in the first round. The verifier replies with a uniformly random challenge, and then the prover responds to the challenge in the third round. Finally, the verifier decides

[1] According to the recent study [22], class groups of 3392-bit order can barely achieve 128-bit security as 256-bit elliptic curve groups.

whether to accept or reject based on the conversation. Flashproofs have perfect completeness, computational witness-extended emulation and perfect special honest verifier zero-knowledge under the typical DL assumption that applies to elliptic curve groups. We follow the transparent approach [13] without resorting to a trusted setup with elliptic curve groups. Besides, our arguments can be made non-interactive via Fiat-Shamir heuristic [25], where provers can generate random challenges by computing the hashes of the initial messages instead of verifiers, with a collision-resistant hash function modelled as a random oracle.

Range Arguments. We put forth a new type of gas-efficient zero-knowledge range arguments to prove that a committed value lies in the range $[0, 2^N - 1]$, where N indicates the bit length. Our range arguments involve $O(N^{\frac{2}{3}})$ group exponentiations for verification and achieve $O(N^{\frac{2}{3}})$ communication cost. Besides, as illustrated in Fig. 1, our arguments with optimisation use a sub-linear number of group exponentiations for proving (Please refer to Sect. 3.2 for optimisation). They are highly suitable for confidential transactions on blockchain platforms. In a nutshell, our work achieves sub-linearly overall efficiency without resorting to a trusted setup while maintaining a negligible soundness error. Especially, our arguments greatly reduce the verification gas costs to a practically affordable level on smart contract platforms.

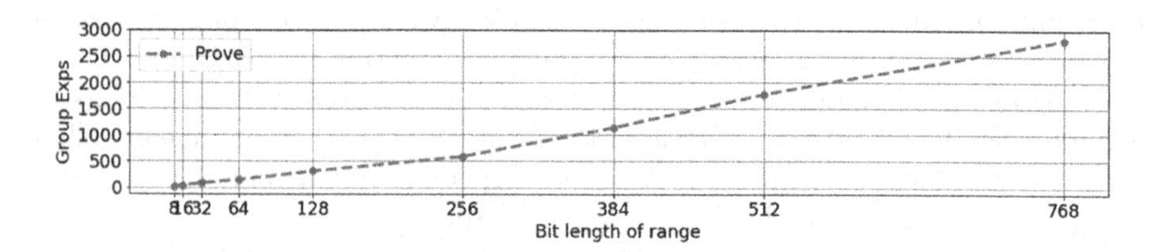

Fig. 1. Proving computational costs of our range arguments with optimisation.

Techniques. Our range arguments are based upon the bit-decomposition approach to proving that a committed value can be represented in binary form. We devise a new strategy to achieve superior computational efficiency compared to conventional works. The intuition is to fold the sequence of the bits of a committed value as a matrix. Then we prove each element in the matrix is either 0 or a certain power of 2 by using a *quadratic-term cancellation* technique. Finally, we flatten the two-dimension matrix to a one-dimension vector in a column-wise manner and prove that the committed value is the sum of the vector values. We introduce an optimisation technique to refine the efficiency in both computation and communication. Besides, the aggregation of multiple arguments is supported for further efficiency improvement.

Comparisons with State-of-the-art Range Proofs. Verifying our range arguments consumes about 237K and 318K gas for general 32-bit and 64-bit ranges. The gas costs are comparable to 220K gas incurred by verifying the most efficient zkSNARK (Groth16) [28], which requires three elliptic curve pairing operations

Table 1. Efficiency comparison of range arguments for the range $[0, 2^N - 1]$, where N is the bit length of the range, $\mathbb{G}$ indicates a cyclic group of prime order p and $\mathbb{Z}_p$ is the ring of integers modulo p. We essentially compare the involved group exponentiations as they dominate the computational cost. The number of group exponentiations required by Bulletproofs proving and unoptimised verification is estimated based on their original Java implementation [9]. Please refer to the original paper for accurate data. Besides, we take the nearest integer $\lceil N^{\frac{1}{3}} \rfloor$ as the cubic root of N and $N^{\frac{2}{3}}$ can thus be obtained by computing $N \cdot \lceil N^{-\frac{1}{3}} \rfloor$. $F(N^{\frac{1}{3}})$ is a function that yields constant values based on $N^{\frac{1}{3}}$, where $F(2) = 3,\ F(3) = 6,\ F(4) = 8,\ F(5) = 11,\ F(6) = 13\ , F(7) = 20,\ F(8) = 27,\ F(9) = 32,\ F(10) = 37$. Please refer to Sect. 3.2 for the details of $F(N^{\frac{1}{3}})$.

Type	Bulletproof	This work (Sect. 3.2)	This work with optimisation (Sect. 3.2)
Prover No. of Exp ($\mathbb{G}$)	$14N + 4\log N + 12$	$\frac{1}{2}(N^{\frac{4}{3}} + 3N^{\frac{2}{3}} + 5N^{\frac{1}{3}} + N + 6)$	$(N^{\frac{2}{3}} + 1) \cdot F(N^{\frac{1}{3}}) + 2N^{\frac{1}{3}} + 2$
Verifier No. of Exp ($\mathbb{G}$)	$4N + 2\log N + 11$	$\frac{3}{2}(N^{\frac{2}{3}} + N^{\frac{1}{3}} + 2)$	$N^{\frac{2}{3}} + N^{\frac{1}{3}} + F(N^{\frac{1}{3}}) + 2$
Proof Size No. of Elements	$2\log N + 4$ ($\mathbb{G}$) 5 ($\mathbb{Z}_p$)	$N^{\frac{2}{3}} + 2$ ($\mathbb{G}$) $\frac{1}{2}(N^{\frac{2}{3}} + 3N^{\frac{1}{3}} + 4)$ ($\mathbb{Z}_p$)	$N^{\frac{2}{3}} + 2$ ($\mathbb{G}$) $N^{\frac{1}{3}} + F(N^{\frac{1}{3}}) + 1$ ($\mathbb{Z}_p$)

Table 2. Detailed efficiency comparison of Bulletproof with our optimised work, where N is the bit length of the range. Note that our range arguments are more succinct in proof size when $N \leq 22$.

	N	8	10	12	14	16	18	20	22	32	52	64
Prover	Bulletproof	136	252	252	252	252	480	480	480	480	932	932
No. of Exp ($\mathbb{G}$)	This work	21	24	27	30	33	36	39	42	80	122	146
Verifier	Bulletproof	49	83	83	83	83	149	149	149	149	279	279
No. of Exp ($\mathbb{G}$)	This work	11	12	13	14	15	16	17	18	22	27	30
Proof Size	Bulletproof	482	546	546	546	546	610	610	610	610	674	674
(Byte)	This work	**385**	**417**	**449**	**481**	**513**	**545**	**577**	**609**	738	898	994

for any arithmetic circuits with the aid of a trusted setup. For the aggregation of 16 of our range arguments, it is estimated that the allocated gas costs per argument would be reduced by 20% to about 188K and 254K. Thus, with respect to proving ranges, our arguments can be a suitable alternative to the zkSNARKs for confidential transactions on blockchain platforms. Bulletproofs [13] are generic-purpose arguments in the DL setting for any arithmetic circuits with a transparent setup, which can instantiate range arguments. Bulletproof[2] is designed to pursue $O(\log N)$ communication efficiency at the expense of using $O(N)$ number of group exponentiations in computation for the range $[0, 2^N - 1]$. Table 1 and 2 show efficiency comparisons with Bulletproof. Our arguments achieve 6.4× and 9.3× improvement in proving and verification efficiency for $N = 64$, respectively, while incurring only 50% additional communication cost. Accordingly, the gas cost incurred by Bulletproof' verification reaches 3703K for a 64-bit range, which

[2] We will call the range instance of Bulletproofs by "Bulletproof" in the following.

is 11.7× of ours (Please see Table 6 for more details on gas costs). For smaller 52-bit ranges[3], the advantage of our arguments in computational efficiency is even greater, whereas the discrepancy in communication efficiency is smaller. Moreover, our range arguments are more sensitive to N, resulting in finer-grained performance and more flexible usage in different scenarios. Another range proof in the DL setting is CKLR21 [20]. It applies Legendre's three squares theorem [36] to achieve constant efficiency in computation and communication by leveraging a bounded integer commitment scheme. However, it suffers an inherent trade-off between the range size and the soundness error (sometimes called "knowledge error") for a certain group. Soundness errors indicate the probability of a malicious prover cheating a verifier into accepting false proofs. Confidential transactions typically have stringent security requirements, demanding highly negligible soundness errors. As for the mainstream 256-bit elliptic curve groups in confidential transactions, CKLR21 achieves a soundness error 2^{-80} for 32-bit ranges at the risk of a re-run with a 65% probability. The errors would rise to 2^{-70} on smart contract platforms due to the 256-bit word limit[4]. Besides, for 64-bit and larger ranges, the errors would surge to no less than 2^{-48}. Thus, current CT platforms must increase the number of sequential iterations or use larger groups to obtain negligible soundness errors. Moving to larger groups is undesirable as it may require a major change to their infrastructure. Moreover, both ways would increase the computational and communication costs. Our arguments tend to be more efficient for verification and communication at a comparable level of soundness errors. For example, iterating CKLR21 three times helps achieve a negligible soundness error 2^{-240} for a 32-bit range but increases the proof size to about 827 bytes. Accordingly, the computational cost also grows. By comparison, our arguments have 738 bytes with a soundness error 2^{-256}. Please see Table 6 for a detailed efficiency comparison.

Polynomial Evaluation Arguments. Based on the techniques of BG13 [3], we present two zero-knowledge arguments, which are optimised for the polynomials $y = P(x; D)$ of lower-degree ($D \in [3, 2^9]$)[5] and higher-degree ($D > 2^9$), respectively. Two arguments are distinguished based on the proof size, with the higher-degree one outperforming the lower-degree one when the degree D exceeds 2^9. Our arguments essentially leverage the *quadratic-term cancellation* technique to greatly reduce the number of group exponentiations and elements for superior efficiency in computation and communication. To the best of our knowledge, our arguments instantiate the most communication-efficient zero-knowledge arguments of membership and non-membership in the DL setting among those not requiring trusted setups. Furthermore, we propose an aggregation optimisation, where multiple arguments satisfying different polynomials with the same degree and inputs can be aggregated such that the efficiency in verification (group exponentiations per argument) and communication is asymptotically increased from $O(\log D)$ to $O(\sqrt{\log D})$. In addition, our range arguments can adapt the poly-

[3] A 52-bit range can cover all the values from 1 satoshi up to 21 million bitcoins.
[4] The size of one field element in CKLR21 is larger than 256 bits for 32-bit ranges.
[5] We skip the protocol for $D \in \{1, 2\}$, which is simpler than the lower-degree one.

Table 3. Efficiency comparison of polynomial evaluation arguments with a transparent setup in the DL setting, where N is the polynomial degree. Note that $\log N$ should be rounded up if N is not a power of 2.

Type	Bulletproofs	BG13	This Work (Sect. 4.2) Lower-Deg $N \in [3, 2^9]$	This Work (Sect. 4.3) Higher-Deg $N > 2^9$
Prover No. of Exp ($\mathbb{G}$)	$15N+2\log N-10$	$8\log N - 4$	$4\log N + 2$	$3\log N + 3\sqrt{\log N} + 2$
Verifier No. of Exp ($\mathbb{G}$)	$5N+2\log N+10$	$7\log N - 1$	$2\log N + 7$	$\log N + 3\sqrt{\log N} + 6$
Proof Size No. of Elements	$2\log N + 8$ ($\mathbb{G}$) 5 ($\mathbb{Z}_p$)	$4\log N - 2$ ($\mathbb{G}$) $3\log N$ ($\mathbb{Z}_p$)	$\log N + 3$ ($\mathbb{G}$) $\log N + 3$ ($\mathbb{Z}_p$)	$2\sqrt{\log N} + 3$ ($\mathbb{G}$) $\log N + \sqrt{\log N} + 4$ ($\mathbb{Z}_p$)

nomial evaluation arguments for scenarios where y is even secretly committed without losing the sub-linear computational efficiency. For example, with the aid of the Maclaurin series [44], the polynomial evaluation arguments can satisfy complex mathematical relations between two committed values, e.g., trigonometric and exponential functions. The range arguments help confine the input x to a specific range to ensure y is in the safe range $[-\frac{p-1}{2}, \frac{p-1}{2}]$ without overflow, where p is the group order.

Comparisons with State-of-the-art Polynomial Evaluation Proofs. Table 3 shows an efficiency comparison of polynomial evaluation arguments in the DL setting with a transparent setup. As compared to BG13, it is observed that our arguments achieve a significant improvement in the efficiency of computation and communication without a trusted setup. More concretely, for polynomials of degree $D = 2^{16} - 1$, our arguments incur 1122 bytes over a 256-bit elliptic curve group, yielding a 3.1× reduction in proof size. The allocated communication cost per argument would decrease by 72.4% to about 310 bytes for the aggregation of 16 distinct arguments. In addition, the efficiency in proving and verification is raised by a factor of 2 and 3.3, respectively. An alternative type of communication-efficient arguments with a transparent setup in the DL setting is the generic-purpose Bulletproofs, which require $2\log N + 13$ elements for any arithmetic circuits, where N is the number of multiplication gates. On the one hand, our arguments outperform Bulletproofs in the efficiency of computation and communication regarding the polynomial evaluation. On the other hand, our arguments only need three rounds, while Bulletproofs require $\log N$ rounds.

1.2 Outline of Our Paper

Our paper is organised as follows. First, we introduce the cryptographic preliminaries in Sect. 2. We elaborate on the core techniques of the range arguments and polynomial evaluation arguments as well as some optimisations in Sects. 3 and 4. A comprehensive evaluation of performance is given in Sect. 5. We provide the full protocols of our arguments and the security proofs in Sect. 6. We describe the related work in Sect. 7.

2 Preliminaries

We follow the definitions in [13,29] to formalise homomorphic commitment schemes and zero-knowledge arguments of knowledge.

Let λ and $\mathsf{negl}(\lambda)$ be the security parameter and the negligible function. PPT means probabilistic polynomial time. Denote a cyclic group of prime order p by $\mathbb{G}$, and the ring of integers modulo p by $\mathbb{Z}_p$. Let $\mathbb{Z}_p^*$ be $\mathbb{Z}_p \backslash \{0\}$. Let $g, h \xleftarrow{\$} \mathbb{G}, (g_i)_{i=0}^{n-1} \xleftarrow{\$} \mathbb{G}^n$ be uniformly random generators from $\mathbb{G}$. Let $x \xleftarrow{\$} \mathbb{Z}_p^*$ be uniformly random element from $\mathbb{Z}_p^*$. Denote the vector spaces of dimension n over $\mathbb{G}$ and $\mathbb{Z}_p$ by $\mathbb{G}^n$ and $\mathbb{Z}_p^n$, respectively.

2.1 Homomorphic Commitment Schemes

Homomorphic commitment schemes are a crucial building block for zero-knowledge proofs. A homomorphic commitment allows to commit to a value with a negligible chance of altering it before opening the commitment. A homomorphic commitment scheme is, hiding if a commitment does not reveal the value and, binding if a commitment can only be opened to one value.

A homomorphic commitment scheme is a pair of PPT algorithms $(\mathcal{G}, \mathsf{Cm})$, where the setup algorithm $\mathcal{G}(\lambda)$ generates a commitment key ck and the commitment algorithm Cm defines a function $\mathsf{Cm}_{\mathsf{ck}} : \mathsf{M}_{\mathsf{ck}} \times \mathsf{R}_{\mathsf{ck}} \rightarrow \mathsf{C}_{\mathsf{ck}}$ for a message space M_{ck}, a randomness space R_{ck} and a commitment space C_{ck}. For a message $m \in \mathsf{M}_{\mathsf{ck}}$, a uniformly randomness $r \in \mathsf{R}_{\mathsf{ck}}$ can be picked to produce a commitment $c = \mathsf{Cm}_{\mathsf{ck}}(m; r)$. The commitments are homomorphic for all well-formed commitment keys ck and $m_0, m_1 \in \mathsf{M}_{\mathsf{ck}}, r_0, r_1 \in \mathsf{R}_{\mathsf{ck}}$:

$$\begin{aligned} \mathsf{Cm}_{\mathsf{ck}}(m_0; r_0) \cdot \mathsf{Cm}_{\mathsf{ck}}(m_1; r_1) &= \mathsf{Cm}_{\mathsf{ck}}(m_0 + m_1; r_0 + r_1) \\ \mathsf{Cm}_{\mathsf{ck}}(m_0; r_0)^{m_1} &= \mathsf{Cm}_{\mathsf{ck}}(m_0 \cdot m_1; r_0 \cdot m_1) \end{aligned}$$

Definition 1 (Hiding). *A commitment scheme $(\mathcal{G}, \mathsf{Cm})$ is hiding if a commitment does not reveal the value for all PPT adversaries $\mathcal{A}$:*

$$Pr\left[\begin{array}{l|l} c = \mathsf{Cm}_{\mathsf{ck}}(m_b),\ b \in \{0,1\}, & \mathsf{ck} \leftarrow \mathcal{G}(\lambda), \\ b' \leftarrow \mathcal{A}(c),\ b = b' & (m_0, m_1 \in \mathsf{M}_{\mathsf{ck}}) \leftarrow \mathcal{A}(\mathsf{ck}) \end{array}\right] \approx \frac{1}{2}$$

The scheme is perfectly hiding if the probability is equal to $\frac{1}{2}$.

Definition 2 (Binding). *A commitment scheme $(\mathcal{G}, \mathsf{Cm})$ is binding if a commitment can only be opened to one value for all PPT adversaries $\mathcal{A}$:*

$$Pr\left[\begin{array}{l|l} \mathsf{Cm}_{\mathsf{ck}}(m_0; r_0) = \mathsf{Cm}_{\mathsf{ck}}(m_1; r_1), & \mathsf{ck} \leftarrow \mathcal{G}(\lambda), \\ m_0 \neq m_1 & (m_0, m_1 \in \mathsf{M}_{\mathsf{ck}}, r_0, r_1 \in \mathsf{R}_{\mathsf{ck}}) \leftarrow \mathcal{A}(\mathsf{ck}) \end{array}\right] \leq \mathsf{negl}(\lambda)$$

The scheme is perfectly binding if the probability is equal to 0.

We define the Pedersen commitment and Pedersen vector commitment as below, both of which are perfect hiding and computationally binding:

Definition 3 (Pedersen Commitment). *Given* $\mathsf{M_{ck}} = \mathbb{Z}_p, \mathsf{R_{ck}} = \mathbb{Z}_p^*$, $\mathsf{C_{ck}} = \mathbb{G}$ *of order* p *and* $g, h \xleftarrow{\$} \mathbb{G}$*:*

$$\mathsf{Cm}(m; r) = g^m h^r \ (mod\ p)$$

Definition 4 (Pedersen Vector Commitment). *Given* $\mathsf{M_{ck}} = \mathbb{Z}_p^n, \mathsf{R_{ck}} = \mathbb{Z}_p^*$, $\mathsf{C_{ck}} = \mathbb{G}$ *of order* p *and* $(g_0, ..., g_{n-1}) \xleftarrow{\$} \mathbb{G}^n, h \xleftarrow{\$} \mathbb{G}$*:*

$$\mathsf{Cm}(m_0, ..., m_{n-1}; r) = h^r \prod_{i=0}^{n-1} g_i^{m_i} \ (mod\ p)$$

2.2 Zero-Knowledge Arguments of Knowledge

Based upon the discrete logarithm assumption, Flashproofs are public-coin honest-verifier zero-knowledge arguments of knowledge. A zero-knowledge argument is comprised of three interactive probabilistic polynomial-time algorithms $(\mathcal{G}, \mathcal{P}, \mathcal{V})$, where the setup algorithm $\mathcal{G}(\lambda)$ returns a common reference string σ. $\mathcal{P}$ and $\mathcal{V}$ are the prover and verifier algorithms, which produce the public transcript, $tr \leftarrow \langle \mathcal{P}(v), \mathcal{V}(t) \rangle$ on inputs v and t. Denote a polynomial-time decidable tertiary relation by $\mathcal{R} \subset \{0,1\}^* \times \{0,1\}^* \times \{0,1\}^*$. A CRS-dependent language can be defined as $L_\sigma = \{u \mid \exists \omega : (\sigma, u, \omega) \in \mathcal{R}\}$, where ω is a witness for a statement u in the relation $(\sigma, u, \omega) \in \mathcal{R}$.

Definition 5 (Argument of Knowledge). *The triple* $(\mathcal{G}, \mathcal{P}, \mathcal{V})$ *is called an argument of knowledge for the relation* $\mathcal{R}$ *if it satisfies the perfect completeness and computational witness-extended emulation.*

Definition 6 (Perfect Completeness). *An argument of knowledge* $(\mathcal{G}, \mathcal{P}, \mathcal{V})$ *has perfect completeness if for all PPT adversaries* $\mathcal{A}$*:*

$$Pr\Big[(\sigma, u, \omega) \notin \mathcal{R} \ or \ \langle \mathcal{P}(\sigma, u, \omega), \mathcal{V}(\sigma, u) \rangle = 1 \ \Big| \ \sigma \leftarrow \mathcal{G}(\lambda), (u, \omega) \leftarrow \mathcal{A}(\sigma)\Big] = 1$$

Definition 7 (Computational Witness-Extended Emulation). *An argument of knowledge* $(\mathcal{G}, \mathcal{P}, \mathcal{V})$ *has witness-extended emulation if for all deterministic polynomial time* $\mathcal{P}^*$*, there exists an expected polynomial time emulator* $\mathcal{E}$ *such that for all PPT adversaries* $\mathcal{A}$*:*

$$Pr\left[\mathcal{A}(tr) = 1 \;\middle|\; \begin{array}{c} \sigma \leftarrow \mathcal{G}(\lambda) \\ (u, s) \leftarrow \mathcal{A}(\sigma), \\ tr \leftarrow \mathcal{O} \end{array}\right] \approx Pr\left[\begin{array}{l} \mathcal{A}(tr) = 1 \\ \wedge \text{ tr is accepting} \\ \rightarrow (\sigma, u, w) \in \mathcal{R} \end{array} \;\middle|\; \begin{array}{l} \sigma \leftarrow \mathcal{G}(\lambda), \\ (u, s) \leftarrow \mathcal{A}(\sigma), \\ (tr, \omega) \leftarrow \mathcal{E}^{\mathcal{O}}(\sigma, u) \end{array}\right]$$

where the oracle is defined as $\mathcal{O} = \langle \mathcal{P}^*(\sigma, u, s), \mathcal{V}(\sigma, u) \rangle$.

Soundness can be defined based on the witness-extended emulation. Informally, whenever $\mathcal{P}^*$ makes a convincing argument in state s, there exists a knowledge emulator $\mathcal{E}$ that can extract a witness for $(\sigma, u, \omega) \in \mathcal{R}$ by rewinding the interaction to any specific points and running again with the same state for the prover, but fresh randomness for the verifier.

Definition 8 (Public Coin). *An argument of knowledge ($\mathcal{G}$, $\mathcal{P}$, $\mathcal{V}$) is called public coin if the verifier chooses her messages uniformly at random and independently of the messages sent by the prover.*

Definition 9 (Perfect Special Honest Verifier Zero-Knowledge, SHVZK). *A public coin argument of knowledge ($\mathcal{G}$, $\mathcal{P}$, $\mathcal{V}$) is called perfect special honest verifier zero-knowledge argument of knowledge for $\mathcal{R}$ if there exists a PPT simulator $\mathcal{S}$ such that for all interactive PPT adversaries $\mathcal{A}$:*

$$Pr\left[\begin{array}{c|c} (\sigma, u, \omega) \in \mathcal{R} & \sigma \leftarrow \mathcal{G}(\lambda), \\ \wedge\, \mathcal{A}(tr) = 1 & (u, \omega, e) \leftarrow \mathcal{A}(\sigma), \\ & tr \leftarrow \langle \mathcal{P}(v), \mathcal{V}(t) \rangle \end{array}\right] = Pr\left[\begin{array}{c|c} (\sigma, u, \omega) \in \mathcal{R} & \sigma \leftarrow \mathcal{G}(\lambda), \\ \wedge\, \mathcal{A}(tr) = 1 & (u, \omega, e) \leftarrow \mathcal{A}(\sigma), \\ & tr \leftarrow \mathcal{S}(u, e) \end{array}\right]$$

where e is a public coin challenge, $v = (\sigma, u, \omega)$ and $t = (\sigma, u, e)$.

An argument is zero-knowledge if no extra information except the witness can be inferred from the statement. A general approach to proving that an argument has special honest verifier zero-knowledge is to construct a simulator that knows the challenge and can simulate the whole transcript of the argument without knowing the witness.

3 Range Arguments

3.1 Overview of Bit-Decomposition Approach

Bit-decomposition is a folklore approach for constructing range proofs. The challenge consists in seeking an efficient method to prove that a committed value can be represented in binary form. Bulletproof employs a variant of the bit-decomposition approach by using an inner product argument [10] (Please refer to their original paper [13] for more details). The intuition is that a prover prepares one vector commitment, which commits to the bit vector $\mathbf{b}$ of the target value y and to the vector $\mathbf{a} = \mathbf{b} - \mathbf{1^N}$. The prover constructs an equation in Eqn. (1) to prove the three constraints: (I) $\langle \mathbf{b}, \mathbf{2^N} \rangle = y$, (II) $\langle \mathbf{b} - \mathbf{1^N} - \mathbf{a}, \mathbf{r} \rangle = 0$ and (III) $\langle \mathbf{b}, \mathbf{a} \circ \mathbf{r} \rangle = 0$.

$$z^2 \cdot \langle \mathbf{b}, \mathbf{2^N} \rangle + z \cdot \langle \mathbf{b} - \mathbf{1^N} - \mathbf{a}, \mathbf{r} \rangle + \langle \mathbf{b}, \mathbf{a} \circ \mathbf{r} \rangle = z^2 \cdot y \tag{1}$$

where $z \in \mathbb{Z}_p^*$ is a random value and $\mathbf{r} \in \mathbb{Z}_p^{*N}$ is a vector of random values provided by the verifier. $\mathbf{1^N} = (1, 1, ..., 1)$ is a vector of 1 and $\mathbf{2^N} = (2^0, 2^1, ..., 2^{N-1})$ is a vector of powers of 2. $\langle \cdot, \cdot \rangle$ and $\circ$ denote the inner product and the Hadamard product, respectively.

Then the prover takes advantage of the inner product argument to recursively compress the equation in $O(\log N)$ rounds. The compression technique helps achieve $O(\log N)$ communication efficiency but exposes two limitations:

- The process is computationally expensive, demanding $O(N)$ group exponentiations for proving and verification.
- To a degree, the recursion impedes a parallel acceleration of proof generation.

3.2 Our Techniques

We devise a new variant of the bit-decomposition approach that only needs three rounds. Our technique is highly lightweight in computation and does not require pairing operations. Compared to Bulletproof, our arguments involve far fewer group exponentiations in both proving and verification and also allow for a speedup of proof generation by parallelisation. In this section, we mainly concentrate on the core techniques of our arguments, whereas the full protocol is given in Sect. 6.1. Our techniques work as follows:

1. Given a commitment $c_y = g^y h^{r_y}$, we express the committed value $y = \sum_{i=0}^{N-1} 2^i b_i$ as a sequence of terms $(w_0, w_1, ..., w_{N-1})$ for the range $[0, 2^N - 1]$, where $b_i \in \{0,1\}$ and $w_i = 2^i b_i$, $i \in \{0, 1, ..., N-1\}$. Then we fold the sequence and arrange all the terms $(w_i)_{i=0}^{N-1}$ in an $L \times K$ matrix in Eqn. (2), where L and K indicate the number of rows and columns, respectively. If N is a prime integer, additional zeros of size $\gamma \in \mathbb{Z}^+$ can be padded onto the high-order bits to make $N + \gamma = K \cdot L$.
2. We prove each coefficient w_{lK+k} is 0 or 2^{lK+k}.
3. We flatten the two-dimension matrix to a one-dimension vector and prove that y is the sum of K values, such that $y = \sum_{k=0}^{K-1} s_k$, where $s_k = \sum_{l=0}^{L-1} w_{lK+k}$ is the sum of L coefficients $(w_{lK+k})_{l=0}^{L-1}$ in the k-th column.

$$\begin{pmatrix} 2^0 b_0 & \cdots & 2^{K-1} b_{K-1} \\ 2^K b_K & \cdots & 2^{K+K-1} b_{K+K-1} \\ \vdots & \ddots & \vdots \\ 2^{(L-1)K} b_{(L-1)K} & \cdots & 2^{(L-1)K+K-1} b_{(L-1)K+K-1} \end{pmatrix} = \begin{pmatrix} w_0 & \cdots & w_{K-1} \\ w_K & \cdots & w_{K+K-1} \\ \vdots & \ddots & \vdots \\ w_{(L-1)K} & \cdots & w_{(L-1)K+K-1} \end{pmatrix} \quad (2)$$

where the i-th term w_i in the l-th row and the k-th column is also denoted by w_{lK+k}, $k \in \{0, ..., K-1\}$ and $l \in \{0, ..., L-1\}$.

Next, we describe the intuition in more details. Instead of proving each bit $b_i \in \{0,1\}$ as Bulletproof, we turn to prove $w_{lK+k} \in \{0, 2^{lK+k}\}$ for each $(i = lK + k)$. In the third round of the protocol, the prover computes and sends a value $v_l = \sum_{k=0}^{K-1} w_{lK+k} e_k + r_l$ to the verifier for each l after acquiring a challenge vector $(e_0, ..., e_{K-1})^\intercal$ from the verifier. v_l is a randomised inner product of the l-th row and the challenge vector, where $r_l \in \mathbb{Z}_p^*$ is used to prevent v_l from leaking any information about the coefficients. The essence of our technique is an effective use of v_l for verifying $w_{lK+k} \in \{0, 2^{lK+k}\}$. Unlike Bulletproof, which requires the prover to satisfy the constraint (II) in Eqn. (1), we design a new technique to relieve the prover of this burden, which greatly reduces proving computational costs. The technique allows the verifier to compute a value f_l by subtracting v_l from $\sum_{k=0}^{K-1} 2^{lK+k} e_k$ for each l:

$$f_l = \sum_{k=0}^{K-1} 2^{lK+k} e_k - v_l = \sum_{k=0}^{K-1} (2^{lK+k} - w_{lK+k}) e_k - r_l$$

For the case where N is a prime number, it suffices for the verifier to use 0 rather than $2^{lK+k} e_k$ for the padded bits. Then computing $f_l \cdot v_l$ for each l will generate a series of cross-terms in the challenges:

$$f_l \cdot v_l \stackrel{?}{=} \underbrace{\sum_{k=0}^{K-1} w_{lK+k}(2^{lK+k} - w_{lK+k}) e_k^2}_{=\,0,\text{ if } w_{lK+k} \in \{0, 2^{lK+k}\}} + \sum_{k=0,j=1}^{k=K-2,j=K-1} t_{l,k,j} e_{k,j} + \sum_{k=0}^{K-1} q_{l,k} e_k + q_{l,K} \tag{3}$$

where $t_{l,k,j} = w_{lK+k}(2^{lK+j} - w_{lK+j}) + w_{lK+j}(2^{lK+k} - w_{lK+k})$ and $e_{k,j} = e_k \cdot e_j$ for $k, j \in \{0, ..., K-1\} \wedge k \neq j$. $q_{l,k} = 2r_l(2^{lK+k-1} - w_{lK+k})$ for $k \in \{0, ..., K-1\}$ and $q_{l,K} = -r_l^2$. The number of terms $e_{k,j}$ is $\frac{K(K-1)}{2}$.

The verifier needs to ensure that the quadratic terms $(e_k^2)_{k=0}^{K-1}$ are all cancelled out by only using the commitments to the coefficients of the remaining terms in Eqn. (3) for verification. Before obtaining the challenges, the prover must provide these commitments in the first round. Thus, by the binding property of Pedersen commitment and the Schwartz-Zippel lemma, it is with an overwhelming probability that the coefficient of the k-th quadratic term satisfies the constraint below:

$$w_{lK+k}(2^{lK+k} - w_{lK+k}) = 0 \Longrightarrow w_{lK+k} \in \{0, 2^{lK+k}\}$$

The prover also needs to provide the commitments $(c_{s_k})_{k=0}^{K}$ in the first round so that the verifier can check the validity of $(s_k)_{k=0}^{K}$ based upon the equation below:

$$\sum_{l=0}^{L-1} v_l \stackrel{?}{=} \sum_{k=0}^{K-1} s_k e_k + s_K, \quad s_K = \sum_{l=0}^{L-1} r_l \tag{4}$$

Finally, the verifier can be convinced that y lies in the range $[0, 2^N - 1]$ by checking the equation $y \stackrel{?}{=} \sum_{k=0}^{K-1} s_k$. As we use elliptic curve groups to instantiate the argument, where the group and field elements have roughly the same size, then the total number of elements would be:

$$|\Pi| = L + 2K + \frac{K(K-1)}{2} + 4 = \lceil \frac{N}{K} \rceil + \frac{K^2}{2} + \frac{3K}{2} + 4$$

The number of group exponentiations for verification is $|\Pi| - 1$. We calculate the derivative $\Delta_{|\Pi|} = K - \frac{N}{K^2} + \frac{3}{2}$, such that when $K \approx \lceil N^{\frac{1}{3}} \rfloor$, both $|\Pi|$ and verification complexity achieve the minimum. Table 4a provides a set of (L, K) values for different ranges.

Table 4. Comparison of range arguments

(a) Values of (L, K)

N	8-bit	16-bit	32-bit	64-bit
L	4	8	11	16
K	2	2	3	4

(b) Comparison of range arguments for 64-bit

Type	Prover No. of Exp ($\mathbb{G}$)	Verifier No. of Exp ($\mathbb{G}$)	Proof Size (Byte)
Original Work	197	33	1090
Optimised Work	146	30	994
Saving	51 (25.9%)	3 (9.1%)	96 (8.8%)

Optimisation. We propose an optimisation technique to improve the overall efficiency. We change the way that the challenge vectors are generated at the expense of amplifying the soundness error from $\frac{(p-K)!}{p!}$ to $\frac{1}{p}$, which is still sufficiently negligible with a large p. The high-level idea is to allow the verifier to randomly produce a challenge e, such that the other challenges in the vector will be produced by taking different powers of e. This change opens the possibility of merging the terms of the same orders to reduce the number of group exponentiations in both proving and verification. We exemplify a concrete case with $K = 4$ and consider the 4 challenges $(e_k)_{k=0}^{3} = (e^{-1}, e, e^4, e^5)$ for a simpler interpretation. To check whether the witness y is correctly represented in binary form, the verifier needs to ensure that none of the terms $(e^{-2}, e^2, e^8, e^{10})$ will appear on the right-hand side of Eqn. (3). Computing $f_l \cdot v_l$ will generate a polynomial with only 8 terms instead of the original $0.5 \cdot 16 + 0.5 \cdot 4 + 1 = 11$:

$$P(e) = w_9 e^9 + w_6 e^6 + w_5 e^5 + w_4 e^4 + w_3 e^3 + w_1 e + w_{-1} e^{-1} + w_0$$

where w_* indicates the coefficients of the corresponding terms.

The coefficients of the combined terms $e \cdot e^{-1}$, $e \cdot e^4$ and $e^{-1} \cdot e^5$ are respectively merged into w_0, w_5 and w_4. As shown in Table 4b, this optimisation saves 51 and 3 group exponentiations for proving and verification, respectively, and 3 group elements for communication when $K = 4$. Notably, the optimisation increases the proving efficiency by 25.9%. Note that a particular choice of K challenges can yield $F(K)$ number of terms for computing $f_l \cdot v_l$. We provide a possible combination of the challenge exponents for $F(K)$ as below and let the readers discover more possible combinations.

K=2: $\{-1, 1\}$, K=3: $\{-1, 1, 4\}$, K=4: $\{-1, 1, 4, 5\}$, K=5: $\{-1, 1, -4, 4, 5\}$
K=6: $\{-1, 1, -4, 4, -5, 5\}$, K=7: $\{-1, 1, -4, 4, -5, 5, 16\}$
K=8: $\{-1, 1, -4, 4, -5, 5, -16, 16\}$, K=9: $\{-1, 1, -4, 4, -5, 5, -16, 16, 17\}$
K=10: $\{-1, 1, -4, 4, -5, 5, -16, 16, -17, 17\}$

3.3 Aggregate Range Arguments

Multiple arguments for the same range created by one prover can be aggregated for further efficiency gains. Given M witnesses $(y_m)_{m=0}^{M-1}$, the prover creates two unique sets $(v_l^{(m)})_{l=0}^{L-1}$ and $(s_k^{(m)})_{k=0}^{K}$ for each $m \in \{0, ..., M-1\}$. The prover utilises $M \cdot L$ generators, where the (m, l)-th generator is in charge of computing $f_l^{(m)} \cdot v_l^{(m)}$. Hence, the M coefficients of each term on the right-hand side of Eq. (3) can be compacted in one commitment. Then we can apply the batch verification technique [4] to reduce the number of group exponentiations by simultaneously checking the equations in Eq. (4) for these arguments. The technique is based on the principle that checking $a = 0 \wedge b = 0$ is equivalent to checking $a + \rho b = 0$ with high probability, where $\rho \in \mathbb{Z}_p^*$ is a random value. Thus, the verifier can produce a new random challenge $z \in \mathbb{Z}_p^*$ and use the equation below to validate $s_k^{(m)}$ in batches:

$$\sum_{m=0}^{M-1}(\sum_{l=0}^{L-1} v_l^{(m)})z^m \stackrel{?}{=} \sum_{k=0}^{K-1}(\sum_{m=0}^{M-1} s_k^{(m)} z^m)e_k + \sum_{m=0}^{M-1} s_K^{(m)} z^m$$

Finally, the verifier can check $y_m \stackrel{?}{=} \sum_{k=0}^{K-1} s_k^{(m)}$ for each m. The total number of elements is $|\Pi_{\text{total}}| = M \cdot (\lceil \frac{N}{K} \rceil + K + 1) + \frac{K^2+K}{2} + 3$. When $K \approx \lceil (MN)^{\frac{1}{3}} \rfloor \wedge \frac{N}{K} \geq 1$, the complexity of both communication and verification achieves the minimum. Then for aggregating M optimised range arguments, we can use the formula $\frac{F(K)+2}{M} + \lceil \frac{N}{K} \rceil + K + 1$ to calculate the number of elements for communication cost or the allocated number of group exponentiations for verification per argument.

4 Polynomial Evaluation Arguments

Built upon the techniques of Bayer & Groth (BG13) [3], our polynomial evaluation arguments aim to prove that two committed values x and y satisfy a public polynomial relation $y = P(x; D)$, where D is the degree. They achieve non-trivial efficiency gains in computation and communication thanks to the *quadratic-term cancellation* technique. We give two protocols, which respectively excel in handling the polynomials of lower-degree $D \in [3, 2^9]$ and higher-degree $D > 2^9$. We essentially focus on the core techniques of our arguments, whereas the full protocols are given in Sects. 6.2 and 6.3.

4.1 Overview of BG13

We begin with an overview of BG13 (Please refer to their original paper [3] for more details). Consider a polynomial function $P(x; D) = \sum_{d=0}^{D} a_d x^d$, where we assume $D = 2^{J+1} - 1$ for $J \in \{1, 2, ...\}$ without loss of generality by padding with zero-coefficients. First, the polynomial $P(x; D)$ can be re-written as below by substituting the d-th term x^d with $x^{\sum_{j=0}^{J} 2^j b_d^{(j)}} = \prod_{j=0}^{J} x^{2^j b_d^{(j)}}$, where $d = \sum_{j=0}^{J} 2^j b_d^{(j)}$, $b_d^{(j)} \in \{0, 1\}$ and $J + 1 = \lceil \log D \rceil$:

$$P(x; D) = \sum_{d=0}^{D} a_d x^d = \sum_{d=0}^{D} a_d x^{\sum_{j=0}^{J} 2^j b_d^{(j)}} = \sum_{d=0}^{D} a_d \prod_{j=0}^{J} x^{2^j b_d^{(j)}}$$

Then BG13 defines a new polynomial $Q(e; J + 1)$ by substituting x^{2^j} with a masking value $z_j = x^{2^j} e + m_j$ for each j, such that the coefficient of the leading term e^{J+1} is equal to $P(x;D)$, where m_j is a random value, e is the verifier's random challenge and w_j is the coefficient of the term e^j.

$$Q(e;J+1) = \sum_{d=0}^{D}(a_d \prod_{j=0}^{J} e^{1-b_d^{(j)}} z_j^{b_d^{(j)}}) = P(x;D)e^{J+1} + \sum_{j=0}^{J} w_j e^j \tag{5}$$

The prover must provide the commitment to $P(x;D)$ and the commitments to the coefficients $(w_j)_{j=0}^{J}$ before acquiring the challenge e to prove that the polynomial $Q(e;J+1)$ is well formed. In a nutshell, there are three constraints to satisfy:

1. $P(x;D)$ is the coefficient of the leading term e^{J+1}.
2. The linearity between x^{2^j} and $z_j = x^{2^j} e + m_j$ for $j \in \{0,...,J\}$.
3. The quadratic relations between x^{2^j} hidden in z_j and $x^{2^{j+1}}$ hidden in z_{j+1} for $j \in \{0,...,J-1\}$.

BG13 creates three sets of group elements $(c_{x^{2^j}})_{j=1}^{J}$, $(c_{m_j})_{j=0}^{J}$, $(c_{(x^{2^j} m_j)})_{j=0}^{J-1}$ and two sets of field elements $(r_j)_{j=0}^{J}$, $(\xi_j)_{j=0}^{J-1}$. Then it utilises two equations to fulfil the constraints 2 and 3 for each j:

$$z_j \stackrel{?}{=} x^{2^j} e + m_j \Longrightarrow \mathsf{Cm}(z_j; r_j) \stackrel{?}{=} c_{x^{2^j}}^{e} \cdot c_{m_j}$$

$$0 \stackrel{?}{=} x^{2^{j+1}} e - x^{2^j} z_j + x^{2^j} m_j \Longrightarrow \mathsf{Cm}(0;\xi_j) \stackrel{?}{=} c_{x^{2^{j+1}}}^{e} \cdot c_{x^{2^j}}^{-z_j} \cdot c_{(x^{2^j} m_j)}$$

4.2 Techniques of Lower-Degree (LD) Protocol

In this protocol, we aim for optimisations to fulfil the constraint 2 and 3 for better computational and communication efficiency. Our technique is a new equation in Eq. (6) that effectively leverages the field elements $(z_j)_{j=0}^{J}$ rather than the group elements as in BG13 to achieve the verification, which significantly improves the computational efficiency by reducing the number of group exponentiations. The two equations for simultaneously satisfying the constraint 2 and 3 are:

$$z_0 \stackrel{?}{=} xe + m_0, \quad z_j^2 - z_{j+1}e \stackrel{?}{=} (2x^{2^j} m_j - m_{j+1})e + m_j^2,\ j \in \{0,...,J-1\} \tag{6}$$

In Eqn. (6), first, we must ensure the linearity between the input x and z_0. Then computing $z_j^2 - z_{j+1}e$ for $j \in \{0,...,J-1\}$ will cancel out quadratic terms e^2 and leave the first-order term $(2x^{2^j} m_j - m_{j+1})e$ and the constant term m_j^2. Our techniques only require the prover to provide the vector commitments to the coefficients of these two terms before acquiring the challenge e. This not only ensures the quadratic relations between x^{2^j} and $x^{2^{j+1}}$ but also justifies the linearity between x^{2^j} and $z_j = x^{2^j} e + m_j$ for $j \in \{1,...,J-1\}$. Otherwise, the quadratic terms e^2 must have appeared on the right-hand side with overwhelming probability. Compared with the techniques of BG13, ours entail far fewer computationally expensive group operations. With respect to the communication cost, the reduction by $5\log D$ elements is essentially attributed to the use of vector commitments. Moreover, our new equation in Eq. (6) also contributes to decreasing the proof size.

4.3 Techniques of Higher-Degree (HD) Protocol

On top of the lower-degree protocol, we aim for a further optimisation to fulfil the constraint 1. We attempt to trade $\log D$ group elements in Eq. (5) for $3\sqrt{\log D}$ group and field elements by applying the technique of the polynomial commitment [10]. Intuitively, we can factor out common polynomial factors from the polynomial $\sum_{j=0}^{J} w_j e^j$. First, we rewrite $\sum_{j=0}^{J} w_j e^j$ as $\sum_{l=0}^{L-1} e^{lK} \sum_{k=0}^{K-1} w_{lK+k} e^k$ without loss of generality by padding with zero coefficients, where $J+1 = L \cdot K$ and $l \in \{0,..,L-1\}$, $k \in \{0,...,K-1\}$. L polynomials $(\sum_{k=0}^{K-1} w_{lK+k} e^k)_{l=0}^{L-1}$ can be factored out to build a matrix in a way that each row contains the coefficients of the factored polynomials, and each column is a vector of the coefficients of the same-order of e:

$$\begin{pmatrix} w_0 + \theta_0 & w_1 & \dots & w_{K-1} \\ w_K + \theta_1 & w_{K+1} & \dots & w_{2K-1} \\ \vdots & \vdots & \ddots & \vdots \\ w_{(L-1)K} + \theta_{L-1} & w_{(L-1)K+1} & \dots & w_{LK-1} \end{pmatrix}$$

The prover commits to all the columns as $(c_{w_k})_{k=0}^{K-1}$ using vector commitments and creates a field value $f_l = \sum_{k=0}^{K-1} w_{lK+k} e^k + \theta_l$ for each l, which is a randomised inner product of the l-th row and the challenge vector $(1, e, ..., e^{K-1})^\intercal$, where $\theta_l \in \mathbb{Z}_p^*$ is a random value to prevent leaking information about the coefficients $(w_{lK+k})_{k=0}^{K-1}$.

$$c_{w_0} = \prod_{l=0}^{L-1} g_l^{w_{lK}+\theta_l} \cdot h^{r_{w_0}} \; (c_{w_k} = \prod_{l=0}^{L-1} g_l^{w_{lK+k}} \cdot h^{r_{w_k}})_{k=1}^{K-1}$$

where $(g_l)_{l=0}^{L-1} \xleftarrow{\$} \mathbb{G}^L, h \xleftarrow{\$} \mathbb{G}$ are distinct generators and $(r_{w_k} \xleftarrow{\$} \mathbb{Z}_p^*)_{k=0}^{K-1}$ are random values.
The verifier computes $\prod_{l=0}^{L-1} g_l^{f_l} \cdot h^s \stackrel{?}{=} \prod_{k=0}^{K-1} c_{w_k}^{e^k}$ to check the correctness of $(f_l)_{l=0}^{L-1}$, where $s = \sum_{k=0}^{K-1} r_{w_k} e^k$, and constructs a new equation in Eqn. (7) to replace Eqn. (5) for the constraint 1:

$$Q(e; J+1) - \sum_{l=0}^{L-1} f_l e^{lK} \stackrel{?}{=} P(x; D) e^{J+1} - \sum_{l=0}^{L-1} \theta_l e^{lK} \tag{7}$$

The prover is required to provide the commitments to $(\theta_l)_{l=0}^{L-1}$ before obtaining the challenge e. In addition to the proof size reduction, this technique greatly reduces the number of group exponentiations, which improves the efficiency in both communication and verification.

4.4 Aggregate Polynomial Evaluation Arguments

The aggregation of multiple arguments is supported for a significant efficiency improvement. Recall that our techniques enable a non-trivial reduction in the communication cost to $\log D + 3\sqrt{\log D} + 7$ elements for higher-degree polynomials, where $J+1$ field elements $(z_j = x^{2^j}e + m_j)_{j=0}^{J}$ dominate the whole argument. Thus, multiple arguments satisfying different polynomials with the same degree and inputs can split the communication cost of these field elements. Given M polynomials $\left(P(x;D)^{(m)}\right)_{m=0}^{M-1}$ of the same degree D, the prover utilises $M \cdot L$ generators to create K commitments $(c_{w_k})_{k=0}^{K-1}$ by compacting the coefficients of all M arguments. Then the prover provides two unique sets of $(f_l^{(m)})_{l=0}^{L-1}$ and $(\theta_l^{(m)})_{l=0}^{L-1}$ for each $m \in \{0, ..., M-1\}$. Similar to the aggregate range argument, the verifier uses the equation below to check the constraint 1 for multiple arguments in batches, where $z \in \mathbb{Z}_p^*$ is a new random challenge provided by the verifier:

$$\sum_{m=0}^{M-1} \left(Q(e;J+1)^{(m)} - \sum_{l=0}^{L-1} f_l^{(m)} e^{lK}\right) z^m \stackrel{?}{=} \sum_{m=0}^{M-1} P(x;D)^{(m)} z^m e^{J+1} - \sum_{l=0}^{L-1}\left(\sum_{m=0}^{M-1} \theta_l^{(m)} z^m\right) e^{lK}$$

For aggregating M arguments, we can use the formula $\frac{\log D + \sqrt{\log D} + 7}{M} + 2\sqrt{\log D}$ to calculate the number of elements for communication cost or the allocated number of group exponentiations for verification per argument. For a certain degree D, the efficiency in verification (group exponentiations) and communication asymptotically approaches $O(\sqrt{\log D})$ when M increases.

4.5 Limitation and Extension

Limitation. Overall, our techniques aim to reduce the number of group exponentiations and elements for superior efficiency in computation and communication. Based on the techniques of BG13, unfortunately, our protocols still inherit its limitation of using a linear number of field multiplications in verification for evaluating the worse-case polynomials with few zero terms. The field multiplications would dominate the computational costs over the group exponentiations when the degrees are fairly large, even the latter ones are far more computationally expensive. However, the computational costs of high-order polynomials with quite a few zero terms are less subject to this limitation. Hence, the more zero terms, the less subject to this limitation.

Extension. Our arguments can be extended to satisfy multi-variate polynomial relations, e.g., the inner-product of two vectors. The efficiency in communication and computation would be linear in the number of variates.

5 Empirical Experiments

In our experiments, we measured verification gas costs of the range proofs on Ethereum, one of the most popular blockchain platforms supporting smart contracts. We employed the 254-bit elliptic curve *BN-128* [18][6] that ensures 127-bit

[6] Gas costs would be significantly reduced if precompiled contracts for non-pairing curves, e.g., secp256k1, are supported in future on smart contract platforms.

security as Ethereum provides gas-efficient precompiled contracts for BN-128 curve operations. We adopted *keccak256* (Ethereum-SHA-3) as the hash function modelling the random oracle. Our empirical evaluation was conducted with the processor Intel Core i7-8700 CPU @3.2GHz.

For range arguments, we conducted a full-scale performance comparison with several state-of-the-art range proofs with respect to the computational costs and gas costs on Ethereum. For polynomial evaluation arguments, we essentially compare the computational efficiency between ours and BG13. We skipped the measurement of Bulletproofs as its running time of both proving and verification is considerably greater than those two.

Computational Cost. We measured running time in milliseconds as an evaluation metric of the computational costs. We used the well-known Bouncy Castle Crypto APIs [12] to implement the BN-128 elliptic curve since they were initially used in the Java implementation[7] of Bulletproofs [9], which facilitates a fair comparison. All the experiments were executed on the Java Virtual Machine 15 in a single thread, with results averaged over 50 instances. Note that the Java implementation was aimed at performance comparison. Rust programming language is more suited to commercial usage for high efficiency.

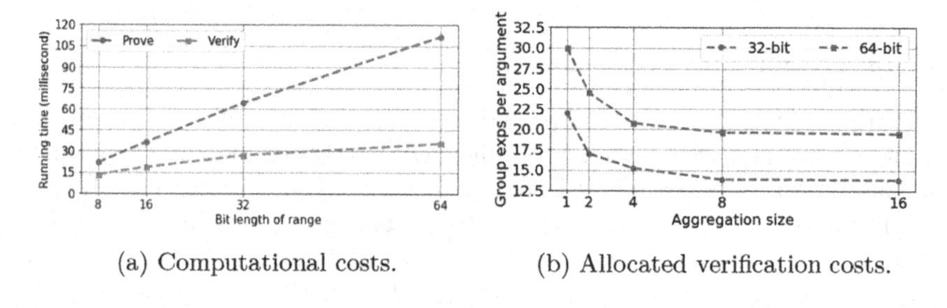

(a) Computational costs.

(b) Allocated verification costs.

Fig. 2. Computational cost of our range arguments.

Figure 2a describes the running time of proving and verification in milliseconds of our optimised range arguments. The verification running time is $O(N^{\frac{2}{3}})$ sub-linear in the range size. The proving running time is slightly sub-linear when $N \leq 64$, which corresponds to the holistic sub-linearity in Fig. 1. Table 5 shows a detailed running time comparison with other state-of-the-art proofs. Our range arguments outperform Bulletproof in both proving and verification. Moreover, at a comparable level of soundness errors, our range arguments do not perform as efficiently as CKLR21 in proving but present higher efficiency in verification. Figure 2b illustrates the allocated number of group exponentiations per argument for verifying aggregate range arguments with the increased aggregation size. The costs are reduced asymptotically as the aggregation size grows. About

[7] The Java code [9] was implemented by the first author of Bulletproofs paper.

Table 5. Running time of range proofs in milliseconds, where CKLR21 was respectively run 3 and 5 iterations for 32-bit and 64-bit ranges to achieve a soundness error 2^{-240}, which is practically close to 2^{-254} of ours. For CKLR21, we considered the additional 54% of the proving computational costs caused by re-runs (mentioned in their paper).

	Type	8-bit	16-bit	32-bit	64-bit
Prove	This work	21.8	36.4	64.4	111.5
	CKLR21	-	-	55.1	73.9
	Bulletproof	132.2	251.4	482	950.4
Verify	This work	13.4	18.7	27.1	35.5
	CKLR21	-	-	37.9	50.8
	Bulletproof	61.3	104.2	187.2	355.9

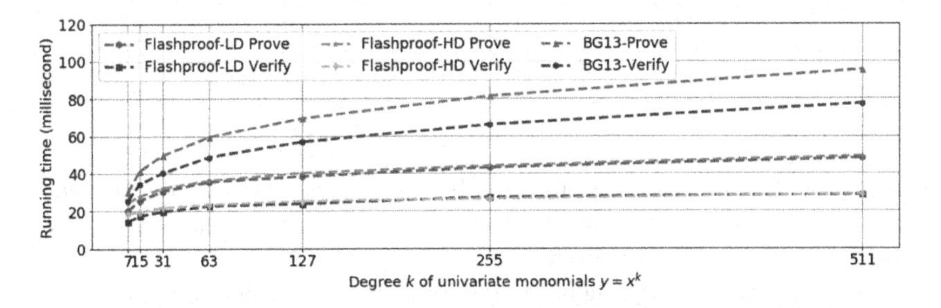

Fig. 3. Computational costs of polynomial evaluation arguments.

35% of the group exponentiations per argument are saved when 16 arguments of the 64-bit range are aggregated.

Figure 3 shows a running time comparison between our polynomial evaluation arguments and BG13 for monomials of different degrees[8]. The computational costs grow logarithmically with the increased degrees. The higher-degree and lower-degree arguments significantly outperform BG13 in proving and verification. Besides, the running time discrepancy between higher-degree and lower-degree arguments diminishes with the increased degrees. It is foreseeable that the higher-degree ones would be more competitive for the degrees over 2^9.

Gas Cost. We used the Solidity programming language [32] and the Truffle development framework [39] to measure the gas costs of verifying range proofs on Ethereum. We set 500,000 to the *optimize-runs*[9] parameter of the Solidity compiler with version 0.8.0. We ran the solidity-based code [1] to measure the gas costs of Bulletproof. We also measured the gas costs of verifying a zkSNARK (Groth16) [28] and a zkSNARK (BCTV14) [7] by running the solidity code from [30] and [23]. Note that the code of two zkSNARKs may not be used for verifying

[8] Note that the arguments may not be sound when $y = x^k$ is greater than the group order p. We use these monomials only for measuring the computational costs.

[9] The number of runs specifies how often each opcode will be executed across the contract's lifetime [38]. The larger the value, the more gas efficient code is generated.

Table 6. Gas costs of verification on Ethereum in ascending order. SONIC* indicates that the gas costs are estimated based on the data in SONIC [35]. We used the latest standard prices of gas and ether for reference at the time of writing, which were 15 GWei and $1745 USD, respectively, taken from [24] and [19] at UTC 11:15 am 12 September 2022. Note that the prices are subject to market fluctuations, but the gas costs tend to be stable and more meaningful.

Type	Transparent setup	Gas Cost	Ether	USD	Proof size (Byte)
zkSNARK (Groth16)	✗	220,100	0.0033	$5.8	192
This work (32-bit)	✓	236,584	0.00355	$6.2	738
This work (64-bit)	✓	317,474	0.00476	$8.3	994
zkSNARK (SONIC, Helped)*	✗	492,000	0.00738	$12.9	385
zkSNARK (SONIC, Unhelped)*	✗	655,000	0.00983	$17.2	1155
zkSNARK (BCTV14)	✗	773,124	0.0116	$20.2	288
Bulletproofs (32-bit)	✓	2,046,252	0.03069	$53.6	610
Bulletproofs (64-bit)	✓	3,703,549	0.05555	$96.9	674

range proofs. But we feel it is meaningful to provide the results for reference as the zkSNARKs benefit from trusted setups to achieve constant verification efficiency for any arithmetic circuits.

Table 6 shows a comprehensive comparison of verification gas costs on Ethereum in ascending order. Benefitting from a trusted setup, the zkSNARK (Groth16) ranks first. Our range arguments incur a comparable amount of gas costs to Groth16 and the least gas costs among those not requiring trusted setups. Notably, there is hardly any discrepancy in gas costs between Groth16 and our 32-bit range argument. We also roughly estimated the gas costs of SONIC, a typical zkSNARK with an updatable structured reference string setup. The helped and unhelped arguments consume approximately 492K and 655K, where helped means their proofs use an additional "helper" batch verification technique to improve the verification efficiency. The zkSNARK (BCTV14) consumes a constant 773K gas with the second smallest proof size. However communication efficient, Bulletproof is the most gas-consuming proof, which incurs 2046K and 3703K gas for 32-bit and 64-bit ranges. Moreover, from Table 2b, the aggregation of 16 of our range arguments saves an average of 8.2 (49.2K gas) and 10.6 (63.6K gas) group exponentiations per argument for 32-bit and 64-bit ranges, respectively, where one group exponentiation costs 6K gas [16] for BN-128 elliptic curve on Ethereum. Thus, it is estimated that the allocated gas costs per argument can be reduced to about 187,384 gas (0.00281 ETH, $4.9) and 253,874 gas (0.00381 ETH, $6.7).

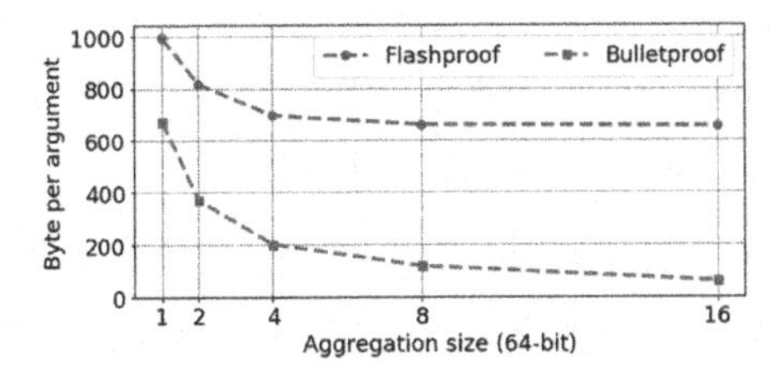

Fig. 4. Allocated communication costs of aggregate range arguments.

Communication Cost. We measured proof sizes as communication costs over a 256-bit field, the standard word size on Ethereum. We used the compressed form of elliptic curve points, where one point can be stored as a 256-bit value plus one extra bit indicating one of the two possible y coordinates. In Table 6, Bulletproof is the most communication-efficient among those not requiring trusted setups for general 32-bit and 64-bit ranges. Our range arguments pursue superior computational efficiency through minor trade-offs in communication efficiency but still offer a slight advantage over CKLR21 at a comparable level of soundness errors. Figure 4 shows a comparison of the communication costs of 64-bit aggregate range arguments[10] between Bulletproof and ours. Despite being less efficient than Bulletproof, our range arguments still achieve satisfactory performance, whose allocated communication cost per argument is asymptotically reduced to 656 bytes for the aggregation of 16 arguments. For instance, regarding 50 million UTXOs from 22 million transactions with 52-bit bitcoins, the aggregate Bulletproof and ours would take up about 17GB [13] and 42GB. The communication cost is still a factor of 3.8× reduction in size, compared to the 160GB data[11] of less succinct proofs in the current systems. Please see Table 3 for the communication cost comparison of polynomial evaluation arguments.

6 Protocols & Security Proofs

6.1 Range Argument

We describe the full protocol of our range arguments. Given a witness $y \in \mathbb{Z}_p$, a random $r_y \xleftarrow{\$} \mathbb{Z}_p^*$, a commitment $c_y = g^y h^{r_y} \in \mathbb{G}$ and the generators $g, h \xleftarrow{\$} \mathbb{G}, (g_l)_{l=0}^{L-1} \xleftarrow{\$} \mathbb{G}^L$, the protocol aims to prove $y \in [0, 2^N - 1]$:

Prover :

$$y = \sum_{i=0}^{N-1} 2^i b_i, \quad b_i \in \{0,1\}, \quad N + \gamma = L \cdot K, \ L, \ K \geq 2, \ \text{for some } \gamma \in \mathbb{Z}^{0+} \tag{8}$$

[10] We did not find the aggregate proofs of CKLR21 in the DL setting [20].
[11] The data refers to the 50 million UTXOs mentioned in Bulletproofs [13].

$$\sum_{i=0}^{N-1} 2^i b_i \rightarrow \begin{pmatrix} w_0 & \cdots & w_{K-1} \\ w_K & \cdots & w_{K+K-1} \\ \vdots & \ddots & \vdots \\ w_{(L-1)K} & \cdots & w_{(L-1)K+K-1} \end{pmatrix}, \tag{9}$$

where $w_{lK+k} = 2^{lK+k} b_{lK+k}$ for $l \in \{0, ..., L-1\}$, $k \in \{0, ..., K-1\}$

$$(r_l \xleftarrow{\$} \mathbb{Z}_p^*)_{l=0}^{L-1}, \quad (r_{s_k} \xleftarrow{\$} \mathbb{Z}_p^*)_{k=1}^{K}, \quad (r_{q_k} \xleftarrow{\$} \mathbb{Z}_p^*)_{k=0}^{K}, \quad (r_{t_{k,j}} \xleftarrow{\$} \mathbb{Z}_p^*)_{k=0,j=1}^{k=K-2,j=K-1} \tag{10}$$

Prover $\Longrightarrow$ Verifier :

$$(c_{s_k} = g^{\sum_{l=0}^{L-1} w_{lK+k}} h^{r_{s_k}})_{k=0}^{K-1}, \quad c_{s_K} = g^{\sum_{l=0}^{L-1} r_l} h^{r_{s_K}}, \text{ where } r_{s_0} = r_y - \sum_{k=1}^{K-1} r_{s_k} \tag{11}$$

$$(c_{t_{k,j}} = \prod_{l=0}^{L-1} g_l^{t_{l,k,j}} \cdot h^{r_{t_{k,j}}})_{k=0,j=1}^{k=K-2,j=K-1}, \text{ for } k \neq j \tag{12}$$

where $t_{l,k,j} = w_{lK+k}(2^{lK+j} - w_{lK+j}) + w_{lK+j}(2^{lK+k} - w_{lK+k})$

$$\left(c_{q_k} = \prod_{l=0}^{L-1} g_l^{q_{l,k}} \cdot h^{r_{q_k}}\right)_{k=0}^{K} \tag{13}$$

where $\left(q_{l,k} = 2r_l(2^{lK+k-1} - w_{lK+k})\right)_{k=0}^{K-1}$, $q_{l,K} = -r_l^2$

Prover $\Longleftarrow$ Verifier : $\quad (e_k \xleftarrow{\$} \mathbb{Z}_p^*)_{k=0}^{K-1}$

Prover $\Longrightarrow$ Verifier :

$$(v_l = \sum_{k=0}^{K-1} w_{lK+k} e_k + r_l)_{l=0}^{L-1} \tag{14}$$

$$u = \sum_{k=0,j=1}^{k=K-2,j=K-1} r_{t_{k,j}} e_{k,j} + \sum_{k=0}^{K-1} r_{q_{l,k}} e_k + r_{q_{l,K}}, \quad \epsilon = \sum_{k=0}^{K-1} r_{s_k} e_k + r_{s_K} \tag{15}$$

where $e_{k,j} = e_k e_j$, for $k \neq j$

Verifier :

$$\prod_{l=0}^{L-1} g_l^{f_l v_l} \cdot h^u \stackrel{?}{=} \prod_{k=0,j=1}^{k=K-2,j=K-1} c_{t_{k,j}}^{e_{k,j}} \cdot \prod_{k=0}^{K-1} c_{q_k}^{e_k} \cdot c_{q_K}, \text{ where } f_l = \sum_{k=0}^{K-1} 2^{lK+k} e_k - v_l \tag{16}$$

$$g^{\sum_{l=0}^{L-1} v_l} \cdot h^{\epsilon} \stackrel{?}{=} \prod_{k=0}^{K-1} c_{s_k}^{e_k} \cdot c_{s_K} \tag{17}$$

$$c_y \stackrel{?}{=} \prod_{k=0}^{K-1} c_{s_k} \tag{18}$$

Theorem 1. *Our range arguments have perfect completeness, computational witness-extended emulation and perfect special honest verifier zero-knowledge (SHVZK).*

Proof. Perfect completeness follows by a careful inspection of the protocol. Then we describe a perfect SHVZK simulation. Given a challenge vector $(e_k)_{k=0}^{K-1}$, a simulator randomly chooses group elements $(c_{t_{k,j}})_{k=0,j=1}^{k=K-2,j=K-1}$, $(c_{s_k})_{k=1}^{K-1}$, $(c_{q_k})_{k=1}^{K}$ and field elements $(v_l)_{l=0}^{L-1}$, u, ϵ. By the perfect hiding property, the commitments in a real argument are uniformly random as in the simulation. The field elements in a real argument are also uniformly random due to the random choices of $(r_l)_{l=0}^{L-1}$, r_{q_K} and r_{s_K}. Hence, in both real argument and simulation, the random elements uniquely determine the values c_{q_K} in Eqn. (16), c_{s_0} in Eqn. (18) and c_{s_K} in (17). This means we have identical distributions of real and simulated arguments with the given challenge vector.

Finally, we prove witness-extended emulation. An emulator $\mathcal{E}$ runs the argument with uniformly random challenges and rewinds the prover until it acquires $T = \frac{K^2+K+2}{2}$ accepting transcripts. We expect $\mathcal{E}$ to rewind $\frac{T}{\delta} \cdot \delta = T$ times, where δ is the probability of a prover making a convincing argument. Thus, $\mathcal{E}$ runs in expected polynomial time. Then we can obtain the openings of the commitments $(c_{t_{k,j}})_{k=0,j=1}^{k=K-2,j=K-1}$ and $(c_{q_k})_{k=0}^{K}$ by computing:

$$\begin{pmatrix} t_{l,0,1} & r_{t_{0,1}} \\ \vdots & \vdots \\ t_{l,K-2,K-1} & r_{t_{K-2,K-1}} \\ q_{l,0} & r_{q_0} \\ \vdots & \vdots \\ q_{l,K-1} & r_{q_{K-1}} \\ q_{l,K} & r_{q_K} \end{pmatrix} = \begin{pmatrix} e_{0,1}^{(1)} & \dots & e_{K-2,K-1}^{(1)} & e_0^{(1)} & \dots & e_{K-1}^{(1)} & 1 \\ \vdots & \ddots & \vdots & \vdots & \ddots & \vdots & \vdots \\ e_{0,1}^{(T)} & \dots & e_{K-2,K-1}^{(T)} & e_0^{(T)} & \dots & e_{K-1}^{(T)} & 1 \end{pmatrix}^{-1} \cdot \begin{pmatrix} f_l^{(1)} v_l^{(1)} & u^{(1)} \\ \vdots & \vdots \\ f_l^{(T)} v_l^{(T)} & u^{(T)} \end{pmatrix}$$

We can also extract the openings of the commitments $(c_{s_k})_{k=0}^{K}$ by computing:

$$\begin{pmatrix} \sum_{l=0}^{L-1} w_{lK} & r_{s_0} \\ \vdots & \vdots \\ \sum_{l=0}^{L-1} w_{lK+K-1} & r_{s_{K-1}} \\ \sum_{l=0}^{L-1} r_l & r_{s_K} \end{pmatrix} = \begin{pmatrix} e_0^{(1)} & \dots & e_{K-1}^{(1)} & 1 \\ \vdots & \ddots & \vdots & \vdots \\ e_0^{(K+1)} & \dots & e_{K-1}^{(K+1)} & 1 \end{pmatrix}^{-1} \cdot \begin{pmatrix} \sum_{l=0}^{L-1} v_l^{(1)} & \epsilon^{(1)} \\ \vdots & \vdots \\ \sum_{l=0}^{L-1} v_l^{(K+1)} & \epsilon^{(K+1)} \end{pmatrix}$$

Both two left multiplying matrices on the right-hand side consist of uniformly random challenges. They are invertible for being full-rank matrices, where all the rows and columns are linearly independent. Finally, the witness y can be obtained by summing up the openings of $(c_{s_k})_{k=0}^{K-1}$.

6.2 Polynomial Evaluation Arguments for Lower Degree

We describe the full protocol of our lower-degree polynomial evaluation arguments. Given two witnesses $x, y \in \mathbb{Z}_p$, two randoms $r_x, r_y \xleftarrow{\$} \mathbb{Z}_p^*$, two commitments $c_x = g^x h^{r_x}, c_y = g^y h^{r_y} \in \mathbb{G}$ and the generators $g, h \xleftarrow{\$} \mathbb{G}$, $(g_j)_{j=0}^{J-1} \xleftarrow{\$} \mathbb{G}^J$, the protocol aims to prove $y = P(x; D) = \sum_{d=0}^{D} a_d x^d$, $D = 2^{J+1} - 1$, $J \in \{1, 2, ...\}$:

Prover :

$$y = \sum_{d=0}^{D} a_d x^d = \sum_{d=0}^{D} a_d \prod_{j=0}^{J} x^{2^j b_d^{(j)}}, \ d = \sum_{j=0}^{J} 2^j b_d^{(j)}, \ b_d^{(j)} \in \{0,1\}, \ J+1 = \lceil \log D \rceil \quad (19)$$

$$(m_j \xleftarrow{\$} \mathbb{Z}_p^*)_{j=0}^{J}, \ (r_{w_j} \xleftarrow{\$} \mathbb{Z}_p^*)_{j=0}^{J}, \ r_m, \ r_{v_0}, \ r_{v_1}, \ \hat{e} \xleftarrow{\$} \mathbb{Z}_p^*, \ (\hat{z}_j = x^{2^j} \hat{e} + m_j)_{j=0}^{J} \quad (20)$$

$$Q(\hat{e}; J+1) = \sum_{d=0}^{D}(a_d \prod_{j=0}^{J} \hat{e}^{1-b_d^{(j)}} \cdot \hat{z}_j^{b_d^{(j)}}) = y\hat{e}^{J+1} + \sum_{j=0}^{J} w_j \hat{e}^j \tag{21}$$

Prover $\Longrightarrow$ Verifier :

$$c_m = g^{m_0} \cdot h^{r_m} \tag{22}$$

$$c_{v0} = \prod_{j=0}^{J-1} g_j^{m_j^2} \cdot h^{r_{v0}}, \quad c_{v1} = \prod_{j=0}^{J-1} g_j^{2m_j x^{2^j} - m_{j+1}} \cdot h^{r_{v1}} \tag{23}$$

$$(c_{w_j} = g^{w_j} \cdot h^{r_{w_j}})_{j=0}^{J} \tag{24}$$

Prover $\Longleftarrow$ Verifier : $e \xleftarrow{\$} \mathbb{Z}_p^*$

Prover $\Longrightarrow$ Verifier :

$$\left(z_j = x^{2^j} e + m_j\right)_{j=0}^{J} \tag{25}$$

$$t = r_x e + r_m, \quad u = r_{v1} e + r_{v0}, \quad s = r_y e^{J+1} + \sum_{j=0}^{J} r_{w_j} e^j \tag{26}$$

Verifier :

$$g^{z_0} \cdot h^t \stackrel{?}{=} c_x^e \cdot c_m \tag{27}$$

$$\prod_{j=0}^{J-1} g_j^{z_j^2 - z_{j+1} e} \cdot h^u \stackrel{?}{=} c_{v_1}^e \cdot c_{v0} \tag{28}$$

$$g^{Q(e;J+1)} \cdot h^s \stackrel{?}{=} c_y^{e^{J+1}} \cdot \prod_{j=0}^{J} c_{w_j}^{e^j} \tag{29}$$

Theorem 2. *Our polynomial evaluation arguments of lower-degree have perfect completeness, computational witness-extended emulation and perfect special honest verifier zero-knowledge (SHVZK).*

Proof. Perfect completeness follows by carefully inspecting the protocol. Next, we depict a perfect SHVZK simulation. Given a challenge e, a simulator randomly picks up group elements c_{v_1}, $(c_{w_j})_{j=1}^{J}$ and field elements $(z_j)_{j=0}^{J}$, t, u, s. By the perfect hiding property and the random choices of $(m_j)_{j=0}^{J}$, r_m, r_{v0}, r_{w0}, the group and field elements are identically distributed in both real and simulated arguments. Therefore, in both real argument and simulation, the random elements uniquely determine the values c_m, c_{v_0} and c_{w_0} in Eqn. (27), (28), (29).

Finally, we prove witness-extended emulation. An emulator $\mathcal{E}$ runs the argument in expected polynomial time and rewinds the prover until it acquires $J+2$ accepting transcripts. With the first two transcripts, $\mathcal{E}$ is able to extract the witness $x = \frac{z_0^{(1)} - z_0^{(0)}}{e_1 - e_0}$ and the random $r_x = \frac{t_1 - t_0}{e_1 - e_0}$. We can also get the openings of c_{v_1} and c_{v_0} by computing:

$$\begin{pmatrix} 2m_j x^{2^j} - m_{j+1} & r_{v_1} \\ m_j^2 & r_{v_0} \end{pmatrix} = \begin{pmatrix} e_0 & 1 \\ e_1 & 1 \end{pmatrix}^{-1} \cdot \begin{pmatrix} z_j^2 - z_{j+1} e_0 & u_0 \\ z_j^2 - z_{j+1} e_1 & u_1 \end{pmatrix}$$

Similarly, for Eqn. (29), we obtain the openings of c_y and $(c_{w_j})_{j=0}^{J-1}$ by computing:

$$\begin{pmatrix} y & r_y \\ w_J & r_{w_J} \\ \vdots & \vdots \\ w_1 & r_{w_1} \\ w_0 & r_{w_0} \end{pmatrix} = \begin{pmatrix} e_0^{J+1} & e_0^J & \dots & e_0 & 1 \\ \vdots & \vdots & \ddots & \vdots & \vdots \\ e_{J+1}^{J+1} & e_{J+1}^J & \dots & e_{J+1} & 1 \end{pmatrix}^{-1} \cdot \begin{pmatrix} Q(e;J+1)_0 & s_0 \\ \vdots & \vdots \\ Q(e;J+1)_{J+1} & s_{J+1} \end{pmatrix}$$

where the left multiplying matrix is invertible for being a Vandermonde matrix. Thanks to the binding property of Pedersen commitment, we can conclude that $P(x;D)$, as the coefficient of the leading term of $Q(e;J+1)$, is the opening of c_y.

6.3 Polynomial Evaluation Arguments for Higher Degree

We describe the full protocol of our higher-degree polynomial evaluation arguments, where the witnesses are the same as those of lower-degree ones except using different generators $g, h \xleftarrow{\$} \mathbb{G}, (g_j)_{j=0}^{J-1} \xleftarrow{\$} \mathbb{G}^J, (g_l)_{l=0}^{L-1} \xleftarrow{\$} \mathbb{G}^L$:

Prover :

$$(m_j \xleftarrow{\$} \mathbb{Z}_p^*)_{j=0}^J,\ (r_{w_k} \xleftarrow{\$} \mathbb{Z}_p^*)_{k=0}^{K-1},\ (\theta_l, r_{\theta_l} \xleftarrow{\$} \mathbb{Z}_p^*)_{l=0}^{L-1},\ r_m,\ r_{v_0},\ r_{v_1},\ \hat{e} \xleftarrow{\$} \mathbb{Z}_p^* \tag{30}$$

$$\sum_{j=0}^{J} w_j \hat{e}^j = \sum_{l=0}^{L-1} \hat{e}^{lK} \sum_{k=0}^{K-1} w_{lK+k} \hat{e}^k, \quad J+1 = \lceil \log D \rceil = L \cdot K,\ L, K \geq 2 \tag{31}$$

$$\sum_{l=0}^{L-1} \theta_l + \sum_{l=0}^{L-1} \sum_{k=0}^{K-1} w_{lK+k} \hat{e}^k = \begin{pmatrix} w_0 + \theta_0 & w_1 & \dots & w_{K-1} \\ w_K + \theta_1 & w_{K+1} & \dots & w_{2K-1} \\ \vdots & \vdots & \ddots & \vdots \\ w_{(L-1)K} + \theta_{L-1} & w_{(L-1)K+1} & \dots & w_{LK-1} \end{pmatrix} \cdot \begin{pmatrix} 1 \\ \hat{e} \\ \vdots \\ \hat{e}^{K-1} \end{pmatrix} \tag{32}$$

Prover $\Longrightarrow$ Verifier :

$$c_m = g^{m_0} \cdot h^{r_m} \tag{33}$$

$$c_{v_0} = \prod_{j=0}^{J-1} g_j^{m_j^2} \cdot h^{r_{v_0}}, \quad c_{v_1} = \prod_{j=0}^{J-1} g_j^{2m_j x^{2^j} - m_{j+1}} \cdot h^{r_{v_1}} \tag{34}$$

$$c_{w_0} = \prod_{l=0}^{L-1} g_l^{w_{lK} + \theta_l} \cdot h^{r_{w_0}}, \quad (c_{w_k} = \prod_{l=0}^{L-1} g_l^{w_{lK+k}} \cdot h^{r_{w_k}})_{k=1}^{K-1} \tag{35}$$

$$(c_{\theta_l} = g^{-\theta_l} \cdot h^{r_{\theta_l}})_{l=0}^{L-1} \tag{36}$$

Prover $\Longleftarrow$ Verifier : $e \xleftarrow{\$} \mathbb{Z}_p^*$

Prover $\Longrightarrow$ Verifier :

$$(z_j = x^{2^j} e + m_j)_{j=0}^J, \quad (f_l = \sum_{k=0}^{K-1} w_{lK+k} e^k + \theta_l)_{l=0}^{L-1} \tag{37}$$

$$t = r_x e + r_m, \quad u = r_{v_1} e + r_{v_0}, \quad s = \sum_{k=0}^{K-1} r_{w_k} e^k, \quad q = r_y e^{J+1} + \sum_{l=0}^{L-1} r_{\theta_l} e^{lK} \tag{38}$$

Verifier :

$$g^{z_0} \cdot h^t \stackrel{?}{=} c_x^e \cdot c_m \tag{39}$$

$$\prod_{j=0}^{J-1} g_j^{z_j^2 - z_{j+1}e} \cdot h^u \stackrel{?}{=} c_{v_1}^e \cdot c_{v_0} \tag{40}$$

$$\prod_{l=0}^{L-1} g_l^{f_l} \cdot h^s \stackrel{?}{=} \prod_{k=0}^{K-1} c_{w_k}^{e^k} \tag{41}$$

$$g^{\zeta} \cdot h^q \stackrel{?}{=} c_y^{e^{J+1}} \cdot \prod_{l=0}^{L-1} c_{\theta_l}^{e^{lK}}, \quad \text{where } \zeta = Q(e; J+1) - \sum_{l=0}^{L-1} f_l e^{lK} \tag{42}$$

Theorem 3. *Our polynomial evaluation arguments of higher-degree have perfect completeness, computational witness-extended emulation and perfect special honest verifier zero-knowledge (SHVZK).*

Proof. Perfect completeness follows by a careful inspection of the protocol. Then, we provide a perfect SHVZK simulation. Given a challenge e, a simulator randomly picks up group elements c_{v_1}, $(c_{w_k})_{k=1}^{K-1}$, $(c_{\theta_l})_{l=1}^{L-1}$ and field elements $(z_j)_{j=0}^{J}$, $(f_l)_{l=0}^{L-1}$, t, u, s, q. By the perfect hiding property and the random choices of $(m_j)_{j=0}^{J}$, r_m, r_{v_0}, r_{w_0}, $(\theta_l)_{l=0}^{L-1}$, the group and field elements are identically distributed in both real and simulated arguments. Therefore, in both real argument and simulation, the random elements uniquely determine the values c_m, c_{v_0}, c_{w_0} and c_{θ_0} in Eqn. (39), (40), (41) and (42).

Finally, we prove witness-extended emulation. We essentially describe the soundness of Eqn. (41) and (42) in this section. Please refer to Theorem 2 for the soundness of Eqn. (39) and (40). An emulator $\mathcal{E}$ runs the argument and rewinds the prover until it acquires K accepting transcripts. We have the openings of $(c_{w_k})_{k=0}^{K-1}$ by computing:

$$\begin{pmatrix} w_{lK+K-1} & r_{w_{K-1}} \\ \vdots & \vdots \\ w_{lK+1} & r_{w_1} \\ w_{lK} + \theta_l & r_{w_0} \end{pmatrix} = \begin{pmatrix} e_0^{K-1} & \dots & e_0 & 1 \\ \vdots & \ddots & \vdots & \vdots \\ e_{K-1}^{K-1} & \dots & e_{K-1} & 1 \end{pmatrix}^{-1} \cdot \begin{pmatrix} f_l^{(0)} & s_0 \\ \vdots & \vdots \\ f_l^{(K-1)} & s_{K-1} \end{pmatrix}$$

$\mathcal{E}$ rewinds the prover to acquire $L+1$ accepting transcripts for the openings of c_y and $(c_{\theta_l})_{l=0}^{L-1}$:

$$\begin{pmatrix} y & r_y \\ -\theta_{L-1} & r_{\theta_{L-1}} \\ \vdots & \vdots \\ -\theta_0 & r_{\theta_0} \end{pmatrix} = \begin{pmatrix} e_0^{J+1} & e_0^{(L-1)K} & \dots & 1 \\ \vdots & \vdots & \ddots & \vdots \\ e_L^{J+1} & e_L^{(L-1)K} & \dots & 1 \end{pmatrix}^{-1} \cdot \begin{pmatrix} \zeta_0 & q_0 \\ \vdots & \vdots \\ \zeta_L & q_L \end{pmatrix}$$

7 Related Work

Range Proofs. In 2003, Lipmaa [33] used Lagrange's four-square theorem [43] to create a constant 1700-byte range proof with an arbitrary range. Groth [27] improved the proof by using Legendre's three-square theorem. Deng et al. [21] also designed a constant-size range proof based on the RSA assumption by adapting Bulletproof for Lagrange's four-square theorem. However, these proofs rely on the RSA assumption, which requires a trusted setup to generate the RSA modulus. In 2008, Camenisch et al. [15] proposed a range proof based on the signature approach that depends on the q-Strong Diffie-Hellman assumption. Their method has $O(N)$ communication cost and requires a trusted setup to make the proof non-interactive, where N is the bit length of the range. AZTEC protocol [45] also provided a signature-based range proof, which uses a trusted-setup protocol to build a huge signature database that contains every acceptable integer in the range. However, the security relies on trusting the parties that would destroy the private keys for generating the signatures. Bootle & Groth [11] presented a range argument under the DL assumption based on the bit-decomposition. Nonetheless, their approach achieves $O(N)$ complexity in communication and computation with a trusted setup. Besides, one could use the asymptotically efficient STARKS [5] to avoid a trusted setup. Nevertheless, the proof size is quite large at 45KB [31]. Supersonic [14] achieves efficient logarithmic efficiency in verification and communication based on class groups with a transparent setup. Nevertheless, class groups demand large groups to meet current security requirements, which are less commonly applied in practical systems.

Polynomial Evaluation Proofs. Table 1 lists a series of state-of-the-art generic-purpose zero-knowledge proofs with transparent setups. Most of them build on general NP-complete languages, which can be used for polynomial evaluation. Based on the hardness of the RSA assumption, Supersonic [14] is one of the most efficient proofs, which has $O(\log N)$ efficiency in verification time and proof size. However, for a polynomial of degree $D = 2^{20}$, it still needs 10.1KB and 60 group exponentiations for verification, whereas our argument only needs 1.25KB and 40 group exponentiations. Bootle and Groth [11] also proposed a polynomial evaluation argument based on BG13. However, it relies on common reference strings as a trusted setup to achieve efficient $O(\frac{\log N}{\log \log N})$ complexity for proving and verification.

Membership Proofs. In this section, we provide a brief related work on membership proofs. Most membership proofs require trusted setups, exposing vulnerabilities that malicious provers can exploit. Proposed by Camenisch et al. [15] in 2008, the most classical membership argument is based on a bilinear-group signature scheme. Based on the q-Strong Diffie-Hellman assumption, the argument has $O(1)$ communication cost but requires $O(N)$ group elements as signatures of all elements in the given set for a preliminary procedure. Therefore, the argument needs a trusted setup to accomplish this procedure for non-interactivity. Furthermore, the authors also proposed an alternative approach using an RSA-based accumulator for short signatures. However, this approach does not remove the trusted setup, either. Recently, Benarroch et al. [8] presented an accumulator-based membership proof based on class groups without a trusted setup. For 128-bit security, the proof uses a 6000-bit discriminant class group to achieve a constant 6.4KB proof size. However, our membership argument requires a tremendous set of $2^{169} \approx 7.5E50$ elements for this proof size, which tends to be more communication-efficient for general scenarios (Table 7).

Table 7. An efficiency comparison [37] of generic-purpose zero-knowledge proofs with transparent setups for NP statements, where N is the statement size.

Type	Ligero [2]	Bulletproofs [13]	STARKs [5]	Aurora [6]	Fractal [17]	Supersonic [14]	Spartan [37]
Prover Running time	$O(N \log N)$	$O(N)$	$O(N \log^2 N)$	$O(N \log N)$	$O(N \log N)$	$O(N \log N)$	$O(N \log N)$
Verifier Running time	$O(N)$	$O(N)$	$O(N \log^2 N)$	$O(N)$	$O(\log^2 N)$	$O(\log N)$	$O(\log^2 N)$
Proof Size	$O(\sqrt{N})$	$O(\log N)$	$O(\log^2 N)$	$O(\log^2 N)$	$O(\log^2 N)$	$O(\log N)$	$O(\log^2 N)$

8 Conclusion

In this paper, we proposed Flashproofs, a new type of efficient special honest verifier zero-knowledge arguments of knowledge with a transparent setup in the DL setting. First, we put forth new gas-efficient range arguments that achieve $O(N^{\frac{2}{3}})$ communication cost, and involve $O(N^{\frac{2}{3}})$ group exponentiations for verification and a slightly sub-linear number of group exponentiations for proving with respect to the range $[0, 2^N - 1]$. Our range arguments achieve a comparable amount of gas costs to the most efficient zkSNARK on blockchain platforms without resorting to a trusted setup. Second, we presented polynomial evaluation arguments based on the techniques of Bayer & Groth. We provided two zero-knowledge protocols that excel in handling lower-degree ($D \in [3, 2^9]$) and higher-degree ($D > 2^9$) polynomials, respectively. Our arguments make a significant improvement in the efficiency of computation and communication. To the best of our knowledge, our arguments instantiate the most communication-efficient zero-knowledge arguments of membership and non-membership in the DL setting among those not requiring trusted setups. In future work, we will incorporate Flashproofs in more real-world blockchain-based applications, e.g., energy sharing and sharing economy [34,42].

References

1. Alex, V., Sergey, V.: Solidity implementation of bulletproof (2018). https://github.com/BANKEX/BulletproofJS
2. Ames, S., Hazay, C., Ishai, Y., Venkitasubramaniam, M.: Ligero: lightweight sublinear arguments without a trusted setup. In: Proceedings of the 2017 ACM SIGSAC Conference on Computer and Communications Security, CCS 2017 (2017)
3. Bayer, S., Groth, J.: Zero-knowledge argument for polynomial evaluation with application to blacklists. In: Johansson, T., Nguyen, P.Q. (eds.) EUROCRYPT 2013. LNCS, vol. 7881, pp. 646–663. Springer, Heidelberg (2013). https://doi.org/10.1007/978-3-642-38348-9_38
4. Bellare, M., Garay, J.A., Rabin, T.: Fast batch verification for modular exponentiation and digital signatures. In: Nyberg, K. (ed.) EUROCRYPT 1998. LNCS, vol. 1403, pp. 236–250. Springer, Heidelberg (1998). https://doi.org/10.1007/BFb0054130
5. Ben-Sasson, E., Bentov, I., Horesh, Y., Riabzev, M.: Scalable, transparent, and post-quantum secure computational integrity. IACR Cryptol. ePrint Arch. (2018)

6. Ben-Sasson, E., Chiesa, A., Riabzev, M., Spooner, N., Virza, M., Ward, N.P.: Aurora: transparent succinct arguments for R1CS. In: Ishai, Y., Rijmen, V. (eds.) EUROCRYPT 2019. LNCS, vol. 11476, pp. 103–128. Springer, Cham (2019). https://doi.org/10.1007/978-3-030-17653-2_4
7. Ben-Sasson, E., Chiesa, A., Tromer, E., Virza, M.: Succinct non-interactive zero knowledge for a von Neumann architecture. In: 23rd USENIX Security Symposium (USENIX Security 2014) (2014)
8. Benarroch, D., Campanelli, M., Fiore, D., Gurkan, K., Kolonelos, D.: Zero-knowledge proofs for set membership: efficient, succinct, modular. In: Financial Cryptography and Data Security (2021)
9. Benedikt, B.: Java implementation of bulletproof (2017). https://github.com/bbuenz/BulletProofLib
10. Bootle, J., Cerulli, A., Chaidos, P., Groth, J., Petit, C.: Efficient zero-knowledge arguments for arithmetic circuits in the discrete log setting. In: Fischlin, M., Coron, J.-S. (eds.) EUROCRYPT 2016. LNCS, vol. 9666, pp. 327–357. Springer, Heidelberg (2016). https://doi.org/10.1007/978-3-662-49896-5_12
11. Bootle, J., Groth, J.: Efficient batch zero-knowledge arguments for low degree polynomials. In: Public-Key Cryptography - PKC 2018 (2018)
12. BouncyCastle: Bouncycastle. https://www.bouncycastle.org/
13. Bunz, B., Bootle, J., Boneh, D., Poelstra, A., Wuille, P., Maxwell, G.: Bulletproofs: Short proofs for confidential transactions and more, pp. 315–334, May 2018
14. Bünz, B., Fisch, B., Szepieniec, A.: Transparent SNARKs from DARK compilers. In: Canteaut, A., Ishai, Y. (eds.) EUROCRYPT 2020. LNCS, vol. 12105, pp. 677–706. Springer, Cham (2020). https://doi.org/10.1007/978-3-030-45721-1_24
15. Camenisch, J., Chaabouni, R., shelat: Efficient protocols for set membership and range proofs. In: Pieprzyk, J. (ed.) ASIACRYPT 2008. LNCS, vol. 5350, pp. 234–252. Springer, Heidelberg (2008). https://doi.org/10.1007/978-3-540-89255-7_15
16. Cardozo, A.S., Williamson, Z.: https://eips.ethereum.org/EIPS/eip-1108
17. Chiesa, A., Ojha, D., Spooner, N.: FRACTAL: post-quantum and transparent recursive proofs from holography. In: Canteaut, A., Ishai, Y. (eds.) EUROCRYPT 2020. LNCS, vol. 12105, pp. 769–793. Springer, Cham (2020). https://doi.org/10.1007/978-3-030-45721-1_27
18. Christian, R.: EIP-196: Precompiled contracts for addition and scalar multiplication on the elliptic curve alt_bn128 (2017). https://eips.ethereum.org/EIPS/eip-196
19. coindesk (2022). https://www.coindesk.com/price/ethereum
20. Couteau, G., Klooß, M., Lin, H., Reichle, M.: Efficient range proofs with transparent setup from bounded integer commitments. In: Canteaut, A., Standaert, F.-X. (eds.) EUROCRYPT 2021. LNCS, vol. 12698, pp. 247–277. Springer, Cham (2021). https://doi.org/10.1007/978-3-030-77883-5_9
21. Deng, C., Tang, X., You, L., Hu, G.: Cuproof: a novel range proof with constant size. IACR Cryptol. ePrint Arch. (2021)
22. Dobson, S., Galbraith, S., Smith, B.: Trustless unknown-order groups. Math. Cryptol. **1**(2), 25–39 (2022). https://journals.flvc.org/mathcryptology/article/view/130579
23. Etherscan. https://ropsten.etherscan.io/address/0xa1f11d83a5222692c0eff9eca32254a7452c4f29#code#L1
24. Etherscan: https://etherscan.io/gasTracker (2022)
25. Fiat, A., Shamir, A.: How to prove yourself: practical solutions to identification and signature problems. In: Odlyzko, A.M. (ed.) CRYPTO 1986. LNCS, vol. 263, pp. 186–194. Springer, Heidelberg (1987). https://doi.org/10.1007/3-540-47721-7_12

26. Gregory, M.: Confidential transactions (2016). https://elementsproject.org/features/confidential-transactions/investigation
27. Groth, J.: Non-interactive zero-knowledge arguments for voting. In: Ioannidis, J., Keromytis, A., Yung, M. (eds.) ACNS 2005. LNCS, vol. 3531, pp. 467–482. Springer, Heidelberg (2005). https://doi.org/10.1007/11496137_32
28. Groth, J.: On the size of pairing-based non-interactive arguments. In: Fischlin, M., Coron, J.-S. (eds.) EUROCRYPT 2016. LNCS, vol. 9666, pp. 305–326. Springer, Heidelberg (2016). https://doi.org/10.1007/978-3-662-49896-5_11
29. Groth, J., Kohlweiss, M.: One-out-of-many proofs: or how to leak a secret and spend a coin. In: Oswald, E., Fischlin, M. (eds.) EUROCRYPT 2015. LNCS, vol. 9057, pp. 253–280. Springer, Heidelberg (2015). https://doi.org/10.1007/978-3-662-46803-6_9
30. HarryR: https://github.com/HarryR/ethsnarks
31. matter labs: Awesome zero knowledge proofs. https://github.com/matter-labs/awesome-zero-knowledge-proofs
32. Language, S.P.: https://docs.soliditylang.org
33. Lipmaa, H.: On Diophantine complexity and statistical zero-knowledge arguments. In: Laih, C.-S. (ed.) ASIACRYPT 2003. LNCS, vol. 2894, pp. 398–415. Springer, Heidelberg (2003). https://doi.org/10.1007/978-3-540-40061-5_26
34. Lyu, L., Chau, S.C.K., Wang, N., Zheng, Y.: Cloud-based privacy-preserving collaborative consumption for sharing economy. IEEE Trans. Cloud Comput. **10**(3), 1647–1660 (2022)
35. Maller, M., Bowe, S., Kohlweiss, M., Meiklejohn, S.: Sonic: Zero-knowledge snarks from linear-size universal and updatable structured reference strings. In: Proceedings of the 2019 ACM SIGSAC Conference on Computer and Communications Security, pp. 2111–2128 (2019)
36. Michaud-Rodgers, P.: Sum of three squares (2019). https://warwick.ac.uk/fac/sci/maths/people/staff/michaud/threesquarestalk.pdf
37. Setty, S.: Spartan: efficient and general-purpose zkSNARKs without trusted setup. In: Micciancio, D., Ristenpart, T. (eds.) CRYPTO 2020. LNCS, vol. 12172, pp. 704–737. Springer, Cham (2020). https://doi.org/10.1007/978-3-030-56877-1_25
38. Solidity: Solidity optimizer (2022). https://docs.soliditylang.org/en/v0.8.14/internals/optimizer.html#optimizer-parameter-runs
39. Suite, T.: https://www.trufflesuite.com
40. TornadoCash: Tornadocash (2021). https://tornado.cash/
41. Wahby, R., Tzialla, I., Shelat, A., Thaler, J., Walfish, M.: Doubly-efficient zksnarks without trusted setup, pp. 926–943, May 2018
42. Wang, N., Chau, S.C.K., Zhou, Y.: Privacy-preserving energy storage sharing with blockchain and secure multi-party computation. ACM SIGENERGY Energy Inform. Rev. **1**(1), 32–50 (2022). https://doi.org/10.1145/3508467.3508471
43. Weisstein, E.W.: Lagrange's four-square theorem (2021). https://mathworld.wolfram.com/LagrangesFour-SquareTheorem.html
44. Weisstein, E.W.: Maclaurin series (2021). https://mathworld.wolfram.com/MaclaurinSeries.html
45. Williamson, Z.J.: The Aztec protocol (2018). https://github.com/AztecProtocol/AZTEC/blob/master/AZTEC.pdf
46. Zhang, J., Xie, T., Zhang, Y., Song, D.X.: Transparent polynomial delegation and its applications to zero knowledge proof. In: 2020 IEEE Symposium on Security and Privacy (SP), pp. 859–876 (2020)

Counting Vampires: From Univariate Sumcheck to Updatable ZK-SNARK

Helger Lipmaa[1], Janno Siim[1(✉)], and Michał Zając[2(✉)]

[1] Simula UiB, Bergen, Norway
helger.lipmaa@gmail.com , jannosiim@gmail.com
[2] Nethermind, London, UK
m.p.zajac@gmail.com

Abstract. We propose a univariate sumcheck argument $\mathfrak{Count}$ of essentially optimal communication efficiency of one group element. While the previously most efficient univariate sumcheck argument of Aurora is based on polynomial commitments, $\mathfrak{Count}$ is based on inner-product commitments. We use $\mathfrak{Count}$ to construct a new pairing-based updatable and universal zk-SNARK $\mathfrak{Vampire}$ with the shortest known argument length (four group and two finite field elements) for NP. In addition, $\mathfrak{Vampire}$ uses the aggregated polynomial commitment scheme of Boneh et al.

Keywords: Aggregatable polynomial commitment · Inner-product commitment · Sumcheck · Updatable and universal zk-SNARK

1 Introduction

Zero-knowledge succinct non-interactive arguments of knowledge (zk-SNARKs, [14,15,21,25]) are zero-knowledge argument systems for NP with succinct argument length and efficient verification. In many applications, one can describe the desired NP language instance as an instance $\mathcal{R}$ of the rank-1 constraint system (R1CS) [14], and the task of the verifier is to check that $\mathcal{R}$ is satisfied on the partially-public input. Zk-SNARKs are immensely popular due to applications in, say, verifiable computation and blockchain.

Non-interactive zero-knowledge arguments, and thus also zk-SNARKs, are impossible in the plain model. To overcome this, one gives all parties access to a trusted common reference string (CRS). The most efficient zk-SNARKs have a relation-specific structured CRS (SRS). That is, they assume that there exists a trusted third party who, given the description of $\mathcal{R}$ as an input, generates an SRS $\mathsf{srs}_{\mathcal{R}}$. The most efficient zk-SNARK by Groth [16] for R1CS with a relation-specific SRS has an argument that consists of only three group elements.

A significant practical downside of such "non-universal" SNARKs is that one has to construct a new SRS for every instance of the constraint system. This observation has spurred an enormous effort to design universal zk-SNARKs, i.e., zk-SNARKs with an SRS that only depends on an upper bound on $\mathcal{R}$'s size.

S. Agrawal and D. Lin (Eds.): ASIACRYPT 2022, LNCS 13792, pp. 249–278, 2022.
https://doi.org/10.1007/978-3-031-22966-4_9

In addition, it is crucial to decrease the amount of trust in the SRS creator. A popular approach is to design *updatable and universal zk-SNARKs* [17,24], where the universal SRS is updated sequentially by several parties such that the soundness holds if at least one of the updaters is honest. For brevity, by "updatable" we will sometimes mean "updatable and universal".

Plonk [13] and Marlin [10] are the first efficient universal zk-SNARKs. Marlin and many subsequent updatable and universal zk-SNARKs [9,26] work for sparse R1CS instances, where the underlying matrices contain a linear (instead of quadratic) number of non-zero elements. Chiesa et al. [10] define an information-theoretic model, algebraic holographic proof (AHP). An AHP is an interactive protocol, where at each step, the prover sends polynomial oracles, and the verifier sends to the prover random field elements. Polynomial oracles are usually implemented using polynomial commitments [19]. In the end, the verifier queries the polynomial oracles and performs low-degree tests. Then, [10] proposes a new AHP for sparse R1CS, and then compiles it to a zk-SNARK named Marlin.

Marlin relies crucially on a univariate sumcheck. A sumcheck argument aims to prove that the given polynomial sums to the given value over the given domain. The first sumcheck arguments [23] were for multivariate polynomials but small domains. Ben-Sasson et al. [5] proposed a univariate sumcheck argument for large domains and used it to construct a new zk-SNARK Aurora. Suppose the domain is a multiplicative subgroup of the given finite field. In that case, Aurora's sumcheck argument requires the prover to forward two different polynomial oracles and use a low-degree test on one of the polynomials.

Lunar [9] improves on Marlin. It defines PHPs (Polynomial Holographic IOPs), a generalization of AHPs. Lunar notes that instead of opening all the polynomial commitments, the verifier can often perform verification equations on commitments themselves, thus obtaining better efficiency. It also defines a simpler version of R1CS called R1CSLite, with one of the three characterizing matrices of $\mathcal{R}$ being the identity matrix. Moreover, it provides a more fine-grained analysis of the zero-knowledge property and several additional optimizations.

Basilisk [26] gains additional efficiency by using a different technique to obtain zero-knowledge and constructing a "free" low-degree test. In addition, [26] constructs even more efficient zk-SNARKs for somewhat more limited constraint systems. Both Lunar and Basilisk introduce new theoretical frameworks; e.g., Basilisk introduces checkable subspace sampling (CSS) arguments as a separate primitive. For simplicity (of reading), we opted not to use such frameworks in the context of the current paper.

In parallel to our work, Zhang et al. [28] proposed Vector Oracle Proofs (VOProofs), a new information-theoretic model based on vector operations. They use it to construct efficient zk-SNARKs for several well-known constraint systems such as R1CS (VOR1CS) and Plonk's constraint system (VOPlonk).

In Table 1, we overview the argument lengths of the most efficient updatable and universal zk-SNARKs. Here, $|X|$ denotes the representation length of an element from X in bits, given the BLS12-381 curve, with $|\mathbb{G}_1| = 384$, $|\mathbb{G}_2| = 768$, and $|\mathbb{F}| = 256$. Thus, even the most efficient updatable and universal zk-SNARK has an approximately two times longer argument than Groth16 [16].

Table 1. Comparison of some known updatable and universal zk-SNARKs.

Scheme	Argument length		Arithmetization
	Elements	Bits	
Updatable and universal zk-SNARKs			
Sonic [24]	$20\|\mathbb{G}_1\| + 16\|\mathbb{F}\|$	11776	[8] constraints
Marlin [10]	$13\|\mathbb{G}_1\| + 8\|\mathbb{F}\|$	7040	R1CS, sparse matrices
Basilisk [26]	$10\|\mathbb{G}_1\| + 3\|\mathbb{F}\|$	4608	R1CSLite, sparse matrices
Plonk [13]	$7\|\mathbb{G}_1\| + 7\|\mathbb{F}\|$	4480	Plonk constraints
LunarLite [9]	$10\|\mathbb{G}_1\| + 2\|\mathbb{F}\|$	4352	R1CSLite, sparse matrices
Basilisk [26]	$8\|\mathbb{G}_1\| + 4\|\mathbb{F}\|$	4096	Plonk constraints
VOR1CS* [28]	$9\|\mathbb{G}_1\| + 2\|\mathbb{F}\|$	3968	R1CS, sparse matrices
VOPlonk* [28]	$7\|\mathbb{G}_1\| + 2\|\mathbb{F}\|$	3200	Plonk constraints
Basilisk (full version, [27])	$6\|\mathbb{G}_1\| + 2\|\mathbb{F}\|$	2816	Weighted R1CS with bounded fan-out
$\mathfrak{Vampire}$ (this work)	$4\|\mathbb{G}_1\| + 2\|\mathbb{F}\|$	2048	R1CSLite, sparse matrices
Non-universal zk-SNARKs (relation-specific SRS)			
Groth16 [16]	$2\|\mathbb{G}_1\| + 1\|\mathbb{G}_2\|$	1536	R1CS

Moreover, Groth16 works for QAP [14] (i.e., full R1CS), while the most efficient variant of Basilisk works for instances of R1CS where the relation-defining matrices are limited to have a small constant number of elements per row (this corresponds to arithmetic circuits of bounded fan-out). Thus, there is still a non-trivial difference between the communication efficiency of relation-specific zk-SNARKs and updatable and universal zk-SNARKs.

Our Contributions. The current paper has three related contributions:

1. The combined use of polynomial commitments and inner-product commitments in the sumcheck and updatable and universal zk-SNARK design. The use of polynomial commitment schemes in zk-SNARKs has dramatically increased their popularity, and we hope the same will happen with inner-product commitments. In particular, ILV inner-product commitments [18] use a SRS made of non-consequent monomial powers.[1]
2. A new updatable (and universal) univariate sumcheck argument $\mathfrak{Count}$ that uses inner-product commitments to achieve optimal computation complexity of a single group element. Since sumchecks are used in many different zk-SNARKs (and elsewhere), we believe $\mathfrak{Count}$ will have wider interest.
3. A new updatable and universal zk-SNARK $\mathfrak{Vampire}$ for sparse R1CSLite with the smallest argument length among all known updatable and universal zk-SNARKs for NP-complete languages. (See Table 1.) $\mathfrak{Vampire}$ uses $\mathfrak{Count}$ and thus inner-product commitments.

[1] Inner-product commitments and arguments are commonly used in the zk-SNARK design. However, the way we use them is markedly different from the prior work.

1.1 Our Techniques

Non-Consequent Monomial SRSs. Groth et al. [17] proved that the SRS of an updatable zk-SNARK cannot contain non-monomial polynomials. Moreover, the SRS's correctness must be verifiable. For example, if the SRS contains[2] $[1, \sigma, \sigma^3, \sigma^4]_1 \in \mathbb{G}_1^4$ for a trapdoor σ, it must also contain $[\sigma, \sigma^2]_2 \in \mathbb{G}_2^2$, so that one can verify the consistency of the SRS elements by using pairing operations. We observe that $[\sigma^2]_1$ does not have to belong to the SRS, and thus, an updatable SRS may contain gaps. Similarly, the SRS can contain multivariate monomials. However, most of the known updatable and universal zk-SNARKs ([17,24] being exceptions) use SRSs that consist of consequent univariate monomials only, i.e., are of the shape $([(\sigma^i)_{i=0}^{m_1}]_1, [(\sigma^i)_{i=0}^{m}]_2)$ for some m_i.

One reason why efficient updatable and universal zk-SNARKs use a consequent monomial SRS is their reliance on polynomial commitment schemes like KZG [19] that have such SRSs. While many other polynomial commitment schemes are known, up to our knowledge, no efficient one uses non-consequent monomial SRSs.[3] In particular, AHP [10] and PHP [9] model polynomial commitments as polynomial oracles and allow the parties to perform operations (e.g., queries to committed oracles and low-degree tests) related to such oracles. Low-degree tests model consequent monomial SRSs: a committed polynomial is a degree-$\leq m$ polynomial iff it is in the span of X^i for $i \leq m$.

One can use non-consequent monomial SRSs to efficiently construct protocols like broadcast encryption and inner-product commitments [18,20]. We use non-consequent monomial SRSs in the context of sumchecks and updatable and universal zk-SNARKs. We will not define an information-theoretic model, but we mention two possible approaches that both have their limitations. First, the pairing-based setting can be modeled as linear interactive proofs (LIPs, [6]) or non-interactive LIPs [16]. However, either model has to be tweaked to our setting: namely, we allow the generation of updatable SRS for multi-round protocols, with the restrictions natural in such a setting (e.g., one can efficiently "span test" that a committed element is in the span of the SRS). Such a model is tailor-fit to pairings and might not be suitable in other algebraic settings. Second, one can generalize PHPs by adding an abstract model of inner-product commitment schemes and allowing for span tests. Such a model is independent of the algebraic setting but restricts one to a limited number of cryptographic tools (polynomial and inner-product commitment schemes), with a need to redefine the model when more tools are found to be helpful.

We have chosen to remain agnostic on this issue by defining new arguments without an intermediate information-theoretic model.

---

[2] We rely on the pairing-based setting and use the by now standard additive bracket notation, see Sect. 2 for more details.

[3] A *monomial* SRS is a SRS of the form $[(\sigma^i)_{i \in I_1}]_1, [(\sigma^i)_{i \in I_2}]_2$, where I_1, I_2 are subsets of $[1, m]$. A SRS is *consequent* if both I_1 and I_2 are intervals and non-consequent otherwise. The definition generalizes naturally to the multivariate case.

New Univariate Sumcheck Argument $\mathfrak{Count}$. Let $\mathbb{F}$ be a finite field and let $\mathbb{H} \subset \mathbb{F}$ be a fixed multiplicative subgroup. In a *univariate sumcheck argument* (for multiplicative subgroups), the prover convinces the verifier that the committed polynomial $f(X) \in \mathbb{F}[X]$ sums to the given value $v_M \in \mathbb{F}$ over $\mathbb{H}$.

Let $n_h := |\mathbb{H}|$ and $\mathcal{Z}_\mathbb{H}(X) := \prod_{\chi \in \mathbb{H}}(X - \chi)$. Aurora's sumcheck [5] relies on the fact that $\sum_{\chi \in \mathbb{H}} f(\chi) = n_h f(0)$, when $f \in \mathbb{F}_{\leq n_h - 1}[X]$ is a polynomial with $\deg f \leq n_h - 1$. Then, for $f \in \mathbb{F}[X]$ of arbitrarily large degree, $\sum_{\chi \in \mathbb{H}} f(\chi) = v_f$ iff there exist polynomials $R, Q \in \mathbb{F}[X]$, such that (1) $\deg R \leq n_h - 2$, and (2) $f(X) = v_f / n_h + XR(X) + Q(X)\mathcal{Z}_\mathbb{H}(X)$. In a cryptographic implementation of Aurora's sumcheck argument in say Marlin [10], the prover uses KZG [19] to commit to R and Q; this means the communication of two group elements. In addition, the prover uses a low-degree test to convince the verifier that (1) holds.

Based on the ILV inner-product commitment [18], we construct a new sumcheck argument $\mathfrak{Count}$ for $f \in \mathbb{F}_{\leq d}[X]$. ILV's non-consequent monomial SRS contains $([(\sigma^i)_{i=0:i\neq N+1}^{2N}]_1, [(\sigma^i)_{i=0}^{N}]_2)$, where σ is a trapdoor and N is a large integer. In ILV, the prover P commits to $\boldsymbol{\mu} \in \mathbb{Z}_p^N$ as $[\mu(\sigma)]_1 \leftarrow \sum_{j=1}^{N} \mu_j [\sigma^j]_1$. When the verifier outputs $\boldsymbol{\nu} \in \mathbb{Z}_p^N$, P returns the inner product $v \leftarrow \boldsymbol{\mu}^\top \boldsymbol{\nu}$ together with a short evaluation proof (a single group element $[\mathsf{op}]_1$) that v is correctly computed. ILV's security relies on $[\sigma^{N+1}]_1$ not belonging to the SRS.

We present an alternative extension of the equality $\sum_{\chi \in \mathbb{H}} f(\chi) = n_h f(0)$ to the case when $d = \deg f$ is arbitrarily large. Namely, we prove that if $f(X) = \sum_{i=0}^{d} f_i X^i \in \mathbb{F}_{\leq d}[X]$, then $\sum_{\chi \in \mathbb{H}} f(\chi) = n_h \cdot (\sum_{i=0}^{\lfloor d/n_h \rfloor} f_{n_h i})$. (See Lemma 1.) Alternatively, $\sum_{\chi \in \mathbb{H}} f(\chi) = v_f$ iff $\boldsymbol{f}^\top \boldsymbol{s} = v_f$, where $\boldsymbol{f} = (f_i)$ and $\boldsymbol{s}$ is a Boolean vector that has ones in positions $n_h \cdot i$ for $i \leq \lfloor d/n_h \rfloor$.

In $\mathfrak{Count}$, the prover first ILV-commits to $\boldsymbol{f}$ and then ILV-opens the commitment to $\boldsymbol{f}^\top \boldsymbol{s}$. Thus, the prover has to output one ILV commitment (one group element) instead of two polynomial commitments (two group elements) in Aurora's sumcheck. Moreover, there is no need for a low-degree test, making $\mathfrak{Count}$ even more efficient. In addition, in the application to $\mathfrak{Vampire}$, $\boldsymbol{s}$ has a small constant number of non-zero elements. Thus, differently from Aurora's sumcheck, the prover's computation is linear in both field operations and group operations. Importantly, the prover does not have to use FFT or polynomial division. An explicit cost of using ILV is that the SRS becomes larger: if the SRS, without $\mathfrak{Count}$, contains $[(\sigma^i)_{i=0}^{d}]_1$ (where d is some constant, fixed by the rest of the zk-SNARK), it now has to contain also $[(\sigma^i)_{i=d+2}^{2d}]_1$ and $[(\sigma^i)_{i=0}^{d}]_2$. (Although, in our construction, we will add significantly less elements to $\mathbb{G}_2$.)

Since sumchecks have ubiquitous applications, $\mathfrak{Count}$ is of independent interest because of both excellent communication and linear-time prover. Linear-time sumchecks are important per se. In particular, univariate sumcheck is used in both updatable and universal zk-SNARKs and transparent zk-SNARKs. As an important application, we will design a new updatable and universal zk-SNARK. We leave it an open question to apply $\mathfrak{Count}$ in transparent zk-SNARKs.

New zk-SNARK. We use $\mathfrak{Count}$ to design a new pairing-based updatable and universal zk-SNARK $\mathfrak{Vampire}$ for the sparse R1CSLite constraint system [9].

𝔙𝔞𝔪𝔭𝔦𝔯𝔢's argument length is four elements of $\mathbb{G}_1$ and two elements of $\mathbb{F}$, which is less than in any known updatable and universal zk-SNARK. While Basilisk [26] (as improved in the full version, [27]) has just 37.5% larger communication than 𝔙𝔞𝔪𝔭𝔦𝔯𝔢, it works for a version of R1CSLite with additional restrictions on the underlying matrices; the version of Basilisk for the arithmetization handled by 𝔙𝔞𝔪𝔭𝔦𝔯𝔢 is less communication-efficient than LunarLite or VOR1CS*.

Let us now give a very brief glimpse to the structure of 𝔙𝔞𝔪𝔭𝔦𝔯𝔢. (The real description, with a very long intuition behind 𝔙𝔞𝔪𝔭𝔦𝔯𝔢's construction, is given in Sect. 4.) Following Lunar and Basilisk, we use the R1CSLite constraint system, where an instance consists of two matrices L and R (the left and right inputs to all constraints) over $\mathbb{F}$ instead of three in the case of R1CS. Let m be the number of constraints. Following Marlin, Lunar, and Basilisk, we use the setting of sparse matrices, where L and R have together at most $|\mathbb{K}| = \Theta(m)$ non-zero entries. Here, $\mathbb{K}$ is a multiplicative subgroup of $\mathbb{F}$.

Let z be the interpolating polynomial of $(\mathbb{x}, \mathbb{w}, \boldsymbol{r}_z)$, where $\boldsymbol{r}_z$ is a short random vector needed for zero-knowledge. The prover starts by committing to $\tilde{z}$, where $\tilde{z}$ is a polynomial related to z. Using $\tilde{z}$ helps one efficiently check that the prover used the correct public input. The verifier replies with a random field element α. We reformulate the check that $(\mathbb{x}, \mathbb{w})$ (where $\mathbb{w}$ is encoded in $\tilde{z}$) satisfies the R1CSLite instance as a univariate sumcheck argument that $\sum_{y \in \mathbb{H}} \psi_\alpha(y) = 0$, for a well-chosen polynomial ψ_α. We then run ℭ𝔬𝔲𝔫𝔱, letting the prover send an ILV-opening $[\psi_{\mathsf{ipc}}(\sigma)]_1$ of ψ_α to the verifier. The verifier replies with another random field element β. The prover's final message consists of two field elements and two group elements. These elements are needed to batch-open three polynomial commitments at different locations, two of which are related to β. It involves a complicated but by now standard step of proving the correctness of the arithmetization of a sparse matrix. This step involves using a univariate sumcheck the second time. However, since here the summed polynomial is of a small degree, we do not need to use ℭ𝔬𝔲𝔫𝔱. We refer to Sect. 4 for more details.

𝔙𝔞𝔪𝔭𝔦𝔯𝔢 is based on the ideas of Marlin (e.g., we use a similar arithmetization of sparse matrices), but it uses optimizations of both Lunar [9] and Basilisk [26]. These optimizations (together with an apparently novel combination of the full witness to a single commitment) result in the argument length of 7 elements of $\mathbb{G}_1$ and 2 finite field elements, which is already comparable to prior shortest updatable and universal zk-SNARKs for any NP-complete constraint system.

ℭ𝔬𝔲𝔫𝔱 helps to remove one more group element from the argument of 𝔙𝔞𝔪𝔭𝔦𝔯𝔢. This step is not trivial: the sumcheck argument requires that the sumchecked polynomial f is committed to, which is not the case in 𝔙𝔞𝔪𝔭𝔦𝔯𝔢. We solve this issue using a batching technique similar to Lunar and Basilisk, asking the prover to open two polynomial commitments. The second committed polynomial is a linear combination of other polynomial commitments with coefficients known to the prover and the verifier after opening the first polynomial.

Our second innovation is the use of polynomial commitment aggregation at different points [7,13]. Intuitively, we commit to a single polynomial $\tilde{z}$ that encodes both the left and right inputs of all constraints; this allows us to save one more group element. When combining the result with the batching technique of the previous paragraph, we need to open three polynomials at different points. In particular, we aggregate the commitment of the second sumcheck, further reducing the proof size by one group element. For batching, we use a technique of [7,13]. However, differently from [7,13], our batching is not randomized since the two opening points are different.

In Theorem 1, we prove that 𝔙𝔞𝔪𝔭𝔦𝔯𝔢 is knowledge-sound in the Algebraic Group Model (AGM, [12]). The proof structure is standard, involving two branches depending on whether the verifier's equations hold as polynomials (we get a reduction to the well-known Power Discrete Logarithm assumption if not). However, the proof of the former case is quite complicated, partially since one has to consider several different polynomials sent by the prover, which depend on different verifier's challenge values.

We prove that 𝔙𝔞𝔪𝔭𝔦𝔯𝔢 is perfectly zero-knowledge by constructing a simulator that uses the trapdoor to make the sumcheck argument acceptable for any, even an all-zero witness. For a simulated argument to be indistinguishable from the real one, we add random terms ($\boldsymbol{r}_z$) to polynomial $\tilde{z}(X)$ which, in the case of real argument, encodes the witness, and, in the case of a simulated argument, encodes a (mostly) zero vector. This assures that even an unbounded adversary who knows the instance and witness cannot tell apart commitments to $\tilde{z}(X)$ in real and simulated arguments. In the full version [22], we prove that 𝔙𝔞𝔪𝔭𝔦𝔯𝔢 is also Sub-ZK (i.e., zero-knowledge even if the SRS generation is compromised, [1,2,4,11]) under the BDH-KE knowledge assumption [1].

On Efficiency. We study how much the argument length can be reduced in updatable and universal SNARKs while only allowing minimal relaxations in other efficiency parameters. We achieve the shortest argument by far. The SRS size of our zk-SNARK is a constant factor larger than in the previous work, which we believe is a reasonable compromise as the SRS needs to be transferred only once. Importantly, the verifier has only to execute $O(|\mathbb{x}|)$ field operations as opposed to $O(|\mathbb{x}|)$ group operations in Groth's zk-SNARK [16].

However, differently from the prior work, prover's computation time in 𝔙𝔞𝔪𝔭𝔦𝔯𝔢 depends on the largest supported R1CSLite size. We discuss this issue further and give a thorough efficiency comparison in the full version [22].

Demaking 𝔙𝔞𝔪𝔭𝔦𝔯𝔢. It is possible to "demake" 𝔙𝔞𝔪𝔭𝔦𝔯𝔢 by removing some of the aggressive length-optimization to obtain a larger argument size but better (say) the SRS size. We leave it as an open question about which optimization should be removed first or whether this is needed at all.

2 Preliminaries

Let $\mathbb{F} = \mathbb{Z}_p$ be a finite field of prime order p, and let $\mathbb{F}_{\leq d}[X] \subset \mathbb{F}[X]$ be the set of degree $\leq d$ polynomials. Define the set of (d, d_{gap})-*punctured* univariate polynomials over $\mathbb{F}$ as

$$\mathsf{PolyPunc}_{\mathbb{F}}(d, d_{\mathsf{gap}}, X) := \{f(X) = \textstyle\sum_{i=0}^{d_{\mathsf{gap}}+d} f_i X^i \in \mathbb{F}_{\leq d_{\mathsf{gap}}+d}[X] : f_{d_{\mathsf{gap}}} = 0\} .$$

Let $\boldsymbol{x} \circ \boldsymbol{y}$ be the elementwise product of vectors $\boldsymbol{x}$ and $\boldsymbol{y}$, $\forall i.(\boldsymbol{x} \circ \boldsymbol{y})_i = x_i y_i$. Let $\mathbf{I}_n \in \mathbb{F}^{n \times n}$ be the n-dimensional identity matrix. Denote matrix and vector elements by using square brackets as in $\mathbf{A}[i,j]$ and $\boldsymbol{a}[i]$.

Interpolation. Let ω be the n_h-th primitive root of unity in $\mathbb{F}$ and let $\mathbb{H} = \{\omega^j : 0 \leq j < n_h\}$ be a multiplicative subgroup of $\mathbb{F}$. Then,

- For any $T \subset \mathbb{F}$, the *vanishing polynomial* $\mathcal{Z}_T(X) := \prod_{i \in T}(X - i)$ is the degree-$|T|$ monic polynomial, such that $\mathcal{Z}_T(i) = 0$ for all $i \in T$. $\mathcal{Z}_{\mathbb{H}}(Y) = Y^{n_h} - 1$ can be computed in $\Theta(\log n_h)$ field operations.
- For $i \in [1, n_h]$, $\ell_i^{\mathbb{H}}(Y)$ is the *ith Lagrange polynomial*, i.e., the unique degree $n_h - 1$ polynomial, such that $\ell_i^{\mathbb{H}}(\omega^{i-1}) = 1$ and $\ell_i^{\mathbb{H}}(\omega^{j-1}) = 0$ for $i \neq j$. It is well known that

$$\ell_i^{\mathbb{H}}(Y) = \frac{\mathcal{Z}_{\mathbb{H}}(Y)}{(\mathcal{Z}'_{\mathbb{H}}(\omega^{i-1}) \cdot (Y - \omega^{i-1}))} = \frac{\mathcal{Z}_{\mathbb{H}}(Y)\omega^{i-1}}{(n_h(Y - \omega^{i-1}))} .$$

  Here, $\mathcal{Z}'_{\mathbb{H}}(X) = d\mathcal{Z}_{\mathbb{H}}(X)/dX$.
- $L_X^{\mathbb{H}}(Y) := \mathcal{Z}_{\mathbb{H}}(Y)X/\left(n_h(Y - X)\right) \in \mathbb{F}(X, Y)$ (a lifted Lagrange rational function), with $L_{\omega^{i-1}}(Y) = \ell_i^{\mathbb{H}}(Y)$ for $i \in [1, n_h]$.

For $f \in \mathbb{F}[X]$, let $\widehat{f}^{\mathbb{H}}(X) := \sum_{i=1}^{n_h} f(\omega^{i-1})\ell_i^{\mathbb{H}}(X)$ be its low-degree extension. To simplify notation, we often omit the accent $\widehat{\cdot}$ and the superscript $\mathbb{H}$.

R1CSLite. R1CSLite [9,26] is a variant of the Rank 1 Constraint System [10,14]. An R1CSLite instance $\mathcal{I} = (\mathbb{F}, m, m_0, \mathbf{L}, \mathbf{R})$ consists of a field $\mathbb{F}$, instance size m, input size m_0, and matrices $\mathbf{L}, \mathbf{R} \in \mathbb{F}^{m \times m}$. An R1CSLite instance is *sparse* if $\mathbf{L}$ and $\mathbf{R}$ have $O(m)$ non-zero elements.

$\mathcal{I} = (\mathbb{F}, m, m_0, \mathbf{L}, \mathbf{R})$ defines the following relation $\mathcal{R} = \mathcal{R}_{\mathcal{I}}$:

$$\mathcal{R} := \left\{ \begin{array}{l} (\mathtt{x}, \mathtt{w}) \colon \mathtt{x} = (z_1, \ldots, z_{m_0})^\top \wedge \mathtt{w} = \left(\begin{smallmatrix} \boldsymbol{z}_{\mathsf{a}} \\ \boldsymbol{z}_{\mathsf{b}} \end{smallmatrix}\right) \wedge \boldsymbol{z}_{\mathsf{a}}, \boldsymbol{z}_{\mathsf{b}} \in \mathbb{F}^{m - m_0 - 1} \wedge \\ \boldsymbol{z}_{\mathsf{l}} = \begin{pmatrix} 1 \\ \mathtt{x} \\ \boldsymbol{z}_{\mathsf{a}} \end{pmatrix} \wedge \boldsymbol{z}_{\mathsf{r}} = \left(\begin{smallmatrix} \mathbf{1}_{m_0+1} \\ \boldsymbol{z}_{\mathsf{b}} \end{smallmatrix}\right) \wedge \boldsymbol{z}_{\mathsf{l}} = \mathbf{L}(\boldsymbol{z}_{\mathsf{l}} \circ \boldsymbol{z}_{\mathsf{r}}) \wedge \boldsymbol{z}_{\mathsf{r}} = \mathbf{R}(\boldsymbol{z}_{\mathsf{l}} \circ \boldsymbol{z}_{\mathsf{r}}) \end{array} \right\} .$$

Equivalently, $\mathbf{W}\boldsymbol{z}^* = \mathbf{0}$, where

$$\mathbf{W} = \left(\begin{smallmatrix} \mathbf{I}_m & \mathbf{0} & -\mathbf{L} \\ \mathbf{0} & \mathbf{I}_m & -\mathbf{R} \end{smallmatrix}\right) \in \mathbb{F}^{2m \times 3m} , \quad \boldsymbol{z}^* = \left(\begin{smallmatrix} \boldsymbol{z}_{\mathsf{l}} \\ \boldsymbol{z}_{\mathsf{r}} \\ \boldsymbol{z} = \boldsymbol{z}_{\mathsf{l}} \circ \boldsymbol{z}_{\mathsf{r}} \end{smallmatrix}\right) . \tag{1}$$

Basic Cryptography. We denote the security parameter by λ. For any algorithm $\mathcal{A}$, $r \leftarrow_\$ \mathsf{RND}_\lambda(\mathcal{A})$ samples random coins of sufficient length for $\mathcal{A}$ for fixed λ. By $y \leftarrow \mathcal{A}(x; r)$, we denote that $\mathcal{A}$ outputs y on input x and random coins r. PPT means probabilistic polynomial time.

Pairings. A bilinear group generator $\mathsf{Pgen}(1^\lambda)$ returns $\mathsf{p} = (p, \mathbb{G}_1, \mathbb{G}_2, \mathbb{G}_T, \hat{e}, [1]_1, [1]_2)$, where p is a prime, $\mathbb{G}_1$, $\mathbb{G}_2$, and $\mathbb{G}_T$ are three additive cyclic groups of order p, $\hat{e} : \mathbb{G}_1 \times \mathbb{G}_2 \to \mathbb{G}_T$ is a non-degenerate efficiently computable bilinear pairing, and $[1]_\iota$ is a generator of $\mathbb{G}_\iota$ for $\iota \in \{1, 2, T\}$ with $[1]_T = \hat{e}([1]_1, [1]_2)$. In this paper, $\mathbb{F} = \mathbb{Z}_p$ has always two large multiplicative subgroups $\mathbb{H}$ and $\mathbb{K}$. Thus, we assume implicitly that $|\mathbb{H}|, |\mathbb{K}| \mid (p-1)$. We require the bilinear pairing to be Type-3, that is, not to have an efficient isomorphism between $\mathbb{G}_1$ and $\mathbb{G}_2$. In practice, one uses a fixed pairing-friendly curve like BLS-381; then, $|\mathbb{K}|, |\mathbb{H}| \mid 2^{32}$.

We use the by now standard additive bracket notation, by writing $[a]_\iota$ to denote $a[1]_\iota$ for $\iota \in \{1, 2, T\}$. We denote $\hat{e}([x]_1, [y]_2)$ by $[x]_1 \bullet [y]_2$. Thus, $[x]_1 \bullet [y]_2 = [xy]_T$. We freely use the bracket notation together with matrix notation; for example, if $\mathbf{A} \cdot \mathbf{B} = \mathbf{C}$ then $[\mathbf{A}]_1 \bullet [\mathbf{B}]_2 = [\mathbf{C}]_T$.

Polynomial Commitment Schemes. In a polynomial commitment scheme [19], the prover commits to a polynomial $f \in \mathbb{F}_{\leq d}[X]$ and later opens it to $f(\beta)$ for $\beta \in \mathbb{F}$ chosen by the verifier. The (non-randomized) KZG [19] polynomial commitment scheme consists of the following algorithms:

Setup: Given 1^λ, return $\mathsf{p} \leftarrow \mathsf{Pgen}(1^\lambda)$.

Commitment key generation: Given a system parameter p and an upper-bound d on the polynomial degree, compute the trapdoor $\mathsf{tk} = \sigma \leftarrow_\$ \mathbb{Z}_p^*$ and the commitment key $\mathsf{ck} \leftarrow (\mathsf{p}, [(\sigma^i)_{i=0}^d]_1, [1, \sigma]_2)$. Return $(\mathsf{ck}, \mathsf{tk})$.

Commitment: Given a commitment key ck and a polynomial $f \in \mathbb{F}_{\leq d}[X]$, return the commitment $[f(\sigma)]_1 \leftarrow \sum_{j=0}^{d} f_j [\sigma^j]_1$.

Opening: Given a commitment key ck, a commitment $[f(\sigma)]_1$, an evaluation point $\beta \in \mathbb{F}$, and a polynomial $f \in \mathbb{F}_{\leq d}[X]$, set $v \leftarrow f(\beta)$ and $f_{\mathsf{pc}}(X) \leftarrow (f(X) - v)/(X - \beta)$. The evaluation proof is $[f_{\mathsf{pc}}(\sigma)]_1 \leftarrow \sum_{j=0}^{d-1} (f_{\mathsf{pc}})_j [\sigma^j]_1$. Return $(v, [f_{\mathsf{pc}}(\sigma)]_1)$.

Verification: Given a commitment key ck, a commitment $[f(\sigma)]_1$, an evaluation point β, a purported evaluation $v = f(\beta)$, and an evaluation proof $[f_{\mathsf{pc}}(\sigma)]_1$, check $[f(\sigma) - v]_1 \bullet [1]_2 = [f_{\mathsf{pc}}(\sigma)]_1 \bullet [\sigma - \beta]_2$.

KZG's security is based on the fact that $(X - \beta) \mid (f(X) - v) \Leftrightarrow f(\beta) = v$.

Inner-Product Commitment Schemes. In an inner-product commitment scheme [18,20], the prover commits to a vector $\boldsymbol{\mu} \in \mathbb{F}^N$ and later opens it to the inner product $\boldsymbol{\mu}^\top \boldsymbol{\nu}$ for $\boldsymbol{\nu} \in \mathbb{F}^N$ chosen by the verifier. The (non-randomized) ILV [18] inner-product commitment scheme consists of the following algorithms:

Setup: Given 1^λ, return $\mathsf{p} \leftarrow \mathsf{Pgen}(1^\lambda)$.

Commitment key generation: Given a system parameter p and a vector dimension N, compute the trapdoor $\mathsf{tk} = \sigma \leftarrow_\$ \mathbb{Z}_p^*$ and the commitment key $\mathsf{ck} \leftarrow ([(\sigma^i)_{i=0:i \neq N+1}^{2N}]_1, [(\sigma^i)_{i=0}^N]_2)$. Return $(\mathsf{ck}, \mathsf{tk})$.

Commitment: Given a commitment key ck and a vector $\boldsymbol{\mu} \in \mathbb{F}^N$, compute the coefficients of $\mu(X) \leftarrow \sum_{j=1}^N \mu_j X^j \in \mathbb{F}_{\leq N}[X]$; $[\mu(\sigma)]_1 = \sum_{j=1}^N \mu_j [\sigma^j]_1$. Return the commitment $[\mu(\sigma)]_1$.

Opening: Given a commitment key ck, a commitment $[\mu(\sigma)]_1$, the vector $\boldsymbol{\mu}$, and a vector $\boldsymbol{\nu}$, let $v \leftarrow \boldsymbol{\mu}^\top \boldsymbol{\nu}$. Set $\nu^*(X) \leftarrow \sum_{j=1}^{N} \nu_j X^{N+1-j} \in \mathbb{F}_{\leq N}[X]$, and $\mu_{\mathsf{ipc}}(X) \leftarrow \mu(X)\nu^*(X) - vX^{N+1} \in \mathsf{PolyPunc}_{\mathbb{F}}(N-1, N+1, X)$. The evaluation proof is $[\mu_{\mathsf{ipc}}(\sigma)]_1 \leftarrow \sum_{i=1, i\neq N+1}^{2N} \mu_{\mathsf{ipc}}[\sigma^i]_1$. Return $(v, [\mu_{\mathsf{ipc}}(\sigma)]_1)$.

Verification: Given a commitment key ck, a commitment $[\mu(\sigma)]_1$, a vector $\boldsymbol{\nu}$, a purported inner product $v = \boldsymbol{\mu}^\top \boldsymbol{\nu}$, and an evaluation proof $[\mu_{\mathsf{ipc}}(\sigma)]_1$, check $[\mu_{\mathsf{ipc}}(\sigma)]_1 \bullet [1]_2 = [\mu(\sigma)]_1 \bullet \sum_{j=1}^{N} \nu_j [\sigma^{N+1-j}]_2 - v[\sigma^N]_1 \bullet [\sigma]_2$.

ILV's security follows since the coefficient of X^{N+1} in $\mu_{\mathsf{ipc}}(X)$ is $\boldsymbol{\mu}^\top \boldsymbol{\nu} - v = 0$ iff v is correctly computed. In this paper, the vector $\boldsymbol{\nu}$ is public and known in advance. Then, the verifier only has to compute two pairings and no exponentiations.

Succinct Zero-Knowledge Arguments. The following definition is based on [9]. Groth et al. [17] introduced the notion of (preprocessing) zk-SNARKs with specializable universal structured reference string (SRS). This notion formalizes the idea that the key generation for $\mathcal{R} \in \mathcal{UR}$, where $\mathcal{UR}$ is a universal relation, can be seen as the sequential combination of two steps. First, a probabilistic algorithm generating an SRS for $\mathcal{UR}$ and second, a deterministic algorithm specializing this universal SRS into one for a specific $\mathcal{R}$.

We consider relation families $(\mathsf{Pgen}, \{\mathcal{UR}_{\mathsf{p},N}\}_{\mathsf{p}\in \mathsf{range}(\mathsf{Pgen}), N\in\mathbb{N}})$ parametrized by $\mathsf{p} \in \mathsf{Pgen}(1^\lambda)$ and a size bound $N \in \mathsf{poly}(\lambda)$.[4] A *succinct zero-knowledge argument* $\Pi = (\mathsf{Pgen}, \mathsf{KGen}, \mathsf{Derive}, \mathsf{P}, \mathsf{V})$ *with specializable universal SRS for a relation family* $(\mathsf{Pgen}, \{\mathcal{UR}_{\mathsf{p},N}\}_{\mathsf{p}\in\{0,1\}^*, N\in\mathbb{N}})$ consists of the following algorithms.

Setup: Given 1^λ, return $\mathsf{p} \leftarrow \mathsf{Pgen}(1^\lambda)$.

Universal SRS Generation: a probabilistic algorithm $\mathsf{KGen}(\mathsf{p}, N) \rightarrow (\mathsf{srs}, \mathsf{td})$ that takes as input public parameters p and an upper bound N on the relation size, and outputs $\mathsf{srs} = (\mathsf{ek}, \mathsf{vk})$ together with a trapdoor. We assume implicitly that elements like ek and vk contain p.

SRS Specialization: a deterministic algorithm $\mathsf{Derive}(\mathsf{srs}, \mathcal{R}) \rightarrow (\mathsf{ek}_\mathcal{R}, \mathsf{vk}_\mathcal{R})$ that takes as input a universal SRS srs and a relation $\mathcal{R} \in \mathcal{UR}_{\mathsf{p},N}$, and outputs a specialized SRS $\mathsf{srs}_\mathcal{R} := (\mathsf{ek}_\mathcal{R}, \mathsf{vk}_\mathcal{R})$.

Prover/Verifier: a pair of interactive algorithms $\langle \mathsf{P}(\mathsf{ek}_\mathcal{R}, \mathbb{x}, \mathbb{w}), \mathsf{V}(\mathsf{vk}_\mathcal{R}, \mathbb{x})\rangle \rightarrow b$, where P takes a proving key $\mathsf{ek}_\mathcal{R}$ for a relation $\mathcal{R}$, a statement $\mathbb{x}$, and a witness $\mathbb{w}$, s.t. $(\mathbb{x}, \mathbb{w}) \in \mathcal{R}$, and V takes a verification key for a relation $\mathcal{R}$ and a statement $\mathbb{x}$, and either accepts $(b = 1)$ or rejects $(b = 0)$ the argument.

Π must satisfy the following four requirements.

Completeness. For all $\mathsf{p} \in \mathsf{range}(\mathsf{Pgen})$, $N \in \mathbb{N}$, $\mathcal{R} \in \mathcal{UR}_{\mathsf{p},N}$, and $(\mathbb{x}, \mathbb{w}) \in \mathcal{R}$,

$$\Pr\left[\langle \mathsf{P}(\mathsf{ek}_\mathcal{R}, \mathbb{x}, \mathbb{w}), \mathsf{V}(\mathsf{vk}_\mathcal{R}, \mathbb{x})\rangle = 1 \,\middle|\, \begin{array}{c} (\mathsf{srs}, \mathsf{td}) \leftarrow \mathsf{KGen}(\mathsf{p}, N); \\ (\mathsf{ek}_\mathcal{R}, \mathsf{vk}_\mathcal{R}) \leftarrow \mathsf{Derive}(\mathsf{srs}, \mathcal{R}) \end{array}\right] = 1 \; .$$

Succinctness. Π is *succinct* if the running time of V is $\mathsf{poly}(\lambda + |\mathbb{x}| + \log |\mathbb{w}|)$ and the communication size is $\mathsf{poly}(\lambda + \log |\mathbb{w}|)$.

[4] Count and Vampire have several size bounds. The definitions generalize naturally.

Knowledge-Soundness. Π is *knowledge-sound*, if for every non-uniform PPT adversary $\mathcal{A} = (\mathcal{A}_1, \mathcal{A}_2)$, there exists a non-uniform PPT extractor $\mathsf{Ext}_{\mathcal{A}}$[5], s.t.

$$\Pr\left[\begin{array}{c|c} \langle \mathcal{A}_2(st; r), \mathsf{V}(\mathsf{vk}_{\mathcal{R}}, \mathbb{x})\rangle = 1 & \mathsf{p} \leftarrow \mathsf{Pgen}(1^\lambda); (\mathsf{srs}, \mathsf{td}) \leftarrow \mathsf{KGen}(\mathsf{p}, N); \\ \wedge \neg \mathcal{R}(\mathbb{x}, \mathbb{w}) & r \leftarrow\!\!\$\ \mathsf{RND}_\lambda(\mathcal{A}); (\mathcal{R}, \mathbb{x}, st) \leftarrow \mathcal{A}_1(\mathsf{srs}; r); \\ & \mathbb{w} \leftarrow \mathsf{Ext}_{\mathcal{A}}(\mathsf{srs}; r); \\ & (\mathsf{ek}_{\mathcal{R}}, \mathsf{vk}_{\mathcal{R}}) \leftarrow \mathsf{Derive}(\mathsf{srs}, \mathcal{R}) \end{array}\right] = \mathsf{negl}(\lambda)\ .$$

Zero-Knowledge. Π is (statistical) *zero-knowledge* if there exists a PPT simulator Sim, s.t. for all unbound $\mathcal{A} = (\mathcal{A}_1, \mathcal{A}_2)$, all $\mathsf{p} \in \mathrm{range}(\mathsf{Pgen})$, all $N \in \mathsf{poly}(\lambda)$,

$$\Pr\left[\begin{array}{c|c} \langle \mathsf{P}(\mathsf{ek}_{\mathcal{R}}, \mathbb{x}, \mathbb{w}), \mathcal{A}_2(st)\rangle = 1 \wedge & (\mathsf{srs}, \mathsf{td}) \leftarrow \mathsf{KGen}(\mathsf{p}, N); \\ \mathcal{R}(\mathbb{x}, \mathbb{w}) \wedge \mathcal{R} \in \mathcal{UR}_{\mathsf{p},N} & (\mathcal{R}, \mathbb{x}, \mathbb{w}, st) \leftarrow \mathcal{A}_1(\mathsf{srs}); \\ & (\mathsf{ek}_{\mathcal{R}}, \mathsf{vk}_{\mathcal{R}}) \leftarrow \mathsf{Derive}(\mathsf{srs}, \mathcal{R}) \end{array}\right] \approx_s$$

$$\Pr\left[\begin{array}{c|c} \langle \mathsf{Sim}(\mathsf{srs}, \mathsf{td}, \mathcal{R}, \mathbb{x}), \mathcal{A}_2(st)\rangle = 1 \wedge & (\mathsf{srs}, \mathsf{td}) \leftarrow \mathsf{KGen}(\mathsf{p}, N); \\ \mathcal{R}(\mathbb{x}, \mathbb{w}) \wedge \mathcal{R} \in \mathcal{UR}_{\mathsf{p},N} & (\mathcal{R}, \mathbb{x}, \mathbb{w}, st) \leftarrow \mathcal{A}_1(\mathsf{srs}); \\ & (\mathsf{ek}_{\mathcal{R}}, \mathsf{vk}_{\mathcal{R}}) \leftarrow \mathsf{Derive}(\mathsf{srs}, \mathcal{R}) \end{array}\right]\ .$$

Here, $\approx_s$ denotes the statistical distance as a function of λ. Π is *perfect zero-knowledge* if the above probabilities are equal.

Π is *subversion zero-knowledge* (Sub-ZK, [4]), if it is zero-knowledge even in the case the SRS is maliciously generated. For perfect zero-knowledge arguments, Sub-ZK follows from the usual zero-knowledge (with trusted SRS), SRS verifiability (there exists a PPT algorithm that checks that the SRS belongs to range(KGen)), and a SNARK-specific knowledge assumption, [1,2]. We will provide the formal definition in the full version [22].

Π is *updatable* [17], if the SRS can be sequentially updated by many updaters, such that knowledge-soundness holds if either the original SRS creator or one of the updaters is honest. Groth et al. [17] showed that an updatable SRS cannot contain non-monomial polynomial evaluations. Moreover, an updatable SRS must be verifiable in the same sense as in the case of Sub-ZK.

Since 𝔙𝔞𝔪𝔭𝔦𝔯𝔢 is public-coin and has a constant number of rounds, we can apply the Fiat-Shamir heuristic to obtain a zk-SNARK.

Sumcheck Arguments. In a sumcheck argument [23] over $\mathbb{F}$, the prover convinces the verifier that for $\mathbb{H} \subseteq \mathbb{F}$, $f \in \mathbb{F}[X_1, \dots, X_c]$, and $v_f \in \mathbb{F}$, it holds that $\sum_{(x_1,\dots,x_c)\in\mathbb{H}^c} f(x_1, \dots, x_c) = v_f$. Multivariate sumcheck has many applications, with usually relatively small $|\mathbb{H}|$ but large c. In the context of efficient updatable zk-SNARKs, one is often interested in *univariate sumcheck*, where $c = 1$ but $|\mathbb{H}|$ is large. Univariate sumcheck arguments are most efficient when $\mathbb{H}$ is either an affine subspace or a multiplicative subgroup [5].

The univariate sumcheck relation for multiplicative subgroups is the set of all pairs $\mathcal{R}_{\mathsf{sum}} := \{((\mathbb{F}, d, \mathbb{H}, v_f), f)\}$, where $\mathbb{F}$ is a finite field, d is a positive integer, $\mathbb{H}$ is a multiplicative subgroup of $\mathbb{F}$, $v_f \in \mathbb{F}$, $f \in \mathbb{F}_{\leq d}[X]$, and $\sum_{\chi\in\mathbb{H}} f(\chi) = v_f$.

[5] Note that although the protocol is interactive, extraction is done non-interactively. This is sometimes called straight-line extractability.

Aurora's Sumcheck. As a part of the zk-SNARK Aurora, Ben-Sasson et al. [5] proposed an efficient univariate sumcheck ("Aurora's sumcheck") for multiplicative subgroups. Since the new univariate sumcheck relies on similar techniques, we next recall Aurora's sumcheck.

As before, let $\mathbb{H} = \langle \omega \rangle = \{\omega^i : i \in [0, n_h - 1]\}$ be a cyclic multiplicative subgroup of order $n_h = |\mathbb{H}|$. Fact 1 underlies Aurora's sumcheck.

Fact 1. *Let* $f \in \mathbb{F}[X]$ *with* $\deg f \leq n_h - 1$. *Then* $\sum_{\chi \in \mathbb{H}} f(\chi) = n_h f(0)$.

In the case of a large-degree f, Ben-Sasson et al. [5] used Fact 2 to construct Aurora's sumcheck argument for proving that $\sum_{\chi \in \mathbb{H}} f(\chi) = v_f$.

Fact 2 (Core Lemma of Aurora's Sumcheck). *Let* $f \in \mathbb{F}[X]$ *with* $d = \deg f \geq n_h$. *Then,* $\sum_{\chi \in \mathbb{H}} f(\chi) = v_f$ *iff there exist* $R \in \mathbb{F}_{\leq n_h - 2}[X]$ *and* $Q \in \mathbb{F}_{\leq d - n_h}[X]$, *such that* $f(X) = v_f / n_h + R(X)X + Q(X)\mathcal{Z}_{\mathbb{H}}(X)$.

Assume that $d = \deg f = \mathsf{poly}(\lambda)$ while $p = 2^{\Theta(\lambda)}$. In Aurora's sumcheck argument, the prover sends to the verifier polynomial commitments to f, R, and Q. The verifier accepts if (1) R has a low degree $\leq n_h - 2$ and (2) $f(X) = v_f / n_h + R(X)X + Q(X)\mathcal{Z}_{\mathbb{H}}(X)$.

On top of two polynomial commitments (two group elements), one has to implement a low-degree test to check that $\deg R \leq n_h - 2$. As the low-degree test, Aurora uses an interactive oracle proof for testing proximity to the Reed-Solomon code, resulting in additional costs. The full version of Basilisk [27] implementes a low-degree test in a partially costless way (without added argument size or verifier's computation); however, one may need to add a large number of elements to the SRS for their low-degree test to succeed.

Assumptions. Let $d_1(\lambda), d_2(\lambda) \in \mathsf{poly}(\lambda)$. Pgen is (d_1, d_2)-*PDL (Power Discrete Logarithm* [21]*) secure* if for any non-uniform PPT $\mathcal{A}$, $\mathsf{Adv}^{\mathrm{pdl}}_{d_1, d_2, \mathsf{Pgen}, \mathcal{A}}(\lambda) :=$

$$\Pr\left[\mathcal{A}\left(\mathsf{p}, [(x^i)_{i=0}^{d_1}]_1, [(x^i)_{i=0}^{d_2}]_2\right) = x \middle| \mathsf{p} \leftarrow \mathsf{Pgen}(1^\lambda); x \leftarrow_{\$} \mathbb{F}^*\right] = \mathsf{negl}(\lambda)\ .$$

Algebraic Group Model (AGM). AGM is an idealized model [12] for security proofs. In the AGM, adversaries are restricted to be *algebraic* in the following sense: if $\mathcal{A}$ inputs some group elements and outputs a group element, it provides an algebraic representation of the latter in terms of the former. More precisely, if $\mathcal{A}$ has received group elements $[\boldsymbol{x}_1]_1, [\boldsymbol{x}_2]_2$ so far and outputs $[y_1]_1, [y_2]_2$, then there exists an extractor $\mathsf{Ext}_{\mathcal{A}}$ which on the same input and random coins outputs integer vectors $\boldsymbol{\gamma}_1, \boldsymbol{\gamma}_2$ such that $[y_1]_1 = \sum_i \gamma_{1,i}[\boldsymbol{x}_{1,i}]_1$ and $[y_2]_2 = \sum_j \gamma_{2,j}[\boldsymbol{x}_{2,j}]_2$.

3 $\mathfrak{Count}$: New Univariate Sumcheck Argument

In this section, we propose $\mathfrak{Count}$, a new sumcheck argument with improved online efficiency (including the argument size) but a larger SRS size than Aurora's univariate sumcheck. We first prove the following generalization of Fact 1, an alternative to Fact 2 in the case f has degree larger than $n_h - 1$.

Lemma 1. *Let* $f(X) = \sum_{i=0}^{d} f_i X^i$ *for* $d \geq 0$. *Then,* $\sum_{\chi \in \mathbb{H}} f(\chi) = n_h \cdot \sum_{i=0}^{\lfloor d/n_h \rfloor} f_{n_h i}$.

Proof. Write $f(X) = R(X) + Q(X)\mathcal{Z}_{\mathbb{H}}(X)$ for $\deg R \leq n_h - 1$. Based on Fact 1, $\sum_{\chi \in \mathbb{H}} f(\chi) = \sum_{\chi \in \mathbb{H}} R(\chi) = n_h R(0)$. Since $X^{n_h} \equiv 1 \pmod{\mathcal{Z}_{\mathbb{H}}(X)}$, $f(X) = \sum_{i=0}^{d} f_i X^i \equiv \sum_{j=0}^{n_h-1} (\sum_{i=0:n_h|(i-j)}^{d} f_i) X^j \pmod{\mathcal{Z}_{\mathbb{H}}(X)}$. Since $f(X) \equiv R(X) \pmod{\mathcal{Z}_{\mathbb{H}}(X)}$, $R(0) = \sum_{i=0}^{\lfloor d/n_h \rfloor} f_{n_h i}$. Thus, $\sum_{\chi \in \mathbb{H}} f(\chi) = n_h \cdot \sum_{i=0}^{\lfloor d/n_h \rfloor} f_{n_h i}$. □

𝔆𝔬𝔲𝔫𝔱 is based on the following result.

Lemma 2 (Core Lemma of 𝔆𝔬𝔲𝔫𝔱). *Let* $\mathbb{H}$ *be an order-*$n_h > 1$ *multiplicative subgroup of* $\mathbb{F}^*$. *Let* $d_{\mathsf{gap}}, d > 0$ *with* $d_{\mathsf{gap}} \geq n_h \cdot \lfloor d/n_h \rfloor$, *and* $f \in \mathsf{PolyPunc}_{\mathbb{F}}(d, d_{\mathsf{gap}}, X)$. *Define*

$$S(X) := \sum_{i=0}^{\lfloor d/n_h \rfloor} X^{d_{\mathsf{gap}} - n_h i} \in \mathbb{F}_{\leq d_{\mathsf{gap}}}[X] .$$

Then, $\sum_{\chi \in \mathbb{H}} f(\chi) = v_f$ *and* $\deg f \leq d$ *iff there exists* $f_{\mathsf{ipc}} \in \mathsf{PolyPunc}_{\mathbb{F}}(d, d_{\mathsf{gap}}, X)$, *s.t.*

$$f(X)S(X) - f_{\mathsf{ipc}}(X) = \frac{v_f}{n_h} \cdot X^{d_{\mathsf{gap}}} . \tag{2}$$

Here, d_{gap} is a parameter fixed by the master protocol (in our case, 𝔙𝔞𝔪𝔭𝔦𝔯𝔢) that uses 𝔆𝔬𝔲𝔫𝔱 as a subroutine.

Proof Clearly, we need $d_{\mathsf{gap}} \geq n_h \cdot \lfloor d/n_h \rfloor$ for S to be a polynomial.

($\Rightarrow$) Define $f_{\mathsf{ipc}}(X) := f(X)S(X) - v_f/n_h \cdot X^{d_{\mathsf{gap}}}$. We must only show that $f_{\mathsf{ipc}} \in \mathsf{PolyPunc}_{\mathbb{F}}(d, d_{\mathsf{gap}}, X)$. Since $\deg f \leq d$ and $\deg S = d_{\mathsf{gap}}$, we have $\deg f_{\mathsf{ipc}} \leq d_{\mathsf{gap}} + d$. Since $f(X)S(X) = (\sum_{i=0}^{d} f_i X^i)(\sum_{i=0}^{\lfloor d/n_h \rfloor} X^{d_{\mathsf{gap}} - n_h i})$, the coefficient of $X^{d_{\mathsf{gap}}}$ in $f(X)S(X)$ is $\sum_{i=0}^{\lfloor d/n_h \rfloor} f_{n_h i}$. By Lemma 1, $\sum_{i=0}^{\lfloor d/n_h \rfloor} f_{n_h i} = v_f/n_h$. Thus, the coefficient of $X^{d_{\mathsf{gap}}}$ in f_{ipc} is 0 and $f_{\mathsf{ipc}} \in \mathsf{PolyPunc}_{\mathbb{F}}(d, d_{\mathsf{gap}}, X)$.

($\Leftarrow$) Suppose Eq. (2) holds for $f_{\mathsf{ipc}} \in \mathsf{PolyPunc}_{\mathbb{F}}(d, d_{\mathsf{gap}}, X)$. Since $\deg S = d_{\mathsf{gap}}$ and $\deg f_{\mathsf{ipc}} \leq d_{\mathsf{gap}} + d$, we have $\deg f \leq d$. As in ($\Rightarrow$), the coefficient of $X^{d_{\mathsf{gap}}}$ in $f(X)S(X)$ is $\sum_{i=0}^{\lfloor d/n_h \rfloor} f_{n_h i}$, which is equal to $(\sum_{\chi \in \mathbb{H}} f(\chi))/n_h$ due to Lemma 1. Since f_{ipc} is missing the monomial $X^{d_{\mathsf{gap}}}$, we get that $v_f = \sum_{\chi \in \mathbb{H}} f(\chi)$. □

It is important that f_{ipc} has degree $\leq d_{\mathsf{gap}} + d$. Thus, one cannot add elements $[\sigma^i]_1$ for $i > d_{\mathsf{gap}} + d$ to the SRS of a master argument that uses 𝔆𝔬𝔲𝔫𝔱.

Description of 𝔆𝔬𝔲𝔫𝔱. Next, we describe 𝔆𝔬𝔲𝔫𝔱 as a zk-SNARK for the sumcheck relation; if needed, it is straightforward to modify it to the language of polynomial oracles. In 𝔆𝔬𝔲𝔫𝔱, the common input is $([f(\sigma)]_1, v_f)$. The prover sends to the verifier a polynomial commitment to $[f_{\mathsf{ipc}}(\sigma)]_1$, and the verifier accepts that $\sum_{\chi \in \mathbb{H}} f(\chi) = v_f$ iff a naturally modified version of Eq. (2) holds on committed polynomials. See Fig. 1 for the full argument. Here, Derive does only preprocessing and does not do any specialization.

Since we only use 𝔆𝔬𝔲𝔫𝔱 as a sub-argument of 𝔙𝔞𝔪𝔭𝔦𝔯𝔢, we do not formally have to prove that it is knowledge-sound or zero-knowledge. Nevertheless, for the sake of completeness, we provide proof sketches.

$\mathsf{Pgen}(\mathsf{p})$: generate p as usually. We implicitly assume $n_h \mid (p-1)$.

$\mathsf{KGen}(\mathsf{p}, n_h, d, d_{\mathsf{gap}})$: $\mathcal{S}_1(X) \leftarrow \{(X^i)_{i=0:i\neq d_{\mathsf{gap}}}^{d_{\mathsf{gap}}+d}\}$; $\mathcal{S}_2(X) \leftarrow \{1, X, (X^{d_{\mathsf{gap}}-n_h i})_{i=0}^{\lfloor d/n_h \rfloor}\}$;
$\sigma \leftarrow_\$ \mathbb{F}^*$; $\mathsf{td} \leftarrow \sigma$; $\mathsf{srs} \leftarrow (\mathsf{p}, n_h, d, d_{\mathsf{gap}}, [g(\sigma) : g \in \mathcal{S}_1(X)]_1, [g(\sigma) : g \in \mathcal{S}_2(X)]_2)$

$\mathsf{Derive}(\mathsf{srs})$: $S(X) \leftarrow \sum_{i=0}^{\lfloor d/n_h \rfloor} X^{d_{\mathsf{gap}}-n_h i} \in \mathbb{F}_{\leq d_{\mathsf{gap}}}[X]$; $\mathsf{ek}_{\mathcal{R}} \leftarrow \mathsf{srs}$;
$\mathsf{vk}_{\mathcal{R}} \leftarrow (\mathsf{srs}, [S(\sigma)]_2, [\sigma^{d_{\mathsf{gap}}}]_T)$; return $(\mathsf{ek}_{\mathcal{R}}, \mathsf{vk}_{\mathcal{R}})$;

$\mathsf{P}(\mathsf{ek}_{\mathcal{R}}, \mathbb{x}, \mathbb{w} = f)$ /* $\mathbb{x} = ([f(\sigma)]_1, v_f)$ */ $\mathsf{V}(\mathsf{vk}_{\mathcal{R}}, \mathbb{x})$

..........Online phase..........

$S(X) \leftarrow \sum_{i=0}^{\lfloor d/n_h \rfloor} X^{d_{\mathsf{gap}}-n_h i} \in \mathbb{F}_{\leq d_{\mathsf{gap}}}[X]$; $f_{\mathsf{ipc}}(X) \leftarrow f(X)S(X) - v_f/n_h \cdot X^{d_{\mathsf{gap}}}$

$\xrightarrow{[f_{\mathsf{ipc}}(\sigma)]_1}$

Check $[f(\sigma)]_1 \bullet [S(\sigma)]_2 - [f_{\mathsf{ipc}}(\sigma)]_1 \bullet [1]_2 = v_f/n_h \cdot [\sigma^{d_{\mathsf{gap}}}]_T$

Fig. 1. The new univariate sumcheck zk-SNARK $\mathfrak{Count}$ for $\sum_{\chi \in \mathbb{H}} f(\chi) = v_f$.

Lemma 3. *The sumcheck zk-SNARK* $\mathfrak{Count}$ *in Eq. (2) is complete and perfectly zero-knowledge. Additionally, the probability that any algebraic* $\mathcal{A}$ *can break knowledge-soundness is bounded by* $\mathsf{Adv}^{\mathrm{pdl}}_{d_1,d_2,\mathsf{Pgen},\mathcal{B}}(\lambda)$, *where* $\mathcal{B}$ *is some PPT adversary,* $d_1 = d_{\mathsf{gap}} + d$, *and* $d_2 = d_{\mathsf{gap}}$.

Proof. Completeness follows from Lemma 2.

We sketch a knowledge-soundness proof in the AGM [12]. Since $\mathcal{A}$ is algebraic, $f(X), f_{\mathsf{ipc}}(X)$ are in the span of X^i for $i \in \mathcal{S}_1(X)$, i.e., $f, f_{\mathsf{ipc}} \in \mathsf{PolyPunc}_{\mathbb{F}}(d, d_{\mathsf{gap}}, X)$. If Eq. (2) holds, then by Lemma 2, the prover is honest. Otherwise, we have a non-zero polynomial $\mathcal{V}(X) := f(X)S(X) - f_{\mathsf{ipc}}(X) - v_f/n_h \cdot X^{d_{\mathsf{gap}}}$ (its coefficients are known since the adversary is algebraic), such that (since the verifier accepts) σ is a root of $\mathcal{V}$. We construct a (d_1, d_2)-PDL adversary $\mathcal{B}$ that gets $(\mathsf{p}, [(\sigma^i)_{i=0}^{d_1}]_1, [(\sigma^i)_{i=0}^{d_2}]_2)$ as an input. $\mathcal{B}$ constructs srs from the challenge input, and runs $\mathcal{A}$ and its extractor $\mathsf{Ext}_{\mathcal{A}}$ to obtain $\mathcal{V}(X)$. Whenever $\mathcal{V}(X) \neq 0$, $\mathcal{B}$ can find the root σ and break the PDL assumption.

We construct a simulator that on input $(\mathsf{srs}, \mathsf{td} = \sigma, ([f(\sigma)]_1, v_f))$ outputs an argument indistinguishable from the real argument. The simulator just computes $[f_{\mathsf{ipc}}(\sigma)]_1$, such that the verification equation holds. That is, $[f_{\mathsf{ipc}}(\sigma)]_1 \leftarrow S(\sigma)[f(\sigma)]_1 - v_f/n_h \cdot \sigma^{d_{\mathsf{gap}}}[1]_1$. Zero-knowledge follows since in the real argument, $[f_{\mathsf{ipc}}(\sigma)]_1$ is computed the same way. □

SRS Verifiability. As noted in Sect. 2, for both Sub-ZK and updatability, it is required that the SRS is verifiable, i.e., that there exists a PPT algorithm that checks that the SRS belongs to the span of KGen. One can verify $\mathfrak{Count}$'s SRS by checking that $[\sigma]_1 \bullet [1]_2 = [1]_1 \bullet [\sigma]_2$, $[\sigma^i]_1 \bullet [1]_2 = [\sigma^{i-1}]_1 \bullet [\sigma]_2$ for $i \in [1, d_{\mathsf{gap}} + d] \setminus \{d_{\mathsf{gap}}, d_{\mathsf{gap}} + 1\}$, $[\sigma^{d_{\mathsf{gap}}+1}]_1 \bullet [1]_2 = [\sigma]_1 \bullet [\sigma^{d_{\mathsf{gap}}}]_2$, $[\sigma^{d_{\mathsf{gap}}-1}]_1 \bullet [\sigma]_2 = [1]_1 \bullet [\sigma^{d_{\mathsf{gap}}}]_2$, and $[\sigma^{n_h i}]_1 \bullet [\sigma^{d_{\mathsf{gap}}-n_h i}]_2 = [1]_1 \bullet [\sigma^{d_{\mathsf{gap}}}]_2$ for $i \in [1, \lfloor d/n_h \rfloor]$. Since, in addition, $\mathfrak{Count}$'s SRS consists of monomial evaluations only, $\mathfrak{Count}$ is updatable.

Efficiency. In $\mathfrak{Count}$, the prover outputs a single group element instead of two in Aurora's univariate sumcheck argument. The latter also requires one to implement a low-degree test, while there is no need for a low-degree test in $\mathfrak{Count}$.

Another important aspect of $\mathfrak{Count}$ is the prover's computation. In Aurora's univariate sumcheck, the prover computes polynomials R and Q, such that $f(X) = v_f/n_h + XR(X) + Q(X)\mathcal{Z}_{\mathbb{H}}(X)$; this can be done in quasilinear number of field operations. On the other hand, since in $\mathfrak{Vampire}$, S only has a small number of non-zero coefficients, the prover of $\mathfrak{Count}$ only executes a linear number of field operations. Both univariate sumchecks however require the prover to use a linear number of $\mathbb{G}_1$ operations. Linear-time *multivariate* sumchecks are well-known, and important in applications.

We emphasize that d_{gap} needs to satisfy $d_{\mathsf{gap}} \geq n_h \cdot \lfloor d/n_h \rfloor$, but it can be bigger. In $\mathfrak{Vampire}$, $d_{\mathsf{gap}} = d$.

As a drawback, $\mathfrak{Count}$'s SRS contains more elements than in Aurora's sumcheck. This is a consequence of using the ILV inner-product commitment scheme.

4 $\mathfrak{Vampire}$: New Updatable and Universal Zk-SNARK

In this section, we will use $\mathfrak{Count}$ to construct an efficient updatable and universal zk-SNARK $\mathfrak{Vampire}$ for the sparse R1CSLite constraint system. At a very high level, we use the general approach of Marlin [10], taking into account optimizations of Lunar [9] and Basilisk [26]. On top of already aggressive optimization, we use three novel techniques.

First, Marlin uses Aurora's univariate sumcheck twice. We replace it with $\mathfrak{Count}$ in one of the instantiations. (In another one, the sumcheck is for a low-degree polynomial; thus, we just use Fact 1.) Second, we use a variant of the aggregated polynomial commitment scheme of Boneh et al. [7] to batch the openings of three different polynomials at different points. While Boneh et al. [7] proposed only a randomized batch-opening protocol, we observe that in our case, it can be deterministic. Third, we use a single commitment to commit to left and right inputs of each constraint. All the techniques together remove four group elements from the communication. In the end, $\mathfrak{Vampire}$ is the most communication-efficient updatable and universal zk-SNARK for any NP-complete constraint system. (See Table 1 and the full version [22] for an efficiency comparison.)

4.1 Formulating R1CSLite as Sumcheck

Let $\mathbb{F} = \mathbb{Z}_p$. As in [9,10,26], let $\mathbb{H} = \langle \omega \rangle$ and $\mathbb{K}$ be two multiplicative subgroups of $\mathbb{F}$. We use $\mathbb{H}$ to index the rows (and columns) and $\mathbb{K}$ to index the non-zero elements of specific matrices. From now on, we assume that the R1CSLite instance $\mathcal{I} = (\mathbb{F}, \mathbb{H}, \mathbb{K}, m, m_0, \mathbf{L}, \mathbf{R})$ includes descriptions of $\mathbb{H}$ and $\mathbb{K}$.

We want to demonstrate the satisfiability of $\mathcal{I}$. Recall from Eq. (1) that for this we need to show that $\mathbf{W} \cdot \boldsymbol{z}^* = \mathbf{0}$, where $\mathbf{W} = (\mathbf{I}_{2m} \| - \mathbf{M})$, $\mathbf{M} = \binom{\mathbf{L}}{\mathbf{R}}$, and $\boldsymbol{z}^* = (\boldsymbol{z}_{\mathsf{l}}^\top \| \boldsymbol{z}_{\mathsf{r}}^\top \| (\boldsymbol{z}_{\mathsf{l}} \circ \boldsymbol{z}_{\mathsf{r}})^\top)^\top$, where $\boldsymbol{z}_{\mathsf{l}}$ and $\boldsymbol{z}_{\mathsf{r}}$ are the vectors of all left and right inputs of all R1CSLite constraints.

Zero-Knowledge. To obtain zero-knowledge, we use a technique motivated by [27]. Let $|\mathbb{H}| = n_h := 2m + b$, for a randomizing parameter $b \in \mathbb{N}$ (to be fixed to $b = 4$ in Theorem 2) that helps us to achieve zero knowledge. We add new random elements to $\boldsymbol{z}^*$ and zero elements to $\mathbf{W}$; the latter are needed not to disturb the knowledge-soundness proof. More precisely, for $\boldsymbol{r}_z \leftarrow\$ \mathbb{F}^b$, let

$$\boldsymbol{z}_\mathsf{l} := \begin{pmatrix} 1 \\ \mathbf{x} \\ \boldsymbol{z}_\mathsf{a} \end{pmatrix} \in \mathbb{F}^m, \boldsymbol{z}_\mathsf{r} := \begin{pmatrix} \mathbf{1}_{m_0+1} \\ \boldsymbol{z}_\mathsf{b} \end{pmatrix} \in \mathbb{F}^m, \text{ and } \boldsymbol{z} := \begin{pmatrix} \boldsymbol{z}_\mathsf{l} \\ \boldsymbol{z}_\mathsf{r} \\ \boldsymbol{r}_z \end{pmatrix}.$$

Let $\mathbf{I}^b := \begin{pmatrix} \mathbf{I}_m & \mathbf{0} & \mathbf{0} \\ \mathbf{0} & \mathbf{I}_m & \mathbf{0} \\ \mathbf{0} & \mathbf{0} & \mathbf{0} \end{pmatrix}$ and $\mathbf{M}^b := \begin{pmatrix} \mathbf{L} & \mathbf{0} \\ \mathbf{R} & \mathbf{0} \\ \mathbf{0} & \mathbf{0} \end{pmatrix}$ be $n_h \times n_h$ matrices. Let $\boldsymbol{z}' := \begin{pmatrix} \boldsymbol{z}_\mathsf{r} \\ \mathbf{0}_{n_h-m} \end{pmatrix}$. Our goal is to show

$$\mathbf{W}^b \cdot \begin{pmatrix} \boldsymbol{z} \\ \boldsymbol{z} \circ \boldsymbol{z}' \end{pmatrix} = \mathbf{0} , \tag{3}$$

where $\mathbf{W}^b := \left(\mathbf{I}^b \| - \mathbf{M}^b\right)$. Clearly, Eq. (3) is equivalent to $\mathbf{W} \cdot \boldsymbol{z}^* = \mathbf{0}$.

Next, Eq. (3) holds iff $\mathbf{I}^b \boldsymbol{z} - \mathbf{M}^b(\boldsymbol{z} \circ \boldsymbol{z}') = \mathbf{0}$, i.e.,

$$\forall x \in \mathbb{H}. P[x] := \textstyle\sum_{y \in \mathbb{H}} \left(\mathbf{I}^b[x,y] - \mathbf{M}^b[x,y] z'[y]\right) z[y] = 0 .$$

Language of Polynomials. Next, we replace vectors with their low-degree encodings, with say $z(Y) := \sum_{\chi \in \mathbb{H}} z[\chi] L_\chi^\mathbb{H}(Y) \in \mathbb{F}_{\leq n_h - 1}[Y]$. Let $\Lambda_\mathbb{H}^b(X,Y)$ and M^b be polynomials, fixed later, that interpolate the matrices $\mathbf{I}^b$ and $\mathbf{M}^b$. That is, $\Lambda_\mathbb{H}^b(x,y) = \mathbf{I}^b[x,y]$ and $M^b(x,y) = \mathbf{M}^b[x,y]$ for $x, y \in \mathbb{H}$. Thus, $\mathbf{I}^b[x,y]z[y] = \Lambda_\mathbb{H}^b(x,y)z(y)$ for any $x, y \in \mathbb{H}$. Moreover, since $z(y\omega^m) = z[y\omega^m] = z'[y]$ for $y \in \{\omega^0, \dots, \omega^{m-1}\}$, we get $\mathbf{M}^b[x,y]z'[y]z[y] = M^b(x,y)z(y\omega^m)z(y)$. On the other hand, for $x \in \mathbb{H}$ and $y \in \{\omega^m, \dots, \omega^{n_h-1}\}$, the value of $z[y\omega^m]$ does not matter since we multiply it by $M^b(x,y) = 0$.

Thus, Eq. (3) is equivalent to $\forall x \in \mathbb{H}. P(x) = 0$, where

$$P(X) := \textstyle\sum_{y \in \mathbb{H}} \psi(X,y), \tag{4}$$

$$\psi(X,Y) := \left(\Lambda_\mathbb{H}^b(X,Y) - M^b(X,Y)z(Y\omega^m)\right) z(Y) . \tag{5}$$

To simplify it further, $\Lambda_\mathbb{H}^b(X,Y)$ and $M^b(X,Y)$ have to satisfy additional conditions that we define in the rest of this subsection.

Interpolating $\mathbf{I}^b$. Following Lunar [9], we interpolate $\mathbf{I}$ with the function

$$\Lambda_\mathbb{H}(X,Y) := \frac{\mathcal{Z}_\mathbb{H}(X)Y - \mathcal{Z}_\mathbb{H}(Y)X}{n_h(X-Y)} . \tag{6}$$

$\Lambda_\mathbb{H}$ satisfies the following properties: (1) $\Lambda_\mathbb{H}(x,y)$ is PPT computable, (2) $\Lambda_\mathbb{H}$ is a polynomial (this follows since $\mathcal{Z}_\mathbb{H}(X)Y - \mathcal{Z}_\mathbb{H}(Y)X = X - Y + XY(X^{n_h-1} - Y^{n_h-1}) = (X-Y)(1 + XY(\sum_{i=0}^{n_h-2} X^{n_h-2-i}Y^i))$ divides by $X - Y$), (3) $\Lambda_\mathbb{H}$ is symmetric, $\Lambda_\mathbb{H}(X,Y) = \Lambda_\mathbb{H}(Y,X)$, (4) $\Lambda_\mathbb{H}(x,y)$ interpolates $\mathbf{I}$ over $\mathbb{H}^2$, i.e., $\forall x, y \in \mathbb{H}. \Lambda_\mathbb{H}(x,y) = \mathbf{I}[x,y]$ (this follows since $\mathcal{Z}_\mathbb{H}(x)y - \mathcal{Z}_\mathbb{H}(y)x = 0$ for all $x \neq y \in \mathbb{H}$ and $1 + XY(\sum_{i=0}^{n_h-2} X^{n_h-2-i}Y^i) = 1 + (n_h - 1)x^{n_h} = 1 + n_h - 1 = n_h$ when $X = Y = x \in \mathbb{H}$), (5) $\Lambda_\mathbb{H}(x,y) = L_x^\mathbb{H}(y)$ for any $x \in \mathbb{H}, y \in \mathbb{F}$. Thus, $\{\Lambda_\mathbb{H}(x,Y)\}_{x \in \mathbb{H}}$ is a basis of $\mathbb{F}_{\leq |\mathbb{H}|-1}[Y]$.

It is natural to define the interpolating polynomial of $\mathbf{I}^b$ as

$$\Lambda^b_{\mathbb{H}}(X,Y) := \Lambda_{\mathbb{H}}(X,Y) - \sum_{i=1}^{b} \ell^{\mathbb{H}}_{n_h-b+i}(X)\ell^{\mathbb{H}}_{n_h-b+i}(Y) .$$

Clearly, if b is small, then $\Lambda^b_{\mathbb{H}}(X,Y)$ is efficiently computable. Moreover, $\Lambda^b_{\mathbb{H}}(X,Y)$ is symmetric since $\Lambda_{\mathbb{H}}(X,Y)$ is symmetric.

Interpolating $\mathbf{M}^b$. We use the sparse matrix encoding of $\mathbf{M}^b$ from Marlin [10] that keeps track of the matrix's non-zero entries. Let $\mathcal{NZ} := \{(i,j) \in \mathbb{H} \times \mathbb{H} : \mathbf{M}^b[i,j] \neq 0\}$ be the set of indices where $\mathbf{M}^b$ is non-zero. Let $\mathbb{K}$ be the minimum-size multiplicative subgroup of $\mathbb{F}$ such that $n_k := |\mathbb{K}| \geq |\mathcal{NZ}|$.[6] We encode $\mathbf{M}^b$ by using polynomials row and col to keep track of the indices of its non-zero entries while using a polynomial val for the values of these entries. That is, $\forall \kappa \in \mathbb{K}$, $\mathsf{row}(\kappa) \in \mathbb{H}$ is the row index of the κth element (by using the natural ordering of $\mathbb{H}^2$) of $\mathcal{NZ}$, $\mathsf{col}(\kappa) \in \mathbb{H}$ is the column index of the κth element of $\mathcal{NZ}$, and $\mathsf{val}(\kappa) = \mathbf{M}^b[\mathsf{row}(\kappa), \mathsf{col}(\kappa)] \in \mathbb{F}$ is the corresponding matrix entry. Let

$$\mathsf{row}(Z) := \sum_{\kappa\in\mathbb{K}} \mathsf{row}(\kappa) L^{\mathbb{K}}_{\kappa}(Z) \in \mathbb{F}_{\leq n_k-1}[Z]$$

be the low-degree extension of the vector $(\mathsf{row}(\kappa))_{\kappa\in\mathbb{K}}$. Let $\mathsf{col}(Z)$ and $\mathsf{val}(Z)$ be the low-degree extensions of $(\mathsf{col}(\kappa))_{\kappa\in\mathbb{K}}$ and $(\mathsf{val}(\kappa))_{\kappa\in\mathbb{K}}$. Let $\mathsf{zcv}(Z)$, $\mathsf{rcv}(Z)$, $\mathsf{zrow}(Z)$, $\mathsf{zcol}(Z)$, $\mathsf{rc}(Z)$, and $\mathsf{zrc}(Z)$ be the low-degree encodings of $Z\mathsf{col}(Z)\mathsf{val}(Z)$, $\mathsf{row}(Z)\mathsf{col}(Z)\mathsf{val}(Z)$, $Z\mathsf{row}(Z)$, $Z\mathsf{col}(Z)$, $\mathsf{row}(Z)\mathsf{col}(Z)$, and $Z\mathsf{row}(Z)\mathsf{col}(Z)$. For example,

$$\mathsf{rcv}(Z) := \sum_{\kappa\in\mathbb{K}} \mathsf{row}(\kappa)\mathsf{col}(\kappa)\mathsf{val}(\kappa) L^{\mathbb{K}}_{\kappa}(Z) \in \mathbb{F}_{\leq n_k-1}[Z] .$$

We define $M^b \in \mathbb{F}[X,Y]$ that interpolates $\mathbf{M}^b$, as the low-degree extension of

$$\forall x,y \in \mathbb{H}. M^b(x,y) := \mathbf{M}^b[x,y] = \sum_{\kappa\in\mathbb{K}} \mathsf{val}(\kappa)\Lambda_{\mathbb{H}}(\mathsf{row}(\kappa),x)\Lambda_{\mathbb{H}}(\mathsf{col}(\kappa),y) .$$

Next, $\Lambda_{\mathbb{H}}(\mathsf{row}(\kappa),x) = (\mathcal{Z}_{\mathbb{H}}(\mathsf{row}(\kappa))x - \mathcal{Z}_{\mathbb{H}}(x)\mathsf{row}(\kappa))/(n_h(\mathsf{row}(\kappa) - x))$. Since $\mathcal{Z}_{\mathbb{H}}(\mathsf{row}(\kappa)) = 0$, $\Lambda_{\mathbb{H}}(\mathsf{row}(\kappa),x) = \mathcal{Z}_{\mathbb{H}}(x)\mathsf{row}(\kappa)/(n_h(x - \mathsf{row}(\kappa)))$. Similarly, $\Lambda_{\mathbb{H}}(\mathsf{col}(\kappa),y) = \mathcal{Z}_{\mathbb{H}}(y)\mathsf{col}(\kappa)/(n_h(y - \mathsf{col}(\kappa)))$. Thus,

$$\begin{aligned}\forall x,y \in \mathbb{H}. M^b(x,y) &= \sum_{\kappa\in\mathbb{K}} \mathsf{val}(\kappa) \cdot \frac{\mathcal{Z}_{\mathbb{H}}(x)\mathsf{row}(\kappa)}{n_h(x-\mathsf{row}(\kappa))} \cdot \frac{\mathcal{Z}_{\mathbb{H}}(y)\mathsf{col}(\kappa)}{n_h(y-\mathsf{col}(\kappa))} \\ &= \frac{\mathcal{Z}_{\mathbb{H}}(x)\mathcal{Z}_{\mathbb{H}}(y)}{n_h^2} \sum_{\kappa\in\mathbb{K}} \frac{\mathsf{rcv}(\kappa)}{(x-\mathsf{row}(\kappa))(y-\mathsf{col}(\kappa))} \\ &\overset{(*)}{=} \frac{\mathcal{Z}_{\mathbb{H}}(x)\mathcal{Z}_{\mathbb{H}}(y)}{n_h^2} \sum_{\kappa\in\mathbb{K}} \frac{\mathsf{rcv}(\kappa)}{xy-x\mathsf{col}(\kappa)-y\mathsf{row}(\kappa)+\mathsf{rc}(\kappa)} ,\end{aligned}$$

where $(*)$ follows from $\forall \kappa \in \mathbb{K}. \mathsf{rc}(\kappa) = \mathsf{col}(\kappa)\mathsf{row}(\kappa)$. Thus, we define

$$M^b(X,Y) := \frac{\mathcal{Z}_{\mathbb{H}}(X)\mathcal{Z}_{\mathbb{H}}(Y)}{n_h^2} \sum_{\kappa\in\mathbb{K}} \frac{\mathsf{rcv}(\kappa)}{XY-X\mathsf{col}(\kappa)-Y\mathsf{row}(\kappa)+\mathsf{rc}(\kappa)} . \tag{7}$$

Since $\deg_X M^b(X,Y) \leq |\mathbb{H}| - 1$, $\forall y \in \mathbb{H}. M^b(X,y) = \sum_{\chi\in\mathbb{H}} M^b(\chi,y)\Lambda_{\mathbb{H}}(\chi,X)$. Clearly, M^b interpolates $\mathbf{M}^b$.

[6] $\mathbb{H}$ and $\mathbb{K}$ can be arbitrary subsets of $\mathbb{F}$, but the most efficient algorithms are known when they are multiplicative subgroups. One can assume $\mathbb{K} = \mathbb{H}$ by adding all-zero rows and columns to the matrix, but we generally do not need that $\mathbb{K} = \mathbb{H}$. Keeping $|\mathbb{K}|$ and $|\mathbb{H}|$ flexible allows us to achieve different trade-offs.

Getting to Sumcheck. Next, we show that, under mild conditions on interpolating matrices that the above encodings satisfy, $\forall x \in \mathbb{H}. P(x) = 0$ (and thus also Eq. (3)) is equivalent to $\sum_{y \in \mathbb{H}} \psi(X, y) = 0$.

Lemma 4. *Assume* $\deg_X \Lambda_{\mathbb{H}}(X,Y), \deg_X M^b(X,Y) \leq |\mathbb{H}| - 1$. *Then,* $\forall x \in \mathbb{H}. P(x) = 0$ *iff* $\sum_{y \in \mathbb{H}} \psi(X, y) = 0$.

Proof. ($\Rightarrow$) Assume $\forall x \in \mathbb{H}. P(x) = 0$. Recall from Eq. (5) that $\psi(X, y) = (\Lambda^b_{\mathbb{H}}(X, y) - M^b(X, y) z(y\omega^m)) z(y)$. Since $\deg_X \Lambda_{\mathbb{H}}(X,Y), \deg_X M^b(X,Y) \leq |\mathbb{H}| - 1$, then also $\deg_X \psi(X, y) \leq |\mathbb{H}| - 1$. Thus,

$$\sum_{y \in \mathbb{H}} \psi(X, y) = \sum_{y \in \mathbb{H}} \sum_{x \in \mathbb{H}} \psi(x, y) L_x(X) \stackrel{4}{=} \sum_{x \in \mathbb{H}} P(x) L_x(X) \stackrel{(*)}{=} 0 ,$$

where (*) follows from $\forall x \in \mathbb{H}. P(x) = 0$.
($\Leftarrow$) Let $\sum_{y \in \mathbb{H}} \psi(X, y) = 0$. By Eq. (4), $\forall x \in \mathbb{H}. P(x) = \sum_{y \in \mathbb{H}} \psi(x, y) = 0$. $\square$

To enable efficient verification that the public input was correctly computed, the prover transmits $[\tilde{z}(\sigma)]_1$, for the polynomial $\tilde{z}(Y)$ defined as follows. Let

$$\begin{aligned} \mathsf{Z}_{\mathsf{inp}}(Y) :=& \prod_{i=1}^{m_0+1} (Y - \omega^{i-1})(Y - \omega^{m+i-1}) \in \mathbb{F}_{\leq 2(m_0+1)}[Y] , \\ \mathsf{inp}(Y) :=& \ell_1^{\mathbb{H}}(Y) + \sum_{i=1}^{m_0} \mathbb{x}_i \ell_{i+1}^{\mathbb{H}}(Y) + \sum_{i=1}^{m_0+1} \ell_{m+i}^{\mathbb{H}}(Y) \in \mathbb{F}_{\leq n_h - 1}[Y] , \\ \tilde{z}(Y) :=& \sum_{i=1}^{m-m_0-1} \boldsymbol{z}_{\mathsf{a}}[i] \frac{\ell_{m_0+1+i}^{\mathbb{H}}(Y)}{\mathsf{Z}_{\mathsf{inp}}(Y)} + \sum_{i=1}^{m-m_0-1} \boldsymbol{z}_{\mathsf{b}}[i] \frac{\ell_{m+m_0+1+i}^{\mathbb{H}}(Y)}{\mathsf{Z}_{\mathsf{inp}}(Y)} + \\ & \sum_{i=1}^{b} \boldsymbol{r}_z[i] \frac{\ell_{2m+i}^{\mathbb{H}}(Y)}{\mathsf{Z}_{\mathsf{inp}}(Y)} . \end{aligned} \tag{8}$$

Since $\ell_i^{\mathbb{H}}(Y) = \prod_{j \neq i} (Y - \omega^{j-1}) / (\omega^{i-1} - \omega^{j-1})$, $\tilde{z}(Y) \in \mathbb{F}_{\leq n_h - 2m_0 - 3}[Y]$. Thus, $\mathsf{Z}_{\mathsf{inp}}(Y) \tilde{z}(Y) = \sum_{i=1}^{m-m_0-1} \boldsymbol{z}_{\mathsf{a}}[i] \ell_{m_0+1+i}^{\mathbb{H}}(Y) + \sum_{i=1}^{m-m_0-1} \boldsymbol{z}_{\mathsf{b}}[i] \ell_{m+m_0+1+i}^{\mathbb{H}}(Y) + \sum_{i=1}^{b} \boldsymbol{r}_z[i] \ell_{2m+i}^{\mathbb{H}}(Y)$ interpolates $(\mathbf{0}_{m_0+1}^\top \| \boldsymbol{z}_{\mathsf{a}}^\top \| \mathbf{0}_{m_0+1}^\top \| \boldsymbol{z}_{\mathsf{b}}^\top \| \boldsymbol{r}_z^\top)^\top$. Moreover,

$$z(Y) = \mathsf{Z}_{\mathsf{inp}}(Y) \tilde{z}(Y) + \mathsf{inp}(Y) \in \mathbb{F}_{\leq n_h - 1}[Y] . \tag{9}$$

Thus, the existence of a polynomial $\tilde{z}(Y)$, such that Eq. (9) holds, guarantees that $z(Y)$ interpolates $(1 \| \mathbb{x}^\top \| \boldsymbol{z}_{\mathsf{a}}^\top \| \mathbf{1}_{m_0+1}^\top \| \boldsymbol{z}_{\mathsf{b}}^\top \| \boldsymbol{r}_z^\top)^\top$ for some $\boldsymbol{z}_{\mathsf{a}}$, $\boldsymbol{z}_{\mathsf{b}}$, and $\boldsymbol{r}_z$.

4.2 From Sumcheck to Vampire

According to the preceding discussion, one can handle R1CSLite by proving that $\sum_{y \in \mathbb{H}} \psi(X, y) = 0$. In the current subsection, we construct an argument for the latter. We replace X with a random α chosen by the verifier, obtaining the polynomial $\psi_\alpha(Y) := \psi(\alpha, Y)$. We use Count to show that $\sum_{y \in \mathbb{H}} \psi_\alpha(y) = 0$. For this, as in Sect. 3, the prover computes the polynomial ψ_{ipc} and the verifier checks $\varphi(Y) := \psi_\alpha(Y) S(Y) - \psi_{\mathsf{ipc}}(Y)$ is a zero polynomial. The latter can be done by KZG-opening all involved polynomials (e.g., $\tilde{z}(Y)$; see Eq. (5)), but this is inefficient. Instead, the prover KZG-opens $\tilde{z}(Y)$ at $Y = \beta\omega^m$ and $\Phi(Y)$, $M^b(\alpha, Y)$ at $Y = \beta$, where (1) Φ is a polynomial defined so that $\Phi(\beta) = \varphi(\beta) = 0$, and (2) one can verify efficiently the correctness, given $v_z \leftarrow \tilde{z}(\beta\omega^m)$ and $v_M \leftarrow$

$M^b(\alpha, \beta)$. This requires us to open a polynomial related to the ILV-opening of $\psi_\alpha(Y)$. We aggregate two KZG-openings by using the technique of Boneh et al. [7]. Finally, we use a univariate sumcheck to check the correctness of v_M; this step is complicated, but it follows closely [9,10]. Importantly, we also show that one of the two commitments from the second sumcheck can be considered an aggregated KZG-opening and thus batched with other KZG-openings.

To simplify some formulas, we assume always $n_h > 3$. This is w.l.o.g., since $n_h = 2m + b$, $m \geq 1$, and $b \geq 2$.

Details. Let $\alpha \leftarrow_\$ \mathbb{F} \backslash \mathbb{H}$ be sampled by the verifier. (We explain later why $\alpha \notin \mathbb{H}$.) To test that $\sum_{y \in \mathbb{H}} \psi(X, y) = 0$, define

$$\psi_\alpha(Y) := \psi(\alpha, Y) \in \mathbb{F}_{\leq d}[Y] .$$

From Eqs. (5) and (9), we get $\psi_\alpha(Y) = \left(\Lambda^b_{\mathbb{H}}(\alpha, Y) - M^b(\alpha, Y) z(Y\omega^m)\right) \cdot \left(\mathcal{Z}_{\mathsf{inp}}(Y)\tilde{z}(Y) + \mathsf{inp}(Y)\right)$. Clearly, one can set

$$d := \deg \psi_\alpha = 3(n_h - 1) . \tag{10}$$

We use $\mathfrak{Count}$ to prove that $\sum_{y \in \mathbb{H}} \psi_\alpha(y) = 0$. As in Lemma 2, we define

$$\begin{aligned} S(Y) &:= \textstyle\sum_{i=0}^{\lfloor d/n_h \rfloor} Y^{d_{\mathsf{gap}} - n_h i} \in \mathbb{F}_{\leq d_{\mathsf{gap}}}[Y] , \\ \psi_{\mathsf{ipc}}(Y) &:= \psi_\alpha(Y) S(Y) \in \mathsf{PolyPunc}_{\mathbb{F}}(d, d_{\mathsf{gap}}, Y) . \end{aligned} \tag{11}$$

Here, $d_{\mathsf{gap}} \in \mathbb{N}$ is some integer, such that $S(Y)$ and $\psi_{\mathsf{ipc}}(Y)$ are polynomials, i.e., $d_{\mathsf{gap}} \geq n_h \cdot \lfloor d/n_h \rfloor = n_h \cdot \lfloor 3(n_h - 1)/n_h \rfloor = 2n_h$. (This holds for $n_h \geq 3$.) Taking into account later considerations, we set

$$d_{\mathsf{gap}} := 3(n_h - 1) . \tag{12}$$

Thus, $S(Y) = Y^{d_{\mathsf{gap}}} + Y^{d_{\mathsf{gap}} - n_h} + Y^{d_{\mathsf{gap}} - 2n_h} = Y^{3n_h - 3} + Y^{2n_h - 3} + Y^{n_h - 3}$.

According to Lemma 2, we need to check that the coefficient of $Y^{d_{\mathsf{gap}}}$ in $\psi_\alpha(Y)S(Y)$ is 0. We do it by checking that

(i) $\psi_{\mathsf{ipc}}(Y) \in \mathsf{PolyPunc}_{\mathbb{F}}(d, d_{\mathsf{gap}}, Y)$, and
(ii) $\psi_{\mathsf{ipc}}(Y)$ is the correct ILV-opening polynomial, i.e.,

$$\begin{aligned} \varphi(Y) :=& \psi_\alpha(Y) S(Y) - \psi_{\mathsf{ipc}}(Y) \\ =& \left(\Lambda^b_{\mathbb{H}}(\alpha, Y) - M^b(\alpha, Y) z(Y\omega^m)\right) \left(\mathcal{Z}_{\mathsf{inp}}(Y)\tilde{z}(Y) + \mathsf{inp}(Y)\right) \cdot S(Y) - \psi_{\mathsf{ipc}}(Y) \end{aligned}$$

is a zero polynomial.

The prover sends to the verifier KZG-commitments to $\tilde{z}(Y)$ and $\psi_{\mathsf{ipc}}(Y)$. Checking i is free in the pairing-based setting. To check ii, we verify that $\varphi(\beta) = 0$, where $\beta \in C_\beta \subset \mathbb{F} \backslash \mathbb{H}$ is sampled by the verifier. (We will define and motivate C_β later.) More precisely, we verify that $\varphi(\beta) = 0$, where $M^b(\alpha, \beta)$ is substituted by a value v_M computed by the prover. (The latter means that the verifier does not have to compute $M^b(\alpha, \beta)$ itself.) We first describe how to check that $\varphi(\beta) = 0$, assuming v_M is correct. After that, we use another sumcheck instantiation to prove that v_M is correctly computed.

First: checking $\varphi(\beta) = 0$. A straightforward check that $\varphi(\beta) = 0$ requires, on top of sending v_M, the prover to KZG-open $\tilde{z}(Y)$ both at $Y = \beta$ and $Y = \beta\omega^m$ and $\psi_{\mathsf{ipc}}(Y)$ at $Y = \beta$. (The verifier can efficiently evaluate other polynomials like $\Lambda^b_{\mathbb{H}}(X, Y)$, $\mathcal{Z}_{\mathsf{inp}}(Y)$, and $S(Y)$ at $(X, Y) = (\alpha, \beta)$ itself.)

To improve on efficiency, we *implicitly* KZG-commit to Φ, where

$$\begin{aligned} \Phi(Y) :=& (\Psi(Y)S(Y) - \psi_{\mathsf{ipc}}(Y))/S(Y) = \Psi(Y) - \psi_\alpha(Y) \in \mathbb{F}_{\leq d}[Y] \text{ , and} \\ \Psi(Y) :=& \left(\Lambda^b_{\mathbb{H}}(\alpha, \beta) - v_M \cdot z(\beta\omega^m)\right) (\mathcal{Z}_{\mathsf{inp}}(\beta)\tilde{z}(Y) + \mathsf{inp}(\beta)) \in \mathbb{F}_{\leq n_h - 2m_0 - 3}[Y] \ . \end{aligned} \quad (13)$$

Ψ is obtained from ψ_α by replacing $M^b(\alpha, \beta)$ with v_M and all but one occurrences of Y with β. Φ is a low-degree polynomial satisfying $\Phi(\beta) = \varphi(\beta) = 0$.

We open KZG-commitments to $\tilde{z}(Y)$ at $Y = \beta\omega^m$ (in order to compute $z(\beta\omega^m)$) and $\Phi(Y)$ at $Y = \beta$. For this, the prover sends

$$v_z \leftarrow \tilde{z}(\beta\omega^m) \in \mathbb{F} \ .$$

Since $\Phi(\beta) = 0$, $\Phi(\beta)$ is not transferred. We can open and verify the KZG-commitment to Φ (see Eq. (13)) since we have KZG-commitments to $\tilde{z}$ and ψ_{ipc} (the need for the latter becomes apparent soon), KZG is homomorphic, and the verifier knows all other information present in Φ like $\mathsf{inp}(\beta)$ and v_M. More precisely, the prover batch-opens the two KZG-commitments by computing the KZG-opening polynomials

$$\begin{aligned} \tilde{z}_{\mathsf{pc}}(Y) :=& \tfrac{\tilde{z}(Y) - \tilde{z}(\beta\omega^m)}{Y - \beta\omega^m} \in \mathbb{F}_{\leq n_h - 2m_0 - 4}[Y] \ , \\ \Phi_{\mathsf{pc}}(Y) :=& \tfrac{\Phi(Y) - \Phi(\beta)}{Y - \beta} = \tfrac{\Psi(Y) - \psi_\alpha(Y)}{Y - \beta} \in \mathbb{F}_{\leq d-1}[Y] \ . \end{aligned}$$

Since the prover batches these openings together with one more opening, we will explain the batching process later.

Second (correctness of v_M). We modify a technique from [9,10] by using batching. Recall that M^b satisfies Eq. (7). Moreover, $\deg_X M^b(X, Y)$, $\deg_Y M^b(X, Y) \leq n_h - 1$. Thus, $M^b(\alpha, \beta) = \sum_{\kappa \in \mathbb{K}} T(\kappa) \in \mathbb{F}$, where

$$\begin{aligned} \mathsf{num}(Z) :=& \mathcal{Z}_{\mathbb{H}}(\alpha)\mathcal{Z}_{\mathbb{H}}(\beta)/n_h^2 \cdot \mathsf{rcv}(Z) \in \mathbb{F}_{\leq n_k - 1}[Z] \ , \\ \mathsf{den}(Z) :=& \alpha\beta - \alpha \cdot \mathsf{col}(Z) - \beta \cdot \mathsf{row}(Z) + \mathsf{rc}(Z) \in \mathbb{F}_{\leq n_k - 1}[Z] \ , \\ T(Z) :=& \tfrac{\mathsf{num}(Z)}{\mathsf{den}(Z)} \in \mathbb{F}(Z) \ . \end{aligned} \quad (14)$$

Here, we need $\mathsf{den}(\kappa) = (\alpha - \mathsf{row}(\kappa))(\beta - \mathsf{col}(\kappa)) \neq 0$ for any $\kappa \in \mathbb{K}$. This explains why we chose $\alpha, \beta \notin \mathbb{H}$.

We use a sumcheck to check that $v_M = M^b(\alpha, \beta)$. Since this sumcheck is over a low-degree polynomial, we do not need to use $\mathfrak{Count}$'s full power. Let

$$\widehat{T}(Z) := \textstyle\sum_{\kappa \in \mathbb{K}} T(\kappa) L^{\mathbb{K}}_\kappa(Z) \in \mathbb{F}_{\leq n_k - 1}[Z] \ .$$

Clearly, $\mathsf{num}(Z) - \widehat{T}(Z)\mathsf{den}(Z) \equiv 0 \pmod{\mathcal{Z}_{\mathbb{K}}(Z)}$. Since $\sum_{\kappa \in \mathbb{K}} \widehat{T}(\kappa) = v_M$, by Fact 1, $\widehat{T}(Z) = ZR(Z) + v_M/n_k$ for

$$R(X) \leftarrow (\widehat{T}(Z) - v_M/n_k)/Z \in \mathbb{F}_{\leq n_k - 2}[Z] \ . \ .$$

Thus, $\mathsf{num}(Z) - (ZR(Z) + v_M/n_k)\mathsf{den}(Z) \equiv 0 \pmod{\mathcal{Z}_{\mathbb{K}}(Z)}$. Since this equality has to hold only when $Z \in \mathbb{K}$, we modify it as follows. Let

$$Q(Z) \leftarrow (\mathsf{num}(Z) - R(Z) \cdot \mathsf{zden}(Z) - v_M/n_k \cdot \mathsf{den}(Z))/\mathcal{Z}_{\mathbb{K}}(Z) \in \mathbb{F}_{\leq n_k - 3}[Z]$$

be such that

$$\mathsf{num}(Z) - R(Z) \cdot \mathsf{zden}(Z) - v_M/n_k \cdot \mathsf{den}(Z) = Q(Z)\mathcal{Z}_{\mathbb{K}}(Z) \text{ , where} \quad (15)$$

$$\mathsf{zden}(Z) := \alpha\beta Z - \alpha\mathsf{zcol}(Z) - \beta\mathsf{zrow}(Z) + \mathsf{zrc}(Z) \in \mathbb{F}_{\leq n_k - 1}[Z] \text{ .} \quad (16)$$

Thus, $\mathsf{zden}(\kappa) = \kappa\mathsf{den}(\kappa)$ for $\kappa \in \mathbb{K}$. This rewriting minimizes the degree of polynomials (e.g., $\mathsf{zcol}(Z) \in \mathbb{F}_{\leq n_k - 1}[Z]$ while $Z\mathsf{col}(Z) \in \mathbb{F}_{\leq n_k}[Z]$).

Marlin and Lunar [9,10] now transferred polynomial commitment to $Q(Z)$. We improve on it, by interpreting Eq. (15) as saying that the polynomial $\mathsf{num}(Z) - R(Z) \cdot \mathsf{zden}(Z) - v_M/n_k \cdot \mathsf{den}(Z)$ opens to 0 at all points $Z \in \mathbb{K}$. Thus, $Q(Z)$ is an aggregated polynomial *opening* of the left-hand side of Eq. (15) at all points of $\mathbb{K}$. Importantly, we can aggregate this opening with the openings $\tilde{z}_{\mathsf{pc}}(Z)$ and $\Phi_{\mathsf{pc}}(Z)$ from before. Hence, we can save an additional one group element. (We will explain batching in a few paragraphs.)

Thus, the prover only commits to R. When we add to $\mathsf{srs}_{\mathcal{R}}$ elements like $[\mathsf{rcv}(\sigma), \mathsf{col}(\sigma)]_2$, the verifier can compute the $\mathbb{G}_2$ elements in the last equation since he knows α and β. Thus, polynomials like $[\mathsf{rcv}(\sigma)]_2$ need to be in $\mathsf{srs}_{\mathcal{R}}$, while monomials, needed for the V to be able to compute $\mathsf{srs}_{\mathcal{R}}$, need to be in srs. This explains the definition of $\mathsf{srs}_{\mathcal{R}}$ in Fig. 2.

One needs to check that $\deg R \leq n_k - 2$. To perform this test without increasing the argument size, we use a second trapdoor $\tau \leftarrow\!\!\$\ \mathbb{F}^*$. We add $[(\sigma^i\tau)_{i=0}^{n_k-2}]_2$ to the SRS and use $[R(\sigma)\tau, Q(\sigma)\tau]_1$ instead of $[R(\sigma), Q(\sigma)]_1$. This modifies the verification equations. The idea is that if the SRS contains $[(\sigma^i)_{i\in\mathcal{S}}, (\sigma^i\tau)_{i\in\mathcal{S}'}]_1$, then a verification $[a]_1 \bullet [1]_2 = [b]_1 \bullet [\tau]_2$ guarantees in the AGM that $a \in \mathrm{span}(\sigma^i\tau)_{i\in\mathcal{S}'}$.

Batching. The prover batches the openings of $\tilde{z}(Y)$ at $Y = \beta\omega^m$, $\Phi(Y)$ at $Y = \beta$, and the left-hand side of Eq. (15) at all $Y \in \mathbb{K}$ as $[B_{\mathsf{pc}}(\sigma, \tau)]_1 \leftarrow [\tilde{z}_{\mathsf{pc}}(\sigma) + \Phi_{\mathsf{pc}}(\sigma) + Q(\sigma)\tau]_1$. Notably, since the polynomial openings are at different locations (β, $\beta\omega^m$, and all points of $\mathbb{K}$, correspondingly), one does not have to randomize this check. (See Sect. 5.1 for formal proof.) The latter is a general fact, not mentioned in [7,13] and is thus an independent contribution.

Following [7,13], the verifier must check that $[\tilde{z}(\sigma) - v_z]_1 \bullet [(\sigma - \beta)\mathcal{Z}_{\mathbb{K}}(\sigma)]_2 + [\Phi(\sigma)]_1 \bullet [(\sigma - \beta\omega^m)\mathcal{Z}_{\mathbb{K}}(\sigma)]_2 + [\mathsf{num}(\sigma) - R(\sigma)\mathsf{zden}(\sigma) - v_M/n_k \cdot \mathsf{den}(\sigma)]_1 \bullet [(\sigma - \beta)(\sigma - \beta\omega^m)]_2 = [B_{\mathsf{pc}}(\sigma)]_1 \bullet [(\sigma - \beta)(\sigma - \beta\omega^m)\mathcal{Z}_{\mathbb{K}}(\sigma)]_2$, where $[\Phi(\sigma)]_1 = [\Psi(\sigma)]_1 - [\psi_\alpha(\sigma)]_1$. Since the verifier does not know $[\psi_\alpha(\sigma)]_1$ but knows $[\psi_{\mathsf{ipc}}(\sigma)]_1 = [\psi_\alpha(\sigma)S(\sigma)]_1$, we multiply each term of the verification equation by $S(\sigma)$. We also modify the last addend on the left-hand side to allow the prover and the verifier to compute it given the terms given in the SRS. Finally, we use the trapdoor τ because we need to do a low-degree test.

As part of $[B_{\mathsf{pc}}(\sigma)]_1$, the prover has to compute $[\Phi_{\mathsf{pc}}(\sigma)]_1 \leftarrow [(\Phi(\sigma) - \psi_\alpha(\sigma))/(\sigma - \beta)]_1$, where $\Phi_{\mathsf{pc}} \in \mathbb{F}_{\leq d-1}[Y]$ and σ is a trapdoor. For $\mathfrak{Count}$ to

$\mathsf{Pgen}(1^\lambda)$: generate p as usually, assuming that $n_h, n_k \mid (p-1)$ and $3 \nmid n_k$;

$\mathsf{KGen}(\mathsf{p}, n_h, n_k)$: $\mathcal{S}_1(X, X_\tau) = \{(X^i)_{i=0:i\neq d_{\mathsf{gap}}}^{d_{\mathsf{gap}}+d}, (X^i X_\tau)_{i=0}^{n_k-2}\}$;
$\mathcal{S}_2(X) = \{1, X, X^2, X^{n_k}, X^{n_k+1}, (X^{d_{\mathsf{gap}}-jn_h+i})_{j\in\{0,1,2\}, i\in[0,n_k+2]}\}$;
$\sigma, \tau \leftarrow\!\!\$\, \mathbb{F}^*$; $\mathsf{td} \leftarrow (\sigma, \tau)$;
$\mathsf{srs} \leftarrow (\mathsf{p}, n_h, n_k, [g(\sigma,\tau) : g \in \mathcal{S}_1(X, X_\tau)]_1, [g(\sigma) : g \in \mathcal{S}_2(X)]_2)$;

$\mathsf{Derive}(\mathsf{srs}, \mathcal{I})$: $\mathsf{ek}_\mathcal{R} \leftarrow (\mathsf{p}, \mathcal{I}, [g(\sigma,\tau) : g \in \mathcal{S}_1(X, X_\tau)]_1)$;

$$\mathsf{srs}_\mathcal{R} \leftarrow \begin{pmatrix} \left[(\sigma^i S(\sigma))_{i=0}^3, \mathsf{rcv}(\sigma)S(\sigma), \mathsf{col}(\sigma)S(\sigma), \mathsf{row}(\sigma)S(\sigma), \mathsf{rc}(\sigma)S(\sigma), \mathcal{Z}_\mathbb{K}(\sigma)\right]_2, \\ \left[\sigma\mathcal{Z}_\mathbb{K}(\sigma), (\sigma^i \mathsf{zcol}(\sigma)S(\sigma), \sigma^i \mathsf{zrow}(\sigma)S(\sigma), \sigma^i \mathsf{zrc}(\sigma)S(\sigma), \sigma^i \mathcal{Z}_\mathbb{K}(\sigma)S(\sigma))_{i=0}^2\right]_2 \end{pmatrix}$$

$\mathsf{vk}_\mathcal{R} \leftarrow (\mathsf{p}, \mathcal{I}, [1, \tau, \sigma\tau, \sigma^2\tau]_1, [1]_2, \mathsf{srs}_\mathcal{R})$;

Fig. 2. 𝔙𝔞𝔪𝔭𝔦𝔯𝔢's parameter and SRS generation, where $\mathcal{I} = (\mathbb{F}, \mathbb{H}, \mathbb{K}, m, m_0, \mathbf{L}, \mathbf{R})$.

be secure, the SRS cannot contain $[\sigma^{d_{\mathsf{gap}}}]_1$. Hence, we need to assume $d \leq d_{\mathsf{gap}}$. This motivates the choice of $d_{\mathsf{gap}} = 3(n_h - 1)$ in Eq. (10). The batch opening reduces the communication by two group elements.

4.3 Description of 𝔙𝔞𝔪𝔭𝔦𝔯𝔢

In Figs. 2 and 3, we describe interactive 𝔙𝔞𝔪𝔭𝔦𝔯𝔢, the new succinct interactive zero-knowledge argument with a specializable universal SRS. For the sake of completeness, Figs. 2 and 3 define all used polynomials. Since this argument is public-coin and has a constant number of rounds, we can apply the Fiat-Shamir heuristic (we omit the details) to obtain the zk-SNARK 𝔙𝔞𝔪𝔭𝔦𝔯𝔢.

We sample the challenge β from the set

$$C_\beta = \left\{ \beta \in \mathbb{F} \;\middle|\; \begin{array}{c} \beta \notin (\mathbb{H} \cup \mathbb{K} \cup \{0, \sigma, \sigma/\omega^m\}) \wedge \\ S(\beta) \neq 0 \wedge S(\beta\omega^m) \neq 0 \wedge \beta\omega^m \notin \mathbb{K} \end{array} \right\}.$$

We need $\beta \notin \{\sigma, \sigma/\omega^m\}$ to get perfect zero-knowledge (see the proof of Theorem 2). One can efficiently verify that $\beta \notin \{\sigma, \sigma/\omega^m\}$, given $[\sigma]_1$ from the SRS. In addition, in the knowledge-soundness proof we need that $S(Y)$, $\mathcal{Z}_\mathbb{K}(Y)$, $Y - \beta$, and $Y - \beta\omega^m$ are coprime. Hence, we need that (1) $S(\beta) \neq 0$, $S(\beta\omega^m) \neq 0$, $\mathcal{Z}_\mathbb{K}(\beta) \neq 0$, $\mathcal{Z}_\mathbb{K}(\beta\omega^m) = 0$ (the latter two conditions hold iff $\beta \notin \mathbb{K}$ and $\beta\omega^m \notin \mathbb{K}$) for coprimeness with $Y - \beta$ and $Y - \beta\omega^m$, and (2) $\beta \neq 0$ (otherwise $\beta = \beta\omega^m$, and thus $Y - \beta$ and $Y - \beta\omega^m$ cannot be coprime). As mentioned previously, $\alpha, \beta \notin \mathbb{H}$ since otherwise $\mathsf{den}(\kappa) = 0$ for any $\kappa \in \mathbb{K}$. Note that if n_h and d_{gap} are much smaller than $|\mathbb{F}|$ (which is typically the case), then $\beta \leftarrow\!\!\$\, \mathbb{F}$ is contained in C_β with an overwhelming probability. Thus, in practice, β can be sampled from $\mathbb{F}$, resulting in only a negligible security risk.

Since $\mathcal{S}_1(X, X_\tau)$ and $\mathcal{S}_2(X)$ consist of monomials and one can verify the correctness of its SRS efficiently, 𝔙𝔞𝔪𝔭𝔦𝔯𝔢 is updatable. We will prove the latter in the full version [22]. See the full version [22] for a thorough efficiency analysis.

$\mathsf{P}(\mathsf{ek}_{\mathcal{R}}, \mathbb{x}, \mathbb{w})$ .... Init .... $\mathsf{V}(\mathsf{vk}_{\mathcal{R}}, \mathbb{x})$

$\mathcal{Z}_{\mathsf{inp}}(Y) \leftarrow \prod_{i=1}^{m_0+1}(Y - \omega^{i-1})(Y - \omega^{m+i-1}) \in \mathbb{F}_{\leq 2m_0+2}[Y]$;

$\mathsf{inp}(Y) \leftarrow \ell_1^{\mathbb{H}}(Y) + \sum_{i=1}^{m_0} \mathbb{x}_i \ell_{i+1}^{\mathbb{H}}(Y) + \sum_{i=1}^{m_0+1} \ell_{m+i}^{\mathbb{H}}(Y) \in \mathbb{F}_{\leq n_h-1}[Y]$; $\boldsymbol{r}_z \leftarrow_\$ \mathbb{F}^b$;

$\tilde{z}(Y) \leftarrow \sum_{i=1}^{m-m_0-1} \boldsymbol{z}_{\mathsf{a}}[i] \frac{\ell_{m_0+1+i}^{\mathbb{H}}(Y)}{\mathcal{Z}_{\mathsf{inp}}(Y)} + \sum_{i=1}^{m-m_0-1} \boldsymbol{z}_{\mathsf{b}}[i] \frac{\ell_{m+m_0+1+i}^{\mathbb{H}}(Y)}{\mathcal{Z}_{\mathsf{inp}}(Y)} + \sum_{i=1}^{b} \boldsymbol{r}_z[i] \frac{\ell_{2m+i}^{\mathbb{H}}(Y)}{\mathcal{Z}_{\mathsf{inp}}(Y)}$;

$z(Y) \leftarrow \mathcal{Z}_{\mathsf{inp}}(Y)\tilde{z}(Y) + \mathsf{inp}(Y)$; // $\tilde{z}(Y) \in \mathbb{F}_{\leq n_h-2m_0-3}[Y]$; $z(Y) \in \mathbb{F}_{\leq n_h-1}[Y]$

$\xrightarrow{[\tilde{z}(\sigma)]_1}$

$\xleftarrow{\alpha}$ $\qquad \alpha \leftarrow_\$ \mathbb{F} \setminus \mathbb{H}$

Abort if $\alpha \notin \mathbb{F} \setminus \mathbb{H}$

...... **Count**: $\sum_{y \in \mathbb{H}} \psi_\alpha(y) = 0$ for $\psi_\alpha(Y) = \left(\Lambda_{\mathbb{H}}^b(\alpha, Y) - M^b(\alpha, Y) z(Y\omega^m)\right) z(Y)$ ......

$S(Y) \leftarrow \sum_{i=0}^{\lfloor d/n_h \rfloor} Y^{d_{\mathsf{gap}} - n_h i} \in \mathbb{F}_{\leq d_{\mathsf{gap}}}[Y]$; $\psi_{\mathsf{ipc}}(Y) \leftarrow \psi_\alpha(Y) S(Y) \in \mathsf{PolyPunc}_{\mathbb{F}}(d, d_{\mathsf{gap}}, Y)$;

$\xrightarrow{[\psi_{\mathsf{ipc}}(\sigma)]_1}$

$\xleftarrow{\beta}$ $\qquad \beta \leftarrow_\$ C_\beta$

.... Low-degree sumcheck for $\sum_{\kappa \in \mathbb{K}} (\mathsf{num}(\kappa)/\mathsf{den}(\kappa)) = v_M = M^b(\alpha, \beta)$ ....

Abort if $\beta \notin C_\beta$; $v_M \leftarrow M^b(\alpha, \beta) \in \mathbb{F}$; $v_z \leftarrow \tilde{z}(\beta\omega^m) \in \mathbb{F}$;

$\mathsf{num}(Z) \leftarrow \mathcal{Z}_{\mathbb{H}}(\alpha)\mathcal{Z}_{\mathbb{H}}(\beta)/n_h^2 \cdot \mathsf{rcv}(Z) \in \mathbb{F}_{\leq n_k-1}[Z]$;

$\mathsf{den}(Z) \leftarrow \alpha\beta - \alpha \cdot \mathsf{col}(Z) - \beta \cdot \mathsf{row}(Z) + \mathsf{rc}(Z) \in \mathbb{F}_{\leq n_k-1}[Z]$;

$T(Z) \leftarrow \mathsf{num}(Z)/\mathsf{den}(Z) \in \mathbb{F}(Z)$; $\widehat{T}(Z) \leftarrow \sum_{\kappa \in \mathbb{K}} T(\kappa) L_\kappa^{\mathbb{K}}(Z) \in \mathbb{F}_{\leq n_k-1}[Z]$;

$R(Z) \leftarrow (\widehat{T}(Z) - v_M/n_k)/Z \in \mathbb{F}_{\leq n_k-2}[Z]$;

$Q(Z) \leftarrow (\mathsf{num}(Z) - R(Z) \cdot \mathsf{zden}(Z) - v_M/n_k \cdot \mathsf{den}(Z))/\mathcal{Z}_{\mathbb{K}}(Z) \in \mathbb{F}_{\leq n_k-3}[Z]$;

$z(\beta\omega^m) \leftarrow \mathcal{Z}_{\mathsf{inp}}(\beta\omega^m)v_z + \mathsf{inp}(\beta\omega^m)$;

$\Psi(Y) \leftarrow \left(\Lambda_{\mathbb{H}}^b(\alpha, \beta) - v_M \cdot z(\beta\omega^m)\right)\left(\mathcal{Z}_{\mathsf{inp}}(\beta)\tilde{z}(Y) + \mathsf{inp}(\beta)\right) \in \mathbb{F}_{\leq n_h-m_0-3}[Y]$;

$\tilde{z}_{\mathsf{pc}}(Y) \leftarrow (\tilde{z}(Y) - v_z)/(Y - \beta\omega^m) \in \mathbb{F}_{\leq n_h-m_0-4}[Y]$;

$\Phi_{\mathsf{pc}}(Y) \leftarrow (\Psi(Y) - \psi_\alpha(Y))/(Y - \beta) \in \mathbb{F}_{\leq d-1}[Y]$;

$B_{\mathsf{pc}}(Y, X_\tau) \leftarrow \tilde{z}_{\mathsf{pc}}(Y) + \Phi_{\mathsf{pc}}(Y) + Q(Y)X_\tau \in \mathbb{F}_{\leq d-1}[Y] \cup (\mathbb{F}_{\leq n_k-3}[Y])[X_\tau]$;

$\xrightarrow{v_z, v_M, [R(\sigma)\tau, B_{\mathsf{pc}}(\sigma, \tau)]_1}$

$[B_1(\sigma)]_2 \leftarrow [(\sigma - \beta)\mathcal{Z}_{\mathbb{K}}(\sigma)S(\sigma)]_2$; $[B_2(\sigma)]_2 \leftarrow [(\sigma - \beta\omega^m)\mathcal{Z}_{\mathbb{K}}(\sigma)S(\sigma)]_2$;

$[B_3(\sigma)]_2 \leftarrow [(\sigma - \beta\omega^m)\mathcal{Z}_{\mathbb{K}}(\sigma)]_2$; $[B_4(\sigma)\tau]_1 \leftarrow [(\sigma - \beta)(\sigma - \beta\omega^m)\tau]_1$;

$[\zeta_1(\sigma)]_2 \leftarrow \mathcal{Z}_{\mathbb{H}}(\alpha)\mathcal{Z}_{\mathbb{H}}(\beta)/n_h^2 \cdot [\mathsf{rcv}(\sigma)S(\sigma)]_2$; // $= [\mathsf{num}(\sigma)S(\sigma)]_2$

$[\zeta_2(\sigma)]_2 \leftarrow \alpha\beta[S(\sigma)]_2 - \alpha[\mathsf{col}(\sigma)S(\sigma)]_2 - \beta[\mathsf{row}(\sigma)S(\sigma)]_2 + [\mathsf{rc}(\sigma)S(\sigma)]_2$; // $= [\mathsf{den}(\sigma)S(\sigma)]_2$

$[\zeta_3(\sigma)]_2 \leftarrow \alpha\beta[(\sigma - \beta)(\sigma - \beta\omega^m)\sigma S(\sigma)]_2 - \alpha[(\sigma - \beta)(\sigma - \beta\omega^m)\mathsf{zcol}(\sigma)S(\sigma)]_2 -$
$\beta[(\sigma - \beta)(\sigma - \beta\omega^m)\mathsf{zrow}(\sigma)S(\sigma)]_2 + [(\sigma - \beta)(\sigma - \beta\omega^m)\mathsf{zrc}(\sigma)S(\sigma)]_2$;
// $= [(\sigma - \beta)(\sigma - \beta\omega^m)\mathsf{zden}(\sigma)S(\sigma)]_2$

$\mathsf{inp}(\beta\omega^m) \leftarrow \ell_1^{\mathbb{H}}(\beta\omega^m) + \sum_{i=1}^{m_0} \mathbb{x}_i \ell_{i+1}^{\mathbb{H}}(\beta\omega^m) + \sum_{i=1}^{m_0+1} \ell_{m+i}^{\mathbb{H}}(\beta\omega^m)$;

$\mathcal{Z}_{\mathsf{inp}}(\beta\omega^m) \leftarrow \prod_{i=1}^{m_0+1}(\beta\omega^m - \omega^{i-1})(\beta\omega^m - \omega^{m+i-1})$;

$z(\beta\omega^m) \leftarrow \mathcal{Z}_{\mathsf{inp}}(\beta\omega^m)v_z + \mathsf{inp}(\beta\omega^m)$;

$[\Psi(\sigma)]_1 \leftarrow \left(\Lambda_{\mathbb{H}}^b(\alpha, \beta) - v_M \cdot z(\beta\omega^m)\right)\left(\mathcal{Z}_{\mathsf{inp}}(\beta)[\tilde{z}(\sigma)]_1 + \mathsf{inp}(\beta)[1]_1\right)$;

(♯♯) Check $\left([\tilde{z}(\sigma) - v_z]_1 \bullet [B_1(\sigma)]_2\right) + \left([\Psi(\sigma)]_1 \bullet [B_2(\sigma)]_2 - [\psi_{\mathsf{ipc}}(\sigma)]_1 \bullet [B_3(\sigma)]_2\right) +$
$\left([B_4(\sigma)\tau]_1 \bullet [\zeta_1(\sigma) - v_M/n_k \cdot \zeta_2(\sigma)]_2 - [R(\sigma)\tau]_1 \bullet [\zeta_3(\sigma)]_2\right)$
$=^? [B_{\mathsf{pc}}(\sigma, \tau)]_1 \bullet [(\sigma - \beta)(\sigma - \beta\omega^m)\mathcal{Z}_{\mathbb{K}}(\sigma)S(\sigma)]_2$;

Fig. 3. 𝔙𝔞𝔪𝔭𝔦𝔯𝔢's online phase: $\mathcal{I} = (\mathbb{F}, \mathbb{H}, \mathbb{K}, m, m_0, \mathbf{L}, \mathbf{R})$ and $\mathbb{w} = \binom{z_a}{z_b} \in \mathbb{F}^{2(m-m_0-1)}$.

5 Security Proofs

We first provide additional preliminaries, needed to prove $\mathfrak{Vampire}$'s security.

Fact 3 (Schwartz-Zippel Lemma). *Let $f(X_1, \ldots, X_c) \neq 0$ be a total degree-d polynomial over a field $\mathbb{F}$ and let $\mathcal{S} \subseteq \mathbb{F}^c$. Then, $\Pr[\boldsymbol{x} \leftarrow\!\!\$\, \mathcal{S} : f(\boldsymbol{x}) = 0] \leq d/|\mathcal{S}|$.*

Fact 4 (Bauer et al. [3]). *Let $\mathcal{V}(X_1, \ldots, X_c) \in \mathbb{F}[X_1, \ldots, X_c]$ be a non-zero polynomial of total degree d. Define $\mathcal{P}(Z) \in (\mathbb{F}[S_1, \ldots, S_c, R_1, \ldots, R_c])[Z]$ as $\mathcal{P}(Z) := \mathcal{V}(S_1 Z + R_1, \ldots, S_c Z + R_c)$. Then the coefficient of the leading term in $\mathcal{P}(Z)$ is a polynomial in $\mathbb{F}[S_1, \ldots, S_c]$ of degree d.*

The following lemma (based on [7,13,19]) allows to batch-open several polynomials in distinct points. The prior work [7,13] had a more general version where the points do not have to be distinct; the cost of it is a randomized verification that involves a value $\gamma \leftarrow\!\!\$\, \mathbb{F}$ sampled by the verifier. On the other hand, [7,13] did not involve the polynomial $S(Y)$ and worked only with univariate polynomials.

Lemma 5 (Aggregation lemma). *Let $f_i \in \mathbb{F}[Y, X_\tau]$, $T_i \subset \mathbb{F}$ be mutually disjoint sets, and let $T := \cup_i T_i$. Let $S(Y) \in \mathbb{F}[Y]$ be such that $\forall s \in T. S(s) \neq 0$. Fix $v_s \in \mathbb{F}$ for all $s \in T$. Let $\hat{v}_i \in \mathbb{F}[Y]$ be a polynomial, such that $\hat{v}_i(s) = v_s$ for all $s \in T_i$. Let $b_i \in \{0, 1\}$. If there exists a polynomial $B_{\mathsf{pc}} \in \mathbb{F}[Y, X_\tau]$, such that*

$$\textstyle\sum_i (f_i(Y, X_\tau) - \hat{v}_i(Y)) \mathcal{Z}_{T \setminus T_i}(Y) S(Y)^{b_i} = B_{\mathsf{pc}}(Y, X_\tau) \mathcal{Z}_T(Y) S(Y) \ , \qquad (17)$$

then $\forall i. \forall s \in T_i. f_i(s, X_\tau) = v_s$.

Proof. Since T_i are disjoint and the roots of $S(Y)$ are not in T, Eq. (17) implies that $\forall i. (\mathcal{Z}_{T_i}(Y) \mid (f_i(Y, X_\tau) - \hat{v}_i(Y)))$. The lemma follows. □

In our use, $\hat{v}_i(Y)$ is either constant or the unique monic polynomial (e.g., Lagrange's polynomial) of degree $|T_i| - 1$, such that $\hat{v}_i(s) = v_s$ for all $s \in T_i$.

Remark 1. When $T_i \cap T_j \neq \emptyset$, $\forall i. (\mathcal{Z}_{T_i}(Y) \mid (f_i(Y, X_\tau) - \hat{v}_i(Y)))$ does not follow. However, if we introduce another variable Z to Eq. (17), changing Eq. (17) to $\sum_i (f_i(Y, X_\tau) - \hat{v}_i(Y)) \mathcal{Z}_{T \setminus T_i}(Y) S(Y)^{b_i} Z^{i-1} = B_{\mathsf{pc}}(Z, Y, X_\tau) \mathcal{Z}_T(Y) S(Y)$, then the claim will again follow. This is essentially how the randomized batching in [7] works (Z is substituted by a random β).

5.1 Knowledge-Soundness Proof

We start by proving two lemmas about coprimeness of some of the polynomials used in $\mathfrak{Vampire}$. We need them later in the knowledge soundness proof.

Lemma 6. *Recall that $\mathcal{Z}_{\mathbb{K}}(Y) = \prod_{\kappa \in \mathbb{K}} (Y - \kappa)$ and $S(Y) = Y^{d_{\mathsf{gap}}} + Y^{d_{\mathsf{gap}} - n_h} + Y^{d_{\mathsf{gap}} - 2n_h}$. If $\operatorname{char}(\mathbb{F}) \neq 3$, $n_h \geq 3$, and $3 \nmid n_k$, then $\gcd(S(Y), \mathcal{Z}_{\mathbb{K}}(Y)) = 1$.*

Proof. Clearly, $\gcd(S(Y), \mathcal{Z}_{\mathbb{K}}(Y)) = 1$ iff $\mathbb{K}$ does not contain roots of $S(Y)$. Since $S(Y) = Y^{3n_h-3} + Y^{2n_h-3} + Y^{n_h-3} = Y^{n_h-3}(Y^{2n_h} + Y^{n_h} + 1)$, roots of $S(Y)$ are 0 (when $n_h > 3$), which is not in $\mathbb{K}$, and roots of $S^*(Y) := Y^{2n_h} + Y^{n_h} + 1$.

Consider the polynomial $P(X) = X^2 + X + 1$ where Y^{n_h} from $S^*(Y)$ is substituted by X. Let a be a root of $P(X)$. Since $a^2 = -a - 1$, we have $a^3 = -a^2 - a = a + 1 - a = 1$. Thus, the order of a divides three. The order cannot be one since then $a^1 = a = 1$, but $P(1) = 1 + 1 + 1 \neq 0$ when $\mathrm{char}(\mathbb{F}) \neq 3$. Thus, the order of a is three. If $a \in \mathbb{K}$, then by Lagrange's theorem, $3 \mid n_k$, violating the assumption $3 \nmid n_k$. Thus, $a \notin \mathbb{K}$. Finally, suppose that b is a root of $Y^{2n_h} + Y^{n_h} + 1$. If $b \in \mathbb{K}$, then $b^{n_h} \in \mathbb{K}$ and $P(b^{n_h}) = 0$. We already showed that $P(X)$ does not have roots in $\mathbb{K}$ and thus, $S(Y)$ does not have roots in $\mathbb{K}$. □

Lemma 7. *If* $\mathrm{char}(\mathbb{F}) \neq 3$, $n_h \geq 3$, $3 \nmid n_k$, *and* $\beta \in C_\beta$, *then* $S(Y)$, $\mathcal{Z}_{\mathbb{K}}(Y)$, $Y - \beta$, *and* $Y - \beta\omega^m$ *are pair-wise coprime.*

Proof. Let us look at all the pairs one-by-one.

1. We proved in Lemma 6 that $S(Y)$ and $\mathcal{Z}_{\mathbb{K}}(Y)$ are coprime assuming $\mathrm{char}(\mathbb{F}) \neq 3$, $n_h \geq 3$, and $3 \nmid n_k$.
2. Suppose that $\beta = \beta\omega^m$. Then, $\beta(\omega^m - 1) = 0$ and thus either $\beta = 0$ or $\omega^m = 1$. However, $0 \notin C_\beta$. Moreover, $\omega^m \neq 1$ since $m < n_h$. Thus, $Y - \beta$ and $Y - \beta\omega^m$ are coprime.
3. $\mathcal{Z}_{\mathbb{K}}(Y)$ is coprime with $Y - \beta$ and $Y - \beta\omega^m$ since β and $\beta\omega^m$ are not roots of $\mathcal{Z}_{\mathbb{K}}(Y)$ by the definition of C_β.
4. For the same reason, $S(Y)$ is coprime with $Y - \beta$ and $Y - \beta\omega^m$. □

Theorem 1. *Assume that* $\mathrm{char}(\mathbb{F}) \neq 3$, $n_h \geq 3$ *and* $3 \nmid n_k$. *Then,* 𝔙𝔞𝔪𝔭𝔦𝔯𝔢 *is knowledge-sound in the AGM under the PDL assumption. More precisely, an algebraic* $\mathcal{A}$ *breaks the knowledge-soundness of* 𝔙𝔞𝔪𝔭𝔦𝔯𝔢 *with probability at most*

$$\mathsf{Adv}^{\mathrm{pdl}}_{d_1,d_2,\mathsf{Pgen},\mathcal{B}}(\lambda) \cdot \frac{|\mathbb{F}|^2}{|\mathbb{F}|^2 - q} + \frac{16n_h + 4m_0 - 12}{|C_\beta|} + \frac{n_h - 1}{|\mathbb{F}| - n_h} , \tag{18}$$

where $\mathcal{B}$ *is some PPT adversary,* $d_1 = \max(d_{\mathsf{gap}} + d, n_k - 1)$, $d_2 = n_k + d_{\mathsf{gap}} + 2$, *and* $q \leq 2 + n_k + d_{\mathsf{gap}} + d_{\max}$ *such that* $d_{\max} = \max(d_{\mathsf{gap}} + d, n_k - 1)$.

Proof. Let $\mathcal{A} = (\mathcal{A}_1, \mathcal{A}_2)$ be an arbitrary algebraic adversary in the knowledge soundness game and $\mathsf{Ext}_\mathcal{A}$ its extractor. In each round, $\mathcal{A}$ sends some elements of either $\mathbb{G}_1$ or $\mathbb{F}$. For the elements of $\mathbb{G}_1$, $\mathsf{Ext}_\mathcal{A}$ outputs coefficients of a polynomial where its monomials belong to $\mathcal{S}_1(X, X_\tau)$. We denote polynomials that the adversary sends as $\tilde{z}(Y, X_\tau)$, $\psi_{\mathsf{ipc}}(Y, X_\tau)$, $R(Y, X_\tau)$, and $B_{\mathsf{pc}}(Y, X_\tau)$, where each of the polynomials is in the span of $\mathcal{S}_1(Y, X_\tau)$. We denote the field elements $v_z, v_M \in \mathbb{F}$, sent by the prover, as in the honest protocol description.

In Fig. 4, we depict the knowledge extractor Ext. Ext runs $\mathsf{Ext}_\mathcal{A}$[7] to obtain coefficients of $\tilde{z}(Y, X_\tau)$. Ext then evaluates $\tilde{z}(Y, 0) \cdot \mathcal{Z}_{\mathsf{inp}}(Y)$ at points of $Y \in \mathbb{H}$, corresponding to $\boldsymbol{z}_\mathsf{a}$ and $\boldsymbol{z}_\mathsf{b}$ in the honest argument. Ext then returns those vectors. In the rest of this proof, we show that the value outputted by Ext is a valid witness for $\mathbb{x}$ with an overwhelming probability.

[7] Even though $\mathcal{A}$ is interactive, since we extract only from the first round message of $\mathcal{A}$, the knowledge soundness extractor is still non-interactive.

$\mathsf{Ext}(\mathsf{srs}, \mathsf{aux}; r)$

$\tilde{z}(Y, X_\tau) \leftarrow \mathsf{Ext}_{\mathcal{A}}(\mathsf{srs}, \mathsf{aux}; r)$;
$\boldsymbol{z}_\mathsf{a} \leftarrow \left(\tilde{z}(\omega^{m_0+1}, 0) \cdot \mathcal{Z}_{\mathsf{inp}}(\omega^{m_0+1}), \ldots, \tilde{z}(\omega^{m-1}, 0) \cdot \mathcal{Z}_{\mathsf{inp}}(\omega^{m-1})\right)^\top$;
$\boldsymbol{z}_\mathsf{b} \leftarrow \left(\tilde{z}(\omega^{m+m_0+1}, 0) \cdot \mathcal{Z}_{\mathsf{inp}}(\omega^{m+m_0+1}), \ldots, \tilde{z}(\omega^{2m-1}, 0) \cdot \mathcal{Z}_{\mathsf{inp}}(\omega^{2m-1})\right)^\top$;
return $\mathrm{w} = \binom{\boldsymbol{z}_\mathsf{a}}{\boldsymbol{z}_\mathsf{b}}$;

Fig. 4. The knowledge-soundness extractor Ext for $\mathfrak{Vampire}$ zk-SNARK where $\mathcal{A}$ is an algebraic adversary and $\mathsf{Ext}_{\mathcal{A}}$ its extractor.

We have one verification check that guarantees $\mathcal{V}(\sigma, \tau) = 0$, where

$$\begin{aligned}\mathcal{V}(Y, X_\tau) := &(\tilde{z}(Y, X_\tau) - v_z) \cdot (Y - \beta)\mathcal{Z}_{\mathbb{K}}(Y)S(Y) + \\ &(\Psi(Y, X_\tau)S(Y) - \psi_{\mathsf{ipc}}(Y, X_\tau)) \cdot (Y - \beta\omega^m)\mathcal{Z}_{\mathbb{K}}(Y) + \\ &\left(\left(\mathsf{num}(Y) - \tfrac{v_M}{n_k}\mathsf{den}(Y)\right)X_\tau - R(Y, X_\tau)\mathsf{zden}(Y)\right) \cdot (Y - \beta)(Y - \beta\omega^m)S(Y) - \\ &B_{\mathsf{pc}}(Y, X_\tau) \cdot (Y - \beta)(Y - \beta\omega^m)\mathcal{Z}_{\mathbb{K}}(Y)S(Y) ,\end{aligned}$$

where $\Psi(Y, X_\tau) = \left(\Lambda^b_{\mathbb{H}}(\alpha, \beta) - v_M \cdot z(\beta\omega^m)\right)\left(\mathcal{Z}_{\mathsf{inp}}(\beta)\tilde{z}(Y, X_\tau) + \mathsf{inp}(\beta)\right)$ for $z(\beta\omega^m) = \mathcal{Z}_{\mathsf{inp}}(\beta\omega^m)v_z + \mathsf{inp}(\beta\omega^m)$. ($\mathcal{V}(\sigma, \tau) = 0$ follows from ($\sharp\sharp$) in Fig. 3 when one allows polynomials like $\tilde{z}(Y, X_\tau)$ to be maliciously chosen.)

Clearly, $\Pr[\mathcal{A} \text{ wins}] \leq \Pr[\mathcal{A} \text{ wins} \mid \mathcal{V}(Y, X_\tau) = 0] + \Pr[\mathcal{A} \text{ wins} \mid \mathcal{V}(Y, X_\tau) \neq 0]$. Below, we will analyze both conditional probabilities.

Lemma 8. *Assume* $\mathrm{char}(\mathbb{F}) \neq 3$, $n_h \geq 3$, *and* $3 \nmid n_k$. *For an algebraic* $\mathcal{A}$, $\Pr[\mathcal{A}$ *wins* $\mid \mathcal{V}(Y, X_\tau) = 0] \leq (16n_h + 4m_0 - 12)/|\mathcal{C}_\beta| + (n_h - 1)/(|\mathbb{F}| - n_h)$.

Proof. Assume $\mathcal{V}(Y, X_\tau) = 0$. Recall that by Lemma 7, $S(Y)$, $\mathcal{Z}_{\mathbb{K}}(Y)$, $Y - \beta$, and $Y - \beta\omega^m$ are pair-wise coprime. Hence, we can use Lemma 5 with $f_1(Y) = \tilde{z}(Y, X_\tau)S(Y)$, $f_2(Y) = \Psi(Y, X_\tau)S(Y) - \psi_{\mathsf{ipc}}(Y, X_\tau)$, $f_3(Y) = (\mathsf{num}(Y) - v_M/n_k \cdot \mathsf{den}(Y))X_\tau - R(Y, X_\tau)\mathsf{zden}(Y)$, $T_1 = \{\beta\omega^m\}$, $T_2 = \{\beta\}$, $T_3 = \mathbb{K}$, $v_{\beta\omega^m} = v_z$, $v_\beta = 0$, and $v_y = 0$ for $y \in \mathbb{K}$. It follows from $\mathcal{V} = 0$ and Lemma 5 that

$$\tilde{z}(\beta\omega^m, X_\tau) = v_z \; , \tag{19}$$

$$\Psi(\beta, X_\tau)S(\beta) - \psi_{\mathsf{ipc}}(\beta, X_\tau) = 0 \; , \tag{20}$$

$$\forall y \in \mathbb{K}. \left(\mathsf{num}(y) - \tfrac{v_M}{n_k}\mathsf{den}(y)\right)X_\tau - R(y, X_\tau)\mathsf{zden}(y) = 0 \; . \tag{21}$$

We analyze each of the three equations separately.

Equation (19). Denote $\tilde{z}(Y, X_\tau) = \tilde{z}'(Y)X_\tau + \tilde{z}''(Y)$. It follows from Eq. (19) that $\tilde{z}'(\beta\omega^m)X_\tau + \tilde{z}''(\beta\omega^m) = v_z$. Thus, $\tilde{z}''(\beta\omega^m) = v_z$ and $\tilde{z}'(\beta\omega^m) = 0$.

Equation (21). Write $R(Y, X_\tau) = R'(Y)X_\tau + R''(Y)$ and $Q(Y, X_\tau) = Q'(Y)X_\tau + Q''(Y)$. In particular, $\deg R'(Y) \leq n_k - 2$ since the only X_τ-dependent monomials in $\mathcal{S}_1(Y)$ are $(Y^i X_\tau)_{i=0}^{n_k-2}$. Thus, from Eq. (21),

$$\forall y \in \mathbb{K}. \left(\mathsf{num}(y) - \tfrac{v_M}{n_k}\mathsf{den}(y) - R'(Y)\mathsf{zden}(y)\right)X_\tau - R''(y)\mathsf{zden}(y) = 0.$$

Hence, $\forall y \in \mathbb{K}.\mathsf{num}(y) - v_M/n_k \cdot \mathsf{den}(y) - yR'(y)\mathsf{den}(y) = 0$, that is, $\forall y \in \mathbb{K}.T(y) := \mathsf{num}(y)/\mathsf{den}(y) = v_M/n_k + yR'(y)$. Since $\widehat{T}(Z) := \sum_{y\in\mathbb{K}} T(y)L_y^{\mathbb{K}}(Z)$ has degree $\leq n_k - 1$, we get that $\widehat{T}(Z) = ZR'(Z) + v_M/n_k$. By Fact 1,

$$M^b(\alpha, \beta) = \sum_{y\in\mathbb{K}} T(y) = \sum_{y\in\mathbb{K}} \widehat{T}(y) = v_M \ . \tag{22}$$

Equation (20). Denote $\psi_{\mathsf{ipc}}(Y, X_\tau) = \psi'_{\mathsf{ipc}}(Y)X_\tau + \psi''_{\mathsf{ipc}}(Y)$. Observe that $\psi''_{\mathsf{ipc}}(Y) \in \mathsf{PolyPunc}_{\mathbb{F}}(d, d_{\mathsf{gap}}, Y)$. We express $\Psi(Y, X_\tau)$ as

$$\begin{aligned}\Psi(Y, X_\tau) &= \left(\Lambda^b_{\mathbb{H}}(\alpha, \beta) - v_M \cdot z(\beta\omega^m)\right) \cdot (\mathcal{Z}_{\mathsf{inp}}(\beta)\tilde{z}(Y, X_\tau) + \mathsf{inp}(\beta))\\ &= \left(\Lambda^b_{\mathbb{H}}(\alpha, \beta) - v_M \cdot z(\beta\omega^m)\right) \cdot (\mathcal{Z}_{\mathsf{inp}}(\beta)(\tilde{z}'(Y)X_\tau + \tilde{z}''(Y)) + \mathsf{inp}(\beta))\\ &= \Psi'(Y)X_\tau + \Psi''(Y) \ ,\end{aligned}$$

where $\Psi'(Y) := \left(\Lambda^b_{\mathbb{H}}(\alpha, \beta) - v_M \cdot z(\beta\omega^m)\right)\mathcal{Z}_{\mathsf{inp}}(\beta)\tilde{z}'(Y)$ and $\Psi''(Y) = \left(\Lambda^b_{\mathbb{H}}(\alpha, \beta) - v_M \cdot z(\beta\omega^m)\right) \cdot (\mathcal{Z}_{\mathsf{inp}}(\beta)\tilde{z}''(Y) + \mathsf{inp}(\beta))$.

Thus, Eq. (20) implies $(\Psi'(\beta)S(\beta) - \psi'_{\mathsf{ipc}}(\beta))X_\tau + \Psi''(\beta)S(\beta) - \psi''_{\mathsf{ipc}}(\beta) = 0$. Hence, $\Psi''(\beta)S(\beta) = \psi''_{\mathsf{ipc}}(\beta)$.

Denote $\psi(Y) := \left(\Lambda^b_{\mathbb{H}}(\alpha, Y) - M^b(\alpha, Y) \cdot z(Y\omega^m)\right) \cdot (\mathcal{Z}_{\mathsf{inp}}(Y)\tilde{z}''(Y) + \mathsf{inp}(Y))$. Let $\mathcal{V}_3(Y) := \psi(Y)S(Y) - \psi''_{\mathsf{ipc}}(Y)$. By Eq. (22), $\psi(\beta) = \Psi''(\beta)$ and thus $\mathcal{V}_3(\beta) = 0$. Since $\psi(Y)$ and $\psi_{\mathsf{ipc}}(Y)$ were fixed before the adversary received β, we can apply the Schwartz-Zippel lemma to $\mathcal{V}_3$. Recall that (1) $\deg \tilde{z}'' \leq d_{\mathsf{gap}} + d$, (2) $\deg \mathsf{inp} \leq n_h - 1$, (3) $\deg \mathcal{Z}_{\mathsf{inp}} \leq 2(m_0 + 1)$, (4) $\deg z \leq d_{\mathsf{gap}} + d + 2(m_0 + 1)$, (5) $\deg_Y \Lambda_{\mathbb{H}}(\alpha, Y) \leq n_h - 1$, $\deg_Y M^b(\alpha, Y) \leq n_h - 1$, (6) $\deg \psi''_{\mathsf{ipc}} \leq d_{\mathsf{gap}} + d$, (7) $\deg \psi \leq (n_h - 1) + 2\left(d_{\mathsf{gap}} + d + 2(m_0 + 1)\right) = 13n_h + 4m_0 - 9$. Thus, $\deg \mathcal{V}_3 \leq \max(\deg \psi + d_{\mathsf{gap}}, \deg \psi''_{\mathsf{ipc}}) \leq \max(16n_h + 4m_0 - 12, 6(n_h - 1)) = 16n_h + 4m_0 - 12$. If $\mathcal{V}_3(Y) \neq 0$, then the verifier's acceptance implies that $\mathcal{V}_3(\beta) = 0$, which according to Schwartz-Zippel lemma can only happen with probability $(16n_h + 4m_0 - 12)/|\mathcal{C}_\beta|$.

Let us consider the case $\mathcal{V}_3(Y) = 0$. Since $\psi(Y)S(Y) = \psi''_{\mathsf{ipc}}(Y)$, $\deg \psi''_{\mathsf{ipc}} \leq d_{\mathsf{gap}} + d$ and $\deg S = d_{\mathsf{gap}}$, then $\deg \psi(Y) \leq d$. Since $Y^{d_{\mathsf{gap}}} \notin \mathcal{S}_1(Y, X_\tau)$, the coefficient of $Y^{d_{\mathsf{gap}}}$ in $\psi(Y)S(Y) = \psi''_{\mathsf{ipc}}(Y) = \sum_{i=0}^{d_{\mathsf{gap}}+d} (\psi''_{\mathsf{ipc}})_i Y^i$ is 0. But this coefficient is $\psi_0 + \psi_{n_h} + \psi_{2n_h} = 0$. Thus, from Lemma 1, it follows that $\sum_{y\in\mathbb{H}} \psi(y) = 0$.

Let us express $\psi(Y)$ as $\psi(X, Y)$, where X corresponds to α. We established that $\sum_{y\in\mathbb{H}} \psi(\alpha, y) = 0$. For any $y \in \mathbb{H}$, $\deg \psi(X, y) = n_h - 1$. If $\sum_{y\in\mathbb{H}} \psi(X, y) \neq 0$, then by the Schwartz-Zippel lemma, $\sum_{y\in\mathbb{H}} \psi(\alpha, y) = 0$ with probability at most $(n_h - 1)/(|\mathbb{F}| - n_h)$. Assume that $\sum_{y\in\mathbb{H}} \psi(X, y) = 0$. By Lemma 4, $\forall x \in \mathbb{H}.P(x) = 0$, where $P(x)$ is as in Eq. (4). In the beginning of Sect. 4, we established that this equation is equivalent to R1CSLite. Since $z(Y) = \mathcal{Z}_{\mathsf{inp}}(Y)\tilde{z}''(Y) + \mathsf{inp}(Y) = \tilde{z}''(Y)\prod_{i=1}^{m_0+1}(Y - \omega^{i-1})(Y - \omega^{m+i-1}) + \ell_1^{\mathbb{H}}(Y) + \sum_{i=1}^{m_0} \mathbb{x}_i \ell_{i+1}^{\mathbb{H}}(Y) + \sum_{i=1}^{m_0+1} \ell_{m+i}^{\mathbb{H}}(Y)$, then $z(\omega^{i-1})$ for $i \in \{1, \dots, m_0 + 1\}$ correctly encodes $(1, \mathbb{x}_1, \dots, \mathbb{x}_{m_0})$. The extractor extracts $z(\omega^{i-1})$ for $i \in \{m_0 + 2, \dots, m\} \cup \{m + m_0 + 2, \dots, 2m\}$ which indeed corresponds to the R1CSLite witness. □

Lemma 9. *Let* $d_1 := \max(d_{\mathsf{gap}} + d, n_k - 1)$, $d_2 := n_k + d_{\mathsf{gap}} + 2$, *and* $q \leq 2 + n_k + d_{\mathsf{gap}} + d_{\max}$ *for* $d_{\max} := \max(d_{\mathsf{gap}} + d, n_k - 1)$. *For an algebraic* $\mathcal{A}$ *and*

$\mathcal{V}(Y, X_\tau)$ as above, there exists a PPT $\mathcal{B}$, such that $\Pr[\mathcal{A} \text{ wins} \mid \mathcal{V}(Y, X_\tau) \neq 0] \leq \mathsf{Adv}^{\mathsf{pdl}}_{d_1,d_2,\mathsf{Pgen},\mathcal{B}}(\lambda) \cdot |\mathbb{F}|^2/(|\mathbb{F}|^2 - q)$.

Proof. The proof is standard and similar to [12]'s proof for Groth16 SNARK. We sketch the main idea. We construct an adversary $\mathcal{B}$ that breaks the (d_1, d_2)-PDL assumption if $\mathcal{A}$ wins in the knowledge soundness game and $\mathcal{V}(Y) \neq 0$.

$\mathcal{B}$ gets as an input $(\mathsf{p}; [(x^i)_{i=0}^{d_1}]_1, [(x^i)_{i=0}^{d_2}]_2)$. $\mathcal{B}$ samples s_1, s_2, r_1, r_2 and defines $\sigma = s_1 x + r_1$ and $\tau = s_2 x + r_2$. Although $\mathcal{B}$ does not know σ or τ (they depend on the challenge x), $\mathcal{B}$ is able to homomorphically compute elements of the form $[\sigma^i]_\iota$ and $[\sigma^i \tau]_\iota$ (e.g., $[\sigma]_1 = s_1[x]_1 + r_1[1]_1$). The degrees d_1 and d_2 are sufficiently high so that $\mathcal{B}$ can compute srs where σ and τ are the trapdoors. Next, $\mathcal{B}$ runs $\mathcal{A}$ and $\mathsf{Ext}_\mathcal{A}$ on this srs to obtain the argument and related argument polynomials. $\mathcal{B}$ now knows coefficients of verification polynomial $\mathcal{V}(Y, X_\tau)$.

When $\mathcal{A}$ wins, $\mathcal{V}(\sigma, \tau) = 0$. Let $\mathcal{P}(X) := \mathcal{V}(S_1 X + R_1, S_2 X + R_2) \in (\mathbb{F}[S_1, S_2, R_1, R_2])[X]$. From Fact 4, if $\mathcal{V}(Y, X_\tau) \neq 0$ has degree q, the coefficient of the maximal degree of $\mathcal{P}(X)$ is some $C(S_1, S_2) \in \mathbb{F}[S_1, S_2]$ of degree q. Thus, the coefficient of the leading term of $\mathcal{P}'(X) := \mathcal{V}(s_1 X + r_1, s_2 X + r_2) \in \mathbb{F}[X]$ is $C(s_1, s_2)$. Since s_1 and s_2 are information-theoretically hidden from $\mathcal{A}$ (they are masked by r_1 and r_2), by the Schwartz-Zippel lemma, $C(s_1, s_2) = 0$ at most with probability $q/|\mathbb{F}|^2$. Thus, with an overwhelming probability, $C(s_1, s_2) \neq 0$ and $\mathcal{P}'(X) \neq 0$. Thus, $\mathcal{B}$ can find the roots of $\mathcal{P}'(X)$. One of the roots must be σ since $\mathcal{P}'(\sigma) = \mathcal{V}(s_1\sigma + r_1, s_2\sigma + r_2) = \mathcal{V}(\sigma, \tau) = 0$. Finally, $\mathcal{B}$ outputs σ.

The total degree q of $\mathcal{V}$ is $\leq 2 + d_{\mathsf{gap}} + n_k + d_{\max}$, where $d_{\max} := \max(d_{\mathsf{gap}} + d, n_k - 2)$. Thus, $\Pr[\mathcal{A} \text{ wins} \mid \mathcal{V}(Y) \neq 0](1 - q/|\mathbb{F}|^2) \leq \mathsf{Adv}^{\mathsf{pdl}}_{d_1,d_2,\mathsf{Pgen},\mathcal{B}}(\lambda)$. Hence, $\Pr[\mathcal{A} \text{ wins} \mid \mathcal{V}(Y) \neq 0] \leq \mathsf{Adv}^{\mathsf{pdl}}_{d_1,d_2,\mathsf{Pgen},\mathcal{B}}(\lambda) \cdot |\mathbb{F}|^2/(|\mathbb{F}|^2 - q)$. □

It follows from these lemmas that Eq. (18) holds. This proves the claim. □

5.2 Zero-Knowledge Proof

Theorem 2. *Let $b = 4$. Then, 𝔙𝔞𝔪𝔭𝔦𝔯𝔢 is perfectly zero-knowledge.*

We prove zero-knowledge (and subversion zero-knowledge) in the full version.

Acknowledgment. Most of the work was done when Janno Siim was employed by the University of Tartu and Michał Zając by Clearmatics Technologies. Janno Siim was supported by the Estonian Research Council grant (PRG49).

References

1. Abdolmaleki, B., Baghery, K., Lipmaa, H., Zając, M.: A subversion-resistant SNARK. In: Takagi, T., Peyrin, T. (eds.) ASIACRYPT 2017. LNCS, vol. 10626, pp. 3–33. Springer, Cham (2017). https://doi.org/10.1007/978-3-319-70700-6_1
2. Abdolmaleki, B., Lipmaa, H., Siim, J., Zajac, M.: On subversion-resistant SNARKs. J. Cryptol. **34**(3), 17 (2021). https://doi.org/10.1007/s00145-021-09379-y

3. Bauer, B., Fuchsbauer, G., Loss, J.: A classification of computational assumptions in the algebraic group model. In: Micciancio, D., Ristenpart, T. (eds.) CRYPTO 2020. LNCS, vol. 12171, pp. 121–151. Springer, Cham (2020). https://doi.org/10.1007/978-3-030-56880-1_5
4. Bellare, M., Fuchsbauer, G., Scafuro, A.: NIZKs with an untrusted CRS: security in the face of parameter subversion. In: Cheon, J.H., Takagi, T. (eds.) ASIACRYPT 2016. LNCS, vol. 10032, pp. 777–804. Springer, Heidelberg (2016). https://doi.org/10.1007/978-3-662-53890-6_26
5. Ben-Sasson, E., Chiesa, A., Riabzev, M., Spooner, N., Virza, M., Ward, N.P.: Aurora: transparent succinct arguments for R1CS. In: Ishai, Y., Rijmen, V. (eds.) EUROCRYPT 2019. LNCS, vol. 11476, pp. 103–128. Springer, Cham (2019). https://doi.org/10.1007/978-3-030-17653-2_4
6. Bitansky, N., Chiesa, A., Ishai, Y., Paneth, O., Ostrovsky, R.: Succinct non-interactive arguments via linear interactive proofs. In: Sahai, A. (ed.) TCC 2013. LNCS, vol. 7785, pp. 315–333. Springer, Heidelberg (2013). https://doi.org/10.1007/978-3-642-36594-2_18
7. Boneh, D., Drake, J., Fisch, B., Gabizon, A.: Efficient polynomial commitment schemes for multiple points and polynomials. Cryptology ePrint Archive, Report 2020/081 (2020). https://eprint.iacr.org/2020/081
8. Bootle, J., Cerulli, A., Chaidos, P., Groth, J., Petit, C.: Efficient zero-knowledge arguments for arithmetic circuits in the discrete log setting. In: Fischlin, M., Coron, J.-S. (eds.) EUROCRYPT 2016. LNCS, vol. 9666, pp. 327–357. Springer, Heidelberg (2016). https://doi.org/10.1007/978-3-662-49896-5_12
9. Campanelli, M., Faonio, A., Fiore, D., Querol, A., Rodríguez, H.: Lunar: a toolbox for more efficient universal and updatable zkSNARKs and commit-and-prove extensions. In: Tibouchi, M., Wang, H. (eds.) ASIACRYPT 2021. LNCS, vol. 13092, pp. 3–33. Springer, Cham (2021). https://doi.org/10.1007/978-3-030-92078-4_1
10. Chiesa, A., Hu, Y., Maller, M., Mishra, P., Vesely, N., Ward, N.: Marlin: preprocessing zkSNARKs with universal and updatable SRS. In: Canteaut, A., Ishai, Y. (eds.) EUROCRYPT 2020. LNCS, vol. 12105, pp. 738–768. Springer, Cham (2020). https://doi.org/10.1007/978-3-030-45721-1_26
11. Fuchsbauer, G.: Subversion-zero-knowledge SNARKs. In: Abdalla, M., Dahab, R. (eds.) PKC 2018. LNCS, vol. 10769, pp. 315–347. Springer, Cham (2018). https://doi.org/10.1007/978-3-319-76578-5_11
12. Fuchsbauer, G., Kiltz, E., Loss, J.: The algebraic group model and its applications. In: Shacham, H., Boldyreva, A. (eds.) CRYPTO 2018. LNCS, vol. 10992, pp. 33–62. Springer, Cham (2018). https://doi.org/10.1007/978-3-319-96881-0_2
13. Gabizon, A., Williamson, Z.J., Ciobotaru, O.: PLONK: Permutations over lagrange-bases for oecumenical noninteractive arguments of knowledge. Cryptology ePrint Archive, Report 2019/953 (2019). https://eprint.iacr.org/2019/953
14. Gennaro, R., Gentry, C., Parno, B., Raykova, M.: Quadratic span programs and succinct NIZKs without PCPs. In: Johansson, T., Nguyen, P.Q. (eds.) EUROCRYPT 2013. LNCS, vol. 7881, pp. 626–645. Springer, Heidelberg (2013). https://doi.org/10.1007/978-3-642-38348-9_37
15. Groth, J.: Short pairing-based non-interactive zero-knowledge arguments. In: Abe, M. (ed.) ASIACRYPT 2010. LNCS, vol. 6477, pp. 321–340. Springer, Heidelberg (2010). https://doi.org/10.1007/978-3-642-17373-8_19
16. Groth, J.: On the size of pairing-based non-interactive arguments. In: Fischlin, M., Coron, J.-S. (eds.) EUROCRYPT 2016. LNCS, vol. 9666, pp. 305–326. Springer, Heidelberg (2016). https://doi.org/10.1007/978-3-662-49896-5_11

17. Groth, J., Kohlweiss, M., Maller, M., Meiklejohn, S., Miers, I.: Updatable and universal common reference strings with applications to zk-SNARKs. In: Shacham, H., Boldyreva, A. (eds.) CRYPTO 2018. LNCS, vol. 10993, pp. 698–728. Springer, Cham (2018). https://doi.org/10.1007/978-3-319-96878-0_24
18. Izabachène, M., Libert, B., Vergnaud, D.: Block-wise P-signatures and non-interactive anonymous credentials with efficient attributes. In: Chen, L. (ed.) IMACC 2011. LNCS, vol. 7089, pp. 431–450. Springer, Heidelberg (2011). https://doi.org/10.1007/978-3-642-25516-8_26
19. Kate, A., Zaverucha, G.M., Goldberg, I.: Constant-size commitments to polynomials and their applications. In: Abe, M. (ed.) ASIACRYPT 2010. LNCS, vol. 6477, pp. 177–194. Springer, Heidelberg (2010). https://doi.org/10.1007/978-3-642-17373-8_11
20. Libert, B., Yung, M.: Concise mercurial vector commitments and independent zero-knowledge sets with short proofs. In: Micciancio, D. (ed.) TCC 2010. LNCS, vol. 5978, pp. 499–517. Springer, Heidelberg (2010). https://doi.org/10.1007/978-3-642-11799-2_30
21. Lipmaa, H.: Progression-free sets and sublinear pairing-based non-interactive zero-knowledge arguments. In: Cramer, R. (ed.) TCC 2012. LNCS, vol. 7194, pp. 169–189. Springer, Heidelberg (2012). https://doi.org/10.1007/978-3-642-28914-9_10
22. Lipmaa, H., Siim, J., Zajac, M.: Counting vampires: From univariate sumcheck to updatable ZK-SNARK. Cryptology ePrint Archive, Report 2022/406 (2022). https://eprint.iacr.org/2022/406
23. Lund, C., Fortnow, L., Karloff, H.J., Nisan, N.: Algebraic methods for interactive proof systems. In: 31st FOCS, pp. 2–10. IEEE Computer Society Press (1990). https://doi.org/10.1109/FSCS.1990.89518
24. Maller, M., Bowe, S., Kohlweiss, M., Meiklejohn, S.: Sonic: Zero-knowledge SNARKs from linear-size universal and updatable structured reference strings. In: Cavallaro, L., Kinder, J., Wang, X., Katz, J. (eds.) ACM CCS 2019, pp. 2111–2128. ACM Press (2019). https://doi.org/10.1145/3319535.3339817
25. Parno, B., Howell, J., Gentry, C., Raykova, M.: Pinocchio: nearly practical verifiable computation. In: 2013 IEEE Symposium on Security and Privacy, pp. 238–252. IEEE Computer Society Press (2013). https://doi.org/10.1109/SP.2013.47
26. Ràfols, C., Zapico, A.: An algebraic framework for universal and updatable SNARKs. In: Malkin, T., Peikert, C. (eds.) CRYPTO 2021. LNCS, vol. 12825, pp. 774–804. Springer, Cham (2021). https://doi.org/10.1007/978-3-030-84242-0_27
27. Ràfols, C., Zapico, A.: An Algebraic Framework for Universal and Updatable SNARKs. Technical Report 2021/590, IACR (2021). https://eprint.iacr.org/2021/590, Accessed 19 Aug 2021
28. Zhang, Y., Szepeniec, A., Zhang, R., Sun, S.F., Wang, G., Gu, D.: VOProof: efficient zkSNARKs generation for algebra dummies. In: ACM CCS 2022. ACM, Los Angeles (2022). accepted

Improved Straight-Line Extraction in the Random Oracle Model with Applications to Signature Aggregation

Yashvanth Kondi[1(✉)] and Abhi Shelat[2]

[1] Aarhus University, Aarhus, Denmark
ykondi@cs.au.dk
[2] Northeastern University, Boston, USA
abhi@neu.edu

Abstract. The goal of this paper is to *improve the efficiency and applicability* of straightline extraction techniques in the random oracle model. *Straightline extraction in the random oracle model* refers to the existence of an extractor, which given the random oracle queries made by a prover $P^*(x)$ on some theorem x, is able to produce a witness w for x with roughly the same probability that P^* produces a verifying proof. This notion applies to both zero-knowledge protocols and verifiable computation where the goal is *compressing* a proof.

Pass (CRYPTO '03) first showed how to achieve this property for NP using a *cut-and-choose* technique which incurred a λ^2-bit overhead in communication where λ is a security parameter. Fischlin (CRYPTO '05) presented a more efficient technique based on "proofs of work" that sheds this λ^2 cost, but only applies to a limited class of Sigma Protocols with a "quasi-unique response" property, which for example, does not necessarily include the standard OR composition for Sigma protocols.

With *Schnorr/EdDSA signature aggregation* as a motivating application, we develop new techniques to improve the computation cost of straight-line extractable proofs. Our improvements to the state of the art range from *70*×*-200*× for the best compression parameters. This is due to a uniquely suited polynomial evaluation algorithm, and the insight that a proof-of-work that relies on multicollisions and the birthday paradox is faster to solve than inverting a fixed target.

Our collision based proof-of-work more generally improves the Prover's random oracle query complexity when applied in the NIZK setting as well. In addition to reducing the query complexity of Fischlin's Prover, for a special class of Sigma protocols we can for the first time closely match a new lower bound we present.

Finally we extend Fischlin's technique so that it applies to a more general class of *strongly-sound* Sigma protocols, which includes the OR com-

Y. Kondi—The full version of this paper is available at http://eprint.iacr.org/2022/393.pdf.
This work was done while the author was at Northeastern University.

S. Agrawal and D. Lin (Eds.): ASIACRYPT 2022, LNCS 13792, pp. 279–309, 2022.
https://doi.org/10.1007/978-3-031-22966-4_10

position. We achieve this by carefully randomizing Fischlin's technique—we show that its current deterministic nature prevents its application to certain multi-witness languages.

1 Introduction

A Sigma protocol is a three move public coin proof for a language L that allows for efficient sampling of transcripts without a witness (honest-verifier zero-knowledge), and has the property that any pair of accepting conversations that share the same first message will yield a witness for the statement (two-special soundness). Sigma protocols are a useful abstraction in multiple regards, as many algebraic languages admit highly efficient sigma protocols [Sch91], compilers for more complex languages have been constructed [CDS94], and analysis of whether a protocol does indeed meet the definition of a Sigma protocol is usually straightforward.

In the many settings where a non-interactive zero-knowledge proof (NIZK) suits the network constraints, a Sigma protocol can be efficiently compiled to a NIZK in the Random Oracle model [FS87, Pas03, Fis05]. The Fiat-Shamir compiler [FS87] is the most efficient with essentially no overhead in computation or communication, however the extractor induced for the proof-of-knowledge property requires rewinding a malicious prover in order to extract a witness. This extraction technique known as "forking" the adversary is due to Pointcheval and Stern [PS96] and incurs a substantial penalty in the *tightness* of the security reduction.

Moreover while a rewinding extractor is conducive to proving sequential composition, when arbitrary concurrent composition is desired, an *online* or *straight-line* extractor vastly simplifies matters. Straightline extraction refers to the notion of soundness by which the witness for a theorem can be extracted from a prover without rewinding. Early work in this area [SG02, CF01] established its benefits for composition and tight security, and that protocols which support straightline extraction require some setup such as a common random string or a random oracle. The later choice is particularly useful in more practical protocols.

Signature Aggregation. A recent application of straight-line extraction techniques is in the aggregation of Schnorr/EdDSA signatures [CGKN21]. Signature schemes based on the discrete logarithm problem alone have not traditionally been known to support aggregation methods, unlike say pairing based constructions [BLS01]. Chalkias et al. [CGKN21] construct a Sigma protocol by which one can prove knowledge of a collection of Schnorr signatures rather than transmit them naively. The Sigma protocol is compressing, as its transcript is only half the size of a naive concatenation of the signatures. Compiling this Sigma protocol to a non-interactive proof (i.e. an *aggregate signature*) via the Fiat-Shamir transformation is efficient but problematic as it incurs a quadratic security loss due to the forking lemma—doubling the size of the underlying elliptic curve (to retain the same security level as the original signature) entirely erases the compression due to aggregation. Using a straight-line extractable compiler to produce a non-interactive proof yields a tight reduction, and therefore has the scope to retain the compression of the Sigma protocol while maintaining the same security level as the signature itself.

1.1 Existing Approaches to Straight Line Extraction

Pass [Pas03] showed that the random oracle model could be used to achieve efficient and easily implementable protocols that were *straightline extractable*, deniable, and concurrently secure. The main idea in Pass is to apply a *cut and choose* technique to a Sigma protocol wherein a Prover commits to the transcripts of 2^ℓ invocations of the protocol with the same first message but different challenges. These commitments are implemented using a Merkle tree consisting of random oracle evaluations. The Merkle tree root is itself used as a random oracle query, and the result determines the index of the transcript that is to be decommitted to the verifier. Intuitively a prover that succeeds in this protocol must have committed to at least two accepting transcripts with probability greater than $2^{-\ell}$; these two transcripts can then be used by the extractor (without rewinding) to extract a witness due to the two-special soundness property of the original Sigma protocol. This basic unit is repeated $r = \lambda/\ell$ times to amplify the soundness to a λ-bit security level. This technique applies to any two-special sound Sigma protocol, and thus shows the universal straightline extractability for any language in NP via Blum's Hamiltonicity protocol. Unruh [Unr15] shows how to adapt this technique to construct a non-interactive zero-knowledge proof of knowledge that is secure against polynomial-time quantum adversaries[1].

The drawbacks of this approach are two-fold: first, the Prover must compute $r \cdot 2^\ell$ protocol transcripts and hash them, and second, there is large overhead in opening the leaves of the Merkle tree in each repetition of the basic unit. Concretely revealing a single leaf costs $\ell\lambda$ bits, and r leaves have to be revealed, bringing the total overhead to $r\ell\lambda = \lambda^2$ bits for the openings alone.

To partially address this inefficiency, Fischlin [Fis05] suggested a different method for achieving straightline extraction that relies on the Prover using a *proof of work* to find a suitable protocol transcript. Intuitively, the Prover must compute a protocol transcript that, for example, hashes to zero for a suitably chosen hash function. This is equivalent to 'inverting' the hash function at a fixed target, i.e. finding a pre-image x so that $H(x) = 0$. The proof of work intuitively forces the Prover compute several valid protocol transcripts (all starting with the same first message), and thus allows an extractor to find a witness simply by reading the different queries to the random oracle. This method avoids the overhead of having to commit to many protocol instances and opening only one. The main advantage of this approach is an asymptotically smaller transcript because it entirely sheds the λ^2 bits required for the Merkle tree openings, which in many situations could be the dominant asymptotic term[2].

---

[1] The Unruh transformation removes the Merkle tree alltogether and thus incurs a large overhead penalty; however the aim in that work is security against quantum adversaries (which, e.g., cannot be rewound).

[2] If a single Sigma protocol transcript is of size S, then a proof by [Pas03] is of size $S \cdot \frac{\lambda}{\log \lambda} + \lambda^2$. Assuming $S \in O(\lambda)$, the λ^2 Merkle opening cost dominates asymptotically.

Inadequacies in the State of the Art. While the method of Fischlin achieves a lower communication complexity, it also has two drawbacks.

- **Prover Computation Overhead.** The prover must hash roughly the same number of transcripts in expectation as Pass in order to find a proof. Fischlin provides some justification as to why the Prover of any NIZKPoK with a straight-line extractor that does not program the random oracle must incur a cost of $\omega(\log \lambda)$ queries made to the random oracle [Fis05, Proposition 2] however the gap between *optimal* performance and the performance of Fischlin's scheme (if there is one) remains unexplored. This aspect is particularly evident in the signature aggregation application, as the construction that Chalkias et al. obtained upon applying Fischlin's transformation suffered from a high computation cost for the prover/aggregator.
- **Limited Applicability Due To Quasi-unique Responses.** For technical reasons in their proof, Fischlin's method only applies to a subset of three-move protocols which satisfy a "quasi unique responses" property. Roughly this means that no efficient prover can output a theorem x and a, e, z, z' such that (a, e, z) and (a, e, z') are both accepting transcripts for x. This excludes Sigma protocols such as logical compositions and proof of knowledge of Pedersen commitment openings. While it is folklore that this property is not necessary for the extractor to succeed, to our knowledge it is unknown at present if this property is strictly necessary for zero-knowledge.

1.2 This Work

We advance the study of straight-line extraction in the random oracle model on the fronts of *computation cost*, as well as the *applicability of Fischlin's transform*. We make orthogonal but compatible improvements in both dimensions.

Computation Cost of Straight-Line Extraction. Our motivating application in which to improve computation cost is signature aggregation, and so we first develop our new techniques in this context and subsequently examine implications that are of more general interest. Roughly, the prover/aggregator in Chalkias et al.'s construction evaluates a polynomial f that encodes the signatures, in order to find points $x_i, f(x_i)$ such that $H(x_i, f(x_i)) = 0$. The computation cost can be broken into two components: the cost $\mathsf{C}_{\mathsf{qry}}$ per evaluation of f, and the *prover query complexity*, i.e. number $\mathsf{T}_{\mathsf{Agg}}$ of evaluations of f that must be hashed before a solution is found—we improve both components in this work.

- **Better $\mathsf{C}_{\mathsf{qry}}$ via Improved Polynomial Evaluation.** We make use of an $O(n^{1.5})$ polynomial evaluation algorithm that performs over an order of magnitude better than the $O(n^2)$ naive method for practically relevant parameters. After diligently searching the literature for this simple technique, we are unaware of any previous application of this observation—perhaps because it was already folklore. Nonetheless, we are the first to discover its unique suitability to straight-line extraction especially for the parameters and elliptic curve groups relevant to signature aggregation.

Theorem 1. *(Informal) For $\mathbb{Z}_q$ such that $q-1$ has a few small factors, there is an algorithm to evaluate a degree n polynomial at n points using $2n^{1.5}$ multiplications in $\mathbb{Z}_q$.*

Polynomial evaluation algorithms with significantly better asymptotic costs are known [vzGG13,BCKL21], however they are either concretely inferior in the relevant parameter ranges, or outright incompatible with commonly used signing curve groups.

- **Collision Predicates Improve Prover Query Complexity.** We replace the inversion based proof-of-work predicate with a *collision* based one. In particular the prover must now find $x_i, f(x_i)$ values such that $H(x_1, f(x_1)) = \cdots = H(x_r, f(x_r))$, which is significantly faster (up to 2×) than finding inversions at the same security level.

Theorem 2. *(Informal) Let r be an integer, and H_1 and H_2 be random oracles with output lengths ℓ_1 and ℓ_2 bits respectively. Let* inv *and* col *be predicates such that $\mathsf{inv}^{H_1}(x_1, \cdots, x_r) = 1$ iff $H_1(x_1) = \cdots = H_1(x_r) = 0^{\ell_1}$, and $\mathsf{col}^{H_2}(x_1, \cdots, x_r) = 1$ iff $H_2(x_1) = \cdots = H_2(x_r)$. If r, ℓ_1, ℓ_2 are constrained so that $\Pr[\mathsf{inv}^{H_1}(1, \cdots, r)] = \Pr[\mathsf{col}^{H_2}(1, \cdots, r)]$, then finding a satisfying assignment for col^{H_2} is faster than finding one for inv^{H_1}.*

We find that the principle of collision finding having superior combinatorics as compared to inversions more generally improves prover query complexity—Fischlin's NIZKPoK construction is sped up by 10 – 15% by directly applying this insight. For a special class of Sigma protocols, the prover query complexity improvement due to the collision predicate idea is up to 2×.

- **Lower Bound on Query Complexity.** We tighten Fischlin's asymptotic lower bound on prover query complexity to obtain a concrete one under certain conditions.

Lemma 1. *(Informal) If a NIZKPoK scheme for a hard relation with a straight-line extractor (in the non-programmable ROM) induces a verifier to make V queries to the RO for a λ-bit security level, then the prover must on average make at least $P_{\mathsf{OPT}}[V, \lambda] = (V! \cdot 2^{\lambda})^{\frac{1}{V}}$ queries in generating a proof.*

This bound is not met by any existing constructions for non-trivial parameters. However the special class of Sigma protocols mentioned above with the collision predicate idea achieves the optimal query complexity for a range of non-trivial parameters—this also serves to inspire confidence in the tightness of the bound.

Lemma 2. *(Informal) There is a NIZPoK for the* DLog *relation with a straight-line extractor (in the non-programmable ROM) where the prover makes roughly $P_{\mathsf{OPT}}[V, \lambda]$ queries on average for V up to 5, and $\lambda = 128$ onwards.*

We tighten the parameters and benchmark our improved aggregation construction, the result of which report in Table 1. We obtain up to a 200× improvement in prover computation over Chalkias et al. [CGKN21] for practically relevant parameters, at the same compression rate. This makes provably secure parameters for signature aggregation accessible in many real-world settings.

Applicability of Fischlin's Transform. We revisit (and eliminate) the role of quasi-unique responses in Fischlin's transform. To our knowledge, it is folklore that the extractor does not strictly need this property, and it is unclear as to whether it is really necessary for zero-knowledge. In fact, Fischlin even suggested informally [Fis05, pg. 13] that their construction works for Sigma protocols for languages with multiple witnesses (such as logical combinations [CDS94]) where achieving quasi-unique responses appears to be simply a matter of adjusting syntax. We find this intuition to be false; in particular we show by means of an attack that *witness indistinguishability* is not preserved upon applying Fischlin's transformation to a natural Sigma protocol (i.e. logical OR composition [CDS94]) in a context that appears to be conducive to quasi-unique responses. Intuitively this stems from the deterministic nature of Fischlin's Prover which leads to a subtle trace of the witness in compiled proofs.

Theorem 3. *(Informal) Fischlin's transformation does not preserve Witness Indistinguishability when applied to the Sigma protocol to prove knowledge of one of two Discrete Logarithms.*

Through a new proof, we show how a simple randomization of Fischlin's method allows it to be safely applied to any *strong* special sound Sigma protocol, where strong special soundness—which we introduce—is a simpler property of a Sigma protocol and does not require context-specific reasoning (i.e. dependence on setup parameters) like quasi-unique responses. Requiring strong special soundness rather than quasi-unique responses strictly increases the applicability of Fischlin's transform.

Theorem 4. *(Informal) Any Strong Special Sound Sigma protocol can be compiled to a straight-line extractable NIZKPoK in the ROM, with the same computation and bandwidth efficiency as applying Fischlin's transformation.*

Our attack on WI appears to uncover an interesting aspect of the role of randomness in straight-line extractable zero-knowledge proofs. Pass' transformation is randomized (due to its use of a commitment scheme), and naively derandomizing it would result in a similar attack. An interesting and natural question for future work would be to identify the class of languages for which "well-behaved" transforms that make black-box use of an underlying zero-knowledge protocol and compile them into a straightline extractable one in the random oracle model *must* be randomized.

We therefore demonstrate conclusively that one can do better than generic cut-and-choose (i.e. Pass [Pas03]) for straight-line extractable NIZKs for many algebraic languages in the random oracle model. Such languages include logical combinations [CDS94], openings to Pedersen commitments, among many others that are used in non-trivial cryptographic systems such as the anonymous survey protocol [HMPs14].

2 Our Techniques

We first recall Fischlin's transformation in order to build intuition for our techniques. The base unit of the transformation is the following: for the instance x, the Prover computes a first message a of the Sigma protocol, and finds second and third messages e, z such that $V_x(a, e, z) = 1$ and $H(a, e, z) = 0$ for some ℓ-bit hash function[3] H, where $\ell \in O(\log \lambda)$. This is done by starting with $e = 0$ (and the corresponding response z) and computing $H(a, e, z)$, iteratively stepping through e, z candidates which verify until the first e, z pair is found such that $H(a, e, z)$ evaluates to the all-zero string 0. An adversarial prover is able to produce (a, e, z) such that $H(a, e, z) = 0$ without querying more than one transcript to H only if it gets lucky with its first query, which happens with probability $2^{-\ell}$. This base unit is therefore repeated $r = \lambda/\ell$ times to achieve λ bits of soundness; specifically, to bind these instances together and prevent independent grinding, all of the a messages for the repeated instances are incorporated into the input to the hash function. For example, for 2 repetitions, the Prover must produce $a_1, a_2, e_1, e_2, z_2, z_2$ such that $H(a_1, a_2, e_1, z_1) = 0$ and $H(a_1, a_2, e_2, z_2) = 0$ and of course $V_x(a_1, e_1, z_1) = 1$ and $V_x(a_2, e_2, z_2) = 1$.

Prover Query Complexity. We refer to the (expected) number of queries that the prover makes to the random oracle as the *prover query complexity*. For instance, the Prover query complexity of Fischlin's construction as described above is $r \cdot 2^{\ell} = r \cdot 2^{\frac{\lambda}{r}}$, which implies a tradeoff between r (which governs proof size and verification cost) and the query complexity. We develop the study of prover query complexity in this work, as part of our study on the computation cost of straight-line extraction.

Fischlin presents a variant of their transformation where the verifier accepts 'near' inversions. This is is not relevant for our work, as discussed in the full version.

2.1 Schnorr/EdDSA Signature Aggregation and Computation Cost

Our motivating practical application is that of aggregating Schnorr/EdDSA signatures with tight security. Chalkias et al. construct a compressing Sigma protocol to prove knowledge of n Schnorr signatures, to which they apply Fischlin's transformation to obtain a non-interactive proof. As mentioned earlier, their scheme is roughly to have the prover encode the n signatures as the coefficients of a degree $n-1$ polynomial f, and output a proof consisting of $(x_1, f(x_1)), \cdots, (x_r, f(x_r))$ such that each $H(x_i, f(x_i)) = 0$. They find producing such a proof to be computationally intensive, for instance over a minute to aggregate even hundreds of signatures at a 53% compression ratio[4] which induces a prohibitively high latency for many applications.

[3] The instance x is also included in the hash, but omitted for clarity.

[4] The r parameter governs a tradeoff between query complexity and compression ratio—a lower ratio is better compression, and 50% is the lowest possible [CGKN21].

Faster Polynomial Evaluation with Curve25519. If we denote the prover query complexity as $\mathsf{T}_{\mathsf{Agg}}$, the prover must evaluate f at $\mathsf{T}_{\mathsf{Agg}}$ points. The first aspect of the prover's computation cost that we improve is the cost of producing $\mathsf{T}_{\mathsf{Agg}}$ evaluations of f. The naive method to evaluate a degree n polynomial costs n multiplications in $\mathbb{Z}_q$, meaning that the prover performs $n\mathsf{T}_{\mathsf{Agg}}$ multiplications. The Fast Fourier Transform (FFT) is a well-known method to speed up polynomial evaluation to $O(\mathsf{T}_{\mathsf{Agg}} \log n)$, and is used in straight-line extractable proofs for general statements [AHIV17,BCR+19]. Unfortunately the most common variant of Schnorr in practice—EdDSA—uses Curve25519, whose corresponding base field does not have a sufficiently large multiplicative subgroup to support the FFT.

We instead make use of a method (Theorem 5) by which we can derive a randomly chosen polynomial h of degree $k < n$, such that it agrees with f on k points. Deriving h costs n multiplications, and evaluating h at each point costs k multiplications, which means that we can obtain k evaluations of f at roughly $n + k^2$ cost rather than the naive nk—a substantial improvement when $k \approx \sqrt{n}$. A prerequisite to use this method is that $\mathbb{Z}_q$ must have a multiplicative subgroup of size k, however unlike the FFT this method is *randomized* and can be invoked multiple times using the same subgroup, with negligible probability of producing redundant evaluations. Curve25519 has multiplicative subgroups of size up to 132, which provides nearly optimal values of $k \approx \sqrt{n}$ for the parameters relevant to signature aggregation (n up to 2^{12} or so).

The intuition for the method is as follows: we decompose f into k different degree n/k polynomials f_i such that $f(x) = \sum_{i\in[k]} x^i \cdot f_i(x^k)$. We then sample $\alpha \leftarrow \mathbb{Z}_q$, and derive $h(x) = \sum_{i\in[k]} x^i \cdot f_i(\alpha^k)$. Observe that for any primitive k^{th} root of unity $\omega \in \mathbb{Z}_q$ and for any $j \in [k]$, it holds that $f_i((\alpha\omega^j)^k) = f_i(\alpha^k)$ for every f_i. Consequently, h agrees with f on the points $\{\alpha \cdot \omega^j\}_{j\in[k]}$.

Better Prover Query Complexity via Collisions. We change the underlying proof of work predicate to that of finding collisions rather than inversions of the hash function. In particular, the prover outputs a proof consisting of $(x_1, f(x_1)), \cdots, (x_r, f(x_r))$ such that $H(x_1, f(x_1)) = \cdots = H(x_r, f(x_r))$. For the same r and soundness level (note that ℓ has to be adjusted), analytical estimates on multicollision running times [vM39,Pre93] place the query complexity $\mathsf{T}_{\mathsf{Agg}}$ induced by this collision predicate at up to $2\times$ better than that of inversions.

Combining these improvements (along with a tighter analysis that makes the proof of work easier by 2–8×) yields an improvement of a *factor of 70×–200×* for the most aggressive compression settings reported in prior work (see Table 1).

Collisions Improve Fischlin's NIZK. We generalize this principle and apply it to Fischlin's transform for NIZKPoKs as well, by using a collision pair base unit as a drop-in replacement for inversion base units. In particular, a collision pair base unit instructs the prover to find pairs of accepting Sigma protocol transcripts (a, e, z) and (a', e', z') such that $H((a, a'), e, z) = H((a, a'), e', z')$. A forgery requires a collision within the first two queries to the random oracle, which happens with probability $2^{-\ell}$ for an ℓ-bit hash function. This serves as a drop-in replacement for a pair of inversion base units that achieve a combined ℓ bits of soundness. Analyzing the query complexity is difficult as this is a *chosen prefix* collision [SLdW07], and so we test the new proof-of-work problem empirically and observe an $11\% - 15\%$ improvement for common practical parameters.

A Query Complexity Lower Bound. We tighten Fischlin's asymptotic lower bound on hash queries for a NIZK with a non-programming extractor [Fis05, Proposition 2] to derive Lemma 3 and subsequently Corollary 1, which characterizes the optimal prover query complexity $P_{\mathsf{OPT}}[V]$ for a given verifier query complexity V. Intuitively if the prover makes P queries of which V are checked by the verifier, $\binom{P}{V}$ must be at least 2^{λ} to achieve a $2^{-\lambda}$ soundness error. We note that this bound applies to schemes with perfect completeness, and while Lemma 3 is sufficiently general to derive a strict bound for probabilistic schemes, P_{OPT} serves as a useful reference point, and will be the quantity that we refer to as 'optimal' prover query complexity.

We show via Claim 6 that the expected query complexity of Fischlin's construction is never better than $\sqrt{2}P_{\mathsf{OPT}}$ in any non-trivial parameter regime.

We note that Pass' transform (and equivalently Unruh's transform[5] [Unr15]) has a (strict) query complexity that is twice that of the expected prover complexity of Fischlin in any non-trivial parameter regime, and so we do not consider Pass/Unruh going forward.

Achieving P_{OPT}. For a special class of r-simulatable Sigma protocols (i.e. r transcripts are simulatable at once) we show that a NIZKPoK with prover query complexity P_{OPT} can be achieved for a range of non-trivial parameters. We construct this NIZK by applying a multicollision predicate akin to our signature aggregation construction, where the prover must produce transcripts $(\boldsymbol{a}, e_1, z_1), \cdots, (\boldsymbol{a}, e_r, z_r)$ such that $H(\boldsymbol{a}, e_1, z_1) = \cdots = H(\boldsymbol{a}, e_r, z_r)$. We make use of classic results on multicollision complexities [vM39, Pre93] to analyze the expected prover query complexities. Note that this transform is limited in applicability—we show how Schnorr's proof of knowledge of discrete logarithm can be made r-simulatable, but leave it as an interesting problem for future work to expand the scope of this transform.

Wider Application of Our Techniques. Our techniques for improving the computation cost of Signature Aggregation can be applied directly to the threshold cryptography context for the same signature schemes. For example, the most expensive component of Distributed Key Generation (DKG) for the canonical (t, n) threshold Schnorr scheme [Lin22, Protocol 6.1] is the NIZKPoK to prove knowledge of a polynomial that is committed in the curve group. The instantiation for this NIZKPoK suggested by Lindell [Lin22] is the batch PoK of Discrete Log [GLSY04] compiled to a NIZK using Fischlin's transform—i.e. exactly the

[5] For the purpose of prover query complexity, Unruh's transform can be seen as Pass' transform without the Merkle trees to reduce the number of repetitions of the base Sigma protocol.

same as EdDSA signature aggregation (with an extra blinding factor). Consequently, DKG for (t, n) EdDSA can benefit from roughly the same speedup that we report for signature aggregation. We briefly discuss other applications related to threshold cryptography with Curve25519 and secp256k1 in the full version.

Is Better (e.g. Sublinear) Aggregation Possible? Unfortunately, any aggregation technique that is blackbox in the Schnorr hash function (such as ours) is inherently limited to a 50% aggregation rate [CGKN21, Theorem 9]. The only known aggregation methods that are non-blackbox in the hash function involve expressing the hash function as an arithmetic circuit and invoking a generic SNARK, which is much too slow for standard hash functions like SHA2—on the order of 10s–100s of milliseconds per signature being aggregated, as opposed to our technique which can process each signature in a fraction of a millisecond.

2.2 Extending the Applicability of Fischlin's Transform

A technicality in Fischlin's transformation arises when it is possible for the Prover to iterate through verifying transcripts *without* having to change the challenge message e. Consider a Sigma protocol that permits an adversary without a witness to sample $(a, e), z_1, z_2, \cdots z_n$ such that each (a, e, z_i) is a valid transcript. Applying Fischlin's transformation will not produce a sound NIZK because an adversary can simply step through $H(a, e, z_1), \cdots, H(a, e, z_n)$ to find a pre-image of 0 whereas an extractor may not be able to extract a witness from this sequence of queries because they do not satisfy the requirements for 2-special soundness.

Although it is folklore that many Sigma protocols allow for extraction even given accepting transcripts $(a, e, z_1), (a, e, z_2)$ (examples include the famous logical OR composition [CDS94], opening of a Pedersen commitment, etc. for which this is simply a matter of adjusting syntax), Fischlin's transform only applies to protocols that support a *quasi-unique response* property, given below.

Definition 1. *[Fis05, Definition 1] A Sigma protocol has quasi-unique responses if for every PPT algorithm $\mathcal{A}$, for system parameter k and $(x, a, e, z_1, z_2) \leftarrow \mathcal{A}(k)$, we have as a function of k that the following probability is negligible:*

$$\Pr\left[V_x(a, e, z_1) = V_x(a, e, z_2) = 1 \wedge z_1 \neq z_2\right]$$

Here the system parameter k can be an arbitrarily structured object sampled according to some distribution, for e.g. an RSA modulus or $h \in \mathbb{G}$ such that $\mathsf{DLog}_g(h)$ is unknown, as required in Okamoto's identification protocols [Oka93].

Interestingly, Fischlin's proof also uses this property to argue *zero-knowledge*. It is less obvious as to why quasi-unique responses is relevant for this purpose. In the absence of an explicit attack on the zero-knowledge property when quasi-unique responses does not hold, one may even conclude that it is simply an artefact leveraged to prove the simulation secure.

We show this intuition to be *false*. In particular, we construct an explicit attack on *Witness Indistinguishability* when Fischlin's transformation is applied to a common Sigma protocol for a language with two witnesses. This attack is the result of combining two facts:

- **Fischlin's Transformation is Deterministic.** Once the Sigma protocol first messages have been sampled, the prover's algorithm is deterministic.
- **Some Sigma Protocols Reveal the Prover's Randomness.** In particular Schnorr's proof of knowledge of discrete logarithm reveals a linear combination of the witness and the prover's randomness—knowledge of the witness therefore allows an attacker to reconstruct the prover's randomness.

It is therefore possible for an attacker to *retrieve* the prover's random tape when given a Fischlin-compiled Schnorr proof, and *replay* the prover's steps and reconstruct the proof string. To demonstrate why this is problematic, we examine the effect of this retrieve-and-replay strategy given a Fischlin-compiled proof of knowledge of one-out-of-two discrete logarithms [CDS94]. In particular if a prover uses one of x_0, x_1 to prove knowledge of $x_0 \cdot G \vee x_1 \cdot G$, an attacker with knowledge of say x_0 can execute the retrieve-and-replay strategy to test if x_0 was indeed used in producing the proof string. We show that if the attacker uses x_0 to execute this strategy on a proof that was actually produced using x_1, there is a non-negligible chance that the proof string that the attacker reconstructs will be *different* from the given one (as opposed to a proof string produced using x_0, which always matches the reconstruction). Intuitively, this is because the proof string serves as a record of how many Sigma protocol transcripts had to be hashed before a solution to the proof of work was found—recomputing the proof using a different witness might result in finding a solution by hashing fewer transcripts.

We note that our attack runs entirely in the random oracle model and does not exploit concrete instantiations of the hash function, unlike previous work that studies the concrete instantiability of Fischlin's transform [ABGR13].

Randomization Fixes the Problem. We formalize a notion of *strong special soundness* to capture the folklore notion that accepting transcripts of the form (a, e, z_1),(a, e, z_2) yield a witness. This is a subtle change in the definition of special soundness; luckily many natural Sigma protocols (including those with multiple witnesses for which Fischlin's transformation is shown not to work as above) satisfy this property, including every regular special sound Sigma protocol that supports quasi-unique responses.

We then show how to randomize Fischlin's transformation to erase all traces of the witness from the compiled proof strings, and prove that zero-knowledge is guaranteed unconditionally for any strong special sound Sigma protocol. Intuitively this is achieved by having the prover step randomly through the challenge space to find a solution to the proof of work, and this form of randomization is directly compatible with a collision-based proof of work.

3 Preliminaries

A Sigma protocol is a three move public coin protocol between a prover $P_\Sigma(x, w)$ and a verifier $V_\Sigma(x)$. We further use $(\mathsf{state}, a) \leftarrow P_{\Sigma,a}(x, w)$ to denote the internal state and first message output by P_Σ respectively. Subsequently $z \leftarrow P_{\Sigma,z}(\mathsf{state}, e)$ denotes the response of P_Σ upon being given the previously produced internal state, and the verifier's challenge respectively. We omit the formal definitions of Sigma protocols and straight-line extraction due to space constraints, and defer them to the full version.

4 Signature Aggregation with a Tight Reduction

We first explore aggregating EdDSA signatures as a motivating practical application. In particular, we are focused on obtaining a tight reduction for the unforgeability of the aggregate signature to that of the underlying signatures, which at its core is a problem of straight-line extraction. We briefly recap the work of Chalkias et al. [CGKN21] who recently constructed an aggregation scheme for Schnorr (of which EdDSA is a widely used instantiation) that achieves factor 2 compression in the random oracle model.

Sigma Protocol and Non-interactive Compilation. Their first step is to construct an n-special sound Sigma protocol to prove knowledge of n Schnorr signatures. For signatures instantiated over a field of order q, the transcript of the Sigma protocol is of size $(n + 1)|q|$ bits, as opposed to naive transmission of n signatures which would require $2n|q|$ bits.

They subsequently apply Fischlin's transformation to their Sigma protocol in order to construct a non-interactive proof of knowledge that enjoys a tight reduction (yielding *provably secure* parameters, unlike Fiat-Shamir) while achieving a compression rate that can be arbitrarily close to 2. However the proximity to factor 2 compression comes at the expense of prover computation.

Concretely as per [CGKN21, Figure 2] aggregating EdDSA[6] signatures with Fischlin's transformation incurs an amortized cost of 4.2ms per signature when compressing by a factor of 1.33, and 39.7ms for factor 1.81 compression. This is multiple orders of magnitude slower than the Fiat-Shamir compiled proof (which incurs a fraction of a microsecond per signature on the same hardware) and processing even hundreds of signatures at once becomes prohibitively expensive.

Faster Straight-Line Extraction. In this section we will develop the tools to substantially speed up the aggregation of EdDSA signatures with straight-line extraction in the random oracle model. Our improved aggregation algorithm is up to 200× faster for practically relevant parameters, and potentially within the performance envelope of real-world applications.

[6] We use EdDSA to refer to Ed25519 [BDL+12] in particular, which is believed to instantiate a 128-bit security level.

4.1 Recap of [CGKN21] Construction

Schnorr Compression Sigma Protocol [CGKN21]. Recall that a Schnorr signature on a message $m \in \{0,1\}^*$ under a public key $\mathsf{pk} \in \mathbb{G}$ consists of a nonce $R \in \mathbb{G}$ and a scalar $s \in \mathbb{Z}_q$ such that $z \cdot G = H_{\mathsf{Sch}}(\mathsf{pk}, R, m) \cdot \mathsf{pk} + R$. Informally the Sigma protocol is the combination of two ideas:

1. Once m, pk, R are determined there is a unique $s \in \mathbb{Z}_q$ that 'completes' the signature, and this is the discrete logarithm of the publicly computable group element $S = H_{\mathsf{Sch}}(\mathsf{pk}, R, m) \cdot \mathsf{pk} + R$. Proving knowledge of the discrete logarithm of S is therefore equivalent to proving knowledge of the missing component of the signature.
2. There is an n-special sound Sigma protocol to simultaneously prove knowledge of the discrete logarithms of n public group elements at the same bandwidth cost of a single PoK of DLog [GLSY04].

Upon fixing n messages m_i and signatures $(R_i, s_i)_{i\in[n]}$ under respective public keys pk_i, the prover is given a challenge $e \in \mathbb{Z}_q$, to which it computes the response $z = \sum_{i\in[n]} s_i \cdot e^i$. The verifier is given the statement $(\mathsf{pk}_i, R_i, m_i)_{i\in[n]}$, challenge e, and the putative Prover's response z, and validates them by verifying that $z \cdot G = \sum_{i\in[n]} e^i \cdot (H_{\mathsf{Sch}}(\mathsf{pk}_i, R_i, m_i) \cdot \mathsf{pk} + R_i)$.

Applying Fischlin's Transformation. Chalkias et al. directly apply Fischlin's transformation to the above Sigma protocol to obtain a non-interactive proof. In particular, a 'base unit' of the proof is a challenge-response pair (e_j, z_j) such that $H(, e_j, z_j) = 0$ where H is an ℓ-bit random oracle, and this unit is repeated r times in order to achieve a λ-bit soundness level. These parameters are set so that a successful prover must query the random oracle with at least n accepting transcripts except with probability $2^{-\lambda}$.

Breaking Down the Cost. We can express the prover's computation cost in producing a proof as $\mathsf{T}_{\mathsf{Agg}} \cdot \mathsf{C}_{\mathsf{qry}}$, where $\mathsf{T}_{\mathsf{Agg}}$ is the prover query complexity, i.e. the number of (e, z) values the prover queries to the random oracle, and $\mathsf{C}_{\mathsf{qry}}$ is the cost of generating each (e, z) value. We discuss below how to improve on both of these dimensions.

4.2 Reducing $\mathsf{C}_{\mathsf{qry}}$ via Improved Polynomial Evaluation

The efficiency of polynomial evaluation algorithms is usually tied to the degree of the polynomial being evaluated. In our case, the degree of the polynomial corresponds to the number of signatures being aggregated. As the signature batch size can be small in practice (e.g. number of transactions in a block, which is around 2000 for Bitcoin [Blo]) asymptotically efficient polynomial evaluation algorithms [vzGG13,BCKL21] may not be relevant to our setting (Fig. 1).

Theorem 5. *Given a prime q, degree n polynomial $f \in \mathbb{Z}_q[X]$, and primitive k^{th} root of unity $\omega \in \mathbb{Z}_q$, Algorithm* PolyEval *outputs a list of k distinct points that lie on f at a cost of $k^2+n+2\log k$ multiplications and $k(k-1)+n$ additions in $\mathbb{Z}_q$.*

Algorithm PolyEval

This algorithm is parameterized by a finite field $\mathbb{Z}_q$ where q is prime, a primitive k^{th} root of unity $\omega \in \mathbb{Z}_q$, and a degree n polynomial $f \in \mathbb{Z}_q[X]$. For simplicity we assume that k divides n. The output of this algorithm is a list of points $\{(x_i, f(x_i))\}_{i\in[k]}$.

PolyEval(q, k, f, n):

1. Parse the coefficients of f, with c_i as the coefficient of x^i
2. For each $i \in [0..k-1]$, define polynomial $f_i(x) = \sum_{j\in[0..n/k]} x^j \cdot c_{jk+i}$
3. Sample $\alpha \leftarrow \mathbb{Z}_q^*$ and for each $i \in [0..k-1]$ compute $\vec{\alpha}_i = f_i(\alpha^k)$
4. Define the degree $k-1$ polynomial $h(x) = \sum_{i\in[0..k-1]} \vec{\alpha}_i x^i$
5. Let points denote the (initially empty) list of output points
6. For each $i \in [0..k-1]$, append $\left(\alpha \cdot \omega^i, h(\alpha \cdot \omega^i)\right)$ to points
7. Output points

Fig. 1. Improved polynomial evaluation

We defer the proof of this theorem to the full version.

While this is a significant improvement over the naive polynomial evaluation algorithm (which requires nk $\mathbb{Z}_q$ multiplications), in our application we need to evaluate f over a large set of points, and PolyEval only produces a batch of k evaluations. A simple extension to produce a batch of say $m \cdot k$ evaluations is to invoke PolyEval m times independently. However it is possible that there may be some redundancy across the multiple evaluations, i.e. independent instances may evaluate f at the same point. We show in the full version that for the parameters relevant to our setting, the probability of there being any redundancy is negligible.

Efficiency. As per Theorem 5, PolyEval achieves the best improvement when $k \approx \sqrt{n}$. In this case, evaluating a degree n polynomial at $\sqrt{n}$ points costs roughly $2n$ multiplications, which is a factor $\sqrt{n}/2$ improvement over the naive method. This improvement is subject to the availability of appropriate k in the field in question. The setting that we consider in this paper involves the EdDSA signature scheme, which uses Curve25519 [Ber06], which in turn is of order q such that $q-1$ is divisible by 4, 3, and 11. Given that we are interested in $n < 2^{12}$ or so, we are able to find a nearly optimal k for any value of n in our range. We plot the improvement achieved by PolyEval in Fig. 2.

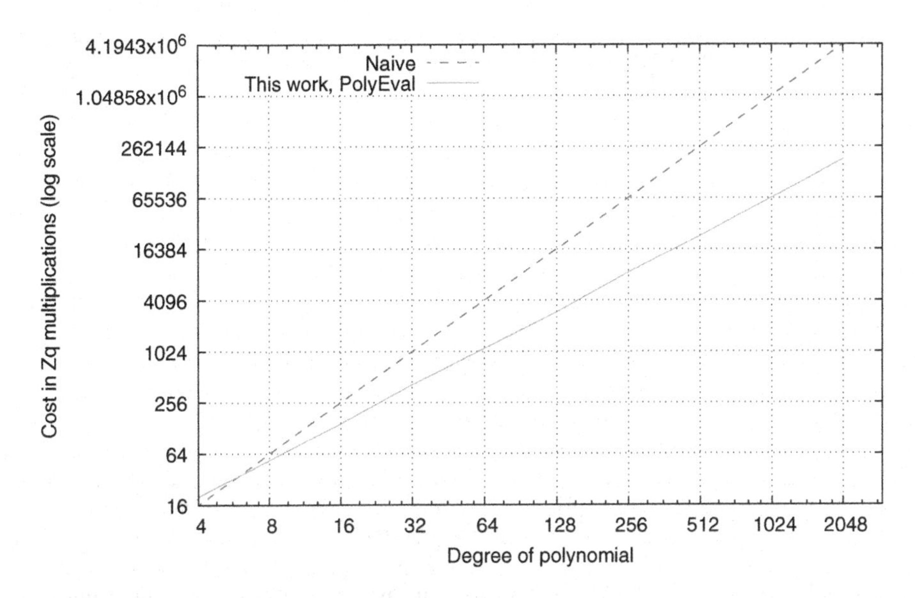

Fig. 2. This graph plots the computation cost of evaluating a polynomial of degree n up to 2^{12} at n points in $\mathbb{Z}_q$, where q is the order of the elliptic curve Curve25519 used for EdDSA. The cost is derived analytically.

Comparison with ECFFT. The very recent work of Ben-Sasson et al. [BCKL21] introduces a method to enable an FFT-like recursive evaluation of a polynomial in any arbitrary $\mathbb{Z}_q$, by using isogenies of elliptic curves. Their algorithm achieves impressive asymptotic as well as concrete performance in the preprocessing model, and can be applied to our setting. In particular, their $O(n \log^2(n))$ complexity is asymptotically superior to our $O(n^{1.5})$ PolyEval algorithm. However for our parameter range, we find our PolyEval algorithm to perform better, as we show in Fig. 3.

4.3 Improving Prover Query Complexity $\mathsf{T}_{\mathsf{Agg}}$

First we note that tightening the parameters of [CGKN21] via a better analysis yields an improvement of 2 to 8× in the hardness setting for the proof-of-work problem. Intuitively this is because of Chalkias et al.'s direct application of Fischlin's transform by repeating a base unit sufficiently many times for the desired soundness level, whereas one can prove better parameters by directly analyzing the final construction, i.e. the event that a malicious prover finds r inversions within n queries.

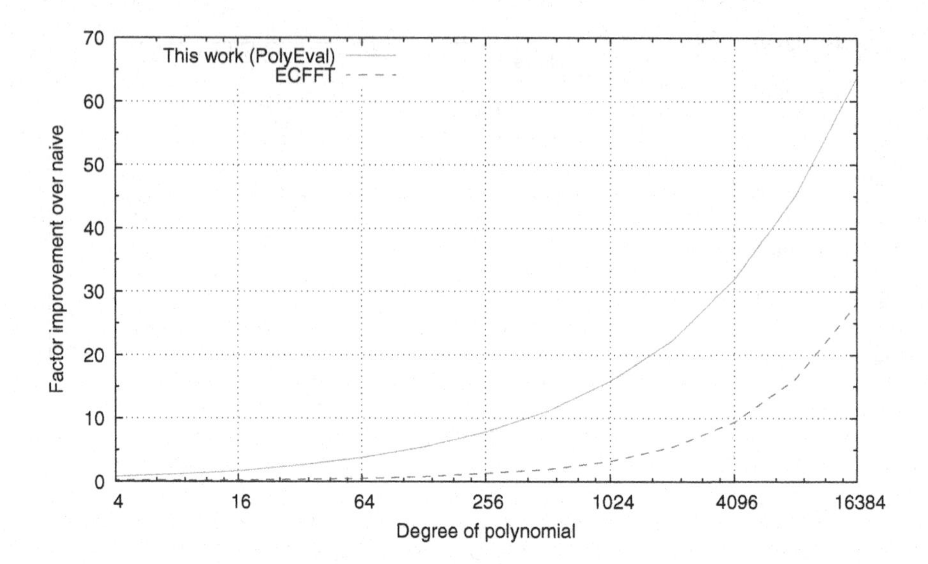

Fig. 3. This graph plots the factor improvement over the naive method, in evaluating a polynomial of degree n up to 2^{14} at n points in $\mathbb{Z}_q$, where q is the order of the BN-254 elliptic curve. The improvement factor for ECFFT is taken from a public Rust implementation [wbo]. We did not re-implement PolyEval for this curve, however our Rust implementation for Ed25519 is faithful to our analytical estimate, and so we derived the improvement factor for PolyEval analytically.

Our Idea. We change the underlying 'proof of work problem' solved by the prover from finding r inversions to finding an r-collision. In particular the prover now searches for $(e_j, z_j)_{j\in[r]}$ such that $H(, e_1, z_1) = \cdots = H(, e_r, z_r)$, where H is a random oracle with output bit length $\ell \geq (\lambda + r\log_2(n) - \log(r!))/(r-1)$. This yields a ≈ 1.5 to $2\times$ improvement in $\mathsf{T}_{\mathsf{Agg}}$ corresponding to the ratio of the costs of finding an r-collision to that of finding r inversions at the same security level (even with the improved analysis).

We give the full protocol and justify its parameterization below. However we defer a more precise analytical justification of why finding an r-collision is faster than finding an equivalent number of inversions at the same security level to Sect. 5.3.

Caveat: Memory Complexity. We note that keeping track of collisions consumes more memory—$O(\mathsf{T}_{\mathsf{Agg}})$—than the inversion construction which only needs $O(\lambda)$. In practice, however, this is quite a small amount (up to 30MB for benchmarked parameters).

Further Applications. The superior combinatorial characteristics of the collision problem over the inversion problem has interesting implications for the computation complexity of straight-line extraction even in the zero-knowledge setting. In Sects. 5.1 and 5.3, we show how to improve the prover's query complexity when compiling *any* standard Sigma protocol to a NIZKPoK by 10–15%, and for some special Sigma protocols by up to a factor of 2. The latter is particularly significant as it matches a new lower bound that we prove.

4.4 Putting It Together – Improved EdDSA Aggregation

We combine our improvements to $\mathsf{T}_{\mathsf{Agg}}$ and $\mathsf{C}_{\mathsf{qry}}$ to obtain an EdDSA signature aggregation algorithm π_{Aggr} with substantially improved prover computation complexity, which we give below in Fig. 4. We further justify its performance improvements with our benchmarks in Table 1. We postpone the security theorem to the full version.

Protocol π_{Aggr}

The prover P and verifier V are both given the public instance $(\mathsf{pk}_i, m_i, R_i)_{i\in[n]} \in (\mathbb{G}\times\{0,1\}^*\times\mathbb{G})^n$ while the prover also has witness $(s_i)_{i\in[n]} \in \mathbb{Z}_q^n$ for the statement $s_i \cdot G = H_{\mathsf{Sch}}(\mathsf{pk}_i, R_i, m_i)\cdot \mathsf{pk}_i + R_i\ \forall i \in [n]$. Both parties have access to an ℓ-bit Random Oracle $H : \{0,1\}^* \mapsto \{0,1\}^\ell$ where $\ell \geq (\lambda + r\log_2(n) - \log_2(r!))/(r-1)$.

$\mathsf{P}^H((\mathsf{pk}_i, m_i, R_i, s_i)_{i\in[n]})$:

1. Find k closest to $\sqrt{n}$ such that $k \mid q-1$
2. Set $\boldsymbol{a} = (\mathsf{pk}_i, m_i, R_i)_{i\in[n]}$, and define polynomial $f(x) = \sum_{i\in[n]} x^i \cdot s_i$
3. Initialize $\mathcal{Z} = \emptyset$ and do the following until an output is produced:
   (a) Obtain $\mathsf{points} \leftarrow \mathsf{PolyEval}(q, k, f, n)$ and append each $(e, z) \in \mathsf{points}$ to $\mathcal{Z}$
   (b) If $\exists (e_1, z_1), (e_2, z_2), \cdots, (e_r, z_r) \in \mathcal{Z}$ such that
   $$H(\boldsymbol{a}, e_1, z_1) = H(\boldsymbol{a}, e_2, z_2) = \cdots = H(\boldsymbol{a}, e_r, z_r)$$
   then set $\boldsymbol{e} = (e_i)_{i\in[r]}$ and $(z_i)_{i\in[r]}$ and output $\pi = (\boldsymbol{a}, \boldsymbol{e}, \boldsymbol{z})$

$\mathsf{V}^H((\mathsf{pk}_i, m_i, R_i)_{i\in[n]}, \pi)$:

1. Parse $(\boldsymbol{a}, \boldsymbol{e}, \boldsymbol{z}) = \pi$, and $(e_i)_{i\in[r]} = \boldsymbol{e}$, and $(z_i)_{i\in[r]} = \boldsymbol{z}$.
2. Check that $H(\boldsymbol{a}, e_1, z_1) = H(\boldsymbol{a}, e_2, z_2) = \cdots = H(\boldsymbol{a}, e_r, z_r)$
3. For each $i \in [n]$, compute $S_i = H_{\mathsf{Sch}}(\mathsf{pk}, R, m)\cdot \mathsf{pk} + R$
4. For each $i \in [r]$, check that $z_i \cdot G = \sum_{i\in[n]} e^i \cdot S_i$, aborting with output 0 if not
5. Accept by outputting 1

Fig. 4. Collision based aggregation of n signatures

Table 1. Comparing the computation cost for aggregation and aggregate-verification of n Ed25519 signatures with SHA-256 hash function used for H_1 on the same parameters from [CGKN21]. The benchmarks were run using the publically available code for [CGKN21], and a new Rust implementation of our method and the Criterion rust framework; times show a 95% confidence interval over at least 30 runs on one Intel i7-10710U core running at 3.9 Ghz with 32 GB of memory. Intervals are omitted when less than 1ms. While the aggregation methods can easily be parallelized, each of these benchmarks only use 1-core to properly compare against the implementation from [CGKN21]. The best compression ratios are achieved on the first row at roughly 53%; the last row in the table achieves the worst ratio around 75%. Both constructions have nearly the same bit size, with [CGKN21] slightly better due to smaller sized polynomial evaluation points—the difference is around 1.5% at the better compression rates.

n	r	Chalkias et al.		Our work		Improvement
		AggVer(ms)	AggSign	AggVer(ms)	AggSign	
512	16	137	167 ± 13.0 s	134	2.2 ± 0.07 s	76x
1024	32	485	85.5 ± 4.8 s	452 ± 6	350 ± 10 ms	244x
256	16	78	40.6 ± 2.8 s	72	901 ± 36 ms	45x
512	32	258	20.1 ± 1.4 s	255	136 ± 3 ms	147x
128	16	43	9.9 ± 0.74 s	42	363 ± 8 ms	27x
256	32	147	5.5 ± 0.31 s	143	54 ± 1 ms	101x
32	8	5.7	84.2 ± 11.6 s	5.6	7.8 ± 0.5s	11x
64	16	21	2.9 ± 0.25 s	23	78 ± 1 ms	37x
128	32	80	1.4 ± 0.08 s	84.5	20 ms	70x

5 Applying the Collision Predicate to NIZKPoK

We apply the principle of replacing hash inversions in Fischlin's transformation with hash collisions to the original NIZKPoK transform, and observe improved prover query complexity in this setting as well. We begin by considering the hash collision predicate as a *drop-in replacement* to any Sigma protocol for which Fischlin's transformation can be applied, and observe an 11–15% improvement in the prover's query complexity.

To our knowledge this is the best query complexity achieved for NIZKs so far, however a natural question is to ask to what extent such techniques can be extended. To this end, we show a lower bound on the query complexity of *any* NIZK that has a straight-line non-programming extractor in Sect. 5.2. We find that Fischlin's construction (which is the most query efficient straight-line extractable scheme) never meets this lower bound for any non-trivial parameters.

We show in Sect. 5.3 that it is indeed feasible to meet this lower bound for some non-trivial parameters, by means of a new transformation based on our collision predicate. Unfortunately this transformation only applies to a special class of Sigma protocols that have an r-simulatability property. We show in the full version how to construct such a Sigma protocol by extending Schnorr's proof of knowledge of discrete logarithm.

5.1 Unconditionally Improving Fischlin's Query Complexity

Recall that the prover in Fischlin's transformation is required to invert a fixed target of the random oracle. In particular, a proof consists of a base unit where the prover is required to find a Sigma protocol transcript (a, e, z) such that $H(, a, e, z) = 0^\ell$, and this unit is repeated r times to achieve $\lambda = r \cdot \ell$ bits of security. We can replace this inversion based unit by a collision based one as follows: the prover is required to find a pair of independent transcripts (a_1, e_1, z_1) and (a_2, e_2, z_2) such that $H(, a_1, e_1, z_1) = H(, a_2, e_2, z_2)$. Note that just as in the case of Fischlin, includes a_1, a_2 to prevent trivial attacks. Additionally, the output length of the hash function is 2ℓ, i.e. doubled as compared to the inversion predicate.

Security. Upon fixing , a prover is successful in finding an accepting pair (a_1, e_1, z_1) and (a_2, e_2, z_2) in their first attempt with probability no more than $2^{-2\ell}$. Repeating this base unit $r/2$ times achieves security $2\ell \cdot r/2 = \lambda$ bits.

Efficiency. A base unit of the collision based construction is equivalent to two base units of the inversion construction; in both cases two Sigma protocol transcripts are transmitted, and they achieve 2ℓ bits of security. With regards to computation cost, both constructions have the same cost per query made to the random oracle (i.e. computing a fresh Sigma protocol response), and therefore the difference comes down to the number of queries made per proof, i.e. the prover query complexity.

What Query Complexity Does This Induce? Consider $\mathcal{Z}_1, \mathcal{Z}_2$ to be domains from which (e_1, z_1) and (e_2, z_2) are drawn respectively, and observe that $\mathcal{Z}_1, \mathcal{Z}_2$ are entirely disjoint when $a_1 \neq a_2$. If we consider $(, a_1, e_1, z_1)$ and $(, a_2, e_2, z_2)$ to be the 'left' and 'right' halves of the collision respectively, this means that any given $(, a_i, e_i, z_i)$ can be a candidate pre-image for either the left or right half, but not both. This is because any given e_i, z_i can be a verifying transcript with at most one of a_1 or a_2. This task therefore becomes that of finding a *chosen prefix* collision [SLdW07]. The combinatorics of chosen prefix collisions are considerably more complex to analyze than regular collisions, making the derivation of the exact query complexity of the above construction difficult. We instead measure the query complexity induced by this predicate empirically, and report on the results in Table 2.

As our experiments show, this chosen prefix collision predicate works for the exact same Sigma protocols as Fischlin's transformation, and improves on its query complexity. A natural question for future work is if we can obtain further improvements by considering multicollisions rather than pairs of collisions.

Table 2. Comparing the computation cost of Fischlin's approach to our chosen prefix, pairwise collision approach. The reported value is the expected number of queries for finding either one preimage, or 2 collisions taken over 500–2000 experiments. Parameters for r and ℓ are set for the same 128 bit security.

r	ℓ	Fischlin	Pairwise collisions		
		Expected queries	ℓ	Exp queries	Improvement
8	2^{16}	64,877	2^{32}	58,190	1.11
10	2^{13}	8,233	2^{26}	7,293	1.13
12	2^{11}	2,038	2^{22}	1,824	1.12
14	2^{9}	509	2^{18}	448	1.13
16	2^{8}	267	2^{16}	232	1.15

5.2 Lower Bound on Prover Query Complexity

Fischlin [Fis05] proved via a meta reduction that any NIZKPoK scheme (with a non-programming extractor) for a language with a hard instance generator, must have a super-logarithmic number of queries V in λ made by the verifier to the random oracle. Fischlin's proof demonstrated asymptotic bounds due to its reliance on the hardness of the underlying language; in this work we are concerned with tight parameters for concrete security as guaranteed in the random oracle model, independently of the hardness of the underlying language. We therefore initiate a study of concrete query complexity, in particular we express this as the optimal prover query complexity P upon fixing V.

Caveat. We make a simplifying assumption, namely that the language L has a hard instance generator $\mathcal{I}$ such that the probability that any PPT algorithm is able to find a witness w for theorem $x \leftarrow \mathcal{I}(\lambda)$ is bounded by $\varepsilon_\lambda \ll 2^{-\lambda}$.

This assumption frequently does not hold as in practice one can instantiate the NIZKPoK with a concrete soundness level comparable to the hardness of instances generated by $\mathcal{I}$, however making this simplification allows us to focus on the random oracle query complexity of the NIZKPoK (which is given by parameters independent of the language) without having to account for concrete hardness of the language (which is very specific to each language and seldom leveraged by the extractor of a NIZKPoK scheme).

We begin with the following lemma, which is a tightening of [Fis05, Proposition 2]:

Lemma 3. *If* (P, V) *is a straight-line extractable NIZKPoK scheme for a* ε_λ*-hard language* L *in the random oracle model with the following characteristics for security parameter* λ*:*

- *Perfect zero-knowledge simulator* Sim
- ℓ*-bit output random oracle* H

- *P queries made by* P *to H in generating a proof*
- *Probability $p_C > 0$ of producing an accepting proof*
- *V queries made by deterministic* V *to H in verifying a proof, is a strict subset of the queries made by* P
- *Non-programming extractor* Ext *with error $\leq 2^{-\lambda}$ for an adversary that makes $\leq V$ queries to the random oracle*

Then it must hold that:

$$\binom{P}{V} \geq \frac{p_C}{2^{-\lambda} + \varepsilon_\lambda}$$

We can use the above lemma to derive the optimal prover query complexity for proofs that are non-trivially secure, i.e. when $V \ll \binom{P}{V}$. We define $P_{\mathsf{OPT}}[\lambda, V]$ to be the smallest prover query complexity for a given verifier query complexity V at a λ-bit security level.

Corollary 1. *If* (P, V) *is a perfectly complete straight-line extractable NIZKPoK scheme for ε_λ-hard language L in the random oracle model with all the characteristics required by Lemma 3 with the additional constraints that $V < \lambda$ and $2^{-\lambda} \gg \varepsilon_\lambda$, then its prover query complexity is at least:*

$$P_{\mathsf{OPT}}[\lambda, V] \approx \left(V! \cdot 2^{\lambda}\right)^{\frac{1}{V}}$$

We defer both proofs to the full version.

In subsequent text we drop the argument $[\lambda, V]$ when it is obvious. Note that P_{OPT} only characterizes the optimal prover query complexity for *perfectly complete* schemes. Since Lemma 3 accounts for schemes with arbitrary completeness errors, it is possible to amend Corollary 1 accordingly if desired. However we will see that P_{OPT} serves as a useful benchmark for our study. Interestingly Fischlin's scheme, which has the lowest prover query complexity in the literature, performs worse than P_{OPT} for all $V > 1$.

Claim 6. *Let r parameterize the number of repetitions of a Sigma protocol used to instantiate Fischlin's NIZK [Fis05] at a λ-bit security level. Then the average prover query complexity of the resulting scheme $\mathsf{T}_{\mathsf{Fis}}$ is a factor of $r/(r!)^{1/r}$ worse than the corresponding P_{OPT}. Therefore $\mathsf{T}_{\mathsf{Fis}} > P_{\mathsf{OPT}}$ for every $r > 1$.*

Proof. The average prover query complexity $\mathsf{T}_{\mathsf{Fis}}$ is given by the complexity of finding r inversions of the all-zero string of r independent λ/r-bit random oracles. This task requires $r \cdot 2^{\lambda/r}$ tries in expectation. Since $V = r$, the optimal prover complexity is given by $P_{\mathsf{OPT}} = (r! \cdot 2^{\lambda})^{1/r}$. The ratio of the average prover complexity to the optimal is therefore:

$$\frac{\mathsf{T}_{\mathsf{Fis}}}{P_{\mathsf{OPT}}} = \frac{r \cdot 2^{\lambda/r}}{(r! \cdot 2^{\lambda})^{1/r}} = \frac{r}{(r!)^{1/r}}$$

□

The ratio $\mathsf{T}_{\mathsf{Fis}}/P_{\mathsf{OPT}} = 1$ only when $r = 1$, which is of no use as the average complexity of computing a proof honestly matches the average complexity of forging a proof when $r = 1$. This ratio is $\sqrt{2} \approx 1.41$ when $r = 2$, and continues to increase as r grows, ultimately converging[7] at $e \approx 2.71$. Given this it is natural to ask, is it possible to meet P_{OPT} for any non-trivial parameters?

5.3 Special Case: $r+1$-Special Sound Sigma Protocols

Given a Sigma protocol that is $r+1$-special sound and r simulatable (i.e. given r challenges, a simulator can produce r accepting transcripts) we are able to apply a multicollision predicate and reduce the prover's query complexity as compared with Fischlin's inversion predicate even further—to the point where we can meet P_{OPT} for a non-trivial parameter range.

Note that we present a randomized construction here—this aspect is orthogonal to query complexity. The purpose is to avoid dependence on 'quasi-unique responses', which we will discuss in detail in Sect. 6.

We begin by refining the standard definition of Sigma protocols [Dam02] to incorporate a weaker notion of soundness and simulatability. This notion essentially requires (1) $r+1$-special soundness, which guarantees the success of an extractor upon being given $r+1$ accepting conversations that begin with the same first message, and (2) r-simulatability, which requires that for any statement, r accepting conversations (with the same first message) can be simulated for any r given challenges. We defer a formal definition and instantiation to the full version. We describe our NIZK transformation in Fig. 5.

Theorem 7. *If Σ is a strongly $r+1$-special sound Sigma protocol and $\ell(r-1) = \lambda$, the protocol π_{NIZK} is a straight-line extractable NIZKPoK in the random oracle model, with an extractor that does not program the random oracle and achieves extraction error $Q/2^\lambda$ for an adversary making Q queries to the random oracle.*

Proof. (Sketch) We defer the full proof to the full version. Completeness follows from the pigeonhole principle, as any function that maps a domain of size $r \cdot 2^\ell$ to a range of size 2^ℓ will produce at least one r-collision. Zero-knowledge comes from the fact that the challenges $\boldsymbol{e}$ are distributed uniformly in $\{0,1\}^{t \cdot r}$, and the rest of the transcripts $\boldsymbol{a}, \boldsymbol{z}$ can be simulated by invoking $\mathsf{Sim}_\Sigma(x, r, \boldsymbol{e})$. Proof-of-knowledge follows from the fact that in order for an adversary to compute a proof by querying fewer than $r+1$ accepting Sigma protocol transcripts to H, the first r accepting transcripts it queries to H must all evaluate to the same ℓ-bit string. This happens with probability $(2^{-\ell})^{r-1} = 2^{-\lambda}$. □

Query Complexity. We make use of the analysis of multicollision running times by von Mises [vM39] and revisited by Preneel [Pre93, Appendix B].

[7] $\lim_{r \to \infty} r/(r!)^{1/r} = e$.

Protocol π_{NIZK}

The prover P and verifier V are both given the statement x while the prover also has a witness w for the statement $x \in L$. Both parties have access to an ℓ-bit Random Oracle $H : \{0,1\}^* \mapsto \{0,1\}^\ell$. The underlying Strongly $r+1$-special sound sigma protocol is given by $\Sigma = ((P_{\Sigma,a}, P_{\Sigma,z}), \mathsf{V}_\Sigma)$. Define $t = \ell + \lceil \log r \rceil$.

$\mathsf{P}^H(x, w)$:

1. Run $P_{\Sigma,a}(x, w)$ to obtain $\boldsymbol{a}$ and state
2. Set $\mathcal{E} = \mathcal{Z} = \emptyset$ and do the following until an output is produced:
   (a) Uniformly sample $e \leftarrow \{0,1\}^t \setminus \mathcal{E}$
   (b) Set $z = P_{\Sigma,z}(\mathsf{state}, e)$ and append (e, z) to $\mathcal{Z}$ and e to $\mathcal{E}$
   (c) If $\exists (e_1, z_1), (e_2, z_2), \cdots, (e_r, z_r) \in \mathcal{Z}$ such that

$$H(\boldsymbol{a}, e_1, z_1) = H(\boldsymbol{a}, e_2, z_2) = \cdots = H(\boldsymbol{a}, e_r, z_r)$$

   then set $\boldsymbol{e} = (e_i)_{i\in[r]}$ and $(z_i)_{i\in[r]}$ and output $\pi = (\boldsymbol{a}, \boldsymbol{e}, \boldsymbol{z})$

$\mathsf{V}^H(x, \pi)$:

1. Parse $(\boldsymbol{a}, \boldsymbol{e}, \boldsymbol{z}) = \pi$, and $(e_i)_{i\in[r]} = \boldsymbol{e}$, and $(z_i)_{i\in[r]} = \boldsymbol{z}$.
2. Check that $H(\boldsymbol{a}, e_1, z_1) = H(\boldsymbol{a}, e_2, z_2) = \cdots = H(\boldsymbol{a}, e_r, z_r)$
3. For each $i \in [r]$, check that $\mathsf{V}_\Sigma(x, (\boldsymbol{a}, e_i, z_i)) = 1$, aborting with output 0 if not
4. Accept by outputting 1

Fig. 5. Collision based NIZK

Corollary 2. *[vM39, Pre93][Theorem B.2 and pg. 283] If T balls are randomly distributed over n urns, the number T required to have at least one urn with r balls with probability $1 - \exp(-\alpha_r)$ is given by the following equation:*

$$T \cdot \exp\left(-\frac{T}{r \cdot n}\right) = \left(\alpha_r \cdot n^{(r-1)} \cdot r!\right)^{1/r}$$

In order to obtain the time $\mathsf{T}_{\mathsf{Col}}$ required to find an r-collision in expectation, one must solve for T when the parameter $\alpha_r = 1$. Substituting $n = 2^{\lambda/(r-1)}$ for our context, we get that:

$$\mathsf{T}_{\mathsf{Col}} \cdot \exp\left(-\frac{\mathsf{T}_{\mathsf{Col}}}{r \cdot 2^{\lambda/(r-1)}}\right) = \left(2^\lambda \cdot r!\right)^{1/r} = P_{\mathsf{OPT}}$$

This equation is non-trivial to analyze relative to that of Fischlin, and so for ease of understanding we plot the ratio T/P_{OPT} for both π_{NIZK} and Fischlin's construction in Fig. 6. This plot shows that for some reasonable parameterizations around $r \sim 5$, our construction achieves roughly 2x factor improvement in Prover complexity.

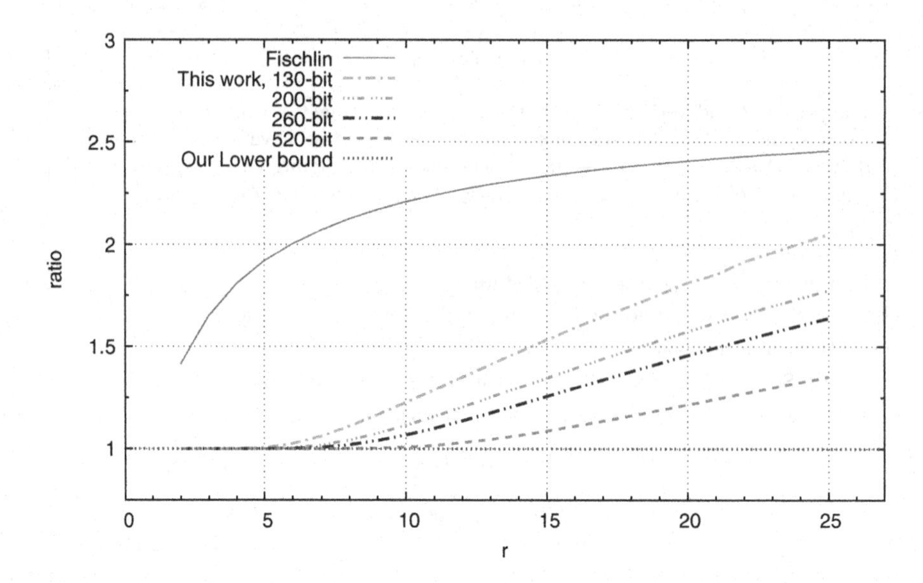

Fig. 6. Ratio of prover query complexities $\mathsf{T}_{\mathsf{Col}}$ and $\mathsf{T}_{\mathsf{Fis}}$ to the optimal P_{OPT} (y-axis) for different r parameters (x-axis), where $\mathsf{T}_{\mathsf{Col}}[r]$ and $\mathsf{T}_{\mathsf{Fis}}[r]$ are the number of oracle queries required to compute a proof in expectation upon fixing parameter r. Note that $\mathsf{T}_{\mathsf{Col}}/P_{\mathsf{OPT}}$ depends on the security parameter, whereas $\mathsf{T}_{\mathsf{Fis}}/P_{\mathsf{OPT}}$ is essentially invariant of it. Consequently we plot $\mathsf{T}_{\mathsf{Col}}/P_{\mathsf{OPT}}$ for a range of security parameters, where "λ-bit Col" denotes a λ-bit security level.

Finally, we note that Fig. 6 only plots the ratio of Fischlin/Collision/optimal but does not convey the actual prover query complexities at those parameter choices.

6 Expanding the Applicability of Fischlin's Transform

As mentioned in Sect. 1, Fischlin's transformation applies to only a limited class of Sigma protocols that satisfy a *quasi-unique responses* constraint. Fischlin relied on this property to prove both zero-knowledge as well as proof of knowledge. While it is folklore that this property is not strictly necessary for the extractor, its necessity for zero-knowledge has remained thus far unclear.

We begin by showing in Sect. 6.1 a concrete attack on Witness Indistinguishability when Fischlin's transformation is applied to the Sigma protocol used to prove knowledge of one of two discrete logarithms [CDS94]. We then formalize a *strong special soundness* property for Sigma protocols that suffices for extraction, which includes languages that do not by default support the quasi-unique responses property, such as the logical OR Sigma protocol mentioned above. Finally we show how appropriately randomizing Fischlin's construction can achieve ZK unconditionally, for any strong special sound Sigma protocol.

6.1 Testing Witness Use in Fischlin's Transformation

Our distinguisher will not rely on the ability to query multiple accepting transcripts for the same challenge. For reference, we first recall the underlying Sigma protocol (due to Cramer et al. [CDS94]) in Fig. 7.

Protocol $\Sigma_{\mathsf{DL}}^{\vee}$

The prover P and verifier V are both given the statement $(X_0, X_1) = (w_0 \cdot G, w_1 \cdot G) \in \mathbb{G}^2$ while the prover also has $w_b \in \mathbb{Z}_q$ for $b \in \{0,1\}$.

$\mathsf{P}^a_{\Sigma_{\mathsf{DL}}^{\vee}}((X_0, X_1), w_b)$:

1. Simulate a transcript for DLog proof of knowledge of X_{1-b}:
   - Sample $e_{1-b} \leftarrow \{0,1\}^\lambda$ and compute $(a_{1-b}, z_{1-b}) \leftarrow \mathsf{Sim}_{\Sigma_{\mathsf{DL}}}(X_{1-b}, e_{1-b})$
2. Sample $r_b \leftarrow \mathbb{Z}_q$ and compute $a_b = r_b \cdot G$
3. Publish commitment $a = (a_0, a_1)$ and output $\mathsf{state} = w_b, r_b, (a_{1-b}, e_{1-b}, z_{1-b})$

$\mathsf{P}^z_{\Sigma_{\mathsf{DL}}^{\vee}}(\mathsf{state}, e)$: Compute $e_b = e \oplus e_{1-b}$ and $z_b = w_b \cdot e_b + r_b$, and Output (e_0, e_1, z_0, z_1)

$\mathsf{V}(X, a, e, z)$:

1. Parse $a = (a_0, a_1)$ and $z = (e_0, e_1, z_0, z_1)$ and verify $e_0 \oplus e_1 = e$
2. Verify $z_b \cdot G = e_b \cdot X_b + a_b$ for each $b \in \{0,1\}$

Fig. 7. Proving knowledge of one of two discrete logarithms [CDS94]

An adversary attacking Witness Indistinguishability conventionally possesses two witnesses to the theorem and is given a proof π, and must determine which witness was used to produce it. We construct a more powerful type of attack, which makes use of a single witness and determines whether π was created using this witness or the opposite one. This fact will be useful when examining the protocol contexts in which our attack applies.

As we briefly discussed in Sect. 2.2, the attack strategy is to exploit the deterministic nature of Fischlin's prover by retrieving the Sigma protocol randomness and retracing the prover's steps. Concretely with Schnorr-style proofs, the messages z and c and the witness determine the randomness. The attacker can therefore retrieve this randomness, and simply replay the honest prover's algorithm and see if the resulting proof string is the same as the given one. The main subtle step in this attack's analysis is to argue that when this retrieve-and-retrace procedure is applied using a different witness from the one used to produce the proof string originally, there is a noticeable probability of producing a different proof string.

While the regular Witness Indistinguishability definition allows the adversary to supply both witnesses, in order to stay within the constraints of quasi-unique responses we formulate a stronger version of the WI experiment for our specific setting. In our definition the challenger samples both witnesses and gives the adversary only one of them (the other witness represents the trapdoor for the system parameter k). We define our experiment as follows:
$\mathsf{Expt}^{\mathsf{DL\text{-}WI}}_{\mathcal{A},\mathsf{P}}(1^\lambda)$:

1. The adversary $\mathcal{A}$ submits a bit $b \in \{0,1\}$ to the challenger
2. The challenger samples $w_0, w_1 \leftarrow \mathbb{Z}_q$ and sets $X_0 = g^{w_0}, X_1 = g^{w_1}$
3. The challenger tosses a coin $\beta \leftarrow \{0,1\}$, and computes $\pi \leftarrow \mathsf{P}((X_0, X_1), w_\beta)$
4. The challenger sends X_0, X_1, w_b, π to $\mathcal{A}$
5. $\mathcal{A}$ outputs a bit

The advantage $\mathsf{AdvDL\text{-}WI}[\mathcal{A}, \mathsf{P}]$ of an adversary $\mathcal{A}$ is defined as:

$$|\Pr[\mathcal{A}(b, w_b, X_{1-b}, \pi) = 1 \mid \beta = 0] - \Pr[\mathcal{A}(b, w_b, X_{1-b}, \pi) = 1 \mid \beta = 1]|$$

Clearly any Witness Indistinguishable scheme will guarantee that the above advantage is negligible. We now give our concrete attack and analysis.

Lemma 4. *Let* P *be the prover's algorithm obtained by applying Fischlin's transformation [Fis05] to the Sigma protocol to prove knowledge of one of two discrete logarithms [CDS94]. Then there is an efficient adversary* $\mathcal{A}$ *such that* $\mathsf{AdvDL\text{-}WI}[\mathcal{A}, \mathsf{P}]$ *is non-negligible.*

Equipped with this non-negligibly successful adversary $\mathcal{A}$, in the full version we will show how a natural protocol scenario that appears to enable quasi-unique responses in fact structurally resembles the $\mathsf{Expt}^{\mathsf{DL\text{-}WI}}_{\mathcal{A},\mathsf{P}}$ experiment. This allows us to deploy our $\mathsf{Expt}^{\mathsf{DL\text{-}WI}}_{\mathcal{A},\mathsf{P}}$ adversary $\mathcal{A}$ to break the security of the larger protocol.

Proof. For simplicity, we consider only a single base unit, i.e. assume that there is only one repetition in the transformed Sigma protocol.

Consider an attacker, that on input a proof $\pi = ((a_0, a_1), e, (e_0, e_1, z_0, z_1))$ obtained by applying Fischlin's transformation to $\Sigma^{\vee}_{\mathsf{DL}}$ using ℓ-bit output hash function H, and witness w_b, does the following:

1. Compute $r_b = z_b - w_b \cdot e_b$ and set $\mathsf{state}_b = w_b, r_b, (a_{1-b}, e_{1-b}, z_{1-b})$
2. Starting with $e = 0$, increment e until $H((a_0, a_1), e, (e_0, e_1, z_0, z_1)) = 0^\ell$ is found, where $(e_0, e_1, z_0, z_1) = \mathsf{P}^z_{\Sigma^{\vee}_{\mathsf{DL}}}(\mathsf{state}_b, e)$
3. Set $\pi_b = (a_0, a_1), e', (e'_0, e'_1, z'_0, z'_1)$
4. If $\pi_b = \pi$ output b, otherwise output $1 - b$.

Denote the witness used by the challenger to produce the proof as w_β. When $\beta = b$ the attacker outputs the correct bit with certainty since the honest prover's steps are perfectly reconstructed to produce $\pi_b = \pi$. The interesting case to analyze is when $\beta = 1-b$. There are two possible outcomes triggered in this case, i.e., $\pi_b = \pi$ and $\pi_b \neq \pi$. The latter outcome is induced by the attacker finding an accepting transcript (a, e', z') with $e' < e$ that resulted in $H(a, e', z') = 0^\ell$

(note that $e' > e$ is impossible as we know that $H(a, e, z) = 0^\ell$, and so the prover never increments past e). The implication in this event is that π was certainly not produced using w_b; this is because had the honest prover started with witness w_b and state state_b, it would have terminated with output $\pi' = (a, e', z')$ rather than the given π.

It remains to show that this distinguishing event (call it $\mathsf{diffProof}$) occurs with non-negligible probability. Note that since the attack is always successful when $\beta = b$, the value $\Pr[\mathsf{diffProof}]$ characterizes the distinguishing advantage of this attack. This is because $\mathsf{AdvDL\text{-}WI}[\mathcal{A}, \mathsf{P}]$ can be simplified as follows, given that b is fixed:

$$\begin{aligned}|\Pr[\mathcal{A}(w_b, X_{1-b}, \pi) = b \mid \beta = b] - \Pr[\mathcal{A}(w_b, X_{1-b}, \pi) = b \mid \beta = 1 - b]|\\ = |1 - (1 - \Pr[\mathsf{diffProof}])| = \Pr[\mathsf{diffProof}]\end{aligned}$$

Let $Q_{b,i}$ be the query made by the attacker that corresponds to responding to the ith challenge using witness w_b; in particular

$$Q_{b,i} = (a_0, a_1), i, \mathsf{P}^z_{\Sigma^\vee_{\mathsf{DL}}}(\mathsf{state}_b, i)$$

and thus $\pi_b = Q_{b,i}$ for the smallest i such that $H(Q_{b,i}) = 0^\ell$. Define $Q_{1-b,i}$ the same way using $\mathsf{state}_{1-b} = w_{1-b}, r_{1-b}, (a_b, e_b, z_b)$, except that the query is made by the challenger rather than the attacker in this experiment (since $\beta = 1 - b$).

Claim 8. *$\forall e' \neq e$, it holds that $Q_{0,e'} \neq Q_{1,e'}$.*

Proof. Consider any $e' \neq e$. Let $e'_0 = e' \oplus e_1$ and $e'_1 = e' \oplus e_0$. Clearly $e'_0 \neq e_0$ and $e'_1 \neq e_1$ as $e' \neq e = e_0 \oplus e_1$. By the structure of $\mathsf{P}^z_{\Sigma^\vee_{\mathsf{DL}}}(\mathsf{state}_b, e')$, the queries $Q_{b,e'}$ are correspondingly constructed as follows:

$$Q_{0,e'} = (\cdots e'_0, e_1, \cdots) \text{ and } Q_{1,e'} = (\cdots e_0, e'_1, \cdots)$$

Clearly $Q_{0,e'} \neq Q_{1,e'}$ as $e_0 \neq e'_0$ and $e_1 \neq e'_1$. □

Corollary 3. *$\forall e' \neq e$, the values $H(Q_{0,e'})$ and $H(Q_{1,e'})$ are independently distributed.*

Recall that the event $\mathsf{diffProof}$ is precisely the event that the attacker finds an accepting proof $\pi_b = (a, e', z')$ such that $e' < e$. Rather than characterizing $\mathsf{diffProof}$ in its entirety, we analyze a simpler special case. In particular, the event $H(Q_{\beta,0}) \neq 0^\ell$ (implying $e > 0$ in π) and $H(Q_{1-\beta,0}) = 0^\ell$ (implying $e' = 0$ and hence $\pi_b \neq \pi$) induces $\mathsf{diffProof}$. Then applying Corollary 3 we can therefore lower bound $\Pr[\mathsf{diffProof}]$ as follows:

$$\begin{aligned}\Pr[\mathsf{diffProof}] &\geq \Pr[H(Q_{\beta,0}) \neq 0^\ell \wedge H(Q_{1-\beta,0}) = 0^\ell]\\ &= \Pr[H(Q_{\beta,0}) \neq 0^\ell] \cdot \Pr[H(Q_{1-\beta,0}) = 0^\ell]\\ &= \frac{2^\ell - 1}{2^\ell} \cdot \frac{1}{2^\ell} = \frac{2^\ell - 1}{2^{2\ell}}\end{aligned}$$

As we know that $\ell \in O(\log \lambda)$ is necessary for completeness, the denominator of the above value $2^{2\ell} \in \mathsf{poly}(\lambda)$. We therefore conclude that $\Pr[\mathsf{diffProof}]$ is non-negligible in λ, and this completes the analysis.

6.2 Strong Special Soundness

Before describing how to patch the above attack, we present an easily verifiable property of Sigma protocols for which our transformation applies. Rather than attempting to quantify the ability of an adversary to induce a bad event, we take a constructive approach in our definition; i.e., it is easier to evaluate precise deterministic conditions (such as special soundness) rather than reason about probabilistic/computational system parameters (as in quasi-unique responses).

Our definition is a mild strengthening of the two-special soundness notion for Sigma protocols [Dam02], and so we call it *strong* two-special soundness—also in homage to the similar concept of *strong* unforgeability for signature schemes. Informally stated, a strongly two-special sound sigma protocol has an extractor which when given two distinct accepting transcripts (a, e, z) and (a, e', z') that share the same first message, outputs a witness for the statement with certainty (note that $e = e'$ is allowed). The standard two-special soundness notion enforces that $e \neq e'$ for the extractor's success. We give the formal definition in the full version.

Many natural sigma protocols (including logical compositions [CDS94], Okamoto's identification protocol [Oka93], etc.) satisfy this definition (but may not satisfy quasi-unique responses). There are two notable natural examples that may not meet this definition: (1) Blum's protocol to prove knowledge of a Hamiltonian cycle [Blu86] allows the prover to open any cycle in the graph and it is unclear as to how an extractor for strong special soundness can deal with such a situation, and (2) the Sigma protocol that underlies EdDSA [BDL+12], which is Schnorr's scheme implemented over an elliptic curve group of composite order. The lax verification equation in the original specification means that the verifier accepts multiple discrete logarithms for the same curve point. However we stress that this is due to lax realization of the abstraction required for Schnorr's sigma protocol, and is easily fixed in works that succeeded the original spec [CGN20,BCJZ21]. Note that both cases will not support quasi-unique responses either, if they are not strong special sound.

Note that any standard Sigma protocol that is not strongly two-special sound can not have quasi-unique responses. In particular by definition the only way to retain standard special soundness while violating strong two-special soundness is by presenting accepting transcripts $(a, e, z_1), (a, e, z_2)$ that do not yield a witness for the theorem when given to the extractor. Any notion of *efficient* adversaries being unable to find such transcripts in the case of quasi-unique responses is captured by amending the theorem for the strong two-special sound Sigma protocol to include a disjunctive clause for knowledge of the system parameter trapdoor.

With our definition in place, we study how to compile such Sigma protocols to NIZKPoKs using Fischlin's technique.

6.3 Randomization Extends Fischlin's Technique

The issue in Fischlin's transformation is that the prover's algorithm is deterministic and consequently re-traceable. Indeed, if one were to instantiate the transformation of Pass [Pas03] by simply constructing a hash tree of accepting protocol transcripts instead of a Merkle tree of *commitments* to such transcripts, the same issue as described above would present itself more directly: given a proof and candidate witness for the statement, one could simply extract the prover's randomness and test if recomputing the proof once again yields the given one. This issue is implicitly avoided by Pass (at constant factor overhead) by constructing the Merkle tree with commitments to protocol transcripts. However it is unclear how to make such an approach work with Fischlin's transform; using randomized commitments appears to be at odds with obtaining soundness.

We show that an alternate method of randomization can be used to extend Fischlin's technique to any strong special sound Sigma protocol. The idea is to randomize the NIZK prover's algorithm so that the prover randomly steps through the challenge space until an accepting transcript that hashes to the all-zero string is found. Intuitively, proofs produced with this modified transformation do not leak any information about how many queries the prover had to make in order to find an accepting transcript. This makes it impossible for a distinguisher to retrace the steps of a prover even given all witnesses as it does not have access to the random sequence in which the prover queried the random oracle. We give a formal description of the modified transformation in the full version, along with a proof of security.

Acknowledgements. The authors would like to thank Jack Doerner and François Garillot for helpful discussions, and the anonymous reviewers for useful comments. The authors are supported in part by NSF grants 1816028 and 1646671.

References

[ABGR13] Ananth, P., Bhaskar, R., Goyal, V., Rao, V.: On the (in)security of Fischlin's paradigm. In: Sahai, A. (ed.) TCC 2013. LNCS, vol. 7785, pp. 202–221. Springer, Heidelberg (2013). https://doi.org/10.1007/978-3-642-36594-2_12

[AHIV17] Ames, S., Hazay, C., Ishai, Y., Venkitasubramaniam, M.: Ligero: lightweight sublinear arguments without a trusted setup. In: ACM CCS 2017 (2017)

[BCJZ21] Brendel, J., Cremers, C., Jackson, D., Zhao, M.: The provable security of ed25519: theory and practice. In IEEE S&P 2021 (2021)

[BCKL21] Ben-Sasson, E., Carmon, D., Kopparty, S., Levit, D.: Elliptic curve fast fourier transform (ECFFT) part I: fast polynomial algorithms over all finite fields. In: ECCC, p. 103 (2021)

[BCR+19] Ben-Sasson, E., Chiesa, A., Riabzev, M., Spooner, N., Virza, M., Ward, N.P.: Aurora: transparent succinct arguments for R1CS. In: Ishai, Y., Rijmen, V. (eds.) EUROCRYPT 2019. LNCS, vol. 11476, pp. 103–128. Springer, Cham (2019). https://doi.org/10.1007/978-3-030-17653-2_4

[BDL+12] Bernstein, D.J., Duif, N., Lange, T., Schwabe, P., Yang, B.-Y.: High-speed high-security signatures. J. Cryptogr. Eng. **2**(2), 77–89 (2012)

[Ber06] Bernstein, D.J.: Curve25519: new Diffie-Hellman speed records. In: PKC 2006 (2006)

[Blo] Average transactions per block – blockchain.com. www.blockchain.com/charts/n-transactions-per-block. Accessed 11 Feb 2022

[BLS01] Boneh, D., Lynn, B., Shacham, H.: Short signatures from the weil pairing. In: Boyd, C. (ed.) ASIACRYPT 2001. LNCS, vol. 2248, pp. 514–532. Springer, Heidelberg (2001). https://doi.org/10.1007/3-540-45682-1_30

[Blu86] Blum, M.: How to prove a theorem so no one else can claim it. In: Proceedings of the International Congress of Mathematicians, vol. 1, p. 2. Citeseer (1986)

[CDS94] Cramer, R., Damgård, I., Schoenmakers, B.: Proofs of partial knowledge and simplified design of witness hiding protocols. In: Desmedt, Y.G. (ed.) CRYPTO 1994. LNCS, vol. 839, pp. 174–187. Springer, Heidelberg (1994). https://doi.org/10.1007/3-540-48658-5_19

[CF01] Canetti, R., Fischlin, M.: Universally composable commitments. In: Kilian, J. (ed.) CRYPTO 2001. LNCS, vol. 2139, pp. 19–40. Springer, Heidelberg (2001). https://doi.org/10.1007/3-540-44647-8_2

[CGKN21] Chalkias, K., Garillot, F., Kondi, Y., Nikolaenko, V.: Non-interactive half-aggregation of EdDSA and variants of Schnorr signatures. In: Paterson, K.G. (ed.) CT-RSA 2021. LNCS, vol. 12704, pp. 577–608. Springer, Cham (2021). https://doi.org/10.1007/978-3-030-75539-3_24

[CGN20] Chalkias, K., Garillot, F., Nikolaenko, V.: Taming the many EdDSAs. In: van der Merwe, T., Mitchell, C., Mehrnezhad, M. (eds.) SSR 2020. LNCS, vol. 12529, pp. 67–90. Springer, Cham (2020). https://doi.org/10.1007/978-3-030-64357-7_4

[Dam02] Damgård, I.: On Σ-protocols. In: Lecture Notes, University of Aarhus, Department for Computer Science (2002)

[Fis05] Fischlin, M.: Communication-efficient non-interactive proofs of knowledge with online extractors. In: Shoup, V. (ed.) CRYPTO 2005. LNCS, vol. 3621, pp. 152–168. Springer, Heidelberg (2005). https://doi.org/10.1007/11535218_10

[FS87] Fiat, A., Shamir, A.: How to prove yourself: practical solutions to identification and signature problems. In: Odlyzko, A.M. (ed.) CRYPTO 1986. LNCS, vol. 263, pp. 186–194. Springer, Heidelberg (1987). https://doi.org/10.1007/3-540-47721-7_12

[GLSY04] Gennaro, R., Leigh, D., Sundaram, R., Yerazunis, W.: Batching schnorr identification scheme with applications to privacy-preserving authorization and low-bandwidth communication devices. In: Lee, P.J. (ed.) ASIACRYPT 2004. LNCS, vol. 3329, pp. 276–292. Springer, Heidelberg (2004). https://doi.org/10.1007/978-3-540-30539-2_20

[HMPs14] Hohenberger, S., Myers, S., Pass, R., Shelat, A.: ANONIZE: a large-scale anonymous survey system. In: IEEE S&P (2014)

[Lin22] Lindell, Y.: Simple three-round multiparty schnorr signing with full simulatability. IACR Cryptology ePrint Archive, p. 374 (2022)

[Oka93] Okamoto, T.: Provably secure and practical identification schemes and corresponding signature schemes. In: Brickell, E.F. (ed.) CRYPTO 1992. LNCS, vol. 740, pp. 31–53. Springer, Heidelberg (1993). https://doi.org/10.1007/3-540-48071-4_3

[Pas03] Pass, R.: On deniability in the common reference string and random oracle model. In: Boneh, D. (ed.) CRYPTO 2003. LNCS, vol. 2729, pp. 316–337. Springer, Heidelberg (2003). https://doi.org/10.1007/978-3-540-45146-4_19

[Pre93] Preneel, B.: Analysis and design of cryptographic hash functions. Ph.D. thesis, Katholieke Universiteit te Leuven (1993)

[PS96] Pointcheval, D., Stern, J.: Security proofs for signature schemes. In: Maurer, U. (ed.) EUROCRYPT 1996. LNCS, vol. 1070, pp. 387–398. Springer, Heidelberg (1996). https://doi.org/10.1007/3-540-68339-9_33

[Sch91] Schnorr, C.-P.: Efficient signature generation by smart cards. J. Cryptol. **4**(3), 161–174 (1991)

[SG02] Shoup, V., Gennaro, R.: Securing threshold cryptosystems against chosen ciphertext attack. J. Cryptol. **15**(2), 75–96 (2002)

[SLdW07] Stevens, M., Lenstra, A., de Weger, B.: Chosen-prefix collisions for MD5 and colliding X.509 certificates for different identities. In: Naor, M. (ed.) EUROCRYPT 2007. LNCS, vol. 4515, pp. 1–22. Springer, Heidelberg (2007). https://doi.org/10.1007/978-3-540-72540-4_1

[Unr15] Unruh, D.: Non-interactive zero-knowledge proofs in the quantum random oracle model. In: Oswald, E., Fischlin, M. (eds.) EUROCRYPT 2015. LNCS, vol. 9057, pp. 755–784. Springer, Heidelberg (2015). https://doi.org/10.1007/978-3-662-46803-6_25

[vM39] von Mises, R.: Über Aufteilungs-und Besetzungswahrscheinlichkeiten. na (1939)

[vzGG13] von zur Gathen, J., Gerhard, J.: Modern Computer Algebra, 3rd edn. Cambridge University Press, Cambridge (2013)

[wbo] ECFFT algorithms on the BN254 base field. https://github.com/wborgeaud/ecfft-bn254. Accessed 12 Feb 2022

SIDH Proof of Knowledge

Luca De Feo[1](✉), Samuel Dobson[2], Steven D. Galbraith[2], and Lukas Zobernig[2]

[1] IBM Research Europe, Zürich, Switzerland
asiacrypt22@defeo.lu
[2] Mathematics Department, University of Auckland, Auckland, New Zealand
{s.galbraith,lukas.zobernig}@auckland.ac.nz

Abstract. We show that the soundness proof for the De Feo–Jao–Plût identification scheme (the basis for supersingular isogeny Diffie–Hellman (SIDH) signatures) contains an invalid assumption, and we provide a counterexample for this assumption—thus showing the proof of soundness is invalid. As this proof was repeated in a number of works by various authors, multiple pieces of literature are affected by this result. Due to the importance of being able to prove knowledge of an SIDH key (for example, to prevent adaptive attacks), soundness is a vital property.

Surprisingly, the problem of proving knowledge of a specific isogeny turns out to be considerably more difficult than was perhaps anticipated. The main results of this paper are a sigma protocol to prove knowledge of a walk of specified length in a supersingular isogeny graph, and a second one to additionally prove that the isogeny maps some torsion points to some other torsion points (as seen in SIDH public keys). Our scheme also avoids the SIDH identification scheme soundness issue raised by Ghantous, Pintore and Veroni. In particular, our protocol provides a non-interactive way of verifying correctness of SIDH public keys, and related statements, as protection against adaptive attacks.

Post-scriptum: Some months after this work was completed and made public, the SIDH assumption was broken in a series of papers by several authors. Hence, in the standard SIDH setting, some of the statements studied here now have trivial polynomial time non-interactive proofs. Nevertheless our first sigma protocol is unaffected by the attacks, and our second protocol may still be useful in present and future variants of SIDH that escape the attacks.

Keywords: Post-quantum cryptography · Isogenies · Zero-knowledge · Proofs of knowledge

1 Introduction

While Supersingular Isogeny Diffie-Hellman (SIDH) [9,20] is a fast and efficient post-quantum key exchange candidate, it has been hampered by the existence of practical adaptive attacks on the scheme—the first of these given by Galbraith,

S. Agrawal and D. Lin (Eds.): ASIACRYPT 2022, LNCS 13792, pp. 310–339, 2022.
https://doi.org/10.1007/978-3-031-22966-4_11

Petit, Shani, and Ti [13] (the GPST attack), followed by other variations [12,29]. These attacks mean it is not safe to re-use a static key across multiple SIDH exchanges without other forms of protection. As such, various countermeasures have been proposed—though each with its unique drawbacks.

The first of these is to require one participant to use a one-time ephemeral key in the exchange, accompanied by a Fujisaki–Okamoto-type transform [19] revealing the corresponding secret to the other party. This allows the recipient to verify the public key is well-formed, ensuring an adaptive attack was not used. This is what was done in SIKE [1], and converts the scheme to a secure key encapsulation mechanism (KEM). But it is of limited use in cases where both parties wish to use a long-term key.

The second countermeasure is to use many SIDH exchanges in parallel, combining all the resulting secrets into a single value, as proposed by Azarderakhsh, Jao, and Leonardi [2]. This scheme is known as k-SIDH, where k is the number of keys used by each party in the exchange. The authors suggest $k = 92$ is required for a secure key exchange. Dobson, Galbraith, LeGrow, Ti, and Zobernig [10] demonstrate how the GPST adaptive attack can be ported to $k = 2$ and above. Note that the number of SIDH instances grows as k^2, so this scheme is very inefficient. Urbanik and Jao's [31] proposal attempted to improve the efficiency of this protocol by making use of the special automorphisms on curves with j-invariant 0 or 1728, but it was shown by Basso, Kutas, Merz, Petit, and Weitkämper [3] that Urbanik and Jao's proposal is vulnerable to a more efficient adaptive attack and actually scales worse in efficiency than k-SIDH itself (although the public keys are approximately 4/5 of the size, it requires around twice as many SIDH instances for the same security).

Finally, adaptive attacks can also be prevented by providing a non-interactive proof that a public key is well-formed or honestly generated. Generic NIZK techniques would make this possible, but in a very inefficient manner. Urbanik and Jao [31] claim a method for doing so using a similar idea to their k-SIDH improvement mentioned above. Their scheme is based on the SIDH-based identification scheme by De Feo, Jao, and Plût [9], which is a fairly simple proof with single bit challenges.

We briefly recall the De Feo, Jao, and Plût proof here, for full details see Sect. 4.1. Let $\phi : E_0 \to E_1$ be the isogeny of degree $\ell_1^{e_1}$ we wish to prove knowledge of. Let P_0, Q_0 be a basis of the torsion subgroup $E_0[\ell_2^{e_2}]$, and let $(P_1, Q_1) = (\phi(P_0), \phi(Q_0))$. The prover chooses a pair of integers (a, b), and sends to the verifier $E_2 = E_0/\langle [a]P_0 + [b]Q_0 \rangle$ and $E_3 = E_1/\langle [a]P_1 + [b]Q_1 \rangle$. The verifier sends a single bit challenge chall. When $\mathsf{chall} = 0$ the prover responds with (a, b), and when $\mathsf{chall} = 1$ the prover responds with an isogeny $\phi' : E_2 \to E_3$ of degree $\ell_1^{e_1}$. The protocol is repeated until the verifier is satisfied.

We show a counterexample to the soundness of the original De Feo–Jao–Plût scheme. Because this scheme (and proof) has since been used to build an undeniable signature by Jao and Soukharev [21], a signature scheme by Yoo, Azarderakhsh, Jalali, Jao, and Soukharev [33], and also by Galbraith, Petit, and Silva [14], all of these subsequent papers suffer from the same issue. Our counterexample does not immediately apply to Urbanik and Jao's scheme, but we show other problems with that scheme in Sect. 4.4.

Ghantous, Pintore, and Veroni [17] have demonstrated that the soundness property for the De Feo–Jao–Plût scheme (and those based on it) fails for a different reason—namely the existence of multiple isogenies of the same degree between some curves. The protocols we propose in this paper are not vulnerable to the same issue, as we briefly discuss in Remark 2.

We stress that the flaw in the De Feo–Jao–Plût soundness argument does not mean, *per se*, that previous isogeny signature schemes [14,33] are insecure. Forgery for these schemes still requires an attacker to compute an isogeny between two given elliptic curves, which, in full generality, is believed to be a hard problem. However, a recent series of pre-prints [6,23,26] has shown that the isogeny problem underlying SIDH itself can be solved in (classical) polynomial time. As a consequence, SIDH, SIKE, the derived signature schemes, and several other protocols are all subject to very efficient key recovery attacks.

Nevertheless, the variation on the SIDH problem we study in Sect. 5 (specifically in Fig. 3 of Sect. 5.3), by virtue of not revealing any torsion point information to the attacker, is still widely believed to be secure. In particular, our sigma protocol can be converted into a secure signature scheme using the Fiat-Shamir transform. Additionally, the problem of computing a secret isogeny from some torsion point information is still believed to be secure in some settings other than standard SIDH/SIKE; for example when the order of the known torsion is much smaller than the degree of the isogeny, when the degree of the secret isogeny is unknown [25], or when the action on the torsion basis is masked [11]. Thus the protocol we introduce in Sect. 6 may still be adapted to prove non-trivial statements.

1.1 Our Contributions

We present three new sigma protocols for SIDH. They all prove, for a pair (E_0, E_1) of publicly known supersingular curves, knowledge of an isogeny $\phi : E_0 \to E_1$ of the correct degree (the private key or *witness*). But they have some key differences we summarize next.

First, in Sect. 5.1, we propose a modification to the De Feo–Jao–Plût scheme that ensures that there is an extractor for the witness $\phi : E_0 \to E_1$. The first key idea in this protocol is the provision of bases (P_2, Q_2) for $E_2[\ell_2^{e_2}]$ and (P_3, Q_3) for $E_3[\ell_2^{e_2}]$. This allows the verifier to check that $(P_3, Q_3) = (\phi'(P_2), \phi'(Q_2))$ in the $\mathsf{chall} = 1$ case, and in the $\mathsf{chall} = 0$ case, to check that the isogenies from E_2 to E_0 and E_3 to E_1 are "parallel". The second key idea is, in the 2-special soundness proof, to view the transcript as an SIDH square where E_2 is treated as the "base curve" (instead of E_0), and where E_0 and E_3 play the roles of the participants' two public-key curves in SIDH. It then follows that there is a witness ϕ as required.

This protocol is simple, and sound, but there is a minor problem with zero-knowledge: In the $\mathsf{chall} = 0$ case, contrary to the De Feo–Jao–Plût scheme, the data $(E_2, P_2, Q_2, E_3, P_3, Q_3)$ appears to be difficult to simulate without knowledge of the secret witness. We solve this issue in Sect. 5.3 by moving from binary to ternary challenges, thus making the protocol 3-special sound: The $\mathsf{chall} = 0$ case is split into two different challenges, so that only one of (E_2, P_2, Q_2) or (E_3, P_3, Q_3) needs to be revealed at a time. Plugging a statistically hiding commitment scheme in, we obtain a zero-knowledge Proof of Knowledge for what we call the *weak SIDH relation*, i.e. the existence of $\phi : E_0 \rightarrow E_1$ of degree $\ell_1^{e_1}$. Ternary challenges and commitment schemes have been used in this context by Boneh, Kogan and Woo [5] for a variant of SIDH with three coprime subgroups.

Finally, in Sect. 6, we give a new sigma protocol that convinces a verifier not only that there is an isogeny $\phi : E_0 \rightarrow E_1$ of the correct degree, but also that the torsion points provided in an SIDH public key are the correct images of the public parameter points under ϕ. We call this stronger relation the *SIDH relation*. Boneh, Kogan and Woo [5] also give a solution to this problem in the non-standard case of SIDH with three coprime subgroups. Our scheme works with any base elliptic curve, rather than being restricted to the two curves with j-invariant 0 or 1728 as in [31].

The SIDH relation was recently proven to be decidable in polynomial time [6, 23, 26], when parameters are set like in standard SIDH/SIKE. Thus our last protocol has arguably lost most of its usefulness. Nevertheless, more general variants of the SIDH relation are still believed to be secure [11, 25]. Adapting our sigma protocol and making it non-interactive using the Fiat-Shamir heuristic gives a secure method for proving well-formedness of public keys, which is needed if one wants to prevent adaptive attacks.

The scheme in Sect. 6 builds on the protocols of Sect. 5. However, it requires assurance that the ephemeral isogenies used in the commitments by the prover are "independent enough". To achieve this, we "double" the protocol, by essentially running two sessions of the protocol from Sect. 5.3 for each challenge bit. The prover shows that the two instances are consistent with each other by providing images of a random torsion basis in both squares, which the verifier can check are correct. The verifier also checks that the two instances are independent. This allows us to construct an extractor that outputs a correct witness.

Because both of our two protocols are 3-special sound, the probability of successful cheating is 2/3—indeed a forger who does not know the witness can simultaneously construct valid responses to any two challenges. This would have implications on tightness if they were used for signature schemes. We do not recommend our protocols as bases for signatures.

Commitments in the original De Feo–Jao–Plût scheme were just j-invariants of curves, but our new proofs require committing to various points on curves as well. This makes the proofs considerably larger. As with the original De Feo–Jao–Plût scheme, it is non-trivial in the $\mathsf{chall} = 1$ case to simulate valid protocol transcripts without knowing the witness and so we only achieve computational zero-knowledge.

We explain in Sect. 7 that our scheme gives an asymptotically more efficient non-interactive key exchange (NIKE) than the k-SIDH proposal by Azarderakhsh, Jao and Leonardi [2]. But we stress that NIKE is not the only application of our work.

1.2 Plan of the Paper

Section 2 recalls the SIDH protocol and gives some useful lemmas that are used in our soundness proofs. Section 3 presents some isogeny-based hardness assumptions and reductions, including the new decisional assumptions we need for our zero-knowledge proofs. We then recall the De Feo–Jao–Plût identification scheme in Sect. 4.1 and outline the issue with its proof of soundness in Sect. 4.2. In Sect. 5 we present our protocols for the weak SIDH relation: A sound but potentially insecure protocol first, then a zero-knowledge modification afterwards. Section 6 presents a protocol to prove correctness of the points in the SIDH public key. In Sect. 7, we conclude with some standard discussion on how a NIZK scheme which is a Proof of Knowledge (PoK) of an SIDH secret key can be constructed from our last scheme—the first such scheme that is sound and proves correctness of the points in the public key (a protection mechanism against adaptive attacks [10,13]). Section 8 describes some open problems and future directions.

2 Preliminaries

Notation. As a convention, we will use K_ϕ to denote a point which generates the kernel of a cyclic isogeny ϕ. Let $[t]$ denote the set $\{1, \ldots, t\}$. All isogenies in this paper are assumed to be separable. The notation $\hat{\psi}$ denotes the dual isogeny of ψ.

2.1 SIDH

We now provide a brief refresher on the Supersingular Isogeny Diffie-Hellman (SIDH) key exchange protocol [9,20] by De Feo, Jao, and Plût.

As public parameters, we have a prime $p = \ell_1^{e_1} \cdot \ell_2^{e_2} \cdot f \pm 1$, where ℓ_1, ℓ_2 are small primes, f is an integer cofactor, and $\ell_1^{e_1} \approx \ell_2^{e_2}$. We work over the finite field $\mathbb{F}_{p^2}$. Additionally we fix a base supersingular elliptic curve E and bases $\{P_1, Q_1\}$, $\{P_2, Q_2\}$ for both the $\ell_1^{e_1}$ and $\ell_2^{e_2}$-torsion subgroups of $E(\mathbb{F}_{p^2})$ respectively (such that $E[\ell_i^{e_i}] = \langle P_i, Q_i \rangle$). Typically $\ell_1 = 2$ and $\ell_2 = 3$.

It is well known that knowledge of an isogeny (up to isomorphism) and knowledge of its kernel are equivalent, and we can convert between them at will, via Vélu's formulae [32]. In SIDH, the secret keys of Alice and Bob are isogenies $\phi_A : E(\mathbb{F}_{p^2}) \to E_A(\mathbb{F}_{p^2})$, $\phi_B : E(\mathbb{F}_{p^2}) \to E_B(\mathbb{F}_{p^2})$ of degree $\ell_1^{e_1}$ and $\ell_2^{e_2}$, respectively. These isogenies are generated by randomly choosing secret integers $a_i, b_i \in \mathbb{Z}/\ell_i^{e_i}\mathbb{Z}$ (not both divisible by ℓ_i) and computing the isogeny with kernel generated by $K_i = [a_i]P_i + [b_i]Q_i$. We thus unambiguously refer to the isogeny, its kernel, and such integers a, b, as "the secret key."

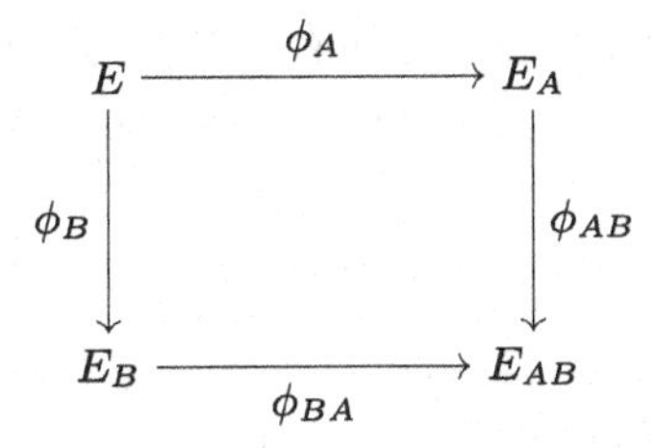

Fig. 1. Commutative diagram of SIDH, where $\ker(\phi_{BA}) = \phi_B(\ker(\phi_A))$ and $\ker(\phi_{AB}) = \phi_A(\ker(\phi_B))$.

Figure 1 depicts the commutative diagram making up the key exchange. In order to make the diagram commute, Alice and Bob are required to not only give their image curves E_A and E_B in their respective public keys, but also the images of the basis points of the other participant's kernel on E. That is, Alice provides E_A, $P_2' = \phi_A(P_2), Q_2' = \phi_A(Q_2)$ as her public key. This allows Bob to "transport" his secret isogeny to E_A and compute ϕ_{AB} whose kernel is $\langle [a_2]P_2' + [b_2]Q_2' \rangle$. Both Alice and Bob will arrive along these transported isogenies at isomorphic image curves E_{AB}, E_{BA} (using Vélu's formulae, they will actually arrive at exactly the same curve [22]). Two elliptic curves are isomorphic over $\overline{\mathbb{F}}_p$ if and only if their j-invariants are equal, $j(E_{AB}) = j(E_{BA})$, hence this j-invariant may be used as the shared secret of the SIDH key exchange.

Some cryptographic hardness assumptions related to isogenies and SIDH are discussed in Sect. 3.

2.2 Isogeny Squares

We collect here some basic definitions and lemmas that we will use repeatedly throughout the paper. In the statements below, all elliptic curves are defined over a field of characteristic p.

Definition 1 (Independent points, isogenies). *Let E be an elliptic curve, let $\ell \neq p$ be a prime and e an integer, let (P, Q) be a basis of $E[\ell^e]$. Let $R = [a]P + [b]Q$ and $S = [c]P + [d]Q$. The following conditions are equivalent:*

(a) (R, S) form a basis of $E[\ell^e]$.
(b) ℓ does not divide $ad - bc$, i.e., the matrix $\left(\begin{smallmatrix} a & b \\ c & d \end{smallmatrix}\right)$ is invertible modulo ℓ^e.
(c) The value of the ℓ^e-th Weil pairing $\zeta = e(R, S)$ has order ℓ^e, i.e., $\zeta^{\ell^{e-1}} \neq 1$.

When R, S satisfy any of these, we say they are independent *of one another. Similarly, we say that two cyclic groups of order ℓ^e are independent whenever any of their generators are. Finally, we say that two isogenies of degree ℓ^e are independent if their kernels are.*

Proof. (a) $\Rightarrow$ (b): Both P, Q and R, S are bases of the same torsion subgroup $E[\ell^e]$. Hence, $A = \left(\begin{smallmatrix} a & b \\ c & d \end{smallmatrix}\right)$ is a change-of-basis from P, Q to R, S and there must be an inverse change-of-basis A^{-1} from R, S to P, Q. Then A is necessarily invertible, and therefore, so too is its determinant $ad - bc$ modulo ℓ^e.

$(b) \Rightarrow (c)$: We have that

$$\zeta = e(R, S) = e([a]P + [b]Q, [c]P + [d]Q).$$

Then since e is bilinear, $\zeta = e(P, Q)^{ad-bc}$. Now $e(P, Q)$ has order ℓ^e because e is surjective onto the group of ℓ^e-th roots of unity (c.f. [27, Corollary III.8.1.1]), and since $\ell \nmid ad - bc$, then ζ must also have order ℓ^e.

$(c) \Rightarrow (a)$: Recall that $E[\ell^e] \simeq \mathbb{Z}/\ell^e\mathbb{Z} \times \mathbb{Z}/\ell^e\mathbb{Z}$ [27, Corollary III.6.4b]. Thus, in order for R, S to form a basis, we must show $\langle R\rangle \cap \langle S\rangle = \{\mathcal{O}_E\}$.

Suppose $[w]R = [z]S \neq \mathcal{O}_E$ for some integers w, z. By assumption, it must be that $\ell^e \nmid w$ and $\ell^e \nmid z$. Now consider $e([w]R - [z]S, S) = 1$, since $e(\mathcal{O}_E, T) = 1$ for any T. By the bilinearity of the pairing, this gives

$$e([w]R - [z]S, S) = e(R, S)^w e(S, S)^{-z} = 1.$$

Then, because $e(S, S) = 1$, we arrive at the conclusion $e(R, S)^w = 1$, which is a contradiction since $e(R, S)$ has order ℓ^e and $\ell^e \nmid w$. Thus, there can exist no such integers w, z, and therefore $\langle R\rangle \cap \langle S\rangle = \{\mathcal{O}_E\}$. □

Lemma 1. *Let $\phi : E \to E/\langle R\rangle$ be an isogeny of kernel $\langle R\rangle$ and degree ℓ^e, let S be a point of order ℓ^e independent to R. Then $\phi(S)$ has order ℓ^e and generates* $\ker(\widehat{\phi})$.

Proof. Because R and S are independent (Definition 1), the subgroups generated by R and S intersect trivially. Thus, since ϕ has kernel $\langle R\rangle$, no non-trivial point in $\langle S\rangle$ is in the kernel of ϕ. Furthermore, we know that $\widehat{\phi} \circ \phi = [\ell^e]$ has kernel $E[\ell^e]$, and that $S \in E[\ell^e]$. Thus $\widehat{\phi}(\phi(S)) = \mathcal{O}$, implying $\phi(S)$ is in the kernel of $\widehat{\phi}$. The same holds for all elements $S' = [\lambda]S \in \langle S\rangle$, and since $\phi(S') \neq \mathcal{O}$ for all non-trivial S', $\phi(S)$ has order ℓ^e and generates $\ker(\widehat{\phi})$. □

The following lemma is the main tool we are going to use, repeatedly, to design all proofs of knowledge.

Lemma 2. *Let ℓ_1, ℓ_2 be distinct primes different from p, let e_1, e_2 be integers. Let $\phi_A : E \to E_A$ be an isogeny of degree $\ell_1^{e_1}$. Let $\phi_B : E \to E_B$ and $\phi_{AB} : E_A \to E_{AB}$ be isogenies of degree $\ell_2^{e_2}$ such that* $\ker(\phi_{AB}) = \phi_A(\ker(\phi_B))$. *Then there exists an isogeny $\phi_{BA} : E_B \to E_{AB}$ of degree $\ell_1^{e_1}$.*

Proof. Let K_A be a generator of $\ker(\phi_A)$. Then because the degrees of ϕ_A, ϕ_B are coprime, $\phi_B(K_A)$ also has order $\ell_1^{e_1}$ and generates the kernel of some isogeny

$$\chi : E_B \to E_B/\langle\phi_B(K_A)\rangle.$$

Observe that E_{AB} is defined as the codomain of $\phi_{AB} \circ \phi_A$. We thus have that $E_{AB} \cong E/\langle K_A, K'\rangle$ for a point K' of order $\ell_2^{e_2}$ such that $\langle\phi_A(K')\rangle = \ker(\phi_{AB})$. Because $\ker(\phi_{AB}) = \phi_A(\ker(\phi_B))$, we conclude $\langle K'\rangle = \ker(\phi_B)$. Therefore, $E_B/\langle\phi_B(K_A)\rangle \cong E_{AB}$ as required. □

2.3 Sigma Protocols

A sigma protocol Π_Σ for a relation $\mathcal{R} = \{(X, W)\}$ is a public-coin three-move interactive proof system consisting of two parties: A verifier V and a prover P. Recall that public-coin informally means that there are no secret sources of randomness—the verifier's coin tosses are accessible to the prover. In practice this means the challenge sent by the verifier to the prover is uniformly random. For our purposes, a witness W can be thought of as a secret key, while the statement X is the corresponding public key. Thus, proving $(X, W) \in \mathcal{R}$ is equivalent to saying that X is a valid public key for which a corresponding secret key exists. We use the security parameter κ to parametrize the length of the secret keys involved.

Definition 2 (Sigma protocol). *A sigma protocol Π_Σ for a family of relations $\{\mathcal{R}\}_\kappa$ parametrized by security parameter κ consists of PPT algorithms $((P_1, P_2), (V_1, V_2))$ where V_2 is deterministic and we assume P_1, P_2 share states. The protocol proceeds as follows:*

1. *Round 1: The prover, on input $(X, W) \in \mathcal{R}$, returns a commitment $\mathsf{com} \leftarrow P_1(X, W)$ which is sent to the verifier.*
2. *Round 2: The verifier, on receipt of com, runs $\mathsf{chall} \leftarrow V_1(1^\kappa)$ to obtain a random challenge, and sends this to the prover.*
3. *Round 3: The prover then runs $\mathsf{resp} \leftarrow P_2(X, W, \mathsf{chall})$ and returns resp to the verifier.*
4. *Verification: The verifier runs $V_2(X, \mathsf{com}, \mathsf{chall}, \mathsf{resp})$ and outputs either $\top$ (accept) or $\perp$ (reject).*

A transcript $(\mathsf{com}, \mathsf{chall}, \mathsf{resp})$ is said to be valid if $V_2(X, \mathsf{com}, \mathsf{chall}, \mathsf{resp})$ outputs $\top$. Let $\langle P, V\rangle$ denote the transcript for an interaction between prover P and verifier V. The main requirements of a sigma protocol are:

Correctness: If the prover P knows $(X, W) \in \mathcal{R}$ and behaves honestly, then the verifier V accepts.

n-special Soundness: There exists a polynomial-time extraction algorithm that, given a statement X and n valid transcripts

$$(\mathsf{com}, \mathsf{chall}_1, \mathsf{resp}_1), \dots, (\mathsf{com}, \mathsf{chall}_n, \mathsf{resp}_n)$$

where $\mathsf{chall}_i \neq \mathsf{chall}_j$ for all $1 \leq i < j \leq n$, outputs a witness W such that $(X, W) \in \mathcal{R}$ with probability at least $1 - \varepsilon$ for soundness error ε.

A sound sigma protocol for $\mathcal{R}$ is also called a **Proof of Knowledge (PoK)** for $\mathcal{R}$.

Special Honest Verifier Zero-knowledge (SHVZK): If there exists a polynomial-time simulator that, given a statement X and a challenge chall, outputs a valid transcript $(\mathsf{com}, \mathsf{chall}, \mathsf{resp})$ that is indistinguishable from a real transcript.

Definition 3. *A sigma protocol (P, V) is computationally special honest verifier zero-knowledge if there exists a probabilistic polynomial time simulator* Sim *such that for all probabilistic polynomial time stateful adversaries $\mathcal{A}$*

$$\Pr\left[\mathcal{A}(\mathsf{com}, \mathsf{chall}, \mathsf{resp}) = 1 \;\middle|\; \begin{array}{l} (X, W, \mathsf{chall}) \leftarrow \mathcal{A}(1^\kappa); \\ \mathsf{com} \leftarrow P_1(X, W); \\ \mathsf{resp} \leftarrow P_2(X, W, \mathsf{chall}) \end{array}\right]$$
$$\approx \Pr\left[\mathcal{A}(\mathsf{com}, \mathsf{chall}, \mathsf{resp}) = 1 \;\middle|\; \begin{array}{l} (X, W, \mathsf{chall}) \leftarrow \mathcal{A}(1^\kappa); \\ (\mathsf{com}, \mathsf{resp}) \leftarrow \mathsf{Sim}(X, \mathsf{chall}) \end{array}\right]. \quad (1)$$

Although SHVZK is not a particularly strong flavour of zero-knowledge, there exist efficient transformations to full zero-knowledge that incur only a small overhead in communication and computation [7,8,16]. In particular, it is well known that SHVZK is sufficient to obtain full non-interactive zero-knowledge in the random oracle model [4].

An earlier version of our paper proposed schemes with binary challenges whose security required a certain computational assumption. It turned out that with respect to Definition 3 this assumption did not hold. To resolve this we have modified the schemes to use ternary challenges.

3 SIDH Problems and Assumptions

In this section, we recall some standard isogeny-based hardness assumptions of relevance to this work. We then introduce a new decisional assumption which will be useful for the proof of zero-knowledge in Sect. 6. The first two are computational isogeny-finding problems.

Definition 4 (General isogeny problem). *Given j-invariants $j, j' \in \mathbb{F}_{p^2}$, find an isogeny $\phi : E \to E'$ if one exists, where $j(E) = j$ and $j(E') = j'$.*

This is the foundational hardness assumption of isogeny-based cryptography, that it is hard to find an isogeny between two given curves. Note the decisional version, determining whether an isogeny exists, is easy—an isogeny exists if and only if $\#E(\mathbb{F}_{p^2}) = \#E'(\mathbb{F}_{p^2})$.

Definition 5 (Computational Supersingular Isogeny (CSSI) problem). *For fixed SIDH prime p, base curve E_0, and $\ell_2^{e_2}$-torsion basis $P_0, Q_0 \in E_0$, let $\phi : E_0 \to E_1$ be an isogeny of degree $\ell_1^{e_1}$. Given an SIDH public key $(E_1, P_1 = \phi(P_0), Q_1 = \phi(Q_0))$, find an isogeny $\phi' : E_0 \to E_1$ of degree $\ell_1^{e_1}$ such that P_1, $Q_1 = \phi'(P_0), \phi'(Q_0)$.*

This is problem 5.2 of [9] and essentially states that it is hard to find the secret key corresponding to a given public key. This problem is also called the SIDH isogeny problem by [15, Definition 2]. The recent attacks [6,23,26] show that this problem, as stated, can be solved in polynomial time. Some generalizations [11, 25] may still be hard, though.

At the heart of the GPST adaptive attack is the problem that, given a public key (E_1, P_1, Q_1), we cannot validate that P_1, Q_1 are indeed the correct images of basis points P_0, Q_0 under the secret isogeny ϕ. The best we know how to do is to check they are indeed a basis of the correct order, and use the Weil pairing check

$$e_{\ell_2^{e_2}}(P_1, Q_1) = e_{\ell_2^{e_2}}(P_0, Q_0)^{\deg \phi}.$$

Unfortunately this holds for many different choices of basis points. Indeed, if (P_1, Q_1) are the correct images, then any pair $([a]P_1 + [b]Q_1, [c]P_1 + [d]Q_1)$ such that $ad - bc = 1 \bmod \ell_2^{e_2}$ also passes the check. So this is not enough to uniquely determine ϕ, and, in particular, is insufficient to protect against the GPST adaptive attack.

The following decisional problem follows Definition 3 of [15] and is also very similar to the key validation problem of Urbanik and Jao [30, Problem 3.4] (the key validation problem asks whether a ϕ of degree *dividing* $\ell_1^{e_1}$ exists). However, the previous definitions did not take the Weil pairing check into account, which would serve as a distinguisher.

Definition 6 (Decisional SIDH isogeny (DSIDH) problem). *The decisional SIDH problem is to distinguish between the following two distributions:*

- $\mathcal{D}_0 = \{(E_0, P_0, Q_0, E_1, P_1, Q_1)\}$ *such that* E_0 *is a supersingular elliptic curve defined over* $\mathbb{F}_{p^2}$*,* P_0, Q_0 *a basis such that* $E_0[\ell_2^{e_2}] = \langle P_0, Q_0 \rangle$*,* $\phi : E_0 \to E_1$ *is an isogeny of degree* $\ell_1^{e_1}$*, and* $P_1 = \phi(P_0)$ *and* $Q_1 = \phi(Q_0)$*.*
- $\mathcal{D}_1 = \{(E_0, P_0, Q_0, E_1, P_1, Q_1)\}$ *such that* E_0 *is a supersingular elliptic curve defined over* $\mathbb{F}_{p^2}$*,* P_0, Q_0 *a basis such that* $E_0[\ell_2^{e_2}] = \langle P_0, Q_0 \rangle$*,* E_1 *is any supersingular elliptic curve over* $\mathbb{F}_{p^2}$ *with the same cardinality as* E_0*, and* P_1, Q_1 *is a basis of* $E_1[\ell_2^{e_2}]$ *satisfying the Weil pairing check* $e_{\ell_2^{e_2}}(P_1, Q_1) = e_{\ell_2^{e_2}}(P_0, Q_0)^{\ell_1^{e_1}}$*.*

As shown by Galbraith and Vercauteren [15], Thormarker [28], and Urbanik and Jao [30], being able to solve this decisional problem is as hard as solving the computational (CSSI) problem, so, assuming CSSI is hard, key validation is fundamentally difficult. This is done by testing ℓ_1-isogeny neighboring curves of E_1 and learning the correct path one bit at a time.

Definition 7 (Decisional Supersingular Product (DSSP) problem). *Given an isogeny* $\phi : E_0 \to E_1$ *of degree* $\ell_1^{e_1}$*, the decisional supersingular product problem is to distinguish between the following two distributions:*

- $\mathcal{D}_0 = \{(E_2, E_3, \phi')\}$ *such that there exists a cyclic subgroup* $G \subseteq E_0[\ell_2^{e_2}]$ *of order* $\ell_2^{e_2}$ *and* $E_2 \cong E_0/G$ *and* $E_3 \cong E_1/\phi(G)$*, and* $\phi' : E_2 \to E_3$ *is a degree* $\ell_1^{e_1}$ *isogeny.*
- $\mathcal{D}_1 = \{(E_2, E_3, \phi')\}$ *such that* E_2 *is a random supersingular curve with the same cardinality as* E_0*, and* E_3 *is the codomain of a random isogeny* $\phi' : E_2 \to E_3$ *of degree* $\ell_1^{e_1}$*.*

This is problem 5.5 of [9] and intuitively states that it is hard to determine whether there exist valid "vertical sides" to an SIDH square given the corners and the bottom horizontal side. It is not known to be affected by the recent attacks on SIDH.

3.1 Double Variant

In Sect. 6, we propose a scheme which uses two independent SIDH squares in each round of the sigma protocol. For the zero-knowledge proof in that section, we require a "double" variant of the DSSP problem.

The Double-DSSP problem differs from the "single" version by the introduction of two bases U_i', V_i' of the $\ell_1^{e_1}$-torsion subgroups on $E_{2,i}$, for $i \in \{0, 1\}$. As we shall see in Sect. 6, these extra points will be used to verify that the two independent SIDH squares in the "double" protocol both use consistent isogenies ϕ_i'.

Definition 8 (Double-DSSP Problem). *Given an isogeny $\phi : E_0 \to E_1$ of degree $\ell_1^{e_1}$, let $\mathcal{D}_0$ and $\mathcal{D}_1$ denote the two distributions in the DSSP problem. The double decisional supersingular product problem is to distinguish between the following two distributions:*

- $\mathcal{D}_0' = \{(\mathsf{inst}_i, U_i', V_i')_{i\in\{0,1\}}\}$ *where* $\mathsf{inst}_i = (E_{2,i}, E_{3,i}, \phi_i') \leftarrow \mathcal{D}_0$, *and additionally, if $\psi_i : E_0 \to E_{2,i}$ are the respective isogenies of degree $\ell_2^{e_2}$, then ψ_0 and ψ_1 are independent and $U_i', V_i' = \psi_i(U), \psi_i(V)$ where $\{U, V\}$ is a random (secret) basis of $E_0[\ell_1^{e_1}]$.*
- $\mathcal{D}_1' = \{(\mathsf{inst}_i, U_i', V_i')_{i\in\{0,1\}}\}$ *where* $\mathsf{inst}_i = (E_{2,i}, E_{3,i}, \phi_i') \leftarrow \mathcal{D}_1$, *and U_i', V_i' is a random basis of the $\ell_1^{e_1}$ torsion subgroup on $E_{2,i}$ such that $e_{\ell_1^{e_1}}(U_0', V_0') = e_{\ell_1^{e_1}}(U_1', V_1')$ and for any generator K_i of* $\ker(\phi_i')$

$$e_{\ell_1^{e_1}}(U_0', K_0) e_{\ell_1^{e_1}}(K_1, V_1') = e_{\ell_1^{e_1}}(K_0, V_0') e_{\ell_1^{e_1}}(U_1', K_1).$$

The extra points in Double-DSSP make its hardness more dubious than that of DSSP. Indeed, one strategy to distinguish $\mathcal{D}_0'$ from $\mathcal{D}_1'$ would be to compute the isogeny $\psi_1 \circ \widehat{\psi_0} : E_{2,0} \to E_{2,1}$ of degree $\ell_2^{2e_2}$ from the knowledge of its action on (U_0', V_0'). One could imagine using the recent attacks on SIDH for this task, however in a standard SIDH setting they do not apply, because $\ell_2^{2e_2} \gg \ell_1^{e_1}$. There exist parameter regimes, though, where DSSP is still thought to be hard, whereas Double-DSSP is clearly not. At any rate, since Double-DSSP is meant to be used in contexts where a variant of CSSI is hard, it is reasonable to assume the extra points do not affect security.

4 Previous SIDH Identification Scheme and Soundness Issue

4.1 De Feo–Jao–Plût Scheme

Let p be a large prime of the form $\ell_1^{e_1} \cdot \ell_2^{e_2} \cdot f \pm 1$, where ℓ_1, ℓ_2 are small primes. We start with a supersingular elliptic curve E_0 defined over $\mathbb{F}_{p^2}$ with $\#E_0(\mathbb{F}_{p^2}) =$

$(\ell_1^{e_1}\ell_2^{e_2}f)^2$. The private key is a uniformly random point $K_\phi \in E_0(\mathbb{F}_{p^2})$ of exact order $\ell_1^{e_1}$. Define $E_1 = E_0/\langle K_\phi \rangle$ and denote the corresponding $\ell_1^{e_1}$-isogeny by $\phi : E_0 \to E_1$.

Let P_0, Q_0 be a basis of the torsion subgroup $E_0[\ell_2^{e_2}] = \langle P_0, Q_0 \rangle$. The fixed public parameters are $pp = (p, E_0, P_0, Q_0)$. The public key is $(E_1, \phi(P_0), \phi(Q_0))$. The private key is the kernel generator K_ϕ (equivalently, the isogeny ϕ). The interaction goes as follows:

1. The prover chooses a random primitive $\ell_2^{e_2}$-torsion point K_ψ as $K_\psi = [a]P_0 + [b]Q_0$ for some integers $0 \leq a, b < \ell_2^{e_2}$ not both divisible by ℓ_2. Note that $\phi(K_\psi) = [a]\phi(P_0) + [b]\phi(Q_0)$. The prover defines the curves $E_2 = E_0/\langle K_\psi \rangle$ and $E_3 = E_1/\langle \phi(K_\psi) \rangle = E_0/\langle K_\psi, K_\phi \rangle$, and uses Vélu's formulae to compute the following diagram.

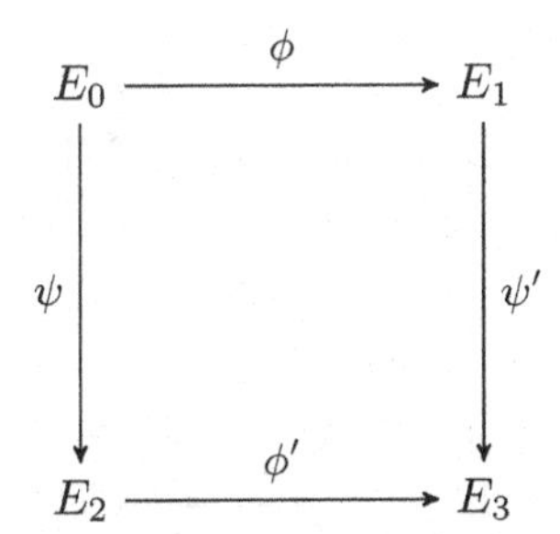

   The prover sends commitment $\mathsf{com} = (E_2, E_3)$ to the verifier.
2. The verifier challenges the prover with a uniformly random bit $\mathsf{chall} \leftarrow \{0, 1\}$.
3. If $\mathsf{chall} = 0$, the prover reveals $\mathsf{resp} = (a, b)$ from which K_ψ and $\phi(K_\psi) = K_{\psi'}$ can be reconstructed. If $\mathsf{chall} = 1$, the prover reveals $\mathsf{resp} = (\psi(K_\phi) = K_{\phi'})$.

In both cases, the verifier accepts the proof if the points revealed have the correct order and generate kernels of isogenies between the correct curves. We iterate this process t times to reduce the cheating probability (where t is chosen based on the security parameter κ). Note that in an honest execution of the proof, we have

$$\widehat{\psi'} \circ \phi' \circ \psi = [\ell_2^{e_2}]\phi.$$

Note that in this basic scheme (and all protocols known in the literature) honest transcripts involve responses like K_ψ and $\phi(K_\psi)$. Hence it is natural to allow the proof to reveal $\phi(P_0), \phi(Q_0)$ where $\{P_0, Q_0\}$ is a basis for $E_0[\ell_2^{e_2}]$.

4.2 Issue with Soundness Proofs for the de Feo–Jao–Plût Scheme

A core component of the security proof of the De Feo–Jao–Plût identification scheme is the soundness proof. A proof of soundness was given by multiple previous works [9,14,33]. A sketch of it is as follows:

Suppose $\mathcal{A}$ is an adversary that takes as input the public key and succeeds in the identification protocol (all t iterations) with noticeable probability ϵ. Given a challenge instance $(E_0, E_1, R_0, S_0, \phi(R_0), \phi(S_0))$ for the CSSI problem, we run $\mathcal{A}$ on the tuple $(E_1, \phi(R_0), \phi(S_0))$ as the public key. In the first round, $\mathcal{A}$ outputs commitments $(E_{i,2}, E_{i,3})$ for $1 \le i \le t$. We then send a challenge $b \in \{0,1\}^t$ to $\mathcal{A}$ and, with probability ϵ, $\mathcal{A}$ outputs a response that satisfies the verification algorithm. Now, we use the standard replay technique: Rewind $\mathcal{A}$ to the point where it had output its commitments and then respond with a different challenge $b' \in \{0,1\}^t$. With probability ϵ, $\mathcal{A}$ outputs a valid response. This gives exactly the 2-special soundness requirement of two valid transcripts with the same commitment but different challenges.

Now, choose some index i such that $b_i \neq b'_i$. We now restrict our focus to the components (E_2, E_3) for that index, and the two responses. It means $\mathcal{A}$ sent E_2, E_3 and can answer both challenges $b = 0$ and $b = 1$ successfully. Hence $\mathcal{A}$ has provided the maps ψ, ϕ', ψ' in the following diagram.

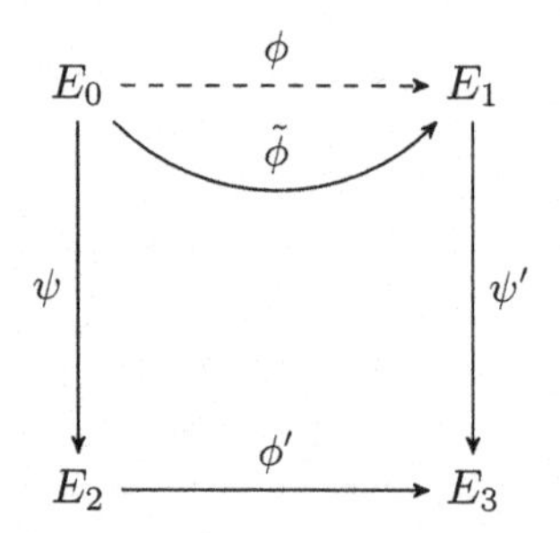

The argument proceeds as follows: We have an explicit description of an isogeny $\tilde{\phi} = \widehat{\psi'} \circ \phi' \circ \psi$ from E_0 to E_1. The degree of $\tilde{\phi}$ is $\ell_1^{e_1}\ell_2^{2e_2}$. One can determine $\ker(\tilde{\phi}) \cap E_0[\ell_1^{e_1}]$ by iteratively testing points in $E_0[\ell_1^j]$ for $j = 1, 2, \ldots$. Hence, one determines the kernel of ϕ, as desired.

However, the important issue with this argument which has so far gone unnoticed, is that it assumes $\ker(\phi) = \ker(\tilde{\phi}) \cap E_0[\ell_1^{e_1}]$. This assumption has no basis, and we will provide a simple counterexample to this argument in the following section. While we always recover an isogeny, it may not be ϕ at all—it is entirely possible the isogeny we recover does not even have codomain E_1 so this proof of 2-special soundness is not valid.

4.3 Counterexample to Soundness

Fix a supersingular curve E_0 as above. Generate a random $\ell_2^{e_2}$-torsion point $K_\psi \in E_0(\mathbb{F}_{p^2})$ as $K_\psi = [a]P_0 + [b]Q_0$ for some integers $0 \le a, b < \ell_2^{e_2}$ not both divisible by ℓ_2. Let $\psi : E_0 \to E_2$ have kernel generated by K_ψ. Then choose a random isogeny $\phi' : E_2 \to E_3$ of degree $\ell_1^{e_1}$ with kernel generated by $K_{\phi'}$. Then choose a random isogeny $\psi' : E_3 \to E_1$ of degree $\ell_2^{e_2}$. Choose points $P'_0, Q'_0 \in E_1(\mathbb{F}_{p^2})$ such that $\ker(\widehat{\psi'}) = \langle [a]P'_0 + [b]Q'_0 \rangle$. Then publish

$$(E_0, E_1, P_0, Q_0, P'_0, Q'_0)$$

as a public key. In other words, we have

$$E_0 \xrightarrow{\psi} E_2 \xrightarrow{\phi'} E_3 \xrightarrow{\psi'} E_1$$

Now there is no reason to believe that there exists an isogeny from E_0 to E_1 of degree $\ell_1^{e_1}$, yet we can respond to both challenge bits 0 and 1 in a single round of the identification scheme. Pulling back the kernel of ϕ' via ψ to E_0 will result in the kernel of an isogeny which, in general, will not have codomain E_1 (but instead a random other curve). This is because ψ' is entirely unrelated to ψ in this case (they are not "parallel"), so we have no SIDH square.

The key observation is that a verifier could be fooled into accepting this public key by a prover who always uses the same curves (E_2, E_3) instead of randomly chosen ones. When $\mathsf{chall} = 0$ the prover responds with the pair (a, b) corresponding to the kernel of ψ and $\widehat{\psi'}$, and when $\mathsf{chall} = 1$ the prover responds with $K_{\phi'}$. The verifier will agree that all responses are correct and will accept the proof.

It is true that the verifier could test whether the commitments (E_2, E_3) are being re-used, but this has never been stated as a requirement in any of the protocol descriptions. To tweak the verification protocol we need to know how "random" the pairs (E_2, E_3) (or, more realistically, the pairs (a, b)) need to be. One may think that the original scheme seems to be secure despite the issue with the proof, as long as the commitment (E_2, E_3) is not reused every time. However, in experiments with small primes, it is entirely possible to construct instances[1] where even with multiple different commitments, a secret isogeny of the correct degree between E_0 and E_1 does not exist. We expect that this extrapolates to large primes too, although one could potentially argue that finding enough such instances is computationally infeasible.

It is also true that repeating (E_2, E_3) means the protocol is no longer zero-knowledge. We emphasize that soundness and zero-knowledge are independent security properties, which are proved separately (and affect different parties: One gives an assurance to the verifier and the other to the prover). The counterexample we have provided is a counterexample to the soundness proof. The fact that the counterexample is not consistent with the proof that the protocol is zero-knowledge is irrelevant.

Finally, one could consider basing security of the protocol on the general isogeny problem (Definition 4) because, even in our counterexample, an isogeny $E_0 \to E_1$ exists and can be extracted—it just doesn't have degree $\ell_1^{e_1}$. We find it interesting that none of the previous authors chose to do it that way. However, some applications may require using the identification/signature protocols to prove that an SIDH public key is well-formed, implying the secret isogeny has the correct degree. For such applications we need soundness to be rigorously proved.

The issue in the security proofs in the literature is not only that it is implicitly assumed that there is an isogeny of degree $\ell_1^{e_1}$ between E_0 and E_1. The key issue

[1] Thank you to Lorenz Panny for demonstrating this.

is that it is implicitly assumed that the pullback under ψ of $\ker(\phi')$ is the kernel of this isogeny. Our counterexample calls these assumptions into question, and shows that the proofs are incorrect as written.

To make this very clear, consider the soundness proof from De Feo, Jao, and Plût [9]. The following diagram is written within the proof. It implicitly assumes that the horizontal isogeny ϕ' has kernel given by $\psi(S)$, so that the image curve is $E/\langle S, R\rangle$.

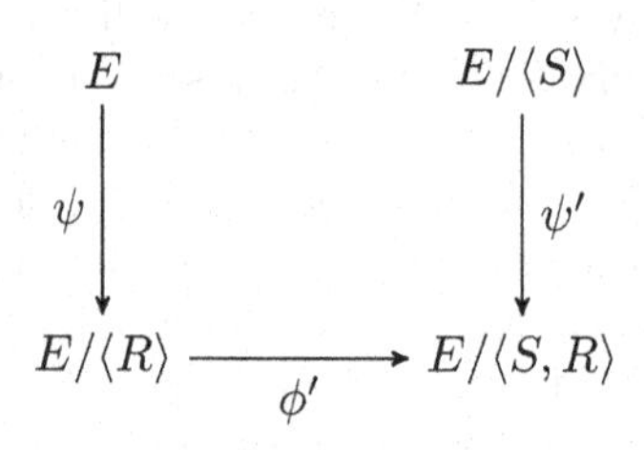

This implicit assumption seems to have been repeated in all subsequent works, such as [33] and [14].

4.4 Soundness of UJ20

Urbanik and Jao [31] give a variant of SIDH that exploits automorphisms and gets essentially three SIDH keys out of single protocol messages. Section 5 of their paper claims an isogeny-based zero-knowledge identification protocol that validates all elements of an SIDH key.

The statement being proved is $(E, P_B, Q_B, E_A, P'_B, Q'_B)$ and the witness is an isogeny $\phi : E \to E_A = E/A$ with $P'_B = \phi(P_B), Q'_B = \phi(Q_B)$. (Here the symbol A is overloaded to signify "Alice" and also Alice's subgroup that is the kernel of the isogeny.) Here the base curve E has a non-trivial automorphism η of order 6.

The proof works by sending E/B such that there are three SIDH keys that can be computed by Alice and Bob: $E_1 = E/\langle A, B\rangle, E_2 = E/\langle \eta(A), B\rangle, E_3 = E/\langle \eta^2(A), B\rangle$. More precisely, the prover picks $B = \langle [a]P_B + [b]Q_B\rangle$ and commits to the three related squares. The verifier makes a challenge $\mathsf{chall} \in \{0, 1, 2, 3\}$. When $\mathsf{chall} = 0$ the prover reveals (a, b), and the verifier can check all three isogenies $E \to E_B, E_A \to E_i$ for $i \in \{1, 2, 3\}$. When $\mathsf{chall} \geq 1$ the prover reveals the kernel of an isogeny $E_B \to E_{\mathsf{chall}}$.

There is no formal proof of soundness given in [31].

First, it is easy to see that if P'_B and Q'_B are the correct image points, then replacing them with $[z]P'_B$ and $[z]Q'_B$ for any invertible z modulo the order of P'_B is also accepted by the verifier. So it is clear that the protocol is at most giving an assurance of a weaker statement than claimed.

However, the protocol fails more drastically due to a similar issue to the problem discussed in Sect. 5.2. Briefly, because (a, b) is chosen by the prover, the prover can "hide" their cheating. For example, suppose a dishonest prover sets

$P'_B = \phi(P_B), Q'_B = \phi(Q_B) + T$ where T is a point of order ℓ_2 (a divisor of the order of P_B and Q_B). Then as long as b is chosen to be a multiple of ℓ_2 we have

$$[a]P'_B + [b]Q'_B = [a]\phi(P_B) + [b]\phi(Q_B)$$

and so the cheating is not detected by the verifier.

5 Steps Towards an SIDH Proof – The Weak SIDH Relation

The purpose of this section is to present a protocol to prove in zero-knowledge a natural but weaker statement than the knowledge of an SIDH secret key. In the next section we will augment this protocol to prove the full SIDH statement.

5.1 A Sound but Insecure Protocol

We start with a simple protocol which follows the blueprint of De Feo–Jao–Plût, but fixes its soundness issue. Unfortunately, the fix breaks zero-knowledge, and we will need to change the protocol again to achieve our goal.

Let public parameters $pp = (p, \ell_1, \ell_2, e_1, e_2, E_0)$ be such that $\#E_0(\mathbb{F}_{p^2}) = (\ell_1^{e_1}\ell_2^{e_2}f)^2$. As before, suppose a user has a secret isogeny $\phi : E_0 \to E_1$ of degree $\ell_1^{e_1}$ with kernel $\ker(\phi) = \langle K_\phi \rangle$. In this section we are only interested in proving knowledge of ϕ, thus we will not consider the public torsion basis (P_0, Q_0) and its image (P_1, Q_1) by ϕ.

Our simple (but insecure) protocol is presented in Fig. 2. It includes some basic functions:

- IsogenyFromKernel is a function taking a point $S \in E$ and outputting a (normalised) isogeny with kernel $\langle S \rangle$ and codomain curve $E/\langle S \rangle$.
- $\mathsf{RandomBasis}_i$ is a function taking a curve and outputting a uniformly random pair of points U, V which generate the $\ell_i^{e_i}$-torsion subgroup on the given curve, for $i = 1, 2$.
- DualKernel is a function taking an isogeny ψ and outputting a generator $K_{\widehat{\psi}}$ of the kernel of the dual isogeny $\widehat{\psi}$.

Intuitively, the sigma protocol follows Sect. 4.1, with a single bit challenge—if the challenge is 0, we reveal the vertical isogenies ψ, ψ', while if the challenge is 1, we reveal the horizontal ϕ'. The difference is the introduction of additional points on E_3 to the commitment, which force ψ, ψ' to be, in some sense, "compatible" or "parallel". This restriction lets us prove 2-special soundness by extracting the secret ϕ from two accepting transcripts.

Theorem 1. *The sigma protocol in Fig. 2 for relation*

$$\mathcal{R}_{\mathsf{weakSIDH}} = \{(E_1, \phi) \mid \phi : E_0 \to E_1, \deg \phi = \ell_1^{e_1}\}$$

is correct and 2-special sound. Repeated with κ iterations, it is thus a Proof of Knowledge for $\mathcal{R}_{\mathsf{weakSIDH}}$ with knowledge error $2^{-\kappa}$.

Proof. We prove the properties of Theorem 1 separately below.

Correctness: Following the protocol honestly will result in an accepting transcript. This is clear for the $\mathsf{chall} = 1$ case. For the $\mathsf{chall} = 0$ case, observe that

$$\phi'(K_{\widehat{\psi}}) = \phi'([c]P_2 + [d]Q_2) = [c]P_3 + [d]Q_3 = K_{\widehat{\psi'}},$$

thus $K_{\widehat{\psi'}}$ generates the kernel of $\widehat{\psi}'$.

round 1 (commitment)

1: Sample uniformly random $\ell_2^{e_2}$-isogeny kernel $\langle K_\psi \rangle \subset E_0$
2: $\psi, E_2 \leftarrow \mathsf{IsogenyFromKernel}(K_\psi)$
3: $P_2, Q_2 \leftarrow \mathsf{RandomBasis}_2(E_2)$
4: $K_{\phi'} \leftarrow \psi(K_\phi) \in E_2$
5: $\phi', E_3 \leftarrow \mathsf{IsogenyFromKernel}(K_{\phi'})$
6: $P_3, Q_3 \leftarrow \phi'(P_2), \phi'(Q_2) \in E_3$
7: Prover sends $\mathsf{com} \leftarrow (E_2, P_2, Q_2, E_3, P_3, Q_3)$ to Verifier.

round 2 (challenge)

1: Verifier sends $\mathsf{chall} \leftarrow \{0, 1\}$ to Prover.

round 3 (response)

1: **if** $\mathsf{chall} = 1$ **then**
2: $\quad \mathsf{resp} \leftarrow K_{\phi'}$
3: **else**
4: $\quad K_{\widehat{\psi}} \leftarrow \mathsf{DualKernel}(\psi)$
5: $\quad$ Write $K_{\widehat{\psi}} = [c]P_2 + [d]Q_2$ for $c, d \in \mathbb{Z}/\ell_2^{e_2}\mathbb{Z}$
6: $\quad \mathsf{resp} \leftarrow (c, d)$
7: Prover sends resp to Verifier.

Verification

1: $(E_2, P_2, Q_2, E_3, P_3, Q_3) \leftarrow \mathsf{com}$
2: **if** $\mathsf{chall} = 1$ **then**
3: $\quad K_{\phi'} \leftarrow \mathsf{resp}$
4: $\quad$ Check $K_{\phi'}$ has order $\ell_1^{e_1}$ and lies on E_2, otherwise output reject
5: $\quad \phi', E_3' \leftarrow \mathsf{IsogenyFromKernel}(K_{\phi'})$
6: $\quad$ Verify $E_3 = E_3'$ and $(P_3, Q_3) = (\phi'(P_2), \phi'(Q_2))$, otherwise output reject
7: **else**
8: $\quad (c, d) \leftarrow \mathsf{resp}$
9: $\quad K_{\widehat{\psi}} \leftarrow [c]P_2 + [d]Q_2$
10: $\quad K_{\widehat{\psi'}} \leftarrow [c]P_3 + [d]Q_3$
11: $\quad$ Check $K_{\widehat{\psi}}, K_{\widehat{\psi'}}$ have order $\ell_2^{e_2}$, otherwise output reject
12: $\quad \widehat{\psi}, E_0' \leftarrow \mathsf{IsogenyFromKernel}(K_{\widehat{\psi}})$
13: $\quad \widehat{\psi}', E_1' \leftarrow \mathsf{IsogenyFromKernel}(K_{\widehat{\psi'}})$
14: $\quad$ Check $E_0 = E_0'$ and $E_1 = E_1'$, otherwise output reject
15: Output accept

Fig. 2. One iteration of the simple but insecure sigma protocol for SIDH. The public parameters are $pp = (p, \ell_1, \ell_2, e_1, e_2, E_0)$. The public key is E_1, and the corresponding secret isogeny is ϕ.

2-special Soundness: Without loss of generality, suppose we obtain two transcripts $(\mathsf{com}, 0, \mathsf{resp})$, $(\mathsf{com}, 1, \mathsf{resp}')$. Then recover $(c, d) \leftarrow \mathsf{resp}$ and $K_{\phi'} \leftarrow \mathsf{resp}'$, and let ϕ' be an isogeny whose kernel is generated by $K_{\phi'}$. Applying Lemma 2, with

$(\phi_A, \phi_B, \phi_{AB}) = (\phi', \widehat{\psi}, \widehat{\psi'})$, we obtain an isogeny $\chi : E_0 \to E_1$ of degree $\ell_1^{e_1}$. The conditions of the lemma on the kernels of $\widehat{\psi}$ and $\widehat{\psi'}$ are satisfied because $\phi'(K_{\widehat{\psi}}) = K_{\widehat{\psi'}}$, as above. This shows the protocol is 2-special sound, and that it is a Proof of Knowledge of an isogeny corresponding to the given public key curve. □

5.2 Why This Protocol Does Not Prove Correctness of the Points (P_1, Q_1)

We briefly explain why the protocol in this section does not convince a verifier that $(P_1, Q_1) = (\phi(P_0), \phi(Q_0))$. The first observation is that Fig. 2 does not actually use P_1 or Q_1 anywhere, so of course, nothing is proved. But one could tweak the protocol in the $\mathsf{chall} = 0$ case to use the isogenies $\widehat{\psi} : E_2 \to E_0$ and $\widehat{\psi'} : E_3 \to E_1$ to test the points. For example, using the duals of these isogenies, one could compute integers (a, b) such that $\ker(\psi) = \langle [a]P_0 + [b]Q_0 \rangle$ and then test whether or not $\ker(\psi') = \langle [a]P_1 + [b]Q_1 \rangle$.

The problem for the verifier is that this is not enough to deduce that $(P_1, Q_1) = (\phi(P_0), \phi(Q_0))$. For example, a dishonest prover who wants to perform an attack might set $(P_1, Q_1) = (\phi(P_0), \phi(Q_0) + T)$ where T is a point of order ℓ_2. If the prover always uses integers b that are multiples of ℓ_2 (and remember, the prover does choose (a, b)) then this cheating will not be detected by the verifier. Hence, the protocol needs to be changed so that the verifier can tell that the kernels of the isogenies $\widehat{\psi}$ are sufficiently independent across the executions of the protocol. This is the fundamental problem that we solve in Sect. 6.

5.3 Making the Proof Zero-Knowledge

There is an obvious reason why the protocol is not zero-knowledge: We already noted that it is not sufficient to prove that $P_1 = \phi(P_0)$ and $Q_1 = \phi(Q_0)$, even if we try some minor tweaks. However, a honest prover leaks a random pair $(K_\psi, \phi(K_\psi))$ every time it is challenged with $\mathsf{chall} = 0$. Thus, after less than three iterations on average, it leaks the action of ϕ on the full $E_0[\ell_2^{e_2}]$, and in particular it leaks P_1 and Q_1. This fact was already observed by De Feo, Jao and Plût, who instead sketched a proof of how their protocol is zero-knowledge with respect to the stronger SIDH relation, which includes (P_1, Q_1) in the language (see definition in Sect. 6).

But there is a second reason why our protocol fails to be zero-knowledge, even with respect to the SIDH relation. When challenged with $\mathsf{chall} = 0$ a simulator can perfectly simulate the isogenies ψ and ψ', however it will not be able to compute the associated ϕ', and thus the correct points (P_3, Q_3). On the other hand, the adversary of Definition 3 knows ϕ, and after seeing ψ and ψ' it can easily compute ϕ' and then P_3 and Q_3, thus unmasking the simulator. We stress this is not an issue limited to SHVZK: All other definitions of computational zero-knowledge we are aware of have the protocol fall, in one way or another, into the same trap.

We solve both issues at once by moving to ternary challenges $\{-1, 0, 1\}$, splitting the $\mathsf{chall} = 0$ case into two separate flows: $\mathsf{chall} = -1$ corresponding to revealing ψ, and $\mathsf{chall} = 0$ corresponding to revealing ψ'. However, now the information on E_2, E_3 and the respective torsion bases may not be fully revealed when $\mathsf{chall} \in \{-1, 0\}$: To hide it but still commit to it, we introduce a binding and hiding commitment scheme that we denote by $\mathsf{C}(x; y)$. We need statistical hiding, so that $\mathsf{C}(\mathsf{com}; r)$, where r is a sufficiently long random string, can in principle be a commitment to any of the possible values for com. We also need it to be (computationally) hard for a malicious prover to open $\mathsf{C}(\mathsf{com}; r)$ to a different value $(\mathsf{com}'; r')$. As an example, we can take $\mathsf{C}(x; y) = H(x\|y)$ where H is a cryptographic hash function and y is considerably longer than the output length of H (e.g., H hashes to n bits and y is $2n$ bits, chosen uniformly at

round 1 (commitment)

1: Run **commitment** from Figure 2, giving commitment $\mathsf{com}_0 = (E_2, P_2, Q_2, E_3, P_3, Q_3)$
2: Let ψ be the isogeny from Line 2 of Figure 2
3: $K_{\widehat{\psi}} \leftarrow \mathsf{DualKernel}(\psi)$
4: Compute $c, d \in \mathbb{Z}/\ell_2^{e_2}\mathbb{Z}$ such that $K_{\widehat{\psi}} = [c]P_2 + [d]Q_2$ (and $K_{\widehat{\psi'}} = [c]P_3 + [d]Q_3$)
5: Set $\mathsf{com}_L = (E_2, P_2, Q_2)$ and $\mathsf{com}_R = (E_3, P_3, Q_3)$
6: Choose random nonces r_L, r_R, r
7: Output $\mathsf{com} \leftarrow (\mathsf{C}_L = \mathsf{C}(\mathsf{com}_L; r_L), \mathsf{C}_R = \mathsf{C}(\mathsf{com}_R; r_R), \mathsf{C} = \mathsf{C}(c, d; r))$.

round 3 (response)

1: **if** $\mathsf{chall} = 1$ **then**
2: Let $K_{\phi'}$ be the kernel generator computed at Line 4 of Figure 2
3: Output $\mathsf{resp} \leftarrow (\mathsf{com}_L, r_L, K_{\phi'}, \mathsf{com}_R, r_R)$
4: **else**
5: **if** $\mathsf{chall} = 0$ **then**
6: Output $\mathsf{resp} \leftarrow (\mathsf{com}_R, r_R, c, d, r)$
7: **else**
8: Output $\mathsf{resp} \leftarrow (\mathsf{com}_L, r_L, c, d, r)$

Verification

1: $(\mathsf{C}_L, \mathsf{C}_R, \mathsf{C}) \leftarrow \mathsf{com}$
2: **if** $\mathsf{chall} = 1$ **then**
3: $(\mathsf{com}_L, r_L, K_{\phi'}, \mathsf{com}_R, r_R) \leftarrow \mathsf{resp}$
4: Check that the commitments C_L and C_R are well-formed, if not output reject
5: $\mathsf{com}' \leftarrow (E_2, P_2, Q_2, E_3, P_3, Q_3)$
6: Verify $(\mathsf{com}', \mathsf{chall}, K_{\phi'})$ as in Figure 2 **verification**
7: If verification fails, output reject.
8: **else**
9: $(\mathsf{com}_X, r_X, c, d, r) \leftarrow \mathsf{resp}$
10: Check that the commitments C and C_X are well-formed, if not output reject
11: **if** $\mathsf{chall} = -1$ **then**
12: $K_{\widehat{\psi}} \leftarrow [c]P_2 + [d]Q_2$
13: Check $K_{\widehat{\psi}}$ has order $\ell_2^{e_2}$, otherwise output reject
14: $\widehat{\psi}, E_0' \leftarrow \mathsf{IsogenyFromKernel}(K_{\widehat{\psi}})$
15: Check $E_0 = E_0'$, otherwise output reject
16: **else**
17: $K_{\widehat{\psi'}} \leftarrow [c]P_3 + [d]Q_3$
18: Check $K_{\widehat{\psi'}}$ has order $\ell_2^{e_2}$, otherwise output reject
19: $\widehat{\psi'}, E_1' \leftarrow \mathsf{IsogenyFromKernel}(K_{\widehat{\psi'}})$
20: Check $E_1 = E_1'$, otherwise output reject
21: Output accept if all the above conditions hold.

Fig. 3. Sigma protocol to prove the weak SIDH relation $\mathcal{R}_{\mathsf{weakSIDH}}$.

random at the time of the commitment). The resulting scheme is presented in Fig. 3.

Theorem 2. *For a fixed security parameter κ, a proof consisting of κ iterations of the sigma protocol in Fig. 3 is a computationally SHVZK Proof of Knowledge for $\mathcal{R}_{\mathsf{weakSIDH}}$ with knowledge error $(2/3)^\kappa$, assuming the DSSP problem is hard and the commitment scheme $\mathsf{C}()$ is computationally binding and statistically hiding.*

Proof. Because the protocol only adds a few commitments to the protocol in Fig. 2, correctness follows immediately from Theorem 1.

Soundness: We prove 3-special soundness by reducing to the 2-special soundness of the simplified protocol. From three transcripts $(\mathsf{com}, -1, \mathsf{resp}_{-1})$, $(\mathsf{com}, 0, \mathsf{resp}_0)$ and $(\mathsf{com}, 1, \mathsf{resp}_1)$, we recover $\mathsf{com}_0 = (E_2, P_2, Q_2, E_3, P_3, Q_3)$, $K_{\phi'}$ and (c, d), like in the simplified protocol. Because C is binding, these values are (computationally) uniquely determined by com, so they must be consistent across the three transcripts. Joining together the verifications of cases $\mathsf{chall} = -1, 0$, we see that the verifier does the exact same computations as in the simplified protocol. Hence, Theorem 1 shows that there exists an isogeny $\chi : E_0 \to E_1$ of degree $\ell_1^{e_1}$, and thus the protocol is sound.

A cheating prover has 1/3 chance of being caught, as they may prepare commitments in a way that lets them answer any two out of the three challenges. We conclude that the protocol has knowledge error $(2/3)^\kappa$.

Zero-Knowledge: We only need to prove that a single execution of the protocol is SHVZK, then SHVZK of κ repetition follows by the hybrid technique of Goldreich, Micali, and Wigderson [18]. We define the simulator Sim as follows.

Case $\mathsf{chall} = -1$: Sim follows the honest protocol by choosing a random generator $K_\psi \in E_0[\ell_2^{e_2}]$, then picking $P_2, Q_2 \leftarrow \mathsf{RandomBasis}_2(E_2)$ and computing c, d such that $\ker(\widehat{\psi}) = \langle [c]P_2 + [d]Q_2 \rangle$. It finally commits to $\mathsf{C}_L = \mathsf{C}(E_2, P_2, Q_2; r_L)$ and $\mathsf{C} = \mathsf{C}(c, d; r)$, while taking a uniformly random value for C_R. The responses are the openings to C_L and C, it is clear that this transcript is valid.

Observe that the commitments C_L and C are identical to the honest commitments, thus the only way for an adversary $\mathcal{A}$ to distinguish Sim from a real transcript is to distinguish C_R from a commitment to (E_3, P_3, Q_3), but this is impossible since we assumed that $\mathsf{C}()$ is statistically hiding.

Case $\mathsf{chall} = 0$: This is nearly identical to the previous case. Sim chooses a random kernel generator $K_{\psi'} \in E_1[\ell_2^{e_2}]$, picks a random basis (P_3, Q_3) of $E_3[\ell_2^{e_2}]$, and computes c, d such that $\ker(\widehat{\psi}) = \langle [c]P_3 + [d]Q_3 \rangle$. It then computes the commitments C_R and C like in the honest protocol, and takes a random value for C_L.

We only need to observe that in the honest protocol both $K_{\psi'}$ and (P_3, Q_3) are uniformly random, thus C_R and C are distributed identically to the honest protocol. We conclude again using the fact that $\mathsf{C}()$ is statistically hiding.

Case chall = 1: Sim chooses a random supersingular elliptic curve[2] E_2. It then chooses uniformly a random kernel generator $K_{\phi'} \in E_2$ of order $\ell_1^{e_1}$ and computes the isogeny $\phi' : E_2 \to E_3$. Next, Sim generates a basis $P_2, Q_2 \leftarrow \mathsf{RandomBasis}_2(E_2)$ and computes $P_3, Q_3 \leftarrow \phi'(P_2), \phi_i'(Q_2)$. Finally, it commits to $\mathsf{C}_L = \mathsf{C}(E_2, P_2, Q_2; r_L)$ and $\mathsf{C}_R = \mathsf{C}(E_3, P_3, Q_3; r_R)$, while taking a uniformly random value for C. The responses are the openings to C_L and C_R, it is clear that this transcript is valid.

Like before, because $\mathsf{C}()$ is statistically hiding the adversary cannot use C to gain an advantage in distinguishing Sim. But now the curves E_2 and E_3 and the isogeny ϕ' are not distributed identically to the honest protocol, but rather like in distribution $\mathcal{D}_1$ of the DSSP problem (Definition 7). It is then clear that an adversary that has a non-negligible advantage in distinguishing Sim from the real protocol can be used as a distinguisher for DSSP. □

Remark 1. There are certainly improvements that can be made to increase efficiency and compress the size of signatures, but these are standard and we will not explore them here. For example, in practice the information (E_2, P_2, Q_2) would be replaced with a triplet of x-coordinates, as in SIKE [1].

6 Correctness of the Points in an SIDH Public Key

Section 5 gave a simple protocol, which can be shown to be a Proof of Knowledge of a degree $\ell_1^{e_1}$ isogeny from E_0 to E_1. However, an SIDH public key (E_1, P_1, Q_1) also consists of the two torsion points, and these points are the cause of issues such as the adaptive attack [13], as discussed in Sect. 3. In this section, we show that the choice of points P_1, Q_1 by a malicious prover is severely restricted if they must keep them consistent with "random enough" values of a, b (i.e., random choices of ψ)—preventing adaptive attacks entirely.

Fix E_0 and a basis $\{P_0, Q_0\}$ for $E_0[\ell_2^{e_2}]$. We define the strong[3] SIDH relation to be

$$\mathcal{R}_{\mathsf{SIDH}} = \left\{ ((E_1, P_1, Q_1), \phi) \middle| \begin{array}{l} \phi : E_0 \to E_1, \deg \phi = \ell_1^{e_1}, \\ P_1 = \phi(P_0), Q_1 = \phi(Q_0) \end{array} \right\}.$$

Figure 4 presents our protocol for proving this strong relation. We also provide a visual representation in Fig. 5, in the hope that it may help understand its algebraic structure.

This protocol is reminiscent of the one in Sect. 5 in that it "flips the SIDH square upside down": We view E_2 as the "starting curve" in SIDH, and use the fact that the verifier can check $\widehat{\psi} : E_2 \to E_0$ and $\phi' : E_2 \to E_3$. The verifier also

[2] One way to do so is to take a random ℓ_2-isogeny walk from E_0. To ensure a distribution close to uniform, we take a walk of length $\gtrsim \log(p) \approx 2e_2$. However a walk of length e_2 is sufficient to get a variant of DSSP that is also believed to be hard.

[3] The word "strong" here indicates that we confirm not only the correctness of the degree of the isogeny, but the correct images of points.

checks that $\ker(\widehat{\psi}') = \phi'(\ker(\widehat{\psi}))$, and from this the curve E_1 is well-defined and the existence of an isogeny $\phi : E_0 \to E_1$ with $\ker(\phi) = \widehat{\psi}(\ker(\phi'))$ follows.

But this is not enough, since there might be multiple isogenies from E_0 to E_1. The key idea we introduce here is to require pairs of points $R_{1,0}, R_{1,1} = \phi(R_{0,0}), \phi(R_{0,1})$ that are "independent" (in the sense that they generate the full torsion). Hence the action of ϕ on the whole $\ell_2^{e_2}$ torsion is determined. This is why we "double" the protocol. So in each round of our new sigma protocol, we commit to two SIDH squares rather than just one, and require that the kernel generators of ψ in these two squares are independent from each other. We add this independence as an extra check during verification. We also require an assurance that both squares use consistent isogenies ϕ'. For this purpose we use a uniformly random $\ell_1^{e_1}$-torsion basis (U, V) on E_0 and compute the image of this basis on both curves $E_{2,i}$—if both ϕ'_i are the images of ϕ under the vertical isogenies ψ_i, then both should be representable in terms of $(\psi_i(U), \psi_i(V))$ using the same coefficients. These extra checks achieve a 3-special sound protocol for the strong SIDH relation above.

We stress that the points (U, V) are not made public in the commitment. In the protocol the function $\mathsf{RandomBasis}_1$ is called many times on the same curve E_0 during t rounds of the protocol and it is important that the outputs are independent and not known to the verifier in the $\mathsf{chall} = 1$ case.

Theorem 3. *For a fixed security parameter κ, a proof consisting of κ iterations of the sigma protocol in Fig. 4 is a computationally SHVZK Proof of Knowledge for $\mathcal{R}_{\mathsf{SIDH}}$ with knowledge error $(2/3)^\kappa$, assuming the Double-DSSP problem is hard and the commitment scheme $\mathsf{C}()$ is computationally binding and statistically hiding.*

Proof. We prove correctness, soundness, and zero-knowledge individually.

Correctness: The point $R_{0,i}$ will always be an invertible scalar multiple of the point K_ψ used by the prover in the commitment round (in the i-th SIDH square) of the protocol because both K_ψ and $R_{0,i}$ are generators of the kernel of ψ in the i-th SIDH square. Hence, because the honest prover will use commitments such that ψ_0 and ψ_1 are independent, then a_i, b_i necessarily exist such that $a_0 b_1 - a_1 b_0$ is invertible in line 8 of commitment. Also note that because $K_{\phi',i} = [e]U'_i + [f]V'_i = [e]\psi_i(U) + [f]\psi_i(V)$ for both $i \in \{0, 1\}$, and U, V have order coprime to the degree of ψ_i, the checks involving U'_i, V'_i, e, and f will also succeed. Correctness of the rest of the protocol can also be verified in a straightforward way.

Zero-Knowledge: We start from the simulator described in Theorem 2, and extend it to simulate the parts of the transcript that are specific to Fig. 4: Namely, the bases U'_i, V'_i and the coefficients c'_i, d'_i, a_i, b_i.

Case $\mathsf{chall} = -1$: For $i = 0, 1$, Sim constructs $K_{\psi_i} \in E_0[\ell_2^{e_2}]$, $P_{2,i}, Q_{2,i}$ and c_i, d_i like in Theorem 2, while ensuring that ψ_0 and ψ_1 are independent.

Additionally, Sim samples $U, V \leftarrow \mathsf{RandomBasis}_1(E_0)$ and computes $U'_i = \psi_i(U)$ and $V'_i = \psi_i(V)$. Then it takes c'_i, d'_i such that $c'_i d_i - d'_i c_i$ is invertible

round 1 (commitment)

1: Run **commitment** from Figure 3, giving commitment $\mathsf{com}^0 = (\mathsf{C}^0_L = \mathsf{C}(\mathsf{com}^0_L; r^0_L), \mathsf{C}^0_R = \mathsf{C}(\mathsf{com}^0_R; r^0_R), \mathsf{C}^0 = \mathsf{C}(c_0, d_0; r^0))$.
2: Let ψ_0 be the isogeny from Line 2 of Figure 3
3: Run **commitment** from Figure 3 again, subject to one extra condition:
 – If ψ_1 is the isogeny from Line 2 of Figure 3, then ψ_0 and ψ_1 must be independent. Otherwise repeat the commitment phase.
 Let $\mathsf{com}^1 = (\mathsf{C}^1_L = \mathsf{C}(\mathsf{com}^1_L; r^1_L), \mathsf{C}^1_R = \mathsf{C}(\mathsf{com}^1_R; r^1_R), \mathsf{C}^1 = \mathsf{C}(c_1, d_1; r^1))$ be the commitment returned by this execution.
4: $U, V \leftarrow \mathsf{RandomBasis}_1(E_0)$
5: **for** $i \in \{0, 1\}$ **do**
6: Choose $c'_i, d'_i \in \mathbb{Z}/\ell_2^{e_2}\mathbb{Z}$ such that $c'_i d_i - d'_i c_i$ is invertible modulo $\ell_2^{e_2}$
7: Set $R_{0,i} \leftarrow \widehat{\psi}_i([c'_i]P_{2,i} + [d'_i]Q_{2,i})$ and $R_{1,i} \leftarrow \widehat{\psi}'_i([c'_i]P_{3,i} + [d'_i]Q_{3,i})$
8: Compute $a_i, b_i \in \mathbb{Z}/\ell_2^{e_2}\mathbb{Z}$ such that, simultaneously, $R_{0,i} = [a_i]P_0 + [b_i]Q_0$ and $R_{1,i} = [a_i]P_1 + [b_i]Q_1$
9: Let $U'_i = \psi_i(U)$ and $V'_i = \psi_i(V)$
10: Choose random nonces r^0_m, r^1_m
11: Output $\mathsf{com}_i \leftarrow (U'_i, V'_i, \mathsf{C}^i_L, \mathsf{C}^i_R, \mathsf{C}^i, \mathsf{C}^i_m = \mathsf{C}(c'_i, d'_i, a_i, b_i; r^i_m))$ for $i \in \{0, 1\}$.

round 3 (response)

1: **if** $\mathsf{chall} = 1$ **then**
2: Write $K_\phi = [e]U + [f]V$ for $e, f \in \mathbb{Z}/\ell_1^{e_1}\mathbb{Z}$
3: Output $\mathsf{resp} \leftarrow ((e, f), \mathsf{com}^0_L, r^0_L, \mathsf{com}^1_L, r^1_L, \mathsf{com}^0_R, r^0_R, \mathsf{com}^1_R, r^1_R)$
4: **else**
5: **if** $\mathsf{chall} = 0$ **then**
6: Output $\mathsf{resp} \leftarrow (\mathsf{com}^0_R, r^0_R, \mathsf{com}^1_R, r^1_R, c_0, d_0, r^0, c_1, d_1, r^1, c'_0, d'_0, a_0, b_0, r^0_m, c'_1, d'_1, a_1, b_1, r^1_m)$
7: **else**
8: Output $\mathsf{resp} \leftarrow (\mathsf{com}^0_L, r^0_L, \mathsf{com}^1_L, r^1_L, c_0, d_0, r^0, c_1, d_1, r^1, c'_0, d'_0, a_0, b_0, r^0_m, c'_1, d'_1, a_1, b_1, r^1_m)$

Verification

1: $(U'_0, V'_0, \mathsf{C}^0_L, \mathsf{C}^0_R, \mathsf{C}^0, \mathsf{C}^0_m), (U'_1, V'_1, \mathsf{C}^1_L, \mathsf{C}^1_R, \mathsf{C}^1, \mathsf{C}^1_m) \leftarrow \mathsf{com}^0, \mathsf{com}^1$
2: **if** $\mathsf{chall} = 1$ **then**
3: $((e, f), \mathsf{com}^0_L, r^0_L, \mathsf{com}^1_L, r^1_L, \mathsf{com}^0_R, r^0_R, \mathsf{com}^1_R, r^1_R) \leftarrow \mathsf{resp}$
4: **for** $i \in \{0, 1\}$ **do**
5: $\mathsf{com}'_i \leftarrow (\mathsf{C}^i_L, \mathsf{C}^i_R, \mathsf{C}^i)$
6: Compute $K_{\phi'_i} = [e]U'_i + [f]V'_i$
7: $\mathsf{resp}'_i \leftarrow (\mathsf{com}^i_L, r^i_L, K_{\phi'_i}, \mathsf{com}^i_R, r^i_R)$
8: Verify $(\mathsf{com}'_i, \mathsf{chall}, \mathsf{resp}'_i)$ as in Figure 3 **verification**
9: If verification fails, output reject.
10: **else**
11: $(\mathsf{com}^0_X, r^0_X, \mathsf{com}^1_X, r^1_X, c_0, d_0, r^0, c_1, d_1, r^1, c'_0, d'_0, a_0, b_0, r^0_m, c'_1, d'_1, a_1, b_1, r^1_m) \leftarrow \mathsf{resp}$
12: **for** $i \in \{0, 1\}$ **do**
13: $\mathsf{com}'_i \leftarrow (\mathsf{C}^i_L, \mathsf{C}^i_R, \mathsf{C}^i)$
14: $\mathsf{resp}'_i \leftarrow (\mathsf{com}^i_X, r^i_X, c_i, d_i, r^i)$
15: Verify $(\mathsf{com}'_i, \mathsf{chall}, \mathsf{resp}'_i)$ as in Figure 3 **verification**
16: **if** $\mathsf{chall} = -1$ **then**
17: $R_{0,i} \leftarrow \widehat{\psi}_i([c'_i]P_{2,i} + [d'_i]Q_{2,i})$
18: Check $R_{0,i} = [a_i]P_0 + [b_i]Q_0$, otherwise output reject
19: **else**
20: $R_{1,i} \leftarrow \widehat{\psi}'_i([c'_i]P_{3,i} + [d'_i]Q_{3,i})$
21: Check $R_{1,i} = [a_i]P_1 + [b_i]Q_1$, otherwise output reject
22: If $\mathsf{chall} = -1$ check $\widehat{\psi}_0(U'_0) = \widehat{\psi}_1(U'_1)$ and $\widehat{\psi}_0(V'_0) = \widehat{\psi}_1(V'_1)$, otherwise output reject.
23: Check that $a_0 b_1 - a_1 b_0$ is invertible modulo $\ell_2^{e_2}$, otherwise output reject.
24: Output accept if all the above conditions hold.

Fig. 4. Sigma protocol to prove the strong SIDH relation $\mathcal{R}_{\mathsf{SIDH}}$.

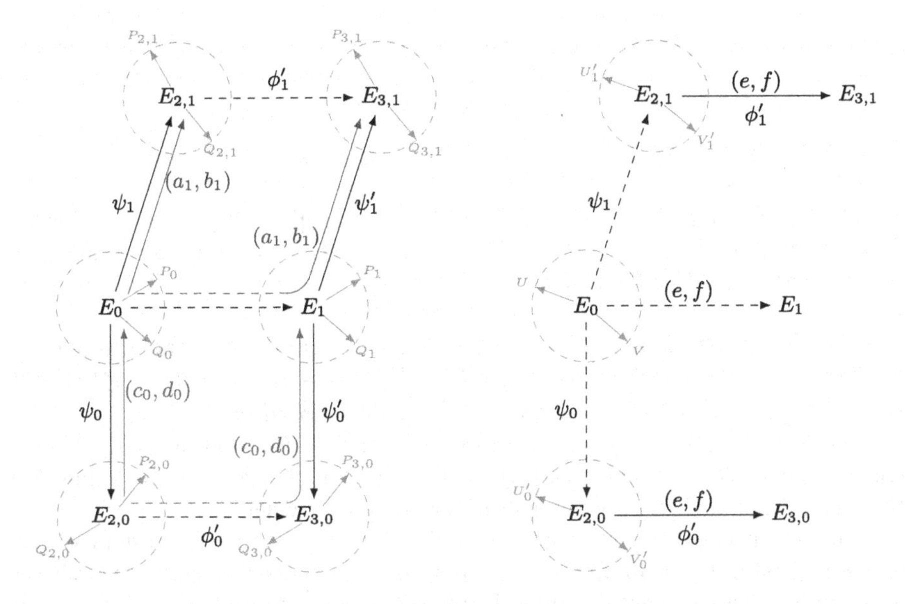

Fig. 5. Visual representation of the protocol for the strong SIDH relation. Black arrows represent isogenies computed by the prover; only the continuous arrows are revealed to the verifier. Dashed circles represent torsion subgroups, the radial arrows within represent torsion generators. The torsion generators have the same order as the degree of the continuous arrows, and are mapped consistently by the dashed arrows. **Left:** consistency checks performed by the verifier in the cases *chall* $= -1, 0$: the blue and the red arrows represent isogenies recomputed by the verifier from the opening of the torsion bases and of (a_i, b_i, c_i, d_i). For readability, a set of red arrows (associated to (a_0, b_0)) in the top square, and a set of blue arrows (associated to (c_1, d_1)) in the bottom square are omitted. The verifier must also check that the bases (U'_0, V'_0) and (U'_1, V'_1) (see right) are mapped consistently. **Right:** consistency checks in the case *chall* $= 1$: the verifier recomputes ϕ'_i from the opening of the torsion bases and of (e, f). The verifier must also check that the bases $(P_{2,i}, Q_{2,i})$ and $(P_{3,i}, Q_{3,i})$ (see left) are mapped consistently. (Color figure online)

and computes $R_{0,i}, a_i, b_i$ like in the honest protocol. Finally it computes all commitments like in the honest protocol, except for C_R^i which are taken at random.

It is clear that the distribution of $U'_i, V'_i, c'_i, d'_i, a_i, b_i$ is identical to the honest protocol, thus this simulation is indistiguishable following the same argument as in Theorem 2.

Case $\mathsf{chall} = 0$: This case is similar to the previous one, however Sim needs to compute both ψ_i and ψ'_i in order to simulate U'_i, V'_i. Because the image points $P_1 = \phi(P_0)$ and $Q_1 = \phi(Q_0)$ are part of the SIDH relation, Sim can choose $a', b' \in \mathbb{Z}/\ell_2^{e_2}\mathbb{Z}$ and compute $K_{\psi_i} = [a']P_0 + [b']Q_0$ and $K_{\psi'_i} = [a']P_1 + [b']Q_1$.

It then proceeds like in Theorem 2, but also computes U, V, U'_i, V'_i as above using the knowledge of ϕ_i. After taking c'_i, d'_i with the usual condition, it computes $R_{1,i}$ and then a_i, b_i. Finally, it computes all commitments honestly, except for C_L^i. Again, the simulation is perfect except for C_L^i, and is thus indistinguishable thanks to the hiding property of $\mathsf{C}()$.

Case $\mathsf{chall} = 1$: The simulator twice chooses a random supersingular elliptic curve $E_{2,i}$ for $i \in \{0,1\}$.

The simulator then chooses uniformly a random point $K_{\phi_0'} \in E_{2,0}$ of order $\ell_1^{e_1}$ and computes the isogeny $\phi_0' : E_{2,0} \to E_{3,0}$ with kernel $K_{\phi_0'}$. Sim chooses a random basis $\{U_0', V_0'\}$ for $E_{2,0}[\ell_1^{e_1}]$, and writes $K_{\phi_0'} = [e]U_0' + [f]V_0'$ for integers e, f.

Next, Sim will randomly generate a basis $\{U_1', V_1'\}$ of the $\ell_1^{e_1}$-torsion subgroup on $E_{2,1}$, such that $e_{\ell_1^{e_1}}(U_1', V_1') = e_{\ell_1^{e_1}}(U_0', V_0')$. It sets $K_{\phi_1'} = [e]U_1' + [f]V_1'$ and lets $\phi_1' : E_{2,1} \to E_{3,1}$ be an isogeny with kernel generated by $K_{\phi_1'}$.

Next, the simulator generates basis $P_{2,i}, Q_{2,i} \leftarrow \mathsf{RandomBasis}_2(E_{2,i})$, and computes $P_{3,i}, Q_{3,i} \leftarrow \phi_i'(P_{2,i}), \phi_i'(Q_{2,i})$. Finally, Sim chooses random values for the commitments $\mathsf{C}^i, \mathsf{C}_m^i$, which will never be opened when $\mathsf{chall} = 1$.

Like in Theorem 2, this is not a perfect simulation of the honest protocol. However, thanks to the hiding property of $\mathsf{C}()$, the adversary is reduced to solving precisely an instance of the Double-DSSP problem (Definition 8).[4]

3-special Soundness: Suppose we obtain three accepting transcripts ($\mathsf{com}, -1, \mathsf{resp}_{-1}$), ($\mathsf{com}, 0, \mathsf{resp}_0$), and ($\mathsf{com}, 1, \mathsf{resp}_1$). The secret isogeny corresponding to the public key $X = (E_1, P_1, Q_1)$ can be recovered as follows, hence we can extract a valid witness W for the statement X such that $(X, W) \in \mathcal{R}_{\mathsf{SIDH}}$.

Consider just one of the isogeny squares (e.g., $i = 0$). We have (c, d) which defines a point $K_{\widehat{\psi}} = [c]P_{2,0} + [d]Q_{2,0}$ and hence an isogeny $\widehat{\psi} : E_{2,0} \to E_0$. We also have $K_{\phi'} \in E_{2,0}$ which defines an isogeny $\phi' : E_{2,0} \to E_{3,0}$ whose kernel is generated by $K_{\phi'}$. Applying Lemma 2, with $(\phi_A, \phi_B, \phi_{AB}) = (\phi', \widehat{\psi}, \widehat{\psi}')$, we obtain an isogeny $\phi_0 : E_0 \to E_1$ of degree $\ell_1^{e_1}$. The conditions of the lemma on the kernels of $\widehat{\psi}$ and $\widehat{\psi}'$ are satisfied because $\phi'(K_{\widehat{\psi}}) = K_{\widehat{\psi}'}$, as above. Hence we have extracted an isogeny as required.

Repeating the argument for $i = 1$ provides another isogeny $\phi_1 : E_0 \to E_1$ of degree $\ell_1^{e_1}$. The next step is to prove that these isogenies are equivalent (i.e., have the same kernel). This is where the points U_0', V_0', U_1', V_1' are needed. We have

$$\begin{aligned}
\ker(\phi_0) &= \widehat{\psi}_0(\ker(\phi_0')) \\
&= \langle \widehat{\psi}_0([e]U_0' + [f]V_0') \rangle \\
&= \langle \widehat{\psi}_1([e]U_1' + [f]V_1') \rangle \\
&= \widehat{\psi}_1(\ker(\phi_1')) \quad = \ker(\phi_1).
\end{aligned}$$

[4] Note that the second pairing condition in Definition 8 is equivalent to the existence of K_0, K_1 such that $K_0 = [e]U_0' + [f]V_0'$ and $K_1 = [e]U_1' + [f]V_1'$.

Therefore, we recover the same[5] isogeny $\phi_0 = \phi_1 = \phi$ from both squares.

It remains to prove that the isogeny ϕ we have extracted does map (P_0, Q_0) to (P_1, Q_1) and so is a correct witness.

Recall we are provided with points $R_{j,i}$ and integers a_i, b_i such that $R_{0,i} = [a_i]P_0 + [b_i]Q_0$. Define

$$B = \begin{pmatrix} a_0 & b_0 \\ a_1 & b_1 \end{pmatrix}.$$

Since B is invertible, $\langle R_{0,0}, R_{0,1} \rangle$ is another basis for $\langle P_0, Q_0 \rangle = E_0[\ell_2^{e_2}]$. Recall that $R_{0,i} = \widehat{\psi}_i([c_i']P_{2,i} + [d_i']Q_{2,i})$, $R_{1,i} = \widehat{\psi}_i'([c_i']P_{3,i} + [d_i']Q_{3,i})$, and $P_{3_i}, Q_{3,i} = \phi'(P_{2,i}), \phi'(Q_{2,i})$. It follows from $\phi \circ \widehat{\psi}_i = \widehat{\psi}_i' \circ \phi'$ that $\phi(R_{0,i}) = R_{1,i}$. Hence we have

$$\begin{pmatrix} R_{0,0} \\ R_{0,1} \end{pmatrix} = B \begin{pmatrix} P_0 \\ Q_0 \end{pmatrix}$$

$$\begin{pmatrix} R_{1,0} \\ R_{1,1} \end{pmatrix} = \begin{pmatrix} \phi(R_{0,0}) \\ \phi(R_{0,1}) \end{pmatrix} = B \begin{pmatrix} \phi(P_0) \\ \phi(Q_0) \end{pmatrix}$$

$$\begin{pmatrix} R_{1,0} \\ R_{1,1} \end{pmatrix} = B \begin{pmatrix} P_1 \\ Q_1 \end{pmatrix},$$

therefore

$$B \begin{pmatrix} \phi(P_0) \\ \phi(Q_0) \end{pmatrix} = B \begin{pmatrix} P_1 \\ Q_1 \end{pmatrix},$$

and since B is invertible, we must have that $P_1 = \phi(P_0)$ and $Q_1 = \phi(Q_0)$, as required. □

Note that the protocol in Fig. 4 runs the previous protocol (in Fig. 3) twice, hence the transcripts produced by this Proof of Knowledge for $\mathcal{R}_{\mathsf{SIDH}}$ will be (at least) twice the size. We expect that improvements to the efficiency and size of the scheme are possible with more analysis, but leave this for future work.

Remark 2. Ghantous, Pintore, and Veroni [17] discuss issues with extraction of a witness in two different scenarios. Their first scenario ("single collision") involves two distinct isogenies $\phi' : E_2 \to E_3$ in the SIDH square of the identification scheme. Neither of our new identification schemes are impacted by such collisions because the provision of points $P_3, Q_3 \in E_3$ uniquely determines the isogeny ϕ', as shown by Martindale and Panny [24]. Their second scenario ("double collision") involves two distinct (non-equivalent) isogenies $\phi, \tilde{\phi} : E_0 \to E_1$, both of degree $\ell_1^{e_1}$ and a point $R \in E_0$ such that

$$E_1/\langle \phi(R) \rangle \cong E_1/\langle \tilde{\phi}(R) \rangle.$$

[5] They could differ by an automorphism, but this does not matter. Fix one of them and call it ϕ.

Our second protocol, for the relation $\mathcal{R}_{\mathsf{SIDH}}$, ensures that the witness extracted is a valid witness for the public key used (including the torsion points). Hence, this second collision scenario does not have any impact on the soundness of our protocol either.

7 Non-interactive Proof of Knowledge

We conclude with some brief remarks about the use of the new protocols proposed above.

It is standard to construct a non-interactive Proof of Knowledge from an interactive protocol using the Fiat-Shamir transformation (secure in the random oracle model). This works by making the challenge chall for the t rounds of the ID scheme a random-oracle output from input the commitment com and a message M. That is, for message M,

$$V_1^{\mathcal{O}}(\mathsf{com}) = \mathcal{O}(\mathsf{com} \parallel M).$$

In some situations one should include the instance $(E_0, P_0, Q_0, E_1, P_1, Q_1)$ in the hash too. Thus the prover does not need to interact with a verifier and can compute a non-interactive transcript. Because the sigma protocol described in Sect. 6 not only proves knowledge of the secret isogeny between two curves, but also correctness of the torsion points in the public key, we obtain a non-interactive Proof of Knowledge of the secret key corresponding to a given SIDH public key, which proves that the SIDH public key is well-formed. This provides protection against adaptive attacks.

Such a NIZK of an SIDH secret key can, among other applications, be used to achieve a secure non-interactive key exchange scheme based on SIDH.

Currently the only other method known to get a NIKE from SIDH is the k-SIDH proposal by Azarderakhsh, Jao and Leonardi [2]. This requires both parties to publish k SIDH keys and to compute $O(k^2)$ shared SIDH keys, and so requires k^2 isogeny computations to construct the shared key. It is known [3,10] that one can attack the scheme in $\tilde{O}(16^k)$ oracle queries and time. For a given security parameter λ it is therefore natural to suppose k grows linearly in λ, in which case the complexity of the protocol grows quadratically in λ. In contrast, the soundess of our NIZK protocol means the number of rounds grows linearly in λ, and the key exchange protocol itself is a single SIDH exchange. So asymptotically the cost of our scheme will be less than k-SIDH.

8 Conclusions

We have shown a counterexample to the soundness of the De Feo–Jao–Plût sigma protocol. We have described a new sigma protocol that addresses this issue, and also allows to prove that an SIDH key is correctly generated. Our protocol also solves the soundness issue raised by Ghantous, Pintore and Veroni.

The problem of proving correctness of an isogeny turns out to be considerably more difficult than was anticipated (at least, by us!), and there are several open problems for future work. First it would be good to have a protocol with 2-special soundness for the SIDH relation. The 3-special soundness and ternary challenges seem to be necessary for the weak SIDH relation, preventing leakage of torsion point information, and thus protecting against the recent attacks on SIDH.

However, in cases where the torsion point information is public, our protocols use ternary challenges only to bypass the difficulty in simulating the torsion bases (P_2, Q_2) and (P_3, Q_3). A protocol with statistical zero-knowledge instead of computational zero-knowledge would therefore help with this issue. Second, the protocol seems extremely complex and it would be wonderful to have a simpler and more elegant one.

We have not considered ways to make the protocol more compact. There are some trivial modifications that would reduce the communication (such as replacing pairs (c_i, d_i) with projective points $(c_i : d_i)$) and there is scope for more sophisticated compression of the protocol messages. However, we feel that progress at the conceptual level to reduce the communication cost is more relevant than applying standard implementation tricks.

Acknowledgements. We thank David Jao, Jason LeGrow, and Yi-Fu Lai for useful discussion about this work. We also thank Paulo Barreto for catching some typos in this paper, and Simon-Philipp Merz for valuable comments. We thank Javad Doliskani for important observations that inspired significant improvements to this work. We thank the anonymous reviewers for very helpful comments, including about the correct formulation of computational zero knowledge. Finally, we would like to thank those involved with the BIRS Supersingular Isogeny Graphs in Cryptography workshop for great discussion on some questions this work raised—especially Lorenz Panny and his work analyzing SIDH squares in small fields.

References

1. Azarderakhsh, R., et al.: Supersingular isogeny key encapsulation. Submission to the NIST Post-Quantum Standardization project (2017)
2. Azarderakhsh, R., Jao, D., Leonardi, C.: Post-quantum static-static key agreement using multiple protocol instances. In: Adams, C., Camenisch, J. (eds.) SAC 2017. LNCS, vol. 10719, pp. 45–63. Springer, Cham (2018). https://doi.org/10.1007/978-3-319-72565-9_3
3. Basso, A., Kutas, P., Merz, S.-P., Petit, C., Weitkämper, C.: On adaptive attacks against Jao-Urbanik's isogeny-based protocol. In: Nitaj, A., Youssef, A. (eds.) AFRICACRYPT 2020. LNCS, vol. 12174, pp. 195–213. Springer, Cham (2020). https://doi.org/10.1007/978-3-030-51938-4_10
4. Bellare, M., Rogaway, P.: Random oracles are practical: a paradigm for designing efficient protocols. In: Denning, D.E., Pyle, R., Ganesan, R., Sandhu, R.S., Ashby, V. (eds.) ACM CCS 1993, pp. 62–73. ACM Press (1993). https://doi.org/10.1145/168588.168596
5. Boneh, D., Kogan, D., Woo, K.: Oblivious pseudorandom functions from isogenies. In: Moriai, S., Wang, H. (eds.) ASIACRYPT 2020. LNCS, vol. 12492, pp. 520–550. Springer, Cham (2020). https://doi.org/10.1007/978-3-030-64834-3_18

6. Castryck, W., Decru, T.: An efficient key recovery attack on SIDH (preliminary version). Cryptology ePrint Archive, Paper 2022/975 (2022). https://eprint.iacr.org/2022/975
7. Damgård, I.: Efficient concurrent zero-knowledge in the auxiliary string model. In: Preneel, B. (ed.) EUROCRYPT 2000. LNCS, vol. 1807, pp. 418–430. Springer, Heidelberg (2000). https://doi.org/10.1007/3-540-45539-6_30
8. Damgård, I., Goldreich, O., Okamoto, T., Wigderson, A.: Honest verifier vs dishonest verifier in public coin zero-knowledge proofs. In: Coppersmith, D. (ed.) CRYPTO 1995. LNCS, vol. 963, pp. 325–338. Springer, Heidelberg (1995). https://doi.org/10.1007/3-540-44750-4_26
9. De Feo, L., Jao, D., Plût, J.: Towards quantum-resistant cryptosystems from supersingular elliptic curve isogenies. J. Math. Cryptol. **8**(3), 209–247 (2014). https://doi.org/10.1515/jmc-2012-0015. https://www.degruyter.com/view/j/jmc.2014.8.issue-3/jmc-2012-0015/jmc-2012-0015.xml
10. Dobson, S., Galbraith, S.D., LeGrow, J., Ti, Y.B., Zobernig, L.: An adaptive attack on 2-SIDH. Int. J. Comput. Math. Comput. Syst. Theory **5**(4), 282–299 (2020)
11. Fouotsa, T.B.: SIDH with masked torsion point images. Cryptology ePrint Archive, Paper 2022/1054 (2022). https://eprint.iacr.org/2022/1054
12. Fouotsa, T.B., Petit, C.: A new adaptive attack on SIDH. In: Galbraith, S.D. (ed.) CT-RSA 2022. LNCS, vol. 13161, pp. 322–344. Springer, Cham (2022). https://doi.org/10.1007/978-3-030-95312-6_14
13. Galbraith, S.D., Petit, C., Shani, B., Ti, Y.B.: On the security of supersingular isogeny cryptosystems. In: Cheon, J.H., Takagi, T. (eds.) ASIACRYPT 2016. LNCS, vol. 10031, pp. 63–91. Springer, Heidelberg (2016). https://doi.org/10.1007/978-3-662-53887-6_3
14. Galbraith, S.D., Petit, C., Silva, J.: Identification protocols and signature schemes based on supersingular isogeny problems. J. Cryptol. **33**(1), 130–175 (2020)
15. Galbraith, S.D., Vercauteren, F.: Computational problems in supersingular elliptic curve isogenies. Quantum Inf. Process. **17**(10), 1–22 (2018). https://doi.org/10.1007/s11128-018-2023-6
16. Garay, J.A., MacKenzie, P., Yang, K.: Strengthening zero-knowledge protocols using signatures. J. Cryptol. **19**(2), 169–209 (2005). https://doi.org/10.1007/s00145-005-0307-3
17. Ghantous, W., Pintore, F., Veroni, M.: Collisions in supersingular isogeny graphs and the SIDH-based identification protocol. Cryptology ePrint Archive, Report 2021/1051 (2021). https://eprint.iacr.org/2021/1051
18. Goldreich, O., Micali, S., Wigderson, A.: Proofs that yield nothing but their validity or all languages in NP have zero-knowledge proof systems. J. ACM (JACM) **38**(3), 690–728 (1991)
19. Hofheinz, D., Hövelmanns, K., Kiltz, E.: A modular analysis of the Fujisaki-Okamoto transformation. In: Kalai, Y., Reyzin, L. (eds.) TCC 2017. LNCS, vol. 10677, pp. 341–371. Springer, Cham (2017). https://doi.org/10.1007/978-3-319-70500-2_12
20. Jao, D., De Feo, L.: Towards quantum-resistant cryptosystems from supersingular elliptic curve isogenies. In: Yang, B.-Y. (ed.) PQCrypto 2011. LNCS, vol. 7071, pp. 19–34. Springer, Heidelberg (2011). https://doi.org/10.1007/978-3-642-25405-5_2
21. Jao, D., Soukharev, V.: Isogeny-based quantum-resistant undeniable signatures. In: Mosca, M. (ed.) PQCrypto 2014. LNCS, vol. 8772, pp. 160–179. Springer, Cham (2014). https://doi.org/10.1007/978-3-319-11659-4_10
22. Leonardi, C.: A note on the ending elliptic curve in SIDH. Cryptology ePrint Archive, Report 2020/262 (2020). https://ia.cr/2020/262

23. Maino, L., Martindale, C.: An attack on SIDH with arbitrary starting curve. Cryptology ePrint Archive, Paper 2022/1026 (2022). https://eprint.iacr.org/2022/1026
24. Martindale, C., Panny, L.: How to not break SIDH. CFAIL (2019). https://ia.cr/2019/558
25. Moriya, T.: Masked-degree SIDH. Cryptology ePrint Archive, Paper 2022/1019 (2022). https://eprint.iacr.org/2022/1019
26. Robert, D.: Breaking SIDH in polynomial time. Cryptology ePrint Archive, Paper 2022/1038 (2022). https://eprint.iacr.org/2022/1038
27. Silverman, J.H.: The Arithmetic of Elliptic Curves. GTM, vol. 106, 2nd edn. Springer, New York (2009). https://doi.org/10.1007/978-0-387-09494-6
28. Thormarker, E.: Post-quantum cryptography: supersingular isogeny Diffie-Hellman key exchange. Thesis, Stockholm University (2017)
29. Ueno, R., Xagawa, K., Tanaka, Y., Ito, A., Takahashi, J., Homma, N.: Curse of re-encryption: a generic power/EM analysis on post-quantum KEMs. IACR Transactions on Cryptographic Hardware and Embedded Systems, pp. 296–322 (2022)
30. Urbanik, D., Jao, D.: SoK: the problem landscape of SIDH. In: Proceedings of the 5th ACM on ASIA Public-Key Cryptography Workshop, pp. 53–60 (2018)
31. Urbanik, D., Jao, D.: New techniques for SIDH-based NIKE. J. Math. Cryptol. **14**(1), 120–128 (2020)
32. Vélu, J.: Isogénies entre courbes elliptiques. C. R. Acad. Sci. Paris Sér. A-B **273**, A238–A241 (1971)
33. Yoo, Y., Azarderakhsh, R., Jalali, A., Jao, D., Soukharev, V.: A post-quantum digital signature scheme based on supersingular isogenies. In: Kiayias, A. (ed.) FC 2017. LNCS, vol. 10322, pp. 163–181. Springer, Cham (2017). https://doi.org/10.1007/978-3-319-70972-7_9

DAG-Σ: A DAG-Based Sigma Protocol for Relations in CNF

Gongxian Zeng[1], Junzuo Lai[2(✉)], Zhengan Huang[1(✉)], Yu Wang[1(✉)], and Zhiming Zheng[1,3]

[1] Peng Cheng Laboratory, Shenzhen, China
gxzeng@cs.hku.hk, zhahuang.sjtu@gmail.com, wangy12@pcl.ac.cn, zzheng@pku.edu.cn

[2] College of Information Science and Technology, Jinan University, Guangzhou, China
laijunzuo@gmail.com

[3] Institute of Artificial Intelligence, LMIB, NLSDE, Beijing Advanced Innovation Center for Future Blockchain and Privacy Computing, Beihang University, Beijing, China

Abstract. At CRYPTO 1994, Cramer, Damgård and Schoenmakers proposed a general method to construct proofs of knowledge (PoKs), especially for k-out-of-n partial knowledge, of which relations can be expressed in disjunctive normal form (DNF). Since then, proofs of k-out-of-n partial knowledge have attracted much attention and some efficient constructions have been proposed. However, many practical scenarios require efficient PoK protocols for partial knowledge in other forms.

In this paper, we mainly focus on PoK protocols for k-conjunctive normal form (k-CNF) relations, which have n statements and can be expressed as follows: (i) k statements constitute a clause via "OR" operations, and (ii) the relation consists of multiple clauses via "AND" operations. We propose an alternative Sigma protocol (called DAG-Σ protocol) for k-CNF relations (in the discrete logarithm setting), by converting these relations to directed acyclic graphs (DAGs). Our DAG-Σ protocol achieves less communication cost and smaller computational overhead compared with Cramer et al.'s general method.

Keywords: Sigma protocol · Proof of partial knowledge · Conjunctive normal form · Directed acyclic graph · Disjunctive normal form

1 Introduction

Proofs of partial knowledge demonstrate the possession of certain subsets of witnesses for a given collection of statements. In 1994, Cramer, Damgård and Schoenmakers [14] showed a *general* method with access structures to construct proofs of partial knowledge for compound statements, from "atomic" *Sigma protocols* for the individual statements.

S. Agrawal and D. Lin (Eds.): ASIACRYPT 2022, LNCS 13792, pp. 340–370, 2022.
https://doi.org/10.1007/978-3-031-22966-4_12

During the last decades, most works of proofs of partial knowledge [1,2,5,20] focus on k-out-of-n partial knowledge (i.e., proving knowledge of witnesses for k out of n statements). The relations of k-out-of-n partial knowledge can be expressed in the following *disjunctive normal form (DNF)* on n statements: every k different statements are combined with operation "AND" (we call such a combination of k statements a "Type-$\wedge$ clause"), and C_n^k different Type-$\wedge$ clauses are combined with operation "OR". An informal expression when $k = 2$ and $n = 3$ is $(y_1 \wedge y_2) \vee (y_1 \wedge y_3) \vee (y_2 \wedge y_3)$, where y_1, y_2, y_3 are 3 statements, and $(y_1 \wedge y_2)$, $(y_1 \wedge y_3)$, $(y_2 \wedge y_3)$ are 3 Type-$\wedge$ clauses. We call this kind of relations *complete k-DNF relations*, since each of them contains C_n^k Type-$\wedge$ clauses for some specific k and n.

However, many practical scenarios require proofs of partial knowledge in other forms, such as a variant of the aforementioned DNF relations, which are very similar to complete k-DNF relations but the number of Type-$\wedge$ clauses is smaller than C_n^k (e.g., when $k = 2$ and $n = 3$, $(y_1 \wedge y_2) \vee (y_1 \wedge y_3)$). We call this kind of relations *incomplete k-DNF relations.*

Relations expressed in *conjunctive normal form (CNF)* are another important collection of relations in practice. For instance, many access control policies are naturally set in CNF and they have been discussed in some attribute-based encryption schemes [8,25,27,33]. Another class of examples is the collection of instances of the k-SAT problem [24], e.g., a start-up company wants to show the investors a business plan (building at least a shopping mall in every k neighbouring blocks) in a zero-knowledge manner, avoiding the business roadmap being leaked. Some other applications about relations in CNF are also mentioned in [2], e.g., proof of possession of white money, where given a transaction graph, a user proves that the money are transferred among some white organizations while preserving the organizations' pseudonymity.

In this paper, we mainly focus on *k-CNF relations*[1]: k different statements are combined with operation "OR" (similarly, we call such a combination a "Type-$\vee$" clause), and many Type-$\vee$ clauses are combined with operation "AND". An example expression when $k = 2$ and $n = 3$ is $(y_1 \vee y_2) \wedge (y_1 \vee y_3)$, where $(y_1 \vee y_2)$ and $(y_1 \vee y_3)$ are 2 Type-$\vee$ clauses.

Note that given some witnesses and statements, in order to determine whether they belongs to a k-CNF relation, one has to check every Type-$\vee$ clause. But if for a k-DNF relation, once a Type-$\wedge$ clause is satisfied, the other Type-$\wedge$ clauses do not need to be checked anymore. It seems that the above difference results in the failure of applying most approaches of Sigma protocols for complete k-DNF relations to k-CNF relations.

To the best of our knowledge, only Cramer et al. [14] shows constructions of Sigma protocols for k-CNF relations. However, it may lead to super-polynomial communication cost. Acyclicity program, proposed by Abe et al. [2], also works for k-CNF relations, but it is designed for non-interactive zero-knowledge proofs

[1] In this paper, when we refer to k-CNF relations, we usually mean incomplete k-CNF relations (i.e., the number of Type-$\vee$ clauses num is smaller than C_n^k), since complete k-CNF relations (i.e., $num = C_n^k$) can be trivially converted to complete $(n - k + 1)$-DNF relations.

(NIZK), not Sigma protocols. More importantly, it seems impossible to transfer their scheme [2] into a standard Sigma protocol, so acyclicity program [2] does not have the strengths of Sigma protocols. For example, Sigma protocols often enjoy low soundness error by design, have high efficiency relative to their generic counterparts, and are more flexible. Using the Fiat-Shamir transform [15], Sigma protocols can be transferred to NIZK, so they are widely adopted in both non-interactive algorithms [4,7,31] and interactive protocols [10,18]. Some protocols [10,18] even enjoy round complexity improvement benefit from delayed-input Sigma protocols, which can be transferred from ordinary Sigma protocols using the method in [11]. But the acyclicity program does not enjoy these advantages.

Therefore, a question is raised naturally: *Is it possible to construct a more efficient Sigma protocol for k-CNF relations?*

Our Contributions. This paper gives an affirmative answer to the above question in the discrete-logarithm (DL) setting. More concretely, we systematically study proofs of partial knowledge for k-CNF relations, showing constructions of Sigma protocols for these relations and extensions.

We firstly formally define *partial knowledge for k-CNF relations.* Then, we propose a construction of a Sigma protocol for k-CNF relations and we call it DAG-Σ protocol. More specifically, we first put forth an efficient deterministic algorithm kCNFtoDAG to convert a k-CNF relation to a directed acyclic graph (DAG). Then, we construct the DAG-Σ protocol by composing a collection of Schnorr's Sigma protocols [32] according to the DAG. With this approach, we succeed in reducing the size of the transcripts and improving the efficiency.

As an extension, we apply our DAG-Σ protocols to construct Sigma protocols for incomplete k-DNF relations. We prove theoretically that a Sigma protocol for incomplete k-DNF relations can be obtained from two Sigma protocols: one for k-CNF relations and the other one for complete k-DNF relations. Then we construct a Sigma protocol for incomplete k-DNF relations in the DL setting, by restricting the choices of statements.

A comparison of communication costs of some existing protocols for three kinds of relations (k-CNF, incomplete k-DNF and complete k-DNF) is shown in Table 1. To compare these schemes, we consider them in the DL setting where given a group $\mathbb{G}$ of order p, the secret (or witness) of each statement is the corresponding discrete logarithm. For the Sigma protocols (i.e., except [2]), we consider the size of the data transmitted during the communication between the prover and the verifier. For the others (i.e., [2]), we consider the proof size.

For k-CNF relations, the communication cost of our protocol (in Sect. 5.2) is $O(n-k)|\mathbb{G}| + O(|V|)|\mathbb{Z}_p^*|$. Note that V in Table 1 denotes the vertices of the DAG in our DAG-Σ protocol. A discussion on upper bound of $|V|$ shows that the size of our solution is smaller (actually is much smaller in most cases) than that of [14], which implies that our solution enjoys a better performance when compared with [14]. Although the communication cost of [2] is linear in n, it is a non-interactive protocol, so it lacks some general extensions for standard Sigma protocols as discussed before.

For incomplete k-DNF relations, only a few protocols work for them. As shown in Table 1, the communication costs of our protocol (in Sect. 6) and [1]

Table 1. Comparison of some existing protocols (in the DL setting)*

Schemes	Σ protocol?	k-CNF	Incomplete k-DNF	Complete k-DNF
Cramer et al. [14]	Yes	$O(k \cdot num)(\lvert\mathbb{G}\rvert + \lvert\mathbb{Z}_p^*\rvert)$	$O(k \cdot num)(\lvert\mathbb{G}\rvert + \lvert\mathbb{Z}_p^*\rvert)$	$O(n)(\lvert\mathbb{G}\rvert + \lvert\mathbb{Z}_p^*\rvert)$
Groth et al. [20]**	Yes	\	\	$O(\log n)(\lvert\mathbb{G}\rvert + \lvert\mathbb{Z}_p^*\rvert)$
Abe et al. [1]	Yes	\	$O(n)\lvert\mathbb{G}\rvert + O(num)\lvert\mathbb{Z}_p^*\rvert$	$O(n)\lvert\mathbb{G}\rvert + O(C_n^k)\lvert\mathbb{Z}_p^*\rvert$
Abe et al. [2]	No	$O(n)(\lvert\mathbb{G}\rvert + \lvert\mathbb{Z}_p^*\rvert)$	\	\
Attema et al. [5]	Yes	\	\	$O(\log(2n-k))\lvert\mathbb{G}\rvert + 4 \times \lvert\mathbb{Z}_p^*\rvert$
Goel et al. [17]	Yes	\	\	$O(k \cdot n)^{***}$
Ours (Sect. 5.2)	Yes	$O(n-k)\lvert\mathbb{G}\rvert + O(\lvert V\rvert)\lvert\mathbb{Z}_p^*\rvert$	\	$O(k)\lvert\mathbb{G}\rvert + O(\lvert V\rvert)\lvert\mathbb{Z}_p^*\rvert^{\dagger}$
Ours (Sect. 6)‡	Yes	\	$O(n)\lvert\mathbb{G}\rvert + O(\lvert V\rvert)\lvert\mathbb{Z}_p^*\rvert$	\

* The results here are obtained by trivially applying the corresponding protocols. There are n statements and num clauses in the expression of the k-CNF or (in)complete k-DNF relations, where each clause contains k different statements. V denotes the vertices of the DAG in our DAG-Σ protocol ($|V| \leq k \cdot num$).
** The solution in [20] only works for $k = 1$.
*** [17] presents a discussion on this kind of relation and the result is directly obtained from the discussion. It involves a special commitment scheme, so we do not have $|\mathbb{G}|$ and $|\mathbb{Z}_p^*|$ here.
† The result is obtained from Remark 1.
‡ Our solution in Sect. 6 only works for special language.

are both less than [14]. In the case of $|V| < num$, our protocol (in Sect. 6) has less communication cost than that of [1].

Compared with those protocols for complete k-DNF relations with general k ([5,14]), [5] does not consider k-CNF relations, and the protocol in [14] for k-CNF relations has more communication cost than ours.

Finally, we provide an implementation of our DAG-Σ protocol based on elliptic curve groups with key size of 512 bits. It shows that our DAG-Σ protocol saves more than 95% communication costs and more than 90% running time, compared with [14], when proving the relations in our experiments.

Discussion: Non-discrete-Logarithm Setting. In this paper, we mainly focus on the DL setting (exactly running Schnorr's Sigma protocol [32] for each statement). Our solution can be extended to non-discrete-logarithm setting. We describe the DAG-Σ protocol by using many algorithm interfaces of a modified Schnorr's Sigma protocol. If similar modification can also be applied to other non-discrete-logarithm-based Sigma protocols [9,23,29], then using the framework of our DAG-Σ protocol and embedding other non-discrete-logarithm Sigma protocols, the new protocol can work in non-discrete-logarithm setting.

Technical Overview. Recall that a Sigma protocol is an interactive protocol run by a prover $\mathcal{P}$ and a verifier $\mathcal{V}$, and during the execution, a commitment a, a challenge c and a response z are sent in turn by $\mathcal{P}$ and $\mathcal{V}$, where c is randomly picked by $\mathcal{V}$. In the literature, a composite Sigma protocol for compound NP relations is constructed by composing "atomic" Sigma protocols for the individual relations securely. Our DAG-Σ protocol follows this general idea. Generally, to run the composite Sigma protocol, $\mathcal{P}$ firstly runs each of the "atomic" Sigma protocols to generate the individual commitment a_{atm}, and then sends a to $\mathcal{V}$, where a derives from all the a_{atm}'s as per the rule of the composite protocol. After receiving a randomly sampled c from $\mathcal{V}$, $\mathcal{P}$ prepares the challenges c_{atm}'s, based on what she sees (including c), for all the "atomic" Sigma protocols to generate the responses z_{atm}'s for all statements. Finally, $\mathcal{P}$ packs the responses z_{atm}'s and some c_{atm}'s as z (e.g., [1,14]) and sends z to $\mathcal{V}$. Correctness usually requires that having c and z, $\mathcal{V}$ can compute a result a' that equals a.

Our starting point is the most trivial solution, i.e., a contains all commitments a_{atm}'s, and z contains all challenges c_{atm}'s and all responses z_{atm}'s. Then, we show step by step how to reduce the size of the communication, i.e., reducing the numbers of a_{atm}'s in a, and the number of c_{atm}'s and z_{atm}'s in z.

Step I: Reduce the Number of a_{atm}'s and c_{atm}'s. Inspired by the ring signature [4], in a Type-$\vee$ clause with k statements, we take the hash value of the commitment for the $(j+1)^{th}$ statement as the challenge for the jth $(1 \leq j < k)$ statement, i.e., $c_j = \mathsf{Hash}(a_{j+1})$, where c_j denotes one of c_{atm}'s and a_{j+1} denotes one of a_{atm}'s. Further, all Type-$\vee$ clauses share the challenge c picked by $\mathcal{V}$, and for each Type-$\vee$ clause, the kth statement takes c as the challenge. In this way, $\mathcal{V}$ can also compute all the challenges by himself when verification. Hence, only *one* challenge (i.e., c) needs to be transmitted, reducing the number of c_{atm}'s in z. Moreover, we informally require that the underlying "atomic" Sigma protocols can have the verifier compute a_{atm} from the corresponding c_{atm} and z_{atm}. Then for each clause, considering the property that "$c_j = \mathsf{Hash}(a_{j+1})$ $(1 \leq j < k)$", the commitment a_{atm} of the first statement essentially can be computed by c and corresponding z_{atm}'s. Thus, we just put the a_{atm}'s of the first statement of all "Type-$\vee$" clauses in a to reduce the number of a_{atm}'s. To guarantee the correctness, we employ a variant of Schnorr's Sigma protocol and following we take the proof of 1-out-of-k partial knowledge (i.e., there is only one Type-$\vee$ clause) for example to highlight the main idea.

An example relation in the DL setting is in Fig. 1, where $\mathbf{x} = (x_1, \ldots, x_k)$ and $\mathbf{y} = (y_1, \ldots, y_k)$ denote the witnesses and statements respectively, and the witness x_μ for statement y_μ is known by the prover. In Fig. 1, the prover in the first step of the Sigma protocol (i.e., $\mathcal{P}_1$) randomly picks $(z_1, \ldots, z_{k-1}, r)$ to compute $(a_1, \ldots, a_k)$, and then sends only a_1 as the commitment a to the verifier. Note that except the last statement, we take the hash value of commitment a_{j+1} $(1 \leq j < k)$ as the challenge for the jth statement, i.e., $c_j = \mathsf{H}(a_{j+1})$, where $\mathsf{H} : \mathbb{G} \to \mathbb{Z}_p^*$ is a collision-resistance hash function. After receiving the challenge c from the verifier, the prover in the third step of the Sigma protocol (i.e., $\mathcal{P}_2$) re-computes the commitments by randomly picking $z'_k, \ldots, z'_{\mu+1}$ until the μth statement y_μ, of which $\mathcal{P}_2$ knows the discrete logarithm x_μ. For the μth statement, when given a_μ and x_μ, we can re-compute z'_μ for y_μ by the property of *Chameleon Σ-protocol* [12] (Schnorr's Sigma protocol is also a Chameleon Σ-protocol and more details are in Sect. 5.1) , such that the value of z'_μ guarantees $a_\mu = a'_\mu$. Then when $1 \leq i < \mu$, we just set $z'_i = z_i$. By induction on $1 \leq i < \mu$ (i.e., $\mathsf{H}(a_{i+1}) = \mathsf{H}(a'_{i+1})$ and $z_i = z'_i$ imply $a_i = a'_i$, and the latter further implies $\mathsf{H}(a_i) = \mathsf{H}(a'_i)$), we have $a = a_1 = a'_1$. Hence, the verifier will accept the proof. The detailed algorithm can be found in Sect. 5.1.

If applying the above method directly to each Type-$\vee$ clause of a k-CNF relation, then the size of the response z (resp., the commitment a) would be $O(k \cdot$

$$\mathcal{R} = \{(\mathbf{x}, \mathbf{y}) : y_1 = g^{x_1} \vee \ldots \vee y_k = g^{x_k}\}$$

$$\mathcal{P}_1 \quad a_1 = g^{z_1}/y_1^{\mathsf{H}(a_2)} \leftarrow \ldots \leftarrow a_\mu = g^{z_\mu}/y_\mu^{\mathsf{H}(a_{\mu+1})} \ldots \leftarrow a_{k-1} = g^{z_{k-1}}/y_{k-1}^{\mathsf{H}(a_k)} \leftarrow a_k = g^r$$

$$\mathcal{P}_2 \quad \underbrace{a'_1 = g^{z'_1}/y_1^{\mathsf{H}(a'_2)} \leftarrow \ldots \leftarrow a'_\mu = g^{z'_\mu}/y_\mu^{\mathsf{H}(a'_{\mu+1})}}_{a_i = a'_i (1 \leq i \leq \mu)} \ldots \leftarrow a'_{k-1} = g^{z'_{k-1}}/y_{k-1}^{\mathsf{H}(a'_k)} \leftarrow a'_k = g^{z'_k}/y_k^{\mathsf{c}}$$

$$(z'_1 = z_1 \,,\ \ldots \,, z'_{\mu-1} = z_{\mu-1} \,,\ \boxed{z'_\mu = z_\mu + (\mathsf{H}(a'_{\mu+1}) - \mathsf{H}(a_{\mu+1}))x_u} \,,\ z'_{\mu+1} \leftarrow \mathbb{Z}_p^* \,,\ \ldots \,,\ z'_k \leftarrow \mathbb{Z}_p^*)$$

Fig. 1. An example of the proof of 1-out-of-k partial knowledge

num) (resp., $O(num)$), where num is the number of Type-$\vee$ clauses. Hence, the complexity is theoretically equal to that of [14] as shown in Table 1. Therefore, we further consider to reduce the number of a_{atm}'s and z_{atm}'s.

Step II: Reduce the Number of a_{atm}'s and z_{atm}'s. Given a k-CNF relation, there may be many duplicate statements in different Type-$\vee$ clauses. If these duplicate statements can share the commitments a_{atm}'s and responses z_{atm}'s, then we can reduce the numbers. To this end, we convert the relation to a DAG, requiring that (i) every Type-$\vee$ clause is converted to a directed path with k vertices and each vertex represents a statement; (ii) the maximum length of paths is k, and the number of paths with length k equals the number of the Type-$\vee$ clauses num. We merge the vertices in the graph while the above requirements are preserved. For the details of the rules of merging, please refer to the transfer algorithm kCNFtoDAG in Sect. 4. Our composite Sigma protocol is run over the DAG. As a result, the size of the commitment a is $O(n-k)$, and the size of the response z is $O(|V|)$, where V is the vertex set of the DAG. Through a theoretic analysis, we will show that $|V| \leq (k \cdot num)$, even $|V| \ll (k \cdot num)$ in most cases.

To illustrate the idea more clearly, we take the k-CNF relation in Eq. (1) for example and the relation is informally denoted as

$$(y_1 \vee y_2) \wedge (y_2 \vee y_3) \wedge (y_3 \vee y_4) \wedge (y_1 \vee y_4). \tag{1}$$

Figure 2 is the DAG output by kCNFtoDAG when inputting the relation in Eq. (1), which has 4 directed paths, just equal to the number of the Type-$\vee$ clauses in Eq. (1). Node i, i' ($i \in [1,4]$) represents the corresponding statement y_i. For each Type-$\vee$ clause, we have a corresponding directed path with length k (e.g., for $(y_1 \vee y_2)$, we have path $2 \rightarrow 1$). There are 4 different statements and each has 2 duplicates in Eq. (1). Note that in Fig. 2, there is only one node representing y_1 (similar for y_4), because we merge some nodes by the algorithm kCNFtoDAG. We also note that not all nodes corresponding to the duplicate statements can be merged, e.g., node 3 and node $3'$ for y_3.

Based on the DAG output by kCNFtoDAG, we compose the "atomic" Sigma protocols for individual relations. Informally, we run a "atomic" Sigma protocol over each node in the DAG. In a nutshell, for each node, we generate a commitment for the corresponding statement of the node, and then generate a response after receiving the challenge.

Note that the DAG affects the generation of the challenges for statements. In Fig. 1, we note that the challenges are generated sequentially and only one

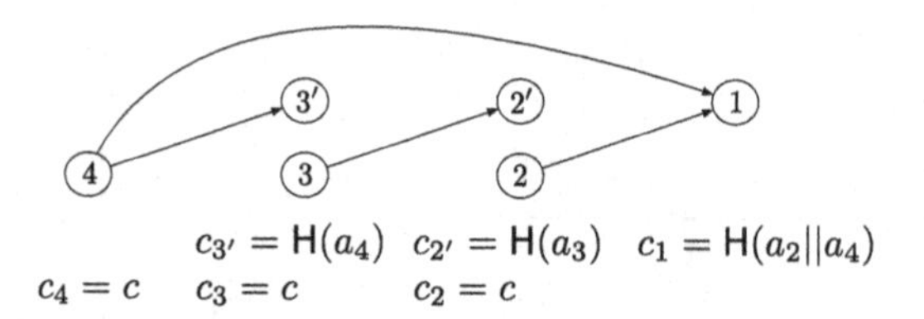

Fig. 2. An example of our scheme

commitment influences the computation of a challenge (i.e., informally, $c_j = \mathsf{H}(a_{j+1})$). However, in Fig. 2, there may be multiple arrows pointing to a node v (e.g., node 1). For convenience, we call the nodes that these arrows point from *the predecessor nodes* of node v. So here we have the challenge for the corresponding statement of node v being influenced by multiple commitments, which are generated for the statements of the predecessor nodes of v. More exactly, to compute the challenge, the hash function will take these commitments as the input (e.g., $c_1 = \mathsf{H}(a_2||a_4)$). For those nodes that no arrows point to, we directly take c as the challenge for their corresponding statements (e.g., $c_4 = c$). With this approach, we preserve the effect of Step I for reducing the number of a_{atm}'s and c_{atm}'s.

Related Works. A general composition technique of Sigma protocol was proposed by Cramer, Damgård and Schoenmakers [14]. The idea is to secret-share the challenge according to the access structure and then use the shares as challenges in the corresponding Sigma protocols for each of the "atomic" statements. Another composition technique, to sequentially generate the challenge as we do in Step I, is introduced in [4] and recently revisited in [2,16]. Some more discussion on constructing proofs for k-CNF relations using the techniques of [14] and [2] can be found in the full version of this paper.

Composition is also a hot topic in NIZKs in the common reference string model. Numbers of works [3,19,21,28,30] are proposed to implement disjunctive relations for the Groth-Sahai proofs [22] and Quasi-Adaptive NIZKs [26].

Composite Sigma protocol for 1-out-of-n partial knowledge (or complete k-DNF relations) have been studied for a long time, since Cramer et al. [14] achieves linear communication complexity. Later, Groth and Kohlweiss [20] show how to achieve logarithmic (in n) communication when $k = 1$, while Attema, Cramer and Fehr [5] achieve logarithmic communication for general k and n in the DL setting. Recently, Aarushi Goel et al. [17] propose stacking Sigmas to compose Sigma protocols for disjunctions. The resulting Sigma protocol has communication complexity proportional to the communication required by the largest clause.

Roadmap. The rest of paper is organised as follows. We review preliminaries in Sect. 2. The definition of k-CNF relations is introduced in Sect. 3 and a transfer algorithm $\mathsf{kCNFtoDAG}$ is presented in Sect. 4. We formally present the DAG-Σ protocol in Sect. 5 and an extension on incomplete k-DNF relations in Sect. 6. Finally, we show the experimental results in Sect. 7.

2 Preliminary

Notations. Throughout this paper, let λ denote the security parameter. For any $k \in \mathbb{N}$, let $[k] := \{1, 2, \cdots, k\}$. For a finite set S, we denote by $a \leftarrow S$ the process of uniformly sampling a from S. For a distribution X, we denote by $a \leftarrow X$ the process of sampling a from X. For any probabilistic polynomial-time (PPT) algorithm Alg, we write $\mathsf{Alg}(x; r)$ for the process of Alg on input x and with inner randomness r, and use $y \leftarrow \mathsf{Alg}(x)$ to denote the process of running Alg on input x and with uniformly sampled inner randomness r, and assigning y the result. We also use the symbol "$\leftarrow$" to assign the value of a variable or the result of a formula on the right-hand side to the variable on the left-hand side. We write vectors in $\mathbb{Z}_q^n$ or $\mathbb{G}^n$ in boldface, e.g., $\mathbf{x} = (x_1, \ldots, x_n) \in \mathbb{Z}_q^n$. In addition, let $(a||b)$ denote the concatenation of a and b.

Sigma Protocol. Let $\mathcal{R}$ be a polynomial-time-decidable binary relation. The corresponding language L consists of statement y such that there exists a witness x satisfying $(x, y) \in \mathcal{R}$. We specify L as an NP language. A Sigma protocol $\Sigma = (\mathcal{P}, \mathcal{V})$ for polynomial-time-decidable relation $\mathcal{R}$ is a three-move protocol and consists of two efficient interactive protocol algorithms $(\mathcal{P}, \mathcal{V})$, where $\mathcal{P} = (\mathcal{P}_1, \mathcal{P}_2)$ is the prover and $\mathcal{V} = (\mathcal{V}_1, \mathcal{V}_2)$ is the verifier, associated with a challenge space $\mathcal{CL}$. Specifically, for any $(x, y) \in \mathcal{R}$, the commitment a, the challenge c and the response z are sent in turn by the prover and verifier, where c is randomly picked over $\mathcal{CL}$ by the verifier. It enjoys completeness if for any $(x, y) \in \mathcal{R}$ and any transcript (a, c, z) output by the protocol, the verifier (i.e., $\mathcal{V}_2$) outputs 1. It also has the security requirements of knowledge soundness, special honest verifier zero knowledge (special HVZK) and witness indistinguishability. In this paper, we relax the requirement of knowledge soundness to *computational* knowledge soundness. Due to page limitations, formal definitions of these security requirements will be given in the full version of this paper. Without loss of generality, when there are multiple Sigma protocols, for $\Sigma = (\mathcal{P}, \mathcal{V})$, we use $\Sigma.\mathcal{P}$ and $\Sigma.\mathcal{V}$ to specify the prover and verifier of Σ, respectively.

Graphs. A directed graph is a tuple $G = (V, E)$ where V is a set of elements called vertices (or nodes) and E is a set of vertices pairs, $E \subseteq V \times V$, called directed edges or arrows. Given an edge $e = (u, v)$, it is pointed from vertex u to vertex v, and u is called the head of e and v is called the tail of e. A cycle in G is a finite sequence of edges $(e_1, \ldots, e_l)$ satisfying that the tail of edge e_i is the head of edge e_{i+1} for $\forall i \in [l]$ (we set $e_{l+1} = e_1$). A graph with no cycles is called acyclic. Given an acyclic graph G, we define a vertex sequence $(v_1, \ldots, v_l)$ as a path, where there is an edge $e = (v_i, v_{i+1})$ for every pair of neighboring vertices (v_i, v_{i+1}) for $i \in [l-1]$. The number of edges pointed to vertex v is called the in-degree of vertex v and we denote it as $\mathsf{in\text{-}deg}(v)$. Similarly, the number of edges pointed from vertex v is called the out-degree of vertex v and we denote it as $\mathsf{out\text{-}deg}(v)$. Given a vertex v, we call it a *source* if $\mathsf{in\text{-}deg}(v) = 0$ and call it a *sink* if $\mathsf{out\text{-}deg}(v) = 0$. In addition, we define some operations for a directed acyclic graph G: (1) $\mathsf{sink}(G)$ outputs a vertex set S^{sink} that contains all sinks; (2) similarly, $\mathsf{source}(G)$ outputs a vertex set S^{source} that contains all sources;

(3) for any vertex v, $\mathsf{pred}(v)$ outputs a vertex set S_v^{pred} where the elements are the head of the edges that are pointed to vertex v.

3 Definition of k-CNF Relations

In this section, we formally define partial knowledge for k-CNF relations. Let y denote a statement, and S_k denote the universal set of which the elements are k-size subsets of $[n]$, i.e., $S_k := \{\{i_1, \ldots, i_k\} | \ 1 \leq i_1 < \ldots < i_k \leq n, \{i_1, \ldots, i_k\} \subset [n]\}$. Besides, $(x_l, y_l) \in \mathcal{R}_l$ $(l \in [n])$ denotes a valid witness-statement pair belonging to a relation $\mathcal{R}_l$. Then, we define the following partial knowledge for compound statements.

Definition 1. (Partial knowledge for k-CNF). *Given n different statements $(y_l)_{l\in[n]}$, n sub-relations $(\mathcal{R}_l)_{l\in[n]}$, and $S'_k \subsetneqq S_k$, the prover proves that for all $\{i_1, \ldots, i_k\} \in S'_k$, she knows the witnesses for at least one of $y_{i_1}, \cdots, y_{i_k}$.*

The relation can be presented in CNF as follows,

$$\mathcal{R}_{k\text{-CNF},S'_k} = \{(\mathbf{x}, \mathbf{y}) : \wedge_{\{i_1,\ldots,i_k\}\in S'_k} (\vee_{j\in[k]} (x_{i_j}, y_{i_j}) \in \mathcal{R}_{i_j})\}, \tag{2}$$

where $\mathbf{x}$, $\mathbf{y}$ are two n-dimension vectors, and $\mathcal{R}_{i_j} \in \{\mathcal{R}_l \mid l \in [n]\}$ is a sub-relation. We call $(\vee_{j\in[k]}(x_{i_j}, y_{i_j}) \in \mathcal{R}_{i_j})$ a "Type-$\vee$" clause, where $\{i_1, \ldots, i_k\} \in S_k$. Let *num* denote the number of Type-$\vee$ clauses in $\mathcal{R}_{k\text{-CNF},S'_k}$, i.e., $num = |S'_k|$. Note that $num \leq C_n^k$, and we only consider polynomial-time relation, so it is required that the membership of $(\mathbf{x}, \mathbf{y})$ to $\mathcal{R}_{k\text{-CNF},S'_k}$ can be determined in polynomial time in $|\mathbf{y}|$. We denote the *(polynomial-time)* relation defined in Eq. (2) as a **k-CNF relation**.

We stress that *not* all the $\mathcal{R}_{k\text{-CNF},S'_k}$ defined in Eq. (2) can be decided in polynomial time. For example, when k is about $\frac{n}{3}$ and num is close to C_n^k, generally the complexity of determining whether $(\mathbf{x}, \mathbf{y}) \in \mathcal{R}_{k\text{-CNF},S'_k}$ is $O(k \cdot num) = O(\frac{n}{3} \cdot C_n^{\frac{n}{3}})$, so it is super-polynomial.

In this paper, we focus on k-CNF relations that can be determined in polynomial time, e.g., (i) $|S'_k|$ is polynomial in $|\mathbf{y}|$, and (ii) k is a constant. Specifically, when $|S'_k|$ is polynomial in $|\mathbf{y}|$, the time for determining $\mathcal{R}_{k\text{-CNF},S'_k}$ is linear in $|S'_k|$, so it is also polynomial. On the other hand, when k is a constant, $O(k \cdot num) = O(num)$, where num is polynomial in n in the worst case.

Remark 1. When $num = C_n^k$, a proof for a k-CNF relation can be transferred into a proof of $(n - k + 1)$-out-of-n partial knowledge. Then there exists some trivial and efficient solutions, e.g., [5]. Thus, without loss of generality, when we refer to k-CNF relations, we usually mean "incomplete" k-CNF relations (i.e., $num < C_n^k$). It also can be inferred that a proof of k-out-of-n partial knowledge can be transferred into a proof for a $(n - k + 1)$-CNF relation with C_n^{n-k+1} clauses.

Throughout this paper, we mainly focus on the discrete logarithm (DL) setting. In other words, the prover aims to convince the verifier that she knows the discrete logarithms of some statements (i.e., the group elements). Formally, let $\mathbb{G}$ be a cyclic group of order p, and g be a generator of $\mathbb{G}$. Following Definition 1 and the DL setting, we define the relation $\mathcal{R}^{\mathrm{dl}}_{k\text{-CNF},S'_k}$ as follows:

$$\mathcal{R}^{\mathrm{dl}}_{k\text{-CNF},S'_k} = \{(\mathbf{x}, \mathbf{y}) : \wedge_{\{i_1,\ldots,i_k\}\in S'_k}(\vee_{j\in[k]} y_{i_j} = g^{x_{i_j}})\}, \tag{3}$$

where $\mathbf{x} \in (\mathbb{Z}_p^* \cup \{\perp\})^n \backslash \{(\perp)^n\}$, $\mathbf{y} \in \mathbb{G}^n$, S'_k is defined as in Definition 1, and for all $\{i_1, \ldots, i_k\} \in S'_k$, $1 \leq i_1 < \ldots < i_k \leq n$. Furthermore, for any $\mathbf{x} \in (\mathbb{Z}_p^* \cup \{\perp\})^n \backslash \{(\perp)^n\}$, let $S^{\mathrm{w}}_{\mathbf{x}} := \{i \in [n] \mid y_i = g^{x_i}\}$. In other words, $S^{\mathrm{w}}_{\mathbf{x}}$ contains the indices that prover knows the corresponding witnesses.

4 Converting *k*-CNF Relations into DAGs

Before constructing our Sigma protocol for k-CNF relations, we firstly introduce a deterministic transfer algorithm kCNFtoDAG, which can convert a k-CNF relation $\mathcal{R}_{k\text{-CNF},S'_k}$ (in Eq. (2)) to a directed acyclic graph (DAG). In Sect. 5, we will show a Sigma protocol (DAG-Σ) based on the DAG output by the algorithm kCNFtoDAG.

We require that the DAG output by kCNFtoDAG should have the following properties:

- **Property-(i):** Each node in some path corresponds to a statement in the corresponding Type-∨ clause.
- **Property-(ii):** The number of paths from the nodes in S^{source} to the nodes in S^{sink} equals the number of Type-∨ clauses in the expression of $\mathcal{R}_{k\text{-CNF},S'_k}$, and the lengths of these paths are k.

Furthermore, we require that the number of vertices in the DAG should be *as few as possible.* That's because in Sect. 5, we will show that the communication complexity of our DAG-Σ protocol depends on the number of the vertices of the DAG output by kCNFtoDAG.

Now, we turn to the details of algorithm kCNFtoDAG.

For simplicity, we require that the statements in each Type-∨ clause are sorted from the smallest index to the largest, e.g., $\mathcal{R}_1$ in Eq. (4) (for simplicity, we use Σ to denote $(x, y) \in \mathcal{R}$).

$$\begin{aligned}\mathcal{R}_1 = \{(\mathbf{x}, \mathbf{y}) : (\Sigma_1 \vee \Sigma_2 \vee \Sigma_3) \wedge (\Sigma_1 \vee \Sigma_2 \vee \Sigma_4)\\ \wedge (\Sigma_2 \vee \Sigma_3 \vee \Sigma_5) \wedge (\Sigma_3 \vee \Sigma_4 \vee \Sigma_5)\}\end{aligned} \tag{4}$$

A simple idea to implement kCNFtoDAG is to build a separate directed path for each Type-∨ clause. However, it would result in $(k \cdot num)$ nodes in the graph, where num is the number of Type-∨ clauses. As shown in Fig. 3, we draw a DAG for $\mathcal{R}_1$ in Eq. (4), using the simple idea. It is clear that the DAG has the above two properties, and there are totally $3 \times 4 = 12$ nodes in the graph.

To reduce the number of nodes, we consider the following method first. We scan the relation and let every statement have at most three states, i.e., beginning, middle, ending. The beginning state shows that the statement is the last statement of some Type-$\vee$ clause so the corresponding node is the head of some path. The middle state indicates that the statement is placed in the middle of some Type-$\vee$ clause. The ending state is that the statement is the first statement of some Type-$\vee$ clause (note that in Sect. 5, the prover will compute a commitment for each node, and only the commitments for the nodes indicating statements with ending state will be sent to the verifier). Then for every Type-$\vee$ clause, we have a path in G from a node indicating the beginning state of some statement to a node indicating the ending state of some statement.

Thus, we merge the nodes with the same state in Fig. 3, then obtain another DAG in Fig. 4. We use a_l, b_l, e_l ($l \in [1, 5]$) to denote the beginning, middle, ending state of the lth statement respectively. When describing the DAG here, for convenience, we also use these notations (i.e., a_l, b_l and e_l) to represent the head nodes, middle nodes and tail nodes respectively. In addition, we may use superscripts to indicate different duplicate nodes (e.g., nodes b_3^1 and b_3^2 in Fig. 6 represent the different duplicates). When talking about the paths in the DAG, we sometimes write the path with nodes and arrows (e.g., for the path (a_3, b_2, e_1) in Fig. 4, we write it as $a_3 \to b_2 \to e_1$). In Fig. 4, the number of vertices is 9, which is smaller than that in Fig. 3.

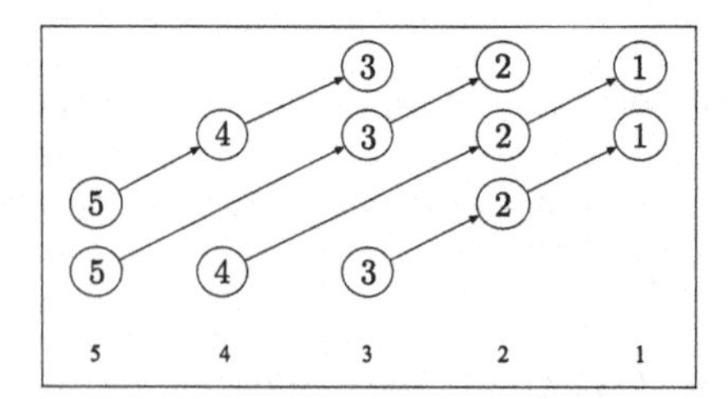

Fig. 3. A simple idea

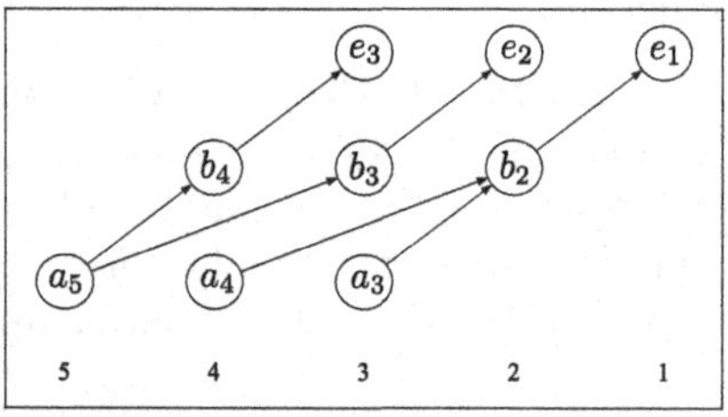

Fig. 4. An example for CNF

However, the above approach cannot handle all cases. A counter example is

$$\mathcal{R}_2 = \{(\mathbf{x}, \mathbf{y}) : (\Sigma_1 \vee \Sigma_2 \vee \Sigma_3) \wedge (\Sigma_1 \vee \Sigma_2 \vee \Sigma_4) \wedge (\Sigma_1 \vee \Sigma_3 \vee \Sigma_4) \\ \wedge (\Sigma_2 \vee \Sigma_3 \vee \Sigma_5) \wedge (\Sigma_3 \vee \Sigma_4 \vee \Sigma_5)\} \tag{5}$$

and we try to draw a DAG as shown in Fig. 5, using the above approach.

Compared with relation $\mathcal{R}_1$ in Eq. (4), one more Type-$\vee$ clause is added in Eq. (5) (i.e., $(\Sigma_1 \vee \Sigma_3 \vee \Sigma_4)$), and we use the dashed arrows in Fig. 5 to show the difference compared with Fig. 4. Note that there is a "crossing edge" (i.e., in node b_3) in Fig. 5. It implies two more directed paths (i.e., $a_4 \to b_3 \to e_2$ and $a_5 \to b_3 \to e_1$) are introduced in Fig. 5, while $(\Sigma_2 \vee \Sigma_3 \vee \Sigma_4)$ and $(\Sigma_1 \vee \Sigma_3 \vee \Sigma_5)$ are not in Eq. (5). Hence, the obtaining DAG does not have the above two properties. Essentially, a "wrong" crossing edge may introduce nonexistent Type-$\vee$ clauses. Thus, to output a correct DAG, a duplicate node for b_3 is needed in this case, as shown in Fig. 6.

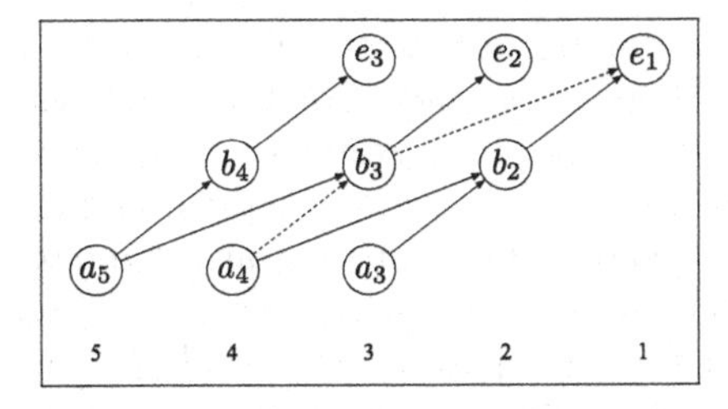

Fig. 5. A counter exam

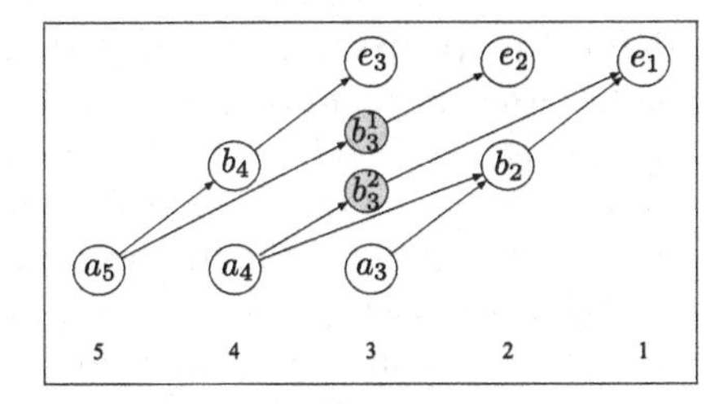

Fig. 6. A fixed graph

Next, we present the formal description of algorithm kCNFtoDAG, which is constructed with the above approach. We also take relation $\mathcal{R}_2$ in Eq. (5) as an example, to show how kCNFtoDAG works step by step.

Algorithm Description. Inputting a k-CNF relation $\mathcal{R}_{k\text{-CNF},S'_k}$ (in Eq. (2)), the deterministic transfer algorithm kCNFtoDAG runs in the following steps and finally outputs a DAG $G = (V, E)$:

1. **Preparing nodes.** For each Type-$\vee$ clause in $\mathcal{R}_{k\text{-CNF},S'_k}$, draw a separate directed path $(v_1, \ldots, v_k)$ with length k and each node represents a statement. For each path, we require that the indices of their corresponding statements are from the largest to the smallest. In other words, given a function $f : V \rightarrow [n]$, mapping the nodes to the indices of the corresponding statements, we have $f(v_1) > \ldots > f(v_k)$.
   As shown in Fig. 7, for every Type-$\vee$ clause of the expression of $\mathcal{R}_2$ in Eq. (5), we draw a path. There are 5 paths and 15 nodes in total. The numbers in the bottom of Fig. 7 (i.e., $5, \ldots, 1$) indicate the statements that the above nodes map to, e.g., node a_3 represents statement y_3. It is clear that given any path (v_1, v_2, v_3) in Fig. 7, the indices of the corresponding statements are in descending order, e.g., for the path which is denoted as $a_3 \rightarrow b_2^2 \rightarrow e_1^3$, we have $f(v_1) = 3 > f(v_2) = 2 > f(v_3) = 1$.

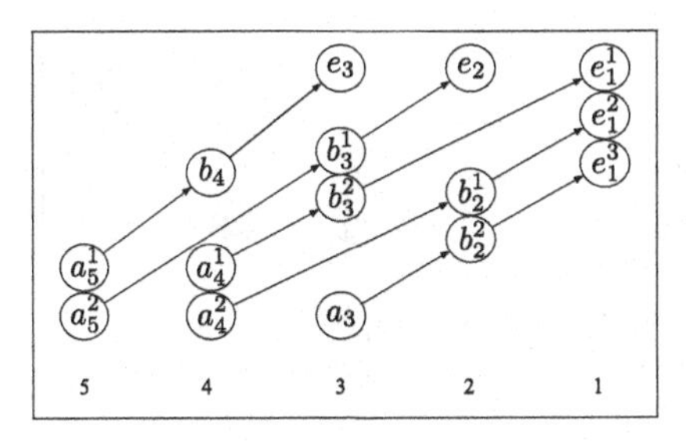

Fig. 7. Graph after step 1

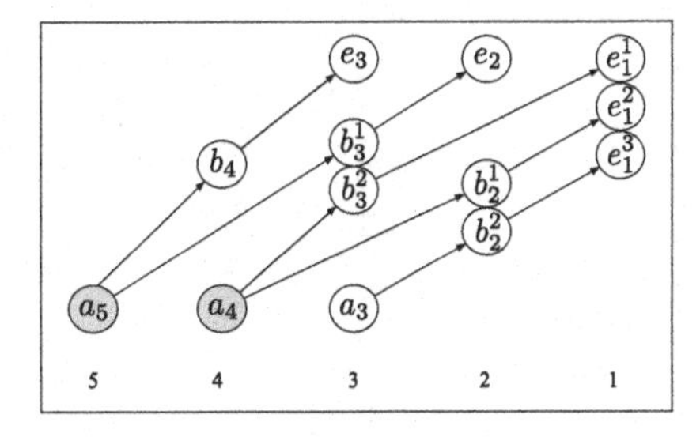

Fig. 8. Graph after step 2

2. **Merging prefixes.** For any node v_l ($l \in [k]$) in some path $(v_1, \ldots, v_k)$, we define the *prefix* of v_l as $(v_1, \ldots, v_{l-1})$. For any v_l and v'_l, if their prefixes $(v_1, \ldots, v_{l-1})$ and $(v'_1, \ldots, v'_{l-1})$ correspond to the same statements, then for all $i \in [l-1]$, we merge v_i and v'_i into one node. Here, we merge the nodes in descending order of the indices of the statements, i.e., from the largest index to the least index.
For example, in Fig. 7, node b_4 (in path $a_5^1 \to b_4 \to e_3$) and node b_3^1 (in path $a_5^2 \to b_3^1 \to e_2$) have the same prefix (i.e., node a_5^1 and node a_5^2). Thus, we merge them into one node (i.e., the blue node a_5 in Fig. 8). Similarly, we merge node a_4^1 and node a_4^2 into another blue node a_4 in Fig. 8. Finally, we obtain Fig. 8 after merging prefixes and there are totally 5 paths and 13 nodes.
3. **Merging suffixes.** For any node v_l ($l \in [k]$) in some path $(v_1, \ldots, v_k)$, we define the *suffix* of v_l as $(v_{l+1}, \ldots, v_k)$. Note that a node may have multiple suffixes after merging prefixes. For any v_l and v'_l, we will merge them into one node, if they satisfy the following conditions: i) they correspond to the same statement; ii) the numbers of suffixes of v_l and v'_l are the same (if the suffix is empty, the number of suffixes is 0); iii) when the numbers of suffixes are greater than 0, for each suffix of v_l, there is suffix of v'_l such that the corresponding statements of the suffixes are the same. Here, we merge the nodes in ascending order of the indices of the statements, i.e., from the least index to the largest index. Finally, output the graph G.
In Fig. 8, the suffix of the node e_1^1 in path $a_4 \to b_3^2 \to e_1^1$, the suffix of node e_1^2 in path $a_4 \to b_2^1 \to e_1^2$ and the suffix of node e_1^3 in path $a_3 \to b_2^2 \to e_1^3$, are all empty. Thus, we merge them into one node, as the blue node e_1 in Fig. 9. After that, node b_2^1 (in path $a_4 \to b_2^1 \to e_1$) and node b_2^2 (in path $a_3 \to b_2^2 \to e_1$) share the same suffixes (i.e., node e_1). Thus, we merge node b_2^1 and node b_2^2 into one node (i.e., the blue node b_2 in Fig. 10). Finally, we can see that the graphs in Fig. 10 and Fig. 6 are identical. There are 5 paths and 10 nodes in total in Fig. 10, and the number of the nodes in Fig. 10 are much smaller than that in Fig. 7.

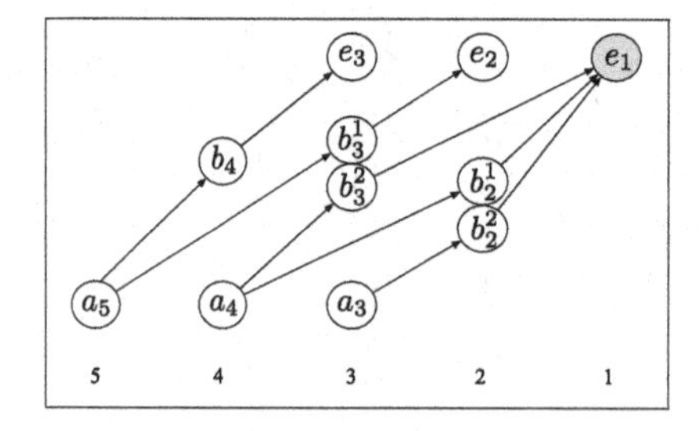

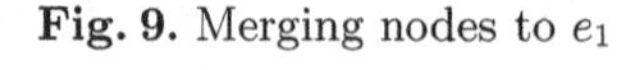
Fig. 9. Merging nodes to e_1

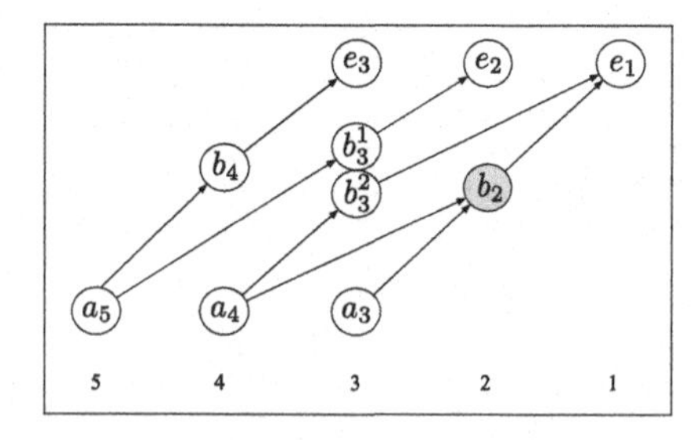

Fig. 10. Graph after step 3

That's the description of the deterministic transfer algorithm kCNFtoDAG.

Now we turn to discuss the properties that kCNFtoDAG has. Formally, we have the following two theorems. Due to space limitations, the proofs of these two theorems are provided in the full version of this paper.

Theorem 1. *Given a k-CNF relation, the DAG output by algorithm* kCNFtoDAG *has the aforementioned Property-(i) and Property-(ii).*

Theorem 2. *Given a k-CNF relation $\mathcal{R}_{k\text{-CNF},S'_k}$ for n statements, the number of vertices $|V|$ in the DAG, output by the above transfer algorithm* kCNFtoDAG*, satisfies that $|V| \leq \mathsf{Min}(V_{\text{bound}}, (k \cdot num))$, where num is the number of the clauses in the expression of $\mathcal{R}_{k\text{-CNF},S'_k}$, and*

$$V_{\text{bound}} = 2^d + 2(n-2d+1) + (n-2d+2)C_n^{\lfloor \frac{d}{2} \rfloor + 1} \begin{cases} d = k & (2 \leq k < \frac{n+1}{2}) \\ d = n-k+1 & (\frac{n+1}{2} \leq k \leq n-1) \end{cases} \tag{6}$$

In addition, if we just prepare as many nodes as the theoretical result (i.e., V_{bound}), then we can further reduce the running time and memory space when invoking kCNFtoDAG. An improved algorithm can be found in the full version of this paper.

5 DAG-Σ Protocol for *k*-CNF

In this section, we construct a Sigma protocol for k-CNF relations. Specifically, we first show a Sigma protocol for k-CNF relations based on a Sigma protocol for 1-out-of-k relations in Sect. 5.1. Further, we convert the k-CNF relations to directed acyclic graphs (DAGs), and then show a DAG-based Sigma protocol (DAG-Σ protocol) in Sect. 5.2.

5.1 Warm-Up

Here we describe a Sigma protocol for k-CNF relations. Part of the ideas will be adopted in our later DAG-Σ protocol.

Framework. Let $\mathcal{R}_{1\text{-OR}}$ be a 1-out-of-k relation in the DL setting, i.e.,

$$\mathcal{R}_{1\text{-OR}} = \{(\mathbf{x}, \mathbf{y}) : y_1 = g^{x_1} \vee \ldots \vee y_k = g^{x_k}\}, \tag{7}$$

where $\mathbf{x} \in (\mathbb{Z}_p^* \cup \{\perp\})^k \backslash \{(\perp)^k\}$ and $\mathbf{y} \in \mathbb{G}^k$. We will firstly construct a Sigma protocol $\Sigma^{\mathcal{R}_{1\text{-OR}}}$ for $\mathcal{R}_{1\text{-OR}}$. Then, with $\Sigma^{\mathcal{R}_{1\text{-OR}}}$ as an ingredient, we construct a composite Sigma protocol $\Sigma_{\text{plain}}^{\mathcal{R}^{\text{dl}}_{k\text{-CNF},S'_k}}$ for $\mathcal{R}^{\text{dl}}_{k\text{-CNF},S'_k}$ (Eq. (3)) in this way:

1. For each Type-$\vee$ clause in $\mathcal{R}^{\text{dl}}_{k\text{-CNF},S'_k}$, the prover $\mathcal{P}_1$ calls $\Sigma^{\mathcal{R}_{1\text{-OR}}}.\mathcal{P}_1$ to generate a commitment; then she sends all the commitments to the verifier.
2. The verifier $\mathcal{V}_1$ picks a random number from $\mathbb{Z}_p^*$ as a challenge and sends it to the prover.

3. The prover $\mathcal{P}_2$ calls $\Sigma^{\mathcal{R}_{1\text{-OR}}}.\mathcal{P}_2$ to generate responses and then sends them to the verifier.

Finally, the verifier $\mathcal{V}_2$ outputs 1 if and only if $\Sigma^{\mathcal{R}_{1\text{-OR}}}.\mathcal{V}_2$ accepts all the transcripts (for all the Type-$\vee$ clauses in $\mathcal{R}^{\text{dl}}_{k\text{-CNF},S'_k}$).

Completeness, computational knowledge soundness and special HVZK property of this composite Sigma protocol are trivially based on that of $\Sigma^{\mathcal{R}_{1\text{-OR}}}$. So we omit the analysis here, and turn to the construction of $\Sigma^{\mathcal{R}_{1\text{-OR}}}$.

Sigma Protocol $\Sigma^{\mathcal{R}_{1\text{-OR}}}$. Before describing the protocol $\Sigma^{\mathcal{R}_{1\text{-OR}}}$, we firstly recall Schnorr's Sigma protocol [32] $\Sigma^{\mathcal{R}}_{\text{Sch}} = (\mathcal{P}, \mathcal{V})$ for relation $\mathcal{R} = \{(x, y) : y = g^x\}$ in Fig. 11, where the description of the HVZK simulator Sim is also presented. Observe that the witness x is not needed for $\Sigma^{\mathcal{R}}_{\text{Sch}}.\mathcal{P}_1$, so we write $\Sigma^{\mathcal{R}}_{\text{Sch}}.\mathcal{P}_1(\perp, y)$ directly in Fig. 11. Note that Schnorr's Sigma protocol $\Sigma^{\mathcal{R}}_{\text{Sch}}$ is a *Chameleon* Σ-protocol [12] (the definition will be recalled in the full version of this paper). Generally, in a Chameleon Σ-protocol, the prover can compute the commitment a by using the simulator (taking a statement y and an arbitrary challenge c' as input). Once the challenge c has been received, the prover can compute the response z by using the witness x and the randomness which is used by the simulator to compute a. Thus, a Chameleon Σ-protocol for $\mathcal{R}$ has two modes: standard mode when $\mathcal{P}$ runs $\mathcal{P}_1$ and $\mathcal{P}_2$, and a Chameleon mode when $\mathcal{P}$ runs the simulator. It is required that for all $(x, y) \in \mathcal{R}$, the transcript output in the standard mode and that output in the Chameleon mode are indistinguishable. As pointed out in [12], $\Sigma^{\mathcal{R}}_{\text{Sch}}$ is a Chameleon Σ-protocol, so we provide another proving algorithm $\mathcal{P}' = (\mathcal{P}'_1, \mathcal{P}'_2)$ for $\Sigma^{\mathcal{R}}_{\text{Sch}}$ in Fig. 11.

In fact, Schnorr's Sigma protocol is a perfect Chameleon Σ-protocol, so for all $(x, y) \in \mathcal{R}$, the transcripts generated by $(\mathcal{P}, \mathcal{V})$ and that generated by $(\mathcal{P}', \mathcal{V})$ are distributed identically.

Standard mode:	$\mathcal{V}_2(y, a, c, z)$:	Chameleon mode:
(1) $\mathcal{P}_1(\perp, y)$ $r \leftarrow \mathbb{Z}_p^*$, $a \leftarrow g^r$ Send a to $\mathcal{V}$ (2) $\mathcal{V}_1(a)$: $c \leftarrow \mathbb{Z}_p^*$ Send c to $\mathcal{P}$ (3) $\mathcal{P}_2(a, c, x, y)$ $z \leftarrow r + cx$ Send z to $\mathcal{V}$	$a' \leftarrow g^z / y^c$ Return $(a' \stackrel{?}{=} a)$ Simulator $\mathsf{Sim}(y, c)$: $z \leftarrow \mathbb{Z}_p^*$, $a \leftarrow g^z / y^c$ Return (a, z)	(1) $\mathcal{P}'_1(\perp, y)$: $c' \leftarrow \mathbb{Z}_p^*$ $r \leftarrow \mathbb{Z}_p^*$, $a \leftarrow g^r / y^{c'}$ $//\Sigma^{\mathcal{R}}_{\text{Sch}}.\mathsf{Sim}(y, c')$ Send a to $\mathcal{V}$ (2) $\mathcal{V}_1(a)$: $c \leftarrow \mathbb{Z}_p^*$, Send c to $\mathcal{P}$ (3) $\mathcal{P}'_2(a, c, c', x, y)$: $z \leftarrow r + (c - c')x$ Send z to $\mathcal{V}$

Fig. 11. Schnorr's Sigma protocol $\Sigma^{\mathcal{R}}_{\text{Sch}}$

Now, we turn to the construction of Sigma protocol $\Sigma^{\mathcal{R}_{1\text{-OR}}}$.

Let $\Sigma^{\mathcal{R}}_{\text{Sch}}$ be Schnorr's Sigma protocol as shown in Fig. 11, and $\varphi : \{0, 1\}^* \rightarrow \mathbb{Z}_p^*$ be a collision-resistant hash function. The Sigma protocol $\Sigma^{\mathcal{R}_{1\text{-OR}}} = (\mathcal{P}, \mathcal{V})$ for $\mathcal{R}_{1\text{-OR}}$ is as follows (and the detailed algorithms are shown in Fig. 12).

1. $\underline{\mathcal{P} \to \mathcal{V}.}$ The prover $\mathcal{P}_1$ computes the commitment as follows. First, $\mathcal{P}_1$ calls $\Sigma_{\text{Sch}}^{\mathcal{R}}.\mathcal{P}_1(\perp, y_k)$ to generate a random commitment a_k for the kth statement y_k. Then for $l = k-1$ to 1, $\mathcal{P}_1$ invokes the HVZK simulator $\Sigma_{\text{Sch}}^{\mathcal{R}}.\mathsf{Sim}$, feeding it with $\varphi(a_{l+1})$ as the challenge, to generate a_l for the lth statement y_l. Finally, $\mathcal{P}_1$ sends $a = a_1$ to the verifier $\mathcal{V}$.
2. $\underline{\mathcal{V} \to \mathcal{P}.}$ Receiving a, $\mathcal{V}_1$ samples $c \leftarrow \mathbb{Z}_p^*$ and sends it to $\mathcal{P}$.
3. $\underline{\mathcal{P} \to \mathcal{V}.}$ Receiving c, $\mathcal{P}_2$ proceeds to compute the response. We denote the largest component in $S_{\mathbf{x}}^{\text{w}}$ as μ, i.e., the witness x_μ for y_μ is known by the prover. For every $l > \mu$, $\mathcal{P}_2$ invokes the HVZK simulator $\Sigma_{\text{Sch}}^{\mathcal{R}}.\mathsf{Sim}$ to generate another commitment a'_l for each statement y_l. Then, for $l = \mu$, $\mathcal{P}_2$ calls $\Sigma_{\text{Sch}}^{\mathcal{R}}.\mathcal{P}'_2(a_\mu, \varphi(a'_{\mu+1}), \varphi(a_{\mu+1}), x_\mu, y_\mu)$ (or $\Sigma_{\text{Sch}}^{\mathcal{R}}.\mathcal{P}_2(a_k, c, x_k, y_k)$ if $\mu = k$) to generate a valid response. For every $l < \mu$, we just set the responses equal to those responses output by the HVZK simulator in the first step. Finally, $\mathcal{P}_2$ sends $z = \{z_l\}_{l \in [k]}$ to the verifier.

The verification is as follows. The verifier $\mathcal{V}_2$ invokes the codes in $\Sigma_{\text{Sch}}^{\mathcal{R}}.\mathcal{V}_2$ to compute the commitments for every statement. Then he compares the computed commitment of the first statement with the commitment a sent by $\mathcal{P}_1$. If they are equal, $\mathcal{V}_2$ outputs 1.

Completeness. Now we analyze the completeness of $\Sigma^{\mathcal{R}_{\text{1-OR}}}$. For any $(\mathbf{x}, \mathbf{y}) \in \mathcal{R}_{\text{1-OR}}$, denote the largest component in $S_{\mathbf{x}}^{\text{w}}$ as μ. If $\mu = k$, we have $a''_k = g^{z_k}/y_k^c = g^{r+x_k c}/y_k^c = g^r = a_k = a'_k$. If $\mu < k$, we have $a''_k = g^{z_k} y_k^c = a'_k$ and then by mathematical induction we have $a''_{\mu+1} = a'_{\mu+1}$. Further, we have

$$\begin{aligned} a''_\mu &= g^{z_\mu}/y_\mu^{\varphi(a''_{\mu+1})} = g^{z_\mu}/y_\mu^{\varphi(a'_{\mu+1})} \\ &= g^{\hat{z}_\mu + (\varphi(a'_{\mu+1}) - \varphi(a_{\mu+1}))x_\mu}/y_\mu^{\varphi(a'_{\mu+1})} = g^{\hat{z}_\mu}/y_\mu^{\varphi(a_{\mu+1})} = a_\mu = a'_\mu. \end{aligned}$$

Therefore, when $l < \mu$, we can prove the following recursively: $a''_l = g^{z_l}/y_l^{\varphi(a''_{l+1})} = g^{z_l}/y_l^{\varphi(a'_{l+1})} = g^{\hat{z}_l}/y_l^{\varphi(a_{l+1})} = a_l = a'_l$. It implies that $a''_1 = a'_1 = a_1 = a$, so $\mathcal{V}_2$ outputs 1.

The completeness implies some special features of $\Sigma^{\mathcal{R}_{\text{1-OR}}}$:

1. For every statement, the commitment computed by $\mathcal{P}_2$ equals that computed by $\mathcal{V}_2$, i.e., $a'_l = a''_l$ $(l \in [k])$.
2. For the statement of which the prover knows the witness, the corresponding commitments in different steps are the same, i.e., $a_\mu = a'_\mu = a''_\mu$.
3. If $a_{l+1} \neq a''_{l+1}$ $(l \in [k-1])$ and the prover does not know the witness of y_l, then it holds that $a_l \neq a''_l$ with overwhelming probability.

Due to page limitations, the analysis of computational knowledge soundness, special HVZK and witness indistinguishability of $\Sigma^{\mathcal{R}_{\text{1-OR}}}$ will be given in the full version of this paper.

With this Sigma protocol $\Sigma^{\mathcal{R}_{\text{1-OR}}}$ as a building block, we can obtain a composite Sigma protocol $\Sigma_{\text{plain}}^{\mathcal{R}^{\text{dl}}_{k\text{-CNF},S'_k}}$ for $\mathcal{R}^{\text{dl}}_{k\text{-CNF},S'_k}$ (Eq. (3)) following the framework

(1) $\mathcal{P}_1(x_\mu, \mathbf{y})$:
  $r \leftarrow \mathbb{Z}_p^*$, $a_k \leftarrow g^r$ // $\Sigma_{\text{Sch}}^{\mathcal{R}}.\mathcal{P}_1(\perp, y_k)$
  For $l = k-1$ to 1:
    $\hat{z}_l \leftarrow \mathbb{Z}_p^*$, $a_l \leftarrow g^{\hat{z}_l}/y_l^{\varphi(a_{l+1})}$ // $\Sigma_{\text{Sch}}^{\mathcal{R}}.\mathsf{Sim}(y_l, \varphi(a_{l+1}))$
  Send $a = a_1$ to $\mathcal{V}$
(2) $\mathcal{V}_1(a)$:
  $c \leftarrow \mathbb{Z}_p^*$, Send c to $\mathcal{P}$
(3) $\mathcal{P}_2(a, c, x_\mu, \mathbf{y})$:
  If $\mu = k$:
    $z_k \leftarrow r + x_k c$, $a'_k \leftarrow a_k$ // $\Sigma_{\text{Sch}}^{\mathcal{R}}.\mathcal{P}_2(a_k, c, x_k, y_k)$
  Else:
    $z_k \leftarrow \mathbb{Z}_p^*$, $a'_k \leftarrow g^{z_k}/y_k^c$ // $\Sigma_{\text{Sch}}^{\mathcal{R}}.\mathsf{Sim}(y_k, c)$
    For $l = k-1$ to $\mu+1$:
      $z_l \leftarrow \mathbb{Z}_p^*$, $a'_l \leftarrow g^{z_l}/y_l^{\varphi(a'_{l+1})}$ // $\Sigma_{\text{Sch}}^{\mathcal{R}}.\mathsf{Sim}(y_l, \varphi(a'_{l+1}))$
    $z_\mu \leftarrow \hat{z}_\mu + (\varphi(a'_{\mu+1}) - \varphi(a_{\mu+1}))x_\mu$, $a'_\mu \leftarrow a_\mu$
      // $\Sigma_{\text{Sch}}^{\mathcal{R}}.\mathcal{P}'_2(a_l, \varphi(a'_{l+1}), \varphi(a_{l+1}), x_l, y_l)$
  For $l = \mu - 1$ to 1: $a'_l \leftarrow a_l$, $z_l \leftarrow \hat{z}_l$
  Send $z = \{z_l\}_{l \in [k]}$ to $\mathcal{V}$

$\mathcal{V}_2(\mathbf{y}, a, c, z)$:
  $\{z_l\}_{l \in [k]} \leftarrow z$, $a''_k \leftarrow g^{z_k}/y_k^c$
  For $l = k-1$ to 1: $a''_l \leftarrow g^{z_l}/y_l^{\varphi(a''_{l+1})}$
  Return $(a''_1 \stackrel{?}{=} a)$

Fig. 12. Algorithms of $\Sigma^{\mathcal{R}_{1\text{-OR}}}$ (μ is the largest component in $S_{\mathbf{x}}^{\mathsf{w}}$, i.e., the prover knows x_μ for y_μ.)

as mentioned before. We note that the communication complexity of the composite Sigma protocol for $\mathcal{R}^{\text{dl}}_{k\text{-CNF},S'_k}$ is $O(k \cdot num)$, which theoretically equals the complexity of [14].

5.2 Description of DAG-Σ Protocols

Here, we construct a more efficient Sigma protocol for $\mathcal{R}^{\text{dl}}_{k\text{-CNF},S'_k}$ in Eq. (3). Informally, we construct this protocol following the main idea of $\Sigma^{\mathcal{R}_{1\text{-OR}}}$, except that (i) we firstly convert the relation to a directed acyclic graph (DAG), and generate a commitment for each node v of the DAG (instead of generating a_l for each statement y_l in $\Sigma^{\mathcal{R}_{1\text{-OR}}}$), and (ii) the value of commitment for node v depends on all the commitments for the nodes in S_v^{pred} (while the value of commitment a_l depends on a single statement a_{l+1} for statement y_{l+1}). Furthermore, the communication complexity of the DAG-based protocol depends on the number of vertices of the DAG.

Building Blocks. Let $\Sigma^{\mathcal{R}}_{\text{Sch}}$ be Schnorr's Sigma protocol as shown in Fig. 11, and $\varphi : \{0,1\}^* \rightarrow \mathbb{Z}_p^*$ be a collision-resistant hash function. Let kCNFtoDAG be the deterministic transfer algorithm presented in Sect. 4, which takes a k-CNF relation $\mathcal{R}_{k\text{-CNF},S'_k}$ (i.e., relation of the form like Eq. (2)) as input and outputs a directed acyclic graph $G = (V, E)$. As in the description of kCNFtoDAG, we can have a function $f : V \rightarrow [n]$ such that if there is an edge from v_1 to v_2 in the graph, then $f(v_1) > f(v_2)$.

Overview. We firstly run the transfer algorithm kCNFtoDAG to convert the relation $\mathcal{R}^{\text{dl}}_{k\text{-CNF},S'_k}$ to a DAG $G = (V, E)$. Note that a node in G represents only one statement, while a statement may correspond to multiple nodes, since there are multiple Type-$\vee$ clauses in the expression of $\mathcal{R}^{\text{dl}}_{k\text{-CNF},S'_k}$. Recall that in the Sigma protocol $\Sigma^{\mathcal{R}_{1\text{-OR}}}$ in Fig. 12, for each statement y_l, a corresponding commitment a_l is generated. Here, with similar approach, for each node of G, we compute a commitment for the corresponding statement. For a node v, the commitment computed with the algorithm $\mathcal{P}_1$ of the DAG-Σ protocol is denoted as a_v if $v \in S^{\text{source}}$, or b_v if $(v \notin S^{\text{source}}) \wedge (v \notin S^{\text{sink}})$, or e_v if $v \in S^{\text{sink}}$. In other words, it is denoted according to the in-degree and out-degree of node v. Note that the in-degree and out-degree cannot both be zero when $k \geq 2$ (it is a trivial problem when $k = 1$). In addition, the values of these commitments will not be changed once they are assigned.

On the other hand, recall that in $\Sigma^{\mathcal{R}_{1\text{-OR}}}$ (as shown in Fig. 12), commitment a_l is computed based on $\varphi(a_{l+1})$, i.e., the underlying hash function φ takes only one commitment as input. In our DAG-Σ protocol, when computing the commitment for the statement corresponding to node v (hereinafter, we sometimes directly write it as the commitment for node v for simplicity), the hash function φ would take all the commitments for the nodes in S^{pred}_v as input. Specifically, for the algorithm $\mathcal{P}_1$ of the DAG-Σ protocol, we provide an algorithm $\mathsf{msg}(G, v)$ to "splice" the commitments computed by $\mathcal{P}_1$, denoting the output of $\mathsf{msg}(G, v)$ as m_v, such that φ will directly take m_v as input. We assume that msg always "splice" the commitments from the smallest index to the largest one. So for any fixed node v in G, $\mathsf{msg}(G, v)$ is also a fixed value. The detailed description of msg will be given in Fig. 14.

Analogously, in the description of the DAG-Σ protocol (which will be shown in Fig. 13 and Fig. 14), the commitments computed by $\mathcal{P}_2$ (resp., $\mathcal{V}_2$) are denoted as a'_v, b'_v or e'_v (resp., a''_v, b''_v or e''_v). Respectively, we also provide msg' and msg'', and the detailed descriptions will be given in Fig. 14.

Note that in $\Sigma^{\mathcal{R}_{1\text{-OR}}}$ (as shown in Fig. 12), the corresponding commitments computed in $\Sigma^{\mathcal{R}_{1\text{-OR}}}.\mathcal{P}_1$ and in $\Sigma^{\mathcal{R}_{1\text{-OR}}}.\mathcal{P}_2$ are equal (i.e., $a_l = a'_l$ in Fig. 12), only when the prover knows the witness x_l or $a_{l+1} = a'_{l+1}$. Comparatively, in our DAG-Σ protocol, the commitments (for a node v) computed in $\mathcal{P}_1$ and in $\mathcal{P}_2$ are equal, only when the prover knows the witness (of the statement corresponding to v) or $\mathsf{msg}(G, v) = \mathsf{msg}'(G, v)$.

In addition, as described in $\Sigma_{\text{plain}}^{\mathcal{R}^{\text{dl}}_{k\text{-CNF},S'_k}}$ in Sect. 5.1, $\Sigma_{\text{plain}}^{\mathcal{R}^{\text{dl}}_{k\text{-CNF},S'_k}}.\mathcal{P}_1$ sends all the a_1's of different Type-$\vee$ clauses to $\Sigma_{\text{plain}}^{\mathcal{R}^{\text{dl}}_{k\text{-CNF},S'_k}}.\mathcal{V}_1$, and then $\Sigma_{\text{plain}}^{\mathcal{R}^{\text{dl}}_{k\text{-CNF},S'_k}}.\mathcal{V}_2$

computes all the corresponding (a_1'')'s and compare them with a_1's for verification. Comparatively, in our DAG-Σ protocol, $\mathcal{P}_1$ sends all the $\{e_v\}_{v \in S^{\mathsf{sink}}}$ to $\mathcal{V}_1$, and then $\mathcal{V}_2$ computes all the $\{e_v''\}_{v \in S^{\mathsf{sink}}}$ and compares them with $\{e_v\}_{v \in S^{\mathsf{sink}}}$ for verification.

Next, we turn to the detailed description of our DAG-Σ protocol.

<u>*Description.*</u> Our DAG-based Sigma protocol $\Sigma_{\mathrm{DAG}}^{\mathcal{R}^{\mathrm{dl}}_{k\text{-CNF},S_k'}}$ for relation $\mathcal{R}^{\mathrm{dl}}_{k\text{-CNF},S_k'}$ is as follows. The detailed algorithms are shown in Fig. 13 and Fig. 14.

1. <u>$\mathcal{P} \rightarrow \mathcal{V}$.</u> The prover $\mathcal{P}_1$ first calls $\mathsf{kCNFtoDAG}(\mathcal{R}^{\mathrm{dl}}_{k\text{-CNF},S_k'})$ to get a directed acyclic graph $G = (V, E)$, and then generates the commitment a as follows: for every node v in G,
   (a) if v is a source (i.e., $\mathsf{in\text{-}deg}(v) = 0$), then $\mathcal{P}_1$ calls $\Sigma^{\mathcal{R}}_{\mathsf{Sch}}.\mathcal{P}_1$ to generates a commitment for this node, i.e., $a_v = g^{r_v}$, where $r_v \leftarrow \mathbb{Z}_p^*$.
   (b) if v is neither a source nor a sink (i.e., $\mathsf{in\text{-}deg}(v) \neq 0$ and $\mathsf{out\text{-}deg}(v) \neq 0$), $\mathcal{P}_1$ invokes the HVZK simulator $\Sigma^{\mathcal{R}}_{\mathsf{Sch}}.\mathsf{Sim}$ to generate the commitment b_v for node v (i.e., $b_v \leftarrow \Sigma^{\mathcal{R}}_{\mathsf{Sch}}.\mathsf{Sim}(y_{f(v)}, \varphi(m_v)))$, where $m_v \leftarrow \mathsf{msg}(G, v)$.
   (c) if v is a sink (i.e., $\mathsf{out\text{-}deg}(v) = 0$), $\mathcal{P}_1$ computes a commitment for node v similar to step (*b*), and the only difference is that we denote the commitment as e_v here.

   Finally, $\mathcal{P}_1$ sends $a = \{e_v\}_{v \in S^{\mathsf{sink}}}$ to the verifier $\mathcal{V}$.
2. <u>$\mathcal{V} \rightarrow \mathcal{P}$.</u> Receiving a, $\mathcal{V}_1$ samples $c \leftarrow \mathbb{Z}_p^*$ and sends it to $\mathcal{P}$.
3. <u>$\mathcal{P} \rightarrow \mathcal{V}$.</u> Receiving c, $\mathcal{P}_2$ proceeds to compute the response. In a nutshell, for every $v \in V$: if the prover knows $x_{f(v)}$ of the corresponding statement $y_{f(v)}$, she calls $\Sigma^{\mathcal{R}}_{\mathsf{Sch}}.\mathcal{P}_2$ to compute a response if $v \in S^{\mathsf{source}}$, or calls $\Sigma^{\mathcal{R}}_{\mathsf{Sch}}.\mathcal{P}_2'$ if $(v \notin S^{\mathsf{source}}) \wedge (m_v \neq m_v')$; otherwise (i.e., the prover does not know any witness of the corresponding statement), she calls $\Sigma^{\mathcal{R}}_{\mathsf{Sch}}.\mathsf{Sim}$ to generate a response and re-generate the commitment once $v \in S^{\mathsf{source}}$ or $m_v \neq m_v'$. In the above cases, if $(v \notin S^{\mathsf{source}}) \wedge (m_v = m_v')$, then we just set the response equal to that output by the simulator in $\mathcal{P}_1$. Note that if for some $v \in S^{\mathsf{sink}}$, the prover does not know $x_{f(v)}$, and $m_v \neq m_v'$, then the protocol aborts, because we can find a Type-$\vee$ clause such that the prover does not know any witness of the statements in it, which implies that $(\mathbf{x}, \mathbf{y}) \notin \mathcal{R}^{\mathrm{dl}}_{k\text{-CNF},S_k'}$.

   Finally, $\mathcal{P}_2$ sends $z = \{z_v\}_{v \in V}$ to $\mathcal{V}$.

The verification is as follows. $\mathcal{V}_2$ invokes the codes in $\Sigma^{\mathcal{R}}_{\mathsf{Sch}}.\mathcal{V}_2$ to compute the commitments for every node in G according to the edges in G. If the commitments of the nodes in S^{sink} are equal to the corresponding commitments sent by $\mathcal{P}_1$, then $\mathcal{V}_2$ accepts, otherwise he rejects.

We provide some more explanations about the algorithms here.

Given a node v, $\mathsf{msg}(G, v)$ will always succeed in returning the same value, because (i) G is a directed acyclic graph, there are no inter-dependent nodes, i.e., no endless loops exist; (ii) its predecessor nodes can have correct assignments, which can be achieved by adopting recursion or a special node sequence (for the code "For $v \in V$" in $\mathcal{P}_1$ and we omit the details here). In addition, the "For loops" in the msg are executed following a deterministic sequence of nodes, e.g.,

(1) $\mathcal{P}_1(\mathbf{x}, \mathbf{y})$:
  $G = (V, E) \leftarrow \mathsf{kCNFtoDAG}(\mathcal{R}^{\mathrm{dl}}_{k\text{-CNF}, S'_k})$ // convert the relation into a DAG
  For $v \in V$:
    If $\mathsf{in\text{-}deg}(v) = 0$: $r_v \leftarrow \mathbb{Z}_p^*$, $a_v \leftarrow g^{r_v}$ // $\Sigma^{\mathcal{R}}_{\mathsf{Sch}}.\mathcal{P}_1(\perp, y_{f(v)})$
    Else If $\mathsf{out\text{-}deg}(v) \neq 0$:
      $m_v \leftarrow \mathsf{msg}(G, v)$, $\hat{z}_v \leftarrow \mathbb{Z}_p^*$, $b_v \leftarrow g^{\hat{z}_v} / y_{f(v)}^{\varphi(m_v)}$ //$\Sigma^{\mathcal{R}}_{\mathsf{Sch}}.\mathsf{Sim}(y_{f(v)}, \varphi(m_v))$
    Else $m_v \leftarrow \mathsf{msg}(G, v)$, $\hat{z}_v \leftarrow \mathbb{Z}_p^*$, $e_v \leftarrow g^{\hat{z}_v} / y_{f(v)}^{\varphi(m_v)}$ //$\Sigma^{\mathcal{R}}_{\mathsf{Sch}}.\mathsf{Sim}(y_{f(v)}, \varphi(m_v))$
  Send $a = \{e_v\}_{v \in S^{\mathsf{sink}}}$ to $\mathcal{V}$
(2) $\mathcal{V}_1(a)$: $c \leftarrow \mathbb{Z}_p^*$, Send c to $\mathcal{P}$
(3) $\mathcal{P}_2(a, c, \mathbf{x}, \mathbf{y})$:
  For $v \in V$:
    If $f(v) \in S^{\mathrm{w}}_{\mathbf{x}}$: //$\mathcal{P}$ knows witness of $y_{f(v)}$
      If $\mathsf{in\text{-}deg}(v) = 0$: $z_v \leftarrow r_v + x_{f(v)}c$, $a'_v \leftarrow a_v$ //$\Sigma^{\mathcal{R}}_{\mathsf{Sch}}.\mathcal{P}_2(a_v, c, x_{f(v)}, y_{f(v)})$
      Else If $(m'_v \leftarrow \mathsf{msg}'(G, v), m_v \neq m'_v)$:
        $z_v \leftarrow \hat{z}_v + (\varphi(m'_v) - \varphi(m_v))x_{f(v)}$ //$\Sigma^{\mathcal{R}}_{\mathsf{Sch}}.\mathcal{P}'_2(a_v, \varphi(m'_v), \varphi(m_v), x_{f(v)}, y_{f(v)})$
        Else $z_v \leftarrow \hat{z}_v$
        If $\mathsf{out\text{-}deg}(v) \neq 0$: $b'_v \leftarrow b_v$
        Else $e'_v \leftarrow e_v$
    Else //$\mathcal{P}$ does not know witness of $y_{f(v)}$
      If $\mathsf{in\text{-}deg}(v) = 0$: $z_v \leftarrow \mathbb{Z}_p^*$, $a'_v \leftarrow g^{z_v} / y_{f(v)}^{c}$ //$\Sigma^{\mathcal{R}}_{\mathsf{Sch}}.\mathsf{Sim}(y_{f(v)}, c)$
      Else If $(m'_v \leftarrow \mathsf{msg}'(G, v), m_v \neq m'_v)$:
          If $\mathsf{out\text{-}deg}(v) \neq 0$:
            $z_v \leftarrow \mathbb{Z}_p^*$, $b'_v \leftarrow g^{z_v} / y_{f(v)}^{\varphi(m'_v)}$ //$\Sigma^{\mathcal{R}}_{\mathsf{Sch}}.\mathsf{Sim}(y_{f(v)}, \varphi(m'_v))$
          Else Return $\perp$
        Else
          If $\mathsf{out\text{-}deg}(v) \neq 0$: $b'_v \leftarrow b_v$, $z_v \leftarrow \hat{z}_v$
          Else $e'_v \leftarrow e_v$, $z_v \leftarrow \hat{z}_v$
  Send $z = \{z_v\}_{v \in V}$ to $\mathcal{V}$

Fig. 13. Generation algorithms of $\Sigma_{\mathrm{DAG}}^{\mathcal{R}^{\mathrm{dl}}_{k\text{-CNF}, S'_k}}$ (Assume that the "For loops" are executed following a deterministic sequence of nodes).

from the smallest index to the largest. Similar explanations are also applied to $\mathcal{P}_2$ and $\mathcal{V}_2$ with msg' and msg'' respectively.

For all $v \in V$, a_v (or b_v or e_v) and $\hat{z}_v$ are generated by $\mathcal{P}_1$, a'_v (or b'_v or e'_v) and z_v are generated by $\mathcal{P}_2$, and a''_v (or b''_v or e''_v) is generated by $\mathcal{V}_2$. $\mathcal{P}$ knows some witness of $y_{f(v)}$ if and only if $f(v) \in S^{\mathrm{w}}_{\mathbf{x}}$. Moreover, algorithm $\mathcal{P}_2$ has the following properties.

(I): For any $v \in V$, if $f(v) \in S^{\mathrm{w}}_{\mathbf{x}}$, then $a'_v = a_v$ or $b'_v = b_v$ or $e'_v = e_v$. In other words, if $a'_v \neq a_v$ or $b'_v \neq b_v$ or $e'_v \neq e_v$, then $f(v) \notin S^{\mathrm{w}}_{\mathbf{x}}$.
(II): For any $v \in V \setminus S^{\mathsf{source}}$, if $f(v) \notin S^{\mathrm{w}}_{\mathbf{x}}$, and for all $v' \in S^{\mathsf{pred}}_v$, $a'_{v'} = a_{v'}$ or $b'_{v'} = b_{v'}$ (i.e., $m_v = m'_v$), then $b'_v = b_v$ or $e'_v = e_v$.

```
V_2(y, a, c, z):
  G = (V, E) ← kCNFtoDAG(R^dl_{k-CNF,S'_k})
  {e_v}_{v∈S^sink} ← a, {z_v}_{v∈V} ← z
  For v ∈ V:
    If in-deg(v) = 0: a''_v ← g^{z_v}/y^c_{f(v)}
    Else If out-deg(v) ≠ 0:
        m''_v ← msg''(G, v)
        b''_v ← g^{z_v}/y^{φ(m''_v)}_{f(v)}
      Else
        m''_v ← msg''(G, v)
        e''_v ← g^{z_v}/y^{φ(m''_v)}_{f(v)}
  If ∀v ∈ S^sink, e''_v = e_v:
    Return 1
  Else
    Return 0

msg(G, v):
  m_v ←⊥, S^pred_v ← pred(v)
  For v' ∈ S^pred_v:
    If in-deg(v') = 0: m_v ← (m_v||a_{v'})
    Else m_v ← (m_v||b_{v'})
  Return m_v

msg'(G, v):
  m'_v ←⊥, S^pred_v ← pred(v)
  For v' ∈ S^pred_v:
    If in-deg(v') = 0: m'_v ← (m'_v||a'_{v'})
    Else m'_v ← (m'_v||b'_{v'})
  Return m'_v

msg''(G, v):
  m''_v ←⊥, S^pred_v ← pred(v)
  For v' ∈ S^pred_v:
    If in-deg(v') = 0: m''_v ← (m''_v||a''_{v'})
    Else m''_v ← (m''_v||b''_{v'})
  Return m''_v
```

Fig. 14. Verification algorithm of $\Sigma_{\mathrm{DAG}}^{\mathcal{R}^{\mathrm{dl}}_{k\text{-CNF},S'_k}}$ and other auxiliary algorithms (Assume that the "For loops" are executed following a deterministic sequence of nodes).

***(III)*:** Implied by *(I)* and *(II)*, if $a'_v \neq a_v$ or $b'_v \neq b_v$ or $e'_v \neq e_v$ for some $v \in V \setminus S^{\mathsf{source}}$, then there must be some $v' \in S^{\mathsf{pred}}_v$ such that $a'_{v'} \neq a_{v'}$ or $b'_{v'} \neq b_{v'}$ (which further implies $f(v') \notin S^{\mathrm{w}}_{\mathbf{x}}$ according to Property *(I)*).
***(IV)*:** Implied by *(III)* and by induction on path, if $a'_{\tilde{v}} \neq a_{\tilde{v}}$ or $b'_{\tilde{v}} \neq b_{\tilde{v}}$ or $e'_{\tilde{v}} \neq e_{\tilde{v}}$ for some $\tilde{v} \in V$, then there must be some path such that for any vertex v in the path from a source to $\tilde{v}$, $f(v) \notin S^{\mathrm{w}}_{\mathbf{x}}$.
***(V)*:** As a special case of *(IV)*, if $e'_{\tilde{v}} \neq e_{\tilde{v}}$ for some $\tilde{v} \in S^{\mathsf{sink}}$, there must be some path such that for any vertex v in this path, $f(v) \notin S^{\mathrm{w}}_{\mathbf{x}}$, which also implies that there is a Type-$\vee$ clause $\vee_{j\in[k]} y_{i_j}$ such that $\mathcal{P}$ does not know any witness of $(y_{i_j})_{j\in[k]}$, i.e., $(\mathbf{x}, \mathbf{y}) \notin \mathcal{R}^{\mathrm{dl}}_{k\text{-CNF},S'_k}$.

Note that when the event mentioned in Property *(V)* occurs, $\mathcal{P}_2$ will return $\perp$, as shown in Fig. 13.

Completeness. For any $(\mathbf{x}, \mathbf{y}) \in \mathcal{R}^{\mathrm{dl}}_{k\text{-CNF},S'_k}$, let (a, c, z) denote the transcript generated by the protocol. Now we consider the computation of $\mathcal{V}_2(\mathbf{y}, a, c, z)$. Note that for all $v \in S^{\mathsf{source}}$, $a''_v = g^{z_v}/y^c_{f(v)} = a'_v$. By induction on path, we have the following claim, the formal proof of which can be found in the full version of this paper.

Claim. For all $v \in V \backslash S^{\mathsf{sink}}$, $a''_v = a'_v$ or $b''_v = b'_v$.

According to above claim, for any $v \in V$, $m''_v = m'_v$. For each $v \in S^{\mathsf{sink}}$ satisfying $f(v) \in S^{\mathrm{w}}_{\mathbf{x}}$, we have:

(1) If $m_v \neq m'_v$, then

$$e''_v = g^{z_v}/y_{f(v)}^{\varphi(m''_v)} = g^{z_v}/y_{f(v)}^{\varphi(m'_v)}$$
$$= g^{\hat{z}_v+(\varphi(m'_v)-\varphi(m_v))x_{f(v)}}/y_{f(v)}^{\varphi(m'_v)} = g^{\hat{z}_v}/y_{f(v)}^{\varphi(m_v)} = e_v.$$

(2) If $m_v = m'_v$, then according to the procedures of $\mathcal{P}_2$, we have $z_v = \hat{z}_v$, so $e''_v = g^{z_v}/y_{f(v)}^{\varphi(m''_v)} = g^{z_v}/y_{f(v)}^{\varphi(m'_v)} = g^{\hat{z}_v}/y_{f(v)}^{\varphi(m_v)} = e_v$.

For each $v \in S^{\mathsf{sink}}$ satisfying $f(v) \notin S^{\mathrm{w}}_{\mathbf{x}}$, we have:

(1) If $m_v \neq m'_v$, then according to Property *(IV)*, there is some path such that for any vertex $\tilde{v}$ in the path from a source to v', $f(\tilde{v}) \notin S^{\mathrm{w}}_{\mathbf{x}}$ (we denote these $k-1$ vertices as S_{pa}). Note that $v \in S^{\mathsf{sink}}$ and $f(v) \notin S^{\mathrm{w}}_{\mathbf{x}}$, so $S_{\mathsf{pa}} \cup \{v\}$ constitute a path such that for any vertex $\tilde{v}$ in the path, $f(\tilde{v}) \notin S^{\mathrm{w}}_{\mathbf{x}}$. According to Property *(V)*, $(\mathbf{x}, \mathbf{y}) \notin \mathcal{R}^{\mathrm{dl}}_{k\text{-CNF},S'_k}$, contradicting the assumption that $(\mathbf{x}, \mathbf{y}) \in \mathcal{R}^{\mathrm{dl}}_{k\text{-CNF},S'_k}$. So we don't need to consider this case in completeness analysis.
(2) If $m_v = m'_v$ then according to the procedures of $\mathcal{P}_2$, we have $e'_v = e_v$ and $z_v = \hat{z}_v$. Since $m''_v = m'_v$, we derive $e''_v = g^{z_v}/y_{f(v)}^{\varphi(m''_v)} = g^{\hat{z}_v}/y_{f(v)}^{\varphi(m_v)} = e_v$.

Other Properties. For computational knowledge soundness and special HVZK property, we have the following theorem. Due to space limitations, we provide the proof in the full version of this paper.

Theorem 3. *If φ is a collision-resistant hash function, $\Sigma_{\mathrm{DAG}}^{\mathcal{R}^{\mathrm{dl}}_{k\text{-CNF},S'_k}}$ provides computational knowledge soundness and is special HVZK.*

Communication Complexity. It is clear that there are $|S^{\mathsf{sink}}|$ group elements and $(|V|+1)$ elements in $\mathbb{Z}_p^*$ in the communication of the 3-move Sigma protocol $\Sigma_{\mathrm{DAG}}^{\mathcal{R}^{\mathrm{dl}}_{k\text{-CNF},S'_k}}$. If we apply Fiat-Shamir transform [15], the total proof would be $|V|$ elements in $\mathbb{Z}_p^*$.

According to Theorem 2, $|V| \leq \mathsf{Min}(V_{\mathsf{bound}}, (k \cdot num))$, which implies that $|V| \leq k \cdot num$. Note that the communication complexity of [14] is $O(k \cdot num)$, so we can draw such a conclusion that the communication complexity of $\Sigma_{\mathrm{DAG}}^{\mathcal{R}^{\mathrm{dl}}_{k\text{-CNF},S'_k}}$ is better than that of [14]. A further analysis of V_{bound} (which can be found in the full version of this paper) will show that *generally* $V_{\mathsf{bound}} \ll k \cdot num$. It implies that *generally* $\Sigma_{\mathrm{DAG}}^{\mathcal{R}^{\mathrm{dl}}_{k\text{-CNF},S'_k}}$ protocol based on $\mathsf{kCNFtoDAG}$ has a remarkable performance improvement on proving k-CNF relations, when compared with [14].

6 Extension: Incomplete *k*-DNF Relations

In Sect. 5.2, we have shown a Sigma protocol for k-CNF relations. However, in some scenarios, the required relations of partial knowledge are formalized in disjunctive normal form (DNF) [5,13], i.e., each clause combines the statements using "AND" operation, and then the formula of the relation combines the clauses using "OR" operation. If every clause has k statement, we call it k-DNF relations and then we further classify them into *complete* ones and *incomplete* ones. In this section, we show a construction of Sigma protocols for incomplete k-DNF relations, partially based on DAG-Σ protocol in Sect. 5.

6.1 Problem Definition

First, please refer to Sect. 3 for the notations of S_k and $\mathcal{R}_l$ ($l \in [n]$). Then, we define the following partial knowledge for compound statements.

Definition 2. (Complete k-out-of-n partial knowledge for DNF). *Given n different statements $\{y_l\}_{l\in[n]}$ and n sub-relations $\{\mathcal{R}_l\}_{l\in[n]}$, the prover proves that she knows k witnesses among the n statements. In other words, she knows some $(y_{i_1}, \cdots, y_{i_k})$ are true, where $\{i_1, \cdots, i_k\} \in S_k$.*

The relation can be presented in DNF as follows,

$$\mathcal{R}^{\text{com}}_{k\text{-DNF},S_k} = \{(\mathbf{x}, \mathbf{y}) : \vee_{\{i_1,\dots,i_k\}\in S_k}(\wedge_{j\in[k]}(x_{i_j}, y_{i_j}) \in \mathcal{R}_{i_j})\}, \tag{8}$$

where $\mathbf{x}, \mathbf{y}$ are two n-dimension vectors, and $\mathcal{R}_{i_j} \in \{\mathcal{R}_l\}_{l\in[n]}$ is a sub-relation. For simplicity, we denote the relation in disjunctive normal form where every clause has k statements as **complete k-DNF relation**. Furthermore, we stress that $|S_k| = C^k_n$.

Then similarly, we define the incomplete k-out-of-n partial knowledge relation in DNF as follows.

Definition 3. (Incomplete k-out-of-n partial knowledge for DNF). *Given n different statements $\{y_l\}_{l\in[n]}$, n sub-relations $\{\mathcal{R}_l\}_{l\in[n]}$, and a subset $S''_k \subsetneq S_k$, the prover proves that she knows some $(y_{i_1}, \cdots, y_{i_k})$ are true, where $\{i_1, \cdots, i_k\} \in S''_k$.*

Similarly, the relation can be presented in DNF as follows,

$$\mathcal{R}^{\text{incom}}_{k\text{-DNF},S''_k} = \{(\mathbf{x}, \mathbf{y}) : \vee_{\{i_1,\dots,i_k\}\in S''_k}(\wedge_{j\in[k]}(x_{i_j}, y_{i_j}) \in \mathcal{R}_{i_j})\}, \tag{9}$$

where $\mathbf{x}, \mathbf{y}$ are two n-dimension vectors, and $\mathcal{R}_{i_j} \in \{\mathcal{R}_l\}_{l\in[n]}$ is a sub-relation. Note that $|S''_k| < C^k_n$. We denote the relation in Eq. (9) as **incomplete k-DNF relation** and we also focus on the incomplete k-DNF relations that can be decided in polynomial time.

6.2 A Transfer for Special Cases

Following $\mathcal{R}^{\text{com}}_{k\text{-DNF},S_k}$ (Eq. (8)) and $\mathcal{R}^{\text{incom}}_{k\text{-DNF},S''_k}$ (Eq. (9)), we further consider the following relations,

$$\mathcal{R}^{\text{not}}_{k\text{-CNF},S_k\setminus S''_k} = \{(\mathbf{x}, \mathbf{y}) : \wedge_{\{i_1,\dots,i_k\}\in S_k\setminus S''_k}(\vee_{j\in[k]}(x_{i_j}, y_{i_j}) \notin \mathcal{R}_{i_j})\}, \tag{10}$$

$$\mathcal{R}^{\text{tsf}} = \mathcal{R}^{\text{com}}_{k\text{-DNF},S_k} \cap \mathcal{R}^{\text{not}}_{k\text{-CNF},S_k\setminus S''_k}, \tag{11}$$

where $\mathbf{x}$ and $\mathbf{y}$ are two n-dimension vectors, $S''_k \subsetneq S_k$, and we assume that $1 \leq i_1 < \ldots < i_k \leq n$ without loss of generality. Obviously, we have that $\mathcal{R}^{\text{tsf}} \subset \mathcal{R}^{\text{not}}_{k\text{-CNF},S_k \setminus S''_k}$.

Now we show $\mathcal{R}^{\text{tsf}} \subset \mathcal{R}^{\text{incom}}_{k\text{-DNF},S''_k}$. Specifically, for any pair $(\mathbf{x},\mathbf{y})$ belonging to $\mathcal{R}^{\text{tsf}}$, $(\mathbf{x},\mathbf{y}) \in \mathcal{R}^{\text{com}}_{k\text{-DNF},S_k}$ and $(\mathbf{x},\mathbf{y}) \in \mathcal{R}^{\text{not}}_{k\text{-CNF},S_k \setminus S''_k}$. In other words, at least one clause labeled in S_k with respect to $\mathcal{R}^{\text{com}}_{k\text{-DNF},S_k}$, e.g., $(\wedge_{j\in[k]}(x_{i_j}, y_{i_j}) \in \mathcal{R}_{i_j})$, is true, while the clauses labeled in $S_k \setminus S''_k$ with respect to $\mathcal{R}^{\text{not}}_{k\text{-CNF},S_k \setminus S''_k}$, e.g., $(\vee_{j\in[k]}(x_{i_j}, y_{i_j}) \notin \mathcal{R}_{i_j})$, are all true. It means that the clauses labeled in $S_k \setminus S''_k$ with respect to $\mathcal{R}^{\text{com}}_{k\text{-DNF},S_k}$ are all false. In all, at least one clause labeled in S''_k with respect to $\mathcal{R}^{\text{com}}_{k\text{-DNF},S_k}$ is true, which implies that $(\mathbf{x},\mathbf{y}) \in \mathcal{R}^{\text{incom}}_{k\text{-DNF},S''_k}$.

We claim that a Sigma protocol $\Sigma^{\mathcal{R}^{\text{tsf}}}$ for relation $\mathcal{R}^{\text{tsf}}$ can be transferred to a Sigma protocol for relation $\mathcal{R}^{\text{incom}}_{k\text{-DNF},S''_k}$. Given a witness-statement pair $(\mathbf{x},\mathbf{y}) \in \mathcal{R}^{\text{incom}}_{k\text{-DNF},S''_k}$, we know that one of the clauses with respect to $\mathcal{R}^{\text{incom}}_{k\text{-DNF},S''_k}$ is true. The prover chooses one among the true clauses, and then she only preserves the witnesses for the statements in this clause and set the others empty. Therefore, we get an $\mathbf{x}'$. It is clear that $(\mathbf{x}',\mathbf{y}) \in \mathcal{R}^{\text{incom}}_{k\text{-DNF},S''_k}$ and $(\mathbf{x}',\mathbf{y}) \in \mathcal{R}^{\text{tsf}}$. Thus, if $\Sigma^{\mathcal{R}^{\text{tsf}}}$ with the input $(\mathbf{x}',\mathbf{y})$ outputs a proof and the verifier accepts the proof together with input $\mathbf{y}$, then the accepting proof indicates that the prover knows the partial knowledge of $\mathbf{y}$ as per the relation $\mathcal{R}^{\text{tsf}}$, which implies that the prover knows the partial knowledge of $\mathbf{y}$ as per the relation $\mathcal{R}^{\text{incom}}_{k\text{-DNF},S''_k}$.

The Sigma protocol $\Sigma^{\mathcal{R}^{\text{tsf}}}$ can be obtained from $\Sigma^{\mathcal{R}^{\text{com}}_{k\text{-DNF},S_k}}$ and $\Sigma^{\mathcal{R}^{\text{not}}_{k\text{-CNF},S_k \setminus S''_k}}$ using "AND"-proof construction [6]. Therefore, we have the following theorem.

Theorem 4. *The proof for an incomplete k-DNF relation $\mathcal{R}^{\text{incom}}_{k\text{-DNF},S''_k}$ can be obtained from a proof for a complete k-DNF relation $\mathcal{R}^{\text{com}}_{k\text{-DNF},S_k}$ and a proof for a k-*CNF *relation $\mathcal{R}^{\text{not}}_{k\text{-CNF},S_k \setminus S''_k}$.*

In other words, a Sigma protocol $\Sigma^{\mathcal{R}^{\text{incom}}_{k\text{-DNF},S''_k}}$ can be obtained from $\Sigma^{\mathcal{R}^{\text{com}}_{k\text{-DNF},S_k}}$ and $\Sigma^{\mathcal{R}^{\text{not}}_{k\text{-CNF},S_k \setminus S''_k}}$. Since there are some efficient constructions for $\Sigma^{\mathcal{R}^{\text{com}}_{k\text{-DNF},S_k}}$, e.g., [14], what remains is to construct $\Sigma^{\mathcal{R}^{\text{not}}_{k\text{-CNF},S_k \setminus S''_k}}$ efficiently. However, it seems difficult to prove a "NOT" statement (e.g., $(x_{i_j}, y_{i_j}) \notin \mathcal{R}_{i_j}$) generally.

Here, we discuss this problem in the *discrete logarithm* setting for some special cases. More specifically, in the following, we show a construction of a Sigma protocol for $\mathcal{R}^{\text{incom}}_{k\text{-DNF},S''_k}$ *under the conditions (defined by Eq.* (12)*–*(13)*) in the discrete logarithm setting.*

We firstly introduce the definition of ρ-type pairs as follows.

Definition 4 (ρ-type pair). *Let $\mathbb{G}$ be a cyclic group of prime order p generated by $g \in \mathbb{G}$. Let $h \in \mathbb{G}$ be some arbitrary non-identity element and $\log_g h$ is unknown. Then we call $(x, y = g^x h^\rho) \in \mathbb{Z}_p \times \mathbb{G}$ a ρ-type pair, where $\rho \in \mathbb{Z}_p$.*

We stress that for any distinct ρ_1, ρ_2, when $x_1, x_2 \leftarrow \mathbb{Z}_p$, $y_1 = g^{x_1} h^{\rho_1}$ and $y_2 = g^{x_2} h^{\rho_2}$ are distributed identically.

Then, we consider the following two conditions for relations: 1) every statement is obtained from a 0-type or 1-type pair, as shown in Eq. (12); 2) further there are only k 0-type pairs among all witness-statement pairs, as shown in Eq. (12)–(13).

$$\mathcal{R}_{\text{con1}} = \{(\mathbf{x}, \mathbf{y}) : \wedge_{l\in[n]}(y_l = g^{x_l} \vee y_l/h = g^{x_l})\}, \tag{12}$$

$$\mathcal{R}_{\text{con2}} = \{(\mathbf{x}, \mathbf{y}) : (\prod_{l=1}^{n} y_l)/h^{n-k} = g^{\sum_{l=1}^{n} x_l}\}. \tag{13}$$

In the discrete logarithm setting, $\mathcal{R}^{\text{incom}}_{k\text{-DNF},S''_k}$, $\mathcal{R}^{\text{com}}_{k\text{-DNF},S_k}$ and $\mathcal{R}^{\text{not}}_{k\text{-CNF},S_k\backslash S''_k}$ can be written as

$$\mathcal{R}^{\text{incom,dl}}_{k\text{-DNF},S''_k} = \{(\mathbf{x}, \mathbf{y}) : \vee_{\{i_1,\ldots,i_k\}\in S''_k}(\wedge_{j\in[k]}\ y_{i_j} = g^{x_{i_j}})\}, \tag{14}$$

$$\mathcal{R}^{\text{com,dl}}_{k\text{-DNF},S_k} = \{(\mathbf{x}, \mathbf{y}) : \vee_{\{i_1,\ldots,i_k\}\in S_k}(\wedge_{j\in[k]}\ y_{i_j} = g^{x_{i_j}})\}, \tag{15}$$

$$\mathcal{R}^{\text{not,dl}}_{k\text{-CNF},S_k\backslash S''_k} = \{(\mathbf{x}, \mathbf{y}) : \wedge_{\{i_1,\ldots,i_k\}\in S_k\backslash S''_k}(\vee_{j\in[k]}\overline{y_{i_j} = g^{x_{i_j}}})\}. \tag{16}$$

Under the conditions defined by Eq. (12)–(13), $\mathcal{R}^{\text{incom,dl}}_{k\text{-DNF},S''_k}$ further becomes

$$\mathcal{R}^{\text{incom}}_{k} = \mathcal{R}^{\text{incom,dl}}_{k\text{-DNF},S''_k} \cap \mathcal{R}_{\text{con1}} \cap \mathcal{R}_{\text{con2}}. \tag{17}$$

Note that $\mathcal{R}^{\text{incom,dl}}_{k\text{-DNF},S''_k}$ indicates that at least one clause labeled in S''_k is true, and $\mathcal{R}^{\text{incom}}_{k}$ means that only one clause labeled in S''_k is true.

Now we turn to $\mathcal{R}^{\text{not,dl}}_{k\text{-CNF},S_k\backslash S''_k}$ in Eq. (16) under the conditions defined by Eq. (12)–(13). Firstly, because of Eq. (12), a "NOT" statement, i.e., $\overline{y_{i_j} = g^{x_{i_j}}}$ here, can be transferred into $y_{i_j}/h = g^{x_{i_j}}$. Secondly, Eq. (12)–(13) guarantee that once $(\mathbf{x}, \mathbf{y}) \in \mathcal{R}^{\text{incom}}_{k}$, for every $\{i_1, \ldots, i_k\} \in S_k\backslash S''_k$, there is at least one of the indices of the $(n-k)$ 1-type pairs falling in $\{i_1, \ldots, i_k\}$. Therefore, $\mathcal{R}^{\text{not,dl}}_{k\text{-CNF},S_k\backslash S''_k}$ in Eq. (16) under the conditions defined by Eq. (12)–(13) becomes

$$\mathcal{R}^{\text{not},\rho\text{-type}}_{k\text{-CNF},S_k\backslash S''_k} = \{(\mathbf{x}, \mathbf{y}) : \wedge_{\{i_1,\ldots,i_k\}\in S_k\backslash S''_k}(\vee_{j\in[k]}\ y_{i_j}/h = g^{x_{i_j}})\}. \tag{18}$$

Considering relation

$$\mathcal{R}^{\text{tsf}}_{k} = \mathcal{R}^{\text{com,dl}}_{k\text{-DNF},S_k} \cap \mathcal{R}^{\text{not},\rho\text{-type}}_{k\text{-CNF},S_k\backslash S''_k} \cap \mathcal{R}_{\text{con1}} \cap \mathcal{R}_{\text{con2}}, \tag{19}$$

it is easy to see that $\mathcal{R}^{\text{tsf}}_{k} = \mathcal{R}^{\text{incom}}_{k}$. We note that $\mathcal{R}^{\text{com,dl}}_{k\text{-DNF},S_k}$ in Eq. (15) indicates that at least one clause labeled in S_k is true, while $\mathcal{R}^{\text{tsf}}_{k}$ in Eq. (19) implies that only one clause labeled in S_k is true and it is not labeled in $S_k\backslash S''_k$.

Hence, in order to construct a Sigma protocol for $\mathcal{R}^{\text{incom}}_{k}$ in Eq. (17), we need to construct a Sigma protocol for $\mathcal{R}^{\text{tsf}}_{k}$, which can be obtained from $\Sigma^{\mathcal{R}^{\text{com,dl}}_{k\text{-DNF},S_k}}$, $\Sigma^{\mathcal{R}^{\text{not},\rho\text{-type}}_{k\text{-CNF},S_k\backslash S''_k}}$, $\Sigma^{\mathcal{R}_{\text{con1}}}$ and $\Sigma^{\mathcal{R}_{\text{con2}}}$ using "AND" operation [6]. Moreover, $\Sigma^{\mathcal{R}_{\text{con1}}}$ and $\Sigma^{\mathcal{R}_{\text{con2}}}$ can be obtained from Schnorr's Sigma protocol and "AND/OR" proof construction. As for $\Sigma^{\mathcal{R}^{\text{com,dl}}_{k\text{-DNF},S_k}}$, there are existing constructions, e.g. [5,14]. As for $\Sigma^{\mathcal{R}^{\text{not},\rho\text{-type}}_{k\text{-CNF},S_k\backslash S''_k}}$, note that for each sub-relation with respect to $\mathcal{R}^{\text{not},\rho\text{-type}}_{k\text{-CNF},S_k\backslash S''_k}$, Schnorr's Sigma protocol can be applied; then $\Sigma^{\mathcal{R}^{\text{not},\rho\text{-type}}_{k\text{-CNF},S_k\backslash S''_k}}$ can be obtained from the Sigma protocol in Sect. 5.2.

Thus, we obtain an efficient Sigma protocol for $\mathcal{R}^{\text{incom}}_k$ in Eq. (17), i.e., the incomplete k-DNF relation $\mathcal{R}^{\text{incom}}_{k\text{-DNF},S''_k}$ under the conditions defined by Eq. (12)–(13).

Remark 2. Note that besides ρ-type pairs, the statements can be other kinds of elements, e.g., DDH and OneNDH in [13]. Roughly, we only require that they are indistinguishable and the conditions will be modified accordingly.

7 Experiments

In this section, we show the performance of our DAG-Σ protocol $\Sigma_{\text{DAG}}^{\mathcal{R}^{\text{dl}}_{k\text{-CNF},S'_k}}$ and to have a more straight view, we compare it with that of [14]. Note that we implement [14] in its simplest way as mentioned in the introduction section.

We implement our experiments in Golang language (version 16.6) based on elliptic curve groups with key size of 512 bits. The experiments are conducted on a docker, over Pengcheng Cloud Brain[2], running Ubuntu 16.04 on two Intel® Xeon™ Gold 6248 CPUs@2.50 GHz and using 64 GB memory in total. We are interested in the space overhead in communications as well as the timing overhead in running the Sigma protocols. To this end, we present microbenchmarks to evaluate the overhead costs. There are two factors k and n, that will affect the performance greatly. For simplicity, we have n vary from 10 to 50 and we choose $4 \leq k \leq n/3$ in most cases (if $n/3 < 4$, we just set $k = 4$, e.g., in Fig. 15, there is only one data when $n = 10$). Since we find no k-CNF relations in use in the real world, we construct some different relations in the DL setting for our experiments. Given n and k, the number of clauses in a k-CNF relation expression num also has an influence on the performance, but the range of num is large. Similar to the theoretical analysis, here we set $num = C_n^k - \chi$, where χ is a random number in $[50, 200]$, which is nearly the worst case and can reflect the worst performance (i.e., the most space and running time that the tested Sigma protocols need). In the full version of this paper, we draw some 3D figures to show the complete and thorough influence of k and n over the performance. Here, we pick some experimental data and draw some 2D figures, e.g., stacked bar charts and line charts, for better comparison. Following are the experimental analysis.

Communication Costs. The communication costs are measured by the bit length of all the messages between the prover and the verifier when running the Sigma protocols. A theoretical comparison is displayed in Table 1 in Sect. 1. Here,

[2] https://cloudbrain.pcl.ac.cn/.

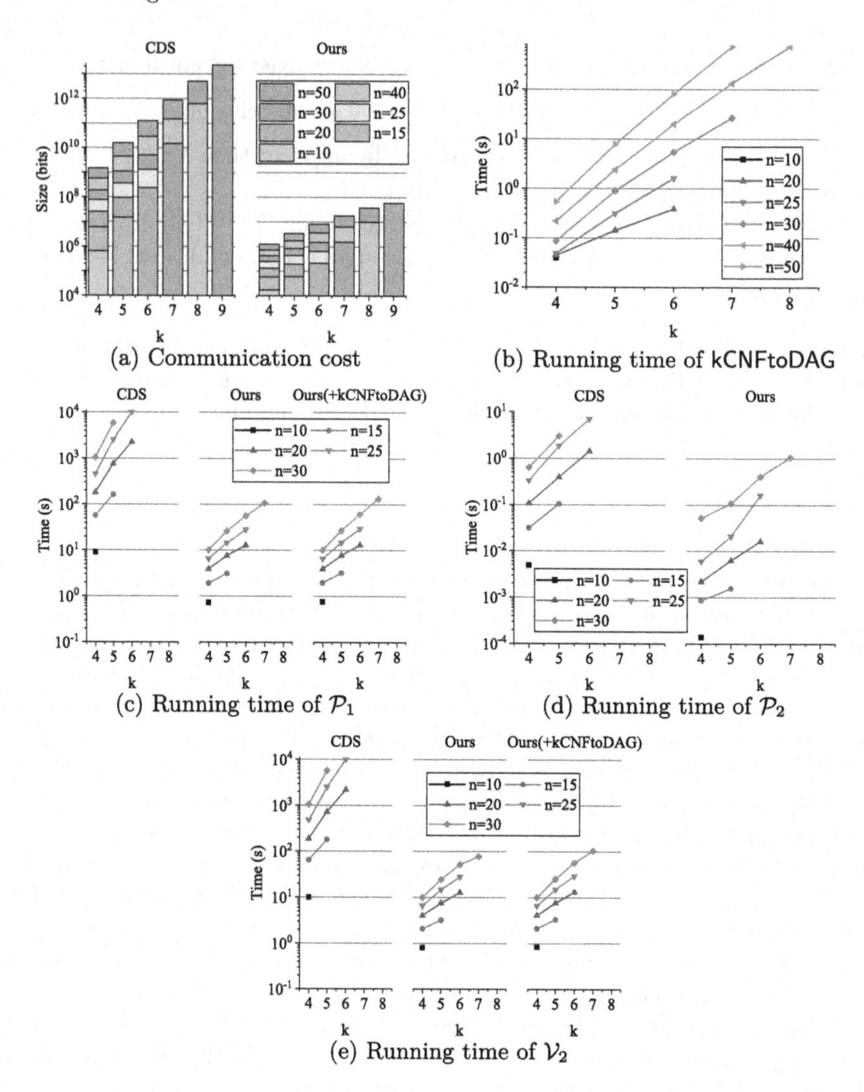

Fig. 15. Figures for the experiments (CDS is the solution [14] proposed by Cramer, Damgård and Schoenmakers. The number of clauses in one relation is $C_n^k - \chi$, where χ is a random number in $[50, 200]$.)

we make a quantitative comparison. In Table 2, we show that the communication size when $k = 4$. It is clear that our scheme saves more than 97% space overhead compared with [14].

For more cases, we draw a stacked bar chart as shown in Fig. 15a, where k varies from 4 to 9. It is clear that our solution has a remarkable decrease on the communication costs compared with [14]. In addition, the figure shows that the effect on decrease would be better as n and k get larger.

Table 2. Communication cost when $k = 4$ ($\times 10^4$ bits) (ratio $= 1 - \frac{\text{bits of our scheme}}{\text{bits of [14]}} \times 100\%$)

n	[14]	Our scheme	Ratio
10	65.54	1.72	97.37% ↓
15	538.62	4.07	99.24% ↓
20	1964.03	7.45	99.62% ↓
25	5160.96	11.90	99.77% ↓
30	11204.6	17.48	99.84% ↓
40	37412.9	31.92	99.91% ↓
50	94310.4	50.92	99.94% ↓

Running Time. We evaluate the running time of $\mathcal{P}_1$, $\mathcal{P}_2$ and $\mathcal{V}_2$ in Fig. 15. Note that when testing our solution, we also record the running time of kCNFtoDAG for special interest. In fact, the directed acyclic graphs can be pre-computed. Thus, when recording the running time of $\mathcal{P}_1$ or $\mathcal{V}_2$ in our scheme, we have two versions: one includes the running time of kCNFtoDAG and the other one does not. Here we implement kCNFtoDAG using the improved algorithm as mentioned in Sect. 4.

We planned to evaluate both schemes with the same range of n and k. However, the running time of [14] grows so fast that the program was killed when n and k are set relatively large numbers. Therefore, in the experiment of [14], we set n from 10 to 33 and k from 4 to 7. In the experiment of our scheme, n varies from 10 to 50 and k varies from 4 to 10. More detailed experimental results can be found in the full version of this paper. Here, we just pick some data for analysis.

The running time of kCNFtoDAG is presented in Fig. 15b. It can be expected that as k and n get larger, the running time increases very quickly, since the number of vertices grows fast. If we compare it with the running time of $\mathcal{P}_1$ and $\mathcal{V}_2$ of our scheme (as shown in Fig. 15c and Fig. 15e), kCNFtoDAG performs reasonably well.

For the running time of $\mathcal{P}_1$, $\mathcal{P}_2$ and $\mathcal{V}_2$, we draw a table (Table 3) to present the running time when $k = 4$. The table tells that our scheme saves more than 90% running time, compared with [14]. More cases (i.e., n varies from 10 to 30 and the range of k is $[4, 8]$) are shown in Fig. 15 (Fig. 15c - Fig. 15e). They also indicates that the running time of $\mathcal{P}_1$, $\mathcal{P}_2$ and $\mathcal{V}_2$ of our scheme outperforms [14]. Note that counting in the running time of kCNFtoDAG or not does not affect the performance a lot, since it only occupies a limited percentage of the total running time and the time of commitment generation in $\mathcal{P}_1$ and verification in $\mathcal{V}_2$ of our scheme dominate the whole performance. In addition, Table 3, Fig. 15c and Fig. 15e show that the running time of $\mathcal{P}_1$ and $\mathcal{V}_2$ have similar performance. It is because in both [14] and our scheme, $\mathcal{P}_1$ and $\mathcal{V}_2$ have similar computation for the commitments.

Table 3. Running time when $k = 4$ (s) (Here, we count in the running time of $\mathsf{kCNFtoDAG}$ when running $\mathcal{P}_1$ and $\mathcal{V}_2$ in our scheme. ratio $= 1 - \frac{\text{time of our scheme}}{\text{time of [14]}} \times 100\%$).

n	$\mathcal{P}_1$			$\mathcal{P}_2$			$\mathcal{V}_2$		
	[14]	Ours	Ratio	[14]	Ours	Ratio	[14]	Ours	Ratio
10	8.91	0.72	91.87% ↓	0.0049	1.40×10^{-4}	97.11% ↓	10.04	0.85	91.56% ↓
15	57.47	1.92	96.66% ↓	0.033	8.63×10^{-4}	97.27% ↓	65.08	2.13	96.72% ↓
20	182.23	3.91	97.85% ↓	0.11	2.20×10^{-3}	97.95% ↓	187.41	4.13	97.80% ↓
25	456.37	6.54	98.57% ↓	0.33	5.97×10^{-3}	98.20% ↓	477.74	6.66	98.61% ↓
30	1046.45	10.09	99.04% ↓	0.63	5.21×10^{-2}	91.78% ↓	1058.25	10.08	99.05% ↓

In all, according to the experiment results, when compared with [14], our scheme achieves a remarkable performance improvement on proving k-CNF relations, no matter from the view of communication costs or running time.

Acknowledgements. We would like to express our sincere appreciation to the anonymous reviewers for their valuable comments and suggestions! Junzuo Lai was supported by National Natural Science Foundation of China (Grant Nos. 61922036, U2001205), Major Program of Guangdong Basic and Applied Research Project (Grant No. 2019B030302008), National Joint Engineering Research Center of Network Security Detection and Protection Technology, and Guangdong Key Laboratory of Data Security and Privacy Preserving.

References

1. Abe, M., Ambrona, M., Bogdanov, A., Ohkubo, M., Rosen, A.: Non-interactive composition of sigma-protocols via share-then-hash. In: Moriai, S., Wang, H. (eds.) ASIACRYPT 2020. LNCS, vol. 12493, pp. 749–773. Springer, Cham (2020). https://doi.org/10.1007/978-3-030-64840-4_25
2. Abe, M., Ambrona, M., Bogdanov, A., Ohkubo, M., Rosen, A.: Acyclicity programming for sigma-protocols. In: Nissim, K., Waters, B. (eds.) TCC 2021. LNCS, vol. 13042, pp. 435–465. Springer, Cham (2021). https://doi.org/10.1007/978-3-030-90459-3_15
3. Abe, M., Chase, M., David, B., Kohlweiss, M., Nishimaki, R., Ohkubo, M.: Constant-size structure-preserving signatures: generic constructions and simple assumptions. J. Cryptol. **29**(4), 833–878 (2016)
4. Abe, M., Ohkubo, M., Suzuki, K.: 1-out-of-n signatures from a variety of keys. In: Zheng, Y. (ed.) ASIACRYPT 2002. LNCS, vol. 2501, pp. 415–432. Springer, Heidelberg (2002). https://doi.org/10.1007/3-540-36178-2_26
5. Attema, T., Cramer, R., Fehr, S.: Compressing proofs of k-out-of-n partial knowledge. In: Malkin, T., Peikert, C. (eds.) CRYPTO 2021. LNCS, vol. 12828, pp. 65–91. Springer, Cham (2021). https://doi.org/10.1007/978-3-030-84259-8_3
6. Boneh, D., Shoup, V.: A graduate course in applied cryptography. Draft 0.5 (2020)

7. Camenisch, J.: Efficient and generalized group signatures. In: Fumy, W. (ed.) EUROCRYPT 1997. LNCS, vol. 1233, pp. 465–479. Springer, Heidelberg (1997). https://doi.org/10.1007/3-540-69053-0_32
8. Canard, S., Trinh, V.C.: Constant-size ciphertext attribute-based encryption from multi-channel broadcast encryption. In: Ray, I., Gaur, M.S., Conti, M., Sanghi, D., Kamakoti, V. (eds.) ICISS 2016. LNCS, vol. 10063, pp. 193–211. Springer, Cham (2016). https://doi.org/10.1007/978-3-319-49806-5_10
9. Chaum, D., Pedersen, T.P.: Wallet databases with observers. In: Brickell, E.F. (ed.) CRYPTO 1992. LNCS, vol. 740, pp. 89–105. Springer, Heidelberg (1993). https://doi.org/10.1007/3-540-48071-4_7
10. Rai Choudhuri, A., Ciampi, M., Goyal, V., Jain, A., Ostrovsky, R.: Round optimal secure multiparty computation from minimal assumptions. In: Pass, R., Pietrzak, K. (eds.) TCC 2020. LNCS, vol. 12551, pp. 291–319. Springer, Cham (2020). https://doi.org/10.1007/978-3-030-64378-2_11
11. Ciampi, M., Parisella, R., Venturi, D.: On adaptive security of delayed-input sigma protocols and Fiat-Shamir NIZKs. In: Galdi, C., Kolesnikov, V. (eds.) SCN 2020. LNCS, vol. 12238, pp. 670–690. Springer, Cham (2020). https://doi.org/10.1007/978-3-030-57990-6_33
12. Ciampi, M., Persiano, G., Scafuro, A., Siniscalchi, L., Visconti, I.: Improved OR-composition of sigma-protocols. In: Kushilevitz, E., Malkin, T. (eds.) TCC 2016. LNCS, vol. 9563, pp. 112–141. Springer, Heidelberg (2016). https://doi.org/10.1007/978-3-662-49099-0_5
13. Ciampi, M., Persiano, G., Scafuro, A., Siniscalchi, L., Visconti, I.: Online/offline OR composition of sigma protocols. In: Fischlin, M., Coron, J.-S. (eds.) EUROCRYPT 2016. LNCS, vol. 9666, pp. 63–92. Springer, Heidelberg (2016). https://doi.org/10.1007/978-3-662-49896-5_3
14. Cramer, R., Damgård, I., Schoenmakers, B.: Proofs of partial knowledge and simplified design of witness hiding protocols. In: Desmedt, Y.G. (ed.) CRYPTO 1994. LNCS, vol. 839, pp. 174–187. Springer, Heidelberg (1994). https://doi.org/10.1007/3-540-48658-5_19
15. Fiat, A., Shamir, A.: How to prove yourself: practical solutions to identification and signature problems. In: Odlyzko, A.M. (ed.) CRYPTO 1986. LNCS, vol. 263, pp. 186–194. Springer, Heidelberg (1987). https://doi.org/10.1007/3-540-47721-7_12
16. Fischlin, M., Harasser, P., Janson, C.: Signatures from sequential-OR proofs. In: Canteaut, A., Ishai, Y. (eds.) EUROCRYPT 2020. LNCS, vol. 12107, pp. 212–244. Springer, Cham (2020). https://doi.org/10.1007/978-3-030-45727-3_8
17. Goel, A., Green, M., Hall-Andersen, M., Kaptchuk, G.: Stacking sigmas: a framework to compose σ-protocols for disjunctions. Cryptology ePrint Archive (2021)
18. Goyal, V., Richelson, S.: Non-malleable commitments using Goldreich-Levin list decoding. In: FOCS 2019, pp. 686–699. IEEE (2019)
19. Groth, J.: Simulation-sound NIZK proofs for a practical language and constant size group signatures. In: Lai, X., Chen, K. (eds.) ASIACRYPT 2006. LNCS, vol. 4284, pp. 444–459. Springer, Heidelberg (2006). https://doi.org/10.1007/11935230_29
20. Groth, J., Kohlweiss, M.: One-out-of-many proofs: or how to leak a secret and spend a coin. In: Oswald, E., Fischlin, M. (eds.) EUROCRYPT 2015. LNCS, vol. 9057, pp. 253–280. Springer, Heidelberg (2015). https://doi.org/10.1007/978-3-662-46803-6_9
21. Groth, J., Ostrovsky, R., Sahai, A.: Perfect non-interactive zero knowledge for NP. In: Vaudenay, S. (ed.) EUROCRYPT 2006. LNCS, vol. 4004, pp. 339–358. Springer, Heidelberg (2006). https://doi.org/10.1007/11761679_21

22. Groth, J., Sahai, A.: Efficient non-interactive proof systems for bilinear groups. In: Smart, N. (ed.) EUROCRYPT 2008. LNCS, vol. 4965, pp. 415–432. Springer, Heidelberg (2008). https://doi.org/10.1007/978-3-540-78967-3_24
23. Guillou, L.C., Quisquater, J.-J.: A practical zero-knowledge protocol fitted to security microprocessor minimizing both transmission and memory. In: Barstow, D., et al. (eds.) EUROCRYPT 1988. LNCS, vol. 330, pp. 123–128. Springer, Heidelberg (1988). https://doi.org/10.1007/3-540-45961-8_11
24. Impagliazzo, R., Paturi, R.: On the complexity of k-sat. J. Comput. Syst. Sci. **62**(2), 367–375 (2001)
25. Junod, P., Karlov, A.: An efficient public-key attribute-based broadcast encryption scheme allowing arbitrary access policies. In: Proceedings of the Tenth Annual ACM Workshop on Digital Rights Management, pp. 13–24 (2010)
26. Jutla, C.S., Roy, A.: Shorter quasi-adaptive NIZK proofs for linear subspaces. J. Cryptol. **30**(4), 1116–1156 (2017)
27. Lai, J., Deng, R.H., Li, Y.: Fully secure cipertext-policy hiding CP-ABE. In: Bao, F., Weng, J. (eds.) ISPEC 2011. LNCS, vol. 6672, pp. 24–39. Springer, Heidelberg (2011). https://doi.org/10.1007/978-3-642-21031-0_3
28. Malkin, T., Teranishi, I., Vahlis, Y., Yung, M.: Signatures resilient to continual leakage on memory and computation. In: Ishai, Y. (ed.) TCC 2011. LNCS, vol. 6597, pp. 89–106. Springer, Heidelberg (2011). https://doi.org/10.1007/978-3-642-19571-6_7
29. Okamoto, T.: An efficient divisible electronic cash scheme. In: Coppersmith, D. (ed.) CRYPTO 1995. LNCS, vol. 963, pp. 438–451. Springer, Heidelberg (1995). https://doi.org/10.1007/3-540-44750-4_35
30. Ràfols, C.: Stretching Groth-Sahai: NIZK proofs of partial satisfiability. In: Dodis, Y., Nielsen, J.B. (eds.) TCC 2015. LNCS, vol. 9015, pp. 247–276. Springer, Heidelberg (2015). https://doi.org/10.1007/978-3-662-46497-7_10
31. Rivest, R.L., Shamir, A., Tauman, Y.: How to leak a secret. In: Boyd, C. (ed.) ASIACRYPT 2001. LNCS, vol. 2248, pp. 552–565. Springer, Heidelberg (2001). https://doi.org/10.1007/3-540-45682-1_32
32. Schnorr, C.P.: Efficient signature generation by smart cards. J. Cryptol. **4**(3), 161–174 (1991). https://doi.org/10.1007/BF00196725
33. Tsabary, R.: Fully secure attribute-based encryption for t-CNF from LWE. In: Boldyreva, A., Micciancio, D. (eds.) CRYPTO 2019. LNCS, vol. 11692, pp. 62–85. Springer, Cham (2019). https://doi.org/10.1007/978-3-030-26948-7_3

Zero-Knowledge Protocols for the Subset Sum Problem from MPC-in-the-Head with Rejection

Thibauld Feneuil[1,2](✉), Jules Maire[3], Matthieu Rivain[1], and Damien Vergnaud[3,4]

[1] CryptoExperts, Paris, France
thibauld.feneuil@cryptoexperts.com
[2] Sorbonne Université, CNRS, INRIA, Institut de Mathématiques de Jussieu-Paris Rive Gauche, Ouragan, Paris, France
[3] Sorbonne Université, CNRS, LIP6, 75005 Paris, France
[4] Institut Universitaire de France, Paris, France

Abstract. We propose (honest verifier) zero-knowledge arguments for the modular *subset sum problem*. Previous combinatorial approaches, notably one due to Shamir, yield arguments with cubic communication complexity (in the security parameter). More recent methods, based on the *MPC-in-the-head* technique, also produce arguments with cubic communication complexity.

We improve this approach by using a secret-sharing over small integers (rather than modulo q) to reduce the size of the arguments and remove the prime modulus restriction. Since this sharing may reveal information on the secret subset, we introduce the idea of *rejection* to the MPC-in-the-head paradigm. Special care has to be taken to balance completeness and soundness and preserve zero-knowledge of our arguments. We combine this idea with two techniques to prove that the secret vector (which selects the subset) is well made of binary coordinates.

Our new protocols achieve an asymptotic improvement by producing arguments of quadratic size. This improvement is also practical: for a 256-bit modulus q, the best variant of our protocols yields 13 KB arguments while previous proposals gave 1180 KB arguments, for the best general protocol, and 122 KB, for the best protocol restricted to prime modulus. Our techniques can also be applied to vectorial variants of the subset sum problem and in particular the *inhomogeneous short integer solution* (ISIS) problem for which they provide an efficient alternative to state-of-the-art protocols when the underlying ring is not small and NTT-friendly. We also show the application of our protocol to build efficient zero-knowledge arguments of plaintext and/or key knowledge in the context of *fully-homomorphic encryption*. When applied to the TFHE scheme, the obtained arguments are more than 20 times smaller than those obtained with previous protocols. Eventually, we use our technique to construct an efficient digital signature scheme based on a pseudo-random function due to Boneh, Halevi, and Howgrave-Graham.

S. Agrawal and D. Lin (Eds.): ASIACRYPT 2022, LNCS 13792, pp. 371–402, 2022.
https://doi.org/10.1007/978-3-031-22966-4_13

1 Introduction

The *(modular) subset sum* problem is to find, given integers $w_1, \dots, w_n$, t and q, a subset of the w_i's that sum to t modulo q, i.e. to find bits $x_1, \dots, x_n \in \{0, 1\}$ such that

$$\sum_{i=1}^{n} x_i w_i = t \bmod q. \tag{1}$$

It was shown to be NP-complete (in its natural decision variant) in 1972 by Karp [Kar72] and was considered in cryptography as an interesting alternative to hardness assumptions based on number theory. Due to its simplicity, it was notably used in the 1980s, following [MH78], for the construction of several public-key encryption schemes.

Most of these proposals (if not all) were swiftly broken using lattice-based techniques (see [Odl90]), but the problem itself remains intractable for appropriate parameters and is even believed to be so for quantum computers. For instance, when the so-called density $d = n/\log_2(q)$ of the subset sum instance is close to 1 (i.e. $q \simeq 2^n$), the fastest known (classical and quantum) algorithms have complexity $2^{O(n)}$ (see [BBSS20] and references therein) and one can reach an alleged security level of λ bits with $n = \Theta(\lambda)$. Many cryptographic constructions were proposed whose security relies on the hardness of the subset sum problem: pseudo-random generators [IN96], bit commitments [IN96], public-key encryption [LPS10], ...

The concept of *zero-knowledge* proofs and arguments introduced in [GMR89] has become a fundamental tool in cryptography. It enables a prover to convince a verifier that some mathematical statement is true without revealing any additional information. Zero-knowledge proofs or arguments of knowledge, in which a prover demonstrates that they knows a "witness" of the validity of the statement, have found numerous applications in cryptography (notably for privacy-preserving constructions or to enforce honest behaviour of parties in complex protocols). The main goal of the present paper is to present new efficient zero-knowledge arguments of knowledge for the subset sum problem.

1.1 Prior Work

Given integers $w_1, \dots, w_n$, t and q, an elegant zero-knowledge proof system due to Shamir [Sha86] (see also [BGKW90]) allows a prover to convince a verifier that they knows $x_1, \dots, x_n \in \{0, 1\}$ such that the relation (1) holds. The proof system is combinatorial in nature and it requires $\Theta(\lambda)$ rounds of communication to achieve soundness error $2^{-\lambda}$ where each round requires $\Theta(n^2)$ bits of communication. For an alleged security level of λ bits, the overall communication complexity of Shamir's proof system is thus of $\Theta(\lambda^3)$. In [LNSW13], Ling, Nguyen, Stehlé, and Wang proposed a proof of knowledge of a solution for the infinity norm *inhomogeneous small integer solution* (ISIS) problem which is a vectorial variant of the subset sum problem. It is based on Stern's zero-knowledge proof of knowledge for the *syndrome decoding* problem [Ste94] and is also combinatorial.

It thus requires a large number of rounds of communication and when specialized to the subset sum problem it also yields proofs with $\Theta(\lambda^3)$-bit communication complexity for an alleged security level of λ bits.

A secure multi-party computation (MPC) protocol allows a set of mutually distrusting parties to jointly evaluate a function f over their inputs while keeping those inputs private. An elegant approach to constructing zero-knowledge protocols has gained particular attention over the last years: the *MPC-in-the-head* paradigm of Ishai, Kushilevitz, Ostrovsky, and Sahai [IKOS09] in which a prover secretly shares their secret input, simulates the execution of an MPC protocol on these shares (in "their head"), commits to this execution and partially reveals it to the verifier on some challenge subset of parties. The verifier can then check that the partial execution is consistent and accepts or rejects accordingly. This approach was at first stood in the realm of theoretical cryptography (with a focus on the asymptotic performance for any problem in NP), but it was subsequently demonstrated to be also of practical relevance [GMO16, KKW18]. In [BD10], Bendlin and Damgård were the first to use the MPC-in-the-head paradigm in lattice-based cryptography. They proposed a zero-knowledge proof of knowledge of the plaintext contained in a given ciphertext from Regev's cryptosystem [Reg05] (and a variant they proposed). More recently, Baum and Nof [BN20] proposed an efficient zero-knowledge argument of knowledge of the *short integer solution* (SIS) problem (incorporating the *sacrificing* principle in the MPC-in-the-head paradigm). Beullens also recently proposed such arguments obtained from sigma protocols *with helper* [Beu20]. When applied to the subset sum problem itself, all (variants of) these protocols yield proofs with $\Theta(\lambda^3)$-bit communication complexity for an alleged security level of λ bits.

There exist numerous other protocols for (vectorial variants of) the subset sum problem from lattice-based cryptography. Until recently, they all introduce some slack in the proof, i.e. there is a difference between the language used for completeness and the language that the soundness guarantees (see, e.g. [BDLN16] for a generic argument of knowledge of a pre-image for *homomorphic one-way functions over integer vectors*). In particular, the witness that can be extracted from a proof is larger than the one that an honest prover uses (and in the subset sum problem, the extractor will not output a binary vector). This slack forces to use larger parameters for the underlying cryptosystem and induces some loss in efficiency. Conversely, we shall only consider exact arguments for the subset-sum problem in the present paper. Finally, new exact arguments were proposed recently [BLS19, ENS20, LNS21] but they require to use a modulus q of a special form (namely a prime number as in [BN20, Beu20] but with additional arithmetic constraints to make it "NTT-friendly").

1.2 Contributions

In the MPC-in-the-head paradigm, the prover wants to convince a verifier that they know a (secret) pre-image x of $y = f(x)$ for some one-way function f where the function f is represented as an arithmetic circuit. For the subset sum problem, the function f is defined *via* (1) and it is thus natural to consider the simple inner-product arithmetic circuit defined over $\mathbb{Z}_q$. The prover's secret input is the binary vector $x = (x_1, \ldots, x_n) \in \{0,1\}^n$ and they have to perform some secret-sharing of x in $\mathbb{Z}_q$ in such a way that the shares of any unauthorized set of parties should reveal no information about the secret. This approach has the major disadvantage that sharing a single bit requires several elements of $\mathbb{Z}_q$ each of size $\Theta(\lambda)$ bits.

We adapt this paradigm using a secret sharing scheme done directly over the integers. This approach was already used in cryptography (e.g. for multi-party computation modulo a shared secret modulus [CGH00]). To additively share a secret t in a given interval $[-T, T]$ for $T \in \mathbb{N}$, among $n \geq 2$ parties, a dealer may pick uniformly at random $t_1, \ldots, t_n \in [-T2^\rho, T2^\rho]$ under the constraint that $t = t_1 + \cdots + t_n$ (over the integers), for some parameter ρ. However, given $(n-1)$ shares, $t_2, \ldots, t_n$ for instance, the value $t_1 = t - (t_2 + \cdots t_n)$ is not randomly distributed in $[-T2^\rho, T2^\rho]$ and this may reveal information on the secret t. It is thus necessary to sample the shares in an interval sufficiently large in such a way that their distributions for distinct secrets are statistically indistinguishable. For a security level λ, this requires $\rho = \Omega(\lambda)$ and thus the additive sharing of bits involves shares of size $\Omega(\lambda)$. To overcome this limitation and use additive secret sharing over *small* integers, we will rely on *rejection*. The computation being actually simulated by the prover, they can abort the protocol whenever the sharing leaks information on the secret vector $x = (x_1, \ldots, x_n) \in \{0,1\}^n$. In some cases, the prover cannot respond to the challenge from the verifier and must abort the protocol. A similar idea was used for lattice-based signatures by Lyubashevsky [Lyu09] but using different methods.

Our technique also allows overcoming the second disadvantage of the previous tentatives to use the MPC-in-the-head paradigm for lattice-based problems. Indeed, using our additive secret sharing over the integers, we can prove the knowledge of some integer vector $x = (x_1, \ldots, x_n)$ satisfying relation (1) (for any q) and further prove that $x_i \in \{0,1\}$ for $i \in \{1, \ldots, n\}$. This is achieved by simulating a (single) non-linear operation modulo some arbitrary prime number q' (independent from q and much smaller than q). We also introduce another technique to prove that the solution $x = (x_1, \ldots, x_n)$ indeed lies in $\{0,1\}^n$ using some masking and a *cut-and-choose* strategy. Both methods yield zero-knowledge proofs with $\Theta(\lambda^2)$-bit communication complexity for an alleged security level of λ bits. This improvement is not only of theoretical interest since for $q \simeq 2^{256}$, our protocol can produce proof of size 13KB where Shamir's protocol [Sha86] (updated with modern tips) produces proof of size 1186KB and [LNSW13] produces proofs of size 2350 KB.

Our protocols are particularly efficient for the subset sum problem where the modulus q is large. However, we show that our method has applications in other contexts in cryptography. We show that it can be used for the (binary) ISIS problem in lattice-based cryptography and that the resulting protocols are competitive with state-of-the-art protocols for this problem. We also present applications of our techniques to the context of *fully-homomorphic encryption* (FHE). Specifically, adaptations of our protocols provide efficient zero-knowledge arguments of plaintext and/or key knowledge for the so-called *Torus Fully Homomorphic*

Encryption (TFHE) scheme from [CGGI20]. Eventually, we use our technique to construct an efficient digital signature scheme based on a pseudo-random function due to Boneh, Halevi, and Howgrave-Graham [BHH01].

2 Preliminaries

2.1 Zero-Knowledge Proofs

A zero-knowledge (ZK) protocol for some polynomial-time decidable binary relation $\mathcal{R}$ (i.e., a relation that defines a language in NP) is defined by two probabilistic polynomial time (PPT) interactive algorithms, a prover $\mathcal{P}$ and a verifier $\mathcal{V}$: both $\mathcal{V}$ and $\mathcal{P}$ are given a common input x and $\mathcal{P}$ is given in addition a witness w such that $(x, w) \in \mathcal{R}$. Then, $\mathcal{P}$ and $\mathcal{V}$ exchange a sequence of messages alternatively until $\mathcal{V}$ outputs a bit b (with $b = 1$ indicating that $\mathcal{V}$ accepts $\mathcal{P}$'s claim and $b = 0$ indicating that $\mathcal{V}$ rejects the claim). The entire sequence of messages exchanged by $\mathcal{P}$ and $\mathcal{V}$, along with the answer b, is called a *transcript.*

A zero-knowledge argument for $\mathcal{R}$ with *soundness error* ϵ, *completeness error* α and (t, ζ)*-zero-knowledge* satisfies the following properties:

1. **Completeness:** if $(x, w) \in \mathcal{R}$, and $\mathcal{P}$ knows a witness w for x, they will succeed in convincing $\mathcal{V}$ (except with probability α), i.e.,

$$\Pr[\langle \mathcal{P}(x, w), \mathcal{V}(x) \rangle = 1] \geq 1 - \alpha.$$

2. **Soundness:** if there exists a PPT algorithm $\tilde{\mathcal{P}}$ such that

$$\tilde{\epsilon} := \Pr\ [\langle \tilde{\mathcal{P}}(x), \mathcal{V}(x) \rangle = 1] > \epsilon,$$

   then there exists a PPT algorithm $\mathcal{E}$ (called the *extractor*) which, given rewindable black-box access to $\tilde{\mathcal{P}}$ outputs a witness w' for x in time in time $\mathsf{poly}(\lambda, (\tilde{\epsilon} - \epsilon)^{-1})$ with probability at least $1/2$.
3. **Zero-knowledge:** for every PPT algorithm $\tilde{\mathcal{V}}$, there exists a PPT algorithm $\mathcal{S}$ (called the *simulator*) which, given the input statement x and rewindable black-box access to $\tilde{\mathcal{V}}$, outputs a simulated transcript which is (t, ζ)-indistinguishable from $\mathrm{View}(\mathcal{P}(x, w), \tilde{\mathcal{V}}(x))$ (see the full version [FMRV22] for a formal definition).

Remark 1. The soundness property ensures that a PPT algorithm $\tilde{\mathcal{P}}$ without knowledge of the witness cannot convince $\mathcal{V}$ with probability greater than ϵ assuming that the underlying problem is hard. Otherwise, the existence of $\mathcal{E}$ implies that $\tilde{\mathcal{P}}$ can be used to compute a valid witness w' for x. If the zero-knowledge property holds only for the genuine verifier $\mathcal{V}$, then the protocol is deemed *honest-verifier* zero-knowledge.

2.2 MPC-in-the-Head and Batch Product Verification

The MPC-in-the-Head (MPCitH) paradigm [IKOS09] constructs ZK proofs from MPC protocols. Efficient instances of this paradigm have been published for the first time these last years starting with a protocol called ZKBoo [GMO16] and has found numerous applications (e.g. [GMO16, KKW18, BN20]).

We consider a prover $\mathcal{P}$ and a verifier $\mathcal{V}$ engaging a two-party interactive protocol for some public circuit C over a finite field $\mathbb{F}$ and some value $t \in \mathbb{F}$ such that $\mathcal{P}$ wants to convince $\mathcal{V}$ that they knows an $x \in \mathbb{F}$ satisfying $C(x) = t$.

In the MPCitH paradigm, the prover $\mathcal{P}$ usually decomposes their secret x into N shares $[\![x]\!]_1, ..., [\![x]\!]_N$ using some additive secret sharing over $\mathbb{F}$. Then, $\mathcal{P}$ simulates an N-party MPC protocol for evaluating C. At the end of the MPC protocol, using a commitment scheme (see definition in the full version [FMRV22]), $\mathcal{P}$ commits to the N views of the parties resulting from the MPC protocol simulation. $\mathcal{V}$ then challenges $\mathcal{P}$ to open a subset of the views. $\mathcal{P}$ answers by opening these views and $\mathcal{V}$ checks that these views are consistent with the MPC process as well as valid openings of the commitments. In the basic setting where $N-1$ out of N parties are opened, the resulting zero-knowledge protocol achieves a soundness error of $1/N$.

Batch Product Verification. Using the MPCitH approach the linear operations over $\mathbb{F}$ (i.e. addition in $\mathbb{F}$ and multiplication by constants in $\mathbb{F}$) can be handled easily and are almost free in terms of computation and communication. The most cumbersome part of the MPCitH method is to handle non-linear operations and in particular multiplications in $\mathbb{F}$. The authors of [BN20] propose an MPC protocol to verify the correctness of a product in $\mathbb{F}$ by "sacrificing" another one. This construction enables to check that a triple of sharings $([\![x]\!], [\![y]\!], [\![z]\!])$ is such that $x \cdot y = z$, by using a second random triple $([\![a]\!], [\![b]\!], [\![c]\!])$ satisfying $a \cdot b = c$. The second triple can be used a single time (to preserve the zero-knowledge property), hence the "sacrifice".

Recently [KZ22] has adapted and optimized this method to build an efficient MPC protocol which check simultaneously many products by sacrificing a dot-product (see the full version [FMRV22]).

Additive Sharing. In most recent MPCitH schemes, in order to decrease the communication costs, when the prover splits their secret x into N shares $[\![x]\!]_1, ..., [\![x]\!]_N$, the first $N-1$ shares are generated using a pseudo-random generator and only the N-th share $[\![x]\!]_N$ is computed in such a way that $x = [\![x]\!]_1 + \cdots + [\![x]\!]_N$ in $\mathbb{F}$. In this paper, since our sharings will not be defined over some additive group, we will generate the N shares $[\![x]\!]_1, ..., [\![x]\!]_N$ from N seeds using a pseudo-random generator and we will introduce an auxiliary value Δx (not distributed over the same set) such that $x = [\![x]\!]_1 + \cdots + [\![x]\!]_N + \Delta x$ over the integers.

3 General Idea

We consider an instance $(w, t) \in \mathbb{Z}_q^n \times \mathbb{Z}_q$ of the subset sum problem (SSP) and denote x one solution. We have $x \in \{0,1\}^n$ and $\sum_{j=1}^{n} x_j \cdot w_j = t \bmod q$.

We want to use the MPCitH paradigm to build a zero-knowledge protocol that proves the knowledge of a solution for the instance (w, t). To proceed, we need to build an MPC protocol with honest-but-curious parties taking as inputs shares of the secret x, and possibly shares of other data, and which computation can only succeed if x is a valid solution of the SSP instance. As a first ingredient, we need a method to share the secret x between the different parties.

3.1 The Naive Approach

The SSP instance is defined on $\mathbb{Z}_q$, so a natural sharing of x would be defined as:

$$\begin{cases} [\![x]\!]_i \xleftarrow{\$} (\mathbb{Z}_q)^n \text{ for all } i \in [N], \\ \Delta x \leftarrow x - \sum_{i=1}^{N} [\![x]\!]_i \bmod q \end{cases}.$$

In the MPCitH paradigm, the communication cost of a sharing is the cost to send the auxiliary values, *i.e.* the vector Δx. Here, the natural sharing of x costs

$$n \cdot \log_2(q) \text{ bits.}$$

If we take $n = 256$ and $q = 2^{256}$, the cost is about 2^{16} bits $= 8$ KB. To achieve a soundness error of 2^{-128} with $N = 256$, we need to repeat the protocol at least 16 times, so the communication cost of the protocol would be already more than 128 KB for the sole sharing of x (some communication being further required for the MPCitH protocol). Asymptotically, the parameters for the subset sum problem are chosen such that $n = \Theta(\lambda)$ and $\log_2 q = \Theta(\lambda)$, the communication cost of this sharing is thus about $\Theta(\lambda^2)$ bytes per protocol repetition. Since we need to repeat the protocol about $\Theta(\lambda)$ times to achieve a $2^{-\lambda}$ soundness error the global communication cost is then of at least $\Theta(\lambda^3)$ (for the sharing only).

We present hereafter an alternative strategy for the sharing of x, which achieves better practical and asymptotic communication costs.

3.2 Sharing on the Integers and Opening with Abort

We propose another way to share the secret x to achieve lower communication. We know that x is a binary vector (*i.e.* $x \in \{0,1\}^n$), so instead of the natural sharing, we suggest to use a sharing defined on the integers, that is

$$\begin{cases} [\![x]\!]_i \xleftarrow{\$} \{0, \ldots, A-1\}^n \text{ for all } i \in [N], \\ \Delta x \leftarrow x - \sum_{i=1}^{N} [\![x]\!]_i. \end{cases}$$

However, this sharing leaks information about the secret x. The distribution Δx_j is not the same depending on whether $x_j = 0$ or $x_j = 1$ as illustrated on Fig. 1. To solve this issue, the prover must abort the protocol in some cases.

To see how this leakage can be effectively exploited to (partly) recover x, let us recall that at the end of the protocol, the verifier shall ask the prover to open

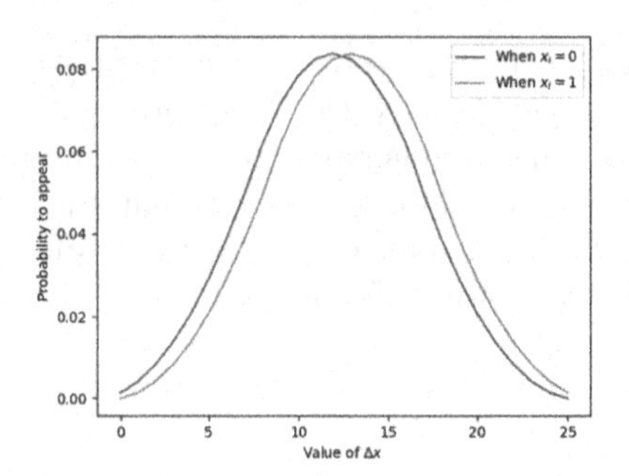

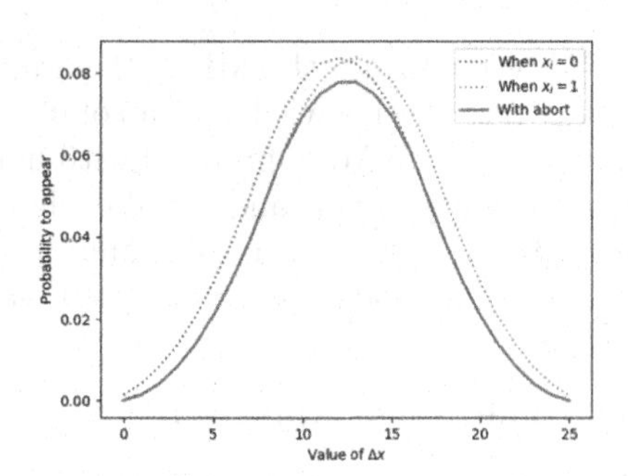

Fig. 1. Probability mass function of Δx_j when $x_j = 0$ and when $x_j = 1$ (on the left) and of Δx_j with abort (on the right), for $N = 3$ and $A = 9$.

the views of all parties except one. Let us denote i^* the index of the unopened party. It means the verifier will have access to

$$\{[\![x]\!]_i\}_{i \neq i^*} \quad \text{and} \quad \Delta x.$$

For the sake of simplicity, let us first consider the case $n = 1$, *i.e.* $x \in \{0, 1\}$ and $[\![x]\!]$ is the sharing of a single integer. With the opened values, the verifier can compute

$$x - [\![x]\!]_{i^*} \text{ as } \Delta x + \sum_{i \neq i^*} [\![x]\!]_i.$$

Now let us denote $Y = x - [\![x]\!]_{i^*}$ the underlying random variable over the uniform random sampling of $[\![x]\!]_{i^*}$. We have

$$\Pr(Y = -A+1) = \begin{cases} \frac{1}{A} & \text{if } x = 0 \\ 0 & \text{if } x = 1 \end{cases} \quad \text{and} \quad \Pr(Y = 1) = \begin{cases} 0 & \text{if } x = 0 \\ \frac{1}{A} & \text{if } x = 1 \end{cases}$$

while

$$\Pr(Y = y) = \frac{1}{A} \quad \text{for every } y \in \{-A+2, \dots, 0\}.$$

So by observing $x - [\![x]\!]_{i^*} = -A+1$ one learns $(x, [\![x]\!]_{i^*}) = (0, -A+1)$. Similarly, by observing $x - [\![x]\!]_{i^*} = 1$ one learns $(x, [\![x]\!]_{i^*}) = (1, 0)$. To avoid this flaw, the prover must abort the protocol before revealing $\{[\![x]\!]_i\}_{i \neq i^*}$ and Δx whenever one of these two cases occurs. This notably implies that Δx must not be revealed before receiving the challenge i^*, but it should still be committed beforehand in order to ensure the soundness of the protocol. Doing so, we modify the distribution of the revealed auxiliary value which does not leak any information about x anymore as illustrated in Fig. 1, and the probability to abort does not leak information about x since it is $1/A$ in the both cases ($x = 0$ and $x = 1$).

Let us now come back to the general case of $n \geq 1$. The prover applies the above abortion strategy for all the coordinates of x, namely

- if there exists $j \in [n]$ such that $x_j = 0$ and $[\![x_j]\!]_{i^*} = A - 1$, the prover aborts;
- if there exists $j \in [n]$ such that $x_j = 1$ and $[\![x_j]\!]_{i^*} = 0$, the prover aborts;
- otherwise the prover proceeds.

The probability to abort, which we call *rejection rate*, is

$$1 - \left(1 - \frac{1}{A}\right)^n \leq \frac{n}{A}.$$

We note that the rejection rate can be tightly approximated by the n/A upper bound when A is sufficiently large. In order to achieve a small (constant) rejection rate, we should hence choose A greater than n. Asymptotically, we then have $A = \Theta(n) = \Theta(\lambda)$, which represents an exponential improvement compared to $q = 2^{\Theta(\lambda)}$.

Let us now analyze the computation cost of our strategy for sharing x. In the absence of rejection, Δx_j belongs to $\{-N \cdot (A-1)+1, \ldots, 0\}$, therefore sending the auxiliary value Δx would cost $n \cdot \log_2(N \cdot (A-1))$ bits. However, the prover can save communication by sending $x - [\![x]\!]_{i^*}$ instead, which is strictly equivalent in terms of revealed information by the relation $x - [\![x]\!]_{i^*} = \Delta x + \sum_{i \neq i^*} [\![x]\!]_i$. Since each coordinate of $x - [\![x]\!]_{i^*}$ is uniformly distributed over $\{-A+2, \ldots, 0\}$, sending it only costs

$$n \cdot \log_2(A-1) \text{ bits.}$$

With $x - [\![x]\!]_{i^*}$, the verifier can recover Δx by computing $\Delta x = (x - [\![x]\!]_{i^*}) - \sum_{i \neq i^*} [\![x]\!]_i$. The cost of this sharing has the advantage of being independent of the modulus q on which the SSP instance is defined. The value of A will be chosen according to the desired trade-off between communication cost and rejection rate. If $n = 256$ and $A = 2^{16}$, we have a cost of 0.5 KB for a rejection rate of 0.0038, which is much better than the 8 KB of the naive approach.

Let us remark that adding an abort event does not impact the soundness of the protocol. A malicious prover can abort as many times she wants claiming that it would leak information, but an abortion does not help to convince the verifier. The soundness theorem will state that someone who does not know the secret can only answer with a probability smaller than the constant value called soundness error, and adding an abort event cannot increase this probability. The prover could sample a random party i' and give to i' a wrong share and she may indeed decide to abort if the verifier challenge is not i', but this does not change the fact that the probability for the prover to convince the verifier is the probability that the prover guesses the verifier challenge a priori.

Now that we have defined the sharing of x, we need to demonstrate two properties of the shared SSP instance through multi-party computation. The first one is the SSP relation which in the shared setting translates to

$$\sum_{j=1}^{n} [\![x_j]\!] \cdot w_j = [\![t]\!] \bmod q$$

for a sharing $[\![t]\!]$ of t. The linearity of this relation makes it easy to deal with: the share $[\![t]\!]_i$ can simply be computed as $[\![t]\!]_i := \sum_{j=1}^{n} [\![x_j]\!]_i \cdot w_j \bmod q$ and committed to the verifier by each party. The verifier can then check that the open parties have correctly computed their shares $[\![t]\!]_i$ and that the relation $\sum_{i=1}^{N}[\![t]\!]_i = [\![t]\!] \bmod q$ well holds. The second property which must be demonstrated through multi-party computation is that the solution x corresponding to the sharing $[\![x]\!]$ is a binary vector. This is not a priori guaranteed to the verifier since the shares of the coordinate of x are defined over $\{0, \ldots, A-1\}$ and the correctness of the linear relation does not imply that x is indeed binary. We present two different solutions to this issue in the following.

3.3 Binarity Proof from Batch Product Verification

Our first solution relies on standard MPC-in-the-Head techniques to prove the relation

$$x \circ (x-1) = 0$$

where $\circ$ denotes the coordinate-wise product, 0 and 1 are to be interpreted as the all-0 and all-1 vectors. To this aim, we can use the MPC-in-the-Head batch product verification suggested in [LN17, BN20] and recently improved in [KZ22] (see Sect. 2.2). However, we can do better than a straight application of those techniques.

The relation $x \circ (x-1) = 0$ is defined in $\mathbb{Z}_q$ and the above techniques imply to send at least one field element per product, that is n elements from $\mathbb{Z}_q$. To save communication and since the sharing $[\![x]\!]$ is defined on the integers, we can work on a smaller field. We previously explained that the verifier receives $\{[\![x]\!]_i\}_{i \neq i^*}$ and Δx from the prover, so they can check that, for all $j \in [n]$,

$$-A + 2 \leq x_j - [\![x_j]\!]_{i^*} \leq 0.$$

They further trusts $[\![x_j]\!]_{i^*} \in \{0, \ldots, A-1\}$ (which is verified for the open parties). Thus the verifier can deduce that, for all $j \in [n]$,

$$-A + 2 \leq x_j \leq A - 1. \tag{2}$$

Let q' be a prime such that $q' \geq A$. If the prover convinces the verifier that $x_j(x_j - 1) = 0 \bmod q'$, then the latter deduces that $x_j \in \{0, 1\}$ because

$$\begin{aligned} q' | x_j(x_j - 1) &\Rightarrow (q' | x_j) \text{ or } (q' | x_j - 1) \\ &\Rightarrow (x_j = 0) \text{ or } (x_j = 1) \quad \text{by (2)} \end{aligned}$$

The prover hence just needs to prove $x \circ (x-1) = 0 \bmod q'$ for some prime q' such that $q' \geq A$. To this purpose, we apply the batch product verification of [KZ22] as follows (see also the full version [FMRV22]).

The prover first samples $a \in (\mathbb{Z}_{q'})^n$ with its sharing

$$[\![a]\!]_i \overset{\$}{\leftarrow} (\mathbb{Z}_{q'})^n \text{ for } i \in [N].$$

The value a is hence defined as a uniform random element of $(\mathbb{Z}_{q'})^n$ and no auxiliary value Δa is necessary. The prover then computes $c = \langle a, x \rangle$ and its sharing as

$$\begin{cases} [\![c]\!]_i \xleftarrow{\$} \mathbb{Z}_{q'} \text{ for all } i \in [N], \\ \Delta c \xleftarrow{\$} c - \sum_{i=1}^{N} [\![c]\!]_i \bmod q' \end{cases}.$$

The prover gives the shares of x, a and c as inputs to the parties and runs the following MPC protocol:

1. the parties get a random challenge $\varepsilon \in (\mathbb{Z}_{q'})^n$ from the verifier;
2. the parties locally set $[\![\alpha]\!] = \varepsilon \circ (1 - [\![x]\!]) + [\![a]\!]$;
3. the parties open $[\![\alpha]\!]$ to get α;
4. the parties locally set $[\![v]\!] = \langle \alpha, [\![x]\!] \rangle - [\![c]\!]$;
5. the parties open $[\![v]\!]$ to get v;
6. the parties accept iff $v = 0$.

Besides the input shares and commitments, the prover-to-verifier communication cost of the corresponding MPCitH zero-knowledge protocol only results from the size of $[\![\alpha]\!]_{i^*}$ (the broadcasted vector of the unopened party i^*), which is of

$$n \cdot \log_2(q') \text{ bits.}$$

We stress that the prover does not need to send $[\![v]\!]_{i^*}$ because the verifier knows that v must be zero and will deduce $[\![v]\!]_{i^*} = -\Delta v - \sum_{i \neq i^*} [\![v]\!]_i$

As described in Sect. 2.2, the batch product MPC verification produces false positives with probability $1/q'$. Thus the soundness error of the obtained zero-knowledge protocol is

$$1 - \left(1 - \frac{1}{N}\right)\left(1 - \frac{1}{q'}\right) < \frac{1}{N} + \frac{1}{q'}.$$

On the other hand, the protocol has a rejection rate of $1 - (1 - \frac{1}{A})^n$ and a prover-to-verifier communication cost (in bits) of

$$2 \cdot (2\lambda) + \underbrace{n \cdot \log_2(A-1)}_{x - [\![x]\!]_{i^*}} + \underbrace{n \cdot \log_2(q')}_{\Delta \alpha} + \underbrace{\log_2(q')}_{\Delta c} + \lambda \log_2 N + 2\lambda.$$

3.4 Binarity Proof from Masking and Cut-and-Choose Strategy

Our second solution to prove that $[\![x]\!]$ encodes a binary vector relies on a masking of x and a cut-and-choose strategy. The idea is to generate a random vector r from $\{0,1\}^n$ and to apply the sharing described in Sect. 3.2 to r. In addition, the prover computes (and commits) $\tilde{x} := x \oplus r \in \{0,1\}^n$ where $\oplus$ represents the XOR operation. Instead of giving the shares $[\![x]\!]$ of x as inputs of the MPC protocol, the idea is now to send the shares $[\![r]\!]$ of r. Then using $\tilde{x}$, the parties can locally deduce a sharing of x as

$$[\![x]\!] = (1 - \tilde{x}) \circ [\![r]\!] + \tilde{x} \circ (1 - [\![r]\!])$$

which is a linear relation in $[\![r]\!]$, and the verifier can further deduce the auxiliary value Δx from Δr as

$$\Delta x = (1 - \tilde{x}) \circ \Delta r + \tilde{x} \circ (1 - \Delta r).$$

By replacing $[\![x]\!]$ with $[\![r]\!]$ the parties' input is made independent of the secret. The interest of doing so is to enable a cut-and-choose strategy to prove that $[\![r]\!]$ encodes a binary vector, which in turns implies that $x = \tilde{x} \oplus r$ is a binary vector. More precisely, at the beginning of the zero-knowledge protocol, the prover produces M binary vectors $r^{[\ell]}$ and their corresponding shares $[\![r^{[\ell]}]\!]$ (in practice these vectors and their sharings are pseudo-randomly derived from some seeds). Then the prover commits those sharings $[\![r^{[\ell]}]\!]$ as well as the corresponding masked vectors $\tilde{x}^{[\ell]} := x \oplus r^{[\ell]}$. Then the verifier asks to open all the sharings $r^{[\ell]}$ except one and checks that they correspond to binary vectors. The verifier will hence trust that the unopened sharing encodes also a binary vector with a soundness error of $1/M$. We stress that all the values $\tilde{x}^{[\ell]}$ for which $r^{[\ell]}$ is opened must remain hidden (otherwise x could be readily recovered). The obtained zero-knowledge protocol has a soundness error of

$$\max\left\{\frac{1}{M}, \frac{1}{N}\right\},$$

a rejection rate of $1 - (1 - \frac{1}{A})^n$ and a prover-to-verifier communication cost (in bits) of

$$2 \cdot (2\lambda) + \underbrace{\lambda \log_2 M}_{\text{Cost of C\&C}} + \underbrace{n \cdot \log_2(A-1)}_{r - [\![r]\!]_{i^*}} + \underbrace{n}_{\tilde{x}} + \lambda \log_2 N + 2\lambda.$$

3.5 Asymptotic Analysis

We analyze hereafter the asymptotic complexity of the two variants of our protocol. We show that for a security parameter λ both variants have an asymptotic communication cost of $\Theta(\lambda^2)$ and an asymptotic computation time of $\Theta(\lambda^4)$.

For the binarity proof based on masking and cut-and-choose, we assume $M = N$ (which is optimal for the communication cost given the soundness error). For the other parameters, let us recall that

- for a security parameter λ, one must take $n \approx \log_2 q = \Theta(\lambda)$,
- the prime q' can be chosen as the smallest prime greater than A, which implies $q' \approx A$.

For both variants, the asymptotic communication cost for one repetition of the protocol is then of

$$\Theta(\lambda \log_2 A + \lambda \log_2 N).$$

Since each repetition has a soundness error of $\Theta(1/N)$, the protocol must be repeated $\tau = \Theta(\lambda / \log_2 N)$ times to reach a global soundness error of $2^{-\lambda}$. The probability that any of these τ repetitions aborts is given by

$$1 - \left(1 - \frac{1}{A}\right)^{n \cdot \tau} \approx \frac{n \cdot \tau}{A}$$

where the approximation is tight when A is sufficiently large. Thus for a small constant rejection probability, one must take $A = \Theta(n \cdot \tau) = \Theta(\lambda^2 / \log_2 N)$. We have a communication cost for the τ iterations in

$$\Theta\left(\lambda^2 \frac{\log_2 A}{\log_2 N} + \lambda^2\right) = \Theta\left(\frac{\lambda^2}{\log_2 N} \log_2\left(\frac{\lambda^2}{\log_2 N}\right) + \lambda^2\right)$$

and we hence obtain a minimal asymptotic communication cost of $\Theta(\lambda^2)$ by taking $N = \Theta(\lambda)$.

The asymptotic computation time for one repetition of the protocol is of $\Theta(Nn(\log_2 q)(\log_2 A))$, where the term $(\log_2 q)(\log_2 A)$ arises from the complexity of the multiplication between an element of $\mathbb{Z}_q$ and a value smaller than A. We hence get a computation time of $\Theta(\lambda^3 \log_2 \lambda)$ per repetition which makes $\Theta(\lambda^4)$ for τ repetitions.

4 Protocols and Security Proofs

In this section, we formally describe our two protocols and state their security. We further introduce a method to decrease the rejection rate.

4.1 Protocol with Batch Product Verification

Protocol description. In Sect. 3.3, we proposed an MPC protocol that proves that the sharing $[\![x]\!]$ encodes a binary vector. We then add the checking of the linear relation as described in Sect. 3.2 and we transform the multi-party computation into a zero-knowledge protocol which proves the knowledge of a solution of an SSP instance. We give the formal description of our protocol in Protocol 1. The protocol makes use of a pseudo-random generator PRG, a tree-based pseudo-random generator TreePRG (see definition in [KKW18]), two collision-resistant hash functions Hash_i for $i \in \{1, 2\}$ and a commitment scheme (Com, Verif) as defined in the full version [FMRV22]. In this description, the procedure Check returns 0 if the evaluated condition is false (*i.e.* the equality does not hold) and the execution continues otherwise.

Security Proofs. The following theorems state the completeness, zero-knowledge and soundness of Protocol 1. The proofs of Theorems 1, 2 and 3 are provided in appendix of the full version [FMRV22].

Theorem 1 (Completeness). *A prover $\mathcal{P}$ who knows a solution x to the subset sum instance $(w, t) \in \mathbb{Z}_q^n \times \mathbb{Z}_q$ and who follows the steps of Protocol 1 convinces the verifier $\mathcal{V}$ with probability*

$$\left(1 - \frac{1}{A}\right)^n.$$

Prover $\mathcal{P}$		Verifier $\mathcal{V}$
$x \in \{0,1\}^n$		
$w \in \mathbb{Z}_q^n, t = \langle w, x \rangle$		w, t
$\mathsf{mseed} \xleftarrow{\$} \{0,1\}^\lambda$		
Compute parties' seeds		
$(\mathsf{seed}_1, \rho_1), \ldots, (\mathsf{seed}_N, \rho_N)$		
with TreePRG(mseed)		
For each party $i \in \{1, \ldots, N\}$:		
$[\![a]\!]_i, [\![x]\!]_i, [\![c]\!]_i \leftarrow \mathrm{PRG}(\mathsf{seed}_i)$		$\triangleright\, a \in \mathbb{Z}_{q'}^n,\ c \in \mathbb{Z}_{q'},\ [\![x]\!]_i \in \{0, \ldots, A-1\}^n$
$\mathsf{com}_i = \mathrm{Com}(\mathsf{seed}_i; \rho_i)$		
$\Delta x = x - \sum_i [\![x]\!]_i$		
$\Delta c = \langle a, x \rangle - \sum_i [\![c]\!]_i$		
$h = \mathrm{Hash}_1(\Delta x, \Delta c, \mathsf{com}_1, \ldots, \mathsf{com}_N)$		
	$\xrightarrow{h}$	
		$\varepsilon \xleftarrow{\$} \mathbb{Z}_{q'}^n$
	$\xleftarrow{\varepsilon}$	
The parties locally set		
- $[\![t]\!] = \langle w, [\![x]\!] \rangle$		$\triangleright\, t \in \mathbb{Z}_q$
- $[\![\alpha]\!] = \varepsilon \circ (1 - [\![x]\!]) + [\![a]\!]$		$\triangleright\, \alpha \in \mathbb{Z}_{q'}^n$ (computation in $\mathbb{Z}_{q'}$)
The parties open $[\![\alpha]\!]$ to get α.		
The parties locally set		
$[\![v]\!] = \langle \alpha, [\![x]\!] \rangle - [\![c]\!]$		$\triangleright\, v \in \mathbb{Z}_{q'}$ (computation in $\mathbb{Z}_{q'}$)
$h' = \mathrm{Hash}_2([\![t]\!], [\![\alpha]\!], [\![v]\!])$		
	$\xrightarrow{h'}$	
		$i^* \xleftarrow{\$} \{1, \ldots, N\}$
	$\xleftarrow{i^*}$	
If there exists $j \in [n]$ such that:		
- either $[\![x_j]\!]_{i^*} = 0$ with $x_j = 1$		
- or $[\![x_j]\!]_{i^*} = A - 1$ with $x_j = 0$,		
then abort.		
$y = x - [\![x]\!]_{i^*}$		
	$(\mathsf{seed}_i, \rho_i)_{i \neq i^*},\ \mathsf{com}_{i^*},$ $y,\ \Delta c,\ [\![\alpha]\!]_{i^*}$ $\longrightarrow$	
		For all $i \neq i^*$,
		$[\![a]\!]_i, [\![x]\!]_i, [\![c]\!]_i \leftarrow \mathrm{PRG}(\mathsf{seed}_i)$
		$\Delta x = y - \sum_{i \neq i^*} [\![x]\!]_i$
		$\Delta \alpha = \varepsilon \cdot (1 - \Delta x)$
		For all $i \neq i^*$,
		Rerun the party i as the prover
		and compute the commitment com_i.
		$\Delta t = \langle w, \Delta x \rangle$
		$\Delta v = \langle \alpha, \Delta x \rangle - \Delta c$
		$[\![t]\!]_{i^*} = t - \Delta t - \sum_{i \neq i^*} [\![t]\!]_i$
		$[\![v]\!]_{i^*} = -\Delta v - \sum_{i \neq i^*} [\![v]\!]_i$
		Check $h = \mathrm{Hash}_1(\Delta x, \Delta c, \mathsf{com}_1, \ldots, \mathsf{com}_N)$
		Check $h' = \mathrm{Hash}_2([\![t]\!], [\![\alpha]\!], [\![v]\!])$
		Return 1

Protocol 1: Zero-knowledge argument for Subset Sum Problem via MPC-in-the-head with rejection, using batch product verification to prove binarity.

Theorem 2 (Zero-Knowledge). *Let the PRG used in Protocol 1 be (t, ε_{PRG})-secure and the commitment scheme* Com *be (t, ε_{Com})-hiding. There exists an* *efficient simulator $\mathcal{S}$ which outputs a transcript which is $(t, \varepsilon_{PRG} + \varepsilon_{Com})$-indistingui-shable from a real transcript of Protocol 1.*

Theorem 3 (Soundness). *Suppose that there is an efficient prover $\tilde{\mathcal{P}}$ that, on input (w,t), convinces the honest verifier $\mathcal{V}$ on input H, y to accept with probability*

$$\tilde{\epsilon} := \Pr[\langle \tilde{\mathcal{P}}(w,t), \mathcal{V}(w,t)\rangle = 1] > \epsilon$$

for a soundness error ϵ equal to

$$\frac{1}{q'} + \frac{1}{N} - \frac{1}{q'} \cdot \frac{1}{N}.$$

Then, there exists an efficient probabilistic extraction algorithm $\mathcal{E}$ that, given rewindable black-box access to $\tilde{\mathcal{P}}$, produces either a witness x such that $t = \langle w, x\rangle$ and $x \in \{0,1\}^n$, or a commitment collision, by making an average number of calls to $\tilde{\mathcal{P}}$ which is upper bounded by

$$\frac{4}{\tilde{\epsilon} - \epsilon} \cdot \left(1 + \tilde{\epsilon} \cdot \frac{2 \cdot \ln(2)}{\tilde{\epsilon} - \epsilon}\right).$$

Proof Size. To achieve a targeted soundness error $2^{-\lambda}$, we can perform τ parallel executions of the protocol such that $\epsilon^\tau \leq 2^{-\lambda}$. Such parallel repetition does not preserve (general) zero-knowledge and the resulting scheme achieves *honest verifier* zero knowledge. And instead of sending τ values for h and h', the prover can merge them together to send a single h and a single h'. Moreover, instead to sending the $N-1$ seeds and commitment randomness of $(\mathsf{seed}_i, \rho_i)_{i \neq i^*}$ for each execution, we can instead send the sibling path from $(\mathsf{seed}_{i^*}, \rho_{i^*})$ to the tree root, it costs at most $\lambda \cdot \log_2(N)$ bits (we need to reveal $\log_2(N)$ nodes of the tree) by execution. The communication cost (in bits) of the protocol with τ repetitions is

$$\text{SIZE} = 4\lambda + \tau \cdot [n \cdot (\log_2(A-1) + \log_2(q')) + \log_2(q') + \lambda \log_2 N + 2\lambda]$$

while the soundness error and rejection rate scale as

$$\left(\frac{1}{q'} + \frac{1}{N} - \frac{1}{q'} \cdot \frac{1}{N}\right)^\tau \quad \text{and} \quad 1 - \left(1 - \frac{1}{A}\right)^{\tau \cdot n}$$

respectively. Let us stress that the obtained size is independent of the modulus q (and of the size of the integers $\{w_j\}, t$).

4.2 Protocol with Cut-and-Choose Strategy

Protocol description. As described in Sect. 3.4, we can also use a cut-and-choose strategy to prove that the vector $[\![x]\!]$ is binary. It is possible since we can remplace the input $[\![x]\!]$ of the multi-party computation by a sharing $[\![r]\!]$ *independent* of the secret, where r is a mask uniformly sampled in $\{0,1\}^n$. To achieve a targeted soundness error $2^{-\lambda}$, we can perform τ parallel executions of the protocol such that $\epsilon^\tau \leq 2^{-\lambda}$. Like [KKW18], instead of performing τ independent cut-and-choose phases each resulting in trusting one sharing $[\![r]\!]$ among M, we can perform a global cut-and-choose phase resulting in τ trusted sharings $[\![r]\!]$ among a larger M (see [KKW18] for more details). We give the formal description of this zero-knowledge protocol in Protocol 2. The protocol makes use of a pseudo-random generator PRG, a tree-based pseudo-random generator TreePRG (see definition in [KKW18]), four collision-resistant hash functions Hash_i for $i \in \{1,2,3,4\}$ and a commitment scheme (Com, Verif) as defined in the full version [FMRV22]. In this description, the procedure Check returns 0 if the evaluated condition is false (*i.e.* the equality does not hold) and the execution continues otherwise.

Security Proofs. The following theorems state the completeness, zero-knowledge and soundness of Protocol 2. The proofs of Theorems 4, 5 and 6 are provided in appendix of the full version [FMRV22].

Theorem 4 (Completeness). *A prover $\mathcal{P}$ who knows a solution x to the subset sum instance $(w,t) \in \mathbb{Z}_q^n \times \mathbb{Z}_q$ and who follows the steps of Protocol 2 convinces the verifier $\mathcal{V}$ with probability*

$$\left(1 - \frac{1}{A}\right)^{\tau \cdot n}.$$

Theorem 5 (Honest-Verifier Zero-Knowledge). *Let the PRG used in Protocol 2 be (t, ε_{PRG})-secure and the commitment scheme* Com *be (t, ε_{Com})-hiding. There exists an efficient simulator $\mathcal{S}$ which, given random challenges J and L outputs a transcript which is $(t, \tau \cdot \varepsilon_{PRG} + \tau \cdot \varepsilon_{Com})$-indistinguishable from a real transcript of Protocol 2.*

Theorem 6 (Soundness). *Suppose that there is an efficient prover $\tilde{\mathcal{P}}$ that, on input (w,t), convinces the honest verifier $\mathcal{V}$ on input H, y to accept with probability*

$$\tilde{\epsilon} := \Pr[\langle \tilde{\mathcal{P}}(w,t), \mathcal{V}(w,t)\rangle = 1] > \epsilon$$

for a soundness error ϵ equal to

$$\max_{M-\tau \leq k \leq M} \left\{ \frac{\binom{k}{M-\tau}}{\binom{M}{M-\tau} \cdot N^{k-M+\tau}} \right\}.$$

Then, there exists an efficient probabilistic extraction algorithm $\mathcal{E}$ that, given rewindable black-box access to $\tilde{\mathcal{P}}$, produces either a witness x such that $t = \langle w, x\rangle$ and $x \in \{0,1\}^n$, or a commitment collision, by making an average number of calls to $\tilde{\mathcal{P}}$ which is upper bounded by

$$\frac{4}{\tilde{\epsilon} - \epsilon} \cdot \left(1 + \tilde{\epsilon} \cdot \frac{8 \cdot M}{\tilde{\epsilon} - \epsilon}\right).$$

Prover $\mathcal{P}$		Verifier $\mathcal{V}$
$x \in \{0,1\}^n$		
$w \in \mathbb{Z}_q^n, t = \langle w, x \rangle$		w, t
$\mathsf{mseed}^{[0]} \xleftarrow{\$} \{0,1\}^\lambda$		
$(\mathsf{mseed}^{[e]})_{e\in[M]} \leftarrow \mathrm{TreePRG}(\mathsf{mseed}^{[0]})$		
For each $e \in \{1,\dots,M\}$:		
$r^{[e]} \leftarrow \mathrm{PRG}(\mathsf{mseed}^{[e]})$		$\triangleright\ r^{[e]} \in \{0,1\}^n$
$(\mathsf{seed}_i^{[e]}, \rho_i^{[e]})_{i\in[N]} \leftarrow \mathrm{TreePRG}(\mathsf{mseed}^{[e]})$		
For each $i \in \{1,\dots,N\}$:		
$[\![r^{[e]}]\!]_i \leftarrow \mathrm{PRG}(\mathsf{seed}_i^{[e]})$		$\triangleright\ [\![r^{[e]}]\!]_i \in \{0,\dots,A-1\}^n$
$\mathsf{com}_i^{[e]} = \mathrm{Com}(\mathsf{seed}_i^{[e]}; \rho_i^{[e]})$		
$\Delta r^{[e]} = r^{[e]} - \sum_i [\![r^{[e]}]\!]_i$		
$h_e = \mathrm{Hash}_1(\Delta r^{[e]}, \mathsf{com}_1^{[e]}, \dots, \mathsf{com}_n^{[e]})$		
$h = \mathrm{Hash}_2(h_1, \dots, h_M)$		
	$\xrightarrow{\ h\ }$	
		$J \xleftarrow{\$} \{J \subset [M]\ ;\ \lvert J\rvert = \tau\}$
	$\xleftarrow{\ J\ }$	
For each $e \in J$:		
$\tilde{x}^{[e]} = x \oplus r^{[e]}$		$\triangleright\ \oplus$ is the XOR operation ($\tilde{x} \in \{0,1\}^n$)
The parties locally set		
$[\![x^{[e]}]\!] = (1 - \tilde{x}^{[e]}) \circ [\![r^{[e]}]\!]$		
$+\tilde{x}^{[e]} \circ (1 - [\![r^{[e]}]\!])$		
and they set $[\![t^{[e]}]\!] = \langle w, [\![x^{[e]}]\!] \rangle$.		
$h'_e = \mathrm{Hash}_3(\tilde{x}^{[e]}, [\![t^{[e]}]\!])$		
$h' = \mathrm{Hash}_4((h'_e)_{e\in J})$		
	$\xrightarrow{\ h',\ (\mathsf{mseed}^{[e]})_{e\in[M]\setminus J}\ }$	
		$L = \{\ell_e\}_{e\in J} \xleftarrow{\$} \{1,\dots,N\}^\tau$
	$\xleftarrow{\ L\ }$	
If there exists $(e,j) \in J \times [n]$ such that:		
- either $[\![r_j^{[e]}]\!]_{\ell_e} = 0$ with $r_j^{[e]} = 1$		
- or $[\![r_j^{[e]}]\!]_{\ell_e} = A-1$ with $r_j^{[e]} = 0$,		
then abort.		
$y = r^{[e]} - [\![r^{[e]}]\!]_{\ell_e}$		
	$\xrightarrow{\ \begin{pmatrix} (\mathsf{seed}_i^{[e]}, \rho_i^{[e]})_{i\neq\ell_e} \\ y, \tilde{x}^{[e]},\ \mathsf{com}_{\ell_e}^{[e]} \end{pmatrix}_{e\in J}\ }$	
		For each $e \notin J$:
		Compute h_e using $\mathsf{mseed}^{[e]}$
		For each $e \in J$:
		For all $i \neq \ell_e$
		$\mathsf{com}_i^{[e]} = \mathrm{Com}(\mathsf{seed}_i^{[e]}; \rho_i^{[e]})$
		Rerun the party i
		as the prover to get $[\![t^{[e]}]\!]_i$
		$\Delta r^{[e]} = y - \sum_{i\neq\ell_e} [\![r^{[e]}]\!]$
		$h_e = \mathrm{Hash}_1(\Delta r^{[e]}, \mathsf{com}_1^{[e]}, \dots, \mathsf{com}_n^{[e]})$
		From $\Delta r^{[e]}$, deduce $\Delta t^{[e]}$.
		$[\![t^{[e]}]\!] = t - \Delta t^{[e]} - \sum_{i\neq\ell_e} [\![t^{[e]}]\!]_i$
		$h'_e = \mathrm{Hash}_3(\tilde{x}^{[e]}, [\![t^{[e]}]\!])$
		Check $h = \mathrm{Hash}_2(h_1, \dots, h_M)$
		Check $h' = \mathrm{Hash}_4((h'_e)_{e\in J})$
		Return 1

Protocol 2: Zero-knowledge argument for Subset Sum Problem via MPC-in-the-head with rejection, using cut-and-choose strategy to prove binarity.

Proof Size. Let us recall that the couples $(\mathsf{seed}_i, \rho_i)$ are sampled using a tree PRG, sending $(\mathsf{seed}_i^{[e]}, \rho_i^{[e]})_{i \neq \ell_e}$ costs at most $\lambda \cdot \log_2(N)$ bits by iteration. The communication cost (in bits) of the protocol is then

$$\textsc{Size} = 4\lambda + \lambda \cdot \tau \cdot \log_2 \frac{M}{\tau} + \tau \cdot [n \cdot \log_2(A-1) + n + \lambda \log_2 N + 2\lambda].$$

Here again, the obtained size is independent of the modulus q (and of the size of the integers $\{w_j\}, t$).

4.3 Decreasing the Rejection Rate

The two above protocols have a rejection rate around $\tau n/A$ which implies that we must take $A = \Theta(\tau n)$ to obtain a constant (small) rejection rate. In practice, this results in a significant increase in the communication cost. Let us for instance consider Protocol 1 with $(\tau, N, A) = (16, 280, 2^{13})$. For this setting, the proof size is about 15.6 KB for a rejection rate of 0.394. If we increased A to get a rejection rate below 0.003, we should take $A = 2^{21}$ and the proof size would be 23.6 KB.

A better strategy consists in allowing the prover to abort a few of the τ iterations. Let us assume that the verifier accepts the proof if the prover can answer to $\tau - \eta$ challenges among the τ iterations. This slightly increases the soundness error, but it can also significantly decrease the global rejection rate. If we denote p_{rej} the probability that an iteration aborts, then the global rejection rate of this strategy is given by

$$1 - \sum_{i=0}^{\eta} \binom{\tau}{i} \cdot (1 - p_{\text{rej}})^{\tau - i} \cdot p_{\text{rej}}^{i}. \tag{3}$$

At the same time, the soundness error for Protocol 1 becomes

$$\sum_{i=0}^{\eta} \binom{\tau}{i} \cdot (1-\epsilon)^{i} \cdot \epsilon^{\tau - i}$$

where $\epsilon = \frac{1}{N} + \frac{1}{q'} - \frac{1}{q'} \cdot \frac{1}{N}$ is the soundness error of a single iteration. Using this strategy with $\tau = 20$ and $\eta = 3$, the proof size is of 16.7 KB for a rejection rate of 0.003 (instead of 23.6 KB with the naive strategy).

The same strategy also applies to Protocol 2. The rejection rate is also given by Eq. (3) while the soundness error becomes

$$\max_{M-\tau \leq k \leq M} \left\{ \frac{\binom{k}{M-\tau}}{\binom{M}{M-\tau}} \cdot \sum_{i=0}^{\eta} \left[\binom{k-M+\tau}{i} \left(1 - \frac{1}{N}\right)^{i} \left(\frac{1}{N}\right)^{k-M+\tau-i} \right] \right\}.$$

In any case, the prover always answers to at most $\tau - \eta$ challenges of the verifier (even if the prover aborts less than η among the τ iterations) so that the communication cost is roughly that of $\tau - \eta$ iterations. Additionally, for each unanswered challenge, the prover must further send two hash digests to enable the verifier to recompute and check h and h'. Thus the new proof size (in bits) for Protocol 1 is

$$\begin{aligned} \text{SIZE}_\eta &= 4\lambda + \eta \cdot 4\lambda \\ &\quad + (\tau - \eta) \cdot [n \cdot (\log_2(A-1) + \log_2(q')) + \log_2(q') + \lambda \log_2 N + 2\lambda], \end{aligned}$$

while the new proof size (in bits) for Protocol 2 is

$$\begin{aligned} \text{SIZE}_\eta = 4\lambda + \eta \cdot 4\lambda + \lambda{\cdot}\tau \cdot \log_2 \frac{M}{\tau} \\ + (\tau - \eta) \cdot [n \cdot \log_2(A-1) + n + \lambda \log_2 N + 2\lambda]. \end{aligned}$$

We note that in practice, given a target security level and a target rejection probability, one needs to use a slightly increased τ (or N) to compensate for the loss in terms of soundness. While this shall slightly increase the proof size, the above approach (with $\eta > 0$) still provides better trade-offs than the original approach ($\eta = 0$).

5 Instantiations and Performances

5.1 Subset Sum Instances

We recall in this section known techniques to solve the modular subset sum problem (SSP) defined by (1). It is well-known that the hardness of an SSP instance depends greatly on its *density* defined as $d = n/\log_2 q$. If the SSP instance is too sparse (e.g. $d < 1/n$) or too dense (e.g. $d > n/\log^2 n$) then the problem can be solved in polynomial time (see e.g. [CJL+92] and references therein). We shall therefore only consider SSP instances with density $d \simeq 1$ (i.e. $q \simeq 2^n$) which are arguably the hardest ones [IN96].

In this case, simple algorithms exist based on brute force enumeration at $O(2^n)$ time and constant space, or time-space tradeoff [HS74] with $O(2^{n/2})$ time and space complexities. The first non-trivial algorithm was published by Schroeppel and Shamir [SS81] with time complexity $O(2^{n/2})$ and space complexity $O(2^{n/4})$. Later, faster algorithms were proposed with similar time and space complexities, e.g. $\tilde{O}(2^{0.337n})$ by Howgrave-Graham and Joux [HJ10] and $\tilde{O}(2^{0.283n})$ by Bonnetain, Bricout, Schrottenloher and Shen [BBSS20]. The latter algorithms neglect the cost to access an exponential memory but even with this optimistic assumption, for $n = 256$, all known algorithms require at least a time complexity lower-bounded by 2^{128} operations or memory of size at least 2^{72} bits. There also exists a vast literature on quantum algorithms for solving the SSP (see [BBSS20] and references therein). The best (heuristic) quantum complexity from [BBSS20] has time complexity $\tilde{O}(2^{0.216n})$ and thus requires about 2^{64} quantum operations and quantum memory for $n = 256$. In the following, we, therefore, consider the efficiency of our protocols for $n = 256$.

5.2 Zero Knowledge Protocols

Let us consider the subset sum problem with $n = 256$. We propose in Table 1 several sets of parameters for our two protocols which target a security of 128 bits. We provide two kinds of instantiations to give the reader an idea of the obtained performance while changing the number of parties. The first ones correspond to instantiations with fast computation. The second ones correspond to instantiations that achieve smaller communication costs but slower computation. For each setting, we suggest two parameter sets: one achieving a rejection rate around 0.4 and the other one achieving a rejection rate between 0.001 and 0.004.

Table 1. Comparison of state-of-the-art zero-knowledge protocols for proving the knowledge of an SSP instance (with $n = 256$ and $q \approx 2^{256}$).

Protocol	Parameters					Proof size	Rej. rate	Soundness err.
	τ	η	N	A	M			
Shamir [Sha86]	219	–	–	–	–	1186 KB	–	128 bits
[LNSW13]	219	–	–	–	–	2350 KB	–	128 bits
Beullens [Beu20]	14	–	1024	–	4040	122 KB	–	128 bits
Protocol 1 (batching)	26	0	32	2^{14}	–	25.7 KB	0.334	130 bits
Protocol 1 (batching)	31	3	32	2^{14}	–	27.9 KB	0.001	128 bits
Protocol 2 (C&C)	27	0	32	2^{14}	462	17.4 KB	0.344	128 bits
Protocol 2 (C&C)	33	3	32	2^{14}	470	19.6 KB	0.002	128 bits
Protocol 1 (batching)	17	0	256	2^{13}	–	16.6 KB	0.412	135 bits
Protocol 1 (batching)	21	3	256	2^{13}	–	17.7 KB	0.004	133 bits
Protocol 2 (C&C)	19	0	256	2^{13}	954	13.0 KB	0.448	128 bits
Protocol 2 (C&C)	24	3	256	2^{14}	952	15.4 KB	0.001	128 bits

We provide in Table 1 the performance of the other zero-knowledge protocols proving the knowledge of an SSP solution. The only other protocol designed for the subset sum problem is Shamir's one [Sha86]. We can also compare these protocols with [LNSW13] which is an adaptation of Stern's protocol to the ISIS (inhomogeneous short integer solution) problem. The remaining articles in the literature about proofs for the ISIS problem are restricted to the case where the modulus q is prime. We add Beullens' protocol [Beu20] for ISIS with prime q to the comparison.

We provide in the full version [FMRV22] the performances of the obtained signatures when applying the Fiat-Shamir transform [FS87] to our protocols.

5.3 Comparison with Generic Techniques

In this section, we compare our scheme with efficient generic techniques to prove the knowledge of an SSP solution. Among those techniques, we consider SNARKs (e.g. [Gro16]), "compressed" proof systems such as *Bulletproofs* [BBB+18] and STARKs (e.g. [BBHR18]). For the sake of accuracy, we split the notation for the security level of the subset sum instance, denoted κ, and of the zero-knowledge argument, denoted λ. Adapting the analysis of Sect. 3.5 to this setting, we get a communication cost of $\Theta(\lambda^2 + \lambda \cdot \kappa)$ for our protocols.

The asymptotic size of [Gro16] arguments is roughly[1] $\Omega(\lambda^3)$ which is asymptotically larger than ours, but for $\kappa = \lambda = 128$, these arguments will be shorter than ours (within the range of 700–800 bytes). Using *Bulletproofs* [BBB+18], one can obtain an asymptotic communication cost of $\Omega(\log(\kappa)(\lambda+\kappa))$, and about 600 bytes for $\kappa = \lambda = 128$. Although SNARKs and "compressed" proof systems give shorter arguments than ours for $\kappa = \lambda = 128$, they both require stronger and non post-quantum computational assumptions. In particular, [Gro16] requires a trusted setup and a non-falsifiable assumption, while Bulletproofs rely on the algebraic group model in their non-interactive version [GOP+21]. In comparison, the security of our arguments only relies on weak post-quantum assumptions (PRG, collision-resistant hash functions).

Regarding STARKs [BBHR18], their security assumptions are similar to ours. When applying STARKs to the subset sum problem, one gets arguments of size $\Omega(\lambda^2 \cdot \log^2 \kappa)$, which is larger than ours.[2]

6 Further Applications

As illustrated on the subset sum problem, our technique of sharing over the integers with rejection is –more generally– instrumental to a context of a secret vector $s \in \mathbb{Z}_q^n$ with small coefficients. Since the communication cost of our protocols is independent of the size q of the ring $\mathbb{Z}_q$, the gain in communication is higher when the modulus q is high. But it does not need to have a modulus as high as in the subset sum problem to be interesting. In the three subsections, we present the performance of our schemes with the sharing over the integers on three other applications with moderate-size modulus:

- to prove the knowledge of a solution of an ISIS problem instance,
- to prove the knowledge of a secret key and plaintext(s) matching a (set of) FHE ciphertext(s),
- to construct an efficient digital signature based on Boneh-Halevi-Howgrave-Graham pseudo-random function.

Another advantage of the sharing on the integers is that we can perform any operation on it with any modulus. We used this property in one of our protocols to check multiplication triples in a smaller field. This property can be also useful when we want to prove that the same secret vector verifies many relations using distinct modulus.

[1] This is due to sub-exponential attacks on the discrete logarithm in the target group which also impacts the size of elements of the second group of the bilinear structure.

[2] The λ^2 factor is obtained by λ for the hash digest size times λ for the number of evaluation points in the FRI protocol (which scales with the soundness error). The $\log^2 \kappa$ factor comes from the size κ of the program verifying the SSP instance.

6.1 Short Integer Solution Problem

Given a matrix $A \in \mathbb{Z}^{m \times n}$ and a vector $u \in \mathbb{Z}_m$, the inhomogenous short integer solution (ISIS) problem consists in finding a vector $s \in \mathbb{Z}^n$ with small coefficients such that

$$As = u \bmod q.$$

The Ling-Nguyen-Stehlé-Wang protocol [LNSW13], which is an adaptation of Stern's protocol, has been for a long time the only zero-knowledge exact protocol which proves the knowledge of a solution of an ISIS instance. Other protocols existed but they were only relaxed proofs, *i.e.* they prove the knowledge of an s' and c satisfying $As' = cu \bmod q$. These protocols can be useful in some contexts, but they are not suited to prove the exact statement.

Recently, new exact proofs [BLS19,ENS20,LNS21,BN20,Beu20] have been published. However, all these new protocols require an assumption on the modulus q to work: some of them only require that q is a prime number when the others require that q is an NTT-friendly prime number. In the state of the art, the only protocol which works for any q (even when q is not a prime) is [LNSW13].

We can adapt our protocols of Sect. 4 to the case of the ISIS problem. The linear constraint "$As = u$" is free in communication as it was the case for "$t = \langle w, x \rangle$" for the subset sum problem (see Sect. 3.2). The hard part is to prove that the secret s satisfies $\|s\|_\infty \leq \beta$ for some bound β. To proceed, we decompose s as $k := \lceil \log_2(2\beta + 1) \rceil$ vectors $(s_0, \ldots, s_{k-1})$ of $\{0,1\}^n$ such that

$$s = \sum_{i=0}^{k-2} 2^i s_i + (2\beta - 2^{k-1} + 1)s_{k-1} - \beta. \quad (4)$$

If all vectors s_i belong to $\{0,1\}$, the above relation gives that $\|s\|_\infty \leq \beta$. So we just need to give the sharing $\{[\![s_i]\!]\}_{i \in \{0,\ldots,k-1\}}$ to the MPC protocol instead of $[\![s]\!]$. The latter can then check that $\{[\![s_i]\!]\}_{i \in \{0,\ldots,k-1\}}$ are binary vectors and that $A[\![s]\!]$ corresponds to u modulo q where $[\![s]\!]$ is recovered by linearity of Eq. (4). The proof sizes of the resulting protocols are given by the formulae as before, we just need to consider that the length of the secret is $n \cdot k$ (instead of n).

We compare our protocols with the state of the art in Table 2 on the two following ISIS problems:

1. $\|s\|_\infty \leq 1$, $m = 1024$, $n = 2048$, $q \approx 2^{32}$
2. Binary s, $m = 512$, $n = 4096$, $q \approx 2^{61}$

For both instances, we have $k \cdot n = 4096$. For our protocols, we choose the following parameters:

- Protocol 1 (batch product verification):

$$A = 2^{16}, \ N = 128, \ q' \approx A, \ \tau = 23, \ \eta = 3.$$

– Protocol 2 (cut-and-choose strategy):

$$A = 2^{16},\ N = 256,\ q' \approx A,\ M = 952,\ \tau = 24,\ \eta = 3.$$

We can remark that our protocols have the same communication cost for both instances. It comes from the fact that their proof size is independent of the modulus q. Even when q is prime (and larger than 2^{32}), our Protocol 2 (with the cut-and-choose phase) has smaller communication cost than Beullens' protocol and this while taking less aggressive parameters towards size against speed (the parameters used in [Beu20] are $(\tau, M, N) = (14, 4040, 2^{10})$). We also observe that our protocols achieve proof sizes which are more than 10 times smaller than those of [LNSW13], the only previous protocol supporting any modulus q.

Table 2. Comparison with the existing exact protocols which prove the knowledge of the solution of a ISIS instance.

Protocol	Year	Any q	Instance 1		Instance 2	
			Proof size	Rej. rate	Proof size	Rej. rate
[LNSW13]	2013	✓	3600 KB	–	8988 KB	–
[BN20]	2020	q prime	–	–	4077 KB	–
[Beu20]	2020	q prime	233 KB	–	444 KB	–
Our Protocol 1	2022	✓	291 KB	0.04	291 KB	0.04
Our Protocol 2	2022	✓	184 KB	0.05	184 KB	0.05
[BLS19]	2019	q prime + NTT	384 KB	0.92		
[ENS20]	2020	q prime + NTT	47 KB	0.95		
[LNS21]	2021	q prime + NTT	33.3 KB	0.85		
Aurora [BCR+19]	2019	q prime + NTT	71 KB	–		
Ligero [AHIV17]	2017	q prime + NTT	157 KB	–		

6.2 Fully Homomorphic Encryption

Our zero-knowledge protocols also find application to fully homomorphic encryption (FHE). We can indeed adapt our protocols to prove the knowledge of a secret key matching a (set of) FHE-encrypted plaintext(s). We elaborate on this application hereafter for the particular case of TFHE (Torus FHE) [CGGI20] which is currently one of the FHE schemes with the best performances in practice.

For some $q \in \mathbb{N}$, let $\mathbb{T}_q = q^{-1}\mathbb{Z}/\mathbb{Z}$ be the discretized torus with q elements, i.e. the submodule of the real torus with representative $\{i/q\ ;\ i \in \mathbb{Z}_q\}$ [Joy21]. In practice, q is often chosen to be 2^{32} or 2^{64} in order to match the word-size and arithmetic operations of common CPUs. For this reason, we shall consider that q is a power of 2 in the following (although the described application can be easily generalized to any q). TFHE relies on so called TLWE (Torus Learning With Error) encryption. Let $p \mid q$ and $\delta = q/p$. The plaintext space is defined as $\mathbb{Z}_p$ while the key space is defined as $\{0,1\}^n \subset \mathbb{Z}^n$. Let $s = (s_1, \ldots, s_n) \in \{0,1\}^n$

be a secret key. The TLWE encryption of a plaintext $\mu \in \mathbb{Z}_p$ under the secret key s and with *error* $e \in \mathbb{Z}$ is defined as

$$c = (a_1, \ldots, a_n, b) \in \mathbb{T}_q^{n+1} \quad \text{where} \quad \begin{cases} \mu^* = \frac{\delta\mu + e \bmod q}{q} \in \mathbb{T}_q \\ b = \sum_{j=1}^{n} s_j \cdot a_j + \mu^* \end{cases}$$

The a_i's are random elements of $\mathbb{T}_q$ which are sampled at encryption time or which arise from the homomorphic operations between other ciphertexts. The value $e \in \mathbb{Z}$ is the error which must satisfies $|e| < \delta/2$ to ensure the correctness of the decryption.

Proving the knowledge of a key s and plaintext μ for which $c = (a_1, \ldots, a_n, b)$ is a correct TLWE encryption of μ under s can be achieved by proving the knowledge of a binary vector

$$x = (s_1, \ldots, s_n) \mid (\mu_1, \ldots, \mu_{\ell_p}) \mid (e_1, \ldots, e_{\ell_e})$$

where $\ell_p = \log_2 p$ and ℓ_e is such that $e \in \{-2^{\ell_e - 1}, \ldots, 2^{\ell_e - 1} - 1\}$, and which satisfies

$$\sum_{i=1}^{n} \bar{a}_i s_i + \sum_{i=1}^{\ell_p} (2^{i-1}\delta)\mu_i + \sum_{i=1}^{\ell_e} (2^{i-1}) e_i = \bar{b} + 2^{\ell_e - 1} \pmod{q}$$

where $\bar{a}_i \in \mathbb{Z}$ (resp. $\bar{b} \in \mathbb{Z}$) is the integer such that $a_i = \bar{a}_i/q \in \mathbb{T}_q$ (resp. $b = \bar{b}/q \in \mathbb{T}_q$) and where the error is $e := -2^{\ell_e - 1} + \sum_{i=1}^{\ell_e} (2^{i-1}) e_i$. The application of our protocols to this context is immediate. We note that the secret binary vector is of size $n' = n + \ell_p + \ell_e$ when the underlying plaintext must remain secret while it is of size $n' = n + \ell_e$ if the plaintext is public. In the latter case, the value of the sum is $t = \bar{b} + 2^{\ell_e - 1} - \mu$. We can also use our protocols to prove the knowledge of a secret key and a set of plaintexts matching a set of ciphertexts. For m ciphertexts, we obtain m linear relations with a binary vector of size $n' = n + m \cdot (\ell_p + \ell_e)$ (or $n' = n + m \cdot \ell_e$ in the public plaintext setting).

Remark 2. Proving the knowledge of a single key-plaintext pair matching a given ciphertext might not be relevant on its own. Indeed, for the typical parameters given above, the obtained SSP instance might not be hard (*i.e.* finding *a* solution is not hard while finding the original key-plaintext pair is still hard). However, such proof is still useful whenever proving additional properties involving the underlying secret key and/or plaintext. In such contexts, finding a solution to the SSP instance which does not match the original key-plaintext pair is useless.

According to [Joy21], typical parameters for a TLWE encryption are $q = 2^{32}$ or $q = 2^{64}$ and $n = 630$. Depending on the exact message space and error space, we have $n' \in (n, n + \log_2 q]$. Table 3 gives the obtained communication cost for proving the knowledge of the key (and plaintexts) corresponding to 1, 64 and 1024 TLWE ciphertexts using our protocols (assuming $q = 2^{64}$ and $\ell_e + \ell_p = 64$). For the sake of comparison, we also give the communication obtained with Shamir's protocol [Sha86]. We note that the latter and the LNSW protocol [LNSW13] are the only previous protocols which can work with such values of q and the LNSW protocol is always heavier than Shamir's in this context. We observe that our protocols always gain more than a factor 10 (for Protocol 1) and 20 (for Protocol 2) for the obtained communication cost compared to Shamir's protocol.

Table 3. Comparison of ZK protocols for TFHE decryption.

Protocol	Parameters					Proof size	Rej. rate	Soundness err.
	τ	η	N	A	M			
1 ciphertext								
Shamir [Sha86]	219	–	–	–	–	845 KB	–	128 bits
Protocol 1 (batching)	19	2	256	2^{15}	–	46.1 KB	0.007	128 bits
Protocol 2 (C&C)	24	3	256	2^{15}	952	34.0 KB	0.002	128 bits
64 ciphertexts								
Shamir [Sha86]	219	–	–	–	–	8.48 MB	–	128 bits
Protocol 1 (batching)	19	2	256	2^{18}	–	356 KB	0.005	129 bits
Protocol 2 (C&C)	24	3	256	2^{18}	952	236 KB	0.001	128 bits
1024 ciphertexts								
Shamir [Sha86]	219	–	–	–	–	77.9 MB	–	128 bits
Protocol 1 (batching)	19	2	256	2^{22}	–	5.90 MB	0.003	129 bits
Protocol 2 (C&C)	24	3	256	2^{21}	952	3.65 MB	0.006	128 bits

6.3 Digital Signatures from Boneh-Halevi-Howgrave-Graham PRF

As another application, we present a short and efficient candidate post-quantum signature scheme based on an elegant pseudo-random function (PRF) proposed by Boneh, Halevi, and Howgrave-Graham in 2001 [BHH01].

Let p be a public m-bit prime number that defines the PRF message space as $\mathbb{Z}_p$. A secret key for the PRF is an element $x \in \mathbb{Z}_p$ picked uniformly at random. We denote $\text{MSB}_\delta(t)$ the δm most significant bits of an m-bit element $t \in \mathbb{Z}_p$.[3] The value of the PRF on the message $m \in \mathbb{Z}_p$ for the secret-key $x \in \mathbb{Z}_p$ is $F_x(m) = \text{MSB}_\delta((x+m)^{-1} \bmod p)$.

Our signature scheme follows the blueprint of most signatures based on the MPCitH paradigm since the proposal of Picnic [CDG+17]: the public key is made of the outputs of Boneh *et al.*'s PRF on t public messages in $\{1,\ldots,t\}$, i.e. the δm-bit elements $y_1,\ldots,y_t$ such that

$$y_i := \text{MSB}_\delta((x+i)^{-1} \bmod p) \text{ for } i \in \{1,\ldots,t\}$$

[3] We assume hereafter that $\delta m \in \mathbb{Z}$. Otherwise, one should take the nearest integer $\lfloor \delta m \rceil$ instead.

and the signature consists of a non-interactive proof of knowledge of $x, z_1, \ldots, z_t$ (parametrized by the signed message using the Fiat-Shamir heuristic) such that

$$(x+1)(2^{(1-\delta)m}y_1 + z_1) \equiv \cdots \equiv (x+t)(2^{(1-\delta)m}y_t + z_t) \equiv 1 \bmod p \quad (5)$$

$$\text{and} \qquad z_1, \ldots, z_t \in \{0, \ldots, 2^{(1-\delta)m} - 1\} \quad (6)$$

where $z_1, \ldots, z_t$ are the $(1-\delta)m$ least significant bits of $(x+1)^{-1} \bmod p, \ldots, (x+t)^{-1} \bmod p$. Note that the condition (6) on the size of the z_i's is fundamental since otherwise, it is easy for an attacker to find a witness.

In our applications, the values of t and δ are chosen to prevent all known classical attacks and target a 128-bit security level.

Let's fix t, the number of outputs of the PRF. Then, to ensure that the equations (5) and (6) have a unique witness, we add the constraint $\delta \geq 1/t$ so that the t PRF outputs define (heuristically) the secret x uniquely. To avoid brute-force attacks from a single output of the PRF, the hidden most significant bits of one output should be at least 128 bits, thus $\log p \geq \frac{128}{1-\delta}$. Otherwise, an attacker could reconstruct a possible key for the PRF and then evaluate the other outputs with this candidate to test it.

It is possible to apply generically the MPCitH paradigm to prove (5) and (6), but proving (6) seems inefficient (e.g. by using a binary decomposition and proving consistency). Instead, we can use our secret sharing over the integers for proving the knowledge of small z_i's by sharing them as a sum of "small" integers which directly proves that the z_i's are indeed small.

Proving Eq. (5). Instead of proving the t products of (5) separately, the prover can batch them into a linear combination where coefficients $\gamma_1, \ldots, \gamma_t$ are provided by the verifier, *i.e.* the prover proves the equation

$$\sum_{i=1}^{t} \gamma_i \cdot \Big((x+i)(2^{(1-\delta)m}y_i + z_i) - 1 \Big) = 0 \bmod p,$$

or equivalently,

$$x \cdot \left(\sum_{i=1}^{t} \gamma_i z_i \right) = -\sum_{i=1}^{t} \gamma_i \left(x \cdot 2^{(1-\delta)m}y_i + i \cdot 2^{(1-\delta)m}y_i + i \cdot z_i - 1 \right) \bmod p. \quad (7)$$

If one of the products is not equal to 1 in (5), then (7) is satisfied only with a probability of $\frac{1}{p}$. And to prove (7), one can use the protocol of [BN20] with a single multiplication on $\mathbb{Z}_p$ (for the left-hand side of (7), the right-hand side being a linear combination of the witness). The resulting MPC protocol produces false positives with probability $1/p + (1-1/p) \cdot 1/p := 2/p + 1/p^2$, and thus the obtained zero-knowledge argument has a soundness error of

$$\epsilon = \frac{1}{N} + \left(1 - \frac{1}{N}\right)\left(\frac{2}{p} + \frac{1}{p^2}\right).$$

Proving Eq. (6). It remains to prove that z_i is in $\{0, \dots, B-1\}$ with $B = 2^{(1-\delta)m}$ in (6) for $i \in \{1, \dots, t\}$. To share z_i, we use our secret sharing over the integers of Sect. 3.2. Since the z_i are not binary but in a larger range, we need to adapt the rejection rules. Following exactly the same reasoning as in Sect. 3.2, we get that the prover must abort if there exists an index $j \in [t]$ for which $z_j - [\![z_j]\!]_{i^*} \geq 1$ or $z_j - [\![z_j]\!]_{i^*} \leq -A + B - 1$. The resulting rejection rate is given by

$$p_{\text{rej}} = 1 - \left(1 - \frac{B-1}{A}\right)^{t \cdot \tau} \approx t \cdot \tau \cdot \frac{B-1}{A}.$$

Even without proving anything on the range of z_j, the verifier knows that

$$\forall j \in [t], -A + B \leq z_j \leq A - 1$$

thanks to (2) (generalized). In practice, we settle this range, implying that there is a slack between the underlying hard problem and the proven statement. A malicious prover can use bigger values for z_i, and this is equivalent to ignoring some bits of y_i. A malicious prover can ignore up to $\log_2 \frac{A}{B} \approx \log_2 \frac{t \cdot \tau}{p_{\text{rej}}}$ bits for each PRF output, and thus it reduces the security of $t \cdot \log_2 \frac{t \cdot \tau}{p_{\text{rej}}}$ bits. A way to fix this security loss without increasing the size of p (and of the key) is to reveal a few more PRF outputs to guarantee that the key is still heuristically unique. In theory, this decreases the security but for state-of-the-art algorithms, this stays beyond the capacity of the best-known algorithms for small t. In fact, we need to reveal $\tilde{t} \geq t$ outputs of the PRF such that

$$\tilde{t} \cdot \delta \cdot m - \tilde{t} \cdot \log\left(\frac{\tilde{t} \cdot \tau}{p_{\text{rej}}}\right) > m.$$

In other words, since $\delta \geq \frac{1}{t}$, we adapt this constraint as

$$\delta \geq \frac{1}{\tilde{t}} + \frac{1}{m} \log_2\left(\frac{\tilde{t} \cdot \tau}{p_{\text{rej}}}\right).$$

This leads to a scheme (formally described in the full version [FMRV22]) with the communication cost (in bits):

$$4\lambda + \tau \cdot (\log_2 p + \tilde{t} \cdot \log_2 A + \log_2 p + \log_2 p + \lambda \cdot \log_2 N + 2\lambda),$$

with soundness error (if interactive)

$$\epsilon = \frac{1}{N} + \left(1 - \frac{1}{N}\right)\left(\frac{2}{p} + \frac{1}{p^2}\right),$$

and with forgery security (if non-interactive)

$$\text{cost}_{\text{forge}} = \min_{\tau_1, \tau_2 : \tau_1 + \tau_2 = \tau} \left\{ \frac{1}{\sum_{i=\tau_1}^{\tau} \binom{\tau}{i} p'^i (1-p')^{\tau-i}} + N^{\tau_2} \right\},$$

with $p' := 2/p + 1/p^2$.

We propose in Table 4 some parameters which target 128-bit security (based on the hardness of the so-called *modular inverse hidden number problem*) according to the current cryptanalysis state-of-the-art for Boneh *et al.*'s PRF. We can remark that the achieved signature sizes are competitive with Rainier scheme [DKR+21] (which can produce signatures that are around 5 KB in size too) and outperform all the other signatures based on MPC-in-the-Head paradigm (Picnic4 [KZ22], PorcRoast [Bd20], SDitH [FJR22], ...).

Table 4. Parameter sets and achieved performances of the signature based on Boneh *et al.*'s PRF, for a 128-bit security.

Parameters							Size	p_{rej}
$p \approx 2^m$	$\tilde{t}$	δ	B	A	N	τ		
$\approx 2^{229}$	3	88/229	2^{141}	2^{141+12}	256	16	4 916 B	0.012
$\approx 2^{186}$	4	58/186	2^{128}	2^{128+12}	256	16	4 860 B	0.016
$\approx 2^{175}$	5	47/175	2^{128}	2^{128+12}	256	16	5 074 B	0.019

Regarding the cryptanalysis, the security of Boneh *et al.*'s PRF has been extensively analyzed since 20 years [BHH01,LSSW12,BVZ12,XSH+19] and relies strongly on δ and the number of known PRF outputs. In [XSH+19], Xu, Sarkar, Hu, Wang, and Pan presented a heuristic attack based on Coppersmith's method that breaks Boneh *et al.*'s PRF (for a sufficiently large modulus p) if the number of outputs of the PRF is large enough (depending on δ). However, this polynomial-time attack is not practical and hides *galactic* constant factors. For instance, for $\delta = 1/3$, this attack requires 45 outputs of the PRF and uses a lattice of dimension 209899 in Coppersmith's method.

The best known lattice-based attacks with a small number of PRF outputs are described in [BHH01,BVZ12] and require larger δ's than the ones we use. In order to mount them, an adversary has thus to perform an exhaustive search on the missing bits on several outputs. A precise security analysis is given in the full version of the paper [FMRV22]. For all parameters provided in Table 4 an exhaustive search on (at least) 128 bits has to be performed by the adversary in order to run the attacks from [BHH01,BVZ12].

To the best of our knowledge, the quantum security of Boneh *et al.*'s PRF has not been analyzed yet. Our signature protocol is thus a post-quantum candidate and requires further analysis of its security by quantum algorithm specialists.

Acknowledgements. The authors are supported in part by the French ANR SANGRIA project (ANR-21-CE39-0006). The authors would like to thank Charles Bouillaguet for suggesting investigation of zero-knowledge proofs for the subset sum problem.

References

[AHIV17] Ames, S., Hazay, C., Ishai, Y., Venkitasubramaniam, M.: Ligero: Lightweight sublinear arguments without a trusted setup. In: Thuraisingham, B.M., Evans, D., Malkin, T., Xu, D. (eds.) ACM CCS 2017, pp. 2087–2104. ACM Press (2017)

[BBB+18] Bünz, B., Bootle, J., Boneh, D., Poelstra, A., Wuille, P., Maxwell, G.: BulletProofs: short proofs for confidential transactions and more. In: 2018 IEEE Symposium on Security and Privacy, pp. 315–334. IEEE Computer Society Press (2018)

[BBHR18] Ben-Sasson, E., Bentov, I., Horesh, Y., Riabzev, M.: Scalable, transparent, and post-quantum secure computational integrity. Cryptology ePrint Archive, Report 2018/046 (2018)

[BBSS20] Bonnetain, X., Bricout, R., Schrottenloher, A., Shen, Y.: Improved classical and quantum algorithms for subset-sum. In: Moriai, S., Wang, H. (eds.) ASIACRYPT 2020, Part II. LNCS, vol. 12492, pp. 633–666. Springer, Cham (2020). https://doi.org/10.1007/978-3-030-64834-3_22

[BCR+19] Ben-Sasson, E., Chiesa, A., Riabzev, M., Spooner, N., Virza, M., Ward, N.P.: Aurora: transparent succinct arguments for R1CS. In: Ishai, Y., Rijmen, V. (eds.) EUROCRYPT 2019, Part I. LNCS, vol. 11476, pp. 103–128. Springer, Cham (2019). https://doi.org/10.1007/978-3-030-17653-2_4

[BD10] Bendlin, R., Damgård, I.: Threshold decryption and zero-knowledge proofs for lattice-based cryptosystems. In: Micciancio, D. (ed.) TCC 2010. LNCS, vol. 5978, pp. 201–218. Springer, Heidelberg (2010). https://doi.org/10.1007/978-3-642-11799-2_13

[Bd20] Beullens, W., Delpech de Saint Guilhem, C.: LegRoast: efficient post-quantum signatures from the Legendre PRF. In: Ding, J., Tillich, J.-P. (eds.) PQCrypto 2020. LNCS, vol. 12100, pp. 130–150. Springer, Cham (2020). https://doi.org/10.1007/978-3-030-44223-1_8

[BDLN16] Baum, C., Damgård, I., Larsen, K.G., Nielsen, M.: How to prove knowledge of small secrets. In: Robshaw, M., Katz, J. (eds.) CRYPTO 2016, Part III. LNCS, vol. 9816, pp. 478–498. Springer, Heidelberg (2016). https://doi.org/10.1007/978-3-662-53015-3_17

[Beu20] Beullens, W.: Sigma protocols for MQ, PKP and SIS, and fishy signature schemes. In: Canteaut, A., Ishai, Y. (eds.) EUROCRYPT 2020, Part III. LNCS, vol. 12107, pp. 183–211. Springer, Cham (2020). https://doi.org/10.1007/978-3-030-45727-3_7

[BGKW90] Ben-Or, M., Goldwasser, S., Kilian, J., Wigderson, A.: Efficient identification schemes using two prover interactive proofs. In: Brassard, G. (ed.) CRYPTO 1989. LNCS, vol. 435, pp. 498–506. Springer, New York (1990). https://doi.org/10.1007/0-387-34805-0_44

[BHH01] Boneh, D., Halevi, S., Howgrave-Graham, N.: The modular inversion hidden number problem. In: Boyd, C. (ed.) ASIACRYPT 2001. LNCS, vol. 2248, pp. 36–51. Springer, Heidelberg (2001). https://doi.org/10.1007/3-540-45682-1_3

[BLS19] Bootle, J., Lyubashevsky, V., Seiler, G.: Algebraic techniques for short(er) exact lattice-based zero-knowledge proofs. In: Boldyreva, A., Micciancio, D. (eds.) CRYPTO 2019, Part I. LNCS, vol. 11692, pp. 176–202. Springer, Cham (2019). https://doi.org/10.1007/978-3-030-26948-7_7

[BN20] Baum, C., Nof, A.: Concretely-efficient zero-knowledge arguments for arithmetic circuits and their application to lattice-based cryptography. In: Kiayias, A., Kohlweiss, M., Wallden, P., Zikas, V. (eds.) PKC 2020, Part I. LNCS, vol. 12110, pp. 495–526. Springer, Cham (2020). https://doi.org/10.1007/978-3-030-45374-9_17

[BVZ12] Bauer, A., Vergnaud, D., Zapalowicz, J.-C.: Inferring sequences produced by nonlinear pseudorandom number generators using coppersmith's methods. In: Fischlin, M., Buchmann, J., Manulis, M. (eds.) PKC 2012. LNCS, vol. 7293, pp. 609–626. Springer, Heidelberg (2012). https://doi.org/10.1007/978-3-642-30057-8_36

[CDG+17] Chase, M., et al.: Post-quantum zero-knowledge and signatures from symmetric-key primitives. In: Thuraisingham, B.M., Evans, D., Malkin, T., Xu, D. (eds.) ACM CCS 2017, pp. 1825–1842. ACM Press (2017)

[CGGI20] Chillotti, I., Gama, N., Georgieva, M., Izabachène, M.: TFHE: fast fully homomorphic encryption over the torus. J. Cryptol. **33**(1), 34–91 (2020)

[CGH00] Catalano, D., Gennaro, R., Halevi, S.: Computing inverses over a shared secret modulus. In: Preneel, B. (ed.) EUROCRYPT 2000. LNCS, vol. 1807, pp. 190–206. Springer, Heidelberg (2000). https://doi.org/10.1007/3-540-45539-6_14

[CJL+92] Coster, M.J., Joux, A., LaMacchia, B.A., Odlyzko, A.M., Schnorr, C., Stern, J.: Improved low-density subset sum algorithms. Comput. Complex. **2**, 111–128 (1992)

[DKR+21] Dobraunig, C., Kales, D., Rechberger, C., Schofnegger, M., Zaverucha, G.: Shorter signatures based on tailor-made minimalist symmetric-key crypto. Cryptology ePrint Archive, Report 2021/692 (2021)

[ENS20] Esgin, M.F., Nguyen, N.K., Seiler, G.: Practical exact proofs from lattices: new techniques to exploit fully-splitting rings. In: Moriai, S., Wang, H. (eds.) ASIACRYPT 2020. LNCS, vol. 12492, pp. 259–288. Springer, Cham (2020). https://doi.org/10.1007/978-3-030-64834-3_9

[FJR22] Feneuil, T., Joux, A., Rivain, M.: Syndrome decoding in the head: Shorter signatures from zero-knowledge proofs. Cryptology ePrint Archive, Report 2022/188 (2022)

[FMRV22] Feneuil, T., Maire, J., Rivain, M., Vergnaud, D.: Zero-knowledge protocols for the subset sum problem from MPC-in-the-head with rejection. Cryptology ePrint Archive, Report 2022/223 (2022)

[FS87] Fiat, A., Shamir, A.: How to prove yourself: practical solutions to identification and signature problems. In: Odlyzko, A.M. (ed.) CRYPTO 1986. LNCS, vol. 263, pp. 186–194. Springer, Heidelberg (1987). https://doi.org/10.1007/3-540-47721-7_12

[GMO16] Giacomelli, I., Madsen, J., Orlandi, C.: ZKBoo: faster zero-knowledge for Boolean circuits. In: Holz, T., Savage, S. (eds.) 25th USENIX Security Symposium, USENIX Security 2016, Austin, TX, USA, 10–12 August 2016, pp. 1069–1083. USENIX Association (2016)

[GMR89] Goldwasser, S., Micali, S., Rackoff, C.: The knowledge complexity of interactive proof systems. SIAM J. Comput. **18**(1), 186–208 (1989)

[GOP+21] Ganesh, C., Orlandi, C., Pancholi, M., Takahashi, A., Tschudi, D.: Fiat-Shamir bulletproofs are non-malleable (in the algebraic group model). Cryptology ePrint Archive, Report 2021/1393 (2021)

[Gro16] Groth, J.: On the size of pairing-based non-interactive arguments. In: Fischlin, M., Coron, J.-S. (eds.) EUROCRYPT 2016, Part II. LNCS, vol.

9666, pp. 305–326. Springer, Heidelberg (2016). https://doi.org/10.1007/978-3-662-49896-5_11

[HJ10] Howgrave-Graham, N., Joux, A.: New generic algorithms for hard knapsacks. In: Gilbert, H. (ed.) EUROCRYPT 2010. LNCS, vol. 6110, pp. 235–256. Springer, Heidelberg (2010). https://doi.org/10.1007/978-3-642-13190-5_12

[HS74] Horowitz, E., Sahni, S.: Computing partitions with applications to the knapsack problem. J. ACM **21**(2), 277–292 (1974)

[IKOS09] Ishai, Y., Kushilevitz, E., Ostrovsky, R., Sahai, A.: Zero-knowledge proofs from secure multiparty computation. SIAM J. Comput. **39**(3), 1121–1152 (2009)

[IN96] Impagliazzo, R., Naor, M.: Efficient cryptographic schemes provably as secure as subset sum. J. Cryptol. **9**(4), 199–216 (1996). https://doi.org/10.1007/BF00189260

[Joy21] Joye, M.: Guide to fully homomorphic encryption over the [discretized] torus. Cryptology ePrint Archive, Report 2021/1402 (2021)

[Kar72] Karp, R.M.: Reducibility among combinatorial problems. In: Miller, R.E., Thatcher, J.W. (eds.) Proceedings of a symposium on the Complexity of Computer Computations, Held 20–22 March 1972, at the IBM Thomas J. Watson Research Center, Yorktown Heights, New York, USA, The IBM Research Symposia Series, pp. 85–103. Plenum Press, New York (1972)

[KKW18] Katz, J., Kolesnikov, V., Wang, X.: Improved non-interactive zero knowledge with applications to post-quantum signatures. In: Lie, D., Mannan, M., Backes, M., Wang, X. (eds.) ACM CCS 2018, pp. 525–537. ACM Press (2018)

[KZ22] Kales, D., Zaverucha, G.: Efficient lifting for shorter zero-knowledge proofs and post-quantum signatures. Cryptology ePrint Archive, Paper 2022/588 (2022)

[LN17] Lindell, Y., Nof, A.: A framework for constructing fast MPC over arithmetic circuits with malicious adversaries and an honest-majority. In: Thuraisingham, B.M., Evans, D., Malkin, T., Xu, D. (eds.) ACM CCS 2017, pp. 259–276. ACM Press (2017)

[LNS21] Lyubashevsky, V., Nguyen, N.K., Seiler, G.: Shorter lattice-based zero-knowledge proofs via one-time commitments. In: Garay, J.A. (ed.) PKC 2021, Part I. LNCS, vol. 12710, pp. 215–241. Springer, Cham (2021). https://doi.org/10.1007/978-3-030-75245-3_9

[LNSW13] Ling, S., Nguyen, K., Stehlé, D., Wang, H.: Improved zero-knowledge proofs of knowledge for the ISIS problem, and applications. In: Kurosawa, K., Hanaoka, G. (eds.) PKC 2013. LNCS, vol. 7778, pp. 107–124. Springer, Heidelberg (2013). https://doi.org/10.1007/978-3-642-36362-7_8

[LPS10] Lyubashevsky, V., Palacio, A., Segev, G.: Public-key cryptographic primitives provably as secure as subset sum. In: Micciancio, D. (ed.) TCC 2010. LNCS, vol. 5978, pp. 382–400. Springer, Heidelberg (2010). https://doi.org/10.1007/978-3-642-11799-2_23

[LSSW12] Ling, S., Shparlinski, I.E., Steinfeld, R., Wang, H.: On the modular inversion hidden number problem. J. Symb. Comput. **47**(4), 358–367 (2012)

[Lyu09] Lyubashevsky, V.: Fiat-Shamir with aborts: applications to lattice and factoring-based signatures. In: Matsui, M. (ed.) ASIACRYPT 2009. LNCS, vol. 5912, pp. 598–616. Springer, Heidelberg (2009). https://doi.org/10.1007/978-3-642-10366-7_35

[MH78] Merkle, R.C., Hellman, M.E.: Hiding information and signatures in trapdoor knapsacks. IEEE Trans. Inf. Theory **24**(5), 525–530 (1978)

[Odl90] Odlyzko, A.M.: The rise and fall of knapsack cryptosystems. Cryptol. Comput. Number Theory. **42**, 75–88 (1990). Lecture Notes AMS Short Course, Boulder/CO (USA) 1989, Proceedings of Symposium on Applied Mathematics

[Reg05] Regev, O.: On lattices, learning with errors, random linear codes, and cryptography. In: Gabow, H.N., Fagin, R. (eds.) 37th ACM STOC, pp. 84–93. ACM Press (2005)

[Sha86] Shamir, A.: A zero-knowledge proof for knapsacks. Presented at a Workshop on Probabilistic Algorithms, Marseille (1986)

[SS81] Schroeppel, R., Shamir, A.: A $T=O(2^{n/2})$, $S=O(2^{n/4})$ algorithm for certain NP-complete problems. SIAM J. Comput. **10**(3), 456–464 (1981)

[Ste94] Stern, J.: A new identification scheme based on syndrome decoding. In: Stinson, D.R. (ed.) CRYPTO 1993. LNCS, vol. 773, pp. 13–21. Springer, Heidelberg (1994). https://doi.org/10.1007/3-540-48329-2_2

[XSH+19] Xu, J., Sarkar, S., Hu, L., Wang, H., Pan, Y.: New results on modular inversion hidden number problem and inversive congruential generator. In: Boldyreva, A., Micciancio, D. (eds.) CRYPTO 2019, Part I. LNCS, vol. 11692, pp. 297–321. Springer, Cham (2019). https://doi.org/10.1007/978-3-030-26948-7_11

Efficient Zero-Knowledge Arguments in Discrete Logarithm Setting: Sublogarithmic Proof or Sublinear Verifier

Sungwook Kim[1], Hyeonbum Lee[2], and Jae Hong Seo[2](✉)

[1] Department of Information Security, Seoul Women's University, Seoul 01797, Republic of Korea
kim.sungwook@swu.ac.kr

[2] Department of Mathematics and Research Institute for Natural Sciences, Hanyang University, Seoul 04763, Republic of Korea
{leehb3706,jaehongseo}@hanyang.ac.kr

Abstract. We propose three interactive zero-knowledge arguments for arithmetic circuit of size N in the common random string model, which can be converted to be non-interactive by Fiat-Shamir heuristics in the random oracle model. First argument features $O(\sqrt{\log N})$ communication and round complexities and $O(N)$ computational complexity for the verifier. Second argument features $O(\log N)$ communication and $O(\sqrt{N})$ computational complexity for the verifier. Third argument features $O(\log N)$ communication and $O(\sqrt{N}\log N)$ computational complexity for the verifier. Contrary to first and second arguments, the third argument is free of reliance on pairing-friendly elliptic curves. The soundness of three arguments is proven under the standard discrete logarithm and/or the double pairing assumption, which is at least as reliable as the decisional Diffie-Hellman assumption.

1 Introduction

A zero-knowledge (ZK) argument is a protocol between two parties, the prover and the verifier, such that the prover can convince the verifier that a particular statement is true without revealing anything else about the statement itself. ZK arguments have been used in numerous applications such as verifiable outsourced computation, anonymous credentials, and cryptocurrencies.

Our goal is to build an efficient ZK argument for arithmetic circuit (AC) in the common random string model that is sound under well-established standard assumptions, such as the discrete logarithm (DL) assumption: Compared to q-type strong assumptions such as q-DLOG [27,38], the standard assumptions will provide strong security guarantees as well as a good efficiency with smaller group size due to Cheon's attack on q-type assumptions [20]. To this end, we propose three inner-product (IP) arguments with the same properties (standard assumption, common random string model), where an IP argument is

S. Agrawal and D. Lin (Eds.): ASIACRYPT 2022, LNCS 13792, pp. 403–433, 2022.
https://doi.org/10.1007/978-3-031-22966-4_14

a proof system that convinces the verifier of an inner-product relation between committed integer vectors. Then, we can apply well-established reductions from IP argument to ZK argument for AC [13,17,18,46].

The first sublinear ZK argument for AC solely based on the hardness of the DL problem is due to Groth [29] and improved by Seo [44]. These works feature constant round complexity as well. Groth [31] gives a ZK argument with a cubic root communication complexity using pairing-based two-tiered homomorphic commitment scheme whose binding property is based on the double pairing (DPair) assumption [1]. The first logarithmic ZK argument for AC solely from the DL assumption is due to Bootle, Cerulli, Chaidos, Groth, and Petit [13] and improved by Bünz, Bootle, Boneh, Poelstra, Wuille, and Maxwell [17], which is called Bulletproofs. Hoffmann, Klooß, and Rupp [34] revisited and improved Bulletproofs by showing that it can cover systems of quadratic equations, of which rank-1 constraint systems is a special case. These logarithmic ZK argument systems [13,17,34] have linear verifiers. Other DL-based ZK argument systems with different asymptotic performance, in particular sublinear verifier, have been proposed. e.g., Hyrax [46] and Spartan [45]. Recently, Bünz, Maller, Mishra, Tyagi, and Vesely [19] achieved a logarithmic ZK argument with a sublinear verifier under the DPair assumption.

Focusing on specific languages, there are more researches achieving logarithmic communication complexity [3,33] prior to Bulletproofs. Logarithmic communication complexity in these works is attained with relatively large round complexity, compared to [29,44].

Relying on the non-standard but reliable assumptions, there exists a ZK argument system with better asymptotic performance due to Bünz, Fisch, and Szepieniec [18] that achieve logarithmic communications and logarithmic verifier simultaneously, but it relies on a rather stronger assumption such as the strong RSA assumption and the adaptive root assumption. A lot of important research for succinct non-interactive argument (SNARG) [6,9–11,21,27,28,30,32,33,37,38,40,47] have been proposed on the top of bilinear groups, where an argument consists of a constant number of group elements. However, the soundness of these works relies on non-falsifiable knowledge extractor assumptions and/or the structured reference string (SRS) that requires a trusted setup, which is not required in the aforementioned DL-based protocols. There is another important line of works [5,7,22,48] for SNARG without using pairings, but based on interactive oracle proofs [8]. These works are strong candidates for post-quantum ZK arguments and simultaneously minimizing communication cost and verifier computation. However, their communication cost is proportional to $\log^2 N$ for the circuit size N, which is larger than that of the DL based approach [13,17].

Our Results. We propose three IP arguments between two integer vectors of length N in the common random string model. We refer to [13,17,18,46] or Sect. 6 for a constant round reduction from ZK arguments for AC of size N with fan-in 2 gates to IP arguments. We summarize our results as follows.

1. We propose the first IP argument with *sublogarithmic communication*. We prove its soundness under the DL assumption and the DPair assumption.

Table 1. Comparison for transparent ZK arguments N: circuit size, d: circuit depth, w: input size, $(\mathbb{G}_1, \mathbb{G}_2, \mathbb{G}_t)$: bilinear groups, $(\mathbb{G}_p, \mathbb{G}_q)$: elliptic curve groups of order p and q, $\mathbb{G}_U$: group of unknown order, $\mathbb{H}$: hash function, m, p, h, τ_i, u: operation of field, pairing, hash, $\mathbb{G}_i$, $\mathbb{G}_U$, UOGroup: unknown-order group (strong RSA & adaptive root assumptions), CR hash: collision-resistant hashes, $\mathrm{DL}^\dagger$: DL assumption over pairing-friendly elliptic curves All arguments in the table are public coin (Definition 1), so that they achieve non-interactivity in the random oracle model using the Fiat-Shamir heuristic [25].

Scheme	Communication	$\mathcal{P}$'s comp.	$\mathcal{V}$'s comp.	Assump.
Groth [29] and Seo [44]	$O(\sqrt{N})\mathbb{G}_1$	$O(N)\tau_1$	$O(N)\tau_1$	DL
Groth [31]	$O(\sqrt[3]{N})\mathbb{G}_1$	$O(N)\tau_1$	$O(\sqrt[3]{N})\tau_1$	DPair
BP [13,17] and HKR [34]	$O(\log N)\mathbb{G}_1$	$O(N)\tau_1$	$O(N)\tau_1$	DL
Hyrax [46]	$O(\sqrt{w} + d\log N)\mathbb{G}_1$	$O(N\log N)\tau_1$	$O(\sqrt{w} + d\log N)\tau_1$	DL
Spartan DL [45]	$O(\sqrt{N})\mathbb{G}_1$	$O(N)\tau_1$	$O(\sqrt{N})\tau_1$	DL
BMMTV [19]	$O(\log N)\mathbb{G}_t$	$O(N)\tau_1$	$O(\sqrt{N})\tau_2$	DPair
Supersonic [18]	$O(\log N)\mathbb{G}_U$	$O(N\log N)\mathsf{u}$	$O(\log N)\mathsf{u}$	UOGroup
Spartan CL [45]	$O(\log^2 N)\mathbb{G}_U$	$O(N\log N)\mathsf{u}$	$O(\log^2 N)\mathsf{u}$	UOGroup
Ligero [2]	$O(\sqrt{N})\mathbb{H}$	$O(N\log N)\mathsf{h}$	$O(N)\mathsf{h}$	CR hash
STARK [5]	$O(\log^2 N)\mathbb{H}$	$O(N\log^2 N)\mathsf{h}$	$O(\log^2 N)\mathsf{h}$	CR hash
Aurora [7]	$O(\log^2 N)\mathbb{H}$	$O(N\log N)\mathsf{h}$	$O(N)\mathsf{h}$	CR hash
Fractal [22]	$O(\log^2 N)\mathbb{H}$	$O(N\log N)\mathsf{h}$	$O(\log^2 N)\mathsf{h}$	CR hash
Virgo [48]	$O(d\log N)\mathbb{H}$	$O(N\log N)\mathsf{h}$	$O(d\log N)\mathsf{h}$	CR hash
BCGGHJ [14]	$O(\sqrt{N})\mathbb{H}$	$O(N)\mathsf{m}$	$O(N)\mathsf{m}$	CR hash
BCL [15]	$\mathsf{polylog}(N)\mathbb{H}$	$O(N)\mathsf{m}$	$\mathsf{polylog}(N)\mathsf{m}$	CR hash
Our IP arguments + Sect. 6				
Protocol2 (Sect. 3.2)	$O(\sqrt{\log N})\mathbb{G}_t$	$O(N2^{\sqrt{\log N}})\tau_1$	$O(N)\tau_1$	$\mathrm{DL}^\dagger$&DPair
Protocol3 (Sect. 4.3)	$O(\log N)\mathbb{G}_t$	$O(N)\tau_1$	$O(\sqrt{N})\tau_2$	$\mathrm{DL}^\dagger$
Protocol4 (Sect. 5.3)	$O(\log N)\mathbb{G}_q$	$O(N)\tau_p$	$O(\sqrt{N}\log N)\tau_q$	DL

2. We present the first IP argument with $O(\log N)$ communication and $O(\sqrt{N})$ verifier computation such that its soundness is *based on the DL assumption.*
3. We introduce a novel method to achieve the IP argument with a similar performance to the second argument, especially *without the reliance of pairings.*

We provide a comparison for transparent ZK arguments in Table 1[1]. Note that there are more efficient arguments in the DL setting [9,21,24,27,36,38] if we rely on a trusted setup or non-standard, non-falsifiable assumptions.

[1] We often use a terminology 'transparent' in the meaning of 'without trusted setup'.

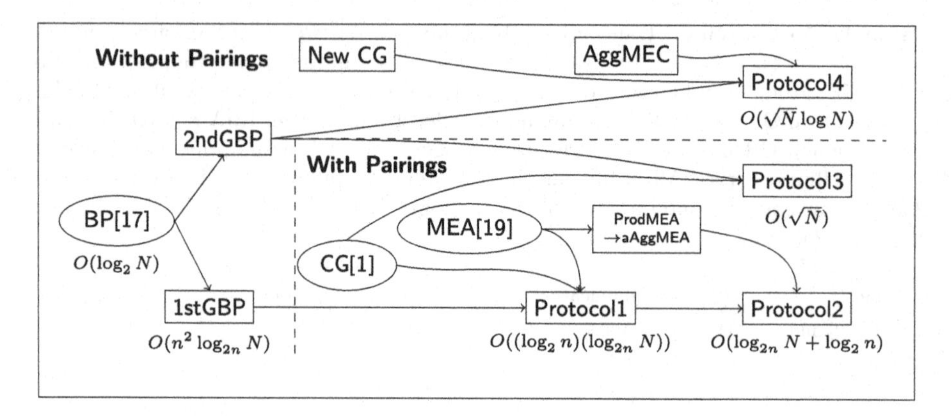

Fig. 1. Overview of Our Approach toward Sublogarithmic Proofs or Sublinear Verifier

Each arrow links between the underlying and the advanced protocols. The big-O notation under each protocol indicates communication complexity, except for Protocol3 and Protocol4 that indicate verifier's computational complexity. The oval nodes indicate known results; BP: Bulletproofs [13,17], MEA: multi-exponentiation argument [19], CG: Commitment to group elements [1]. The rectangle nodes indicate the proposed protocols; New CG: Commitment to Elliptic Curve Points, 1stGBP & 2stGBP: generalizations of Bulletproofs, aAggMEA & AggMEC: aggregations of multi-exponentiations & multi-elliptic curve operations. Protocol1: an intermediate protocol. Protocol2: Sublogarithmic IP argument, Protocol3 & Protocol4: Sublinear Verifier IP arguments. N is the dimension of witness vectors. n is a positive integer parameter for 1stGBP, where $n = 1$ implies the original Bulletproofs.

Our starting point is Bünz et al.'s Bulletproofs IP argument (BP-IP) [17] that features $O(\log N)$ communication and $O(N)$ computation in the common random string model and is sound under the DL assumption. For shorter proofs or faster verification, we first generalize BP-IP in two different ways. A pictorial overview of our approach is given in Fig. 1.

Sublogarithmic Communications. BP-IP consists of $\log N$ recursive steps such that the prover sends two group elements per each round. The goal of each recursive step is to halve the length of witness. Our first generalization of BP-IP reduces the length of witness one $2n$-th per each recursive round if N is a power of $2n$ for any positive integer n. If need be, one can easily pad the inputs to ensure that the requirement for the format of N holds, like in BP-IP. Then, the recursive steps are finished in $\log_{2n} N$ rounds and the prover sends $2n(2n-1)$ group elements in each round, so that the overall communication cost is $O((\log_{2n} N) \times n^2)$, which becomes minimal when $n = 1$. That is, this generalization has no advantage over BP-IP in terms of communications.

Nevertheless, we observe that the commit-and-prove approach can reduce transmission overhead; the prover can commit to $2n(2n-1)$ group elements instead of sending them all, and then proves that the openings satisfy what the verifier should have checked with the openings. To this end, we use a pairing-based commitment scheme to group elements (e.g., AFGHO [1]). This process of committing and proving can be achieved using a multi-exponentiation argument (e.g., [19]). Unfortunately, this naïve commit-and-prove approach ends up with asymptotically the same proof size as BP-IP since we must prove several multi-exponentiation arguments for every round. We call this protocol Protocol1.

To further reduce the communication cost, we aggregate multiple multi-exponentiation arguments. Although there are well-known aggregating techniques for multiple arguments with homomorphic commitment scheme (e.g., aggregating range proofs [17], linear combinations of protocols [34]), these aggregating techniques are not well applicable to the case including ours such that bases and exponents are distinct for multiple arguments. We try to reduce multiple relations to a single relation by multiplying all relations and then employ a recursive proof technique like BP-IP. However, we find that this strategy does not work well. The detailed explanation about the difficulty we faced is given in Sect. 3.2. Instead, we devise a novel aggregating technique using newly proposed *augmented aggregated multi-exponentiation argument* aAggMEA and product argument ProdMEA. The final protocol, called Protocol2, using aAggMEA and ProdMEA achieves sublogarithmic communication overhead.

Sublinear Verifier. The soundness of BP-IP is based on the discrete logarithm relation assumption (DLR), which is equivalent to the DL assumption, such that no adversary can find non-trivial relation among *uniformly* chosen group elements. We observe that the uniform condition in sampling group elements is not necessary in the soundness proof of BP-IP, but the hardness of finding non-trivial relation among the CRS is sufficient. From this observation, we first generalize the DLR assumption by removing the uniform condition and then propose and prove that a new assumption with non-uniform distribution holds. More precisely, we combine this generalization with the AFGHO commitments; Let $e : \mathbb{G}_1 \times \mathbb{G}_2 \to \mathbb{G}_t$ be a bilinear map, where $\mathbb{G}_1$ and $\mathbb{G}_2$ are source groups and $\mathbb{G}_t$ is the target group. $g_1, \ldots, g_{\sqrt{N}} \in \mathbb{G}_1$ and $H_1, \ldots, H_{\sqrt{N}} \in \mathbb{G}_2$ are uniformly chosen. We prove that no adversary can find a non-trivial vector $(a_{11}, \ldots, a_{\sqrt{N}\sqrt{N}}) \in \mathbb{Z}_p^N$ satisfying $\prod_{i,j=1}^{\sqrt{N}} e(g_i, H_j)^{a_{ij}}$ if the DL assumptions in the source groups hold. That is, $e(g_i, H_j)$'s are not uniformly distributed but hard to find non-trivial relation among them. Therefore, if we set $e(g_i, H_j)$'s as the CRS of BP-IP, then the actual CRS becomes g_i's and H_j's of $2\sqrt{N}$ size while keeping the soundness proof under the DL assumption in the source group.

Nevertheless, a naïve approach using the above idea will keep linear verifier computation in N since we still keep the same verification process as that of BP-IP. We introduce a trick to track verifier's computation with $O(\sqrt{N})$ computation. For example, in the first recursive step of BP-IP, the verifier should update the public parameter $g_1, \ldots, g_N$ to $g_1^x g_{N/2+1}^{x^{-1}}, \ldots, g_{N/2}^x g_N^{x^{-1}}$ for a challenge integer x, which requires $O(N)$ computation. In our setting, the public parameter $e(g_1, H_1), \ldots, e(g_{\sqrt{N}}, H_{\sqrt{N}})$ can be halved to $e(g_1^x g_{\sqrt{N}/2+1}^{x^{-1}}, H_i), \ldots,$

$e(g^x_{\sqrt{N}/2} g^{x^{-1}}_{\sqrt{N}}, H_i)$ for all $i = 1, \ldots, \sqrt{N}$. Therefore, the verifier can track this computation by computing only $g_i^x g^{x^{-1}}_{\sqrt{N}/2+i}$ for $i = 1, \ldots, \sqrt{N}$, which require $O(\sqrt{N})$ exponentiations in $\mathbb{G}_1$. Note that this trick does not increase the prover's overhead, so that we sacrifice neither the other complexities nor assumptions to achieve sublinear verifier. The resulting protocol with sublinear verifier is called Protocol3.

Sublinear Verifier without Pairings. The core of the above second generalization of BP-IP is to employ *two-tiered homomorphic commitment scheme*: Pedersen commitment scheme to integers in the 1st layer + pairing-based AFGHO commitment scheme to group elements in the 2nd layer. We propose another IP argument with sublinear verifier, particularly not relying on pairing-friendly elliptic curves. To circumvent the use of AGFHO scheme, we propose a new two-tiered commitment scheme built on a usual elliptic curve with a mild condition. Although the proposed two-tiered commitment scheme is not homomorphic, we emphasize that it has a similar-but-weakened property, *friendly to proving homomorphic operations* of the underlying mathematical structure, particularly the group law of elliptic curve over finite fields. Second, we show that this weakened property is sufficient to construct an IP argument protocol with sublinear verifier. After replacing pairing-based two-tiered homomorphic commitment scheme with the new commitment scheme, the prover performs the verifier computation, proves the integrity of the computation, and sends the verifier the computation along with a proof. In order to raise efficiency of this approach, we also bring in the aggregation technique used for the protocol with sublogarithmic communications. The resulting protocol without pairings is called Protocol4.

Related Works and Organization. Additional related works that were not mentioned before are provided in the full version [35]. After providing necessary definitions in the next section, we present our first generalization of BP-IP and then reduce its communication overhead by using the aggregation technique in Sect. 3. We present another generalization that achieves sublinear CRS size and verifier computation in Sect. 4 (with Pairings) and Sect. 5 (without Pairings). In Sect. 6, we extend our IP arguments to ZK arguments for AC.

2 Definitions

Argument System for Relation $\mathcal{R}$. Let $\mathcal{K}$ be the common reference string (CRS) generator that takes the security parameter as input and outputs the CRS σ. In this paper, the CRS consists of randomly generated group elements, so that indeed we are in the common random string model, where an argument consists of two interactive PPT algorithms $(\mathcal{P}, \mathcal{V})$ such that $\mathcal{P}$ and $\mathcal{V}$ are called the prover and the verifier, respectively. The transcript produced by an interaction between $\mathcal{P}$ and $\mathcal{V}$ on inputs x and y is denoted by $tr \leftarrow \langle \mathcal{P}(x), \mathcal{V}(y) \rangle$. Since we are in the common random string model, for the sake of simplicity, we omit the process of running $\mathcal{K}$ and assume the CRS is given as common input to both $\mathcal{P}$

and $\mathcal{V}$. At the end of transcript, the verifier $\mathcal{V}$ outputs b, which is denoted by $\langle \mathcal{P}(x), \mathcal{V}(y) \rangle = b$, where $b = 1$ if $\mathcal{V}$ accepts and $b = 0$ if $\mathcal{V}$ rejects.

Let $\mathcal{R}$ be a polynomial time verifiable ternary relation consisting of tuples of the CRS σ, a statement x, and a witness w. We define a CRS-dependent language L_σ as the set of statements x that have a witness w such that $(\sigma, x, w) \in \mathcal{R}$. That is, $L_\sigma = \{ x \mid \exists\ w \text{ satisfying } (\sigma, x, w) \in \mathcal{R} \}$. For a ternary relation $\mathcal{R}$, we use the format $\{(\text{common input}; \text{witness}) : \mathcal{R}\}$ to denote the relation $\mathcal{R}$ using specific common input and witness.

Argument of Knowledge. Informally, the argument of knowledge means the argument system satisfying the completeness and the soundness with extractability. Due to space constraints, we provide definitions in the full version [35].

Transparent and Non-interactive Argument in the Random Oracle Model. A protocol in the common random string model can be converted into a protocol without a trusted setup in the random oracle model [4]; if $\mathcal{K}$ outputs random group elements of an elliptic curve group $\mathbb{G}$ of prime order, then the CRS can be replaced with hash values of a small random seed, where the hash function mapping from $\{0, 1\}^*$ to $\mathbb{G}$ is modeled as a random oracle as in [12].

Any public coin interactive argument protocol defined in Definition 1 can be converted into a non-interactive one by applying the Fiat-Shamir heuristic [25] in the random oracle model; all $\mathcal{V}$'s challenges can be replaced with hash values of the transcript up to that point.

Definition 1. *An argument $(\mathcal{P}, \mathcal{V})$ is called* public coin *if all $\mathcal{V}$'s challenges are chosen uniformly at random and independently of $\mathcal{P}$'s messages.*

All interactive arguments proposed in this paper can be converted to transparent non-interactive arguments in the random oracle model.

Assumptions. Let $\mathcal{G}$ be a group generator such that $\mathcal{G}$ takes 1^λ as input and outputs $(p, \mathbb{G}, g)$, where λ is the security parameter, $\mathbb{G}$ is the description of a group of order p, and g is a generator of G, which is used to sample an element of $\mathbb{G}$ with uniform distribution. Let $negl(\lambda)$ be a negligible function in λ.

Definition 2 (Discrete Logarithm (DL) Assumption). *We say that the group generator $\mathcal{G}$ satisfies the discrete logarithm assumption if for all non-uniform polynomial-time adversaries $\mathcal{A}$, the following inequality holds.*

$$\Pr\left[g^a = h \;\middle|\; (p, \mathbb{G}, g) \leftarrow \mathcal{G}(1^\lambda),\ \ h \xleftarrow{\$} \mathbb{G};\ a \leftarrow \mathcal{A}(p, g, h, \mathbb{G})\right] < negl(\lambda).$$

Definition 3 (Discrete Logarithm Relation (DLR) Assumption). *We say that the group generator $\mathcal{G}$ satisfies the discrete logarithm relation assumption if for all non-uniform polynomial-time adversaries $\mathcal{A}$, the following inequality holds.*

$$\Pr\left[\boldsymbol{a} \neq \boldsymbol{0} \wedge \boldsymbol{g}^{\boldsymbol{a}} = 1_{\mathbb{G}} \;\middle|\; (p, \mathbb{G}, g) \leftarrow \mathcal{G}(1^\lambda), \boldsymbol{g} \xleftarrow{\$} \mathbb{G}^n; \boldsymbol{a} \leftarrow \mathcal{A}(p, \mathbb{G}, g, \boldsymbol{g})\right] < negl(\lambda),$$

where $1_{\mathbb{G}}$ *is the identity of* $\mathbb{G}$.

Although the equivalence between DLR and DL assumptions is well-known, to be self-contained, we provide the complete reductions in the full version [35].

Let $\mathcal{G}_b$ be an asymmetric bilinear group generator such that $\mathcal{G}_b$ takes 1^λ as input and outputs $(p, g, H, \mathbb{G}_1, \mathbb{G}_2, \mathbb{G}_t, e)$, where $\mathbb{G}_1, \mathbb{G}_2, \mathbb{G}_t$ are the descriptions of distinct cyclic groups of order p of length λ, g and H are generators of $\mathbb{G}_1, \mathbb{G}_2$, respectively, and e is a non-degenerate bilinear map from $\mathbb{G}_1 \times \mathbb{G}_2$ to $\mathbb{G}_t$.

Definition 4 (Double Pairing Assumption). *We say that the asymmetric bilinear group generator* $\mathcal{G}_b$ *satisfies the double pairing assumption if for all non-uniform polynomial-time adversaries* $\mathcal{A}$, *the following inequality holds.*

$$\Pr\left[\begin{array}{c} e(g', G) = e(g'', G^a) \\ \wedge\ (g', g'') \neq (1_{\mathbb{G}_1}, 1_{\mathbb{G}_1}) \end{array} \middle| \begin{array}{c} (p, g, H, \mathbb{G}_1, \mathbb{G}_2, \mathbb{G}_t, e) \leftarrow \mathcal{G}_b(1^\lambda), \\ G \xleftarrow{\$} \mathbb{G}_2,\ a \xleftarrow{\$} \mathbb{Z}_p; \\ (g', g'') \leftarrow \mathcal{A}((G, G^a), (p, g, H, \mathbb{G}_1, \mathbb{G}_2, \mathbb{G}_t, e)) \end{array}\right] < negl(\lambda)$$

Abe et al. [1] proved that the double pairing assumption is as reliable as the decisional Diffie-Hellman assumption in $\mathbb{G}_2$.

Groups, Vectors, and Operations. We introduce some notations for succinct description of protocols. $[m]$ denotes a set of continuous integers from 1 to m, $\{1, \ldots, m\}$. For elements in groups $\mathbb{G}_1$ and $\mathbb{G}_2$ obtained by $\mathcal{G}_b$, we separately use lower case letters for $\mathbb{G}_1$ and upper case letters for $\mathbb{G}_2$. A vector is denoted by a bold letter, e,g., $\boldsymbol{g} = (g_1, ..., g_m) \in \mathbb{G}_1^m$ and $\boldsymbol{a} = (a_1, ..., a_m) \in \mathbb{Z}_p^m$. For a vector $\boldsymbol{a} \in \mathbb{Z}_p^m$, its separation to the left half vector $\boldsymbol{a}_1 \in \mathbb{Z}_p^{m/2}$ and the right half vector $\boldsymbol{a}_{-1} \in \mathbb{Z}_p^{m/2}$ is denoted by $\boldsymbol{a} = \boldsymbol{a}_1 \| \boldsymbol{a}_{-1}$. Equivalently, the notation $\|$ is used when sticking two vectors $\boldsymbol{a}_1$ and $\boldsymbol{a}_{-1}$ to $\boldsymbol{a}$ and can be sequentially used when sticking several vectors.[2] We use several vector operations denoted as follows.

Component-wise Operations. The component-wise multiplication between several vectors is denoted by $\circ$ e.g., for $\boldsymbol{g}_k = (g_{k,1}, \ldots, g_{k,n}) \in \mathbb{G}_i^n$, $i \in \{1, 2, t\}$, and $k \in [m]$, $\circ_{k \in [m]} \boldsymbol{g}_k = (\prod_{k \in [m]} g_{k,1} \ldots, \prod_{k \in [m]} g_{k,n})$. If $k = 2$, we simply denote it by $\boldsymbol{g}_1 \circ \boldsymbol{g}_2$.

Bilinear Functions & Scalar-Vector Operations.

1. The standard inner-product in $\mathbb{Z}_p^n$ is denoted by $\langle\ ,\ \rangle$ and it satisfies the following bilinearity. $\langle \sum_{k \in [m]} \boldsymbol{a}_k, \sum_{j \in [n]} \boldsymbol{b}_j \rangle = \sum_{k \in [m]} \sum_{j \in [n]} \langle \boldsymbol{a}_k, \boldsymbol{b}_j \rangle \in \mathbb{Z}_p$.
2. For $\boldsymbol{g} = (g_1, \ldots, g_n) \in \mathbb{G}_i^n$, $i \in \{1, 2, t\}$ and $\boldsymbol{a} = (a_1, \ldots, a_n) \in \mathbb{Z}_p^n$, the multi-exponentiation is denoted by $\boldsymbol{g}^{\boldsymbol{a}} := \prod_{k \in [n]} g_k^{a_k} \in \mathbb{G}_i$ and it satisfies the following bilinearity. $(\circ_{k \in [m]} \boldsymbol{g}_k)^{\sum_{j \in [\ell]} \boldsymbol{z}_j} = \prod_{k \in [m]} \prod_{j \in [\ell]} \boldsymbol{g}_k^{\boldsymbol{z}_j} \in \mathbb{G}_i$.

[2] Note that we use the indices $(1, -1)$ instead of $(1, 2)$ since it harmonizes well with the usage of the challenges in Bulletproofs and our generalization of Bulletproofs. e.g., let $\boldsymbol{a} = \boldsymbol{a}_1 \| \boldsymbol{a}_{-1}$ be a witness and x be a challenge, and then $\boldsymbol{a}$ is updated to $\sum_{i=\pm 1} \boldsymbol{a}_i x^i$, a witness for the next recursive round.

3. For $\boldsymbol{g} = (g_1, \ldots, g_n) \in \mathbb{G}_1^n, \boldsymbol{H} = (H_1, \ldots, H_n) \in \mathbb{G}_2^n$, the inner-pairing product is denoted by $\boldsymbol{E}(\boldsymbol{g}, \boldsymbol{H}) := \prod_{k \in [n]} e(g_k, H_k) \in \mathbb{G}_t$ and it satisfies the following bilinearity. $\boldsymbol{E}(\circ_{k\in[m]} \boldsymbol{g}_k, \circ_{j\in[\ell]} \boldsymbol{H}_j) = \prod_{k\in[m]} \prod_{j\in[\ell]} \boldsymbol{E}(\boldsymbol{g}_k, \boldsymbol{H}_j) \in \mathbb{G}_t$.
4. For $c \in \mathbb{Z}_p$ and $\boldsymbol{a} \in \mathbb{Z}_p^m$, the scalar multiplication is denoted by $c \cdot \boldsymbol{a} := (c \cdot a_1, \ldots, c \cdot a_n) \in \mathbb{Z}_p^m$.
5. For $c \in \mathbb{Z}_p$ and $\boldsymbol{g} \in \mathbb{G}_i^m$, $i \in \{1, 2, t\}$ the scalar exponentiation is denoted by $\boldsymbol{g}^c := (g_1^c, \ldots, g_m^c) \in \mathbb{G}_i^m$.
6. For $\boldsymbol{c} \in \mathbb{Z}_p^m$ and $g \in \mathbb{G}_i$, $i \in \{1, 2, t\}$ the vector exponentiation is denoted by $g^{\boldsymbol{c}} := (g^{c_1}, \ldots, g^{c_m}) \in \mathbb{G}_i^m$.

3 Sublogarithmic Proofs via Generalization of BP-IP

In this section, we present our first generalization of BP-IP for the following IP relation $\mathcal{R}_{\mathsf{IP}}$ and then reduce its communication cost using the newly proposed aggregation technique.

$$\mathcal{R}_{\mathsf{IP}} = \left\{ (\boldsymbol{g}, \boldsymbol{h} \in \mathbb{G}^N, u, P \in \mathbb{G}; \boldsymbol{a}, \boldsymbol{b}) : \ P = \boldsymbol{g}^{\boldsymbol{a}} \boldsymbol{h}^{\boldsymbol{b}} u^{\langle \boldsymbol{a}, \boldsymbol{b} \rangle} \in \mathbb{G} \right\} \tag{1}$$

where $\mathbb{G}$ is an arbitrary cyclic group of order p satisfying the DL assumption, and $\boldsymbol{g}, \boldsymbol{h}$, and u are uniformly selected common inputs.

The BP-IP consists of $\log N$ recursive steps that halves the size of witness and the parameters. In each recursive round of BP-IP, each vector in the CRS and a witness are split into two equal-length subvectors. We generalize BP-IP by splitting a vector of length N into $2n$ subvectors of length $N/2n$ in each round, where $n = 1$ implies the original BP-IP. Similar to BP-IP, we assume N is a power of $2n$ for the sake of simplicity. Let $\widehat{N} = \frac{N}{2n}$ and the prover begins with parsing the witness $\boldsymbol{a}, \boldsymbol{b}$ and the parameter $\boldsymbol{g}, \boldsymbol{h}$ to

$$\begin{aligned} \boldsymbol{a} &= \boldsymbol{a}_1 \| \boldsymbol{a}_{-1} \| \cdots \boldsymbol{a}_{2n-1} \| \boldsymbol{a}_{-2n+1}, & \boldsymbol{b} &= \boldsymbol{b}_1 \| \boldsymbol{b}_{-1} \| \cdots \boldsymbol{b}_{2n-1} \| \boldsymbol{b}_{-2n+1}, \\ \boldsymbol{g} &= \boldsymbol{g}_1 \| \boldsymbol{g}_{-1} \| \cdots \boldsymbol{g}_{2n-1} \| \boldsymbol{g}_{-2n+1}, & \text{and } \boldsymbol{h} &= \boldsymbol{h}_1 \| \boldsymbol{h}_{-1} \| \cdots \boldsymbol{h}_{2n-1} \| \boldsymbol{h}_{-2n+1}. \end{aligned}$$

Let $I_n = \{\pm 1, \pm 3, \ldots, \pm(2n-1)\}$ be a $2n$-size index set. In each recursive round of BP-IP, the prover computes and sends two group elements L and R. In our generalization, instead of L and R, $\mathcal{P}$ calculates $v_{i,j} = \boldsymbol{g}_i^{\boldsymbol{a}_j} \boldsymbol{h}_j^{\boldsymbol{b}_i} u^{\langle \boldsymbol{a}_j \boldsymbol{b}_i \rangle} \in \mathbb{G}$ for all distinct $i, j \in I_n$, and then sends $\{v_{i,j}\}_{\substack{i,j \in I_n \\ i \neq j}}$ to $\mathcal{V}$. Note that if $n = 1$, then $v_{1,-1}$ and $v_{-1,1}$ are equal to L and R in BP-IP, respectively. $\mathcal{V}$ chooses $x \xleftarrow{\$} \mathbb{Z}_p^*$ and returns it to $\mathcal{P}$. Finally, both $\mathcal{P}$ and $\mathcal{V}$ compute

$$\widehat{\boldsymbol{g}} = \circ_{i \in I_n} \boldsymbol{g}_i^{x^{-i}} \in \mathbb{G}^{\widehat{N}}, \ \widehat{\boldsymbol{h}} = \circ_{i \in I_n} \boldsymbol{h}_i^{x^i} \in \mathbb{G}^{\widehat{N}}, \text{ and } \widehat{P} = P \cdot \prod_{\substack{i,j \in I_n \\ i \neq j}} v_{i,j}^{x^{j-i}} \in \mathbb{G}$$

and $\mathcal{P}$ additionally computes a witness for the next round argument

$$\widehat{\boldsymbol{a}} = \sum_{i \in I_n} \boldsymbol{a}_i x^i \in \mathbb{Z}_p^{\widehat{N}} \text{ and } \widehat{\boldsymbol{b}} = \sum_{i \in I_n} \boldsymbol{b}_i x^{-i} \in \mathbb{Z}_p^{\widehat{N}}.$$

We can verify that this process is a reduction to a one $2n$-th length IP argument by checking $(\widehat{\boldsymbol{g}}, \widehat{\boldsymbol{h}}, u, \widehat{P}; \widehat{\boldsymbol{a}}, \widehat{\boldsymbol{b}})$ satisfies the relation $\mathcal{R}_{\mathsf{IP}}$. The concrete descriptions of BP-IP and the above generalized BP-IP and their proofs for the perfect completeness and the soundness are relegated to the full version [35].

Efficiency Analysis. The prover repeats the $(N > 1)$ case $\log_{2n} N$ times and then runs the $(N = 1)$ case. For each $(N > 1)$ case, $\mathcal{P}$ sends $v_{i,j}$'s of size $2n(2n-1)$ and two integers in the $(N = 1)$ case, so that the communication overhead sent by $\mathcal{P}$ is $2n(2n-1)\log_{2n} N$ group elements and 2 integers. The verifier updates $\widehat{\boldsymbol{g}}$, $\widehat{\boldsymbol{h}}$ and $\widehat{P}$ that cost $O(N + n^2 \log_{2n} N)$ group exponentiation. For sufficiently small $n < \sqrt{N}$, it becomes $O(N)$. The prover should compute $v_{i,j}$ for all i, j for each round, so that the prover's computation overhead is $O(Nn^2)$. The overall complexities are minimized when n has the smallest positive integer (that is, $n = 1$), which is identical to the BP-IP protocol.

3.1 Proof Size Reduction Using Multi-exponentiation Argument

We improve our generalization of BP-IP by using the pairing-based homomorphic commitment scheme to group elements [1]. We first slightly extend our target relation by adding the commitment key of [1] into the common random string in our argument as follows.

$$\left\{ \begin{array}{l} (\boldsymbol{g}, \boldsymbol{h} \in \mathbb{G}_1^N, u \in \mathbb{G}_1, \boldsymbol{F}_1, \ldots, \boldsymbol{F}_m \in \mathbb{G}_2^{2n(2n-1)}, \boldsymbol{H} \in \mathbb{G}_2^m, P \in \mathbb{G}_1; \boldsymbol{a}, \boldsymbol{b}) \\ : P = \boldsymbol{g}^{\boldsymbol{a}} \boldsymbol{h}^{\boldsymbol{b}} u^{\langle \boldsymbol{a}, \boldsymbol{b} \rangle} \in \mathbb{G}_1 \end{array} \right\} \quad (2)$$

where $\boldsymbol{g}, \boldsymbol{h}, u, \boldsymbol{F}_k$, and $\boldsymbol{H}$ are the common random string. Here, $\boldsymbol{F}_k$ and $\boldsymbol{H}$ are not necessary to define the relation $P = \boldsymbol{g}^{\boldsymbol{a}} \boldsymbol{h}^{\boldsymbol{b}} u^{\langle \boldsymbol{a}, \boldsymbol{b} \rangle}$. However, our IP protocols will use them to run a subprotocol for multi-exponentiation arguments given in the following subsections.

The generalized BP-IP with $n > 1$ carries larger communication overhead than that of BP-IP. In order to reduce the communication cost in each round, we can use a commitment to group elements. That is, the prover sends a commitment to group elements $v_{i,j}$'s instead of sending all $v_{i,j}$'s. This approach will reduce communication cost in each round. Then, however, the verifier cannot directly compute the update $\widehat{P}$ of P, $\prod_{\substack{i,j \in I_n \\ i \neq j}} v_{i,j}^{x^{j-i}}$, by himself, and thus the prover sends it along with its proof of validity, which is exactly a multi-exponentiation argument proving the following relation.

$$\left\{ (\boldsymbol{F} \in \mathbb{G}_2^N, \boldsymbol{z} \in \mathbb{Z}_p^N, P \in \mathbb{G}_t, q \in \mathbb{G}_1; \boldsymbol{v} \in \mathbb{G}_1^N) : P = \boldsymbol{E}(\boldsymbol{v}, \boldsymbol{F}) \wedge q = \boldsymbol{v}^{\boldsymbol{z}} \right\}, \quad (3)$$

where $\boldsymbol{F}$ is the common random string such that their discrete logarithm relation is unknown to both $\mathcal{P}$ and $\mathcal{V}$ and $\boldsymbol{z}$ is an arbitrary public vector.

We will omit the detailed description for the multi-exponentiation argument for the relation in (3), but provide an intuitive idea for it. In fact, BP-IP argument can be naturally extended to this proof system due to the resemblance between the standard IP and the inner-pairing product. More precisely, the additive homomorphic binding commitment to an integer vector (e.g., $\boldsymbol{g}^{\boldsymbol{a}}$) is changed with the multiplicative homomorphic commitment to a group element vector (e.g., $\boldsymbol{E}(\boldsymbol{v}, \boldsymbol{F})$) and the standard IP between two integer vectors (e.g., $\langle \boldsymbol{a}, \boldsymbol{b} \rangle$) can be substituted with multi-exponentiation (e.g., $\boldsymbol{v}^{\boldsymbol{z}}$).[3] This type of extension is well formalized by Bünz, Maller, Mishra, Tyagi, and Vesely [19] in terms of two-tiered homomorphic commitment scheme [31]. The multi-exponentiation argument in [19] costs the same complexities as those of BP-IP; $O(\log N)$ communication overhead and $O(N)$ computational costs for the prover and the verifier.

For our purpose, we can use the commitment scheme to group elements [31] and the multi-exponentiation argument in [19] so that we can construct a protocol with shorter communications, denoted by Protocol1. We provide full description of our generalized BP-IP with Multi-Exponentiation Argument, denoted by Protocol1 in Fig. 2. In the protocol, we add the state information for the prover and the verifier, denoted by st_P and st_V, respectively. Both st_P and st_V are initialized as empty lists and used to stack the inputs of the multi-exponentiation argument for each recursive round. At the final stage, the prover and the verifier can run several multi-exponentiation argument protocols in parallel.

Efficiency Analysis. Although this approach reduces communication overheads, compared to the generalized BP-IP, it is not quite beneficial for our purpose. More precisely, the communication overhead $O(n^2 \log_{2n} N)$ of the generalized BP-IP is reduced to $O((\log n) \cdot (\log_{2n} N))$ since the communication overhead per round $O(n^2)$ is reduced to its logarithm $O(\log n)$ by the multi-exponentiation argument. Although the communication overhead is reduced to $O((\log n) \cdot (\log_{2n} N))$ compared with the generalized BP-IP ($n > 1$), the resulting complexity is equal to $O(\log N)$, which is asymptotically the same as the communication overhead of BP-IP. Therefore, this protocol is no better than BP-IP, at least in terms of communication complexity. Nevertheless, this protocol is a good basis for our sublogarithmic protocol presented in the next subsection.

3.2 Sublogarithmic Protocol from Aggregated Multi-exponentiation Arguments

We build a protocol, denoted by Protocol2, for sublogarithmic transparent IP arguments on the basis of Protocol1 described in the previous subsection. To this end, we develop an aggregation technique to prove multiple multi-exponentiation arguments at once, which proves the following aggregated relation.

$$\mathcal{R}_{AggMEA} = \left\{ \begin{array}{l} \left(\begin{array}{l} \boldsymbol{F}_k \in \mathbb{G}_2^{2n(2n-1)}, \boldsymbol{z}_k \in \mathbb{Z}_p^{2n(2n-1)}, P_k \in \mathbb{G}_t, q_k \in \mathbb{G}_1 \\ ; \boldsymbol{v}_k \in \mathbb{G}_1^{2n(2n-1)} \text{ for } k \in [m] \end{array} \right) \\ : \bigwedge_{k \in [m]} \left(P_k = \boldsymbol{E}(\boldsymbol{v}_k, \boldsymbol{F}_k) \wedge q_k = \boldsymbol{v}_k^{\boldsymbol{z}_k} \right) \end{array} \right\}$$

[3] The BP-IP is about two witness vectors $\boldsymbol{a}$ and $\boldsymbol{b}$ and it can be easily modified with one witness vector $\boldsymbol{a}$ and a public $\boldsymbol{b}$. e.g., [46]. Our multi-exponentiation argument corresponds to this variant.

Protocol1($\boldsymbol{g}, \boldsymbol{h}, u, \boldsymbol{F}_k$ for $k \in [m], P \in \mathbb{G}_1, st_V; \boldsymbol{a}, \boldsymbol{b}, st_P$), where $m = \log_{2n} N$

If $N = 1$:

Step 1: $\mathcal{P}$ sends $\mathcal{V}$ a and b.

Step 2: $\mathcal{V}$ proceeds the next step if $P = g^a h^b u^{a \cdot b}$ holds. Otherwise, $\mathcal{V}$ outputs *Reject*.

Step 3: If st_P is empty, then $\mathcal{V}$ outputs *Accept*. Otherwise, let $(u_k, v_k, \boldsymbol{x}_k; \boldsymbol{v}_k)$ be the k-th row in st_P.

Step 4: $\mathcal{P}$ and $\mathcal{V}$ run MEA($\boldsymbol{F}_k, \boldsymbol{x}_k, u_k, v_k; \boldsymbol{v}_k$) for $k \in [m]$.

Else ($N > 1$): Let $\widehat{N} = \frac{N}{2n}$ and parse $\boldsymbol{a}, \boldsymbol{b}, \boldsymbol{g}$, and $\boldsymbol{h}$ to

$$\boldsymbol{a} = \boldsymbol{a}_1 \| \boldsymbol{a}_{-1} \| \cdots \boldsymbol{a}_{2n-1} \| \boldsymbol{a}_{-2n+1}, \qquad \boldsymbol{b} = \boldsymbol{b}_1 \| \boldsymbol{b}_{-1} \| \cdots \boldsymbol{b}_{2n-1} \| \boldsymbol{b}_{-2n+1},$$
$$\boldsymbol{g} = \boldsymbol{g}_1 \| \boldsymbol{g}_{-1} \| \cdots \boldsymbol{g}_{2n-1} \| \boldsymbol{g}_{-2n+1}, \qquad \text{and } \boldsymbol{h} = \boldsymbol{h}_1 \| \boldsymbol{h}_{-1} \| \cdots \boldsymbol{h}_{2n-1} \| \boldsymbol{h}_{-2n+1}.$$

Step 1: $\mathcal{P}$ calculates for all distinct $i \neq j \in I_n = \{\pm 1, \pm 3, \ldots, \pm(2n-1)\}$,

$$v_{i,j} = \boldsymbol{g}_i^{\boldsymbol{a}_j} \boldsymbol{h}_j^{\boldsymbol{b}_i} u^{\langle \boldsymbol{a}_j, \boldsymbol{b}_i \rangle} \in \mathbb{G}_1$$

sets $\boldsymbol{v} = (v_{i,j}) \in \mathbb{G}_1^{2n(2n-1)}$ in the lexicographic order and sends $\mathcal{V}$ $\boldsymbol{E}(\boldsymbol{v}, \boldsymbol{F}_m)$.

Step 2: $\mathcal{V}$ chooses $x \overset{\$}{\leftarrow} \mathbb{Z}_p^*$ and returns it to $\mathcal{P}$.

Step 3: $\mathcal{P}$ computes $v = \boldsymbol{v}^{\boldsymbol{x}} = \prod_{\substack{i,j \in I_n \\ i \neq j}} v_{i,j}^{x^{j-i}} \in \mathbb{G}_1$, where $\boldsymbol{x}$ is the vector consisting of x^{j-i}, and then sends it to $\mathcal{V}$.

Step 4: Both $\mathcal{P}$ and $\mathcal{V}$ compute

$$\widehat{\boldsymbol{g}} = \circ_{i \in I_n} \boldsymbol{g}_i^{x^{-i}} \in \mathbb{G}_1^{\widehat{N}}, \quad \widehat{\boldsymbol{h}} = \circ_{i \in I_n} \boldsymbol{h}_i^{x^i} \in \mathbb{G}_1^{\widehat{N}} \quad \text{and} \quad \widehat{P} = P \cdot v \in \mathbb{G}_1.$$

Additionally, $\mathcal{P}$ computes $\widehat{\boldsymbol{a}} = \sum_{i \in I_n} \boldsymbol{a}_i x^i \in \mathbb{Z}_p^{\widehat{N}}$ and $\widehat{\boldsymbol{b}} = \sum_{i \in I_n} \boldsymbol{b}_i x^{-i} \in \mathbb{Z}_p^{\widehat{N}}$.

Step 5: $\mathcal{V}$ updates st_V by adding a tuple $(\boldsymbol{E}(\boldsymbol{v}, \boldsymbol{F}_m), v, \boldsymbol{x})$ into the bottom. $\mathcal{P}$ updates st_P by adding a tuple $(\boldsymbol{E}(\boldsymbol{v}, \boldsymbol{F}_m), v, \boldsymbol{x}; \boldsymbol{v})$ into the bottom. Both $\mathcal{P}$ and $\mathcal{V}$ run Protocol1($\widehat{\boldsymbol{g}}, \widehat{\boldsymbol{h}}, u, \boldsymbol{F}_k$ for $k \in [m-1], \widehat{P}, st_V; \widehat{\boldsymbol{a}}, \widehat{\boldsymbol{b}}, st_P$).

Fig. 2. Protocol1

Failed Naïve approach: linear combination. One may try to employ a random linear combination technique, which is widely used to aggregate multiple relations using homomorphic commitment schemes. For example, it is called *linear combination of protocols* in [34]. To this end, one may also try to use one $\boldsymbol{F}$ instead of distinct $\boldsymbol{F}_k$'s for every pairing equation and employ homomorphic property of pairings and multi-exponentiations to apply a random linear combination technique. Unfortunately, however, the relation $\mathcal{R}_{AggMEA}$ consists of two distinct types of equations P_k and q_k containing *distinct* $\boldsymbol{z}_k$'s, so that such a random linear combination technique is not directly applicable to $\mathcal{R}_{AggMEA}$ even with one $\boldsymbol{F}$.

Why we use distinct $\boldsymbol{F}_k$'s? Our basic strategy for aggregation is to merge multiple equations into a single equation by product. Later, we will present a reduction for it (Theorem 2). To this end, it is necessary to use distinct $\boldsymbol{F}_k$'s for each equation since it prevents the prover from changing opening vectors between committed vectors in the product.

A difficulty when we use several F_k's. As we mentioned, we use different $\boldsymbol{F}_k$'s for each commitment P_k. In this case, it is not easy to efficiently prove that the equation that $P_k = \boldsymbol{E}(\boldsymbol{v}_k, \boldsymbol{F}_k)$ holds. The CRS contains all $\boldsymbol{F}_k$'s, and thus, in order to prove $P_k = \boldsymbol{E}(\boldsymbol{v}_k, \boldsymbol{F}_k)$, we have to prove that only one $\boldsymbol{F}_k$ is used and the others are not used in the equation. Proving unusedness of the other $\boldsymbol{F}_j$ for $j \neq k$ with high performance is rather challenging. Let us consider the following simplified aggregation relation to clarify this difficulty.

$$\mathcal{R}_{2agg} = \left\{(\boldsymbol{F}_k, P_k; \boldsymbol{v}_{k,j} \text{ for } k \in [2]) : \wedge_{k \in [2]} P_k = \boldsymbol{E}(\boldsymbol{v}_k, \boldsymbol{F}_k)\right\}$$

In order to merge two equations into a single equation by product, we might construct a reduction as follows; The verifier chooses a challenge y, both the players set $\tilde{\boldsymbol{F}}_1 = \boldsymbol{F}_1, \tilde{\boldsymbol{F}}_2 = \boldsymbol{F}_2^y$, and $\tilde{P} = P_1 P_2^y$, and then run a product argument convincing that the knowledge of $\tilde{\boldsymbol{v}}_k$ satisfying

$$\tilde{P} = \boldsymbol{E}(\tilde{\boldsymbol{v}}_1, \tilde{\boldsymbol{F}}_1)\boldsymbol{E}(\tilde{\boldsymbol{v}}_2, \tilde{\boldsymbol{F}}_2). \tag{4}$$

Here, one may expect that an equality Eq. (4) guarantees two equalities in $\mathcal{R}_{2agg}$ by a random challenge y. Unfortunately, this is not true since fake P_k' passing the protocol can be created by $\boldsymbol{E}(\boldsymbol{v}_{k1}, \boldsymbol{F}_1)\boldsymbol{E}(\boldsymbol{v}_{k2}, \boldsymbol{F}_2)$ for $k = 1, 2$. That is, this reduction failed to show the unusedness of $\boldsymbol{F}_2$ in P_1 and $\boldsymbol{F}_1$ in P_2.

Our Solution: Augmented Aggregate Multi-exponentiation Argument. Although the above approach is failed to prove the unusedness of $\boldsymbol{F}_2$ in P_1 and $\boldsymbol{F}_1$ in P_2, it can be still used to prove that P_k's are of the form $\boldsymbol{E}(\boldsymbol{v}_1, \boldsymbol{F}_1)\boldsymbol{E}(\boldsymbol{v}_2, \boldsymbol{F}_2)$ for some witness $\boldsymbol{v}_1$ and $\boldsymbol{v}_2$. Therefore, instead of devising a protocol for the unusedness, we keep using the above approach of reducing to a product equation but change the target relation; we add redundant relations so that the final relation contains our target relation, multiple multi-exponentiations. That is, by adding some redundant values, we can further generalize the relation $\mathcal{R}_{AggMEA}$ and obtained the following relation $\mathcal{R}_{aAggMEA}$ for *augmented* aggregation of multi-exponentiations.

$$\left\{\begin{array}{l}\left(\begin{array}{l}\boldsymbol{F}_k \in \mathbb{G}_2^{2n(2n-1)}, \boldsymbol{z}_k \in \mathbb{Z}_p^{2n(2n-1)}, H_k \in \mathbb{G}_2, P_k \in \mathbb{G}_t, q_k \in \mathbb{G}_1 \\ ; \boldsymbol{v}_{k,j} \in \mathbb{G}^{2n(2n-1)} \text{ for } k, j \in [m]\end{array}\right) \\ : \bigwedge_{k \in [m]} \left(P_k = \prod_{j \in [m]} \boldsymbol{E}(\boldsymbol{v}_{k,j}, \boldsymbol{F}_j) \wedge q_k = \boldsymbol{v}_{k,k}^{\boldsymbol{z}_k} \wedge (\boldsymbol{v}_{k,j}^{\boldsymbol{z}_j} = 1_{\mathbb{G}_1} \text{ for } j \neq k)\right)\end{array}\right\} \tag{5}$$

Here, P_k is a commitment to $\boldsymbol{v}_{k,j}$'s and q_k is a multi-exponentiation of the committed value $\boldsymbol{v}_{k,k}$ and a public vector $\boldsymbol{z}$. In particular, P_k is defined by using all $\boldsymbol{F}_k$'s to avoid the difficulty of proving unusedness. Although there are redundant $\boldsymbol{v}_{k,j}$'s in P_k $(j \neq k)$, the above relation is sufficient to guarantee q_k is a multi-exponentiation of a committed value $\boldsymbol{v}_{k,k}$. In addition, H_k's are not necessary in the above relation, but we will use H_k's in the product argument, where we reduce from the augmented aggregation multi-exponentiation protocol.

The full description of $\mathsf{Protocol2}$ using $\mathsf{aAggMEA}$ is given in Fig. 3.

Protocol2($\boldsymbol{g}, \boldsymbol{h}, u, \boldsymbol{F}_k$ for $k \in [m], \boldsymbol{H}, P \in \mathbb{G}_1, st_V; \boldsymbol{a}, \boldsymbol{b}, st_P$), where $m = \log_{2n} N$

If $N = 1$:

Step 1: $\mathcal{P}$ sends $\mathcal{V}$ a and b.

Step 2: $\mathcal{V}$ proceeds the next step if $P = g^a h^b u^{a \cdot b}$ holds. Otherwise, $\mathcal{V}$ outputs *Reject*.

Step 3: If st_P is empty, then $\mathcal{V}$ outputs *Accept*. Otherwise, let $(u_k, v_k, \boldsymbol{x}_k; \boldsymbol{v}_k)$ be the k-th row in st_P and

$$\boldsymbol{v}_{k,j} = \begin{cases} \mathbf{1}_{\mathbb{G}_1} & \text{if } j \neq k \\ \boldsymbol{v}_k & \text{if } j = k \end{cases}$$

Step 4: $\mathcal{P}$ and $\mathcal{V}$ run aAggMEA($\boldsymbol{F}_k, \boldsymbol{x}_k, H_k, u_k, v_k; \boldsymbol{v}_{k,j}$ for $k, j \in [m]$).

Else ($N > 1$): Let $\widehat{N} = \frac{N}{2n}$ and parse $\boldsymbol{a}, \boldsymbol{b}, \boldsymbol{g}$, and $\boldsymbol{h}$ to

$$\boldsymbol{a} = \boldsymbol{a}_1 \| \boldsymbol{a}_{-1} \| \cdots \boldsymbol{a}_{2n-1} \| \boldsymbol{a}_{-2n+1}, \qquad \boldsymbol{b} = \boldsymbol{b}_1 \| \boldsymbol{b}_{-1} \| \cdots \boldsymbol{b}_{2n-1} \| \boldsymbol{b}_{-2n+1},$$
$$\boldsymbol{g} = \boldsymbol{g}_1 \| \boldsymbol{g}_{-1} \| \cdots \boldsymbol{g}_{2n-1} \| \boldsymbol{g}_{-2n+1}, \qquad \text{and } \boldsymbol{h} = \boldsymbol{h}_1 \| \boldsymbol{h}_{-1} \| \cdots \boldsymbol{h}_{2n-1} \| \boldsymbol{h}_{-2n+1}.$$

Step 1: $\mathcal{P}$ calculates for all distinct $i, j \in I_n = \{\pm 1, \pm 3, \ldots, \pm(2n-1)\}$,

$$v_{i,j} = \boldsymbol{g}_i^{\boldsymbol{a}_j} \boldsymbol{h}_j^{\boldsymbol{b}_i} u^{\langle \boldsymbol{a}_j, \boldsymbol{b}_i \rangle} \in \mathbb{G}_1$$

sets $\boldsymbol{v} = (v_{i,j}) \in \mathbb{G}_1^{2n(2n-1)}$ in the lexicographic order and sends $\mathcal{V}$ $\boldsymbol{E}(\boldsymbol{v}, \boldsymbol{F}_m)$.

Step 2: $\mathcal{V}$ chooses $x \xleftarrow{\$} \mathbb{Z}_p^*$ and returns it to $\mathcal{P}$.

Step 3: $\mathcal{P}$ computes $v = \boldsymbol{v}^{\boldsymbol{x}} = \prod_{\substack{i,j \in I_n \\ i \neq j}} v_{i,j}^{x^{j-i}} \in \mathbb{G}_1$, where $\boldsymbol{x}$ is the vector consisting of x^{j-i}, and then send v to $\mathcal{V}$.

Step 4: Both $\mathcal{P}$ and $\mathcal{V}$ compute

$$\widehat{\boldsymbol{g}} = \circ_{i \in I_n} \boldsymbol{g}_i^{x^{-i}} \in \mathbb{G}_1^{\widehat{N}}, \quad \widehat{\boldsymbol{h}} = \circ_{i \in I_n} \boldsymbol{h}_i^{x^i} \in \mathbb{G}_1^{\widehat{N}}, \quad \text{and} \quad \widehat{P} = P \cdot v \in \mathbb{G}_1.$$

In addition, $\mathcal{P}$ computes

$$\widehat{\boldsymbol{a}} = \sum_{i \in I_n} \boldsymbol{a}_i x^i \in \mathbb{Z}_p^{\widehat{N}} \quad \text{and} \quad \widehat{\boldsymbol{b}} = \sum_{i \in I_n} \boldsymbol{b}_i x^{-i} \in \mathbb{Z}_p^{\widehat{N}}.$$

Step 5: $\mathcal{V}$ updates st_V by adding a tuple $(\boldsymbol{E}(\boldsymbol{v}, \boldsymbol{F}_m), v, \boldsymbol{x})$ into the bottom. $\mathcal{P}$ updates st_P by adding a tuple $(\boldsymbol{E}(\boldsymbol{v}, \boldsymbol{F}_m), v, \boldsymbol{x}; \boldsymbol{v})$ into the bottom. Both $\mathcal{P}$ and $\mathcal{V}$ run Protocol2($\widehat{\boldsymbol{g}}, \widehat{\boldsymbol{h}}, u, \boldsymbol{F}_k$ for $k \in [m-1], \boldsymbol{H}, \widehat{P}, st_V; \widehat{\boldsymbol{a}}, \widehat{\boldsymbol{b}}, st_P$).

Fig. 3. Protocol2: Sublogarithmic IP Argument

Theorem 1. *The IP argument in Fig. 3 has perfect completeness and computational witness-extended-emulation under the discrete logarithm relation assumption in* $\mathbb{G}_1$ *and the double pairing assumption.*

Due to space constraints, the proof is provided in the full version [35].

Efficiency Analysis A main difference between Protocol1 and Protocol2 is the aggregating process for $\log_{2n} N$ multi-exponentiation arguments; Our proposal for aAggMEA in the next subsection has logarithmic communication overhead in the size of witness. For each round of Protocol2, $2n(2n-1)$ group elements are committed and thus total $\log_{2n} N \times 2n(2n-1)$ group elements are committed. Therefore, the overall communication overhead is $O(\log_{2n} N)$ for the main recursive rounds and $O(\log(\log_{2n} N \times 2n(2n-1))) = O(\log n + \log(\log_{2n} N))$ for aAggMEA. That is, $O(\log n + \log_{2n} N)$. If n satisfies $O(\log_{2n} N) = O(\log n)$, then the communication complexity becomes $O(\log n + \log_{2n} N) = O(\sqrt{\log N})$.

As for the computational overhead, compared to generalized BP-IP, only a run of aAggMEA protocol is imposed. Our proposal for the aAggMEA protocol is an extended variant of BP-IP, so that its computational complexity is still linear in the length of witness vector that is $O(n^2 \log_{2n} N)$. Therefore, for sufficiently small $n < \sqrt{N}$, this does not affect on the overall complexity, so that the total prover's computational overhead is $O(Nn^2)$ and the verifier's computational overhead is $O(N + n^2 \log_{2n} N)$ that are equal to those of general BP-IP.[4]

3.3 Aggregating Multi-exponentiation Argument

In this section, we propose an augmented aggregation of multi-exponentiation arguments aAggMEA for the relation in Eq. (5). Vectors in Eq. (5) are of dimension $2n(2n-1)$. For the sake of simplicity, we set the dimension of vectors N in this section and, by introducing dummy components, we can without loss of generality assume that N is a power of 2. The proposed protocol consists of two parts.

First, the aAggMEA is reduced to a proof system, denoted by ProdMEA, for the following relation $\mathcal{R}_{PMEA}$ for a product of multi-exponentiation.

$$\mathcal{R}_{PMEA} = \left\{ \begin{array}{l} (\boldsymbol{F}_k \in \mathbb{G}_2^N, \boldsymbol{z}_k \in \mathbb{Z}_p^N, H_k \in \mathbb{G}_2, P \in \mathbb{G}_t; \boldsymbol{v}_k \in \mathbb{G}_1^N \text{ for } k \in [m]) \\ : P = \prod_{k \in [m]} \boldsymbol{E}(\boldsymbol{v}_k, \boldsymbol{F}_k) e(\boldsymbol{v}_k^{\boldsymbol{z}_k}, H_k) \end{array} \right\}$$

The reduction is provided in Fig. 4 and its security property is given in the following theorem.

Theorem 2. *The* aAggMEA *protocol in Fig. 4 has perfect completeness and computational witness-extended-emulation if the* ProdMEA *protocol used in Fig. 4 has perfect completeness and computational witness-extended-emulation and the double pairing assumption holds.*

Due to space constraints, the proof is relegated to the full version [35].

Second part of aAggMEA is to run ProdMEA. The idea for the construction of ProdMEA is to use the resemblance between $\mathcal{R}_{PMEA}$ and $\mathcal{R}_{IP}$; $\mathcal{R}_{IP}$ is the relation about the inner-product between integer vectors, that is, a sum

[4] Note that when the communication complexity is evaluated, we set $n = 2^{\sqrt{\log N}}$ that is much smaller than $\sqrt{N} = 2^{\frac{1}{2}\log N}$, and thus our estimation for computational cost makes sense.

$\mathsf{aAggMEA}(\boldsymbol{F}_k \in \mathbb{G}_2^N, \boldsymbol{z}_k \in \mathbb{Z}_p^N, H_k \in \mathbb{G}_2, P_k \in \mathbb{G}_t, q_k \in \mathbb{G}_1; \boldsymbol{v}_{k,j} \in \mathbb{G}_1^N \text{ for } k, j \in [m])$

Step 1: $\mathcal{V}$ chooses and sends $y \xleftarrow{\$} \mathbb{Z}_p$ to $\mathcal{P}$.
Step 2: Both $\mathcal{P}$ and $\mathcal{V}$ set

$$\tilde{\boldsymbol{z}}_k = y^{k-1}\boldsymbol{z}_k,\ \tilde{\boldsymbol{F}}_k = \boldsymbol{F}_k^{y^{k-1}},\ \tilde{H}_k = H_k^{y^m},\ \text{ and } \tilde{P} = \prod_{k\in[m]} \left(P_k^{y^{k-1}} \cdot e(q_k^{y^{k-1}}, \tilde{H}_k)\right),$$

and $\mathcal{P}$ additionally sets $\tilde{\boldsymbol{v}}_k = \circ_{j\in[m]} \boldsymbol{v}_{j,k}^{y^{j-k}}$.
Step 3: $\mathcal{P}$ and $\mathcal{V}$ run $\mathsf{ProdMEA}(\tilde{\boldsymbol{F}}_k, \tilde{\boldsymbol{z}}_k, \tilde{H}_k, \tilde{P}; \tilde{\boldsymbol{v}}_k \text{ for } k \in [m])$

Fig. 4. Reduction from aAggMEA to ProdMEA

of component-wise products. $\mathcal{R}_{PMEA}$ is the relation about a product of exponentiation between a vector of group element $(\boldsymbol{v}_1, \ldots, \boldsymbol{v}_m)$ and an integer vector $(\boldsymbol{z}_1, \ldots, \boldsymbol{z}_m)$. In particular, P is a product of $\prod_{k\in[m]} \boldsymbol{E}(\boldsymbol{v}_k, \boldsymbol{F}_k)$ a commitment to $(\boldsymbol{v}_1, \ldots, \boldsymbol{v}_m)$, and $\prod_{k\in[m]} e(\boldsymbol{v}_k^{\boldsymbol{z}_k}, H_k)$ a commitment to the product of component-wise exponentiation between $(\boldsymbol{v}_1, \ldots, \boldsymbol{v}_m)$ and $(\boldsymbol{z}_1, \ldots, \boldsymbol{z}_m)$. The homomorphic property of commitment to group elements enables us to construct ProdMEA similarly to BP-IP using the homomorphic Pedersen commitment to integers. We provide the construction and the detailed explanation of the protocol ProdMEA in the full version [35].

The computational costs of ProdMEA for the prover and the verifier are linear and the communication cost is logarithmic in the size of witness, like BP-IP. The reduction from aAggMEA to ProdMEA requires a constant communication cost and linear computational costs for both prover and verifier in the size of witness. Therefore, aAggMEA requires linear computational complexity and logarithmic communication complexity in the size of witness.

4 Sublinear Verifier via Second Generalization

In this section, we propose an IP argument with logarithmic communication and sublinear verifier computation, solely based on the DL assumption.

4.1 Matrices and Operations

For succinct exposition, we additionally define notations using matrices. Similar to a vector, a matrix is denoted by a bold letter and a vector is considered a row matrix. For a matrix $\boldsymbol{a} \in \mathbb{Z}_p^{m\times n}$, its separation to the upper half matrix $\boldsymbol{a}_1 \in \mathbb{Z}_p^{m/2\times n}$ and the lower half matrix $\boldsymbol{a}_{-1} \in \mathbb{Z}_p^{m/2\times n}$ is denoted by $\boldsymbol{a} = [\![\boldsymbol{a}_1 \| \boldsymbol{a}_{-1}]\!]$. We define three matrix operations as follows.

Inner-Product. For $\boldsymbol{a}, \boldsymbol{b} \in \mathbb{Z}_p^{m\times n}$, the inner-product between $\boldsymbol{a}$ and $\boldsymbol{b}$ is defined as $\langle \boldsymbol{a}, \boldsymbol{b}\rangle := \sum_{r\in[m],s\in[n]} a_{r,s} b_{r,s} \in \mathbb{Z}_p$.

Multi-exponentiation. For $\boldsymbol{g} \in \mathbb{G}_i^{m \times n}$, $i \in \{1, 2, t\}$ and $\boldsymbol{a} \in \mathbb{Z}_p^{m \times n}$, the multi-exponentiation is defined as $\boldsymbol{g}^{\boldsymbol{a}} := \prod_{r \in [m], s \in [n]} g_{r,s}^{a_{r,s}} \in \mathbb{G}_i$.

Outer-Pairing Product. For $\boldsymbol{g} \in \mathbb{G}_1^m$ and $\boldsymbol{H} \in \mathbb{G}_2^n$, the outer-pairing product[5] is defined as

$$\boldsymbol{g} \otimes \boldsymbol{H} := \begin{bmatrix} e(g_1, H_1) & \dots & e(g_1, H_n) \\ \vdots & \ddots & \vdots \\ e(g_m, H_1) & \dots & e(g_m, H_n) \end{bmatrix} \in \mathbb{G}_t^{m \times n}.$$

Note that we set the output of the outer-pairing product to be a matrix instead of a vector, unlike an usual vector-representation of a tensor product since the matrix-representation is useful when separating it into two parts.

4.2 General Discrete Logarithm Relation Assumption

We restate the DLR assumption in terms of problem instance sampler to generalize it. Let GDLRsp be a sampler that takes the security parameter λ as input and outputs $(p, g_1, \dots, g_n, \mathbb{G})$, where $\mathbb{G}$ is a group $\mathbb{G}$ of λ-bit prime-order p and $g_1, \dots, g_n$ are generators of $\mathbb{G}$.

Definition 5 (General Discrete Logarithm Relation Assumption). *Let* GDLRsp *be a sampler. We say that* GDLRsp *satisfies the general discrete logarithm relation (GDLR) assumption if all non-uniform polynomial-time adversaries* $\mathcal{A}$*, the following inequality holds.*

$$\Pr\left[\boldsymbol{a} \neq \boldsymbol{0} \ \wedge \ \boldsymbol{g}^{\boldsymbol{a}} = 1_{\mathbb{G}} \ \middle| \ \begin{matrix} (p, \boldsymbol{g} \in \mathbb{G}^n, \mathbb{G}) \leftarrow \mathsf{GDLRsp}(1^\lambda) \\ \boldsymbol{a} \leftarrow \mathcal{A}(p, \boldsymbol{g}, \mathbb{G}) \end{matrix}\right] < negl(\lambda),$$

where $1_{\mathbb{G}}$ *is the identity of* $\mathbb{G}$ *and* $negl(\lambda)$ *is a negligible function in* λ.

Definition 6. *For a fixed integer* N*, the sampler* GDLRsp_{Rand} *is defined as follows.*

$$\mathsf{GDLRsp}_{Rand}(1^\lambda) : \textit{Choose a group } \mathbb{G} \textit{ of } \lambda\textit{-bit prime-order } p;\ \boldsymbol{g} \xleftarrow{\$} \mathbb{G}^N; \\ \textit{Output } (p, \boldsymbol{g}, \mathbb{G}).$$

Theorem 3. GDLRsp_{Rand} *satisfies the GDLR assumption if the DL assumption holds for the same underlying group* $\mathbb{G}$.

The soundness theorem of BP-IP holds under the GDLR assumption; it uses only the fact that no adversary can find a non-trivial relation, regardless of the distribution of generators $\boldsymbol{g}$. We restate the soundness theorem of BP-IP below.

Theorem 4 [17]**.** *The BP-IP has perfect completeness and computational witness-extended-emulation under the GDLR assumption.*

---

[5] Note that this operation is also called "projecting bilinear map" in the context of converting composite-order bilinear groups to prime-order bilinear groups [26].

We propose another sampler that satisfies the GDLR assumption.

Definition 7. *For $m, n \in \mathbb{N}$, the sampler* GDLRsp_{BM} *is defined as follows.*

$$\mathsf{GDLRsp}_{BM}(1^\lambda) : (p, g, H, \mathbb{G}_1, \mathbb{G}_2, \mathbb{G}_t, e) \leftarrow \mathcal{G}(1^\lambda); \boldsymbol{g} \xleftarrow{\$} \mathbb{G}_1^m; \boldsymbol{H} \xleftarrow{\$} \mathbb{G}_2^n, u \xleftarrow{\$} \mathbb{G}_t; \\ \textit{Output } (p, \boldsymbol{g} \otimes \boldsymbol{H}, u, \mathbb{G}_t).$$

Theorem 5. GDLRsp_{BM} *satisfies the GDLR assumption if the DL assumption holds on $\mathbb{G}_1$ and $\mathbb{G}_2$.*

Proof. Suppose that there exists a non-uniform polynomial-time adversary $\mathcal{A}$ breaking the GDLR assumption with non-negligible probability. That is, with non-negligible probability, $\mathcal{A}$ outputs a matrix $\boldsymbol{a} \in \mathbb{Z}_p^{m \times n}$ and an integer $c \in \mathbb{Z}_p$ such that $(\boldsymbol{g} \otimes \boldsymbol{H})^{\boldsymbol{a}} u^c = 1_{\mathbb{G}_t}$ and $\boldsymbol{a}$, c are not all zeros, where $1_{\mathbb{G}_t}$ is the identity of $\mathbb{G}_t$. We separate the adversarial types according to the output distribution. Let $\boldsymbol{a}_i \in \mathbb{Z}_p^n$ be the i-th row vector of $\boldsymbol{a}$ for $i \in [m]$.

- (Type 1) $c \neq 0$
- (Type 2) Not Type-1. $\forall i \in [m]$, $\boldsymbol{H}^{\boldsymbol{a}_i} = 1_{\mathbb{G}_2}$.
- (Type 3) Neither Type-1 or Type-2.

It is straightforward that $\mathcal{A}$ should be at least one of the above 3 types. For each adversary, we show how to break one of the DL assumption on $\mathbb{G}_1$, $\mathbb{G}_2$, and $\mathbb{G}_t$.[6]

Type-1 adversary. Given a DL instance $h_t \in \mathbb{G}_t$, we construct a simulator finding $Dlog_{e(g,H)} h_t$. First, choose $\boldsymbol{x}$ and $\boldsymbol{z} \xleftarrow{\$} \mathbb{Z}_p^n$ and set $\boldsymbol{g} = g^{\boldsymbol{x}}$, $\boldsymbol{H} = H^{\boldsymbol{z}}$, and $u = h_t$. Then, the distribution of $(\boldsymbol{g}, \boldsymbol{H}, u)$ is identical to the real GDLR instance. The type-1 adversary outputs $\boldsymbol{a}$ and c such that $c \neq 0$ and $\boldsymbol{a} \neq \boldsymbol{0}$. From the necessary condition for $\boldsymbol{a}$ and c, we know the following equality holds.

$$\langle \boldsymbol{x} \otimes \boldsymbol{z}, \boldsymbol{a} \rangle + c \cdot Dlog_{e(g,H)} h_t = 0 \pmod{p}$$

Since we know all components except for $Dlog_{e(g,H)} h_t$ and $c \neq 0$, we can find $Dlog_{e(g,H)} h_t$ by solving the above modular equation.

Type-2 adversary. This type of adversary can be used as an attacker breaking the GDLR assumption on $\mathbb{G}_2$ with a sampler GDLRsp_{Rand}. Theorem 3 guarantees that there is no type-2 adversary breaking the GDLR assumption with GDLRsp_{BM} under the DL assumption on $\mathbb{G}_2$.

Type-3 adversary. Given a DL instance $\hat{g} \in \mathbb{G}_1$, we construct a simulator finding $DL_g \hat{g}$. First, choose an index $k \xleftarrow{\$} [m]$, integer vectors $\boldsymbol{x} = (x_1, \ldots, x_m) \xleftarrow{\$} \mathbb{Z}_p^m$, $\boldsymbol{z} \xleftarrow{\$} \mathbb{Z}_p^n$, and $w \xleftarrow{\$} \mathbb{Z}_p$, and set $\boldsymbol{g} = (g^{x_1}, \ldots, g^{x_{k-1}}, \hat{g}, g^{x_{k+1}}, \ldots, g^{x_m})$, $\boldsymbol{H} = H^{\boldsymbol{z}}$, and $u = e(g, H)^w$. Then, the distribution of $(\boldsymbol{g}, \boldsymbol{H}, u)$ is identical to the real GDLR instance. Let $\hat{\boldsymbol{x}} = (x_1, \ldots, x_{k-1}, Dlog_g \hat{g}, x_{k+1}, \ldots, x_m)$. Then, $\boldsymbol{g} = g^{\hat{\boldsymbol{x}}}$.

[6] Note that the DL assumption on $\mathbb{G}_1$ implies the DL assumption on $\mathbb{G}_t$ by the MOV attack [39].

The type-3 adversary outputs $\boldsymbol{a}$ and c such that $c = 0$ and $\boldsymbol{H}^{\boldsymbol{a}_i} \neq 1_{\mathbb{G}_2}$ for some $i \in [n]$. From the necessary condition for $\boldsymbol{a}$ and c, we know the following equality holds.

$$\begin{aligned}\langle \hat{\boldsymbol{x}} \otimes \boldsymbol{z}, \boldsymbol{a} \rangle + c \cdot w &= x_1 \langle \boldsymbol{z}, \boldsymbol{a}_1 \rangle + \cdots + (Dlog_g \hat{g}) \langle \boldsymbol{z}, \boldsymbol{a}_k \rangle + \cdots + x_m \langle \boldsymbol{z}, \boldsymbol{a}_m \rangle + c \cdot w \\ &= 0 \pmod p\end{aligned}$$

Since the index k is completely hidden from the viewpoint of $\mathcal{A}$, $i = k$ with non-negligible $1/m$ probability. If $i = k$, then $\langle \boldsymbol{z}, \boldsymbol{a}_k \rangle \neq 0$, so that we can recover $(Dlog_g \hat{g})$ by solving the above modular equation, since we know all components except for $Dlog_g \hat{g}$. □

4.3 Another Generalization of BP-IP with Sublinear Verifier

In BP-IP, most of the common input for $\mathcal{P}$ and $\mathcal{V}$ are uniformly selected group elements, which is the common random string. What we expect from these group elements is that their discrete logarithms are unknown, so that the DLR assumption holds. The DL assumption implies the GDLR assumption with uniform sampler and this assumption is the root of the soundness of BP-IP. We can generalize BP-IP while keeping the soundness proof by using an arbitrary sampler satisfying the GDLR assumption, instead of GDLRsp_{Rand} to create the CRS.

Sublinear Common Inputs. We uniformly generate $\boldsymbol{g}, \boldsymbol{h} \in \mathbb{G}_1^m$ and $\boldsymbol{H} \in \mathbb{G}_2^n$ and use $\boldsymbol{g} \otimes \boldsymbol{H}$ and $\boldsymbol{h} \otimes \boldsymbol{H} \in \mathbb{G}_t^{m \times n}$ instead of the CRS in BP-IP. That is, we construct a proof system for the following relation.

$$\left\{ \begin{array}{l} (\boldsymbol{g}, \boldsymbol{h} \in \mathbb{G}_1^m, \boldsymbol{H} \in \mathbb{G}_2^n, u, P \in \mathbb{G}_t;\ \boldsymbol{a}, \boldsymbol{b} \in \mathbb{Z}_p^{m \times n}) \\ :\ P = (\boldsymbol{g} \otimes \boldsymbol{H})^{\boldsymbol{a}} (\boldsymbol{h} \otimes \boldsymbol{H})^{\boldsymbol{b}} u^{\langle \boldsymbol{a}, \boldsymbol{b} \rangle} \in \mathbb{G}_t \end{array} \right\} \tag{6}$$

Note that this modification does not require the structured reference string since $\boldsymbol{g} \otimes \boldsymbol{H}$ and $\boldsymbol{h} \otimes \boldsymbol{H}$ are publicly computable from the common random string $\boldsymbol{g}$, $\boldsymbol{h}$ and $\boldsymbol{H}$. Furthermore, the proof system is still sound since, like the CRS in BP-IP, $\boldsymbol{g} \otimes \boldsymbol{H}$ and $\boldsymbol{h} \otimes \boldsymbol{H}$ hold the GDLR assumption under the DL assumption on $\mathbb{G}_1$ and $\mathbb{G}_2$ by Theorem 5.

Sublinear Verification. If we set $m = n = \sqrt{N}$, the above modification can reduce the CRS size to be a square root of BP-IP. Nevertheless, computing $\boldsymbol{g} \otimes \boldsymbol{H}$ requires linear computation in N so that the verification cost is still linear in N. We arrange the order of witness $\boldsymbol{a}$ and $\boldsymbol{b}$ in each round, and thus we can go through the process without exactly computing $\boldsymbol{g} \otimes \boldsymbol{H}$ and $\boldsymbol{h} \otimes \boldsymbol{H}$. We explain how to avoid a full computation of $\boldsymbol{g} \otimes \boldsymbol{H}$ and $\boldsymbol{h} \otimes \boldsymbol{H}$. Without loss of generality, we assume that m and n are powers of 2.[7] If $m > 1$, then let $\widehat{m} = \frac{m}{2}$ and parse $\boldsymbol{a}, \boldsymbol{b} \in \mathbb{Z}_p^{m \times n}, \boldsymbol{g}, \boldsymbol{h} \in \mathbb{G}_1^m$ to

[7] If needed, we can appropriately pad zeros in the vectors since zeros do not affect the result of inner-product.

$$\boldsymbol{a} = [\![\boldsymbol{a}_1 \| \boldsymbol{a}_{-1}]\!] \quad \boldsymbol{b} = [\![\boldsymbol{b}_1 \| \boldsymbol{b}_{-1}]\!], \quad \boldsymbol{g} = \boldsymbol{g}_1 \| \boldsymbol{g}_{-1}, \text{ and } \boldsymbol{h} = \boldsymbol{h}_1 \| \boldsymbol{h}_{-1}.$$

Then, the bases $\boldsymbol{g} \otimes \boldsymbol{H} \in \mathbb{G}_t^{m \times n}$ and $\boldsymbol{h} \otimes \boldsymbol{H} \in \mathbb{G}_t^{m \times n}$ are able to be implicitly parsed to $[\![\boldsymbol{g}_1 \otimes \boldsymbol{H} \| \boldsymbol{g}_{-1} \otimes \boldsymbol{H}]\!]$ and $[\![\boldsymbol{h}_1 \otimes \boldsymbol{H} \| \boldsymbol{h}_{-1} \otimes \boldsymbol{H}]\!]$, respectively. Let $\tilde{\boldsymbol{g}}_i = \boldsymbol{g}_i \otimes \boldsymbol{H} \in \mathbb{G}_t^{\widehat{m} \times n}$ and $\tilde{\boldsymbol{h}}_i = \boldsymbol{h}_i \otimes \boldsymbol{H} \in \mathbb{G}_t^{\widehat{m} \times n}$ for $i \in \{1, -1\}$. Next, $\mathcal{P}$ calculates

$$L = \tilde{\boldsymbol{g}}_{-1}^{\boldsymbol{a}_1} \ \tilde{\boldsymbol{h}}_1^{\boldsymbol{b}_{-1}} u^{\langle \boldsymbol{a}_1, \boldsymbol{b}_{-1} \rangle} \text{ and } R = \tilde{\boldsymbol{g}}_1^{\boldsymbol{a}_{-1}} \tilde{\boldsymbol{h}}_{-1}^{\boldsymbol{b}_1} \ u^{\langle \boldsymbol{a}_{-1}, \boldsymbol{b}_1 \rangle} \in \mathbb{G}_t$$

and sends them to $\mathcal{V}$. This computation of $\mathcal{P}$ is equivalent to BP-IP with CRS $\boldsymbol{g} \otimes \boldsymbol{H}$ and $\boldsymbol{h} \otimes \boldsymbol{H}$. $\mathcal{V}$ returns a random challenge $x \overset{\$}{\leftarrow} \mathbb{Z}_p^*$ to $\mathcal{P}$. Finally, both $\mathcal{P}$ and $\mathcal{V}$ compute

$$\widehat{\boldsymbol{g}} = \boldsymbol{g}_1^{x^{-1}} \circ \boldsymbol{g}_{-1}^{x} \in \mathbb{G}_1^{\widehat{m}}, \quad \widehat{\boldsymbol{h}} = \boldsymbol{h}_1^{x} \circ \boldsymbol{h}_{-1}^{x^{-1}} \in \mathbb{G}_1^{\widehat{m}}, \quad \text{and } \widehat{P} = L^{x^2} P \, R^{x^{-2}} \in \mathbb{G}_t$$

and $\mathcal{P}$ additionally computes $\widehat{\boldsymbol{a}} = \boldsymbol{a}_1 x + \boldsymbol{a}_{-1} x^{-1}$ and $\widehat{\boldsymbol{b}} = \boldsymbol{b}_1 x^{-1} + \boldsymbol{b}_{-1} x \in \mathbb{Z}_p^{\widehat{m} \times n}$. Then, $\widehat{P}$ is well computed since L and R are equivalent to those in BP-IP. In BP-IP, however, $\tilde{\boldsymbol{g}}_1^{x^{-1}} \circ \tilde{\boldsymbol{g}}_{-1}^{x}$ and $\tilde{\boldsymbol{h}}_1^{x} \circ \tilde{\boldsymbol{h}}_{-1}^{x^{-1}}$ should be computed as the new bases for the next round argument with witness $\widehat{\boldsymbol{a}}$ and $\widehat{\boldsymbol{b}}$. Instead, in Protocol3, we use the equality $\widehat{\boldsymbol{g}} \otimes \boldsymbol{H} = \tilde{\boldsymbol{g}}_1^{x^{-1}} \circ \tilde{\boldsymbol{g}}_{-1}^{x}$ and $\widehat{\boldsymbol{h}} \otimes \boldsymbol{H} = \tilde{\boldsymbol{h}}_1^{x} \circ \tilde{\boldsymbol{h}}_{-1}^{x^{-1}}$ such that $\widehat{\boldsymbol{g}}$ and $\widehat{\boldsymbol{h}}$ are the bases for the next argument with $\widehat{\boldsymbol{a}}$ and $\widehat{\boldsymbol{b}}$. Therefore, both $\mathcal{P}$ and $\mathcal{V}$ can run the protocol with $(\widehat{\boldsymbol{g}}, \widehat{\boldsymbol{h}}, \boldsymbol{H}, u, \widehat{P}; \widehat{\boldsymbol{a}}, \widehat{\boldsymbol{b}})$. If $m = 1$, the CRS is of the form $e(g, \boldsymbol{H})$ and $e(h, \boldsymbol{H})$, which is uniform in $\mathbb{G}_t$, so that we can directly run BP-IP over $\mathbb{G}_t$. We present the full description of our protocol, denoted by Protocol3, in Fig. 5. The number of rounds and the communication cost in Protocol3 are the same as those of BP-IP over $\mathbb{G}_t$. The verification cost is $O(\sqrt{N})$ when setting $m = n$. Note that a naïve verification in the ($m = 1$) case requires $O(\sqrt{N})$ expensive pairing computation for calculating $e(g, \boldsymbol{H})$ and $e(h, \boldsymbol{H})$, but using a similar trick in the case ($m > 1$), the verifier can update $\boldsymbol{H}$ only instead of $e(g, \boldsymbol{H})$ and $e(h, \boldsymbol{H})$ and then perform constant pairing operations only at the final stage.

Linear Prover and Logarithmic Communication. In terms of the prover's computation and communication overheads, Protocol3 is asymptotically the same as BP-IP since we can consider Protocol3 as BP-IP with CRS $\boldsymbol{g} \otimes \boldsymbol{H}$ and $\boldsymbol{h} \otimes \boldsymbol{H}$. That is, $O(N)$ and $O(\log_2 N)$ for computation and communication, respectively.

Theorem 6. *The argument presented in Fig. 5 for the relation* (6) *has perfect completeness and computational witness-extended-emulation under the GDLR assumption with the sampler* GDLRsp_{BM}.

Proof. Although the verification cost in Protocol3 is reduced compared with BP-IP, both players' computation in Protocol3 is equivalent to that of BP-IP with the CRS $\boldsymbol{g} \otimes \boldsymbol{H}$ and $\boldsymbol{h} \otimes \boldsymbol{H}$. Therefore, the proof of this theorem should be exactly the same as the proof of BP-IP [35], except that the GDLR assumption is guaranteed by Theorem 5 instead of Theorem 3. □

$\mathsf{Protocol3}(\boldsymbol{g}, \boldsymbol{h} \in \mathbb{G}_1^m, \boldsymbol{H} \in \mathbb{G}_2^n, u, P; \boldsymbol{a}, \boldsymbol{b})$

If $m = 1$: $\mathcal{P}$ and $\mathcal{V}$ run $\mathsf{BP}_{\mathsf{IP}}(e(g, \boldsymbol{H}), e(h, \boldsymbol{H}), u, P; \boldsymbol{a}, \boldsymbol{b})$.
Else ($m > 1$): Let $\widehat{m} = \frac{m}{2}$. Parse $\boldsymbol{a}, \boldsymbol{b}, \boldsymbol{g}$, and $\boldsymbol{h}$ to

$$\boldsymbol{a} = [\![\boldsymbol{a}_1 \| \boldsymbol{a}_{-1}]\!] \quad \boldsymbol{b} = [\![\boldsymbol{b}_1 \| \boldsymbol{b}_{-1}]\!], \quad \boldsymbol{g} = \boldsymbol{g}_1 \| \boldsymbol{g}_{-1}, \text{ and } \boldsymbol{h} = \boldsymbol{h}_1 \| \boldsymbol{h}_{-1}.$$

Step 1: $\mathcal{P}$ calculates

$$L = (\boldsymbol{g}_{-1} \otimes \boldsymbol{H})^{\boldsymbol{a}_1} \ (\boldsymbol{h}_1 \ \otimes \boldsymbol{H})^{\boldsymbol{b}_{-1}} u^{\langle \boldsymbol{a}_1, \boldsymbol{b}_{-1} \rangle} \in \mathbb{G}_t$$
$$\text{and } R = (\boldsymbol{g}_1 \ \otimes \boldsymbol{H})^{\boldsymbol{a}_{-1}} (\boldsymbol{h}_{-1} \otimes \boldsymbol{H})^{\boldsymbol{b}_1} \ u^{\langle \boldsymbol{a}_{-1}, \boldsymbol{b}_1 \rangle} \in \mathbb{G}_t$$

and sends them to $\mathcal{V}$.
Step 2: $\mathcal{V}$ chooses $x \stackrel{\$}{\leftarrow} \mathbb{Z}_p^*$ and returns it to $\mathcal{P}$.
Step 3: Both $\mathcal{P}$ and $\mathcal{V}$ compute

$$\widehat{\boldsymbol{g}} = \boldsymbol{g}_1^{x^{-1}} \circ \boldsymbol{g}_{-1}^{x} \in \mathbb{G}_1^{\widehat{m}}, \quad \widehat{\boldsymbol{h}} = \boldsymbol{h}_1^{x} \circ \boldsymbol{h}_{-1}^{x^{-1}} \ \in \mathbb{G}_1^{\widehat{m}}, \quad \text{and } \widehat{P} = L^{x^2} P \, R^{x^{-2}} \in \mathbb{G}_t.$$

Additionally, $\mathcal{P}$ computes $\widehat{\boldsymbol{a}} = \boldsymbol{a}_1 x + \boldsymbol{a}_{-1} x^{-1}$ and $\widehat{\boldsymbol{b}} = \boldsymbol{b}_1 x^{-1} + \boldsymbol{b}_{-1} x \in \mathbb{Z}_p^{\widehat{m}}$.
Step 4: Both $\mathcal{P}$ and $\mathcal{V}$ run the protocol with $(\widehat{\boldsymbol{g}}, \widehat{\boldsymbol{h}}, \boldsymbol{H}, u, \widehat{P}; \widehat{\boldsymbol{a}}, \widehat{\boldsymbol{b}})$.

Fig. 5. Protocol3: Another Generalization of BP-IP

4.4 Practical Verification of Protocol 3

When it comes to asymptotic complexity, Protocol3 is definitely better than BP-IP. However, for practical performance, we need to consider the computation time of group operations which depends on the choice of elliptic curves. Actually, BP-IP and Protocol3 are built on different elliptic curves. Current implementations of BP-IP use two curves, i.e., secp256k1 and ed25519 curves. The dalek project has reported that the use of ed25519 provides approximately 2x speepup [23]. However, Protocol3 cannot use ed25519 because it requires pairing operations. Therefore, we take ed25519 for BP-IP and BLS12-381 for Protocol3 in the below estimation.

We consider a typical parameter setting $N = 2^{20}$ in 128-bits security which both secp256k1 and ed25519 curves provide. BP-IP requires 2×2^{20} group operations for verification. Protocol3 requires 2×2^{10} $\mathbb{G}_1$ operations and 2×2^{10} $\mathbb{G}_2$ operations for verification. According to the implementation results from [43], the execution times of operations in $\mathbb{G}_1$ and $\mathbb{G}_2$ of BLS12-381 are roughly $5\times$ and $10\times$ slower than that of ed25519, respectively. Thus, we expect that Protocol3's verifier is significantly faster (approximately $70\times$) than that of BP-IP.

5 Sublinear Verifier Without Pairing

We propose another IP argument with sublinear verifier, particularly without pairings. The crucial ingredient for Protocol3 is pairing-based homomorphic commitments to group elements [1], which is employed as the second layer scheme of the two-tiered commitment scheme. For example, L in **Step 1** of Protocol3 contains a factor $(\boldsymbol{g}_{-1} \otimes \boldsymbol{H})^{\boldsymbol{a}_1}$, which can be considered as a vector of homomorphic commitments to $\boldsymbol{g}_{-1}^{\boldsymbol{a}_1} \in \mathbb{G}_1^n$, where $\boldsymbol{g}_{-1}^{\boldsymbol{a}_1}$ is a vector of the first layer commitments to columns of $\boldsymbol{a}_1$ and $\boldsymbol{g}_{-1} \in \mathbb{G}_1^m$ and $\boldsymbol{H} \in \mathbb{G}_2^n$ are the commitment keys of first and second layer schemes, respectively. When the verifier checks $\widehat{P} = L^{x^2} P\, R^{x^{-2}} \in \mathbb{G}_t$ in **Step 3** of Protocol3, the homomorphic property of the second layer scheme guarantees a vector of linear group equations $(\boldsymbol{g}_{-1}^{\boldsymbol{a}_1})^{x^2} \cdot (\boldsymbol{g}^{\boldsymbol{a}} \boldsymbol{h}^{\boldsymbol{b}}) \cdot (\boldsymbol{h}_1^{\boldsymbol{b}_{-1}})^{x^{-2}} \in \mathbb{G}_1^n$ holds, where $(\boldsymbol{g}_{-1}^{\boldsymbol{a}_1})$, $(\boldsymbol{g}^{\boldsymbol{a}} \boldsymbol{h}^{\boldsymbol{b}})$, and $(\boldsymbol{h}_1^{\boldsymbol{b}_{-1}})$ are second layer openings of L, R, and P. Since the first layer scheme is homomorphic, these n equations in $\mathbb{G}_1^n$ similarly guarantee that mn linear equations hold.

In order to circumvent the necessity of using the pairing-based primitive, we propose a new two-tiered commitment scheme such that the first layer scheme is still Pedersen commitment scheme mapping from integers to group elements and the second layer scheme for committing to group elements is replaced with the new one. We show that although the new second layer scheme is not homomorphic in group operations, it facilitates efficient proving group operations.

Indeed the integrity of homomorphic operation is sufficient to build an argument system. For example, if the prover computes L and R in **Step 1** by using the new two-tiered commitments, the verifier cannot compute $\widehat{P}$ by herself in **Step 3**, so that the prover should send $\widehat{P}$ along with its integrity proof. As mentioned above, the relation for the integrity proof is exactly a vector of linear group equations between the second layer openings. Since the new commitment scheme facilitates proving this type of relation, the new argument system still has the benefit of sublinear verifier.

Unfortunately, this approach increases the proof size due to additional integrity proofs for each round. Finally, we bring in the aggregation technique used for the sublogarithmic proofs in Sect. 3, so that we can simultaneously attain both logarithmic proof size and sublinear verifier.

Notation. We use a pair of elliptic curve groups, denoted by $(\mathbb{G}_p, \mathbb{G}_q)$, of distinct prime order p and q such that $\mathbb{G}_p := E(\mathbb{Z}_q)$. In order to avoid confusion, we use lower case letters to denote elements in $\mathbb{G}_p$ and upper case letters to denote elements in $\mathbb{G}_q$. For example, $g \in \mathbb{G}_p$ and $G \in \mathbb{G}_q$. In our protocol, we repeatedly use parallel multi-exponentiations with the same base $\boldsymbol{g} \in \mathbb{G}_p^m$. For example, given an integer matrix $\boldsymbol{a} \in \mathbb{Z}_p^{m \times n}$, we often compute $\boldsymbol{g}^{\boldsymbol{a}_i}$ for $i \in [n]$, that are n multi-exponentiations, where $\boldsymbol{a}_i$ is the i-th column of $\boldsymbol{a}$. This computation is compactly denoted by $\overrightarrow{\boldsymbol{g}^{\boldsymbol{a}}} := (\boldsymbol{g}^{\boldsymbol{a}_1}, \ldots, \boldsymbol{g}^{\boldsymbol{a}_n})$.

5.1 Projective Presentation for Elliptic Curve Group

Affine coordinates are the conventional way of expressing elliptic curve points. However, there is no complete addition formula in affine coordinates, i.e., affine coordinates require special addition formulas for exceptional cases such as doubling and operations with the point at infinity or the inverse point. In our construction, it is desirable to have an arithmetic circuit which correctly computes the operation between any two points in the elliptic curve group. Thus, we make use of complete addition formulas for prime order elliptic curves in projective coordinates, which have been proposed by Renes et al. [41] based on the work of Bosma and Lenstra [16].

Let $E(\mathbb{Z}_q)$ with $q \geq 5$ be a prime order elliptic curve group given by the short Weierstrass equation in two-dimensional projective space $\mathbb{P}^2(\mathbb{Z}_q)$, i.e.,

$$\{(X, Y, Z) \in \mathbb{Z}_q^3 | Y^2 Z = X^3 + aXZ^2 + bZ^3\}.$$

Two points (X_1, Y_1, Z_1) and (X_2, Y_2, Z_2) are equal in $\mathbb{P}^2(\mathbb{Z}_q)$ if and only if $(X_2, Y_2, Z_2) = (\lambda X_1, \lambda Y_1, \lambda Z_1)$ for some $\lambda \in \mathbb{Z}_q^*$. The point at infinity is equal to $(0, 1, 0)$. Because $E(\mathbb{Z}_q)$ has prime order, there is no $\mathbb{Z}_q$-rational point of order 2. In this setting, for any two pair of points (X_1, Y_1, Z_1) and (X_2, Y_2, Z_2), Bosma and Lenstra gave the complete formulas to compute $(X_3, Y_3, Z_3) = (X_1, Y_1, Z_1) + (X_2, Y_2, Z_2)$ where X_3, Y_3, and Z_3 are expressed as polynomials in X_1, Y_1, Z_1, X_2, Y_2, and Z_2. Later, Renes et al. presented the algorithm [41, Algorithm 1] for the optimized version of Bosma and Lenstra' addition formula. The algorithm covers both doubling and addition operations without exceptional cases using 12 multiplications, 5 multiplications by constant, and 23 additions over $\mathbb{Z}_q$. Thus, we consider the arithmetic circuit from this formula for group operations of $E(\mathbb{Z}_q)$ in our construction. For the convenience of readers, we provide the algorithm given by Renes et al. in the full version [35].

5.2 Two-Tiered Commitment Scheme and Proof for Second Layer

We introduce a two-tiered commitment scheme for handing columns of a matrix $\boldsymbol{a} \in \mathbb{Z}_p^{m \times n}$. The first layer commitment is for committing to a vector in $\mathbb{Z}_p^m$. The second layer commitment is for committing to the multiple, say n, first layer commitments. Therefore, the final two-tiered commitment scheme is for committing to a matrix $\boldsymbol{a} \in \mathbb{Z}_p^{m \times n}$.

We begin with a pair of elliptic curve groups $(\mathbb{G}_p = E(\mathbb{Z}_q), \mathbb{G}_q)$ of respective order p and q such that the discrete logarithm assumption holds in both $\mathbb{G}_p$ and $\mathbb{G}_q$. Note that there are efficient methods to generate such a pair of prime order elliptic curves $(\mathbb{G}_p = E(\mathbb{Z}_q), \mathbb{G}_q)$ of given primes p and q whose sizes are both 2λ for the security parameter λ [42]. In the first layer, we use the Pedersen commitment scheme with commitment key $\boldsymbol{g} \in \mathbb{G}_p^m$ to commit to columns of $\boldsymbol{a}$.[8] That is, the commitment is $\overrightarrow{\boldsymbol{g}^{\boldsymbol{a}}} \in \mathbb{G}_p^n$, which is an n-tuple of Pedersen commitments to columns of $\boldsymbol{a}$. Since it consists of elliptic curve group elements, it can be represented by n sequences of 3-element tuples $(X_i, Y_i, Z_i)_{i=1}^n \in \mathbb{Z}_q^{3n}$, where (X_i, Y_i, Z_i) is the projective representation of the i-th component of $\overrightarrow{\boldsymbol{g}^{\boldsymbol{a}}}$. For the second layer, we again use the Pedersen commitment with a *different* commitment key $\boldsymbol{G} = (G_1, \ldots, G_{3n}) \in \mathbb{G}_q^{3n}$ so that the commitment to $\overrightarrow{\boldsymbol{g}^{\boldsymbol{a}}} = (X_i, Y_i, Z_i)_{i=1}^n$ is defined as $\prod_{i=1}^n G_{3i-2}^{X_i} G_{3i-1}^{Y_i} G_{3i}^{Z_i}$, denoted by $\mathsf{Com}(\overrightarrow{\boldsymbol{g}^{\boldsymbol{a}}}; \mathbf{G})$.

---

[8] More precisely, we use a slightly modified Pedersen commitment scheme in the sense that (1) opening is not an integer but a vector and (2) the random element is always set to be zero since the hiding property is not required.

Note that we often consider $\overrightarrow{\boldsymbol{g}^{\boldsymbol{a}}}$ as an element in $\mathbb{Z}_q^{3n}$ since we always use the projective representation for $\mathbb{G}_p = E(\mathbb{Z}_q)$ throughout the paper. The binding property of the proposed commitment scheme holds under the discrete logarithm assumption in $\mathbb{G}_p$ and $\mathbb{G}_q$.

Proving for Relation Between Second Layer Opening. The second layer opening is $\overrightarrow{\boldsymbol{g}^{\boldsymbol{a}}} \in \mathbb{G}_p^n$, a vector of group elements, which can be considered as a vector of $\mathbb{Z}_q^{3n}$. As aforementioned in the first part of this section, we should prove a relation among the second layer openings that consist of a vector of group operations. As shown in Sect. 5.1, the group law of $E(\mathbb{Z}_q)$ can be represented by an arithmetic circuit over $\mathbb{Z}_q$ of constant size. Therefore, we eventually need a proof system for arithmetic circuits over $\mathbb{Z}_q$ such that the input of the circuit is given as commitments. In fact, the bulletproofs for arithmetic circuit (BP-AC) [17] allows to take Pedersen commitments as input. However, BP-AC uses the ordinary Pedersen commitment to an integer, so that it is not directly applicable with the generalized Pedersen commitment to a vector of integers. We generalize BP-AC for handling the general Pedersen commitments and provide the protocol, denoted by $\mathsf{Comp.BP}_{AC}$, and the security and efficiency analysis in the full version [35]. If we prove $O(\ell)$ group operations, then the circuit size is $O(\ell \cdot n)$, so that both the computational cost for the prover and the verifier are $O(\ell \cdot n)$ and the cost for round and communication is $O(\log n + \log \ell)$.

In fact, the new commitment scheme can take any sequence of 3-integer tuples $(X_i, Y_i, Z_i) \in \mathbb{Z}_q^3$ as input. Although we normally take (X_i, Y_i, Z_i) from $\mathbb{G}_p = E(\mathbb{Z}_q)$, to prevent abnormal usages, we need a proof that $(X_i, Y_i, Z_i) \in \mathbb{Z}_q^3$ is on the elliptic curve, equivalently, it satisfies $Y^2Z = Z^3 + aXZ^2 + bZ^3$ for some $a, b \in \mathbb{Z}_q$. Since the relation for the membership proof consists of low degree polynomials, it can be performed by $\mathsf{Comp.BP}_{AC}$ whose cost is cheaper than that for elliptic curve operations.

5.3 Sublinear Verifier from New Two-Tiered Commitment Scheme

We propose a new IP argument with the sublinear verifier, denoted by Protocol4, that proves the following IP relation.

$$\mathcal{R}_{\mathsf{IP}}^{m,n} = \left\{ \begin{array}{l} (\boldsymbol{g}, \boldsymbol{h} \in \mathbb{G}_p^m, \boldsymbol{F} \in \mathbb{G}_q^{6n}, P \in \mathbb{G}_q, c \in \mathbb{Z}_p; \boldsymbol{a}, \boldsymbol{b} \in \mathbb{Z}_p^{m \times n}) : \\ P = \mathsf{Com}(\overrightarrow{\boldsymbol{g}^{\boldsymbol{a}}} \parallel \overrightarrow{\boldsymbol{h}^{\boldsymbol{b}}}; \boldsymbol{F}) \wedge c = \langle \boldsymbol{a}, \boldsymbol{b} \rangle, \end{array} \right\} \tag{7}$$

where $\langle \boldsymbol{a}, \boldsymbol{b} \rangle$ is the Frobenius inner product between matrices $\boldsymbol{a}$ and $\boldsymbol{b}$. Similarly to Protocol3, Protocol4 consists of two parts, the row-reduction and the column-reduction. The row-reduction part is denoted by Protocol4.Row and reduces from the relation $\mathcal{R}_{\mathsf{IP}}^{m,n}$ to $\mathcal{R}_{\mathsf{IP}}^{1,n}$. The column-reduction part is denoted by Protocol4.Col and reduces from the relation $\mathcal{R}_{\mathsf{IP}}^{1,n}$ to $\mathcal{R}_{\mathsf{IP}}^{1,1}$.

Let $\ell = \log m$. For each $(\ell+1-k)$-th row-reduction[9] round in Protocol4.Row the prover sends the verifier a commitment S_k by using the new commitment scheme in Sect. 5.2. However, contrary to Protocol3, the verifier cannot compute a valid instance P_k for the next round by himself, due to lack of homomorphic property. Instead, the prover sends a new instance for the next round along with a proof for its integrity. For the column-relation $\mathcal{R}_{\mathsf{IP}}^{1,n}$, both the prover and the verifier can similarly perform a column-reduction protocol Protocol4.Col and the corresponding integrity proof at the final step of the protocol. In a nutshell, Protocol4 resembles Protocol3 except that Protocol4 uses a different commitment scheme and additionally requires the integrity proof. The full description of Protocol4.Row is provided in the full version [35].

In general, this *commit-first-and-prove-later* approach indeed ends up with low efficiency if the relation is not algebraic (e.g., non-polynomial relations) or we do not use homomorphic commitment scheme (e.g., collision-resistant hash functions). Our new two-tiered commitment scheme helps to circumvent such efficiency degradation since it is friendly to proving homomorphic operations and the prover's computation in Protocol4 exactly consists of elliptic curve operations that can be represented by polynomials as we already investigated in Sect 5.1.

Although the new two-tiered commitment scheme contributes for the sublinear verifier, the naïve approach for the integrity proof increases the proof size $O(\log(N)^2)$, which is larger than $O(\log N)$ of Protocol3, where $N = mn$. Therefore, we bring in another technique to make the proof size compact. We apply the aggregation techniques as in Sect 3.3 such that the integrity of the prover's computation in all reduction rounds is relegated to the final round and then proven in aggregate. More concretely, the integrity proof should guarantee that the openings $\boldsymbol{p}_{k+1} \in \mathbb{G}_p^{2n}$, $\boldsymbol{l}_k \| \boldsymbol{r}_k \in \mathbb{G}^{4n}$, and $\boldsymbol{p}_k \in \mathbb{G}_p^{2n}$ of P_{k+1}, S_k, and P_k satisfies $\boldsymbol{p}_k = \boldsymbol{l}_k^{x^2} \circ \boldsymbol{p}_{k+1} \circ \boldsymbol{r}_k^{x^{-2}}$, which is essentially equivalent to the relation between openings of $\widehat{P} = L^{x^2} P R^{x^{-2}}$ in **Step 3** of Protocol3. The formal relation for the aggregated integrity proof is given in Eq. (8) (for Protocol4.row) and Eq. (9) (for Protocol4.col), where x_k is a challenge chosen by the verifier and the others are the common random strings. Using the protocol for $\mathcal{R}_{\mathsf{AggMEC.Row}}$ ($\mathcal{R}_{\mathsf{AggMEC.Col}}$, resp.), denoted by AggMEC.Row (AggMEC.Col, resp.), Protocol4.Row (Protocol4.Col, resp.) reduces from the relation $\mathcal{R}_{\mathsf{IP}}^{m,n}$ ($\mathcal{R}_{\mathsf{IP}}^{1,n}$, resp.) to the relation $\mathcal{R}_{\mathsf{IP}}^{1,n}$ ($\mathcal{R}_{\mathsf{IP}}^{1,1}$, resp.).

$$\mathcal{R}_{\mathsf{AggMEC.Row}} = \left\{ \begin{array}{l} \left(\begin{bmatrix} (\boldsymbol{S}_k, \boldsymbol{F}_k, S_k, P_k, x_k) \\ (\,\cdot\,, \boldsymbol{F}_{\ell+1}, \cdot\,, P_{\ell+1}, \cdot\,) \end{bmatrix}; \begin{bmatrix} (\boldsymbol{l}_k, \boldsymbol{r}_k, \boldsymbol{p}_k) \\ (\,\cdot,\ \cdot, \boldsymbol{p}_{\ell+1}) \end{bmatrix} \text{ for } k \in [\ell] \right) : \\ \wedge_{j=1}^{\ell+1} \left(P_j = \mathsf{Com}(\boldsymbol{p}_j; \boldsymbol{F}_j)\right) \\ \wedge_{k=1}^{\ell} \left(S_k = \mathsf{Com}(\boldsymbol{l}_k \,\|\, \boldsymbol{r}_k; \boldsymbol{S}_k) \wedge \boldsymbol{p}_k = \boldsymbol{l}_k^{x_k^2} \circ \boldsymbol{p}_{k+1} \circ \boldsymbol{r}_k^{x_k^{-2}} \right) \\ \boxed{\wedge_{k=1}^{\ell} \boldsymbol{l}_k, \boldsymbol{r}_k \in \mathbb{G}_p^{2n} \wedge \boldsymbol{p}_{\ell+1} \in \mathbb{G}_p^{2n}} \end{array} \right\} \quad (8)$$

[9] Notice that we use a subscript k in reverse order from $k = \ell$ to $k = 1$. That is, Protocol4.Row reduces an instance from P_{k+1} to P_k.

where $((\boldsymbol{S}_k, \boldsymbol{F}_k, S_k, P_k, x_k); (\boldsymbol{l}_k, \boldsymbol{r}_k, \boldsymbol{p}_k)) \in ((\mathbb{G}_q^{12n} \times \mathbb{G}_q^{6n} \times \mathbb{G}_q \times \mathbb{G}_q \times \mathbb{Z}_p) \times (\mathbb{Z}_q^{6n} \times \mathbb{Z}_q^{6n} \times \mathbb{Z}_q^{6n}))$.

$$\mathcal{R}_{\mathsf{AggMEC.Col}} = \left\{ \begin{array}{l} \left(\begin{bmatrix} (\boldsymbol{D}_k, P_k, x_k) \\ (\boldsymbol{D}_{\ell+1}, P_{\ell+1}, \ \cdot \ ) \end{bmatrix}; \begin{bmatrix} (\boldsymbol{p}_k) \text{ for } k \in [\ell] \\ (\boldsymbol{p}_{\ell+1}) \end{bmatrix} \right) : \\ \wedge_{j=1}^{\ell+1} (P_j = \mathsf{Com}(\boldsymbol{p}_j; \boldsymbol{D}_j)) \wedge \boxed{\boldsymbol{p}_{\ell+1} \in \mathbb{G}_p^{2^{\ell+1}}} \\ \wedge_{k=1}^{\ell} (\boldsymbol{p}_k = (\boldsymbol{p}_{1,k+1} \parallel \boldsymbol{p}_{4,k+1})^{x_k} \circ (\boldsymbol{p}_{2,k+1} \parallel \boldsymbol{p}_{3,k+1})^{x_k^{-1}}) \\ \text{where } \boldsymbol{p}_{k+1} = \boldsymbol{p}_{1,k+1} \parallel \boldsymbol{p}_{2,k+1} \parallel \boldsymbol{p}_{3,k+1} \parallel \boldsymbol{p}_{4,k+1} \end{array} \right\} \tag{9}$$

where $((\boldsymbol{D}_k, P_k, x_k); (\boldsymbol{p}_k)) \in ((\mathbb{G}_q^{3\cdot 2^k} \times \mathbb{G}_q \times \mathbb{Z}_p) \times (\mathbb{Z}_q^{3\cdot 2^k}))$.

The concrete descriptions of the four protocols Protocol4.Row, Protocol4.Col, AggMEC.Row, and AggMEC.Col and the proofs for proving argument systems are given in the full version [35].

We remark that $\mathcal{R}_{\mathsf{AggMEC.Row}}$ and $\mathcal{R}_{\mathsf{AggMEC.Col}}$ contain the group membership relations of the openings, which are marked with the block boxes. As for the group membership proof, it is sufficient to prove only memberships of $\boldsymbol{l}_k, \boldsymbol{r}_k$ for $k \in [\ell]$ and $\boldsymbol{p}_{\ell+1}$ since $\boldsymbol{p}_k$ for $k \in [\ell]$ are defined as a result of the group operations among $\boldsymbol{l}_k, \boldsymbol{r}_k$ for $k \in [\ell]$ and $\boldsymbol{p}_{\ell+1}$.

Efficiency Analysis. We analyze the efficiency of Protocol4 at a high level. The detailed analysis is given in the full version [35]. Below, we denote group operations in a group G by G-operations. The efficiency of Protocol4 is basically equivalent to that of Protocol3 except for using a different commitment scheme and the most computational cost of $\mathcal{V}$ shifts to the column reduction part (Protocol4.Col). In the row-reduction part (Protocol4.Row), the computation cost for $\mathcal{P}$ is dominated by $O(mn \log p)$ $\mathbb{G}_p$-operations for computing two-tiered commitments with $N = mn$ integers, the computation cost for $\mathcal{V}$ is $O(m \log p)$ $\mathbb{G}_p$-operations, and $\mathcal{P}$ and $\mathcal{V}$ communicate with $O(\log m)$ $\mathbb{G}_q$-elements. The complexity of the column-reduction part is dominated by proving the following relations, which can be represented by small-degree polynomials, by running the arithmetic circuit argument $\mathsf{Comp.BP}_{AC}$ given in Sect. 5.2:

$$\boldsymbol{l}_k^{x_k^2} \circ \boldsymbol{p}_{k+1} \circ \boldsymbol{r}_k^{x_k^{-2}} - \boldsymbol{p}_k = \boldsymbol{0} \text{ for } k \in [\ell] \tag{10}$$

$$(\boldsymbol{p}_{1,k+1} \parallel \boldsymbol{p}_{4,k+1})^{x_k} \circ (\boldsymbol{p}_{2,k+1} \parallel \boldsymbol{p}_{3,k+1})^{x_k^{-1}} - \boldsymbol{p}_k = \boldsymbol{0} \in \mathbb{G}_p^{2k} \text{ for } k \in [\ell]. \tag{11}$$

Arithmetic circuits for computing Eq. (10) and Eq. (11) consist of $O(n\ell \log p)$ and $O(2^\ell \log p)$ $\mathbb{G}_p$-operations, respectively. Finally, $\mathsf{Comp.BP}_{AC}$ for the above arithmetic circuits cost $O((n\ell + 2^\ell) \log p \log q)$ $\mathbb{G}_q$-operations for each $\mathcal{P}$ and $\mathcal{V}$ and transmissions of $O(\log n + \ell + \log \log p)$ $\mathbb{G}_q$-elements. Setting $\ell \leftarrow \log m$, $\mathcal{P}$'s computation complexity is $O(mn \log p)$ $\mathbb{G}_p$-operations, $\mathcal{V}$'s computation complexity is $O(m \log p)$ $\mathbb{G}_p$-operations and $O(n \log m \log p \log q)$ $\mathbb{G}_q$-operations, and the communication complexity is $O(\log n + \log m + \log \log p)$ $\mathbb{G}_q$-elements.

6 Extensions

6.1 Transparent Polynomial Commitment Scheme

Informally, using the polynomial commitment scheme (PCS), a committer first commits to a polynomial $f(X)$, and then later opens $f(x)$ at some point x (mostly chosen by a verifier) and convinces a verifier of correctness of $f(x)$. Due to space constraint, we provide the definition of the PCS, a way to use the proposed IP arguments as PCS, and a comparison table in the full version [35].

6.2 Zero-Knowledge Argument for Arithmetic Circuits

There is a well-established approach toward the argument for arithmetic circuits via polynomial commitment scheme; an IP argument is firstly reduced to polynomial commitment schemes as in 6.1 and then combined with polynomial IOPs [18]. This reduction increases constant times the complexity, where linear preprocessing is required for the verifier. Therefore, the final argument for the arithmetic circuit of size N has the same complexity as those of our IP arguments between vectors of length N, where the online verifier's complexity is unchanged, but the offline verifier's complexity is linear in N.

The perfect special honest verifier zero-knowledge (SHVZK) means that given the challenge values, it is possible to simulate the whole transcript even without knowing the witness. If the polynomial commitment scheme is hiding and the proof of evaluation is SHVZK, then the resulting argument for arithmetic circuit is SHVZK as well. Although the proposed IP protocols do not have these properties yet, there is a simple method to add ZK into IP arguments [18,46]. For example, we can extend commitment schemes used in the paper to have hiding factors like the original Pedersen commitment scheme.

There is another approach for converting from an IP argument without SHVZK to the SHVZK argument for arithmetic circuit [13,17]. We can apply this reduction to our IP arguments. We provide the details in the full version [35].

7 Discussion on Best of Two Generalizations

It would be interesting to devise a technique for combining two generalizations.

First, we find that naïve combining $\mathsf{Protocol2}$ and $\mathsf{Protocol3}$ is difficult because each of them uses a bilinear map for a different purpose. In $\mathsf{Protocol2}$, the bilinear map is used in the first step for compressing multiple group elements by sending a commitment instead of multiple group elements. In the first step of $\mathsf{Protocol3}$, the $\mathcal{P}$ sends L and R to the verifier, where L and R are elements in $\mathbb{G}_t$. We can generalize $\mathsf{Protocol3}$ like $\mathsf{Protocol1}$, but we cannot put L and R into a homomorphic commitment scheme directly since L and R are already in the target group of the bilinear map.

Although $\mathsf{Protocol4}$ does not use the bilinear map, combining $\mathsf{Protocol2}$ and $\mathsf{Protocol4}$ will be challenging as well. Since both protocols use two-tier commitment schemes, we may need three-tier commitment scheme such as $\mathsf{C}_3 \circ \mathsf{C}_2 \circ \mathsf{C}_1$, where C_3 is pairing-based AFGHO scheme, C_2 is a commitment to elliptic curve point, and C_1 is Pedersen commitment scheme. Protocol4 requires to prove small-degree polynomial relations over C_1 and C_2 supports an efficient protocol for it. C_3 may support to prove a small-degree polynomial relation over C_2. However, since C_1 is an opening of an opening of C_3, the small-degree polynomial relation over C_1 might be represented as a complicated relation over C_2 of higher-degree. We leave achieving the best of both generalizations as an open problem.

Acknowledgement. We thank Taechan Kim for discussion on complete addition formulas for elliptic curves. This work was supported in part by the Institute of Information and Communications Technology Planning and Evaluation (IITP) grant funded by the Korea Government (MSIT) (A Study on Cryptographic Primitives for SNARK, 50%) under Grant 20210007270012002, and in part by the National Research Foundation of Korea (NRF) grant funded by the Korean Government (MSIT), 50%, under Grant 2020R1C1C1A0100696812.

References

1. Abe, M., Fuchsbauer, G., Groth, J., Haralambiev, K., Ohkubo, M.: Structure-preserving signatures and commitments to group elements. J. Cryptol. **29**(2), 363–421 (2016)
2. Ames, S., Hazay, C., Ishai, Y., Venkitasubramaniam, M.: Ligero: lightweight sublinear arguments without a trusted setup. In ACM CCS 2017, pp. 2087–2104. ACM (2017)
3. Bayer, S., Groth, J.: Zero-knowledge argument for polynomial evaluation with application to blacklists. In: Johansson, T., Nguyen, P.Q. (eds.) EUROCRYPT 2013. LNCS, vol. 7881, pp. 646–663. Springer, Heidelberg (2013). https://doi.org/10.1007/978-3-642-38348-9_38
4. Bellare M., Rogaway, P.: Random oracles are practical: A paradigm for designing efficient protocols. In: ACM CCS 1993, pp. 62–73. ACM (1993)
5. Ben-Sasson, E., Bentov, I., Horesh, Y., Riabzev, M.: Scalable, transparent, and post-quantum secure computational integrity. Cryptology ePrint Archive, Report 2018/046 (2018). https://eprint.iacr.org/2018/046
6. Ben-Sasson, E., Chiesa, A., Genkin, D., Tromer, E., Virza, M.: SNARKs for C: verifying program executions succinctly and in zero knowledge. In: Canetti, R., Garay, J.A. (eds.) CRYPTO 2013. LNCS, vol. 8043, pp. 90–108. Springer, Heidelberg (2013). https://doi.org/10.1007/978-3-642-40084-1_6
7. Ben-Sasson, E., Chiesa, A., Riabzev, M., Spooner, N., Virza, M., Ward, N.P.: Aurora: transparent succinct arguments for R1CS. In: Ishai, Y., Rijmen, V. (eds.) EUROCRYPT 2019. LNCS, vol. 11476, pp. 103–128. Springer, Cham (2019). https://doi.org/10.1007/978-3-030-17653-2_4
8. Ben-Sasson, E., Chiesa, A., Spooner, N.: Interactive oracle proofs. In: Hirt, M., Smith, A. (eds.) TCC 2016. LNCS, vol. 9986, pp. 31–60. Springer, Heidelberg (2016). https://doi.org/10.1007/978-3-662-53644-5_2
9. Ben-Sasson, E., Chiesa, A., Tromer, E., Virza, M.: Succinct non-interactive zero knowledge for a von Neumann architecture. In: USENIX Security, vol. 2014, pp. 781–796 (2014)

10. Bitansky, N., Canetti, R., Chiesa, A., Tromer, E.: From extractable collision resistance to succinct non-interactive arguments of knowledge, and back again. In: ITCS 2012, pp. 326–349. Springer (2012)
11. Bitansky, N., Canetti, R., Chiesa, A., Tromer, E.: Recursive composition and bootstrapping for snarks and proof-carrying data. In: Symposium on Theory of Computing Conference, STOC 2013, pp. 111–120. ACM(2013)
12. Boneh, D., Lynn, B., Shacham, H.: Short signatures from the weil pairing. J. Cryptol. **17**(4), 297–319 (2004)
13. Bootle, J., Cerulli, A., Chaidos, P., Groth, J., Petit, C.: Efficient zero-knowledge arguments for arithmetic circuits in the discrete log setting. In: Fischlin, M., Coron, J.-S. (eds.) EUROCRYPT 2016. LNCS, vol. 9666, pp. 327–357. Springer, Heidelberg (2016). https://doi.org/10.1007/978-3-662-49896-5_12
14. Bootle, J., Cerulli, A., Ghadafi, E., Groth, J., Hajiabadi, M., Jakobsen, S.K.: Linear-time zero-knowledge proofs for arithmetic circuit satisfiability. In: Takagi, T., Peyrin, T. (eds.) ASIACRYPT 2017. LNCS, vol. 10626, pp. 336–365. Springer, Cham (2017). https://doi.org/10.1007/978-3-319-70700-6_12
15. Bootle, J., Chiesa, A., Liu, S.: Zero-knowledge IOPs with linear-time prover and polylogarithmic-time verifier. In: EUROCRYPT 2022, vol. 13276. LNCS, pp. 275–304. Springer, Cham (2022) https://doi.org/10.1007/978-3-031-07085-3_10
16. Bosma, W., Lenstra, H.W.: Complete systems of two addition laws for elliptic curves. J. Number Theory **53**, 229–240 (1995)
17. Bünz, B., Bootle, J., Boneh, D., Poelstra, A., Wuille, P., Maxwell, G.: Bulletproofs: Short proofs for confidential transactions and more. In: IEEE Symposium on Security and Privacy 2018, pp 315–334. IEEE Computer Society (2018)
18. Bünz, B., Fisch, B., Szepieniec, A.: Transparent SNARKs from DARK compilers. In: Canteaut, A., Ishai, Y. (eds.) EUROCRYPT 2020. LNCS, vol. 12105, pp. 677–706. Springer, Cham (2020). https://doi.org/10.1007/978-3-030-45721-1_24
19. Bünz, B., Maller, M., Mishra, P., Tyagi, N., Vesely, P.: Proofs for inner pairing products and applications. In: Tibouchi, M., Wang, H. (eds.) ASIACRYPT 2021. LNCS, vol. 13092, pp. 65–97. Springer, Cham (2021). https://doi.org/10.1007/978-3-030-92078-4_3
20. Cheon, J.H.: Discrete logarithm problems with auxiliary inputs. J. Cryptol. **23**(3), 457–476 (2010)
21. Chiesa, A., Hu, Y., Maller, M., Mishra, P., Vesely, N., Ward, N.: Marlin: preprocessing zkSNARKs with universal and updatable SRS. In: Canteaut, A., Ishai, Y. (eds.) EUROCRYPT 2020. LNCS, vol. 12105, pp. 738–768. Springer, Cham (2020). https://doi.org/10.1007/978-3-030-45721-1_26
22. Chiesa, A., Ojha, D., Spooner, N.: Fractal: post-quantum and transparent recursive proofs from holography. In: Canteaut, A., Ishai, Y. (eds.) EUROCRYPT 2020. LNCS, vol. 12105, pp. 769–793. Springer, Cham (2020). https://doi.org/10.1007/978-3-030-45721-1_27
23. dalek cryptography:Bulletproofs (2018). https://github.com/dalek-cryptography/bulletproofs
24. Daza, V., Ràfols, C., Zacharakis, A.: Updateable inner product argument with logarithmic verifier and applications. In: Kiayias, A., Kohlweiss, M., Wallden, P., Zikas, V. (eds.) PKC 2020. LNCS, vol. 12110, pp. 527–557. Springer, Cham (2020). https://doi.org/10.1007/978-3-030-45374-9_18
25. Fiat, A., Shamir, A.: How to prove yourself: practical solutions to identification and signature problems. In: Odlyzko, A.M. (ed.) CRYPTO 1986. LNCS, vol. 263, pp. 186–194. Springer, Heidelberg (1987). https://doi.org/10.1007/3-540-47721-7_12

26. Freeman, D.M.: Converting pairing-based cryptosystems from composite-order groups to prime-order groups. In: Gilbert, H. (ed.) EUROCRYPT 2010. LNCS, vol. 6110, pp. 44–61. Springer, Heidelberg (2010). https://doi.org/10.1007/978-3-642-13190-5_3
27. Gabizon, A., Williamson, Z.J., Ciobotaru, O.: Plonk: Permutations over lagrange-bases for oecumenical noninteractive arguments of knowledge. Cryptology ePrint Archive, Report 2019/953 (2019). https://eprint.iacr.org/2019/953.pdf
28. Gennaro, R., Gentry, C., Parno, B., Raykova, M.: Quadratic span programs and succinct NIZKs without PCPs. In: Johansson, T., Nguyen, P.Q. (eds.) EUROCRYPT 2013. LNCS, vol. 7881, pp. 626–645. Springer, Heidelberg (2013). https://doi.org/10.1007/978-3-642-38348-9_37
29. Groth, J.: Linear algebra with sub-linear zero-knowledge arguments. In: Halevi, S. (ed.) CRYPTO 2009. LNCS, vol. 5677, pp. 192–208. Springer, Heidelberg (2009). https://doi.org/10.1007/978-3-642-03356-8_12
30. Groth, J.: Short pairing-based non-interactive zero-knowledge arguments. In: Abe, M. (ed.) ASIACRYPT 2010. LNCS, vol. 6477, pp. 321–340. Springer, Heidelberg (2010). https://doi.org/10.1007/978-3-642-17373-8_19
31. Groth, J.: Efficient zero-knowledge arguments from two-tiered homomorphic commitments. In: Lee, D.H., Wang, X. (eds.) ASIACRYPT 2011. LNCS, vol. 7073, pp. 431–448. Springer, Heidelberg (2011). https://doi.org/10.1007/978-3-642-25385-0_23
32. Groth, J.: On the size of pairing-based non-interactive arguments. In: Fischlin, M., Coron, J.-S. (eds.) EUROCRYPT 2016. LNCS, vol. 9666, pp. 305–326. Springer, Heidelberg (2016). https://doi.org/10.1007/978-3-662-49896-5_11
33. Groth, J., Kohlweiss, M.: One-out-of-many proofs: or how to leak a secret and spend a coin. In: Oswald, E., Fischlin, M. (eds.) EUROCRYPT 2015. LNCS, vol. 9057, pp. 253–280. Springer, Heidelberg (2015). https://doi.org/10.1007/978-3-662-46803-6_9
34. Hoffmann, M., Klooß, M., Rupp, A.: Efficient zero-knowledge arguments in the discrete log setting, revisited. In: ACM CCS, vol. 2019, pp. 2093–2110 (2019)
35. Kim, S., Lee, H., Seo, J.H.: Efficient zero-knowledge argument in discrete logarithm setting: Sublogarithmic proof or sublinear verifier. Cryptology ePrint Archive, Paper 2021/1450 (2021). https://eprint.iacr.org/2021/1450
36. libsnark (2017). https://github.com/scipr-lab/libsnark
37. Lipmaa, H.: Progression-free sets and sublinear pairing-based non-interactive zero-knowledge arguments. In: Cramer, R. (ed.) TCC 2012. LNCS, vol. 7194, pp. 169–189. Springer, Heidelberg (2012). https://doi.org/10.1007/978-3-642-28914-9_10
38. Maller, M., Bowe, S., Kohlweiss, M., Meiklejohn, S.: Sonic: Zero-knowledge snarks from linear-size universal and updatable structured reference strings. In ACM CCS 2019, pp. 2111–2128. Association for Computing Machinery (2019)
39. Menezes, A., Okamoto, T., Vanstone, S.A.: Reducing elliptic curve logarithms to logarithms in a finite field. IEEE Trans. Inf. Theory **39**(5), 1639–1646 (1993)
40. Parno, B., Howell, J., Gentry, C., Raykova, M.: Pinocchio: Nearly practical verifiable computation. In: IEEE Symposium on Security and Privacy 2013, pp. 238–252. IEEE (2013)
41. Renes, J., Costello, C., Batina, L.: Complete addition formulas for prime order elliptic curves. In: Fischlin, M., Coron, J.-S. (eds.) EUROCRYPT 2016. LNCS, vol. 9665, pp. 403–428. Springer, Heidelberg (2016). https://doi.org/10.1007/978-3-662-49890-3_16

42. Savaş, E., Schmidt, T.A., Koç, Ç.K.: Generating elliptic curves of prime order. In: Koç, Ç.K., Naccache, D., Paar, C. (eds.) CHES 2001. LNCS, vol. 2162, pp. 142–158. Springer, Heidelberg (2001). https://doi.org/10.1007/3-540-44709-1_13
43. Scott, M.: On the deployment of curve based cryptography for the internet of things. Cryptology ePrint Archive, Report 2020/514 (2020). https://eprint.iacr.org/2020/514
44. Seo, J.H.: Round-efficient sub-linear zero-knowledge arguments for linear algebra. In: Catalano, D., Fazio, N., Gennaro, R., Nicolosi, A. (eds.) PKC 2011. LNCS, vol. 6571, pp. 387–402. Springer, Heidelberg (2011). https://doi.org/10.1007/978-3-642-19379-8_24
45. Setty, S.: Spartan: efficient and general-purpose zkSNARKs without trusted setup. In: Micciancio, D., Ristenpart, T. (eds.) CRYPTO 2020. LNCS, vol. 12172, pp. 704–737. Springer, Cham (2020). https://doi.org/10.1007/978-3-030-56877-1_25
46. Wahby, R.S., Tzialla, I., Shelat, A., Thaler, J., Walfish, M.: Doubly-efficient zkSNARKs without trusted setup. In: IEEE Symposium on Security and Privacy 2018, pp. 926–943. IEEE (2018)
47. Xie, T., Zhang, J., Zhang, Y., Papamanthou, C., Song, D.: Libra: succinct zero-knowledge proofs with optimal prover computation. In: Boldyreva, A., Micciancio, D. (eds.) CRYPTO 2019. LNCS, vol. 11694, pp. 733–764. Springer, Cham (2019). https://doi.org/10.1007/978-3-030-26954-8_24
48. Zhang, J., Xie, T., Zhang, Y., Song., D.: Transparent polynomial delegation and its applications to zero knowledge proof. In: IEEE Symposium on Security and Privacy 2020, pp. 859–876. IEEE (2019)

Non Interactive Zero Knowledge

Unconditionally Secure NIZK in the Fine-Grained Setting

Yuyu Wang[1(✉)] and Jiaxin Pan[2]

[1] University of Electronic Science and Technology of China, Chengdu, China
wangyuyu@uestc.edu.cn

[2] Department of Mathematical Sciences, NTNU - Norwegian University of Science and Technology, Trondheim, Norway
jiaxin.pan@ntnu.no

Abstract. Non-interactive zero-knowledge (NIZK) proof systems are often constructed based on cryptographic assumptions. In this paper, we propose the *first* unconditionally secure NIZK system in the AC^0-fine-grained setting. More precisely, our NIZK system has perfect soundness for all adversaries and unconditional zero-knowledge for AC^0 adversaries, namely, an AC^0 adversary can only break the zero-knowledge property with negligible probability unconditionally. At the core of our construction is an OR-proof system for satisfiability of 1 out of polynomial many statements.

Keywords: Non-interactive zero-knowledge · Fine-grained cryptography · AC^0 · Unconditional security

1 Introduction

Constructing non-interactive zero-knowledge (NIZK) proof systems [7] is one of the central topics in cryptography, since NIZK is a fundamental primitive that can convince a verifier the validity of a statement with minimum communication round.

Most NIZK systems are constructed based on various cryptographic assumptions, such as Discrete-Logarithm-like (e.g., [10,11]) and Learning With Errors (LWE, e.g., [17]) assumptions. Recent development of succinct NIZK systems [2,6,8,9,16] even base their security on rather strong, non-falsifiable assumptions, such as knowledge assumptions and assuming generic groups. Although there are many cryptanalysis results on assumptions, such as Discrete Logarithm and LWE, it is natural to consider whether it is possible to construct NIZK from much mild assumptions.

Y. Wang—Supported by the National Natural Science Foundation for Young Scientists of China under Grant Number 62002049, the Natural Science Foundation of Sichuan under Grant Number 2023NSFSC0472, the Sichuan Science and Technology Program under Grant Number 2022YFG0037, and the Fundamental Research Funds for the Central Universities under Grant Number ZYGX2020J017.

J. Pan—Supported by the Research Council of Norway under Project No. 324235.

S. Agrawal and D. Lin (Eds.): ASIACRYPT 2022, LNCS 13792, pp. 437–465, 2022.
https://doi.org/10.1007/978-3-031-22966-4_15

NIZK Based on Mild Assumptions. Very recently, Wang and Pan [19] put forth this direction in the fine-grained setting. Here fine-grained setting (or fine-grained cryptography) [3] means that adversaries can only have bounded resources and honest users have no more resources than adversaries. More precisely, the work of Wang and Pan considers that all parties are in NC^1. In this setting, they obtained a NIZK system under a rather mild assumption, $\mathsf{NC}^1 \subsetneq \oplus\mathsf{L/poly}$. Their system is very efficient since only simple operations such as AND, OR, and PARITY for bits are involved. The assumption, $\mathsf{NC}^1 \subsetneq \oplus\mathsf{L/poly}$, also yields the security of proof systems in [1,5,20].

However, in complexity theory, it has not been proven that $\mathsf{NC}^1 \subsetneq \oplus\mathsf{L/poly}$, although it is widely accepted. It is desirable to further push this direction and study whether it is possible to construct an *unconditionally secure* NIZK system in the fine-grained setting.

We suppose that in the classical setting it seems not possible to have unconditional security for NIZK. The reason is that for proving the zero-knowledge property, the common reference string (CRS) is often related to the simulation trapdoor, and given the CRS an (unbounded) adversary may recover the simulation trapdoor and break the soundness. Meanwhile, it is promising to construct unconditionally secure NIZK in the fine-grained setting, since it restricts the capability of an adversary. However, this will also limit the resources of an honest user, which makes it particularly difficult to instantiate a scheme. Our technical goal is to resolve this tension.

1.1 Our Contributions

We consider the AC^0-fine-grained setting, namely, all adversaries, honest provers, and verifiers are in AC^0. In this setting, we construct the *first* unconditionally secure NIZK proof system for circuit satisfiability (SAT). More precisely, it is perfectly sound and has zero-knowledge against any adversaries in AC^0. Our system only involves simple operations in $GF(2)$ and does not require any cryptographic group operations or assumptions such as Discrete Logarithm and Factoring.

Our NIZK only supports statements verifiable in AC^0 given witnesses, since if a statement circuit is beyond AC^0 then an honest prover in AC^0 cannot decide its truth with the witness. However, we stress that our method is not limited to AC^0 statements. For instance, if we allow polynomial-time honest provers as in [1], our constructions naturally support statement circuits with polynomial-size. Moreover, any polynomial-size statement circuit can be represented as one verifiable in AC^0. Specifically, if a witness contains the bits of all wires in the circuit, then an AC^0 algorithm can efficiently verify the validity of an input/output pair of each gate in parallel and check whether the bit for the final output wire is 1. In this sense, the prover of our NIZK works for any NP statement, given a witness containing "enough information".

Applications of Security Against AC^0. Security against AC^0 naturally captures adversaries with limited resources. Moreover, an AC^0-fine-grained NIZK works well in systems requiring "online security", where attacks are valid only if they succeed immediately. For instance, our NIZK with composable zero-knowledge against AC^0 and perfect soundness can be used to protect secrets only valuable in a short period of time. Also, its dual mode enjoys everlasting security. Namely, its perfect zero-knowledge continuously prevents the adversary from learning information on secrets and its soundness guarantees security in a system requiring users to provide proofs in a short time.

Impacts of Our Work. Our work gives us interesting insights to the minimum hardness assumptions required by NIZK and the landscape of AC^0-fine-grained cryptography. Before our work, it seemed that cryptographic assumptions, in particular, those imply public-key encryption (PKE), were necessary for NIZK in the standard model. Putting it in Impagliazzo's view of complexity landscape [14], NIZK seemed to be in the Cryptomania. Examples are Diffie-Hellman-based NIZKs [10,11]. Even in the NC^1-fine-grained setting, NIZK systems [19] require the assumption $\mathsf{NC}^1 \subsetneq \oplus\mathsf{L}/\mathsf{poly}$, which implies PKE schemes [3].

Our work shows that those assumptions implying PKE are not necessary, since in the AC^0-fine-grained setting, it is not known whether there is a PKE scheme yet.[1] Up until now, only "minicrypt primitives" such as one-way function, weak pseudorandom function, secret-key encryption, and collision-resistant hash function are known to exist [3,12] in this setting, and we were not aware of any impossibility or possibility results showing that assumptions implying PKE are necessary for NIZK, in particular, in the AC^0-fine-grained setting, or not. As a further direction left open, we will explore how to extend our techniques in the classical setting and construct a NIZK from weaker assumptions (e.g., Discrete Logarithms) that are not known to imply PKE.

Extensions. While all the aforementioned NIZKs are in the CRS model, we can further extend them to the uniform random string (URS) model, where a trust setup only samples public coins. We also prove that our NIZKs have verifiable correlated key generations [10], which lead to a conversion from our NIZKs to unconditionally secure non-interactive zaps [4] (i.e., non-interactive witness-indistinguishability proof systems in the plain model) [10] against AC^0.

1.2 Technical Overview

In this section, we give more details about our techniques. Our approach is divided into three intermediate steps. We firstly construct a simple NIZK for linear languages, and then compile it to an OR-proof scheme for 1-out-of-ℓ disjunction, where ℓ can be any polynomial. Both schemes run in NC^0, which is a subset of AC^0. Thirdly, we use this OR-proof scheme to construct a NIZK system for circuit SAT.

A main technical hurdle throughout our work is that in the AC^0-fine-grained setting, many standard operations, such as computing the sum of a polynomial number of random elements and multiplication of two random matrices, are

[1] How to construct a provably secure PKE scheme in the AC^0-fine-grained setting is left as an open problem in [3].

not allowed. These operations can be easily performed in NC^1 and thus previous fine-grained NIZKs under complexity assumptions [1,19] are not confronted with this problem. As a result, it is more challenging to construct a NIZK (or any cryptographic scheme, in general) in AC^0, compared to the work of Wang and Pan [19].

NIZK for Linear Languages in AC^0. Our starting point is a simple NIZK that is computable in NC^0 and has perfect soundness and composable zero-knowledge against adversaries in AC^0 under no assumption. The linear languages we consider are of the form

$$\mathsf{L}_{\mathbf{M}} = \{\mathbf{t} : \exists \mathbf{w} \in \{0,1\}^t, \text{ s.t. } \mathbf{t} = \mathbf{M}\mathbf{w}\},$$

where each row vector in $\mathbf{M} \in \{0,1\}^{n \times t}$ is sparse. Here, by sparse we mean that each row vector in $\mathbf{M}$ has only constant Hamming weight. This restriction is inherent, since otherwise even the multiplication of $\mathbf{M}$ and $\mathbf{w}$ cannot be performed in NC^0.[2] However, this is still sufficient for our final NIZK for circuit SAT.

The technique behind our scheme is based on the fact that an AC^0 adversary cannot tell the parity of a random string with the size being the security parameter λ [13,15]. For our purpose, we explain it as the indistinguishability between the following distributions:

$$\underbrace{\{\mathbf{E}_\lambda \widetilde{\mathbf{r}} | \widetilde{\mathbf{r}} \stackrel{\$}{\leftarrow} \{0,1\}^{\lambda-1}\}}_{=D_0} \text{ and } \underbrace{\{\mathbf{E}_\lambda \widetilde{\mathbf{r}} + \mathbf{e}_\lambda^\lambda | \widetilde{\mathbf{r}} \stackrel{\$}{\leftarrow} \{0,1\}^{\lambda-1}\}}_{=D_1},$$

where $\mathbf{e}_\lambda^\lambda \in \{0,1\}^\lambda$ denotes constant vector with the parity being 1 and $\mathbf{E}_\lambda \in \{0,1\}^{\lambda \times (\lambda-1)}$ denotes a fixed constant matrix (see Sect. 2 for the formal definitions). More specifically, we prove that a vector sampled from D_0 (respectively, D_1) is uniformly distributed conditioned on the parity being 0 (respectively 1). A useful property of $\mathbf{E}_\lambda$ we will exploit is that each row and column vector in it has constant Hamming weight, which implies that multiplication between $\mathbf{E}_\lambda$ and $\widetilde{\mathbf{r}}$ or other matrices can be performed in NC^0.

For the aforementioned linear language $\mathsf{L}_{\mathbf{M}}$, we set the binding CRS as a vector $\mathbf{r}$ sampled from D_1. The prover computes $\mathbf{C} = \mathbf{M}\mathbf{R}$ and $\mathbf{D} = (\mathbf{R}||\mathbf{w}) \begin{pmatrix} \mathbf{E}_\lambda^\top \\ \mathbf{r}^\top \end{pmatrix}$, where $\mathbf{R} \stackrel{\$}{\leftarrow} \{0,1\}^{t \times (\lambda-1)}$, and the verifier accepts iff $(\mathbf{C}||\mathbf{x}) \begin{pmatrix} \mathbf{E}_\lambda^\top \\ \mathbf{r}^\top \end{pmatrix} = \mathbf{M}\mathbf{D}$. For each multiplication of matrices (or vectors) involved, one can see that either the row vectors of the left hand side matrix or the column vectors of the right hand side matrix have only constant Hamming weight. Hence, all the operations can be performed in NC^0. Roughly speaking, soundness follows from the fact that, for a valid proof, either $\mathbf{x}$ being in the span of $\mathbf{M}$ or $\mathbf{r}$ being in the span of $\mathbf{E}_\lambda$ must hold, while all $\mathbf{r} \in D_1$ are outside the span of $\mathbf{E}_\lambda$. To prove zero-knowledge, we switch the binding CRS to a hiding CRS by replacing the distribution of $\mathbf{r}$

[2] An NC^0 circuit cannot compute the inner product of two vectors unless one of them is sparse.

by D_0. In this case, seeing $\mathbf{C}$ and $\mathbf{D}$ simultaneously reveals no information on $\mathbf{w}$ except for $\mathbf{x}$. Due to this CRS switching, we call this zero-knowledge composable, and this change does not modify the view of an AC^0 adversary.

OR-Proof for One Disjunction. Following a fine-grained version of the "OR-proof techniques" [10,18], the above NIZK can be transformed to an OR-proof for the 1-out-of-2 disjunction (namely, satisfiability of 1 out of 2 statements). Let $\mathbf{r}$ be a binding CRS sampled from D_1. Assuming the prover knows the witness $\mathbf{w}$ of statement $\mathbf{x}_j$ for some $j \in \{0,1\}$, it generates a hiding CRS $\mathbf{r}_{1-j}$ with a trapdoor $\widetilde{\mathbf{r}}_{1-j}$ and a binding CRS $\mathbf{r}_j$ such that $\mathbf{r}_j = \mathbf{r} - \mathbf{r}_{1-j}$. Then the prover generates proofs for $\mathbf{x}_j$ and $\mathbf{x}_{1-j}$ with $\mathbf{w}$ and $\widetilde{\mathbf{r}}_{1-j}$ respectively. The verifier receives $\mathbf{r}_0$ and generates $\mathbf{r}_1$ by itself for verification. Soundness follows from the fact that for any pair of $(\mathbf{r}_0, \mathbf{r}_1)$ such that $\mathbf{r} = \mathbf{r}_0 + \mathbf{r}_1$, at least one of $(\mathbf{r}_0, \mathbf{r}_1)$ must be a binding CRS with the parity being 1. Composable zero-knowledge follows from that switching the distribution of $\mathbf{r}$ to D_0 leads both $\mathbf{r}_0$ and $\mathbf{r}_1$ to become hiding CRSs.

OR-Proof for Multiple Disjunctions. While the above construction works for the 1-out-of-2 disjunction, our NIZK for all AC^0 circuit SAT requires 1-out-of-ℓ disjunction for any polynomial ℓ. This is due to the fact that an AC^0 circuit may contain unbounded fan-in AND or OR gates. A natural idea is to let the prover "split" $\mathbf{r}$ into ℓ CRSs $(\mathbf{r}_i)_{i\in[\ell]}$ instead of two, among which one is binding and $\ell - 1$ ones are hiding. However, this will result in workload beyond AC^0 for both the prover and the verifier. Especially, a prover with a witness for the jth statement will have to compute $\mathbf{r}_j = \mathbf{r} - \sum_{i \neq j} \mathbf{r}_i$ and the verifier will have to compute $\mathbf{r}_\ell = \mathbf{r} - \sum_{i=1}^{\ell-1} \mathbf{r}_i$. Neither of them can be performed in AC^0.

To overcome the above problems, we develop a new framework of OR-proof for multiple disjunctions. At the core of our framework is a verifiable "double layer" sampling procedure.

In the first layer, we adopt a distribution, say D_0', which is the same as D_0 except that it outputs vectors with size ℓ. By running D_0' for $\lambda - 1$ times, we immediately achieve a matrix in $\{0,1\}^{\ell \times (\lambda - 1)}$, which can be parsed as ℓ random vectors in $\{0,1\}^{\lambda - 1}$ with the sum being a $\mathbf{0}$-vector. In the second layer, we sample ℓ vectors from D_0, while using the vectors generated in the first layer as the internal randomness. This results in ℓ random vectors conditioned on the sum being a $\mathbf{0}$-vector and the parities being 0's. Assuming that the witness for the jth statement is known, we add the jth vector with the original CRS $\mathbf{r}$ from D_1 to obtain a binding CRS and use the rest $\ell - 1$ vectors as the hiding CRSs. Notice that when switching $\mathbf{r}$ to a hiding CRS sampled from D_0, the ℓ split CRSs are all randomly distributed in D_0 conditioned on the sum being $\mathbf{r}$. In this case, information on the index j is information-theoretically hidden, which preserves the zero-knowledge.

For verification, we propose a method to extract a matrix from the internal randomness used in the first layer. We then use the matrix as a witness to prove that the sum of the CRSs generated by the prover is exactly $\mathbf{r}$, via our NIZK for linear languages. In this way, we can convince the verifier that at least one of the CRSs must be binding, and thus soundness can be guaranteed.

In conclusion, the above sampling procedure gives rise to ways to split a CRS into multiple ones and to convince the verifier that some of the resulting CRSs is binding, while all the operations involved can be performed in AC^0. Combining this sampling procedure with our OR-proof for one disjunction, we achieve an OR-proof for multiple disjunction, which plays a key component of our NIZK for circuit SAT.

NIZK for Circuit SAT. We now give an overview on how we construct a NIZK for all statements verifiable in AC^0 (given a witness) by using our NIZK for linear languages and our OR-proof.

For a valid witness, we extend it to contain bits of all wires in the statement circuit and commit each bit w_i as $\mathsf{cm}_i = \mathbf{E}_\lambda \mathbf{r}_i + \mathbf{t}\mathsf{w}_i$, where $\mathbf{r}_i$ is a random vector in $\{0,1\}^{\lambda-1}$ and $\mathbf{t} \xleftarrow{\$} D_1$ is in the CRS. For the final output, we commit it as $\mathbf{t}$. Note that the commitment is additively homomorphic and $\mathbf{t}$ is a commitment to 1. For each NOT gate with input commitments $(\mathsf{cm}_{i1}, \mathsf{cm}_{i2})$, we use the NIZK for linear languages to prove that $\mathsf{cm}_{i1} + \mathsf{cm}_{i2} + \mathbf{t}$ is in the span of $\mathbf{E}_\lambda$, i.e., it commits to 0. For each AND gate with input commitments $(\mathsf{cm}_{ij})_{j\in[\ell]}$ and output commitments $\mathsf{cm}_{i(\ell+1)}$, we use an OR-proof for 1-out-of-$(\ell+1)$ disjunction to prove that either both cm_{ij} and $\mathsf{cm}_{i(\ell+1)}$ commit to 0 for some $j \in [\ell]$ or $\mathsf{cm}_{ij} - \mathbf{t}$ commits to 0 for all $j \in [\ell+1]$. Proofs for OR gates are generated analogously. Notice that when generating the proof of compliance for each AND (respectively, OR) gate, the prover needs to find the index of the lexicographically first 0-bit (respectively, 1-bit) of its input from the extended witness. While common ways may go beyond AC^0 due to the unbounded fan-in of each gate, we prove that this can indeed be performed in AC^0 by proposing concrete circuits (See Theorem 5 for details).

Due to the perfect soundness of the underlying OR-proof and NIZK for linear languages, if there exist valid proofs for all gates, we can extract a witness leading the circuit to output 1 by computing the parities of all commitments for the input wires of the circuit. Notice that the statement here is information-theoretical, and thus the extraction procedure is not necessarily runnable in AC^0. Moreover, when switching the distribution of $\mathbf{t}$ to D_0, all the commitments are just random vectors with parities being 0 and the proofs of the underlying NIZKs reveal no useful information.

If we only treat statements verifiable in NC^0, which consists only of fan-in 2 gates, rather than AC^0, we can further reduce the proof size by instantiating the underlying OR-proof with our warm-up construction for one disjunction.

Overview of Extensions. Due to the fact that a random string falls into D_0 and D_1 with half-half probability, we can also implement our construction in the URS model by running it for multiple times in parallel. Composable zero-knowledge of the resulting construction follows from that of the original NIZK and statistical soundness follows from the fact that at least one CRS falls into D_1 with overwhelming probability.

Moreover, we can merge each CRS of all our NIZKs into one vector sampled from D_1. In this case, switching a binding CRS to a hiding one can be efficiently done by changing a single bit, and for any two CRSs with the sum being a constant vector where only one entry is 1, at least one of them must be binding. This implies that our NIZKs have verifiable correlated key generation. Based on this observation, we can convert our NIZKs into unconditionally secure non-interactive ZAPs in AC^0, following the conversion technique in [10].

2 Preliminaries

Notations. We note that all arithmetic computations are over $GF(2)$ in this work. Namely, all arithmetic computations are performed with a modulus of 2, and addition and subtraction are equivalent. We write $a \xleftarrow{\$} \mathcal{A}(b)$ (respectively, $a = \mathcal{A}(b)$) to denote the random variable output by a probabilistic (respectively, deterministic) algorithm (or circuit) $\mathcal{A}$ on input b. By $x \xleftarrow{\$} \mathcal{S}$ we denote the process of sampling an element x from a set or distribution $\mathcal{S}$ uniformly at random. By $[n]$ we denote the set $\{1, \cdots, n\}$. By negl we denote an unspecified negligible function.

By $\mathbf{x} \in \{0,1\}^n$ we denote a column vector with size n, and by x_i we denote the ith element of a vector $\mathbf{x}$. By $\mathbf{x}_1 \circ \cdots \circ \mathbf{x}_\ell$ for some ℓ, we denote $(\mathbf{x}_1^\top, \cdots, \mathbf{x}_\ell^\top)^\top$, i.e., the concatenation of $(\mathbf{x}_i)_{i \in [\ell]}$.

For a matrix $\mathbf{A} \in \{0,1\}^{n \times t}$ with rank $t' \leq n$, we denote the sets $\{\mathbf{y} \mid \exists \mathbf{x} \text{ s.t. } \mathbf{y} = \mathbf{A}\mathbf{x}\}$ and $\{\mathbf{x} \mid \mathbf{A}\mathbf{x} = \mathbf{0}\}$ by $\mathrm{Span}(\mathbf{A})$ (i.e., the span of $\mathbf{A}$) and $\mathrm{Ker}(\mathbf{A})$ respectively. By $\mathbf{A}^\perp \in \{0,1\}^{n \times (n-t')}$ we denote a matrix of rank $n - t'$ in $\mathrm{Ker}(\mathbf{A}^\top)$. Note that for any $\mathbf{y} \notin \mathrm{Span}(\mathbf{A})$, we have $\mathbf{y}^\top \mathbf{A}^\perp \neq \mathbf{0}$. By $\overline{\mathbf{A}}$ (respectively, $\underline{\mathbf{A}}$) we denote the upper $(n-1) \times t$ matrix (respectively, lower $1 \times t$ vector) of $\mathbf{A}$.

By $\mathbf{I}_n$ we denote an identity matrix in $\{0,1\}^{n \times n}$. By $\mathbf{e}_n^i$ we denote the column vector in $\{0,1\}^n$ with the ith element being 1 and the other elements being 0. By $\mathbf{0}$ we denote a zero vector or matrix. By $\mathbf{f}_n^i$ we denote the vector in $\{0,1\}^n$ such that the first $i-1$ entries are 0's and the other entries are 1's. By $\mathbf{E}_n$ we denote the following $n \times (n-1)$ matrix, where the entries of the two main diagonals are 1's and the other entries are 0's.

$$\mathbf{E}_n = \begin{pmatrix} 1 & & & \\ 1 & 1 & & \\ & & \ddots & \\ & & & 1\ 1 \\ & & & 1 \end{pmatrix} \in \{0,1\}^{n \times (n-1)}.$$

One can check that $\mathbf{f}_n^1 \in \mathrm{Ker}(\mathbf{E}_n^\top)$ and $\mathbf{E}_n \mathbf{f}_{n-1}^i = \mathbf{e}_n^i + \mathbf{e}_n^n$ for $i \in [n-1]$.

2.1 Circuits in AC^0

We now recall the definitions of function family, NC^0, and AC^0.

Definition 1 (Function family). *A* function family *is a family of (possibly randomized) functions $\mathcal{F} = \{f_\lambda\}_{\lambda \in \mathbb{N}}$, where for each λ, f_λ has a domain D^f_λ and a range R^f_λ.*

Definition 2 (NC^0). *The class of (non-uniform) AC^0 function families is the set of all function families $\mathcal{F} = \{f_\lambda\}_{\lambda \in \mathbb{N}}$ for which there is a polynomial $p(\cdot)$ and constant d such that for each λ, f_λ can be computed by a (randomized) circuit of size $p(\lambda)$, depth d, and fan-in 2 using* AND, OR, *and* NOT *gates.*

Definition 3 (AC^0). *The class of (non-uniform) AC^0 function families is the set of all function families $\mathcal{F} = \{f_\lambda\}_{\lambda \in \mathbb{N}}$ for which there is a polynomial $p(\cdot)$ and constant d such that for each λ, f_λ can be computed by a (randomized) circuit of size $p(\lambda)$, depth d, and unbounded fan-in using* AND, OR, *and* NOT *gates.*

One can easily see that NC^0 is a subset of AC^0, and for any polynomial $n = n(\lambda)$ and $\mathbf{x}, \mathbf{y} \in \{0,1\}^n$ where either $\mathbf{x}$ or $\mathbf{y}$ has only constant Hamming weight, the inner product of $\mathbf{x}$ and $\mathbf{y}$ is computable in NC^0.

Let $\{\mathsf{PARITY}_\lambda\}_{\lambda \in \mathbb{N}}$ be the function family such that for all $\lambda \in \mathbb{N}$, PARITY_λ on input any $\mathbf{x} \in \{0,1\}^\lambda$ outputs $\sum_{i=1}^{\lambda} x_i$. The following theorem states that any AC^0 circuit has very small correlation with PARITY_λ.

Theorem 1 ([13,15]). *For any $\mathcal{A} = \{a_\lambda\}_{\lambda \in \mathbb{N}} \in \mathsf{AC}^0$ with size p and constant depth d and any $\lambda \in \mathbb{N}$, we have*

$$\left| \Pr_{\mathbf{x} \xleftarrow{\$} \{0,1\}^\lambda} [a_\lambda(\mathbf{x}) = 1 | \mathsf{PARITY}_\lambda(\mathbf{x}) = 1] - \Pr_{\mathbf{x} \xleftarrow{\$} \{0,1\}^\lambda} [a_\lambda(\mathbf{x}) = 1 | \mathsf{PARITY}_\lambda(\mathbf{x}) = 0] \right| \leq 2^{-\Omega(\lambda / \log^{d-1}(p))}.$$

One can see that for any polynomial p in λ, $2^{-\Omega(\lambda/\log^{d-1}(p))} = 2^{-\Omega(\lambda/\log^{d-1}(\lambda))}$ is negligible.

2.2 Proof Systems

Definition 4 (Non-interactive zero-knowledge (NIZK) proof). *A $\mathcal{C}_1$-*NIZK *for a family of relations $\{\mathsf{R}_\lambda\}_{\lambda \in \mathbb{N}}$ is a function family $\mathsf{NIZK} = \{\mathsf{Gen}_\lambda, \mathsf{Prove}_\lambda, \mathsf{Ver}_\lambda\}_{\lambda \in \mathbb{N}} \in \mathcal{C}_1$ with the following properties.*

- Gen_λ *returns a binding CRS* crs.
- $\mathsf{Prove}_\lambda(\mathsf{crs}, \mathsf{x}, \mathsf{w})$ *returns a proof* π.
- $\mathsf{Ver}_\lambda(\mathsf{crs}, \mathsf{x}, \pi)$ *deterministically returns* 1 *(accept) or* 0 *(reject).*

Completeness *is satisfied if for all $\lambda \in \mathbb{N}$, all (x, w) such that $\mathsf{R}_\lambda(\mathsf{x}, \mathsf{w}) = 1$, all $\mathsf{crs} \in \mathsf{Gen}_\lambda$, and all $\pi \in \mathsf{Prove}_\lambda(\mathsf{crs}, \mathsf{x}, \mathsf{w})$, we have $\mathsf{Ver}_\lambda(\mathsf{crs}, \mathsf{x}, \pi) = 1$.*

$\mathcal{C}_2$-composable zero-knowledge *is satisfied if there exists a simulator $\{\mathsf{TGen}_\lambda, \mathsf{Sim}_\lambda\}_{\lambda \in \mathbb{N}} \in \mathcal{C}_1$ such that for any adversary $\mathcal{A} = \{a_\lambda\}_{\lambda \in \mathbb{N}} \in \mathcal{C}_2$, we have*

$$|\Pr[1 \xleftarrow{\$} a_\lambda(\mathsf{crs}) | \mathsf{crs} \xleftarrow{\$} \mathsf{Gen}_\lambda] - \Pr[1 \xleftarrow{\$} a_\lambda(\mathsf{crs}) | (\mathsf{crs}, \mathsf{td}) \xleftarrow{\$} \mathsf{TGen}_\lambda]| \leq \mathsf{negl}(\lambda),$$

and for all $\lambda \in \mathbb{N}$ *and all* (x, w) *such that* $\mathsf{R}_\lambda(\mathsf{x}, \mathsf{w}) = 1$*, the following distributions are identical.*

$$\pi \xleftarrow{\$} \mathsf{Prove}_\lambda(\mathsf{crs}, \mathsf{x}, \mathsf{w}) \text{ and } \pi \xleftarrow{\$} \mathsf{Sim}_\lambda(\mathsf{crs}, \mathsf{td}, \mathsf{x}),$$

where $(\mathsf{crs}, \mathsf{td}) \xleftarrow{\$} \mathsf{TGen}_\lambda$.

Perfect soundness *is satisfied if for all* $\lambda \in \mathbb{N}$*, all* $\mathsf{crs} \in \mathsf{Gen}_\lambda$*, all* $\mathsf{x} \notin \mathsf{L}_\lambda$*, and all* π*, we have* $\mathsf{Ver}_\lambda(\mathsf{crs}, \mathsf{x}, \pi) = 0$.

URS Model. In the above definition, if Gen_λ only returns a public string $\mathsf{crs} \xleftarrow{\$} \{0,1\}^{p(\lambda)}$ uniformly at random for some polynomial p, then we say that NIZK is in the *URS model.*

Non-interactive Zap. A non-interactive zap is a witness-indistinguishable non-interactive proof system in the plain model, where there is no trusted setup. The definition is as follows.

Definition 5 (Non-interactive zap). *A* $\mathcal{C}_1$-non-interactive zap *for a family of relations* $\{\mathsf{R}_\lambda\}_{\lambda \in \mathbb{N}}$ *is a function family* $\mathsf{ZAP} = \{\mathsf{ZProve}_\lambda, \mathsf{ZVer}_\lambda\}_{\lambda \in \mathbb{N}} \in \mathcal{C}_1$ *with the following properties.*

- $\mathsf{ZProve}_\lambda(\mathsf{x}, \mathsf{w})$ *returns a proof* π.
- $\mathsf{ZVer}_\lambda(\mathsf{x}, \pi)$ *deterministically returns* 1 *(accept) or* 0 *(reject).*

Completeness *is satisfied if for all* $\lambda \in \mathbb{N}$ *and all* (x, w) *such that* $\mathsf{R}_\lambda(\mathsf{x}, \mathsf{w}) = 1$*, and all* $\pi \in \mathsf{ZProve}_\lambda(\mathsf{x}, \mathsf{w})$*, we have* $\mathsf{ZVer}_\lambda(\mathsf{x}, \pi) = 1$.

$\mathcal{C}_2$-witness indistinguishability *is satisfied if for all* $\lambda \in \mathbb{N}$*, all* $(\mathsf{x}, \mathsf{w}_0, \mathsf{w}_1)$ *such that* $\mathsf{R}_\lambda(\mathsf{x}, \mathsf{w}_0) = \mathsf{R}_\lambda(\mathsf{x}, \mathsf{w}_1) = 1$*, and any adversary* $\mathcal{A} = \{a_\lambda\}_{\lambda \in \mathbb{N}} \in \mathcal{C}_2$*, we have*

$$|\Pr[1 \xleftarrow{\$} a_\lambda(\mathsf{x}, \pi) | \pi \xleftarrow{\$} \mathsf{ZProve}_\lambda(\mathsf{x}, \mathsf{w}_0)] - \Pr[1 \xleftarrow{\$} a_\lambda(\mathsf{x}, \pi) | \pi \xleftarrow{\$} \mathsf{ZProve}_\lambda(\mathsf{x}, \mathsf{w}_1)]| \leq \mathsf{negl}(\lambda).$$

Perfect soundness *is satisfied if for all* $\lambda \in \mathbb{N}$*, all* $\mathsf{x} \notin \mathsf{L}_\lambda$*, and all* π*, we have* $\mathsf{ZVer}_\lambda(\mathsf{x}, \pi) = 0$.

3 NIZK for Linear Languages

In this section, we propose an NC^0-NIZK for linear languages with perfect soundness and AC^0-composable zero-knowledge. Before giving our construction, we prove the following lemma, which says that the uniform distribution in and out of the span of $\mathbf{E}_\lambda$ are indistinguishable for an AC^0 adversary.

Lemma 1. *For any* $\mathcal{A} = \{a_\lambda\}_{\lambda \in \mathbb{N}} \in \mathsf{AC}^0$ *and any* $\lambda \in \mathbb{N}$*, we have*

$$\left| \Pr_{\mathbf{r} \xleftarrow{\$} \{0,1\}^{\lambda-1}} [a_\lambda(\mathbf{E}_\lambda \mathbf{r}) = 1] - \Pr_{\mathbf{r} \xleftarrow{\$} \{0,1\}^{\lambda-1}} [a_\lambda(\mathbf{E}_\lambda \mathbf{r} + \mathbf{e}_\lambda^\lambda) = 1] \right| \leq \mathsf{negl}(\lambda).$$

Proof. We first note that for $\mathbf{r} \xleftarrow{\$} \{0,1\}^{\lambda-1}$, the first $\lambda-1$ bits of $\mathbf{y} = \mathbf{E}_\lambda \mathbf{r} + \mathbf{e}_\lambda^\lambda b$ are uniformly distributed for $b \in \{0,1\}$, due to the fact that $\overline{\mathbf{E}}_\lambda$ is of full rank. Moreover, the last bit of $\mathbf{y}$ is uniquely determined by the first $\lambda-1$ ones conditioned on $\mathsf{PARITY}_\lambda(\mathbf{y}) = {\mathbf{f}_\lambda^1}^\top \mathbf{y} = b$. Thus, $\mathbf{y}$ is uniformly distributed conditioned on $\mathsf{PARITY}_\lambda(\mathbf{y}) = b$. Then Lemma 1 follows immediately from Theorem 1. □

Our Construction. Let $\mathbf{M}$ be a matrix from $\{0,1\}^{n \times t}$, where $n = n(\lambda)$, $t = t(\lambda)$, and $t' = t'(\lambda)$ are polynomials in λ and the Hamming weight of each row vector in $\mathbf{M}$ is constant. We define the associated language as

$$\mathsf{L}_\mathbf{M} = \{\mathbf{x} : \exists \mathbf{w} \in \{0,1\}^t, \text{ s.t. } \mathbf{x} = \mathbf{M}\mathbf{w}\}.$$

For the associated relation $\mathsf{R}_\mathbf{M}$, we have $\mathsf{R}_\mathbf{M}(\mathbf{x}, \mathbf{w}) = 1$ iff $\mathbf{x} = \mathbf{M}\mathbf{w}$. We give the construction of a NIZK LNIZK for $\{\mathsf{L}_\mathbf{M}\}_{\lambda \in \mathbb{N}}$ and its simulator in Figs. 1 and 2 respectively.

Gen_λ:	$\mathsf{Prove}_\lambda(\mathsf{crs}, \mathbf{x}, \mathbf{w})$:	$\mathsf{Ver}_\lambda(\mathsf{crs}, \mathbf{x}, \pi)$:
$\widetilde{\mathbf{r}} \xleftarrow{\$} \{0,1\}^{\lambda-1}$ $\mathbf{r} = \mathbf{E}_\lambda \widetilde{\mathbf{r}} + \mathbf{e}_\lambda^\lambda \in \{0,1\}^\lambda$ Return $\mathsf{crs} = \mathbf{r}$	$\mathbf{R} \xleftarrow{\$} \{0,1\}^{t \times (\lambda-1)}$ $\mathbf{C} = \mathbf{M}\mathbf{R} \in \{0,1\}^{n \times (\lambda-1)}$ $\mathbf{D} = (\mathbf{R} \Vert \mathbf{w}) \begin{pmatrix} \mathbf{E}_\lambda^\top \\ \mathbf{r}^\top \end{pmatrix} \in \{0,1\}^{t \times \lambda}$ Return $\pi = (\mathbf{C}, \mathbf{D})$	Return 1 iff $(\mathbf{C} \Vert \mathbf{x}) \begin{pmatrix} \mathbf{E}_\lambda^\top \\ \mathbf{r}^\top \end{pmatrix} = \mathbf{M}\mathbf{D}$

Fig. 1. Definition of $\mathsf{LNIZK} = \{\mathsf{Gen}_\lambda, \mathsf{Prove}_\lambda, \mathsf{Ver}_\lambda\}_{\lambda \in \mathbb{N}}$.

TGen_λ:	$\mathsf{Sim}_\lambda(\mathsf{crs}, \mathsf{td}, \mathbf{x})$:
$\widetilde{\mathbf{r}} \xleftarrow{\$} \{0,1\}^{\lambda-1}$ $\mathbf{r} = \mathbf{E}_\lambda \widetilde{\mathbf{r}}$ Return $\mathsf{crs} = \mathbf{r}$ and $\mathsf{td} = \widetilde{\mathbf{r}}$	$\mathbf{R}' \xleftarrow{\$} \{0,1\}^{t \times (\lambda-1)}$ $\mathbf{C} = \mathbf{M}\mathbf{R}' - \mathbf{x} \cdot \widetilde{\mathbf{r}}^\top$, $\mathbf{D} = \mathbf{R}' \mathbf{E}_\lambda^\top$ Return $\pi = (\mathbf{C}, \mathbf{D})$

Fig. 2. Definition of the simulator $\{\mathsf{TGen}_\lambda, \mathsf{Sim}_\lambda\}_{\lambda \in \mathbb{N}}$ of LNIZK.

Theorem 2. LNIZK *in Fig. 1 is an* NC^0-*NIZK with perfect soundness and* AC^0-*composable zero-knowledge.*

Proof. **Complexity.** First, we note that in Figs. 1 and 2, the Hamming weight of each row vector in $\mathbf{E}_\lambda$, $\mathbf{M}$, and $\mathbf{x}$ and each column vector in $\begin{pmatrix} \mathbf{E}_\lambda^\top \\ \mathbf{r}^\top \end{pmatrix}$ is constant.[3] Thus, the multiplication of matrices involved can be performed in NC^0. Since

[3] Notice that $\mathbf{x}$ can be treated as a matrix with row vectors with Hamming weight at most 1.

addition of a constant number of matrices can be performed in NC^0 as well, we have $\{\mathsf{Gen}_\lambda, \mathsf{Prove}_\lambda, \mathsf{Ver}_\lambda, \mathsf{TGen}_\lambda, \mathsf{Sim}_\lambda\}_{\lambda \in \mathbb{N}} \in \mathsf{NC}^0$.

Completeness. Completeness follows from the fact that for $\mathbf{x} = \mathbf{Mw}$, $\mathbf{C} = \mathbf{MR}$, and $\mathbf{D} = (\mathbf{R}||\mathbf{w}) \begin{pmatrix} \mathbf{E}_\lambda^\top \\ \mathbf{r}^\top \end{pmatrix}$, we have

$$(\mathbf{C}||\mathbf{x}) \begin{pmatrix} \mathbf{E}_\lambda^\top \\ \mathbf{r}^\top \end{pmatrix} = (\mathbf{MR}||\mathbf{Mw}) \begin{pmatrix} \mathbf{E}_\lambda^\top \\ \mathbf{r}^\top \end{pmatrix} = \mathbf{M}(\mathbf{R}||\mathbf{w}) \begin{pmatrix} \mathbf{E}_\lambda^\top \\ \mathbf{r}^\top \end{pmatrix} = \mathbf{MD}.$$

AC^0-Composable Zero-Knowledge. The indistinguishability between CRSs generated by Gen_λ and TGen_λ follows immediately from Lemma 1.

For $\mathbf{r} = \mathbf{E}_\lambda \widetilde{\mathbf{r}} \in \mathsf{TGen}_\lambda$ and $\mathbf{x} = \mathbf{Mw}$, we have $\mathbf{MR} = \mathbf{M}(\mathbf{R} + \mathbf{w} \cdot \widetilde{\mathbf{r}}^\top) - \mathbf{x} \cdot \widetilde{\mathbf{r}}^\top$ and

$$(\mathbf{R}||\mathbf{w}) \begin{pmatrix} \mathbf{E}_\lambda^\top \\ \mathbf{r}^\top \end{pmatrix} = (\mathbf{R}||\mathbf{w}) \begin{pmatrix} \mathbf{E}_\lambda^\top \\ \widetilde{\mathbf{r}}^\top \mathbf{E}_\lambda^\top \end{pmatrix} = (\mathbf{R} + \mathbf{w} \cdot \widetilde{\mathbf{r}}^\top) \mathbf{E}_\lambda^\top.$$

Moreover, for $\mathbf{R} \overset{\$}{\leftarrow} \{0,1\}^{t \times (\lambda-1)}$, the distribution of $\mathbf{R} + \mathbf{w} \cdot \widetilde{\mathbf{r}}^\top$ is uniformly random in $\{0,1\}^{t \times (\lambda-1)}$. Thus, for any valid statement, the simulator perfectly simulates honest proofs, completing the proof of composable zero-knowledge.

Perfect Soundness. Recall that $\mathbf{f}_\lambda^1$ denotes the vector consisting only of 1's and $\mathbf{f}_\lambda^1 \in \mathrm{Ker}(\mathbf{E}_\lambda^\top)$. When $\mathbf{r}$ is generated as $\mathbf{r} \overset{\$}{\leftarrow} \mathsf{Gen}_\lambda$, we have $\mathbf{r} \notin \mathrm{Span}(\mathbf{E}_\lambda)$ since ${\mathbf{f}_\lambda^1}^\top \mathbf{r} = 1$. Moreover, for any valid statement/proof pair $(\mathbf{x}, (\mathbf{C}, \mathbf{D}))$ such that $(\mathbf{C}||\mathbf{x}) \begin{pmatrix} \mathbf{E}_\lambda^\top \\ \mathbf{r}^\top \end{pmatrix} = \mathbf{MD}$, we have ${\mathbf{M}^\perp}^\top (\mathbf{C}||\mathbf{x}) \begin{pmatrix} \mathbf{E}_\lambda^\top \\ \mathbf{r}^\top \end{pmatrix} = \mathbf{0}$, i.e., $\mathbf{E}_\lambda(\mathbf{C}^\top \mathbf{M}^\perp) = \mathbf{r}(\mathbf{x}^\top \mathbf{M}^\perp)$. When $\mathbf{r} \notin \mathrm{Span}(\mathbf{E}_\lambda)$, we must have $\mathbf{x}^\top \mathbf{M}^\perp = \mathbf{0}$, which in turn implies $\mathbf{x} \in \mathsf{L}_\mathbf{M}$, completing the proof of statistical soundness. Notice that in this part, the arguments are information-theoretical and the equations are not necessarily efficiently computable.

Putting all the above together, Theorem 2 immediately follows. □

Remark. By replacing Gen_λ by TGen_λ in LNIZK, we immediately achieve a fine-grained NIZK with perfect zero-knowledge and computational soundness. Similar arguments can also be made for our OR-proofs and NIZK for circuit SAT given in the following sections.

4 NIZK for OR-Languages

In this section, we extend the NIZK LNIZK in Sect. 3 to an OR-proof system. We first give an efficient warm-up construction for 1-out-of-2 disjunction languages, and then show how to extend it to a fully-fledged one for the disjunction of polynomial number of linear languages.

4.1 A Warm-Up Construction

Let $n_0 = n_0(\lambda)$, $n_1 = n_1(\lambda)$, $t_0 = t_0(\lambda)$, and $t_1 = t_1(\lambda)$ be any polynomials in λ. We define the following language

$$\mathsf{L}^{\mathsf{or}}_{(\mathbf{M}_0,\mathbf{M}_1)} = \{(\mathbf{x}_0, \mathbf{x}_1) : \exists \mathbf{w} \text{ s.t. } \mathbf{x}_0 = \mathbf{M}_0\mathbf{w} \vee \mathbf{x}_1 = \mathbf{M}_1\mathbf{w}\},$$

where $\mathbf{M}_i \in \{0,1\}^{n_i \times t_i}$ and the Hamming weight of each row vector in $\mathbf{M}_i$ is constant for $i \in \{0,1\}$. For the associated relation $\mathsf{R}^{\mathsf{or}}_{(\mathbf{M}_0,\mathbf{M}_1)}$, we have $\mathsf{R}^{\mathsf{or}}_{(\mathbf{M}_0,\mathbf{M}_1)}((\mathbf{x}_0, \mathbf{x}_1), \mathbf{w}) = 1$ iff $\mathbf{x}_j = \mathbf{M}_j\mathbf{w}$ for some $j \in \{0,1\}$. The OR-proof and its simulator are given in Figs. 3 and 4 respectively. Roughly, the prover splits the original binding CRS $\mathbf{r}$ into a binding one $\mathbf{r}_j$ and a hiding one $\mathbf{r}_{1-j}$ for some $j \in \{0,1\}$, and respectively uses the witness and trapdoor to generate proofs for the two linear statements. The verifer on receiving $\mathbf{r}_0$ recovers $\mathbf{r}_1$ as $\mathbf{r}_1 = \mathbf{r} - \mathbf{r}_0$ and executes the verification procedure.

$\underline{\mathsf{ORGen}_\lambda:}$
$\widetilde{\mathbf{r}} \xleftarrow{\$} \{0,1\}^{\lambda-1}$, $\mathbf{r} = \mathbf{E}_\lambda\widetilde{\mathbf{r}} + \mathbf{e}^\lambda_\lambda \in \{0,1\}^\lambda$
Return $\mathsf{crs} = \mathbf{r}$

$\underline{\mathsf{ORProve}_\lambda(\mathsf{crs}, (\mathbf{x}_0, \mathbf{x}_1), \mathbf{w}):}$
Let $j \in \{0,1\}$ s.t. $\mathbf{x}_j = \mathbf{M}_j\mathbf{w}$
Sample $\widetilde{\mathbf{r}}_{1-j} \xleftarrow{\$} \{0,1\}^{\lambda-1}$ and compute $\mathbf{r}_{1-j} = \mathbf{E}_\lambda\widetilde{\mathbf{r}}_{1-j}$ and $\mathbf{r}_j = \mathbf{r} - \mathbf{r}_{1-j}$
Sample $\mathbf{R}'_{1-j} \xleftarrow{\$} \{0,1\}^{t_{1-j}\times(\lambda-1)}$ and compute

$$\mathbf{C}_{1-j} = \mathbf{M}_{1-j}\mathbf{R}'_{1-j} - \mathbf{x}_{1-j}\cdot\widetilde{\mathbf{r}}^\top_{1-j} \in \{0,1\}^{n_{1-j}\times(\lambda-1)}, \mathbf{D}_{1-j} = \mathbf{R}'_{1-j}\mathbf{E}^\top_\lambda \in \{0,1\}^{t_{1-j}\times\lambda}$$

Sample $\mathbf{R}_j \xleftarrow{\$} \{0,1\}^{t_j\times(\lambda-1)}$ and compute

$$\mathbf{C}_j = \mathbf{M}_j\mathbf{R}_j, \mathbf{D}_j = (\mathbf{R}_j||\mathbf{w}) \begin{pmatrix} \mathbf{E}^\top_\lambda \\ \mathbf{r}^\top_j \end{pmatrix}$$

Return $\pi = ((\mathbf{C}_i, \mathbf{D}_i)_{i\in\{0,1\}}, \mathbf{r}_0)$

$\underline{\mathsf{ORVer}_\lambda(\mathsf{crs}, (\mathbf{x}_0, \mathbf{x}_1), \pi):}$
$\mathbf{r}_1 = \mathbf{r} - \mathbf{r}_0$
Return 1 iff $(\mathbf{C}_i||\mathbf{x}_i) \begin{pmatrix} \mathbf{E}^\top_\lambda \\ \mathbf{r}^\top_i \end{pmatrix} = \mathbf{M}_i\mathbf{D}_i$ for all $i \in \{0,1\}$

Fig. 3. Definition of $\mathsf{ORNIZK}_{\mathsf{wm}} = \{\mathsf{ORGen}_\lambda, \mathsf{ORProve}_\lambda, \mathsf{ORVer}_\lambda\}_{\lambda\in\mathbb{N}}$.

Theorem 3. $\mathsf{ORNIZK}_{\mathsf{wm}}$ *in Fig. 3 is an* NC^0*-NIZK with perfect soundness and* AC^0*-composable zero-knowledge.*

Proof. **Complexity.** First, we note that in Figs. 3 and 4, the Hamming weight of each row vector in $\mathbf{E}_\lambda$, $\mathbf{M}_i$, and $\mathbf{x}_i$ and each column vector in $\begin{pmatrix} \mathbf{E}^\top_\lambda \\ \mathbf{r}^\top_i \end{pmatrix}$ is constant

$\underline{\mathsf{ORTGen}_\lambda}$:
$\widetilde{\mathbf{r}} \xleftarrow{\$} \{0,1\}^{\lambda-1}$, $\mathbf{r} = \mathbf{E}_\lambda \widetilde{\mathbf{r}}$
Return $\mathsf{crs} = \mathbf{r}$ and $\mathsf{td} = \widetilde{\mathbf{r}}$

$\underline{\mathsf{ORSim}_\lambda(\mathsf{crs}, \mathsf{td}, (\mathbf{x}_0, \mathbf{x}_1))}$:
Sample $\widetilde{\mathbf{r}}_0 \xleftarrow{\$} \{0,1\}^\lambda$ and compute $\widetilde{\mathbf{r}}_1 = \widetilde{\mathbf{r}} - \widetilde{\mathbf{r}}_0$, $\mathbf{r}_0 = \mathbf{E}_\lambda \widetilde{\mathbf{r}}_0$, and $\mathbf{r}_1 = \mathbf{E}_\lambda \widetilde{\mathbf{r}}_1$
For all $i \in \{0,1\}$, compute

$$\mathbf{R}'_i \xleftarrow{\$} \{0,1\}^{t_i \times (\lambda-1)}, \mathbf{C}_i = \mathbf{M}_i \mathbf{R}'_i - \mathbf{x}_i \cdot \widetilde{\mathbf{r}}_i^\top, \mathbf{D}_i = \mathbf{R}'_i \mathbf{E}_\lambda^\top$$

Return $\pi = ((\mathbf{C}_i, \mathbf{D}_i)_{i=0,1}, \mathbf{r}_0)$

Fig. 4. Definition of the simulator $\{\mathsf{ORTGen}_\lambda, \mathsf{ORSim}_\lambda\}_{\lambda \in \mathbb{N}}$ of $\mathsf{ORNIZK}_{\mathsf{wm}}$.

for all $i \in \{0,1\}$. Thus, the multiplication of matrices involved can be performed in NC^0. Also, addition of a constant number of matrices can be performed in NC^0. Hence, we have $\{\mathsf{ORGen}_\lambda, \mathsf{ORProve}_\lambda, \mathsf{ORVer}_\lambda, \mathsf{ORTGen}_\lambda, \mathsf{ORSim}_\lambda\}_{\lambda \in \mathbb{N}} \in \mathsf{NC}^0$.

Completeness. Completeness follows from the fact that for $\mathbf{x}_j = \mathbf{M}_j \mathbf{w}$, $\mathbf{C}_j = \mathbf{M}_j \mathbf{R}_j$, and $\mathbf{D}_j = (\mathbf{R}_j || \mathbf{w}) \begin{pmatrix} \mathbf{E}_\lambda^\top \\ \mathbf{r}_j^\top \end{pmatrix}$, we have

$$(\mathbf{C}_j || \mathbf{x}_j) \begin{pmatrix} \mathbf{E}_\lambda^\top \\ \mathbf{r}_j^\top \end{pmatrix} = (\mathbf{M}_j \mathbf{R}_j || \mathbf{M}_j \mathbf{w}) \begin{pmatrix} \mathbf{E}_\lambda^\top \\ \mathbf{r}_j^\top \end{pmatrix} = \mathbf{M}_j \mathbf{D}_j,$$

and for $\mathbf{C}_{1-j} = \mathbf{M}\mathbf{R}'_{1-j} - \mathbf{x}_{1-j} \cdot \widetilde{\mathbf{r}}_{1-j}^\top$ and $\mathbf{D}_{1-j} = \mathbf{R}'_{1-j} \mathbf{E}_\lambda^\top$, we have

$$\begin{aligned}(\mathbf{C}_{1-j} || \mathbf{x}_{1-j}) \begin{pmatrix} \mathbf{E}_\lambda^\top \\ \mathbf{r}_{1-j}^\top \end{pmatrix} &= ((\mathbf{M}\mathbf{R}'_{1-j} - \mathbf{x}_{1-j} \cdot \widetilde{\mathbf{r}}_{1-j}^\top) || \mathbf{x}_{1-j}) \begin{pmatrix} \mathbf{E}_\lambda^\top \\ \mathbf{r}_{1-j}^\top \end{pmatrix} \\ &= \mathbf{M}\mathbf{R}'_{1-j} \mathbf{E}_\lambda = \mathbf{M}\mathbf{D}_{1-j}.\end{aligned}$$

AC^0-Composable Zero-Knowledge. The indistinguishability between CRSs generated by Gen_λ and TGen_λ follows immediately from Lemma 1.

When the CRS is generated as $\mathbf{r} = \mathbf{E}_\lambda \widetilde{\mathbf{r}}$ where $\widetilde{\mathbf{r}} \xleftarrow{\$} \{0,1\}^{\lambda-1}$, $\mathbf{r}_0$ and $\mathbf{r}_1$ generated by both $\mathsf{ORProve}_\lambda$ and ORSim_λ are uniformly distributed in $\mathrm{Span}(\mathbf{E}_\lambda)$, conditioned on $\mathbf{r} = \mathbf{r}_0 + \mathbf{r}_1$. Moreover, we have

$$\mathbf{M}_j \mathbf{R}_j = \mathbf{M}_j (\mathbf{R}_j + \mathbf{w} \cdot \widetilde{\mathbf{r}}^\top) - \mathbf{x}_j \cdot \widetilde{\mathbf{r}}^\top$$

and

$$(\mathbf{R}_j || \mathbf{w}) \begin{pmatrix} \mathbf{E}_\lambda^\top \\ \widetilde{\mathbf{r}}_j^\top \mathbf{E}_\lambda^\top \end{pmatrix} = (\mathbf{R}_j + \mathbf{w} \cdot \widetilde{\mathbf{r}}_j^\top) \mathbf{E}_\lambda^\top$$

for $\mathbf{x}_j = \mathbf{M}_j \mathbf{w}$. Since the distribution of $\mathbf{R}_j + \mathbf{w} \cdot \widetilde{\mathbf{r}}_j^\top$ for $\mathbf{R}_j \xleftarrow{\$} \{0,1\}^{t_j \times (\lambda-1)}$ is uniform in $\{0,1\}^{t_j \times (\lambda-1)}$, the simulator perfectly simulates honest proofs, completing the proof of composable zero-knowledge.

Perfect Soundness. Recall that $\mathbf{f}_\lambda^1$ denotes the vector consisting only of 1's and $\mathbf{f}_\lambda^1 \in \mathrm{Ker}(\mathbf{E}_\lambda^\top)$. For $\mathbf{r} \in \mathsf{Gen}_\lambda$, we have ${\mathbf{f}_\lambda^1}^\top \mathbf{r} = 1$, i.e., $\mathbf{r} \notin \mathrm{Span}(\mathbf{E}_\lambda)$. Hence, for a valid statement/proof pair (x, π) where $\mathsf{x} = (\mathbf{x}_0, \mathbf{x}_1)$ and $\pi = ((\mathbf{C}_i, \mathbf{D}_i)_{i\in\{0,1\}}, \mathbf{r}_0)$, we must have $\mathbf{r}_j \notin \mathrm{Span}(\mathbf{E}_\lambda)$ and $(\mathbf{C}_j||\mathbf{x}_j)\begin{pmatrix}\mathbf{E}_\lambda^\top \\ \mathbf{r}_j^\top\end{pmatrix} = \mathbf{M}_j\mathbf{D}_j$ for some $j \in \{0,1\}$, where $\mathbf{r}_1 = \mathbf{r} - \mathbf{r}_0$. For such j, we have $(\mathbf{M}_j^\perp)^\top(\mathbf{C}_j||\mathbf{x}_j)\begin{pmatrix}\mathbf{E}_\lambda^\top \\ \mathbf{r}_j^\top\end{pmatrix} = \mathbf{0}$, i.e., $\mathbf{r}_j(\mathbf{x}_j^\top \mathbf{M}_j^\perp) = \mathbf{E}_\lambda(\mathbf{C}_j^\top \mathbf{M}_j^\perp)$. Since $\mathbf{r}_j \notin \mathrm{Span}(\mathbf{E}_\lambda)$, we must have $\mathbf{x}_j^\top \mathbf{M}_j^\perp = 0$, which in turn implies $\mathsf{x} \in \mathsf{L}^{\mathsf{or}}_{\mathbf{M}_0,\mathbf{M}_1}$, completing the proof of perfect soundness. Notice that this part of arguments is information-theoretical and thus the equations are not necessarily computable in AC^0.

Putting all the above together, Theorem 3 immediately follows. □

Remark. As discussed in Sect. 1.2, the above construction can not be naturally extended to 1-out-of-ℓ disjunction for any polynomial ℓ, due to the fact that an AC^0 algorithm cannot compute the sum of a polynomial number of random vectors (even conditioned on the parity being fixed). Specifically, if we extend the construction in a straightforward way, the prover and the verifier will have to compute $\mathbf{r}_j = \mathbf{r} - \sum_{i\neq j} \mathbf{r}_i$ and $\mathbf{r}_\ell = \mathbf{r} - \sum_{i=1}^{\ell-1} \mathbf{r}_i$ respectively, while neither can be performed in AC^0. In the next section, we propose a new method to overcome this problem.

4.2 A Fully-Fledged Construction

We now extend the warm-up OR-proof to a fully-fledged one for 1-out-of-ℓ disjunction.

Let $\ell = \ell(\lambda)$, $(n_i = n_i(\lambda))_{i\in[\ell]}$, $(t_i = t_i(\lambda))_{i\in[\ell]}$ be any polynomials in λ. We define the following languages:

$$\mathsf{L}_{\mathbf{E}_\ell} = \{\mathbf{Y} : \exists \mathbf{W} \in \{0,1\}^{(\ell-1)\times\lambda}, \text{ s.t. } \mathbf{Y} = \mathbf{E}_\ell \mathbf{W}\}.$$

and

$$\mathsf{L}^{\mathsf{or}}_{(\mathbf{M}_i)_{i\in[\ell]}} = \{(\mathbf{x}_i)_{i=1}^{\ell} : \exists \mathbf{w} \in \{0,1\}^{t_i}, \text{ s.t. } \bigvee_{i\in[\ell]} \mathbf{x}_i = \mathbf{M}_i \mathbf{w}\},$$

where $\mathbf{M}_i \in \{0,1\}^{n_i \times t_i}$ and the Hamming weight of each row vector in $\mathbf{M}_i$ is constant for $i \in [\ell]$. One can easily see that $\{\mathsf{L}_{\mathbf{E}_\ell}\}_{\lambda\in\mathbb{N}}$ is supported by our NIZK for linear languages given in Sect. 3, since $\mathsf{L}_{\mathbf{E}_\ell}$ is equivalent to the following linear language:

$$\mathsf{L}'_{\mathbf{E}_\ell} = \{(\mathbf{y}_i)_{i\in[\ell]} : \exists \mathbf{w} \in \{0,1\}^{(\ell-1)\lambda}, \text{ s.t. } \mathbf{y}_1 \circ \cdots \circ \mathbf{y}_\ell = \mathbf{M}\mathbf{w}\}$$

where $\mathbf{Y} = (\mathbf{y}_i)_{i\in[\ell]}$ and

$$\mathbf{M} = \begin{pmatrix} \mathbf{E}_\ell & \mathbf{0} & \cdots & \mathbf{0} \\ \mathbf{0} & \ddots & \ddots & \vdots \\ \vdots & \ddots & \ddots & \mathbf{0} \\ \mathbf{0} & \cdots & \mathbf{0} & \mathbf{E}_\ell \end{pmatrix} \in \{0,1\}^{\ell\cdot\lambda\times(\ell-1)\lambda}$$

contains $\mathbf{E}_\lambda$'s in the main diagonal and $\mathbf{0}$ in the other positions. Here recall that $\mathbf{y}_1 \circ \cdots \circ \mathbf{y}_\ell$ denotes the concatenation of $(\mathbf{y}_i)_{i\in[\ell]}$. It is easy to see that the Hamming weight of each row vector in $\mathbf{M}$ is constant.

Let $\mathsf{LNIZK} = \{\mathsf{Gen}_\lambda, \mathsf{Prove}_\lambda, \mathsf{Ver}_\lambda\}_{\lambda\in\mathbb{N}}$ be a NIZK with a simulator $\{\mathsf{TGen}_\lambda, \mathsf{Sim}_\lambda\}_{\lambda\in\mathbb{N}}$ for $\{\mathsf{L}_{\mathbf{E}_\ell}\}_{\lambda\in\mathbb{N}}$, we give an OR-proof for $\{\mathsf{L}^{\mathsf{or}}_{(\mathbf{M}_i)_{i\in[\ell]}}\}_{\lambda\in\mathbb{N}}$ and its simulator in Figs. 5 and 6 respectively.

Roughly, we adopt a verifiable sampling procedure with double layers to split the original CRS into $\ell-1$ hiding CRSs and one binding CRS. In the first layer, we sample ℓ vectors with a trapdoor $\mathbf{S}$, and in the second layer, we in turn use the ℓ vectors as trapdoors to sample ℓ random hiding CRSs with the sum being 0, and add one of them with $\mathbf{r}$ to make it binding. Later, we use a NIZK for linear languages to prove that the sum of the ℓ CRSs is $\mathbf{r}$, where the witness can be extracted from $\mathbf{S}$. In this way, a verifier in AC^0 can check that at least one of the split CRSs is binding, without learning any useful information.

Theorem 4. *If* LNIZK *is an* NC^0*-NIZK with perfect soundness and* AC^0*-composable zero-knowledge, then* ORNIZK *in Fig. 5 is an* NC^0*-NIZK with perfect soundness and* AC^0*-composable zero-knowledge.*

Proof. **Complexity.** First, we note that in Figs. 5 and 6, the Hamming weight of each row vector in $\mathbf{E}_\lambda$, $\mathbf{E}_{\ell-1}$, $\mathbf{M}_i$, and $\mathbf{x}_i$ and each column vector in $\begin{pmatrix}\mathbf{E}_\lambda^\top \\ \mathbf{r}_i^\top\end{pmatrix}$ is constant for all $i \in [\ell]$. Thus, the multiplication of matrices involved can be performed in NC^0. Since addition of a constant number of matrices and running LNIZK and its simulator can be performed in NC^0 as well, we have $\{\mathsf{ORGen}_\lambda, \mathsf{ORProve}_\lambda, \mathsf{ORVer}_\lambda, \mathsf{ORTGen}_\lambda, \mathsf{ORSim}_\lambda\}_{\lambda\in\mathbb{N}} \in \mathsf{NC}^0$.

Completeness. For $\mathbf{x}_j = \mathbf{M}_j\mathbf{w}$, $\mathbf{C}_j = \mathbf{M}_j\mathbf{R}_j$, and $\mathbf{D}_j = (\mathbf{R}_j||\mathbf{w})\begin{pmatrix}\mathbf{E}_\lambda^\top \\ \mathbf{r}_j^\top\end{pmatrix}$, we have

$$(\mathbf{C}_j||\mathbf{x}_j)\begin{pmatrix}\mathbf{E}_\lambda^\top \\ \mathbf{r}_j^\top\end{pmatrix} = (\mathbf{M}_j\mathbf{R}_j||\mathbf{M}_j\mathbf{w})\begin{pmatrix}\mathbf{E}_\lambda^\top \\ \mathbf{r}_j^\top\end{pmatrix} = \mathbf{M}_j\mathbf{D}_j.$$

For $(\mathbf{r}_i)_{i\in[\ell]} = \mathbf{R} = \mathbf{E}_\lambda\widetilde{\mathbf{R}} + \mathbf{r}\cdot{\mathbf{e}_\ell^j}^\top$, we have $\mathbf{r}_i = \mathbf{E}_\lambda\widetilde{\mathbf{r}}_i$ for all $i \in [\ell]\backslash\{j\}$. Then, for $\mathbf{C}_i = \mathbf{M}\mathbf{R}'_i - \mathbf{x}_i\cdot\widetilde{\mathbf{r}}_i^\top$ and $\mathbf{D}_i = \mathbf{R}'_i\mathbf{E}_\lambda^\top$ where $i \in [\ell]\backslash\{j\}$, we have

$$(\mathbf{C}_i||\mathbf{x}_i)\begin{pmatrix}\mathbf{E}_\lambda^\top \\ \mathbf{r}_i^\top\end{pmatrix} = ((\mathbf{M}\mathbf{R}'_i - \mathbf{x}_i\cdot\widetilde{\mathbf{r}}_i^\top)||\mathbf{x}_i)\begin{pmatrix}\mathbf{E}_\lambda^\top \\ \mathbf{r}_i^\top\end{pmatrix} = \mathbf{M}\mathbf{R}'_i\mathbf{E}_\lambda = \mathbf{M}\mathbf{D}_i.$$

$\underline{\mathsf{ORGen}_\lambda}$:
$\widetilde{\mathbf{r}} \xleftarrow{\$} \{0,1\}^{\lambda-1}$, $\mathbf{r} = \mathbf{E}_\lambda \widetilde{\mathbf{r}} + \mathbf{e}_\lambda^\lambda \in \{0,1\}^\lambda$, $\mathsf{crs} \xleftarrow{\$} \mathsf{Gen}_\lambda$
Return $\mathsf{crs}_{\mathsf{or}} = (\mathsf{crs}, \mathbf{r})$

$\underline{\mathsf{ORProve}_\lambda(\mathsf{crs}_{\mathsf{or}}, (\mathbf{x}_i)_{i \in [\ell]}, \mathbf{w})}$:
Let $\mathbf{x}_j = \mathbf{M}_j \mathbf{w}$ for some $j \in [\ell]$
Sample $\mathbf{S} \xleftarrow{\$} \{0,1\}^{(\ell-1)\times(\lambda-1)}$
Compute $\widetilde{\mathbf{R}}^\top = \mathbf{E}_\ell \mathbf{S} \in \{0,1\}^{\ell\times(\lambda-1)}$ and $\mathbf{R} = \mathbf{E}_\lambda \widetilde{\mathbf{R}} + \mathbf{r} \cdot \mathbf{e}_\ell^{j\top} \in \{0,1\}^{\lambda\times\ell}$
Parse $\mathbf{R} = (\mathbf{r}_i)_{i\in[\ell]}$ and $\widetilde{\mathbf{R}} = (\widetilde{\mathbf{r}}_i)_{i\in[\ell]}$
For all $i \in [\ell]\backslash\{j\}$, sample $\mathbf{R}'_i \xleftarrow{\$} \{0,1\}^{t_i\times(\lambda-1)}$ and compute

$$\mathbf{r}_i = \mathbf{E}_\lambda \widetilde{\mathbf{r}}_i \in \{0,1\}^\lambda, \mathbf{C}_i = \mathbf{M}_i \mathbf{R}'_i - \mathbf{x}_i \cdot \widetilde{\mathbf{r}}_i^\top \in \{0,1\}^{n_i\times(\lambda-1)}, \mathbf{D}_i = \mathbf{R}'_i \mathbf{E}_\lambda^\top \in \{0,1\}^{t_i\times\lambda}$$

Sample $\mathbf{R}_j \xleftarrow{\$} \{0,1\}^{t_j\times(\lambda-1)}$ and compute

$$\mathbf{C}_j = \mathbf{M}_j \mathbf{R}_j \text{ and } \mathbf{D}_j = (\mathbf{R}_j || \mathbf{w}) \begin{pmatrix} \mathbf{E}_\lambda^\top \\ \mathbf{r}_j^\top \end{pmatrix}$$

Compute

$$\pi \xleftarrow{\$} \mathsf{Prove}_\lambda(\mathsf{crs}, \mathbf{R}^\top - \mathbf{e}_\ell^\ell \mathbf{r}^\top, \mathbf{S}\mathbf{E}_\lambda^\top + \mathbf{f}_{\ell-1}^j \mathbf{r}^\top)$$

Return $\pi_{\mathsf{or}} = ((\mathbf{C}_i, \mathbf{D}_i)_{i\in[\ell]}, \mathbf{R}, \pi)$

$\underline{\mathsf{ORVer}_\lambda(\mathsf{crs}, (\mathbf{x}_i)_{i\in[\ell]}, \pi_{\mathsf{or}})}$:
Parse $\mathbf{R} = (\mathbf{r}_i)_{i\in[\ell]}$
Return 1 iff $(\mathbf{C}_i || \mathbf{x}_i) \begin{pmatrix} \mathbf{E}_\lambda^\top \\ \mathbf{r}_i^\top \end{pmatrix} = \mathbf{M}_i \mathbf{D}_i$ for all $i \in [\ell]$ and

$$\mathsf{Ver}_\lambda(\mathsf{crs}, \mathbf{R}^\top - \mathbf{e}_\ell^\ell \mathbf{r}^\top, \pi) = 1$$

Fig. 5. Definition of $\mathsf{ORNIZK} = \{\mathsf{ORGen}_\lambda, \mathsf{ORProve}_\lambda, \mathsf{ORVer}_\lambda\}_{\lambda\in\mathbb{N}}$. Recall that by $\mathbf{f}_{\ell-1}^j \in \{0,1\}^{\ell-1}$ we denote the vector such that the first $j-1$ entries are 0's and the last $\ell - j$ ones are 1's.

Moreover, since $\mathbf{E}_\ell \mathbf{f}_{\ell-1}^j = \mathbf{e}_\ell^j + \mathbf{e}_\ell^\ell$, for $\widetilde{\mathbf{R}}^\top = \mathbf{E}_\ell \mathbf{S}$ and $\mathbf{R} = \mathbf{E}_\lambda \widetilde{\mathbf{R}} + \mathbf{r} \cdot \mathbf{e}_\ell^{j\top}$, we have

$$\begin{aligned} \mathbf{R}^\top &= \widetilde{\mathbf{R}}^\top \mathbf{E}_\lambda^\top + \mathbf{e}_\ell^j \cdot \mathbf{r}^\top \\ &= \mathbf{E}_\ell \mathbf{S} \mathbf{E}_\lambda^\top + \mathbf{e}_\ell^j \cdot \mathbf{r}^\top \\ &= \mathbf{E}_\ell \mathbf{S} \mathbf{E}_\lambda^\top + (\mathbf{e}_\ell^\ell \mathbf{r}^\top + \mathbf{e}_\ell^j \cdot \mathbf{r}^\top) + \mathbf{e}_\ell^\ell \cdot \mathbf{r}^\top \\ &= \mathbf{E}_\ell \mathbf{S} \mathbf{E}_\lambda^\top + \mathbf{E}_\ell \mathbf{f}_{\ell-1}^j \mathbf{r}^\top + \mathbf{e}_\ell^\ell \mathbf{r}^\top \\ &= \mathbf{E}_\ell (\mathbf{S} \mathbf{E}_\lambda^\top + \mathbf{f}_{\ell-1}^j \mathbf{r}^\top) + \mathbf{e}_\ell^\ell \mathbf{r}^\top, \end{aligned}$$

i.e., $\mathbf{R}^\top - \mathbf{e}_\ell^\ell \mathbf{r}^\top = \mathbf{E}_\ell (\mathbf{S}\mathbf{E}_\lambda^\top + \mathbf{f}_{\ell-1}^j \mathbf{r}^\top)$. Then the completeness of ORNIZK follows immediately from that of LNIZK.

AC^0-Composable Zero-Knowledge. The indistinguishability between CRSs generated by ORGen_λ and ORTGen_λ follows immediately from the composable zero-knowledge of LNIZK and Lemma 1.

$\underline{\mathsf{ORTGen}_\lambda}$:
$\widetilde{\mathbf{r}} \xleftarrow{\$} \{0,1\}^{\lambda-1}$, $\mathbf{r} = \mathbf{E}_\lambda \widetilde{\mathbf{r}} \in \{0,1\}^\lambda$, $(\mathsf{crs}, \mathsf{td}) \xleftarrow{\$} \mathsf{TGen}_\lambda$
Return $\mathsf{crs}_{\mathsf{or}} = ((\mathsf{crs}, \mathbf{r}), \mathsf{td}_{\mathsf{or}} = (\mathsf{td}, \widetilde{\mathbf{r}}))$

$\underline{\mathsf{ORSim}_\lambda(\mathsf{crs}, \mathsf{td}, (\mathbf{x}_i)_{i\in[\ell]})}$:
Sample $\mathbf{S} \xleftarrow{\$} \{0,1\}^{(\ell-1)\times(\lambda-1)}$
Compute $\widetilde{\mathbf{R}}^\top = \mathbf{E}_\ell \mathbf{S} \in \{0,1\}^{\ell\times(\lambda-1)}$ and $\mathbf{R} = \mathbf{E}_\lambda \widetilde{\mathbf{R}} + \mathbf{r}\cdot \mathbf{e}_\ell^{\ell\top} \in \{0,1\}^{\ell\times\lambda}$
Parse $\mathbf{R} = (\mathbf{r}_i)_{i\in[\ell]}$ and $\widetilde{\mathbf{R}} = (\widetilde{\mathbf{r}}_i)_{i\in[\ell]}$
For $i \in [\ell]$, sample $\mathbf{R}'_i \xleftarrow{\$} \{0,1\}^{t_i\times(\lambda-1)}$ and compute $\mathbf{D}_i = \mathbf{R}'_i \mathbf{E}_\lambda^\top$
Compute $\mathbf{C}_i = \mathbf{M}_i \mathbf{R}'_i - \mathbf{x}_i \cdot \widetilde{\mathbf{r}}_i^\top$ for $i \in [\ell-1]$ and $\mathbf{C}_\ell = \mathbf{M}_\ell \mathbf{R}'_\ell - \mathbf{x}_\ell \cdot (\widetilde{\mathbf{r}}_\ell + \widetilde{\mathbf{r}})^\top$
Compute
$$\pi \xleftarrow{\$} \mathsf{Sim}_\lambda(\mathsf{crs}, \mathsf{td}, \mathbf{R}^\top - \mathbf{e}_\ell^\ell \mathbf{r}^\top)$$
Return $\pi_{\mathsf{or}} = ((\mathbf{C}_i, \mathbf{D}_i)_{i\in[\ell]}, \mathbf{R}, \pi)$

Fig. 6. Definition of the simulator $\{\mathsf{ORTGen}_\lambda, \mathsf{ORSim}_\lambda\}_{\lambda\in\mathbb{N}}$ of ORNIZK.

Next we define a modified prover $\mathsf{ORProve}_\lambda{}'$, which is exactly the same as $\mathsf{ORProve}_\lambda$ except that π is generated as $\pi \xleftarrow{\$} \mathsf{Sim}_\lambda(\mathsf{crs}, \mathsf{td}, \mathbf{R}^\top - \mathbf{e}_\ell^\ell \mathbf{r}^\top)$. The following distributions are identical due to the composable zero-knowledge of ORNIZK.

$$\Pi \xleftarrow{\$} \mathsf{ORProve}_\lambda(\mathsf{crs}_{\mathsf{or}}, (\mathbf{x}_i)_{i\in[\ell]}, \mathbf{w}) \text{ and } \Pi \xleftarrow{\$} \mathsf{ORProve}_\lambda{}'(\mathsf{crs}_{\mathsf{or}}, (\mathbf{x}_i)_{i\in[\ell]}, \mathbf{w}),$$

for $(\mathsf{crs}_{\mathsf{or}}, \mathsf{td}_{\mathsf{or}}) \xleftarrow{\$} \mathsf{ORTGen}_\lambda$ and any $((\mathbf{x}_i)_{i\in[\ell]}, \mathbf{w})$ such that $\mathbf{x}_j = \mathbf{M}_j \mathbf{w}$ for some $j \in [\ell]$.

Next we note that for $\mathbf{S} \xleftarrow{\$} \{0,1\}^{(\ell-1)\times(\lambda-1)}$, $\widetilde{\mathbf{R}}^\top = \mathbf{E}_\ell \mathbf{S}$ is uniformly distributed conditioned on $\sum_{i=1}^{\ell} \widetilde{\mathbf{r}}_i = \mathbf{0}$ for $\widetilde{\mathbf{R}}^\top = (\widetilde{\mathbf{r}}_i)_{i\in[\ell]}$. The reason is that $(\widetilde{\mathbf{r}}_i)_{i\in[\ell-1]}$ are randomly distributed (since $\overline{\mathbf{E}}_\ell$ is of full rank) and $\widetilde{\mathbf{r}}_\ell$ is uniquely determined conditioned on $\sum_{i=1}^{\ell} \widetilde{\mathbf{r}}_i = \mathbf{0}$. Thus, for any $\mathbf{r} = \mathbf{E}_\lambda \widetilde{\mathbf{r}}$ where $\widetilde{\mathbf{r}} \in \{0,1\}^{\lambda-1}$, both $\widetilde{\mathbf{R}} + \widetilde{\mathbf{r}} \cdot \mathbf{e}_\ell^{j\top}$ and $\widetilde{\mathbf{R}} + \widetilde{\mathbf{r}} \cdot \mathbf{e}_\ell^{\ell\top}$ are uniformly distributed conditioned on the sum of the column vectors being $\widetilde{\mathbf{r}}$. In this case, the distributions of $\mathbf{R} = \mathbf{E}_\lambda \widetilde{\mathbf{R}} + \mathbf{r} \cdot \mathbf{e}_\ell^{j\top}$ and $\mathbf{R} = \mathbf{E}_\lambda \widetilde{\mathbf{R}} + \mathbf{r} \cdot \mathbf{e}_\ell^{\ell\top}$ (generated by $\mathsf{ORProve}_\lambda$ and ORSim_λ respectively) are identical as well. Moreover, we have

$$\mathbf{M}_j \mathbf{R}_j = \mathbf{M}_j (\mathbf{R}_j + \mathbf{w} \cdot \widetilde{\mathbf{r}}_j^\top) - \mathbf{x}_j \cdot \widetilde{\mathbf{r}}_j^\top$$

and

$$(\mathbf{R}_j || \mathbf{w}) \begin{pmatrix} \mathbf{E}_\lambda^\top \\ \widetilde{\mathbf{r}}_j^\top \mathbf{E}_\lambda^\top \end{pmatrix} = (\mathbf{R}_j + \mathbf{w} \cdot \widetilde{\mathbf{r}}_j^\top) \mathbf{E}_\lambda^\top$$

for $\mathbf{x}_j = \mathbf{M}_j \mathbf{w}$. Since the distribution of $\mathbf{R}_j + \mathbf{w} \cdot \widetilde{\mathbf{r}}_j^\top$ for $\mathbf{R}_j \xleftarrow{\$} \{0,1\}^{t_j\times(\lambda-1)}$ is uniform in $\{0,1\}^{t_j\times(\lambda-1)}$, the following distributions are identical.

$$\Pi \xleftarrow{\$} \mathsf{ORProve}_\lambda{}'(\mathsf{crs}_{\mathsf{or}}, (\mathbf{x}_i)_{i\in[\ell]}, \mathbf{w}) \text{ and } \Pi \xleftarrow{\$} \mathsf{ORSim}_\lambda(\mathsf{crs}_{\mathsf{or}}, \mathsf{td}_{\mathsf{or}}, (\mathbf{x}_i)_{i\in[\ell]}),$$

for $(\mathsf{crs}_{\mathsf{or}}, \mathsf{td}_{\mathsf{or}}) \stackrel{\$}{\leftarrow} \mathsf{ORTGen}_\lambda$ and any $((\mathbf{x}_i)_{i\in[\ell]}, \mathbf{w})$ such that $\mathbf{x}_j = \mathbf{M}_j\mathbf{w}$ for some $j \in [\ell]$, completing the proof of composable zero-knowledge.

Perfect Soundness. Due to the perfect soundness of LNIZK, for a valid proof $\pi_{\mathsf{or}} = ((\mathbf{C}_i, \mathbf{D}_i)_{i=0,1}, \mathbf{R}, \pi)$, we have $\mathbf{R}^\top = \mathbf{E}_\ell\mathbf{W} + \mathbf{e}_\ell^\ell\mathbf{r}^\top$ for some $\mathbf{W} \in \{0,1\}^{(\ell-1)\times\lambda}$. Hence, we have

$$\sum_{i=1}^{\ell} \mathbf{r}_i^\top = {\mathbf{f}_\ell^1}^\top \mathbf{R}^\top = {\mathbf{f}_\ell^1}^\top(\mathbf{E}_\ell\mathbf{W} + \mathbf{e}_\ell^\ell\mathbf{r}^\top) = {\mathbf{f}_\ell^1}^\top \mathbf{e}_\ell^\ell\mathbf{r}^\top = \mathbf{r}^\top.$$

Here, recall that $\mathbf{f}_\ell^1$ denotes a vector in $\{0,1\}^\ell$ consisting only of 1's and $\mathbf{f}_\ell^1 \in \mathrm{Span}(\mathbf{E}_\ell^\top)$. Since we have $\mathbf{r} \notin \mathrm{Span}(\mathbf{E}_\lambda)$ in any CRS generated by Gen_λ, we must have $\mathbf{r}_j \notin \mathrm{Span}(\mathbf{E}_\lambda)$ for some $j \in [\ell]$. For such $j \in [\ell]$, we have $(\mathbf{C}_j||\mathbf{x}_j)\begin{pmatrix}\mathbf{E}_\lambda^\top \\ \mathbf{r}_j^\top\end{pmatrix} = \mathbf{M}_j\mathbf{D}_j$, i.e., $(\mathbf{M}_j^\perp)^\top(\mathbf{C}_j||\mathbf{x}_j)\begin{pmatrix}\mathbf{E}_\lambda^\top \\ \mathbf{r}_j^\top\end{pmatrix} = \mathbf{0}$. Hence, $\mathbf{r}_j(\mathbf{x}_j^\top\mathbf{M}_j^\perp) = \mathbf{E}_\lambda(\mathbf{C}_j^\top\mathbf{M}_j^\perp)$ must hold. Since $\mathbf{r}_j \notin \mathrm{Span}(\mathbf{E}_\lambda)$, we must have $\mathbf{x}_j^\top\mathbf{M}_j^\perp = 0$, which implies $\mathsf{x} \in \mathsf{L}^{\mathsf{or}}_{(\mathbf{M}_i)_{i\in[\ell]}}$, completing the proof of perfect soundness. Notice that this part of arguments is information-theoretical and thus the equations are not necessarily computable in AC^0.

Putting all the above together, Theorem 4 immediately follows. □

Remark on the CRS. When instantiating LNIZK in ORNIZK with our NIZK given in Sect. 3, both crs and $\mathbf{r}$ in $\mathsf{crs}_{\mathsf{or}}$ are uniformly distributed conditioned on the parities being 1. Hence, we can reduce the length of $\mathsf{crs}_{\mathsf{or}}$ by merging crs and $\mathbf{r}$ in $\mathsf{crs}_{\mathsf{or}}$ as a single vector in $\mathrm{Span}(\mathbf{E}_\lambda)$.

5 NIZK for Circuit SAT

In this section, we propose a fine-grained NIZK for AC^0 circuit SAT running in AC^0 and secure against adversaries in AC^0.

Before giving our construction, we prove the following theorem, which is necessary to show that our NIZK can be executed in AC^0.

Theorem 5. *There exists a family of circuits* $\{\mathsf{ZeroF}_\lambda\}_{\lambda\in\mathbb{N}} \in \mathsf{AC}^0$ *(respectively,* $\{\mathsf{OneF}_\lambda\}_{\lambda\in\mathbb{N}} \in \mathsf{AC}^0$*) such that* ZeroF_λ *(respectively,* OneF_λ*) on input a bit-string* $(b_1, \ldots, b_n)$ *(for some polynomial* $n = n(\lambda)$*) outputs the index* i^* *of the lexicographically first* 0*-bit (respectively,* 1*-bit) of* $(b_i)_{i\in[n]}$*.*

Proof. We first define ZeroF_λ as in Fig. 7.

$\mathsf{ZeroF}_\lambda(b_1, , b_n)$:
For each $i \in [n]$, we compute $\mathbf{x}_i = \mathbf{i} \cdot (1 - b_i)$ in parallel
For each $i \in [n]$, we compute $\mathbf{y}_i = \mathbf{x}_i \cdot (1 - \mathsf{OR}_{1 \leq k \leq (1-i), 1 \leq j \leq \ell}(x_{k,j}))$
Compute $\mathbf{y}_{i^*} = \mathsf{OR}_{1 \leq i \leq n}(y_{i,1}) \| \| \| \mathsf{OR}_{1 \leq i \leq n}(y_{i,\ell})$

Fig. 7. Definition of ZeroF_λ. By $\mathbf{i} \in \{0,1\}^\ell$ we denote the bit-string representing the index i, where we assume that the bit-representation of n has ℓ bits. By $y_{i,j}$ we denote the j-th bit of $\mathbf{y}_i$.

Complexity. The first step can be done by running the NOT and AND gates in parallel with depth 2. The second step can be done by running the NOT, OR, and AND gates in parallel with depth 3. The third step can be done in parallel by running the OR gates with depth 1. Hence, ZeroF_λ can be performed in AC^0 with constant depth 6 by using unbounded fan-in AND, OR, and NOT gates.

Correctness. We now show that ZeroF_λ correctly finds the index of the lexicographically first 0-bit of its input. Via the first step, we can obtain a sequence of strings $(\mathbf{x}_i)_{i \in [n]}$ such that $\mathbf{x}_i = \mathbf{i}$ if $b_i = 0$ and $\mathbf{x}_i = \mathbf{0}$ otherwise. This step is to pick up indices corresponding to 0-bits.

The second step is to cancel all the indices larger than i^*, where i^* is the index of the first 0-bit in $(b_1, \ldots, b_n)$. Specifically, we use the OR gate to compute $\mathbf{y}_i$ such that $\mathbf{y}_i = \mathbf{x}_i$ if all $\mathbf{x}_1, \ldots, \mathbf{x}_{i-1}$ are 0^ℓ, and $\mathbf{y}_i = 0^\ell$ otherwise.

After the second step, we have obtained $(\mathbf{y}_i)_{i \in [n]}$ such that $\mathbf{y}_{i^*} = \mathbf{i}^*$ and $\mathbf{y}_i = \mathbf{0}$ for all $i \neq i^*$, where i^* is the index of the first 0-bit in $(b_1, \ldots, b_n)$. Then we can conclude that the final step outputs each bit of $\mathbf{y}_{i^*} = \mathbf{i}^*$ correctly by using the OR gate.

Construction of OneF_λ. One can see that by generating $\mathbf{x}_i$ as $\mathbf{x}_i = \mathbf{i} \cdot b_i$ instead of $\mathbf{x}_i = \mathbf{i} \cdot (1 - b_i)$, we immediately obtain a circuit OneF_λ running in AC^0 and outputting the first 1-bit of a bit string.

Putting all the above together, Theorem 5 immediately follows. □

An Example for ZeroF_λ. For ease of understanding, we now give an example of the running procedure of ZeroF_λ. Assuming that the string is 10100. In the first step, the circuit outputs 000 – 010 – 000 – 100 – 101 by using the NOT and AND gates. In the second step, for each block, the circuit checks wether all its left bits are 0 by using the NOT and OR gates. We can see that the check only works for the block 010. Hence, the circuit now outputs 000 – 010 – 000 – 000 – 000. In the third step, the circuit outputs $(\mathsf{OR}(0,0,0,0,0), \mathsf{OR}(0,1,0,0,0), \mathsf{OR}(0,0,0,0,0)) = 010 = 2$, which is exactly the index of the first $b_i = 0$.

Construction of Our NIZK. We now define the following languages

$$\mathsf{L}_\lambda = \{\mathbf{x} : \exists \mathbf{w} \in \{0,1\}^{\lambda-1}, \text{ s.t. } \mathbf{x} = \mathbf{E}_\lambda \mathbf{w}\}$$

and

$$\mathsf{L}_\lambda^{\mathsf{or}} = \{(\mathbf{x}_i)_{i\in[\ell]} : \exists \mathbf{w} \in \{0,1\}^{2\lambda} \text{ s.t. } \bigvee_{i\in[\ell]} \mathbf{x}_i = \mathbf{M}_1\mathbf{w}$$
$$\text{or } \exists \mathbf{w} \in \{0,1\}^{(\ell+1)\cdot\lambda} \text{ s.t. } \mathbf{x}_{(\ell+1)} = \mathbf{M}_2\mathbf{w}\}$$

where

$$\mathbf{M}_1 = \begin{pmatrix} \mathbf{E}_\lambda & \mathbf{0} \\ \mathbf{0} & \mathbf{E}_\lambda \end{pmatrix} \in \{0,1\}^{2\lambda\times 2(\lambda-1)}$$

and

$$\mathbf{M}_2 = \begin{pmatrix} \mathbf{E}_\lambda & \mathbf{0} & \cdots & \mathbf{0} \\ \mathbf{0} & \ddots & \ddots & \vdots \\ \vdots & \ddots & \ddots & \mathbf{0} \\ \mathbf{0} & \cdots & \mathbf{0} & \mathbf{E}_\lambda \end{pmatrix} \in \{0,1\}^{(\ell+1)\cdot\lambda\times(\ell+1)\cdot(\lambda-1)},$$

i.e., $\mathbf{M}_1$ and $\mathbf{M}_2$ contain $\mathbf{E}_\lambda$'s in the main diagonal and $\mathbf{0}$ in the other positions. One can see that $\{\mathsf{L}_\lambda\}_{\lambda\in\mathbb{N}}$ and $\{\mathsf{L}_\lambda^{\mathsf{or}}\}_{\lambda\in\mathbb{N}}$ are supported by our NIZK for linear languages in Sect. 3 and our OR-proof given in Sect. 4.2 respectively.

Let $\{\mathsf{L}_\lambda^{\mathsf{AC}^0}\}_{\lambda\in\mathbb{N}}$ be any family of languages such that for all $\mathsf{x} \in \mathsf{L}_\lambda^{\mathsf{AC}^0}$, we can run $\mathsf{R}_\lambda^{\mathsf{AC}^0}(\mathsf{x},\cdot)$ in AC^0, where $\mathsf{R}_\lambda^{\mathsf{AC}^0}(\mathsf{x},\cdot)$ is the associated relation.[4] Without loss of generality, we assume that all the AND and OR gates have fan-in of some polynomial $\ell = \ell(\lambda)$. Let $\mathsf{LNIZK} = \{\mathsf{Gen}_\lambda, \mathsf{Prove}_\lambda, \mathsf{Ver}_\lambda\}_{\lambda\in\mathbb{N}}$ and $\mathsf{ORNIZK} = \{\mathsf{ORGen}_\lambda, \mathsf{ORProve}_\lambda, \mathsf{ORVer}_\lambda\}_{\lambda\in\mathbb{N}}$ be NIZKs with simulators $\{\mathsf{TGen}_\lambda, \mathsf{Sim}_\lambda\}_{\lambda\in\mathbb{N}}$ and $\{\mathsf{ORTGen}_\lambda, \mathsf{ORSim}_\lambda\}_{\lambda\in\mathbb{N}}$ for $\{\mathsf{L}_\lambda\}_{\lambda\in\mathbb{N}}$ and $\{\mathsf{L}_\lambda^{\mathsf{or}}\}_{\lambda\in\mathbb{N}}$ respectively. We give our NIZK for $\{\mathsf{L}_\lambda^{\mathsf{AC}^0}\}_{\lambda\in\mathbb{N}}$ and its simulator in Figs. 8 and 9 respectively.

Theorem 6. *If* LNIZK *and* ORNIZK *are* NC^0*-NIZKs with perfect soundness and* AC^0*-composable zero-knowledge, then* ACNIZK *is an* AC^0*-NIZK with perfect soundness and* AC^0*-composable zero-knowledge.*

Proof. **Complexity.** First, we note that the Hamming weight of each row vector in $\mathbf{E}_\lambda$, $\mathbf{M}_1$, and $\mathbf{M}_2$ is constant. Thus, the multiplication of matrices involved in Figs. 8 and 9 and running NIZK and ORNIZK and their simulators can be performed in NC^0. Also, addition of a constant number of matrices can be performed in NC^0, and extending the witness to contain the bits of all wires can be performed in AC^0. Moreover, finding the lexicographically first $j \in [\ell]$ such that $\mathsf{w}_{ij} = 0$ (respectively $\mathsf{w}_{ij} = 1$) for each AND (respectively, OR) gate can also be performed in AC^0 according to Theorem 5. As a result, we have $\{\mathsf{ACGen}_\lambda, \mathsf{ACProve}_\lambda, \mathsf{ACVer}_\lambda, \mathsf{ACTGen}_\lambda, \mathsf{ACSim}_\lambda\}_{\lambda\in\mathbb{N}} \in \mathsf{AC}^0$. Notice that after extending the witness, the prover can generate commitments and run ORNIZK for each wire and gate in parallel and the verifier can check the proofs in parallel.

[4] We can assume that each $\mathsf{R}_\lambda^{\mathsf{AC}^0}(\mathsf{x},\cdot)$ consists only of AND and OR gates, since by De Morgan Rules, we can move all NOT gates to just the inputs and the resulting circuit is still in AC^0. However, this may cause loss on efficiency.

$\underline{\mathsf{ACGen}_\lambda}$:
$\mathsf{crs} \xleftarrow{\$} \mathsf{Gen}_\lambda$, $\mathsf{crs}_{\mathsf{or}} \xleftarrow{\$} \mathsf{ORGen}_\lambda$, $\widetilde{\mathbf{r}} \xleftarrow{\$} \{0,1\}^{\lambda-1}$, $\mathbf{t} = \mathbf{E}_\lambda \widetilde{\mathbf{r}} + \mathbf{e}_\lambda^\lambda$
Return $\mathsf{CRS} = (\mathsf{crs}, \mathsf{crs}_{\mathsf{or}}, \mathbf{t})$

$\underline{\mathsf{ACProve}_\lambda(\mathsf{CRS}, \mathsf{x}, \mathsf{w})}$:
Extend w to $(\mathsf{w}_1, \cdots, \mathsf{w}_{\mathsf{out}})$ containing the bits of all wires in the circuit $\mathsf{R}_\lambda^{\mathsf{AC}^0}(\mathsf{x}, \cdot)$
Compute $\mathbf{r}_i \xleftarrow{\$} \{0,1\}^{\lambda-1}$ and $\mathsf{cm}_i = \mathbf{E}_\lambda \mathbf{r}_i + \mathbf{t}\mathsf{w}_i$ for each bit w_i
Set $\mathbf{r}_{\mathsf{out}} = \mathbf{0}$ and $\mathsf{cm}_{\mathsf{out}} = \mathbf{e}_\lambda^\lambda$ for the output wire
For each NOT gate with input commitment $\mathsf{cm}_{i1} = \mathbf{E}_\lambda \mathbf{r}_{i1} + \mathbf{t}\mathsf{w}_{i1}$ and output commitment $\mathsf{cm}_{i2} = \mathbf{E}_\lambda \mathbf{r}_{i2} + \mathbf{t}\mathsf{w}_{i2}$, compute $\pi_i \xleftarrow{\$} \mathsf{Prove}_\lambda(\mathsf{crs}, \mathsf{x}_i, \mathbf{r}_{i1} + \mathbf{r}_{i2})$ where $\mathsf{x}_i = \mathsf{cm}_{i1} + \mathsf{cm}_{i2} + \mathbf{t}$
For each AND or OR gate with input commitments $(\mathsf{cm}_{ij} = \mathbf{E}_\lambda \mathbf{r}_{ij} + \mathbf{t}\mathsf{w}_{ij})_{j \in [\ell]}$ and the output commitment $\mathsf{cm}_{i(\ell+1)} = \mathbf{E}_\lambda \mathbf{r}_{i(\ell+1)} + \mathbf{t}\mathsf{w}_{i(\ell+1)}$,
- if the gate is an AND gate,
  - if $\mathsf{w}_{ij} = 1$ for all $j \in [\ell+1]$, set $\mathbf{r} = \mathbf{r}_1 \circ \cdots \circ \mathbf{r}_{\ell+1}$
  - otherwise, find the lexicographically first $j \in [\ell]$ such that $\mathsf{w}_{ij} = 0$ and set $\mathbf{r} = \mathbf{r}_i \circ \mathbf{r}_{\ell+1}$
  - compute $\pi_i \xleftarrow{\$} \mathsf{ORProve}_\lambda(\mathsf{crs}_{\mathsf{or}}, (\mathsf{x}_{ij})_{j \in [\ell+1]}, \mathbf{r})$ where $\mathsf{x}_{ij} = \mathsf{cm}_{ij} \circ \mathsf{cm}_{i(\ell+1)}$ for all $j \in [\ell]$ and $\mathsf{x}_{i(\ell+1)} = (\mathsf{cm}_{i1} - \mathbf{t}) \circ \cdots \circ (\mathsf{cm}_{i(\ell+1)} - \mathbf{t})$
- if the gate is an OR gate,
  - if $\mathsf{w}_{ij} = 0$ for all $j \in [\ell+1]$, set $\mathbf{r} = \mathbf{r}_1 \circ \cdots \circ \mathbf{r}_{\ell+1}$
  - otherwise, find the lexicographically first $j \in [\ell]$ such that $\mathsf{w}_{ij} = 1$ and set $\mathbf{r} = \mathbf{r}_i \circ \mathbf{r}_{\ell+1}$
  - compute $\pi_i \xleftarrow{\$} \mathsf{ORProve}_\lambda(\mathsf{crs}_{\mathsf{or}}, (\mathsf{x}_{ij})_{j \in [\ell+1]}, \mathbf{r})$ where $\mathsf{x}_{ij} = (\mathsf{cm}_{ij} - \mathbf{t}) \circ (\mathsf{cm}_{i(\ell+1)} - \mathbf{t})$ for all $j \in [\ell]$ and $\mathsf{x}_{i(\ell+1)} = \mathsf{cm}_{i1} \circ \cdots \circ \mathsf{cm}_{i(\ell+1)}$

Return Π consisting of all the commitments and proofs

$\underline{\mathsf{ACVer}_\lambda(\mathsf{CRS}, \mathsf{x}, \Pi)}$:
Check that all wires have a corresponding commitment and $\mathsf{cm}_{\mathsf{out}} = \mathbf{t}$
Check that all NAND gates have a valid NIZK proof of compliance
Return 1 iff all checks pass

Fig. 8. Definition of $\mathsf{ACNIZK} = \{\mathsf{ACGen}_\lambda, \mathsf{ACProve}_\lambda, \mathsf{ACVer}_\lambda\}_{\lambda \in \mathbb{N}}$. Recall that for any vectors $(\mathbf{x}_i)_{i \in [\ell]}$, by $\mathbf{x}_1 \circ \cdots \circ \mathbf{x}_\ell$ we denote $(\mathbf{x}_1^\top, \cdots, \mathbf{x}_\ell^\top)^\top$.

Completeness. Let $(\mathsf{w}_{i1}, \mathsf{w}_{i2})$ be an input/output pair of a NOT gate and $(\mathsf{cm}_{ib} = \mathbf{E}_\lambda \mathbf{r}_{ib} + \mathbf{t}\mathsf{w}_{ib})_{b \in [2]}$ be the corresponding commitments, we must have

$$\mathsf{cm}_{i1} + \mathsf{cm}_{i2} + \mathbf{t} = \mathbf{E}_\lambda(\mathbf{r}_{i1} + \mathbf{r}_{i2}) + \mathbf{t}(\mathsf{w}_{i1} + \mathsf{w}_{i2} + 1) = \mathbf{E}_\lambda(\mathbf{r}_{i1} + \mathbf{r}_{i2}).$$

Let $((\mathsf{w}_{ij})_{j \in [\ell]}, \mathsf{w}_{i(\ell+1)})$ be a valid input/output pair of an AND or OR gate in the statement circuit and $(\mathsf{cm}_{ij} = \mathbf{E}_\lambda \mathbf{r}_{ij} + \mathbf{t}\mathsf{w}_{ij})_{j \in [\ell+1]}$ be the corresponding commitments.

If the gate is an AND gate, we must have $\mathsf{w}_{ij} = 0 \wedge \mathsf{w}_{i(\ell+1)} = 0$ for some $j \in [\ell]$ or $\mathsf{w}_{ij} = 1$ for all $j \in [\ell+1]$, which implies

$$\mathsf{cm}_{ij} \circ \mathsf{cm}_{i(\ell+1)} = \mathbf{M}_1(\mathbf{r}_{ij} \circ \mathbf{r}_{\ell+1})$$

ACTGen_λ:
$(\mathsf{crs}, \mathsf{td}) \xleftarrow{\$} \mathsf{TGen}_\lambda(\lambda)$, $(\mathsf{crs}_{\mathsf{or}}, \mathsf{td}_{\mathsf{or}}) \xleftarrow{\$} \mathsf{ORTGen}_\lambda(\lambda)$, $\widetilde{\mathbf{r}} \xleftarrow{\$} \{0,1\}^{\lambda-1}$, $\mathbf{t} = \mathbf{E}_\lambda \widetilde{\mathbf{r}}$
Return $\mathsf{CRS} = (\mathsf{crs}, \mathsf{crs}_{\mathsf{or}}, \mathbf{t})$ and $\mathsf{TD} = (\mathsf{td}, \mathsf{td}_{\mathsf{or}})$

$\mathsf{ACSim}_\lambda(\mathsf{CRS}, \mathsf{TD}, \mathsf{x})$:
Compute $\mathbf{r}_i \xleftarrow{\$} \{0,1\}^{\lambda-1}$ and $\mathsf{cm}_i = \mathbf{E}_\lambda \mathbf{r}_i$ for each wire in the circuit $\mathsf{R}_\lambda^{\mathsf{AC}^0}(\mathsf{x}, \cdot)$
For each NOT gate with input commitment cm_{i1} and output commitment cm_{i2}, run $\pi_i \xleftarrow{\$} \mathsf{Sim}_\lambda(\mathsf{crs}, \mathsf{td}, \mathsf{x}_i)$ where $\mathsf{x}_i = \mathsf{cm}_{i1} + \mathsf{cm}_{i2} + \mathbf{t}$
For each AND or NOT gate with input commitments $(\mathsf{cm}_{ij})_{j\in[\ell]}$ and the output commitment $\mathsf{cm}_{i(\ell+1)}$, run $\pi_i \xleftarrow{\$} \mathsf{ORSim}_\lambda(\mathsf{crs}_{\mathsf{or}}, \mathsf{td}_{\mathsf{or}}, (\mathsf{x}_{ij})_{j\in[\ell+1]})$, where
- $\mathsf{x}_{ij} = \mathsf{cm}_{ij} \circ \mathsf{cm}_{i(\ell+1)}$ for all $j \in [\ell]$ and $\mathsf{x}_{\ell+1} = (\mathsf{cm}_{i1} - \mathbf{t}) \circ \cdots \circ (\mathsf{cm}_{i(\ell+1)} - \mathbf{t})$ if the gate is an AND gate
- $\mathsf{x}_{ij} = (\mathsf{cm}_{ij} - \mathbf{t}) \circ (\mathsf{cm}_{i(\ell+1)} - \mathbf{t})$ for all $j \in [\ell]$ and $\mathsf{x}_{\ell+1} = \mathsf{cm}_{i1} \circ \cdots \circ \mathsf{cm}_{i(\ell+1)}$ if the gate is an OR gate

Return Π consisting of all the commitments and proofs

Fig. 9. Definition of the simulator $\{\mathsf{ACTGen}_\lambda, \mathsf{ACSim}_\lambda\}_{\lambda\in\mathbb{N}}$ of ACNIZK.

for some $j \in [\ell]$ or

$$(\mathsf{cm}_{i1} - \mathbf{t}) \circ \cdots \circ (\mathsf{cm}_{i(\ell+1)} - \mathbf{t}) = \mathbf{M}_2(\mathbf{r}_1 \circ \cdots \circ \mathbf{r}_{\ell+1}).$$

If the gate is an OR gate, we must have $\mathsf{w}_{ij} = 1 \wedge \mathsf{w}_{i(\ell+1)} = 1$ for some $i \in [\ell]$ or $\mathsf{w}_{ij} = 0$ for all $j \in [\ell+1]$, which implies

$$(\mathsf{cm}_{ij} - \mathbf{t}) \circ (\mathsf{cm}_{i(\ell+1)} - \mathbf{t}) = \mathbf{M}_1(\mathbf{r}_i \circ \mathbf{r}_{\ell+1})$$

for some $i \in [\ell]$ or

$$\mathsf{cm}_{i1} \circ \cdots \circ \mathsf{cm}_{i(\ell+1)} = \mathbf{M}_2(\mathbf{r}_1 \circ \cdots \circ \mathbf{r}_{\ell+1}).$$

Then the completeness of ACNIZK follows from that of LNIZK and that of ORNIZK.

AC^0-Composable Zero-Knowledge. The indistinguishability of CRSs generated by ACGen_λ and ACTGen_λ follows immediately from Lemma 1 and the composable zero-knowledge of LNIZK and ORNIZK.

Next we define a modified prover $\mathsf{ACProve}'_\lambda$, which is exactly the same as $\mathsf{ACProve}_\lambda$ except that for each NOT gate, π_i is generated as

$$\pi_i \xleftarrow{\$} \mathsf{Sim}_\lambda(\mathsf{crs}, \mathsf{td}, \mathsf{x}_i),$$

and for each AND or OR gate, π_i is generated as

$$\pi_i \xleftarrow{\$} \mathsf{ORSim}_\lambda(\mathsf{crs}_{\mathsf{or}}, \mathsf{td}_{\mathsf{or}}, (\mathsf{x}_{ij})_{j\in[\ell+1]}).$$

The following distributions are identical due to the composable zero-knowledge of LNIZK and ORNIZK.

$$\Pi \xleftarrow{\$} \mathsf{ACProve}_\lambda(\mathsf{CRS}, \mathsf{x}, \mathsf{w}) \text{ and } \Pi \xleftarrow{\$} \mathsf{ACProve}'_\lambda(\mathsf{CRS}, \mathsf{x}, \mathsf{w}),$$

for $(\mathsf{CRS}, \mathsf{TD}) \xleftarrow{\$} \mathsf{TGen}_\lambda$ and any (x, w) such that $\mathsf{R}_\lambda^{\mathsf{AC}^0}(\mathsf{x}, \mathsf{w}) = 1$.

Moreover, since the distribution of $\mathsf{cm}_i = \mathbf{E}_\lambda \mathbf{r}_i$ is identical to that of $\mathsf{cm}_i = \mathbf{E}_\lambda \mathbf{r}_i + \mathbf{t}\mathsf{w}_i$ for $\mathbf{r}_i \xleftarrow{\$} \{0,1\}^\lambda$ when $\mathbf{t} \in \mathrm{Span}(\mathbf{E}_\lambda)$, the distributions of

$$\Pi \xleftarrow{\$} \mathsf{ACProve}'_\lambda(\mathsf{CRS}, \mathsf{x}, \mathsf{w}) \text{ and } \Pi \xleftarrow{\$} \mathsf{ACSim}_\lambda(\mathsf{CRS}, \mathsf{TD}, \mathsf{x}),$$

where $(\mathsf{CRS}, \mathsf{TD}) \xleftarrow{\$} \mathsf{ACTGen}_\lambda$ and $\mathsf{R}_\lambda^{\mathsf{AC}^0}(\mathsf{x}, \mathsf{w}) = 1$, are identical as well, completing the proof of composable zero-knowledge.

Perfect Soundness. Due to the perfect soundness of LNIZK and ORNIZK, for each NOT gate with input/output commitments $(\mathsf{cm}_{i0}, \mathsf{cm}_{i1})$, we have $\mathsf{cm}_{i0} + \mathsf{cm}_{i1} = \mathbf{t}$. For each AND gate with input commitments $(\mathsf{cm}_{ij})_{i \in [\ell]}$ and an output commitment $\mathsf{cm}_{i(\ell+1)}$ in a valid proof, we have

$$\mathsf{x}_{ij} = (\mathsf{cm}_{ij} \circ \mathsf{cm}_{i(\ell+1)}) \in \mathrm{Span}(\mathbf{M}_1)$$

for some $j \in [\ell]$ or

$$\mathsf{x}_k = (\mathsf{cm}_{i1} - \mathbf{t}) \circ \cdots \circ (\mathsf{cm}_{i(\ell+1)} - \mathbf{t}) \in \mathrm{Span}(\mathbf{M}_2).$$

Similarly, for each OR gate, we have

$$\mathsf{x}_{ij} = (\mathsf{cm}_{ij} - \mathbf{t} \circ \mathsf{cm}_{i(\ell+1)} - \mathbf{t}) \in \mathrm{Span}(\mathbf{M}_1)$$

for some $j \in [\ell]$ or

$$\mathsf{x}_k = \mathsf{cm}_{i1} \circ \cdots \circ \mathsf{cm}_{i(\ell+1)} \in \mathrm{Span}(\mathbf{M}_2).$$

Recall that $\mathbf{f}_\lambda^1$ denotes a vector in $\{0,1\}^\lambda$ consisting only of 1's and $\mathbf{f}_\lambda^1 \in \mathrm{Ker}(\mathbf{E}_\lambda^\top)$. For $\mathbf{t} = \mathbf{E}_\lambda \tilde{\mathbf{r}} + \mathbf{e}_\lambda^\lambda$ where $\tilde{\mathbf{r}} \in \{0,1\}^{\lambda-1}$, we have ${\mathbf{f}_\lambda^1}^\top \mathbf{t} = 1$. For a NOT gate, we must have

$${\mathbf{f}_\lambda^1}^\top \mathsf{cm}_{i1} + {\mathbf{f}_\lambda^1}^\top \mathsf{cm}_{i2} + 1 = 0.$$

For an AND gate, we must have

$${\mathbf{f}_\lambda^1}^\top \mathsf{cm}_{ij} = 0 \text{ and } {\mathbf{f}_\lambda^1}^\top \mathsf{cm}_{i(\ell+1)} = 0 \text{ for some } j \in [\ell]$$

or

$${\mathbf{f}_\lambda^1}^\top \mathsf{cm}_{ij} = 1 \text{ for all } j \in [\ell+1].$$

For an OR gate, we must have

$${\mathbf{f}_\lambda^1}^\top \mathsf{cm}_{ij} = 1 \text{ and } {\mathbf{f}_\lambda^1}^\top \mathsf{cm}_{i(\ell+1)} = 1 \text{ for some } j \in [\ell]$$

or

$${\mathbf{f}_\lambda^1}^\top \mathsf{cm}_{ij} = 0 \text{ for all } j \in [\ell+1].$$

For the output wire, we have

$${\mathbf{f}_\lambda^1}^\top \mathsf{cm}_{\mathsf{out}} = {\mathbf{f}_\lambda^1}^\top \mathbf{t} = 1.$$

As a result, we can extract valid values of all the wires with the final output being 1, completing the proof of perfect soundness. Notice that the extraction procedure is not necessarily in AC^0 since the arguments in this part are information-theoretical.

Putting all the above together, Theorem 6 immediately follows. □

Remark. If we only treat statement circuits in NC^0, we can further reduce the proof size by instantiating the underlying OR-proof with our warm-up construction for one disjunction given in Sect. 4.1.

Similar to previous fine-grained NIZKs [1,19], our construction also works in the "inefficient prover setting". Namely, if we allow the prover to run in polynomial-time, we immediately have an unconditionally secure NIZK for all NP against AC^0 adversaries.

Extension to NIZK in the URS model. As remarked in Sect. 4.2, the CRS of the underlying OR-proof can be generated as a single vector uniformly distributed conditioned on the parity being 1. For ACNIZK, we can further merge $\mathsf{crs}_{\mathsf{or}}$ and $\mathbf{t}$ in the same way. Moreover, by running ACNIZK in parallel for the same statement and generating each CRS as a uniformly random string, we immediately achieve a NIZK with perfect soundness and composable zero-knowledge in the URS model. The reason is that a random string is a binding and a hiding CRS with "half-half" probability. Composable zero-knowledge of the resulting scheme follows immediately from Lemma 1, and statistical soundness follows from that at least one string is a binding CRS with overwhelming probability.

6 Non-interactive Zap

In this section, we show that our NIZKs have verifiable correlated key generation and exploit the framework in [10] to convert our NIZKs into non-interactive zaps.

6.1 Verifiable Correlated Key Generation

The definition of verifiable correlated key generation is as follows.

Definition 6 (Verifiable correlated key generation). *A $\mathcal{C}_1$-NIZK* $\mathsf{NIZK} = \{\mathsf{Gen}_\lambda, \mathsf{Prove}_\lambda, \mathsf{Ver}_\lambda\}_{\lambda \in \mathbb{N}}$ *with a simulator* $\{\mathsf{TGen}_\lambda, \mathsf{Sim}_\lambda\}_{\lambda \in \mathbb{N}}$ *has* verifiable correlated key generation *if there exists a function family* $\{\mathsf{Convert}_\lambda, \mathsf{Check}_\lambda\}_{\lambda \in \mathbb{N}} \in \mathcal{C}_1$ *such that*

1. *the distribution of* $\mathsf{Convert}_\lambda(\mathsf{crs}_0)$ *is identical to that of* crs_1*, where* $\mathsf{crs}_0 \xleftarrow{\$} \mathsf{Gen}_\lambda$ *and* $(\mathsf{crs}_1, \mathsf{td}_1) \xleftarrow{\$} \mathsf{TGen}_\lambda$*,*
2. $\mathsf{Check}_\lambda(\mathsf{crs}_0, \mathsf{Convert}_\lambda(\mathsf{crs}_0)) = 1$ *for all* $\mathsf{crs}_0 \in \mathsf{Gen}_\lambda$*, and*
3. *for any* crs_0 *and* crs_1 *(not necessarily in the support of* Gen_λ *or* TGen_λ*) such that* $\mathsf{Check}_\lambda(\mathsf{crs}_0, \mathsf{crs}_1) = 1$*, we have* $\mathsf{crs}_0 \in \mathsf{Gen}_\lambda$ *or* $\mathsf{crs}_1 \in \mathsf{Gen}_\lambda$*.*

Lemma 2. LNIZK *in Sect. 3 (see Fig. 1) has verifiable correlated key generation.*

$\mathsf{Convert}_\lambda(\mathbf{r}_0)$:	$\mathsf{Check}_\lambda(\mathbf{r}_0, \mathbf{r}_1)$:
$\mathbf{r}_1 = \mathbf{r}_0 + \mathbf{e}_\lambda^\lambda$	Return 1 iff $\mathbf{e}_\lambda^\lambda = \mathbf{r}_0 + \mathbf{r}_1$

Fig. 10. Definition of $\{\mathsf{Convert}_\lambda, \mathsf{Check}_\lambda\}_{\lambda\in\mathbb{N}}$.

Proof. For LNIZK where a binding (respectively, hiding) CRS consists only of a vector uniformly sampled conditioned on the parity being 1 (respectively, 0), we define $\{\mathsf{Check}_\lambda\}_{\lambda\in\mathbb{N}}$ and $\{\mathsf{Convert}_\lambda\}_{\lambda\in\mathbb{N}}$ as in Fig. 10.

First we note that $\{\mathsf{Convert}_\lambda\}_{\lambda\in\mathbb{N}} \in \mathsf{NC}^0$ and $\{\mathsf{Check}_\lambda\}_{\lambda\in\mathbb{N}} \in \mathsf{NC}^0$ since they only involve addition of two vectors.

For $\mathbf{r}_0 \xleftarrow{\$} \mathsf{Gen}_\lambda$ and $\mathbf{r}_1 \xleftarrow{\$} \mathsf{TGen}_\lambda$, the distributions of $\mathbf{r}_0 + \mathbf{e}_\lambda^\lambda$ and $\mathbf{r}_1$ are identical. Hence, the first condition in Definition 6 is satisfied. The second condition is satisfied since for $\mathbf{r}_1 = \mathbf{r}_0 + \mathbf{e}_\lambda^\lambda$, we have $\mathbf{r}_0 + \mathbf{r}_1 = \mathbf{r}_0 + (\mathbf{r}_0 + \mathbf{e}_\lambda^\lambda) = \mathbf{e}_\lambda^\lambda$. For $\mathbf{r}_0$ and $\mathbf{r}_1$ such that $\mathbf{e}_\lambda^\lambda = \mathbf{r}_0 + \mathbf{r}_1$, we must have $\mathsf{PARITY}_\lambda(\mathbf{r}_0) = 1$ or $\mathsf{PARITY}_\lambda(\mathbf{r}_1) = 1$, i.e., $\mathbf{r}_0 \in \mathsf{Gen}_\lambda$ or $\mathbf{r}_1 \in \mathsf{Gen}_\lambda$. Hence, the third condition is also satisfied, completing the proof of Lemma 2. □

As remarked in Sects. 4.2 and 5, the CRSs of our OR-proof and our NIZK for circuit SAT can be generated in exactly the same way as those of LNIZK. Hence, we have the following corollary.

Corollary 1. ORNIZK *in Sect. 4.2 (see Fig. 5) and* ACNIZK *in Sect. 5 (see Fig. 8) have verifiable correlated key generation.*

6.2 Construction of Non-interactive Zap

We now show how to convert our NIZKs with verifiable correlated key generation to non-interactive zaps by using the technique in [10].

Let $\{\mathsf{L}_\lambda^{\mathsf{AC}^0}\}_{\lambda\in\mathbb{N}}$ be any family of languages such that for all $\lambda \in \mathbb{N}$ and all $\mathsf{x} \in \mathsf{L}_\lambda^{\mathsf{AC}^0}$, we can run $\mathsf{R}_\lambda^{\mathsf{AC}^0}(\mathsf{x}, \cdot)$ in AC^0, where $\mathsf{R}_\lambda^{\mathsf{AC}^0}$ is the associated relation. Let $\mathsf{NIZK} = \{\mathsf{Gen}_\lambda, \mathsf{Prove}_\lambda, \mathsf{Ver}_\lambda\}_{\lambda\in\mathbb{N}}$ be a NIZK with a simulator $\{\mathsf{TGen}_\lambda, \mathsf{Sim}_\lambda\}_{\lambda\in\mathbb{N}}$ and verifiable correlated key converting and checking algorithms $\{\mathsf{Check}_\lambda, \mathsf{Convert}_\lambda\}_{\lambda\in\mathbb{N}}$ for $\{\mathsf{L}_\lambda^{\mathsf{AC}^0}\}_{\lambda\in\mathbb{N}}$. We give a non-interactive zap $\mathsf{ZAP} = \{\mathsf{ZProve}_\lambda, \mathsf{ZVer}_\lambda\}_{\lambda\in\mathbb{N}}$ for $\{\mathsf{L}_\lambda^{\mathsf{AC}^0}\}_{\lambda\in\mathbb{N}}$ in Fig. 11.

$\mathsf{ZProve}_\lambda(\mathsf{x}, \mathsf{w})$:	$\mathsf{ZVer}_\lambda(\mathsf{x}, \pi)$:
$(\mathsf{crs}_0, \mathsf{td}_0) \xleftarrow{\$} \mathsf{TGen}_\lambda$, $\mathsf{crs}_1 = \mathsf{Convert}_\lambda(\mathsf{crs}_0)$	Return 1 iff
$\pi_0 \xleftarrow{\$} \mathsf{Prove}_\lambda(\mathsf{crs}_0, \mathsf{x}, \mathsf{w})$	$\mathsf{Check}_\lambda(\mathsf{crs}_0, \mathsf{crs}_1) = 1$
$\pi_1 \xleftarrow{\$} \mathsf{Prove}_\lambda(\mathsf{crs}_1, \mathsf{x}, \mathsf{w})$	$\mathsf{Ver}_\lambda(\mathsf{crs}_0, \mathsf{x}, \pi_0) = 1$
Return $\pi = (\mathsf{crs}_0, \mathsf{crs}_1, \pi_0, \pi_1)$	$\mathsf{Ver}_\lambda(\mathsf{crs}_1, \mathsf{x}, \pi_1) = 1$

Fig. 11. Definition of $\mathsf{ZAP} = \{\mathsf{ZProve}_\lambda, \mathsf{ZVer}_\lambda\}_{\lambda\in\mathbb{N}}$ for $\{\mathsf{L}_\lambda^{\mathsf{AC}^0}\}_{\lambda\in\mathbb{N}}$.

Theorem 7. *If* NIZK *is an* AC^0*-NIZK with* AC^0*-composable zero-knowledge, perfect soundness, and verifiable correlated key generation, then* ZAP *is an* AC^0*-non-interactive zap with perfect soundness and* AC^0*-witness indistinguishability.*

We refer the reader to Appendix A for the security proof.

By instantiating the underlying NIZK with our NIZK in Sect. 5, we obtain an AC^0-non-interactive zap for AC^0-circuit SAT with AC^0-witness indistinguishability.

Acknowledgement. We are grateful to the anonymous reviewers of ASIACRYPT 2022 for the helpful feedback.

Appendix

A Proof of Theorem 7

We prove Theorem 7 in this section.

Proof. **Complexity.** our ZAP runs in AC^0, since the underlying NIZK runs in AC^0.

Completeness. The completeness of ZAP follows immediately from that of NIZK and the fact that $\mathsf{Check}_\lambda(\mathsf{crs}_0, \mathsf{Convert}_\lambda(\mathsf{crs}_0)) = 1$ for all $\mathsf{crs}_0 \in \mathsf{Gen}_\lambda$ (see Definition 6).

Perfect Soundness. Due to the verifiable correlated key generation of NIZK, we have $\mathsf{crs}_0 \in \mathsf{Gen}_\lambda$ or $\mathsf{crs}_1 \in \mathsf{Gen}_\lambda$ for a valid proof $\pi = (\mathsf{crs}_0, \mathsf{crs}_1, \pi_0, \pi_1)$. Hence, the perfect soundness of ZAP follows immediately from that of NIZK.

AC^0**-Witness Indistinguishability.** We prove the witness indistinguishability of ZAP by a sequence of games as in Fig. 12.

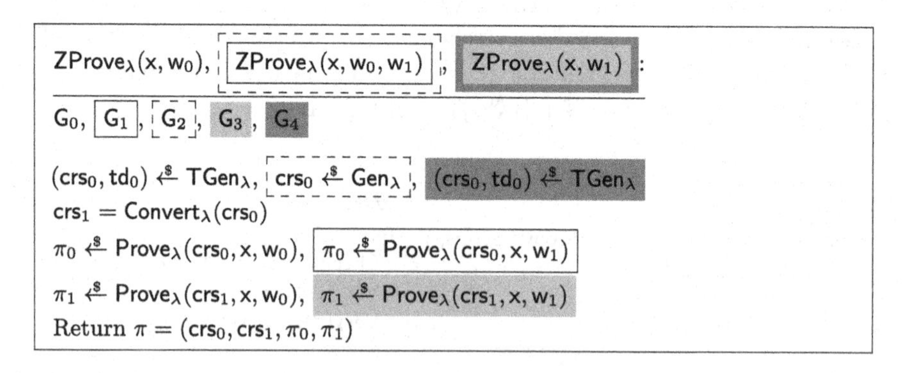

Fig. 12. Modifications on ZProve_λ in the intermediate games.

Let $\mathcal{A} = \{a_\lambda\}_{\lambda \in \mathbb{N}} \in \mathsf{AC}^0$ be an adversary against the witness indistinguishability of ZAP. It receives a proof π generated by the (modified) prover in each game as defined in Fig. 12. Below by ε_i we denote the probability that a_λ outputs 1 in Game G_i for $i = 0, \cdots, 4$.

Games G_0 and G_1. G_0 is the real game where a_λ receives $\pi = (\mathsf{crs}_0, \mathsf{crs}_1, \pi_0, \pi_1) \xleftarrow{\$} \mathsf{ZProve}_\lambda(\mathsf{x}, \mathsf{w}_0)$. G_1 is the same as G_0 except that π_0 is generated as $\pi_0 \xleftarrow{\$} \mathsf{Prove}_\lambda(\mathsf{crs}_0, \mathsf{x}, \mathsf{w}_1)$ instead of $\pi_0 \xleftarrow{\$} \mathsf{Prove}_\lambda(\mathsf{crs}_0, \mathsf{x}, \mathsf{w}_0)$.

Lemma 3. $\varepsilon_0 = \varepsilon_1$.

Proof. Lemma 3 follows immediately from the composable zero knowledge of NIZK. □

Game G_2. This is the same as G_1 except that crs_0 is generated as $\mathsf{crs}_0 \xleftarrow{\$} \mathsf{Gen}_\lambda$ instead of $(\mathsf{crs}_0, \mathsf{td}_0) \xleftarrow{\$} \mathsf{TGen}_\lambda$.

Lemma 4. *There exists an adversary $\mathcal{B}_1 = \{b_\lambda^1\}_{\lambda \in \mathbb{N}} \in \mathsf{AC}^0$ such that b_λ^1 breaks the composable zero-knowledge of* NIZK *with probability $|\varepsilon_2 - \varepsilon_1|$.*

Proof. We build the distinguisher b_λ^1 as follows.

b_λ^1 runs as in G_1 except that now it takes crs_0 as input from the composable zero-knowledge game of NIZK. crs_0 can be generated as $(\mathsf{crs}_0, \mathsf{td}_0) \xleftarrow{\$} \mathsf{TGen}_\lambda$ or $\mathsf{crs}_0 \xleftarrow{\$} \mathsf{Gen}_\lambda$. When a_λ outputs $\beta \in \{0, 1\}$, b_λ^1 outputs β as well.

If crs_0 is generated as $(\mathsf{crs}_0, \mathsf{td}_0) \xleftarrow{\$} \mathsf{TGen}_\lambda$ (respectively, $\mathsf{crs}_0 \xleftarrow{\$} \mathsf{Gen}_\lambda$), the view of a_λ is the same as its view in G_1 (respectively, G_2). Hence, the probability that b_λ^1 breaks the fine-grained matrix linear assumption is $|\varepsilon_2 - \varepsilon_1|$.

Moreover, since all operations in b_λ^1 are performed in AC^0, we have $\mathcal{B}_1 = \{b_\lambda^1\}_{\lambda \in \mathbb{N}} \in \mathsf{AC}^0$, completing this part of proof. □

Game G_3. G_3 is the same as G_2 except that π_1 is generated as $\pi_1 \xleftarrow{\$} \mathsf{Prove}_\lambda(\mathsf{crs}_1, \mathsf{x}, \mathsf{w}_1)$ instead of $\pi_1 \xleftarrow{\$} \mathsf{Prove}_\lambda(\mathsf{crs}_1, \mathsf{x}, \mathsf{w}_0)$.

Lemma 5. $\varepsilon_3 = \varepsilon_2$.

Proof. By the verifiable correlated key generation, the distribution of $\mathsf{Convert}_\lambda(\mathsf{crs}_0)$ is the same as crs_1 for $\mathsf{crs}_0 \xleftarrow{\$} \mathsf{Gen}_\lambda$ and $(\mathsf{crs}_1, \mathsf{td}_1) \xleftarrow{\$} \mathsf{TGen}_\lambda$. Then Lemma 5 follows from the composable zero-knowledge of NIZK. □

Game G_4. G_4 is the same as G_3 except that crs_0 is generated as $(\mathsf{crs}_0, \mathsf{td}_0) \xleftarrow{\$} \mathsf{TGen}_\lambda$ instead of $\mathsf{crs}_0 \xleftarrow{\$} \mathsf{Gen}_\lambda$.

Lemma 6. *There exists an adversary $\mathcal{B}_2 = \{b_\lambda^2\}_{\lambda \in \mathbb{N}} \in \mathsf{AC}^0$ such that b_λ^2 breaks the composable zero-knowledge of* NIZK *with probability $|\varepsilon_4 - \varepsilon_3|$.*

Proof. We build the distinguisher b_λ^2 as follows.

b_λ^2 runs as in G_3 except that crs_0 is taken as input from its composable zero-knowledge challenger, namely, crs_0 can be generated as $\mathsf{crs}_0 \xleftarrow{\$} \mathsf{Gen}_\lambda$ or $(\mathsf{crs}_0, \mathsf{td}_0) \xleftarrow{\$} \mathsf{TGen}_\lambda$. When a_λ outputs $\beta \in \{0,1\}$, b_λ^2 outputs β as well.

If crs_0 is generated as $\mathsf{crs}_0 \xleftarrow{\$} \mathsf{Gen}_\lambda$ (respectively, $(\mathsf{crs}_0, \mathsf{td}_0) \xleftarrow{\$} \mathsf{TGen}_\lambda$), the view of a_λ is the same as its view in G_3 (respectively, G_4). Hence, the probability that b_λ^2 breaks the composable zero-knowledge of NIZK is $|\varepsilon_4 - \varepsilon_3|$.

Moreover, since all operations in b_λ^2 are performed in AC^0, we have $\mathcal{B}_2 = \{b_\lambda^2\}_{\lambda \in \mathbb{N}} \in \mathsf{AC}^0$, and this completes the proof. □

Putting all the above together, Theorem 7 immediately follows. □

Remark on Non-interactive Zap for NP**.** Similar to the work of Wang and Pan [19], our transformation from NIZK to the non-interactive zap also works for polynomial-time provers, namely, we have an unconditionally secure non-interactive zap for all NP against AC^0 adversaries if we allow polynomial-time provers. In our transformation, generating a zap proof (see Fig. 11) involves two proofs of the underlying NIZK. In this case, we have to show that the above reductions run in AC^0, i.e., we need to ensure that they can generate proofs of the underlying NIZK in AC^0. This is possible for our NIZK in Fig. 8. More precisely, to generate a NIZK proof for an NP statement, AC^0-reductions can perform all the steps except for extending the witness (since the commitments and OR-proofs can be generated in parallel). Extending the witness is not necessary, since the extended witness can be hard-wired in an AC^0-reduction beforehand, due to the fact that any statement x and its two witnesses w_0 and w_1 are a-prior fixed in the hybrid games.

References

1. Ball, M., Dachman-Soled, D., Kulkarni, M.: New techniques for zero-knowledge: leveraging inefficient provers to reduce assumptions, interaction, and trust. In: Micciancio, D., Ristenpart, T. (eds.) CRYPTO 2020. LNCS, vol. 12172, pp. 674–703. Springer, Cham (2020). https://doi.org/10.1007/978-3-030-56877-1_24
2. Danezis, G., Fournet, C., Groth, J., Kohlweiss, M.: Square span programs with applications to succinct NIZK arguments. In: Sarkar, P., Iwata, T. (eds.) ASIACRYPT 2014. LNCS, vol. 8873, pp. 532–550. Springer, Heidelberg (2014). https://doi.org/10.1007/978-3-662-45611-8_28
3. Degwekar, A., Vaikuntanathan, V., Vasudevan, P.N.: Fine-grained cryptography. In: Robshaw, M., Katz, J. (eds.) CRYPTO 2016. LNCS, vol. 9816, pp. 533–562. Springer, Heidelberg (2016). https://doi.org/10.1007/978-3-662-53015-3_19
4. Dwork, C., Naor, M.: Zaps and their applications. In: 41st FOCS, pp. 283–293. IEEE Computer Society Press, November 2000
5. Egashira, S., Wang, Y., Tanaka, K.: Fine-grained cryptography revisited. J. Cryptol. **34**(3), 23 (2021)
6. Gennaro, R., Gentry, C., Parno, B., Raykova, M.: Quadratic span programs and succinct NIZKs without PCPs. In: Johansson, T., Nguyen, P.Q. (eds.) EUROCRYPT 2013. LNCS, vol. 7881, pp. 626–645. Springer, Heidelberg (2013). https://doi.org/10.1007/978-3-642-38348-9_37

7. Goldwasser, S., Micali, S., Rackoff, C.: The knowledge complexity of interactive proof systems. SIAM J. Comput. **18**(1), 186–208 (1989)
8. Groth, J.: Short non-interactive zero-knowledge proofs. In: Abe, M. (ed.) ASIACRYPT 2010. LNCS, vol. 6477, pp. 341–358. Springer, Heidelberg (2010). https://doi.org/10.1007/978-3-642-17373-8_20
9. Groth, J.: On the size of pairing-based non-interactive arguments. In: Fischlin, M., Coron, J.-S. (eds.) EUROCRYPT 2016. LNCS, vol. 9666, pp. 305–326. Springer, Heidelberg (2016). https://doi.org/10.1007/978-3-662-49896-5_11
10. Groth, J., Ostrovsky, R., Sahai, A.: New techniques for noninteractive zero-knowledge. J. ACM **59**(3), 11:1–11:35 (2012)
11. Groth, J., Sahai, A.: Efficient non-interactive proof systems for bilinear groups. In: Smart, N. (ed.) EUROCRYPT 2008. LNCS, vol. 4965, pp. 415–432. Springer, Heidelberg (2008). https://doi.org/10.1007/978-3-540-78967-3_24
12. Håstad, J.: One-way permutations in NC0. Inf. Process. Lett. **26**(3), 153–155 (1987)
13. Håstad, J.: On the correlation of parity and small-depth circuits. SIAM J. Comput. **43**(5), 1699–1708 (2014)
14. Impagliazzo, R.: A personal view of average-case complexity. In: Computational Complexity Conference, pp. 134–147. IEEE Computer Society (1995)
15. Impagliazzo, R., Matthews, W., Paturi, R.: A satisfiability algorithm for ac0. CoRR abs/1107.3127 (2011)
16. Lipmaa, H.: Progression-free sets and sublinear pairing-based non-interactive zero-knowledge arguments. In: Cramer, R. (ed.) TCC 2012. LNCS, vol. 7194, pp. 169–189. Springer, Heidelberg (2012). https://doi.org/10.1007/978-3-642-28914-9_10
17. Peikert, C., Shiehian, S.: Noninteractive zero knowledge for NP from (plain) learning with errors. In: Boldyreva, A., Micciancio, D. (eds.) CRYPTO 2019. LNCS, vol. 11692, pp. 89–114. Springer, Cham (2019). https://doi.org/10.1007/978-3-030-26948-7_4
18. Ràfols, C.: Stretching Groth-Sahai: NIZK proofs of partial satisfiability. In: Dodis, Y., Nielsen, J.B. (eds.) TCC 2015. LNCS, vol. 9015, pp. 247–276. Springer, Heidelberg (2015). https://doi.org/10.1007/978-3-662-46497-7_10
19. Wang, Y., Pan, J.: Non-interactive zero-knowledge proofs with fine-grained security. In: Eurocrypt 2022, Trondheim, Norway, 2022, Proceedings. Lecture Notes in Computer Science (2022). https://eprint.iacr.org/2022/548
20. Wang, Y., Pan, J., Chen, Yu.: Fine-grained secure attribute-based encryption. In: Malkin, T., Peikert, C. (eds.) CRYPTO 2021. LNCS, vol. 12828, pp. 179–207. Springer, Cham (2021). https://doi.org/10.1007/978-3-030-84259-8_7

Triply Adaptive UC NIZK

Ran Canetti[1(✉)], Pratik Sarkar[1], and Xiao Wang[2]

[1] Boston University, Boston, USA
{canetti,pratik93}@bu.edu
[2] Northwestern University, Evanston, USA
wangxiao@cs.northwestern.edu

Abstract. Non-interactive zero knowledge (NIZK) enables proving the validity of NP statement without leaking anything else. We study multi-instance NIZKs in the common reference string (CRS) model, against an adversary that adaptively corrupts parties and chooses statements to be proven. We construct the first such *triply adaptive* NIZK that provides full adaptive soundness, as well as adaptive zero-knowledge, assuming either LWE or else LPN and DDH (previous constructions rely on non-falsifiable knowledge assumptions). In addition, our NIZKs are universally composable (UC). Along the way, we:

- Formulate an ideal functionality, $\mathcal{F}_{\mathsf{NICOM}}$, which essentially captures *non-interactive* commitments, and show that it is realizable by existing protocols using standard assumptions.
- Define and realize, under standard assumptions, Sigma protocols which satisfy triply adaptive security with access to $\mathcal{F}_{\mathsf{NICOM}}$.
- Use the Fiat-Shamir transform, instantiated with correlation intractable hash functions, to compile a Sigma protocol with triply adaptive security with access to $\mathcal{F}_{\mathsf{NICOM}}$ into a triply adaptive UC-NIZK argument in the CRS model with access to $\mathcal{F}_{\mathsf{NICOM}}$, assuming LWE (or else LPN and DDH).
- Use the UC theorem to obtain UC-NIZK in the CRS model.

1 Introduction

Non-Interactive zero knowledge (NIZK) [BFM90, BSMP91] is a magical primitive: with the help of a trusted reference string, it allows parties to publicly assert knowledge of sensitive data and prove statements regarding the data while keeping the data itself secret. Proofs are written once and for all, to be inspected and verified by anyone at any time.

R. Canetti—Supported by NSF Awards 1931714, 1801564, 1414119, and by DARPA under Agreement No. HR00112020023.

P. Sarkar—Supported by NSF Awards 1931714, 1414119, and the DARPA SIEVE program.

X. Wang—Supported by DARPA under Contract No. HR001120C0087, NSF award #2016240, and research awards from Facebook and Google.

S. Agrawal and D. Lin (Eds.): ASIACRYPT 2022, LNCS 13792, pp. 466–495, 2022.
https://doi.org/10.1007/978-3-031-22966-4_16

However, harnessing this magic in a concrete and realizable set of security requirements has turned out to be non trivial. A first thrust provides basic formulations of soundness and zero knowledge in the presence of a reference string, and constructions that satisfy them under standard assumptions [BSMP91,FLS99, GR13]. Indeed, even these basic requirements turn out to be non-trivial to formulate and obtain, especially in the case of multiple proofs that use the same reference string and where the inputs and witnesses are chosen adversarially in an adaptive way.

A second thrust addresses malleability attacks [SCO+01,DDN91], and more generally universally composable (UC) security [CLOS02] in a multi-party setting. In particular, UC NIZK has been used as a mainstay for incorporating NIZK proofs in cryptographic protocols and systems - actively secure MPC [GMW87], CCA secure encryption [NY90,DDN91], signatures [BMW03,BKM06] and cryptocurrencies [BCG+14].

A third thrust is to construct NIZK protocols that are secure in a multi-party setting where the adversary can corrupt parties adaptively [CLOS02,CSW20a, AMPS21,CGPS21] as the computation proceeds. Here the traditional definition (which requires that the attacker does not gain any advantage towards breaking the security of the overall system beyond the ideal case where the NIZK is replaced by a trusted party) is extended to the case where the attacker obtains the hidden internal state of some provers *after* the proof was sent. Indeed, this extended guarantee is essential whenever NIZK is used as a primitive within larger protocols that purport to obtain security against adaptive corruptions[1].

The first protocol that provides security against adaptive corruptions is that of Groth, Ostrovsky, and Sahai [GOS06,GOS12] (GOS). That protocol is also UC secure, even in a multi-proof, multi-party setting. However it only guarantees *culpable soundness*, namely that the sequence of instances proven to be in a language L during an execution of the protocol is indistinguishable (given the reference string) from a sequence of instances that are actually in L. The works of [KNYY19,KNYY20] have similar characteristics: they provide security against adaptive corruptions, but only culpable adaptive soundness.

Abe and Fehr [AF07] show how to prove full adaptive soundness of a variant of the GOS protocol, under a knowledge-of-exponent (KOE) assumption[2]. However, their analysis is incompatible with UC security [KZM+15], since KOE-style assumptions require existence of a knowledge extractor that has full access to, and whose code is larger than the code of the environment, In contrast, in the UC framework a single extractor/simulator would have to handle arbitrary poly-time environments. The recent work of [KKK21] investigated composable security for knowledge assumptions in the generic group model. They rule out general composition but demonstrate that it is possible under restricted settings.

[1] In cases where the prover is able to immediately erase all records of its sensitive state - specifically the witness and randomness used in generating the proof - adaptive security is easy to obtain. However such immediate and complete erasure of local state is not always practical.

[2] [AF07] provides adaptive soundness and adaptive zero knowledge and claims security against adaptive corruptions in Remark 11 of their paper.

We refer to their paper for more details. Proving composable security of [AF07] in their model is still an open question.

We are thus left with the following natural question: Can we have triply adaptive NIZK protocols, namely full-fledged UC NIZK protocols in the multi-party, multi-proof setting, in the case of adaptive corruptions without erasures, and with full adaptive soundness? And if so, under what assumptions?

1.1 Our Contributions

We develop a general methodology for obtaining triply adaptive NIZKs, namely UC NIZKs with full adaptive soundness, withstanding adaptive corruptions with no erasures. Using this methodology, we obtain triply adaptive NIZK protocols from statically secure Sigma protocols. The NIZK protocols reuse a single crs for multiple NIZK instances between different pairs of parties. Moreover, one of the NIZK protocols also avoids expensive Karp reductions. Upon concrete instantiation based on either Learning With Errors (LWE), or Decisional Diffie Hellman (DDH) plus Learning Parity with Noise (LPN) assumption, we obtain the following result:

Theorem 1. *(Informal) Assuming either 1) LWE assumption holds or 2) both DDH and LPN assumptions hold, there exists a multi-theorem NIZK protocol that UC-securely implements the NIZK functionality (Fig. 2) against adaptive corruptions in the crs model for multiple instances. Furthermore, it is adaptively sound and adaptively zero knowledge.*

As an independent result we also obtain a compiler that (assuming either LWE or DDH) transforms a given NIZK protocol, where the length of the crs can depend on the NP relation to be asserted, to a NIZK protocol where the length of the crs depends only on the security parameter. Furthermore, we do so while preserving triple adaptive security. Previous such compilers [GGI+15,CsW19] were known only from LWE:

Theorem 2. *(Informal) Assuming either 1) LWE assumption holds or 2) both DDH and LPN assumptions hold, there exists a multi-theorem NIZK protocol that UC-securely implements the NIZK functionality (Fig. 2) against adaptive corruptions with short crs (i.e. $|\mathsf{crs}| = poly(\kappa)$ and κ is the computational security parameter) for multiple instances. Furthermore, it is adaptively sound and adaptively zero knowledge.*

Furthermore, by plugging our NIZK protocol in the compiler of [CsW19] we can obtain a triply adaptive NIZK protocol from LWE, where the reference string size depends only on the security parameter and the proof size depends on the witness size and the security parameter.

1.2 Our Techniques

Our approach follows the general paradigm of applying the Fiat-Shamir transform (instantiated via correlation in tractable hash functions) to Sigma protocols, as developed in [CGH98,HL18,CCH+19,PS19,BKM20,HLR21]. However, to preserve triple adaptivity the transform should be applied with some care.

Starting Point. Let us briefly recall the definition of a Sigma protocol: A Sigma protocol is a 3 round protocol for proving validity of an NP statement $x \in \mathcal{L}$ (where $\mathcal{L}$ is the language) using the knowledge of an accepting witness w. The prover sends the first message a, the verifier samples a random challenge c, and based on the challenge $c \in \mathcal{C}$ the prover computes the response z. The verifier accepts an honest proof when $x \in \mathcal{L}$. Soundness ensures that the verifier rejects cheating proofs with $\frac{1}{|\mathcal{C}|}$ probability. Honest verifier zero knowledge (HVZK) ensures that the simulator constructs an honest proof given a random challenge c and the simulated proof is indistinguishable from an honest proof. However, the usual Sigma protocols [FLS99, Blu86] are only secure against static corruption of prover, i.e. upon post-execution corruption of prover the HVZK simulator obtains witness w and is unable to provide randomness such that it is consistent with the proof (a, c, z) constructed by the HVZK simulator.

New UC-Commitment Functionality $\mathcal{F}_{\mathsf{NICOM}}$. To solve the above issue in a modular fashion, we first introduce a new non-interactive UC commitment functionality, $\mathcal{F}_{\mathsf{NICOM}}$, that enables modular analyzing of NIZK protocols that use commitments as an underlying primitive. Specifically, $\mathcal{F}_{\mathsf{NICOM}}$ returns a commitment string and a decommitment to the committer as an output of the commit phase, where the committer commits to a message. The open phase allows non-interactive verification of the commitment, decommitment and message tuple by a verifier. Moreover, the functionality is provided with an explicit simulation algorithm $\mathcal{S}_C$ which extracts committed messages from maliciously generated commitments and permits equivocation of simulated commitments. Looking ahead, the CI-hash function would be equipped with the $\mathcal{S}_C$ algorithm to run the bad challenge function and yet we would argue security of the NIZK protocol in the $\mathcal{F}_{\mathsf{NICOM}}$ model. Hence, $\mathcal{F}_{\mathsf{NICOM}}$ provides a cleaner abstraction of non-interactive UC commitments. The formal description of the $\mathcal{F}_{\mathsf{NICOM}}$ functionality can be found in Fig. 1. We also show that the [CF01] protocol satisfies $\mathcal{F}_{\mathsf{NICOM}}$.

Strengthening Sigma Protocols in $\mathcal{F}_{\mathsf{NICOM}}$ Model. Now, we define the notion of an *adaptively secure Sigma protocol* in the $\mathcal{F}_{\mathsf{NICOM}}$ model as a stepping stone towards security against adaptive corruptions. These are Sigma protocols which provide security against adaptive corruption of prover in the $\mathcal{F}_{\mathsf{NICOM}}$ model. To attain constructions of such Sigma protocols, we replace the underlying commitment scheme in the *commit-and-open* protocols of [Blu86, FLS99, HV16] with $\mathcal{F}_{\mathsf{NICOM}}$. Then we prove that these Sigma protocols are adaptively secure in the $\mathcal{F}_{\mathsf{NICOM}}$ model, while preserving special soundness. Furthermore, these protocols satisfies full adaptive soundness and provides adaptive ZK in the $\mathcal{F}_{\mathsf{NICOM}}$ model. If $\mathcal{F}_{\mathsf{NICOM}}$ is concretely instantiated using an adaptively secure non-interactive commitment in non-programmable crs model[3] then the protocol also preserves full adaptive soundness and adaptive ZK.

Removing Interaction. It is now tempting to apply the Fiat-Shamir (FS) transform [FS87] using correlation intractable (CI) hash functions [CGH98,

[3] The crs distribution in the real world is statistically close to the crs distribution in the ideal world.

HL18,CCH+19,PS19,BKM20,HLR21], and conclude that the resulting protocol is a NIZK. However, it is not clear how the transform would actually work: the bad challenge function for the CI hash function cannot be defined given blackbox access to a and the challenge space can be exponentially large, for example consider Schnorr's protocol [Sch90]. The current CI-based NIZKs [CGH98,HL18,CCH+19,PS19] consider specific Sigma protocols to construct NIZKs. We take a different route to solve this problem by relying on special soundness property. Special soundness property of a Sigma protocol ensures that given two accepting transcripts (a, c_0, z_0) and (a, c_1, z_1) for different challenges $c_0 \neq c_1$ there exists an extractor which extracts a valid witness from the transcripts. If the statement $x \notin \mathcal{L}$ is not in the language then the prover cannot construct two such accepting transcripts for the same a.

We generalize the framework of [CD00] to construct our compiler. In our compiler, the prover computes a, samples two challenges c_0 and c_1, computes responses z_0 and z_1 and commits to (c_0, z_0) and (c_1, z_1) in $\mathcal{F}_{\mathsf{NICOM}}$ model. This step is repeated for $\tau = \mathcal{O}(\kappa)$ times, where κ is the security parameter. Let $\mathbf{Y}$ denote the commitments to (c_0, c_1, z_0, z_1) for the τ iterations. The CI-hash function is defined in the statistical mode equipped with the extraction algorithm $\mathcal{S}_C$ for $\mathcal{F}_{\mathsf{NICOM}}$. The hash function is CI for the bad challenge function - for each iteration (a, c_0, c_1, z_0, z_1) it outputs 0 if (a, c_0, z_0) is accepting. The prover invokes the CI hash function on $(a, \mathbf{Y})$ to obtain a challenge bit e for each iteration. For each iteration, the prover computes the response as the decommitment to (c_0, c_1, z_e). Special soundness of the Sigma protocol ensures that a malicious prover is unable to compute two such valid transcripts (a, c_0, z_0) and (a, c_1, z_1) for a false statement $x \notin \mathcal{L}$.

CI-Based NIZK Transformations for Arguments. Now we would like to apply the analysis of [CCH+19] to argue soundness of the NIZK protocol, which says that if the malicious prover is able to construct an accepting proof for $x \notin \mathcal{L}$ then it breaks correlation intractability. However, now we are faced with another barrier: The [CCH+19] analysis for CI crucially needs the underlying Sigma protocol to be statistically sound. In contrast, our Sigma protocols are only computationally sound since it relies on the special soundness property (which can be computational) of the Sigma protocol and the computational binding property of the commitment scheme. Furthermore, this is inherent: Statistically sound ZK protocols cannot possibly be secure against adaptive corruptions. In particular, this means that we cannot "switch the crs in the hybrids to make the sigma protocol statistically sound": As soon as we do so, the protocol (in that hybrid) stops being secure against adaptive corruptions.

We get around this barrier[4] as follows: with each commitment made during the interaction we can associate an event B, determined at the time of

[4] The recent work of [CJJ21] also applied the Fiat-Shamir paradigm on an interactive protocol which is not statistically sound using CI hash functions. However, their protocol is not adaptively sound. Meanwhile, the plain-model sigma protocol that [CCH+19] start from is statistically sound.).

commitment, such that: (a) event B can be shown to occur only with negligible probability, and (b) conditioned on event B not occurring, the commitment is statistically binding. Event B is the event where the adversary successfully evades the extraction algorithm $\mathcal{S}_C$ of $\mathcal{F}_{\mathsf{NICOM}}$ and yet the corresponding decommitment is accepted. Given that event B does not occur, we then associate an event D with each of the τ adaptively secure Sigma protocol executions, such that: (a) event D can be shown to occur only with negligible probability, and (b) conditioned on event D not occurring, the Sigma protocol is statistically sound. The event D is the event where the adversary breaks special soundness property of the Sigma protocol. The [CCH+19] analysis can now be resurrected, conditioned on event B not occurring for any of the commitments made, and event D not occurring for the Sigma protocols. Initializing the hash function in the statistical mode ensures that soundness of the protocol is reduced to breaking statistical correlation intractability of the hash function, provided event B and event D does not occur.

Adaptive soundness of our protocol follows in a straightforward way from the fact that the entire proof is performed without changing the distribution of the crs in the $\mathcal{F}_{\mathsf{NICOM}}$ model. (Indeed, this important feature allows us to avoid the main obstacle that prevents the [GOS12] protocol from being adaptively sound.) Adaptive zero knowledge follows from the adaptive security of the Sigma protocol in the $\mathcal{F}_{\mathsf{NICOM}}$ model. If $\mathcal{F}_{\mathsf{NICOM}}$ is concretely instantiated using an adaptively secure non-interactive commitment in non-programmable crs model[5] then the protocol also preserves full adaptive soundness and adaptive ZK.

Instantiations of Adaptively Secure Sigma Protocols in $\mathcal{F}_{\mathsf{NICOM}}$ Model. We demonstrate that a wide variety of Sigma protocols satisfy (in $\mathcal{F}_{\mathsf{NICOM}}$ model) adaptive security with special soundness and adaptive soundness - Schnorr's protocol, Sigma protocol of [FLS99] (FLS), Blum's Hamiltonicity protocol and garbled circuit (GC) based protocol of [HV16]. Furthermore, the GC based protocol avoids expensive Karp reduction.

Instantiating the CI-Hash and $\mathcal{F}_{\mathsf{NICOM}}$. The CI function can be instantiated from LWE [PS19], or it can be replaced by a CI-Approx [BKM20] function based on LPN+DDH. $\mathcal{F}_{\mathsf{NICOM}}$ is instantiated using the protocol of [CF01] from equivocal commitments and CCA-2 secure public key encryption with oblivious ciphertext sampling property in the non-programmable crs model.

Reducing crs Size. By applying techniques from GOS, we obtain a compiler which *reduces the crs size* of a NIZK argument. Assuming reusable non-interactive equivocal commitments with additive homomorphism and PKE (with oblivious ciphertext sampleability) we compile any triply adaptive NIZK argument with a long multi-proof crs, i.e. $|\mathsf{crs}| = \text{poly}(\kappa, |\mathcal{C}|)$ to obtain a triply adaptive NIZK argument with a short multi-proof common reference string scrs, where $|\mathsf{scrs}| = \text{poly}(\kappa)$, $\mathcal{C}$ is the NP verification circuit and κ is the computational security parameter. The prover commits to each wire value (of the circuit) and proves that

[5] The crs distribution in the real world is statistically close to the crs distribution in the ideal world.

they are bit commitments using the NIZK. In addition, the prover applies some homomorphic operation on the input wire and output wire commitments for each gate. If the input and output wire values are consistent with the gate evaluation then the homomorphically evaluated commitment will be a bit commitment. The prover proves this using NIZK for every gate in the circuit. Each NIZK statement is short and depends only on the committer's algorithm ($= \mathrm{poly}(\kappa)$) and not on $|\mathcal{C}|$. As a result the crs size of the NIZK can be short. The commitment can be instantiated from DDH (Pedersen commitment or [CSW20a]) or LWE/SIS [GVW15]. The encryption scheme can be instantiated from DDH assumption using Elgamal encryption or LWE [GSW13] assumption.

Obtaining Multi-session UC Security. We add non-malleability to our NIZK argument using standard techniques from GOS to obtain the multi-session UC-secure NIZK in the short crs model. It relies on a tag-based simulation-sound trapdoor commitment scheme and a strong one-time signature scheme. The tag-based commitment can be instantiated from UC-commitments - DDH [CSW20a] and LWE [CsW19]. Strong one-time signatures can be constructed from one-way functions. This transformation also preserves triply adaptive security.

1.3 Related Work

The works of [GOS06,KNYY19,KNYY20] construct NIZKs which are secure against adaptive corruptions but they lack adaptive soundness. The works of [CCH+19,BKM20] construct statically secure NIZKs which attain adaptive soundness and adaptive ZK. A concurrent work by [CPV20] compiled delayed input Sigma protocol into a Sigma protocol which satisfies adaptive zero knowledge. Upon applying the result of [CPS+16] they obtain adaptive soundness. The Fiat-Shamir transform is applied using CI hash function to obtain NIZKs, but they lack security against adaptive corruptions. The only work which achieves triple adaptive security is [AF07] based on knowledge assumptions; which is incompatible with the UC framework.

The literature consists of work [GGI+15,CsW19] that make the crs size independent of $|\mathcal{C}|$ but those approaches are instantiatable only from LWE. Whereas, our compiler can be instantiated from non-lattice based assumptions like DDH.

Paper Organization. In Sect. 2, we present the key intuitions behind our protocols. We introduce some notations and important concepts used in this paper in Sect. 3. This is followed by our triply adaptively-secure NIZK compiler in Sect. 4. We present our compiler to reduce the crs length in Sect. 5. Finally, we conclude with our multi-session UC-NIZK protocol in the short crs model in Sect. 6. Throughout the paper we refer to *security against adaptive corruptions* as *adaptive security.*

2 Technical Overview

In this section we provide an overview of our protocols. As discussed in the Introduction, a key component in our approach is to break the Fiat-Shamir transformation into two steps: A first step that uses an ideal UC commitment fucntionality, and a second step of instantiating this functionality with an adaptively secure protocol. Validity of the approach would follow from the UC theorem and the special soundness of the sigma protocol.

We first overview the new formulation of ideal UC commitments, $\mathcal{F}_{\mathsf{NICOM}}$, that enables our two-step approach, and argue that known protocols, that UC realize the traditional ([CF01]) formulation of ideal commitment, realize $\mathcal{F}_{\mathsf{NICOM}}$ as well. Next, we overview our notion of fully adaptive Sigma protocols that use $\mathcal{F}_{\mathsf{NICOM}}$, followed by the first step of the Fiat-Shamir transform. We demonstrate that the resulting NIZKs satisfy triply adaptive security in the $\mathcal{F}_{\mathsf{NICOM}}$-hybrid model, and that triple adaptivity is preserved even after replacing $\mathcal{F}_{\mathsf{NICOM}}$ with a protocol that realizes it. Next, we show instantiations of adaptive Sigma protocol. Finally we show how to reduce the crs size of our NIZK protocols to poly(κ) by assuming homomorphic equivocal commitments. Till this point, all our protocols are triply adaptive and single-prover UC-secure. Finally, we make them UC-secure in the general, multi-prover sense by adding non-malleability.

2.1 Formalizing UC Non-interactive Commitment

Our new UC-commitment functionality $\mathcal{F}_{\mathsf{NICOM}}$ can be found in Fig. 1. The functionality receives an algorithm $\mathcal{S}_C$ algorithm from the adversary $\mathcal{S}$. When an honest committer P wants to commit to a message m for subsession ssid, the functionality invokes $\mathcal{S}_C$ for a commitment string π and an internal state st. π is independent of the message m. The functionality then invokes $\mathcal{S}_C$ with the message m and the state st to obtain a decommitment d and an updated state st. The functionality stores $(\mathsf{ssid}, \mathsf{P}, m, \pi, d, \mathsf{st})$ and returns the commitment string π and the decommitment d to the committer. The committer sends π as the commitment to message m. An honest committer decommits to a commitment string π' by sending (m', d') to the verifier V. The verifier locally verifies the decommitment by invoking $\mathcal{F}_{\mathsf{NICOM}}$ on the tuple (m', π', d'). The functionality returns $\mathsf{verified}$ if the tuple is stored in memory corresponding to the subsession and the same committer P. If the same commitment string π' is stored but with different messages/decommitments/committers/ssid then the functionality rejects the opening by sending $\mathsf{verification\text{-}failed}$. Finally, if the commitment string has never been stored in the memory of $\mathcal{F}_{\mathsf{NICOM}}$ then $\mathcal{F}_{\mathsf{NICOM}}$ invokes $\mathcal{S}_C$ to extract a valid message m'' from the commitment string π'. If $m'' == m'$ then the functionality invokes $\mathcal{S}_C$ with the opening (m', π', d') to verify the decommitment. If the decommitment correctly verifies then the functionality stores the tuple in the memory and returns $\mathsf{verified}$ to V. Else, it rejects the decommitment.

Our model allows a prover to send a commitment that was not computed by invoking the $\mathcal{F}_{\mathsf{NICOM}}$ functionality. Furthermore, access to the $\mathcal{S}_C$ algorithm enables extraction from a maliciously generated commitment and equivocating

- At first activation, obtain algorithm $\mathcal{S}_C$ from $\mathcal{S}$.
- **Commit:** On input $(\mathsf{Com}, \mathsf{ssid}, \mathsf{P}, m)$ from committer P:
  - obtain commitment π and internal state st as $(\pi, \mathsf{st}) \leftarrow \mathcal{S}_C(\mathsf{Com}, \mathsf{ssid}, \mathsf{P})$
  - obtain decommitment d and state st as $(d, \mathsf{st}) \leftarrow \mathcal{S}_C(\mathsf{Equiv}, \mathsf{ssid}, \mathsf{P}, \pi, \mathsf{st}, m)$
  - store $(\mathsf{ssid}, \mathsf{P}, m, \pi, d, \mathsf{st})$ and output $(\mathsf{Receipt}, \mathsf{ssid}, \mathsf{P}, \pi, d)$ to P.

  Ignore future $(\mathsf{Com}, \mathsf{ssid}, \cdot)$ inputs with the same ssid.
- **Open:** On input $(\mathsf{Open}, \mathsf{ssid}, \mathsf{P}, m', \pi', d')$ from verifier V:
  - If $(\mathsf{ssid}, \mathsf{P}, m', \pi', d', \mathsf{st})$ is stored for some st, then return $(\mathsf{verified}, \mathsf{ssid}, \mathsf{P})$ to V.
  - If $(\mathsf{ssid}, \mathsf{P}, m'', \pi', d'', \mathsf{st})$ is stored, and $m'' \neq m'$ or $d'' \neq d'$ then return $(\mathsf{verification\text{-}failed}, \mathsf{ssid}, \mathsf{P})$ to V.
  - Else (i.e., no record $(\mathsf{ssid}, ...)$ is stored, or there is a stored record of the form $(\mathsf{ssid}, \mathsf{P}, m'', \pi'', d'', \mathsf{st})$ where $\pi'' \neq \pi'$):
    - Obtain $(m'', \mathsf{st}) \leftarrow \mathcal{S}_C(\mathsf{Ext}, \mathsf{ssid}, \mathsf{P}, \pi')$.
    - If $m'' \neq m'$, set $v = \mathsf{verification\text{-}failed}$.
    - If $m'' = m'$, set $v \leftarrow \mathcal{S}_C(\mathsf{Verify}, \mathsf{ssid}, \mathsf{P}, \pi', d', \mathsf{st})$.
    - If $v == \mathsf{verified}$, then store the tuple $(\mathsf{ssid}, \mathsf{P}, m', \pi', d', \mathsf{st})$ and return $(v, \mathsf{ssid}, \mathsf{P})$ to V. Else return $(\mathsf{verification\text{-}failed}, \mathsf{ssid}, \mathsf{P})$ to V.
- **Corruption:** When receiving $(\mathsf{Corrupt}, \mathsf{ssid})$ from $\mathcal{S}$, mark ssid as corrupted. Send all the stored tuples of the form $(\mathsf{ssid}, \ldots)$ to $\mathcal{S}$. If there does not exist any tuple then send $(\mathsf{ssid}, \perp)$ to $\mathcal{S}$.

  On input $(\mathsf{corrupt\text{-}check}, \mathsf{sid}, \mathsf{ssid})$, return whether $(\mathsf{sid}, \mathsf{ssid})$ is marked as corrupted.

Fig. 1. Non-interactive UC-commitment functionality $\mathcal{F}_{\mathsf{NICOM}}$

a simulated commitment. The $\mathcal{S}_C(\mathsf{Equiv}, \mathsf{ssid}, \mathsf{P}, \pi, \mathsf{st}, m)$ command is used to equivocate a commitment string π such that it opens to m. The $\mathcal{S}_C(\mathsf{Ext}, \mathsf{ssid}, \mathsf{P}, \pi)$ command is used to extract a message from the commitment π. These algorithms come in handy for simulation purposes when $\mathcal{F}_{\mathsf{NICOM}}$ is used in bigger protocols.

Implementing $\mathcal{F}_{NICOM}$. We implement $\mathcal{F}_{\mathsf{NICOM}}$ in the full version [CSW20c] using the non-interactive commitment scheme of [CF01] based on equivocal commitments and CCA-2 secure public key encryption with oblivious ciphertext sampleability. The committer P commits to a bit message m as $c = \mathsf{Com}(m; r)$. The commitment randomness is encrypted via a pair of encryptions. The committer encrypts the corresponding randomness r, subsession id ssid and committer id P using a CCA-2 secure PKE as $E_m = \mathsf{Enc}(\mathsf{pk}, (r, \mathsf{ssid}, \mathsf{P}); s_m)$ with randomness s_m. The other encryption E_{1-m} is obliviously sampled using randomness s_{1-m}. The commitment consists of (c, E_0, E_1) and the opening information is (m, r, s_0, s_1). The verifier performs the canonical verification by reconstructing the commitment. The equivocal commitment can be instantiated from Pedersen Commitment and the obliviously sampleable encryption scheme can be instantiated from Cramer Shoup encryption [CS98], yielding a protocol from DDH. Similarly, we can instantiate the equivocal commitment from LWE [CsW19] and the obliviously sampleable encryption scheme from LWE [MP12].

2.2 Adaptively Secure Sigma Protocols in the $\mathcal{F}_{\mathsf{NICOM}}$ Model

We recall the definition of a Sigma protocol and then we introduce the notion of adaptively Sigma protocols in the $\mathcal{F}_{\mathsf{NICOM}}$ model.

Sigma Protocol. A Sigma protocol consists of a prover possessing an NP statement $x \in \mathcal{L}$ (for language $\mathcal{L}$) and witness w which validates the statement. The verifier possesses the statement x. The prover constructs a first message a and the honest verifier challenges the prover with a random challenge $c \leftarrow_R \mathcal{C}$ from the challenge space $\mathcal{C}$. Based on the challenge, the prover computes a response z and sends it to the verifier. Completeness ensures that an honest verifier always accepts the proof (a, c, z). Soundness ensures that the verifier accepts a proof corresponding to an invalid statement $x' \notin \mathcal{L}$ with probability $\frac{1}{|\mathcal{C}|}$. The protocol is repeated κ times to obtain negligible (in κ) soundness error. We also require special soundness which guarantees a witness extractor given two accepting transcripts (a, c, z) and (a, c', z') corresponding to the same first message but different challenges $c \neq c' \in \mathcal{C}$. Finally, we need honest verifier zero knowledge which allows a simulator to simulate an accepting proof given an honestly sampled challenge c. The simulated proof should be indistinguishable from an honestly generated proof.

Limitations of a Sigma Protocol. A Sigma protocol does not necessarily guarantee security against adaptive corruptions. The adversary can choose to corrupt the prover after obtaining the simulated proof. In such a case, the simulator obtains the witness and needs to provide prover's randomness such that the simulated proof is consistent with the witness. This problem crops up especially when the first message of the Sigma protocol [FLS99] is statistically binding and doesn't allow equivocation later on. To tackle this issue, we introduce the notion of adaptively secure Sigma protocols in the ideal UC commitment functionality (for multiple subsessions) $\mathcal{F}_{\mathsf{NICOM}}$ model. The traditional UC commitment functionality of [CF01] is not compatible with non-interactive commitments since the functionality is required to interact with the parties during Commit and open phases. So we use our new commitment functionality $\mathcal{F}_{\mathsf{NICOM}}$ which allows non-interactive Commit and Open phases.

Adaptively Secure Sigma Protocols. As seen above, the traditional Sigma protocols does not necessarily guarantee security against adaptive corruptions. In the light of this, we consider Sigma protocols in the $\mathcal{F}_{\mathsf{NICOM}}$ model. The prover sends the first message a to the verifier, the verifier sends a random challenge c to the prover and the prover computes the response z based on c. The prover and verifier has access to the $\mathcal{F}_{\mathsf{NICOM}}$ functionality during the protocol execution. In addition to HVZK and special soundness properties, we also require that the simulator is able to produce consistent randomness for a simulated proof and a valid witness when the prover gets corrupted post-execution. Looking ahead, the first message a will consist of commitments that are obtained by invoking $\mathcal{F}_{\mathsf{NICOM}}$ functionality. This enables the simulator to construct an HVZK proof during protocol execution - where it opens few of the commitments in a which are required for verification. The other commitments in a remain unopened during the protocol. When the prover gets corrupted post-execution, the simulator obtains the witness w, and it equivocates the unopened commitments in a to produce a simulated prover's randomness such that it is indistinguishable from honestly sampled prover randomness (in the real world execution).

We also require special soundness property from our adaptively secure Sigma protocol to construct a NIZK protocol. We say that the protocol satisfies special soundness if there exists a extractor which extracts the witness given two transcripts (a, c_0, z_0) and (a, c_1, z_1) corresponding to the same a.

2.3 Compiling to an Adaptively-Secure NIZK

Next, we implement the $\mathcal{F}_{\mathsf{NIZK}}$ functionality for a single session by using the Fiat-Shamir transform on $\tau = \mathcal{O}(\kappa)$ iterations of the adaptively secure Sigma protocol. We instantiate the hash function in the Fiat-Shamir Transform using a correlation intractable hash function H [PS19, CCH+19, BKM20].

Correlation Intractability. A correlation intractable hash function H has the following property: For every efficient function f, given a hash function $H \leftarrow \mathcal{H}$ from the hash family $\mathcal{H}$, it is computationally hard to find an x s.t. $f(x) = H(x)$. Based on the first message $\mathbf{a}$ of a trapdoor-Sigma Protocol, the Fiat-Shamir challenge $\mathbf{e}$ can be generated using the hash function as $\mathbf{e} = H(\mathbf{a})$. The prover computes the third message $\mathbf{z}$ using $\mathbf{e}$. Trapdoor-Sigma protocol ensures that for every statement not in the language there can be only one bad challenge $\mathbf{e} = g(\mathbf{a})$ s.t. $(\mathbf{a}, \mathbf{e}, \mathbf{z})$ is an accepting transcript. By setting the function $f = g$ as the bad challenge function in H it is ensured that a malicious prover who constructs a bad challenge $\mathbf{e} = H(\mathbf{a})$ can be used to break correlation intractability since $\mathbf{e} = g(\mathbf{a}) = f(\mathbf{a})$. This guarantees soundness of the NIZK protocol.

Protocol. We compile our adaptively secure Sigma protocol into an adaptively secure NIZK in the $\mathcal{F}_{\mathsf{NICOM}}$ model (the $\mathcal{F}_{\mathsf{NICOM}}$ functionality is later instantiated using an adaptively secure non-interactive commitment scheme [CF01]). The prover computes the first message a^j of the adaptively secure Sigma protocol for the jth iteration where $j \in [\tau]$. It samples two challenges c_0^j and c_1^j from the challenge space such that $c_0^j \neq c_1^j$. The prover computes the responses z_0^j and z_1^j corresponding to both challenges c_0^j and c_1^j respectively. The prover commits to the challenges c_0^j and c_1^j, and the responses z_0^j and z_1^j. Let us denote the set of commitments as Y^j. The prover repeats the above protocol for τ iterations. Let $\mathbf{Y} = \{Y^j\}_{j \in [\tau]}$ denote the complete set of commitments and let $\mathbf{a} = \{a^j\}_{j \in [\tau]}$ denote the complete set of first messages. The prover computes the challenge bit-vector $\mathbf{e} = H(\mathsf{k}, (\mathbf{a}, \mathbf{Y}))$ (where k is the hash key) by invoking the hash function on the commitments $\mathbf{Y}$. The hash function is initialized in the statistical mode and the hash key contains the algorithm $\mathcal{S}_C$ obtained from $\mathcal{F}_{\mathsf{NICOM}}$. The hash function internally runs $\mathcal{S}_C$ to extract from the commitments. The hash key k is provided as part of the crs and it is computed as follows.

$$\mathsf{k} = \mathcal{H}.\mathsf{StatGen}(\mathcal{C}_{\mathsf{sk}}).$$

$\mathcal{C}_{\mathsf{sk}}$ is a poly-size circuit that takes $\mathbf{Y}$ as input and $\mathsf{sk} = \mathcal{S}_C$ is the secret algorithm of $\mathcal{F}_{\mathsf{NICOM}}$. $\mathcal{C}_{\mathsf{sk}}(\mathbf{a}, \mathbf{Y})$ is the circuit computing the function $f_{\mathsf{sk}}(\mathbf{a}, \mathbf{Y}) = \mathbf{e}$ s.t. for $j \in [\tau]$, $e^j = 0$ iff (a^j, c_0^j, z_0^j) is an accepting proof where $\mathcal{C}_{\mathsf{sk}}$ extracts the challenges (c_0^j, c_1^j), and the responses (z_0^j, z_1^j) by running $\mathcal{S}_C$. Setting the hash function in the statistical mode ensures that the hash function H is correlation intractable for all relations of the form:

$$\mathcal{R}_{\mathsf{sk}} = \{(\mathbf{a}, \mathbf{Y}, \mathbf{e}) : \mathbf{e} = f_{\mathsf{sk}}(\mathbf{a}, \mathbf{Y})\}$$

In the jth iteration, upon obtaining e as the challenge bit the prover decommits to (c_0^j, c_1^j, z_e^j). The NIZK proof for the jth iteration is $(a^j, c_0^j, c_1^j, z_e^j)$ and the decommitments corresponding to (c_0^j, c_1^j, z_e^j). The verifier checks that - 1) the decommitments are correct, 2) the challenges are different, i.e. $c_0^j \neq c_1^j$, 3) the proof - (a^j, c_e^j, z_e^j) verifies. The verifier runs the verification protocols for every iteration $j \in [\tau]$. The verifier outputs accept if all the τ proofs verify correctly. Correctness of the protocol follows from the correctness of the commitment scheme and correctness of the sigma protocol.

Soundness and Proof of Knowledge. The soundness and proof of knowledge argument follows through a sequence of hybrids. The correlation intractability does not hold in the real world since we start off with an argument and not a proof. The proof starts off with the real world protocol in the first hybrid. In the second hybrid the proof relies on the binding and extractability property of the commitment scheme to ensure that the committed messages can be either correctly extracted or the commitment fails to open correctly. In the next hybrid, we rely on the special soundness property of the Sigma protocol to ensure that if for any jth iteration (for $j \in [\tau]$) if the prover constructs an accepting proof for both $e^j = 0$ and $e^j = 1$ then the witness extractor of the sigma protocol correctly extracts the underlying witness. In the final hybrid, if the prover has evaded the witness extractor and yet succeeded in creating an accepting proof then it has predicted the challenge vector $\mathbf{e}$ correctly by breaking the correlation intractability of the hash function. However, we know that there does not exist $\mathbf{e}$ such that the following holds due to statistical correlation intractability and the underlying Sigma protocol in this hybrid is a proof. This ensures that either the witness extractor extracts an accepting witness from atleast one of the iterations or the proof does not verify. This completes our soundness argument.

Adaptive Soundness. Adaptive Soundness follows along the same lines provided the underlying the sigma protocol satisfies adaptive soundness. The distribution of the crs is identical in the real and ideal world. Hence, we argue that the proof fails to verify for a statement $x \notin \mathcal{L}$ since there does not exist any valid witness.

Security against Adaptive Corruptions and Adaptive ZK. The ZK property crucially relies on the adaptive security of the Sigma protocol and security against adaptive corruptions of the commitment scheme. The ZK simulator of the NIZK protocol invokes the HVZK simulator the sigma protocol to obtain a simulated proof (a^j, c^j, z^j) corresponding to a random ZK challenge c^j for the jth iteration. The simulator constructs the commitments $\mathbf{Y}$ in the equivocal mode and invokes the hash function to obtain the challenge string $\mathbf{e}$. Upon obtaining the challenge bits e^j (for $j \in [\tau]$) the simulator opens the commitments corresponding to e^j to the simulated proof (a^j, z^j, c^j). It also equivocates the commitment for the ZK challenge corresponding to bit $1 - e^j$ to open to a different challenge $c^{j'}$ as part of the protocol. The proof verifies correctly due to the HVZK property of the Sigma protocol and equivocal property of the commitment scheme. Upon post-execution corruption of the prover, the NIZK simulator obtains the correct witness w and it invokes the simulator of the adaptively secure Sigma protocol with w to obtain the internal prover state. Using these information the NIZK simulator constructs the response corresponding to challenge $c^{j'}$ for choice bit $1 - e^j$. The simulator equivocates the commitments in $\mathbf{Y}$ (mainly the commitment to the jth response for challenge bit $1 - e^j$) such that the proofs corresponding to challenge bits $1 - e^j$ verify for every jth proof. Indistinguishability follows from the adaptive security of the Sigma protocol and the adaptive security of the commitment scheme. Adaptive zero-knowledge also follows along the same lines provided the sigma protocol satisfies adaptive zero-knowledge.

2.4 Constructing Adaptively Secure Sigma Protocols with Special Soundness

Next, we show various instantiations of our adaptively sigma protocol which also satisfies special soundness. Plugging these protocols in a blackbox manner into our above compiler would yield a triply adaptive NIZK protocol.

Schnorr's [Sch90] **Protocol.** The classic Schnorr's identification protocol provides HVZK and satisfies special soundness. It also provides security against adaptive corruption. Let us recall the protocol and demonstrate that the Sigma protocol trivially satisfies adaptive security.

In the Schnorr's protocol the prover has a witness $w \in \mathbb{Z}_q$ and statement $x \in \mathbb{G}$ such that $x = g^w$, where $g \in \mathbb{G}$ is a generator of the cyclic group $\mathbb{G}$ where Discrete Log problem holds. The prover samples a random $r \in \mathbb{Z}_q$ and sets $a = g^r$. Upon obtaining a random challenge $c \in \mathbb{Z}_q$ from the verifier the prover sends $z = r + wc$ as the response. The verifier checks that $g^z \stackrel{?}{=} a \cdot x^c$. Given two accepting transcripts (a, c, z) and (a, c', z') the witness w can be extracted as $w = \frac{(z-z')}{c-c'}$. On the other hand, for HVZK the simulator samples a random $c \in \mathbb{Z}_q$ and a random $z \in Zq$ and computes $a = \frac{g^z}{x^c}$. Upon post-execution corruption of prover, the simulator obtains w and sets $r = z - wc$ as the internal state. It is straightforward to see that adaptive security follows.

Adaptive Soundness and Adaptive ZK. Adaptive soundness cannot be defined for Schnorr's protocol since every statement $x' \in \mathbb{G}$ lies in the language corresponding to the witness $w' \in \mathbb{Z}_q$ where $x' = g^{w'}$. Adaptive ZK follows from the HVZK property of the protocol.

Sigma Protocol of [FLS99]**.** We briefly recall the Sigma protocol of [FLS99] (FLS) for the sake of completeness. Let $\mathcal{R}_{\mathsf{Ham}}$ be the set of Hamiltonian graphs. The prover P proves that an n-node graph G is Hamiltonian, i.e. $G \in \mathcal{R}_{\mathsf{Ham}}$, given a Hamiltonian cycle σ as a witness. P samples a random n-node cycle H and commits to the adjacency matrix of the cycle as the first message a. The matrix contains n^2 entries, and P commits to the edges as $\mathsf{Com}(1)$, and non-edges as $\mathsf{Com}(0)$. The prover sends these commitments to the verifier V. V samples a random challenge bit e and sends it to the prover. If $c = 0$, then P decommits to the cycle H. Else, it computes a random permutation π s.t. $H = \pi(\sigma)$ and decommits to the non-edges in $\pi(G)$ and sends π. P sends the decommitments as its response z. Upon obtaining z, the verifier performs the following check:

- $c = 0$: Verify that z contains decommitments to 1, and they form a valid cycle, i.e. the prover must have committed to a valid n-node cycle.
- $c = 1$: Verify that z contains decommitments to 0, and the decommitted edges correspond to non-edges in $\pi(G)$.

Special Soundness. There are only two possible challenges in the boolean challenge space. Given the transcripts $(a, 0, z_0)$ and $(a, 1, z_1)$ where a_c and a'_c are computed as described above, the witness extractor obtains H from z_0 and π from z_1. The extractor computes the witness cycle as $\sigma = \pi^{-1}(H)$. This proves special soundness property of the Sigma protocol.

Honest Verifier Zero Knowledge. The FLS protocol achieves honest verifier zero knowledge. The ZK simulator samples a random challenge $e \in \{0, 1\}$ and based on that he computes (a, z) as follows.

- $c = 0$: The simulator samples a random n-node cycle H and commits to the adjacency matrix of the cycle as a. It sets z as the decommitment to the cycle.
- $c = 1$: The simulator sets all the commitments to 0 in a, i.e. commits to a null graph. It computes a random permutation π and decommits to the non-edges in $\pi(G)$. It sets z as π and the decommitments to the non-edges in $\pi(G)$.

Let us denote a proof as $\gamma = (a, e, z)$. It can be observed that an honest γ is identically distributed to a simulated γ when $e = 0$. When $e = 1$, an honestly γ contains a committed cycle whereas γ contains commitments to 0. The two proofs are indistinguishable due to the hiding of the commitment scheme.

Adaptive Security in $\mathcal{F}_{\mathsf{NICOM}}$ Model. We observe that the FLS protocol satisfies adaptive security if the commitments in a are computed in the $\mathcal{F}_{\mathsf{NICOM}}$ model. We consider the simulated ZK proof and adaptive corruption of prover as follows:

- $c = 0$: The HVZK simulator samples a random n-node cycle H and commits to the adjacency matrix of the cycle as a by invoking $\mathcal{F}_{\mathsf{NICOM}}$. It sets z as the decommitment to the cycle.
  Upon post execution corruption of prover, the simulator obtains the witness cycle σ and it computes the permutation π such that $H = \pi(\sigma)$. The internal state of the prover is set as a, permutation π and the internal state of the committer returned by $\mathcal{F}_{\mathsf{NICOM}}$ (for computing the commitments in a).
- $c = 1$: The HVZK simulator sets a as the commitments to 0 in the $\mathcal{F}_{\mathsf{NICOM}}$ model, i.e. the simulator commits to a null graph. It computes a random permutation π, and sets z as the random permutation π and the decommitments to the non-edges in $\pi(G)$.
  Upon post execution corruption of prover, the simulator obtains the witness cycle σ and it computes the permutation π such that $H = \pi(\sigma)$. The simulator equivocates the unopened commitments in a by invoking the $\mathcal{F}_{\mathsf{NICOM}}$ simulator, such that the unopened commitments decommit to H. The internal state of the prover is set to the permutation π and the commitment randomness returned by $\mathcal{F}_{\mathsf{NICOM}}$ for all the commitments.

For the case of $c == 0$, it can be observed that the simulated internal state is identical to the honest prover internal state. When $c == 1$, the simulated proof consists of commitments to 0 and the simulated prover internal state consists of equivocation randomness which was returned by $\mathcal{F}_{\mathsf{NICOM}}$. Hence, the real and ideal world views are identically distributed in the $\mathcal{F}_{\mathsf{NICOM}}$ model. This shows that the FLS protocol can be plugged into our NIZK compiler to obtain a NIZK protocol which is secure against adaptive corruptions.

Adaptive Soundness and Adaptive ZK. In FLS, the first message a of the prover is computed based on the parameter n without the knowledge of the graph or the witness. After obtaining c from V, the prover requires the input graph G and the witness cycle σ to construct the response. Thus, only the last message in this protocol depends on the input. This property is called delayed-input property. And hence the FLS protocol trivially satisfies adaptive soundness and adaptive ZK in the $\mathcal{F}_{\mathsf{NICOM}}$ model where the input statement can be adversarially chosen after observing the setup string distribution. This allows our NIZK protocol to be adaptively sound and satisfy adaptive ZK when the FLS Sigma protocol is plugged into the triply adaptive NIZK compiler.

Blum's Protocol for Hamiltonicity. Following the above idea, it can be shown that the Blum's protocol [Blu86] for hamiltonicity also satisfies adaptive security and special soundness in the $\mathcal{F}_{\mathsf{NICOM}}$ model. The protocol itself does not satisfy delayed input property since the first message of the prover depends on the statement. However, the protocol does achieve adaptive soundness since a malicious prover would be unsuccessful in generating an accepting proof for a statement $x \notin \mathcal{L}$ in the $\mathcal{F}_{\mathsf{NICOM}}$ model.

Garbled Circuit Based Protocol of [HV16]**.** Next, we modify the GC based protocol of [HV16] to obtain an adaptively secure sigma protocol with special soundness in the $\mathcal{F}_{\mathsf{NICOM}}$ model. We recall their protocol and then discuss the bottlenecks involved.

Protocol of [HV16]. The protocol of [HV16] constructs an adaptively secure ZK proof from one-way functions in the plain model. Their protocol relies on a special commitment scheme called adaptive-instance dependent commitment (AIDCS) schemes. It depends on the statement being proven. AIDCS is statistically binding when the statement (being proven) is not in the language. AIDCS is equivocal when the statement is in the language. The committer can open a commitment to any message given an accepting witness for the statement. In [HV16], the prover constructs a garbled circuit computing the NP relation on the statement x. The prover commits to the garbled circuit $\mathbf{GC}$ (garbling notations can be found in [HV16,CSW20c]), encoding information $\mathbf{u}$ and the decoding information $\mathbf{v}$ using the AIDCS. These commitments are jointly denoted as the first message a. The verifier sends the challenge bit c. If the bit is $c = 0$ then the prover decommits to $(\mathbf{GC}, \mathbf{u}, \mathbf{v})$. The verifier checks that the garbled circuit was correctly constructed. If the bit is $c = 1$ then the prover computes the input wire labels W corresponding to the witness w and decommits to W, the decoding information $\mathbf{v}$ and the path of the computation as $\mathsf{path} = \Pi_{\mathsf{Ev}}(\mathbf{GC}, \mathsf{W})$ in the $\mathbf{GC}$ which corresponds to evaluation of $\mathbf{GC}$ on W. The verifier accepts if the computation of the garbled circuit on W along the path outputs 1. When x is not in the language the AIDCS is statistically binding and hence the prover has to guess the verifier's bit. For ZK, the ZK simulator will guess the random challenge bit of verifier and it will rewind if the guess is wrong. When the prover gets corrupted post-execution, the simulator can equivocate the commitments given the witness w using the equivocal property of AIDCS.

Bottlenecks in Obtaining NIZK. The proof is not binding when $x \in \mathcal{L}$ and a corrupt prover knows the witness since the AIDCS is equivocal given the witness. A malicious prover evades the special soundness property using the following adversarial strategy: The adversary constructs the AIDCS in the equivocal mode as the first message a and it constructs the responses as follows:

- $c_0 == 0$ *:* It samples a garbled circuit as $(\mathbf{GC}, \mathbf{u}, \mathbf{v})$ and sets z_0 as $(\mathbf{GC}, \mathbf{u}, \mathbf{v})$ and the decommitment of a to $(\mathbf{GC}, \mathbf{u}, \mathbf{v})$.
- $c_1 == 1$ *:* It invokes the privacy simulator of the garbled circuit on output 1 to obtain a simulated GC and input wire labels for evaluation. The adversary sets the response z_1 as these wire labels and the path of GC evaluation. The response z_1 also contains the decommitments of a to the wire labels and the evaluation path.

The adversary is able to equivocate the AIDCS to open to different values and this hampers witness extraction from the two accepting transcripts (a, c_0, z_0) and (a, c_1, z_1). This hampers the special soundness property.

Our Solution. We solve this issue by replacing the AIDCS with the $\mathcal{F}_{\mathsf{NICOM}}$ model and demonstrate that the new Sigma protocol in the $\mathcal{F}_{\mathsf{NICOM}}$ model satisfies adaptive security and special soundness property. The prover constructs a garbled circuit computing the NP relation on the statement x. The prover sets a as the commitment to garbled circuit $\mathbf{GC}$, encoding information $\mathbf{u}$ and the decoding information $\mathbf{v}$ in the $\mathcal{F}_{\mathsf{NICOM}}$ model. The prover sends a to the verifier. The verifier sends the challenge bit c. The prover performs the following based on challenge c:

- $c = 0$: The prover decommits to the garbled circuit $\mathbf{GC}$, encoding information $\mathbf{u}$ and decoding information $\mathbf{v}$ as the response z_0.
- $c = 1$: The prover decommits to the input wire labels and the evaluation path in the garbled circuit as the response z_1.

The verifier performs verification using the original verifier algorithm of [HV16]. Completeness is straightforward. We show that the above Sigma protocol satisfies special soundness property and adaptive security in $\mathcal{F}_{\mathsf{NICOM}}$ model.

Special Soundness. There are only two possible challenges in the boolean challenge space. Given two accepting transcripts $(a, 0, z_0)$ and $(a, 1, z_1)$, the witness extractor obtains the encoding information $\mathbf{u}$ and the input wire labels W. Assuming the garbling scheme is projective (for every input wire in the circuit the encoding information consists of two possible wire labels corresponding to bit values 0 and 1), it maps the wire labels with the encoding information to extract the witness w. This proves special soundness property of the Sigma protocol.

Adaptive Security in $\mathcal{F}_{\mathsf{NICOM}}$ Model. We describe the HVZK simulator and then extend it to satisfy adaptive security in the $\mathcal{F}_{\mathsf{NICOM}}$ model. We crucially rely on the reconstructability property of the garbling scheme to argue adaptive security. Reconstructability property says that given a path of computation, the input wire labels and the input to a garbled circuit for circuit C it is possible to reconstruct the rest of the garbled circuit as being honestly generated by the garbling algorithm. We define the HVZK simulator as follows based on the challenge c:

- $c = 0$: The HVZK simulator computes a fresh garbled circuit as $(\mathbf{GC}, \mathbf{u}, \mathbf{v})$ and commits to it using $\mathcal{F}_{\mathsf{NICOM}}$ as the first message a. It sets a as the commitment to $(\mathbf{GC}, \mathbf{u}, \mathbf{v})$. The simulator sends z_0 as $(\mathbf{GC}, \mathbf{u}, \mathbf{v})$ and the decommitments to a.

  When the prover gets adaptively corrupted, the simulator obtains the witness w and it sets the randomness used to garble $\mathbf{GC}$ and the commitment randomness as the internal randomness.

- $c = 1$: The HVZK simulator invokes the GC privacy simulator on output 1 and circuit C to obtain a simulated garbled circuit, input wire label, decoding information and internal state - $(\mathbf{GC}', \mathsf{W}', \mathbf{v}', \mathsf{st}')$. The HVZK simulator sets a as the commitment to $(\mathbf{GC}', 0^{|\mathbf{u}|}, \mathbf{v}')$ in the $\mathcal{F}_{\mathsf{NICOM}}$ model. The simulator computes the path of computation as $\mathsf{path} = \Pi_{\mathsf{Ev}}(\mathbf{GC}', \mathsf{W}')$ on wire labels W'. The simulator sends z_1 as $(\mathsf{path}, \mathsf{W}')$ and decommitment to $(\mathsf{path}, \mathsf{W}')$ from the set of commitments in a.
  When the prover gets adaptively corrupted, the simulator obtains the witness w. Using input w, simulated input wire labels W' and the computation path path, it uses the reconstructability property of the garbling scheme to reconstruct a fresh garbled $\mathbf{GC}$, encoding information $\mathbf{u}$ and decoding information $\mathbf{v}$ and the corresponding garbling randomness. It sets the garbling randomness as the internal state and invokes the $\mathcal{F}_{\mathsf{NICOM}}$ simulator to equivocate the commitments in a such that they open to $(\mathbf{GC}, \mathbf{u}, \mathbf{v})$.

For the case of $c == 0$, it can be observed that the simulated internal state is identical to the honest prover internal state. When $c == 1$, the proof contains the evaluation path, the input wire labels and their decommitments. Upon post execution corruption the simulator relies on the reconstructability property of the garbling scheme to construct the garbled circuit. The distribution of the simulated a in the ideal world is indistinguishable from the honestly constructed a in the real world in the $\mathcal{F}_{\mathsf{NICOM}}$ model due to the reconstructability property. The garbling scheme of [LP09] based on one-way functions satisfies all the required properties for the Sigma protocol. This was shown in the work of [HV16].

Adaptive Soundness and Adaptive ZK. The protocol achieves adaptive soundness and adaptive ZK even when the functionality $\mathcal{F}_{\mathsf{NICOM}}$ is implemented by an adaptively secure commitment protocol [CF01] in the crs model. The distribution of crs is identical in the real and ideal world. A malicious prover fails to prove a false statement $x \notin \mathcal{L}$ without breaking the binding of the commitment scheme (implementing $\mathcal{F}_{\mathsf{NICOM}}$ functionality). Adaptive ZK follows from the adaptive security of the protocol.

3 Preliminaries

Notations. We denote by $a \leftarrow D$ a uniform sampling of an element a from a distribution D. The set of elements $\{1, 2, \ldots, n\}$ is represented by $[n]$. A function $\mathsf{neg}(\cdot)$ is said to be negligible, if for every polynomial $p(\cdot)$, there exists a constant c, such that for all $n > c$, it holds that $\mathsf{neg}(n) < \frac{1}{p(n)}$. We denote a probabilistic polynomial time algorithm as PPT. We denote the computational and statistical security parameters by κ by μ respectively. We denote computational and statistical indistinguishability by $\overset{c}{\approx}$ and $\overset{s}{\approx}$ respectively. When a party $\mathcal{P}$ gets corrupted we denote it by $\mathcal{P}^*$. Let $\mathcal{R}_{\mathsf{Ham}}$ denote the set of n-node Hamiltonian graphs for $n > 1$. We prove security of our protocol in the Universal Composability (UC) model. We refer to the original paper [Can01] for details. Our protocols are in the common reference string model where the parties of a session $(\mathsf{sid}, \mathsf{ssid})$ have access to a public reference string crs sampled from a distribution. In the one-time crs model, each crs is local to each $(\mathsf{sid}, \mathsf{ssid})$. In the reusable crs model, the same crs can be reused across different sessions by different parties. The simulator knows the trapdoors of the crs in both cases. We refer to [CLOS02] for more details.

Definition 1 *[DN00]* **(*PKE with Oblivious Ciphertext Sampling*).** *A public key encryption scheme* PKE $= (\mathsf{KeyGen}, \mathsf{Enc}, \mathsf{Dec})$ *over message space* $\mathcal{M}$*, ciphertext space* $\mathcal{C}$ *and randomness space* $\mathcal{R}$ *satisfies oblivious ciphertext sampling property if there exists PPT algorithms* $(\mathsf{oEnc}, \mathsf{Inv})$ *s.t. for any message* $m \in \mathcal{M}$*, the following two distributions are computationally indistinguishable to a PPT adversary* $\mathcal{A}$*:*

$$\Big| \Pr[\mathcal{A}(m, c, r) = 1 | m \leftarrow \mathcal{A}(\mathsf{pk}), c \leftarrow \mathsf{Enc}(\mathsf{pk}, m; r'), r \leftarrow \mathsf{Inv}(\mathsf{pk}, c)]$$

$$- \Pr[\mathcal{A}(m, \tilde{c}, r) = 1 | m \leftarrow \mathcal{A}(\mathsf{pk}), \tilde{c} \leftarrow \mathsf{oEnc}(\mathsf{pk}; r)] \Big| \leq \mathsf{neg}(\kappa),$$

where $(\mathsf{pk}, \mathsf{sk}) \leftarrow \mathsf{KeyGen}(1^\kappa)$.

We instantiate CCA-2 secure PKE with oblivious ciphertext sampling from DDH [CS98] and LWE [MP12].

3.1 Non-interactive Zero Knowledge

We provide the ideal UC-NIZK functionality in Fig. 2 for a single prover and a single proof. It also considers the case for adaptive corruption of parties where the prover gets corrupted after outputting the proof π. In such a case, the adversary receives the internal state of the prover.

$\mathcal{F}_{\mathsf{NIZK}}$ is parametrized by an NP relation $\mathcal{R}$. (The code treats $\mathcal{R}$ as a binary function.)

- **Proof:** On input $(\mathsf{prove}, \mathsf{sid}, x, w)$ from party P: If $\mathcal{R}(x, w) = 1$ then send $(\mathsf{prove}, P, \mathsf{sid}, x)$ to $\mathcal{S}$. Upon receiving $(\mathsf{proof}, \mathsf{sid}, \pi)$ from $\mathcal{S}$, store $(\mathsf{sid}, x, w, \pi)$ and send $(\mathsf{proof}, \mathsf{sid}, \pi)$ to P.
- **Verification:** On input $(\mathsf{verify}, \mathsf{sid}, x, \pi)$ from a party V: If $(\mathsf{sid}, x, w, \pi)$ is stored, then return $(\mathsf{verification}, \mathsf{sid}, x, \pi, \mathcal{R}(x, w))$ to V. Else, send $(\mathsf{verify}, V, \mathsf{sid}, x, \pi)$ to $\mathcal{S}$. Upon receiving $(\mathsf{witness}, \mathsf{sid}, w)$ from $\mathcal{S}$, store $(\mathsf{sid}, x, w, \pi)$, and return $(\mathsf{verification}, \mathsf{sid}, x, \pi, \mathcal{R}(x, w))$ to V.
- **Corruption:** When receiving $(\mathsf{corrupt}, \mathsf{sid})$ from $\mathcal{S}$, mark sid as corrupted. If there is a stored tuple $(\mathsf{sid}, x, w, \pi)$, then send it to $\mathcal{S}$.

Fig. 2. Single-proof non-interactive zero-knowledge functionality $\mathcal{F}_{\mathsf{NIZK}}$

We also consider $\mathcal{F}^{\mathsf{m}}_{\mathsf{NIZK}}$ (Fig. 3) functionality where a single prover can parallelly prove multiple statements in a single session. The verifier verifies each of them separately. It is a weaker notion than multi-session UC NIZK since $\mathcal{F}^{\mathsf{m}}_{\mathsf{NIZK}}$

$\mathcal{F}_{\mathsf{NIZK}}$ is parametrized by an NP relation $\mathcal{R}$. (The code treats $\mathcal{R}$ as a binary function.)

- **Proof:** On input $(\mathsf{prove}, \mathsf{sid}, \mathsf{ssid}, x, w, P)$ from party P: If there exists $(\mathsf{sid}, P') \in \mathcal{Q}$ and $P \neq P'$ or $\mathcal{R}(x, w) \neq 1$ then ignore the input. Else record $\mathcal{Q} = (\mathsf{sid}, \mathsf{ssid}, P)$. Send $(\mathsf{prove}, P, \mathsf{sid}, \mathsf{ssid}, x)$ to $\mathcal{S}$. Upon receiving $(\mathsf{proof}, \mathsf{sid}, \mathsf{ssid}, \pi)$ from $\mathcal{S}$, store $(\mathsf{sid}, \mathsf{ssid}, x, w, \pi)$ and send $(\mathsf{proof}, \mathsf{sid}, \mathsf{ssid}, \pi)$ to P.
- **Verification:** On input $(\mathsf{verify}, \mathsf{sid}, \mathsf{ssid}, x, \pi)$ from a party V: If $(\mathsf{sid}, \mathsf{ssid}, x, w, \pi)$ is stored, then return $(\mathsf{verification}, \mathsf{sid}, \mathsf{ssid}, x, \pi, \mathcal{R}(x, w))$ to V. Else, send $(\mathsf{verify}, V, \mathsf{sid}, \mathsf{ssid}, x, \pi)$ to $\mathcal{S}$. Upon receiving $(\mathsf{witness}, \mathsf{sid}, \mathsf{ssid}, w)$ from $\mathcal{S}$, store $(\mathsf{sid}, \mathsf{ssid}, x, w, \pi)$, and return $(\mathsf{verification}, \mathsf{sid}, \mathsf{ssid}, x, \pi, \mathcal{R}(x, w))$ to V.
- **Corruption:** When receiving $(\mathsf{corrupt}, \mathsf{sid}, \mathsf{ssid})$ from $\mathcal{S}$, mark $(\mathsf{sid}, \mathsf{ssid})$ as corrupted. If there are stored tuples of the form $(\mathsf{sid}, \mathsf{ssid}, x, w, \pi)$, then send it to $\mathcal{S}$.
  On input $(\mathsf{corrupt\text{-}check}, \mathsf{sid}, \mathsf{ssid})$, return whether $(\mathsf{sid}, \mathsf{ssid})$ is marked as corrupted.

Fig. 3. Non-interactive zero-knowledge functionality $\mathcal{F}^{\mathsf{m}}_{\mathsf{NIZK}}$ for single prover multi-proof setting

considers only a single session between a pair of parties with roles preserved. Different provers have to use different instances of $\mathcal{F}^{\mathsf{m}}_{\mathsf{NIZK}}$ to prove statements.

Next, we define the notion of triple adaptive security for NIZK protocols and provide the property-based definitions of NIZK for completeness. UC-secure NIZKs in the crs model imply adaptive ZK since an environment can statically corrupt the verifier, obtain the crs of the protocol and then choose the statement x to be proven by the honest prover. The simulator against a corrupt verifier ensures that it constructs an accepting simulated proof which is indistinguishable from an honestly generated proof. Hence, UC-NIZK implies adaptive ZK if the environment is allowed to choose the statement being proven after corrupting the verifier.

Definition 2. *A non-interactive zero-knowledge argument system (NIZK) for an NP-language $\mathcal{L}$ consists of three PPT machines $\Pi_{\mathsf{NIZK}} = (\mathsf{Gen}, \mathsf{P}, \mathsf{V})$, that have the following properties:*

- ***Completeness:*** *For all $\kappa \in \mathsf{N}$, and all $(x, w) \in \mathcal{R}$, it holds that:*

$$\Pr[\mathsf{V}(\mathsf{crs}, x, \mathsf{P}(\mathsf{crs}, x, w)) = 1 | (\mathsf{crs}, \mathsf{td}) \leftarrow \mathsf{Gen}(1^\kappa, 1^{|x|})] = 1.$$

- ***Soundness:*** *For all PPT provers P^* and $x \notin \mathcal{L}$ the following holds for all $\kappa \in \mathsf{N}$:*

$$\Pr[\mathsf{V}(\mathsf{crs}, x, \pi) = 1 | (\mathsf{crs}, \mathsf{td}) \leftarrow \mathsf{Gen}(1^\kappa, 1^{|x|}), \pi \leftarrow \mathsf{P}^*(\mathsf{crs})] \leq \mathsf{neg}(\kappa).$$

- ***Zero knowledge:*** *There exists a PPT simulator $\mathcal{S}$ such that for every $(x, w) \in \mathcal{R}$, the following distribution ensembles are computationally indistinguishable:*

$$\{(\mathsf{crs}, \pi) | (\mathsf{crs}, \mathsf{td}) \leftarrow \mathsf{Gen}(1^\kappa, 1^{|x|}), \pi \leftarrow \mathsf{P}(\mathsf{crs}, x, w)\}_{\kappa \in \mathsf{N}}$$

$$\approx \{(\mathsf{crs}, \{\mathcal{S}(1^\kappa, x, \mathsf{td})\})|(\mathsf{crs}, \mathsf{td}) \leftarrow \mathsf{Gen}(1^\kappa, 1^{|x|}\}_{\kappa \in \mathrm{N}}$$

Definition 3 *(Full Adaptive Soundness). Π_{NIZK} is adaptively sound if for every PPT cheating prover P^* the following holds:*

$$\Pr[x \notin \mathcal{L} \wedge \mathsf{V}(\mathsf{crs}, x, \pi) = 1|(\mathsf{crs}, \mathsf{td}) \leftarrow \mathsf{Gen}(1^\kappa, 1^{|x|}), (x, \pi) \leftarrow \mathsf{P}^*(\mathsf{crs})] < \mathsf{neg}(\kappa).$$

Definition 4 *(Adaptive Zero-Knowledge). Π_{NIZK} is adaptively zero-knowledge if for all PPT verifiers V^* there exists a PPT simulator $\mathcal{S}$ such that the following distribution ensembles are computationally indistinguishable:*

$$\{(\mathsf{crs}, \mathsf{P}(\mathsf{crs}, x, w), \mathsf{aux})\} \overset{c}{\approx} \{\mathcal{S}(\mathsf{crs}, \mathsf{td}, 1^\kappa, x)\}_{\kappa \in \mathrm{N}}$$

where $(\mathsf{crs}, \mathsf{td}) \leftarrow \mathsf{Gen}(1^\kappa, 1^{|x|})$ and $(x, w, \mathsf{aux}) \leftarrow \mathsf{V}^*(\mathsf{crs})$.

The Gen algorithm takes the $|x|$ (length of the statement) as input to generate the crs. This shows that the crs size depends on $|x|$. When the crs is independent of $|x|$, the Gen algorithm only takes 1^κ as input.

Definition 5 *(Triple Adaptive Security for a single instance). Let $\Pi_{\mathsf{NIZK}} = (\mathsf{Gen}, \mathsf{P}, \mathsf{V})$ be a NIZK protocol in the crs model. Then Π_{NIZK} satisfies triple adaptive security for a single instance if it securely implements $\mathcal{F}_{\mathsf{NIZK}}$ functionality for a single instance and provides adaptive soundness and adaptive zero knowledge.*

Definition 6 *(Triple Adaptive Security for multiple instances). Let $\Pi_{\mathsf{NIZK}} = (\mathsf{Gen}, \mathsf{P}, \mathsf{V})$ be a NIZK protocol in the crs model. Then Π_{NIZK} satisfies triple adaptive security for multiple instances if it UC-securely implements $\mathcal{F}_{\mathsf{NIZK}}$ functionality for multiple instances and provides adaptive soundness and adaptive zero knowledge.*

3.2 Commitment Schemes

A commitment scheme $\mathsf{Com} = (\mathsf{Gen}, \mathsf{Com}, \mathsf{Ver}, \mathsf{Equiv})$ allows a committing party C to compute a commitment c to a message m, using randomness r, towards a party V in the Com phase. Later in the open phase, C can open c to m by sending the decommitment to V who verifies it using Ver. It should be binding, hiding and equivocal using Equiv algorithm given trapdoor td of the crs. Moreover, we require our commitment scheme to be additively homomorphic for message domain of size at least four, i.e. $\mathsf{Com}(m_1; r_1) + \mathsf{Com}(m_2; r_2) = \mathsf{Com}(m_1 + m_2; r_1 + r_2)$. We also need a tag-based simulation sound commitment consists of $\mathsf{Com}_{\mathsf{SST}} = (\mathsf{KeyGen}, \mathsf{Com}, \mathsf{Ver}, \mathsf{TCom}, \mathsf{TOpen})$ for our protocols. Formal definitions can be found in the full version [CSW20c].

$\mathcal{F}_{\mathsf{NICOM}}$-model. We also provide a new non-interactive UC-commitment functionality in Fig. 1. The $\mathcal{F}_{\mathsf{NICOM}}$ functionality (Fig. 1) is implemented against adaptive adversaries using adaptively secure non-interactive UC commitments [CF01] in the crs model. We perform this using equivocal commitments and CCA-2 secure PKE with oblivious ciphertext sampleability in the non-programmable crs model. It can be found in the full version [CSW20c]. We also prove that this new functionality implies the old UC commitment functionality (of [CF01]) but our new functionality is more compatible with non-interactive protocols.

3.3 Correlation Intractability

As in [CCH+19, PS19, BKM20] we define efficiently searchable relations and recall the definitions of correlation intractability, in their computational and statistical versions.

Definition 7. *We say that a relation $R \subseteq X \times Y$ is searchable in size S if there exists a function $f : X \to Y$ that is implementable as a boolean circuit of size S, such that if $(x, y) \in R$ then $y = f(x)$. (In other words, $f(x)$ is the unique witness for x, if such a witness exists.)*

Definition 8. *Let $R = \{\mathcal{R}_\kappa\}$ be a relation class, i.e., a set of relations for each κ. A hash function family $\mathcal{H} = (\mathsf{Gen}, H)$ is correlation intractable for R if for every non-uniform PPT adversary $\mathcal{A} = \{\mathcal{A}_\kappa\}$ and every $R \in \mathcal{R}_\kappa$ the following holds:*

$$\Pr[(x, H(k, x)) \in R : k \leftarrow \mathsf{Gen}(1^\kappa), x = \mathcal{A}_\kappa(k)] \leq \mathsf{neg}(\kappa)$$

Definition 9. *Let $R = \{\mathcal{R}_\kappa\}$ be a relation class. A hash function family $\mathcal{H} = (\mathsf{Gen}, H)$ with a fake-key generation algorithm $\mathsf{StatGen}$ is somewhere statistically correlation intractable for R if for every $R \in R_\kappa$ and circuits $\exists z_R \in Z_\kappa$ s.t:*

$$\Pr[\exists x \text{ s.t. } (x, H(k, x)) \in R : k \leftarrow \mathsf{StatGen}(1^\kappa, z_R)] \leq \mathsf{neg}(\kappa).$$

and for every $z_\kappa \in Z_\kappa$ if the following distributions the indistinguishable:

$$\{\mathsf{StatGen}(1^\kappa, z_\kappa)\}_\kappa \overset{c}{\approx} \{\mathsf{Gen}(1^\kappa)\}_\kappa.$$

Definition 10. *A hash family $\mathcal{H} = (\mathsf{Gen}, H)$, with input and output length $n := n(\kappa)$ and, resp., $m := m(\kappa)$, is said to be programmable if the following two conditions hold:*

- *1-Universality: For every $\kappa \in \mathsf{N}, x \in \{0,1\}^n$ and $y \in \{0,1\}^m$, the following holds: $\Pr[H(k, x) = y : k \leftarrow \mathsf{Gen}(1^\kappa)] = 2^{-m}$.*
- *Programmability: There exists a PPT algorithm $\mathsf{Gen}'(1^\kappa, x, y)$ that samples from the conditional distribution $Sample(1^\kappa) | H(k, x) = y$.*

4 Triply Adaptive NIZK Argument in the crs Model

In this section, we present our NIZK protocol. First, we recall the definition of Sigma protocol in the crs model and then build upon it to define adaptively Sigma protocol in the $\mathcal{F}_{\mathsf{NICOM}}$ model. Finally, we compile adaptively Sigma protocols into NIZKs using the Fiat-Shamir transform.

4.1 Sigma Protocol

We consider Sigma protocol [CPV20] $\Sigma = (\mathsf{Setup}, \mathsf{P}_1, \mathsf{V}_1, \mathsf{P}_2, \mathsf{V}_2)$ for relation $\mathcal{R}$ between a prover P and a verifier V that receive a common input statement x. P receives an additional private input a witness w for x. The protocol has the following form:

- $\mathsf{Setup}(1^\kappa)$: The Setup algorithm runs on security parameter κ and generates a common reference string crs and a trapdoor td. The crs is published as the public setup string.
- $\mathsf{P}_1(\mathsf{crs}, x, w, 1^\kappa; \mathsf{st})$: The prover runs algorithm P_1 on common input x, crs, private input w, security parameter κ and randomness st obtaining $a = \mathsf{P}_1(x, w, 1^\kappa; \mathsf{st})$ and sends a to verifier.
- $\mathsf{V}_1(\mathsf{crs}, a)$: Verifier samples random challenge $c \leftarrow_R \mathcal{C}$ and sends c to prover.
- $\mathsf{P}_2(\mathsf{crs}, x, w, \mathsf{st}, c)$: The prover runs algorithm P_2 on input $x, w, \mathsf{crs}, \mathsf{st}, c$ and obtain z. It sends z to verifier.
- $\mathsf{V}_2(\mathsf{crs}, x, a, c, z)$: The verifier outputs 1 if it accepts the proof else it outputs 0 to reject the proof.

The above protocol should satisfy completeness, honest verifier zero knowledge and special soundness. We refer to the full version [CSW20c] for the property definitions of Sigma protocol.

4.2 Fully Adaptive Sigma Protocol in $\mathcal{F}_{\mathsf{NICOM}}$ Model

The traditional Sigma protocols are not secure against adaptive corruption of parties. Hence, we introduce the notion of fully adaptive Sigma protocols in the UC-commitment functionality $\mathcal{F}_{\mathsf{NICOM}}$ model. Consider the above Sigma protocol transcript (a, c, z). In the fully adaptive Sigma protocol, the prover has access to the $\mathcal{F}_{\mathsf{NICOM}}$ functionality while computing the first message a. The prover sends a to the verifier. Upon obtaining the challenge c, the prover computes the response z and sends it to the verifier.

Definition 11. *Let $\Sigma = (\mathsf{Setup}, \mathsf{P}_1, \mathsf{V}_1, \mathsf{P}_2, \mathsf{V}_2)$ be a Sigma protocol for relation $\mathcal{R}$ over corresponding domains $(\mathcal{A}, \mathcal{C}, \mathcal{Z})$, where parties make use of an instance of $\mathcal{F}_{\mathsf{NICOM}}$ where the prover is the commiter, and where the first message consists exclusively of a sequence of commitment strings that the prover obtains from $\mathcal{F}_{\mathsf{NICOM}}$. Then Σ is* fully adaptive *in the $\mathcal{F}_{\mathsf{NICOM}}$ model if the following requirements hold:*

1. ***Completeness.*** *If $(x, w) \in \mathcal{R}$, then honest transcripts of the form (x, a, c, z) obtained by the verifier for (x, w) are accepting.*
2. ***Computational Special soundness.*** *There exists a PPT algorithm Ext such that for any polytime adversarial prover P^* and two transcripts (a, c, z) and (a, c', z'), such that $P^*(\kappa) \rightarrow (S_C, x, a)$ where S_C is the adversarial code used by $\mathcal{F}_{\mathsf{NICOM}}$, $P^*(\kappa, c) \rightarrow z$, $P^*(\kappa, c') \rightarrow z'$, $c' \neq c$, and such that the verifier accepts both transcripts when given access to $\mathcal{F}_{\mathsf{NICOM}}^{S_C}$, it holds that:*

$$\Pr[\mathsf{Ext}(\mathsf{crs}, S_C, x, a, c, z, c', z') = w \ \&\ (x, w) \notin \mathcal{R}] < \mathsf{neg}(\kappa)$$

3. ***Adaptive Honest-verifier zero knowledge.*** *There exists PPT algorithm* $\mathcal{S} = (\mathcal{S}_1, \mathcal{S}_2)$ *such that, for any* $(x, w) \in \mathcal{R}$*, any PPT distinguisher* $\mathcal{A}$*, and any PPT adversarial code* $\mathcal{S}_C$ *for* $\mathcal{F}_{\mathsf{NICOM}}$*:*

$$\Big| \Pr\left[(a, c, z, st) \leftarrow \mathcal{S}_1(\mathit{crs}, \mathcal{S}_C, x; \mathit{td}), r \leftarrow \mathcal{S}_2(st, w) : \mathcal{A}^{\mathcal{F}^{\mathcal{S}_C}_{\mathsf{NICOM}}}(a, c, z, r) = 1\right] - \Pr\left[r \leftarrow \{0,1\}^\kappa, (a, st) \leftarrow P_1^{\mathcal{F}^{\mathcal{S}_C}_{\mathsf{NICOM}}}(x, w, r), c \leftarrow \mathcal{C}, z \leftarrow P_2^{\mathcal{F}^{\mathcal{S}_C}_{\mathsf{NICOM}}}(x, w, st, c) : \mathcal{A}^{\mathcal{F}^{\mathcal{S}_C}_{\mathsf{NICOM}}}(a, c, z, r) = 1\right] \Big| \leq \mathit{neg}(\kappa)$$

where $(\mathit{crs}, \mathit{td}) \leftarrow \mathit{Setup}(1^\kappa)$.

4.3 Our NIZK Compiler in the $\mathcal{F}_{\mathsf{NICOM}}$ Model

We apply the Fiat-Shamir transform on the Sigma protocol using correlation intractable hash functions H to remove interaction and obtain our NIZK protocol. The CI hash function is provided with the description of the $\mathcal{S}_C$ algorithm to extract the prover's view and compute the bad challenge function. Our compiler can be found in Fig. 4.

A corrupt prover breaks soundness of the protocol if it breaks the special soundness of the adaptively secure Sigma protocol or it breaks the binding property of the commitment scheme. In the former case, the witness can be extracted by invoking the witness extractor algorithm Ext (according Definition 11) of the Sigma protocol on the proof. We show that our NIZK protocol Π_{NIZK} implements $\mathcal{F}_{\mathsf{NIZK}}$ functionality against adaptive corruption of parties by proving Theorem 3 in the full version [CSW20c]. It can be further shown that the same protocol implements the single prover multi-proof NIZK functionality $\mathcal{F}^{\mathsf{m}}_{\mathsf{NIZK}}$.

Theorem 3. *If* $\mathcal{H}$ *is a somewhere statistically correlation intractable hash function family with programmability,* $\Sigma = (\mathsf{Setup}, P_1, V_1, P_2, V_2)$ *is an adaptively secure Sigma protocol (in the* $\mathcal{F}_{\mathsf{NICOM}}$ *model) with computational special soundness then* Π_{NIZK} *implements* $\mathcal{F}_{\mathsf{NIZK}}$ *functionality in* $(\mathsf{crs}_{\mathsf{NIZK}}, \mathcal{F}_{\mathsf{NICOM}})$ *model against adaptive corruption of parties.*

Adaptive Soundness and Adaptive Zero knowledge. The NIZK protocol can be made triply adaptive secure by adding adaptive soundness and adaptive zero-knowledge. The NIZK protocol satisfies adaptive soundness if the underlying Sigma protocol satisfies adaptive soundness and $\mathcal{F}_{\mathsf{NICOM}}$ is implemented using a non-interactive UC-commitment Com in the non-programmable $\mathsf{crs}_{\mathsf{Com}}$ model Com, whose real and ideal world $\mathsf{crs}_{\mathsf{Com}}$ distribution are identical. Moreover, the NIZK protocol satisfies adaptive zero knowledge if the underlying Sigma protocol satisfies adaptive zero knowledge and Com is a non-interactive adaptively secure commitment in the non-programmable crs model. This is summarized in Theorem 4 and proven in the full version [CSW20c].

- **Primitives:** Adaptively-secure Sigma Protocol $\Sigma = (\mathsf{Setup}, \mathsf{P}_1, \mathsf{V}_1, \mathsf{P}_2, \mathsf{V}_2)$, that uses functionality $\mathcal{F}_{\mathsf{NICOM}}$ (with algorithm $\mathcal{S}_C$). Correlation Intractable hash function family $\mathcal{H} = (\mathsf{Gen}, \mathsf{StatGen}, H)$.
- **Public Inputs:** Setup string $\mathsf{crs}_{\mathsf{NIZK}} = (\mathsf{k}, \mathsf{crs}_\Sigma)$ where $(\mathsf{crs}_\Sigma, \mathsf{td}_\Sigma) \leftarrow \Sigma.\mathsf{Setup}(1^\kappa)$ and $\mathsf{k} \leftarrow \mathcal{H}.\mathsf{StatGen}(1^\kappa, C_{\mathsf{sk}})$ where $\mathsf{sk} = (\mathsf{td}_\Sigma, \mathcal{S}_C)$. [a] The Sigma protocol is repeated for $\tau = \mathcal{O}(\kappa)$ times.
- **Private Inputs:** V has input statement x. P has the same input statement x and secret witness w such that $\mathcal{R}(x, w) = 1$.

$\mathsf{P}(\mathsf{crs}_{\mathsf{NIZK}}, x, w, 1^\kappa)$:
Upon invoked with command $(\mathsf{prove}, \mathsf{sid}, x, w)$ the prover performs the following for $j \in [\tau]$:

- $(a^j, \mathsf{st}^j_\Sigma) \leftarrow \Sigma.\mathsf{P}_1(\mathsf{crs}_\Sigma, x, w, 1^\kappa)$.
- Sample $c^j_0, c^j_1 \leftarrow_R \mathcal{C}$ such that $c^j_0 \neq c^j_1$. Commit to challenges as $(\mathsf{Receipt}, C^j, \mathsf{st}^j_C) \leftarrow \mathcal{F}_{\mathsf{NICOM}}(\mathsf{Com}, 3j+2, \mathsf{P}, (c^j_0, c^j_1))$.
- For $\delta \in \{0, 1\}$, the prover performs the following:
  - Compute $z^j_\delta \leftarrow \Sigma.\mathsf{P}_2(\mathsf{crs}_\Sigma, x, w, \mathsf{st}^j_\Sigma, c^j_\delta)$.
  - Commit to the responses as follows: $(\mathsf{Receipt}, 3j + \delta, \mathsf{P}, Z^j_\delta, \mathsf{st}^j_{Z,\delta}) \leftarrow \mathcal{F}_{\mathsf{NICOM}}(\mathsf{Com}, 3j + \delta, \mathsf{P}, z^j_\delta)$.
- The commitments for the jth run are denoted as $Y^j = (C^j, Z^j_0, Z^j_1)$.

Assemble the commitments as $\mathbf{Y} = \{Y^j\}_{j\in[\tau]}$ and and the first messages as $\mathbf{a} = \{a^j\}_{j\in[\tau]}$. Compute the challenge as $\mathbf{e} = \{e^j\}_{j\in[\tau]} = H(\mathsf{k}, (\mathbf{a}, \mathbf{Y}))$. The prover performs the following for $j \in [\tau]$:

- Set the challenge as $\delta = e^j \in \{0, 1\}$.
- Construct the response as $U^j = (c^j_0, c^j_1, z^j_\delta, \mathsf{st}^j_C, \mathsf{st}^j_{Z,\delta})$ by decommitting to the challenges and the response z^j_δ.

The prover sends the NIZK proof $\gamma = (\mathbf{a}, \mathbf{Y}, \mathbf{U})$ where $\mathbf{U} = \{U^j\}_{j\in[\tau]}$ to the verifier.
$\mathsf{V}(\mathsf{crs}_{\mathsf{NIZK}}, x, \gamma)$:
Upon invoked with command $(\mathsf{verify}, \mathsf{sid}, x, \gamma)$ the verifier performs the following:

- Parse the proof $\gamma = (\mathbf{a}, \mathbf{Y}, \mathbf{U}) = \{a^j, Y^j, U^j\}_{j\in[\tau]}$.
- Compute the challenge string as $\mathbf{e} = \{e^j\}_{j\in[\tau]} = \mathcal{H}.H(\mathsf{k}, (\mathbf{a}, \mathbf{Y}))$ where $\mathbf{e} \in \{0, 1\}^\tau$.
- For $j \in [\tau]$, the verifier performs the following :
  - The verifier sets $\delta = e^j \in \{0, 1\}$.
  - Parse the proof as $Y^j = (C^j, Z^j_0, Z^j_1)$ and $U^j = (c^j_0, c^j_1, z^j, \mathsf{st}^j_Z, \mathsf{st}^j_C)$.
  - Verifies the provided decommitments and proofs. Output $(\mathsf{verification}, \mathsf{sid}, x, \gamma, 0)$ if any of the following occurs:
    1. If $\mathcal{F}_{\mathsf{NICOM}}(\mathsf{Open}, 3j + 2, \mathsf{P}, (c^j_0, c^j_1), C^j, \mathsf{st}^j_C)$ returns verification-failed.
    2. If $\mathcal{F}_{\mathsf{NICOM}}(\mathsf{Open}, 3j + \delta, \mathsf{P}, z^j, Z^j_\delta, \mathsf{st}^j_Z)$ returns verification-failed.
    3. If $\Sigma.\mathsf{V}_2(\mathsf{crs}_\Sigma, x, a^j, c^j_\delta, z^j) = 0$.

The verifier outputs $(\mathsf{verification}, \mathsf{sid}, x, \gamma, 1)$ if all the above τ proofs verified correctly and the above decommitments were correct.

[a] C_{sk} is a poly-size circuit computing the function $f_{\mathsf{sk}}(\mathbf{a}, \mathbf{Y}) = \mathbf{e}$, such that for every $j \in [\tau], e^j = 0$ iff $\Sigma.\mathsf{V}_2(\mathsf{crs}_\Sigma, x, a^j, c^j_0, z^j) = 1$ where $(c^j_0, c^j_1) \leftarrow \mathcal{F}_{\mathsf{NICOM}}(\mathcal{S}_C, \mathsf{Ext}, 3j + 2, \mathsf{P}, C^j), z^j \leftarrow \mathcal{F}_{\mathsf{NICOM}}(\mathcal{S}_C, \mathsf{Ext}, 3j, \mathsf{P}, Z^j_0)$.

Fig. 4. Adaptively secure NIZK protocol Π_{NIZK}

Theorem 4. *If $\mathcal{H}$ is a somewhere statistically correlation intractable hash function family, $\Sigma = (\mathsf{Setup}, P_1, V_1, P_2, V_2)$ is a Sigma protocol satisfying adaptive special soundness and adaptive zero knowledge, and $\mathcal{F}_{\mathsf{NICOM}}$ is implemented using an adaptively secure UC commitment in the non-programmable $\mathsf{crs}_{\mathsf{Com}}$ model then Π_{NIZK} satisfies adaptive soundness and adaptive zero knowledge in the $(\mathsf{crs}_{\mathsf{NIZK}}, \mathsf{crs}_{\mathsf{Com}})$ model.*

Instantiations. The adaptively Sigma protocol can be instantiated using the Schnorr's protocol, Sigma protocol of FLS, Blum's Hamiltonicity protocol or the GC-based protocol of [HV16]. Detailed overview can be found in Sect. 2.4. The CI hash function can be instantiated from LWE [PS19,CCH+19], or from DDH+LPN assumption [BKM20]. This is discussed in the full version [CSW20c]. $\mathcal{F}_{\mathsf{NICOM}}$ is constructed from the UC-commitment scheme of [CF01] in the full version [CSW20c] by relying on equivocal commitments and CCA-2 secure public key encryption with oblivious sampleability. The equivocal commitment can be instantiated from Pedersen Commitment and the obliviously sampleable encryption scheme can be instantiated from Cramer Shoup encryption [CS98], yielding a protocol from DDH. Similarly, we can instantiate the equivocal commitment from LWE [CsW19] and the obliviously sampleable encryption scheme from LWE [MP12].

5 Triply Adaptive NIZK Argument in the Short crs Model

In this section we present our compiler Π_{sNIZK} which obtains a triply adaptive NIZK protocol where the crs size is independent of the circuit size and depends only on κ assuming a non-interactive equivocal commitment scheme in the reusable crs model which supports additive homomorphism, PKE with oblivious ciphertext sampleability and a triply adaptively secure NIZK protocol Π_{NIZK} in the crs model. Our compiler is presented in the full version [CSW20c]. We prove triple adaptive security of Π_{sNIZK} by proving Theorem 5 in the full version [CSW20c]. By applying this result, we reduce the crs size of Π_{NIZK}. The homomorphic commitment scheme can be instantiated from DDH (Pedersen commitment or [CSW20a]) or LWE [GVW15] assumptions. The PKE can be instantiated from DDH assumption (Elgamal encryption) or LWE [GSW13] assumptions. This yields our compiler from DDH or LWE assumption.

Theorem 5. *Assuming* PKE *is a public key encryption scheme with oblivious ciphertext sampling,* Com *is an equivocal additively homomorphic commitment scheme in the reusable $\mathsf{crs}_{\mathsf{Com}}$ model and Π_{NIZK} implements $\mathcal{F}^{m}_{\mathsf{NIZK}}$ against adaptive corruption of parties, then Π_{sNIZK} UC-securely implements $\mathcal{F}_{\mathsf{NIZK}}$ functionality for NP languages against adaptive adversaries in the* crs *model where $|\mathsf{crs}| = poly(\kappa)$. Π_{sNIZK} is also adaptively sound and adaptively zero knowledge.*

6 Triply Adaptive, Multi-proof UC-NIZK Argument

In this section, we add non-malleability to our Π_{sNIZK} protocol to obtain our multi-proof UC-NIZK protocol $\Pi_{\mathsf{UC\text{-}NIZK}}$ by using simulation sound tag-based commitments $\mathsf{Com}_{\mathsf{SST}}$ and strong one-time signature scheme SIG. We add non-malleability to our proof by signing the proof using a pair of keys $(\mathsf{vk}, \mathsf{sk})$ from SIG and committing the witness using a $\mathsf{Com}_{\mathsf{SST}}$ where the tag is $(\mathsf{vk}, \mathsf{sid}, \mathsf{ssid}, x)$. The adversary is bound to vk since vk is part of the tag used to encrypt w using $\mathsf{Com}_{\mathsf{SST}}$ in the proof γ. SIG ensures that an adversary cannot forge a signature using vk and this prevents non-malleability. The same crs is used for multiple subsessions and this ensures adaptive soundness and adaptive zero knowledge. The protocol and the proofs can be found in the full version [CSW20c]. Security of $\Pi_{\mathsf{UC\text{-}NIZK}}$ is summarized in Theorem 6.

Theorem 6. *If Π_{sNIZK} UC-realizes $\mathcal{F}_{\mathsf{NIZK}}$ for a single proof,* SIG *is a strong one-time secure signature scheme, $\mathsf{Com}_{\mathsf{SST}}$ is a tag-based simulation-sound trapdoor commitment and* PKE *is a public key encryption scheme with oblivious ciphertext sampling property then $\Pi_{\mathsf{UC\text{-}NIZK}}$ UC-securely implements $\mathcal{F}_{\mathsf{NIZK}}$ for multiple instances against adaptive adversaries. In addition, $\Pi_{\mathsf{UC\text{-}NIZK}}$ is adaptively sound and adaptively zero knowledge.*

References

[AF07] Abe, M., Fehr, S.: Perfect NIZK with adaptive soundness. In: Vadhan, S.P. (ed.) TCC 2007. LNCS, vol. 4392, pp. 118–136. Springer, Heidelberg (2007). https://doi.org/10.1007/978-3-540-70936-7_7

[AMPS21] Alamati, N., Montgomery, H., Patranabis, S., Sarkar, P.: Two-round adaptively secure MPC from isogenies, LPN, or CDH. In: Tibouchi, M., Wang, H. (eds.) ASIACRYPT 2021. LNCS, vol. 13091, pp. 305–334. Springer, Cham (2021). https://doi.org/10.1007/978-3-030-92075-3_11

[BCG+14] Ben-Sasson, E., et al.: ZeroCash: decentralized anonymous payments from bitcoin. In: 2014 IEEE Symposium on Security and Privacy, SP 2014, Berkeley, CA, USA, 18–21 May 2014, pp. 459–474 (2014)

[BFM90] Blum, M., Feldman, P., Micali, S.: Proving security against chosen ciphertext attacks. In: Goldwasser, S. (ed.) CRYPTO 1988. LNCS, vol. 403, pp. 256–268. Springer, New York (1990). https://doi.org/10.1007/0-387-34799-2_20

[BKM06] Bender, A., Katz, J., Morselli, R.: Ring signatures: stronger definitions, and constructions without random oracles. In: Halevi, S., Rabin, T. (eds.) TCC 2006. LNCS, vol. 3876, pp. 60–79. Springer, Heidelberg (2006). https://doi.org/10.1007/11681878_4

[BKM20] Brakerski, Z., Koppula, V., Mour, T.: NIZK from LPN and trapdoor hash via correlation intractability for approximable relations. In: Micciancio, D., Ristenpart, T. (eds.) CRYPTO 2020. LNCS, vol. 12172, pp. 738–767. Springer, Cham (2020). https://doi.org/10.1007/978-3-030-56877-1_26

[Blu86] Blum, M.: How to prove a theorem so no one else can claim it. In: Proceedings of the International Congress of Mathematicians (1986)

[BMW03] Bellare, M., Micciancio, D., Warinschi, B.: Foundations of group signatures: formal definitions, simplified requirements, and a construction based on general assumptions. In: Biham, E. (ed.) EUROCRYPT 2003. LNCS, vol. 2656, pp. 614–629. Springer, Heidelberg (2003). https://doi.org/10.1007/3-540-39200-9_38

[BSMP91] Blum, M., De Santis, A., Micali, S., Persiano, G.: Noninteractive zero-knowledge. SIAM J. Comput. **20**(6), 1084–1118 (1991)

[Can01] Canetti, R.: Universally composable security: a new paradigm for cryptographic protocols. In: 42nd FOCS, pp. 136–145. IEEE Computer Society Press, October 2001

[CCH+19] Canetti, R., et al.: Fiat-Shamir: from practice to theory. In: Charikar, M., Cohen, E. (eds.), 51st ACM STOC, pp. 1082–1090. ACM Press, June 2019

[CD00] Camenisch, J., Damgård, I.: Verifiable encryption, group encryption, and their applications to separable group signatures and signature sharing schemes. In: Okamoto, T. (ed.) ASIACRYPT 2000. LNCS, vol. 1976, pp. 331–345. Springer, Heidelberg (2000). https://doi.org/10.1007/3-540-44448-3_25

[CF01] Canetti, R., Fischlin, M.: Universally composable commitments. In: Kilian, J. (ed.) CRYPTO 2001. LNCS, vol. 2139, pp. 19–40. Springer, Heidelberg (2001). https://doi.org/10.1007/3-540-44647-8_2

[CGH98] Canetti, R., Goldreich, O., Halevi, S.: The random oracle methodology, revisited (preliminary version). In: 30th ACM STOC, pp. 209–218. ACM Press, May 1998

[CGPS21] Chakraborty, S., Ganesh, C., Pancholi, M., Sarkar, P.: Reverse firewalls for adaptively secure MPC without setup. In: Tibouchi, M., Wang, H. (eds.) ASIACRYPT 2021. LNCS, vol. 13091, pp. 335–364. Springer, Cham (2021). https://doi.org/10.1007/978-3-030-92075-3_12

[CJJ21] Choudhuri, A.R., Jain, A., Jin, Z.: Non-interactive batch arguments for NP from standard assumptions. In: Malkin, T., Peikert, C. (eds.) CRYPTO 2021. LNCS, vol. 12828, pp. 394–423. Springer, Cham (2021). https://doi.org/10.1007/978-3-030-84259-8_14

[CLOS02] Canetti, R., Lindell, Y., Ostrovsky, R., Sahai, A.: Universally composable two-party and multi-party secure computation. In: 34th ACM STOC, pp. 494–503. ACM Press, May 2002

[CPS+16] Ciampi, M., Persiano, G., Scafuro, A., Siniscalchi, L., Visconti, I.: Online/Offline OR composition of sigma protocols. In: Fischlin, M., Coron, J.-S. (eds.) EUROCRYPT 2016. LNCS, vol. 9666, pp. 63–92. Springer, Heidelberg (2016). https://doi.org/10.1007/978-3-662-49896-5_3

[CPV20] Ciampi, M., Parisella, R., Venturi, D.: On adaptive security of delayed-input sigma protocols and Fiat-Shamir NIZKs. In: Galdi, C., Kolesnikov, V. (eds.) SCN 2020. LNCS, vol. 12238, pp. 670–690. Springer, Cham (2020). https://doi.org/10.1007/978-3-030-57990-6_33

[CS98] Cramer, R., Shoup, V.: A practical public key cryptosystem provably secure against adaptive chosen ciphertext attack. In: Krawczyk, H. (ed.) CRYPTO 1998. LNCS, vol. 1462, pp. 13–25. Springer, Heidelberg (1998). https://doi.org/10.1007/BFb0055717

[CsW19] Cohen, R., Shelat, A., Wichs, D.: Adaptively secure MPC with sublinear communication complexity. In: Boldyreva, A., Micciancio, D. (eds.) CRYPTO 2019. LNCS, vol. 11693, pp. 30–60. Springer, Cham (2019). https://doi.org/10.1007/978-3-030-26951-7_2

[CSW20a] Canetti, R., Sarkar, P., Wang, X.: Efficient and round-optimal oblivious transfer and commitment with adaptive security. In: Moriai, S., Wang, H. (eds.) ASIACRYPT 2020. LNCS, vol. 12493, pp. 277–308. Springer, Cham (2020). https://doi.org/10.1007/978-3-030-64840-4_10

[CSW20c] Canetti, R., Sarkar, P., Wang, X.: Triply adaptive UC NIZK. IACR Cryptology ePrint Archive, p. 1212 (2020). https://eprint.iacr.org/2020/1212

[DDN91] Dolev, D., Dwork, C., Naor, M.: Non-malleable cryptography (extended abstract). In: 23rd ACM STOC, pp. 542–552. ACM Press, May 1991

[DN00] Damgård, I., Nielsen, J.B.: Improved non-committing encryption schemes based on a general complexity assumption. In: Bellare, M. (ed.) CRYPTO 2000. LNCS, vol. 1880, pp. 432–450. Springer, Heidelberg (2000). https://doi.org/10.1007/3-540-44598-6_27

[FLS99] Feige, U., Lapidot, D., Shamir, A.: Multiple noninteractive zero knowledge proofs under general assumptions. SIAM J. Comput. **29**(1), 1–28 (1999)

[FS87] Fiat, A., Shamir, A.: How to prove yourself: practical solutions to identification and signature problems. In: Odlyzko, A.M. (ed.) CRYPTO 1986. LNCS, vol. 263, pp. 186–194. Springer, Heidelberg (1987). https://doi.org/10.1007/3-540-47721-7_12

[GGI+15] Gentry, C., Groth, J., Ishai, Y., Peikert, C., Sahai, A., Smith, A.D.: Using fully homomorphic hybrid encryption to minimize non-interactive zero-knowledge proofs. J. Cryptol. **28**(4), 820–843 (2015)

[GMW87] Goldreich, O., Micali, S., Wigderson, A.: How to play any mental game or a completeness theorem for protocols with honest majority. In: Aho, A. (ed.) 19th ACM STOC, pp. 218–229. ACM Press, May 1987

[GOS06] Groth, J., Ostrovsky, R., Sahai, A.: Perfect non-interactive zero knowledge for NP. In: Vaudenay, S. (ed.) EUROCRYPT 2006. LNCS, vol. 4004, pp. 339–358. Springer, Heidelberg (2006). https://doi.org/10.1007/11761679_21

[GOS12] Groth, J., Ostrovsky, R., Sahai, A.: New techniques for noninteractive zero-knowledge. J. ACM **59**(3), 11:1–11:35 (2012)

[GR13] Goldreich, O., Rothblum, R.D.: Enhancements of trapdoor permutations. J. Cryptol. **26**(3), 484–512 (2013)

[GSW13] Gentry, C., Sahai, A., Waters, B.: Homomorphic encryption from learning with errors: conceptually-simpler, asymptotically-faster, attribute-based. In: Canetti, R., Garay, J.A. (eds.) CRYPTO 2013. LNCS, vol. 8042, pp. 75–92. Springer, Heidelberg (2013). https://doi.org/10.1007/978-3-642-40041-4_5

[GVW15] Gorbunov, S., Vaikuntanathan, V., Wichs, D.: Leveled fully homomorphic signatures from standard lattices. In: Servedio, R.A., Rubinfeld, R. (eds.) 47th ACM STOC, pp. 469–477. ACM Press, June 2015

[HL18] Holmgren, J., Lombardi, A.: Cryptographic hashing from strong one-way functions (or: One-way product functions and their applications). In: 59th IEEE Annual Symposium on Foundations of Computer Science, FOCS 2018, Paris, France, 7–9 October 2018, pp. 850–858. IEEE Computer Society (2018)

[HLR21] Holmgren, J., Lombardi, A., Rothblum, R.D.: Fiat-Shamir via list-recoverable codes (or: parallel repetition of GMW is not zero-knowledge). In STOC **2021**, 750–760 (2021)

[HV16] Hazay, C., Venkitasubramaniam, M.: On the power of secure two-party computation. In: Robshaw, M., Katz, J. (eds.) CRYPTO 2016. LNCS, vol. 9815, pp. 397–429. Springer, Heidelberg (2016). https://doi.org/10.1007/978-3-662-53008-5_14

[KKK21] Kerber, T., Kiayias, A., Kohlweiss, M.: Composition with knowledge assumptions. In: Malkin, T., Peikert, C. (eds.) CRYPTO 2021. LNCS, vol. 12828, pp. 364–393. Springer, Cham (2021). https://doi.org/10.1007/978-3-030-84259-8_13

[KNYY19] Katsumata, S., Nishimaki, R., Yamada, S., Yamakawa, T.: Exploring constructions of compact NIZKs from various assumptions. In: Boldyreva, A., Micciancio, D. (eds.) CRYPTO 2019. LNCS, vol. 11694, pp. 639–669. Springer, Cham (2019). https://doi.org/10.1007/978-3-030-26954-8_21

[KNYY20] Katsumata, S., Nishimaki, R., Yamada, S., Yamakawa, T.: Compact NIZKs from standard assumptions on bilinear maps. In: Canteaut, A., Ishai, Y. (eds.) EUROCRYPT 2020. LNCS, vol. 12107, pp. 379–409. Springer, Cham (2020). https://doi.org/10.1007/978-3-030-45727-3_13

[KZM+15] Kosba, A.E., et al.: How to use snarks in universally composable protocols. IACR Cryptol. ePrint Arch. **2015**, 1093 (2015)

[LP09] Lindell, Y., Pinkas, B.: A proof of security of Yao's protocol for two-party computation. J. Cryptol. **22**(2), 161–188 (2009)

[MP12] Micciancio, D., Peikert, C.: Trapdoors for lattices: simpler, tighter, faster, smaller. In: Pointcheval, D., Johansson, T. (eds.) EUROCRYPT 2012. LNCS, vol. 7237, pp. 700–718. Springer, Heidelberg (2012). https://doi.org/10.1007/978-3-642-29011-4_41

[NY90] Naor, M., Yung, M.: Public-key cryptosystems provably secure against chosen ciphertext attacks. In: 22nd ACM STOC, pp. 427–437. ACM Press, May 1990

[PS19] Peikert, C., Shiehian, S.: Noninteractive zero knowledge for NP from (Plain) learning with errors. In: Boldyreva, A., Micciancio, D. (eds.) CRYPTO 2019. LNCS, vol. 11692, pp. 89–114. Springer, Cham (2019). https://doi.org/10.1007/978-3-030-26948-7_4

[Sch90] Schnorr, C.P.: Efficient identification and signatures for smart cards. In: Brassard, G. (ed.) CRYPTO 1989. LNCS, vol. 435, pp. 239–252. Springer, New York (1990). https://doi.org/10.1007/0-387-34805-0_22

[SCO+01] De Santis, A., Di Crescenzo, G., Ostrovsky, R., Persiano, G., Sahai, A.: Robust non-interactive zero knowledge. In: Kilian, J. (ed.) CRYPTO 2001. LNCS, vol. 2139, pp. 566–598. Springer, Heidelberg (2001). https://doi.org/10.1007/3-540-44647-8_33

Efficient NIZKs from LWE via Polynomial Reconstruction and "MPC in the Head"

Riddhi Ghosal, Paul Lou(✉), and Amit Sahai

University of California, Los Angeles, CA, USA
{riddhi,pslou,sahai}@cs.ucla.edu

Abstract. All existing works building non-interactive zero-knowledge (NIZK) arguments for NP from the Learning With Errors (LWE) assumption have studied instantiating the Fiat-Shamir paradigm on a *parallel repetition* of an underlying honest-verifier zero knowledge (HVZK) Σ protocol, via an appropriately built correlation-intractable (CI) hash function from LWE. This technique has inherent efficiency losses that arise from parallel repetition.

In this work, we show how to make use of the more efficient "MPC in the Head" technique for building an underlying honest-verifier protocol upon which to apply the Fiat-Shamir paradigm. To make this possible, we provide a new and more efficient construction of CI hash functions from LWE, using efficient algorithms for polynomial reconstruction as the main technical tool.

We stress that our work provides a new and more efficient "base construction" for building LWE-based NIZK arguments for NP. Our protocol can be the building block around which other efficiency-focused bootstrapping techniques can be applied, such as the bootstrapping technique of Gentry et al. (Journal of Cryptology 2015).

1 Introduction

A recent line of work instantiates the Fiat-Shamir heuristic by building correlation-intractable hash functions from the Learning With Errors (LWE) assumption [7,29,34], yielding the first Non-Interactive Zero-Knowledge (NIZK) protocols for NP from LWE. Such protocols are particularly desirable as LWE is believed to be hard even for quantum computers. While this line of work has been exciting in terms of achieving new feasibility based on LWE, our understanding of how to optimize the efficiency of such constructions is still in its infancy.

In particular, before our work, all known papers constructing NIZK arguments for NP from the LWE assumption studied instantiating the Fiat-Shamir paradigm on a *parallel repetition* of an underlying honest-verifier zero knowledge (HVZK) Σ protocol. Unfortunately, parallel repetition entails inherent efficiency loss. Can we do better?

Supplementary Information The online version contains supplementary material available at https://doi.org/10.1007/978-3-031-22966-4_17.

S. Agrawal and D. Lin (Eds.): ASIACRYPT 2022, LNCS 13792, pp. 496–521, 2022.
https://doi.org/10.1007/978-3-031-22966-4_17

Our Work. In this work, we study how to apply the "MPC-in-the-Head" paradigm [30] to the construction of NIZK arguments for NP from the LWE assumption. Moreover, we do so by directly using simple and efficient polynomial reconstruction algorithms [27,37], avoiding the need for more complex coding previously used in [29][1] We note that this paradigm has previously been used to yield practically efficient constructions in other contexts [1,11,18].

The starting point: Zero Knowledge Protocols. A zero knowledge protocol [22] is an interactive protocol which allows a prover to prove to a verifier that an input x is in some NP language L without revealing anything more than the fact that $x \in L$. A classic example of such a protocol was introduced by Goldreich, Micali and Wigderson [21] for *Graph 3-Coloring.* The NP-completeness of Graph 3-Coloring implies that the GMW protocol indeed leads to zero knowledge proofs for all problem in NP. The basic version of this protocol is public coin and has large soundness error, but this error can be made negligible while still preserving *honest-verifier* zero-knowledge by *parallel repetition.* However, such parallel repetition is a source of significant inefficiency, both asymptotically and concretely. This is especially true if the number of parallel repetitions required is large – an issue that we will come back to later!

An alternative to using parallel repetition of such classic protocols is the MPC-in-the-head paradigm introduced by Ishai, Kushilevitz, Ostrovsky and Sahai [30], which allow us to construct highly sound general zero knowledge proof systems for any NP relation $R(x, w)$, where w is a witness to the fact that $x \in L$. Such a protocol makes black box use of an honest-majority MPC protocol Π_f for a functionality f for the circuit for NP relation R. This approach bypasses the computational overhead of a Karp reduction. Moreover, there is a successful line of work on producing highly efficient perfectly-robust MPC with minimal communication [3,13,14,24].

The MPC-in-the-head paradigm avoids the need for parallel repetition entirely. At a high level, the paradigm works by having the prover run the MPC protocol among q virtual servers entirely in the imagination of the prover, and then commit to the views of these virtual servers. The verifier then specifies a small random subset of these servers to the prover. The prover then opens the commitments to the inputs of the chosen servers, and all messages sent and received by those servers. This allows the verifier to check that the prover correctly executed the MPC protocol for almost all servers. It is absolutely crucial that the number of servers that the verifier specifies to open is significantly smaller than the number of servers q, otherwise no security would remain for the prover.

Using the Fiat-Shamir paradigm with Correlation-Intractable Hash Functions to obtain NIZK. A non-interactive zero knowledge protocol (NIZK) [19] lets the

[1] In personal correspondence after the initial posting of our result, Alex Lombardi showed us that it was possible to use the construction in [29] using Parvaresh-Vardy codes over extension fields to achieve parameters compatible with our variant of MPC-in-the-head, albeit at a significant efficiency cost relative to what we achieve here. Refer to Appendix A.1 for a detailed discussion.

prover eliminate the need for interaction by assuming a common random string (CRS[2]) that is given as input to both parties. A beautiful tool for constructing NIZKs is the Fiat Shamir heuristic [15]: it starts with a *public-coin honest-verifier zero knowledge proof* system and transforms it into a NIZK. This works by placing a random hash key in the CRS and replacing each of the verifier's messages in the interactive protocol with the hash of the input and the entire transcript so far. A sequence of works [5,7–9,28,31,34] has shown that if this hash function is *correlation-intractable* for certain relations, then the resulting NIZK is sound.

The recent work of [29,34] constructs such a correlation-intractable hash function from the LWE assumption and demonstrates how to apply the Fiat-Shamir transformation to a broad class of public-coin honest-verifier zero knowledge protocols built using parallel repetition. However, it is worth noting that the *number* of parallel repetitions needed for the technique of [29] to apply is actually a rather large polynomial. Specifically, if k is the security parameter for LWE and if the size of the verifier's challenge set is bounded by any polynomial in k, then the number of repetitions required is roughly $O(k^2)$ (though they note this can be optimized to $O(k^{1+\varepsilon})$). One crucial reason for this polynomial expression being $O(k^c)$, for $c > 1$, is that list-recoverable error correcting codes play a starring role in the work of [29], and unfortunately the best-known such codes require large block lengths to achieve the parameters needed for [29] to work[3].

Our New Idea in a Nutshell. Our starting technical observation is that the correlation that needs to be intractable for the hash function is in fact far *more structured* in the case of a variant of the MPC-in-the-head protocol that we consider, than in the case of parallel repetition based protocols. The looser structure of the correlation behind parallel repetition based protocols is what led to the work of [29] requiring general list-recoverable codes. The greater structure present in the case of MPC-in-the-head protocols allows us to significantly relax the requirements, and in particular lets us use an aggregate size analysis when decoding. As a result, we are able to use standard polynomial reconstruction algorithms [27,37] directly to solve our problem. To highlight this structure, we define a new variant of list-recoverability, that we call Recurrent List-Recoverability, over product sets where each term in the product is the same set.

Definition 1 (Recurrent List-Recoverable Codes). *An ensemble of codes* $\{\mathcal{C}_\lambda \colon \mathcal{M}_\lambda \rightarrow \mathbb{Z}_{q_\lambda}^{n_\lambda}\}$ *is said to be a* $(\ell(\cdot), L(\cdot))$ -recurrent list recoverable *(for* $\ell, L \colon \mathbb{Z}^+ \rightarrow \mathbb{Z}^+$*) if there is a polynomial-time algorithm* Recover *that:*

- *Takes as input* $\lambda \in \mathbb{Z}^+$ *and explicit descriptions of "constraint" sets* $S \subseteq \mathbb{Z}_q^n$ *where* $|S| \leq \ell(\lambda)$*.*

[2] More generally, CRS can also refer to a common reference string, but our work will achieve NIZKs with a common random string.

[3] In particular, the alternative method pointed out to us by Lombardi using Parvaresh-Vardy codes over extension fields would also incur this $O(k^{1+\varepsilon})$, $\varepsilon > 0$ overhead. We show a more detailed computation in Section A.1.

- *Produces as output a list of at most $L(\lambda)$ messages, containing all $m \in \mathcal{M}$ for which $\mathcal{C}(m)_i \in S$ for all $i \in [n]$.*

We show that this aggregate size analysis and polynomial reconstruction algorithms implies the existence of recurrent list-recoverable codes with the desired parameters, resulting in the following theorem.

Theorem 1. *(Restatement of Theorem 6). For arbitrary constants $0 < \eta, \alpha < 1$ and $0 < \delta \leq \varepsilon < 1$, there exists a probabilistic constructible ensemble for codes*

$$\left\{\mathcal{C}_k : \mathbb{Z}_{q^2}^{k+1} \to \mathbb{Z}_q^{\eta q}\right\}$$

such that $\mathcal{C}_k$ is $(\alpha q, T^2)$-Recurrent List Recoverable with probability at least $1 - e^{-\omega(k \log k)}$, where $q = k \log^{1+\varepsilon+\frac{\delta}{2}} k$ and $T = O(k \log^{2\varepsilon - \frac{\delta}{2}} k)$.

Main Technical Milestone: Quasi-linear blocklength. As noted above, the (ordinary) list-recoverable codes constucted in [29] have block length $O(k^{1+\varepsilon})$, for $\varepsilon > 0$, in the number of input symbols k above. In contrast, in our theorem above, we achieve quasi-linear blocklength $\tilde{O}(k)$. This improvement is despite using a qualitatively *weaker* algebraic component (polynomial reconstruction) in our codes compared to the one used previously (Parvaresh-Vardy codes over extension fields). We discuss why this is possible in our technical overview below.

Composing this recurrent list-recoverable code with the Peikert-Shiehian correlation intractable hash function allows us to instantiate the Fiat-Shamir technique with the MPC-in-the-head technique.

Theorem 2. *(Restatement of Theorem 8). Assuming that $\mathsf{LWE}_{\frac{m}{2\log q}, m, q, \chi}$ holds for the particular parameter settings where χ is a B-bounded distribution for $B = q^{\Omega(1)}$, $q = \mathsf{poly}(k)$, k is the security parameter, and a MPC protocol with perfect αn-robustness and perfect, statistical, or computational security exists, where $\alpha \in (0, 1/2)$ is a constant and n is the size of the challenge set in the interactive protocol, there exists NIZKs with computational soundness for all of* NP *whose proof size is*

$$\mathcal{O}(|C| + q \cdot \mathrm{depth}(C)) + \mathsf{poly}(k)$$

where C is an arithmetic circuit for the NP *verification function and $q = k \log^{1+\epsilon} k$ for any $\epsilon > 0$.*

Bootstrapping. A NIZK with proof size $|w| + \mathsf{poly}(\lambda)$ for witness w and security parameter λ can be constructed using Fully Homomorphic Encryption [17] to bootstrap an underlying NIZK. Their construction uses this NIZK to prove that the fully homomorphic encryption key generation and evaluation is performed correctly by the Prover. Our construction provides an efficient base NIZK construction and can be used in conjunction with the construction of [17] to yield a more efficient form of this bootstrapping. Similarly, other (future) methods of bootstrapping for efficiency can potentially make use of our NIZK as a base construction.

1.1 Technical Overview

MPC-in-the-head. An MPC protocol [4,12,20,38] allows us to compute a q-party functionality (a function of their inputs) while maintaining privacy of the inputs and correctness of the output. In a n-private MPC protocol, any adversary that corrupts at most n players is unable to learn any information about the non-corrupted players' private inputs beyond that obtainable from learning the output of the function. Zero-knowledge protocols can be viewed as a special case of secure two-party computation, where the function verifies the validity of a witness held by the prover.

Modifying the IKOS protocol. Recall that we will be using the Fiat-Shamir paradigm (more on this below) to convert a public coin honest-verifier zero knowledge (HVZK) proof into a NIZK argument. All previous work studied using parallel repetition of a HVZK protocol. We aim to avoid this by starting with an HVZK protocol based on the MPC-in-the-head paradigm [30], as we explain next. The HVZK protocol we use slightly modifies the original protocol presented in [30] by asking the Prover to commit to a single copy of the transcript rather than commit to several (possibly overlapping) views. For any party the Verifier specifies to the Prover, the Prover opens up the relevant commitments in the transcript. The modification, not only simplifies the soundness proof, but ensures that each party's view can be independently verified rather than cross checking different party views for consistency of the views, as was the case in the original protocol. In this way, each party that the Verifier specifies constitutes an independently verifiable challenge. This property of independently verifiable challenges is necessary to cleanly define a single fixed bad challenge set S for the correlation-intractable hash function (the bad challenge space is $S \times S \times \ldots \times S$).

Let R_L be a relation corresponding to a NP language L. In other words, $R_L(x, w) = 1$ if and only if $x \in L$ and w is a witness for x. Define a functionality f_L such that $f_L(x, w_1, w_2, ..., w_q) = R_L(x, w_1 \oplus w_2 \oplus \cdots \oplus w_q)$. Thus, f_L can be viewed as a function computed by q parties where x is the public input and w_i is the private input for Player i. The HVZK protocol Π_{ZK} begins with the Prover carrying out all the steps of a q-party MPC protocol Π_{f_L} in her head. First, she secret shares w into $w_1, \ldots, w_q$ and executes the q-party MPC protocol to produce the protocol transcript of inputs, initial randomness, and messages sent. The Prover sends commitments to the transcript of the execution to the Verifier. Now the Verifier picks a random set S of $n < q$ parties, challenging the Prover to open the commitments to the private inputs, their randomness, and all messages sent or received by parties in S. The Verifier accepts if the openings form a consistent MPC protocol (that is, every message sent matches what the MPC's next message function would output given the previous messages received) and every party in the set S outputs 1.

The HVZK property follows from the privacy guarantee of the MPC. Assuming that the underlying MPC protocol Π_{f_L} is perfectly robust, violating the soundness requires a cheating prover to commit to many messages that are not consistent with the rest of the transcript and we show in Lemma 2 that such a cheating prover gets caught with overwhelming probability.

Fiat-Shamir Heuristic. We begin by reviewing the Fiat-Shamir Heuristic, a generic technique that compresses public-coin interactive arguments into non-interactive arguments in the CRS model. The Fiat-Shamir Heuristic is defined with respect to a public hash function family $\mathcal{H}$. Let us consider the following three-round interactive proof between a prover P and verifier V, in which P's goal is to convince V that $x \in \mathcal{L}$, for some language $\mathcal{L} \in \mathsf{NP}$:

1. P sends a first message α.
2. V responds with a uniform randomly chosen string β.
3. P finally sends a message γ to V.

Note that V accepts the proof (α, β, γ) if and only if $x \in \mathcal{L}$. In order to convert this to a non-interactive proof, the CRS consists of a randomly chosen hash function $h \leftarrow \mathcal{H}$. P computes $\beta = h(x, \alpha)$ and uses this compute γ. Finally, V can recompute β using the publicly known h and checks if the transcript $(x, \alpha, \beta, \gamma)$ is accepting.

This technique requires a careful analysis of soundness, because V no longer has the capability to generate uniformly random strings β. One way to ensure that the Fiat-Shamir transform is indeed sound is to instantiate the hash function with one that is *Correlation Intractable* (CI), which we now define.

Suppose $x \notin \mathcal{L}$. Let us define the set of "bad" βs as:

$$\mathsf{Bad}_\alpha = \{\beta \mid \exists \gamma \text{ such that } V(x, \alpha, \beta, \gamma) = 1\},$$

A CI hash requires that it is computationally infeasible for an efficient cheating prover to come up with an α such that $h(x, \alpha) \in \mathsf{Bad}_\alpha$ when given $h \leftarrow \mathcal{H}$ as input, where $\mathcal{H}$ is a Correlation Intractable hash family with respect to Bad_α. Formally, we say that $\mathcal{H}$ is a correlation intractable hash function family for Bad_α if for all PPT adversaries $\mathcal{A}$,

$$\Pr_{h \leftarrow \mathcal{H}}[h(x, \alpha) \in \mathsf{Bad}_\alpha \mid \mathcal{A}(h, x) = \alpha] \leq \mathsf{negl}(\lambda).$$

Peikert and Shiehian [34] constructed a CI hash family when $|\mathsf{Bad}_\alpha| = 1$ from the LWE assumption. In fact, Canetti et. al. [7] have shown that this construction can be extended to settings when $|\mathsf{Bad}_\alpha|$ is polynomially bounded.

Correlation Intractable Hash Functions from List Recoverable Codes. In their recent work, [29] propose a correlation intractable hash function family for any *three round public coin commit and open protocol.* The classical GMW protocol for 3-coloring with parallel repetition falls in the category of the protocols that [29] dealt with. To illustrate the techniques from [29], we briefly review them in the context of parallel repetition of the basic GMW protocol.

In the GMW protocol, the Prover who knows a 3-coloring of a graph G first commits to a randomly chosen permutation on the 3-coloring. The Verifier then randomly picks an edge of G and asks the Prover to open the vertex colors incident to that edge. If the colors differ, the Verifier accepts; otherwise, the verifier rejects. Repeating the interactive protocol in parallel achieves negligible soundness error while keeping the round complexity low. In any iteration of the interactive protocol there are at most $|E|-1$ edges which can allow the prover to cheat (referred to as the "bad" challenge set). We define S_i to be the bad challenge set in the ith iteration of the interactive protocol. In a parallel repetition of the protocol n times, these bad challenge sets form a product of sets $S_1 \times \cdots \times S_n$, where $\forall\, i \in [n], |S_i| \leq |E|-1$. For $G \notin$ 3-COL, a malicious Prover is able to convince the Verifier to accept if for all iterations $i \in [n]$ the challenge edges selected by the Verifier in the ith iteration belong to S_i. This product of sets defines a product relation $\mathcal{R} = S_1 \times \cdots \times S_n$.

The usefulness of CI hash families prior to the work of [29], such as those in [7,34], were limited to functions and polynomially bounded relations. Our relation $\mathcal{R}$ does not fall in this category as there may be exponentially many bad challenges on which an adversary can find the desired correlation. The work of [29] addresses this concern by constructing new correlation intractable hash functions for such product relations that are *efficiently verifiable* (defined in Sect. 6). In order to do so, they use *list recoverable codes* to construct another relation $\mathcal{R}'$ which is "efficiently enumerable" and therefore amenable to the techniques of [7,34].

To build this relation $\mathcal{R}'$, they use a derandomization approach based on list-recoverable error correcting codes. Informally, an error correcting code is a function $\mathcal{C} : \mathcal{M} \rightarrow \mathbb{Z}_q^n$. Here, n is called the block length of the code. We say that an error correcting code $\mathcal{C}$ is (ℓ, L)-list recoverable if for all sets $S_1, S_2, \ldots, S_n \subseteq \mathbb{Z}_q$ each of size at most ℓ, the number of messages v in $\mathcal{M}$ such that $\mathcal{C}(v) \in S_1 \times \cdots \times S_n$ is less than $L+1$. Moreover, there must exist an efficient algorithm $\mathsf{Recover}$ which extracts all such v. This notion was introduced in [26]. The parameters of the codes can be interpreted as follows in the context of the GMW protocol:

- The size of the alphabet q is the maximum size of the Verifier's challenge set, i.e. $q = |E|$.
- The input list size ℓ is $|E|-1$ which corresponds to the maximum size of a bad challenge set for a single execution of the GMW protocol.
- The block length n is the number of parallel repetitions.
- The output list size L must be polynomially bounded.

The new CI Hash function they construct is given by $\mathcal{H}' := \mathcal{C}(\mathcal{H}(\cdot))$ where $\mathcal{C}$ is the list recoverable error correcting code as defined above and $\mathcal{H}$ is the previous CI hash function from [34].

Our recurrent list-recoverable codes achieve a quasi-linear block size of $O(k \log^{1+\epsilon} k)$ for arbitrary $\epsilon > 0$. We emphasize that this block size is not known to be achievable by any previous framework.

Exploiting the MPC-in-the-head Product Relation. We first highlight the structure of the bad challenge set when using MPC-in-the-head to build a zero-knowledge protocol. Consider a cheating Prover that simulates a q-party MPC protocol and corrupts an α fraction of them in an attempt to fool the Verifier. The Prover commits to a transcript of the execution (denoted by com). The Verifier then specifies n parties to the Prover. The Prover must decommit to the corresponding commitments to inputs and the randomness of the specified parties as well as the messages incident (sent or received) to these parties. Let $S_{\mathsf{com}} \subseteq [q]$ be the set of the parties for which the messages sent are consistent with the input, the randomness, and the previous messages received and where the final output of the party is 1. The *bad* challenge set (equivalently the bad challenge relation) that convinces a Verifier to accept, denoted by $\mathcal{R}_{\mathsf{MPC}} \subseteq [q]^n$, is therefore seen to be the product $\underbrace{S_{\mathsf{com}} \times \cdots \times S_{\mathsf{com}}}_{n \text{ times}}$. Observe that this product relation is a specific product relation where each component is the same set S_{com}. The special structure of the bad challenge set in the MPC-in-the-head setting opens up a new avenue for us to exploit in order to construct a CI hash for $\mathcal{R}_{\mathsf{MPC}}$.

Revisiting Random Codes. A common technique in coding theory introduced by Forney in 1966 [16] is that of code concatenation. Code concatenation involves two codes, an inner code $\mathcal{C}_{in}$ and an outer code $\mathcal{C}_{out}$. The code concatenation encoding scheme first encodes a message m with the outer code $\mathcal{C}_{out}$ to produce $e = \mathcal{C}_{out}(m)$. Then it encodes each symbol in e with the inner code $\mathcal{C}_{in}$. We denote the resulting code as $\mathcal{C}_{out} \circ \mathcal{C}_{in}$[4].

This technique was used by [29] to obtain list-recoverable codes. In particular, their list-recoverable codes result from concatenating an inner code, given by a family of random codes, with an outer code, given by an algebraic code instantiated by the Parvaresh-Vardy code [33]. The inner code reduces the size of the lists to be fed as input to the outer code, achieving an overall smaller block length. The question before us is: Can we use the inner code to help us reduce the size of the lists to be fed as input to the outer code, thereby helping us achieve an overall block length that is smaller than the input list size to the outer code?

Suppose we have a random code $\mathcal{C}_{\mathsf{rand}} : \mathbb{Z}_Q \rightarrow \mathbb{Z}_q^m$, where the parameters Q, q, m are all polynomial in the security parameter. Then a list recovery algorithm is trivial to implement by enumerating every codeword and checking to see if the components of the codeword lie in the input lists. If one analyzes the list recoverability of such a code, one immediately encounters a fundamental barrier: If ℓ is the input list size to the list recovery algorithm, then the output list size must also sometimes be at least ℓ. This is simply because the input lists can correspond to the union of ℓ different codewords in $\mathcal{C}_{\mathsf{rand}}$. Indeed, the work of [29] analyzed the list recoverability of a single random code further to show

[4] The standard notation for code concatenation $\mathcal{C}_{out} \circ \mathcal{C}_{in}$ differs in two ways from the standard function composition notation in which $f \circ g(x) = f(g(x))$. Firstly, $\mathcal{C}_{out}$ is used first to encode the message m. Secondly, $\mathcal{C}_{in}$ is applied index-by-index to each symbol in the $\mathcal{C}_{out}(m)$.

that this worst case is close to tight, but as we noted above, their analysis is not good enough for us.

Can we exploit the fact that the inputs lists must all be equal, and equal to S_{com} in particular? Unfortunately the output list size of the random code must be at least ℓ/m, as the worst case S_{com} could be equal to the union of all the symbols found in ℓ/m codewords. This seems to present a fundamental barrier to us regarding the applicability of random codes as "inner" codes in concatenated codes, since the random code blows up the overall blocklength of the concatenated code by a factor of m, while only shrinking the list size by at most a factor of m. In other words, we seem to have made no progress.

Many random codes are better than one. The key insight behind our work is that while the barrier above applies to a *single* random code, a much different picture emerges if we consider the *sum* of the list sizes output by the recover algorithm of *many* random codes.

Indeed, suppose we have t completely independently chosen random codes $\mathcal{C}^{(i)}_{\mathsf{rand}} : \mathbb{Z}_Q \to \mathbb{Z}_q^m$ for $i \in [t]$. While it is true that for *each* code there exist input sets S_{com} that would lead to an output list of size ℓ/m, with overwhelming probability, these input sets would have tiny intersections because of the independence of the choice of each code. For $i \in [t]$, let L_i be the list obtained as output of the list recovery algorithm of $\mathcal{C}^{(i)}_{\mathsf{rand}}$ on input lists all equal to S_{com}. It is hopeless to get a better bound on $\max_i \{|L_i|\}$. So instead we aim to bound $\sum_i |L_i|$.

In our work, we give a new analysis of this quantity for t independently chosen random codes. We formulate a new variant of Chernoff's Bound (see Lemma 1), and use this to give our analysis in Theorem 5. This shows that with suitably chosen parameters, with overwhelming probability. for every input list S_{com}, $\sum_i |L_i|$ will be bounded by roughly $\tilde{O}(t + \ell/m)$. In other words, we get t output lists roughly for the "price" of a single output list!

Using Polynomial Reconstruction to leverage the aggregate list bound. Now that we have this bound, how can we take advantage of it to build a CI Hash function? We do so by departing from the language of list recoverability of error correcting codes, and instead adopting the more basic algebraic tool of polynomial reconstruction.

In the polynomial reconstruction problem, we are given as input a prime Q, a degree bound k, and n distinct pairs $\{(\alpha_i, y_i)\}_{i\in[n]}$ where each $\alpha_i, y_i \in \mathbb{Z}_Q$. The algorithm of Guruswami and Sudan [27] outputs a list of every polynomial f over $\mathbb{Z}_Q$ of degree at most k, such that $f(\alpha_i) = y_i$ for at least $\sqrt{kn}$ indices $i \in [n]$. Furthermore, this output list has size at most n^2. Combining polynomial reconstruction to leverage the aggregate list bound results in a recurrent list-recoverable code with the desired parameter settings.

The existence of this code and the Peikert-Shiehan correlation-intractable hash function gives rise to our final construction of a CI hash function as follows: Let $\mathcal{H}$ be the Peikert-Shiehan correlation-intractable hash and let α be the first message of the protocol (including the instance x being proven). Interpret $\mathcal{H}(\alpha)$ as coefficients for a degree k polynomial over field $\mathbb{Z}_Q$. Then use the evaluation map on this polynomial at t fixed distinct elements in $\mathbb{Z}_Q$ to yield the code $\mathcal{C}_{\mathsf{alg}} : \mathbb{Z}_Q^{k+1} \to \mathbb{Z}_Q^t$ to obtain t field elements in $\mathbb{Z}_Q$. We assume that we have already sampled t independent random codes $\mathcal{C}_{\mathsf{rand}}^{(i)} : \mathbb{Z}_Q \to \mathbb{Z}_q^m$ for $i \in [t]$ at setup time (this is part of the description of the hash function). Then we apply the ith random code $\mathcal{C}_{\mathsf{rand}}^{(i)}$ on the ith element of $\mathcal{C}_{\mathsf{alg}}(\mathcal{H}(\alpha))$. If $\mathscr{C}_{\mathsf{rand}} = \{\mathcal{C}_{\mathsf{rand}}^{(i)}\}_{i\in[t]}$, we denote this operation by $\mathcal{C}_k(\mathcal{H}(\alpha))$ where $C_k = (\mathcal{C}_{\mathsf{alg}} \circ \mathscr{C}_{\mathsf{rand}})$. This operation, $(\mathcal{C}_{\mathsf{alg}} \circ \mathscr{C}_{\mathsf{rand}})(\mathcal{H}(\cdot))$, defines our final construction of a CI hash function.

This construction indeed satisfies correlation-intractability by observing an efficient recovery algorithm for $(\mathcal{C}_{\mathsf{alg}} \circ \mathscr{C}_{\mathsf{rand}})(\mathcal{H}(\cdot))$. Namely a brute force enumeration of the codewords for the random codes in $\mathscr{C}_{\mathsf{rand}}$ gives an output list of size $\tilde{O}(t+\ell/m)$ that consists of pairs $\{(\alpha_i, y_i)\}_i$. Of these, at most t pairs can be consistent with a degree-k polynomial. The polynomial reconstruction algorithm of [27] will succeed as long as $t > \sqrt{k \cdot \tilde{O}(t+\ell/m)}$. This provides us with ample room to set parameters, and indeed we have significant freedom when choosing values of k, t, ℓ, m to make this work. Then the polynomial reconstruction algorithm outputs at most $\tilde{O}(t^2 + \ell^2/m^2)$ many polynomials. Therefore this efficient recovery algorithm produces a polynomial-size set so the Peikert-Shiehian CI hash function can now be applied, yielding a CI hash function for the MPC-in-the-head setting, achieving our goal. In the remainder of the paper, we show how to instantiate parameters precisely and provide all details regarding our analysis.

2 Preliminaries

2.1 Proof Systems

Zero Knowledge: We define the standard notion of zero knowledge as well known in prior work [21,23,30].

An NP Relation $R(x, w)$ is an efficiently decidable binary relation which can be viewed as a boolean function that outputs 0 or 1. Any NP relation defines a language $L = \{x : \exists w, R(x, w) = 1\}$. A zero knowledge proof consists of two PPT algorithms, namely, a prover P and verifier V. The prover is given access to instance x and witness w, whereas the verifier only has the instance w.

Definition 2 (Interactive Honest Verifier Zero Knowledge Proof). *The protocol (P, V) for a language L defined above consists of an interactive P and V with the following requirement:*

- *Completeness: If $x \in L$, and both P, V are honest, then V must always accept.*
- *Statistical Soundness: If $x \notin L$, then for any malicious and computationally unbounded prover P^*, V accepts with a negligible probability only.*

- *Zero Knowledge: If $x \in L$, then for any non-malicious PPT verifier V^*, there exists a PPT simulator* M *such that the view of V^* upon interaction with P is computationally indistinguishable from the output distribution of $M(x)$. Here, view of V^* consists of its input x, its random coins and all incoming messages.*

Definition 3 (Public Coin). *An interactive proof system is said to be public coin if for every $x \in \{0,1\}^n$, and some $l(n)$, the messages sent by an honest verifier V are i.i.d uniform $l(n)$ bit strings. Moreover, the final output of V must be efficiently computable in polynomial time given x and the transcript upon interaction with P.*

Definition 4 (Non-Interactive Zero Knowledge(NIZK) Arguments in the CRS model). *A non interactive zero knowledge argument for a language L in the Common Reference String (CRS) model is defined three PPT algorithms:*

- $\mathsf{Setup}(1^n, 1^\lambda)$ *outputs a uniform random string* crs *given a statement of length n and security parameter λ.*
- *Prover $P(\mathsf{crs}, x, w)$ outputs a proof π given a statement witness pair (x, w) in the NP relation R.*
- *Verifier $V(\mathsf{crs}, x, \pi)$ either accepts or rejects.*

The following properties must be satisfied:

- *Completeness: $V(\mathsf{crs}, x, \pi)$ must always accept if $x \in L$ and $\pi \leftarrow P(\mathsf{crs}, x, w)$.*
- *Computational Soundness: for every non-uniform* poly *time prover P^*, there exists a negligible function $\epsilon(\lambda)$ such that for any $n \in \mathbb{N}$ and $x \notin L$,*

$$\Pr[\mathsf{crs} \leftarrow \mathsf{Setup}(1^n, 1^\lambda), \pi^* \leftarrow P(\mathsf{crs}, x), V(\mathsf{crs}, x, \pi^*) \text{ accepts}] \leq \epsilon(\lambda).$$

- *Non Interactive Zero Knowledge: There exists a PPT simulator* M *such that for every $x \in L$ such that the distribution of the transcript output by* Setup *and P, i.e., $(\mathsf{crs}, P(\mathsf{crs}, x, w)) : \mathsf{crs} \leftarrow \mathsf{Setup}(1^n, 1^\lambda)$ is statistically indistinguishable from the output of $\mathsf{M}(x)$. Note that M is allowed to generate its own CRS.*

2.2 Cryptographic Assumptions and Commitment Schemes

Definition 5 (Decisional Learning with Errors Problem [36]). *Let $n \geq 1$ be a parameter for dimension, and let $q = q(n) \geq 2$ be a modulus. Let $m \geq 1$ be a parameter for number of samples. Let $\chi = \chi(n)$ be an error distribution over $\mathbb{Z}_q$. The decisional learning with errors problem $\mathsf{LWE}_{n,m,q,\chi}$ is to distinguish between the following two distributions:*

$$\left\{(A, As + e) \mid A \xleftarrow{\$} \mathbb{Z}_q^{m \times n}, s \xleftarrow{\$} \mathbb{Z}_q^n, e \xleftarrow{\$} \chi^m\right\}$$

and

$$\left\{(A, u) \mid A \xleftarrow{\$} \mathbb{Z}_q^{m \times n}, u \xleftarrow{\$} \mathbb{Z}_q^m\right\}$$

Definition 6 (Bounded Error Distributions). *Let $B = B(\lambda)$ such that $B(\lambda) \in \mathbb{N}$. We say that a family of distributions $\chi = \{\chi_\lambda\}_{\lambda\in\mathbb{N}}$ over the integers is B-bounded if for all $\lambda \in \mathbb{N}$,*

$$\Pr\left[x \leftarrow \chi_\lambda \mid |x| \leq B(\lambda)\right] = 1.$$

Definition 7 (Statistically Binding Commitment Scheme in the CRS model). *A Statistically binding commitment scheme in the CRS model is a pair of efficiently computable functions* $(\mathsf{Setup}, \mathsf{Com})$*, where,*

- $\mathsf{Setup}(1^\lambda)$ *outputs a common reference string* crs.
- $\mathsf{Com}(\mathsf{crs}, m; r)$ *takes as input* crs*, a message m to be commited, and uses randomness r to output a commitment* com.

They have the following security properties:

- ***Statistical Binding:*** *With high probability over the choice of* $\mathsf{crs} \leftarrow \mathsf{Setup}(1^\lambda)$*, there does not exists r_0, r_1, and messages $m_0 \neq m_1$ such that* $\mathsf{Com}(\mathsf{crs}, m_0; r_0) = \mathsf{Com}(\mathsf{crs}, m_1; r_1)$.
- ***Computational Hiding:*** *For messages $m_0 \neq m_1$, and randomness r_0, r_1 the distribution of* $(\mathsf{crs}, \mathsf{com}_0)$ *is computationally indistinguishable from* $(\mathsf{crs}, \mathsf{com}_1)$*. Here,* $\mathsf{crs} \leftarrow \mathsf{Setup}(1^\lambda), \mathsf{com}_0 \leftarrow \mathsf{Com}(\mathsf{crs}, m_0; r_0)$*, and* $\mathsf{com}_1 \leftarrow \mathsf{Com}(\mathsf{crs}, m_1; r_1)$.

Given a commitment com *and* crs*, a valid corresponding pair (m, r) is known as the* opening *for* com.

Remark 1. [Non-interactive Perfectly Binding Commitment Schemes from LWE-based PKEs] Any PKE with perfect decryption correctness gives a non-interactive commitment. As observed previously [32], this perfect decryption correctness implies perfect binding even though the committer is allowed to choose the public key maliciously. Since LWE with polynomial modulus-to-noise ratio under a bounded error distribution gives Regev encryption with perfect decryption error [2], it also gives non-interactive perfectly binding, computationally hiding non-interactive commitments.

2.3 Error Correcting Codes

Definition 8. *A q-ary* code *is a function $\mathcal{C} \colon \mathcal{M} \to \mathbb{Z}_q^n$, where n is called the* block length*, $\mathcal{M}$ is called the* message space*, and $\mathbb{Z}_q$ is called the* alphabet *of $\mathcal{C}$.*

Definition 9 (List-Recoverable Codes [25–27]). *An ensemble of codes $\{\mathcal{C}_\lambda \colon \mathcal{M}_\lambda \to \mathbb{Z}_{q_\lambda}^{n_\lambda}\}$ is said to be a* $(\ell(\cdot), L(\cdot))$-list recoverable *(for $\ell, L \colon \mathbb{Z}^+ \to \mathbb{Z}^+$) if there is a polynomial-time algorithm* $\mathsf{Recover}$ *that:*

- *Takes as input $\lambda \in \mathbb{Z}^+$ and explicit descriptions of "constraint" sets $S_1, \ldots, S_n \subseteq \mathbb{Z}_q^n$ with each $|S_i| \leq \ell(\lambda)$, and*
- *produces as output a list of at most $L(\lambda)$ messages, containing all $m \in \mathcal{M}$ for which $\mathcal{C}(m)_i \in S_i$ for all $i \in [n]$.*

Definition 10 (N-independent Concatenated Code). *Let* $\mathscr{C} = \left\{\mathcal{C}_1^{(2)}, \ldots, \mathcal{C}_N^{(2)}\right\}$ *be a collection of* N *codes where for* $i \in [N]$, $\mathcal{C}_i^{(2)} : \mathbb{Z}_Q \to \mathbb{Z}_q^m$. *Let* $\mathcal{C}^{(1)} : \mathcal{M} \to \mathbb{Z}_Q^N$ *be a code. The* N-independent concatenated code $\mathcal{C}^{(1)} \circ \mathscr{C} : \mathcal{M} \to \mathbb{Z}_q^{Nm}$ *is defined by*

$$(\mathcal{C}_1 \circ \mathscr{C})(x)_{(i-1)m+j} = \mathcal{C}_i^{(2)}\left(\left(\mathcal{C}^{(1)}(x)\right)_i\right)_j,$$

for all $x \in \mathcal{M}$, $i \in [N]$, *and* $j \in [m]$.

Definition 11 (Reed-Solomon codes [35]). *A Reed-Solomon code* $\mathcal{C}_\lambda$: $\mathbb{Z}_Q^{k+1} \to \mathbb{Z}_Q^t$ *is parameterized by a base field size* $q = q(\lambda)$, *a degree* $d = k(\lambda)$, *a block length* $t = t(\lambda)$, *and a set of values* $Q_\lambda = \{\alpha_1, \ldots, \alpha_t\}$. $\mathcal{C}_\lambda$ *takes as input a polynomial* p *of degree* k *over* $\mathbb{Z}_q$, *represented by its* $k+1$ *coefficients, and outputs the vector of evaluations* $(p(\alpha_1), \ldots, p(\alpha_t))$ *of* p *on each of the points* α_i.

We look into the problem of list recovery for Reed-Solomon Codes for our desired parameters. Note that as mentioned in Sect. 1.1, the primary challenge for us is to have list recoverability of Reed-Solomon with list sizes larger than what is standard in the error correcting codes world. We point out that the problem of list recovery for Reed-Solomon Codes boils down to the following notion of *polynomial reconstruction* due to Sudan's algorithm [37].

Polynomial Reconstruction

- **INPUT:** Integers k_p and n_p distinct pairs $\{(\alpha_i, y_i)\}_{i \in [n_p]}$, where $\alpha_i, y_i \in \mathbb{Z}_Q$.
- **OUTPUT:** A list of all polynomials $p(X) \in \mathbb{Z}_Q[X]$ of degree at most k_p which satisfy $p(\alpha_i) = y_i$, $\forall\, i \in [n_p]$.

This polynomial reconstruction can be performed efficiently by interpolation. We refer readers to Chap. 4 of [25] for a detailed analysis of the algorithm and how to use it for list recovery. In this work we use the following theorem from Guruswami and Sudan [27] as a black-box.

Definition 12 (Agreement Parameter). *For a Reed-Solomon Code* $\mathcal{C}_{\mathsf{alg}}$: $\mathbb{Z}_Q^{k+1} \to \mathbb{Z}_Q^t$, *the* L *many reconstructed polynomials* $\{p_j\}_{j \in [L]}$ *are said to have an agreement parameter* $t_A \leq t$ *if* $\forall j \in [L], p_j(\alpha_i) = y_i$ *for at least* t_A *many pairs* $(\alpha_i, y_i), i \in [t]$.

Note that $t_A = t$ *denotes the case of perfect polynomial reconstruction which is the setting of interest in this work.*

Theorem 3 (Efficient Polynomial Reconstruction of Reed-Solomon Codes).

The polynomial reconstruction problem with n_p *input pairs, degree* k_p, *and* agreement parameter t_A *can be solved in polynomial time as long as* t_A *is at least* $\sqrt{k_p \cdot n_p}$. *Furthermore, at most* n_p^2 *polynomials will be output by the algorithm.*

2.4 Correlation Intractable Hash Function Family and the Fiat-Shamir Transform

We present this section by following the same flavor as [29].

Definition 13 (Hash Family). *A hash family is a collection* $\mathcal{H} = \{h_\lambda : I_\lambda \times X_\lambda \to Y_\lambda\}_\lambda$ *of keyed hash functions such that* $\{I_\lambda\}$ *is uniformly* $\mathsf{poly}(\lambda)$*-time sampleable and* $\{h_\lambda\}$ *is uniformly* $\mathsf{poly}(\lambda)$*-time evaluable. We will also write* $\mathcal{H}_\lambda$ *to denote the distribution on functions* $h_\lambda(i, \cdot)$ *obtained by sampling* $i \in I_\lambda$*.*

Definition 14 (Correlation-Intractability [10]). *For a hash family* $\mathcal{H} = \{h_\lambda : I_\lambda \times X_\lambda \to Y_\lambda\}_\lambda$ *and a relation ensemble* $R = \{R_\lambda \subseteq X_\lambda \times Y_\lambda\}$*, the correlation intractability game is the following game, played by any adversary* $\mathcal{A}$ *against a fixed challenger* $\mathcal{C}$*:*

1. *On input* 1^λ*,* $\mathcal{C}$ *samples* $i \in I_\lambda$ *and sends* i *to* $\mathcal{A}$*.*
2. $\mathcal{A}$ *sends* $x \in X_\lambda$ *to* $\mathcal{C}$*, and wins the game if* $(x, h_\lambda(i, x)) \in R_\lambda$*.*

We say that $\mathcal{H}$ *is correlation intractable for* R *if every nonuniform poly-time* $\mathcal{A}$ *wins the correlation-intractability game only with probability negligible in the security parameter* λ*.*

Definition 15. *Let* Π *be a public coin interactive protocol where the messages exchanged between* P *and* V *are denoted by* $(\alpha_1, \beta_1, \ldots, \alpha_r, \beta_r)$ *for* r *rounds of interaction. Here* α_i *and* β_i *denote messages sent by* P *and* V *respectively. If the verifier's messages are* l *bits long, then for a hash function family* $\mathcal{H} : \{0,1\}^* \to \{0,1\}^l$*, we define* $FS_{\mathcal{H}}[\Pi]$ *to be the non interactive protocol by sampling a common reference string* $h \leftarrow \mathcal{H}$ *and computing the message* β_i *if* V *as* $h(x, \alpha_1, \beta_1, \ldots, \alpha_i)$*. The verifier for* $FS_{\mathcal{H}}(\Pi)$ *accepts iff the verifier for the interactive protocol accepts and all* β_i *are correctly computed.*

Definition 16 (*FS* Compatible). *We say that a hash function family* $\mathcal{H}$ *is* FS*- compatible for an interactive proof* Π *for language* L *if the non interactive protocol* $FS_{\mathcal{H}(\Pi)}$ *defined above is a non interactive argument.*

2.5 Secure Multiparty Computation (MPC)

We define the standard notion of a Multiparty Computation along with some of the necessary properties of a MPC protocol necessary in our work. All the definitions are standard in literature [6,19,30].

Definition 17 (q-Party Protocol). *Let* $P_1, \ldots, P_q$ *be* q *parties, and let each* P_i *each have a shared public input* x*, a private input* w_i*, and private randomness* r_i*. Let* $m_j^{(i)}$ *be the messages received by party* P_i *in the* j^{th} *round. We specify a q-party protocol by its next message function* NEXT *which on input* $(1^\lambda, i, x, w_i, r_i, (m_1^{(i)}, \ldots, m_j^{(i)}))$ *where* λ *is the security parameter, outputs all messages sent or output by* P_i *in round* $j + 1$ *given inputs* x, w_i, r_i *and round messages* $(m_1^{(i)}, \ldots, m_j^{(i)})$*.*

Definition 18 (View of a Party). *The view V_i of a party P_i during protocol Π contains common input x, private input w_i, randomness r_i, its received messages $\{m_j^{(i)}\}$, and all messages sent or output by P_i.*

Definition 19 (Transcript of an Execution). *The transcript Ξ of an execution of a q-party protocol Π is a set containing the public input, every party's randomness r_i, every party's private input w_i, every message sent in each round.*

Definition 20 (Correctness). *Let f be a deterministic functionality that on inputs $(x, w_1, \ldots, w_q)$ outputs $(f(x, w_1, \ldots, w_q))_{i \in q}$. We say that a q-party protocol Π_f realizes f with perfect (respectively statistical) correctness if for all inputs $(x, w_1, \ldots, w_q)$, the probability that there exists an $i \in [q]$ such that the output of party P_i is not equal to $f(x, w_1, \ldots, w_q)$ is 0 (respectively $\mathsf{negl}(\lambda)$).*

Definition 21 (n-Privacy). *Let $1 \le n < q$. We say that Π_f realizes f with perfect (respectively statistical) n-privacy if there is a PPT simulator Sim such that for all inputs $x, w_1, \ldots, w_q$ and every set of corrupted players $T \subseteq [q]$ where $|T| \le n$, the joint views $\{V_i\}_{i \in T}$ of players in T is distributed identically (respectively statistically close) to $\mathsf{Sim}(T, x, (w_i)_{i \in T}, (f_i(x, w_1, \ldots, w_q))_{i \in T})$.*

Definition 22 (n-Robustness (imported from [30]). *We say that Π_f realizes f with perfect (resp., statistical) n-robustness if it is perfectly (resp., statistically) correct in the presence of a semi-honest adversary as in Definition 20, and furthermore for any computationally unbounded malicious adversary corrupting a set T of at most n players, and for any inputs $(x, w_1, \ldots, w_q)$, the following robustness property holds. If there is no $(w_1', \ldots, w_q')$ such that $f(x, w_1', \ldots, w_q') = 1$, then the probability that some uncorrupted player outputs 1 in an execution of Π_f in which the inputs of the honest players are consistent with $(x, w_1, \ldots, w_n)$ is 0 (resp., is negligible in λ).*

Efficiently Instantiable Perfectly Robust MPC Protocol

Remark 2. Several previous works give perfectly robust communication-efficient MPC protocols [3,14,24].

Theorem 4 (Theorem 7 from [24]). *In the client-server model, let c denote the number of clients, and $n = 2s + 1$ denote the number of parties (servers). Let k be the security parameter and let $\mathbb{F}$ denote a finite field. For an arithmetic circuit C over $\mathbb{F}$ and for all $1 \le o \le s$, there exists an information-theoretic MPC protocol which securely computes the arithmetic circuit C in the presence of a semi-honest adversary controlling up to c clients and $s - o + 1$ parties. The communication complexity of this protocol is $\mathcal{O}(|C| \cdot n/k + n \cdot (c + \text{depth}(C)) + n^5 \cdot k)$ elements in $\mathbb{F}$.*

Remark 3. The client-server generalizes the standard MPC model of parties. To translate this communication complexity into the standard MPC model, every party has a single client and single server so if there are q parties there are q clients and q servers. Choose $o = s$, then in the standard MPC model, the communication complexity is given by,

$$\mathcal{O}(|C| + q \cdot \text{depth}(C)) + \mathsf{poly}(k).$$

where $o, k, |C|$ are as defined in the previous theorem.

Remark 4. The protocol defined above was proved to have perfect security in the Universal Composability (UC) Model [6].

3 A Chernoff Bound

In our work, we will analyze the sum of n Bernoulli random variables X_i where the probability p that $X_i = 1$ is much smaller than $1/n$. We derive a "custom" Chernoff bound that is useful for this case:

Lemma 1 (Chernoff for Bernoulli distributions $\mathsf{Ber}(p)$ with small p). *For $i \in [n]$ let $X_i \sim \mathsf{Ber}(p)$ be independent identically distributed Bernoulli random variables for $p = p(n) \in (0, 1]$. Let $X \triangleq \sum_{i=1}^{n} X_i$. Then for $t \geq 0$, we have:*

$$\Pr[X - np \geq t] \leq \left(\frac{1}{e} + \frac{t}{enp}\right)^{-t}$$

Proof. Let $\tau = np + t$. For tidiness, we use the notation $\exp(a)$ to denote e^a for any $a \in \mathbb{R}$. For all $\lambda \geq 0$, by Markov's inequality,

$$\begin{aligned}\Pr[X \geq \tau] &\leq \frac{\mathbb{E}\left[e^{\lambda X}\right]}{e^{\lambda\tau}} \\ &= \frac{\left(pe^{\lambda} + (1-p)\right)^n}{e^{\lambda\tau}} \\ &= \frac{\left(1 + p\left(e^{\lambda} - 1\right)\right)^n}{e^{\lambda\tau}} \\ &\leq \frac{\exp\left(np(e^{\lambda} - 1)\right)}{\exp(\lambda\tau)} \\ &= \exp\left(np\left(e^{\lambda} - 1\right) - \lambda(np + t)\right).\end{aligned}$$

Minimizing for $\lambda \geq 0$, we choose $\lambda = \ln(1 + t/np)$. Plugging in for λ gives,

$$\begin{aligned}\exp\left(np\left(e^{\lambda} - 1\right) - \lambda(np + t)\right) = e^t\left(1 + \frac{t}{np}\right)^{-(t+np)} &\leq e^t\left(1 + \frac{t}{np}\right)^{-t} \\ &= \left(\frac{1}{e} + \frac{t}{enp}\right)^{-t}.\end{aligned}$$

This immediately yields:

Corollary 1. *For $i \in [n]$ let $X_i \sim \mathsf{Ber}(p)$ be independent identically distributed Bernoulli random variables for $p = p(n) \in (0, 1]$. Let $X \triangleq \sum_{i=1}^{n} X_i$. Then for $t > enp$,*

$$\Pr[X - np \geq t] \leq \left(\frac{t}{enp}\right)^{-t}.$$

4 Recurrent List Recoverable Error Correcting Codes

We present a new notion of *Recurrent List Recoverable* error correcting codes by N-independent concatenating Reed Solomon with random codes. This is a special case of general list recoverability of concatenated codes which we shall formally define later in the section. First, we introduce *Aggregate List Recovery* for Random Codes where a collection of independent random codes have identical constraint sets which are input to their corresponding Recover algorithm.

4.1 Aggregate List Recoverability of Random Codes

Definition 23 (Aggregate List Recoverability). *Given a collection of t independent codes $\{C_j : \mathbb{Z}_Q \to \mathbb{Z}_q^n\}_{j=1}^{t}$, we say that they are (t, ℓ, T)-aggregate list recoverable if the constraint sets $S_{j1}, \ldots, S_{jn}$ that the* Recover *algorithm corresponding to the jth code takes as input are such that $\forall i\ \forall j, S_{ji} = S$ and $|S| \leq \ell$. Furthermore the output list for* Recover *of the jth code is of size L_j, where $\sum_{j \in [t]} L_j \leq T$.*

Theorem 5 (Aggregate List Recoverability of t independent random codes). *Let $\{\mathcal{C}_{\mathsf{rand},i} \colon \mathbb{Z}_Q \to \mathbb{Z}_q^m\}_{i \in [t]}$ be a collection of t independent random codes, and assume that there exist $\varepsilon, \delta, \alpha, T$ such that the following hold,*

- $q = k \log^{1+\varepsilon+\frac{\delta}{2}} k$, $\varepsilon > \delta > 0$,
- $t = k \log^{\varepsilon} k$
- $Q = q^2$,
- $l = \alpha q$, *for some constant* $\alpha \in (0, 1)$
- $T \leq \frac{1}{k^2 \log^{2+2\varepsilon+\delta} k} + k \log^{2\varepsilon - \frac{\delta}{2}} k$, *and*
- $\alpha^m \leq \frac{1}{q^4 t}$,

then t of such independent random codes are (t, l, T)-aggregate list recoverable with probability at least $1 - e^{-\omega(k \log k)}$.

Proof. Given a function $\mathcal{C}_{\mathsf{rand},i} \colon \mathbb{Z}_Q \to \mathbb{Z}_q^m$, let $S \subseteq \mathbb{Z}_q$ be a subset of size l. Let $X_{i,x}$ be an indicator variable such that,

$$X_{i,x} = \begin{cases} 1 & \text{if } (\mathcal{C}_{\mathsf{rand},i}(x))_j \in S, \forall, j \in [m], \\ 0 & \text{otherwise} \end{cases}$$

Thus, $T = \sum_{i,x} X_{i,x}$. Now, $\Pr[X_{i,x} = 1] = \frac{|S|}{q} = \alpha^m$, where the probability is taken over the choice of the set S. Thus, $E[T] = Qt\alpha^m$.

A direct application of Corollary 1 immediately gives an upper bound on the size of T. We have,

$$\Pr[T - Qt\alpha^m \geq k_0] \leq \left(\frac{k_0}{eQt\alpha^m}\right)^{-k_0}.$$

Plugging in Q, α^m, t, k_0 as $q^2, \frac{1}{q^4 t}, k\log^{\epsilon} k, k\log^{2\epsilon - \frac{\delta}{2}} k$ respectively, we get,

$$\begin{aligned}\Pr[T \geq \frac{1}{k^2 \log^{2+2\varepsilon+\delta} k} + k\log^{2\varepsilon-\frac{\delta}{2}} k] &\leq \left(\frac{q^2 k_0}{e}\right)^{-k\log^{2\varepsilon-\frac{\delta}{2}} k} \\ &\leq \left(\frac{k^3 \log^{2+4\varepsilon+\frac{\delta}{2}} k}{e}\right)^{-k\log^{2\varepsilon-\frac{\delta}{2}} k}.\end{aligned}$$

Taking a union bound over all choices of S, the probability that there exists a set S for which the size of T is greater than $\frac{1}{k^2 \log^{2+2\varepsilon+\delta} k} + k\log^{2\varepsilon-\frac{\delta}{2}} k$ is upper bounded by,

$$\begin{aligned}&\binom{q}{\alpha q}\left(\frac{k^3 \log^{2+4\varepsilon+\frac{\delta}{2}} k}{e}\right)^{-k\log^{2\varepsilon-\frac{\delta}{2}} k} \\ &\leq \left(\frac{e}{\alpha}\right)^{\alpha q}\left(\frac{k^3 \log^{2+4\varepsilon+\frac{\delta}{2}} k}{e}\right)^{-k\log^{2\varepsilon-\frac{\delta}{2}} k} \\ &= \frac{\exp\{\alpha q - \alpha q \ln\alpha + k\log^{2\varepsilon-\frac{\delta}{2}} k\}}{\left(k^3 \log^{2+4\varepsilon+\frac{\delta}{2}} k\right)^{k\log^{2\varepsilon-\frac{\delta}{2}} k}} \\ &= \frac{\exp\{\alpha' q + k\log^{2\varepsilon-\frac{\delta}{2}} k\}}{\left(k^3 \log^{2+4\varepsilon+\frac{\delta}{2}} k\right)^{k\log^{2\varepsilon-\frac{\delta}{2}} k}} \qquad \text{where, } \alpha' = \alpha(1-\ln\alpha) \\ &= \exp\left\{\alpha' k\log^{1+\varepsilon+\frac{\delta}{2}} k + \tilde{k} - \tilde{k}\ln\tilde{k} - \tilde{k}\ln\left(k^2 \log^{2+2\varepsilon+\delta} k\right)\right\} \\ &\qquad\qquad \text{where, } \tilde{k} = k\log^{2\epsilon-\frac{\delta}{2}} k \\ &= \exp\left\{\tilde{k}\left(\alpha' \log^{1-\varepsilon+\delta} k + 1 - \ln\tilde{k} - \ln\left(k^2 \log^{2+2\varepsilon+\delta} k\right)\right)\right\} \\ &= \exp\left\{\tilde{k}\left(\alpha' \log^{1-\varepsilon+\delta} k + 1 - 3\ln k - \ln\left(\log^{4\varepsilon+2+\frac{\delta}{2}} k\right)\right)\right\} \\ &= \exp\left\{\tilde{k}\left(-\omega(\log k)\right)\right\} \\ &= \exp\left\{-\omega\left(k\log k\right)\right\}\end{aligned}$$

Thus, the probability that $C_{\mathsf{rand},i}$ are $(\alpha q, L_i)$-list recoverable such that $\sum_i L_i \leq \frac{1}{k^2 \log^{2+2\varepsilon+\delta} k} + k \log^{2\varepsilon - \frac{\delta}{2}} k$ is at least $1 - e^{-\omega(k \log k)}$.

4.2 Recurrent List Recoverability

We first define recurrent list-recoverability as a special case of list-recoverability where the sets are identical, $S_1 = \ldots = S_n$.

Definition 24 (Recurrent List-Recoverable Codes). *An ensemble of codes* $\{C_\lambda \colon \mathcal{M}_\lambda \to \mathbb{Z}_{q_\lambda}^{n_\lambda}\}$ *is said to be a* $(\ell(\cdot), L(\cdot))$-recurrent list recoverable *(for* $\ell, L \colon \mathbb{Z}^+ \to \mathbb{Z}^+$*) if there is a polynomial-time algorithm* Recover *that:*

- *Takes as input* $\lambda \in \mathbb{Z}^+$ *and explicit descriptions of "constraint" sets* $S \subseteq \mathbb{Z}_q^n$ *where* $|S| \leq \ell(\lambda)$.
- *Produces as output a list of at most* $L(\lambda)$ *messages, containing all* $m \in \mathcal{M}$ *for which* $C(m)_i \in S$ *for all* $i \in [n]$.

Theorem 6. *For arbitrary constants* $0 < \eta, \alpha < 1$ *and* $0 < \delta \leq \varepsilon < 1$*, there exists a probabilistic constructible ensemble for codes*

$$\left\{C_k : \mathbb{Z}_{q^2}^{k+1} \to \mathbb{Z}_q^{\eta q}\right\}$$

such that C_k *is* $(\alpha q, T^2)$*-Recurrent List Recoverable with probability at least* $1 - e^{-\omega(k \log k)}$*, where* $q = k \log^{1+\varepsilon+\frac{\delta}{2}} k$ *and* $T = O(k \log^{2\varepsilon - \frac{\delta}{2}} k)$

Proof. Let $\mathscr{C}$ be a collection of t independent random codes $\{C_{\mathsf{rand},i} \colon \mathbb{Z}_Q \to \mathbb{Z}_q^m\}_{i \in [t]}$ with $t = k \log^\varepsilon k$, $Q = q^2$ and m such that $\alpha^m \leq \frac{1}{q^4 t}$. Then, Theorem 5 tells us that with parameters set as above, the collection $\mathscr{C}$ is $(t, \alpha q, T)$- aggregate list recoverable with probability at least $1 - e^{-\omega(k \log k)}$, for $T \leq \frac{1}{k^2 \log^{2+2\varepsilon+\delta} k} + k \log^{2\varepsilon - \frac{\delta}{2}} k$.

Let $C_{\mathsf{alg},k} : \mathbb{Z}_Q^{k+1} \to \mathbb{Z}_Q^t$ be a Reed Solomon Code. Theorem 3 tells us that if $C_{\mathsf{alg},k}$ is a Reed Solomon Code, then $O(k^2 \log^{4\varepsilon - \delta} k)$ polynomials can be recovered by polynomial reconstruction as long as $t \geq \sqrt{k \cdot T}$, where T is the total number of input pairs. Choose $T = O(k \log^{2\epsilon - \frac{\delta}{2}} k)$ and $t = k \log^\varepsilon k$,then the necessary condition is satisfied. Thus, we can feed this list T to the polynomial reconstruction algorithm of $C_{\mathsf{alg},k}$.

Combining these two results and our choice of parameters which satisfy the list recoverability constraint for Reed-Solomon in Theorem 3, we get that polynomial reconstruction outputs a list Lst of size $O(k^2 \log^{4\varepsilon - \delta} k)$. Moreover, our choice of parameter ensures that there exists a constant $0 < \eta < 1$ such that $mt = \frac{2k \log^{1+\epsilon} k + 23k \log k \log \log k}{\log \frac{1}{\alpha}} \leq \eta k \log^{1+\epsilon} k$.

Thus, our code ensemble C_k can be constructed by an t-independent concatenation of $C_{\mathsf{alg},k}$ with $\mathscr{C}$, i.e., $C_k = C_{\mathsf{alg},k} \circ \mathscr{C}$. To elaborate further, according to Definition 10, we first apply $C_{\mathsf{alg},k}$ on a message $m \in \mathbb{Z}_{q^2}^{k+1}$. This produces $C_{\mathsf{alg},k}(m) := (m'_1, \ldots, m'_t) \in \mathbb{Z}_Q^t$. The final code output is then $C_k = C_{\mathsf{alg},k} \circ \mathscr{C}(m) := (C_{\mathsf{rand},i}(m'_1), \ldots, C_{\mathsf{rand},t}(m'_t))$.

5 Zero Knowledge from Secure Computation

Definition 25 (Functionality f_L). *For a language $L \in \mathsf{NP}$ and its corresponding relation R_L, let f_L be the functionality for q players $P_1, \ldots, P_q$. Given a public input x and q shares of the witness $w_1, \ldots, w_q$ received from the Prover, the functionality delivers to all players* 1 *if $(x, w) \in R_L$ and* 0 *otherwise.*

Following [30], we slightly modify their zero knowledge protocol which makes "black box" use of an MPC protocol Π_{f_L}. This means that the zero knowledge protocol simply implements the next message function for each party without looking into the details of the circuits that describe these functions. The next message function NEXT is used by the prover and verifier to interact. NEXT determines the next message to be sent based on the inputs and messages received so far. In particular, we commit to a single transcript of the entire protocol rather than committing to views of a party. We also note that Protocol 1 achieves only honest-verifier zero knowledge. Although, the scheme can be extended to obtain a standard zero knowledge proof, it leads to an increase in the number of rounds (cf. Theorem 4.4 in [30]). Hence, we stick to honest-verifier zero knowledge which suffices for the purpose of producing a NIZK argument.

Protocol 1 (Honest Verifier Zero Knowledge Interactive Protocol Π_{HVZK})

1. *Prover picks at random $w_1, \ldots, w_q$ whose exclusive-or equals the witness w. She simulates the execution of the MPC protocol Π_{f_L} on input $(x, w_1, \ldots, w_q)$. The prover then computes the transcript Ξ at the end and commits to each element of Ξ using a* statistically binding commitment scheme $\mathsf{Com}_{\mathsf{SB}}$. *Finally, she sends the commitments to the Verifier. Such a commitment scheme can be instantiated from Remark 1*
2. *Verifier sends to Prover a challenge set of indices $S_{\mathsf{Ch}} \triangleq \{i_1, \ldots, i_\beta\}$.*
3. *Prover opens all commitments to private inputs w_i, and all messages sent or received by players indexed by $i \in S_{\mathsf{Ch}}$ in Ξ.*
4. *Given the public values x, the Verifier accepts if and only if the Prover successfully opens all the requested commitments, all sent messages are consistent with the application of the next-message function* NEXT *on the appropriate set of received messages, and the output of all parties (computed deterministically by the received messages and their inputs) is* 1.

Fig. 1. HVZK Interactive Protocol using MPC.

Completeness and Honest Verifier Zero Knowledge. The correctness property follow directly from an identical argument to that in [30]. However, we present a sketch here for the sake of completeness. If $(x, w) \in R_L$ and the prover is honest and $w_1 \oplus \ldots \oplus w_q = w$, then the perfect correctness of Π_{f_L} implies that all the messages which were a part of the transcript Ξ will always be consistent with the application of the next-message function NEXT, and the outputs of each party must be 1. This implies correctness.

Let x belong to the language L, i.e., the functionality f_L outputs 1. For Honest Verifier Zero Knowledge, we construct a simulator M that simulates the view of an honest verifier as follows: M samples a challenge set of cardinality β of indices chosen uniformly at random among q parties. Let the set be $S'_{\mathsf{Ch}} \triangleq \{i_1, \ldots, i_\beta\}$. Sim simulates the MPC protocol Π_{f_L} in its head using the parties with indices in S'_{Ch}. Hence, M picks strings $w'_1, \ldots, w'_\beta$ uniformly at random and simulates an execution of Π_{f_L} on input $x, w'_1, \ldots, w'_\beta$ by invoking the MPC simulator Sim on input $(S'_{\mathsf{Ch}}, x, (w'_i)_{i \in S'_{\mathsf{Ch}}}, 1)$. Sim outputs a transcript Ξ'. Recall that the transcript Ξ' consists of the public input, every party's randomness, every party's private input, and every message sent in each round. Along with a commitment to the public input, for all $i \in S'_{\mathsf{Ch}}$, M commits to the ith party's input, randomness, private input, and messages sent and received in Ξ'. Let $\mathsf{com}(S'_{\mathsf{Ch}})$ be defined to be the tuple of commitments listed in the previous sentence. For the remaining values in the transcript Ξ', M commits to 0. M sends all commitments, S'_{Ch}, and openings to all commitments in $\mathsf{com}(S'_{\mathsf{Ch}})$. The opened values of the transcript generated by Sim has an identical (statistically-close) distribution to the view of an *Honest*-Verifier due to the perfect (statistical) t-privacy of Π_{f_L}. Moreover, the hiding property of the commitment scheme implies that the Verifier cannot distinguish between the unopened commitments of 0 from commitments to values in transcript Ξ'.

Lemma 2 (Statistical Soundness). *Let $L \in \mathsf{NP}$ be a language. Let $\mathsf{Com}_{\mathsf{SB}}$ be a statistically-binding commitment scheme. Suppose that protocol Π_{f_L} realizes the q-party functionality f_L with perfect β-robustness (in the malicious model), and perfect, statistical or computational β-privacy (in the honest-but-curious model) for $\beta < \lceil q/2 - 1 \rceil$, then the soundness error in ZK protocol Π_{HVZK} is given by $\mathsf{negl}(q)$.*

Proof. Suppose $x \notin L$ so that there does not exist w such that $(x, w) \in R_L$ for relation R_L on NP language L.

If the Prover commits to inputs, randomness, and messages from an honest execution of Π_{f_L}, all parties output 0 and the Verifier will reject for any choice of S_{Ch}.

Otherwise, there exists a message $m_i^{(j)}$ in Ξ that is not consistent with the previous received messages and the next-message function NEXT. For any party P_i who sends an inconsistent message, we say that P_i is a "corrupted" party. There are two cases to consider: If malicious prover P^* corrupts at most β parties and if P^* corrupts strictly more than β parties. For a fixed execution of Π_{f_L} and its corresponding commitments made by malicious Prover P^*, we let B be the set of the indices of all corrupted parties.

In the first case, the β-perfect robustness property guarantees that for all indices $i \notin B$, the output of P_i is 0. If the Verifier chooses any index $i \notin B$, then the Verifier will observe the output of P_i is 0 and the Verifier will catch the Prover cheating. Therefore, with probability at least $1 - 1/\binom{q}{\beta}$, the Verifier will choose a set of indices of size β that is not contained in set B (if $|B| < \beta$ then the probability that Verifier catches the prover is 1).

In the second case, the Prover has chosen strictly more than β parties to corrupt. Here, we argue that the Verifier will ask for the commitment openings to a corrupted party with overwhelming probability. Suppose the Prover has chosen as little as $\beta+1$ many corrupted parties. The probability that the Verifier chooses a subset of size β that does not contain any of these corrupted parties is given by

$$\begin{aligned}\frac{\binom{q-\beta-1}{\beta}}{\binom{q}{\beta}} &= \prod_{i=0}^{\beta} \frac{q-\beta-i}{q-i} \\ &= \prod_{i=0}^{\beta} \left(1 - \frac{\beta}{q-i}\right) \\ &\leq \prod_{i=0}^{\beta} e^{-\beta/(q-i)} \\ &\leq \left(e^{-\beta/(q-\beta)}\right)^{\beta+1}\end{aligned}$$

where we apply the inequality $1 - x \leq e^{-x}$ for all real x. Then observe that by our assumption $\beta = \alpha q$ for some constant $\alpha < 1$, so

$$\left(e^{-\beta/(q-\beta)}\right)^{\beta+1} \leq e^{-c^2 q - c}.$$

Observe this probability forms an upper bound for the probability the Verifier is fooled for when the Prover chooses *at least* $\beta + 1$ many corrupted parties. Formally, for all $i \geq 1$,

$$\binom{q-\beta-i}{\beta} \leq \binom{q-\beta-1}{\beta}.$$

Therefore the probability that the Verifier fails to catch the Prover in this setting is negligible in q and therefore negligible in security parameter λ.

Finally, by a union bound the soundness error is then $e^{-c^2 q - c} + 1/\binom{q}{\beta} = \mathsf{negl}(q)$.

6 Instantiating Fiat-Shamir via Correlation Intractable Hash Functions

We first reintroduce the notions of Efficient Product Verifiability and Product Sparsity from [29].

Definition 26 (Product Relation). *A relation $R \subset \mathcal{X} \times \mathcal{Y}^t$ is a product relation, if for any x, the set $R_x = \{y \mid (x, y) \in R\}$ is the Cartesian product of several sets $S_{1,x}, S_{2,x}, \ldots, S_{t,x}$,*

$$R_x = S_{1,x} \times S_{2,x} \times \ldots \times S_{t,x}.$$

Definition 27 (Efficient Product Verifiability, Definition 3.3). *A relation R is efficiently product verifiable, if there exists a polynomial-sized circuit C such that, for any x, the sets $S_{1,x}, S_{2,x}, \ldots, S_{t,x}$ (in Definition 26) satisfy for any $i, y_i \in S_{i,x}$ if and only if $C(x, y_i, i) = 1$.*

Definition 28 (Product Sparsity, Definition 3.4). *A relation $R \subseteq \mathcal{X} \times \mathcal{Y}^t$ has sparsity ρ, if for any x, the sets $S_{1,x}, S_{2,x}, \ldots, S_{t,x}$ (in Definition 26) satisfies $|S_{i,x}| \leq \rho|\mathcal{Y}|$.*

Definition 29 (Bad Challenge Set). *For Protocol 1, let* com *be a string containing all commitments the prover sends to the verifier and let V_i denote the view of P_i formed by taking the appropriate subset of decommitments to* com. *We say that V_i is consistent if there exists an honest execution of the the q-party Protocol Π_f with P_i's inputs, randomness, and messages sent and received. Then we have the following set of bad challenges*

$$\mathcal{B} = S_{\mathsf{com}}^{|I|} = \underbrace{S_{\mathsf{com}} \times S_{\mathsf{com}} \times \cdots \times S_{\mathsf{com}}}_{|I| \ times}$$

where $S_{\mathsf{com}} = \{i \mid V_i \text{ is consistent}\}$.

Remark 5. The set S_{com} is efficiently verifiable by the MPC next message function. Also, $|S_{\mathsf{com}}| \leq \alpha q$, for some tiny constant $\alpha \in \{0, 1\}$. Here q is the number of parties involved in the MPC-in-the-Head protocol so the size of the *Bad Challenge Set* is the maximum number of parties in the MPC protocol that can be corrupted.

6.1 Construction of CIH Family

Lemma 3 (CIH for Efficient Enumerable Relations [7,34]**).** *Assuming that $\mathsf{LWE}_{\frac{m}{2\log q}, m, q, \chi}$ holds for the particular parameter settings where χ is a B-bounded distribution for $B = q^{\Omega(1)}$, $q = \mathsf{poly}(m)$. Then, for every triplet of polynomials $T = T(\lambda), n = n(\lambda), m = m(\lambda)$, there exists a hash function family $\mathcal{H} : \{0,1\}^n \rightarrow \{0,1\}^{m \log q}$ that is correlation-intractable for relation that is enumerable in time T.*

Lemma 4 ([29]**).** *Let $R \subseteq \times\mathcal{X} \times \mathbb{Z}_q^n$ be an efficiently verifiable product relation with sparsity α. Moreover, let $C : \mathcal{M} \rightarrow \mathbb{Z}_q^n$ be a code that is $(\alpha q, L)$ list recoverable and $\mathcal{H}$ be a hash function family that is correlation intractable for all efficiently enumerable relations $R' \subseteq \mathcal{X} \times \mathcal{M}$, then $C \circ \mathcal{H}$ is correlation intractable for R.*

Theorem 7. *Let $\mathcal{C}_{\mathsf{concat}} = \mathcal{C}_{\mathsf{alg}} \circ \mathscr{C} : \mathbb{Z}_Q^{k+1} \rightarrow \mathbb{Z}_q^{\eta q}$, $\eta < 1$ be the* Recurrent List Recoverable Code *with parameters as in Theorem 6. Let $\mathcal{H}$ be a Correlation Intractable Hash Function Family for an efficiently enumerable relation as in Lemma 3. Then the hash function family $\mathscr{C}_{\mathsf{concat}} \circ \mathcal{H}$ is a correlation intractable hash function family for the efficiently verifiable relation $\mathcal{B}$.*

Proof. From Theorem 6, the recurrent list recovery of $\mathcal{C}_{\mathsf{concat}}$ tells us that a list of size $O(k^2 \log^{4\varepsilon-\delta} k)$, for arbitrary constants $0 < \delta < \varepsilon < 1$ can be efficiently recovered. This is indeed bound by a polynomial, hence is certainly efficiently enumerable. Thus, from Lemma 3 and Lemma 4, we conclude that $\mathscr{C} \circ \mathcal{H}$ is indeed Correlation Intractable for the relation $\mathcal{B}$.

This leads to our final theorem.

Theorem 8. *Assuming that* $\mathsf{LWE}_{\frac{m}{2\log q},m,q,\chi}$ *holds for the particular parameter settings where* χ *is a* B*-bounded distribution for* $B = q^{\Omega(1)}$, $q = \mathsf{poly}(k)$, k *is the security parameter, and a MPC protocol with perfect* αn*-robustness and perfect, statistical, or computational security, where* $\alpha \in (0, 1/2)$ *is a constant and* n *is the size of the challenge set in the interactive protocol, there exists NIZKs with computational soundness for all of* NP *whose proof size is*

$$\mathcal{O}(|C| + q \cdot \mathrm{depth}(C)) + \mathsf{poly}(\lambda)$$

where C *is an arithmetic circuit for the* NP *verification function at* $q = k \log^{1+\epsilon} k$ *for any* $\epsilon > 0$.

This theorem is a direct consequence of the following results:

- Theorems 3 and 7 combine to provide a hash function family which is Fiat-Shamir compatible with parameters aligning with the "MPC-in-the-Head" paradigm.
- Applying the Fiat-Shamir compatible hash to Protocol 1 gives us a computational sound NIZK from the MPC-in-the-Head model without parallel repetition.
- There exists perfect αn-robust MPC protocols with the aforementioned communication complexity for $\alpha < 0.5$ (Theorem 4).

Acknowledgements. This research was supported in part from a Simons Investigator Award, DARPA SIEVE award, NTT Research, NSF Frontier Award 1413955, BSF grant 2012378, a Xerox Faculty Research Award, a Google Faculty Research Award, and an Okawa Foundation Research Grant. This material is based upon work supported by the Defense Advanced Research Projects Agency through Award HR00112020024. This work was done [in part] while PL was visiting the Simons Institute for the Theory of Computing. The authors would like to thank Alexis Korb for useful discussions and help with proof reading.

References

1. Ames, S., Hazay, C., Ishai, Y., Venkitasubramaniam, M.: Ligero: lightweight sublinear arguments without a trusted setup. In: Thuraisingham, B.M., Evans, D., Malkin, T., Xu, D. (eds.) ACM CCS 2017, pp. 2087–2104. ACM Press (2017)
2. Asharov, G., Ephraim, N., Komargodski, I., Pass, R.: On perfect correctness without derandomization. Cryptology ePrint Archive, Report 2019/1025 (2019). https://eprint.iacr.org/2019/1025

3. Beck, G., Goel, A., Jain, A., Kaptchuk, G.: Order-C secure multiparty computation for highly repetitive circuits. In: Canteaut, A., Standaert, F.-X. (eds.) EUROCRYPT 2021. LNCS, vol. 12697, pp. 663–693. Springer, Cham (2021). https://doi.org/10.1007/978-3-030-77886-6_23
4. Ben-Or, M., Goldwasser, S., Wigderson, A.: Completeness theorems for non-cryptographic fault-tolerant distributed computation (extended abstract). In: 20th ACM STOC, pp. 1–10. ACM Press (1988)
5. Brakerski, Z., Koppula, V., Mour, T.: NIZK from LPN and trapdoor hash via correlation intractability for approximable relations. In: Micciancio, D., Ristenpart, T. (eds.) CRYPTO 2020. LNCS, vol. 12172, pp. 738–767. Springer, Cham (2020). https://doi.org/10.1007/978-3-030-56877-1_26
6. Canetti, R.: Universally composable security: a new paradigm for cryptographic protocols. Cryptology ePrint Archive, Report 2000/067 (2000). https://eprint.iacr.org/2000/067
7. Canetti, R., et al.: Fiat-Shamir: from practice to theory. In: Charikar, M., Cohen, E. (eds.) 51st ACM STOC, pp. 1082–1090. ACM Press (2019)
8. Canetti, R., Chen, Y., Reyzin, L.: On the correlation intractability of obfuscated pseudorandom functions. In: Kushilevitz, E., Malkin, T. (eds.) TCC 2016. LNCS, vol. 9562, pp. 389–415. Springer, Heidelberg (2016). https://doi.org/10.1007/978-3-662-49096-9_17
9. Canetti, R., Chen, Y., Reyzin, L., Rothblum, R.D.: Fiat-Shamir and correlation intractability from strong KDM-secure encryption. In: Nielsen, J.B., Rijmen, V. (eds.) EUROCRYPT 2018. LNCS, vol. 10820, pp. 91–122. Springer, Cham (2018). https://doi.org/10.1007/978-3-319-78381-9_4
10. Canetti, R., Goldreich, O., Halevi, S.: The random oracle methodology, revisited (preliminary version). In: 30th ACM STOC, pp. 209–218. ACM Press (1998)
11. Chase, M., et al.: Post-quantum zero-knowledge and signatures from symmetric-key primitives. Cryptology ePrint Archive, Report 2017/279 (2017). https://eprint.iacr.org/2017/279
12. Chaum, D., Crépeau, C., Damgård, I.: Multiparty unconditionally secure protocols (extended abstract). In: 20th ACM STOC, pp. 11–19. ACM Press (1988)
13. Damgård, I., Ishai, Y.: Scalable secure multiparty computation. In: Dwork, C. (ed.) CRYPTO 2006. LNCS, vol. 4117, pp. 501–520. Springer, Heidelberg (2006). https://doi.org/10.1007/11818175_30
14. Damgård, I., Ishai, Y., Krøigaard, M.: Perfectly secure multiparty computation and the computational overhead of cryptography. In: Gilbert, H. (ed.) EUROCRYPT 2010. LNCS, vol. 6110, pp. 445–465. Springer, Heidelberg (2010). https://doi.org/10.1007/978-3-642-13190-5_23
15. Fiat, A., Shamir, A.: How to prove yourself: practical solutions to identification and signature problems. In: Odlyzko, A.M. (ed.) CRYPTO 1986. LNCS, vol. 263, pp. 186–194. Springer, Heidelberg (1987). https://doi.org/10.1007/3-540-47721-7_12
16. Forney, G.D.: Concatenated codes. Research monograph no. 37 (1966)
17. Gentry, C., Groth, J., Ishai, Y., Peikert, C., Sahai, A., Smith, A.: Using fully homomorphic hybrid encryption to minimize non-interative zero-knowledge proofs. J. Cryptol. **28**(4), 820–843 (2015)
18. Giacomelli, I., Madsen, J., Orlandi, C.: ZKBoo: Faster zero-knowledge for Boolean circuits. In: Holz, T., Savage, S. (eds.) USENIX Security 2016, pp. 1069–1083. USENIX Association (2016)
19. Goldreich, O.: Foundations of Cryptography: Basic Tools, vol. 1. Cambridge University Press, Cambridge, UK (2001)

20. Goldreich, O., Micali, S., Wigderson, A.: How to play any mental game or a completeness theorem for protocols with honest majority. In: Aho, A. (ed.) 19th ACM STOC, pp. 218–229. ACM Press (1987)
21. Goldreich, O., Micali, S., Wigderson, A.: How to prove all NP-statements in zero-knowledge, and a methodology of cryptographic protocol design. In: Odlyzko, A.M. (ed.) CRYPTO'86. LNCS, vol. 263, pp. 171–185. Springer, Heidelberg (Aug (1987)
22. Goldwasser, S., Micali, S., Rackoff, C.: The knowledge complexity of interactive proof-systems (extended abstract). In: 17th ACM STOC, pp. 291–304. ACM Press (1985)
23. Goldwasser, S., Micali, S., Rackoff, C.: The knowledge complexity of interactive proof systems. SIAM J. Comput. **18**(1), 186–208 (1989)
24. Goyal, V., Polychroniadou, A., Song, Y.: Unconditional communication-efficient MPC via hall's marriage theorem. In: Malkin, T., Peikert, C. (eds.) CRYPTO 2021. LNCS, vol. 12826, pp. 275–304. Springer, Cham (2021). https://doi.org/10.1007/978-3-030-84245-1_10
25. Guruswami, V.: Algorithmic results in list decoding. Now Publishers Inc. (2007)
26. Guruswami, V., Indyk, P.: Expander-based constructions of efficiently decodable codes. In: FOCS, pp. 658–667. IEEE Computer Society (2001)
27. Guruswami, V., Sudan, M.: Improved decoding of Reed-Solomon and algebraic-geometric codes. In: FOCS, pp. 28–39. IEEE Computer Society (1998)
28. Holmgren, J., Lombardi, A.: Cryptographic hashing from strong one-way functions (or: One-way product functions and their applications). In: Thorup, M. (ed.) 59th FOCS, pp. 850–858. IEEE Computer Society Press (2018)
29. Holmgren, J., Lombardi, A., Rothblum, R.D.: Fiat-shamir via list-recoverable codes (or: Parallel repetition of GMW is not zero-knowledge), STOC (2021). https://eprint.iacr.org/2021/286
30. Ishai, Y., Kushilevitz, E., Ostrovsky, R., Sahai, A.: Zero-knowledge from secure multiparty computation. In: Johnson, D.S., Feige, U. (eds.) 39th ACM STOC, pp. 21–30. ACM Press (2007)
31. Kalai, Y.T., Rothblum, G.N., Rothblum, R.D.: From obfuscation to the security of fiat-shamir for proofs. In: Katz, J., Shacham, H. (eds.) CRYPTO 2017. LNCS, vol. 10402, pp. 224–251. Springer, Cham (2017). https://doi.org/10.1007/978-3-319-63715-0_8
32. Lombardi, A., Schaeffer, L.: A note on key agreement and non-interactive commitments. Cryptology ePrint Archive, Report 2019/279 (2019). https://eprint.iacr.org/2019/279
33. Parvaresh, F., Vardy, A.: Correcting errors beyond the Guruswami-Sudan radius in polynomial time. In: 46th FOCS, pp. 285–294. IEEE Computer Society Press (2005)
34. Peikert, C., Shiehian, S.: Noninteractive zero knowledge for np from (plain) learning with errors. In: Boldyreva, A., Micciancio, D. (eds.) CRYPTO 2019. LNCS, vol. 11692, pp. 89–114. Springer, Cham (2019). https://doi.org/10.1007/978-3-030-26948-7_4
35. Reed, I.S., Solomon, G.: Polynomial codes over certain finite fields. J. Soci. Industr. Appl. Math. **8**(2), 300–304 (1960)
36. Regev, O.: New lattice based cryptographic constructions. In: 35th ACM STOC, pp. 407–416. ACM Press (2003)
37. Sudan, M.: Decoding of reed Solomon codes beyond the error-correction bound. J. Complex. **13**(1), 180–193 (1997)
38. Yao, A.C.C.: How to generate and exchange secrets (extended abstract). In: 27th FOCS, pp. 162–167. IEEE Computer Society Press (1986)

Symmetric Cryptography

Key-Reduced Variants of 3kf9 with Beyond-Birthday-Bound Security

Yaobin Shen[1,2(✉)] and Ferdinand Sibleyras[3(✉)]

[1] Shanghai Jiao Tong University, Shanghai, China
[2] UCLouvain, ICTEAM, Crypto Group, Louvain-la-Neuve, Belgium
yaobins180@gmail.com
[3] NTT Social Informatics Laboratories, Tokyo, Japan
sibleyras.ferdinand.ez@hco.ntt.co.jp

Abstract. 3kf9 is a three-key CBC-type MAC that enhances the standardized integrity algorithm f9 (3GPP-MAC). It has beyond-birthday-bound security and is expected to be a possible candidate in constrained environments when instantiated with lightweight blockciphers. Two variants 2kf9 and 1kf9 were proposed to reduce key size for efficiency, but recently, Leurent et al. (CRYPTO'18) and Shen et al. (CRYPTO'21) pointed out critical flaws on these two variants and invalidated their security proofs with birthday-bound attacks.

In this work, we revisit previous constructions of key-reduced variants of 3kf9 and analyze what went wrong in security analyses. Interestingly, we find that a single doubling near the end restores the intended beyond-birthday-bound security of both 2kf9 and 1kf9. We then propose two new key-reduced variants of 3kf9, called n2kf9 and n1kf9. By leveraging previous attempts, we prove that n2kf9 is secure up to $2^{2n/3}$ queries, and prove that n1kf9 is secure up to $2^{2n/3}$ queries when the message space is prefix-free. We also provide beyond-birthday analysis of n2kf9 in the multi-user setting. Note that compared to EMAC and CBC-MAC, the additional cost to provide a higher security guarantee is expected to be minimal for n2kf9 and n1kf9. It only requires one additional blockcipher call and one doubling.

Keywords: Message authentication code · CBC-MAC · 3kf9 · Beyond-birthday-bound security

1 Introduction

A Message Authentication Code (MAC) is a fundamental symmetric-key primitive used to ensure the authenticity of messages. A MAC is typically built from a blockcipher (e.g., CBC-MAC [1,8], OMAC [23], PMAC [11]), or from a hash function (e.g., HMAC [7], NMAC [7], NI-MAC [4]). At a high level, many of these constructions iterate the underlying primitive with an n-bit internal state size, and thus they are subject to a generic attack using $2^{n/2}$ queries by Preneel and Oorschot [32] exploiting internal state collisions. However, the

S. Agrawal and D. Lin (Eds.): ASIACRYPT 2022, LNCS 13792, pp. 525–554, 2022.
https://doi.org/10.1007/978-3-031-22966-4_18

birthday-bound security $2^{n/2}$ is not always enough in practice, particularly when a MAC is implemented with a lightweight blockcipher. To reduce implementation costs, these blockciphers often offer a block length n of 64 bits or even shorter [3,5,6,12,13,18,35]. In the case of $n = 64$, the birthday-bound becomes 2^{32} and is vulnerable in certain practical applications [10].

DOUBLE-BLOCK HASH-THEN-SUM CONSTRUCTIONS. To overcome the birthday-bound barrier, a series of blockcipher-based MACs has been proposed, including SUM-ECBC [36], PMAC_Plus [37], 3kf9 [38], and LightMAC_Plus [27]. The first one is a rate-2 construction, whereas the last three are rate-1 constructions and thus more efficient in that aspect.[1] [2] These constructions follow a similar paradigm called Double-block Hash-then Sum (DbHtS), where the internal state of the hash function is $2n$-bit and two encrypted values each of n-bit half are xored to generate the tag. Datta et al. [15] formalized this paradigm and proved these DbHtS MACs including their two-key variants are secure up to $2^{2n/3}$ queries. Leurent et al. [26] proposed a generic attack on DbHtS MACs with query complexity $2^{3n/4}$. Later, a matching proof by Kim et al. [25] confirmed that the security of DbHtS MACs stands at $2^{3n/4}$ queries. Shen et al. [34] also proved that two-key variants of DbHtS MACs are secure against $2^{2n/3}$ queries in the multi-user setting.

KEY-SIZE REDUCTION AND FIELD MULTIPLICATIONS. All the above DbHtS MACs require at least three or two blockcipher keys. Although in some practical protocols, the multiple keys can be generated from a master key, it has two drawbacks: (i) the construction inherently requires multiple blockcipher key schedulings, and typically need more invocation time and more energy consumption; (ii) the previous provable results cannot be applied since they are done by assuming independent keys. Hence another popular direction is to study how to reduce the key size of these MACs for better efficiency, while at the same time keeping their high security. Datta et al. [17] showed that the single-key variant of PMAC_Plus dubbed 1k-PMAC_Plus is secure up to $2^{2n/3}$ queries. Naito [28] also showed that the single-key variant of LightMAC_Plus dubbed LightMAC_Plus1k remains secure up to $2^{2n/3}$ queries. Inheriting from their original versions, besides blockcipher invocations, both 1k-PMAC_Plus and LightMAC_Plus1k require at least one additional field multiplication per message block (and totally at least ℓ field multiplications if the message is ℓ-block). On the contrary, as a CBC-type mode, 3kf9 does not need field multiplications, and its key-reduced version is likely to be particularly appealing to applications in serial processing. Yet, reducing its key size appears to be a challenging problem as discussed below.

A BRIEF HISTORY OF KEY-REDUCED VARIANTS OF 3kf9. 3kf9 [38] is designed by combining f9 (3GPP-MAC) [2,22] and EMAC [31]. Datta et al. [16] initialized the study of key-reduced variants of 3kf9 and proposed a single-key variant called 1kf9. Later, Leurent et al. [26] showed a birthday-bound attack on 1kf9 and thus invalidated its security proof. In an other paper, Datta et al. [15] proposed a two-key variant called 2kf9. Very recently, Shen et al. [34] found a flaw in 2kf9

[1] Rate is the average number of blockcipher invocations per message block [19,20].
[2] The rate of LightMAC_Plus will increase with the counter size.

that it can be forged by using a single-block message. They also attempted to fix 2kf9 with several variants, yet all subject to a birthday-bound attack.

Our Contributions. We revisit previous constructions of key-reduced variants of 3kf9 and analyze what went wrong in previous proofs. *Interestingly*, we find that a single doubling near the end (which can be computed efficiently by one-bit shift and one conditional XOR with a constant string) restores the intended beyond-birthday-bound security of both 2kf9 and 1kf9. We then propose two key-reduced variants of 3kf9, namely a two-key variant called n2fk9 and a single-key variant called n1kf9 (illustrated in Fig. 6 and Fig. 7, respectively). Note that to provide a higher security guarantee that is beyond the birthday-bound, the additional cost compared to EMAC and CBC-MAC is expected to be minimal for n2kf9 and n1kf9: it only requires one additional blockcipher call and one finite field doubling.

We then give security analyses for n2kf9 and n1kf9. We prove that n2kf9 is secure up to $2^{2n/3}$ queries, and prove that n1kf9 is secure up to $2^{2n/3}$ queries when the message space is prefix-free. Prefix-free means that no query is a prefix of another as in the case of CBC-MAC, and can be realized by putting the n-bit length encoding of each message as its first block. Note that both our proofs and previous attempts [15,16] use a similar proof strategy: first show that any pair of the final $2n$-bit state (Σ_i, Λ_i) is cover-free, that is at least one of them is fresh, and then apply the lemma of sum of two identical permutations to get to a beyond-birthday-bound security result. Yet, the difficulties lie in how to show that (Σ_i, Λ_i) is cover-free, which is an essential part of the proof and where previous attempts failed. Learning from previous mistakes, we provide detailed analyses to show that (Σ_i, Λ_i) of constructions n2kf9 and n1kf9 is indeed cover-free with the help of doubling, and thus prove that both of them are secure beyond the birthday-bound. These analyses require surmounting some obstacles and are based on the structure graph of CBC-MAC [9,24]. Moreover, the dominant term in our bound is $q^3\ell^2/2^{2n}$ for n2kf9 and $q^3\ell^3/2^{2n}$ for n1kf9 where q is the number of MAC queries and ℓ is the maximal block length among these MAC queries. Both are better than the previous bound $q^3\ell^4/2^{2n}$ of 2kf9 [15] and 1kf9 [16] in terms of length ℓ. The improvement of mitigating the influence of length ℓ on the bound is non-trivial since it requires a fine-grained analysis of cases with multiple 'accidents' (collisions) in CBC-MAC. We also provide a beyond-birthday analysis of n2kf9 in the multi-user setting.

Discussion of Our Bound. Our bound is interesting for beyond-birthday-bound security with practical interest, especially when communicated messages are of limited length. We show that for any adversary making q MAC queries of maximal block length ℓ, the advantages against the PRF security of n2kf9 and n1kf9 are of the order $q^3\ell^2/2^{2n} + q^2\ell^4/2^{2n}$ and $q^3\ell^3/2^{2n} + q^2\ell^4/2^{2n}$ respectively.[3] We compare the later term with the bound $q^2\ell/2^n$ of conventional rate-1 MACs such as CBC-MAC, OMAC and PMAC. With a 64-bit block size and a guarantee

[3] To the best of our knowledge, all security bounds of CBC-like MACs (regardless of beyond the birthday-bound or not) include a similar term $(\ell^2/2^n)^a$ for $a \geq 1$ [9,15, 25,29]. This seems to be inherent that arises from the collision analysis of CBC-like structure.

that adversaries do not forge with probability more than one in a million, one gets a restriction of the form

$$\frac{q^2\ell}{2^{64}} \leq \frac{1}{2^{20}} \text{ or } \frac{q^3\ell^3}{2^{128}} + \frac{q^2\ell^4}{2^{128}} \leq \frac{1}{2^{20}} .$$

If the messages are 2^6 blocks long, then 2^{19} messages can be tagged and total 2^{31} bits = 256 MB of data for the bound $q^2\ell/2^n$, while 2^{29} messages and total 2^{41} bits = 256 GB for the bound $q^3\ell^3/2^{2n} + q^2\ell^4/2^{2n}$. We stress that using 128-bit blockciphers with n2kf9 and n1kf9 can also provide higher security guarantees.

Organization. First, we set useful notations and security notions in Sect. 2. In Sect. 3 we revisit different variants of 3kf9 with their associated proofs, and motivate our constructions n2kf9 and n1kf9. Then, in Sect. 4 and Sect. 5 we give the security proofs for n2kf9. In Sect. 6, we demonstrate the proof for n1kf9.

2 Preliminaries

Notation. Let ε denote the empty string. Let $\{0,1\}^*$ be the set of all finite bit strings including the empty string ε. For a finite set S, we let $x \leftarrow\!\!\$\ S$ denote the uniform sampling from S and assigning the value to x. Let $|x|$ denote the length of string x. Let $|x|_n$ denote the n-bit encoding of the length of string x. Concatenation of strings x and y is written as $x \parallel y$ or simply xy. $x10^*$ denotes the padding that right padded with a single 1 and as few 0 bits so that the length of string to be a multiple of n bits. We let $y \leftarrow A(x_1, \ldots; r)$ denote running algorithm A with randomness r on inputs $x_1, \ldots$ and assigning the output to y. We let $y \leftarrow\!\!\$\ A(x_1, \ldots)$ be the result of picking r at random and letting $y \leftarrow A(x_1, \ldots; r)$. Let $\mathrm{Perm}(n)$ denote the set of all permutations over $\{0,1\}^n$, and let $\mathrm{Func}(*, n)$ denote the set of all functions from $\{0,1\}^*$ to $\{0,1\}^n$. For integer $1 \leq a \leq N$, let $(N)_a$ denote $N(N-1)\ldots(N-a+1)$.

Security Definitions. An adversary $\mathcal{A}$ is an algorithm that always outputs a bit. We write $\mathcal{A}^O = 1$ to denote the event that $\mathcal{A}$ outputs 1 when given access to oracle O. Let $E : \{0,1\}^k \times \{0,1\}^n \to \{0,1\}^n$ be a blockcipher. Let $\pi \leftarrow\!\!\$\ \mathrm{Perm}(n)$ be a random permutation. The advantage of $\mathcal{A}$ against the PRP security of E is defined as

$$\mathsf{Adv}_E^{\mathrm{prp}}(\mathcal{A}) = \Pr\left[\mathcal{A}^{E_K} = 1\right] - \Pr\left[\mathcal{A}^{\pi} = 1\right]$$

where K is chosen uniformly at random from $\{0,1\}^k$.

Let $F : \mathcal{K} \times \{0,1\}^* \to \{0,1\}^n$ be a MAC algorithm. Let $\mathcal{R} \leftarrow\!\!\$\ \mathrm{Func}(*, n)$ be a random function. The advantage of $\mathcal{A}$ against the PRF security of F is defined as

$$\mathsf{Adv}_F^{\mathrm{prf}}(\mathcal{A}) = \Pr\left[\mathcal{A}^{F_K} = 1\right] - \Pr\left[\mathcal{A}^{\mathcal{R}} = 1\right]$$

where K is chosen uniformly at random from $\mathcal{K}$. We note that the above definition captures the security of a MAC as a pseudorandom function (PRF). It is well known that any PRF is a secure MAC [8].

THE H-COEFFICIENT TECHNIQUE. Following from Hoang and Tessaro [21], we consider interactions between an adversary $\mathcal{A}$ and an abstract system $\mathbf{S}$ which answers $\mathcal{A}$'s queries. The resulting interaction can then be recorded with a transcript $\tau = ((x_1, y_1), \ldots, (x_q, y_q))$. Let $\mathsf{p}_\mathbf{S}(\tau)$ denote the probability that $\mathbf{S}$ produces τ. It is known that $\mathsf{p}_\mathbf{S}(\tau)$ is the description of $\mathbf{S}$ and independent of the adversary $\mathcal{A}$. We say that a transcript is attainable for the system $\mathbf{S}$ if $\mathsf{p}_\mathbf{S}(\tau) > 0$.

We now describe the H-coefficient technique of Patarin [14,30]. Generically, it considers an adversary that aims at distinguishing a "real" system $\mathbf{S}_1$ from an "ideal" system $\mathbf{S}_0$. The interactions of the adversary with those systems induce two transcript distributions X_1 and X_0 respectively. It is well known that the statistical distance $\mathsf{SD}(X_1, X_0)$ is an upper bound on the distinguishing advantage of $\mathcal{A}$.

Lemma 2.1. [14,30] *Suppose that the set of attainable transcripts for the ideal system can be partitioned into good and bad ones. If there exists $\epsilon \geq 0$ such that $\frac{\mathsf{p}_{\mathbf{S}_1}(\tau)}{\mathsf{p}_{\mathbf{S}_0}(\tau)} \geq 1 - \epsilon$ for any good transcript τ, then*

$$\mathsf{SD}(X_1, X_0) \leq \epsilon + \Pr[X_0 \text{ is bad}] \ .$$

SUM OF TWO IDENTICAL PERMUTATIONS. The following result of sum of two identical permutations under conditional distribution is helpful in our analysis.

Lemma 2.2. [17] *For any tuple $(T_1, \ldots, T_q)$ such that each $T_i \neq 0^n$, let $U_1, \ldots, U_q$, $V_1, \ldots, V_q$ be $2q$ random variables sampled without replacement from $\{0,1\}^n \setminus \mathcal{Z}$ that can be regarded as the outputs of a random permutation where the subset $\mathcal{Z}$ is of size z, and satisfy $U_i \oplus V_i = T_i$ for $1 \leq i \leq q$. Denote by $\mathcal{S}$ the set of tuples of these $2q$ variables. Then*

$$|\mathcal{S}| \geq \frac{(2^n)_{2q}}{2^{nq}}(1 - \mu) \ ,$$

where $\mu = \frac{4qz^2 + 8q^2z + 6q^3}{2^{2n}}$ by assuming $z + 2q \leq 2^{n-1}$.

3 The n2kf9 and n1kf9 Constructions

In this section, we first go through previous constructions based on f9-hash (see Fig. 1), including 3kf9 [38], 2kf9 [15], 1kf9 [16] and a plausible construction (see Fig. 5) where 2kf9 and 1kf9 are actually broken. We then propose two new constructions called n2kf9 and n1kf9, and show that they are both secure beyond the birthday-bound.

3.1 Previous Constructions

THE 3kf9 CONSTRUCTION uses 3 different keys (see Fig. 2). It processes the message via f9-hash and then compute $T = E_{K_1}(\Sigma) \oplus E_{K_2}(\Lambda)$. It has a provable beyond-birthday-bound security. Intuitively, using two different keys to compute

procedure f9-hash$[E](L, M)$
$M[1] \| \dots \| M[\ell] \leftarrow M$; $Y_0 \leftarrow 0^n$
for $i \leftarrow 1$ **to** ℓ **do**
  $Y_i \leftarrow E_L(Y_{i-1} \oplus M[i])$
$\Sigma = Y_\ell$; $\Lambda = Y_1 \oplus Y_2 \oplus \cdots \oplus Y_\ell$
return (Σ, Λ)

Fig. 1. The f9-hash algorithm producing a $2n$-bit output.

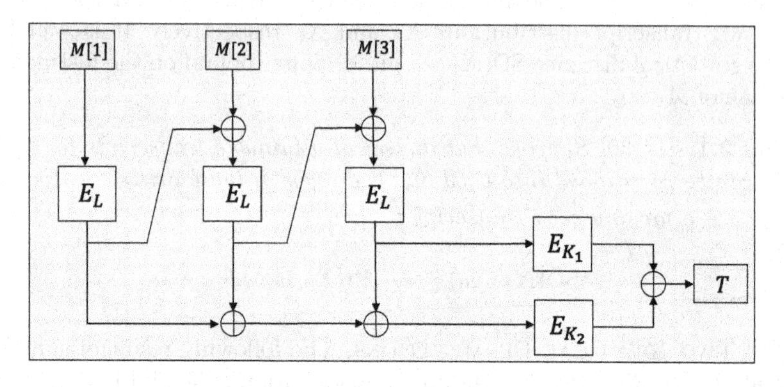

Fig. 2. The 3kf9 construction. It is built on top of a blockcipher $E : \{0,1\}^k \times \{0,1\}^n \rightarrow \{0,1\}^n$ with three keys L, K_1 and K_2.

the tag makes it harder for an attacker to exploit some relations between Σ and Λ. Events like $\Sigma_i = \Lambda_i$ for some message M_i or again $\Sigma_i = \Lambda_j$, $\Sigma_j = \Lambda_i$ for some pair of messages M_i, M_j are hardly detectable by looking at the output tags.

The 1kf9 Construction uses a single-key for both the f9-hash and tag computation ($K = L$) (see Fig. 3). It starts by processing an all-0 block before the message in f9-hash and then finishes by computing $T = E_L(\mathsf{fix0}(2\Sigma)) \oplus E_L(\mathsf{fix1}(2\Lambda))$ where the fix0 and fix1 functions set the least significant bit to 0 and 1 respectively, and multiplication by 2 is done in a Galois field. The fix function acts as a domain-separation ensuring that no $\mathsf{fix0}(2\Sigma)$ values can ever collide with a $\mathsf{fix1}(2\Lambda)$ value. However, there is a birthday-bound attack by Leurent et al. [26] on 1kf9 that actually exploits the fix function. The attack looks for two values x and y such that $E_L(x \oplus E_L(0)) \oplus E_L(y \oplus E_L(0)) = d$, where d is the inverse of 2, as it implies a collision between the tags of messages $x \| 0$ and $y \| d$. Indeed, the Σ parts will be equal as the injection of d cancels the difference, and the Λ parts will differ by d which becomes 1 after multiplication and is absorbed by the fix function. This describes a full-state collision attack with birthday-bound complexity.

The 2kf9 Construction uses two different keys (see Fig. 4), one for f9-hash and the other for the tag computation as $T = E_K(\Sigma) \oplus E_K(\Lambda)$. It doesn't use any fix function or finite field multiplication. However, Shen et al. [34] realized that when f9-hash processes a single-block message then Σ is always equal to Λ and thus the

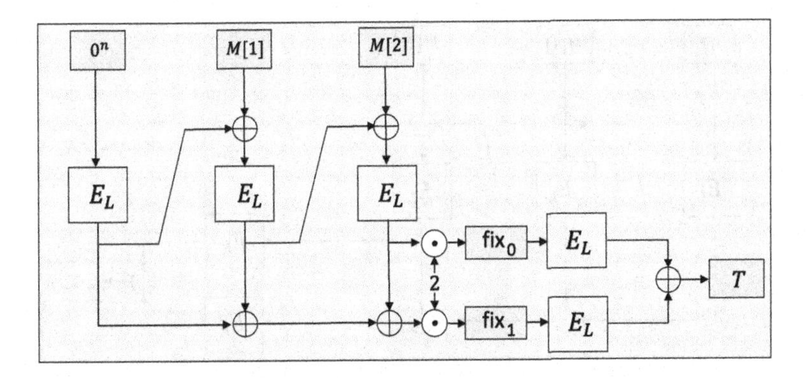

Fig. 3. The 1kf9 construction. It is built on top of a blockcipher $E : \{0,1\}^k \times \{0,1\}^n \rightarrow \{0,1\}^n$ with a single key L.

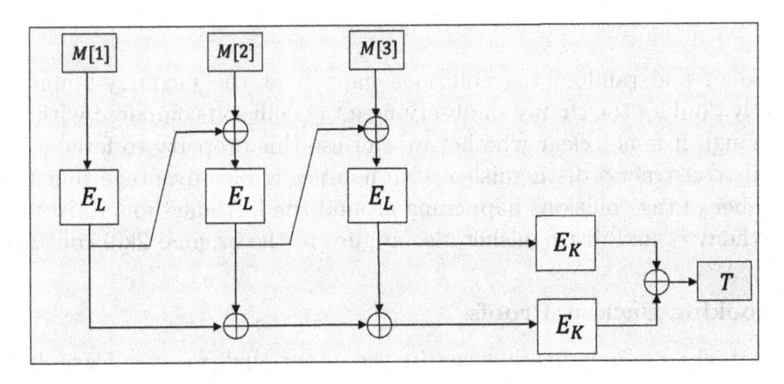

Fig. 4. The 2kf9 Construction. It is built on top of a blockcipher $E : \{0,1\}^k \times \{0,1\}^n \rightarrow \{0,1\}^n$ with two keys L and K.

tag is always 0. This is a single-query forgery attack which clearly demonstrates that one cannot simply use the raw f9-hash to get security beyond the birthday-bound. Shen et al. [34] further realized that adding a fix function and finite field multiplication leads to essentially the same birthday-bound attack as for 1kf9.

A PLAUSIBLE CONSTRUCTION. The 1kf9 construction does not need the fix functions to avoid the one-query attack, thanks to prepending an all-0 block at the beginning which forbids one-block calls to f9-hash. One can wonder if doing the same for 2kf9 would suffice to fix it (see Fig. 5). Unfortunately, in this case, there is still a distinguisher attack with birthday-bound complexity that exploits another undesirable property of f9-hash. For any prefix M (note that Σ_M and Λ_M as the internal state values of f9-hash after processing M), if we query $M||x$ for many x, then the tags should collide about twice often than expected. Indeed, by varying the last block only a new Σ_x value is added to the bottom part to compute $\Lambda_x = \Lambda_M \oplus \Sigma_x$. Therefore, for any value x, the probability that $\Sigma_y = \Lambda_M \oplus \Sigma_x$ is about $1/2^n$ for another value y, which implies $\Sigma_y = \Lambda_x$ and $\Lambda_y = \Sigma_x$ and thus results in a non-random tag collision. Both

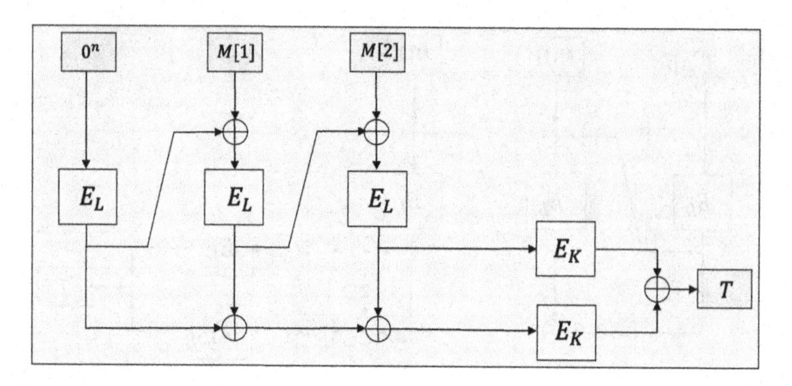

Fig. 5. A plausible construction. It is built on top of a blockcipher $E : \{0,1\}^k \times \{0,1\}^n \rightarrow \{0,1\}^n$ with two keys L and K, and prepends an all-0 block at the beginning.

non-random and random tag collisions happen at the birthday-bound which effectively doubles the chance of observing a tag collision compared with a PRF. Even though it is not clear whether we can use this property to forge a tag, we can easily construct a distinguisher with non-negligible advantage that looks at the number of tag collisions happening around the birthday-bound. Notice that this birthday-bound distinguisher also applies to the original 2kf9 construction.

3.2 Looking Back at Proofs

Those attacks often indicate flaws in the proof that we can learn from. In fact, there are flaws in the original proofs of 3kf9 (see the discussion in [15, Section 6.5]), 2kf9 (attacked by [34]) and 1kf9 (withdrawn by the authors [16] and attacked by [26]). Therefore, it is important to analyze what went wrong before moving forward to fix with new constructions.

The proof of 1kf9 was already known to have flaws and was withdrawn so the attack only confirmed that the proof couldn't be fixed.

The single-query attack on 2kf9 exploits the fact that the event $\Sigma_i = \Lambda_i$ automatically occurs for any single-block message M_i. In the proof of [15], they study the probability of the event $\Sigma_i = \Lambda_i$ as the event that the following equation occurs (namely the intermediate values as in Fig. 1):

$$Y_1^i \oplus \cdots \oplus Y_{l_i-1}^i = 0$$

whose dotted notation may prevent to see that whenever $l_i - 1 = 0$, the case of a one-block message, the equation becomes trivial. Interestingly, even though they pointed out the attack, [34] missed this event from their multi-user setting analysis. While the missing analysis is simple in most cases, it still shows that some terms are missing from the final bound.

The birthday-bound distinguisher of the plausible construction exploits the event that "$\Sigma_i = \Lambda_j$ **and** $\Sigma_j = \Lambda_i$" for two messages M_i and M_j. The analysis of this event is simply missing from [15].

procedure $\mathsf{n2kf9}[E](L, K, M)$
$M[1] \parallel \ldots \parallel M[\ell] \leftarrow M10^*$; $Y_0 \leftarrow 0^n$
for $i \leftarrow 1$ **to** ℓ **do**
  $Y_i \leftarrow E_L(Y_{i-1} \oplus M[i])$
$\Sigma = Y_\ell$; $\Lambda = 2 \cdot (Y_1 \oplus Y_2 \oplus \cdots \oplus Y_\ell)$
$(U, V) \leftarrow (E_K(\Sigma), E_K(\Lambda))$
$T \leftarrow U \oplus V$; **return** T

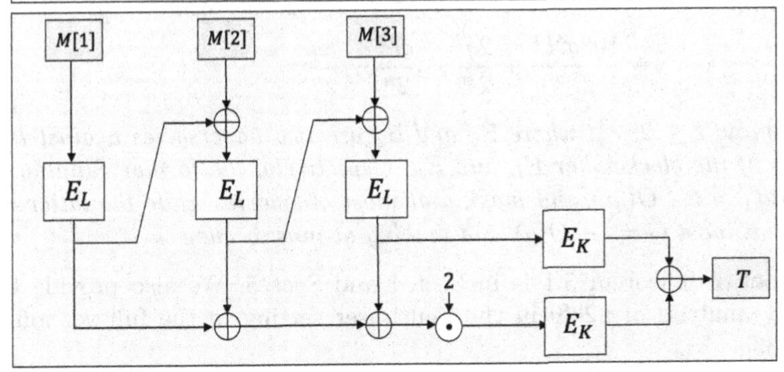

Fig. 6. The $\mathsf{n2kf9}[E]$ **construction.** It is built on top of a blockcipher $E : \{0,1\}^k \times \{0,1\}^n \rightarrow \{0,1\}^n$ with two keys L and K.

3.3 Our Constructions

In the rest of this paper, we will show that a simple doubling (multiply by 2) of the Λ value can fix both 2kf9 and 1kf9 to go beyond the birthday-bound security. We now present the two new constructions n2kf9 and n1kf9.

INTUITION BEHIND THE DESIGNS. Before the presentation of new constructions, we briefly discuss the intuition that the single doubling helps to avoid the problems in previous constructions. The reason is that multiplying the sum of $Y_1 \oplus Y_2 \cdots \oplus Y_\ell$ by 2 can break the relation between Σ and Λ. More concretely, firstly, it avoids the single-query attack as finite field doubling has no fix point except for 0. Secondly, for any prefix M, playing with a single block suffix x will introduce a unique $3 \cdot \Sigma_x$ difference between the top and bottom part and thus avoids the birthday-bound distinguishing attack. Thirdly, the removal of two fix functions fix0 and fix1 avoids the attack in 1kf9. Finally, as evidenced in the proof, for any three messages M_i, M_j and M_k, the probability that $\Sigma_i = \Sigma_j$ or $\Sigma_i = \Lambda_j$, and $\Lambda_i = \Sigma_k$ or $\Lambda_i = \Lambda_k$ is small. Similar argument also holds for the case of two messages M_i and M_j.

THE n2kf9 CONSTRUCTION. Let $E : \{0,1\}^k \times \{0,1\}^n \rightarrow \{0,1\}^n$ be a blockcipher. The n2kf9 is built from a blockcipher E with two keys L and K. Multiplication $\odot$ is done on a finite field. Note that the single doubling (multiply by 2) can be computed efficiently by one-bit shift and one conditional XOR with a constant string. The specification of n2kf9 is illustrated in Fig. 6.

Security of n2kf9. Given that E_L and E_K are two good PRPs, we have the following result.

Theorem 3.1. *For any adversary $\mathcal{A}$ against the PRF security of* n2kf9 *that runs in time at most t and makes at most q queries of block length at most ℓ, we have*

$$\mathsf{Adv}^{\mathrm{prf}}_{\mathsf{n2kf9}[E]}(\mathcal{A}) \leq \mathsf{Adv}^{\mathrm{prp}}_{E}(\mathcal{B}_1) + \mathsf{Adv}^{\mathrm{prp}}_{E}(\mathcal{B}_2) + \frac{60q^3\ell^2}{2^{2n}} + \frac{8q^3}{2^{2n}} + \frac{122q^3\ell^6}{2^{3n}} + \frac{30q^2\ell^4}{2^{2n}} + \frac{108q^3\ell^4}{2^{3n}} + \frac{2q^2}{2^{2n}} + \frac{q\ell^2}{2^n} + \frac{3q}{2^n}$$

by assuming $\ell \leq 2^{n-3}$, where $\mathcal{B}_1$ and $\mathcal{B}_2$ are two adversaries against the PRP security of the blockcipher E_L and E_K respectively, the former running in time at most $t_1 = t + O(q\ell)$ and making at most $q\ell$ queries while the latter running in time at most $t_2 = t + O(q)$ and making at most q queries.

The proof of Theorem 3.1 is in Sect. 4 and Sect. 5. We also provide beyond-birthday analysis of n2kf9 in the multi-user setting in the full version of this paper [33].

The n1kf9 Construction. Let $E : \{0,1\}^k \times \{0,1\}^n \to \{0,1\}^n$ be a blockcipher. The n1kf9 is built from a blockcipher E with a single key K. Multiplication $\odot$ is done on a finite field. The specification of n1kf9 is illustrated in Fig. 7. Note that the first block should always be the n-bit length encoding of the message to realize prefix-free as in the case for CBC-MAC.

Security of n1kf9. Given that E_K is a good PRP, the n1kf9 is a good PRF with beyond-birthday-bound security as shown in the following theorem. The proof of this theorem is in Sect. 6.

Theorem 3.2. *For any adversary $\mathcal{A}$ against the PRF security of* n1kf9 *that runs in time at most t and makes at most q queries of block length at most ℓ, we have*

$$\mathsf{Adv}^{\mathrm{prf}}_{\mathsf{n1kf9}[E]}(\mathcal{A}) \leq \mathsf{Adv}^{\mathrm{prp}}_{E}(\mathcal{B}) + \frac{8q^3(\ell+3)^3}{2^{2n}} + \frac{129q^3(\ell+2)^6}{2^{3n}} + \frac{36q^2(\ell+2)^4}{2^{2n}} + \frac{6q^3}{2^{2n}} + \frac{q(\ell+2)^2}{2^n} + \frac{3q}{2^n}$$

by assuming $\ell \leq 2^{n-3} - 2$, where $\mathcal{B}$ is an adversary against the PRP security of the blockcipher E_K that runs in time at most $t = t + O(q(\ell+3))$ and makes at most $q(\ell+3)$ queries.

Tightness of the Bound. We remark that the provable $2n/3$-bit security for both n2kf9 and n1kf9 may not be tight. Currently we don't find a matching attack with $2^{2n/3}$ queries complexity. On the other hand, intuitively the difficulty of improving the bound lies in how to handle the case when (Σ_i, Λ_i) is not cover-free instead of simply setting bad events since the final two blockciphers use the same key.

procedure $\mathsf{n1kf9}[E](K, M)$
$M[1] \parallel \ldots \parallel M[\ell] \leftarrow M10^*$; $Y_0 \leftarrow E_K(|M|_n)$
for $i \leftarrow 1$ **to** ℓ **do**
  $Y_i \leftarrow E_K(Y_{i-1} \oplus M[i])$
$\Sigma = Y_\ell$; $\Lambda = 2 \cdot (Y_0 \oplus Y_1 \oplus \cdots \oplus Y_\ell)$
$(U, V) \leftarrow (E_K(\Sigma), E_K(\Lambda))$
$T \leftarrow U \oplus V$; **return** T

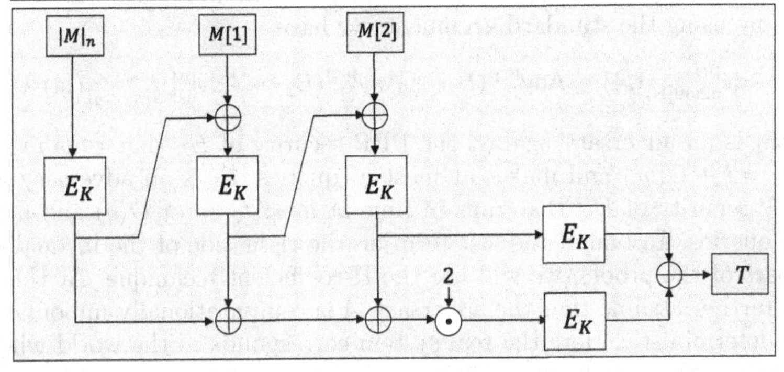

Fig. 7. The $\mathsf{n1kf9}[E]$ construction. It is built on top of a blockcipher $E : \{0,1\}^k \times \{0,1\}^n \rightarrow \{0,1\}^n$ with a single key K.

4 Security Analysis of N2kf9 Construction

In this section, we prove Theorem 3.1, which shows that $\mathsf{n2kf9}$ achieves beyond-birthday-bound security.

Overview of the Proof. In the proof, we first replace blockciphers with random permutations in a standard way, and then adopt the H-coefficient technique as described in Sect. 2 to bound the distance between real world and ideal world.

To upper bound the probability of bad transcripts in the ideal world, we define several bad conditions and grant the adversary simulated values which may be reminiscent of previous attempts [15,34]. Yet, we work on the case of the permutation instead of the key being revealed to the adversary, and some subtleties arise when calculating the ratio of good transcripts. Moreover, to analyze the bad conditions when (Σ_i, Λ_i) is not cover-free and obtain a good bound (beyond birthday-bound), we need to show that the equations related to these two variables have a rank greater than or equal to 2. This analysis requires surmounting some obstacles and is based on the knowledge of structure graph of $\mathsf{CBC\text{-}MAC}$ [9,24]. In particular, to mitigate the influence of length ℓ on the bound, it requires to consider the event when there are two collisions among the computation of a triplet of messages, and show that these equations (including the ones related to variables Σ_i and Λ_i and the ones induced by these two collisions) have a rank greater than or equal to 3. Multiple subcases also occur when analyzing the event of one collision among the computation of a pair of messages. Finally, we conclude the proof by analyzing the ratio of good transcripts.

4.1 Game Description

Proof. Without loss of generality, we assume that the adversary $\mathcal{A}$ never repeats a previous query since otherwise it will receive the same answer. It is helpful to decompose the $2n$-bit hash function H of n2kf9 into two n-bit hash function H^1 and H^2 where $H_L^1(M) = Y_\ell$ and $H_L^2(M) = 2 \cdot (Y_1 \oplus Y_2 \oplus \cdots \oplus Y_\ell)$, and thus $\mathsf{n2kf9}[E](L, K, M) = E_K(H_L^1(M)) \oplus E_K(H_L^2(M))$. We first replace the blockciphers E_L and E_K of n2kf9 with two independent random permutations π_1 and π_2, and by using the standard argument, we have

$$\mathsf{Adv}^{\mathrm{prf}}_{\mathsf{n2kf9}[E]}(\mathcal{A}) \le \mathsf{Adv}^{\mathrm{prp}}_{E}(\mathcal{B}_1) + \mathsf{Adv}^{\mathrm{prp}}_{E}(\mathcal{B}_2) + \mathsf{Adv}^{\mathrm{prf}}_{\mathsf{n2kf9}[\pi_1,\pi_2]}(\mathcal{A}) \ ,$$

where $\mathcal{B}_1$ is an adversary against the PRP security of E_L that runs in time at most $t_1 = t + O(q\ell)$ and makes at most $q\ell$ queries, $\mathcal{B}_1$ is an adversary against the PRP security of E_K that runs in time at most $t_2 = t + O(q)$ and makes at most q queries. To bound the last term on the right side of the inequality (the main part of the proof), we will use the H-coefficient technique. At this stage, we can further assume that the adversary $\mathcal{A}$ is computationally unbounded and thus is deterministic. Here the real system corresponds to the world when $\mathcal{A}$ is interacting with the scheme $\mathsf{n2kf9}[\pi_1, \pi_2]$, and the ideal system corresponds to the world when $\mathcal{A}$ is interacting with a random function $\mathcal{R} \leftarrow \mathrm{Func}(*, n)$.

SETUP. After the adversary $\mathcal{A}$ finishes querying, it obtains a sequence of query-answer entries $(M_1, T_1), \ldots, (M_q, T_q)$ that records the interaction between the adversary and its oracle, where $T_i = \mathsf{n2kf9}[\pi_1, \pi_2](M_i)$ in the real world and $T_i = \mathcal{R}(M_i)$ in the ideal world. In the real world, we denote by Σ_i and Λ_i the internal outputs of H during the computation of entry (M_i, T_i), namely $\Sigma_i = H^1(M_i)$ and $\Lambda_i = H^2(M_i)$. We denote by U_i and V_i the corresponding outputs of permutation π_2, namely $U_i = \pi_2(\Sigma_i)$ and $V_i = \pi_2(\Lambda_i)$. After the interaction, we will reveal the encoding of permutation π_1 to the adversary, and grant it all the internal values U_i and V_i. While in the ideal world, we will instead give the adversary a permutation $\pi_1 \leftarrow\!\!\$\ \mathrm{Perm}(n)$ that is independent of its queries, and grant it q pairs of dummy values U_i and V_i sampled as follows: the simulation oracle $\mathrm{OFF}(q)$ is invoked which is illustrated in Fig. 8 and returns q pairs of (U_i, V_i) to the adversary. Note that this additional information can only help the adversary as it can simply ignore them. In addition, the internal values Σ_i and Λ_i appeared during the computation of $\mathrm{OFF}(q)$ are uniquely determined by message M_i and permutation π_1. Hence a transcript consists of the query-answer pairs (M_i, T_i), the permutation π_1, and the internal values (U_i, V_i).

4.2 Bad Transcripts

DEFINING BAD TRANSCRIPTS. We now give the definition of bad transcripts. The goal of this definition is to ensure that for each query, the corresponding pair of (Σ_i, Λ_i) is always cover-free. That is, at least one of Σ_i and Λ_i is fresh. Formally, we say a transcript is *bad* if at least one of the following conditions is triggered:

(1) There exists an entry (M_i, T_i) such that $T_i = 0^n$. This will force $U_i = V_i$ in the real world even when both Σ_i and Λ_i are fresh, while there is no such constraint in the ideal world.
(2) There exists an entry (M_i, T_i) such that $\Sigma_i = \Lambda_i$. This will force $T_i = 0^n$, while there is no such constraint in the ideal world.
(3) There exists a pair of entries (M_i, T_i) and (M_j, T_j) such that $\Sigma_i = \Sigma_j$ and $\Lambda_i = \Lambda_j$, or $\Sigma_i = \Lambda_j$ and $\Lambda_i = \Sigma_j$. This will force $T_i = T_j$ in the real world, while there is no such constraint in the ideal world.
(4) There exists a pair of entries (M_i, T_i) and (M_j, T_j) such that $\Sigma_i \in \{\Sigma_j, \Lambda_j\}$ and $V_i \in \{V_j, U_j\}$. This guarantees that the outputs of Φ in the simulation oracle $\text{OFF}(q)$ are compatible with a permutation in all good transcripts; namely, when the inputs are distinct the corresponding outputs should also be distinct.
(5) There exists a pair of entries (M_i, T_i) and (M_j, T_j) such that $\Lambda_i \in \{\Sigma_j, \Lambda_j\}$ and $U_i \in \{V_j, U_j\}$. Again, this guarantees that the outputs of Φ in the simulation oracle $\text{OFF}(q)$ are compatible with a permutation in all good transcripts.
(6) There exists a triplet of entries (M_i, T_i), (M_j, T_j) and (M_k, T_k) such that $\Sigma_i \in \{\Sigma_j, \Lambda_j\}$ and $\Lambda_i \in \{\Sigma_k, \Lambda_k\}$. This guarantees that for each query of good transcripts, at least one of Σ_i and Λ_i is fresh, and thus at least one of corresponding outputs U_i and V_i has fresh randomness in the real world.
(7) There exists a triplet of entries (M_i, T_i), (M_j, T_j) and (M_k, T_k) such that $\Sigma_i \in \{\Sigma_j, \Lambda_j\}$ and $V_i \in \{U_k, V_k\}$. This guarantees that the outputs of Φ in the simulation oracle $\text{OFF}(q)$ are compatible with a permutation in all good transcripts; namely, distinct inputs lead to distinct outputs.
(8) There exists a triplet of entries (M_i, T_i), (M_j, T_j) and (M_k, T_k) such that $\Lambda_i \in \{\Sigma_j, \Lambda_j\}$, and $U_i \in \{U_k, V_k\}$. Again, this guarantees that the outputs of Φ in the simulation oracle $\text{OFF}(q)$ are compatible with a permutation in all good transcripts.

If none of above conditions is met, then we say it is a *good* transcript. Denote by X_1 and X_0 the random variables for the transcript distribution in the real and ideal worlds respectively.

PROBABILITY OF BAD TRANSCRIPTS. We now proceed to bound the probability that X_0 is bad in the ideal world. For $1 \le i \le 8$, denote by bad_i the event when the ith condition is triggered. We analyze each event in turn. We begin with the first event. Recall that in the ideal world, each T_i is a random n-bit string. Hence the probability that $T_i = 0^n$ is exactly $1/2^n$. Summing over at most q queries,

$$\Pr[\mathsf{bad}_1] = \frac{q}{2^n} . \tag{1}$$

The probability of events from 2 to 8 is bounded by the following lemma. The proof of this lemma is postponed to Sect. 5, as its analysis is based on the structure graph of CBC-MAC [9,24] and is involved.

Lemma 4.1. *For any adversary that makes at most q queries of block length at most ℓ,*

$$\sum_{j=2}^{8} \Pr[\,bad_j\,] \leq \frac{60q^3\ell^2}{2^{2n}} + \frac{2q^3}{2^{2n}} + \frac{122q^3\ell^6}{2^{3n}} + \frac{22q^2\ell^2}{2^{2n}} + \frac{108q^3\ell^4}{2^{3n}} + \frac{8q^2\ell^4}{2^{2n}} + \frac{2q^2}{2^{2n}} + \frac{q\ell^2}{2^n} + \frac{2q}{2^n}\,.$$

4.3 Good Transcripts

TRANSCRIPT RATIO. Let τ be a good transcript. Note that for any good transcript and for any pair of (Σ_i, Λ_i), at least one of Σ_i and Λ_i is fresh. Hence the set $\mathcal{N}$ in OFF(q) (see Fig. 8) is empty, and the game will not abort. In the set $\mathcal{H}$, there are exactly $q + |\mathcal{F}|$ fresh values ($2|\mathcal{F}|$ fresh values for all indices in $\mathcal{F}$ and additional $(2q-2|\mathcal{F}|)/2$ fresh values for some indices in $\mathcal{G}$), and $q-|\mathcal{F}|$ non-fresh values. For the entries that are recorded by the set $\mathcal{G}$, suppose that there are g classes among the values Σ_i and Λ_i: the elements in the same class are either connected by the equation of $\Phi(\Sigma_i) \oplus \Phi(\Lambda_i) = T_i$, or connected by the equation of $\Sigma_i = \Sigma_j$ or $\Sigma_i = \Lambda_j$, or $\Lambda_i = \Sigma_j$ or $\Lambda_i = \Lambda_j$. That is, the pair (Σ_i, Λ_i) is obviously in the same class. And if $\Sigma_i = \Sigma_j$, then (Σ_i, Λ_i) and (Σ_j, Λ_j) are also in the same class. Note that each class contains at least three elements, and has only one corresponding sampled value since other values will be determined by the equations. On the other hand, since τ is good, the corresponding values U_i and V_i of these g distinct classes are compatible with a permutation. That is, these g sampled values are sampled such that they are distinct from each other and do not collide with other values during the computation of the set $\mathcal{F}$.

We now proceed to compute the transcript ratio. In the ideal world, since τ is good, the event $X_0 = \tau$ is the composition of the following independent events:

- We sample a random permutation $\pi_1 \leftarrow\!\!\$\ \mathrm{Perm}(n)$ to compute the internal Y state values in τ. Let σ the number of unique inputs, this happens with probability $1/(2^n)_\sigma$.
- The answers of these q queries are the same as the values defined in τ. This happens with probability 2^{-qn}. On the other hand, the internal values $(U_i, V_i)_{1\leq i\leq q}$ from OFF(q) (Fig. 8) are the same as the values defined in τ. This happens with probability $1/|\mathcal{S}| \cdot 1/(2^n - 2|\mathcal{F}|)_g$: the variables $(U_i, V_i)_{i\in\mathcal{F}}$ are uniformly at random sampled from the set $\mathcal{S}$, and there are g variables sampled without replacement from the remaining $2^n - 2|\mathcal{F}|$ elements for the rest $(U_i, V_i)_{i\in\mathcal{G}}$.

Therefore,

$$\Pr[\,X_0 = \tau\,] = \frac{1}{(2^n)_\sigma} \cdot \frac{1}{2^{qn}} \cdot \frac{1}{|\mathcal{S}|} \cdot \frac{1}{(2^n - 2|\mathcal{F}|)_g}\,.$$

On the other hand, in the real world, the probability of the event $X_1 = \tau$ entirely comes from the two random permutations:

- For the first permutation $\pi_1 \leftarrow\!\!\$ \ \mathrm{Perm}(n)$, the number of unique inputs appearing in τ is σ as defined in the ideal world analysis. This happens with probability $1/(2^n)_\sigma$.
- The number of unique inputs to the second permutation is the number of unique $(U_i, V_i)_{1\le i\le q}$ as appearing in τ. That is exactly $q + |\mathcal{F}| + g$, because we have a total of $q + |\mathcal{F}|$ fresh input-output tuples, and for each class in $\mathcal{G}$, we have one additional input-output tuple.

Hence,

$$\Pr[X_1 = \tau] = \frac{1}{(2^n)_\sigma} \cdot \frac{1}{(2^n)_{q+|\mathcal{F}|+g}} .$$

Therefore,

$$\begin{aligned}
\frac{\Pr[X_1 = \tau]}{\Pr[X_0 = \tau]} &= \frac{2^{qn} \cdot |\mathcal{S}| \cdot (2^n - 2|\mathcal{F}|)_g}{(2^n)_{q+|\mathcal{F}|+g}} \\
&\ge \frac{2^{(q-|\mathcal{F}|)n} \cdot (2^n)_{2|\mathcal{F}|} \cdot (2^n - 2|\mathcal{F}|)_g}{(2^n)_{q+|\mathcal{F}|+g}} \cdot (1 - \frac{6|\mathcal{F}|^3}{2^{2n}}) \\
&\ge \frac{2^{(q-|\mathcal{F}|)n}}{(2^n - 2|\mathcal{F}| - g)_{q-|\mathcal{F}|}} \cdot (1 - \frac{6|\mathcal{F}|^3}{2^{2n}}) \\
&\ge 1 - \frac{6q^3}{2^{2n}} ,
\end{aligned} \tag{2}$$

where the first inequality comes from Lemma 2.2 by fixing the conditional set to be empty.

4.4 Conclusion

WRAPPING UP. From Lemma 2.1, and combining Eq. (1), Lemma 4.1 and Eq. (2), we obtain

$$\begin{aligned}
\mathsf{Adv}^{\mathrm{prf}}_{\mathsf{n2kf9}[\pi_1,\pi_2]}(\mathcal{A}) \le & \frac{60q^3\ell^2}{2^{2n}} + \frac{8q^3}{2^{2n}} + \frac{122q^3\ell^6}{2^{3n}} + \frac{30q^2\ell^4}{2^{2n}} + \frac{108q^3\ell^4}{2^{3n}} + \frac{2q^2}{2^{2n}} \\
& + \frac{q\ell^2}{2^n} + \frac{3q}{2^n}
\end{aligned}$$

and conclude the proof of Theorem 3.1.

5 Proof of Lemma 4.1

In this section, we analyze the probability of events from 2 to 8 and prove Lemma 4.1. In $\mathsf{n2kf9}[\pi_1, \pi_2]$, the first n-bit hash function $H^1(M)$ is exactly the CBC-MAC on message M, while the second n-bit hash function $H^2(M)$ simply xor-sums all the internal outputs of CBC-MAC and then doubles it. In Appendix B of the full version [33], we recall the definition and properties of a

```
procedure OFF(q)
∀1 ≤ i ≤ q : (Σ_i, Λ_i) ← (H^1(M_i), H^2(M_i))
H = {(Σ_i, Λ_i) : 1 ≤ i ≤ q}
F = {i : both Σ_i and Λ_i are fresh in H}
G = {i : only one of Σ_i and Λ_i is fresh in H}
N = {i : neither Σ_i nor Λ_i is fresh in H}
I: set of tuples of 2|F| distinct values from {0,1}^n
S = {(W_i, X_i)_{i∈F} ∈ I : W_i ⊕ X_i = T_i}
(U_i, V_i)_{i∈F} ←$ S
∀i ∈ F : (Φ(Σ_i), Φ(Λ_i)) ← (U_i, V_i)
∀i ∈ G :
   if Σ_i is not fresh in H then
      if Σ_i ∉ Dom(Φ)
         then U_i ←$ {0,1}^n \ Rng(Φ); Φ(Σ_i) ← U_i
      else U_i ← Φ(Σ_i)
      V_i ← T_i ⊕ U_i; Φ(Λ_i) ← V_i
   else
      if Λ_i ∉ Dom(Φ)
         then V_i ←$ {0,1}^n \ Rng(Φ); Φ(Λ_i) ← V_i
      else V_i ← Φ(Λ_i)
      U_i ← T_i ⊕ V_i; Φ(Σ_i) ← U_i
∃i ∈ N : return ⊥
return (U_i, V_i)_{1≤i≤q}
```

Fig. 8. Offline oracle used in the proof of n2kf9. Here Φ is a partial function that aims to simulate a random permutation. Variables Σ_i and Λ_i are inputs of a random permutation, and U_i and V_i are corresponding outputs of this random permutation. The domain and range of Φ are both initialized to be empty.

combinatorial tool called the structure graph of CBC-MAC [9,24] that is useful in our analysis.

Intuitively, a structure graph $G_\pi^{\boldsymbol{M}}$ is a directed graph that is generated from the computation of CBC-MAC on various inputs $\boldsymbol{M} = \{M_1, M_2, \ldots\}$. The starting node of a structure graph is always the value 0^n, and each output of the permutation π is regarded as a node in the graph. In the structure graph $G_\pi^{\boldsymbol{M}}$, there may be some accidental collisions (called accidents) on the nodes that is captured by the set $\mathsf{Acc}(G_\pi^{\boldsymbol{M}})$. We will first limit the number of accidents, and then analyze the probability of bad events conditioned on it.

Restricting the Accidents. We limit the number of accidents that can arise within any single, pair or triplet of messages. Consider the following event for any distinct messages M_i, M_j, M_k:

$$\mathsf{crash} = |\mathsf{Acc}(G_\pi^{M_i})| \geq 1 \textbf{ or } |\mathsf{Acc}(G_\pi^{\{M_i,M_j\}})| \geq 2 \textbf{ or } |\mathsf{Acc}(G_\pi^{\{M_i,M_j,M_k\}})| \geq 3 \ .$$

From [33, Lemma B.2] and the union bound, and summing over q messages, $\binom{q}{2}$ pairs of messages, $\binom{q}{3}$ triplets of messages:

$$\Pr[\mathsf{crash}] \le \frac{q\ell^2}{2^n} + \binom{q}{2} \cdot \frac{16\ell^4}{2^{2n}} + \binom{q}{3} \cdot \frac{729\ell^6}{2^{3n}} \le \frac{q\ell^2}{2^n} + \frac{8q^2\ell^4}{2^{2n}} + \frac{122q^3\ell^6}{2^{3n}} \ . \quad (3)$$

We now analyze the probability of events from 2 to 8 in conjunction with $\neg\mathsf{crash}$. That is when there is no accident within any single message, at most one accident within any pair of messages, and at most two accidents within any triplet of messages.

Proof Ideas of each Event. We provide some intuition before the formal analysis of each event. For event 2, it involves only one message and is easy to show that the rank of one equation produced by this event is 1. For event 3, it consists of two sub-cases from two messages. The crucial part is to show that the rank of two equations produced by each sub-case is 2 when $|\mathsf{Acc}(G_\pi^{\{M_i,M_j\}})| = 1$. The analyses of event 4 and 5 are a bit easier than the one of event 3 since one of two equations comes from the string T_i which is random and independent of queries in the ideal world. For event 6, it includes totally four sub-cases that are involved three messages. Each sub-case should be analyzed separately but the main idea is similar. The point is to show that the rank of two equations produced by each sub-case is 2 when $|\mathsf{Acc}(G_\pi^{\{M_i,M_j,M_k\}})| = 1$. Moreover, when $|\mathsf{Acc}(G_\pi^{\{M_i,M_j,M_k\}})| = 2$, it requires to show that the rank of two equations produced by each sub-case and the additional equation introduced by accidents is 3. Some details are required in this analysis. Finally, the analyses of event 7 and 8 are analogous to those of event 4 and 5, since one of two equations comes from the random string T_i.

Event 2. For the event 2, it is the same as the equation

$$Y_\ell^i = 2 \cdot (Y_1^i \oplus \cdots \oplus Y_\ell^i) \ ,$$

which is equivalent to

$$3 \cdot Y_\ell^i \oplus 2 \cdot (Y_1^i \oplus \cdots \oplus Y_{\ell-1}^i) = 0 \ .$$

Since the number of accidents of the structure graph $G_\pi^{M_i}$ is 0, $Y_1^i, \ldots, Y_\ell^i$ are all distinct from each other, and thus the rank of this equation is exactly 1. According to [33, Lemma B.3], the probability that this equation holds is at most $1/(2^n - \ell + 1) \le 2/2^n$ by assuming $\ell \le 2^{n-1}$. Summing over at most q queries,

$$\Pr[\mathsf{bad}_2 \wedge \neg\mathsf{crash}] \le \frac{2q}{2^n} \ . \quad (4)$$

Event 3. Next, we bound the probability of event 3. This event consists of two subcases: (i) $\Sigma_i = \Sigma_j \wedge \Lambda_i = \Lambda_j$; (ii)$\Sigma_i = \Lambda_j \wedge \Lambda_i = \Sigma_j$. The first subcase is the same as

$$\begin{cases} Y_{\ell_i}^i = Y_{\ell_j}^j \\ 2 \cdot (Y_1^i \oplus \cdots \oplus Y_{\ell_i}^i) = 2 \cdot (Y_1^j \oplus \cdots \oplus Y_{\ell_j}^j) \ . \end{cases}$$

If the number of accidents of the structure graph $G_\pi^{\{M_i,M_j\}}$ is 0, then this subcase cannot happen since the first equation requires at least one accident. If $|\mathsf{Acc}(G_\pi^{\{M_i,M_j\}})| = 1$, then the rank of the above two equations is 2, which will be justified below. Hence from [33, Lemma B.3]

$$\Pr\left[\,\Sigma_i = \Sigma_j \wedge \Lambda_i = \Lambda_j \wedge |\mathsf{Acc}(G_\pi^{\{M_i,M_j\}})| = 1\,\right] \leq \frac{1}{(2^n - 2\ell + 2)_2} \cdot \binom{2\ell}{2} \leq \frac{8\ell^2}{2^{2n}}$$

where we assume $\ell \leq 2^{n-2}$ and the number of structure graphs $G_\pi^{\{M_i,M_j\}}$ with one accident is at most $\binom{2\ell}{2}$ from [33, Lemma B.1]. We now justify that when $|\mathsf{Acc}(G_\pi^{\{M_i,M_j\}})| = 1$, the rank of above two equations is 2. Without loss of generality, assume that $\ell_i \geq \ell_j$. Let α be the length of common suffix of M_i and M_j. Then the above two equations are the same as

$$\begin{cases} Y^i_{\ell_i-\alpha} \oplus Y^j_{\ell_j-\alpha} = 0 \\ Y^i_1 \oplus \cdots \oplus Y^i_{\ell_i-\alpha-1} \oplus Y^j_1 \oplus \cdots \oplus Y^j_{\ell_j-\alpha-1} = 0 \;. \end{cases}$$

If $\alpha = \ell_j$, namely M_j is a suffix of M_i, then these two equations degenerate to

$$\begin{cases} Y^i_{\ell_i-\ell_j} = 0 \\ Y^i_1 \oplus \cdots \oplus Y^i_{\ell_i-\ell_j-1} = 0 \;. \end{cases}$$

In this case, the first equation cannot hold otherwise it contradicts the assumption that $|\mathsf{Acc}(G_\pi^{M_i})| = 0$. If $\alpha + 1 \leq \ell_j$, then these two equations are the same as

$$\begin{cases} Y^i_{\ell_i-\alpha-1} \oplus Y^j_{\ell_j-\alpha-1} = M_i[\ell_i - \alpha] \oplus M_j[\ell_j - \alpha] \\ Y^i_1 \oplus \cdots \oplus Y^i_{\ell_i-\alpha-1} \oplus Y^j_1 \oplus \cdots \oplus Y^j_{\ell_j-\alpha-1} = 0 \;. \end{cases}$$

If $\ell_i = \alpha+1$, then the first equation cannot hold since $M_i[1] \oplus M_j[1] \neq 0$ (note that $Y^i_0 = Y^j_0 = 0$). If $\ell_i = \alpha+2$, then the second equation degenerates to $Y^i_1 \oplus Y^j_1 = 0$ or $Y^i_1 = 0$, neither of which can hold. Therefore $\ell_i \geq \alpha+2$. Due to $|\mathsf{Acc}(G_\pi^{M_i})| = 0$, all the variables $Y^i_1, \ldots, Y^i_{\ell_i-\alpha-1}$ are distinct, and $Y^i_{\ell_i-\alpha-2} \notin \{Y^j_1, \ldots, Y^j_{\ell_j-\alpha-1}\}$, otherwise it will induce one additional accident on the structure graph $G_\pi^{\{M_i,M_j\}}$. Hence variable $Y_{\ell_i-\alpha-2}$ is unique in the second equation and does not appear in the first equation. Therefore, the rank of these two equations is 2. The first subcase holds with probability at most

$$\Pr\left[\,\Sigma_i = \Sigma_j \wedge \Lambda_i = \Lambda_j \wedge \neg\mathsf{crash}\,\right] \leq \frac{8\ell^2}{2^{2n}} \;.$$

Next, we analyze the subcase ii. This subcase is the same as

$$\begin{cases} Y^i_{\ell_i} = 2 \cdot (Y^j_1 \oplus \cdots \oplus Y^j_{\ell_j}) \\ 2 \cdot (Y^i_1 \oplus \cdots \oplus Y^i_{\ell_i}) = Y^j_{\ell_j} \;, \end{cases}$$

which is equivalent to

$$\begin{cases} Y^i_{\ell_i} \oplus 2 \cdot (Y^j_1 \oplus \cdots \oplus Y^j_{\ell_j}) = 0 \\ 2 \cdot (Y^i_1 \oplus \cdots \oplus Y^i_{\ell_i}) \oplus Y^j_{\ell_j} = 0 \ . \end{cases}$$

If $|\mathsf{Acc}(G_\pi^{\{M_i,M_j\}})| = 0$, then the rank of above two equations is 2. From [33, Lemma B.3], we have

$$\Pr\left[\, \Sigma_i = \Lambda_j \wedge \Lambda_i = \Sigma_j \wedge |\mathsf{Acc}(G_\pi^{\{M_i,M_j\}})| = 0 \,\right] \leq \frac{1}{(2^n - 2\ell + 2)_2} \leq \frac{4}{2^{2n}}$$

by assuming $\ell \leq 2^{n-2}$. If $|\mathsf{Acc}(G_\pi^{\{M_i,M_j\}})| = 1$, then this accident appears between the path of M_i and M_j since $|\mathsf{Acc}(G_\pi^{M_i})| = |\mathsf{Acc}(G_\pi^{M_j})| = 0$. Without loss of generality, assume $\ell_i \geq \ell_j$. Then there exists some variable Y^i_a for $1 \leq a \leq \ell_i$ such that $Y^i_a \notin \{Y^j_1, \ldots, Y^j_{\ell_j}\}$. It can be seen that the rank of these two equations is 2, since Y^i_a is unique and has different coefficients in each equation, and at least one of two equations contains a different variable Y^j_b for $1 \leq b \leq \ell_j$. Hence from [33, Lemma B.3],

$$\Pr\left[\, \Sigma_i = \Lambda_j \wedge \Lambda_i = \Sigma_j \wedge |\mathsf{Acc}(G_\pi^{\{M_i,M_j\}})| = 1 \,\right] \leq \frac{1}{(2^n - 2\ell + 2)_2} \cdot \binom{2\ell}{2} \leq \frac{8\ell^2}{2^{2n}}$$

where we assume $\ell \leq 2^{n-2}$ and the number of structure graphs $G_\pi^{\{M_i,M_j\}}$ with one accident is at most $\binom{2\ell}{2}$ from [33, Lemma B.1]. Thus the probability that subcase ii occurs is at most

$$\Pr\left[\, \Sigma_i = \Lambda_j \wedge \Lambda_i = \Sigma_j \wedge \neg\mathsf{crash} \,\right] \leq \frac{4}{2^{2n}} + \frac{8\ell^2}{2^{2n}} \ .$$

By the union bound, and summing over at most $\binom{q}{2}$ pairs of M_i and M_j,

$$\Pr\left[\, \mathsf{bad}_3 \wedge \neg\mathsf{crash} \,\right] \leq \frac{8q^2\ell^2}{2^{2n}} + \frac{2q^2}{2^{2n}} \ . \tag{5}$$

Events 4 and 5. We then bound the probability of event 4. We begin by analyzing the first two equations. The equations $\Sigma_i = \Sigma_j$ or $\Sigma_i = \Lambda_j$ are the same as

$$Y^i_{\ell_i} = Y^j_{\ell_j} \textbf{ or } Y^i_{\ell_i} = 2 \cdot (Y^j_1 \oplus \cdots \oplus Y^j_{\ell_j}) \ .$$

If $|\mathsf{Acc}(G_\pi^{\{M_i,M_j\}})| = 0$, then the first equation cannot hold since it requires one accident. For the second equation, all these variables are distinct and thus the rank of this equation is 1. By [33, Lemma B.3], this equation holds with probability at most $1/(2^n - \ell) \leq 2/2^n$ by assuming $\ell \leq 2^{n-1}$. If $|\mathsf{Acc}(G_\pi^{\{M_i,M_j\}})| \geq 1$, then by [33, Lemma B.2], this condition itself holds with probability at most $4\ell^2/2^n$. For the last two equations $V_i = V_j$ or $V_i = U_j$, they are the same as

$$U_i \oplus T_i = V_j \textbf{ or } U_i \oplus T_i = U_j$$

which holds with probability at most $2/2^n$ since T_i is a random string and independent of these queries. Summing over at most $\binom{q}{2}$ pairs of queries,

$$\Pr\left[\,\mathsf{bad}_4 \wedge \neg\mathsf{crash}\,\right] \leq \binom{q}{2} \cdot \left(\frac{2}{2^n} + \frac{4\ell^2}{2^n}\right) \cdot \frac{2}{2^n} \leq \frac{6q^2\ell^2}{2^{2n}} \ .$$

From similar arguments,

$$\Pr\left[\,\mathsf{bad}_5 \wedge \neg\mathsf{crash}\,\right] \leq \binom{q}{2} \cdot \left(\frac{4}{2^n} + \frac{4\ell^2}{2^n}\right) \cdot \frac{2}{2^n} \leq \frac{8q^2\ell^2}{2^{2n}}$$

by assuming $\ell \leq 2^{n-2}$.

Event 6. Next, we bound the probability of event 6. This event consists of four subcases, namely (i)$\Sigma_i = \Sigma_j \wedge \Lambda_i = \Sigma_k$; (ii) $\Sigma_i = \Sigma_j \wedge \Lambda_i = \Lambda_k$; (iii)$\Sigma_i = \Lambda_j \wedge \Lambda_i = \Sigma_k$; (iv) $\Sigma_i = \Lambda_j \wedge \Lambda_i = \Lambda_k$. The first subcase is the same as

$$\begin{cases} Y^i_{\ell_i} = Y^j_{\ell_j} \\ 2 \cdot (Y^i_1 \oplus \cdots \oplus Y^i_{\ell_i}) = Y^k_{\ell_k} \end{cases},$$

which is equivalent to

$$\begin{cases} Y^i_{\ell_i} \oplus Y^j_{\ell_j} = 0 \\ 2 \cdot (Y^i_1 \oplus \cdots \oplus Y^i_{\ell_i}) \oplus Y^k_{\ell_k} = 0 \end{cases}.$$

If $|\mathsf{Acc}(G_\pi^{\{M_i,M_j,M_k\}})| = 0$, then the first equation cannot hold since it requires one accident. If $|\mathsf{Acc}(G_\pi^{\{M_i,M_j,M_k\}})| = 1$, then the first equation counts this accident. If $\ell_i = 1$, then obviously these two equations have rank 2 since Y^i_1 has different coefficients in each equation. If $\ell_i > 1$, then we can always find some Y^i_a for $1 \leq a < \ell_i$ such that $Y^i_a \neq Y^i_{\ell_i}$ since $|\mathsf{Acc}(G_\pi^{M_i})| = 0$. Hence the rank of these two equations is 2 since Y^i_a only appears in the second equation. From [33, Lemma B.3],

$$\Pr\left[\,\Sigma_i = \Sigma_j \wedge \Lambda_i = \Sigma_k \wedge |\mathsf{Acc}(G_\pi^{\{M_i,M_j,M_k\}})| = 1\,\right] \leq \frac{1}{(2^n - 3\ell + 2)_2} \cdot \binom{3\ell}{2} \leq \frac{18\ell^2}{2^{2n}}$$

where we assume $\ell \leq 2^{n-3}$ and the number of structure graphs $G_\pi^{\{M_i,M_j,M_k\}}$ with one accident is at most $\binom{3\ell}{2}$ from [33, Lemma B.1]. On the other hand, if $|\mathsf{Acc}(G_\pi^{\{M_i,M_j,M_k\}})| = 2$, then again, the first equation counts one accident. Then the other accident will introduce a third equation $Y^\alpha_a \oplus Y^\beta_b = M_\alpha[a+1] \oplus M_\beta[b+1]$ which is linearly independent from the first equation. The second equation is always linearly independent from the first and the third equation due to the coefficient 2. Hence the rank of these three equations is 3. From [33, Lemma B.3],

$$\Pr\left[\,\Sigma_i = \Sigma_j \wedge \Lambda_i = \Sigma_k \wedge |\mathsf{Acc}(G_\pi^{\{M_i,M_j,M_k\}})| = 2\,\right]$$
$$\leq \frac{1}{(2^n - 3\ell + 2)_3} \cdot \binom{3\ell}{2}^2 \leq \frac{162\ell^4}{2^{3n}},$$

where the number of structure graphs $G_{\pi}^{\{M_i,M_j,M_k\}}$ with two accidents is at most $\binom{3\ell}{2}^2$ from [33, Lemma B.1]. Thus subcase i holds with probability at most

$$\Pr[\Sigma_i = \Sigma_j \wedge \Lambda_i \wedge \neg\mathsf{crash}] \le \frac{18\ell^2}{2^{2n}} + \frac{162\ell^4}{2^{3n}}$$

We then bound the probability of subcase ii. This subcase is the same as

$$\begin{cases} Y_{\ell_i}^i = Y_{\ell_j}^j \\ 2\cdot(Y_1^i \oplus\cdots\oplus Y_{\ell_i}^i) = 2\cdot(Y_1^k \oplus\cdots\oplus Y_{\ell_k}^k) \end{cases},$$

which is equivalent to

$$\begin{cases} Y_{\ell_i-1}^i \oplus Y_{\ell_j-1}^j = M_i[\ell_i] \oplus M_j[\ell_j] \\ Y_1^i \oplus\cdots\oplus Y_{\ell_i}^i \oplus Y_1^k \oplus\cdots\oplus Y_{\ell_k}^k = 0 \end{cases}.$$

If $|\mathsf{Acc}(G_{\pi}^{\{M_i,M_j,M_k\}})| = 0$, then the first equation cannot hold since it requires one accident. If $|\mathsf{Acc}(G_{\pi}^{\{M_i,M_j,M_k\}})| = 1$, then the first equation counts this accident. If $\ell_i = 1$, then $\ell_k \ne 1$ otherwise the second equation cannot hold since M_i and M_k are two distinct messages. Hence we can always find some Y_a^k for $1 \le a \le \ell_k$ such that $Y_a^k \ne Y_1^i$. Then Y_a^k only appears in the second equation, and thus the rank of these two equations is 2. If $\ell_i > 1$, then we can always find some Y_a^i for $1 \le a \le \ell_i$ such that $Y_a^i \ne Y_{\ell_i-1}^i$ since $|\mathsf{Acc}(G_{\pi}^{M_i})| = 0$. Then Y_a^i only appears in the second equation, and thus the rank of these two equations is 2. From [33, Lemma B.3],

$$\Pr\left[\Sigma_i = \Sigma_j \wedge \Lambda_i = \Lambda_k \wedge |\mathsf{Acc}(G_{\pi}^{\{M_i,M_j,M_k\}})| = 1\right] \le \frac{1}{(2^n-3\ell+2)_2}\cdot\binom{3\ell}{2} \le \frac{18\ell^2}{2^{2n}}.$$

On the other hand, if $|\mathsf{Acc}(G_{\pi}^{\{M_i,M_j,M_k\}})| = 2$, then the first equation counts one accident. The other accident will introduce a third equation $Y_a^{\alpha} \oplus Y_b^{\beta} = M_{\alpha}[a+1] \oplus M_{\beta}[b+1]$ which is linearly independent from the first equation. Obviously $(\alpha,\beta) \ne (i,j)$ otherwise $|\mathsf{Acc}(G_{\pi}^{\{M_i,M_j\}})| = 2$ which contradicts $\neg\mathsf{crash}$. We discuss two cases here, namely $(\alpha,\beta) = (i,k)$ or $(\alpha,\beta) = (j,k)$. For $(\alpha,\beta) = (i,k)$, the third equation is $Y_a^i \oplus Y_b^k = M_i[a+1] \oplus M_k[b+1]$. If $\ell_i = \ell_k = 1$, then the second equation cannot hold since M_i and M_k are two distinct messages. If $\ell_k = 1$ and $\ell_i = 2$, then if $a = 1$, Y_2^i only appears in the second equation, and thus the rank of these three equations is 3; and if $a = 0$, then Y_2^i also only appears in the second equation and the rank of these three equations is 3. If $\ell_k = 1$ and $\ell_i \ge 3$, then we can always find some $Y_c^i \notin \{Y_{\ell_i-1}^i, Y_a^i\}$ so that Y_c^i only appears in the second equation, and thus the rank of these three equations is 3. If $\ell_k > 1$, then we can always find some $Y_c^k \ne Y_b^k$ such that Y_c^k only appears in the second equation. Thus the rank of these three equations is 3. On the other hand, for the case of $(\alpha, \beta) = (j, k)$, we can analyze it similarly. Hence the rank of these three equations is 3. From [33, Lemma B.3],

$$\Pr\left[\Sigma_i = \Sigma_j \wedge \Lambda_i = \Lambda_k \wedge |\mathsf{Acc}(G_\pi^{\{M_i,M_j,M_k\}})| = 2\right]$$
$$\leq \frac{1}{(2^n - 3\ell + 2)_3} \cdot \binom{3\ell}{2}^2 \leq \frac{162\ell^4}{2^{3n}} .$$

Thus,

$$\Pr\left[\Sigma_i = \Sigma_j \wedge \Lambda_i = \Lambda_k \wedge \neg\mathsf{crash}\right] \leq \frac{18\ell^2}{2^{2n}} + \frac{162\ell^4}{2^{3n}} .$$

Next, we bound the probability of subcase iii. This subcase is the same as

$$\begin{cases} Y_{\ell_i}^i = 2 \cdot (Y_1^j \oplus \cdots \oplus Y_{\ell_j}^j) \\ 2 \cdot (Y_1^i \oplus \cdots \oplus Y_{\ell_i}^i) = Y_{\ell_k}^k \end{cases} ,$$

which is equivalent to

$$\begin{cases} Y_{\ell_i}^i \oplus 2 \cdot (Y_1^j \oplus \cdots \oplus Y_{\ell_j}^j) = 0 \\ 2 \cdot (Y_1^i \oplus \cdots \oplus Y_{\ell_i}^i) \oplus Y_{\ell_k}^k = 0 \end{cases} .$$

If $|\mathsf{Acc}(G_\pi^{\{M_i,M_j,M_k\}})| = 0$, then the rank of above two equations is 2 due to the coefficient 2. From [33, Lemma B.3], we have

$$\Pr\left[\Sigma_i = \Lambda_j \wedge \Lambda_i = \Sigma_k \wedge |\mathsf{Acc}(G_\pi^{\{M_i,M_j,M_k\}})| = 0\right] \leq \frac{1}{(2^n - 3\ell + 2)_2} \leq \frac{4}{2^{2n}}$$

by assuming $\ell \leq 2^{n-3}$. If $|\mathsf{Acc}(G_\pi^{\{M_i,M_j,M_k\}})| = 1$, then this accident appears between two paths of M_i, M_j and M_k. Suppose this accident introduces a third equation $Y_a^\alpha \oplus Y_b^\beta = M_\alpha[a+1] \oplus M_\beta[b+1]$ for $\alpha \neq \beta$. Then these two equations are linearly independent from this third equation due to the coefficient 2 (note that $Y \oplus 2 \cdot Y = 3 \cdot Y$). Thus the rank of these three equations is at least 2.

From [33, Lemma B.3], we have

$$\Pr\left[\Sigma_i = \Lambda_j \wedge \Lambda_i = \Sigma_k \wedge |\mathsf{Acc}(G_\pi^{\{M_i,M_j,M_k\}})| = 1\right] \leq \frac{1}{(2^n - 3\ell + 2)_2} \cdot \binom{3\ell}{2} \leq \frac{18\ell^2}{2^{2n}}$$

where we assume $\ell \leq 2^{n-3}$ and the number of structure graphs $G_\pi^{\{M_i,M_j,M_k\}}$ with one accident is at most $\binom{3\ell}{2}$ from [33, Lemma B.1]. If $|\mathsf{Acc}(G_\pi^{\{M_i,M_j,M_k\}})| = 2$, then it introduces two linearly independent equations: $Y_a^\alpha \oplus Y_b^\beta = M_\alpha[a+1] \oplus M_\beta[b+1]$ and $Y_c^\gamma \oplus Y_d^\delta = M_\gamma[c+1] \oplus M_\delta[d+1]$ where $\alpha, \beta, \gamma, \delta \in \{i, j, k\}$ and $\alpha \neq \beta, \gamma \neq \delta, (\alpha, \beta) \neq (\gamma, \delta)$. Then these two accidental equations are linearly independent from the above two equations due to the coefficient 2. Thus the rank of these four equations is at least 3. From [33, Lemma B.3],

$$\Pr\left[\Sigma_i = \Lambda_j \wedge \Lambda_i = \Sigma_k \wedge |\mathsf{Acc}(G_\pi^{\{M_i,M_j,M_k\}})| = 2\right]$$
$$\leq \frac{1}{(2^n - 3\ell + 2)_3} \cdot \binom{3\ell}{2}^2 \leq \frac{162\ell^4}{2^{3n}} .$$

Thus subcase iii holds with probability at most

$$\Pr\left[\,\Sigma_i = \Lambda_j \wedge \Lambda_i = \Sigma_k \wedge \neg\mathsf{crash}\,\right] \leq \frac{18\ell^2}{2^{2n}} + \frac{4}{2^{2n}} + \frac{162\ell^4}{2^{3n}} \ .$$

Next, we bound the probability of subcase iv. This subcase is the same as

$$\begin{cases} Y^i_{\ell_i} = 2\cdot(Y^j_1 \oplus \cdots \oplus Y^j_{\ell_j}) \\ 2\cdot(Y^i_1 \oplus \cdots \oplus Y^i_{\ell_i}) = 2\cdot(Y^k_1 \oplus \cdots \oplus Y^k_{\ell_k}) \ , \end{cases}$$

which is equivalent to

$$\begin{cases} Y^i_{\ell_i} \oplus 2\cdot(Y^j_1 \oplus \cdots \oplus Y^j_{\ell_j}) = 0 \\ Y^i_1 \oplus \cdots \oplus Y^i_{\ell_i} \oplus Y^k_1 \oplus \cdots \oplus Y^k_{\ell_k} = 0 \ . \end{cases}$$

Then analogously to the analysis in subcase iii,

$$\Pr\left[\,\Sigma_i = \Lambda_j \wedge \Lambda_i = \Lambda_k \wedge \neg\mathsf{crash}\,\right] \leq \frac{18\ell^2}{2^{2n}} + \frac{4}{2^{2n}} + \frac{162\ell^4}{2^{3n}} \ .$$

By the union bound, and summing over at most $\binom{q}{3}$ triplets of (M_i, M_j, M_k),

$$\Pr\left[\,\mathsf{bad}_6 \wedge \neg\mathsf{crash}\,\right] \leq \frac{12q^3\ell^2}{2^{2n}} + \frac{2q^3}{2^{2n}} + \frac{108q^3\ell^4}{2^{3n}} \ . \quad (6)$$

<u>*Events 7 and 8.*</u> Bounding the probability of event 7 is similar to handling event 4, except that now there are at most q^3 triplets of queries and the probability of $|\mathsf{Acc}(G_\pi^{\{M_i,M_j,M_k\}})| \geq 1$ is bounded by $9\ell^2/2^n$. Hence,

$$\Pr\left[\,\mathsf{bad}_7 \wedge \neg\mathsf{crash}\,\right] \leq q^3 \cdot \left(\frac{2}{2^n} + \frac{9\ell^2}{2^n}\right) \cdot \frac{2}{2^n} \leq \frac{22q^3\ell^2}{2^{2n}} \ .$$

Similarly,

$$\Pr\left[\,\mathsf{bad}_8 \wedge \neg\mathsf{crash}\,\right] \leq q^3 \cdot \left(\frac{4}{2^n} + \frac{9\ell^2}{2^n}\right) \cdot \frac{2}{2^n} \leq \frac{26q^3\ell^2}{2^{2n}} \ .$$

Summing up,

$$\sum_{j=2}^{8} \Pr\left[\,\mathsf{bad}_j\,\right] \leq \Pr\left[\,\mathsf{crash}\,\right] + \sum_{j=2}^{8} \Pr\left[\,\mathsf{bad}_j \wedge \neg\mathsf{crash}\,\right]$$

$$\leq \frac{60q^3\ell^2}{2^{2n}} + \frac{2q^3}{2^{2n}} + \frac{122q^3\ell^6}{2^{3n}} + \frac{22q^2\ell^2}{2^{2n}} + \frac{108q^3\ell^4}{2^{3n}} + \frac{8q^2\ell^4}{2^{2n}} + \frac{2q^2}{2^{2n}} + \frac{q\ell^2}{2^n} + \frac{2q}{2^n}$$

and conclude the proof of Lemma 4.1.

6 Security Analysis of N1kf9 Construction

In this section, we prove Theorem 3.2 that states the beyond-birthday-bound security of n1kf9 (illustrated in Fig. 7).

OVERVIEW OF THE PROOF. The proof idea of n1kf9 mainly follows from the one of n2kf9. Yet, since n1kf9 only requires one key that is both used in the hash part and final encryption, there are some points that are different and non-trivial. This is also the reason that the bound of n1kf9 is slightly worse than the bound of n2kf9. First, the simulation oracle used in the ideal world is adjusted to take into account the relation between the hash part and final encryption. The calculation of good transcripts is changed accordingly. In addition, more bad events emerge since Σ_i and Λ_i may collide with previous inputs of hash part. Moreover, to mitigate the influence of length ℓ on the bound, a fine-grained analysis is again required.

REMARK. It may be interesting to summarize some property of enhanced f9 hash for generalized proof. However, as far as we can see, the analysis of single-key $2n$-bit hash function is case dedicated and requires many insights on the concrete construction.

6.1 Game Description

Proof. Without loss of generality, we assume that the adversary never repeats a prior query since otherwise it will receive the same answer. The $2n$-bit hash function H of n1kf9 consists of two n-bit hash functions H^1 and H^2 where $H^1_K(M) = Y_\ell$ and $H^2_K(M) = 2 \cdot (Y_0 \oplus Y_1 \oplus \cdots \oplus Y_\ell)$, and thus $\mathsf{n1kf9}[E](K, M) = E_K(H^1_K(M)) \oplus E_K(H^2_K(M))$. As usual, we first replace the blockcipher E_K with a random permutation $\pi \leftarrow\!\!\$\ \mathrm{Perm}(n)$, and from the standard argument,

$$\mathsf{Adv}^{\mathrm{prf}}_{\mathsf{n1kf9}[E]}(\mathcal{A}) \leq \mathsf{Adv}^{\mathrm{prp}}_{E}(\mathcal{B}) + \mathsf{Adv}^{\mathrm{prf}}_{\mathsf{n1kf9}[\pi]}(\mathcal{A}) \ ,$$

where $\mathcal{B}$ is an adversary against the PRP security of the blockcipher E_K that runs in time at most $t = t + O(q(\ell + 3))$ and makes at most $q(\ell + 3)$ queries. We will use the H-coefficient technique to bound $\mathsf{Adv}^{\mathrm{prf}}_{\mathsf{n1kf9}[\pi]}(\mathcal{A})$, even when $\mathcal{A}$ is computationally unbounded. The real system and ideal system correspond to the game when $\mathcal{A}$ is interacting with the scheme $\mathsf{n1kf9}[\pi]$ and a random function $\mathcal{R} \leftarrow\!\!\$\ \mathrm{Func}(*, n)$, respectively.

SETUP. After the adversary $\mathcal{A}$ finishes querying, it obtains a sequence of query-answer entries $(M_1, T_1), \ldots, (M_q, T_q)$ that records the interaction with its oracle, where $T_i = \mathsf{n1kf9}[\pi](M_i)$ in the real world and $T_i = \mathcal{R}(M_i)$ in the ideal world. In the real world, let $\Sigma_i = H^1(M_i)$ and $\Lambda_i = H^2(M_i)$ be the internal outputs of H for entry (M_i, T_i). Let $U_i = \pi(\Sigma_i)$ and $V_i = \pi(\Lambda_i)$ be the outputs of permutation π after the hash part. After the interaction, we reveal the random permutation π to the adversary, and grant it all the internal values U_i and V_i. In the ideal world, we instead give the adversary a fresh random permutation π that is independent of its queries, and grant it q pairs of dummy values U_i and V_i sampled as follows: the simulation oracle $\text{OFF}(q)$ is invoked which is illustrated in the full version [33, Fig. 12] and returns (U_i, V_i) to the adversary. These additional information can only help the adversary. In addition, the internal values Σ_i and Λ_i (and also $Y_0^i, \ldots, Y_{\ell_i}^i$) appearing during the computation of $\text{OFF}(q)$ are uniquely determined by message M_i and permutation π. Hence a transcript consists of the query-answer pairs (M_i, T_i), the permutation π, and the internal values (U_i, V_i).

6.2 Bad Transcripts

DEFINING BAD TRANSCRIPTS. We now give the definition of bad transcripts. The goal is to ensure that for each query, the corresponding pair of (Σ_i, Λ_i) is always cover-free. Formally, we say a transcript is *bad* if at least one of the following conditions is triggered:

(1) There exists an entry (M_i, T_i) such that $T_i = 0^n$. This will force $U_i = V_i$ in the real world, while there is no such constraint in the ideal world.
(2) There exists an entry (M_i, T_i) such that $\Sigma_i = \Lambda_i$. This will force $T_i = 0^n$, while there is no such constraint in the ideal world.
(3) There exists an entry (M_i, T_i) such that $\Sigma_i \in \{|M_i|_n, Y_0^i \oplus M_i[1], \ldots, Y_{\ell_i-1}^i \oplus M_i[\ell_i]\}$ and $\Lambda_i \in \{|M_i|_n, Y_0^i \oplus M_i[1], \ldots, Y_{\ell_i-1}^i \oplus M_i[\ell_i]\}$. That is, both Σ_i and Λ_i collide with previous inputs of permutation π for the same query. This guarantees that for each query of all good transcripts, at least one of Σ_i and Λ_i is fresh, and thus at least one of corresponding outputs U_i and V_i has fresh randomness in the real world.
(4) There exists a pair of entries (M_i, T_i) and (M_j, T_j) such that $\Sigma_i \in \{|M_j|_n, Y_0^j \oplus M_j[1], \ldots, Y_{\ell_j-1}^j \oplus M_j[\ell_j], \Sigma_j, \Lambda_j\}$ and $\Lambda_i \in \{|M_j|_n, Y_0^j \oplus M_j[1], \ldots, Y_{\ell_j-1}^j \oplus M_j[\ell_j], \Sigma_j, \Lambda_j\}$. That is, both Σ_i and Λ_i collide with previous inputs of permutation π for another entry (M_j, T_j). Again, this guarantees that for each query of good transcripts, at least one of Σ_i and Λ_i is fresh.
(5) There exists a pair of entries (M_i, T_i) and (M_j, T_j) such that $\Sigma_i \in \{|M_j|_n, Y_0^j \oplus M_j[1], \ldots, Y_{\ell_j-1}^j \oplus M_j[\ell_j], \Sigma_j, \Lambda_j\}$ and $V_i \in \{Y_0^j, \ldots, Y_{\ell_j}^j, U_j, V_j\}$. This guarantees that the outputs of permutation π in the simulation oracle $\text{OFF}(q)$ are compatible with a permutation for all good transcripts, namely when the inputs are distinct, then the corresponding outputs should also be distinct.
(6) There exists a pair of entries (M_i, T_i) and (M_j, T_j) such that $\Lambda_i \in \{|M_j|_n, Y_0^j \oplus M_j[1], \ldots, Y_{\ell_j-1}^j \oplus M_j[\ell_j], \Sigma_j, \Lambda_j\}$ and $U_i \in \{Y_0^j, \ldots, Y_{\ell_j}^j, U_j, V_j\}$. Again, this guarantees that the outputs of permutation π in the simulation oracle $\text{OFF}(q)$ are compatible with a permutation for all good transcripts.
(7) There exists a triplet of entries (M_i, T_i), (M_j, T_j) and (M_k, T_k) such that $\Sigma_i \in \{|M_j|_n, Y_0^j \oplus M_j[1], \ldots, Y_{\ell_j-1}^j \oplus M_j[\ell_j], \Sigma_j, \Lambda_j\}$ and $\Lambda_i \in \{|M_k|_n, Y_0^k \oplus M_k[1], \ldots, Y_{\ell_k-1}^j \oplus M_k[\ell_k], \Sigma_k, \Lambda_k\}$. That is, Σ_i and Λ_i collide with previous inputs of permutation π for two different entries (M_j, T_j) and (M_k, T_k).

(8) There exists a triplet of entries (M_i, T_i), (M_j, T_j) and (M_k, T_k) such that $\Sigma_i \in \{|M_j|_n, Y_0^j \oplus M_j[1], \ldots, Y_{\ell_j-1}^j \oplus M_j[\ell_j], \Sigma_j, \Lambda_j\}$ and $V_i \in \{Y_0^k, \ldots, Y_{\ell_k}^k, U_k, V_k\}$. This guarantees that the outputs of permutation π in the simulation oracle $\text{OFF}(q)$ are compatible with a permutation for all good transcripts, namely distinct inputs produce distinct outputs (and conversely).

(9) There exists a triplet of entries (M_i, T_i), (M_j, T_j) and (M_k, T_k) such that $\Lambda_i \in \{|M_j|_n, Y_0^j \oplus M_j[1], \ldots, Y_{\ell_j-1}^j \oplus M_j[\ell_j], \Sigma_j, \Lambda_j\}$ and $U_i \in \{Y_0^k, \ldots, Y_{\ell_k}^k, U_k, V_k\}$. Again, this guarantees that the outputs of permutation π in the simulation oracle $\text{OFF}(q)$ are compatible with a permutation for all good transcripts.

If none of above conditions is met, then we say it is a *good* transcript. Denote by X_1 and X_0 the random variables for the transcript distribution in the real and ideal worlds respectively. The probability of bad transcripts in the ideal world is bounded by the following lemma; the proof is in [33, Appendix C].

Lemma 6.1. *For any adversary that makes at most q queries of block length at most $\ell \leq 2^{n-3} - 2$,*

$$\Pr[X_0 \text{ is bad}] \leq \frac{5q^3(\ell+3)^3}{2^{2n}} + \frac{3q^3(\ell+3)^2}{2^{2n}} + \frac{24q^2(\ell+2)^4}{2^{2n}} + \frac{122q^3(\ell+2)^6}{2^{3n}} + \frac{7q^3(\ell+3)^5}{2^{3n}} + \frac{q(\ell+2)^2}{2^n} + \frac{3q}{2^n} .$$

6.3 Good Transcripts

TRANSCRIPT RATIO. Let τ be a good transcript. Similarly to the arguments in Sect. 4.3, the set $\mathcal{N}$ in $\text{OFF}(q)$ (illustrated in the full version [33, Fig. 12]) is empty. In the set of Σ_i and Λ_i, there are $q + |\mathcal{F}|$ fresh values and $q - |\mathcal{F}|$ non-fresh values. For the entries that are recorded by the set $\mathcal{G}$, suppose there are g sampled values.

We now proceed to compute the transcript ratio. In the ideal world, since τ is good, the event $X_0 = \tau$ is the composition of the following independent events:

- When we sample a random permutation $\pi \leftarrow\!\!\$\ \text{Perm}(n)$, we use exactly $|\mathcal{H}|$ values which appear in τ. This happens with probability $1/(2^n)_{|\mathcal{H}|}$.
- The answers of these q queries are the same as the values defined in τ. This happens with probability 2^{-qn}. On the other hand, the internal values $(U_i, V_i)_{1 \leq i \leq q}$ from $\text{OFF}(q)$ are the same as the values defined in τ. This happens with probability $1/|\mathcal{S}| \cdot 1/(2^n - |\mathcal{H}| - 2|\mathcal{F}|)_g$: the variables $(U_i, V_i)_{i \in \mathcal{F}}$ are uniformly at random sampled from the set $\mathcal{S}$, and there are g variables sampled without replacement from the remaining $2^n - |\mathcal{H}| - 2|\mathcal{F}|$ elements for the rest $(U_i, V_i)_{i \in \mathcal{G}}$.

Therefore,

$$\Pr[X_0 = \tau] = \frac{1}{(2^n)_{|\mathcal{H}|}} \cdot \frac{1}{2^{qn}} \cdot \frac{1}{|\mathcal{S}|} \cdot \frac{1}{(2^n - |\mathcal{H}| - 2|\mathcal{F}|)_g} .$$

On the other hand, in the real world, the probability of the event $X_1 = \tau$ only comes from the computation of the random permutation π:

- First we draw $|\mathcal{H}|$ values from π to compute the internal Y states values.
- To compute the $(U_i, V_i)_{1\leq i\leq q}$, the number of permutation outputs required is exactly $q + |\mathcal{F}| + g$, because we totally have $q + |\mathcal{F}|$ fresh input-output tuples, and for each class in $\mathcal{G}$, we have one additional input-output tuple.

Hence,

$$\Pr[X_1 = \tau] = \frac{1}{(2^n)_{|\mathcal{H}|+q+|\mathcal{F}|+g}} .$$

Therefore,

$$\begin{aligned}
\frac{\Pr[X_1 = \tau]}{\Pr[X_0 = \tau]} &= \frac{2^{qn} \cdot |\mathcal{S}| \cdot (2^n - |\mathcal{H}| - 2|\mathcal{F}|)_g}{(2^n - |\mathcal{H}|)_{q+|\mathcal{F}|+g}} \\
&\geq \frac{2^{(q-|\mathcal{F}|)n} \cdot (2^n - |\mathcal{H}|)_{2|\mathcal{F}|} \cdot (2^n - |\mathcal{H}| - 2|\mathcal{F}|)_g}{(2^n - |\mathcal{H}|)_{q+|\mathcal{F}|+g}} \cdot \left(1 - \frac{4|\mathcal{F}||\mathcal{H}|^2 + 8|\mathcal{F}|^2|\mathcal{H}| + 6|\mathcal{F}|^3}{2^{2n}}\right) \\
&\geq \frac{2^{(q-|\mathcal{F}|)n}}{(2^n - |\mathcal{H}| - 2|\mathcal{F}| - g)_{q-|\mathcal{F}|}} \cdot \left(1 - \frac{4|\mathcal{F}||\mathcal{H}|^2 + 8|\mathcal{F}|^2|\mathcal{H}| + 6|\mathcal{F}|^3}{2^{2n}}\right) \\
&\geq 1 - \frac{4q(\ell+2)^2 + 8q^2(\ell+2) + 6q^3}{2^{2n}} ,
\end{aligned} \tag{7}$$

where the first inequality comes from Lemma 2.2.

6.4 Conclusion

Wrapping Up. From Lemma 2.1 and combining Lemma 6.1 and Eq. (7), we obtain

$$\begin{aligned}
\mathsf{Adv}^{\mathrm{prf}}_{\mathsf{n1kf9}[\pi]}(\mathcal{A}) \leq \frac{8q^3(\ell+3)^3}{2^{2n}} + \frac{129q^3(\ell+2)^6}{2^{3n}} + \frac{36q^2(\ell+2)^4}{2^{2n}} \\
+ \frac{6q^3}{2^{2n}} + \frac{q(\ell+2)^2}{2^n} + \frac{3q}{2^n}
\end{aligned}$$

and conclude the proof of Theorem 3.2.

Acknowledgments. We thank the reviewers for their useful comments. This work has been funded in parts by the European Union through the ERC consolidator grant SWORD (num. 724725), and by National Key Research and Development Program of China (No. 2019YFB2101601).

References

1. Computer data authentication. National Bureau of Standards, NIST FIPS PUB 113, U.S. Department of Commerce (1985)

2. v 3.1.1, G.T..: Specification of the 3gpp confidentiality and integrity algorithms, document 1: f8 and f9 specification. https://www.3gpp.org/DynaReport/35-series.htm
3. v 3.1.1, G.T..: Specification of the 3gpp confidentiality and integrity algorithms, document 2: Kasumi specification. http://www.3gpp.org/ftp/Specs/html-info/35-series.htm
4. An, J.H., Bellare, M.: Constructing VIL-MACs from FIL-MACs: message authentication under weakened assumptions. In: Wiener, M. (ed.) CRYPTO 1999. LNCS, vol. 1666, pp. 252–269. Springer, Heidelberg (1999). https://doi.org/10.1007/3-540-48405-1_16
5. Banik, S., Pandey, S.K., Peyrin, T., Sasaki, Yu., Sim, S.M., Todo, Y.: GIFT: a small present. In: Fischer, W., Homma, N. (eds.) CHES 2017. LNCS, vol. 10529, pp. 321–345. Springer, Cham (2017). https://doi.org/10.1007/978-3-319-66787-4_16
6. Beaulieu, R., Shors, D., Smith, J., Treatman-Clark, S., Weeks, B., Wingers, L.: The SIMON and SPECK families of lightweight block ciphers. Cryptology ePrint Archive, Report 2013/404 (2013). https://eprint.iacr.org/2013/404
7. Bellare, M., Canetti, R., Krawczyk, H.: Keying hash functions for message authentication. In: Koblitz, N. (ed.) CRYPTO 1996. LNCS, vol. 1109, pp. 1–15. Springer, Heidelberg (1996). https://doi.org/10.1007/3-540-68697-5_1
8. Bellare, M., Kilian, J., Rogaway, P.: The security of the cipher block chaining message authentication code. J. Comput. Syst. Sci. **61**(3), 362–399 (2000)
9. Bellare, M., Pietrzak, K., Rogaway, P.: Improved security analyses for CBC MACs. In: Shoup, V. (ed.) CRYPTO 2005. LNCS, vol. 3621, pp. 527–545. Springer, Heidelberg (2005). https://doi.org/10.1007/11535218_32
10. Bhargavan, K., Leurent, G.: On the practical (in-)security of 64-bit block ciphers: collision attacks on HTTP over TLS and OpenVPN. In: Weippl, E.R., Katzenbeisser, S., Kruegel, C., Myers, A.C., Halevi, S. (eds.) ACM CCS 2016, pp. 456–467. ACM Press (Oct 2016). https://doi.org/10.1145/2976749.2978423
11. Black, J., Rogaway, P.: A block-cipher mode of operation for parallelizable message authentication. In: Knudsen, L.R. (ed.) EUROCRYPT 2002. LNCS, vol. 2332, pp. 384–397. Springer, Heidelberg (2002). https://doi.org/10.1007/3-540-46035-7_25
12. Bogdanov, A., et al.: PRESENT: an ultra-lightweight block cipher. In: Paillier, P., Verbauwhede, I. (eds.) CHES 2007. LNCS, vol. 4727, pp. 450–466. Springer, Heidelberg (2007). https://doi.org/10.1007/978-3-540-74735-2_31
13. Borghoff, J., et al.: PRINCE – a low-latency block cipher for pervasive computing applications. In: Wang, X., Sako, K. (eds.) ASIACRYPT 2012. LNCS, vol. 7658, pp. 208–225. Springer, Heidelberg (2012). https://doi.org/10.1007/978-3-642-34961-4_14
14. Chen, S., Steinberger, J.: Tight security bounds for key-alternating ciphers. In: Nguyen, P.Q., Oswald, E. (eds.) EUROCRYPT 2014. LNCS, vol. 8441, pp. 327–350. Springer, Heidelberg (2014). https://doi.org/10.1007/978-3-642-55220-5_19
15. Datta, N., Dutta, A., Nandi, M., Paul, G.: Double-block hash-then-sum: a paradigm for constructing BBB secure PRF. IACR Trans. Symmetric Cryptol. **2018**(3), 36–92 (2018). https://doi.org/10.13154/tosc.v2018.i3.36-92
16. Datta, N., Dutta, A., Nandi, M., Paul, G., Zhang, L.: Building single-key beyond birthday bound message authentication code. Cryptology ePrint Archive, Report 2015/958 (2015). https://eprint.iacr.org/2015/958
17. Datta, N., Dutta, A., Nandi, M., Paul, G., Zhang, L.: Single key variant of PMAC_Plus. IACR Trans. Symmetric Cryptol. **2017**(4), 268–305 (2017). https://doi.org/10.13154/tosc.v2017.i4.268-305

18. De Cannière, C., Dunkelman, O., Knežević, M.: KATAN and KTANTAN — a family of small and efficient hardware-oriented block ciphers. In: Clavier, C., Gaj, K. (eds.) CHES 2009. LNCS, vol. 5747, pp. 272–288. Springer, Heidelberg (2009). https://doi.org/10.1007/978-3-642-04138-9_20
19. Dodis, Y., Pietrzak, K., Puniya, P.: A new mode of operation for block ciphers and length-preserving MACs. In: Smart, N. (ed.) EUROCRYPT 2008. LNCS, vol. 4965, pp. 198–219. Springer, Heidelberg (2008). https://doi.org/10.1007/978-3-540-78967-3_12
20. Dodis, Y., Steinberger, J.: Message authentication codes from unpredictable block ciphers. In: Halevi, S. (ed.) CRYPTO 2009. LNCS, vol. 5677, pp. 267–285. Springer, Heidelberg (2009). https://doi.org/10.1007/978-3-642-03356-8_16
21. Hoang, V.T., Tessaro, S.: Key-alternating ciphers and key-length extension: exact bounds and multi-user security. In: Robshaw, M., Katz, J. (eds.) CRYPTO 2016. LNCS, vol. 9814, pp. 3–32. Springer, Heidelberg (2016). https://doi.org/10.1007/978-3-662-53018-4_1
22. Iwata, T., Kohno, T.: New security proofs for the 3GPP confidentiality and integrity algorithms. In: Roy, B., Meier, W. (eds.) FSE 2004. LNCS, vol. 3017, pp. 427–445. Springer, Heidelberg (2004). https://doi.org/10.1007/978-3-540-25937-4_27
23. Iwata, T., Kurosawa, K.: OMAC: one-key CBC MAC. In: Johansson, T. (ed.) FSE 2003. LNCS, vol. 2887, pp. 129–153. Springer, Heidelberg (2003). https://doi.org/10.1007/978-3-540-39887-5_11
24. Jha, A., Nandi, M.: Revisiting structure graph and its applications to CBC-MAC and EMAC. Cryptology ePrint Archive, Report 2016/161 (2016). https://eprint.iacr.org/2016/161
25. Kim, S., Lee, B., Lee, J.: Tight security bounds for double-block hash-then-sum MACs. In: Canteaut, A., Ishai, Y. (eds.) EUROCRYPT 2020. LNCS, vol. 12105, pp. 435–465. Springer, Cham (2020). https://doi.org/10.1007/978-3-030-45721-1_16
26. Leurent, G., Nandi, M., Sibleyras, F.: Generic attacks against beyond-birthday-bound MACs. In: Shacham, H., Boldyreva, A. (eds.) CRYPTO 2018. LNCS, vol. 10991, pp. 306–336. Springer, Cham (2018). https://doi.org/10.1007/978-3-319-96884-1_11
27. Naito, Y.: Blockcipher-based MACs: beyond the birthday bound without message length. In: Takagi, T., Peyrin, T. (eds.) ASIACRYPT 2017. LNCS, vol. 10626, pp. 446–470. Springer, Cham (2017). https://doi.org/10.1007/978-3-319-70700-6_16
28. Naito, Y.: Improved security bound of LightMAC_Plus and its single-key variant. In: Smart, N.P. (ed.) CT-RSA 2018. LNCS, vol. 10808, pp. 300–318. Springer, Cham (2018). https://doi.org/10.1007/978-3-319-76953-0_16
29. Nandi, M.: A unified method for improving PRF bounds for a class of Blockcipher based MACs. In: Hong, S., Iwata, T. (eds.) FSE 2010. LNCS, vol. 6147, pp. 212–229. Springer, Heidelberg (2010). https://doi.org/10.1007/978-3-642-13858-4_12
30. Patarin, J.: The Coefficients H technique. In: Avanzi, R.M., Keliher, L., Sica, F. (eds.) SAC 2008. LNCS, vol. 5381, pp. 328–345. Springer, Heidelberg (2009). https://doi.org/10.1007/978-3-642-04159-4_21
31. Petrank, E., Rackoff, C.: CBC MAC for real-time data sources. J. Cryptol. **13**(3), 315–338 (2000). https://doi.org/10.1007/s001450010009
32. Preneel, B., van Oorschot, P.C.: MDx-MAC and building fast MACs from hash functions. In: Coppersmith, D. (ed.) CRYPTO 1995. LNCS, vol. 963, pp. 1–14. Springer, Heidelberg (1995). https://doi.org/10.1007/3-540-44750-4_1

33. Shen, Y., Sibleyras, F.: Key-reduced variants of 3kf9 with beyond-birthday-bound security. Cryptology ePrint Archive, Paper 2022/668 (2022). https://eprint.iacr.org/2022/668 (full version)
34. Shen, Y., Wang, L., Gu, D., Weng, J.: Revisiting the security of DbHtS MACs: beyond-birthday-bound in the multi-user setting. In: Malkin, T., Peikert, C. (eds.) CRYPTO 2021. LNCS, vol. 12827, pp. 309–336. Springer, Cham (2021). https://doi.org/10.1007/978-3-030-84252-9_11
35. Yang, G., Zhu, B., Suder, V., Aagaard, M.D., Gong, G.: The Simeck family of lightweight block ciphers. In: Güneysu, T., Handschuh, H. (eds.) CHES 2015. LNCS, vol. 9293, pp. 307–329. Springer, Heidelberg (2015). https://doi.org/10.1007/978-3-662-48324-4_16
36. Yasuda, K.: The sum of CBC MACs is a secure PRF. In: Pieprzyk, J. (ed.) CT-RSA 2010. LNCS, vol. 5985, pp. 366–381. Springer, Heidelberg (2010). https://doi.org/10.1007/978-3-642-11925-5_25
37. Yasuda, K.: A new variant of PMAC: beyond the birthday bound. In: Rogaway, P. (ed.) CRYPTO 2011. LNCS, vol. 6841, pp. 596–609. Springer, Heidelberg (2011). https://doi.org/10.1007/978-3-642-22792-9_34
38. Zhang, L., Wu, W., Sui, H., Wang, P.: 3kf9: enhancing 3GPP-MAC beyond the birthday bound. In: Wang, X., Sako, K. (eds.) ASIACRYPT 2012. LNCS, vol. 7658, pp. 296–312. Springer, Heidelberg (2012). https://doi.org/10.1007/978-3-642-34961-4_19

Jammin' on the Deck

Norica Băcuieți[1], Joan Daemen[1], Seth Hoffert[3], Gilles Van Assche[2(✉)], and Ronny Van Keer[2]

[1] Radboud University, Nijmegen, The Netherlands
[2] STMicroelectronics, Diegem, Belgium
gilles-iacr@noekeon.org
[3] Lincoln, Nebraska, USA

Abstract. Currently, a vast majority of symmetric-key cryptographic schemes are built as block cipher modes. The block cipher is designed to be hard to distinguish from a random permutation and this is supported by cryptanalysis, while (good) modes can be proven secure if a random permutation takes the place of the block cipher. As such, block ciphers form an abstraction level that marks the border between cryptanalysis and security proofs. In this paper, we investigate a re-factored version of symmetric-key cryptography built not around the block ciphers but rather the deck function: a keyed function with arbitrary input and output length and incrementality properties. This allows for modes of use that are simpler to analyze and still very efficient thanks to the excellent performance of currently proposed deck functions. We focus on authenticated encryption (AE) modes with varying levels of robustness. Our modes have built-in support for sessions, but are also efficient without them. As a by-product, we define a new ideal model for AE dubbed the *jammin cipher*. Unlike the OAE2 security models, the jammin cipher is both a operational ideal scheme and a security reference, and addresses real-world use cases such as bi-directional communication and multi-key security.

Keywords: Deck functions · Authenticated encryption · Wide block cipher · Modes of use · Ideal model

1 Introduction

Currently, a vast majority of symmetric-key cryptographic schemes are built as a mode of use of a block cipher. A block cipher is governed by a secret key and transforms an input block of fixed length into an output block of the same length, and as such its functionality is rather limited. However, the existence of powerful modes of use really unleashes the power of block ciphers: Combining them allows building cryptographic schemes for encryption, authentication and authenticated encryption of messages consisting of arbitrary-length plaintext and associated data. Block ciphers have even been used to build hash functions.

S. Agrawal and D. Lin (Eds.): ASIACRYPT 2022, LNCS 13792, pp. 555–584, 2022.
https://doi.org/10.1007/978-3-031-22966-4_19

1.1 Moving to Deck Functions

Need for PRF Security. Modes of use usually come with a security guarantee: Assuming the underlying block cipher satisfies some security criterion, the cryptographic scheme can be proven secure. Often, this criterion is that the block cipher, when keyed with a uniformly chosen key unknown to the adversary, is hard to distinguish from a random permutation; this is known as the pseudorandom permutation (PRP) security of a block cipher, in the case that an adversary is only allowed to query the block cipher in the forward direction, otherwise it is called strong PRP (SPRP) security. The PRP and SPRP security notions have become so accepted that they are referred to as the *standard model*. Thanks to this split in block ciphers and modes, the assurance of such cryptographic schemes relies on public scrutiny of the block cipher with respect to its (S)PRP security.

The security guarantee of many modes hit the so-called birthday bound and that causes the security of block-cipher based modes to break down as soon as the data complexity reaches $2^{n/2}$, with n the block size. This accounts for the presence, or absence, of collisions in block cipher outputs, depending on the mode.

Hitting this birthday bound is due to the invertibility of the block cipher while most modern block cipher modes do not even use the inverse block cipher.[1] Such modes often rely on the keyed block cipher to behave like a random function rather than a permutation, e.g., see [33], and this is called *pseudorandom function* (PRF) security.

Variable-input and Output Lengths. Block cipher modes parse variable-length inputs as fixed-length blocks. This often comes with considerable complexity, such as dealing with complete last blocks, that propagates to the security proofs. Modes would be simpler if the underlying primitive would *natively* support variable input and output lengths. Moreover, (S)PRP security makes little sense for a primitive with variable input and output lengths, and striving for good PRF security makes more sense.

Such primitives would be a good replacement of block ciphers as a focus point in symmetric key cryptography and they have actually been proposed by Daemen et al. under the name of *deck function* [15]. A construction for building deck functions is called *farfalle*, and the authors showcased an instance of farfalle based on KECCAK-f called KRAVATTE with excellent performance, and later a second one called XOOFFF improving on all aspects over KRAVATTE [8,15]. But *deck function* just specifies an interface and farfalle is not the only way to build a deck function, in the same way that there are multiple ways to build a block cipher: a wide design space is waiting to be explored!

[1] The input and output of a block cipher are often called plaintext and ciphertext, respectively. This may be correct for the ECB mode, but for the majority of today's modes, the input is not the plaintext and/or the output is not the ciphertext.

Performance. We focus on authenticated encryption (AE), i.e., schemes that simultaneously achieve confidentiality and authenticity [7,36]. Next to the simplicity of modes, performance is a clear and natural motivation for exploring AE using deck functions. For instance, KRAVATTE and XOOFFF have excellent reported performance figures and outperform modes using the AES block cipher, sometimes even when the platform has hardware AES support [13]. Even if faster block ciphers can be built, security proofs of their modes rely on their (S)PRP security, and achieving a solid level of (S)PRP security comes at the price of a relatively large number of rounds. Building a variable-input-length function that targets PRF security using the same building blocks can be done more efficiently when the reductionist security argument is dropped. We illustrate this with two MAC functions: CMAC [34] with underlying block cipher AES-128 [18] and Pelican-MAC [19]: for long messages the former costs 10 AES rounds while the latter only 4 (unkeyed) AES rounds per 128-bit block of input. Despite the absence of a reductionist security proof, Pelican-MAC has maintained its security claim, very close to that of CMAC with AES-128, up to this day. A similar argument can be made for functions with variable-length output. Efficient deck functions support both a variable-length input and output and trade reductionist (S)PRP-based security proofs in for security based on cryptanalysis. Clearly, deck function-based cryptography seems like an alternative to block-ciphers that is worth exploring.

1.2 Processing Sessions

Sequences of Messages. Today's applications for cryptography go beyond the encryption or authentication of individual messages. The processing of streams of data, with intermediate tags, and bi-directional communication are common use cases. To this end, we cover as well the traditional authenticated encryption of a single message, i.e., a plaintext-associated data pair, as the authenticated encryption of a sequence of messages. More specifically, we define a *session* as the process of authenticating a message in the context of previously sent ones within the sequence. By extension, we also speak of a session for a sequence of messages that are processed in this way. We envision session-supporting AE as a scheme holding a rolling state that "accumulates" the messages as they are processed.

There exist other techniques for dealing with a sequence of messages. First, *stateful* authenticated encryption (sAE) refers to a scheme that deals with reordering, replay and omission of messages [6,41]. In its most generic definition, it is parameterized with is a set of admissible message numbers. E.g., if the sender emits messages $(1, 2, 3, 4)$, would the receiver accept ciphertext messages arriving the order $(2, 1, 2, 4)$? In a sense, our concept of session is a special case of sAE where the only admissible sequence of ciphertexts is the original sequence.

Then, *online* authenticated encryption refers to the ability to decrypt on the fly with a bounded memory size, see Hoang et al. [25] (HRRV). A typical example would be the encryption of a large message (e.g., a movie) that is cut it into segments (e.g., chunks of a few seconds), each of these being authenticated.

Our concept of session can implement such a use case, although with a diverging definition of a message: One *segment* in HRRV is treated as one *message* in our session. Yet, it is not in HRRV's philosophy to support bi-directional communications as it focuses on sending just one message, even if cut into segments.

If a unique identifier N of the message sequence is available, authenticated encrypting a sequence of messages can be approached in a rather simple way. We can simply encrypt messages under the diversifier (N, n), with n the message number within the sequence, since (N, n) is a nonce. As a rule, the receiver only decrypts and checks message (N, n) if all the previous messages $(N, n' < n)$ were correct.

Adding a rolling state that "accumulates" the messages as they are processed gives additional benefits. First, it provides further robustness. If a message is tampered with at any point in the session, the rest of the session becomes completely corrupted-so if the attacker somehow tricks the implementation into continuing after a bad tag, everything will look like random noise. It forces the implementation to deal with a bad message and it becomes impossible to ignore it. With the previous approach, it was still possible to decrypt message $n + 1$ successfully even if message n was corrupted.

Second, the management of unique diversifiers becomes simpler and more natural. Uniqueness of the diversifier must be ensured at the level of sessions, as individual messages within the session are diversified at least by the number of messages received so far. If a key is bound to only one session, the need of session-level unique diversifiers even vanishes; this can happen, e.g., if the key is the result of a ephemeral Diffie-Hellman key exchange aimed at securing one particular session. Also, with diversifier-reuse-resistant modes, the rest of the session becomes perfectly diversified if any message in the session contains a diversifier.

Sessions and Incrementality. There is another reason for looking at sessions with a rolling state. Several symmetric cryptographic primitives and modes support *incrementality* properties, i.e., by keeping state, appending additional input or requesting further output does not require to re-process everything from the beginning. Note that this is also an explicitly required property of deck functions.

Incrementality comes in handy when defining session-supporting AE schemes: A formal definition specifies that any output of the scheme (keystream or authentication tag) depends on the entire sequence of messages received so far, while the implementation relies on the incrementality and a rolling state to process each message only once. A striking example is the duplex construction that provides an incremental interface to the sponge construction, on top of which it is fairly easy to build session-supporting AE [9].

We could say that the definition of sessions was influenced by the existence of incrementality properties, but in the end sessions and incrementality combine in an elegant and useful way.

1.3 Looking for an Ideal Model

Having set out our goal as to build AE modes on top of a deck function, we need to opt for an ideal model. An obvious choice would be the $(\$, \perp)$ model: The ciphertext looks random and any decryption attempt returns an error. However, this model is referential but not operational:

- *operational*: serves as an ideal scheme for use in higher-level protocols;
- *referential*: serves as an ideal-world model in distinguishability settings for modes or schemes, to prove, or claim, a distinguishing bound.

We aim for an ideal scheme that is both operational and referential. This allows using it in a higher-level protocol, prove that secure, and subsequently instantiate it with a concrete AE scheme; the security of the resulting protocol can then be quantified using the triangle inequality. Some definitions come as a pair of an operational and a referential model, but often with a security gap between the two. For instance, the referential deterministic AE (DAE) is paired with the operational pseudo-random injection (PRI) [40]. In the former encryption gives uniformly distributed ciphertext without replacement and is hence non-deterministic and decryption always returns an error.

The online authenticated encryption 2 (OAE2) security definitions from HRRV are the closest to what we try to achieve [25]. Specifically, OAE2 supports something very close to our sessions and covers streaming applications, where plaintexts and ciphertexts can be processed on the fly. However, they define not a single ideal-world scheme, but a set of three schemes, Ideal2A, Ideal2B and Rand2C. The former two are operational and define the same security concept, but have different interfaces, whereas the third, Rand2C, is referential-only and defines a different security concept. In particular, in Ideal2A and Ideal2B forgery is possible and in Rand2C forgery is impossible by construction. Interestingly, the security gap between Ideal2 and Rand2C is *larger than the one between the modes we define in this paper and our ideal scheme*, see Sect. 2.4.

1.4 Our Contributions

Our two main contributions are an ideal model and a number of deck function modes, both for session-supporting and non-session-supporting authenticated encryption.

The "ultimate" Ideal-world Authenticated Encryption Scheme. We define the *jammin cipher* that is at the same time deterministic, session-supporting, operational and referential. The designation "ultimate" means it achieves the highest security thinkable while behaving deterministically: Forgery is impossible, the cryptograms are as random as injectivity allows and equal inputs give equal outputs in the same context. Our ideal-world scheme supports sessions, although it naturally also covers non-session AE.

Besides combining operational and referential roles in a single scheme, the jammin cipher has several interesting features and compares favorably to OAE2:

- It can serve as a security reference for *both nonce-enforcing and nonce-misuse-resistant schemes.* For OAE2, variants like nOAE or dOAE must be used instead [25].
- It produces cryptograms whose *distribution is intuitive and is as random as allowed while leaving the possibility for decryption.* In contrast, the definition of Ideal2A/B make use of a rather complex building block IdealOAE (τ), called uniformly sampled τ-expanding injective functions.
- It has *ciphertext expansion* as a parameter, required when dealing with schemes that have variable ciphertext expansion due to the use of block encryption.
- It addresses *multi-key security* by supporting multiple instances. While OAE2 focuses on single-key security, Hoang and Shen propose a generalization of nOAE called nOAE2 in the multi-key setting [26].
- It supports unwrap and wrap calls in any order, including *bi-directional communication.* Instead, an instance of Ideal2B can only encipher messages or decipher cryptograms but not both.

Deck Function-Based Session-Supporting Authenticated Encryption. We introduce a number of modes based on deck functions, with different combinations of features, as summarized in Table 1. For the last four modes, we propose a unified approach of achieving several security goals via a Feistel network.

There exist generic modes for building session-supporting AE, like CHAIN and STREAM [25]. However, these build a secure session AE scheme using a secure conventional AE scheme whereas we build both using a deck function. Some other constructions are block-oriented, which is what we try to improve using deck functions [1,5,10,21]. The authenticated streamwise on-line encryption (ASOE) construction explicitly avoids blocks, but it aims for a weaker security notion [42]. Note that Barbosa and Farshim point out that an indifferentiable AE can be realized via a 3-round Feistel network [4].

Table 1. Overview of our AE modes.

Mode	Section	Tolerates nonce misuse	Tolerates release of unverified plaintext	Minimal ciphertext expansion
Deck-PLAIN	4			✓
Deck-BO	5.1	✓		
Deck-BOREE	5.2	✓	✓	
Deck-JAMBO	5.3	✓		✓
Deck-JAMBOREE	5.4	✓	✓	✓

Note that the jammin cipher and the deck function-based modes are efficient for single message AE and can be used in sAE modes.

1.5 Conventions

The set of all bit strings is denoted $\mathbb{Z}_2^*$ and ϵ is the empty string. The length in bits of the string X is denoted $|X|$. The concatenation of two strings X, Y is denoted as $X||Y$ and their bitwise addition as $X + Y$, with the resulting string having length $\min(|X|, |Y|)$. Bit string values are noted with a typewriter font, such as `01101`. The repetition of a bit is noted in exponent, e.g., $0^3 = \mathtt{000}$. In a sequence of m strings, we separate the individual strings with a semicolumn, i.e., $X^{(0)}; X^{(1)}; \ldots; X^{(m-1)}$. The set of all sequences of strings is denoted $(\mathbb{Z}_2^*)^*$ and $\varnothing$ is the sequence containing no strings at all. Similarly, the set of all sequences containing at least one string is denoted $(\mathbb{Z}_2^*)^+$. Finally, $\varnothing$ is the empty set and $\perp$ denotes an error code.

In this paper we perform security analysis in the *distinguishability framework* where one bounds the advantage of an adversary $\mathcal{A}$ in distinguishing a real-world system from an ideal-world system.

Definition 1. *Let $\mathcal{O}, \mathcal{P}$ be two collections of oracles with the same interface. The advantage of an adversary $\mathcal{A}$ in distinguishing $\mathcal{O}$ from $\mathcal{P}$ is defined as*

$$\Delta_{\mathcal{A}}(\mathcal{O} \; ; \; \mathcal{P}) = \left|\Pr\left(\mathcal{A}^{\mathcal{O}} \to 1\right) - \Pr\left(\mathcal{A}^{\mathcal{P}} \to 1\right)\right|.$$

Here $\mathcal{A}$ is an algorithm that returns 0 or 1.

If we can build a real-world system $\mathcal{P}$ that is hard to distinguish from the ideal-world system $\mathcal{O}$, then we can replace $\mathcal{O}$ by $\mathcal{P}$ in the protocol without sacrificing much security. Concretely, if we can prove an upper bound on the distinguishing advantage $\Delta_{\mathcal{A}}(\mathcal{O} \; ; \; \mathcal{P})$ for any adversary $\mathcal{A}$, the attack success probability increases by at most that bound.

1.6 Outline

In Sect. 2, we define the jammin cipher. In Sect. 3, we discuss deck functions and some of their basic applications. In Sect. 4 we define Deck-PLAIN, the simplest of our five AE modes. If using a strong deck function and on the condition that the encryption context is a nonce, Deck-PLAIN can be distinguished from the jammin cipher only through tag guessing. In Sect. 5, we introduce four modes that do not require the encryption context to be a nonce, with different properties.

2 The Jammin Cipher, an Ideal-World AE Scheme

We define the *jammin cipher* in Algorithm 1. We describe it in an object-oriented way, with *object instances* (or *instances* for short) held by the communicating parties. An instance belongs to a given party who initializes it with an object identifier ID. Such an identifier is the counterpart of a secret key in the real world: Encryption and decryption will work consistently only between instances initialized with the same identifier. This setup models independent

Algorithm 1. The jammin cipher $\mathcal{J}^{\text{WrapExpand}(p)}$

1: **Parameter:** WrapExpand, a t-expanding function
2: **Global variables:** codebook initially set to $\perp$ for all, taboo initially set to *empty*

3: **Instance constructor:** init(ID)
4: **return** new instance inst with attribute inst.history = ID

5: **Instance cloner:** inst.clone()
6: **return** new instance inst′ with the history attribute copied from inst

7: **Interface:** inst.wrap(A, P) returns C
8: context ← inst.history; A
9: **if** codebook(context; P) = $\perp$ **then**
10: $\mathcal{C} = \mathbb{Z}_2^{\text{WrapExpand}(|P|)} \setminus (\text{codebook(context}; *) \cup \text{taboo(context)})$
11: **if** $\mathcal{C} = \varnothing$ **then return** $\perp$
12: codebook(context; P) $\xleftarrow{\$} \mathcal{C}$
13: inst.history ← inst.history; A; P
14: **return** codebook(context; P)

15: **Interface:** inst.unwrap(A, C) returns P or $\perp$
16: context ← inst.history; A
17: **if** $\exists! P$: codebook(context; P) = C **then**
18: inst.history ← inst.history; A; P
19: **return** P
20: **else**
21: taboo(context) ← C
22: **return** $\perp$

pairs (or groups) that make use of the AE scheme simultaneously. For example, Alice and Bob may secure their communication each using instances that share the same identifier $\text{ID}_{\text{Alice and Bob}}$, while Edward and Emma use instances initialized with $\text{ID}_{\text{Edward and Emma}}$. We will informally call an *object* the set of instances sharing the same object identifier. This way, all the instances of the same object have indistinguishable behavior, and this justifies that we collectively call them an object, whereas instances of different objects are completely independent.

Our scheme supports two functions: wrap and unwrap. With the wrap function the object computes a cryptogram C from a message that has a plaintext P and associated data A, both arbitrary bit strings. With the unwrap function the object computes the plaintext P from the cryptogram C and A again. The cryptogram C is the encryption of P for a given A.

The jammin cipher is parameterized with a function WrapExpand(p) that specifies the length of the cryptogram given the length p of the plaintext. Typical examples observed in AE schemes in the literature are WrapExpand(p) $= p + t$ with t some fixed length, e.g., 128 for stream encryption followed by a 128-bit tag. For OCB [39], we have WrapExpand(p) $= t \left\lceil \frac{p}{t} + 1 \right\rceil$ with t the block length of the cipher. Both are examples of *t-expanding* functions. For use with the jammin cipher, we require WrapExpand to satisfy this property, defined below.

Definition 2. *A function* $f\colon \mathbb{Z}_{\geq 0} \to \mathbb{Z}_{\geq 0}$ *is* t-expanding *iff (i)* $\forall \ell > 0\colon f(\ell) > f(0)$ *and (ii)* $\forall \ell\colon f(\ell) \geq \ell + t$.

Property (i) is needed in some of the modes to distinguish authentication-only messages from others. Property (ii) allows us to use t as a security parameter: the advantage of distinguishing a real-world scheme from an ideal scheme will be lower bound by an expression in the number of queries multiplied by 2^{-t}.

When two parties communicate, they usually have more than one message to send to each other. And a message is often a response to a previous request, or in general its meaning is to be understood in the context of the previous messages. The jammin cipher is *stateful*, where the sequence of messages exchanged so far is tracked in the attribute history. Initialization sets this attribute to the object identifier and each wrap and (successful) unwrap appends a message (A, P). So history is a sequence with ID followed by zero, one or more messages (A, P).

A *session* is the process in which the history grows with the messages exchanged so far. The wrap and unwrap functions make the history act as associated data, so that a cryptogram authenticates not only the message (A, P) but also the sequence of messages exchanged so far. An important application of this are intermediate tags, which authenticate a long message in an incremental way.

Finally, a jammin cipher object can be cloned. This is the ideal world's equivalent of making a copy of the state of the cipher. This means the user can save the history and restart from it ad libitum.

2.1 Inner Workings

The jammin cipher keeps track of all wrap queries in a global archive called codebook. This is a mapping from tuples $(\mathsf{history}; A; P)$ to a cryptogram or an error code. The data elements history and A together form the *context* for the encryption of P: In different contexts, the jammin cipher encrypts plaintexts independently. We write $\mathsf{context} \leftarrow \mathsf{history}; A$ as the context for encryption in a wrap call, or decryption in an unwrap call, is the history with A appended.

Initially, all the entries of codebook return an error. In the algorithm, the expression $\mathsf{codebook}(\mathsf{context}; P) \xleftarrow{\$} \mathcal{S}$ denotes the assignment of a random element chosen uniformly from $\mathcal{S}$ to the entry $\mathsf{codebook}(\mathsf{context}; P)$, and $\mathsf{codebook}(\mathsf{context}; *)$ denotes the set of the values of $\mathsf{codebook}(\mathsf{context}; P)$ over all P.

Similarly, the jammin cipher keeps track of invalid cryptograms in a global archive called taboo. This is a mapping from (decryption) contexts to a set of cryptograms. Initially taboo is empty and with each attempt at decryption of an invalid cryptogram, it adds the cryptogram to the set of the corresponding context $\mathsf{context} = \mathsf{history}; A$. The expression $\mathsf{taboo}(\mathsf{context}) \leftarrow C$ denotes the addition of C to $\mathsf{taboo}(\mathsf{context})$.

Cryptograms in codebook are never overwritten, as the only place where a cryptogram value is assigned to codebook is on line 12, under the condition that codebook previously contains $\perp$. This makes wrapping deterministic. Similarly, the jammin cipher will unwrap any ciphertext C to the same plaintext value in any given context, i.e., unwrapping is deterministic. This is formalized in the following property.

Proposition 1. *From* codebook *one always recovers at most one plaintext value:*

$$\forall(\mathsf{context}, C), |\{P : \mathsf{codebook}(\mathsf{context}; P) = C\}| \leq 1.$$

Proof. Let $C \in \mathcal{C}$ be the value that is added to $\mathsf{codebook}(\mathsf{context}; P)$ in line 12. If $P' \neq P$ was another plaintext value such that $\mathsf{codebook}(\mathsf{context}; P') = C$, then we would get a contradiction as $C \in \mathsf{codebook}(\mathsf{context}; *)$ and thus $C \notin \mathcal{C}$, proving the proposition. □

We see that in line 11, wrap may return an error and therefore exhibit non-ideal behavior. We will now prove that for reasonable ciphertext expansion this requires an excessive number of specific unsuccessful unwrap queries.

Proposition 2. *If* WrapExpand *is t-expanding with $t \geq 2$,* wrap *is successful unless there were at least 2^t unsuccessful unwrap queries with the same context.*

Proof. A necessary condition for an error to be returned is the following. There exists a context and a cryptogram length n such that the sum of the following two items is at least 2^n:

- the number of calls to $\mathsf{wrap}(A, P)$ with $\mathrm{WrapExpand}(|P|) = n$,
- the number of unsuccessful calls to $\mathsf{unwrap}(A, C)$ with $|C| = n$.

This is because the cardinality of $\mathcal{C}$ in line 10 is at least 2^n minus the number of n-bit strings in $\mathsf{codebook}(\mathsf{context}; *)$ or in $\mathsf{taboo}(\mathsf{context})$.

First, let us consider the case where $n = \mathrm{WrapExpand}(0) \geq t$ with $P = \epsilon$. Given that WrapExpand is t-expanding, only $\mathsf{taboo}(\mathsf{context})$ can exclude possible cryptograms from $\mathcal{C}$ on line 10. It is therefore necessary to have at least $2^n \geq 2^t$ unsuccessful calls to unwrap.

Then, say $n > \mathrm{WrapExpand}(0)$. The number of plaintext values that wrap to ciphertexts of size n is limited to 2^{n-t+1}. The possible plaintext lengths p are such that $\mathrm{WrapExpand}(p) = n$ but they must satisfy $p \leq n - t$. Summing over all such possible lengths, the number of distinct plaintext values is upper bounded by 2^{n-t+1}. For line 11 to return an error, it is therefore necessary to have at least $2^n - 2^{n-t+1}$ unsuccessful calls to unwrap. Since $n > t \geq 2$ this is lower bounded by 2^t. □

2.2 Properties

The jammin cipher enjoys the following properties:

Deterministic wrapping: In a given context, an object wraps equal messages (A, P) to equal cryptograms C. It achieves this by tracking the cryptograms in the codebook archive.

Injective wrapping: An object wraps messages with equal context and A and different P to different cryptograms. It achieves this by excluding cryptogram values that it returned in earlier wrap calls for the same context and A.

Random cryptograms: Except for determinism and injectivity, all cryptograms C are fully random.

Deterministic unwrapping: In a given context, an object unwraps equal cryptograms to equal responses. It achieves this by tracking in taboo cryptogram values that it returns an error to.

Correctness: Thanks to deterministic (un)wrapping and injective wrapping, one jammin cipher object correctly unwraps what another wrapped, whenever their contexts are equal.

Forgery-freeness: In a given context, an object will only unwrap successfully cryptograms C resulting from prior wrap calls in the same context.

2.3 Discussion

Deterministic AE leaks in the sense identical plaintexts map to identical cryptograms. In particular, if the possible plaintexts form a small set, an adversary can recover it from the cryptogram by wrapping all of them. This opens to a family of attacks such as the chosen-prefix secret-suffix (CPSS) attack [20,25].

The countermeasure against these attacks is to make encryption *context-dependent*. If the user can ensure that the encryption context is unique per plaintext, equal plaintexts will give different cryptograms. Usually, this context is a message counter (e.g., in counter mode) or a (random) initial value (e.g., in CBC) and called a *nonce*. This naming is confusing when discussing use cases where the uniqueness of the data element cannot be guaranteed.

The jammin cipher does not enforce the encryption context to be a nonce, this is left up to the higher level protocol or use case.

The jammin cipher takes as encryption context the sequence of messages exchanged so far, including the associated data in the message containing the plaintext to be encrypted (in a message without plaintext, there is no encryption and hence no encryption context). The advantage of doing authenticated encryption in sessions is immediate as this reduces the requirement for global diversifiers of one per session rather than one per message. Session-level diversifiers may even be omitted unless communicating parties wish to start parallel threads or start afresh from the same shared key.

Definition 3. *We say that the* encryption context is a nonce *iff all wrap queries with non-empty plaintext have a different context* context.

In case of re-use of encryption context, the jammin cipher will leak equality of plaintexts given equal cryptograms obtained with equal encryption contexts, but nothing more. In some use cases this may be acceptable. For such use cases, the jammin cipher can serve as a security reference for modes or schemes. A proven upper bound on the distinguishing advantage between such a mode and the jammin cipher, proves that leakage is limited to equal plaintexts and encryption contexts, plus the proven advantage that is typically negligible.

In particular, stream encryption with a keystream that is generated from the encryption context is perfectly secure in use cases where the encryption context is a nonce, but its security completely breaks down when re-using encryption contexts. Therefore, if we wish security in case of repeating encryption contexts, we must use a more elaborate encryption mechanism than stream encryption.

An example of protocol with bi-directional communications can be found in the full version [11].

2.4 Security of the Jammin Cipher in the OAE2 Security Model

We demonstrate the OAE2 security of the jammin cipher by proving an upper bound on the distinguishing advantage between the jammin cipher and OAE2 ideal-world system Rand2C. Concretely, referring to the OAE2c security definition [25, Fig. 6], we prove a tight bound for the case that the ciphertext expansion is t bits.

Theorem 1. *Let* $\mathcal{J}^{+t}$ *be the jammin cipher with* $\mathrm{WrapExpand}(p) = p+t$. *Then, for any adversary* $\mathcal{D}$ *that makes at most* q *queries, we have*

$$\mathbf{Adv}^{\text{oae2-priv}}_{\mathcal{J}^{+t}}(\mathcal{D}) \leq \frac{q}{2^{t+1}} \quad \text{and} \quad \mathbf{Adv}^{\text{oae2-auth}}_{\mathcal{J}^{+t}}(\mathcal{D}) = 0\,.$$

Furthermore, when the encryption context is a nonce, we have

$$\mathbf{Adv}^{\text{oae2-priv}}_{\mathcal{J}^{+t}}(\mathcal{D}) = \mathbf{Adv}^{\text{oae2-auth}}_{\mathcal{J}^{+t}}(\mathcal{D}) = 0\,.$$

The proof can be found in the full version [11].

Our operational jammin cipher is hence fully indistinguishable from the non-operational Rand2C by a nonce-respecting adversary and defines the exact same security concept in that case. In case the encryption context is not a nonce, they can be distinguished only and exclusively by a property of Rand2C that makes it non-operational: non-injective encryption.

In [25, Proposition 2] the authors provide similar bounds for Ideal2B and obtain $\mathbf{Adv}^{\text{oae2-priv}}_{\text{Ideal2B}}(\mathcal{D}) \leq q^2/2^t$ and $\mathbf{Adv}^{\text{oae2-auth}}_{\text{Ideal2B}}(\mathcal{D}) \leq \ell/2^t$ with ℓ the number of messages in a single session. Thus, the jammin cipher is closer to the security definition Rand2C than Ideal2B is.

3 Deck functions

A *deck function* is a keyed function that takes a sequence of strings and returns a pseudorandom string of arbitrary length and that can be computed incrementally. Here *deck* stands for *Doubly-Extendable Cryptographic Keyed* function.

Definition 4 ([15]). *A* deck function F *takes as input a secret key* $K \in \mathcal{K}_F$ *and a sequence of an arbitrary number of strings* $X^{(0)};\ldots;X^{(m-1)} \in (\mathbb{Z}_2^*)^+$, *produces a string of bits of arbitrary length and takes from it the range starting from a specified offset $q \in \mathbb{N}$ and for a specified length $n \in \mathbb{N}$. We denote this as*

$$Z = 0^n + F_K\left(X^{(0)}; \ldots; X^{(m-1)}\right) \ll q \, .$$

A deck function must allow efficient incremental computing, as described below, and typically comes with a security claim, see Sect. 3.1.

By efficient incremental computing we mean the following: by keeping state after computing an output for input $X = X^{(0)}; \ldots; X^{(m-1)}$, computing an output for $X; Y^{(0)}; \ldots; Y^{(n-1)}$ should have cost independent of X. In addition, by keeping state after computing $0^n + F_K\left(X^{(0)}; \ldots; X^{(m-1)}\right) \ll q$, computing $0^m + F_K\left(X^{(0)}; \ldots; X^{(m-1)}\right) \ll (q+n)$ should have cost independent of n or q.

Regarding the notation, we assume that the number of bits that the deck function outputs is determined by the context. For instance, in the expression $X + F_K(\ldots)$, we assume that the deck function outputs $|X|$ bits. Also, in $X + (F_K(\ldots)\,||Y)$, the deck function outputs $|X| - |Y|$ bits so that the string inside the brackets matches X in length.

3.1 Security Claim

A deck function equipped with a fixed unknown random key should behave like a random oracle. We call this pseudorandom function (PRF) security.

Definition 5. *The advantage of an adversary $\mathcal{D}$ in distinguishing a deck function F from a random oracle $\mathcal{RO}$ is:*

$$\boldsymbol{Adv}_F^{\mathrm{prf}}(\mathcal{D}) = \left|\mathbb{P}\left[K \xleftarrow{\$} \mathcal{K}_F : \mathcal{D}^{F_K} = 1\right] - \mathbb{P}\left[\mathcal{D}^{\mathcal{RO}} = 1\right]\right| .$$

Here $\mathcal{RO}$ is a random oracle that takes as input a string sequence. We define the PRF advantage of a deck function $\boldsymbol{Adv}_F^{\mathrm{prf}}$ as

$$\boldsymbol{Adv}_F^{\mathrm{prf}}(\overline{R}) = \sup_{\mathcal{D} \in \mathcal{D}(\overline{R})} \boldsymbol{Adv}_F^{\mathrm{prf}}(\mathcal{D}) ,$$

with $\mathcal{D}(\overline{R})$ the set of all distinguishers with given resource limits $\overline{R}$. Here, we define the resource vector $\overline{R}$ in a rather abstract way, and in practice it typically comprises the data complexity M and the computational complexity N quantified in some well-defined unit.

Expressions for the PRF advantage of a particular deck function is not something that can be measured or proven. Rather, they are useful in security claims. For a particular deck function one can claim an upper bound on the PRF advantage and this serves as a challenge for cryptanalysts. For designers of cryptographic schemes making use of the deck function, they can serve as a security specification: Assuming the bound holds, it allows determining the security strength of the scheme. For the validity of the underlying assumption, one has no choice but to rely on cryptanalysis.

3.2 Multi-key Security

In a multi-user setting with u users, we can adapt Definition 5 and replace the key K with a key array $\vec{K}$ drawn from $\mathcal{K}_F^u$. The adversary has to distinguish between u independently keyed deck functions and u independent random oracles:

$$\mathbf{Adv}_F^{\mathrm{prf}}(\mathcal{D}) = \left|\mathbb{P}\left[\vec{K} \xleftarrow{\$} \mathcal{K}_F^u : \mathcal{D}^{F_{K_1},\ldots,F_{K_u}} = 1\right] - \mathbb{P}\left[\mathcal{D}^{\mathcal{RO}_1,\ldots,\mathcal{RO}_u} = 1\right]\right| .$$

The deck functions are independently keyed, that is, the keys are drawn from $\mathcal{K}_F$ with replacement. Consequently, $\mathbf{Adv}_F^{\mathrm{prf}}(\mathcal{D})$ cannot be smaller than the probability of collision within u draws in $\mathcal{K}_F$, or approximately $\frac{\binom{u}{2}}{|\mathcal{K}_F|}$ if u is small compared to the square root of the key space size.

Exhaustive key search is always possible, limiting the security of the deck function to $\log|\mathcal{K}_F|$ bits. If the adversary has access to the outputs of $F_{K_1}, \ldots, F_{K_u}$ for the same input, a single key guess has u chances of hitting one of the keys, leading to a security degradation of $\log u$ bits. Yet, one can avoid this degradation if the adversary is forced to feed different instances with different inputs, e.g., if the input is prefixed with a unique identifier. Whether adversary $\mathcal{D}$ has such a restriction is part of its resources $\overline{R}$.

3.3 Examples of Deck Functions

Deck functions can be built in many ways and two established constructions for building them from cryptographic permutations are the keyed duplex construction [17] and farfalle [8]. For the former, we can mention Strobe [23] and XOODYAK [14] as concrete instantiations. For the latter, KRAVATTE [8] and XOOFFF [15] are two farfalle instantiations making use of the KECCAK-f and XOODOO permutations respectively. Another example of deck function is Subterranean-deck as part of the Subterranean 2.0 cipher suite [16].

A deck function can be built from other primitives and guarantee a certain PRF security level on the condition that the underlying primitive satisfies some security definition. For instance, we can imagine that a deck function can be fairly naturally built as a mode on top of a tweakable block cipher [29]. First, we compress the input through a secure MAC construction such as PMAC1 [37] or ZMAC [27], with slight adaptations for the multi-string input support. Then, we generate the output by processing the MAC through the tweakable block cipher, for instance with the tweak as a counter albeit in a different domain than during the compression. It is plausible that this construction can be proven PRF-secure assuming the tweakable block cipher to have tweakable PRP security.

3.4 Basic Applications

Deck function can readily be used for stream encryption, authentication, and (nonce-based) AE of single messages.

One can use a deck function for stream encryption by taking as input a *diversifier* D and use the output to encrypt a plaintext P as $C \leftarrow P + F_K(D)$ and decrypt again as $P \leftarrow C + F_K(D)$. If the diversifier D is a nonce and F_K is random oracle, this is one-time pad encryption and so achieves perfect secrecy. Information leakage of this stream cipher is upper bounded by the PRF distinguishing advantage of the deck function. We refer to notion of indistinguishability from random bits under an adaptive chosen-plaintext-and-message-number attack, or IND$ [38]. This shows the following proposition:

Proposition 3. *Let $\mathcal{D}$ be any adversary attacking this stream cipher Π. Then there is an adversary $\mathcal{D}'$ using the same resources as $\mathcal{D}$ such that*

$$\mathbf{Adv}_{\Pi}^{\mathrm{ind\$}}(\mathcal{D}) \leq \mathbf{Adv}_{F}^{\mathrm{prf}}(\mathcal{D}') .$$

One can use a deck function as a MAC function returning a t-bit tag by taking as input the *message* P and truncate the output to t: bits $T \leftarrow 0^t + F_K(P)$. One can verify a tag by taking as input the message P and its tag T and check whether $T + F_K(P)$ equals 0^t. If so, we say (P, T) verifies successfully. We speak of forgery if an adversary can find a (message,tag) pair (P, T), with T not generated in a tag generation query and that verifies successfully. Plugging in a random oracle for F_K would give a forgery success probability of $q/2^t$ with q the number of tag verification queries. It follows that the forgery success probability of our MAC function is at most by $q/2^t$ plus the PRF distinguishing advantage of the deck function. We hence prove the following proposition, see also [28, Section 4.4]:

Proposition 4. *Let $\mathcal{D}$ be any adversary attacking this authentication scheme Π. Then there exists an adversary $\mathcal{D}'$ using equivalent resources as $\mathcal{D}$ such that*

$$\mathbf{Adv}_{\Pi}^{\mathrm{uf\text{-}cma}}(\mathcal{D}) \leq \mathbf{Adv}_{F}^{\mathrm{prf}}(\mathcal{D}') + \frac{q_{\mathrm{ver}}}{2^t} ,$$

with $\mathcal{D}$ making q_{ver} verification queries. The equivalence of resources means that the queries to the tag generation and tag verification methods are translated into queries to F of same length.

From this, AE with a deck function in an encrypt-then-MAC fashion is immediate. The plaintext is encrypted as $Z \leftarrow P + F_K(A)$, with A associated data that should be a nonce (it may contain a diversifier). Then a tag is computed as $T \leftarrow 0^t + F_K(A; Z)$. The cryptogram (Z, T) can be first verified and then decrypted if the tag is correct. Apart from string encoding details, this is a non-session special case of Deck-PLAIN, covered in the next section.

4 Deck-PLAIN

We specify in Algorithm 2 a deck function mode for nonce-based session-supporting AE called Deck-PLAIN. It allows two parties to exchange a sequence of messages, each consisting of associated data and plaintext. At sending end it wraps a message by encrypting the plaintext to a ciphertext and appending a tag that authenticates the sequence of all messages up to that point. At receiving end it unwraps a cryptogram by verifying the tag and, if correct, it decrypts the ciphertext; otherwise, it will return an error.

Deck-PLAIN offers the same interface as the jammin cipher. The only difference is upon initialization, where the jammin cipher takes an identifier as input, while Deck-PLAIN takes a secret key, in particular from an array of keys to be able to model multi-key support. It has two length parameters: the tag length t that determines the security level and an alignment unit length ℓ that is related to an implementation optimization as detailed below.

In the individual messages both associated data and plaintext are optional. We call messages without plaintext *authentication-only* messages and messages without associated data *plaintext-only* messages. Deck-PLAIN even supports empty messages for the purpose of authenticated acknowledgments.

If a key is used more than once, the associated data of the first message of the session **must** be a nonce per key, e.g., a session counter. One may choose to have an authentication-only first message. The corresponding tag is then called a *startup tag*. Verification of a startup tag allows the receiver of the message to authenticate the origin of the session start request including the session counter.

4.1 Inner Workings

Similar to the jammin cipher, Deck-PLAIN accumulates the sequence of messages in a data element called history. Concretely, this is the sequence of associated data and plaintexts of messages received and differs only from history in the jammin cipher by the explicit encoding used.

In a wrap call, Deck-PLAIN encrypts a plaintext by adding to it a keystream that is the output of the underlying deck function with input the *context*. This context is the history followed by A of the message. Clearly, the encryption context is the same as in the jammin cipher. Initialization of a session loads the key in the deck function and initializes the history to an empty sequence.

Deck-PLAIN performs the wrapping of a message in two steps:

1. **Encryption:** It extracts keystream from the deck function and adds it to the plaintext, yielding the ciphertext.
2. **Tag generation:** It appends associated data and ciphertext to the history and extracts the tag from the deck function.

Unwrapping is similar. Tag verification is performed before decryption.

In consecutive plaintext-only wrap or unwrap calls, Deck-PLAIN reserves the first t bits of deck function outputs for tags and the remaining ones for keystream. It takes keystream from an offset that is the smallest multiple of ℓ not shorter than t. So Deck-PLAIN requires only one deck function call per message in this important use case.

For authentication-only messages Deck-PLAIN skips the en(de)cryption step and the absorbing of ciphertext. For plaintext-only messages it skips the absorbing of associated data, except for a blank message where it absorbs the empty

Algorithm 2. Definition of Deck-PLAIN(F, t, ℓ)

Parameters: deck function F, tag length $t \in \mathbb{N}$ and alignment unit length $\ell \in \mathbb{N}$
Let offset $= \ell \lceil \frac{t}{\ell} \rceil$: the smallest multiple of ℓ not smaller than t

Instance constructor: $\mathsf{init}(\vec{K}, i)$ taking key array $\vec{K}$, key index i
$(\mathsf{inst}.K, \mathsf{inst.history}) \leftarrow (\vec{K}[i], \varnothing)$
return Deck-PLAIN instance
Note: in the sequel, K, history denote the attributes of inst

Instance cloner: inst.clone()
return new instance inst′ with all attributes (K, history) copied from inst

Interface: inst.wrap(A, P) returns C
if $|P| = 0$ **then**
  history $\leftarrow$ history; $A||00$
else if $|A| > 0$ or history $= \varnothing$ **then**
  context $\leftarrow$ history; $A||10$
  $Z \leftarrow P + F_K$ (context)
  history $\leftarrow$ context; $Z||1$
else
  context $\leftarrow$ history
  $Z \leftarrow P + F_K$ (context) $\ll$ offset
  history $\leftarrow$ context; $Z||1$
$T \leftarrow 0^t + F_K$ (history)
return $C = Z||T$

Interface: inst.unwrap(A, C) returns P or $\perp$
if $|C| < t$ **then return** $\perp$
Parse C in Z and T
if $|Z| = 0$ **then**
  history′ $\leftarrow$ history; $A||00$
else if $|A| > 0$ or history $= \varnothing$ **then**
  history′ $\leftarrow$ history; $A||10$; $Z||1$
else
  history′ $\leftarrow$ history; $Z||1$
$T' \leftarrow 0^t + F_K$ (history′)
if $T' \neq T$ **then return** $\perp$
if $|A| > 0$ or history $= \varnothing$ **then**
  context $\leftarrow$ history; $A||10$
  $P \leftarrow Z + F_K$ (context)
else
  context $\leftarrow$ history
  $P \leftarrow Z + F_K$ (context) $\ll$ offset
history $\leftarrow$ history′
return P

associated data. To make the mapping from sequences of messages to the history injective, Deck-PLAIN appends frame bits to associated data and ciphertext strings for domain separation before appending to the history. In particular, ciphertext strings end with 1 and associated data strings with 00 (in an authentication-only message) or 10 (otherwise).

4.2 Security Analysis

To be secure, Deck-PLAIN relies on the encryption context to be a nonce, as it otherwise leaks the difference between two plaintexts, as for stream ciphers. If the encryption context is a nonce, Deck-PLAIN can be distinguished from the jammin cipher only by a forgery or by distinguishing the deck function from a random function, as captured in the following theorem. Multi-key security is covered by the $\mathbf{Adv}_F^{\mathrm{prf}}(\mathcal{D}')$ term, see Sect. 3.2. In particular, one can avoid multi-key security degradation by ensuring that the encryption context is different per instance of Deck-PLAIN.

Theorem 2. *Let $\mathcal{D}$ be any fixed deterministic adversary whose goal is to distinguish* Deck-PLAIN(F, t, ℓ) *from $\mathcal{J}^{+t}$, the jammin cipher with* WrapExpand$(p) = p + t$. *If in the queries of $\mathcal{D}$ the encryption context is a nonce, there exists an adversary $\mathcal{D}'$ using the same resources as $\mathcal{D}$ such that*

$$\Delta_{\mathcal{D}}(\text{Deck-PLAIN}(F, t, \ell)\ ;\ \mathcal{J}^{+t}) \leq \frac{q_{\mathsf{unwrap}}}{2^t} + \mathbf{Adv}_F^{\mathrm{prf}}(\mathcal{D}'),$$

with q_{unwrap} the number of unwrap calls $\mathcal{D}$ makes.

We now introduce the proof technique and given the proof in Sect. 4.4.

4.3 The H-coefficient Technique

Our proofs use the H-coefficient technique from Patarin [35]. We will follow the adaptation of Chen and Steinberger [12]. Consider any information-theoretic deterministic adversary $\mathcal{A}$ whose goal is to distinguish $\mathcal{O}$ from $\mathcal{P}$, with its advantage denoted $\Delta_{\mathcal{A}}(\mathcal{O}\ ;\ \mathcal{P})$. The interaction of $\mathcal{A}$ with its oracles, either $\mathcal{O}$ or $\mathcal{P}$, will be recorded in a *transcript* τ. Denote by $D_{\mathcal{O}}$ (resp. $D_{\mathcal{P}}$) the probability distribution of transcripts that can be obtained from interaction with $\mathcal{O}$ (resp. $\mathcal{P}$). Call a transcript τ *attainable* if $\Pr(D_{\mathcal{P}} = \tau) > 0$. Denote by $\mathcal{T}$ the set of attainable transcripts, and consider any partition $\mathcal{T} = \mathcal{T}_{\mathrm{good}} \cup \mathcal{T}_{\mathrm{bad}}$ into "good" and "bad" transcripts. The H-coefficient technique states the following [12].

Lemma 1 (H-coefficient Technique). *Consider a fixed information-theoretic deterministic adversary $\mathcal{A}$ whose goal is to distinguish $\mathcal{O}$ from $\mathcal{P}$. Let ε be such that for all $\tau \in \mathcal{T}_{\mathrm{good}}$: $\Pr(D_{\mathcal{O}} = \tau) / \Pr(D_{\mathcal{P}} = \tau) \geq 1 - \varepsilon$. Then, $\Delta_{\mathcal{A}}(\mathcal{O}\ ;\ \mathcal{P}) \leq \varepsilon + \Pr(D_{\mathcal{P}} \in \mathcal{T}_{\mathrm{bad}})$.*

The H-coefficient technique can thus be used to bound a distinguishing advantage in the terminology of Definition 1. In our proofs below, we use the special case where $\Pr(D_{\mathcal{O}} = \tau) \geq \Pr(D_{\mathcal{P}} = \tau)$ for all $\tau \in \mathcal{T}_{\mathrm{good}}$, so that $\Delta_{\mathcal{A}}(\mathcal{O}\ ;\ \mathcal{P}) \leq \Pr(D_{\mathcal{P}} \in \mathcal{T}_{\mathrm{bad}})$, and we set $\mathcal{O}$ to the jammin cipher and $\mathcal{P}$ to the real world.

4.4 Proof of Theorem 2

Proof. We use a hybrid argument and replace the deck function with a random oracle before comparing Deck-PLAIN with the jammin cipher, i.e.,

$$\begin{aligned}&\Delta_{\mathcal{D}}(\text{Deck-PLAIN}(F,t,\ell)\ ;\ \mathcal{J}^{+t})\\ &\qquad\leq \Delta_{\mathcal{D}''}(\text{Deck-PLAIN}(\mathcal{RO},t,\ell)\ ;\ \mathcal{J}^{+t}) + \mathbf{Adv}_F^{\mathrm{prf}}(\mathcal{D}'),\end{aligned}$$

where $\mathcal{D}''$ has the same resources as $\mathcal{D}$. Here Deck-PLAIN$(\mathcal{RO},t,\ell)$ is a slight abuse of notation. It means that the instance constructor chooses the i-th random oracle from an array and that F_K refers to $\mathcal{RO}_i$ in Algorithm 2.

We then use Lemma 1 with $\mathcal{O} = \mathcal{J}^{+t} \triangleq \mathcal{J}$ and $\mathcal{P} =$ Deck-PLAIN$(\mathcal{RO},t,\ell)$. In this proof, we use the session syntax of the jammin cipher. This is w.l.o.g. as in Deck-PLAIN the history is an encoding of the more abstract history in $\mathcal{J}$.

We define a transcript τ as a sequence of records of the form

$$(\mathsf{wrap/unwrap}, \mathsf{context}, P, C),$$

where the first component indicates the type of call made and the context is the combination of the history as in the definition of $\mathcal{J}$ and A of the wrap/unwrap call. In a wrap record, P is a parameter and C is the returned value, with $C \neq \perp$. In an unwrap record, C is a parameter and P is a return value and may contain an error code $\perp$. We ignore in the transcript wrap records with equal tuple $(\mathsf{context}, P)$ and unwrap records with equal tuple $(\mathsf{context}, C)$. This is w.l.o.g. as both worlds act deterministically. Similarly, we ignore in the transcript unwrap records that have the same tuple $(\mathsf{context}, P, C)$ as a wrap record. This is w.l.o.g. as both worlds behave consistently in this respect. This yields a simple definition of forgery, namely the presence of a successful unwrap record in the transcript.

We have one type of bad event: a successful forgery. $\mathcal{T}_{\mathrm{bad}}$ is the set of transcripts containing a record $(\mathsf{unwrap}, \mathsf{context}, P, C)$ with $P \neq \perp$. In a forgery attempt, unwrap compares a tag to a tag generated with the underlying $\mathcal{RO}$ applied to a unique input. As the latter is a uniformly generated t-bit string, the probability that they are equal is 2^{-t}, hence $\Pr(D_{\mathcal{P}} \in \mathcal{T}_{\mathrm{bad}}) \leq \frac{q_{\mathsf{unwrap}}}{2^t}$ after q_{unwrap} calls to unwrap.

We now prove that, for all $\tau \in \mathcal{T}_{\mathrm{good}}$, we have $\Pr(D_{\mathcal{J}} = \tau) \geq \Pr(D_{\mathcal{P}} = \tau)$, hence $\varepsilon = 0$ in Lemma 1. In both worlds, the cryptogram bits are generated randomly and independently for different contexts, so we can partition the transcript records per $\mathsf{context}$ and take the probability as the product of the probabilities over the different contexts. We will now consider a subset of the transcript for a given $\mathsf{context}$ value.

As the $\mathsf{context}$ is unique per wrap call for non-empty plaintexts, there can be only one of the form $(\mathsf{wrap}, \mathsf{context}, P \neq \epsilon, C)$ and one of the form $(\mathsf{wrap}, \mathsf{context}, \epsilon, C_\epsilon \neq C)$.

Upon an unsuccessful unwrap query, the jammin cipher returns $\perp$ as it avoids forgeries and hence contributes a factor 1 to the probability. Upon a wrap query, the jammin cipher selects C from a set of cardinality at most $2^{|P|+t}$ and hence contributes a factor at least $2^{-(|P|+t)}$ to $\Pr(D_{\mathcal{J}} = \tau)$. It may return an error, but thanks to Proposition 2, this would require $q_{\mathsf{unwrap}} \geq 2^t$.

Upon an unsuccessful unwrap query, $\mathcal{P} = $ Deck-PLAIN$(\mathcal{RO}, t, \ell)$ returns $\perp$ in a good transcript and this contributes at most 1 to $\Pr(D_{\mathcal{P}} = \tau)$. Upon a wrap query, $\mathcal{P}$ computes the value $C = Z||T$ with $Z = P + \mathcal{RO}(\mathsf{context})$, $\mathsf{context} =$ history$; A$ (or $P + \mathcal{RO}(\text{history}) \ll \text{offset}$ when $A = \epsilon$ and history $\neq \varnothing$) and $T = \mathcal{RO}(\text{updated history})$. Thanks to the fact that upon wrap the context is unique and $\mathcal{P}$ takes tags and keystream in different domains or from different parts of the RO output stream, it contributes a factor exactly $2^{-(|P|+t)}$ to $\Pr(D_{\mathcal{P}} = \tau)$. A wrap record with $P = \epsilon$ contributes a factor 2^{-t} to $\Pr(D_{\mathcal{P}} = \tau)$.

This shows that $\Pr(D_{\mathcal{J}} = \tau) \geq \Pr(D_{\mathcal{P}} = \tau)$ and concludes the proof. □

5 Feistel Network Modes

The security of Deck-PLAIN breaks down when the encryption context is not a nonce. In this section, we introduce four different modes of deck functions that are more robust against nonce misuse. Two of the modes make optimal use of the redundancy: for t-bit security they only require a plaintext expansion by t bits. Moreover, two of them provide protection against the accidental release of unverified decrypted ciphertext (a.k.a. release of unverified plaintext or RUP [3]).

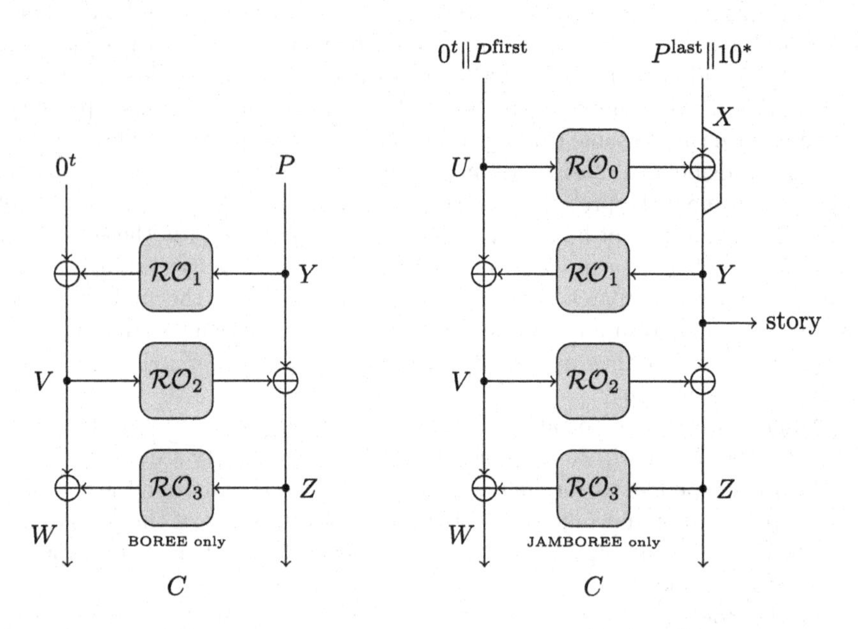

Fig. 1. Feistel network inside the different modes, Deck-BO(REE) on the left and Deck-JAMBO(REE) on the right.

It turns out that different modes like Synthetic Initial Value (SIV) [40], Robust IV (RIV) [2] and wide-block ciphers [30,31] can all be expressed under the hood of a Feistel network. We here give an intuitive overview of these constructions, starting with the simplest case: SIV. Consider Fig. 1 (left) with only the first two rounds. The left branch is initialized with t bits set to zero, while the right branch contains the plaintext. After the first round, V is a pseudorandom function of the plaintext and becomes the tag. We use V also as a synthetic diversifier in the next round, and encrypt the plaintext $Y = P$ by adding to it a keystream that depends on V.

In case the implementation (accidentally) releases unverified decrypted ciphertexts, an adversary can obtain such for chosen values of V.

After querying unwrap with $C_0 = V||Z_0$ and $C_1 = V||Z_1$ and get unverified decrypted ciphertexts P_0 and P_1, she observes that $Z_0 + Z_1 = P_0 + P_1$. The RIV mode avoids this by adding a third round. The ciphertext Z serves as input to a third pseudorandom function to mask V. Compared to SIV, the adversary cannot control V at decryption anymore since she has access to W only.

To avoid collisions in V, SIV and RIV need to have t large enough. In case of unbounded nonce misuse, due to the birthday paradox we must take $t = 2s$ for s bits of security. Consider now Fig. 1 (right). Compared to SIV and RIV, it adds a round at the beginning and the plaintext is spread onto the two branches, with t bits of redundancy on the left branch. This round compresses P into Y, and then we proceed as with SIV and RIV. The left and right branch must be wide enough to avoid collisions in Y, but this is decoupled from the expansion length t and we can now have $t = s$ for s bits of security. If a mode performs the first three rounds but not the last one, we obtain a variant of an SIV mode with optimal redundancy but no resistance to RUP.

We call our modes Deck-BO, Deck-BOREE, Deck-JAMBO and Deck-JAMBOREE and they make use of the Feistel network-based block cipher in Algorithm 3. This algorithm is parameterized with the deck function F and whether the optional first (jam) and last (ree) rounds are performed. A call to the block cipher takes as input a secret key K, a context (tweak) and the input already split into four parts $L_0||L_+||R_0||R_+$. The left branch is $L_0||L_+$ and the right branch is $R_0||R_+$. The first (resp. last) round affects only R_0 (resp. L_0). Additionally, the block cipher returns a history that is the combination of its context and the intermediate value Y. In Deck-BO(REE), Y coincides with the plaintext, while in Deck-JAMBO(REE) it is the compressed plaintext or *plaintext representative*. In all cases, Y needs to be absorbed when evaluating the block cipher and this allow the returned history not to have to be absorbed again, thanks to the incrementality of the deck function.

5.1 Deck-BO

Deck-BO, defined in Algorithm 4, combines the SIV approach [40] with the session support of Deck-PLAIN. Deck-BO wraps a message in three phases:

1. Tag generation: It generates the tag by applying the deck function to the context (history and A) and the plaintext of the message, if non-empty.

2. Encryption: If the plaintext is non-empty, it generates the ciphertext by adding to the plaintext the output of the deck function applied to the context extended with the tag.
3. It updates the history.

Unwrapping is similar. Deck-BO has a single length parameter: the tag length t. It applies domain separation between associated data and plaintext strings in the history, as well as between the generation of keystream and of tag.

Algorithm 3. Definition of block cipher B and its inverse.

Parameters: deck function F and round flags $\subseteq \{\mathsf{jam}, \mathsf{ree}\}$
Note: in the sequel, L is a shortcut notation for $L_0||L_+$ and R for $R_0||R_+$.

Interface: $O = B_{F,\text{flags}}(K, \mathsf{context}, L_0, L_+, R_0, R_+)$
if $\mathsf{jam} \in$ flags **then**
  $R_0 \leftarrow R_0 + F_K\,(\mathsf{context}; L||\mathsf{001})$
$L \leftarrow L + F_K\,(\mathsf{context}; R||\mathsf{011})$
history $\leftarrow \mathsf{context}; R||\mathsf{011}$
$R \leftarrow R + F_K\,(\mathsf{context}; L||\mathsf{101})$
if $\mathsf{ree} \in$ flags **then**
  $L_0 \leftarrow L_0 + F_K\,(\mathsf{context}; R||\mathsf{111})$
return (history, $L||R$)

Interface: $O = B^{-1}_{F,\text{flags}}(K, \mathsf{context}, L_0, L_+, R_0, R_+)$
if $\mathsf{ree} \in$ flags **then**
  $L_0 \leftarrow L_0 + F_K\,(\mathsf{context}; R||\mathsf{111})$
$R \leftarrow R + F_K\,(\mathsf{context}; L||\mathsf{101})$
$L \leftarrow L + F_K\,(\mathsf{context}; R||\mathsf{011})$
history $\leftarrow \mathsf{context}; R||\mathsf{011}$
if $\mathsf{jam} \in$ flags **then**
  $R_0 \leftarrow R_0 + F_K\,(\mathsf{context}; L||\mathsf{001})$
return (history, $L||R$)

In contrast to Deck-PLAIN, leakage of Deck-BO is limited to revealing plaintext equality under equal encryption context. To achieve that, Deck-BO computes the tag over the history with associated data and plaintext attached and then generates the keystream from the encryption context with this tag appended to it. Unless we have colliding tags for equal encryption contexts, keystreams are independent. Therefore, for its security Deck-BO relies on the absence of (rare) tag collisions. The security of Deck-BO is captured in Theorem 3.

Theorem 3. *Let $\mathcal{D}$ be any fixed deterministic adversary whose goal is to distinguish* Deck-BO(F, t) *from $\mathcal{J}^{+t}$, the jammin cipher with* WrapExpand$(p) = p+t$. *Then there exists an adversary $\mathcal{D}'$ using the same resources as $\mathcal{D}$ such that*

$$\Delta_{\mathcal{D}}(\text{Deck-BO}(F, t)\ ;\ \mathcal{J}^{+t}) \leq \frac{q_{\mathsf{unwrap}}}{2^t} + \sum_{\mathsf{context}} \frac{\binom{\sigma(\mathsf{context})}{2}}{2^t} + \mathbf{Adv}^{\mathrm{prf}}_F(\mathcal{D}'),$$

Algorithm 4. Definition of Deck-BO(F, t) and Deck-BOREE(F, t)

Parameters: deck function F and expansion length t
$B = B_{F,\varnothing}$ for Deck-BO or $B = B_{F,\{\mathsf{ree}\}}$ for Deck-BOREE

Constructor: $\mathsf{init}(\vec{K}, i)$ taking key array $\vec{K}$, key index i
$(K, \text{history}) \leftarrow (\vec{K}[i], \varnothing)$
return instance

Interface: $\mathsf{wrap}(A, P)$ returning C
if $|P| = 0$ **then**
  history $\leftarrow$ history; $A||\mathsf{00}$
  return $C \leftarrow 0^t + F_K$ (history)
if $|A| = 0$ **then** context $\leftarrow$ history **else** context $\leftarrow$ history; $A||\mathsf{10}$
$(\text{history}, C) \leftarrow B(K, \mathsf{context}, 0^t, \epsilon, P, \epsilon)$
return C

Interface: $\mathsf{unwrap}(A, C)$ returning P or $\perp$
if $|C| = t$ **then**
  history$'$ $\leftarrow$ history; $A||\mathsf{00}$
  $P \leftarrow \epsilon$
  $C' \leftarrow 0^t + F_K$ (history$'$)
  if $C' \neq C$ **then return** $\perp$
else if $|C| > t$ **then**
  if $|A| = 0$ **then** context $\leftarrow$ history **else** context $\leftarrow$ history; $A||\mathsf{10}$
  $T||Z \leftarrow C$ such that $|T| = t$
  $(\text{history}', P') \leftarrow B^{-1}(K, \mathsf{context}, T, \epsilon, Z, \epsilon)$
  $L||P \leftarrow P'$ such that $|L| = t$
  if $L \neq 0^t$ **then return** $\perp$
else return $\perp$
history $\leftarrow$ history$'$
return P

with q_{unwrap} *the number of unwrap calls that* $\mathcal{D}$ *makes and* $\sigma(\mathsf{context})$ *the number of wrap queries with* $P \neq \epsilon$ *for a given* context *value.*

The second term is due to tags colliding for equal encryption contexts and it determines the length of the tag to achieve a certain security strength s. If the encryption context is a nonce, the term vanishes and it is sufficient to take $t = s$. In case of unbounded nonce misuse, it may reach $\frac{q^2_{\mathsf{wrap}}}{2^{t+1}}$ and we have to set $t \geq 2s - 1$. In use cases where the number of times an encryption context is repeated can be upper bounded by 2^x, we can relax this to $t = s + x - 1$.

The proof can be found in the full version [11].

5.2 Deck-BOREE and Release of Unverified Decrypted Ciphertexts

Deck-BO does not tolerate the release of unverified decrypted ciphertexts when unwrapping. This leads to a distinguisher as detailed earlier. We introduce

Deck-BOREE to address use cases where this is a concern. Deck-BOREE hides the tag value from the adversary by encrypting it using keystream computed from the ciphertext. The distinguisher described above for Deck-BO no longer works as the tag (SIV) depends on the ciphertext and decryption leads to independent keystreams and therefore independent decrypted ciphertexts. We define Deck-BOREE in Algorithm 4.

Theorem 4 formalizes the security of Deck-BOREE. For the release of unverified decrypted ciphertexts, we use an approach similar to indifferentiability [32]. In the real world, we extend the interface of the adversary with the value of the right branch (Y) after processing the unwrap query, as this is where the plaintext appears before the tag is verified. For the ideal world, such a right branch does not exist and we *simulate* it with independently distributed random bits, so without connection to any actual plaintexts. Infeasibility to distinguish the two systems with this extended interface implies that security is preserved even when releasing unverified decrypted ciphertext.

In addition, we grant the adversary the choice per query whether she gets the value of the right branch (or its simulated value). If not, she just receives $\perp$. So Theorem 4 also covers the case where the unverified decrypted ciphertexts are not disclosed, or only a limited number of them.

Theorem 4. *Let $\mathcal{D}$ be any fixed deterministic adversary whose goal is to distinguish* Deck-BOREE(F,t) *from $\mathcal{J}^{+t}$, the jammin cipher with* WrapExpand$(p) = p + t$. *In addition, this adversary has access to the unverified decrypted ciphertexts in the case of Deck-BOREE and to a random string of bits $|C| - t$ bits in the case of the jammin cipher. Then there exists an adversary $\mathcal{D}'$ using the same resources as $\mathcal{D}$ such that*

$$\Delta_{\mathcal{D}}^{\mathrm{RUP}}(\text{Deck-BOREE}(F,t)\ ;\ \mathcal{J}^{+t}) \leq \frac{q_{\mathsf{unwrap}}}{2^t} + \sum_{\mathsf{context}} \frac{\binom{\sigma'(\mathsf{context})}{2}}{2^t} + \mathbf{Adv}_F^{\mathrm{prf}}(\mathcal{D}'),$$

with q_{unwrap} the number of unwrap calls that $\mathcal{D}$ makes and $\sigma'(\mathsf{context})$ the number of wrap (resp. unwrap) queries with $P \neq \epsilon$ (resp. $|C| > t$ and the adversary accesses the unverified decrypted ciphertext) for a given context *value.*

The second term is due to (hidden) tag collisions for wrap call and unwrap calls with leakage for given encryption contexts. As for Deck-BO, it determines the length of the tag to achieve a certain security strength s and the same trade-offs apply. If the adversary does not access unverified decrypted ciphertext, unwrap queries do not contribute to $\sigma'(\mathsf{context})$ and we get the same bound as in Theorem 3 for Deck-BO.

The proof can be found in the full version [11].

5.3 Deck-JAMBO and Optimal Redundancy

Deck-JAMBO is an enhancement of Deck-BO in that it resulting in less required expansion at the cost of an additional round at the beginning in order to protect against chosen plaintext attacks. With Deck-JAMBO, it is possible to take advantage of redundancy that is already present in the plaintext, as long as it resides in the left branch of the Feistel network. We define it in Algorithm 5.

We leave the specifications of how to split the input of the block cipher into left and right parts out of the definition of Deck-JAMBO and Deck-JAMBOREE. The reason is that the most efficient way to do so may vary with the particular deck function in use. For instance, for farfalle-based deck functions, one may wish the left part of the input to fit in exactly one block after padding. Such specific technicalities do not belong in the definition of a general-purpose mode.

The split cuts the expanded plaintext or cryptogram into four parts. We formalize this with three functions that must satisfy some properties: plaintext expansion and extraction and a split function.

First, the expand function takes as input the plaintext P and the expansion length t and returns the expanded plaintext $P' = \text{expand}(P, t)$ of the form $0^t||P||10^*$. The number of zero bits at the end may depend on the length of P but shall not depend on its value. This function must ensure that $|P'| \geq 4t$. The expand function implicitly defines a WrapExpand function, namely,

$$\text{WrapExpand}(|P|) = |\text{expand}(P, t)| \ .$$

For $P = \epsilon$, Deck-JAMBO has a special treatment and the resulting cryptogram has $|C| = t$ bits. So, we can set $\text{WrapExpand}(0) = t$ and therefore the implicitly defined WrapExpand function is t-expanding by construction.

Second, we define a plaintext extraction function called $\text{extract}(P', t)$ that returns $\perp$ if P' does not start with 0^t or cannot be unpadded, and extracts P otherwise. Naturally, we require that $\text{extract}(\text{expand}(P, t)) = P$ for any P. Note that the behavior of this function is fixed and cannot be customized.

Third, the split function takes as input the expanded plaintext P' or ciphertext C and the expansion length t, and it returns a tuple $(L_0, L_+, R_0, R_+) = \text{split}(\alpha, t)$ such that $\alpha = L_0||L_+||R_0||R_+$, $|L_0| \geq 2t$ and $|R_0| \geq 2t$. Here again, the lengths of the four parts may depend on the length of the input string but not on its value. If the input string is shorter than $4t$ bits, it returns an error.

Compared to Deck-BO, we renamed the history to *story* as it is no longer guaranteed that the mapping of the sequence of messages to this sequence of strings is injective. In particular, we do not append plaintexts but rather plaintext representatives. Different plaintexts with colliding plaintext representatives are rare, and we treat them as bad events in the proof.

The security of Deck-JAMBO is captured in the theorem below. Compared to Deck-BO, the expansion parameter t can be equal to the security strength s in all cases. Collisions that happen on the left or right branch are bad events, but as the branches are at least $2t$ bits wide, these are rare.

Theorem 5. *Let $\mathcal{D}$ be any fixed deterministic adversary whose goal is to distinguish* Deck-JAMBO$(F, t, \text{expand}, \text{split})$ *from $\mathcal{J}^{t,\text{expand}}$, the jammin cipher with* WrapExpand *that follows from t and the chosen expand function (or $\mathcal{J}$ for short). Then there is an adversary $\mathcal{D}'$ using the same resources as $\mathcal{D}$ such that*

$$\Delta_{\mathcal{D}}(\text{Deck-JAMBO}(F, \dots) \ ; \ \mathcal{J}) \leq \frac{q_{\mathsf{unwrap}}}{2^t} + \sum_{\mathsf{context}} \frac{\binom{\sigma(\mathsf{context})}{2}}{2^{2t-1}} + \mathbf{Adv}_F^{\mathrm{prf}}(\mathcal{D}'),$$

Algorithm 5. Definition of Deck-JAMBO(REE)$(F, t, \text{expand}, \text{split})$

Parameters: deck function F, expansion length t, expand and split functions
$B = B_{F,\{\mathsf{jam}\}}$ for Deck-JAMBO or $B = B_{F,\{\mathsf{jam},\mathsf{ree}\}}$ for Deck-JAMBOREE

Constructor: $\mathsf{init}(\vec{K}, i)$ taking key array $\vec{K}$, key index i
$(K, \text{story}) \leftarrow (\vec{K}[i], \varnothing)$
return instance

Interface: $\mathsf{wrap}(A, P)$ returning C
if $|P| = 0$ **then**
  story $\leftarrow$ story; $A||\mathsf{00}$
  return $C \leftarrow \mathsf{0}^t + F_K$ (story)
if $|A| = 0$ **then** context $\leftarrow$ story **else** context $\leftarrow$ story; $A||\mathsf{10}$
$P' \leftarrow \text{expand}(P, t)$
$(L_\text{O}, L_+, R_\text{O}, R_+) \leftarrow \text{split}(P', t)$
$(\text{story}, C) \leftarrow B(K, \mathsf{context}, L_\text{O}, L_+, R_\text{O}, R_+)$
return C

Interface: $\mathsf{unwrap}(A, C)$ returning P or $\perp$
story$'$ $\leftarrow$ story
if $|C| = t$ **then**
  story$'$ $\leftarrow$ story$'$; $A||\mathsf{00}$
  $C' \leftarrow \mathsf{0}^t + F_K$ (story$'$)
  if $C' = C$ **then** $P \leftarrow \epsilon$ **else** $P \leftarrow \perp$
else if $\text{split}(C, t) \neq \perp$ **then**
  if $|A| = 0$ **then** context $\leftarrow$ story **else** context $\leftarrow$ story; $A||\mathsf{10}$
  $(L_\text{O}, L_+, R_\text{O}, R_+) \leftarrow \text{split}(C, t)$
  $(\text{story}', P') \leftarrow B^{-1}(K, \mathsf{context}, L_\text{O}, L_+, R_\text{O}, R_+)$
  $P \leftarrow \text{extract}(P', t)$
else $P \leftarrow \perp$
if $P \neq \perp$ **then** story $\leftarrow$ story$'$
return P

with q_{unwrap} *the number of unwrap calls that* $\mathcal{D}$ *makes and* $\sigma(\mathsf{context})$ *the number of wrap queries with* $P \neq \epsilon$ *for a given* context *value.*

The proof can be found in the full version [11].

5.4 Deck-JAMBOREE

Deck-JAMBOREE combines the advantages of Deck-BOREE and Deck-JAMBO in a natural way. For encryption it makes use of a wide tweakable block cipher such as AEZ [24] but rather specified in terms of a deck function, like Double-decker [22]. For authentication, it relies on the redundancy in the expanded plaintext presented to this block cipher.

The security of Deck-JAMBOREE is captured in the theorem below. Like Deck-JAMBO, the expansion parameter t can be equal to the security strength s.

And like Deck-BOREE, it is secure even in the case of the release of unverified decrypted ciphertext. The RUP model is defined similarly, with the difference that there is no clear split anymore between the ciphertext and the tag as in Deck-BOREE. Hence, the adversary has access to the entire unverified decrypted cryptogram, which would contain the expanded plaintext in a successful unwrap.

Theorem 6. *Let $\mathcal{D}$ be any fixed deterministic adversary whose goal is to distinguish* Deck-JAMBOREE$(F, t, \text{expand}, \text{split})$ *from* $\mathcal{J}^{t,\text{expand}}$*, the jammin cipher with* WrapExpand *that follows from t and the chosen expand function (or $\mathcal{J}$ for short). In addition, this adversary has access to the unverified decrypted cryptograms in the case of Deck-JAMBOREE and to a random string of bits $|C|$ bits in the case of the jammin cipher. Then there exists an adversary $\mathcal{D}'$ using the same resources as $\mathcal{D}$ such that*

$$\Delta_{\mathcal{D}}^{\text{RUP}}(\text{Deck-JAMBOREE}(F, \dots)\ ;\ \mathcal{J}) \leq \frac{q_{\mathsf{unwrap}}}{2^t} + \sum_{\mathsf{context}} \frac{\binom{\sigma'(\mathsf{context})}{2}}{2^{2t-1}} + \mathbf{Adv}_F^{\text{prf}}(\mathcal{D}'),$$

with q_{unwrap} the number of unwrap calls that $\mathcal{D}$ makes and $\sigma'(\mathsf{context})$ the number of wrap (resp. unwrap) queries with $P \neq \epsilon$ (resp. $|C| > t$ and the adversary accesses the unverified decrypted cryptogram) for a given context *value.*

The proof can be found in the full version [11].

6 Conclusions

We found that proving the security of the deck function-based modes is relatively easy and gives strong bounds that are tight, as the bounds account only for simple bad events like tag guessing and internal collisions. New modes are relatively easy to design, and this opens the door to more tailored schemes for niche applications, but we leave this as future work.

Acknowledgements. Joan Daemen is supported by the European Research Council under the ERC advanced grant agreement under grant ERC-2017-ADG Nr. 788980 ESCADA.

References

1. Abed, F., et al.: The POET family of on-line authenticated encryption schemes. CAESAR Submission (2014)
2. Abed, F., Forler, C., List, E., Lucks, S., Wenzel, J.: RIV for robust authenticated encryption. In: Peyrin, T. (ed.) FSE 2016. LNCS, vol. 9783, pp. 23–42. Springer, Heidelberg (2016). https://doi.org/10.1007/978-3-662-52993-5_2
3. Andreeva, E., Bogdanov, A., Luykx, A., Mennink, B., Mouha, N., Yasuda, K.: How to securely release unverified plaintext in authenticated encryption. In: Sarkar, P., Iwata, T. (eds.) ASIACRYPT 2014. LNCS, vol. 8873, pp. 105–125. Springer, Heidelberg (2014). https://doi.org/10.1007/978-3-662-45611-8_6

4. Barbosa, M., Farshim, P.: Indifferentiable authenticated encryption. In: Shacham, H., Boldyreva, A. (eds.) CRYPTO 2018. LNCS, vol. 10991, pp. 187–220. Springer, Cham (2018). https://doi.org/10.1007/978-3-319-96884-1_7
5. Bellare, M., Boldyreva, A., Knudsen, L., Namprempre, C.: Online ciphers and the Hash-CBC construction. In: Kilian, J. (ed.) CRYPTO 2001. LNCS, vol. 2139, pp. 292–309. Springer, Heidelberg (2001). https://doi.org/10.1007/3-540-44647-8_18
6. Bellare, M., Kohno, T., Namprempre, C.: Breaking and provably repairing the SSH authenticated encryption scheme: a case study of the encode-then-encrypt-and-mac paradigm. ACM Trans. Inf. Syst. Secur. **7**(2), 206–241 (2004)
7. Bellare, M., Namprempre, C.: Authenticated encryption: relations among notions and analysis of the generic composition paradigm. In: Okamoto, T. (ed.) ASIACRYPT 2000. LNCS, vol. 1976, pp. 531–545. Springer, Heidelberg (2000). https://doi.org/10.1007/3-540-44448-3_41
8. Bertoni, G., Daemen, J., Hoffert, S., Peeters, M., Van Assche, G., Van Keer, R.: Farfalle: parallel permutation-based cryptography. IACR Trans. Symmetric Cryptol. **2017**(4), 1–38 (2017)
9. Bertoni, G., Daemen, J., Peeters, M., Van Assche, G.: Duplexing the sponge: single-pass authenticated encryption and other applications. In: Miri, A., Vaudenay, S. (eds.) SAC 2011. LNCS, vol. 7118, pp. 320–337. Springer, Heidelberg (2012). https://doi.org/10.1007/978-3-642-28496-0_19
10. Boldyreva, A., Taesombut, N.: Online encryption schemes: new security notions and constructions. In: Okamoto, T. (ed.) CT-RSA 2004. LNCS, vol. 2964, pp. 1–14. Springer, Heidelberg (2004). https://doi.org/10.1007/978-3-540-24660-2_1
11. Băcuiei, N., Daemen, J., Hoffert, S., Van Assche, G., Van Keer, R.: Jammin' on the deck. IACR Cryptology ePrint Arch, p. 531 (2022)
12. Chen, S., Steinberger, J.: Tight security bounds for key-alternating ciphers. In: Nguyen, P.Q., Oswald, E. (eds.) EUROCRYPT 2014. LNCS, vol. 8441, pp. 327–350. Springer, Heidelberg (2014). https://doi.org/10.1007/978-3-642-55220-5_19
13. Daemen, J., Hoffert, S., Peeters, M., Van Assche, G., Van Keer, R.: All on Deck! Real World Crypto 2020, New York, USA, 8–10 January 2020. https://rwc.iacr.org/2020/slides/Assche.pdf, https://www.youtube.com/watch?v=CQDsLhf-d-A
14. Daemen, J., Hoffert, S., Peeters, M., Van Assche, G., Van Keer, R.: Xoodyak, a lightweight cryptographic scheme. IACR Trans. Symmetric Cryptol. **2020**(S1), 60–87 (2020)
15. Daemen, J., Hoffert, S., Van Assche, G., Van Keer, R.: The design of Xoodoo and Xoofff. IACR Trans. Symmetric Cryptol. **2018**(4), 1–38 (2018)
16. Daemen, J., Massolino, P.M.C., Mehrdad, A., Rotella, Y.: The subterranean 2.0 cipher suite. IACR Trans. Symmetric Cryptol. **2020**(S1), 262–294 (2020)
17. Daemen, J., Mennink, B., Van Assche, G.: Full-state keyed duplex with built-in multi-user support. In: Takagi, T., Peyrin, T. (eds.) ASIACRYPT 2017. LNCS, vol. 10625, pp. 606–637. Springer, Cham (2017). https://doi.org/10.1007/978-3-319-70697-9_21
18. Daemen, J., Rijmen, V.: The Design of Rijndael: AES - The Advanced Encryption Standard. Information Security and Cryptography. Springer, Heidelberg (2002). https://doi.org/10.1007/978-3-662-04722-4
19. Daemen, J., Rijmen, V.: The pelican MAC function. IACR Cryptol. ePrint Arch. **2005**, 88 (2005)
20. Duong, T., Rizzo, J.: Here come the XOR ninjas. Manuscript (2011)

21. Fouque, P.-A., Joux, A., Martinet, G., Valette, F.: Authenticated on-line encryption. In: Matsui, M., Zuccherato, R.J. (eds.) SAC 2003. LNCS, vol. 3006, pp. 145–159. Springer, Heidelberg (2004). https://doi.org/10.1007/978-3-540-24654-1_11
22. Gunsing, A., Daemen, J., Mennink, B.: Deck-based wide block cipher modes and an exposition of the blinded keyed hashing model. IACR Trans. Symmetric Cryptol. **2019**(4), 1–22 (2019)
23. Hamburg, M.: The STROBE protocol framework. In: Real World Crypto (2017)
24. Hoang, V.T., Krovetz, T., Rogaway, P.: Robust authenticated-encryption AEZ and the problem that it solves. In: Oswald, E., Fischlin, M. (eds.) EUROCRYPT 2015. LNCS, vol. 9056, pp. 15–44. Springer, Heidelberg (2015). https://doi.org/10.1007/978-3-662-46800-5_2
25. Hoang, V.T., Reyhanitabar, R., Rogaway, P., Vizár, D.: Online authenticated-encryption and its nonce-reuse misuse-resistance. In: Gennaro, R., Robshaw, M. (eds.) CRYPTO 2015. LNCS, vol. 9215, pp. 493–517. Springer, Heidelberg (2015). https://doi.org/10.1007/978-3-662-47989-6_24
26. Hoang, V.T., Shen, Y.: Security of streaming encryption in google's tink library. In: Ligatti, J., Ou, X., Katz, J., Vigna, G. (eds.) CCS 2020: 2020 ACM SIGSAC Conference on Computer and Communications Security, Virtual Event, USA, 9–13 November 2020, pp. 243–262. ACM (2020)
27. Iwata, T., Minematsu, K., Peyrin, T., Seurin, Y.: ZMAC: a fast tweakable block cipher mode for highly secure message authentication. In: Katz, J., Shacham, H. (eds.) CRYPTO 2017. LNCS, vol. 10403, pp. 34–65. Springer, Cham (2017). https://doi.org/10.1007/978-3-319-63697-9_2
28. Katz, J., Lindell, Y.: Introduction to Modern Cryptography. Chapman and Hall/CRC Press, Boca Raton (2007)
29. Liskov, M., Rivest, R.L., Wagner, D.: Tweakable block ciphers. In: Yung, M. (ed.) CRYPTO 2002. LNCS, vol. 2442, pp. 31–46. Springer, Heidelberg (2002). https://doi.org/10.1007/3-540-45708-9_3
30. Luby, M., Rackoff, C.: How to construct pseudorandom permutations from pseudorandom functions. SIAM J. Comput. **17**(2), 373–386 (1988)
31. Lucks, S.: Faster Luby-Rackoff ciphers. In: Gollmann, D. (ed.) FSE 1996. LNCS, vol. 1039, pp. 189–203. Springer, Heidelberg (1996). https://doi.org/10.1007/3-540-60865-6_53
32. Maurer, U., Renner, R., Holenstein, C.: Indifferentiability, impossibility results on reductions, and applications to the random oracle methodology. In: Naor, M. (ed.) TCC 2004. LNCS, vol. 2951, pp. 21–39. Springer, Heidelberg (2004). https://doi.org/10.1007/978-3-540-24638-1_2
33. Mennink, B., Neves, S.: Optimal PRFs from blockcipher designs. IACR Trans. Symmetric Cryptol. **2017**(3), 228–252 (2017)
34. NIST: NIST special publication 800–38b, recommendation for block cipher modes of operation: the cmac mode for authentication, June 2016
35. Patarin, J.: The Coefficients H technique. In: Avanzi, R.M., Keliher, L., Sica, F. (eds.) SAC 2008. LNCS, vol. 5381, pp. 328–345. Springer, Heidelberg (2009). https://doi.org/10.1007/978-3-642-04159-4_21
36. Rogaway, P.: Authenticated-encryption with associated-data. In: Atluri, V. (ed.) Proceedings of the 9th ACM Conference on Computer and Communications Security, CCS 2002, Washington, DC, USA, 18–22 November 2002, pp. 98–107. ACM (2002)

37. Rogaway, P.: Efficient instantiations of tweakable blockciphers and refinements to modes OCB and PMAC. In: Lee, P.J. (ed.) ASIACRYPT 2004. LNCS, vol. 3329, pp. 16–31. Springer, Heidelberg (2004). https://doi.org/10.1007/978-3-540-30539-2_2
38. Rogaway, P.: Nonce-based symmetric encryption. In: Roy, B., Meier, W. (eds.) FSE 2004. LNCS, vol. 3017, pp. 348–358. Springer, Heidelberg (2004). https://doi.org/10.1007/978-3-540-25937-4_22
39. Rogaway, P., Bellare, M., Black, J., Krovetz, T.: OCB: a block-cipher mode of operation for efficient authenticated encryption. In: Reiter, M.K., Samarati, P. (eds.) CCS 2001, Proceedings of the 8th ACM Conference on Computer and Communications Security, Philadelphia, Pennsylvania, USA, 6–8 November 2001, pp. 196–205. ACM (2001)
40. Rogaway, P., Shrimpton, T.: A provable-security treatment of the key-wrap problem. In: Vaudenay, S. (ed.) EUROCRYPT 2006. LNCS, vol. 4004, pp. 373–390. Springer, Heidelberg (2006). https://doi.org/10.1007/11761679_23
41. Rogaway, P., Zhang, Y.: Simplifying game-based definitions. In: Shacham, H., Boldyreva, A. (eds.) CRYPTO 2018. LNCS, vol. 10992, pp. 3–32. Springer, Cham (2018). https://doi.org/10.1007/978-3-319-96881-0_1
42. Tsang, P.P., Solomakhin, R., Smith, S.W.: Authenticated streamwise on-line encryption. Dartmouth Computer Science Report TR2009-640 (2009)

A Modular Approach to the Incompressibility of Block-Cipher-Based AEADs

Akinori Hosoyamada[1](✉), Takanori Isobe[2,3,4], Yosuke Todo[1], and Kan Yasuda[1]

[1] NTT Social Informatics Laboratories, Tokyo, Japan
{akinori.hosoyamada.bh,yosuke.todo.xt,kan.yasuda.hy}@hco.ntt.co.jp
[2] University of Hyogo, Hyogo, Japan
takanori.isobe@ai.u-hyogo.ac.jp
[3] National Institute of Information and Communications Technology, Tokyo, Japan
[4] PRESTO, Japan Science and Technology Agency, Tokyo, Japan

Abstract. Incompressibility is one of the most fundamental security goals in white-box cryptography. Given recent advances in the design of efficient and incompressible block ciphers such as SPACE, SPNbox and WhiteBlock, we demonstrate the feasibility of reducing incompressible AEAD modes to incompressible block ciphers. We first observe that several existing AEAD modes of operation, including CCM, GCM(-SIV), and OCB, would be all insecure against white-box adversaries even when used with an incompressble block cipher. This motivates us to revisit and formalize incompressibility-based security definitions for AEAD schemes and for block ciphers, so that we become able to design modes and reduce their security to that of the underlying ciphers. Our new security notion for AEAD, which we name whPRI, is an extension of the pseudo-random injection security in the black-box setting. Similar security notions are also defined for other cryptosystems such as privacy-only encryption schemes. We emphasize that whPRI ensures quite strong authenticity against white-box adversaries: existential unforgeability beyond leakage. This contrasts sharply with previous notions which have ensured either no authenticity or only universal unforgeability. For the underlying ciphers we introduce a new notion of whPRP, which extends that of PRP in the black-box setting. Interestingly, our incompressibility reductions follow from a variant of public indifferentiability. In particular, we show that a practical whPRI-secure AEAD mode can be built from a whPRP-secure block cipher: We present a SIV-like composition of the sponge construction (utilizing a block cipher as its underlying primitive) with the counter mode and prove that such a construction is (in the variant sense) public indifferentiable from a random injection. To instantiate such an AEAD scheme, we propose a 256-bit variant of SPACE, based on our conjecture that SPACE should be a whPRP-secure cipher.

Keywords: Symmetric-key cryptography · White-box cryptography · Incompressibility · Mode of operation · Public indifferentiability

S. Agrawal and D. Lin (Eds.): ASIACRYPT 2022, LNCS 13792, pp. 585–619, 2022.
https://doi.org/10.1007/978-3-031-22966-4_20

1 Introduction

White-box cryptography, which has been introduced by Chow et al. for AES [25] and DES [26], is a technique to protect data in the presence of adversaries who have access to implementations of cryptographic algorithms. For two decades since Chow et al. published the seminal papers, target systems of white-box cryptography have spread out from digital rights management (DRM) to mobile payment and banking services [2,41]. Today white-box cryptography is applied to a wide range of cryptographic algorithms [29], and in this paper we focus on symmetric-key encryption schemes.

Secure white-box implementations must resist key extraction and "code lifting" [29]. While the goal of key extraction is to retrieve a secret key from a white-box implementation, code lifting tries to isolate and copy (a part of) the functionality of the cryptographic algorithm. Security against code lifting is in general stronger than security against key extraction, as key extraction implies code lifting of the full functionality. Preventing code lifting is indispensable to realize secure white-box implementations because arbitrary message can be encrypted or decrypted once the program is copied.

Delerablée et al. [29] have introduced the notion of incompressibility to formalize resistance to code lifting. Roughly, a white-box program of an encryption scheme is incompressible if it is infeasible to compress the encryption program while keeping its functionality. Delerablée et al. have shown that incompressibility is achievable by an RSA-group-based construction. Follow-up work by Fouque et al. [35] has introduced variants of incompressibility regarding privacy (IND-COM) or limited authenticity of universal unforgeability (ENC-COM). They have presented randomized schemes ensuring each of the security notions but not both at the same time.[1] The more recent work by Bock et al. [18] has shown that an incompressible randomized encryption scheme can be built from one-way permutations. Closely related to incompressibility is the work by Bellare et al. on big-key symmetric encryption [9][2], which was later improved by Bellare and Dai [8]. They have provided efficient randomized encryption schemes with a high level of privacy (LIND) and without authenticity, in the setting where information of the key is partially leaked, by making the key big, say, 1GB.

While there exist other white-box security notions, we focus on incompressibility because it is achievable by relatively efficient schemes and without relying on special hardware. True that trusted execution environments are in common use today, but demands for software-only solutions are still high in various scenarios—e.g., cloud servers providing digital rights management based services, mobile phones running cloud-based payment services with host card emulations, and memory-leakage resilient software—as listed by Bogdanov et al. [22].

It should be noted that some pieces of previous work [9,21,22,35] (and we also do) assume that a black-box adversary resides outside the target program and

[1] A scheme in Sect. 2 of the paper [35] achieves authenticity but not privacy in the white-box setting, because its tag-generation part does not depend on keys.

[2] This work focuses on bounded retrieval model rather than white-box cryptography, but as Fouque et al. point out, its security notion almost matches IND-COM.

tries to attack in the conventional sense. More precisely, the white-box adversary, which here we call a *lifter*, tries to isolate and copy the functionality of the encryption program. Then, the black-box adversary tries to break privacy and/or authenticity with the aid of leakage generated by the lifter. Here, the amount of leakage is properly restricted in agreement with the bounded retrieval model [24,27] of leakage-resilient cryptography.

There is another line of research: Designing incompressible block ciphers. Bogdanov and Isobe [21] have introduced the concept of SPACE-hard white-box block ciphers and presented a concrete construction SPACE based on a dedicated design rather than on an obfuscated implementation of an existing cipher (such a direction of adopting dedicated designs for block ciphers was initiated with ASASA [14]). The notion of SPACE hardness is a variant of incompressibility and provides immunity against code lifting. Similar notions include weak white-box security [14] and ENC-TCOM [35]. Bogdanov and Isobe have shown that SPACE achieves SPACE hardness, assuming AES is secure. SPACE is reasonably efficient, running faster than a hundred cycles per byte on modern PCs. A number of follow-up SPACE-hard white-box block ciphers have been proposed, including SPNbox [22] and WhiteBlock [35].

Now our motivation behind this work becomes evident: There is a large gap between the two lines of research. Specifically, we would like to address the following issues:

1. There exist no modes of operation that turn incompressible block ciphers into incompressible authenticated encryption (AE) schemes. As described in Sect. 3 (and in the full version of this paper [40]), existing modes such as GCM [51], GCM-SIV [36], CCM [61], and OCB [46] would not yield incompressible AE even if combined with an incompressible block cipher. The state-of-the-art incompressible block ciphers mentioned above, though secure and reasonably efficient, are not utilized.
2. As mentioned above, there exist no AE schemes that simultaneously ensure both privacy and authenticity against white-box adversaries, unless one relies on special hardware. Moreover, the only type of authenticity that has been achieved in the context of incompressibility is universal unforgeability, which is much weaker than what has been done in the conventional setting. Similar discussions are provided in the previous work by Bock et al. [19] where the authors point out that "the definition of incompressibility does not capture any further security such as confidentiality and authenticity".
3. The lack of secure AE modes or schemes indicates the need for further investigation into the incompressibility notion. Specifically, we would like to come up with a usable definition of incompressible block ciphers as well as a new notion of incompressibility that captures more perfectly the privacy and authenticity requirements on AE schemes. Having done that, we should be able to design a mode that enjoys both privacy and authenticity in a strong sense, by relying on the underlying incompressible cipher.

1.1 Our Contributions

We introduce new incompressibility-based white-box security notions for AEAD schemes and BCs which we name whPRI and whPRP, respectively. Intuitively, with the two notions we attempt to define the best possible security such that any λ-bit leakage from a lifter (e.g., malware) does not allow adversaries to break privacy and/or authenticity, or equivalently indistinguishability, except for λ-bit ciphertexts. In particular, the notions demand authenticity in quite a strong sense: existential unforgeability beyond leakage. Our definition, we believe, should be the first one to formalize this notion concretely. Obviously, this is a much stronger requirement than universal unforgeability. We remark that whPRI and whPRP are extensions of pseudo-random injections (PRI) [58] and pseudo-random permutations (PRP) in the black-box setting, respectively: they exactly match in the extreme case of $\lambda = 0$. The security games for our new definitions involve both of black-box adversaries and lifters. These games become inherently multi-stage.

We properly bound the computational resource t_{lif} of a lifter and the leakage size λ. Especially, no security is guaranteed after either t_{lif} or λ reaches a certain threshold, e.g., $t_{\text{lif}} = 2^{50}$ or $\lambda = 2^{20}$. We expect that an attack (malware activity) should be detectable, before the threshold is reached, by some means, e.g., monitoring active processes and/or outgoing packets. We conjecture that SPACE should satisfy whPRP-security under some reasonable parameter settings.

For completeness we study theoretical possibilities of security reductions of various symmetric-key schemes; we introduce similar notions for keyed functions and conventional (privacy-only) encryption schemes. Our notion for keyed functions, which we call whPRF, is an extension of the standard pseudo-random function (PRF). For conventional encryption schemes, we define two security notions which we name whIND\$-CPA and wh$\widetilde{\text{SPRP}}$. The former is an extension of IND\$-CPA security (for random-IV schemes) in the black-box setting. The latter is obtained as a special case of whPRI where ciphertext lengths are always equal to message lengths. Thus, wh$\widetilde{\text{SPRP}}$ is an extension of the tweakable strong PRP ($\widetilde{\text{SPRP}}$) security for tweakable enciphering schemes [38] in the black-box setting. We observe that meaningful counterparts of MAC security and nonce-based security notions seem unachievable in our context. Table 1 gives comparisons between various security notions for (authenticated) encryption schemes.

We prove that a reduction between the new security notions is possible if the construction in hand satisfies a variant of public indifferentiability [32,63], which we name *weak public indifferentiability.* Then we demonstrate that all the new notions can be reduced to whPRP, by presenting corresponding constructions that are weak public indifferentiable.

Finally, as an example of practical AEAD modes of block ciphers, we show that a composition of the sponge construction [12] and the counter mode (CTR) via SIV [58] is whPRI-secure if the underlying block cipehr E_K is whPRP-secure. Here, the underlying primitive E_K is used both by the sponge and by the CTR. Roughly speaking, if E_K is secure up to λ-bit leakage, the resulting AEAD is

Table 1. Comparison of incompressibility or related notions for symmetric-key (authenticated) encryption schemes. We assume that AEADs always take a nonce (or IV) as a part of input. Especially, a nonce is included into inputs of deterministic AEADs.

Security notion	Target scheme	Leakage	Adversarial goal	
(λ, δ)-incompressibility [18,29]	deterministic or randomized encryption (RSA group or OWP-based schemes [18,29])	whole implementation	δ-functionality with code size $< \lambda$	
			(Privacy)	(Authenticity)
LIND [9]	randomized encryption (Big-Key Encryption [8,9])	via function with output size $= \ell$	distinguishing	—
IND-COM [35]	randomized AE (WhiteKey [35])	via function with entropy left $\geqslant \mu$	distinguishing	—
ENC-COM [35]	randomized AE (WhiteKey+RO)	via function with entropy left $\geq \mu$	—	universal forgery
whPRI [**Sect.** 4.3]	deterministic AE (SIV+CTR (Sect. 7))	via lifter (malware) with output size $\leqslant \lambda$	distinguishing	existential forgery beyond leakage
whIND\$-CPA [**Sect.** 5.3]	randomized encryption (CTR (Sect. 6.3))	via lifter (malware) with output size $\leqslant \lambda$	distinguishing	—
wh$\widetilde{\text{SPRP}}$ [**Sect.** 5.3]	tweakable enciphering scheme (6-round Feistel (Sect. 6.3))	via lifter (malware) with output size $\leqslant \lambda$	distinguishing	—

secure as long as the amount of processed data is $\ll 2^{n/4}$ and leakage is less than λ. To instantiate E_K, we propose to use a 256-bit-block variant of SPACE which we name SPACE256. We conjecture that SPACE256 is secure up to 2^{20} bits of leakage. The resulting AEAD scheme is implemented on an Intel platform for experiments, and we confirm that the performance is practical. The size of the program is in an order of KB or MB, which is reasonably small for mobile applications. Unlike previous schemes achieving incompressibility, our scheme does not need random nonces. This is an advantage in the white-box setting because random number generators may be compromised by adversaries.

Note that our notions do not supersede previous ones but rather coexist with other white-box security approaches such as binding [19,20]. Which security approaches, definitions or solutions one should choose changes depending on use cases and what one wants to achieve. Specifically, when trusted hardware is available or when lifters have much more limited access to programs, other security notions would be more suitable.

1.2 Related Work

Other Security Notions in White-Box Cryptography. The initial goal set by Chow et al. was to protect software implementations of existing block ciphers from key extraction when an attacker is given an unlimited access to a white-box implementation. Many pieces of previous work have proposed such implementations, but none of them remains unbroken [13,47,53,62]. Some of the state-of-the-art work focus on limited white-box adversaries such as DCA and a certain class of algebraic attacks [5,16,17,23].

Several solutions outside incompressibility have been suggested to mitigate code lifting. Chow et al. suggested external encoding [25], which yields a white-box implementation of $E'_K = G \circ E_K \circ F^{-1}$ for some functions F and G instead of E_K. The problem is that even an ordinary user needs a separate implementation of G^{-1} or F to compute E_K. Thus, white-box adversaries would also be able to peel off the external encoding, unless the encoding is stored in trusted hardware. Delerablée et al. suggested one-wayness [29], which formalizes the notion that one is unable to perform decryption even if an encryption program is given. They also suggested traceability [29], which allows a program distributor to trace malicious users who leak their encryption programs. Both are interesting, but they do not encompass resistance to copying encryption programs. Other works have discussed the possibility of binding [1,19,20], where the execution of encryption is bound by trusted hardware or applications. Unfortunately, cryptographically secure binding requires, together with secure hardware, primitives such as indistinguishability obfuscation (iO) or LWE, which are richer than usual symmetric-key primitives.

Symmetrically and Asymmetrically Hard Cryptography. Biryukov and Perrin [15] introduced the HSp mode (and its instantiation WHALE), which can be used to build an incompressible VIL/VOL hash function from a usual sponge hash (like SHA-3) and an FIL/FOL incompressible function. The mode is proven to achieve a universal-unforgeability-like security notion on incompressibility. Their result seems close to ours (in Sect. 6.3) that the sponge construction becomes a VIL/VOL whPRF if the underlying primitive is a whPRP (or FIL/FOL whPRF). Still, there are two differences between theirs and ours. First, they proved only universal-unforgeability-like security while we proved existential-unforgeability-like security (i.e., whPRF-security). Second, their proof is in the random oracle model while ours is in the standard model in that the existence of a whPRP (or a FIL/FOL whPRF) is a falsifiable assumption.

Leakage Resilient Cryptography. An important area related to white-box cryptography is *leakage resilient cryptography*, which aims to achieve provable security against side-channel attacks. Security models in leakage resilient cryptography are roughly classified into two types[3], depending on whether (1) an adversary is allowed to obtain arbitrary leakage from the secret key as long as the leakage length is bounded by a certain parameter, or (2) some form of security is assumed on memory or storage, and/or leakage is obtained only when some computation (e.g., encryption) is performed through a special class of functions such as the Hamming weight of internal states with some noise.

Models of the First Type. A typical model of the first type closely related to our results is the Bounded Retrieval Model (BRM) [27,33], where large (e.g.,

[3] This classification is based on (still not completely the same as) the one in [43,44].

1GB) keys are used to prevent key exfiltration. The BRM and related notions have been studied in a long line of research [3,4,8,9,24,27,33]. Among others, Bellare et al. [9] showed practical symmetric-key encryption schemes achieving confidentiality in the BRM, which was later improved by Bellare and Dai [8].

As pointed out by Fouque et al. [35], the goals of Bellare et al. [8] and incompressibility are quite close. Still, each of the BRM and incompressibility has its own advantages. An advantage of the BRM is that, for well designed schemes such as the one by Bellare et al. [8], bounding the running time of a lifter (malware) is not mandatory (it is mandatory for incompressible ciphers because the secret key sizes are very small). Meanwhile, no previous works on symmetric encryption scheme in the BRM achieve both confidentiality and authenticity simultaneously[4], while we prove that SIV+CTR achieves whPRI.

Models of the Second Type. Major models of the second type include the "only computation leaks information" (OCL) model [52] and wire-probing leakage [42]. In models of the second type, lots of previous works have shown various leakage resilient schemes including AEADs [7,10,11,28,30,31,34,37,45,48,52,55,59]. Especially, Krämer and Struck [45] showed that the security of a leakage-resilient AEAD can be reduced to the security of leakage-resilient PRFs in the "only computation leaks information" model [52]. However, these results are incomparable to ours because they essentially assume that attackers do not have a direct full access to memory or storage that stores the secret key.

A clear advantage of the second type is that the size of implementations can be small, compared to incompressibility and the first type. When we can assume that adversaries do not have a full direct access to memory or storage (e.g., leakage can be obtained only by measuring power consumption of a circuit), models of the second type will be more suitable than incompressibility and the first type. When we cannot, incompressibility or the first type will be suitable.

1.3 Paper Organization

Section 2 introduces basic notations and definitions, and review basics on (public) indifferentiability. Section 3 shows an observation that GCM is unlikely to achieve incompressibility. In Sect. 4, we introduce whPRI, a new security notions for AEADs. New security notions for other schemes are introduced in Sect. 5. Section 6 introduces weak public indifferentiability and shows that weak public indifferentiability implies white-box security reductions. The section also demonstrates that our new notions on various schemes can be reduced to whPRP, by showing (weak) public indifferentiable constructions. In Sect. 7 we show that a practical whPRI-secure AEAD mode of whPRP can be realized as a composition by SIV of the sponge construction and the counter mode.

[4] A scheme by Bellare et al. [9] also achieves authenticity, but only in the absence of leakage (See also Table 1).

2 Preliminaries

Throughout the paper, $\mathrm{len}(M)$ denotes the bit length for a bit string M. Given a positive integer $m < \mathrm{len}(X)$, we write $(A, B) \xleftarrow{m,*} X$ to mean assignment of bit strings, the leftmost m bits of X to A and the remaining bits to B. The variable A or B may be omitted with the symbol "$\cdot$" in which case the corresponding bits are not assigned to any variable. When we write like $(X_1, X_2, \ldots, X_\ell) \xleftarrow{n} X$ we mean partitioning X into n-bit blocks and assigning them to $X_1, X_2, \ldots, X_\ell$ where $\ell = \lceil \mathrm{len}(X)/n \rceil$ and the last X_ℓ is possibly fractional, i.e., $\mathrm{len}(X_\ell) < n$. The symbol $\|$ stands for concatenation of bit strings and the symbol $\oplus$ exclusive OR of two bit stings of the same length. By block length of M we denote $\lceil \mathrm{len}(M)/n \rceil$ when the parameter n is clear from the context. For an invertible function F by $F^{\pm}$ we denote the oracles of F and F^{-1}. We denote the empty bit string by ε and define $\{0,1\}^0 := \{\varepsilon\}$. $\{0,1\}^*$ denotes the set of all bit strings of arbitrary length. For positive integers x and n, by $x \bmod n$ we denote the minimum positive integer i such that $i \equiv x \bmod n$. We say an m-input function $f : (\mathbb{Z}_{\geq 0})^{\times m} \rightarrow \mathbb{R}_{\geq 0}$ is non-decreasing if $f(x_1, \ldots, x_i + z, \ldots, x_m) \geq f(x_1, \ldots, x_m)$ holds for arbitrary $1 \leq i \leq m$, $(x_1, \ldots, x_m) \in (\mathbb{Z}_{\geq 0})^{\times m}$, and $z \in \mathbb{Z}_{\geq 0}$.

Definition 1 (Variable-key and fixed-key random injection). *Let $\tau \geq 0$ be an integer and $\mathrm{Inj}_\tau(\mathbf{K} \times \mathbf{N} \times \mathbf{A} \times \mathbf{M}, \mathbf{C})$ denote the set of functions $F : \mathbf{K} \times \mathbf{N} \times \mathbf{A} \times \mathbf{M} \rightarrow \mathbf{C}$ such that $F_{K,N,A} := F(K, N, A, \cdot)$ is an injection for each (K, N, A) and $\mathrm{len}(F(K, N, A, M)) = \mathrm{len}(M) + \tau$. A* variable-key random injection *F is an injection chosen uniformly at random from $\mathrm{Inj}_\tau(\mathbf{K} \times \mathbf{N} \times \mathbf{A} \times \mathbf{M}, \mathbf{C})$. The inverse $F^{-1} : \mathbf{K} \times \mathbf{N} \times \mathbf{A} \times \mathbf{C} \rightarrow \mathbf{M} \cup \{\bot\}$ is defined so that $F^{-1}(K, N, A, F(N, A, M)) = M$ for each (K, N, A, M) and $F^{-1}(K, N, A, C) = \bot$ for all $C \notin F_{K,N,A}(\mathbf{M})$. If $\mathbf{K}$ is a set that contains exactly a single element, we say F is a* fixed-key random *injection and omit to write $\mathbf{K}$ and K.*

Syntax of Symmetric-Key Cryptosystems and Basic Constructions.

Keyed Functions. A keyed function is a function $f : \{0,1\}^\kappa \times \mathbf{X} \rightarrow \mathbf{Y}$. Here, κ is a positive integer and $\{0,1\}^\kappa$ is called the key space. We write $f_K(M)$ and $f(K, M)$ interchangeably.

Block Ciphers. A block cipher is a keyed function $E : \{0,1\}^\kappa \times \{0,1\}^n \rightarrow \{0,1\}^n$ such that $E(K, \cdot)$ is a permutation for each K. The inverse function $(E_K)^{-1}$ is denoted by D_K, and we write $D_K(C)$ and $D(K, C)$ interchangeably. E and D are called the encryption and decryption functions.

AEADs. An AEAD scheme is a tuple $\Pi = (\mathcal{E}, \mathcal{D})$. The first element of Π is an encryption function $\mathcal{E} : \mathbf{K} \times \mathbf{N} \times \mathbf{A} \times \mathbf{M} \rightarrow \mathbf{C}$. Here, $\mathbf{K}$ is the key space from which the secret key is chosen uniformly at random. The set $\mathbf{N} = \{0,1\}^\nu$ is a nonce space with the nonce length ν being a non-negative integer. The sets $\mathbf{A}, \mathbf{M}, \mathbf{C}$ correspond to the spaces of associated data, plaintext

Algorithm 1: $\text{CTR}(K, IV, M)$

1: $(M_1, M_2, \ldots, M_\ell) \xleftarrow{n} M$
2: **for** $i = 1$ **to** ℓ **do**
3: $\quad y \leftarrow f_K(IV + i - 1)$,
4: $\quad (y', \cdot) \xleftarrow{\text{len}(M_i), *} y$,
5: $\quad C_i \leftarrow M_i \oplus y'$
6: **return** $C_1 \| C_2 \| \cdots \| C_\ell$

Algorithm 2: $\mathcal{E}_{K_1,K_2}(N, A, M)$

1: $IV \leftarrow f_{K_1}(N, A, M)$
2: $C' \leftarrow \mathcal{E}'_{K_2}(IV, M)$
3: **return** $C \leftarrow IV \| C'$

Algorithm 3: $\mathcal{D}_{K_1,K_2}(N, A, C)$

1: $(IV, C') \xleftarrow{\tau, *} C$
2: $M \leftarrow \mathcal{D}_{K_2}(IV, C')$
3: $T \leftarrow f_{K_1}(N, A, M)$
4: **if** $IV = T$ **then**
5: $\quad$ **return** M
6: **else**
7: $\quad$ **return** $\perp$

and ciphertext, respectively, where $\mathbf{M} = \mathbf{C} = \{0,1\}^*$. We write interchangeably $\mathcal{E}(K, N, A, M) = \mathcal{E}_K(N, A, M) = \mathcal{E}_{K,N,A}(M)$. For each $(K, N, A) \in \mathbf{K} \times \mathbf{N} \times \mathbf{A}$ we demand that $\text{len}(\mathcal{E}_{K,N,A}(M)) = \text{len}(M) + \tau$ should hold for all $M \in \mathbf{M}$, where τ a fixed non-negative integer. The second element of Π is a decryption function $\mathcal{D} : \mathbf{K} \times \mathbf{N} \times \mathbf{A} \times \mathbf{C} \rightarrow \mathbf{M} \cup \{\perp\}$. Here, the symbol $\perp$ signifies rejection. We write interchangeably $\mathcal{D}(K, N, A, M) = \mathcal{D}_K(N, A, M) = \mathcal{D}_{K,N,A}(M)$. For each (K, N, A, M) we demand that $\mathcal{D}_{K,N,A}(\mathcal{E}_{K,N,A}(M)) = M$ should hold.

Conventional Encryption Schemes. The syntax for a conventional (privacy-only) encryption scheme is essentially the same as that of AEAD except that it does not take any associated data, i.e., $\mathbf{A} = \{\varepsilon\}$, and $\tau = 0$. In addition, nonce N and nonce space $\mathbf{N}$ are renamed as IV and $\mathbf{IV}$. We assume IV is chosen uniformly at random for every encryption query or arbitrarily chosen by adversary depending on security notions we focus on.

Counter Mode. Counter mode (CTR) is the construction to convert a keyed function into a conventional encryption scheme. Let $f : \{0,1\}^\kappa \times \{0,1\}^m \rightarrow \{0,1\}^n$ be a keyed function. The encryption function of CTR based on f, which we denote by $\text{CTR}(K, IV, M)$, is computed as in Algorithm 1. The key, IV, and message spaces are $\{0,1\}^\kappa$, $\{0,1\}^m$, and $\{0,1\}^*$, respectively. The decryption function is identical to the encryption function.

SIV. SIV is the construction introduced by Rogaway and Shrimpton to realize a deterministic AEAD [58]. Let $\mathbf{N}$ and $\mathbf{A}$ be arbitrarily chosen space of nonces and associated data. (We assume $\mathbf{N} = \{0,1\}^\nu$ for some $\nu \in \mathbb{Z}_{>0}$ and $\mathbf{A} = \{0,1\}^*$ unless otherwise noted.) Let $f : \{0,1\}^{\kappa_1} \times (\mathbf{N} \times \mathbf{A} \times \{0,1\}^*) \rightarrow \{0,1\}^\tau$ be a keyed function and $\Pi' = (\mathcal{E}', \mathcal{D}')$ be a conventional encryption scheme with the key space $\{0,1\}^{\kappa_2}$, IV space $\{0,1\}^\tau$, and message space $\{0,1\}^*$. The SIV construction based on f and Π is an AEAD with key space $\{0,1\}^{\kappa_1} \times \{0,1\}^{\kappa_2}$, nonce space $\mathbf{N}$, associated data space $\mathbf{A}$, and message space $\{0,1\}^*$. The encryption function $\mathcal{E}$ and decryption function $\mathcal{D}$ are defined as in Algorithm 2 and Algorithm 3, respectively. We call an output of f a *tag* and f a tag-generation part.

Programs and White-Box Compilers. We follow the abstraction and notation used by Delerablée et al. [29] for dealing with programs and compilers. A program implements an algorithm, specific to some explicit language and execution model. A program can be read, copied and modified at will. A program can be viewed as a bit string, and its binary code can be executed locally. A program is inherently stateless. A program may, via APIs including system calls, make use of external resources such as random coins and additional functionalities. A white-box compiler $\mathcal{C}_E$ of a block cipher E is an algorithm that takes $K \in \{0,1\}^{\kappa}$ as an input and outputs a program that implements E_K. We use the notation $[\![E_k]\!]$ to denote a white-box implementation of E_K in a context where explicitly indicating the compiler is unnecessary. Moreover, we call $[\![E_K]\!]$ *white-box block cipher* simply. A white-box compiler may be probabilistic, outputting different programs for the same key[5]. White-box compilers of other cryptosystems are defined in the same way.

Indifferentiability. Let T^{P} be an algorithm (a cryptographic scheme, e.g., a VIL hash function) making queries to P, where P is an ideally random primitive (e.g., a FIL random oracle). In addition, let R be an ideally random scheme corresponding to T^{P} with the same input-output interface (e.g., a VIL random oracle). Then, the indifferentiability advantage of $\mathcal{A}$ against $(\mathsf{T}^{\mathsf{P}}, \mathsf{R})$ with respect to a simulator $\mathcal{S}$ is defined as $\mathsf{Adv}^{\mathrm{indiff}}_{\mathsf{T},\mathsf{R},\mathcal{S}}(\mathcal{A}) := \Pr\left[1 \leftarrow \mathcal{A}^{\mathsf{T}^{\mathsf{P}},\mathsf{P}}\right] - \Pr\left[1 \leftarrow \mathcal{A}^{\mathsf{R},\mathcal{S}^{\mathsf{R}}}\right]$. Informally, we say T^{P} is indifferentiable from $\mathcal{R}$ if there is an efficient simulator $\mathcal{S}$ such that the above advantage becomes negligibly small for any efficient $\mathcal{A}$. We call T^{P} (resp., $\mathcal{R}$) a construction oracle and $\mathcal{P}$ a primitive oracle. We call queries to T^{P} or R (resp., P or $\mathcal{S}^{\mathsf{R}}$) construction queries (resp., primitive queries).

The most important feature of indifferentiability is the general "composition theorem" [50,56]: Suppose the following (1)–(3) hold: (1) A scheme (or protocol) Π^{R} depending on the ideal object R is proven secure. (2) T^{P} is indifferentiable from R. (3) The security of Π is defined by single-stage games. Then the composition theorem guarantees that $\Sigma^{\mathsf{T}^{\mathsf{P}}}$ is secure [50]. Note that not only (1) and (2) but also (3) is crucial; the composition theorem does not necessarily hold for schemes of which security is defined by multi-stage games [56]. We do not get into further details because it is not directly related to our results.

Indifferentiability of Sponge. Let $r, c > 0$ and $f : \{0,1\}^{r+c} \to \{0,1\}^{r+c}$ be a function. Let $\mathsf{pad} : \{0,1\}^* \to (\{0,1\}^r)^+$ be an injective padding function such that the last (r-bit) block of $\mathsf{pad}(X)$ is not 0^r for every X.[6] The sponge construction Sponge^f maps bit strings of arbitrary length to bit strings of any

[5] In practice, many white-box implementations of AES are the output of the probabilistic compiler. On the other hand, the dedicated white-box block cipher such as SPACE uses the deterministic compiler in general.

[6] In what follows, we assume the padding function pads "1" and the minimum number of zeroes so that the total length of the padded string becomes multiple of r, i.e., $\mathsf{pad}(X) := X||1||0^{\mathrm{len}(X) \bmod r-1}$.

Algorithm 4: $\mathsf{Sponge}^f(X)$ with requested output length m

1: $(X_1, \ldots, X_\ell) \xleftarrow{r} \mathsf{pad}(X)$, $s \leftarrow 0^{r+c}$, $y \leftarrow \varepsilon$
2: **for** $i = 0$ **to** $\ell - 1$ **do**
3: $\quad s \leftarrow f(s \oplus (X_{i+1} \| 0^c))$
4: **for** $i = \ell$ **to** $\ell + \lceil \frac{m}{r} \rceil - 1$ **do**
5: $\quad y \leftarrow y \|$(the upper r bits of s), $s \leftarrow f(s)$
6: **return** y

requested length as in Algorithm 4 (i.e., Sponge^f can be regarded as a function from $\{0,1\}^* \times \mathbb{N}$ to $\{0,1\}^\infty$). The parameters r and c are called rate and capacity.

Bertoni et al. [12] proved that the sponge construction is indifferentiable from a VIL/VOL random oracle $\mathsf{RO} : \{0,1\}^* \to \{0,1\}^\infty$ if f is an ideally random function. More precisely, they showed the following theorem[7].

Theorem 1 (Theorem 1 of [12]). *Let* $\epsilon(q) := 1 - \prod_{i=1}^{q} \left(1 - \frac{i}{2^c}\right)$. *There exists a simulator* $\mathcal{S}$ *making queries of total length at most* $\lceil \frac{r+c}{r} \rceil q^2$ *such that* $\mathbf{Adv}^{\mathrm{indiff}}_{\mathsf{Sponge},\mathsf{RO},\mathcal{S}}(\mathcal{A}) \le \epsilon(q)$ *holds for any adversary* $\mathcal{A}$ *that calls* f *at most* $q (< 2^c)$ *times in the real world, either directly or indirectly through* Sponge^f.

Indifferentiable AEAD Schemes. Barbosa and Farshim studied indifferentiable AEAD schemes [6], where the ideal oracle is a *variable-key* random injection F and its inverse F^{-1} (see Definition 1)[8]. Note that a variable random injection takes not only nonce, associated data, and message (or ciphertext) but also a key as an input. They especially showed that indifferentiable AEADs cannot be achieved by some generic compositions such as SIV, and that indifferentiable constructions can be built by Encode-then-Encipher (EtE) or 3-round Feistel-based scheme. In particular, by using the sponge construction for round functions of the Feistel-based scheme, an indifferentiable AEAD can be built from a FIL/FOL random function. See the full version of this paper [40] for details.

Public Indifferentiability. Again, let T^{P} be a construction calling an ideal primitive P, and R be an ideal object of which interface is compatible with

[7] The theorem roughly says Sponge^f is secure up to $2^{c/2}$ queries because $\epsilon(q) \approx 1 - e^{-\frac{q(q+1)}{2^{c+1}}} < \frac{q(q+1)}{2^{c+1}}$ holds for $q \ll 2^c$. The original theorem in [12] did not mention the exact number of queries by $\mathcal{S}$ but we can deduce it is at most $\lceil \frac{r+c}{r} \rceil q$ by checking the details of the proof.

[8] The parameter τ (the length of ciphertext-stretch) is also considered as an input to AEADs and random injections in [6], but this paper considers the special case where is τ fixed to a constant.

T^{P}. Public indifferentiability [32,63] is defined in the same way as the original indifferentiability, except that a simulator $\mathcal{S}$ is allowed to observe all the queries by adversaries to R and the responses. (Public-indifferentiability is actually a special case of indifferentiability rather than a variant. However, we regard it as a variant for readability.) More precisely, in the ideal world, there is an additional oracle-query interface to reveal the list of all the queries made so far to R and the responses, and an access to this interface is given to $\mathcal{S}$ (but not to $\mathcal{A}$). We call this interface the *revealing interface*, and denote by Rev[R]. This models the condition that every input to R (and the output) is visible to all the parties involved in a security game, and the general "composition theorem" on public-indifferentiability holds only for schemes of which security games satisfy such a condition. The restriction that the "composition theorem" does not necessarily hold for multi-stage games also applies to public-indifferentiability, but the theorem holds for single-stage games as long as this condition holds. The public indifferentiability advantage is defined as $\mathsf{Adv}^{\text{pub-indiff}}_{\mathsf{T},\mathsf{R},\mathcal{S}}(\mathcal{A}) := \Pr\left[1 \leftarrow \mathcal{A}^{\mathsf{T}^{\mathsf{P}},\mathsf{P}}\right] - \Pr\left[1 \leftarrow \mathcal{A}^{\mathsf{R},\mathcal{S}^{\mathsf{R},\mathsf{Rev}[\mathsf{R}]}}\right]$. Informally, we say T^{P} is public indifferentiable from $\mathcal{R}$ if there exists an efficient simulator $\mathcal{S}$ such that the above advantage becomes negligibly small for any efficient $\mathcal{A}$. The Merkle-Damgård construction is proven public indifferentiable [32].

Remark 1. While it is straightforward to show the composition of two indifferentiable constructions becomes again indifferentiable[9], its seems quite hard (or even impossible) to prove that the composition of two public indifferentiabile constructions becomes again public indifferentiable. (See Sect. 6.1 for details).

3 Code Lifting on GCM

This section briefly explains that GCM [51] is unlikely to achieve incompressibility in the presence of a lifter given an unlimited access to an implementation, even when used with an incompressible block cipher. Recall that GCM is an AEAD mode of 128-bit block cipher composed of CTR and a universal hash function called GHASH (see Fig. 4 of the full version [40] for details). As an input, the encryption function of GCM takes a tuple of a nonce N, associated data A, and a message M. Given an input (N, A, M), CTR first encrypts M into a ciphertext C' with an IV derived from N. Then, a tag value T is computed as $T := \mathrm{GHASH}_{E_K(0^{128})}(A, C') \oplus E_K(N||1)$. The output of the encryption function is $T||C'$. GCM is proven secure in the nonce-respecting scenario where each nonce is never repeated for encryption queries[10]. When a nonce is repeated, GCM is broken even in the black-box setting.

An important feature of GCM is that the authenticity heavily relies on the value $E_K(0^{128})$: Suppose we know $E_K(0^{128})$ in addition to the tag T

[9] If $\mathcal{S}$ (resp., $\mathcal{S}'$) is a simulator for a construction T^{P} (resp., U^{Q}) making the indifferentiability advantage small (and if the interfaces are compatible), then $\mathcal{S}'^{\mathcal{S}}$ makes the advantage for $\mathsf{T}^{\mathsf{U}^{\mathsf{Q}}}$ small.

[10] Note that nonce reuse for *decryption* is allowed.

and the ciphertext C' for an input (N, A, M). Then, for arbitrary $\tilde{A}$ and $\tilde{M}$ with $\text{len}(\tilde{M}) \leq \text{len}(M)$, we can produce the tag $\tilde{T}$ and the ciphertext $\tilde{C}'$ corresponding to $(N, \tilde{A}, \tilde{M})$ *without knowing the secret key* K as $\tilde{C}' = \tilde{M} \oplus$ (the upper $\text{len}(\tilde{M})$ bits of $M \oplus C$) and $\tilde{T} = \text{GHASH}_{E_K(0^{128})}(A, C') \oplus T \oplus \text{GHASH}_{E_K(0^{128})}(\tilde{A}, \tilde{C}')$. This means the universal forgery attack is possible and the authenticity of GCM is completely broken once an adversary retrieves $E_K(0^{128})$.

In the black-box setting, the value $E_K(0^{128})$ is hidden from adversaries and GCM achieves authenticity. However, in the white-box setting where a lifter has an unlimited access to a white-box implementation of GCM, the lifter could copy and leak the value $E_K(0^{128})$ to an attacker to break authenticity[11]. This attack works even if the underlying block cipher E_K is incompressible. Just copying a single 128-bit string $E_K(0^{128})$ would not be difficult no matter how hard copying the full functionality of E_K is.

The above attack shows that GCM fails to inherit incompressibility from E_K: A relatively small amount of data $E_K(0^{128})$ leaks information on an exponentially many input-output pairs of GCM. Similar attacks exist for other AE modes such as CCM, GCM-SIV, and OCB. See the full version [40] for details.

4 New AEAD Security Notion

This section gives us a formal definition of incompressibility-based white-box security of an AEAD implementation. Security notions for other cryptosystems are given later based on the definition for AEADs.

The attack in the previous section (and the ones in the full version of the paper [40]) shows that, with raw implementation of AEAD modes such as GCM, a small amount of leakage from the underlying white-box cipher could lead to giving the adversary a great deal of information concerning valid ciphertext values of the overlying AEAD scheme. Clearly this is an undesirable situation.

Basically, we want that a small amount of leakage would only lead to a small amount of valid ciphertext information, but there is a subtlety. A white-box attacker, or *lifter* (e.g., malware) could locally encrypt a large number of messages and then compute leakage of a small size from the obtained ciphertexts. As a result, the leakage, as a function, may depend on a large number of ciphertext values. Intuitively, we want that:

1. The leakage should not contain information yielding ciphertext values that have not been computed by the lifter, so that the ciphertexts that the adversary can compute from the leakage are limited to those that have been already computed by the lifter, and

[11] The value $E_K(0^{128})$ could be protected from some white-box attacks with software or hardware countermeasures. Still, the effectiveness of such countermeasures would be limited, given that existing white-box implementations of AES ensure security only when adversaries have limited access to implemented algorithms. In addition, our aim is to achieve white-box security without assuming trusted hardware.

2. The number of ciphertexts that the adversary can compute from the leakage should be small likewise the leakage size.

We establish a security notion that formalizes these requirements.

4.1 White-Box AEAD Attack Model

This section shows our attack model on white-box AEADs. We discuss on the security *after* the code lifting because no security can be guaranteed before and during the code lifting.

First, we provide an intuitive observation on what kind of attackers we have to take into account. Assume a white-box AEAD scheme is running on a target device, e.g., a remote server or a smartphone. Real-world attackers will behave as follows: First, an attacker performs advance preparation on the target scheme, making black-box queries to the encryption and decryption functions if possible. Then the attacker creates a lifter, e.g., a malware or an analysis tool, and give the lifter access to the white-box implementation by any means[12]. After analyzing the implementation, the lifter leaks some information on the scheme to the attacker. Finally, the attacker tries to break the privacy or authenticity of the scheme by using the leakage.

Based on the above observation, we reach the following attack model. Formally, let $\Pi = (\mathcal{E}, \mathcal{D})$ be an AEAD and $\mathcal{C}_\Pi$ its compiler. A *white-box adversary* $\mathcal{A} = (\mathcal{A}_{\text{create}}, \mathcal{A}_{\text{dist}})$ is a pair of oracle-aided, probabilistic random-access machines (RAMs.) The adversary $\mathcal{A}$ attacks $\mathcal{C}_\Pi$, running in two stages, as follows:

Initialization. A key K is chosen uniformly at random. Then using this key we put $\mathcal{P} \leftarrow \mathcal{C}_\Pi(K)$.

1st stage: creating a lifter. The first-stage is run by the sub-adversary $\mathcal{A}_{\text{create}}$ which has only black-box access to $\mathcal{P}$, making queries to oracles $\mathcal{E}_K$ and $\mathcal{D}_K$. The goal of $\mathcal{A}_{\text{create}}$ is to output a deterministic RAM $\mathcal{L}$ which we call a *lifter*.

Lifter execution. Once created, the lifter $\mathcal{L}$ gets full access to the AEAD program $\mathcal{P}$. The lifter $\mathcal{L}$ tries to extract some useful information out of the implementation $\mathcal{P}$, for example key material or compressed codes, and sends leakage data L to the adversary. The size of L is restricted to λ bits, which are properly smaller than the description of $\mathcal{P}$.

2nd stage: distinguishing. Upon receiving leakage L from the lifter, the second-stage sub-adversary $\mathcal{A}_{\text{dist}}$ resumes querying to $\mathcal{E}_k$ and $\mathcal{D}_k$, and finally outputs a bit string.

We could consider various sorts of adversarial goals, such as key recovery, plaintext recovery and ciphertext forgery. Of these, we choose the distinguishing

[12] For instance, if the target device is a remote server, the lifter would be a malware that sneaks into the server. If the device is a smartphone, the lifter would be an analysis tool and the attacker may take the advantage of a slight opportunity to analyze the smartphone while the owner does not pay attention to it.

attack, extending the "gold-standard" IND-CCA in the black-box setting: We assume $\mathcal{A}_{\text{dist}}$ finally outputs a bit b. The final goal of the adversary $\mathcal{A}$ is to distinguish between the real world ($b = 1$) and the ideal world ($b = 0$), i.e., whether the oracles $\mathcal{E}_K$ and $\mathcal{D}_K$ and the leakage have been real, or they have been some random and simulated ones.

Of course, white-box implementation is not present in the black-box security definitions, so we shall define how the leakage is computed in the ideal world. Consequently, we shall later introduce a simulator that imitates the behavior of the lifter $\mathcal{L}$.

Even if it is impossible to prevent lifters from getting access to the white-box implementation, we expect it is still possible to notice an attack is being mounted when non-negligible amount of data is sent to a strange and suspicious direction, by monitoring outgoing packets. Hence we define security notions when the leakage size λ is limited, e.g., up to 2^{20} bits. No security is guaranteed after λ reaches the limitation. In addition, basically we assume the running time of the lifter t_{lif} is much smaller than that of the adversary t (e.g., $t_{\text{lif}} = 2^{50}$ while $t = 2^{112}$) and the intrusion of the lifter can be detected after t_{lif} time has passed.

We do not formalize the attack model in such a way $\mathcal{L}$ communicates with $\mathcal{A}$ since $\mathcal{L}$ can do everything $\mathcal{A}$ can do, and thus communications do not help much to break the scheme.

4.2 Ideal Oracles and Simulators

It remains to describe the ideal world in order to give a formal definition of white-box AEAD security.

When *black-box* security of nonce-based AEAD is studied, typically the ideal encryption (resp., decryption) oracle is set to be the one that always returns a random ciphertext (resp., the reject symbol). The adversary is prohibited to forward outputs from the encryption oracle to the decryption oracle to exclude trivial attacks.

On the other hand, in our white-box setting we cannot set the ideal oracles like above because the adversary can distinguish the ideal decryption oracle from the real one if the lifter leaks a valid ciphertext C and the adversary queries C to the decryption oracle.

Thus we set *a fixed-key random injection* F and its inverse F^{-1} as the ideal oracles (see Definition 1), following previous works on pseudorandom injection (PRI) security of AEADs [39,58]. In particular, our security notion will completely match the black-box PRI security when $\lambda = 0$.

Note that the black-box PRI security matches the misuse-resistant AE (MRAE) security [39,58] if the tag length τ is sufficiently long: Roughly speaking, the difference between the PRI advantage and the MRAE advantage of an AEAD scheme is upper-bounded by $O(q^2/2^\tau)$, where q is the number of black-box oracle queries [39, Theorem 1]. Thus our white-box security notion will require a secure scheme to be at least MRAE-secure in the black-box model.

Simulators. Now what remains of the real world is the program $\mathcal{P}$ and the lifter $\mathcal{L}$. $\mathcal{P}$ does not exist in the ideal world and it is non-trivial how we should define the behavior of $\mathcal{L}$. To remedy this, we introduce a simulator that imitates the behavior of $\mathcal{L}$.

Recall our intuition on the property that a secure white-box scheme must meet: Any leakage on a secure scheme does not contain information enabling an adversary to compute ciphertext values that have not been computed by a lifter. In other words, information that a lifter $\mathcal{L}$ can send to an adversary $\mathcal{A}_{\mathsf{dist}}$ (with reasonable computational resources) is only those computable or *simulatable* from some input-output pairs of $\mathcal{E}_K$ and $\mathcal{D}_K$.

We model this situation by existence of a simulator $\mathcal{S}$ working as follows. Given the description of a lifter $\mathcal{L}$[13] and oracle access to F and F^{-1} in the ideal world, $\mathcal{S}$ produces a bit string L_{ideal} which is, to $\mathcal{A}_{\mathsf{dist}}$, indistinguishable from leakage L_{real} by $\mathcal{L}$ in the real world.

Since F is an ideally random object, $\mathcal{S}$ in the ideal world cannot leak more than λ bits of information on $F^{\pm}$ via λ-bit leakage L_{ideal}. Hence, intuitively, if $\mathcal{A}_{\mathsf{dist}}$ cannot L_{real} and L_{ideal}, then $\mathcal{L}$ in the real world cannot leak more than λ bits of information on $\mathcal{E}_K$ and $\mathcal{D}_K$ via λ-bit leakage L_{real}.

More specifically, a simulator $\mathcal{S}$ is an oracle-aided RAM. We give $\mathcal{S}$ the ability to do its job as follows:

1. We give $\mathcal{S}$ as its input the lifter $\mathcal{L}$ just as it is. Then $\mathcal{S}$ can perform static and dynamic analyses on $\mathcal{L}$. The code of $\mathcal{L}$ can be read, dissected and studied, so that $\mathcal{S}$ can determine the functionality of $\mathcal{L}$.
2. Needless to say, we let $\mathcal{S}$ have oracle access to $F^{\pm 1}$.
3. We give $\mathcal{S}$ sufficient computational power and do not explicitly bound its running time. We only demand that the algorithm $\mathcal{S}$ be a finite sequence of well-defined instructions and operations. By doing so, we believe that our security notion should become achievable by a sound portion of AEAD programs while dismissing the rest.

In addition, we assume that $\mathcal{S}$ can observe all the queries to $F^{\pm}$ by $\mathcal{A}_{\mathsf{create}}$ and the responses. The reasons that we assume this is as follows. First, if we define a security notion for conventional encryption schemes similarly *without this assumption*, then a conventional encryption scheme (random-IV CTR) which intuitively seems white-box-secure is deemed insecure (see the full version of this paper [40] for details). However, if the assumption is included in the definition, random-IV CTR can be proven secure (Sect. 6.3). Thus it seems reasonable to include the assumption into the definition for conventional encryption schemes. Second, We would like to make security definitions for various cryptosystems consistent as much as possible. Thus we include this assumption not only for conventional encryption schemes but also for AEADs.

[13] Note that a lifter is also made by a first-stage adversary $\mathcal{A}_{\mathsf{create}}$ in the ideal world, but the black-box oracles given to $\mathcal{A}_{\mathsf{create}}$ are (F, F^{-1}) instead of $(\mathcal{E}_K, \mathcal{D}_K)$.

4.3 Formal Security Notion: whPRI

Now we are ready to define new security notion of AEAD programs. We call our notion *white-box pseudo-random injection security (whPRI)*.

We consider a white-box adversary $\mathcal{A} = (\mathcal{A}_{\text{create}}, \mathcal{A}_{\text{dist}})$ running in two different experiments called games. The real white-box PRI game ($\boxed{\text{PRI}}$-real) is an experiment in the real world as described in Sect. 4.1. We assume that the white-box program $\mathcal{P}$ contains an implementation of not only encryption but also decryption. The ideal white-box PRI game ($\boxed{\text{PRI}}$-ideal) is an experiment in the ideal world, where the oracles and the lifter are replaced with a random injection and a simulator, respectively. These two games are formally defined in Exp. 5 and Exp. 6 (Fig. 1).

Experiment 5: $\mathbf{Exp}^{\boxed{\text{PRI}}\text{-real}}_{\Pi,\mathcal{C}_\Pi,\mathcal{A}}$	**Experiment 6:** $\mathbf{Exp}^{\boxed{\text{PRI}}\text{-ideal}}_{\mathcal{S},\mathcal{A}}$
1: $K \xleftarrow{\$} \mathbf{K}$, $\mathcal{P} \leftarrow \mathcal{C}_\Pi(K)$	1: $F \xleftarrow{\$} \text{Inj}_\tau(\mathbf{N} \times \mathbf{A} \times \mathbf{M}, \mathbf{C})$
2: $(\mathcal{L}, S) \leftarrow \mathcal{A}_{\text{create}}{}^{\mathcal{E}_K,\mathcal{D}_K}()$	2: $(\mathcal{L}, S) \leftarrow \mathcal{A}_{\text{create}}{}^{F,F^{-1}}()$
3: $L \leftarrow \mathcal{L}(\mathcal{P})$	3: $L \leftarrow \mathcal{S}^{F,F^{-1}}(\mathcal{L}, \mathsf{List}_{\text{create}})$
4: $\beta \leftarrow \mathcal{A}_{\text{dist}}{}^{\mathcal{E}_K,\mathcal{D}_K}(S, L)$	4: $\beta \leftarrow \mathcal{A}_{\text{dist}}{}^{F,F^{-1}}(S, L)$
5: **return** β	5: **return** β

Fig. 1. Experiments for whPRI. In the ideal experiment, $\mathsf{List}_{\text{create}}$ denotes the list of queries by $\mathcal{A}_{\text{create}}$ to $F^{\pm}$ and the responses.

Now, given an AEAD scheme Π and its compiler $\mathcal{C}_\Pi$, let us define the *whPRI advantage* of a white-box adversary $\mathcal{A} = (\mathcal{A}_{\text{create}}, \mathcal{A}_{\text{dist}})$ with respect to a simulator $\mathcal{S}$ as $\mathbf{Adv}^{\text{whPRI}}_{\Pi,\mathcal{C}_\Pi,\mathcal{S}}(\mathcal{A}) := \Pr\left[\mathbf{Exp}^{\boxed{\text{PRI}}\text{-real}}_{\Pi,\mathcal{C}_\Pi,\mathcal{A}} = 1\right] - \Pr\left[\mathbf{Exp}^{\boxed{\text{PRI}}\text{-ideal}}_{\mathcal{S},\mathcal{A}} = 1\right]$.

Definition 2 (whPRI). *The pair of an AEAD scheme Π and a compiler $\mathcal{C}_\Pi$ is $(\lambda, t, q, \sigma, t_{\text{lif}}, q_{\text{sim}}, \sigma_{\text{sim}}, \epsilon)$-whPRI-secure white-box AEAD if the following condition is satisfied: Let $\mathcal{A}$ be an arbitrary adversary running in time t and making queries at most q times. The lengths of the queries are at most σ in total*[14]*. In addition, $\mathcal{A}$ creates a lifter that runs in time t_{lif} and outputs at most λ-bit leakage. For arbitrary such $\mathcal{A}$, there exists a simulator $\mathcal{S}$ that makes at most q_{sim} queries of which lengths are at most σ_{sim} in total, and satisfies an inequality $\mathbf{Adv}^{\text{whPRI}}_{\Pi,\mathcal{C}_\Pi,\mathcal{S}}(\mathcal{A}) < \epsilon$.*

[14] The unit of length can be set arbitrarily (e.g., bit or block) depending on the context.

Informally, suppose the following claim holds: For any "efficient" $\mathcal{A}$, there exists a simulator $\mathcal{S}$ that makes a "reasonable amount of" queries and making the whPRI-advantage small[15]. Then we say that Π is whPRI-secure.

The attacks on GCM, GCM-SIV, CCM, OCB in Sect. 3 (or in the full version of this paper [40]) show that, for each of those schemes, there exists a lifter $\mathcal{L}$ that leaks the information on exponentially many number of input-output pairs by only a small amount of leakage. In the ideal world, the information of input-output pairs of the black-box oracle $F^{\pm}$ that a simulator can output by a λ-bit leakage is at most λ-bit. Hence no simulator will be able to mimic the behavior of such $\mathcal{L}$. Therefore those modes are unlikely to achieve whPRI-security.

Experiment 7: $\mathbf{Exp}_{E,\mathcal{C}_E,\mathcal{A}}^{\boxed{\text{PRP}}\text{-real}}$

1: $K \xleftarrow{\$} \{0,1\}^{\kappa}$, $\mathcal{P} \leftarrow \mathcal{C}_E(K)$
2: $(\mathcal{L}, S) \leftarrow \mathcal{A}_{\text{create}}{}^{E_K}()$
3: $L \leftarrow \mathcal{L}(\mathcal{P})$
4: $\beta \leftarrow \mathcal{A}_{\text{dist}}{}^{E_K}(S, L)$
5: **return** β

Experiment 8: $\mathbf{Exp}_{\mathcal{S},\mathcal{A}}^{\boxed{\text{PRP}}\text{-ideal}}$

1: $P \xleftarrow{\$} \text{Perm}(n)$
2: $(\mathcal{L}, S) \leftarrow \mathcal{A}_{\text{create}}{}^{P}()$
3: $L \leftarrow \mathcal{S}^{P,P^{-1}}(\mathcal{L}, \mathsf{List}_{\text{create}})$
4: $\beta \leftarrow \mathcal{A}_{\text{dist}}{}^{P}(S, L)$
5: **return** β

Fig. 2. Experiments for whPRP. $\mathsf{List}_{\text{create}}$ in Experiment 2 denotes the list of queries to P by $\mathcal{A}_{\text{create}}$ and the responses.

5 New White-Box Security Notions for Other Schemes

This section introduces white-box security notions for block ciphers, keyed functions, and conventional encryption schemes.

5.1 whPRP: Secure White-Box Block Ciphers

We call the new security notion for white-box block ciphers *white-box pseudo-random permutation security* (*whPRP*). The definition of whPRP is similar to that of whPRI; the oracles $\mathcal{E}_K$ and $\mathcal{D}_K$ are now just E_K, and its counterpart in the ideal game is a random permutation $P \in \text{Perm}(n)$, where $\text{Perm}(n)$ denotes the set of permutations on $\{0,1\}^n$.

We again consider a white-box adversary $\mathcal{A} = (\mathcal{A}_{\text{create}}, \mathcal{A}_{\text{dist}})$ running in two games: the real white-box PRP game ($\boxed{\text{PRP}}$-real) which is formally defined in Exp. 7 and the ideal white-box PRP game ($\boxed{\text{PRP}}$-ideal) in Exp. 8 (Fig. 2).

[15] We set quantifiers as $\forall\mathcal{A}\exists\mathcal{S}$ rather than $\exists\mathcal{S}\forall\mathcal{A}$ so that the possibility of existence of primitives will increase, and the order of the quantifiers seems to have little impact on whether a practical scheme is judged secure or not. Indeed, our proofs in later sections, in addition to the discussions about the attacks on GCM, GCM-SIV, CCM, OCB mentioned below, work regardless of the order of the quantifiers.

We assume that the white-box program given to a lifter contains an implementation of not only encryption but also decryption. Then, given a block cipher E and its compiler $\mathcal{C}_E$, let us define the *whPRP advantage* of a white-box adversary $\mathcal{A} = (\mathcal{A}_{\text{create}}, \mathcal{A}_{\text{dist}})$ with respect to a simulator $\mathcal{S}$ as $\mathbf{Adv}^{\text{whPRP}}_{E,\mathcal{C}_E,\mathcal{S}}(\mathcal{A}) :=$ $\Pr\left[\mathbf{Exp}^{\boxed{\text{PRP}}\text{-real}}_{E,\mathcal{C}_E,\mathcal{A}} = 1\right] - \Pr\left[\mathbf{Exp}^{\boxed{\text{PRP}}\text{-ideal}}_{\mathcal{S},\mathcal{A}} = 1\right]$.

Definition 3 (whPRP). *The pair of a block cipher E and a compiler $\mathcal{C}_E$ is a $(\lambda, t, q, t_{\text{lif}}, q_{\text{sim}}, \epsilon)$-secure whPRP if the following condition is satisfied: Let $\mathcal{A}$ be an arbitrary adversary running in time t and making at most q queries. $\mathcal{A}$ makes a lifter that runs in time t_{lif} and outputs at most λ-bit leakage. For arbitrary such $\mathcal{A}$, there exists a simulator $\mathcal{S}$ that runs in time t_{sim}, makes at most q_{sim} queries, and satisfies an inequality $\mathbf{Adv}^{\text{whPRP}}_{E,\mathcal{C}_E,\mathcal{S}}(\mathcal{A}) < \epsilon$.*

Informally, suppose the following claim holds: For any "efficient" $\mathcal{A}$, there exists a simulator $\mathcal{S}$ that makes a "reasonable amount of" queries and making the whPRP-advantage small. Then we say that Π is whPRP-secure.

The definition of whPRP is a strengthening of the conventional black-box PRP, as the latter corresponds to the case $\lambda = 0$. It should be noted that we allow the simulator $\mathcal{S}$ to make queries to P^{-1}.

We can also consider the strong PRP version, whSPRP, where $\mathcal{A}$ is given oracle access to not only E_K but also E_K^{-1}. It is strictly stronger than whPRP.

As a candidate of whPRP, we conjecture[16] that SPACE-n_a ($n_a \in \{8, 16, 24, 32\}$) is a $(\lambda, t, q, t_{\text{lif}}, q_{\text{sim}}, \epsilon)$-secure whPRP with $t \approx 2^\kappa$, $q \approx 2^n$, $\lambda \approx (n - n_a) \cdot 2^{n_a - 2}$, and $\epsilon \ll 1$, as long as $t_{\text{lif}} \ll q_{\text{sim}} (< 2^n)$. Here, n and κ denote the block and key length, which are 128. See the full version [40] for more details.

5.2 whPRF: Secure White-Box Keyed Functions

We call the new security notion for white-box keyed functions *white-box pseudorandom function security (whPRF)*[17], which is defined in the same way as whPRP except that the black-box oracle given to the adversary is a random function RF instead of a random permutation P, and that simulators have access to RF instead of P and P^{-1}. Real and ideal experiments in addition to a distinguishing advantage are defined in the same way as those for whPRP.

[16] Note that it is unrealistic to "prove" whPRP-security of SPACE-256-16 in the same sense as proving PRP security of AES is unrealistic. Generally, the only realistic way to be confident with security of a block cipher is to see whether it withstands various attempts of cryptanalysis by experts. Recently, the security of some space-hard block ciphers was reviewed against a similar adversary to whPRP in [60].

[17] We define a white-box version of PRF security but does not for MAC security such as existential unforgeability. This is because a lifter can leak a valid message-tag pair that has not been queried to oracles before, and thus it seems hard to achieve a sound white-box version of existential unforgeability. It might be possible to define a white-box version of weaker notions such as universal unforgeability, but such notions are out of the scope of this paper. Studying weaker notions is a future work.

5.3 White-Box Security of Conventional Encryption Schemes

We define two security notions on conventional IV-based encryption schemes, which we name *tweakable strong PRP security* (wh$\widetilde{\text{SPRP}}$) and *white-box IND$-CPA security* (whIND$-CPA).

wh$\widetilde{\textbf{SPRP}}$. The most natural way to obtain a definition of conventional IV-based encryption schemes is to consider the special case of whPRI where $\mathbf{A} = \{\varepsilon\}$ and $\tau = 0$. This is an extension of (VIL) tweakable strong PRP ($\widetilde{\text{SPRP}}$) security for enciphering schemes in the black-box setting [38], and thus we call it wh$\widetilde{\text{SPRP}}$.

whIND$-CPA. Though wh$\widetilde{\text{SPRP}}$ is naturally derived from whPRI, many popular conventional encryption schemes such as CTR and CBC are not $\widetilde{\text{SPRP}}$-secure even in the black-box setting. Thus we seek for another definition extending ones that CTR and CBC meet in the black-box setting. Since CTR and CBC cannot achieve indistinguishability against CCAs, we focus on security against CPAs.

In the black-box setting, we have three scenarios depending on how IVs for encryption queries are chosen.

1. Arbitrary IV (or, nonce-misuse) scenario: IVs are chosen by adversaries completely arbitrarily.
2. Nonce IV (or, nonce-respecting) scenario: IVs are chosen by adversaries arbitrarily, but repeated uses are prohibited (i.e., once an IV value is used for a query, it is never be used again).
3. Random IV scenario: An IV is chosen uniformly at random for every encryption query.

CTR and CBC cannot achieve indistinguishability in the first scenario. The second scenario is popular in the black-box setting but not suitable in our context since a lifter may leak information on a valid message-ciphertext pair w.r.t. an unused nonce. Thus we focus on the random IV scenario.

We follow [54] for the black-box security notion against CPAs for conventional random-IV encryption scheme. The notion is defined by real and ideal experiments. In the real experiment, an adversary has an access to a modified version of the encryption oracle $\mathcal{E}_K$, which we denote by $\mathcal{E}_{K,\text{rnd}}$. For each encryption query, $\mathcal{E}_{K,\text{rnd}}$ chooses IV uniformly at random, and returns $(IV, \mathcal{E}_K(IV))$. In the ideal experiment, $\mathcal{E}_{K,\text{rnd}}$ is replaced with an oracle $\$(\cdot)$ that just returns a random IV and a random ciphertext of the same length as the message. A scheme is defined to be secure if an adversary with a reasonable amount of computational resources cannot distinguish the two experiments. We call this black-box security notion IND$-CPA[18].

[18] This name is from [57], though it is defined for nonce-based scheme rather than random-IV schemes.

Our new notion whIND\$-CPA is defined by extending IND\$-CPA in the same way as whPRI is defined extending PRI security. In the real world, the black-box oracle given to $\mathcal{A}$ is $\mathcal{E}_{K,\mathrm{rnd}}$ only. In the ideal world, the oracle $\$(\cdot)$ is given to both of $\mathcal{A}$ and $\mathcal{S}$. A complete description of the real and ideal experiments can be found in the full version of this paper [40]. The advantage $\mathbf{Adv}_{\Pi,\mathcal{C}_\Pi,\mathcal{S}}^{\mathrm{whIND\$-CPA}}(\mathcal{A})$ is defined as before. We assume that the white-box program given to a lifter contains an implementation of not only encryption but also decryption.

6 Weak Public Indifferentiability and White-Box Security Reductions

This section first introduces a weaker version of public indifferentiability which we name *weak public indifferentiability*. Second, we show that weak public indifferentiability implies reductions between our white-box security notions introduced in Sects. 4 and 5. Third, we provide feasibility results that our white-box security notions on various schemes can be reduced to whPRP, by showing weak public indifferentiable constructions.

6.1 Weak Public Indifferentiability and Compositions

An important point to be aware of about public indifferentiability is that it seems quite hard to prove a composition of two arbitrary public indifferentiable scheme become again public indifferentiable. This is because the general "composition theorem" is not applicable to show public indifferentiability of composite schemes due to the following reason. Suppose a scheme U^{Q} (Q is an ideally random primitive) is public indifferentiable from a random object P (e.g., a random oracle). Then, what the general "composition theorem" for public indifferentiability says is that we can safely replace P in a protocol or construction with U^{Q} if the security of the protocol/construction is defined by single-stage games satisfying the following condition: Queries to P by any party involved in the security games can be made public without affecting the security. (We denote this condition by (C).) Now, assume that there is another scheme T^{P} that is public indifferentiable from a random object R. If (C) were satisfied by the security games of T^{P} (i.e., by the security games of public indifferentiability), public indifferentiability of U^{Q} and the "composition theorem" would imply public indifferentiability of $\mathsf{T}^{\mathsf{U}^{\mathsf{Q}}}$. However, (C) is not satisfied because queries by a simulator must not be visible to an adversary in the ideal game. Thus the general "composition theorem" is not applicable to prove public indifferentiability of $\mathsf{T}^{\mathsf{U}^{\mathsf{Q}}}$. (See also Remark 2.)

However, infeasibility of compositions is inconvenient because security proofs cannot be provided in a modular way. To remedy this, we introduce a weaker variant which we name *weak public indifferentiability*. Let T^{P} be a construction querying to an ideally random primitive P, and let R be a random object of which input-output interfaces are compatible with T^{P}. Now, let $\mathsf{Rev}'[\mathsf{R}]$ be a variant of the revealing interface $\mathsf{Rev}[\mathsf{R}]$ that returns the list of all the queries made so far by $\mathcal{A}$, but not by $\mathcal{S}$, together with the responses[19]. We define *weak public indifferentiability* in the same way as public indifferentiability is defined except that the revealing interface is $\mathsf{Rev}'[\mathsf{R}]$ instead of $\mathsf{Rev}[\mathsf{R}]$. Weak public indifferentiability advantage is defined as $\mathsf{Adv}^{\text{weak-pub-indiff}}_{\mathsf{T},\mathsf{R},\mathcal{S}}(\mathcal{A}) := \Pr\left[1 \leftarrow \mathcal{A}^{\mathsf{T}^{\mathsf{P}},\mathsf{P}}\right] - \Pr\left[1 \leftarrow \mathcal{A}^{\mathsf{R},\mathcal{S}^{\mathsf{R},\mathsf{Rev}'[\mathsf{R}]}}\right]$.

A public indifferentiable scheme is weak public indifferentiable[20]. This is because a simulator $\mathcal{S}$ for public indifferentiability can be converted into a one for weak public indifferentiability just by recording queries that $\mathcal{S}$ makes to R.

On Compositions of Two Weak Public Indifferentiable Schemes. Here we explain that a composition of two weak public indifferentiable schemes become weak public indifferentiable if a few additional conditions are satisfied. To explain this, we formally define *random-IV schemes.* Note that we say a construction T^{P} is deterministic if, for an arbitrary input X, the output value $\mathsf{T}^{\mathsf{P}}(X)$ is unchanged during each game.

Definition 4. *A construction* T^{P} *is a* random-IV scheme *if it is a public-coin protocol. Namely, there exists a deterministic construction* $\tilde{\mathsf{T}}^{\mathsf{P}}$ *and a set* $\mathbf{IV}$ *such that, on arbitrary input* X, T^{P} *runs as follows: (1) Take a value* IV *from* $\mathbf{IV}$ *uniformly at random. (2) Return* $(IV, \tilde{\mathsf{T}}^{\mathsf{P}}(IV, X))$.

The following lemma shows the composition of two weak public indifferentiable schemes is again weak public indifferentiable if a few additional conditions are satisfied. Here we provide only an informal version due to page limitation. See the full version of this paper [40] for a formal version and a proof.

Lemma 1 (Composition of weak public indifferentiable schemes, informal). *Suppose the following (1)–(3) hold: (1)* T^{P} *is a* deterministic or random-IV *scheme calling an ideally random primitive* P *and is weak public indifferentiable from* R, *(2)* U^{Q} *is another* deterministic *construction calling an ideally random primitive* Q *and is weak public indifferentiable from* P, *and (3)* P *and* Q *are deterministic. Then* $\mathsf{T}^{\mathsf{U}^{\mathsf{Q}}}$ *is also weak public indifferentiable from* R, *regarding* Q *as the primitive oracle.*

All compositions of (weak public) indifferentiable schemes appearing in this paper satisfy (1)–(3).

[19] Note that lists returned by $\mathsf{Rev}'[\mathsf{R}]$ contain more useful information for $\mathcal{S}$ than lists returned by $\mathsf{Rev}[\mathsf{R}]$. This is because (1) $\mathcal{S}$ can record what it has queried to R so far by itself, and (2) Sometimes $\mathcal{S}$ cannot tell which queries recorded in a list by $\mathsf{Rev}[\mathsf{R}]$ have been queried by $\mathcal{A}$: If a value x had been queried to R for the first time by $\mathcal{S}$ but not $\mathcal{A}$, there is no means for $\mathcal{S}$ to know whether $\mathcal{A}$ queried x to R afterwards.

[20] It seems hard to prove weak public indifferentiability implies public indifferentiability, but currently we are not aware of any separation example that is weak public indifferentiable but not public indifferentiable.

Intuition of the Proof. Here we explain a sketch of the proof when all the functions and constructions are deterministic. Suppose the ideal game for T^{U} is being executed with an adversary $\mathcal{A}$.

Let $\mathcal{S}_{\mathsf{T}}$ (resp., $\mathcal{S}_{\mathsf{U}}$) be a "good" simulator for T (resp., U) making the indifferentiability advantage small. Then, a "good" simulator $\mathcal{S}_{\mathsf{T}^{\mathsf{U}}}$ for T^{U} is defined as follows, by using $\mathcal{S}_{\mathsf{T}}$ and $\mathcal{S}_{\mathsf{U}}$ as subroutines: When a value x is queried to $\mathcal{S}_{\mathsf{T}^{\mathsf{U}}}$, it first runs $\mathcal{S}_{\mathsf{U}}$ on the input x as a subroutine. Intuitively, $\mathcal{S}_{\mathsf{T}^{\mathsf{U}}}$ tries to convince the subroutine $\mathcal{S}_{\mathsf{U}}$ that "now $\mathcal{S}_{\mathsf{U}}$ is run as a part of $\mathcal{A}^{\mathsf{T}^{\mathsf{P}},\mathcal{S}_{\mathsf{U}}^{\mathsf{P},\mathsf{Rev}'[\mathsf{P}]}}$". When $\mathcal{S}_{\mathsf{U}}$ returns an output, $\mathcal{S}_{\mathsf{T}^{\mathsf{U}}}$ returns it to $\mathcal{A}$ as its own output. To achieve this, $\mathcal{S}_{\mathsf{T}^{\mathsf{U}}}$ simulates the oracles P and $\mathsf{Rev}'[\mathsf{P}]$ for $\mathcal{S}_{\mathsf{U}}$. P is simulated just by running $\mathcal{S}_{\mathsf{T}}^{\mathsf{R},\mathsf{Rev}'[\mathsf{R}]}$. (Note that $\mathcal{S}_{\mathsf{T}^{\mathsf{U}}}$ is given oracle access to R and $\mathsf{Rev}'[\mathsf{R}]$.) The non-trivial part is how to simulate the oracle $\mathsf{Rev}'[\mathsf{P}]$.

What the subroutine $\mathcal{S}_{\mathsf{U}}$ is expecting to receive when it makes a query to the revealing interface is a list storing queries (and the responses) to P that are made so far by $\mathcal{A}$ through T (but not by $\mathcal{S}_{\mathsf{U}}$) while running $\mathcal{A}^{\mathsf{T}^{\mathsf{P}},\mathcal{S}_{\mathsf{U}}^{\mathsf{P},\mathsf{Rev}'[\mathsf{P}]}}$. Hence, when the subroutine $\mathcal{S}_{\mathsf{U}}$ makes a query to the revealing interface, $\mathcal{S}_{\mathsf{T}^{\mathsf{U}}}$ simulates the oracle $\mathsf{Rev}'[\mathsf{P}]$ as follows. First, $\mathcal{S}_{\mathsf{T}^{\mathsf{U}}}$ queries to $\mathsf{Rev}'[\mathsf{R}]$ to get the list $\mathsf{List}_{\mathcal{A}}[\mathsf{R}]$ of queries made so far to R by $\mathcal{A}$ (but not by $\mathcal{S}_{\mathsf{T}^{\mathsf{U}}}$). Then $\mathcal{S}_{\mathsf{T}^{\mathsf{U}}}$ computes the function $\mathsf{T}^{\mathcal{S}_{\mathsf{T}}^{\mathsf{R},\mathsf{Rev}'[\mathsf{R}]}}$ on the input X for each entry (X, Y) in $\mathsf{List}_{\mathcal{A}}[\mathsf{R}]$, recording all the queries by T to $\mathcal{S}_{\mathsf{T}}^{\mathsf{R},\mathsf{Rev}'[\mathsf{R}]}$ into a list $\mathsf{List}_{\mathrm{prim}}$, together with the responses. Finally, $\mathcal{S}_{\mathsf{T}^{\mathsf{U}}}$ returns $\mathsf{List}_{\mathrm{prim}}$ to $\mathcal{S}_{\mathsf{U}}$ as a response. The simulation works well because $\mathcal{S}_{\mathsf{T}^{\mathsf{U}}}$ can tell which value has been queried to R so far by $\mathcal{A}$ (but not by $\mathcal{S}_{\mathsf{T}^{\mathsf{U}}}$). See the full version of this paper [40] for further details.

Remark 2. The above idea does not work for (original) public indifferentiability. Here we explain which part fails for public indifferentiability. The non-trivial part of the proof is again how to simulate $\mathsf{Rev}[\mathsf{P}]$ for $\mathcal{S}_{\mathsf{U}}$. The issue in simulating $\mathsf{Rev}[\mathsf{P}]$ is also again how to determine the values queried to P through T by $\mathcal{A}$ *but not by* $\mathcal{S}_{\mathsf{U}}$. Now, the procedure "First, $\mathcal{S}_{\mathsf{T}^{\mathsf{U}}}$ queries to $\mathsf{Rev}'[\mathsf{R}]$ to get..." does not work for public indifferentiability due to the property (2) in Footnote 23.

6.2 Weak Public Indifferentiability Implies White-Box Reduction

Let $(\pi, \mathcal{C}_\pi)$ be a white-box symmetric-key scheme that are either of a keyed function, block cipher, AEAD, or a conventional IV-based encryption scheme. In addition, let $(\Sigma^\pi, \mathcal{C}_{\Sigma^\pi})$ be another white-box symmetric-key scheme built on $(\pi, \mathcal{C}_\pi)$. We assume Σ calls π in a black-box manner not only at a level of syntax but also at a level of implementation, i.e., the following conditions are satisfied.

1. The implementation of π (denoted by $[\![\pi]\!]$) is included into the implementation of Σ^π (denoted by $[\![\Sigma^\pi]\!]$). In particular, $[\![\pi]\!]$ and an implementation of an oracle-aided algorithm Σ (which is independent from π) is explicitly separated in $[\![\Sigma^\pi]\!]$.
2. The implementation of Σ calls $[\![\pi]\!]$ in a black-box manner.

Our goal is to reduce the security of $(\Sigma^\pi, \mathcal{C}_{\Sigma^\pi})$ to the security of $(\pi, \mathcal{C}_\pi)$. By sec-const (resp., sec-prim) we denote the security notion corresponding to $(\Sigma^\pi, \mathcal{C}_{\Sigma^\pi})$ (resp., $(\pi, \mathcal{C}_\pi)$), which is whPRI, whPRP, whPRF, wh$\widetilde{\text{SPRP}}$, or whIND\$-CPA[21].

By abuse of notations, we use the same symbols Σ^π and π to denote the corresponding keyed black-box oracles given to $(\mathcal{A}_{\text{create}}, \mathcal{A}_{\text{dist}})$ in the white-box security definitions. We assume Σ^π is a deterministic or random-IV scheme: If it is a random-IV scheme, there exists a scheme $\tilde{\Sigma}^\pi$ and a set $\mathbf{IV}$ such that Σ^π runs as follows on arbitrary input X: (1) IV is chosen uniformly at random from $\mathbf{IV}$. (2) Return $(IV, \tilde{\Sigma}^\pi(IV, X))$.

Let R and P denote the ideal oracles given to a simulator in the ideal games of the security definition of $(\Sigma^\pi, \mathcal{C}_{\Sigma^\pi})$ and $(\pi, \mathcal{C}_\pi)$, respectively. Suppose there exist non-decreasing functions $q_\Sigma(\cdot,\cdot)$ and $\sigma_\Sigma(\cdot,\cdot)$ satisfying the following property: If Σ^π is evaluated on q inputs of which lengths[22] are σ in total during a game, Σ makes at most $q_\Sigma(q,\sigma)$ queries to π and the lengths of the queries are at most $\sigma_\Sigma(q,\sigma)$ in total. In addition, assume we have the following three algorithms.

1. An adversary $\mathcal{A} = (\mathcal{A}_{\text{create}}, \mathcal{A}_{\text{dist}})$ against $(\Sigma^\pi, \mathcal{C}_{\Sigma^\pi})$. The running time is at most $t_{\mathcal{A}}$. The number of black-box oracle queries by $\mathcal{A}$ is at most $q_{\mathcal{A}}$ and the lengths of queries are at most $\sigma_{\mathcal{A}}$ in total. $\mathcal{A}$ creates a lifter running in time t_{lif} and outputs at most λ-bit leakage.
2. A simulator $\mathcal{S}_{\text{prim}}$ for $(\pi, \mathcal{C}_\pi)$ on sec-prim. $\mathcal{S}_{\text{prim}}$ makes at most $q_{\mathcal{S}_{\text{prim}}}$ queries to the ideal oracle P. The lengths of queries are at most $\sigma_{\mathcal{S}_{\text{prim}}}$ in total.
3. A simulator $\mathcal{S}_{\text{indiff}}$ for weak public indifferentiability of Σ^{P} from R[23]. There exist non-decreasing functions $q_{\mathcal{S}_{\text{indiff}}}(\cdot,\cdot,\cdot,\cdot)$ and $\sigma_{\mathcal{S}_{\text{indiff}}}(\cdot,\cdot,\cdot,\cdot)$ satisfying the following properties: If an adversary makes at most q_c (resp., q_p) construction (resp., primitive) queries of which lengths are at most σ_c (resp., σ_p) in total in the ideal game of weak public indifferentiability, $\mathcal{S}_{\text{indiff}}$ makes at most $q_{\mathcal{S}_{\text{indiff}}}(q_c, \sigma_c, q_p, \sigma_p)$ queries to the ideal oracle R. The lengths of the queries are $\sigma_{\mathcal{S}_{\text{indiff}}}(q_c, \sigma_c, q_p, \sigma_p)$ in total.

Theorem 2. *Let $\mathcal{A}$, $\mathcal{S}_{\text{prim}}$, and $\mathcal{S}_{\text{indiff}}$ be as above. Then there exists an adversary $\mathcal{A}' = (\mathcal{A}'_{\text{create}}, \mathcal{A}'_{\text{dist}})$ against $(\pi, \mathcal{C}_\pi)$, a simulator $\mathcal{S}_{\text{const}}$ for $(\Sigma^\pi, \mathcal{C}_{\Sigma^\pi})$, and an algorithm $\mathcal{A}''$ against weak public indifferentiability of Σ such that*

$$\mathbf{Adv}^{\text{sec-const}}_{\Sigma^\pi, \mathcal{C}_{\Sigma^\pi}, \mathcal{S}_{\text{const}}}(\mathcal{A}) = \mathbf{Adv}^{\text{sec-prim}}_{\pi, \mathcal{C}_\pi, \mathcal{S}_{\text{prim}}}(\mathcal{A}') + \mathbf{Adv}^{\text{weak-pub-indiff}}_{\Sigma, \mathsf{R}, \mathcal{S}_{\text{indiff}}}(\mathcal{A}'') \quad (1)$$

[21] We assume the interfaces of π that Σ accesses to are only those given to $\mathcal{A}$ as black-box oracles in the security games of sec-prim. For instance, if π is a block cipher E_K and sec-prim is whPRP, we assume that Σ calls only E_K and does not call E_K^{-1} (though simulators in the ideal game of whPRP access to both of P and P^{-1}).

[22] The unit of length can be set arbitrarily (e.g., bit or block) depending on the context.

[23] Since P is the oracle given to a simulator while π is the black-box oracle given to an adversary in the security games of sec-prim, Σ may access to only a part of the interfaces of P: If sec-prim is whPRP and $\pi = E_K$, P is the pair (P, P^{-1}) (here, P is a random permutation) but Σ accesses only to P (and not to P^{-1}) because the black-box oracle interface given to an adversary $\mathcal{A}$ in the definition of whPRP is only E_K (and E_K^{-1} is not given to $\mathcal{A}$).

holds. Here, we can construct $\mathcal{S}_{\text{const}}$, $\mathcal{A}'$, and $\mathcal{A}''$ so that (a) $\mathcal{A}'$ does not depend on $\mathcal{S}_{\text{prim}}$ and $\mathcal{S}_{\text{indiff}}$, (b) $\mathcal{S}_{\text{const}}$ does not depend on $\mathcal{A}$, (c) $\mathcal{A}''$ does not depend on $\mathcal{S}_{\text{indiff}}$, and the following conditions hold: (1) $\mathcal{S}_{\text{const}}$ makes at most $q_{\mathcal{S}_{\text{indiff}}}(q_{\mathcal{A}}, \sigma_{\mathcal{A}}, q'_{\Sigma}+q_{\mathcal{S}_{\text{prim}}}, \sigma'_{\Sigma}+\sigma_{\mathcal{S}_{\text{prim}}})$ queries to R*. The lengths of the queries are at most $\sigma_{\mathcal{S}_{\text{indiff}}}(q_{\mathcal{A}}, \sigma_{\mathcal{A}}, q'_{\Sigma}+q_{\mathcal{S}_{\text{prim}}}, \sigma'_{\Sigma}+\sigma_{\mathcal{S}_{\text{prim}}})$ in total. Here, $q'_{\Sigma} := q_{\Sigma}(q_{\mathcal{A}}, \sigma_{\mathcal{A}})$ and $\sigma'_{\Sigma} := q_{\Sigma}(q_{\mathcal{A}}, \sigma_{\mathcal{A}})$ (2) $\mathcal{A}'$ runs in time $O(t_{\mathcal{A}} + \sigma'_{\Sigma})$ and makes at most q'_{Σ} queries to a black-box oracle. The lengths of the queries are at most σ'_{Σ} in total. $\mathcal{A}'$ creates a lifter $\mathcal{L}'$ that runs in time $O(t_{\text{lif}})$ and outputs at most λ-bit leakage. (3) $\mathcal{A}''$ makes at most $q_{\mathcal{A}}$ construction queries of which lengths are at most $\sigma_{\mathcal{A}}$ in total, and makes at most $q'_{\Sigma}+q_{\mathcal{S}_{\text{prim}}}$ primitive queries of which lengths are at most $\sigma'_{\Sigma}+\sigma_{\mathcal{S}_{\text{prim}}}$ in total.*

Interpretation of Theorem 2. The above theorem indeed shows that $(\Sigma^{\pi}, \mathcal{C}_{\Sigma^{\pi}})$ is a secure white-box scheme w.r.t. sec-const if the underlying scheme $(\pi, \mathcal{C}_{\pi})$ is secure w.r.t. sec-prim and Σ^{P} is weak public indifferentiable from R: Let $\mathcal{A}$ be an adversary attacking $(\Sigma^{\pi}, \mathcal{C}_{\Sigma^{\pi}})$. Then, we can construct an adversary $\mathcal{A}'$ to attack $(\pi, \mathcal{C}_{\pi})$ as in Theorem 2. If $(\pi, \mathcal{C}_{\pi})$ is secure (w.r.t. sec-prim), then there is a simulator $\mathcal{S}_{\text{prim}}$ for $(\pi, \mathcal{C}_{\pi})$ that makes $\mathbf{Adv}^{\text{sec-prim}}_{\pi,\mathcal{C}_{\pi},\mathcal{S}_{\text{prim}}}(\mathcal{A}')$ small. In addition, if Σ^{P} is weak public indifferentiable from R, then there exists a simulator $\mathcal{S}_{\text{indiff}}$ making $\mathbf{Adv}^{\text{weak-pub-indiff}}_{\Sigma,\mathcal{S}_{\text{indiff}}}(\mathcal{A}'')$ small, where $\mathcal{A}''$ is the adversary built from $\mathcal{A}$ and $\mathcal{S}_{\text{prim}}$ as in the theorem. Again, Theorem 2 assures that we can construct $\mathcal{S}_{\text{const}}$ from $\mathcal{S}_{\text{prim}}$ and $\mathcal{S}_{\text{indiff}}$ such that $\mathbf{Adv}^{\text{sec-const}}_{\Sigma^{\pi},\mathcal{C}_{\Sigma^{\pi}},\mathcal{S}_{\text{const}}}(\mathcal{A})$ satisfies Eq. (1). If all the parameters appearing in Theorem 2 are not so large, the advantage $\mathbf{Adv}^{\text{sec-const}}_{\Sigma^{\pi},\mathcal{C}_{\Sigma^{\pi}},\mathcal{S}_{\text{const}}}(\mathcal{A})$ is sufficiently small.

Intuition of the Proof. Here we provide a rough sketch on why Σ^{π} becomes secure if π is secure and Σ^{P} satisfies the *original* indifferentiability. Let $\mathcal{S}_{\text{indiff}}$ be a simulator making the indifferentiability advantage of Σ^{P} small. We consider the following three games.

1. [The real world (for Σ^{π} on sec-const).] The adversary $\mathcal{A} = (\mathcal{A}_{\text{create}}, \mathcal{A}_{\text{dist}})$ is given a black-box oracle access to Σ^{π}. A lifter L is given a white-box implementation of Σ^{π}.
2. [Intermediate world.] The black-box oracle of π and the lifter L in the real world are replaced with a random permutation P and a simulator $\mathcal{S}_{\text{prim}}$ (for π on sec-prim), respectively. The adversary $\mathcal{A} = (\mathcal{A}_{\text{create}}, \mathcal{A}_{\text{dist}})$ and §prim are given oracle access to Σ^{P} and P, respectively. Especially, this game executes three algorithms $\mathcal{A}^{\Sigma^{\mathsf{P}}}_{\text{create}}$, $\mathcal{S}^{\mathsf{P}}_{\text{prim}}$, and $\mathcal{A}^{\Sigma^{\mathsf{P}}}_{\text{dist}}$.
3. [The ideal world] The black-box oracle given to $\mathcal{A} = (\mathcal{A}_{\text{create}}, \mathcal{A}_{\text{dist}})$ is R. In addition, the simulator (for Σ^{π} on sec-const) is defined to be $\mathcal{S}^{\mathcal{S}_{\text{indiff}}}_{\text{prim}}$. $\mathcal{S}^{\mathcal{S}_{\text{indiff}}}_{\text{prim}}$ is also given an oracle access to R. Especially, this game executes three algorithms $\mathcal{A}^{\mathsf{R}}_{\text{create}}$, $\mathcal{S}^{\mathcal{S}^{\mathsf{R}}_{\text{indiff}}}_{\text{prim}}$, and $\mathcal{A}^{\mathsf{R}}_{\text{dist}}$.

If π is secure, then we can replace π (in Σ^{π}) and a lifter in the real world with P and a simulator $\mathcal{S}_{\text{prim}}$, respectively, with a small security loss. That is, the difference between the first and the second worlds is small. Next, regarding the tuple

$(\mathcal{A}_{\text{create}}, \mathcal{S}_{\text{prim}}, \mathcal{A}_{\text{dist}})$ as a single algorithm, we can regard the intermediate world as a game where a single-stage adversary $(\mathcal{A}_{\text{create}}, \mathcal{S}_{\text{prim}}, \mathcal{A}_{\text{dist}})$ runs relative to the oracles $(\Sigma^{\mathsf{P}}, \mathsf{P})$. Moreover, we can also regard the ideal wold as a game where the single algorithm $(\mathcal{A}_{\text{create}}, \mathcal{S}_{\text{prim}}, \mathcal{A}_{\text{dist}})$ runs relative to the oracles $(\mathsf{R}, \mathcal{S}^{\mathsf{R}}_{\text{indiff}})$. Especially, the difference between the intermediate and ideal worlds matches the indifferentiability advantage of the *single* algorithm $(\mathcal{A}_{\text{create}}, \mathcal{S}_{\text{prim}}, \mathcal{A}_{\text{dist}})$ against T^{P} and R with respect to $\mathcal{S}_{\text{indiff}}$[24]. Since Σ^{P} is indifferentiable from R by $\mathcal{S}_{\text{indiff}}$, the difference between the intermediate world and the ideal world is also small.

In fact there are some subtleties on how to simulate list of queries passed to $\mathcal{S}_{\text{prim}}$. Moreover, when we consider weak public indifferentiability instead of original indifferentiability, we also have to consider how to simulate the revealing interface $\mathsf{Rev}'[\mathsf{R}]$. See the full version of this paper [40] for details.

6.3 Feasibility Results

This section shows feasibility results that various white-box security notions can be reduced to that of block ciphers (whPRP) and FIL/FOL keyed functions (whPRF) like in the black-box setting. We only prove (weak) public indifferentiability of the constructions because Theorem 2 shows white-box security reductions follow from (weak) public indifferentiability.

whPRP-whPRF Switch. Let P be an n-bit random permutation. Then, regarding (P, P^{-1}) as a primitive oracle, P is public indifferentiable from a random function $\mathsf{RF} : \{0,1\}^n \to \{0,1\}^n$. (In the real world, the construction oracle is P and the primitive oracle is (P, P^{-1}).) Specifically, the proposition below holds.

Proposition 1. *There is a simulator $\mathcal{S}$ making at most q_p queries to* RF *satisfying $\mathbf{Adv}^{\text{pub-indiff}}_{P,\mathsf{RF},\mathcal{S}}(\mathcal{A}) \le \frac{(q_c+q_p)^2}{2^n}$ for any adversary $\mathcal{A}$ making at most q_c and q_p queries to the construction and primitive oracles, respectively.*

The proof is quite straightforward. See the full version of this paper [40] for a complete proof. Together with Theorem 2, this proposition implies that a whPRP-secure BC is a whPRF-secure keyed function.

Reduction from whPRP to whPRF. The 6-round Feistel construction is public indifferentiable from a random invertible permutation when round functions are random functions [49]. Thus we can build a whPRP-secure BC from a whPRF-secure keyed function.

---

[24] This is the reason that we can utilize the indifferentiability of Σ^{P} from R to show the security of Σ^{π} although the security games of Σ^{π} are not single-stage games.

Reduction from VIL/VOL-whPRF to FIL/FOL-whPRF. The indifferentiability result of the sponge construction (Theorem 1) implies that we can build VIL/VOL-whPRF from FIL/FOL-whPRF. We can also build VIL/FOL-whPRF from FIL/FOL-whPRF by the Merkle-Damgård construction since it is public indifferentiable [32].

Reduction from whPRI to FIL/FOL-whPRF. By the result of Barbosa and Farshim [6], an indifferentiable AEAD can be constructed from a FIL/FOL random function by a scheme based on (unbalanced) 3-round Feistel that uses the sponge construction as round functions. (See Theorem 5 of the full version of this paper [40] and the explanation below for more details.) Thus we can build a whPRI-secure AEAD from a whPRF-secure FIL/FOL keyed function. In Sect. 7 we show a more practical construction.

Reduction from wh$\widetilde{\text{SPRP}}$ to whPRF. A weak public indifferentiable VIL tweakable ideally random permutation can be built from a FIL/FOL random function f, by a (balanced) 6-round Feistel construction of which round functions are the sponge construction using f as an underlying primitive. See the full version of this paper [40] for more details.

Reduction from whIND$-CPA to whPRF. Let us modify the encryption oracle of CTR in such a way that (1) a uniformly random IV is chosen for each encryption query (rather than IV is chosen by adversary) and IV is returned together with the ciphertext, and (2) the underlying keyed function of CTR is replaced with a random function ρ. We denote the resulting encryption oracle by $\mathcal{E}^{\rho}_{\mathrm{rnd}}$. Then $\mathcal{E}^{\rho}_{\mathrm{rnd}}$ is public indifferentiable from $\$(\cdot)$ that appears in the ideal experiment of whIND$-CPA. More precisely, the following proposition holds.

Proposition 2. *There exists a simulator $\mathcal{S}$ making at most q_c queries to the $\$(\cdot)$, where the lengths of queries are at most σ blocks in total, that satisfies $\mathbf{Adv}^{\text{pub-indiff}}_{\mathcal{E}_{\mathrm{rnd}},\$(\cdot),\mathcal{S}}(\mathcal{A}) \leq \frac{\sigma^2}{2^m} + \frac{\sigma(\sigma+q_p)}{2^m}$ for any adversary $\mathcal{A}$ making at most q_c queries to the construction oracle of which lengths are at most σ blocks in total and q_p queries to the primitive oracle.*

Intuition of the Proof. For simplicity, we assume $\mathrm{len}(M)$ is always a multiple of n and denote the i-th block of M by M_i, i.e., $M = M_1 || \cdots || M_{\mathrm{len}(M)/n}$. Roughly speaking, the simulator $\mathcal{S}$ runs as follows: Let $\mathsf{List}[\$(\cdot)]$ be the list storing queries made so far to $\$(\cdot)$ and the responses. When a fresh value x is queried to the interface corresponding to ρ, the simulator first queries to the revealing interface to get $\mathsf{List}[\$(\cdot)]$. If there exists $(M, (IV, C)) \in \mathsf{List}[\$(\cdot)]$ such that $x = IV + i - 1$ for $1 \leq i \leq \mathrm{len}(M)/n$, the adversary may be trying to compute the i-th block of C itself. Thus the simulator sets the value $\rho(x)$ as $\rho(x) := M_i \oplus C_i$ so that the adversary cannot notice that ρ is simulated. If such $(M, (IV, C))$ does not exist in $\mathsf{List}[\$(\cdot)]$, the value $\rho(x)$ is just randomly sampled.

The simulator may not be able to sample the value $\rho(x)$ in compatible with C and fail if the following (a) or (b) happen: (a) when a message M is queried to

$\$(\cdot)$ and IV is randomly chosen, $IV+i = IV'+j$ holds for some $(M', (IV', C')) \in \mathsf{List}[\$'(\cdot)]$, where $0 \leq i < \mathrm{len}(M)/n$ and $0 \leq j < \mathrm{len}(M')/n$. (b) when a message M is queried to $\$(\cdot)$ and IV is randomly chosen, the value $IV + i$ $(0 \leq i < \mathrm{len}(M)/n)$ collides with a value x on which the output value of ρ is already defined. The events (a) and (b) correspond to the terms $\frac{\sigma^2}{2^m}$ and $\frac{\sigma(\sigma+q_p)}{2^m}$ in the security bound, respectively. If both of (a) and (b) do not happen in the ideal world, then outputs of ρ are appropriately simulated in compatible with ciphertexts, and thus an adversary cannot distinguish the ideal world from the real world. See the full version of this paper [40] for a complete proof.

On Reduction of Pairs and Generic Compositions. We also observe feasibility of reductions of pairs (i.e., providing proof in a modular way), and infeasibility of generic compositions for AEADs. See the full version [40] for details.

7 A Search for a Practical whPRI-Secure AEAD Mode

This section shows a practical AEAD mode to convert whPRP into whPRI. Section 7.1 shows that SIV with CTR is public indifferentiable from a fixed-key random injection when the tag-generation (or, MAC) part is a single VIL/FOL random function f and the underlying keyed function of CTR is a FIL/FOL random function ρ. Then, in Sect. 7.2, we replace ρ and f with keyed functions built from a single whPRP, and observe that the resulting scheme is a whPRI-secure AEAD.

7.1 Public Indifferentiability of SIV+CTR

Let $\mathsf{CTR}^\rho(IV, M)$ denote the encryption function of the counter mode with the underlying keyed function being replaced with a random function $\rho : \{0,1\}^\tau \rightarrow \{0,1\}^n$ $(\tau \leq n)$. In addition, let $\Pi = (\mathcal{E}^{f,\rho}, \mathcal{D}^{f,\rho})$ be the SIV construction of which keyed function for tag-generation is replaced with a random function $f : \mathbf{N} \times \mathbf{A} \times \{0,1\}^* \rightarrow \{0,1\}^\tau$ and conventional encryption scheme is replaced with CTR^ρ. Let $\mathsf{enc} : \mathbf{N} \times \mathbf{A} \times \{0,1\}^* \rightarrow \{0,1\}^*$ be an arbitrary encoding function that encodes each tuple (N, A, X) into a single bit string in a uniquely decodable manner. We let $\mathrm{len}(N, A, X) := \mathrm{len}(\mathsf{enc}(N, A, X))$ and call $\lceil \mathrm{len}(X)/n \rceil$ the block length of a bit string of X. The following theorem shows Π is public indifferentiable from a random injection.

Theorem 3. *Let $F : \mathbf{N} \times \mathbf{A} \times \{0,1\}^* \rightarrow \{0,1\}^*$ be a fixed-key random injection with message space $\{0,1\}^*$ and such that $\mathrm{len}(F(N, A, M)) = \mathrm{len}(M) + \tau$. There exists a simulator $\mathcal{S}$ for public indifferentiability of Π from $F^\pm$, where a primitive oracle is (f, ρ), such that the number of queries by $\mathcal{S}$ to the construction oracle is at most q_f and the block lengths of the queries are at most σ_f in total, and*

$$\mathbf{Adv}^{\text{pub-indiff}}_{\Pi,F^\pm,\mathcal{S}}(\mathcal{A}) \leq \frac{(\sigma_c + \sigma_f)^2}{2^\tau} + \frac{(\sigma_c + \sigma_f)(q_\rho + \sigma_c)}{2^\tau} + \frac{3q_c}{2^\tau} + \frac{(q_c + q_f)^2}{2^\tau} \quad (2)$$

holds for any adversary $\mathcal{A}$ of which computational resources are as follows: To the construction oracle, $\mathcal{A}$ makes at most q_c queries of which block lengths are at most σ_c in total. To the first primitive oracle (corresponding to f), $\mathcal{A}$ makes at most q_f queries of which block lengths are at most σ_f in total. To the second primitive oracle (corresponding to ρ), $\mathcal{A}$ makes at most q_ρ queries. Here, we assume $(q_c + q_f) \leq 2^{\tau-1}$.

Intuition of the Proof. For simplicity, we assume $\text{len}(M)$ is always a multiple of n. For each (N, A, M), we assume $F(N, A, M)$ is divided as $F(N, A, M) = IV||C_1||\cdots||C_\ell$, where $IV \in \{0,1\}^\tau$ and $C_1, \ldots, C_\ell \in \{0,1\}^n$. The simulation of ρ is almost the same as that for the proof of random-IV CTR (See the explanation below Proposition 2. Here, $\$(\cdot)$ in Proposition 2 is replaced with F.). Simulation of $f(N, A, M)$ is done just by querying (N, A, M) to F and return $F_0(N, A, M)$. Intuitively, the simulation does not work well if the simulation of ρ fails (the events (a) and (b) in the explanation below Proposition 2), or (c) an adversary computes $\mathcal{D}^{f,\rho}(N, A, C)$ itself for a tuple (N, A, C) such that C has never been returned from F, and $\mathcal{D}^{f,\rho}(N, A, C)$ happens to be a value that is *not* $\perp$. The events (a) and (b) correspond to the terms $\frac{(\sigma_c+\sigma_f)^2}{2^\tau}$ and $\frac{(\sigma_c+\sigma_f)(q_\rho+\sigma_c)}{2^\tau}$ of Eq. (2), respectively. Due to (c), an additional term $\frac{q_c}{2^\tau}$ is added. Moreover, we need another term $\frac{(q_c+q_f)^2+2q_c}{2^\tau}$ to deal with lazy sampling of a random injection. See the full version of this paper [40] for a complete proof.

7.2 Instantiation with Block Ciphers

This section discusses how to combine the scheme in the previous subsection with a whPRP-secure block cipher to build a whPRI-secure AEAD.

Assume $\tau < n$ and let $P : \{0,1\}^n \to \{0,1\}^n$ a random permutation. Define $P_0 : \{0,1\}^{n-1} \to \{0,1\}^{n-1}$ and $P_1 : \{0,1\}^\tau \to \{0,1\}^n$ by $P_0(x) :=$ (The lower $(n-1)$ bits of $P(0||x)$) and $P_1(x) := P(1^{n-\tau}||x)$. Set $\mathbf{N} = \{0,1\}^{n/2}$. Let enc be an encoding function such that $\mathsf{enc}(N, A, M) = N||A||M||\text{len}(M)$. (We assume $\text{len}(M)$ is represented as an $n/4$-bit string.) In addition, define $\text{MAC}^P(N, A, M) := \mathsf{Sponge}^{P_0}(\mathsf{enc}(N, A, M))$. Replace f (tag generation function) and ρ (underlying function of CTR) of Π in Theorem 3 with MAC^P and P_1, and denote the resulting scheme by $\Pi[P]$.

Then, $\Pi[P]$ is weak public indifferentiable from a fixed-key random injection $F^\pm$ when $P^\pm$ is regarded as a primitive oracle[25]. Furthermore, if we replace P with a whPRP-secure block cipher E_K, the resulting scheme $\Pi[E_K]$ becomes a whPRI-secure AEAD by Theorem 2. (Here, we assume $\Pi[E_K]$ is implemented in such a way that the implementation of the mode is explicitly separated from

[25] This is because (1) an invertible permutation is public indifferentiable from a random function (Proposition 1), (2) the sponge construction is indifferentiable from a random oracle (Theorem 1), (3) the scheme Π in Theorem 3 is public indifferentiable from a fixed-key random injection, (4) composition of deterministic weak public indifferentiable schemes are again weak public indifferentiable (Lemma 1, or its formal version in the full version of this paper [40])..

the implementation of E_K and the former calls the latter in a black-box manner, so that Theorem 2 can be applied.) More precisely, the following corollary holds. (See the full version [40] for more details on how to derive the corollary.)

Corollary 1. *Let $\mathcal{A}$ be an adversary against $(\Pi[E_K], \mathcal{C}_{\Pi[E_K]})$ on whPRI-security. The running time of $\mathcal{A}$ is at most t. The number of queries by $\mathcal{A}$ to a black-box oracle is at most q and the block lengths of the queries are at most σ in total. $\mathcal{A}$ creates a lifter running in time t_{lif} and outputs at most λ-bit leakage. In addition, let $\mathcal{S}_{\text{prim}}$ be a simulator for $(E, \mathcal{C}_E)$ on whPRP-security. $\mathcal{S}_{\text{prim}}$ makes at most q_{sim} queries to $P^{\pm}$. Then there exists a simulator $\mathcal{S}_{\text{const}}$ for $(\Pi[E_K], \mathcal{C}_{\Pi[E_K]})$ on whPRI-security and an adversary $\mathcal{A}'$ against $(E, \mathcal{C}_E)$ on whPRP-security such that $\mathbf{Adv}^{\text{whPRI}}_{\Pi[E_K],\mathcal{C}_{\Pi[E_K]},\mathcal{S}_{\text{const}}}(\mathcal{A})$ is upper bounded by $\mathbf{Adv}^{\text{whPRP}}_{E_K,\mathcal{C}_{E_K},\mathcal{S}_{\text{prim}}}(\mathcal{A}') + \frac{\lceil \frac{n}{r} \rceil^6 (10\lceil \frac{n}{r} \rceil \sigma + q_{\text{sim}})^4}{2^\tau} + \frac{\lceil \frac{n}{r} \rceil^4 (10\lceil \frac{n}{r} \rceil \sigma + q_{\text{sim}})^3}{2^\tau} + \frac{\lceil \frac{n}{r} \rceil^2 (10\lceil \frac{n}{r} \rceil \sigma + q_{\text{sim}})^2}{2^\tau} + \frac{\lceil \frac{n}{r} \rceil^2 (9\lceil \frac{n}{r} \rceil \sigma + 2q_{\text{sim}})^2}{2^n} + \frac{3q_c}{2^\tau} + \epsilon\left(2\left\lceil \frac{n}{r} \right\rceil \left(8\left\lceil \frac{n}{r} \right\rceil \sigma + q_{\text{sim}}\right)\right)$, where $\epsilon(j) = 1 - \Pi_{i=1}^{j}(1 - \frac{1}{2^c})$. $\mathcal{S}_{\text{const}}$ makes at most $\left\lceil \frac{n}{r} \right\rceil \left(9\left\lceil \frac{n}{r} \right\rceil \sigma + q_{\text{sim}}\right)$ queries to $F^{\pm}$ and the lengths of the queries are at most $\left(\left\lceil \frac{n}{r} \right\rceil^3 \left(9\left\lceil \frac{n}{r} \right\rceil \sigma + q_{\text{sim}}\right)^2\right)$ blocks in total. $\mathcal{A}'$ runs in time $O(t + \sigma)$ and makes at most $(2\sigma + \left\lceil \frac{n}{r} \right\rceil q)$ black-box oracle queries. $\mathcal{A}'$ outputs a lifter that runs in time $O(t_{\text{lif}})$ and outputs at most λ bits of leakage.*

Interpretation of Corollary 1. Let us set $\tau = n - 1$ and $(r, c) = (n/2, n/2 - 1)$. Then, Corollary 1 says that $\mathbf{Adv}^{\text{whPRI}}_{\Pi[E_K],\mathcal{C}_{\Pi[E_K]},\mathcal{S}_{\text{const}}}(\mathcal{A})$ becomes small as long as $\mathbf{Adv}^{\text{whPRP}}_{E,\mathcal{C}_E,\mathcal{S}_{\text{prim}}}(\mathcal{A})$ is small and $q_{\text{sim}}, q, \sigma \ll 2^{n/4}$. This means the following: Let λ and t_{lif} be some reasonable parameters ($\ll 2^{n/4}$) and assume the underlying block cipher E_K is a secure whPRP. More concretely, let $\mathcal{A}'$ be an adversary attacking E_K with $t \ll 2^\kappa$ and $q \ll 2^{n/4}$, and $\mathcal{L}$ be a lifter running in time $t_{\text{lif}}(< 2^{n/4})$ that leaks at most λ-bit leakage. Suppose, for any such $\mathcal{A}'$ and $\mathcal{L}$, there exists $\mathcal{S}_{\text{prim}}$ with making $q_{\text{sim}}(\ll 2^{n/4})$ queries such that $\mathbf{Adv}^{\text{whPRP}}_{E,\mathcal{C}_E,\mathcal{S}_{\text{prim}}}(\mathcal{A}')$ is sufficiently small. Then $\Pi[E_K]$ is whPRI-secure against an adversary $\mathcal{A}$ as long as (1) the running time of $\mathcal{A}$ is $\ll 2^\kappa$, (2) the length of messages processed by $\Pi[E_K]$ is $\ll 2^{n/4}$ blocks in total while running $\mathcal{A}$ in the real world, and (3) the running time and leakage of a lifter (output by $\mathcal{A}$) are at most t_{lif} and λ bits[26].

On Underlying Block Cipher. The above discussions show that $\Pi[E_K]$ is whPRI-secure if E_K is whPRP-secure and the amount of data processed by $\Pi[E_K]$ is $\ll 2^{n/4}$. As a candidate of whPRP-secure BC, we conjecture that SPACE is whPRP-secure for some parameter settings (see Sect. 5.1). However, the block length of SPACE is basically $n = 128$ only, when $2^{n/4} = 2^{32}$. In practical use cases, the limitation of 2^{32} is inconvenient and unsatisfactory.

[26] Note that λ does not explicitly appear in the upper bound of $\mathbf{Adv}^{\text{whPRI}}_{\Pi[E_K],\mathcal{C}_{\Pi[E_K]},\mathcal{S}_{\text{const}}}(\mathcal{A})$ in the corollary. This is because we (implicitly) assume $\lambda \leq q_{\text{sim}}$ and the effect of λ is absorbed into q_{sim} in the security bound.

Thus, we propose a 256-bit block variant of SPACE-16, which we name SPACE256-16. Its details are provided in the full version of this paper [40], where we discuss its security against various attacks following the convention of block cipher designs. We conjecture[27] that SPACE256-16 is a $(\lambda, t, q, t_{\text{lif}}, q_{\text{sim}}, \epsilon)$-secure whPRP with $\lambda \approx 2^{20}$, $t \approx 2^{128}$, $q \approx 2^{64}$, $q_{\text{sim}} \approx 2^{64}$, and $\epsilon \ll 1$, as long as $t_{\text{lif}} \ll q_{\text{sim}}$. Assuming our conjecture is true, $\Pi[E_K]$ with E_K instantiated with SPACE256-16 is secure until the amount of processed data is $\ll 2^{64}$ (and the amount of leakage is $< 2^{20}$).

To evaluate the performance, we implemented $\Pi[E_K]$ using SPACE256-16 on a single core in a laptop PC with Intel Core i7-1065G7, being Turbo Boost and hyperthreading disabled. The implementation size is in the order of KB or MB. As a result, the performance reaches about 530 CPB when a 1KB message is processed. Considering the performance of raw SPACE-16 is 305.11 cpb [22], we believe our mode of operation achieves relevant performance.

The limit of leakage for SPACE256-16 is not large. Still, in the same way as (the original, 128-bit-block) SPACE-32 and SPACE-24 provide better security than SPACE-16 does, a better limit could be achieved by 256-bit-block versions of SPACE-32 or SPACE-24 (at the cost of performance). We introduced a 256-bit-block version of SPACE-16 rather than SPACE-32 or SPACE-24 to balance security and performance. Improving the performance and the limit of the leakage is an interesting future work. This could be achieved by improving SPACE-hard block ciphers, modes of operations, or both.

References

1. Agrawal, S., Bock, E.A., Chen, Y., Watson, G.J.: White-box cryptography with device binding from token-based obfuscation and more. IACR Cryptology ePrint Archive 2021/767 (2021)
2. Alliance, S.C.: A smart card alliance mobile & NFC council white paper, host card emulation (HCE) 101 (2014)
3. Alwen, J., Dodis, Y., Naor, M., Segev, G., Walfish, S., Wichs, D.: Public-key encryption in the bounded-retrieval model. In: Gilbert, H. (ed.) EUROCRYPT 2010. LNCS, vol. 6110, pp. 113–134. Springer, Heidelberg (2010). https://doi.org/10.1007/978-3-642-13190-5_6
4. Alwen, J., Dodis, Y., Wichs, D.: Leakage-resilient public-key cryptography in the bounded-retrieval model. In: Halevi, S. (ed.) CRYPTO 2009. LNCS, vol. 5677, pp. 36–54. Springer, Heidelberg (2009). https://doi.org/10.1007/978-3-642-03356-8_3
5. Banik, S., Bogdanov, A., Isobe, T., Jepsen, M.B.: Analysis of software countermeasures for whitebox encryption. IACR Trans. Symmetric Cryptol. **2017**(1), 307–328 (2017)
6. Barbosa, M., Farshim, P.: Indifferentiable authenticated encryption. In: Shacham, H., Boldyreva, A. (eds.) CRYPTO 2018, Part I. LNCS, vol. 10991, pp. 187–220. Springer, Cham (2018). https://doi.org/10.1007/978-3-319-96884-1_7

[27] This conjecture is obtained by changing the settings of n and n_a in our conjecture in Sect. 5.1 to $n = 256$ and $n_a = 16$. κ is still 128.

7. Barwell, G., Martin, D.P., Oswald, E., Stam, M.: Authenticated encryption in the face of protocol and side channel leakage. In: Takagi, T., Peyrin, T. (eds.) ASIACRYPT 2017, Part I. LNCS, vol. 10624, pp. 693–723. Springer, Cham (2017). https://doi.org/10.1007/978-3-319-70694-8_24
8. Bellare, M., Dai, W.: Defending against key exfiltration: efficiency improvements for big-key cryptography via large-alphabet subkey prediction. In: Thuraisingham, B.M., Evans, D., Malkin, T., Xu, D. (eds.) ACM CCS 2017, pp. 923–940. ACM (2017)
9. Bellare, M., Kane, D., Rogaway, P.: Big-key symmetric encryption: resisting key exfiltration. In: Robshaw, M., Katz, J. (eds.) CRYPTO 2016, Part I. LNCS, vol. 9814, pp. 373–402. Springer, Heidelberg (2016). https://doi.org/10.1007/978-3-662-53018-4_14
10. Berti, F., Guo, C., Pereira, O., Peters, T., Standaert, F.: TEDT, a leakage-resist AEAD mode for high physical security applications. IACR Trans. Cryptogr. Hardw. Embed. Syst. **2020**(1), 256–320 (2020)
11. Berti, F., Pereira, O., Peters, T., Standaert, F.: On leakage-resilient authenticated encryption with decryption leakages. IACR Trans. Symmetric Cryptol. **2017**(3), 271–293 (2017)
12. Bertoni, G., Daemen, J., Peeters, M., Van Assche, G.: On the indifferentiability of the sponge construction. In: Smart, N. (ed.) EUROCRYPT 2008. LNCS, vol. 4965, pp. 181–197. Springer, Heidelberg (2008). https://doi.org/10.1007/978-3-540-78967-3_11
13. Billet, O., Gilbert, H., Ech-Chatbi, C.: Cryptanalysis of a white box AES implementation. In: SAC 2004, Revised Selected Papers, pp. 227–240 (2004)
14. Biryukov, A., Bouillaguet, C., Khovratovich, D.: Cryptographic schemes based on the ASASA structure: black-box, white-box, and public-key (extended abstract). In: Sarkar, P., Iwata, T. (eds.) ASIACRYPT 2014, Part I. LNCS, vol. 8873, pp. 63–84. Springer, Heidelberg (2014). https://doi.org/10.1007/978-3-662-45611-8_4
15. Biryukov, A., Perrin, L.: Symmetrically and asymmetrically hard cryptography. In: Takagi, T., Peyrin, T. (eds.) ASIACRYPT 2017, Part III. LNCS, vol. 10626, pp. 417–445. Springer, Cham (2017). https://doi.org/10.1007/978-3-319-70700-6_15
16. Biryukov, A., Udovenko, A.: Attacks and countermeasures for white-box designs. In: Peyrin, T., Galbraith, S. (eds.) ASIACRYPT 2018, Part II. LNCS, vol. 11273, pp. 373–402. Springer, Cham (2018). https://doi.org/10.1007/978-3-030-03329-3_13
17. Biryukov, A., Udovenko, A.: Dummy shuffling against algebraic attacks in white-box implementations. In: Canteaut, A., Standaert, F.-X. (eds.) EUROCRYPT 2021, Part II. LNCS, vol. 12697, pp. 219–248. Springer, Cham (2021). https://doi.org/10.1007/978-3-030-77886-6_8
18. Bock, E.A., Amadori, A., Bos, J.W., Brzuska, C., Michiels, W.: Doubly half-injective PRGs for incompressible white-box cryptography. In: Matsui, M. (ed.) CT-RSA 2019. LNCS, vol. 11405, pp. 189–209. Springer, Cham (2019). https://doi.org/10.1007/978-3-030-12612-4_10
19. Bock, E.A., Amadori, A., Brzuska, C., Michiels, W.: On the security goals of white-box cryptography. IACR Trans. Cryptogr. Hardw. Embed. Syst. **2020**(2), 327–357 (2020)
20. Bock, E.A., Brzuska, C., Fischlin, M., Janson, C., Michiels, W.: Security reductions for white-box key-storage in mobile payments. In: Moriai, S., Wang, H. (eds.) ASIACRYPT 2020, Part I. LNCS, vol. 12491, pp. 221–252. Springer, Cham (2020). https://doi.org/10.1007/978-3-030-64837-4_8

21. Bogdanov, A., Isobe, T.: White-box cryptography revisited: space-hard ciphers. In: Ray, I., Li, N., Kruegel, C. (eds.) ACM CCS 2015, pp. 1058–1069. ACM (2015)
22. Bogdanov, A., Isobe, T., Tischhauser, E.: Towards practical whitebox cryptography: optimizing efficiency and space hardness. In: Cheon, J.H., Takagi, T. (eds.) ASIACRYPT 2016, Part I. LNCS, vol. 10031, pp. 126–158. Springer, Heidelberg (2016). https://doi.org/10.1007/978-3-662-53887-6_5
23. Bos, J.W., Hubain, C., Michiels, W., Teuwen, P.: Differential computation analysis: hiding your white-box designs is not enough. In: Gierlichs, B., Poschmann, A.Y. (eds.) CHES 2016. LNCS, vol. 9813, pp. 215–236. Springer, Heidelberg (2016). https://doi.org/10.1007/978-3-662-53140-2_11
24. Cash, D., Ding, Y.Z., Dodis, Y., Lee, W., Lipton, R., Walfish, S.: Intrusion-resilient key exchange in the bounded retrieval model. In: Vadhan, S.P. (ed.) TCC 2007. LNCS, vol. 4392, pp. 479–498. Springer, Heidelberg (2007). https://doi.org/10.1007/978-3-540-70936-7_26
25. Chow, S., Eisen, P., Johnson, H., Van Oorschot, P.C.: White-box cryptography and an AES implementation. In: Nyberg, K., Heys, H. (eds.) SAC 2002. LNCS, vol. 2595, pp. 250–270. Springer, Heidelberg (2003). https://doi.org/10.1007/3-540-36492-7_17
26. Chow, S., Eisen, P., Johnson, H., van Oorschot, P.C.: A white-box DES implementation for DRM applications. In: Feigenbaum, J. (ed.) DRM 2002. LNCS, vol. 2696, pp. 1–15. Springer, Heidelberg (2003). https://doi.org/10.1007/978-3-540-44993-5_1
27. Di Crescenzo, G., Lipton, R., Walfish, S.: Perfectly secure password protocols in the bounded retrieval model. In: Halevi, S., Rabin, T. (eds.) TCC 2006. LNCS, vol. 3876, pp. 225–244. Springer, Heidelberg (2006). https://doi.org/10.1007/11681878_12
28. Degabriele, J.P., Janson, C., Struck, P.: Sponges resist leakage: the case of authenticated encryption. In: Galbraith, S.D., Moriai, S. (eds.) ASIACRYPT 2019, Part II. LNCS, vol. 11922, pp. 209–240. Springer, Cham (2019). https://doi.org/10.1007/978-3-030-34621-8_8
29. Delerablée, C., Lepoint, T., Paillier, P., Rivain, M.: White-box security notions for symmetric encryption schemes. In: Lange, T., Lauter, K., Lisoněk, P. (eds.) SAC 2013. LNCS, vol. 8282, pp. 247–264. Springer, Heidelberg (2014). https://doi.org/10.1007/978-3-662-43414-7_13
30. Dobraunig, C., Eichlseder, M., Mangard, S., Mendel, F., Unterluggauer, T.: ISAP - towards side-channel secure authenticated encryption. IACR Trans. Symmetric Cryptol. **2017**(1), 80–105 (2017)
31. Dobraunig, C., Mennink, B.: Leakage resilience of the duplex construction. In: Galbraith, S.D., Moriai, S. (eds.) ASIACRYPT 2019, Part III. LNCS, vol. 11923, pp. 225–255. Springer, Cham (2019). https://doi.org/10.1007/978-3-030-34618-8_8
32. Dodis, Y., Ristenpart, T., Shrimpton, T.: Salvaging Merkle-Damgård for practical applications. In: Joux, A. (ed.) EUROCRYPT 2009. LNCS, vol. 5479, pp. 371–388. Springer, Heidelberg (2009). https://doi.org/10.1007/978-3-642-01001-9_22
33. Dziembowski, S.: Intrusion-resilience via the bounded-storage model. In: Halevi, S., Rabin, T. (eds.) TCC 2006. LNCS, vol. 3876, pp. 207–224. Springer, Heidelberg (2006). https://doi.org/10.1007/11681878_11
34. Dziembowski, S., Pietrzak, K.: Leakage-resilient cryptography. In: FOCS 2008, pp. 293–302. IEEE Computer Society (2008)
35. Fouque, P.-A., Karpman, P., Kirchner, P., Minaud, B.: Efficient and provable white-box primitives. In: Cheon, J.H., Takagi, T. (eds.) ASIACRYPT 2016, Part I. LNCS,

vol. 10031, pp. 159–188. Springer, Heidelberg (2016). https://doi.org/10.1007/978-3-662-53887-6_6
36. Gueron, S., Lindell, Y.: GCM-SIV: full nonce misuse-resistant authenticated encryption at under one cycle per byte. In: Ray, I., Li, N., Kruegel, C. (eds.) ACM CCS 2015, pp. 109–119. ACM (2015)
37. Guo, C., Pereira, O., Peters, T., Standaert, F.: Towards low-energy leakage-resistant authenticated encryption from the duplex sponge construction. IACR Trans. Symmetric Cryptol. **2020**(1), 6–42 (2020)
38. Halevi, S., Rogaway, P.: A tweakable enciphering mode. In: Boneh, D. (ed.) CRYPTO 2003. LNCS, vol. 2729, pp. 482–499. Springer, Heidelberg (2003). https://doi.org/10.1007/978-3-540-45146-4_28
39. Hoang, V.T., Krovetz, T., Rogaway, P.: Robust authenticated-encryption AEZ and the problem that it solves. In: Oswald, E., Fischlin, M. (eds.) EUROCRYPT 2015, Part I. LNCS, vol. 9056, pp. 15–44. Springer, Heidelberg (2015). https://doi.org/10.1007/978-3-662-46800-5_2
40. Hosoyamada, A., Isobe, T., Todo, Y., Yasuda, K.: A Modular Approach to the Incompressibility of Block-Cipher-Based AEADs. IACR Cryptology ePrint Archive (2022)
41. intertrust: Intertrust white paper, taking steps to protect financial mobile applications (2018)
42. Ishai, Y., Sahai, A., Wagner, D.: Private circuits: securing hardware against probing attacks. In: Boneh, D. (ed.) CRYPTO 2003. LNCS, vol. 2729, pp. 463–481. Springer, Heidelberg (2003). https://doi.org/10.1007/978-3-540-45146-4_27
43. Kalai, Y.T., Reyzin, L.: A survey of leakage-resilient cryptography. In: Goldreich, O. (ed.) Providing Sound Foundations for Cryptography: On the Work of Shafi Goldwasser and Silvio Micali, pp. 727–794. ACM (2019)
44. Kalai, Y.T., Reyzin, L.: A survey of leakage-resilient cryptography. IACR Cryptology ePrint Archive, p. 302 (2019)
45. Krämer, J., Struck, P.: Leakage-resilient authenticated encryption from leakage-resilient pseudorandom functions. In: Bertoni, G.M., Regazzoni, F. (eds.) COSADE 2020. LNCS, vol. 12244, pp. 315–337. Springer, Cham (2021). https://doi.org/10.1007/978-3-030-68773-1_15
46. Krovetz, T., Rogaway, P.: The software performance of authenticated-encryption modes. In: Joux, A. (ed.) FSE 2011. LNCS, vol. 6733, pp. 306–327. Springer, Heidelberg (2011). https://doi.org/10.1007/978-3-642-21702-9_18
47. Lepoint, T., Rivain, M., Mulder, Y.D., Roelse, P., Preneel, B.: Two Attacks on a White-Box AES Implementation. In: SAC 2013, Revised Selected Papers, pp. 265–285 (2013)
48. Longo, J., Martin, D.P., Oswald, E., Page, D., Stam, M., Tunstall, M.J.: Simulatable leakage: analysis, pitfalls, and new constructions. In: Sarkar, P., Iwata, T. (eds.) ASIACRYPT 2014, Part I. LNCS, vol. 8873, pp. 223–242. Springer, Heidelberg (2014). https://doi.org/10.1007/978-3-662-45611-8_12
49. Mandal, A., Patarin, J., Seurin, Y.: On the public indifferentiability and correlation intractability of the 6-round Feistel construction. In: Cramer, R. (ed.) TCC 2012. LNCS, vol. 7194, pp. 285–302. Springer, Heidelberg (2012). https://doi.org/10.1007/978-3-642-28914-9_16
50. Maurer, U., Renner, R., Holenstein, C.: Indifferentiability, impossibility results on reductions, and applications to the random oracle methodology. In: Naor, M. (ed.) TCC 2004. LNCS, vol. 2951, pp. 21–39. Springer, Heidelberg (2004). https://doi.org/10.1007/978-3-540-24638-1_2

51. McGrew, D.A., Viega, J.: The security and performance of the Galois/Counter Mode (GCM) of operation. In: Canteaut, A., Viswanathan, K. (eds.) INDOCRYPT 2004. LNCS, vol. 3348, pp. 343–355. Springer, Heidelberg (2004). https://doi.org/10.1007/978-3-540-30556-9_27
52. Micali, S., Reyzin, L.: Physically observable cryptography. In: Naor, M. (ed.) TCC 2004. LNCS, vol. 2951, pp. 278–296. Springer, Heidelberg (2004). https://doi.org/10.1007/978-3-540-24638-1_16
53. Mulder, Y.D., Roelse, P., Preneel, B.: Cryptanalysis of the Xiao - Lai white-box AES implementation. In: SAC 2012, Revised Selected Papers, pp. 34–49 (2012)
54. Namprempre, C., Rogaway, P., Shrimpton, T.: Reconsidering generic composition. In: Nguyen, P.Q., Oswald, E. (eds.) EUROCRYPT 2014. LNCS, vol. 8441, pp. 257–274. Springer, Heidelberg (2014). https://doi.org/10.1007/978-3-642-55220-5_15
55. Pietrzak, K.: A leakage-resilient mode of operation. In: Joux, A. (ed.) EUROCRYPT 2009. LNCS, vol. 5479, pp. 462–482. Springer, Heidelberg (2009). https://doi.org/10.1007/978-3-642-01001-9_27
56. Ristenpart, T., Shacham, H., Shrimpton, T.: Careful with composition: limitations of the indifferentiability framework. In: Paterson, K.G. (ed.) EUROCRYPT 2011. LNCS, vol. 6632, pp. 487–506. Springer, Heidelberg (2011). https://doi.org/10.1007/978-3-642-20465-4_27
57. Rogaway, P.: Authenticated-encryption with associated-data. In: Atluri, V. (ed.) ACM CCS 2002, pp. 98–107. ACM (2002)
58. Rogaway, P., Shrimpton, T.: A provable-security treatment of the key-wrap problem. In: Vaudenay, S. (ed.) EUROCRYPT 2006. LNCS, vol. 4004, pp. 373–390. Springer, Heidelberg (2006). https://doi.org/10.1007/11761679_23
59. Standaert, F.-X., Pereira, O., Yu, Yu.: Leakage-resilient symmetric cryptography under empirically verifiable assumptions. In: Canetti, R., Garay, J.A. (eds.) CRYPTO 2013, Part I. LNCS, vol. 8042, pp. 335–352. Springer, Heidelberg (2013). https://doi.org/10.1007/978-3-642-40041-4_19
60. Todo, Y., Isobe, T.: Hybrid code lifting on space-hard block ciphers: application to Yoroi and SPNbox. IACR Trans. Symmetric Cryptol. **2022**(3), 368–402 (2022)
61. Whiting, D., Housley, R., Ferguson, N.: AES Encryption & Authentication Using CTR Mode & CBC-MAC. IEEE P802.11 Wireless LNAs (2002)
62. Wyseur, B., Michiels, W., Gorissen, P., Preneel, B.: Cryptanalysis of white-box DES implementations with arbitrary external encodings. In: SAC 2007, Revised Selected Papers, pp. 264–277 (2007)
63. Yoneyama, K., Miyagawa, S., Ohta, K.: Leaky random oracle. IEICE Trans. Fundam. Electron. Commun. Comput. Sci. **92-A**(8), 1795–1807 (2009)

Security of Truncated Permutation Without Initial Value

Lorenzo Grassi(✉) and Bart Mennink

Radboud University, Nijmegen, The Netherlands
{l.grassi,b.mennink}@cs.ru.nl

Abstract. Indifferentiability is a powerful notion in cryptography. If a construction is proven to be indifferentiable from an ideal object, it can under certain assumptions instantiate that ideal object in higher-level constructions. Indifferentiability is a particularly useful model for cryptographic hash functions, and myriad results are known proving that a hash function behaves like a random oracle under the assumption that the underlying primitive (typically a compression function, a block cipher, or a permutation) is random. Recently, advances have been made in proving indifferentiability of one-way functions with fixed input length. One such example is truncation of a permutation. If one evaluates a random permutation on an input value concatenated with a fixed initial value, and truncates the output, one obtains a construction that is indifferentiable from a random function up to a certain bound (Dodis et al., FSE 2009; Choi et al., ASIACRYPT 2019). Security of this construction, however, is in part determined by the length of the initial value; omission of this fixed value yields an insecure construction.

In this paper, we reconsider truncation of a permutation, and prove that the construction is indifferentiable from a random oracle, even if this fixed initial value is replaced by a randomized value. This randomized value may be the same for different evaluations of the construction, or freshly generated, up to the discretion of the adversary. The security level is the same as that of truncation with fixed initial value, up to collisions in the randomized value.

We show that our construction has immediate implications in the context of parallel variable-length digest generation. In detail, we describe Cascade-MGF, that operates on top of any cryptographic hash function and uses the hash function output as randomized initial value in truncation. We demonstrate that Cascade-MGF compares favorably over earlier parallel variable-length digest generation constructions, namely Counter-MGF and Chained-MGF, in almost all settings.

Keywords: Random permutation · Truncation · Indifferentiability · MGF · Digest generation

1 Introduction

A cryptographic hash function is a one-way function that maps data of arbitrary size to an output of a fixed size. Cryptographic hash functions are amongst the

S. Agrawal and D. Lin (Eds.): ASIACRYPT 2022, LNCS 13792, pp. 620–650, 2022.
https://doi.org/10.1007/978-3-031-22966-4_21

most-studied and most-used cryptographic functions. They are used to provide integrity and authenticity in a large number of applications and protocols, including digital signatures, message authentication codes (MACs), and other forms of authentication.

The first hash functions appeared in the 70s, when Rabin introduced his iterative hash function design [40] and Merkle his ideas on tree hashing [36]. The iterative Merkle-Damgård construction, independently described by Damgård and Merkle [17,35], later became the predominant approach in hash function design. Given a compression function $\mathcal{F}$ that maps $2n$ bits to n bits, the construction first pads and splits an arbitrarily sized input $M \in \{0,1\}^*$ injectively into n-bit blocks $M_0, M_1, \ldots, M_\mu$. The hash value is obtained by compressing these blocks one-by-one into an n-bit state:

$$h_{i+1} = \mathcal{F}(h_i, M_i) \quad \text{for } i = 0, \ldots, \mu\,, \tag{1}$$

where $h_0 = IV \in \{0,1\}^n$ is an initial value. Classical hash functions, including SHA-1, SHA-2, and MD5, are of this form.

In more recent years, the approach of permutation based hashing has gained popularity, mainly due to the rise of the sponge hash function construction [4,6], that is (among others) used as mode in the SHA-3 construction Keccak [8]. The sponge construction accommodates for both arbitrarily sized inputs and arbitrarily sized outputs. Let $\mathcal{P}$ be a permutation over $\{0,1\}^b$, and let $b = r + c$, where c denotes the capacity and r the rate. As before, an input message $M \in \{0,1\}^*$ is first injectively padded and split into r-bit blocks $M_0, M_1, \ldots, M_\mu$. Then, the message blocks are compressed one-by-one into a b-bit state:

$$h_{i+1} = \mathcal{P}(h_i \oplus (M_i \| 0^c)) \quad \text{for } i = 0, \ldots, \mu\,, \tag{2}$$

where $h_0 = IV \in \{0,1\}^b$ is an initial value. Let $h_{i+1} = \mathcal{P}(h_i)$ for $i \geq \mu + 1$. After the absorption of the last message block, the output is of the form

$$\text{left}_r(h_{\mu+1}) \,\|\, \text{left}_r(h_{\mu+2}) \,\|\, \text{left}_r(h_{\mu+3}) \,\|\, \cdots\,,$$

where $\text{left}_r(\cdot)$ denotes the r leftmost bits of its input.

All of these constructions have faced extensive security analysis. Whereas originally the focus was collision resistance, preimage resistance, and second preimage resistance, the current trend is to argue that a hash function construction is secure in the indifferentiability model, described and recalled in detail in Sect. 2.1. This model, introduced by Maurer et al. [29] and tailored to hash functions by Coron et al. [13], considers a security game where an adversary has access to either the hash function construction and an idealized primitive, or it has access to a random oracle and a simulator with the same interface as the hash function primitive. The goal of the simulator is to "mimic" the behavior of the idealized primitive so that any transcript an adversary has from communication with the random oracle and the simulator is hard to distinguish from a transcript that it may obtain from the actual construction and the idealized primitive. Although the plain Merkle-Damgård construction was *not* indifferentiable (see Coron et al. [13]), several variations of it have been proven to be indifferentiable up to around $2^{n/2}$ queries [11,13]. Likewise, Bertoni et al. [6] proved that the sponge construction (based on a random function or a permutation) is indifferentiable from a random oracle up to around $2^{c/2}$ queries.

The Merkle-Damgård indifferentiability result was proven under the assumption that the underlying function $\mathcal{F}$ is a random compression function. In practice, however, compression functions are built from invertible primitives such as block ciphers or permutations, e.g., the PGV compression functions [10,39]. Such compression functions are often easy to differentiate from random, which makes the aforementioned indifferentiable result futile. Instead, the research community had to resort to proving indifferentiability of Merkle-Damgård constructions based on a block cipher directly [13].

1.1 State of the Art on Compression Function Design

Having said that, there *do* exist compression functions based on block ciphers or permutations that are indifferentiable from a random function, up to a proper bound, and that can be used to instantiate $\mathcal{F}$ in the Merkle-Damgård construction. Two notable block cipher based examples are a double block length compression function of Mennink [30,31] and the compression function used in BLAKE2 [2,27]. Both constructions achieve indifferentiability by operating on an internal state that is larger than the block size of the compression function.

A notable permutation based example is the compression function used in the MD6 hash function [41]. Given $\mathcal{P}$ a permutation over $\{0,1\}^b$, the compression function consists of truncating (TRUNC) the output of the permutation:

$$\text{TRUNC}(I) = \text{left}_n\left(\mathcal{P}(IV \| I)\right), \tag{3}$$

where $IV \in \{0,1\}^m$ is an initial value, $I \in \{0,1\}^{b-m}$ is the input, and where $\text{left}_n(\cdot)$ returns the n leftmost bits (where $n < b$). Dodis et al. [18] proved that this compression function is hard to distinguish from random. Choi et al. [12] recently derived an improved bound and proved that (3) is indifferentiable from a random function up to around $\min\left\{2^{\frac{2b-n}{3}}, \frac{2^{b-n}}{b-n}, 2^m\right\}$ queries.

Note that the TRUNC construction is not a compression function in the strict sense of the word: its input may be larger or smaller than its output, or they may be of the same size, depending on the parameter choice, and it should rather be named a one-way function. Another well-known permutation based one-way function design that is proven to be indifferentiable from a random function is the sum of independent permutations (SOP) construction, that operates based on two permutations $\mathcal{P}_1$ and $\mathcal{P}_2$ over $\{0,1\}^b$:

$$\text{SOP}(I) = \mathcal{P}_1(I) \oplus \mathcal{P}_2(I), \tag{4}$$

where $I \in \{0,1\}^b$ is the input. The earliest analysis of a construction of this kind (in which the random permutations are publicly available to the adversary) is by Mandal et al. [28], who proved $2b/3$-bit security. The proof turned out to have a subtle but non-negligible flaw which has been fixed by Mennink and Preneel [32]. Later, Lee [26] proved improved security for the general construction, and Bhattacharya and Nandi [9] improved all these known bounds and proved (full) b-bit indifferentiability of the sum of $k \geq 2$ independent permutations.

1.2 Improving Truncation

Common to all aforementioned compression function constructions is that they operate on an increased internal state and/or make multiple primitive calls to achieve indifferentiability. In addition, TRUNC has the property of additionally taking an initial value $IV \in \{0,1\}^m$ as input. This fixed initial value is, in fact, crucial for the indifferentiability proof: if omitted, the TRUNC construction (3) can be easily distinguished from random. (To wit, also the proven security bound becomes void for $m = 0$.)

Still, intuitively, the initial value is overkill. To see this, assume for the sake of example that we *drop* the initial value. In other words, we consider TRUNC of (3) with $m = 0$. If we set $n = c$, we obtain a compression function from b to c bits, and we can use it in the Merkle-Damgård construction (1) with state c and message block size $b - c$. The resulting construction is very similar to the sponge construction (2), the only difference is that message blocks are not added to the outer part but rather substituted, and this construction is known to be secure [6]. (This is known as the Grindahl construction [25].) Bottom line is that this initial value in TRUNC helps us in proving indifferentiability of the compression function and making it possible to instantiate the Merkle-Damgård construction with TRUNC. On the other hand, it is overkill in the sense that it is not strictly necessary for guaranteeing the security of the hashing scheme (equivalently, its omission does not make the resulting hashing scheme insecure).

1.3 Truncation Without Fixed IV

In this work, we take a closer look at the TRUNC construction, and particularly the role of the initial value IV. Concretely, we consider TRUNC of (3) where the fixed initial value IV is replaced by a random value. The adversary may choose to evaluate TRUNC multiple times for the same random value, it may choose to evaluate TRUNC for a different random value each query, and it may learn all random values used. We prove that this construction is still indifferentiable from a random oracle up to a comparable bound: the only difference occurs in the event of collisions in the random initial values.

More detailed, our proof incorporates an additional random oracle $\mathcal{H}$, and queries that the adversary makes to the TRUNC construction do not just consist of an input value $I \in \{0,1\}^{b-m}$, but also include a message M. The IV is subsequently replaced by $\mathcal{H}(M)$. Formally, for a hash function $\mathcal{H}$ with range $\{0,1\}^m$ and a permutation $\mathcal{P}$ over $\{0,1\}^b$, our construction RTRUNC is defined as

$$\text{RTRUNC}(M, I) = \text{left}_n\left(\mathcal{P}(\mathcal{H}(M) \| I)\right) . \tag{5}$$

Under the assumption that $\mathcal{H}$ is a random oracle and $\mathcal{P}$ is a random permutation, we prove that the RTRUNC construction is indifferentiable from a random oracle up to around

$$\min\left\{2^{\frac{2b-n}{3}}, 2^{\frac{m}{2}}, \frac{2^{b-n}}{b-n}\right\} \approx \min\left\{2^{\frac{2b-n}{3}}, 2^{\frac{m}{2}}, 2^{b-n}\right\} \tag{6}$$

queries. The proof is given in Sect. 4. It is inspired by the proof of Choi et al. for their isolated compression function, but deals with the complicating factor that comes with the presence of the hash function outputs.

1.4 Application: Parallel Digest Generation

Despite the fact that the applicability of earlier compression function indifferentiability results was negligible, mostly due to its expensive internal operation to make the indifferentiability proof work, our construction has direct practical applications. The main application, in fact, immediately comes from the proof approach: RTRUNC allows to extend *any* cryptographic hash function $\mathcal{H}$ into a parallel eXtendable Output Function (XOF) [38] that generates arbitrarily sized outputs. Note that, indeed, the Merkle-Damgård construction only outputs a fixed sized digest; the sponge construction does allow for arbitrarily sized outputs, but this output generation is inherently sequential. Parallel digest generation can lead to a significant speed-up in certain implementations, and would particularly be relevant in use with parallel tree hashing.

The quest for parallel digest generation is not new. Indeed, evaluating several permutations simultaneously in modern CPUs is faster than evaluating them in sequence. Hence, it is desirable to have schemes that can be efficiently parallelized. In the case of PRFs, this goal has been achieved by, e.g., the Farfalle construction proposed by Bertoni et al. [5] at ToSC 2017. For hashing, there already exist several constructions for achieving such a goal, which are commonly called "Mask Generation Functions" (MGFs).

Counter-MGF. To the best of our knowledge, the first construction – denoted as MGF1 ("Mask Generating Function 1") – was introduced by Kaliski and Staddon [24] in 1998 for use in public key cryptography. The majority of existing MGFs [1,22,23,42] follow the counter-based design and have been standardized by ANSI, IEEE, and ISO/IEC. Focusing on the MGF1 construction, it is built on top of a hash function $\mathcal{H} : \{0,1\}^* \to \{0,1\}^m$. It takes as input an arbitrarily sized message M, glues a counter $\langle i \rangle_l$ of fixed size l to it, and outputs

$$\mathcal{H}(M \| \langle 0 \rangle_l) \parallel \mathcal{H}(M \| \langle 1 \rangle_l) \parallel \mathcal{H}(M \| \langle 2 \rangle_l) \parallel \cdots . \tag{7}$$

This construction is also known as Counter-MGF. Its indifferentiability from a (variable output length) random oracle follows from the indifferentiability of $\mathcal{H}$ from a (fixed output length) random oracle. See also Suzuki and Yasuda [43].

Chained-MGF. A comparable approach is Chained-MGF [37]. This mask generation function is built on top of a hash function $\mathcal{H} : \{0,1\}^* \to \{0,1\}^m$ and a one-way function $\mathcal{F} : \{0,1\}^{m+l} \to \{0,1\}^n$. It evaluates $\mathcal{H}$ on the message M, glues a counter $\langle i \rangle_l$ of fixed size l to this digest, and outputs

$$\mathcal{F}(\mathcal{H}(M) \| \langle 0 \rangle_l) \parallel \mathcal{F}(\mathcal{H}(M) \| \langle 1 \rangle_l) \parallel \mathcal{F}(\mathcal{H}(M) \| \langle 2 \rangle_l) \parallel \cdots . \tag{8}$$

This construction is proven to be indifferentiable from a random oracle up to the random oracle security of $\mathcal{H}$ and $\mathcal{F}$ by Suzuki and Yasuda [43]. Note, in particular, that security is capped by $2^{m/2}$ because security breaks in case one finds collisions in the output of $\mathcal{H}$.

Clearly, Chained-MGF has a disadvantage over Counter-MGF in that it uses two independent primitives. On the other hand, it *does* allow for more freedom in the choice of the finalizing one-way function $\mathcal{F}$, and the design is ignorant of the actual hash function in use. This is an advantage that will become clearer if we apply these modes to permutation-based hashing.

Cascade-MGF. The transition of our construction RTRUNC to a new MGF, which we dub Cascade-MGF, is immediate. For a hash function $\mathcal{H} : \{0,1\}^* \to \{0,1\}^m$ and a permutation $\mathcal{P} : \{0,1\}^b \to \{0,1\}^b$, it plainly evaluates RTRUNC on message M and counter $\langle i \rangle_l$ of fixed size $l = b - m$, and outputs

$$\begin{aligned} &\mathrm{RTRUNC}(M, \langle 0 \rangle_l) \parallel \cdots \parallel \mathrm{RTRUNC}(M, \langle i \rangle_l) \parallel \cdots \\ &= \mathrm{left}_n\left(\mathcal{P}(\mathcal{H}(M) \| \langle 0 \rangle_l)\right) \parallel \cdots \parallel \mathrm{left}_n\left(\mathcal{P}(\mathcal{H}(M) \| \langle i \rangle_l)\right) \parallel \cdots , \end{aligned} \tag{9}$$

where $\langle i \rangle_l \in \{0,1\}^l$ denotes the bit representation of $i \in \mathbb{Z}_{2^{b-m}}$. Note that Cascade-MGF of (9) is *exactly* equal to Chained-MGF of (8) instantiated with the construction (3) of Choi et al., *but with the IV removed.*

Comparison. In Sect. 5 we perform a generic comparison of Cascade-MGF with Counter-MGF and Chained-MGF with the focus on parallelizable permutation-based hashing and achieving k-bit security. It appears that Cascade-MGF compares favorably in most cases. An overview of this general comparison is given in Table 1. For the sake of exemplification, we now restrict our focus to $k = 128$-bit security with the use of a 384-bit permutation such as GIMLI [3] or Xoodoo [14]. In this case, the hash function $\mathcal{H}$ outputs digests of size $m = 256$ bits.

It appears that Cascade-MGF now achieves the exact same level of security as Chained-MGF instantiated with TRUNC (3). The only difference is that our construction does not use/need an initial value whereas Chained-MGF with TRUNC requires a $k = 128$-bit initial value. Due to this, our construction allows for a counter of size $l = b - m = 128$ bits whereas Chained-MGF with TRUNC allows for a counter of size $l = b - m - k = 0$ bits. As a concrete application, the squeezing phase in the recent tree-sponge construction proposed by Gunsing [20] can be instantiated via Cascade-MGF instead of Chained-MGF.

Chained-MGF instantiated with SOP (4) allows for the generation of more output blocks. Keeping the security parameters as in above choices,

Chained-MGF with SOP can generate 384-bit digests at a time as opposed to 256-bit digests in Cascade-MGF. The price to pay is that SOP makes two permutation evaluations per digest blocks instead of one, effectively making it less efficient.

The comparison of Cascade-MGF with Counter-MGF is less trivial. The reason is that Cascade-MGF is more versatile and is defined regardless of the hash function $\mathcal{H}$ in use, whereas Counter-MGF processes the counter $\langle i \rangle_l$ by the hash function. This means that a comparison between Cascade-MGF and Counter-MGF can only be made for a specific hash function choice. In Sect. 5.2, we instantiate both constructions with a minimal parallelizable permutation-based tree hash construction that is proven to be indifferentiable [15,21], and argue that even in this case, Cascade-MGF has advantages. First of all, and more importantly, the cost in terms of the number function/permutation calls for generating an output of arbitrary length is independent of the size of the input message for Cascade-MGF, while it depends on it for Counter-MGF. In particular, we show that the cost in term of function/permutation calls of Counter-MGF is *at least double* with respect to the cost necessary for Counter-MGF, but such factor can even be much bigger depending on the size of the input message. Secondly, in Cascade-MGF one can take a smaller permutation for digest generation. On the downside, Counter-MGF would then be based on only one primitive whereas Cascade-MGF takes two. This can be remedied by instantiating the primitives using a single permutation with different round constants.

2 Preliminaries

Notation. For $m, n \in \mathbb{N}$, $\{0,1\}^n$ denotes the set of bit strings of length n. By $\{0,1\}^*$ we denote the set of arbitrarily sized strings, and by $\{0,1\}^\infty$ the set of infinitely long strings. We denote by $\mathrm{Hw}(x)$ the Hamming Weight of a binary string $x \in \{0,1\}^*$. We denote by $\mathrm{func}(m,n)$ the set of all functions from $\{0,1\}^m$ to $\{0,1\}^n$ and by $\mathrm{perm}(n)$ the set of permutations on $\{0,1\}^n$. Abusing notation, we denote by $\mathrm{func}(*,n)$ the set of all functions from $\{0,1\}^*$ to $\{0,1\}^n$. For a finite set $\mathfrak{X}$, $x \xleftarrow{\$} \mathfrak{X}$ denotes the uniform random sampling of an element x from $\mathfrak{X}$. The definition extends to $\mathrm{func}(*,n)$ by lazy sampling.

A random oracle $\mathcal{RO}$ gives access to a function that takes as input binary strings of arbitrary length and returns a random infinite string for each input, that is, $\mathcal{RO} : \{0,1\}^* \to \{0,1\}^\infty$. In a slightly more practical view, $\mathcal{RO}$ gets both a binary string and a length parameter $\ell \in \mathbb{N}$ as inputs, and it outputs a random string of length ℓ. If it is queried twice for the same message but for different length parameters $\ell, \ell' \in \mathbb{N}$, the shorter output is a substring of the longer one.

For $m, n \in \mathbb{N}$ with $m \geq n$, we denote by $\mathrm{left}_n : \{0,1\}^m \to \{0,1\}^n$ the function that outputs the leftmost n bits of the input. Likewise, $\mathrm{right}_n : \{0,1\}^m \to \{0,1\}^n$ outputs the rightmost n bits of the input. For a set $\mathfrak{X} \subseteq \{0,1\}^m$, we write $\mathrm{left}_n(\mathfrak{X}) = \{\mathrm{left}_n(x) \mid x \in \mathfrak{X}\}$, $\mathrm{right}_n(\mathfrak{X}) = \{\mathrm{right}_n(x) \mid x \in \mathfrak{X}\}$, and $\mathfrak{X}\|*^n = \{x\|y \in \{0,1\}^{m+n} \mid x \in \mathfrak{X} \wedge y \in \{0,1\}^n\}$.

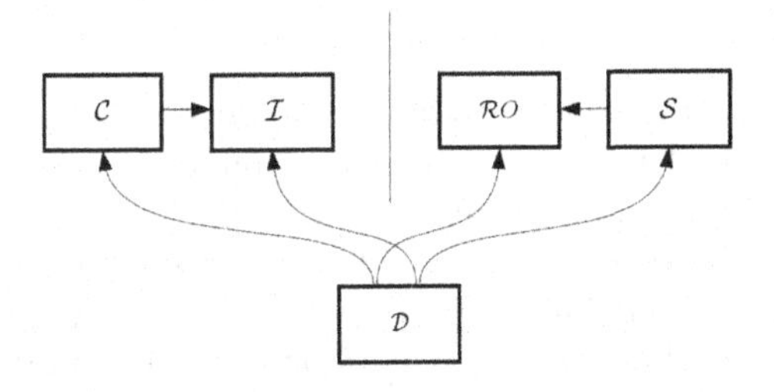

Fig. 1. The indifferentiability model.

2.1 Indifferentiability Model

Consider a hash function construction $\mathcal{C}$ built on top of an ideal component $\mathcal{I}$. To measure how good this hash function behaves like a random oracle $\mathcal{RO}$, we adopt the indifferentiability framework of Maurer et al. [29], and more precisely its version tailored to hash functions by Coron et al. [13]. In this framework, we consider a distinguisher $\mathcal{D}$. This distinguisher has access to either of two worlds: the real world $(\mathcal{C}[\mathcal{I}], \mathcal{I})$ and the simulated world $(\mathcal{RO}, \mathcal{S}[\mathcal{RO}])$, where $\mathcal{S}$ is a *simulator* that has the same interface as $\mathcal{I}$ and that has as goal to mimic its behavior in such a way that transcripts appearing in the ideal world are hard to distinguish from transcripts appearing in the real world. The goal of the distinguisher is to determine, for a given simulator $\mathcal{S}$, which world it is communicating with. If this is computationally hard, we say that $\mathcal{C}[\mathcal{I}]$ behaves like a random oracle, or simply that it is indifferentiable from a random oracle (up to a certain bound). Formally, we have the following definition.

Definition 1. *Let $\mathcal{C}$ by a cryptographic hash function with access to an ideal component $\mathcal{I}$. Let $\mathcal{RO}$ be a random oracle with the same interface as $\mathcal{C}$. We say that $\mathcal{C}$ is (Q, q, ε)-indifferentiable from $\mathcal{RO}$ if there exists a simulator $\mathcal{S}$ such that*

$$Adv_{\mathcal{C},\mathcal{S}}(\mathcal{D}) = \left|\Pr\left(\mathcal{D}^{\mathcal{C}[\mathcal{I}],\mathcal{I}} = 1\right) - \Pr\left(\mathcal{D}^{\mathcal{RO},\mathcal{S}[\mathcal{RO}]} = 1\right)\right| < \varepsilon,$$

for any distinguisher $\mathcal{D}$ making at most Q queries to the outer construction ($\mathcal{C}[\mathcal{I}]$ in the real world and $\mathcal{RO}$ in the simulated world) and at most q queries to the inner construction ($\mathcal{I}$ in the real world and $\mathcal{S}[\mathcal{RO}]$ in the simulated world).

The indifferentiability model is depicted in Fig. 1.

In our work, we will consider hash functions $\mathcal{C}$ built on top of a set of components $\mathcal{I}$, namely a hash function $\mathcal{H}$ *and* a random permutation $\mathcal{P}$. In this case, $\mathcal{S}$ will also consist of two collaborating sub-simulators, and we split the inner complexity q into $q_{\mathcal{H}}$ and $q_{\mathcal{P}}$. Also, as we consider information-theoretic distinguishers and maximize over all of them, we will consider deterministic distinguishers only (without loss of generality).

2.2 χ^2 Method

At Crypto 2017, Dai et al. [16] introduced the *chi-squared method (χ^2 method)*, which can be exploited to obtain an upper bound on the statistical distance between two joint probability distributions.

Let $\mathcal{W}_0$ and $\mathcal{W}_1$ be two random systems over a sample space Ω. Let $\mathcal{D}$ be a deterministic distinguisher that makes ρ oracle queries to one of the two random systems. For each $j \in \{1, \ldots, \rho\}$, we denote by $Z_{\mathcal{W},j}$ the random variable over Ω that follows the distribution of the j-the answer obtained by $\mathcal{D}$ interacting with $\mathcal{W}$. Let

$$\boldsymbol{Z}^j_{\mathcal{W}} = (Z_{\mathcal{W},1}, Z_{\mathcal{W},2}, \ldots, Z_{\mathcal{W},j}),$$

and for each $\boldsymbol{z}_{j-1} = (z_1, z_2, \ldots, z_{j-1}) \in \Omega^{j-1}$, let

$$p^{\boldsymbol{z}_{j-1}}_{\mathcal{W},j}(z) = \Pr\left(Z_{\mathcal{W},j} = z \mid \boldsymbol{Z}^{j-1}_{\mathcal{W}} = \boldsymbol{z}_{j-1}\right).$$

Assume that $\mathcal{W}_0$ and $\mathcal{W}_1$ are such that $p^{\boldsymbol{z}_{j-1}}_{\mathcal{W}_0,j}(z) > 0$ whenever $p^{\boldsymbol{z}_{j-1}}_{\mathcal{W}_1,j}(z) > 0$. Define, for any $j \in \{1, \ldots, \rho\}$ and any $\boldsymbol{z}_{j-1} = (z_1, z_2, \ldots, z_{j-1}) \in \Omega^{j-1}$,

$$\chi^2(\boldsymbol{z}_{j-1}) = \sum_{z\in\Omega \text{ such that } p^{\boldsymbol{z}_{j-1}}_{\mathcal{W}_0,j}(z)>0} \frac{\left(p^{\boldsymbol{z}_{j-1}}_{\mathcal{W}_0,j}(z) - p^{\boldsymbol{z}_{j-1}}_{\mathcal{W}_1,j}(z)\right)^2}{p^{\boldsymbol{z}_{j-1}}_{\mathcal{W}_0,j}(z)}.$$

Dai et al. [16] proved that the distinguishing advantage between $\mathcal{W}_0$ and $\mathcal{W}_1$, denoted $|\boldsymbol{Z}_{\mathcal{W}_0} - \boldsymbol{Z}_{\mathcal{W}_1}|$, is upper bounded as follows:

$$|\boldsymbol{Z}_{\mathcal{W}_0} - \boldsymbol{Z}_{\mathcal{W}_1}| \leq \left(\frac{1}{2}\sum_{j=1}^{\rho} \mathrm{Ex}\left(\chi^2(\boldsymbol{z}_{j-1})\right)\right)^{\frac{1}{2}}.$$

3 The RTRUNC and Cascade-MGF Constructions

In this section, we describe the RTRUNC construction that we are going to analyze, as well as the Cascade-MGF hash function mode that can naturally be built on top of RTRUNC.

Let $b, m, n \in \mathbb{N}$ such that $m, n \leq b$, and let $l = b - m$. Let $\mathcal{H} \in \mathrm{func}(*, m)$ be a hash function and $\mathcal{P} \in \mathrm{perm}(b)$ a permutation. The function RTRUNC is defined as

$$\begin{aligned} \mathrm{RTRUNC}: \{0,1\}^* \times \{0,1\}^l &\to \{0,1\}^n, \\ (M, I) &\mapsto \mathrm{left}_n\left(\mathcal{P}(\mathcal{H}(M)\|I)\right). \end{aligned} \tag{10}$$

As already informally explained in Sect. 1, this construction immediately yields an MGF, which we dub Cascade-MGF. This construction is built on the same primitives, namely a hash function $\mathcal{H} \in \mathrm{func}(*, m)$ and a permutation

$\mathcal{P} \in \text{perm}(b)$, and it consists of concatenating multiple evaluations of RTRUNC for different inputs $I = \langle i \rangle_l$ for $i = 0, 1, 2, \ldots$:

$$\text{RTRUNC}(M, \langle 0 \rangle_l) \parallel \text{RTRUNC}(M, \langle 1 \rangle_l) \parallel \text{RTRUNC}(M, \langle 2 \rangle_l) \parallel \cdots . \tag{11}$$

If we prove that the RTRUNC construction of (10) is indifferentiable from a fixed output length random oracle, then (11) is indifferentiable from a variable length random oracle. It thus suffices to prove the former, and this is the topic of next section.

Before proceeding with that proof, we admit that, even after concatenating outputs, (11) is not variable output length, as the counter can take at most 2^l values. Nevertheless, if l is large enough, for example if l is at least as much as the targeted security parameter, this is sufficient. Note that a similar limitation holds, e.g., for the sponge construction: in theory it can output an arbitrary amount of output blocks, but the security proof dictates that its security cannot be guaranteed once the permutation is evaluated more than $2^{c/2}$ times.

4 Indifferentiability of the RTRUNC Construction

In this section, we prove the indifferentiability of the RTRUNC construction.

Theorem 1. *Let $b, m, n \in \mathbb{N}$ such that $m, n \leq b$, and let $l = b - m$. Let $\mathcal{H} \xleftarrow{\$} \text{func}(*, m)$ be a random hash function and $\mathcal{P} \xleftarrow{\$} \text{perm}(b)$ a random permutation. Consider the* RTRUNC *construction of (10), which we denote by $\mathcal{C}$. Let $\mathcal{RO}$ be a random oracle with the same interface as $\mathcal{C}$. There exists a simulator $\mathcal{S}$, explicitly constructed in the proof, such that*

$$\begin{aligned} Adv_{\mathcal{C},\mathcal{S}}(\mathcal{D}) \leq\ & \frac{\binom{q_{\mathcal{H}}}{2} + 3 \cdot q_{\mathcal{H}} \cdot q_{\mathcal{P}}}{2^m} + \frac{Q \cdot q_{\mathcal{P}}}{2^{b-3}} + \frac{(3 \cdot \ln(Q) + 3n + 1) \cdot q_{\mathcal{P}}}{2^{b-n-1}} \\ & + \left(\frac{6 \cdot (Q + q_{\mathcal{H}} + q_{\mathcal{P}})^3}{2^{2b-n}} + \frac{3 \cdot (Q + q_{\mathcal{H}} + q_{\mathcal{P}})^2}{2^m} + \frac{5 \cdot (Q + q_{\mathcal{H}} + q_{\mathcal{P}})}{2^{b-n}} \right)^{\frac{1}{2}} \end{aligned} \tag{12}$$

for any distinguisher $\mathcal{D}$ making Q queries to the outer construction and $q_{\mathcal{H}}$ and $q_{\mathcal{P}}$ to the inner constructions, where $Q + q_{\mathcal{H}} + q_{\mathcal{P}} \leq 2^{m-1}$ and $1 + q_{\mathcal{P}} \leq 2^{b-n-1}$.

An interpretation of the security bound will be given in Sect. 5.

The first step of the proof will be to design a simulator $\mathcal{S}$. This will be done in Sect. 4.1. Note that, in fact, this simulator must simulate multiple functions: a hash function $\mathcal{S}_{\mathcal{H}}$ as well as the forward and inverse interfaces $\mathcal{S}_{\mathcal{P}}$ and $\mathcal{S}_{\mathcal{P}}^{-1}$. The next step is to bound the distance $\text{Adv}_{\mathcal{C},\mathcal{S}}(\mathcal{D})$ of Definition 1 for the given simulator and for any computationally unbounded distinguisher that can make Q queries to the outer construction and $q_{\mathcal{H}}$ and $q_{\mathcal{P}}$ to the inner constructions. This is done in Sect. 4.2. This bounding itself relies on a triangle inequality with an intermediate world, by bounding the two distances from the real and from the simulated world to this intermediate world. These two bounds are derived in separate lemmas in Sects. 4.3 and 4.4.

4.1 Simulator

The first step is to design a simulator $\mathcal{S}[\mathcal{RO}]$, which consists of three algorithms: $\mathcal{S}_\mathcal{H}$, $\mathcal{S}_\mathcal{P}$, and $\mathcal{S}_\mathcal{P}^{-1}$. These three algorithms are related, i.e., any algorithm might have access to the query history of another algorithm. In addition, they may query $\mathcal{RO}$. The goal is to design algorithms that are hard to distinguish from random functions $\mathcal{H}$, $\mathcal{P}$, and $\mathcal{P}^{-1}$, respectively, and that are consistent with the random oracle $\mathcal{RO}$.

Simulators. To store input-output tuples of $\mathcal{S}_\mathcal{H}, \mathcal{S}_\mathcal{P}$ and $\mathcal{S}_\mathcal{P}^{-1}$, we maintain the following initially empty sets $\mathfrak{C}_\mathcal{H}$ and $\mathfrak{C}_\mathcal{P}$:

$$\mathfrak{C}_\mathcal{H} = \{(M,x) \in \{0,1\}^* \times \{0,1\}^m \mid \mathcal{S}_\mathcal{H}(M) = x\},$$
$$\mathfrak{C}_\mathcal{P} = \{(X,Y) \in \{0,1\}^b \times \{0,1\}^b \mid \mathcal{S}_\mathcal{P}(X) = Y \text{ and } \mathcal{S}_\mathcal{P}^{-1}(Y) = X\}.$$

We additionally define the domain and range values respectively of $\mathfrak{C}_\mathcal{H}$ and $\mathfrak{C}_\mathcal{P}$ as follows:

$$\mathfrak{D}_\mathcal{H} = \{M \in \{0,1\}^* \mid \exists x \in \{0,1\}^m \text{ such that } (M,x) \in \mathfrak{C}_\mathcal{H}\},$$
$$\mathfrak{R}_\mathcal{H} = \{x \in \{0,1\}^m \mid \exists M \in \{0,1\}^* \text{ such that } (M,x) \in \mathfrak{C}_\mathcal{H}\},$$
$$\mathfrak{D}_\mathcal{P} = \{X \in \{0,1\}^b \mid \exists Y \in \{0,1\}^b \text{ such that } (X,Y) \in \mathfrak{C}_\mathcal{P}\},$$
$$\mathfrak{R}_\mathcal{P} = \{Y \in \{0,1\}^b \mid \exists X \in \{0,1\}^b \text{ such that } (X,Y) \in \mathfrak{C}_\mathcal{P}\}.$$

Moreover, for each $y \in \{0,1\}^n$, we define $\mathfrak{R}_\mathcal{P}^y$ as follows:

$$\mathfrak{R}_\mathcal{P}^y = \{y' \in \{0,1\}^{b-n} \mid y \| y' \in \mathfrak{R}_\mathcal{P}\}.$$

Likewise, to store the input-output tuples of $\mathcal{C}$, we maintain the following initially empty set $\mathfrak{C}_\mathcal{C}$:

$$\mathfrak{C}_\mathcal{C} = \{((M,I),y) \in \{0,1\}^* \times \{0,1\}^l \times \{0,1\}^n \mid \mathcal{C}(M,I) = y\}.$$

We additionally define the domain and range values of $\mathfrak{C}_\mathcal{C}$ as follows:

$$\mathfrak{D}_\mathcal{C} = \{(M,I) \in \{0,1\}^* \times \{0,1\}^l \mid \exists x \in \{0,1\}^n \text{ such that } ((M,I),y) \in \mathfrak{C}_\mathcal{C}\},$$
$$\mathfrak{R}_\mathcal{C} = \{y \in \{0,1\}^n \mid \exists (M,I) \in \{0,1\}^* \times \{0,1\}^l \text{ such that } ((M,I),y) \in \mathfrak{C}_\mathcal{C}\}.$$

Note that the simulator has *no* access to $\mathfrak{C}_\mathcal{C}$; we will need it later to bound the indifferentiability advantage.

Based on this, simulator $\mathcal{S}_\mathcal{H}$ is now given in Algorithm 1, simulator $\mathcal{S}_\mathcal{P}$ in Algorithm 2, and simulator $\mathcal{S}_\mathcal{P}^{-1}$ in Algorithm 3.

Discussion. We briefly elaborate on some design choices of the simulator.

Regarding $\mathcal{S}_\mathcal{H}$, the output is chosen from the set $\{0,1\}^m \setminus (\mathfrak{R}_\mathcal{H} \cup \text{left}_m(\mathfrak{D}_\mathcal{P}))$. One of our goals is to avoid a collision at the output of $\mathcal{S}_\mathcal{H}$. The problem is not about collisions itself (note that a collision can also occur in the real world), but

Algorithm 1: Simulator $\mathcal{S}_\mathcal{H}$

Data: input $M \in \{0,1\}^*$
Result: output $x \in \{0,1\}^m$
1 **if** $M \in \mathfrak{D}_\mathcal{H}$ **then**
2   **return** x such that $(M, x) \in \mathfrak{C}_\mathcal{H}$
3 $x \xleftarrow{\$} \{0,1\}^m \setminus (\mathfrak{R}_\mathcal{H} \cup \text{left}_m(\mathfrak{D}_\mathcal{P}))$
4 $\mathfrak{C}_\mathcal{H} \leftarrow \mathfrak{C}_\mathcal{H} \cup \{(M, x)\}$
5 **return** x

Algorithm 2: Simulator $\mathcal{S}_\mathcal{P}$

Data: input $X \in \{0,1\}^b$
Result: output $Y \in \{0,1\}^b$
1 **if** $X \in \mathfrak{D}_\mathcal{P}$ **then**
2   **return** $Y \in \mathfrak{R}_\mathcal{P}$ such that $(X, Y) \in \mathfrak{C}_\mathcal{P}$
3 parse $X = x \| I$ where $x = \text{left}_m(X) \in \{0,1\}^m$
4 **if** $x \in \mathfrak{R}_\mathcal{H}$ **then**
5   let $M \in \{0,1\}^*$ be such that $(M, x) \in \mathfrak{C}_\mathcal{H}$
6     $y \leftarrow \mathcal{RO}(M, I)$
7     $y' \xleftarrow{\$} \{0,1\}^{b-n} \setminus \mathfrak{R}_\mathcal{P}^y$
8     $Y \leftarrow y \| y'$
9 **else**
10     $Y \xleftarrow{\$} \{0,1\}^b \setminus \mathfrak{R}_\mathcal{P}$
11 $\mathfrak{C}_\mathcal{P} \leftarrow \mathfrak{C}_\mathcal{P} \cup \{(X, Y)\}$
12 **return** Y

Algorithm 3: Simulator $\mathcal{S}_\mathcal{P}^{-1}$

Data: input $Y \in \{0,1\}^b$
Result: output $X \in \{0,1\}^b$
1 **if** $Y \in \mathfrak{R}_\mathcal{P}$ **then**
2   **return** $X \in \mathfrak{D}_\mathcal{P}$ such that $(X, Y) \in \mathfrak{C}_\mathcal{P}$
3 $X \xleftarrow{\$} \{0,1\}^b \setminus (\mathfrak{D}_\mathcal{P} \cup \mathfrak{R}_\mathcal{H} \| *^{b-m})$
4 $\mathfrak{C}_\mathcal{P} \leftarrow \mathfrak{C}_\mathcal{P} \cup \{(X, Y)\}$
5 **return** X

rather about the fact that the two outputs of the overall construction $\mathcal{C}[\mathcal{H}, \mathcal{P}]$ would be equal, and this could be problematic when defining $\mathcal{S}_\mathcal{P}$.

In a similar way, we want to avoid that calls to $\mathcal{S}_\mathcal{H}$ create collisions between the outputs of $\mathcal{S}_\mathcal{H}$ and the leftmost m bits of the inputs to $\mathcal{S}_\mathcal{P}$. This type of collisions is also explicitly avoided in calls to $\mathcal{S}_\mathcal{P}^{-1}$. The problem of collisions between the outputs of $\mathcal{S}_\mathcal{H}$ and the inputs to $\mathcal{S}_\mathcal{P}$ is related to the consistency between the inner constructions and the outer one, in this case the random oracle $\mathcal{RO}$. For example, assume that $\mathcal{S}_\mathcal{H}(M)$ returns a value x that already belongs to $\text{left}_m(\mathfrak{D}_\mathcal{P})$, or in a similar way that $\mathcal{S}_\mathcal{P}^{-1}$ returns a value X such that

$\text{left}_m(X) \in \mathfrak{R}_{\mathcal{H}}$. Let $I \in \{0,1\}^l$ be such that $\text{right}_l(X) = I$. In this case, an attacker can check the consistency of these two simulator queries with $\mathcal{RO}$, by verifying if $\mathcal{RO}(M, I) = \text{left}_n(Y)$. This equality would hold with probability 1 in the real world.

Besides these two collisions, no other types of collisions are avoided, and the simulators $\mathcal{S}_{\mathcal{H}}$ and $\mathcal{S}_{\mathcal{P}}^{\pm}$ behave like a random hash function and permutation, respectively, with *one* difference: if the simulator $\mathcal{S}_{\mathcal{P}}$ is queried on an input X such that $\text{left}_m(X) \in \mathfrak{R}_{\mathcal{H}}$, the simulator *must* maintain oracle consistency, i.e., query its random oracle $\mathcal{RO}$ to generate a response to the query.

4.2 Proof of Theorem 1

Let $\mathcal{C}$ be the construction of (10) defined via a random hash function $\mathcal{H}$ and a random permutation $\mathcal{P}$. Let $\mathcal{RO}$ be a random oracle with the same interface as $\mathcal{C}$, and let $\mathcal{S}$ be the simulator of Sect. 4.1. Let $\mathcal{W}_{\text{S}} = (\mathcal{RO}, \mathcal{S}_{\mathcal{H}}[\mathcal{RO}], \mathcal{S}_{\mathcal{P}}^{\pm}[\mathcal{RO}])$ and $\mathcal{W}_{\text{R}} = (\mathcal{C}[\mathcal{H}, \mathcal{P}], \mathcal{H}, \mathcal{P})$ denote the simulated world and the real world, respectively. Let $\mathcal{D}$ be any distinguisher that makes at most Q construction queries (to $\mathcal{RO}$ or $\mathcal{C}[\mathcal{H}, \mathcal{P}]$), $q_{\mathcal{H}}$ queries to the first primitive oracle ($\mathcal{S}_{\mathcal{H}}[\mathcal{RO}]$ or $\mathcal{H}$) and $q_{\mathcal{P}}$ queries to the second primitive oracle ($\mathcal{S}_{\mathcal{P}}[\mathcal{RO}]$ or $\mathcal{P}$). Assume that $\mathcal{D}$ never makes redundant queries, i.e., query an oracle twice on the same input. From Definition 1, our goal is to bound

$$\text{Adv}_{\mathcal{C},\mathcal{S}}(\mathcal{D}) = \left|\Pr\left(\mathcal{D}^{\mathcal{W}_{\text{S}}} = 1\right) - \Pr\left(\mathcal{D}^{\mathcal{W}_{\text{R}}} = 1\right)\right| . \tag{13}$$

Additional World. First, we will consider the differences between the two worlds. Focusing on $\mathcal{S}_{\mathcal{H}}$ and $\mathcal{H}$, it is obvious that the former never results in collisions, but they might occur in the latter. This means that there exist communication transcripts that can occur in $\mathcal{W}_{\text{R}}$ but not in $\mathcal{W}_{\text{S}}$. At the same time, the random oracle $\mathcal{RO}$ in $\mathcal{W}_{\text{S}}$ outputs random strings, whereas in $\mathcal{W}_{\text{R}}$ the outputs of the function $\mathcal{C}[\mathcal{H}, \mathcal{P}]$ depend on the details of the function $\mathcal{H}$ and of the permutation $\mathcal{P}$. Hence, there exist communication transcripts that can occur in $\mathcal{W}_{\text{S}}$ but not in $\mathcal{W}_{\text{R}}$.

As our goal is to apply the chi-squared method, our first step is to introduce an intermediate world $\mathcal{W}_{\text{I}} = (\mathcal{C}[\mathcal{H}^\star, \mathcal{P}^\star], \mathcal{H}^\star, \mathcal{P}^\star)$, which has the same oracle interface as $\mathcal{W}_{\text{S}}$ and $\mathcal{W}_{\text{R}}$. The idea is that the world $\mathcal{W}_{\text{I}}$ behaves closely to $\mathcal{W}_{\text{R}}$, and that $\mathcal{W}_{\text{I}}$ is in the support of $\mathcal{W}_{\text{S}}$, and this world reminds of the intermediate world introduced by Choi et al. [12], though it is more involved as a hash function interface is added. These functions maintain initially empty sets to store input-output tuples $\mathfrak{C}_{\mathcal{H}}^\star, \mathfrak{C}_{\mathcal{P}}^\star$ and $\mathfrak{C}_{\mathcal{C}}^\star$, in a similar vein as in Sect. 4.1, with $\mathfrak{D}_{\mathcal{H}}^\star$, $\mathfrak{R}_{\mathcal{H}}^\star$, $\mathfrak{D}_{\mathcal{P}}^\star$, $\mathfrak{R}_{\mathcal{P}}^\star$, ${\mathfrak{R}_{\mathcal{P}}^\star}^y$, $\mathfrak{D}_{\mathcal{C}}^\star$, and $\mathfrak{R}_{\mathcal{C}}^\star$ defined analogously as before. The algorithms $\mathcal{H}^\star$, $\mathcal{P}^\star$, and $\mathcal{P}^{\star -1}$ are now given in Algorithms 4, 5, 6, respectively.

In a nutshell, the world $\mathcal{W}_{\text{I}}$ operates as $\mathcal{W}_{\text{R}}$ but instantiates it with lazily-sampled primitives $\mathcal{H}^\star$ and $\mathcal{P}^\star$ that slightly deviate from $\mathcal{H}$ and $\mathcal{P}$. In particular, $\mathcal{H}^\star$ never samples any element in $\mathfrak{R}_{\mathcal{H}}^\star \cup \text{left}_m(\mathfrak{D}_{\mathcal{P}}^\star)$, and $\mathcal{P}^{\star -1}$ never samples any element of $\mathfrak{D}_{\mathcal{P}}^\star \cup (\mathfrak{R}_{\mathcal{H}}^\star \| *^{b-m})$. The world uses flags denoted by bad_1, bad_2, and bad_3 (all initialized as false), to mark events in which $\mathcal{W}_{\text{I}}$ differs from $\mathcal{W}_{\text{R}}$.

Algorithm 4: Procedure $\mathcal{H}^\star$ with appended bad events

```
   Data: input M ∈ {0,1}*
   Result: output x ∈ {0,1}^m
 1 x ←$ {0,1}^m
 2 if x ∈ 𝔑*_H or x ∈ left_m(𝔇*_P) then
 3     if x ∈ 𝔑*_H then
 4         bad1 ← true
 5     if x ∈ left_m(𝔇*_P) then
 6         bad2 ← true
 7     x ←$ {0,1}^m \ (𝔑*_H ∪ left_m(𝔇*_P))
 8 ℭ*_H ← ℭ*_H ∪ {(M, x)}
 9 return x
```

Algorithm 5: Procedure $\mathcal{P}^\star$ with appended bad events

```
   Data: input X ∈ {0,1}^b
   Result: output Y ∈ {0,1}^b
 1 Y ←$ {0,1}^b \ 𝔑*_P
 2 ℭ*_P ← ℭ*_P ∪ {(X, Y)}
 3 return Y
```

Algorithm 6: Procedure $\mathcal{P}^{\star-1}$ with appended bad events

```
   Data: input Y ∈ {0,1}^b
   Result: output X ∈ {0,1}^b
 1 parse Y = y||y' where y = left_n(Y) ∈ {0,1}^n
 2 if Y ∉ 𝔑*_P then
 3     X ←$ {0,1}^b \ 𝔇*_P
 4     if left_m(X) ∈ 𝔑*_H then
 5         bad2 ← true
 6         X ←$ {0,1}^b \ (𝔇*_P ∪ 𝔑*_H||*^(b-m))
 7     ℭ*_P ← ℭ*_P ∪ {(X, Y)}
 8 else
 9     bad3 ← true
10     let X' ∈ {0,1}^b be such that (X', Y) ∈ ℭ*_P
11     X ←$ {0,1}^b \ (𝔇*_P ∪ 𝔑*_H||*^(b-m))
12     y' ←$ {0,1}^(b-n) \ 𝔑*_P^y
13     Y' ← y||y'
14     ℭ*_P ← (ℭ*_P \ ({X', Y}) ∪ {(X, Y), (X', Y')}
15 return X
```

A significant change is in the oracle $\mathcal{P}^{\star-1}$, where it makes a distinction between whether or not $Y \notin \mathfrak{R}^\star_\mathcal{P}$. Recall that the adversary never evaluates repeated queries. This means that if $Y \in \mathfrak{R}^\star_\mathcal{P}$ holds, necessarily there had been a query (M, I) to $\mathcal{C}(M, I)$ that returned $y = \text{left}_n(Y)$. In this case, the distinguisher did not obtain any information on the $b - n$ rightmost bits of Y, yet. The only thing it knows, is that there should be an evaluation

$$\mathcal{P}^\star(\hat{*}\|I) = y\|*$$

for unknown $\hat{*} \in \{0,1\}^n$ and $* \in \{0,1\}^{b-m}$. When this inverse query $P^{\star -1}(y\|*)$ is made later during the attack, the rightmost bits $\text{right}_{b-n}(y\|*)$ are replaced by a new element y', and $P^{\star -1}(y\|*)$ is also given a new element X outside $\mathfrak{D}^\star_{\mathcal{P}} \cup \mathfrak{R}^\star_{\mathcal{H}}\|*^{b-m}$.

Triangle Inequality. Using intermediate world $\mathcal{W}_\text{I}$, a triangle inequality yields for (13):

$$\begin{aligned}\text{Adv}_{\mathcal{C},\mathcal{S}}(\mathcal{D}) \leq \\ \left|\Pr\left(\mathcal{D}^{\mathcal{W}_\text{S}} = 1\right) - \Pr\left(\mathcal{D}^{\mathcal{W}_\text{I}} = 1\right)\right| + \left|\Pr\left(\mathcal{D}^{\mathcal{W}_\text{I}} = 1\right) - \Pr\left(\mathcal{D}^{\mathcal{W}_\text{R}} = 1\right)\right| \quad (14)\end{aligned}$$

Bounds on the remaining two terms are derived separately. In Lemma 1, a bound on the distance between $\mathcal{W}_\text{I}$ and $\mathcal{W}_\text{R}$ is derived, and in Lemma 2, a bound on the distance between $\mathcal{W}_\text{S}$ and $\mathcal{W}_\text{I}$ is derived.

Lemma 1. *Let $\mathcal{W}_I = (\mathcal{C}[\mathcal{H}^\star, \mathcal{P}^\star], \mathcal{H}^\star, \mathcal{P}^\star)$ and $\mathcal{W}_R = (\mathcal{C}[\mathcal{H}, \mathcal{P}], \mathcal{H}, \mathcal{P})$ be respectively the intermediate and the real world, as defined before. Then,*

$$\begin{aligned}\left|\Pr\left(\mathcal{D}^{\mathcal{W}_I} = 1\right) - \Pr\left(\mathcal{D}^{\mathcal{W}_R} = 1\right)\right| \leq \frac{\binom{q_\mathcal{H}}{2} + 3 \cdot q_\mathcal{H} \cdot q_\mathcal{P}}{2^m} + \frac{Q \cdot q_\mathcal{P}}{2^{b-3}} \\ + \frac{(3 \cdot \ln(Q) + 3n + 1) \cdot q_\mathcal{P}}{2^{b-n-1}}\end{aligned}$$

for any distinguisher $\mathcal{D}$ making Q queries to the outer construction and $q_\mathcal{H}$ and $q_\mathcal{P}$ to the inner constructions, where $Q + q_\mathcal{H} + q_\mathcal{P} \leq 2^{b-1}$.

Lemma 2. *Let $\mathcal{W}_S = (\mathcal{RO}, \mathcal{S}_\mathcal{H}[\mathcal{RO}], \mathcal{S}^\pm_\mathcal{P}[\mathcal{RO}])$ and $\mathcal{W}_I = (\mathcal{C}[\mathcal{H}^\star, \mathcal{P}^\star], \mathcal{H}^\star, \mathcal{P}^\star)$ be respectively the simulated world and the intermediate world, as defined before.*

$$\begin{aligned}\left|\Pr\left(\mathcal{D}^{\mathcal{W}_S} = 1\right) - \Pr\left(\mathcal{D}^{\mathcal{W}_I} = 1\right)\right| \leq \Bigg(\frac{6 \cdot (Q + q_\mathcal{H} + q_\mathcal{P})^3}{2^{2b-n}} \\ + \frac{3 \cdot (Q + q_\mathcal{H} + q_\mathcal{P})^2}{2^m} + \frac{5 \cdot (Q + q_\mathcal{H} + q_\mathcal{P})}{2^{b-n}}\Bigg)^{\frac{1}{2}}\end{aligned}$$

for any distinguisher $\mathcal{D}$ making Q queries to the outer construction and $q_\mathcal{H}$ and $q_\mathcal{P}$ to the inner constructions, where $Q + q_\mathcal{H} + q_\mathcal{P} \leq 2^{m-1}$ and $1 + q_\mathcal{P} \leq 2^{b-n-1}$.

The proof of Lemma 1 is given in Sect. 4.3, and consists of bounding the probability that a bad event occurs in $\mathcal{W}_\text{I}$. The proof of Lemma 2 is given in Sect. 4.4, and is based on the chi-squared method. The proof of Theorem 1 is immediately completed by plugging the bounds of Lemmas 1 and 2 into (14).

Additional Notation. For world $\mathcal{W}_\text{I}$, and specifically for evaluations of $\mathcal{P}^\star$ and $\mathcal{P}^{\star-1}$, we introduce the following additional notation. Consider any query $\mathcal{P}^{\star-1}(Y)$ with $y = \text{left}_n(Y)$. At the point of making this query,

- V_y counts the number of elements X where $\mathcal{P}^\star(X)$ has been determined by a function query or a distinguisher query such that $\mathcal{P}^\star(X) = y\|y'$ for some $y' \in \{0,1\}^{b-n}$:

$$V_y = |\{X \in \{0,1\}^b \mid \exists y' \in \{0,1\}^{b-n} \text{ such that } \mathcal{P}^\star(X) = y\|y'\}|\,;$$

- S_y counts the number of elements X where $\mathcal{P}^\star(X)$ has been determined *only* by a distinguisher query such that $\mathcal{P}^\star(X) = y\|y'$ for some $y' \in \{0,1\}^{b-n}$;
- F_y counts the number of elements X where $\mathcal{P}^\star(X)$ has been partially determined only by a function query and $\mathcal{P}^\star(X) = y\|\star$ for some unknown $\star \in \{0,1\}^{b-n}$, in such a way that $F_y = V_y - S_y$.

Finally, let $V = \sum_{y\in\{0,1\}^n} V_y$. At any point in time, $V = |\mathfrak{C}^\star_\mathcal{P}|$.

4.3 Upper Bound on Distance Between $\mathcal{W}_\text{I}$ and $\mathcal{W}_\text{R}$ (Lemma 1)

The two worlds behave in the same way until one of the bad events is set to true in $\mathcal{W}_\text{I}$. Hence, we can upper bound this term by computing the probability that one of the bad events is set to true:

$$\begin{aligned}\left|\Pr\left(\mathcal{D}^{\mathcal{W}_\text{I}} = 1\right) - \Pr\left(\mathcal{D}^{\mathcal{W}_\text{R}} = 1\right)\right| &\le \Pr(\mathsf{bad}_1 \cup \mathsf{bad}_2 \cup \mathsf{bad}_3) \\ &\le \Pr(\mathsf{bad}_1) + \Pr(\mathsf{bad}_2) + \Pr(\mathsf{bad}_3)\,.\end{aligned}$$

In the following, we compute $\Pr(\mathsf{bad}_i)$ for each $i \in \{1,2,3\}$. The proof of the lemma is then completed by a simple addition of the three terms.

Probability of bad_1. This event happens if $\mathcal{H}^\star$ returns a value x that already belongs to $\mathfrak{R}^\star_\mathcal{H}$, or equivalently, a value x for which there exists an earlier M' such that $(M', x) \in \mathfrak{C}^\star_\mathcal{H}$. As the distinguisher makes $q_\mathcal{H}$ queries to $\mathcal{H}^\star$, the probability that this occurs is bounded as follows:

$$\Pr(\mathsf{bad}_1) \le \sum_{j=1}^{q_\mathcal{H}} \frac{j-1}{2^m} \le \frac{\binom{q_\mathcal{H}}{2}}{2^m}\,.$$

Probability of bad_2. This event happens if $\mathcal{H}^\star$ returns a value x that already belongs to $\text{left}_m(\mathfrak{D}^\star_\mathcal{P})$ or if $\mathcal{P}^{\star-1}$ returns a value X such that $\text{left}_m(X) \in \mathfrak{R}^\star_\mathcal{H}$. In a query to $\mathcal{H}^\star$, bad_2 is set with probability at most $q_\mathcal{P}/2^m$. In a query to $\mathcal{P}^{\star-1}$, bad_2 is set with probability at most $(q_\mathcal{H} \cdot 2^{b-m})/(2^b - q_\mathcal{P}) \le 2q_\mathcal{H}/2^m$ (provided that $q_\mathcal{P} \le 2^{b-1}$). After $q_\mathcal{H}$ queries to $\mathcal{H}^\star$ and at most $q_\mathcal{P}$ queries to $\mathcal{P}^{\star-1}$, the probability of this event to occur is upper bounded by:

$$\Pr(\mathsf{bad}_2) \le \sum_{j=1}^{q_\mathcal{H}} \frac{q_\mathcal{P}}{2^m} + \sum_{j=1}^{q_\mathcal{P}} \frac{2q_\mathcal{H}}{2^m} = \frac{3 \cdot q_\mathcal{H} \cdot q_\mathcal{P}}{2^m}\,.$$

Probability of bad_3. The event is very similar to bad event E_2 of Choi et al. [12], and we adopt their reasoning. This event happens if a query $Y = y \| y'$ to $\mathcal{P}^{\star-1}$ belongs to $\mathfrak{R}_{\mathcal{C}}^{\star} \| *^{b-m}$, that is if $y = \text{left}_n(Y)$ is the result of a query to the outer construction. Consider any query. Note that this query fixes $y = \text{left}_n(Y)$. The probability, conditioned on the previous queries, that this query with $\text{left}_n(Y) = y$ sets bad_3 is at most $\frac{F_y \cdot 2^n}{2^b - q_{\mathcal{P}}}$, as for any guess there are F_y possible values y' that could set the bad event, and the adversary knows at most $q_{\mathcal{P}}$ earlier outcomes of $\mathcal{P}^{\star}$. Provided that $q_{\mathcal{P}} \leq 2^{b-1}$, and as the adversary can choose y, the conditional probability that the j-th query sets bad_3 is upper bounded by

$$\frac{\max_{y \in \{0,1\}^n} F_y}{2^{b-n-1}} .$$

Thus, summing over all queries we get

$$\Pr(\mathsf{bad}_3) \leq \sum_{j=1}^{q_{\mathcal{P}}} \text{Ex}_j \left(\frac{\max_{y \in \{0,1\}^n} F_y}{2^{b-n-1}} \right) , \tag{15}$$

where $\text{Ex}_j(\cdot)$ denotes the expectation taken over the interaction between $\mathcal{D}$ and $\mathcal{P}^{\star}$ up to the j-th simulator query. Choi et al. [12] derived the following bound:

$$\text{Ex}_j \left(\max_{y \in \{0,1\}^n} F_y \right) \leq \frac{Q}{2^{n-1}} + 3 \cdot \ln(Q) + 3n + 1 , \tag{16}$$

provided that $Q + q_{\mathcal{H}} + q_{\mathcal{P}} \leq 2^{b-1}$. The proof of this bound is included in Supplementary Material [19, App. A] for reference. By combining (15) and (16), we obtain:

$$\Pr(\mathsf{bad}_3) \leq \sum_{j=1}^{q_{\mathcal{P}}} \left(\frac{Q}{2^{b-2}} + \frac{3 \cdot \ln(Q) + 3n + 1}{2^{b-n-1}} \right) = \frac{Q \cdot q_{\mathcal{P}}}{2^{b-3}} + \frac{(3 \cdot \ln(Q) + 3n + 1) \cdot q_{\mathcal{P}}}{2^{b-n-1}} .$$

4.4 Upper Bound on Distance Between $\mathcal{W}_\text{S}$ and $\mathcal{W}_\text{I}$ (Lemma 2)

We will use the chi-squared method (recalled in Sect. 2.2) to provide an upper bound of the distance between the simulated world and the intermediate world. The analysis is inspired by Choi et al. [12], but crucially differs on certain aspects. Most importantly, the elimination of the initial value IV and the subsequent changes to the intermediate world have created significant differences in the distributions between the two worlds $\mathcal{W}_\text{S}$ and $\mathcal{W}_\text{I}$, as we will explain below.

Note that, by design, the support of the intermediate world $\mathcal{W}_\text{I}$ is contained in the support of the simulated world $\mathcal{W}_\text{S}$. Let $\Omega = \{0,1\}^n \times \{0,1\}^m \times \{0,1\}^b$ be the set that contains all possible answers for oracle queries to the simulated world $\mathcal{W}_\text{S}$. For fixed $j \in \{1, \ldots, Q + q_{\mathcal{H}} + q_{\mathcal{P}}\}$ and $\boldsymbol{z}_{j-1} = (z_1, z_2, \ldots, z_{j-1}) \in \Omega^{j-1}$ such that $p_{\mathcal{W}_\text{S}}^{j-1}(\boldsymbol{z}_{j-1}) > 0$, our goal is to compute a bound on

$$\chi^2(\boldsymbol{z}_{j-1}) = \sum_{z \in \Omega \text{ such that } p_{\mathcal{W}_\text{S},j}^{\boldsymbol{z}_{j-1}}(z) > 0} \frac{\left(p_{\mathcal{W}_\text{S},j}^{\boldsymbol{z}_{j-1}}(z) - p_{\mathcal{W}_\text{I},j}^{\boldsymbol{z}_{j-1}}(z) \right)^2}{p_{\mathcal{W}_\text{S},j}^{\boldsymbol{z}_{j-1}}(z)} . \tag{17}$$

Note that the distinguisher can make four types of queries:

- to the outer construction (either the function $\mathcal{RO}$ in world $\mathcal{W}_\mathrm{S}$ or $\mathcal{C}[\mathcal{H}^\star, \mathcal{P}^\star]$ in world $\mathcal{W}_\mathrm{I}$);
- to the first primitive (either the function $\mathcal{S}_\mathcal{H}[\mathcal{RO}]$ in world $\mathcal{W}_\mathrm{S}$ or $\mathcal{H}^\star$ in world $\mathcal{W}_\mathrm{I}$);
- to the forward interface of the second primitive (either the function $\mathcal{S}_\mathcal{P}[\mathcal{RO}]$ in world $\mathcal{W}_\mathrm{S}$ or $\mathcal{P}^\star$ in world $\mathcal{W}_\mathrm{I}$);
- to the forward interface of the second primitive (either the function $\mathcal{S}_\mathcal{P}^{-1}[\mathcal{RO}]$ in world $\mathcal{W}_\mathrm{S}$ or $\mathcal{P}^{\star-1}$ in world $\mathcal{W}_\mathrm{I}$).

To bound $\chi^2(\boldsymbol{z}_{j-1})$ of (17), we will make a case distinction depending on the type of oracle query, below. Afterwards, we will combine the computations and conclude the proof using the chi-squared technique.

Query to Outer Construction. Suppose that the j-th query is an outer construction query. For any $y \in \{0,1\}^n$, we have that

$$p_{\mathcal{W}_\mathrm{S},j}^{\boldsymbol{z}_{j-1}}(y) = \frac{1}{2^n}, \qquad \text{and} \qquad p_{\mathcal{W}_\mathrm{I},j}^{\boldsymbol{z}_{j-1}}(y) = \frac{2^{b-n} - |\mathfrak{R}_\mathcal{P}^{\star\, y}|}{2^b - |\mathfrak{R}_\mathcal{P}^\star|}.$$

For world $\mathcal{W}_\mathrm{S}$, this is obvious as the outer construction is the random oracle. For world $\mathcal{W}_\mathrm{I}$, note that different inputs for $\mathcal{C}$ are mapped into different inputs for $\mathcal{P}^\star$, as the middle state value is drawn $x \xleftarrow{\$} \{0,1\}^m \setminus (\mathfrak{R}_\mathcal{H}^\star \cup \mathrm{left}_m(\mathfrak{D}_\mathcal{P}^\star))$. The resulting output Y of $\mathcal{P}^\star$ is drawn from a set of $2^b - |\mathfrak{R}_\mathcal{P}^\star|$ elements and exactly $2^{b-n} - |\mathfrak{R}_\mathcal{P}^{\star\, y}|$ of them satisfy $\mathrm{left}_n(Y) = y$.

We thus obtain for (17) that, for outer construction queries,

$$\chi^2(\boldsymbol{z}_{j-1}) = \sum_{y\in\{0,1\}^n} \frac{\left(p_{\mathcal{W}_\mathrm{S},j}^{\boldsymbol{z}_{j-1}}(y) - p_{\mathcal{W}_\mathrm{I},j}^{\boldsymbol{z}_{j-1}}(y)\right)^2}{p_{\mathcal{W}_\mathrm{S},j}^{\boldsymbol{z}_{j-1}}(y)} = \sum_{y\in\{0,1\}^n} \frac{(2^n \cdot |\mathfrak{R}_\mathcal{P}^{\star\, y}| - |\mathfrak{R}_\mathcal{P}^\star|)^2}{2^n \cdot (2^b - |\mathfrak{R}_\mathcal{P}^\star|)^2}.$$

Using that $|\mathfrak{R}_\mathcal{P}^\star| \le Q + q_\mathcal{P} \le 2^{b-1}$ and subsequently using that $|\mathfrak{R}_\mathcal{P}^\star| = \sum_{y\in\{0,1\}^n} |\mathfrak{R}_\mathcal{P}^{\star\, y}|$, we can bound this term as follows:

$$\begin{aligned}
\chi^2(\boldsymbol{z}_{j-1}) &\le \frac{4}{2^{2b-n}} \cdot \sum_{y\in\{0,1\}^n} \left(|\mathfrak{R}_\mathcal{P}^{\star\, y}| - \frac{|\mathfrak{R}_\mathcal{P}^\star|}{2^n}\right)^2 \\
&\le \frac{4}{2^{2b-n}} \cdot \left(\sum_{y\in\{0,1\}^n} (|\mathfrak{R}_\mathcal{P}^{\star\, y}|)^2 + \sum_{y\in\{0,1\}^n} \frac{(|\mathfrak{R}_\mathcal{P}^\star|)^2}{2^{2n}}\right) \\
&\le \frac{4}{2^{2b-n}} \cdot \left(\left(\sum_{y\in\{0,1\}^n} |\mathfrak{R}_\mathcal{P}^{\star\, y}|\right)^2 + \frac{(|\mathfrak{R}_\mathcal{P}^\star|)^2}{2^n}\right) = \frac{4 \cdot (|\mathfrak{R}_\mathcal{P}^\star|)^2}{2^{2b-n}} \cdot \left(1 + \frac{1}{2^n}\right) \\
&\le \frac{6 \cdot (Q + q_\mathcal{P})^2}{2^{2b-n}}, \qquad (18)
\end{aligned}$$

using that $1 + \frac{1}{2^n} \le 3/2$.

Query to First Primitive. Suppose that the j-th query is a query to the first primitive. For any $x \in \{0,1\}^m$, we have that

$$p^{z_{j-1}}_{\mathcal{W}_\mathrm{S},j}(x) = \begin{cases} \dfrac{1}{2^m - |\mathfrak{R}_\mathcal{H} \cup \mathrm{left}_m(\mathfrak{D}_\mathcal{P})|} & \text{if } x \in \{0,1\}^m \setminus (\mathfrak{R}_\mathcal{H} \cup \mathrm{left}_m(\mathfrak{D}_\mathcal{P}))\,, \\ 0 & \text{otherwise}\,, \end{cases}$$

$$p^{z_{j-1}}_{\mathcal{W}_\mathrm{I},j}(x) = \begin{cases} \dfrac{1}{2^m - |\mathfrak{R}^\star_\mathcal{H} \cup \mathrm{left}_m(\mathfrak{D}^\star_\mathcal{P})|} & \text{if } x \in \{0,1\}^m \setminus (\mathfrak{R}^\star_\mathcal{H} \cup \mathrm{left}_m(\mathfrak{D}^\star_\mathcal{P}))\,, \\ 0 & \text{otherwise}\,. \end{cases}$$

Note that, despite what intuition suggests, these distributions are *not* the same. In world $\mathcal{W}_\mathrm{I}$, any construction query adds tuples to $\mathfrak{C}^\star_\mathcal{H}$ and $\mathfrak{C}^\star_\mathcal{P}$, whereas this is not the case for $\mathcal{W}_\mathrm{S}$. In the proof of Choi et al., this issue is resolved by restricting world $\mathcal{W}_\mathrm{I}$ in such a way that the differences are annihilated. In our case, with the omission of the initial value, this is not possible.[1]

Nevertheless, we *do* have that $(\mathfrak{R}_\mathcal{H} \cup \mathrm{left}_m(\mathfrak{D}_\mathcal{P})) \subseteq (\mathfrak{R}^\star_\mathcal{H} \cup \mathrm{left}_m(\mathfrak{D}^\star_\mathcal{P}))$. Thus, (17) satisfies, for queries to the first primitive,

$$\begin{aligned} \chi^2(z_{j-1}) &= \sum_{x \in \{0,1\}^m} \frac{\left(p^{z_{j-1}}_{\mathcal{W}_\mathrm{S},j}(x) - p^{z_{j-1}}_{\mathcal{W}_\mathrm{I},j}(x)\right)^2}{p^{z_{j-1}}_{\mathcal{W}_\mathrm{S},j}(x)} \\ &= \sum_{x \in \left(\mathfrak{R}^\star_\mathcal{H} \cup \mathrm{left}_m(\mathfrak{D}^\star_\mathcal{P})\right) \setminus (\mathfrak{R}_\mathcal{H} \cup \mathrm{left}_m(\mathfrak{D}_\mathcal{P}))} p^{z_{j-1}}_{\mathcal{W}_\mathrm{S},j}(x) \\ &\quad + \sum_{x \in \{0,1\}^m \setminus \left(\mathfrak{R}^\star_\mathcal{H} \cup \mathrm{left}_m(\mathfrak{D}^\star_\mathcal{P})\right)} \frac{\left(p^{z_{j-1}}_{\mathcal{W}_\mathrm{S},j}(x) - p^{z_{j-1}}_{\mathcal{W}_\mathrm{I},j}(x)\right)^2}{p^{z_{j-1}}_{\mathcal{W}_\mathrm{S},j}(x)}, \end{aligned}$$

where $p^{z_{j-1}}_{\mathcal{W}_\mathrm{I},j}(x) = 0$ in the first sum. As $|\,(\mathfrak{R}^\star_\mathcal{H} \cup \mathrm{left}_m(\mathfrak{D}^\star_\mathcal{P})) \setminus (\mathfrak{R}_\mathcal{H} \cup \mathrm{left}_m(\mathfrak{D}_\mathcal{P}))\,| \le Q$, we can bound this term as follows:

$$\begin{aligned} \chi^2(z_{j-1}) &\le \frac{Q}{2^m - |\mathfrak{R}_\mathcal{H} \cup \mathrm{left}_m(\mathfrak{D}_\mathcal{P})|} \\ &\quad + 2^m \cdot \frac{\left(|\mathfrak{R}_\mathcal{H} \cup \mathrm{left}_m(\mathfrak{D}_\mathcal{P})| - |\mathfrak{R}^\star_\mathcal{H} \cup \mathrm{left}_m(\mathfrak{D}^\star_\mathcal{P})|\right)^2}{(2^m - |\mathfrak{R}_\mathcal{H} \cup \mathrm{left}_m(\mathfrak{D}_\mathcal{P})|) \cdot (2^m - |\mathfrak{R}^\star_\mathcal{H} \cup \mathrm{left}_m(\mathfrak{D}^\star_\mathcal{P})|)^2} \\ &\le \frac{Q}{2^m - |\mathfrak{R}_\mathcal{H} \cup \mathrm{left}_m(\mathfrak{D}_\mathcal{P})|} + \frac{2^m \cdot Q^2}{(2^m - |\mathfrak{R}^\star_\mathcal{H} \cup \mathrm{left}_m(\mathfrak{D}^\star_\mathcal{P})|)^3} \\ &\le \frac{2 \cdot Q}{2^m} + \frac{8 \cdot Q^2}{2^{2m}}, \end{aligned} \tag{19}$$

where we used that $|\mathfrak{R}^\star_\mathcal{H} \cup \mathrm{left}_m(\mathfrak{D}^\star_\mathcal{P})| \le Q + q_\mathcal{H} + q_\mathcal{P} \le 2^{m-1}$.

[1] Note that Choi et al. did not have a hash primitive, whereas we do, so the drawn parallel here is a bit odd. The comparison with Choi et al.'s proof and the induced difficulties become more apparent when we consider inverse queries, later on.

Forward Query to Second Primitive. Suppose that the j-th query is a forward query $X = x \| I$ to the second primitive. We can distinguish three cases:

1. a query that does not complete a construction evaluation, namely a query X for which $x \notin \mathfrak{R}_{\mathcal{H}}$ (equivalently, for which $\nexists M \in \mathfrak{D}_{\mathcal{H}}$ such that $\mathcal{H}(M) = x$);
2. a forward query on an element related to a previous outer construction query, namely a query X for which there exists $M \in \mathfrak{D}_{\mathcal{H}}$ such that (i) $\mathcal{H}(M) = x$ and (ii) $(M, I) \in \mathfrak{D}_{\mathcal{C}}$;
3. a query that does complete a construction evaluation, namely a query X for which there exists $M \in \mathfrak{D}_{\mathcal{H}}$ such that (i) $\mathcal{H}(M) = x$ and (ii) $(M, I) \notin \mathfrak{D}_{\mathcal{C}}$.

We will analyze these three cases separately.

First Case. For any $Y \in \{0,1\}^b$, we have that

$$p_{\mathcal{W}_{\mathrm{S}},j}^{\boldsymbol{z}_{j-1}}(Y) = \begin{cases} \dfrac{1}{2^b - |\mathfrak{R}_{\mathcal{P}}|} & \text{if } Y \in \{0,1\}^b \setminus \mathfrak{R}_{\mathcal{P}}\,, \\ 0 & \text{otherwise}\,, \end{cases}$$

$$p_{\mathcal{W}_{\mathrm{I}},j}^{\boldsymbol{z}_{j-1}}(Y) = \begin{cases} \dfrac{1}{2^b - |\mathfrak{R}^{\star}_{\mathcal{P}}|} & \text{if } Y \in \{0,1\}^b \setminus \mathfrak{R}^{\star}_{\mathcal{P}}\,, \\ 0 & \text{otherwise}\,. \end{cases}$$

As for the case of queries to the first primitive, these distributions are not the same. Nevertheless, we *do* have that $\mathfrak{R}_{\mathcal{P}} \subseteq \mathfrak{R}^{\star}_{\mathcal{P}}$. Thus, (17) satisfies, for forward queries to the first primitive of type 1,

$$\begin{aligned} \chi^2(\boldsymbol{z}_{j-1}) &= \sum_{Y \in \{0,1\}^b} \frac{\left(p_{\mathcal{W}_{\mathrm{S}},j}^{\boldsymbol{z}_{j-1}}(Y) - p_{\mathcal{W}_{\mathrm{I}},j}^{\boldsymbol{z}_{j-1}}(Y)\right)^2}{p_{\mathcal{W}_{\mathrm{S}},j}^{\boldsymbol{z}_{j-1}}(Y)} \\ &= \sum_{Y \in \mathfrak{R}^{\star}_{\mathcal{P}} \setminus \mathfrak{R}_{\mathcal{P}}} p_{\mathcal{W}_{\mathrm{S}},j}^{\boldsymbol{z}_{j-1}}(Y) + \sum_{Y \in \{0,1\}^b \setminus \mathfrak{R}^{\star}_{\mathcal{P}}} \frac{\left(p_{\mathcal{W}_{\mathrm{S}},j}^{\boldsymbol{z}_{j-1}}(Y) - p_{\mathcal{W}_{\mathrm{I}},j}^{\boldsymbol{z}_{j-1}}(Y)\right)^2}{p_{\mathcal{W}_{\mathrm{S}},j}^{\boldsymbol{z}_{j-1}}(Y)}\,. \end{aligned}$$

where $p_{\mathcal{W}_{\mathrm{I}},j}^{\boldsymbol{z}_{j-1}}(Y) = 0$ in the first sum. As $|\mathfrak{R}^{\star}_{\mathcal{P}} \setminus \mathfrak{R}_{\mathcal{P}}| \leq Q$, we can bound this term as follows:

$$\begin{aligned} \chi^2(\boldsymbol{z}_{j-1}) &\leq \frac{Q}{2^b - |\mathfrak{R}_{\mathcal{P}}|} + 2^b \cdot \frac{(|\mathfrak{R}_{\mathcal{P}}| - |\mathfrak{R}^{\star}_{\mathcal{P}}|)^2}{(2^b - |\mathfrak{R}_{\mathcal{P}}|) \cdot (2^b - |\mathfrak{R}^{\star}_{\mathcal{P}}|)^2} \\ &\leq \frac{Q}{2^b - |\mathfrak{R}_{\mathcal{P}}|} + \frac{2^b \cdot Q^2}{(2^b - |\mathfrak{R}^{\star}_{\mathcal{P}}|)^3} \\ &\leq \frac{2 \cdot Q}{2^b} + \frac{8 \cdot Q^2}{2^{2b}}\,, \end{aligned} \tag{20}$$

where we used that $|\mathfrak{R}^{\star}_{\mathcal{P}}| \leq Q + q_{\mathcal{P}} \leq 2^{b-1}$.

Second Case. Let $M \in \mathfrak{D}_{\mathcal{H}}$ be the *unique* (by design of $\mathcal{S}_{\mathcal{H}}$ and $\mathcal{H}^\star$) value such that $(M, x) \in \mathfrak{C}_{\mathcal{H}}$. Let y be such that $((M, I), y) \in \mathfrak{C}_{\mathcal{C}}$. By design, in both worlds, the response Y will be of the form $y \| y'$ for some $y' \in \{0,1\}^{b-n}$. As a matter of fact, in both worlds, the value y' is randomly drawn in such a way that $y \| y'$ does not collide with a former primitive evaluation. In other words, for any $Y \in \{0,1\}^b$, we have that

$$p^{\boldsymbol{z}_{j-1}}_{\mathcal{W}_{\mathrm{S}},j}(Y) = \begin{cases} \dfrac{1}{2^{b-n} - |\mathfrak{R}^y_{\mathcal{P}}|} & \text{if } Y = y\|y' \text{ with } y' \in \{0,1\}^{b-n} \setminus \mathfrak{R}^y_{\mathcal{P}}\,, \\ 0 & \text{otherwise}\,, \end{cases}$$

$$p^{\boldsymbol{z}_{j-1}}_{\mathcal{W}_{\mathrm{I}},j}(Y) = \begin{cases} \dfrac{1}{2^{b-n} - |\mathfrak{R}^{\star\,y}_{\mathcal{P}}|} & \text{if } Y = y\|y' \text{ with } y' \in \{0,1\}^{b-n} \setminus \mathfrak{R}^{\star\,y}_{\mathcal{P}}\,, \\ 0 & \text{otherwise}\,. \end{cases}$$

The case of world $\mathcal{W}_{\mathrm{I}}$, however, needs some clarification. In principle, procedure $\mathcal{P}^\star$ draws $Y \xleftarrow{\$} \{0,1\}^b \setminus \mathfrak{R}^\star_{\mathcal{P}}$. However, as we condition on the query history, we are *given* the earlier tuple including the value y. Condition on this, Y is drawn uniformly randomly such that $\mathrm{left}_n(Y) = y$ and such that Y hits no other range value. This is equivalent to drawing $y' \xleftarrow{\$} \{0,1\}^{b-n} \setminus \mathfrak{R}^{\star\,y}_{\mathcal{P}}$, for given y. Note, also, that this value might have been given a different value internally in the shuffling of $\mathcal{P}^{\star-1}$, but also here, Y is generated identically.

As for the case of queries to the first primitive, these distributions are not the same. Nevertheless, we *do* have that $\mathfrak{R}^y_{\mathcal{P}} \subseteq \mathfrak{R}^{\star\,y}_{\mathcal{P}}$. Thus, (17) satisfies, for forward queries to the first primitive of type 2,

$$\begin{aligned} \chi^2(\boldsymbol{z}_{j-1}) &= \sum_{Y \in \{0,1\}^b} \frac{\left(p^{\boldsymbol{z}_{j-1}}_{\mathcal{W}_{\mathrm{S}},j}(Y) - p^{\boldsymbol{z}_{j-1}}_{\mathcal{W}_{\mathrm{I}},j}(Y)\right)^2}{p^{\boldsymbol{z}_{j-1}}_{\mathcal{W}_{\mathrm{S}},j}(Y)} \\ &= \sum_{\substack{Y = y\|y' \text{ with} \\ y' \in \mathfrak{R}^{\star\,y}_{\mathcal{P}} \setminus \mathfrak{R}^y_{\mathcal{P}}}} p^{\boldsymbol{z}_{j-1}}_{\mathcal{W}_{\mathrm{S}},j}(Y) + \sum_{\substack{Y = y\|y' \text{ with} \\ y' \in \{0,1\}^{b-n} \setminus \mathfrak{R}^{\star\,y}_{\mathcal{P}}}} \frac{\left(p^{\boldsymbol{z}_{j-1}}_{\mathcal{W}_{\mathrm{S}},j}(Y) - p^{\boldsymbol{z}_{j-1}}_{\mathcal{W}_{\mathrm{I}},j}(Y)\right)^2}{p^{\boldsymbol{z}_{j-1}}_{\mathcal{W}_{\mathrm{S}},j}(Y)}\,. \end{aligned}$$

where $p^{\boldsymbol{z}_{j-1}}_{\mathcal{W}_{\mathrm{I}},j}(Y) = 0$ in the first sum. As $|\mathfrak{R}^{\star\,y}_{\mathcal{P}} \setminus \mathfrak{R}^y_{\mathcal{P}}| \leq 1$ (as in world $\mathcal{W}_{\mathrm{I}}$, $\mathcal{H}^\star$ does not output collisions), we can bound this term as follows:

$$\begin{aligned} \chi^2(\boldsymbol{z}_{j-1}) &\leq \frac{1}{2^{b-n} - |\mathfrak{R}^y_{\mathcal{P}}|} + 2^{b-n} \cdot \frac{(|\mathfrak{R}^y_{\mathcal{P}}| - |\mathfrak{R}^{\star\,y}_{\mathcal{P}}|)^2}{(2^{b-n} - |\mathfrak{R}^y_{\mathcal{P}}|) \cdot (2^{b-n} - |\mathfrak{R}^{\star\,y}_{\mathcal{P}}|)^2} \\ &\leq \frac{1}{2^{b-n} - |\mathfrak{R}^y_{\mathcal{P}}|} + \frac{2^{b-n}}{(2^{b-n} - |\mathfrak{R}^{\star\,y}_{\mathcal{P}}|)^3} \\ &\leq \frac{2}{2^{b-n}} + \frac{8}{2^{2b-2n}}\,, \end{aligned} \tag{21}$$

where we used that $|\mathfrak{R}^{\star\,y}_{\mathcal{P}}| \leq 1 + q_{\mathcal{P}} \leq 2^{b-n-1}$.

Third Case. Let $M \in \mathfrak{D}_{\mathcal{H}}$ be the *unique* (by design of $\mathcal{S}_{\mathcal{H}}$ and $\mathcal{H}^\star$) value such that $(M, x) \in \mathfrak{C}_{\mathcal{H}}$. In world $\mathcal{W}_{\rm S}$, the response Y is generated by calling $y \leftarrow \mathcal{RO}(M, I)$ and generating $y' \xleftarrow{\$} \{0,1\}^{b-n} \setminus \mathfrak{R}^y_{\mathcal{P}}$. Thus, for any $Y \in \{0,1\}^b$, we have that

$$p^{\boldsymbol{z}_{j-1}}_{\mathcal{W}_{\rm S},j}(Y) = \begin{cases} \dfrac{1}{2^n} \cdot \dfrac{1}{2^{b-n} - |\mathfrak{R}^y_{\mathcal{P}}|} & \text{if } Y = y \| y' \text{ with } y \in \{0,1\}^n, y' \in \{0,1\}^{b-n} \setminus \mathfrak{R}^y_{\mathcal{P}}\,, \\ 0 & \text{otherwise}\,. \end{cases}$$

For world $\mathcal{W}_{\rm I}$, the response Y is generated as $Y \xleftarrow{\$} \{0,1\}^b \setminus \mathfrak{R}^\star_{\mathcal{P}}$. Thus, for any $Y \in \{0,1\}^b$, we have that

$$p^{\boldsymbol{z}_{j-1}}_{\mathcal{W}_{\rm I},j}(Y) = \begin{cases} \dfrac{1}{2^b - |\mathfrak{R}^\star_{\mathcal{P}}|} & \text{if } Y \in \{0,1\}^b \setminus \mathfrak{R}^\star_{\mathcal{P}}\,, \\ 0 & \text{otherwise}\,. \end{cases}$$

As for the case of queries to the first primitive, these distributions are not the same. Nevertheless, we *do* have that $\mathfrak{R}^y_{\mathcal{P}} \subseteq \mathfrak{R}^{\star\,y}_{\mathcal{P}}$, and any value $Y \in \{0,1\}^b \setminus \mathfrak{R}^\star_{\mathcal{P}}$ can be written as $Y = y \| y'$ with $y \in \{0,1\}^n$, $y' \in \{0,1\}^{b-n} \setminus \mathfrak{R}^{\star\,y}_{\mathcal{P}}$. Thus, (17) satisfies, for forward queries to the first primitive of type 3,

$$\begin{aligned} \chi^2(\boldsymbol{z}_{j-1}) &= \sum_{Y \in \{0,1\}^b} \frac{\left(p^{\boldsymbol{z}_{j-1}}_{\mathcal{W}_{\rm S},j}(Y) - p^{\boldsymbol{z}_{j-1}}_{\mathcal{W}_{\rm I},j}(Y)\right)^2}{p^{\boldsymbol{z}_{j-1}}_{\mathcal{W}_{\rm S},j}(Y)} \\ &= \sum_{\substack{Y = y\|y' \text{ with} \\ y \in \{0,1\}^n \text{ and} \\ y' \in \mathfrak{R}^{\star\,y}_{\mathcal{P}} \setminus \mathfrak{R}^y_{\mathcal{P}}}} p^{\boldsymbol{z}_{j-1}}_{\mathcal{W}_{\rm S},j}(Y) + \sum_{\substack{Y = y\|y' \text{ with} \\ y \in \{0,1\}^n \text{ and} \\ y' \in \{0,1\}^{b-n} \setminus \mathfrak{R}^{\star\,y}_{\mathcal{P}}}} \frac{\left(p^{\boldsymbol{z}_{j-1}}_{\mathcal{W}_{\rm S},j}(Y) - p^{\boldsymbol{z}_{j-1}}_{\mathcal{W}_{\rm I},j}(Y)\right)^2}{p^{\boldsymbol{z}_{j-1}}_{\mathcal{W}_{\rm S},j}(Y)}\,. \end{aligned}$$

where $p^{\boldsymbol{z}_{j-1}}_{\mathcal{W}_{\rm I},j}(Y) = 0$ in the first sum. As $|\mathfrak{R}^{\star\,y}_{\mathcal{P}} \setminus \mathfrak{R}^y_{\mathcal{P}}| \leq 1$ for any y (as in world $\mathcal{W}_{\rm I}$, $\mathcal{H}^\star$ does not output collisions), we can bound this term as follows:

$$\chi^2(\boldsymbol{z}_{j-1}) \leq \frac{2^n}{2^b - 2^n \cdot |\mathfrak{R}^y_{\mathcal{P}}|} + \sum_{y \in \{0,1\}^n} \frac{(2^n \cdot |\mathfrak{R}^y_{\mathcal{P}}| - |\mathfrak{R}^\star_{\mathcal{P}}|)^2}{(2^b - 2^n \cdot |\mathfrak{R}^y_{\mathcal{P}}|)(2^b - |\mathfrak{R}^\star_{\mathcal{P}}|)^2}\,.$$

Using that $|\mathfrak{R}^\star_{\mathcal{P}}| \leq Q + q_{\mathcal{P}} \leq 2^{b-1}$ and that $|\mathfrak{R}^y_{\mathcal{P}}| \leq |\mathfrak{R}^{\star\,y}_{\mathcal{P}}| \leq 1 + q_{\mathcal{P}} \leq 2^{b-n-1}$, we can bound this term as follows:

$$\begin{aligned} \chi^2(\boldsymbol{z}_{j-1}) &\leq \frac{2}{2^{b-n}} + \frac{8}{2^{3b-2n}} \cdot \sum_{y \in \{0,1\}^n} \left(|\mathfrak{R}^y_{\mathcal{P}}| - \frac{|\mathfrak{R}^\star_{\mathcal{P}}|}{2^n}\right)^2 \\ &\leq \frac{2}{2^{b-n}} + \frac{8}{2^{3b-2n}} \cdot \left(\sum_{y \in \{0,1\}^n} (|\mathfrak{R}^y_{\mathcal{P}}|)^2 + \sum_{y \in \{0,1\}^n} \frac{(|\mathfrak{R}^\star_{\mathcal{P}}|)^2}{2^{2n}}\right) \\ &\leq \frac{2}{2^{b-n}} + \frac{8}{2^{3b-2n}} \cdot \left(\left(\sum_{y \in \{0,1\}^n} |\mathfrak{R}^y_{\mathcal{P}}|\right)^2 + \frac{(|\mathfrak{R}^\star_{\mathcal{P}}|)^2}{2^n}\right) \\ &\leq \frac{2}{2^{b-n}} + \frac{12 \cdot (Q + q_{\mathcal{P}})^2}{2^{3b-2n}}\,, \end{aligned} \tag{22}$$

again using that $1+\frac{1}{2^n}\leq 3/2$.

Inverse Query to Second Primitive. Suppose that the j-th query is an inverse query to the second primitive. For any $X\in\{0,1\}^b$, we have that

$$p^{z_{j-1}}_{\mathcal{W}_S,j}(X)=\begin{cases}\frac{1}{2^b-|\mathfrak{D}_{\mathcal{P}}\cup\mathfrak{R}_{\mathcal{H}}\|*^{b-m}|} & \text{if } X\in\{0,1\}^b\setminus\left(\mathfrak{D}_{\mathcal{P}}\cup\mathfrak{R}_{\mathcal{H}}\|*^{b-m}\right),\\ 0 & \text{otherwise},\end{cases}$$

$$p^{z_{j-1}}_{\mathcal{W}_I,j}(X)=\begin{cases}\frac{1}{2^b-|\mathfrak{D}^\star_{\mathcal{P}}\cup\mathfrak{R}^\star_{\mathcal{H}}\|*^{b-m}|} & \text{if } X\in\{0,1\}^b\setminus\left(\mathfrak{D}^\star_{\mathcal{P}}\cup\mathfrak{R}^\star_{\mathcal{H}}\|*^{b-m}\right),\\ 0 & \text{otherwise}.\end{cases}$$

As for the case of queries to the first primitive, these distributions are not the same. Choi et al. had a comparable case, but they managed to construct $\mathcal{W}_I$ in such a way that the values were drawn identically to world $\mathcal{W}_S$. Due to our omission of the initial value IV, this is (again) not an option for us. Thus, we follow a comparable reasoning as for queries to the first primitive.

We *do* have that $\left(\mathfrak{D}_{\mathcal{P}}\cup\mathfrak{R}_{\mathcal{H}}\|*^{b-m}\right)\subseteq\left(\mathfrak{D}^\star_{\mathcal{P}}\cup\mathfrak{R}^\star_{\mathcal{H}}\|*^{b-m}\right)$. Thus, (17) satisfies, for inverse queries to the second primitive,

$$\begin{aligned}\chi^2(z_{j-1})&=\sum_{X\in\{0,1\}^b}\frac{\left(p^{z_{j-1}}_{\mathcal{W}_S,j}(X)-p^{z_{j-1}}_{\mathcal{W}_I,j}(X)\right)^2}{p^{z_{j-1}}_{\mathcal{W}_S,j}(X)}\\&=\sum_{X\in\left(\mathfrak{D}^\star_{\mathcal{P}}\cup\mathfrak{R}^\star_{\mathcal{H}}\|*^{b-m}\right)\setminus\left(\mathfrak{D}_{\mathcal{P}}\cup\mathfrak{R}_{\mathcal{H}}\|*^{b-m}\right)}p^{z_{j-1}}_{\mathcal{W}_S,j}(X)\\&\quad+\sum_{X\in\{0,1\}^b\setminus\left(\mathfrak{D}^\star_{\mathcal{P}}\cup\mathfrak{R}^\star_{\mathcal{H}}\|*^{b-m}\right)}\frac{\left(p^{z_{j-1}}_{\mathcal{W}_S,j}(X)-p^{z_{j-1}}_{\mathcal{W}_I,j}(X)\right)^2}{p^{z_{j-1}}_{\mathcal{W}_S,j}(X)}.\end{aligned}$$

where $p^{z_{j-1}}_{\mathcal{W}_I,j}(X)=0$ in the first sum. As $|\left(\mathfrak{D}^\star_{\mathcal{P}}\cup\mathfrak{R}^\star_{\mathcal{H}}\|*^{b-m}\right)\setminus\left(\mathfrak{D}_{\mathcal{P}}\cup\mathfrak{R}_{\mathcal{H}}\|*^{b-m}\right)|\leq 2^{b-m}\cdot Q$, we can bound this term as follows:

$$\begin{aligned}\chi^2(z_{j-1})&\leq\frac{2^{b-m}\cdot Q}{2^b-|\mathfrak{D}_{\mathcal{P}}\cup\mathfrak{R}_{\mathcal{H}}\|*^{b-m}|}\\&\quad+2^b\cdot\frac{\left(|\mathfrak{D}_{\mathcal{P}}\cup\mathfrak{R}_{\mathcal{H}}\|*^{b-m}|-|\mathfrak{D}^\star_{\mathcal{P}}\cup\mathfrak{R}^\star_{\mathcal{H}}\|*^{b-m}|\right)^2}{(2^b-|\mathfrak{D}_{\mathcal{P}}\cup\mathfrak{R}_{\mathcal{H}}\|*^{b-m}|)\cdot(2^b-|\mathfrak{D}^\star_{\mathcal{P}}\cup\mathfrak{R}^\star_{\mathcal{H}}\|*^{b-m}|)^2}\\&\leq\frac{2^{b-m}\cdot Q}{2^b-|\mathfrak{D}_{\mathcal{P}}\cup\mathfrak{R}_{\mathcal{H}}\|*^{b-m}|}+\frac{2^{3b-2m}\cdot Q^2}{(2^b-|\mathfrak{D}^\star_{\mathcal{P}}\cup\mathfrak{R}^\star_{\mathcal{H}}\|*^{b-m}|)^3}\\&\leq\frac{2\cdot Q}{2^m}+\frac{8\cdot Q^2}{2^{2m}},\end{aligned}\tag{23}$$

where we used that $|\mathfrak{D}^\star_{\mathcal{P}}\cup\mathfrak{R}^\star_{\mathcal{H}}\|*^{b-m}|\leq 2^{b-m}\cdot Q+2^{b-m}\cdot q_{\mathcal{H}}+q_{\mathcal{P}}\leq 2^{b-1}$.

Conclusion. The j-th query is of either of the four types outlined in the beginning of this section (construction query, first primitive query, forward second primitive query (of any type), or inverse primitive query). We can thus obtain that the term of (17) satisfies

$$\begin{aligned}\chi^2(\boldsymbol{z}_{j-1}) &\leq \max\{(18),(19),(20),(21),(22),(23)\}\\ &\leq \frac{12\cdot(Q+q_{\mathcal{P}})^2}{2^{2b-n}}+\frac{6\cdot Q}{2^m}+\frac{10}{2^{b-n}},\end{aligned}$$

where we summarize that the individual terms held conditioned on the fact that $Q+q_{\mathcal{H}}+q_{\mathcal{P}}\leq 2^{m-1}$ and $1+q_{\mathcal{P}}\leq 2^{b-n-1}$. Using the chi-squared method, we obtain the following bound on the distance between $\mathcal{W}_{\mathrm{S}}$ and $\mathcal{W}_{\mathrm{I}}$:

$$\begin{aligned}\left|\Pr\left(\mathcal{D}^{\mathcal{W}_{\mathrm{S}}}=1\right)-\Pr\left(\mathcal{D}^{\mathcal{W}_{\mathrm{I}}}=1\right)\right| &\leq \left(\frac{1}{2}\sum_{j=1}^{Q+q_{\mathcal{H}}+q_{\mathcal{P}}}\mathrm{Ex}\left(\chi^2(\boldsymbol{z}_{j-1})\right)\right)^{\frac{1}{2}}\\ \leq \left(\frac{6\cdot(Q+q_{\mathcal{H}}+q_{\mathcal{P}})^3}{2^{2b-n}}+\frac{3\cdot(Q+q_{\mathcal{H}}+q_{\mathcal{P}})^2}{2^m}+\frac{5\cdot(Q+q_{\mathcal{H}}+q_{\mathcal{P}})}{2^{b-n}}\right)^{\frac{1}{2}}.\end{aligned}$$

5 Application and Comparison

We will compare the Cascade-MGF construction of (11) with the existing MGF constructions mentioned in Sect. 1, Counter-MGF and Chained-MGF. In this comparison, we aim for a security level k. Note that both Cascade-MGF and Chained-MGF can be compared regardless of the actual hash function $\mathcal{H}$ in use, and we will compare these two schemes in Sect. 5.1. The efficiency of Counter-MGF depends on the actual hash function $\mathcal{H}$ in use, and we will mount a comparison of our scheme with Counter-MGF in Sect. 5.2.

5.1 Cascade-MGF Versus Chained-MGF

The two schemes can be compared regardless of the hash function $\mathcal{H}$ in use, the only thing we require of $\mathcal{H}$ is that it must output digests of size $m=2k$ bits, for both schemes. Likewise, in order to achieve k-bit security, we set $n=2k$ for both schemes. (Strictly seen, we have a $\log_2(k)$ loss in the output, in the sense that digest blocks are of size around $2k-\log_2(k)$ bits. This makes the comparison much harder to grasp, and in addition, the same loss occurs for both schemes.)

For our construction Cascade-MGF, we can conclude from Theorem 1 that we require the width b of the permutation $\mathcal{P}$ to satisfy $b\geq\max\left\{\frac{3k+n}{2},k+n\right\}=3k$. As the permutation $\mathcal{P}$ takes as input the hash result $\mathcal{H}(M)\in\{0,1\}^{2k}$ and the counter $\langle i\rangle_l$, we can conclude that in Cascade-MGF we can take $l=b-2k$.

For fair comparison, we will consider Chained-MGF to be instantiated with a permutation-based $\mathcal{F}$ as well. We will consider it to be instantiated with either TRUNC of (3) or SOP of (4). The comparison is summarized in Table 1.

Table 1. Security of existing methods for variable-length digest generation, tailored to the use of a b-bit permutation with k-bit security. The size of the digest blocks discards logarithmic factors for simplicity – see Sect. 5.1 for details.

Construction	(Underlying) primitive(s)	Size of digest block	# primitive call(s) per digest block	Max # of digest blocks	Reference
Chained-MGF with TRUNC (3)	$\mathcal{H}, \mathcal{P}$	$b-k$	1	$\min\{2^k, 2^{b-3k}\}$	(8), [43]
Chained-MGF with SOP (4)	$\mathcal{H}, \mathcal{P}_1, \mathcal{P}_2$	b	2	$\min\{2^k, 2^{b-2k}\}$	(8), [43]
Cascade-MGF	$\mathcal{H}, \mathcal{P}$	$b-k$	1	$\min\{2^k, 2^{b-2k}\}$	(9)

Comparison to Chained-MGF with TRUNC (3). Also in this case, we require $b \geq 3k$ for the same reason as for Cascade-MGF. In order to achieve k bits of security, it is required that the initial value IV is of size k bits. As the b-bit hash function must absorb the hash output $\mathcal{H}(M) \in \{0,1\}^{2k}$, the initial value $IV \in \{0,1\}^k$, *and* the counter $\langle i \rangle_l$, we can conclude that the construction can only take $l = b - 3k$ bits of counter. (Note that also for this construction, we have omitted the $\log_2(k)$ loss in the output, in the sense that digest blocks are of size around $2k - \log_2(k)$ bits.)

We can observe that Cascade-MGF is exactly as secure and as efficient as Chained-MGF with TRUNC, with the sole difference that our construction allows for the generation of more output blocks: $\min\{2^k, 2^{b-2k}\}$ as opposed to $\min\{2^k, 2^{b-3k}\}$. The difference is particularly significant if one instantiates $\mathcal{P}$ with a small permutation. For example, focusing on $k = 128$-bit security, one can instantiate $\mathcal{P}$ using a 384-bit permutation such as GIMLI [3] or Xoodoo [14]. In this case, Cascade-MGF can be used to generate up to 2^{128} digest blocks, whereas Chained-MGF with TRUNC can only be used to generate 1 digest block (as the counter size is 0).

As a concrete application, Gunsing [20] recently proposed the tree sponge, a generalization of the sequential sponge construction with parallel absorbing and squeezing. Referring to [20, Sect. 5.3], the squeezing phase is set up via a Chained-MGF instantiated with TRUNC. Our results imply that such construction would benefit by replacing Chained-MGF with Cascade-MGF.

Comparison to Chained-MGF with SOP (4). The sum of permutation construction achieves optimal b-bit security, and by using this function as finalization in Chained-MGF, one can output b-bit digest blocks in parallel. This is more than the $(b-k)$-bit (or in fact, $b - k - \log_2(k)$-bit) digest blocks in Cascade-MGF, but the downside is that two permutation calls are made for one output block. Concretely, Cascade-MGF improves over Chained-MGF with SOP if $b/2 \leq b - k$, or equivalently if $2k \leq b$. By construction, this is always the case, recalling that the hash function output is of size $2k$ bits.

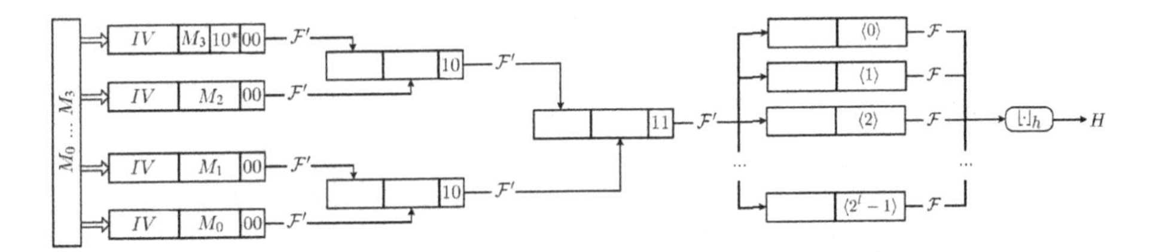

Fig. 2. The Cascade-MGF construction instantiated via a tree hash construction.

5.2 Cascade-MGF Versus Counter-MGF

A comparison between the Counter-MGF and Cascade-MGF constructions cannot be mounted without being specific about the hash function $\mathcal{H} : \{0,1\}^* \rightarrow \{0,1\}^m$ in use, where $m = 2k$ for k-bit security. Since the focus of this work is a parallel digest generation, it makes sense to consider parallelizable hashing as well, and more specifically, tree hashing.

The idea of tree hashing [33,34] is to partition the message into blocks, which are subsequently placed at the leaves of a tree. Each non-leaf node of the tree is then a compression function evaluation of its child notes. The indifferentiability of permutation-based tree hashing was analyzed by Dodis et al. [18] and Bertoni et al. [7], and more recently by Daemen et al. [15] and Gunsing et al. [21].

Let $\mathcal{P}' : \{0,1\}^{b'} \rightarrow \{0,1\}^{b'}$ be a permutation. Define $\mathcal{F}' : \{0,1\}^{b'} \rightarrow \{0,1\}^m$ as $\mathcal{F}'(X) = \text{left}_m(\mathcal{P}'(X))$. The most minimalistic permutation-based tree hashing construction that is proven to be indifferentiable initiates the leaves with an m-bit initial value IV, with message bits (possibly injectively padded), and frame bits 00. Non-leaf nodes consist of chaining bits coming from evaluations of $\mathcal{F}'$ of the children and frame bits 10. The final evaluation takes frame bits 11. The construction is depicted in Fig. 2, where it is already used to instantiate $\mathcal{H}$ in Cascade-MGF.

Daemen et al. [15] and Gunsing et al. [21] proved that if $\mathcal{P}'$ is a random permutation, this tree hash function construction behaves like a random oracle against distinguishers with a complexity of around $\min\{2^{m/2}, 2^{(b'-m)/2}\}$. It follows that k-bit security is achieved for $m \geq 2k$ and $b' \geq 4k$. Strictly seen, putting $m = 2k$, we require $b' = 4k + 2$ for the frame bits $\{00, 10, 11\}$ to be taken into account.

For the permutation $\mathcal{P}$ in Cascade-MGF, the same restrictions as before apply, and most importantly, $b \geq 3k$. This means that one can perform digest generation with a permutation that is approximately 25% smaller than the one used for hashing, without any security sacrifice. If necessary, we expect that Cascade-MGF can also run on a single permutation, or strictly seen two permutations that are similar, possibly instantiated with different round constants.

Comparison to Counter-MGF. By the generic design of the Counter-MGF construction (7), the same truncated permutation is used both in the absorbing

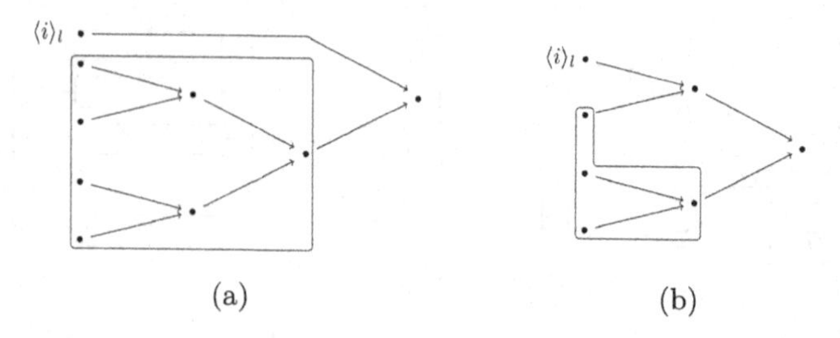

(a) (b)

Fig. 3. The Counter-MGF construction instantiated via a tree hash function. The highlighted sub-trees are independent of the counter $\langle i \rangle_l$. We emphasize that the initial points represent the result of the compression between the initial value IV and the corresponding message block/$\langle i \rangle$.

Algorithm 7: Generation of t output blocks via Counter-MGF instantiated with a tree-hash function

---

Data: input message $M \in \{0,1\}^*$
Result: output $h_0, h_1, \ldots, h_{t-1} \in \{0,1\}^m$ for $t \geq 1$

1 parse $M \| 10^* = M_0 \| M_1 \| \ldots \| M_{z-1}$ for $z \geq 1$ and $M_0, M_1, \ldots, M_{z-1} \in \{0,1\}^m$
2 let $\zeta_0, \zeta_1, \ldots, \zeta_{\lfloor \log_2(z) \rfloor} \in \{0,1\}$ be such that $z = \sum_{i=0}^{\lfloor \log_2(z) \rfloor} \zeta_i \cdot 2^i$
3 let $\mathfrak{S}_0, \mathfrak{S}_1, \ldots, \mathfrak{S}_{\lfloor \log_2(z) \rfloor}$ be empty sets
4 $l \leftarrow 0$
    `// Initially parallelizable phase`
5 **for** i *from 0 to* $\lfloor \log_2(z) \rfloor$ **do**
6   **if** $\zeta_i = 1$ **then**
        `// Computing the hash of the subtrees`
7   **for** j *from 0 to* $2^{\zeta_i} - 1$ **do**
8             $\mathfrak{S}_i \leftarrow \mathfrak{S}_i \cup \{M_l\}$
9             $l \leftarrow l + 1$
10         $h'_i \leftarrow$ tree-hash$(\mathfrak{S}_i)$
    `// Non-parallelizable phase`
11 **for** i *from 0 to* $t - 1$ **do**
12     $h_i \leftarrow$ tree-hash$(\langle i \rangle, IV)$
13   **for** j *from 0 to* $\lfloor \log_2(z) \rfloor$ **do**
14   **if** $\zeta_j = 1$ **then**
15             $h_i \leftarrow$ tree-hash(h'_j, h_i)
16 **return** $h_0, h_1, \ldots, h_{t-1}$

---

and squeezing part. Hence, compared to Cascade-MGF, it is not possible to work with a smaller permutation in the squeezing part.

Secondly, and more importantly, the cost for generating an output of size $n \cdot t$ for $t \geq 1$ could be much higher for Counter-MGF than for Cascade-MGF, depending on the size of the input message M and on the value of $m = 2k$. Consider, for example, the simplified depiction of tree hashing in Fig. 3:

- In case (a), the number of message blocks happens to be a power of 2. In this case, the digest blocks are generated in parallel, since the message is fully absorbed independently of the counter $\langle i \rangle$.
- In case (b), only part of the message can be absorbed independently of the counter $\langle i \rangle$, and the digest blocks are only partially generated in parallel (the extreme case showed in the picture occurs when the number of blocks that composed M is a power of 2 minus 1).

As a result, while the cost in terms of the number of function/permutation calls is the same for Counter-MGF and for Cascade-MGF in the first case (a), the cost is much smaller for Cascade-MGF than for Counter-MGF in the second case (b). In more detail, the cost for Counter-MGF is at least *twice* that of Cascade-MGF. Indeed, given an input message composed of z blocks, the cost for generating t output blocks via Cascade-MGF instantiated via a tree-hash function consists of $2 \cdot z - 1$ $\mathcal{F}'$-calls for the compression part, and t $\mathcal{P}$-calls for the expansion part, for a total of

$$t + 2 \cdot z - 1 \in \mathcal{O}(t)$$

function/permutation calls. In the case of Counter-MGF instantiated via a tree-hash function, the cost is

$$(1 + \mathrm{Hw}(z)) \cdot t + 2 \cdot z - \mathrm{Hw}(z) \in \mathcal{O}\left((1 + \mathrm{Hw}(z)) \cdot t\right)$$

function/permutation calls, based on the algorithm given in Algorithm 7. The difference between the two cases is approximately a factor $(1 + \mathrm{Hw}(z)) \geq 2$, and the maximum is attained when the number of blocks z is a power of 2 minus 1.

Acknowledgments. Lorenzo Grassi is supported by the European Research Council under the ERC advanced grant agreement under grant ERC-2017-ADG Nr. 788980 ESCADA. Bart Mennink is supported by the Netherlands Organisation for Scientific Research (NWO) under grant VI.Vidi.203.099.

References

1. ANSI: ANSI X9.44: Public-Key Cryptography for the Financial Services Industry Key Establishment Using Integer Factorization Cryptography (2002)
2. Aumasson, J.-P., Neves, S., Wilcox-O'Hearn, Z., Winnerlein, C.: BLAKE2: simpler, smaller, fast as MD5. In: Jacobson, M., Locasto, M., Mohassel, P., Safavi-Naini, R. (eds.) ACNS 2013. LNCS, vol. 7954, pp. 119–135. Springer, Heidelberg (2013). https://doi.org/10.1007/978-3-642-38980-1_8
3. Bernstein, D.J., Kölbl, S., Lucks, S., Massolino, P.M.C., Mendel, F., Nawaz, K., Schneider, T., Schwabe, P., Standaert, F.-X., Todo, Y., Viguier, B.: GIMLI: a cross-platform permutation. In: Fischer, W., Homma, N. (eds.) CHES 2017. LNCS, vol. 10529, pp. 299–320. Springer, Cham (2017). https://doi.org/10.1007/978-3-319-66787-4_15
4. Bertoni, G., Daemen, J., Peeters, M., Van Assche, G.: Sponge functions. In: Ecrypt Hash Workshop 2007 (2007)

5. Bertoni, G., Daemen, J., Hoffert, S., Peeters, M., Van Assche, G., Van Keer, R.: Farfalle: parallel permutation-based cryptography. IACR Trans. Symmetric Cryptol. **2017**(4), 1–38 (2017)
6. Bertoni, G., Daemen, J., Peeters, M., Van Assche, G.: On the indifferentiability of the sponge construction. In: Smart, N. (ed.) EUROCRYPT 2008. LNCS, vol. 4965, pp. 181–197. Springer, Heidelberg (2008). https://doi.org/10.1007/978-3-540-78967-3_11
7. Bertoni, G., Daemen, J., Peeters, M., Van Assche, G.: Sufficient conditions for sound tree and sequential hashing modes. Int. J. Inf. Sec. **13**(4), 335–353 (2014)
8. Bertoni, G., Daemen, J., Peeters, M., Van Assche, G.: The KECCAK reference (2011)
9. Bhattacharya, S., Nandi, M.: Full indifferentiable security of the Xor of two or more random permutations using the χ^2 method. In: Nielsen, J.B., Rijmen, V. (eds.) EUROCRYPT 2018. LNCS, vol. 10820, pp. 387–412. Springer, Cham (2018). https://doi.org/10.1007/978-3-319-78381-9_15
10. Black, J., Rogaway, P., Shrimpton, T., Stam, M.: An Analysis of the Blockcipher-Based Hash Functions from PGV. J. Cryptol. **23**(4), 519–545 (2010)
11. Chang, D., Lee, S., Nandi, M., Yung, M.: Indifferentiable security analysis of popular hash functions with prefix-free padding. In: Lai, X., Chen, K. (eds.) ASIACRYPT 2006. LNCS, vol. 4284, pp. 283–298. Springer, Heidelberg (2006). https://doi.org/10.1007/11935230_19
12. Choi, W., Lee, B., Lee, J.: Indifferentiability of truncated random permutations. In: Galbraith, S.D., Moriai, S. (eds.) ASIACRYPT 2019. LNCS, vol. 11921, pp. 175–195. Springer, Cham (2019). https://doi.org/10.1007/978-3-030-34578-5_7
13. Coron, J.-S., Dodis, Y., Malinaud, C., Puniya, P.: Merkle-Damgård revisited: how to construct a hash function. In: Shoup, V. (ed.) CRYPTO 2005. LNCS, vol. 3621, pp. 430–448. Springer, Heidelberg (2005). https://doi.org/10.1007/11535218_26
14. Daemen, J., Hoffert, S., Van Assche, G., Van Keer, R.: The design of Xoodoo and Xoofff. IACR Trans. Symmetric Cryptol. **2018**(4), 1–38 (2018)
15. Daemen, J., Mennink, B., Van Assche, G.: Sound hashing modes of arbitrary functions, permutations, and block ciphers. IACR Trans. Symmetric Cryptol. **2018**(4), 197–228 (2018)
16. Dai, W., Hoang, V.T., Tessaro, S.: Information-theoretic indistinguishability via the chi-squared method. In: Katz, J., Shacham, H. (eds.) CRYPTO 2017. LNCS, vol. 10403, pp. 497–523. Springer, Cham (2017). https://doi.org/10.1007/978-3-319-63697-9_17
17. Damgård, I.B.: A design principle for hash functions. In: Brassard, G. (ed.) CRYPTO 1989. LNCS, vol. 435, pp. 416–427. Springer, New York (1990). https://doi.org/10.1007/0-387-34805-0_39
18. Dodis, Y., Reyzin, L., Rivest, R.L., Shen, E.: Indifferentiability of permutation-based compression functions and tree-based modes of operation, with applications to MD6. In: Dunkelman, O. (ed.) FSE 2009. LNCS, vol. 5665, pp. 104–121. Springer, Heidelberg (2009). https://doi.org/10.1007/978-3-642-03317-9_7
19. Grassi, L., Mennink, B.: Security of Truncated Permutation Without Initial Value. Cryptology ePrint Archive, Paper 2022/508 (2022)
20. Gunsing, A.: Block-cipher-based tree hashing. In: Dodis, Y., Shrimpton, T. (eds.) CRYPTO 2022. LNCS, vol. 13510, pp. 205–233. Springer, Cham. (2022). https://doi.org/10.1007/978-3-031-15985-5_8
21. Gunsing, A., Daemen, J., Mennink, B.: Errata to sound hashing modes of arbitrary functions, permutations, and block ciphers. IACR Trans. Symmetric Cryptol. **2020**(3), 362–366 (2020)

22. IEEE Computer Society: IEEE 1363.1 Standard Specifications For Public-Key Cryptography (2000)
23. ISO/IEC: ISO/IEC 18033–2 Information technology - Security techniques - Encryption algorithms - Part 2: Asymmetric ciphers (2006)
24. Kaliski, B., Staddon, J.: PKCS #1: RSA cryptography specifications version 2.0. RFC 2437, pp. 1–39 (1998)
25. Knudsen, L.R., Rechberger, C., Thomsen, S.S.: The grindahl hash functions. In: Biryukov, A. (ed.) FSE 2007. LNCS, vol. 4593, pp. 39–57. Springer, Heidelberg (2007). https://doi.org/10.1007/978-3-540-74619-5_3
26. Lee, J.: Indifferentiability of the sum of random permutations toward optimal security. IEEE Trans. Inf. Theory **63**(6), 4050–4054 (2017)
27. Luykx, A., Mennink, B., Neves, S.: Security analysis of BLAKE2's modes of operation. IACR Trans. Symmetric Cryptol. **2016**(1), 158–176 (2016)
28. Mandal, A., Patarin, J., Nachef, V.: Indifferentiability beyond the Birthday Bound for the Xor of Two Public Random Permutations. In: Gong, G., Gupta, K.C. (eds.) INDOCRYPT 2010. LNCS, vol. 6498, pp. 69–81. Springer, Heidelberg (2010). https://doi.org/10.1007/978-3-642-17401-8_6
29. Maurer, U., Renner, R., Holenstein, C.: Indifferentiability, impossibility results on reductions, and applications to the random oracle methodology. In: Naor, M. (ed.) TCC 2004. LNCS, vol. 2951, pp. 21–39. Springer, Heidelberg (2004). https://doi.org/10.1007/978-3-540-24638-1_2
30. Mennink, B.: Optimal collision security in double block length hashing with single length key. In: Wang, X., Sako, K. (eds.) ASIACRYPT 2012. LNCS, vol. 7658, pp. 526–543. Springer, Heidelberg (2012). https://doi.org/10.1007/978-3-642-34961-4_32
31. Mennink, B.: Indifferentiability of double length compression functions. In: Stam, M. (ed.) IMACC 2013. LNCS, vol. 8308, pp. 232–251. Springer, Heidelberg (2013). https://doi.org/10.1007/978-3-642-45239-0_14
32. Mennink, B., Preneel, B.: On the XOR of multiple random permutations. In: Malkin, T., Kolesnikov, V., Lewko, A.B., Polychronakis, M. (eds.) ACNS 2015. LNCS, vol. 9092, pp. 619–634. Springer, Cham (2015). https://doi.org/10.1007/978-3-319-28166-7_30
33. Merkle, R.C.: Protocols for public key cryptosystems. In: Proceedings of the 1980 IEEE Symposium on Security and Privacy, pp. 122–134. IEEE Computer Society (1980)
34. Merkle, R.C.: A Digital Signature Based on a Conventional Encryption Function. In: Pomerance, C. (ed.) CRYPTO 1987. LNCS, vol. 293, pp. 369–378. Springer, Heidelberg (1988). https://doi.org/10.1007/3-540-48184-2_32
35. Merkle, R.C.: A certified digital signature. In: Brassard, G. (ed.) CRYPTO 1989. LNCS, vol. 435, pp. 218–238. Springer, New York (1990). https://doi.org/10.1007/0-387-34805-0_21
36. Merkle, R.C.: Secrecy, authentication and public key systems (1979), Ph.D. thesis, UMI Research Press
37. NIST: NIST SP800-108: Recommendation for Key Derivation Using Pseudorandom Functions (2009)
38. NIST: NIST FIPS 202: SHA-3 Standard: Permutation-Based Hash and Extendable-Output Functions (2015)
39. Preneel, B., Govaerts, R., Vandewalle, J.: Hash functions based on block ciphers: a synthetic approach. In: Stinson, D.R. (ed.) CRYPTO 1993. LNCS, vol. 773, pp. 368–378. Springer, Heidelberg (1994). https://doi.org/10.1007/3-540-48329-2_31

40. Rabin, M.O.: Digitalized signatures. Foundations of Secure Computation, pp. 155–166 (1978)
41. Rivest, R., et al.: The MD6 hash function - A proposal to NIST for SHA-3 (2008), submission to NIST's SHA-3 competition
42. RSA Security: PKCS#1 v2.1: RSA Cryptography Standard (2002)
43. Suzuki, K., Yasuda, K.: On the security of the cryptographic mask generation functions standardized by ANSI, IEEE, ISO/IEC, and NIST (2012). NTT Technical Review

Puncturable Key Wrapping and Its Applications

Matilda Backendal(✉), Felix Günther, and Kenneth G. Paterson

Department of Computer Science, ETH Zurich, Zurich, Switzerland
{mbackendal,kenny.paterson}@inf.ethz.ch, mail@felixguenther.info

Abstract. We introduce *puncturable key wrapping* (PKW), a new cryptographic primitive that supports fine-grained forward security properties in symmetric key hierarchies. We develop syntax and security definitions, along with provably secure constructions for PKW from simpler components (AEAD schemes and puncturable PRFs). We show how PKW can be applied in two distinct scenarios. First, we show how to use PKW to achieve forward security for TLS 1.3 0-RTT session resumption, even when the server's long-term key for generating session tickets gets compromised. This extends and corrects a recent work of Aviram, Gellert, and Jager (Journal of Cryptology, 2021). Second, we show how to use PKW to build a protected file storage system with file shredding, wherein a client can outsource encrypted files to a potentially malicious or corrupted cloud server whilst achieving strong forward-security guarantees, relying only on local key updates.

1 Introduction

Key wrapping. Key encryption, or *key wrapping*, is a mechanism often deployed to build symmetric key hierarchies: systems in which the confidentiality and integrity of multiple cryptographic keys are protected by a single (master wrapping) key. The wrapped keys may in turn be used to secure data at a more fine-grained level, e.g., at the level of individual files, messages, or financial transactions. This hierarchical approach eases key management: it allows strong but more expensive protection to be applied to a small number of wrapping keys while limiting the security impact if individual wrapped keys are exposed. Key wrapping is widely used in practice; specific schemes have been standardized by NIST in [24]. Formal foundations for key wrapping were established in [47].

As a pertinent example, when using the pre-shared key (PSK) mode of TLS 1.3 [45] for session resumption, new sessions between client and server are protected by independent, symmetric keys (denoted PSK) established in an earlier session. To reduce storage overhead, servers often use a long-term symmetric encryption key to *wrap* PSKs into so-called *tickets*. These tickets are sent to the client, thereby outsourcing the PSK storage from the server to the client.

Another example of key hierarchies is found in cloud storage systems, where service providers encrypt data before storing it on their servers—so called *encryption at rest*. The encryption is done to meet customer demand and regulatory

S. Agrawal and D. Lin (Eds.): ASIACRYPT 2022, LNCS 13792, pp. 651–681, 2022.
https://doi.org/10.1007/978-3-031-22966-4_22

requirements. To ensure good key-hygiene, best practices stipulate that separate encryption keys be used for separate files (or even parts of large files). To this end, cloud storage providers use a new *data encryption key* (DEK) to encrypt each (part of a) file. The DEK is then wrapped using a *key encryption key* (KEK) and stored together with the encrypted file. Here, using a key hierarchy also allows for a form of *key rotation*, a process in which a key is replaced by a fresh one, and the encrypted data is updated to be secured under the new key. The technique used by all four of Amazon Web Services [4], Google Cloud [30], IBM Cloud [34] and Microsoft Azure [42] is to rotate only the KEK rather than all of the DEKs. This limits the amount of data that needs to be re-encrypted under the new KEK to just the DEKs that were wrapped under the original KEK, rather than the actual files themselves. This approach provides an efficient but security-limited form of key rotation [25].

Forward-Secure Session Resumption and Puncturable Encryption. Aviram, Gellert, and Jager (AGJ) [1,2] observed that the key hierarchy induced by the ticketing mechanism in TLS 1.3 PSK mode can be used to achieve *forward security* for resumed sessions. By updating the Session Ticket Encryption Key (STEK) after accepting the ticket of a resumed session, and deleting the corresponding PSK, the confidentiality of the session is guaranteed even against an attacker who later compromises the STEK. AGJ formalized this idea with their notion of a forward-secure *session resumption protocol.* The per-session forward security enjoyed by such a resumption protocol is reminiscent of the fine-grained forward security achieved by *puncturable encryption* [31], and indeed, AGJ make use of *puncturable* pseudo-random functions (PPRFs) [13,17,36] for their construction. Their innovation naturally begs the question: Can puncturing be combined with key hierarchies to bring fine-grained forward security also to other applications? This work provides the affirmative response.

Our Contributions. We investigate how puncturing can be combined with key wrapping to provide fine-grained forward security in applications using a symmetric key hierarchy. To this end, we introduce a new cryptographic primitive that we call *puncturable key wrapping* (PKW). We provide formal definitions, relations between security notions, and an efficient, generic construction for PKW. We also show how to use PKW in two sample applications: TLS ticketing (inspired by [2], but addressing several shortcomings of that work) and protected file storage. We argue that, while PKW is closely related to existing primitives like PPRFs, it provides a useful abstraction that more intuitively captures what is needed for achieving fine-grained forward security in symmetric key hierarchies. This makes building applications conceptually simpler and less error-prone.[1]

[1] A broad analogy that readers may find useful: PKW is to PPRFs as AEAD is to block ciphers.

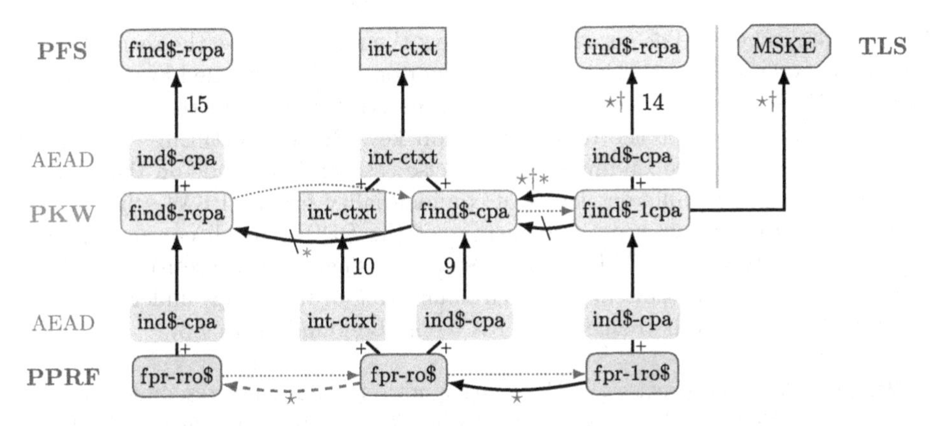

Fig. 1. Security notions and relations for PPRFs, puncturable key-wrapping (PKW), protected file storge (PFS), and TLS ticketing (TLS). Confidentiality/forward security notions are in rounded boxes, integrity notions in rectangular boxes. Solid lines indicate implications, with numbers referencing the respective theorem in this paper (others in [5]) and a plus + when combining several notions. Barred lines denote separations, dotted lines trivial implications, and dashed lines non-tight implications. A star ⋆ or dagger † next to an arrow indicates that the implication holds if puncture invariance (Definitions 2, 5), resp. consistency (Definition 6) is assumed; a ∗ indicates additional assumptions.

Puncturable Key Wrapping. A puncturable key-wrapping scheme provides the basic functionality needed for a symmetric key hierarchy: algorithms to wrap and unwrap data encryption keys under a master secret key. Additionally, a puncturing algorithm allows the master secret key to be updated such that specific wrapped data encryption keys are rendered irrecoverable. Our PKW syntax merges classical key wrapping/deterministic authenticated encryption [47] with tag-based puncturable encryption [31]. The resulting primitive allows authenticated headers and uses tags to enable fine-grained puncturing of ciphertexts. The puncturing tags simplify the exposition of PKW and allow for versatile treatments of the targeted applications: e.g., tags may be chosen via a counter when keeping state or ordering is required, or as random strings when meta-data privacy is a concern (cf. [7]). This contrasts with the foundational work on (non-puncturable) key wrapping [47], where randomness needed for secure wrapping is effectively extracted from the wrapped key in the SIV construction.

We introduce four different security notions for PKW schemes (see Fig. 1), three relating to confidentiality (find$-cpa: a classical "real-or-random" notion, find$-rcpa: additionally allowing "real" wrappings, and find$-1cpa: a one-time challenge notion) and one to integrity (of ciphertexts, int-ctxt). They are developed with an eye towards applications, catering to the needs of key hierarchies found in cloud storage systems and the TLS ticketing mechanism. Hence, all four are in a multi-key (or multi-user) setting [6]. We also provide a simple and generic construction for a PKW scheme based on a PPRF and a nonce-based

AEAD [46] scheme. The core idea is to view the master key as the secret key of a PPRF; wrapping of a selected data encryption key is performed by evaluating the PPRF on the tag to generate a one-time AEAD key, and then using that AEAD key to encrypt the data encryption key. PKW puncturing equates to PPRF puncturing. Depending on the precise assumptions made on the PPRF, we reach our three different levels of confidentiality for the PKW scheme; the integrity notion requires nothing further of the PPRF. In all cases, standard multi-user notions of AEAD security suffice. Using a misuse-resistant AEAD scheme [47] could further enable batch puncturing of wrappings under the same tag. Full details of our treatment of PKW can be found in Sect. 3.

PPRFs. While the precise PPRF security notions we require resemble those in prior work [13,17,36,48], they appear to be, strictly speaking, new. This shows how an application-driven analysis can bring to the surface new requirements on existing primitives. In Sect. 2 (see also Fig. 1), we explore the relations between our different PPRF notions and discuss possible instantiations, e.g., using the GGM construction for PRFs (as adapted to PPRFs in e.g. [36]).

To summarize, we obtain a generic instantiation of PKW, achieving a variety of security notions from standard primitives (AEAD schemes and PRGs).

Application: Forward-Secure Session Resumption. Equipped with our new primitive, we revisit the idea of Aviram, Gellert, and Jager (AGJ) [2] for achieving forward security for the zero round-trip time (0-RTT) data that is immediately sent by clients in the TLS 1.3 PSK resumption mode. In Sect. 4, we show how a find$-1cpa-secure PKW scheme can readily be deployed for TLS ticketing to yield forward-secure TLS 1.3 0-RTT resumption that is secure in the sense of a multi-stage key exchange (MSKE) protocol [27]; see also Fig. 1. Using PKWs in place of PPRFs (as in AGJ) permits us to take a more generic and abstract viewpoint. This not only directly facilitates constructions offering differing functionality and security guarantees, but also enabled us to identify and correct some technical issues arising in the approach of AGJ.

In particular, building TLS ticketing from PKW allows us to seamlessly switch to a more *privacy-friendly* approach, addressing an open problem in [2]: by sampling tags randomly, we are able to make TLS tickets indistinguishable from random, whereas the AGJ proposal uses a counter in the construction, making their tickets potentially linkable to the time of issuance. Thus our approach can alleviate privacy concerns for TLS ticketing, e.g., regarding tracking users on the web by passively observing network traffic.

The integration of a session resumption protocol into the TLS 1.3 resumption handshake is described in [2, Section 4]. Rephrasing the AGJ proposal in the language of puncturable key wrapping led us to discover conceptual and technical issues in the security model, the proposed protocol, and the proof that prevent the proposal of AGJ from being forward secure, as we discuss in Sect. 4. Specifically, the security model used in [2] does not reflect the ticketing mechanism of a key exchange protocol in how pre-shared secrets are sampled, registered with parties, and potentially corrupted. Furthermore, the proposed protocol encrypts the TLS resumption master secret RMS in the session ticket. Since RMS is used to derive multiple PSK values, this violates forward security (an adversary learning RMS from one ticket can use it to decrypt prior sessions using a PSK derived from the same RMS). However, this can be easily fixed by ticketing the respective PSK instead of RMS. Finally, we identified overlooked steps and missing underlying assumptions in the AGJ security proof, which were surfaced when applying our PKW formalism. We address all these points in our treatment of forward-secure session resumption for TLS 1.3, see Sect. 4.

Application: Protected File Storage. As a second application example, we show in Sect. 5 how our new PKW primitive can be used in an encrypted file storage system to give forward security to deleted files. This application is motivated by the current trust assumptions in cloud storage systems, where the confidentiality of the stored data rarely extends to the service provider. Indeed, if the master key in the key hierarchy is managed by the cloud, then the service provider can trivially decrypt any file. The aim of our protected file storage (PFS) system is to provide strong security guarantees for the user, even when encrypted files are outsourced to a malicious or corrupted storage system.

Using a PKW scheme, a client can locally encrypt files under separate data encryption keys, wrap the DEKs with its master key (acting as a KEK) and then outsource both the encrypted files and the wrapped keys to the cloud. In addition to relieving the user of the need to store anything beyond the master key for the PKW scheme, our PFS system also allows secure *shredding* of files: by puncturing the master key such that a specific wrapped DEK is rendered irrecoverable, the file encrypted by the DEK is made permanently inaccessible, even if the ciphertext is not actually deleted by the cloud storage provider when the client requests it to be. This means that a motivated attacker with access both to the encrypted files *and* the secret key of the user will not be able to compromise the contents of files that were shredded before the user key was compromised. The system hence provides very strong forward security guarantees for shredded files. Crucially in our approach, there is no need for the user to trust the storage provider to actually delete the shredded files, an assumption which would seldom hold in practice due to the presence of backups for disaster recovery purposes (see, e.g., [30]) or bugs in the deletion process [44].

An additional feature of our PFS system is that, in line with current industry practice, it supports key rotation at the KEK level. Key rotation extends the lifetime of encrypted data, overcomes usage limits of encryption through rekeying, and supports forward security in practice. It is also important given that the PKW schemes we build have a finite puncturing capability; KEK rotation is then used to restore puncturing capability whenever needed. The multi-key aspect of our PKW security notions readily supports this key rotation.

As core contributions here, we define a syntax for PFS and security notions capturing confidentiality, forward security, and integrity of stored files in a PFS scheme. We show how all of these notions can be achieved by building a PFS scheme from a PKW scheme and an AEAD scheme in a natural and efficient way. We actually provide two different routes to proving our main results on the forward security of PFS, as represented in the first and third column in Fig. 1. These routes rely on different security assumptions on the underlying cryptographic components, specifically the PKW scheme used, and result in security theorems with different tightness properties—using a stronger PKW scheme yields a tighter proof of security for the PFS scheme. This in turn relates to the properties required of the underlying PPRF in each of the two routes. While the left, tighter, route requires a PPRF satisfying the strongest security notion (fpr-rro$) as a basic building block—an assumption which, to the best of our knowledge, generally relies on a non-tight (complexity-leveraging) reduction to weaker PPRF notions—it asks less from the building blocks in terms of other properties. Specifically, it avoids the technical requirements of puncture invariance and consistency which we detail in Sect. 3 and that not all PPRFs may provide, yet which are required for the right, less tight route. The two routes hence show that secure PFS schemes can be constructed from different levels of PKW (and PPRF) schemes; we see this as motivating future work on efficient PKW (or PPRF) constructions that directly fulfill our strong security notions.

We stress that the aim of our PFS system is to showcase how integrating PKWs into existing symmetric key hierarchies can improve security for the *cryptographic core* of secure file storage systems. Building a full-blown system is left to future work.

Further Related Work. The origins of forward security, in the context of key exchange, date back to Günther [32] and Diffie et al. [23]. A helpful systematization is given by Boyd and Gellert [16].

Green and Miers [31] introduced *puncturable* (public-key) encryption as a means of achieving fine-grained forward security. The ideas of [31] were applied to 0-RTT key exchange and session resumption for TLS 1.3 in [2,22,33] as well as symmetric key exchange [3,15]. The treatment of [15] is for general key exchange, where both parties share a key to a PPRF and puncture it in a semi-synchronized manner. By contrast, our approach to achieving forward security for TLS 1.3 PSK resumption mode using session tickets (in common with [2]) targets the use of puncturable primitives in a "one-sided" setting, where only the server holds the key and performs puncturing operations.

Puncturing techniques have further been used in the context of searchable encryption [51,52]. Fine-grained forward security is also targeted in Derived Unique Keys Per Transaction (DUKPT) [18]: keys are derived in a tree structure and used in a one-time manner, with the aim of improving security against side-channel attacks on weakly protected devices, e.g., payment terminals.

The idea of *secure outsourced storage* is not new. Blaze [10] designed a "Cryptographic File System" already in 1993 to empower users to encrypt their files, preventing remote file servers used for storage from gaining plaintext access to user data. A rich body of work followed suit, improving on and expanding the security guarantees in the direction of, for example, data integrity and file sharing [43], group collaboration [26], access pattern and metadata hiding [19,20] and minimizing trust assumptions [41]. There is also a plethora of services running on top of existing storage systems, for example [14,39]. *Key rotation* for symmetric encryption is widely used by outsourced storage systems in practice, but was only recently formally treated, see [25] and follow-up works [37,40] including work using puncturing [50].

Our approach to secure file storage shares the aim of removing the need to trust the storage provider for confidentiality, but we specifically focus on adding *forward security* for individual files. Boneh and Lipton [12] introduced the idea of using key deletion to revoke access to encrypted files, with an emphasis on file backup systems. Their proposal uses linear data structures to store keys, but lacks the fine-grained forward security and key rotation our PFS scheme offers.

A more recent proposal, BurnBox [54], recognizing the difficulty of truly secure file deletion, introduced self-revocable encryption to limit the power of compelled searches of devices. BurnBox achieves fine-grained forward security for deleted files via a tree-based key hierarchy, storing the root in erasable storage. It further hides file metadata in a protected lookup table, an approach we also suggest for our system. On the surface, these properties make BurnBox very similar to our PFS concept. However, the main goal of BurnBox is not forward security, but the much stronger notion of *compelled access security*, which encompasses temporarily revoking file access when device compromise is expected and further goals such as deletion/revocation obliviousness and timing privacy. This forces BurnBox to use highly application-specific approaches, rely on secure storage, and compromise on efficiency (e.g., of file lookups, in favor of privacy). In contrast, our approach is more generic, requires fewer assumptions, and can directly benefit from optimizations of the underlying PKW or PPRF schemes.

Notation and Conventions. For a string $a \in \{0,1\}^*$, $|a|$ denotes its bit length. By $x \leftarrow_{\$} S$, we denote sampling x uniformly at random (u.a.r.) from a set S of size $|S|$. For sets $\mathcal{S}_1, \mathcal{S}_2$, the shorthand $\mathcal{S}_1 \overset{\cup}{\leftarrow} \mathcal{S}_2$ denotes $\mathcal{S}_1 \leftarrow \mathcal{S}_1 \cup \mathcal{S}_2$. We write $X = (x_1, x_2, \ldots, x_n)$ for an n-tuple and $X \mathrel{+}= x$ or $X \mathrel{-}= x$ for adding, resp. removing, an element x to/from a list or set. By $x \| y$ we denote the concatenation of strings or lists x and y. For an algorithm A, we denote by $y \leftarrow A(x_1, \ldots; r)$ running A on inputs $x_1, \ldots$ and random coins r with output y; by $y \leftarrow_{\$} A(x_1, \ldots)$ running A on uniformly random coins. The distinguished output $\perp$ indicates rejecting; by convention we require that any algorithm on input $\perp$ also outputs $\perp$.

We use the game-playing framework of [8]. By $\Pr[\mathbf{G}(\mathcal{A}) \Rightarrow x]$ we denote the probability that game $\mathbf{G}$ interacting with adversary $\mathcal{A}$ outputs x; where $\Pr[\mathbf{G}(\mathcal{A})]$ is a shorthand for $\Pr[\mathbf{G}(\mathcal{A}) \Rightarrow \text{true}]$. In games, adversaries implicitly have access to all described oracles unless otherwise indicated, and integer variables, strings, set variables and boolean variables are initialized, respectively, to 0, the empty string ε, the empty set $\emptyset$, and false, unless otherwise specified.

2 Puncturable PRFs, Security Notions, and Relations

Puncturable PRFs (PPRFs) were conceived of independently in [13,17,36]. We recall the definition from Sahai and Waters [48], but restrict our attention to PPRFs with deterministic puncturing algorithms.

Definition 1 (PPRF). *A puncturable pseudorandom function* $\mathsf{PPRF} = (\mathsf{KeyGen}, \mathsf{Eval}, \mathsf{Punc})$ *is a triple of algorithms with three associated sets; the secret-key space* $\mathcal{SK}$*, the domain* $\mathcal{X}$ *and the range* $\mathcal{Y}$*.*

- *Via* $sk \leftarrow\$ \mathsf{KeyGen}()$*, the probabilistic key generation algorithm* KeyGen*, taking no input, outputs the secret key* $sk \in \mathcal{SK}$*.*
- *Via* $y/\bot \leftarrow \mathsf{Eval}(sk, x)$*, the function evaluation algorithm* Eval*, on input the secret key* sk *and an element* $x \in \mathcal{X}$ *outputs* $y \in \mathcal{Y}$ *or, to indicate failure,* $\bot$*.*
- *Via* $sk' \leftarrow \mathsf{Punc}(sk, x)$*, the deterministic puncturing algorithm* Punc*, on input the secret key* sk *and an element* $x \in \mathcal{X}$ *outputs an updated secret key* $sk' \in \mathcal{SK}$*.*

For correctness *we require that for all* $sk \in \mathcal{SK}$ *and all* $x, y \in \mathcal{X}$*:*

(1) $\Pr[\,\mathsf{Eval}(sk_0, x) \neq \bot \mid sk_0 \leftarrow\$ \mathsf{KeyGen}()\,] = 1$.
(2) If $sk' \leftarrow \mathsf{Punc}(sk, x)$ *and* $y \neq x$*, then* $\mathsf{Eval}(sk, y) = \mathsf{Eval}(sk', y)$.
(3) If $sk' \leftarrow \mathsf{Punc}(sk, x)$*, then* $\mathsf{Eval}(sk', x) = \bot$.

Requirement (1) ensures that for any freshly generated secret key sk_0 *and for any* $x \in \mathcal{X}$*,* $\mathsf{Eval}(sk_0, x)$ *will not be* $\bot$*. Requirement (2) says that puncturing any secret key* sk *on* x *only affects the evaluation of* x*. Requirement (3) demands that the evaluation of a punctured point will always be* $\bot$*.*

Requirement (3)—which goes beyond prior PPRF definitions [2,48]—is needed to achieve integrity in applications like TLS ticketing, as we shall see in Sect. 4. Alternative to phrasing it as a correctness property, one could implicitly demand it in the security games. We find the explicit requirement cleaner and argue that it captures the intuitive understanding that PPRF function evaluation on punctured points should "fail". Alternative concepts such as private puncturable PRFs [11] could achieve similar results, but are harder to construct.

Following [2], we define an additional property of PPRFs called "puncture invariance" which demands that the scheme is insensitive to the order in which punctures are performed. I.e., the puncturing operation is commutative with respect to the resulting secret key. As noted in [2], this property enables reductions that change the order of punctures without an adversary later compromising the secret key noticing; this is necessary for example to have our single-challenge notion (fpr-1ro$) imply our core PPRF notion (fpr-ro$), as we shall see.

Definition 2 (PPRF puncture invariance). *A puncturable pseudorandom function* $\mathsf{PPRF} = (\mathsf{KeyGen}, \mathsf{Eval}, \mathsf{Punc})$ *is* puncture invariant *if for all keys* $sk \in \mathcal{SK}$ *and all* $x_0, x_1 \in \mathcal{X}$ *it holds that* $\mathsf{Punc}(\mathsf{Punc}(sk, x_0), x_1) = \mathsf{Punc}(\mathsf{Punc}(sk, x_1), x_0)$.

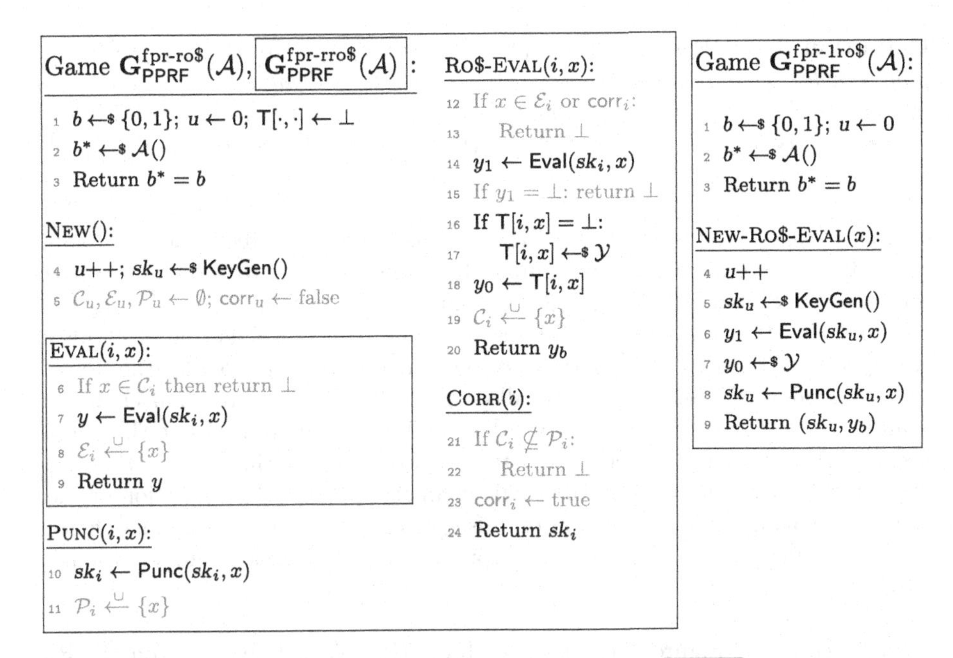

Fig. 2. Left: Games defining real-or-\$ (fpr-ro\$, without the boxed EVAL oracle) and real-and-real-or-\$ (fpr-rro\$, with $\mathcal{A}$ having access to EVAL) forward pseudorandomness. Right: Game defining one-time forward pseudorandomness (fpr-1ro\$) PPRF security. Grey code prevents trivial attacks. (Color figure online)

PPRF Security. We define three security notions for PPRFs, all in the multi-user setting [6], capturing the combined forward security and pseudorandomness goals, or *forward pseudorandomness* (fpr) for short. Let us start with our core *forward pseudorandomness* notion (fpr-ro\$), given in Fig. 2. It is an extension of classical PRF security, where the adversary is given oracle access (RO\$-EVAL) either to the real function evaluated on a hidden key, or a lazily-sampled random function. Forward security is captured through access to a puncturing oracle (PUNC) as well as corruption oracle (CORR), through which the adversary can obtain secret keys that have been punctured on all challenge points.

Our second, stronger notion, *forward pseudorandomness with real evaluations* (fpr-rro\$), in addition gives the adversary access to a real evaluation oracle (EVAL), capturing that real evaluations do not help distinguishing challenge outputs (even post-corruption).

In our third, weaker notion, *single-challenge forward pseudorandomness* (fpr-1ro\$), the adversary only gets a single challenge evaluation under each key. The challenge is obtained from oracle NEW-RO\$-EVAL, which on input a domain point x returns either the real function evaluation of x under the (unpunctured) secret key (in the "real" world), or a string drawn u.a.r. from $\mathcal{Y}$ (in the "ideal" world). Additionally the adversary obtains the secret key punctured on x. As usual, the adversary wins if it can distinguish the real world from the ideal one.

Definition 3 (PPRF security (fpr-ro\$, fpr-rro\$, fpr-1ro\$)**).** *Let* PPRF *be a puncturable pseudorandom function. We define the advantage of an adversary* $\mathcal{A}$ *against the forward pseudorandomness* $X \in \{\text{fpr-ro\$}, \text{fpr-rro\$}, \text{fpr-1ro\$}\}$ *of* PPRF *as* $\mathbf{Adv}^{X}_{\mathsf{PPRF}}(\mathcal{A}) = 2\left|\Pr\left[\mathbf{G}^{X}_{\mathsf{PPRF}}(\mathcal{A}) \Rightarrow \text{true}\right] - \frac{1}{2}\right|$, *where game* $\mathbf{G}^{X}_{\mathsf{PPRF}}(\mathcal{A})$ *is given in Fig. 2.*

Comparison to Prior Work. Our PPRF notions resemble those in prior work, but also differ in several ways. For example, fpr-1ro\$ is similar to the non-adaptive notion in [2,48], but restricted to a single challenge. Through a multi-key hybrid argument [6], their notion implies ours. The adaptive "*rand*" notion of [2] most closely corresponds to our fpr-rro\$ notion, but our notion provides the adversary with more flexibility by both allowing multiple real-or-random challenge evaluations under each key (compared to a single evaluation under the single key in [2]) and giving it access both to a separate puncturing oracle (the *rand* experiment only punctures on the single challenge point) and corruption oracle, thereby allowing multiple key compromises of keys punctured on points chosen by the adversary. Our middle notion fpr-ro\$ is, to the best of our knowledge, new.

PPRF Relations. Figure 1 (on page 3) shows the relations between our PPRF security notions. The trivial implications (dotted lines) immediately arise from restricting the adversary. As an example, fpr-rro\$ implies fpr-ro\$ because an adversary against the fpr-rro\$ security can simply ignore the EVAL-oracle. Similarly fpr-ro\$ implies fpr-1ro\$.

In the other direction, fpr-1ro\$ implies fpr-ro\$ for any puncture-invariant PPRF PPRF. That is, for any adversary $\mathcal{A}$ against the fpr-ro\$ security of PPRF, there exists an adversary $\mathcal{B}$ running in approximately the same time as $\mathcal{A}$ such that $\mathbf{Adv}^{\text{fpr-ro\$}}_{\mathsf{PPRF}}(\mathcal{A}) \leq q_{\text{ro\$}} \cdot \mathbf{Adv}^{\text{fpr-1ro\$}}_{\mathsf{PPRF}}(\mathcal{B})$, via a standard hybrid argument, where puncture invariance ensures that reorderings of punctures do not affect simulation of the later-corrupted secret key.

Via a non-tight reduction, we can also show that fpr-ro\$ implies fpr-rro\$ for a puncture-invariant PPRF. This is again via a hybrid argument, which however now involves guessing the input to the challenge query RO\$-EVAL under each key (so-called complexity leveraging [13,17]), resulting in reduction loss proportional to the size of the PPRF domain.

Instantiations From the Literature. One, by now folklore, way of building a PPRF is to use the GGM PRF construction via a tree of pseudorandom-generator (PRG) evaluations [29], extended with a puncturing algorithm, as first noted by [13,17,36]. The core idea to enable puncturing on a domain point x in a GGM PRF is to update the secret key, removing nodes on the path to x in the PRG tree and adding all nodes on the co-path from the root to x. For a more in-depth description and argument of security we refer to [2,36]. Note that the GGM-based construction is correct and puncture invariant, and hence, via our established relations, yields an fpr-ro\$-secure PPRF. Additionally, for this specific construction, adaptive security can be achieved with a loss factor that is only quasi-polynomial in the input length, improving greatly over the exponential loss of complexity leveraging [28]. An alternative construction for a PPRF with security based on the Strong RSA assumption can be found in [2].

3 Puncturable Key Wrapping

We now present our core cryptographic primitive, *puncturable key wrapping* (PKW). With puncturable key wrapping, we merge the notion of key wrapping, originally extensively studied by Rogaway and Shrimpton [47], with tag-based puncturable encryption [31], adapted to the symmetric setting, to capture forward security through puncturing. Puncturable key wrapping, beyond the key K to be wrapped, hence takes a *tag* T used as a pointer for puncturing, as well as optional associated *header* data H which is authenticated along with the wrapped key (akin to associated data in AEAD). In the following, we give syntax, security, and further notions for this new primitive.

Definition 4 (PKW scheme). *A* puncturable key-wrapping scheme $\mathsf{PKW} = (\mathsf{KeyGen}, \mathsf{Wrap}, \mathsf{Unwrap}, \mathsf{Punc})$ *is a 4-tuple of algorithms with four associated sets; the secret-key space $\mathcal{SK}$, the tag space $\mathcal{T}$, the header space $\mathcal{H}$ and the wrap-key space $\mathcal{K}$. Associated to the scheme is a ciphertext-length function* $\mathsf{cl} : \mathbb{N} \to \mathbb{N}$.

- *Via $sk \leftarrow_{\$} \mathsf{KeyGen}()$, the probabilistic key generation algorithm* KeyGen, *taking no input, outputs a secret key $sk \in \mathcal{SK}$.*
- *Via $C/\bot \leftarrow \mathsf{Wrap}(sk, T, H, K)$, the deterministic wrapping algorithm* Wrap *on input a secret key $sk \in \mathcal{SK}$, a tag $T \in \mathcal{T}$, a header $H \in \mathcal{H}$ and a key $K \in \mathcal{K}$ outputs a ciphertext $C \in \{0,1\}^{\mathsf{cl}(|K|)}$ or, to indicate failure, $\bot$.*
- *Via $K/\bot \leftarrow \mathsf{Unwrap}(sk, T, H, C)$, the deterministic unwrapping algorithm* Unwrap *on input a secret key $sk \in \mathcal{SK}$, a tag $T \in \mathcal{T}$, a header $H \in \mathcal{H}$ and a ciphertext $C \in \{0,1\}^*$ returns a key $K \in \mathcal{K}$ or, to indicate failure, $\bot$.*
- *Via $sk' \leftarrow \mathsf{Punc}(sk, T)$, the deterministic puncturing algorithm* Punc *on input a secret key $sk \in \mathcal{SK}$ and a tag $T \in \mathcal{T}$ returns a potentially updated secret key $sk' \in \mathcal{SK}$.*

Correctness *of a PKW scheme intuitively demands that a wrapped key can be recovered from its wrapping ciphertext unless the secret key has been punctured on the tag used for the wrapping step, i.e., even if the secret key has been punctured on other tags. Formally, we require that for all $T \in \mathcal{T}$, $H \in \mathcal{H}$, $K \in \mathcal{K}$, and all tuples $\bar{T}_1, \bar{T}_2 \in \mathcal{T}^*$ where $T \notin \bar{T}_1$ and $T \notin \bar{T}_2$,*

$$\Pr\left[\mathsf{Unwrap}(sk_{\setminus \bar{T}_1}, T, H, \mathsf{Wrap}(sk_{\setminus \bar{T}_2}, T, H, K)) = K \mid sk \leftarrow_{\$} \mathsf{KeyGen}()\right] = 1.$$

Here $sk_{\setminus(T_1,T_2,\ldots,T_n)} = \mathsf{Punc}(\ldots(\mathsf{Punc}(\mathsf{Punc}(sk, T_1), T_2), \ldots), T_n)$ is shorthand for the secret key obtained via puncturing sk in order on $T_1, \ldots, T_n \in \mathcal{T}$.

Analogously to Definition 2 for PPRFs, we also define *puncture invariance* for PKW schemes, demanding that the order of punctures does not affect the resulting secret key.

Definition 5 (PKW puncture invariance). *A puncturable key-wrapping scheme* $\mathsf{PKW} = (\mathsf{KeyGen}, \mathsf{Wrap}, \mathsf{Unwrap}, \mathsf{Punc})$ *is* puncture invariant *if for all keys* $sk \in \mathcal{SK}$ *and all tags* $T_0, T_1 \in \mathcal{T}$ *it holds that*

$$\mathsf{Punc}(\mathsf{Punc}(sk, T_0), T_1) = \mathsf{Punc}(\mathsf{Punc}(sk, T_1), T_0).$$

Additionally, we introduce a property of PKW schemes which we call *consistency*, inspired by the definition of consistent puncturable signature schemes in [9]. A consistent PKW scheme is one for which the output of algorithm Wrap only depends on the tag, header and wrap-key input, and not on the (puncturing) state of the secret key—except for when the output is $\perp$ due to puncturing.

Definition 6 (PKW consistency). *A puncturable key wrapping scheme* $\mathsf{PKW} = (\mathsf{KeyGen}, \mathsf{Wrap}, \mathsf{Unwrap}, \mathsf{Punc})$ *is* consistent *if for all keys* $K \in \mathcal{K}$, *all headers* $H \in \mathcal{H}$, *all tags* $(T_1, \ldots, T_n) \in \mathcal{T}^*$ *and all* $T \in \mathcal{T} \setminus \{T_1, \ldots, T_n\}$ *it holds that*

$$\Pr\left[\mathsf{Wrap}(sk, T, H, K) = \mathsf{Wrap}(sk_{\setminus(T_1,\ldots,T_n)}, T, H, K) \mid sk \leftarrow\!\!\$\ \mathsf{KeyGen}()\right] = 1.$$

Puncture invariance and consistency guarantee a kind of indifference of the PKW scheme with respect to puncturing, allowing sequences of punctures and wrappings to be flexibly reordered without affecting the scheme's future behavior. As we shall see, these properties are important to consider when deploying PKW schemes in, and proving the security of, higher-level applications.

3.1 PKW Security

Confidentiality. Following Rogaway and Shrimpton [47], we adopt indistinguishability from random bits (ind$) as the appropriate notion to model confidentiality for (puncturable) key-wrapping schemes. Our three confidentiality notions, formalized in Fig. 3, capture forward security in the sense that the confidentiality guarantees hold also after compromise of the secret key, given that it has been appropriately punctured prior to corruption to avoid trivial wins. As before, they are all in the multi-key (or multi-user) setting [6][2]

Our first notion, which we call find$-cpa, can be viewed as a form of ind$-cpa security adapted to the PKW setting. The adversary is given access to a challenge wrapping oracle RO$-WRAP, which on input a key index i, a tag T, a header H and a key K chosen by the adversary, returns either an honest wrapping of K under secret key sk_i, or a random bit-string of length $\mathsf{cl}(|K|)$. Forward security is captured via a corruption oracle CORR which allows the adversary to compromise the current version of a secret key sk_i, given that all tags used

[2] To focus on forward security, we separate confidentiality (with forward security) and integrity (below) into distinct notions, contrasting with the combined notion in [47]. We give a combined notion in the full version [5], also capturing CCA-style active attacks, and show that it is equivalent to the junction of our separate notions.

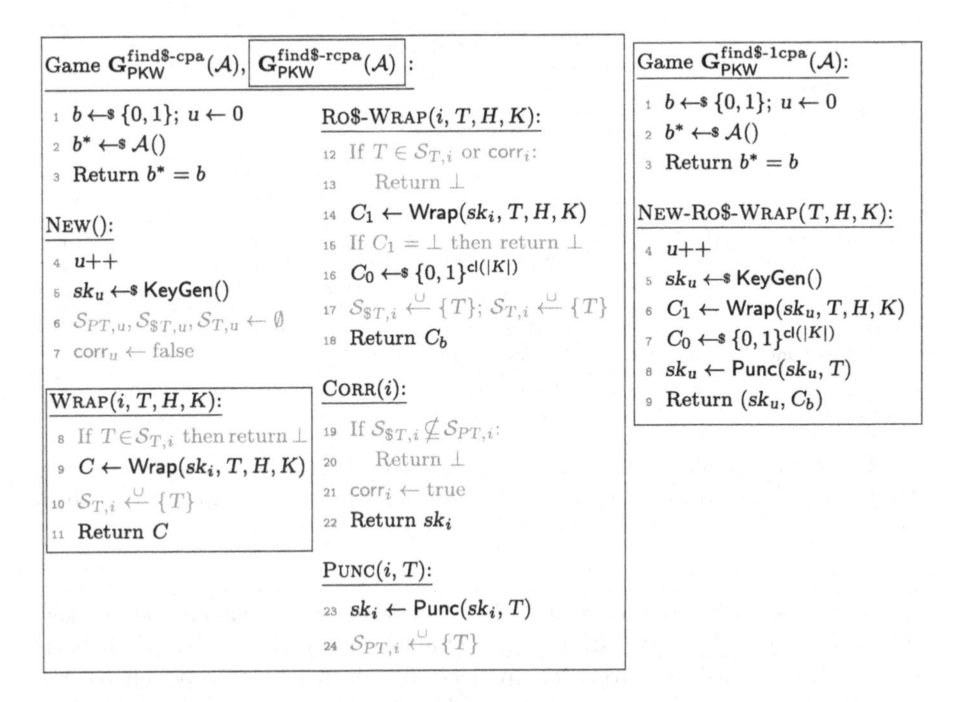

Fig. 3. Left and middle: Forward security and privacy find\$-cpa (without access to the boxed WRAP oracle)/find\$-rcpa (with access to WRAP) of a puncturable key-wrapping scheme PKW. Right: One-time privacy and forward security find\$-1cpa security of a puncturable key-wrapping scheme PKW. Grey code prevents trivial attacks and ensures that unique tags are used for wrapping. (Color figure online)

in challenge queries under sk_i must be punctured on at the time of corruption (via the puncturing oracle PUNC). Focusing on fine-grained forward security, we restrict the adversary to use tags only *once* for wrapping and call this behavior *tag-respecting* (akin to a nonce-respecting adversary in authenticated encryption); this enables puncturing of *individual* ciphertexts.[3]

Guided by the envisioned usage of puncturable key-wrapping schemes, our second, stronger confidentiality notion, find\$-rcpa, additionally gives the adversary access to real wrappings that it does not have to puncture on via an additional oracle WRAP. The rationale behind the notion is that although find\$-cpa provides forward security for all wrapped keys which have been punctured on at the time of compromise, it does not capture the potential leakage from unpunctured ciphertexts which the adversary gains insight into by corrupting.

[3] We note that a stronger formalization is possible where tag reuse is allowed: by storing and checking the whole tuple (T, H, K) in the sets $\mathcal{S}_{T,i}$ instead of only T, one can demand wraps to look random except when this is impossible due to entirely repeating inputs. This could cater to applications interested in "batch puncturing" [31], i.e., revoking access to multiple wrapped keys via a single puncturing call. Such stronger notions would also require stronger building blocks, as we will see below.

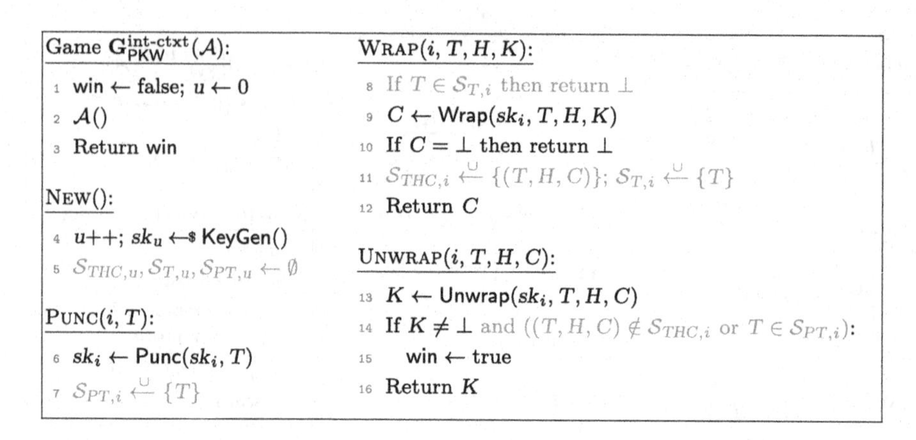

Fig. 4. Integrity of ciphertexts of a puncturable key-wrapping scheme PKW. Grey code prevents trivial attacks and ensures that tags are not repeated in wrap queries. (Color figure online)

That is, we would like to ensure that there is a form of independence across key wrappings produced with distinct tags. This is motivated by what we believe to be realistic attack scenarios for applications which use a PKW scheme for key management—such as our protected file storage system (to be defined in Sect. 5). In such a system, normal usage implies the existence of some unpunctured ciphertexts (corresponding to non-shredded files) at any given time, and hence in particular at the time of a key compromise. The idea of find$-rcpa security is that compromising ciphertexts generated with tags that have not been punctured on, should not give the adversary a higher advantage in distinguishing challenge ciphertexts from random bits.

Lastly, we also introduce a one-time security notion, find$-1cpa, which only provides the adversary with one challenge output and the punctured secret key, per key. As we will see, together with puncture invariance and consistency, find$-1cpa turns out to be sufficiently strong to achieve full security in the applications we are interested in.

Definition 7 (PKW confidentiality (find$-cpa, find$-rcpa, find$-1cpa)**).** *Let* PKW *be a puncturable key-wrapping scheme. We define the advantage of an adversary* $\mathcal{A}$ *against the forward indistinguishability* $X \in \{\text{find\$-cpa}, \text{find\$-rcpa}, \text{find\$-1cpa}\}$ *of* PKW *as* $\mathbf{Adv}^{X}_{\mathsf{PKW}}(\mathcal{A}) = 2\left|\Pr\left[\mathbf{G}^{X}_{\mathsf{PKW}}(\mathcal{A}) \Rightarrow \text{true}\right] - \frac{1}{2}\right|$, *where* $\mathbf{G}^{X}_{\mathsf{PKW}}(\mathcal{A})$ *is defined in Fig. 3.*

Integrity. In addition to the confidentiality notions we also define (multi-key) *integrity of ciphertexts* (int-ctxt) for PKW schemes as shown in Fig. 4. Here, the adversary is given oracle access to wrapping (WRAP), unwrapping (UNWRAP), and puncturing (PUNC). Its goal is to forge a ciphertext (together with a tag and a header) that was not output by WRAP, or for which the tag was punctured on via PUNC, and that unwraps to something other than the error symbol $\bot$.

Note that we particularly treat ciphertexts under punctured tags as valid forgery attempts, even if previously output by WRAP. This ensures that after puncturing on a tag, no ciphertext with that tag will be accepted any more, which is sometimes referred to as *replay protection.*

Definition 8 (PKW integrity (int-ctxt)**).** *Let* PKW *be a puncturable key-wrapping scheme. We define the advantage of an adversary $\mathcal{A}$ against the* integrity of ciphertexts *of* PKW *as* $\mathbf{Adv}^{\text{int-ctxt}}_{\mathsf{PKW}}(\mathcal{A}) = \Pr\left[\mathbf{G}^{\text{int-ctxt}}_{\mathsf{PKW}}(\mathcal{A}) \Rightarrow \text{true}\right]$, *where* $\mathbf{G}^{\text{int-ctxt}}_{\mathsf{PKW}}(\mathcal{A})$ *is defined in Fig. 4.*

Notably, in the integrity setting, forging a valid ciphertext becomes trivial if one would allow the adversary to compromise the secret key. Forward security hence seems to only make sense in scenarios where *two copies* of the key are available simultaneously, one "more punctured" than the other. The challenge then would be to forge a ciphertext on a punctured tag T using access to the compromised, more punctured key, such that the ciphertext unwraps under the less punctured key (which has not been punctured on T). This could be interesting, e.g., in a setting where punctured keys are distributed across servers. We leave extending puncturing to the distributed setting as future work.

Relations Between PKW Notions. We briefly explain how the PKW confidentiality notions are related. See Fig. 1 for an overview of all security notions and their relations, and the full version [5] for details and proofs. Beginning from strong to weak: the trivial implications (dotted arrows) arise directly from restricting the adversary. As an example, find\$-rcpa implies find\$-cpa because an adversary against the find\$-rcpa security can simply ignore the WRAP-oracle.

In the opposite direction the relations are more complex. Generally, find\$-1cpa does not imply find\$-cpa. Showing the separation is straightforward: Modify any find\$-1cpa secure scheme so that Wrap outputs a fixed string when receiving an already-punctured tag as input. This makes challenge wraps on punctured tags—which are available in the find\$-cpa game, but not in find\$-1cpa—easily distinguishable. In contrast, for the special case of a PKW scheme that is puncture invariant and consistent, and additionally for which attempting to wrap using a punctured tag always results in $\perp$ (i.e., $\mathsf{Wrap}(sk_{\setminus \bar{T}}, T, \cdot, \cdot) = \perp$ if $T \in \bar{T} \subseteq \mathsf{PKW}.\mathcal{T}$)[4] , find\$-1cpa implies find\$-cpa via a hybrid argument.

Lastly, assuming a (forward) secure source of pseudorandomness, such as a fpr-ro\$ secure PPRF, find\$-rcpa is strictly stronger than find\$-cpa. The separation relies on the fact that in the find\$-cpa game, an adversary must puncture on all tags which have been used for wrapping before compromising the secret key; a restriction which is not imposed on tags queried to oracle WRAP in the find\$-rcpa game. This can be used to construct a scheme which leaks a copy of the original, unpunctured secret key when punctured *only once* on a hidden, special tag $\hat{T}$, which can only be learned by wrapping under a different, fixed and publicly known tag T_0. Tag $\hat{T}$ is accessible to an adversary in the find\$-

[4] The last assumption is necessary for the reduction to simulate a RO\$-WRAP challenge query on an already punctured tag in the find\$-cpa game.

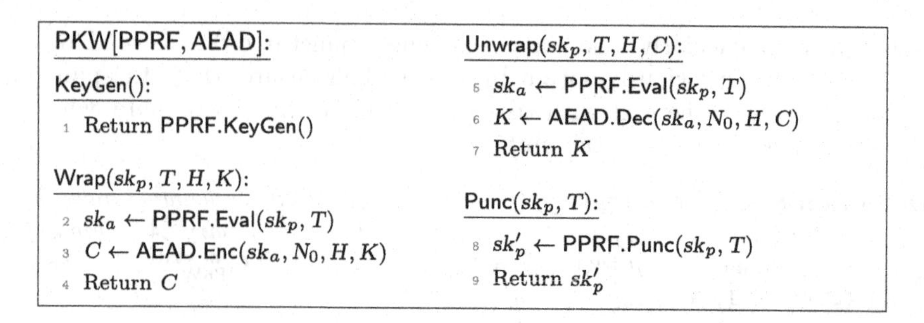

Fig. 5. The PKW[PPRF, AEAD] instantiation of a puncturable key-wrapping scheme based on a puncturable pseudorandom function PPRF and a nonce-based AEAD scheme AEAD (with N_0 a fixed nonce in the nonce space of AEAD).

rcpa game via oracle WRAP, but not to a find$-cpa adversary. The latter can learn $\hat{T}$ only through a RO$-WRAP call on T_0, forcing it to also puncture on T_0 and thereby destroying the key copy.

3.2 Instantiating PKW from PPRF and AEAD

Next, we give a generic construction of a PKW scheme, formalized in Fig. 5. The construction uses an authenticated encryption scheme with associated data AEAD to encrypt (wrap) keys, using a new AEAD key together with a fixed nonce N_0 for each key-wrap. The keys of AEAD are generated by a pseudorandom function PPRF on input the wrap tag, the key of which is the secret key of the PKW scheme. This allows AEAD keys to be "forgotten" via puncturing the PPRF key, thereby rendering the key-wrap ciphertexts unrecoverable. The construction is inspired by, and re-captures, the generic construction of a "0-RTT session resumption protocol" by Aviram, Gellert, and Jager [2], with the difference that we use a *nonce-based* AEAD scheme, following practically deployed schemes like AES-GCM or ChaCha20-Poly1305, rather than a probabilistic one.

The only technical requirement for our construction is that the range of PPRF matches the key space of AEAD. The key space of the resulting PKW scheme is the key space of PPRF, the tag space the PPRF domain, the header space the associated data space of AEAD, and the wrap-key space the message space of AEAD. The ciphertext-length function cl for PKW is that of AEAD.

Our construction PKW[PPRF, AEAD] achieves puncture invariance and consistency (given PPRF is puncture invariant), all levels of forward indistinguishability (find$-cpa, find$-rcpa, and find$-1cpa) given AEAD ind$-cpa security and the corresponding strength (fpr-ro$, fpr-rro$, resp. fpr-1ro$) of the underlying PPRF security, as well as integrity of ciphertexts (given PPRF fpr-ro$ security and AEAD int-ctxt security). For space reasons, we only give security statements for find$-cpa forward indistinguishability and integrity here, deferring the details of the other results to the full version [5].

Theorem 9 (PKW[PPRF, AEAD] **is** find\$-cpa *secure*). *Let* PKW[PPRF, AEAD] *be the PKW scheme in Fig. 5. For every adversary $\mathcal{A}$ against the* find\$-cpa-*security of* PKW[PPRF, AEAD] *making at most q_n, $q_{ro\$}$, q_{corr} and q_p queries to oracles* New, Ro\$-Wrap, Corr *and* Punc, *respectively, there exists adversaries $\mathcal{B}_{\mathsf{pprf}}$ and $\mathcal{B}_{\mathsf{aead}}$ running in approximately the same time as $\mathcal{A}$ such that*

$$\mathbf{Adv}^{\text{find\$-cpa}}_{\mathsf{PKW[PPRF,AEAD]}}(\mathcal{A}) \leq 2 \cdot \mathbf{Adv}^{\text{fpr-ro\$}}_{\mathsf{PPRF}}(\mathcal{B}_{\mathsf{pprf}}) + \mathbf{Adv}^{\text{ind\$-cpa}}_{\mathsf{AEAD}}(\mathcal{B}_{\mathsf{aead}}).$$

Adversary $\mathcal{B}_{\mathsf{pprf}}$ makes at most q_n, $q_{ro\$}$, q_{corr}, and q_p queries to oracles New, Ro\$-Eval, Corr, *resp.* Punc. *Adversary $\mathcal{B}_{\mathsf{aead}}$ makes at most $q_{ro\$}$ queries to oracles* New *and* Ro\$.

Proof. We first leverage the fpr-ro\$ security of PPRF to replace the AEAD keys by random ones, then in a second step apply ind\$-cpa security of AEAD to argue that wrapped PKW[PPRF, AEAD] ciphertexts are indistinguishable from random. The first step consists of a game hop from the original find\$-cpa game, abbreviated $\mathbf{G}_0$, to a game $\mathbf{G}_1$ which replaces the outputs of PPRF by random AEAD keys in the implementation of oracle Ro\$-Wrap. We bound the difference $|\Pr[\mathbf{G}_0] - \Pr[\mathbf{G}_1]|$ by the distinguishing advantage of an adversary $\mathcal{B}_{\mathsf{pprf}}$ against the fpr-ro\$ security of PPRF (cf. Definition 3).

Adversary $\mathcal{B}_{\mathsf{pprf}}$ draws a random bit b' and acts as the challenger in game $\mathbf{G}_0$. When $b' = 1$ adversary $\mathcal{B}_{\mathsf{pprf}}$ simulates the "real world" in the PKW game, wrapping the keys output by adversary $\mathcal{A}$. When $b' = 0$, adversary $\mathcal{B}_{\mathsf{pprf}}$ simulates the "random world" and returns random strings in the ciphertext space of the AEAD scheme in response to challenge queries from $\mathcal{A}$. Finally, when adversary $\mathcal{A}$ halts and outputs bit $b^*_{\mathcal{A}}$, adversary $\mathcal{B}_{\mathsf{pprf}}$ returns 1 if $b^*_{\mathcal{A}} = b'$ and 0 otherwise.

Let b denote the random bit drawn by the challenger in the fpr-ro\$ game. When $b = 1$, adversary $\mathcal{B}_{\mathsf{pprf}}$ simulates game $\mathbf{G}_0$ for $\mathcal{A}$. When $b = 0$, the simulation corresponds to game $\mathbf{G}_1$. This gives $\mathbf{Adv}^{\text{fpr-ro\$}}_{\mathsf{PPRF}}(\mathcal{B}_{\mathsf{pprf}}) = |\Pr[\mathbf{G}_0] - \Pr[\mathbf{G}_1]|$.

It remains to bound $\Pr[\mathbf{G}_1(\mathcal{A})]$. A straightforward reduction to the multi-key ind\$-cpa security of AEAD gives $\Pr\left[\mathbf{G}^{\text{ind\$-cpa}}_{\mathsf{AEAD}}(\mathcal{B}_{\mathsf{aead}})\right] = \Pr[\mathbf{G}_1(\mathcal{A})]$ for an adversary $\mathcal{B}_{\mathsf{aead}}$ which simulates game $\mathbf{G}_1$ for adversary $\mathcal{A}$. Adversary $\mathcal{B}_{\mathsf{aead}}$ acts as the challenger in the game, except for when adversary $\mathcal{A}$ makes a query to oracle Ro\$-Wrap. To respond to such a query Ro\$-Wrap(j, T, H, K), $\mathcal{B}_{\mathsf{aead}}$ first queries oracle New to initiate a new AEAD key. Additionally it increments an internal key counter i by one. It then issues a (single) query Ro\$$(i, N_0, H, K)$, requesting the challenge to be under the new key. The assumption that adversary $\mathcal{A}$ is tag-respecting ensures that this is a sound simulation. □

Note that for all our forward indistinguishability results, *one-time* multi-user AEAD security suffices, since the uniqueness of tags means that each AEAD encryption is performed under a new key. If we wanted to allow tag-reuse to enable *batch puncturing* (cf. Footnote 3), our PKW[PPRF, AEAD] scheme would need to be instantiated with a *misuse-resistant* AEAD scheme [47] to achieve find\$-cpa security. Interestingly, this straightforward modification is insufficient for find\$-rcpa security: the reuse of tags across real and challenge wrap queries creates a key commitment problem which breaks the reduction. This could potentially be addressed in an idealized model, cf. [35], but we leave this to future work.

Theorem 10 (PKW[PPRF, AEAD] **is** int-ctxt **secure).** *Let* PKW[PPRF, AEAD] *be the PKW scheme in Fig. 5. For every adversary* $\mathcal{A}$ *against the* int-ctxt*-security of* PKW[PPRF, AEAD] *(Def. 8) making at most* q_w*,* q_u*,* q_p *and* q_n *to oracles* WRAP, UNWRAP, PUNC *and* NEW, *respectively, there exists adversaries* $\mathcal{B}_{\mathsf{aead}}$ *and* $\mathcal{B}_{\mathsf{pprf}}$ *running in approximately the same time as* $\mathcal{A}$ *such that*

$$\mathbf{Adv}^{\text{int-ctxt}}_{\mathsf{PKW[PPRF,AEAD]}}(\mathcal{A}) \leq \mathbf{Adv}^{\text{fpr-ro\$}}_{\mathsf{PPRF}}(\mathcal{B}_{\mathsf{pprf}}) + \mathbf{Adv}^{\text{int-ctxt}}_{\mathsf{AEAD}}(\mathcal{B}_{\mathsf{aead}}).$$

Adversary $\mathcal{B}_{\mathsf{pprf}}$ *makes at most* $q_w + q_u$*,* q_p*, and* q_n *queries to oracles* RO\$-EVAL, PUNC, *resp.* NEW. *Adversary* $\mathcal{B}_{\mathsf{aead}}$ *makes at most* $q_w + q_u$*,* q_w*, and* q_u *queries to oracles* NEW, ENC, *resp.* DEC.

Proof. We first apply the fpr-ro\$ security of PPRF to replace all AEAD keys by (consistent) random strings, denoting the original game as $\mathbf{G}_0$ and the modified one as $\mathbf{G}_1$. Somewhat similarly to the first step in the proof of Theorem 9, a reduction $\mathcal{B}_{\mathsf{pprf}}$ can bound the introduced difference as $|\Pr[\mathbf{G}_0(\mathcal{A})] - \Pr[\mathbf{G}_1(\mathcal{A})]| = \mathbf{Adv}^{\text{fpr-ro\$}}_{\mathsf{PPRF}}(\mathcal{B}_{\mathsf{pprf}})$. Here, $\mathcal{B}_{\mathsf{pprf}}$ uses its challenge oracle RO\$-EVAL to request AEAD keys upon wrapping and unwrapping, and directly relays NEW and PUNC query from $\mathcal{A}$ to its own corresponding oracles. When $\mathcal{A}$ halts, $\mathcal{B}_{\mathsf{pprf}}$ checks and outputs 1 iff $\mathcal{A}$ produced a valid forgery; this yields the first bound.

The second part of the proof now leverages the independent random AEAD keys to reduce a forgery of $\mathcal{A}$ in $\mathbf{G}_1$ to an AEAD multi-key integrity forgery via the following adversary $\mathcal{B}_{\mathsf{aead}}$. Adversary $\mathcal{B}_{\mathsf{aead}}$ simulates $\mathbf{G}_1$ using its oracles ENC and DEC to wrap, resp. unwrap. Each time $\mathcal{A}$ makes a wrap or unwrap query under a new pair (i, T), $\mathcal{B}_{\mathsf{aead}}$ employs a new key index j in the int-ctxt game which it tracks via some table $\mathsf{T}[i, T] = j$. To track puncturing on (i, T), $\mathcal{B}_{\mathsf{aead}}$ sets $\mathsf{T}[i, T] = \bot$ and responds with $\bot$ to any subsequent WRAP/UNWRAP calls on (i, T). This way, $\mathcal{B}_{\mathsf{aead}}$ perfectly simulates game $\mathbf{G}_1$ for $\mathcal{A}$. Additionally, $\mathcal{B}_{\mathsf{aead}}$ wins game $\mathbf{G}^{\text{int-ctxt}}_{\mathsf{AEAD}}$ precisely when adversary $\mathcal{A}$ submits a valid forgery in $\mathbf{G}_1$, as the latter means $\mathcal{A}$ unwraps a not previously output ciphertext under a non-punctured key (as otherwise that key was set to $\mathsf{T}[i, T] = \bot$, yielding $\bot$ upon unwrapping), which translates to an AEAD forgery in $\mathcal{B}_{\mathsf{aead}}$'s DEC call. This completes the bound, as now $\mathbf{Adv}^{\text{int-ctxt}}_{\mathsf{AEAD}}(\mathcal{B}_{\mathsf{aead}}) \geq \Pr[\mathbf{G}_1(\mathcal{A}) \Rightarrow \mathsf{true}]$. □

4 TLS Ticketing

We now turn our attention to applications and begin with the Transport Layer Security (TLS) protocol. We show how the ticketing approach taken in its resumption handshake protocol can be instantiated with a PKW scheme, increasing forward security of resumed sessions. A TLS connection between clients and servers begins with the establishment of a shared symmetric key through a so called *handshake*. For repeated connections, TLS offers a *resumption* handshake mode with better performance, which bootstraps security from a *pre-shared key* (PSK) established in a prior full handshake.

In order to enable a resumption handshake, the so-called "resumption master secret" RMS is derived in a TLS 1.3 handshake and then used to derive (usually multiple) pre-shared keys for later resumptions. For each such pre-shared key, the TLS 1.3 server sends the client a unique nonce N_T, and both derive the pre-shared key as PSK $\leftarrow$ $\mathsf{HKDF.Expand}(\mathrm{RMS}, \texttt{"tls13 resumption"} \| N_T)$ using the HKDF key derivation function [38]. The client will store all PSKs established, but the server may outsource this storage to the client, e.g., by encrypting PSK under a long-term symmetric key, the so-called Session Ticket Encryption Key (STEK), and sending the resulting ciphertext (as the PSK identifier) to the client. This process of outsourcing the server-side resumption state to the client is commonly referred to as *ticketing* [49], and the identifier hence called a *ticket*.

One issue with TLS ticketing is that the tickets are generally not forward secret: if an attacker compromises the STEK, it will be able to recover the PSKs encrypted in prior resumption handshakes, thereby compromising the security of the concerned sessions. While TLS 1.3 allows for ephemeral Diffie–Hellman secrets to be mixed into the key derivation, the so-called "early" or "zero round-trip time" (0-RTT) data that a client can send immediately does not enjoy this protection, and hence would be exposed if the PSK were to be compromised.

Aviram, Gellert, and Jager (AGJ) [2] recently proposed an approach to achieve forward-secure session ticketing, giving forward security even for 0-RTT data, through what they call "session resumption protocols." In this section we revisit their approach and show how their session resumption mechanism can be viewed more simply through the lens of puncturable key wrapping: First of all, their construction is mimicked by our instantiation $\mathsf{PKW}[\mathsf{PPRF}, \mathsf{AEAD}]$ of a PKW from a puncturable PRF and an AEAD scheme, when tags are chosen (and sent as part of the TLS ticket) as *counters*. More importantly, capturing TLS ticketing through the PKW scheme $\mathsf{PKW}[\mathsf{PPRF}, \mathsf{AEAD}]$ allows us to seamlessly switch to a more *privacy-friendly* variant: by choosing the tags as random values, we make the entire TLS ticket random-looking. This avoids the potentially traceable counter element in the AGJ [2] ticketing proposal, thereby addressing privacy concerns for TLS ticketing, e.g., regarding tracking users on the web by passive network observers (see [53] for a broader discussion).

When rephrasing the AGJ integration of a session resumption protocol into the TLS 1.3 resumption handshake [2, Section 4.2, 4.3] as puncturable key wrapping, we found conceptual and technical issues in their proposed protocol, the security model, and the proof. These prevent their proposal from being (forward-)secure as-is. We rectify this situation through the following corrections:

1. Ticketing the right key. In AGJ, the TLS 1.3 resumption master secret RMS is encrypted in the session ticket(s). However, RMS is used to derive *multiple*

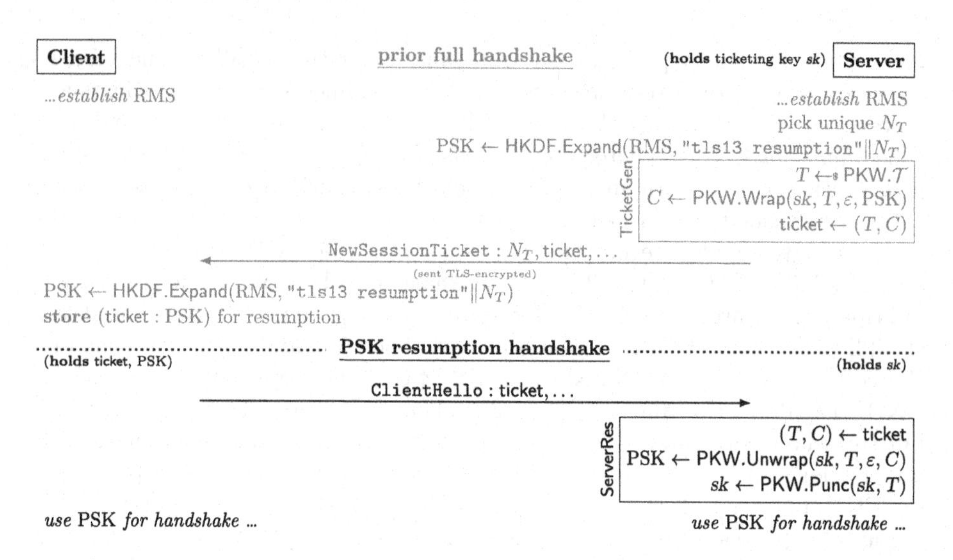

Fig. 6. Forward-secure TLS 1.3 0-RTT pre-shared key (PSK) resumption handshake using a puncturable key-wrapping scheme PKW (bottom part), based on a session ticket generated by the server and stored by the client in a prior full handshake (upper part, in gray). The boxed sections can be read as the PKW-based instantiation of a session resumption protocol [2], with tag sampling and wrapping corresponding to ticket generation (TicketGen) and unwrapping and puncturing corresponding to session resumption (ServerRes); the PKW key sk plays the role of the STEK. (Color figure online)

pre-shared keys PSK for resumption. Ticketing RMS thus violates the goal of forward security: an adversary learning RMS from one ticket can use that value to decrypt prior sessions using a PSK derived from the same RMS. In our protocol integration (cf. Fig. 6), we instead ticket PSK, not RMS, following the TLS 1.3 RFC [45, Section 4.6.1].

2. Accurately modeling tickets and corruption. The security model in AGJ does not reflect the ticketing mechanism of a key exchange protocol in how pre-shared secrets are sampled, registered with parties, and possibly corrupted. This leads to their model, strictly speaking, being unable to capture the ticketing mechanism of TLS resumption. [5] Only allowing server-side corruptions, their model also fails to capture that an adversary might compromise pre-shared secrets stored by clients. In our security model, we integrate the protocol's ticketing mechanism and allow the adversary to corrupt both the ticketing mechanism keys of servers, as well as stored secrets of clients.
3. Rectifying proof steps. The security proof for the protocol integration of AGJ [2, Theorem 4] only uses part of the power of their session resumption

[5] E.g., when setting up new pre-shared keys, their model takes the identifier *psid* of the key as an *adversary-provided* input, while *psid* in fact corresponds to the ticket *(honestly) output* by the protocol's ticketing mechanism. This means that their model is actually unable to capture how tickets are generated by (honest) servers.

primitive (i.e., a single challenge where their primitive provides many), and also misses some preliminary steps (esp. the necessity of puncture invariance and consistency, which our PKW formalism brings to light).
In our proof, we add these missing steps and show that reducing to the weaker one-time PKW security suffices for our integration.
4. Making underlying assumptions precise. The AGJ proof makes two undefined assumptions on the underlying session resumption resp. PPRF scheme. Formally, this leads to an issue with the security proof of their construction, which in turn enables a theoretical violation of the formal integrity claims on their protocol.
Through our formalism for puncturable key wrapping and PPRFs, we make the necessary assumptions (puncture invariance for PKW, resp. demanding $\perp$ output after puncturing for PPRFs) visible and explicit.

Overall, our exposition stays close to the approach by AGJ, focusing on the necessary corrections. We see this not only as an illustration that puncturable key wrapping is readily applicable to achieve forward-secure 0-RTT session resumption, but also that this conceptual framework helps to avoid errors when integrating puncturing techniques into more complex applications. For space reasons, we defer the technical details of our integration of PKW-based ticketing into TLS as well as the accompanying revised security model, proof, and discussion of assumptions to the full version [5].

5 Protected File Storage

We now turn our focus to our second application, file storage, and show how a PKW scheme can be used to provide (forward) security for remotely stored sensitive data. To this end, we design a *protected file storage* (PFS) system, which provides an interface for local encryption, decryption, and secure file shredding to a privacy-concerned user. The system is inspired by the internals of existing cloud storage services, but the final primitive is oblivious to the actual relationship between data owner and storage provider: in a PFS system, all trust lies with the holder of the secret key. This means that our system can cater both to users who wish to maintain control over the security of their data while offloading storage, *and* to storage providers who perform data encryption as a service.

The PFS interface is aimed at the former case, and hence hides internals of the system such as the key hierarchy to minimize the risk of involuntary misuse by an end user. However, it is still designed to support commonplace attributes of cloud storage systems, such as functionality for key rotation, as well as additionally providing fine-grained forward security for deleted files. This makes our approach conformable for use also by cloud service providers who wish to enhance the security guarantees in their existing systems.

5.1 PFS Syntax

We envision a PFS system to be utilized by a user who holds a set of (plaintext) files that they wish to protect and outsource the storage of. The user generates a local secret key sk via the setup algorithm $\mathsf{Setup}()$. They can then encrypt and decrypt files via algorithms $\mathsf{EncFile}$ and $\mathsf{DecFile}$, where encrypted files are associated with an identifier id, a header h, and a ciphertext C, of which the user stores h and C under the "filename" id at the storage service. (The user may keep a local look-up table mapping human-readable filenames to identifiers id, or decide to offload this table as yet another protected file to the storage service, too. In the latter case, the user only needs to store the identifier of the mapping file.) To shred a file, it suffices to locally run the algorithm $\mathsf{ShredFile}(sk, id)$ on the file identifier to be shredded. This will ensure that the corresponding file is irrecoverable (*forward secure*) from this point on; remote deletion at the service provider is not required to ensure its forward security. Finally, a user may rotate its secret key (e.g., for regulatory purposes or to refresh the key once its usage limit has been reached), which is done through calling a RotKey algorithm, taking the current list of file identifiers and headers as input and updating them with new headers to be replaced at the storage provider.

Definition 11 (PFS scheme). *A protected file storage scheme* $\mathsf{PFS} = (\mathsf{Setup}, \mathsf{EncFile}, \mathsf{DecFile}, \mathsf{ShredFile}, \mathsf{RotKey})$ *is a 5-tuple of algorithms with four associated sets; the secret key space* $\mathcal{SK}$*, the file space* $\mathcal{F}$*, the file identifier space* $\mathcal{I}$*, and the header space* $\mathcal{H}$*. Associated to the* PFS *is a ciphertext-length function* $\mathsf{cl}\colon \mathbb{N} \to \mathbb{N}$.

- *Via* $sk \leftarrow_{\$} \mathsf{Setup}()$*, the probabilistic setup algorithm* Setup*, taking no input, produces a secret key* $sk \in \mathcal{SK}$.
- *Via* $(id, h, C)/\bot \leftarrow_{\$} \mathsf{EncFile}(sk, F)$*, the randomized file encryption algorithm* $\mathsf{EncFile}$ *on input the secret key* $sk \in \mathcal{SK}$ *and a plaintext file* $F \in \mathcal{F}$ *produces a file identifier* $id \in \mathcal{I}$*, a header* $h \in \mathcal{H}$ *and a ciphertext* $C \in \{0,1\}^{\mathsf{cl}(|F|)}$ *or, to indicate failure,* $\bot$.
- *Via* $F/\bot \leftarrow \mathsf{DecFile}(sk, id, h, C)$*, the deterministic file decryption algorithm* $\mathsf{DecFile}$ *on input the key* $sk \in \mathcal{SK}$*, a file header* $h \in \mathcal{H}$*, and a ciphertext* $C \in \{0,1\}^*$ *returns a file plaintext* $F \in \mathcal{F}$ *or, to indicate failure,* $\bot$.
- *Via* $sk' \leftarrow \mathsf{ShredFile}(sk, id)$*, the deterministic file shredding algorithm* $\mathsf{ShredFile}$ *on input the secret key* $sk \in \mathcal{SK}$ *and a file identifier* $id \in \mathcal{I}$ *returns the updated secret key* $sk' \in \mathcal{SK}$.
- *Via* $(sk', (h'_1, \ldots, h'_\ell))/(sk', \bot) \leftarrow_{\$} \mathsf{RotKey}(sk, ((id_1, h_1), \ldots, (id_\ell, h_\ell)))$*, the randomized key-rotation algorithm* RotKey *on input the secret key* $sk \in \mathcal{SK}$ *and a list of file identifier-header pairs* $(id_1, h_1), \ldots, (id_\ell, h_\ell) \in (\mathcal{I} \times \mathcal{H})^*$ *returns the potentially updated secret key* $sk' \in \mathcal{SK}$ *and a sequence of updated headers* $(h'_1, \ldots, h'_\ell) \in \mathcal{H}^*$ *or, to indicate failure,* $\bot$.

5.2 Confidentiality and Integrity of PFS

A protected file storage scheme should provide confidentiality of the stored files, including their metadata (file identifiers and headers), as well as forward security when files have been shredded. Additionally, key rotation should allow the scheme to recover from corruption, ensuring security of newly encrypted files.

We capture this form of confidentiality through the notion of *forward indistinguishability from random bits* under *real and chosen-plaintext attack* (find\$-

```
Game G_PFS^{find$-rcpa}(A):
 1  b <-$ {0,1}; sk <-$ Setup()
 2  R <- (); Q <- ()
 3  S_$id <- ∅; corr <- false
 4  b* <-$ A()
 5  Return b* = b

Ro$-Enc(F):
 6  If corr = true then return ⊥
 7  (id_1, h_1, C_1) <-$ EncFile(sk, F)
 8  If (id_1, h_1, C_1) = ⊥:
 9     Return ⊥
10  id_0 <-$ I; h_0 <-$ H
11  C_0 <-$ {0,1}^{cl(|F|)}
12  R += (id_b, h_b)
13  S_$id <-∪ {id_b}
14  Return (id_b, h_b, C_b)

Enc(F):
15  (id, h, C) <-$ EncFile(sk, F)
16  Q += (id, h)
17  Return (id, h, C)

Shred(id):
18  sk <- ShredFile(sk, id)
19  R -= (id, *); Q -= (id, *); S_$id <- S_$id \ {id}

RotKey():
20  ((id_1, h_1), ..., (id_|R|, h_|R|)) <- R
21  ((id_|R|+1, h_|R|+1), ..., (id_|R|+|Q|, h_|R|+|Q|)) <- Q
22  If b = 0:
23     For i = 1 to |R| do h'_i <-$ H
24     (sk, (h'_|R|+1, ..., h'_|R|+|Q|)) <-$ RotKey(sk, Q)
25     If (h'_|R|+1, ..., h'_|R|+|Q|) = ⊥ then return ⊥
26  If b = 1:
27     (sk, (h'_1, ..., h'_|R|+|Q|)) <-$ RotKey(sk, R||Q)
28     If (h'_1, ..., h'_|R|+|Q|) = ⊥ then return ⊥
29  R <- ((id_1, h'_1), ..., (id_|R|, h'_|R|))
30  Q <- ((id_|R|+1, h'_|R|+1), ..., (id_|R|+|Q|, h'_|R|+|Q|))
31  corr <- false
32  Return R||Q

Corr():
33  If S_$id ≠ ∅ then return ⊥
34  corr <- true
35  Return sk
```

Fig. 7. Confidentiality and forward security (find\$-rcpa) game for a protected file storage scheme PFS. Grey code prevents trivial attacks. Lists R and Q keep track of file identifiers and headers currently in the system for the sake of key rotation. (Color figure online)

rcpa). In the find\$-rcpa security game, given in Fig. 7, the adversary is asked to distinguish real from random outputs of a challenge real or \$ encryption oracle Ro\$-Enc. We emphasize that indistinguishability here encompasses *both* the file ciphertext *and* metadata (i.e., identifier and header), encoding a strong form of *privacy*. The game further allows the adversary to shred files (via the oracle Shred) and to rotate keys (via RotKey), leading to an update of the headers of all non-shredded files. We encode forward security via a Corr oracle, through which the adversary may ultimately learn the user's current secret key, provided that it shredded all challenge files (to prevent trivial distinguishing attacks) and does not make further challenge queries on that key. Furthermore, we allow new challenge queries *after* a successful key rotation, which captures security being regained after key rotation in which the adversary remained passive, a form of *post-compromise security* [21]. In order to capture potential leakage from unshredded files in the system which a real-world adversary would gain access to when corrupting a user's secret key, the game additionally includes a real

```
Game G^{int-ctxt}_{PFS}(A):
 1 sk ←$ Setup()
 2 S ← ∅; win ← false
 3 A()
 4 Return win

Enc(F):
 5 (id, h, C) ←$ EncFile(sk, F)
 6 S ∪← {(id, h, C)}
 7 Return (id, h, C)

Dec(id, h, C):
 8 F ← DecFile(sk, id, h, C)
 9 If (id, h, C) ∉ S and F ≠ ⊥:
10   win ← true
11 Return F

Shred(id):
12 sk ← ShredFile(sk, id)
13 S ← S \ {(id, *, *)}

RotKey(((id_1, h_1), ..., (id_ℓ, h_ℓ))):
14 (sk, (h'_1, ..., h'_ℓ)) ←$ RotKey(sk, ((id_1, h_1), ...,
   (id_ℓ, h_ℓ)))
15 If (h'_1, ..., h'_ℓ) = ⊥ then return ⊥
16 S_new ← ∅
17 For (id, h, C) ∈ S do:
18   If ∃i ∈ {1, ..., ℓ} s.t. (id, h) = (id_i, h_i):
19     S_new ∪← {(id_i, h'_i, C)}
20 S ← S_new
21 Return ((id_1, h'_1), ..., (id_ℓ, h'_ℓ))
```

Fig. 8. Integrity of ciphertexts game for a protected file storage scheme PFS. Grey code prevents trivial attacks. (Color figure online)

encryption oracle ENC, which provides the adversary with honest encryptions of plaintexts of its choice that do not need to be shredded prior to corruption.

Definition 12 (PFS confidentiality (find\$-rcpa)**).** *Let* PFS *be a protected file storage scheme and* $\mathbf{G}^{\text{find\$-rcpa}}_{\mathsf{PFS}}$ *be the game defined in Fig. 7. We define the advantage of an adversary* $\mathcal{A}$ *against the* find\$-rcpa *security of* PFS *as* $\mathbf{Adv}^{\text{find\$-rcpa}}_{\mathsf{PFS}}(\mathcal{A}) = 2\left|\Pr\left[\mathbf{G}^{\text{find\$-rcpa}}_{\mathsf{PFS}}(\mathcal{A}) \Rightarrow \text{true}\right] - \frac{1}{2}\right|$.

We also define integrity (of ciphertexts) for a PFS scheme, via the game in Fig. 8. The adversary's goal here is to come up with a file tuple (id, h, C) that was not output by the encryption oracle ENC, or has been shredded (using oracle SHRED), yet successfully decrypts (in the decryption oracle DEC). The game further provides access to a key rotation oracle ROTKEY; in contrast to the find\$-rcpa game, this is strengthened to take adversarially-chosen file identifiers and headers as input. This captures that a malicious storage service might inject forged identifiers and headers into a user's storage or omit files from key rotation.

Definition 13 (PFS integrity (int-ctxt)**).** *Let* PFS *be a protected file storage scheme and* $\mathbf{G}^{\text{int-ctxt}}_{\mathsf{PFS}}$ *be the game defined in Fig. 8. We define the advantage of an adversary* $\mathcal{A}$ *against the* int-ctxt *security of* PFS *as* $\mathbf{Adv}^{\text{int-ctxt}}_{\mathsf{PFS}}(\mathcal{A}) = \Pr\left[\mathbf{G}^{\text{int-ctxt}}_{\mathsf{PFS}}(\mathcal{A}) \Rightarrow \text{true}\right]$.

5.3 Instantiating PFS from PKW and AEAD

We now construct a generic PFS scheme PFS[PKW, AEAD] from a puncturable key-wrapping scheme PKW, which will handle the key management, and an authenticated encryption scheme with associated data AEAD, handling the actual file encryption. The construction, formalized in Fig. 9, works as follows.

- Setup generates a PKW key *sk*, which—for reference to cloud storage and its key-wrapping functionality—we refer to as the key encryption key (KEK).
- EncFile first samples an AEAD "data encryption key" (DEK) and a file identifier *id* at random, and wraps DEK under the KEK into a file header h, using *id* as tag. [6] It then AEAD-encrypts the file plaintext under DEK and a random [7] nonce N into a ciphertext C; $N \| C$ constitutes the PFS file ciphertext.
- DecFile inverts file encryption by first unwrapping the DEK from the header and then using it to decrypt the file ciphertext.
- ShredFile punctures the KEK *sk* on a file identifier *id*, using the PKW puncturing algorithm. This effectively prevents future unwrapping of the DEK wrapped with tag *id*, and hence file decryptions of files with this identifier.
- RotKey first unwraps the DEKs in all headers it is handed, then samples a fresh KEK to re-wrap them. The PKW tags are re-used in this process, ensuring that encrypted files keep their identifiers across key rotations.

For PFS[PKW, AEAD], we establish confidentiality in Theorems 14 and 15 (below) and integrity (in the full version [5]). Notably, our two confidentiality results follow different paths: Theorem 14 employs weak one-time (find$-1cpa) PKW security in a hybrid together with puncture invariance and consistency. Theorem 15 in contrast shows our construction achieves the same goal in a tight manner if the underlying PKW scheme meets the stronger find$-rcpa notion. While the latter notion is currently only known to be achievable from strong (fpr-rro$) PPRF security, the route of Theorem 15 may still be interesting as it does not require puncture invariance and consistency, properties which we expect schemes with non-perfect correctness (e.g., employing Bloom filters), would not achieve. We only give one proof sketch here and provide the full proofs in [5].

Theorem 14 (PFS[PKW, AEAD] **is** find$-rcpa **secure, via PKW** find$-1cpa). *Let* PFS[PKW, AEAD] *be the PFS construction in Fig. 9 with file identifier space* $\mathcal{I} = \{0,1\}^t$. *If* PKW *is puncture invariant and consistent (Definitions 5 and 6), then for every adversary* $\mathcal{A}$ *against the* find$-rcpa *security (Definition 12) of* PFS[PKW, AEAD] *making at most* $q_{ro\$}$, q_e, *resp.* $m-1$ *queries in total to its oracles* Ro$-Enc, Enc, *and* RotKey, *and at most* q_s *queries to oracle* Shred *between each query to the key rotation oracle* RotKey, *there exists adversaries* $\mathcal{B}_{\mathsf{pkw}}$ *and* $\mathcal{B}_{\mathsf{aead}}$ *running in approximately the same time as* $\mathcal{A}$ *such*

[6] Our construction leaves the PKW header empty. In practice, this field may be used to authenticate control data of the DEK, such as expiration date or permitted usage.

[7] Our construction only uses a single AEAD nonce N per any one data encryption key DEK, which would allow using a fixed nonce. We still sample a random nonce to enable file updates/re-encryption as a potential extension to our construction.

```
Setup():
 1 sk ←$ PKW.KeyGen()
 2 Return sk

EncFile(sk, F):
 3 K ←$ {0,1}^k; id ←$ {0,1}^t
 4 h ← PKW.Wrap(sk, id, ε, K)
 5 If h = ⊥ then return ⊥
 6 N ←$ {0,1}^n
 7 C ← AEAD.Enc(K, N, ε, F)
 8 Return (id, h, N||C)

DecFile(sk, id, h, N||C):
 9 K ← PKW.Unwrap(sk, id, ε, h)
10 F ← AEAD.Dec(K, N, ε, C)
11 Return F

ShredFile(sk, id):
12 sk' ← PKW.Punc(sk, id)
13 Return sk'

RotKey(sk_old, (id_1, h_1), ..., (id_ℓ, h_ℓ)):
14 sk_new ←$ PKW.KeyGen()
15 For i = 1 to ℓ do:
16     K_i ← PKW.Unwrap(sk_old, id_i, ε, h_i)
17     h'_i ← PKW.Wrap(sk_new, id_i, ε, K_i)
18     If h'_i = ⊥ then return (sk_old, ⊥)
19 Return (sk_new, (id_1, h'_1), ..., (id_ℓ, h'_ℓ))
```

Fig. 9. Construction of a protected file storage scheme $\mathsf{PFS}[\mathsf{PKW}, \mathsf{AEAD}]$ from a puncturable key-wrapping scheme PKW and an AEAD scheme AEAD. The PKW scheme has wrap-key space $\{0,1\}^k$ and tag space $\{0,1\}^t$. The AEAD scheme has key space $\{0,1\}^k$ and nonce space $\{0,1\}^n$. Hence, for the resulting PFS scheme, $\mathcal{I} = \{0,1\}^t$, $\mathcal{H} = \{0,1\}^{\mathsf{PKW.cl}(k)}$, and $\mathsf{PFS.cl}(|F|) = n + \mathsf{AEAD.cl}(|F|)$.

that $\mathbf{Adv}^{\text{find\$-rcpa}}_{\mathsf{PFS[PKW,AEAD]}}(\mathcal{A}) \leq 2q_{ro\$}\left(\frac{(2q_s+q_e+q_{ro\$}-1)}{2^t} + m\cdot\mathbf{Adv}^{\text{find\$-1cpa}}_{\mathsf{PKW}}(\mathcal{B}_{\mathsf{pkw}}) + m\cdot \mathbf{Adv}^{\text{ind\$-cpa}}_{\mathsf{AEAD}}(\mathcal{B}_{\mathsf{aead}})\right)$. *Adversary* $\mathcal{B}_{\mathsf{pkw}}$ *makes at most* m *queries to oracle* NEW-RO\$-WRAP. *Adversary* $\mathcal{B}_{\mathsf{aead}}$ *makes one query each to its oracles* NEW *and* RO\$.

Proof idea. The proof proceeds by a series of six game hops, starting with game $\mathbf{G}_0 = \mathbf{G}^{\text{find\$-rcpa}}_{\mathsf{PFS[PKW,AEAD]}}$. Let $\mathbf{Adv}_i(\mathcal{A}) := 2\left|\Pr[\mathbf{G}_i(\mathcal{A})] - \frac{1}{2}\right|$ for $i \in \{0,\ldots,6\}$. By *key phase* we denote the period between two consecutive key rotation queries.

$\mathbf{G}_0 \rightarrow \mathbf{G}_1$: We begin by excluding, via a bad event [8], that the (real- or ideal-world) challenge file identifier coincides with one already shredded in the current key phase, since the output of wrapping with such an identifier as tag is undefined and hence possibly distinguishable from the ideal-world behavior. The probability of this happening is upper-bounded by $2q_{ro\$} \cdot \frac{q_s}{2^t}$.

$\mathbf{G}_1 \rightarrow \mathbf{G}_2$: We reduce the $q_{ro\$}$ RO\$-ENC challenge queries to a single one via a hybrid argument, yielding an adversary $\mathcal{A}'$ making a single query to RO\$-ENC and at most $q_e + q_{ro\$} - 1$ queries to ENC, such that $\mathbf{Adv}_1(\mathcal{A}) = q_{ro\$} \cdot \mathbf{Adv}_2(\mathcal{A}')$.

$\mathbf{G}_2 \rightarrow \mathbf{G}_3$: Next, we exclude that PKW tags used for the (at most $q_e + q_{ro\$} - 1$) real encryption queries prior to the challenge query collide with the (single) challenge tag, a bad event occurring with probability at most $\frac{q_e+q_{ro\$}-1}{2^t}$.

$\mathbf{G}_3 \rightarrow \mathbf{G}_4$: The challenger now guesses in which of the at most m key phases the challenge encryption occurs; silencing the output otherwise loses a factor of m.

$\mathbf{G}_4 \rightarrow \mathbf{G}_5$: We can now apply the find\$-1cpa security of PKW through a reduction $\mathcal{B}_{\mathsf{pkw}}$ to replace the header in the challenge encryption by a random string. This step requires PKW's puncture invariance and consistency to reorder the challenge PKW wrap in the reduction; the latter makes at most m queries to oracle NEW-RO\$-WRAP and yields $|\Pr[\mathbf{G}_4] - \Pr[\mathbf{G}_5]| \leq \mathbf{Adv}^{\text{find\$-1cpa}}_{\mathsf{PKW}}(\mathcal{B}_{\mathsf{pkw}})$.

$\mathbf{G}_5 \rightarrow \mathbf{G}_6$: Finally, we replace the challenge file ciphertext with a random string via a reduction $\mathcal{B}_{\mathsf{aead}}$ to the AEAD scheme's ind\$-cpa security, which yields $|\Pr[\mathbf{G}_5] - \Pr[\mathbf{G}_6]| \leq \mathbf{Adv}^{\text{ind\$-cpa}}_{\mathsf{AEAD}}(\mathcal{B}_{\mathsf{aead}})$. After this step, $\mathbf{Adv}_6(\mathcal{A}) = 0$. □

Theorem 15. **(PFS[PKW, AEAD] is find\$-rcpa secure, via PKW find\$-rcpa).** *Let PFS[PKW, AEAD] be the PFS construction in Fig. 9 with file identifier space $\mathcal{I} = \{0,1\}^t$. For every adversary $\mathcal{A}$ against the find\$-rcpa security (Definition 12) of PFS[PKW, AEAD] making at most $q_{ro\$}$, q_e, q_{corr}, resp. q_{rk} queries in total to its oracles RO\$-ENC, ENC, CORR and ROTKEY, and at most q_s queries to oracle SHRED between each query to oracle ROTKEY, there exists adversaries $\mathcal{B}_{\mathsf{pkw}}$ and $\mathcal{B}_{\mathsf{aead}}$ running in approximately the same time as $\mathcal{A}$ such that $\mathbf{Adv}^{\text{find\$-rcpa}}_{\mathsf{PFS[PKW,AEAD]}}(\mathcal{A}) \leq 2 \cdot \left(\frac{2q_{ro\$}q_s}{2^t} + \frac{(q_e+q_{ro\$})^2}{2^{t+1}} + \mathbf{Adv}^{\text{find\$-rcpa}}_{\mathsf{PKW}}(\mathcal{B}_{\mathsf{pkw}}) + \mathbf{Adv}^{\text{ind\$-cpa}}_{\mathsf{AEAD}}(\mathcal{B}_{\mathsf{aead}})\right)$. Adversary $\mathcal{B}_{\mathsf{pkw}}$ makes at most $q_{rk}+1$, $q_{ro\$}(q_{rk}+1)$, $q_e(q_{rk}+1)$, q_{corr} and $q_{rk} \cdot q_s$ queries to oracles NEW, RO\$-WRAP, WRAP, CORR and PUNC, respectively. Adversary $\mathcal{B}_{\mathsf{aead}}$ makes at most $q_{ro\$}$ queries each to its oracles NEW and RO\$.*

6 Discussion and Future Work

Our approach to PKW integrates a flexible tag-based approach [31] with classical key wrapping [47]. We build PKW generically from PPRF and AEAD, focusing on applications which require fine-grained forward security. For applications where batch puncturing might be useful, deploying nonce-misuse resistant AEAD would allow tags to be reused, achieving a stronger version of our main find\$-cpa security notion. Interestingly, proving the (even stronger) find\$-rcpa security of such an instantiation runs into a key commitment problem; whether resolving this needs idealized models (cf. [35]) or can be done in the standard model is an interesting open problem.

Our PKWs and the PPRFs they are built from are not private [11]; we could potentially obtain improved privacy after client compromise for our PFS system if they were, cf. [54]. Finding practically efficient private PPRFs and building private PKW schemes from them is an open problem whose solution would have immediate applications.

Our work on TLS session resumption assumes the server's key is held and operated on by a single server. Yet distributed server environments are common in TLS deployments, to reduce latency and improve scalability. It would be useful to extend our work to this setting. The challenge is to maintain appropriate synchronization amongst the punctured keys held by the servers.

The applications we treat in this work are a sample from the set of possible use-cases for PKW. They already demonstrate that it is a useful abstraction. Examining further potential applications where puncturable key wrapping can be integrated, such as in symmetric key exchange [15] and DUKPT [18], would be interesting future work.

Acknowledgments. We thank the anonymous reviewers for their helpful comments. Felix Günther has been supported in part by Research Fellowship grant GU 1859/1-1 of the German Research Foundation (DFG).

References

1. Aviram, N., Gellert, K., Jager, T.: Session resumption protocols and efficient forward security for TLS 1.3 0-RTT. In: Ishai, Y., Rijmen, V. (eds.) EUROCRYPT 2019. LNCS, vol. 11477, pp. 117–150. Springer, Cham (2019). https://doi.org/10.1007/978-3-030-17656-3_5
2. Aviram, N., Gellert, K., Jager, T.: Session resumption protocols and efficient forward security for TLS 1.3 0-RTT. J. Cryptol. **34**(3), 1–57 (2021). https://doi.org/10.1007/s00145-021-09385-0
3. Avoine, G., Canard, S., Ferreira, L.: Symmetric-key authenticated key exchange (SAKE) with perfect forward secrecy. In: Jarecki, S. (ed.) CT-RSA 2020. LNCS, vol. 12006, pp. 199–224. Springer, Cham (2020). https://doi.org/10.1007/978-3-030-40186-3_10
4. AWS: Protecting data using client-side encryption. http://docs.aws.amazon.com/AmazonS3/latest/dev/UsingClientSideEncryption.html
5. Backendal, M., Günther, F., Paterson, K.G.: Puncturable key wrapping and its applications. Cryptology ePrint Archive, Paper 2022/1209 (2022). https://eprint.iacr.org/2022/1209
6. Bellare, M., Boldyreva, A., Micali, S.: Public-key encryption in a multi-user setting: security proofs and improvements. In: Preneel, B. (ed.) EUROCRYPT 2000. LNCS, vol. 1807, pp. 259–274. Springer, Heidelberg (2000). https://doi.org/10.1007/3-540-45539-6_18
7. Bellare, M., Ng, R., Tackmann, B.: Nonces are noticed: AEAD revisited. In: Boldyreva, A., Micciancio, D. (eds.) CRYPTO 2019. LNCS, vol. 11692, pp. 235–265. Springer, Cham (2019). https://doi.org/10.1007/978-3-030-26948-7_9
8. Bellare, M., Rogaway, P.: The security of triple encryption and a framework for code-based game-playing proofs. In: Vaudenay, S. (ed.) EUROCRYPT 2006. LNCS, vol. 4004, pp. 409–426. Springer, Heidelberg (2006). https://doi.org/10.1007/11761679_25
9. Bellare, M., Stepanovs, I., Waters, B.: New negative results on differing-inputs obfuscation. In: Fischlin, M., Coron, J.-S. (eds.) EUROCRYPT 2016. LNCS, vol. 9666, pp. 792–821. Springer, Heidelberg (2016). https://doi.org/10.1007/978-3-662-49896-5_28
10. Blaze, M.: A cryptographic file system for UNIX. In: Denning, D.E., Pyle, R., Ganesan, R., Sandhu, R.S., Ashby, V. (eds.) ACM CCS 1993, pp. 9–16. ACM Press (1993). https://doi.org/10.1145/168588.168590
11. Boneh, D., Lewi, K., Wu, D.J.: Constraining pseudorandom functions privately. In: Fehr, S. (ed.) PKC 2017. LNCS, vol. 10175, pp. 494–524. Springer, Heidelberg (2017). https://doi.org/10.1007/978-3-662-54388-7_17

12. Boneh, D., Lipton, R.J.: A revocable backup system. In: USENIX Security 1996. USENIX Association (1996)
13. Boneh, D., Waters, B.: Constrained pseudorandom functions and their applications. In: Sako, K., Sarkar, P. (eds.) ASIACRYPT 2013. LNCS, vol. 8270, pp. 280–300. Springer, Heidelberg (2013). https://doi.org/10.1007/978-3-642-42045-0_15
14. Boxcryptor: Boxcryptor security for your cloud. https://www.boxcryptor.com/
15. Boyd, C., Davies, G.T., de Kock, B., Gellert, K., Jager, T., Millerjord, L.: Symmetric key exchange with full forward security and robust synchronization. In: Tibouchi, M., Wang, H. (eds.) ASIACRYPT 2021. LNCS, vol. 13093, pp. 681–710. Springer, Cham (2021). https://doi.org/10.1007/978-3-030-92068-5_23
16. Boyd, C., Gellert, K.: A modern view on forward security. Comput. J. **64**(4), 639–652 (2021). https://doi.org/10.1093/comjnl/bxaa104
17. Boyle, E., Goldwasser, S., Ivan, I.: Functional signatures and pseudorandom functions. In: Krawczyk, H. (ed.) PKC 2014. LNCS, vol. 8383, pp. 501–519. Springer, Heidelberg (2014). https://doi.org/10.1007/978-3-642-54631-0_29
18. Brier, E., Peyrin, T.: A forward-secure symmetric-key derivation protocol. In: Abe, M. (ed.) ASIACRYPT 2010. LNCS, vol. 6477, pp. 250–267. Springer, Heidelberg (2010). https://doi.org/10.1007/978-3-642-17373-8_15
19. Chen, W., Hoang, T., Guajardo, J., Yavuz, A.A.: Titanium: A metadata-hiding file-sharing system with malicious security. In: NDSS 2022. The Internet Society (2022). https://doi.org/10.14722/ndss.2022.24161
20. Chen, W., Popa, R.A.: Metal: a metadata-hiding file-sharing system. In: NDSS 2020. The Internet Society (2020)
21. Cohn-Gordon, K., Cremers, C.J.F., Garratt, L.: On post-compromise security. In: Hicks, M., Köpf, B. (eds.) CSF 2016 Computer Security Foundations Symposium, pp. 164–178. IEEE Computer Society Press (2016). https://doi.org/10.1109/CSF.2016.19
22. Derler, D., Jager, T., Slamanig, D., Striecks, C.: Bloom filter encryption and applications to efficient forward-secret 0-RTT key exchange. In: Nielsen, J.B., Rijmen, V. (eds.) EUROCRYPT 2018. LNCS, vol. 10822, pp. 425–455. Springer, Cham (2018). https://doi.org/10.1007/978-3-319-78372-7_14
23. Diffie, W., van Oorschot, P.C., Wiener, M.J.: Authentication and authenticated key exchanges. Des. Codes Cryptogr. **2**(2), 107–125 (1992)
24. Dworkin, M.: Recommendation for block cipher modes of operation: methods for key wrapping. NIST Special Publication SP 800–38F (2012). https://nvlpubs.nist.gov/nistpubs/SpecialPublications/NIST.SP.800-38F.pdf
25. Everspaugh, A., Paterson, K., Ristenpart, T., Scott, S.: Key rotation for authenticated encryption. In: Katz, J., Shacham, H. (eds.) CRYPTO 2017. LNCS, vol. 10403, pp. 98–129. Springer, Cham (2017). https://doi.org/10.1007/978-3-319-63697-9_4
26. Feldman, A.J., Zeller, W.P., Freedman, M.J., Felten, E.W.: Sporc: group collaboration using untrusted cloud resources. In: OSDI 20210 (2010)
27. Fischlin, M., Günther, F.: Multi-stage key exchange and the case of Google's QUIC protocol. In: Ahn, G.J., Yung, M., Li, N. (eds.) ACM CCS 2014, pp. 1193–1204. ACM Press (2014). https://doi.org/10.1145/2660267.2660308
28. Fuchsbauer, G., Konstantinov, M., Pietrzak, K., Rao, V.: Adaptive security of constrained PRFs. In: Sarkar, P., Iwata, T. (eds.) ASIACRYPT 2014. LNCS, vol. 8874, pp. 82–101. Springer, Heidelberg (2014). https://doi.org/10.1007/978-3-662-45608-8_5

29. Goldreich, O., Goldwasser, S., Micali, S.: How to construct random functions (extended abstract). In: 25th FOCS, pp. 464–479. IEEE Computer Society Press (1984). https://doi.org/10.1109/SFCS.1984.715949
30. Google: Encryption at rest in Google Cloud. https://cloud.google.com/security/encryption/default-encryption
31. Green, M.D., Miers, I.: Forward secure asynchronous messaging from puncturable encryption. In: 2015 IEEE Symposium on Security and Privacy, pp. 305–320. IEEE Computer Society Press (2015). https://doi.org/10.1109/SP.2015.26
32. Günther, C.G.: An identity-based key-exchange protocol. In: Quisquater, J.-J., Vandewalle, J. (eds.) EUROCRYPT 1989. LNCS, vol. 434, pp. 29–37. Springer, Heidelberg (1990). https://doi.org/10.1007/3-540-46885-4_5
33. Günther, F., Hale, B., Jager, T., Lauer, S.: 0-RTT key exchange with full forward secrecy. In: Coron, J.-S., Nielsen, J.B. (eds.) EUROCRYPT 2017. LNCS, vol. 10212, pp. 519–548. Springer, Cham (2017). https://doi.org/10.1007/978-3-319-56617-7_18
34. IBM: Protecting data with envelope encryption. https://cloud.ibm.com/docs/key-protect?topic=key-protect-envelope-encryption
35. Jaeger, J., Tyagi, N.: Handling adaptive compromise for practical encryption schemes. In: Micciancio, D., Ristenpart, T. (eds.) CRYPTO 2020. LNCS, vol. 12170, pp. 3–32. Springer, Cham (2020). https://doi.org/10.1007/978-3-030-56784-2_1
36. Kiayias, A., Papadopoulos, S., Triandopoulos, N., Zacharias, T.: Delegatable pseudorandom functions and applications. In: Sadeghi, A.R., Gligor, V.D., Yung, M. (eds.) ACM CCS 2013, pp. 669–684. ACM Press (2013). https://doi.org/10.1145/2508859.2516668
37. Klooß, M., Lehmann, A., Rupp, A.: (R)CCA secure updatable encryption with integrity protection. In: Ishai, Y., Rijmen, V. (eds.) EUROCRYPT 2019. LNCS, vol. 11476, pp. 68–99. Springer, Cham (2019). https://doi.org/10.1007/978-3-030-17653-2_3
38. Krawczyk, H.: Cryptographic extraction and key derivation: the HKDF scheme. In: Rabin, T. (ed.) CRYPTO 2010. LNCS, vol. 6223, pp. 631–648. Springer, Heidelberg (2010). https://doi.org/10.1007/978-3-642-14623-7_34
39. Lau, B., Chung, S.P., Song, C., Jang, Y., Lee, W., Boldyreva, A.: Mimesis aegis: a mimicry privacy shield-a system's approach to data privacy on public cloud. In: Fu, K., Jung, J. (eds.) USENIX Security 2014, pp. 33–48. USENIX Association (2014)
40. Lehmann, A., Tackmann, B.: Updatable encryption with post-compromise security. In: Nielsen, J.B., Rijmen, V. (eds.) EUROCRYPT 2018. LNCS, vol. 10822, pp. 685–716. Springer, Cham (2018). https://doi.org/10.1007/978-3-319-78372-7_22
41. Mahajan, P., Setty, S., Lee, S., Clement, A., Alvisi, L., Dahlin, M., Walfish, M.: Depot: cloud storage with minimal trust. ACM Trans. Comput. Syst. **29**(4) (2011). https://doi.org/10.1145/2063509.2063512
42. Microsoft: Azure Data Encryption at rest. https://docs.microsoft.com/en-us/azure/security/fundamentals/encryption-atrest
43. Miller, E., Long, D., Freeman, W., Reed, B.: Strong security for distributed file systems. In: Conference Proceedings of the 2001 IEEE International Performance, Computing, and Communications Conference, pp. 34–40 (2001). https://doi.org/10.1109/IPCCC.2001.918633
44. Nichols, S.: Dropbox: Oops, yeah, we didn't actually delete all your files this bug kept them in the cloud (2017). https://www.theregister.com/2017/01/24/dropbox_brings_old_files_back_from_dead/

45. Rescorla, E.: The Transport Layer Security (TLS) Protocol Version 1.3. RFC 8446 (Proposed Standard) (2018). https://www.rfc-editor.org/rfc/rfc8446.txt
46. Rogaway, P.: Authenticated-encryption with associated-data. In: Atluri, V. (ed.) ACM CCS 2002, pp. 98–107. ACM Press (2002). https://doi.org/10.1145/586110.586125
47. Rogaway, P., Shrimpton, T.: A provable-security treatment of the key-wrap problem. In: Vaudenay, S. (ed.) EUROCRYPT 2006. LNCS, vol. 4004, pp. 373–390. Springer, Heidelberg (2006). https://doi.org/10.1007/11761679_23
48. Sahai, A., Waters, B.: How to use indistinguishability obfuscation: deniable encryption, and more. In: Shmoys, D.B. (ed.) 46th ACM STOC, pp. 475–484. ACM Press (2014). https://doi.org/10.1145/2591796.2591825
49. Salowey, J., Zhou, H., Eronen, P., Tschofenig, H.: Transport Layer Security (TLS) Session Resumption without Server-Side State. RFC 5077 (Proposed Standard) (2008). https://www.rfc-editor.org/rfc/rfc5077.txt, obsoleted by RFC 8446, updated by RFC 8447
50. Slamanig, D., Striecks, C.: Puncture 'em all: updatable encryption with no-directional key updates and expiring ciphertexts. Cryptology ePrint Archive, Report 2021/268 (2021). https://eprint.iacr.org/2021/268
51. Sun, S.F., et al.: Practical non-interactive searchable encryption with forward and backward privacy. In: NDSS 2021. The Internet Society (2021)
52. Sun, S., et al.: Practical backward-secure searchable encryption from symmetric puncturable encryption. In: Lie, D., Mannan, M., Backes, M., Wang, X. (eds.) ACM CCS 2018, pp. 763–780. ACM Press (2018). https://doi.org/10.1145/3243734.3243782
53. Sy, E., Burkert, C., Federrath, H., Fischer, M.: Tracking users across the web via TLS session resumption. In: ACSAC 2018, pp. 289–299. ACM (2018). https://doi.org/10.1145/3274694.3274708
54. Tyagi, N., Mughees, M.H., Ristenpart, T., Miers, I.: BurnBox: self-revocable encryption in a world of compelled access. In: Enck, W., Felt, A.P. (eds.) USENIX Security 2018, pp. 445–461. USENIX Association (2018)

Multi-user Security of the Sum of Truncated Random Permutations

Wonseok Choi[1](✉), Hwigyeom Kim[2], Jooyoung Lee[2](✉), and Yeongmin Lee[2]

[1] KIAS, Seoul, Korea
wonseok@kias.re.kr
[2] KAIST, Daejeon, Korea
{buddha93,hicalf,dudals4780}@kaist.ac.kr

Abstract. For several decades, constructing pseudorandom functions from pseudorandom permutations, so-called Luby-Rackoff backward construction, has been a popular cryptographic problem. Two methods are well-known and comprehensively studied for this problem: summing two random permutations and truncating partial bits of the output from a random permutation. In this paper, by combining both summation and truncation, we propose new Luby-Rackoff backward constructions, dubbed SaT1 and SaT2, respectively.

SaT2 is obtained by partially truncating output bits from the sum of two independent random permutations, and SaT1 is its single permutation-based variant using domain separation. The distinguishing advantage against SaT1 and SaT2 is upper bounded by $O(\sqrt{\mu q_{\max}}/2^{n-0.5m})$ and $O(\sqrt{\mu} q_{\max}^{1.5}/2^{2n-0.5m})$, respectively, in the multi-user setting, where n is the size of the underlying permutation, m is the output size of the construction, μ is the number of users, and $q_{\max}$ is the maximum number of queries per user. We also prove the distinguishing advantage against a variant of XORP[3] (studied by Bhattacharya and Nandi at Asiacrypt 2021) using independent permutations, dubbed SoP3-2, is upper bounded by $O(\sqrt{\mu} q_{\max}^{2}/2^{2.5n})$.

In the multi-user setting with $\mu = O(2^{n-m})$, a truncated random permutation provides only the birthday bound security, while SaT1 and SaT2 are fully secure, i.e., allowing $O(2^n)$ queries for each user. It is the same security level as XORP[3] using three permutation calls, while SaT1 and SaT2 need only two permutation calls.

Keywords: Pseudorandom function · Luby-Rackoff backward · Sum of permutations · Truncated random permutation · Multi-user security

W. Choi—Supported by a KIAS Individual Grant CG089501 at Korea Institute for Advanced Study

J. Lee—This work was supported by Institute for Information & communications Technology Planning & Evaluation(IITP) grant funded by the Korea government(MSIT) (No.2022-0-01202 , Regional strategic industry convergence security core talent training business).

S. Agrawal and D. Lin (Eds.): ASIACRYPT 2022, LNCS 13792, pp. 682–710, 2022.
https://doi.org/10.1007/978-3-031-22966-4_23

1 Introduction

Block ciphers are usually considered to be pseudorandom permutations (PRPs) from a cryptographic perspective. That means someone cannot distinguish a secure block cipher from a random permutation before performing a certain number of encryption and decryption queries in a black-box manner. On the other hand, various cryptographic constructions such as the Wegman-Carter message authentication scheme use a pseudorandom function (PRF) as their building primitives to achieve beyond-birthday-bound security. When the underlying PRF is instantiated with a block cipher, the security of the resulting construction (e.g., the Wegman-Carter-Shoup construction) might be degraded down to the birthday bound [2–4].

In order to address the problem of security degradation, there has been a significant amount of research on construction of beyond-birthday-bound secure PRFs from (sufficiently secure) PRPs [1,3,5,9,14,16,19,20,23,30,31]. Among such *Luby-Rackoff backward* constructions, two constructions are well-known and have been comprehensively studied: summing two random permutations and truncating partial bits of the output from a random permutation.

Sum of Random Permutations. Given two n-bit (keyed) PRPs P_1 and P_2, their sum, denoted SoP, maps $x \in \{0,1\}^n$ to

$$\mathsf{SoP}[\mathsf{P}_1, \mathsf{P}_2](x) \stackrel{\text{def}}{=} \mathsf{P}_1(x) \oplus \mathsf{P}_2(x).$$

This construction was first introduced by Bellare et al. [3], and its security has been proved up to $2^{2n/3}$ queries by Lucks [24]. A series of works followed [11, 27,30], culminating with the proof by Dai et al. [14] that the sum of two n-bit random permutations is (fully) secure up to $O(2^n)$ queries.

Sum of Three or More Random Permutations. $\mathsf{SoP}[k]$ is a generalization of SoP. With k random permutations, $\mathsf{SoP}[k]$ returns its output by summing outputs of k random permutations. Lucks [24] showed that $\mathsf{SoP}[k]$ is secure up to $O(2^{kn/(k+1)})$ queries, and Mennink and Preneel [27] showed that $\mathsf{SoP}[k]$ is not weaker than SoP. Since SoP is fully secure in terms of indistinguishability, this problem seemed to be settled. However, a single permutation variant of $\mathsf{SoP}[3]$ with domain separation, originally dubbed $\mathsf{XORP}[3]$, but denoted $\mathsf{SoP3\text{-}1}$ throughout this paper, was revisited by Bhattacharya and Nandi [6], where they proved its n-bit security in the multi-user setting with $O(2^n)$ users.

Truncated Random Permutations. Let n and m be positive integers such that $m < n$. The TRP construction is defined as

$$\mathsf{TRP}[\mathsf{P}] \stackrel{\text{def}}{=} \mathsf{Tr}_m(\mathsf{P}(\cdot)),$$

where P is an n-bit permutation (modeled as a random secret permutation) and

$$\mathsf{Tr}_m : \{0,1\}^n \longrightarrow \{0,1\}^m$$
$$x \longmapsto x_L,$$

when $x \in \{0,1\}^n$ is written as $x_L \| x_R$ for $x_L \in \{0,1\}^m$ and $x_R \in \{0,1\}^{n-m}$. Truncating a random permutation was first considered by Hall et al. [20] and proved secure up to $O(2^{(n+m)/2})$ adversarial queries [16]. Besides, the authors realized that their security bound follows from the result of Stam [32] which was already published in 1978. This bound turns out to be tight as they also present matching attacks. Mennink [25] generalized truncation functions used in TRP and showed that the security of such constructions could not exceed that of the original TRP.

MULTI-USER SECURITY. In the real world, multiple users use the same cryptographic scheme with independent keys. Even if a cryptographic scheme is proved to be secure in the single-user setting, it does not generally guarantee its multi-user security, where an adversary access multiple instances, each of which uses a distinct key. Multi-user security of symmetric-key constructions was firstly considered by Mouha et al. [28], by proving the multi-user security of the Even-Mansour cipher. Since then, various constructions have been analyzed in the multi-user setting [7,21,22,33].

1.1 Related Work

There have been some other approaches to building a PRF on top of PRPs. In this section, P_1 and P_2 are independent n-bit permutations.

ENCRYPTED DAVIS-MEYER. Cogliati and Seurin [12] introduced a PRF construction, dubbed Encrypted Davis-Meyer (EDM), defined as

$$\mathsf{EDM}[\mathsf{P}_1, \mathsf{P}_2](x) \stackrel{\text{def}}{=} \mathsf{P}_2(\mathsf{P}_1(x) \oplus x).$$

They proved PRF-security of EDM up to $O\left(2^{2n/3}\right)$ queries. Later, Dai et al. [14] improved this bound up to $O\left(2^{3n/4}\right)$ via the chi-squared method. Mennink and Neves [26] introduced a dual construction of EDM, dubbed Encrypted Davis-Meyer Dual (EDMD), defined as

$$\mathsf{EDMD}[\mathsf{P}_1, \mathsf{P}_2](x) \stackrel{\text{def}}{=} \mathsf{P}_2(\mathsf{P}_1(x)) \oplus \mathsf{P}_1(x).$$

They claimed both EDM and EDMD are secure up to (almost) 2^n queries. However, the proof depends on Patarin's Mirror theory, which has not been fully verified. Cogliati and Seurin [13] proved that the single permutation variant of EDM is secure up to $2^{2n/3}$ queries.

SUMMATION-TRUNCATION HYBRID. Gunsing and Mennink [19] proposed the so-called Summation Truncation Hybrid (STH) construction. The idea of this construction is concatenating outputs of two independent TRPs and sum of discarded bits from those TRPs. They proved that STH is asymptotically as secure as TRP, which implies that the use of discarded bits does not degrade the security.

Sum of Even-Mansour. Sum of Even-Mansour (SoEM) [8] is a PRF built from public permutations. When P_1 and P_2 are public permutations, the construction is defined as

$$\mathsf{SoEM}[\mathsf{P}_1, \mathsf{P}_2, k_1, k_2](x) \stackrel{\text{def}}{=} \mathsf{P}_1(x \oplus k_1) \oplus k_1 \oplus \mathsf{P}_2(x \oplus k_2) \oplus k_2,$$

where k_1 and k_2 are secret keys. The authors proved that SoEM with independent permutations and keys achieves $2n/3$-bit security, which is tight. They also proposed another PRF construction, dubbed SoKAC, however, Nandi [29] pointed out a flaw from the security proof of SoKAC and this construction is disclaimed.

1.2 Our Contribution

In this paper, we propose new Luby-Rackoff backward constructions: $\mathsf{SaT1}$ and $\mathsf{SaT2}$. Let P, P_1 and P_2 be n-bit permutations. For a positive integer m such that $m < n$, $\mathsf{SaT1}$ and $\mathsf{SaT2}$ are defined as follows (see Fig. 1).

$$\begin{aligned}\mathsf{SaT1}[\mathsf{P}] : \{0,1\}^{n-1} &\longrightarrow \{0,1\}^m \\ x &\longmapsto \mathsf{Tr}_m(\mathsf{P}(0 \,\|\, x) \oplus \mathsf{P}(1 \,\|\, x)), \\ \mathsf{SaT2}[\mathsf{P}_1, \mathsf{P}_2] : \{0,1\}^{n} &\longrightarrow \{0,1\}^m \\ x &\longmapsto \mathsf{Tr}_m(\mathsf{P}_1(x) \oplus \mathsf{P}_2(x)).\end{aligned}$$

We also propose a variant of $\mathsf{SoP}[3]$ using three independent permutations, dubbed $\mathsf{SoP3\text{-}2}$. For n-bit permutations P, P_1, P_2 and P_3, $\mathsf{SoP3\text{-}1}$ and $\mathsf{SoP3\text{-}2}$ are defined as follows (see Fig. 2).

$$\begin{aligned}\mathsf{SoP3\text{-}1}[\mathsf{P}] : \{0,1\}^{n-2} &\longrightarrow \{0,1\}^n \\ x &\longmapsto \mathsf{P}(00 \,\|\, x) \oplus \mathsf{P}(01 \,\|\, x) \oplus \mathsf{P}(10 \,\|\, x), \\ \mathsf{SoP3\text{-}2}[\mathsf{P}_1, \mathsf{P}_2, \mathsf{P}_3] : \{0,1\}^{n} &\longrightarrow \{0,1\}^n \\ x &\longmapsto \mathsf{P}_1(x) \oplus \mathsf{P}_2(x) \oplus \mathsf{P}_3(x).\end{aligned}$$

The multi-user security of $\mathsf{SaT1}$, $\mathsf{SaT2}$, and $\mathsf{SoP3\text{-}2}$ is summarized in Table 1. Note that the single-user security bound of $\mathsf{SaT1}$ and $\mathsf{SaT2}$ can be obtained from our bound by setting $\mu = 1$, while the generic multi-user bound is obtained by multiplying μ to the single-user bound. Our security bound is proportional to $\mu^{1/2}$, which is better than the one from the hybrid argument.

$\mathsf{SaT1}$ and $\mathsf{SaT2}$ can be regarded as the sum of two TRPs. Also, $\mathsf{SaT2}$ (resp. $\mathsf{SaT1}$) can be obtained by truncating SoP (resp. SoP based on a single permutation with domain separation). If we apply our proof technique to TRP, the security bound would be

$$O\left(\frac{\sqrt{\mu} q_{\max}}{2^{n-\frac{m}{2}}}\right).$$

We omit the proof, but proving the above bound would be straightforward. TRP cannot achieve full security with respect to the permutation size in the multi-user setting. For $m = n/2$ and $\mu = O(2^{n/2})$, TRP is secure up to $O(2^{n/2})$ queries

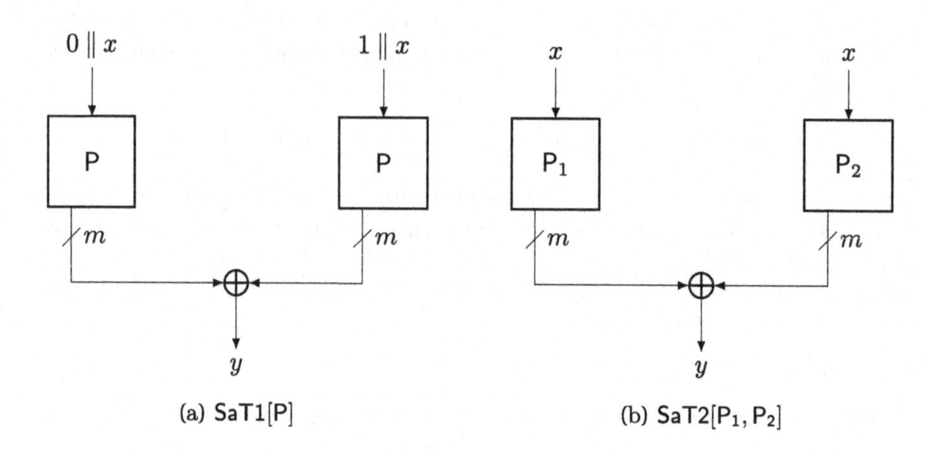

Fig. 1. SaT1 and SaT2 constructions

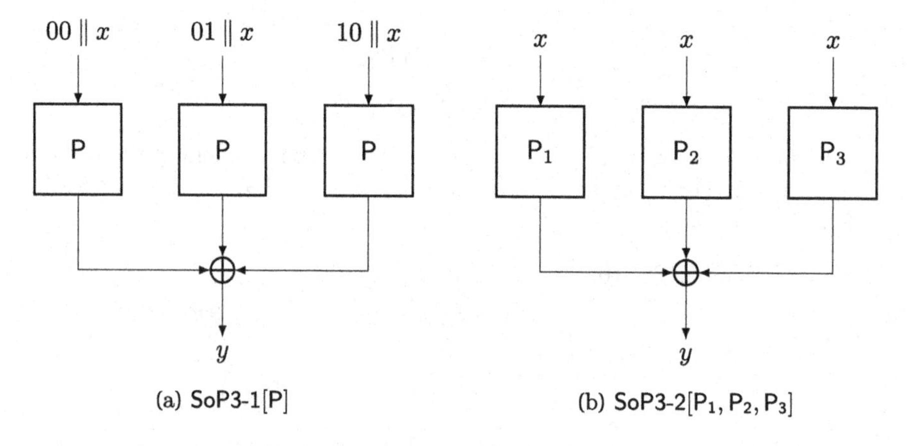

Fig. 2. SoP3-1 and SoP3-2 constructions

Table 1. Multi-user security and efficiency of SaT and SoP[3] constructions. Constants are ignored in the security bounds. μ is the number of users and $q_{\max}$ is the maximum number of queries per user. Rate is the number of output bits per permutation call.

Construction	Security bound	Rate	Number of keys	Reference
SaT1	$\sqrt{\mu q_{\max}}/2^{n-0.5m}$	$m/2$	1	Ours
SaT2	$\sqrt{\mu q_{\max}^{1.5}}/2^{2n-0.5m}$	$m/2$	2	Ours
SoP3-1	$\sqrt{\mu q_{\max}}/2^{n}$	$n/3$	1	[6]
SoP3-2	$\sqrt{\mu q_{\max}^{2}}/2^{2.5n}$	$n/3$	3	Ours

for each user, while SaT1 and SaT2 are secure up to $O(2^n)$ queries for each user. Compared to SoP3-1, SaT1 and SaT2 can be made more secure at the cost of a lower rate, or conversely, can be made more efficient according to the acceptable level of security or the number of users. If $\mu \ll 2^{n/3}$, SaT1 and SaT2 can allow $O(2^n)$ queries per user and the rate is higher than $n/3$ (the rate of SoP3-1) by setting $m = n - \log_2 \mu$.

As a concrete example, when $n = 128$, $m = 64$ and $\mu = 2^{64}$, both SaT1 and SaT2 are optimally secure, i.e., $(128 - \epsilon)$-bit secure for all $\mu = 2^{64}$ users, where ϵ is a small constant from our security bounds. If more output bits are needed, one can truncate only 16 bits (with $m = 112$), in which case SaT1 enjoys 80-bit security, and SaT2 is even better, enjoying 112-bit security. Hence, SaT2 outputs 112-bit blocks with 112-bit security, while SoP3-1 outputs 128-bit blocks with 128-bit security for 2^{64} users, at the cost of two primitive calls and three primitive calls, respectively.

When $\mu \gg O(2^{n-m})$, we note that SaT2 can accept significantly more queries than SaT1. We also see our security bound of SoP3-2 is better than SoP3-1, while the tightness of these security bounds is still open.

Proof Technique. Compared to SoP, it is not straightforward to compute the expectation of the χ^2-divergence for truncated values. We addressed this issue by modifying the domain over which the expectation is taken. Moreover, we had to precisely compute the expectation rather than loosely upper bounding it, which was possible by using more involved counting - we take into account almost all the terms appearing in our computation, and make them cancel out each other.

Application. The key-generation algorithm in AES-GCM-SIV [7,17,18] can be replaced by SaT1 or SaT2. GCM-SIV and other authenticated encryption schemes such as CWC+ [15] and SCM [10] use synthetic IVs derived from secure PRFs. We expect that those constructions would perform better in the multi-user setting when combined with SaT1 or SaT2, while proving their overall security would be an independent topic of interest.

2 Preliminaries

Notation. Throughout this paper, we fix positive integers n, m, and μ such that $m < n$ to denote the block size, the number of output bits (after truncation), and number of users, respectively. We denote 0^m (i.e., m-bit string of all zeros) by $\mathbf{0}$. Given a non-empty finite set $\mathcal{X}$, $x \leftarrow_\$ \mathcal{X}$ denotes that x is chosen uniformly at random from $\mathcal{X}$. $|\mathcal{X}|$ means the number of elements in $\mathcal{X}$. The set of all permutations of $\{0,1\}^n$ is simply denoted $\mathsf{Perm}(n)$. The set of all functions with domain $\{0,1\}^n$ and codomain $\{0,1\}^m$ is simply denoted by $\mathsf{Func}(n,m)$. For a keyed function $F : \mathcal{K} \times \mathcal{X} \to \mathcal{Y}$ with key space $\mathcal{K}$ and non-empty sets $\mathcal{X}$ and $\mathcal{Y}$, we will denote $F(K,\cdot)$ by $F_K(\cdot)$ for $K \in \mathcal{K}$. A truncating function is defined as follows:

$$\begin{aligned} \mathsf{Tr}_m : \{0,1\}^n &\longrightarrow \{0,1\}^m \\ x &\longmapsto x_L, \end{aligned}$$

where $x \in \{0,1\}^n$ is written as $x_L \| x_R$ for $x_L \in \{0,1\}^m$ and $x_R \in \{0,1\}^{n-m}$.

MULTI-USER PSEUDORANDOM FUNCTION. Let $\mathsf{C} : \mathcal{K} \times \{0,1\}^n \rightarrow \{0,1\}^m$ be a keyed function with key space $\mathcal{K}$. We will consider an information theoretic distinguisher $\mathcal{A}$ that makes oracle queries to C, and returns a single bit. The advantage of $\mathcal{A}$ in breaking the mu-prf security of C, i.e., in distinguishing $\mathsf{C}(K_1,\cdot),\ldots,\mathsf{C}(K_\mu,\cdot)$ where $K_1,\ldots,K_\mu \leftarrow_\$ \mathcal{K}$ from uniformly chosen functions $\mathsf{F}_1,\ldots,\mathsf{F}_\mu \leftarrow_\$ \mathsf{Func}(n,m)$, is defined as

$$\mathbf{Adv}_{\mathsf{C}}^{\text{mu-prf}}(\mathcal{A}) = \Big|\Pr\left[K_1,\ldots,K_\mu \leftarrow_\$ \mathcal{K} : \mathcal{A}^{\mathsf{C}_{K_1}(\cdot),\ldots,\mathsf{C}_{K_\mu}(\cdot)} = 1\right] - \Pr\left[\mathsf{F}_1,\ldots,\mathsf{F}_\mu \leftarrow_\$ \mathsf{Func}(n,m) : \mathcal{A}^{\mathsf{F}_1(\cdot),\ldots,\mathsf{F}_\mu(\cdot)} = 1\right]\Big|.$$

We define $\mathbf{Adv}_{\mathsf{C}}^{\text{mu-prf}}(\mu, q_{\max}, t)$ as the maximum of $\mathbf{Adv}_{\mathsf{C}}^{\text{mu-prf}}(\mathcal{A})$ over all the distinguishers against C for μ users making at most $q_{\max}$ queries to each user and running in time at most t. When we consider information theoretic security, we will drop the parameter t.

MULTI-USER PSEUDORANDOM PERMUTATION. Let $\mathsf{E} : \mathcal{K} \times \{0,1\}^n \rightarrow \{0,1\}^n$ be an n-bit block cipher with key space $\mathcal{K}$. We will consider an information theoretic distinguisher $\mathcal{A}$ that makes oracle queries to E, and returns a single bit. The advantage of $\mathcal{A}$ in breaking the mu-prp security of E is defined as

$$\mathbf{Adv}_{\mathsf{E}}^{\text{mu-prp}}(\mathcal{A}) = \Big|\Pr\left[K_1,\ldots,K_\mu \leftarrow_\$ \mathcal{K} : \mathcal{A}^{\mathsf{E}_{K_1}(\cdot),\ldots,\mathsf{E}_{K_\mu}(\cdot)} = 1\right] - \Pr\left[\mathsf{P}_1,\ldots,\mathsf{P}_\mu \leftarrow_\$ \mathsf{Perm}(n) : \mathcal{A}^{\mathsf{P}_1(\cdot),\ldots,\mathsf{P}_\mu(\cdot)} = 1\right]\Big|.$$

Similarly to the mu-prf security, we define $\mathbf{Adv}_{\mathsf{E}}^{\text{mu-prp}}(\mu, q_{\max}, t)$.

THE CHI-SQUARED METHOD. We give here all the necessary background on the chi-squared method [14] that we will use throughout this paper.

We fix a set of random systems, a deterministic distinguisher $\mathcal{A}$ that makes q oracle queries to one of the random systems, and a set Ω that contains all possible answers for oracle queries to the random systems. For a random system $\mathcal{S}$ and $i \in \{1,\ldots,q\}$, let $Z_{\mathcal{S},i}$ be the random variable over Ω that follows the distribution of the i-th answer obtained by $\mathcal{A}$ interacting with $\mathcal{S}$. Let

$$\mathbf{Z}_{\mathcal{S}}^i \stackrel{\text{def}}{=} (Z_{\mathcal{S},1},\ldots,Z_{\mathcal{S},i}),$$

and let

$$\mathsf{p}_{\mathcal{S}}^i(\mathbf{z}) \stackrel{\text{def}}{=} \Pr\left[\mathbf{Z}_{\mathcal{S}}^i = \mathbf{z}\right]$$

for $\mathbf{z} \in \Omega^i$. For $i \le q$ and $\mathbf{z} = (z_1,\ldots,z_{i-1}) \in \Omega^{i-1}$ such that $\mathsf{p}_{\mathcal{S}}^{i-1}(\mathbf{z}) > 0$, the probability distribution of $Z_{\mathcal{S},i}$ conditioned on $\mathbf{Z}_{\mathcal{S}}^{i-1} = \mathbf{z}$ will be denoted $\mathsf{p}_{\mathcal{S},i}^{\mathbf{z}}(\cdot)$, namely for $z \in \Omega$,

$$\mathsf{p}_{\mathcal{S},i}^{\mathbf{z}}(z) \stackrel{\text{def}}{=} \Pr\left[Z_{\mathcal{S},i} = z \mid \mathbf{Z}_{\mathcal{S}}^{i-1} = \mathbf{z}\right].$$

For two random systems $\mathcal{S}_0$ and $\mathcal{S}_1$, and for $i < q$ and $\mathbf{z} = (z_1, \ldots, z_{i-1}) \in \Omega^{i-1}$ such that $\mathsf{p}^{i-1}_{\mathcal{S}_0}(\mathbf{z})$, $\mathsf{p}^{i-1}_{\mathcal{S}_1}(\mathbf{z}) > 0$, the χ^2*-divergence* for $\mathsf{p}^{\mathbf{z}}_{\mathcal{S}_0,i}(\cdot)$ and $\mathsf{p}^{\mathbf{z}}_{\mathcal{S}_1,i}(\cdot)$ is defined as follows.

$$\chi^2\left(\mathsf{p}^{\mathbf{z}}_{\mathcal{S}_1,i}(\cdot), \mathsf{p}^{\mathbf{z}}_{\mathcal{S}_0,i}(\cdot)\right) \stackrel{\text{def}}{=} \sum_{\substack{z\in\Omega \text{ such that} \\ \mathsf{p}^{\mathbf{z}}_{\mathcal{S}_0,i}(z)>0}} \frac{\left(\mathsf{p}^{\mathbf{z}}_{\mathcal{S}_1,i}(z) - \mathsf{p}^{\mathbf{z}}_{\mathcal{S}_0,i}(z)\right)^2}{\mathsf{p}^{\mathbf{z}}_{\mathcal{S}_0,i}(z)}.$$

We will simply write $\chi^2(\mathbf{z}) = \chi^2\left(\mathsf{p}^{\mathbf{z}}_{\mathcal{S}_1,i}(\cdot), \mathsf{p}^{\mathbf{z}}_{\mathcal{S}_0,i}(\cdot)\right)$ when the random systems are clear from the context. If the support of $\mathsf{p}^{i-1}_{\mathcal{S}_1}(\cdot)$ is contained in the support of $\mathsf{p}^{i-1}_{\mathcal{S}_0}(\cdot)$, then we can view $\chi^2\left(\mathsf{p}^{\mathbf{z}}_{\mathcal{S}_1,i}(\cdot), \mathsf{p}^{\mathbf{z}}_{\mathcal{S}_0,i}(\cdot)\right)$ as a random variable, denoted $\chi^2\left(\mathbf{Z}^{i-1}_{\mathcal{S}_1}\right)$, where $\mathbf{z}$ follows the distribution of $\mathbf{Z}^{i-1}_{\mathcal{S}_1}$.

Then $\mathcal{A}$'s distinguishing advantage is upper bounded by the *total variation distance* of $\mathsf{p}^{q}_{\mathcal{S}_0}(\cdot)$ and $\mathsf{p}^{q}_{\mathcal{S}_1}(\cdot)$, denoted $\|\mathsf{p}^{q}_{\mathcal{S}_0}(\cdot) - \mathsf{p}^{q}_{\mathcal{S}_1}(\cdot)\|$, and we also have

$$\|\mathsf{p}^{q}_{\mathcal{S}_0}(\cdot) - \mathsf{p}^{q}_{\mathcal{S}_1}(\cdot)\| \leq \left(\frac{1}{2}\sum_{i=1}^{q} \mathbf{Ex}\left[\chi^2\left(\mathbf{Z}^{i-1}_{\mathcal{S}_1}\right)\right]\right)^{\frac{1}{2}}. \tag{1}$$

See [14] for the proof of (1).

3 Summation-and-Truncation

In this section, we propose new PRF constructions based on PRPs. We will prove that these constructions are fully secure (secure after almost 2^n queries made for each user) with 2^{n-m} users. Let

$$\begin{aligned} \mathsf{SaT1}[\mathsf{P}] : \{0,1\}^{n-1} &\longrightarrow \{0,1\}^m \\ x &\longmapsto \mathsf{Tr}_m(\mathsf{P}(0 \,\|\, x) \oplus \mathsf{P}(1 \,\|\, x)) \end{aligned}$$

where Tr_m is defined in Sect. 2 and P is an n-bit random permutation from $\mathsf{Perm}(n)$. The $\mathsf{mu\text{-}prf}$ security of $\mathsf{SaT1}$ is represented by the following theorem.

Theorem 1. *Let n, m, μ, and q_{max} be positive integers such that $m < n$ and $q_{\max} \leq 2^{n-3}$. Then one has*

$$\mathbf{Adv}^{\mathsf{mu\text{-}prf}}_{\mathsf{SaT1}}(\mu, q_{\max}) \leq \left(\frac{20\mu q^3_{\max}}{2^{4n-m}} + \frac{21\mu q_{\max}}{2^{2n-m}}\right)^{\frac{1}{2}}.$$

The proof is given in Sect. 4.

Remark 1. When $m = n$, it is well known that the $\mathsf{mu\text{-}prf}$ advantage of $\mathsf{SaT1}$ (equivalently, SoP) is about $\mu q_{\max}/2^n$ since $\mathsf{SaT1}$ never outputs $\mathbf{0}$ which is distinguished from a random function.

We also define $\mathsf{SaT2}$ which is a variant of $\mathsf{SaT1}$ on two independent random permutations. Let

$$\begin{aligned}\mathsf{SaT2}[\mathsf{P}_1, \mathsf{P}_2] : \{0,1\}^n &\longrightarrow \{0,1\}^m \\ x &\longmapsto \mathsf{Tr}_m(\mathsf{P}_1(x) \oplus \mathsf{P}_2(x))\end{aligned}$$

where Tr_m is defined in Sect. 2 and P_1 and P_2 are two independent random permutations from $\mathsf{Perm}(n)$. The mu-prf security of $\mathsf{SaT2}$ is represented by the following theorem.

Theorem 2. *Let n, m, μ, and q_{max} be positive integers such that $m \leq n$ and $q_{\max} \leq 2^{n-2}$. Then one has*

$$\mathbf{Adv}^{\mathsf{mu\text{-}prf}}_{\mathsf{SaT2}}(\mu, q_{\max}) \leq \left(\frac{2\mu q_{\max}^3}{2^{4n-m}}\right)^{\frac{1}{2}}.$$

The proof is given in Sect. 5.

One can consider $\mathsf{SaT1}$ and $\mathsf{SaT2}$ based on an n-bit block cipher $\mathsf{E} : \mathcal{K} \times \{0,1\}^n \rightarrow \{0,1\}^n$ with key space $\mathcal{K}$, which is defined as

- For $x \in \{0,1\}^{n-1}$ and $K \in \mathcal{K}$,

$$\mathsf{SaT1}[\mathsf{E}](K, x) = \mathsf{Tr}_m(\mathsf{E}_K(0 \parallel x) \oplus \mathsf{E}_K(1 \parallel x));$$

- For $x \in \{0,1\}^n$ and $K_1, K_2 \in \mathcal{K}$,

$$\mathsf{SaT2}[\mathsf{E}](K_1, K_2, x) = \mathsf{Tr}_m(\mathsf{E}_{K_1}(x) \oplus \mathsf{E}_{K_2}(x)).$$

Up to the mu-prp security of E, one can derive the multi-user security of $\mathsf{SaT1}[\mathsf{E}]$ and $\mathsf{SaT2}[\mathsf{E}]$.

$$\mathbf{Adv}^{\mathsf{mu\text{-}prf}}_{\mathsf{SaT1[E]}}(\mu, q_{\max}, t) \leq \mathbf{Adv}^{\mathsf{mu\text{-}prp}}_{\mathsf{E}}(\mu, 2q_{\max}, t') + \left(\frac{20\mu q_{\max}^3}{2^{4n-m}} + \frac{21\mu q_{\max}}{2^{2n-m}}\right)^{\frac{1}{2}},$$

$$\mathbf{Adv}^{\mathsf{mu\text{-}prf}}_{\mathsf{SaT2[E]}}(\mu, q_{\max}, t) \leq \mathbf{Adv}^{\mathsf{mu\text{-}prp}}_{\mathsf{E}}(2\mu, q_{\max}, t') + \left(\frac{2\mu q_{\max}^3}{2^{4n-m}}\right)^{\frac{1}{2}}$$

where $t' \approx t + 2\mu q_{\max}$.

4 Proof of Theorem 1

Before proving the security of $\mathsf{SaT1}$, we define random experiments to make it possible to prove it with the chi-squared method in Algorithm 1.

Algorithm 1. Experiments for SaT1

Experiment $\mathcal{B}_0$

```
1: for j ← 1 to μ do
2:     for i ← 1 to q_max do
3:         y_i^j ←$ {0,1}^m
4:     Z^j ← (y_1^j, ··· , y_{q_max}^j)
5: return (Z^1, ..., Z^μ)
```

Experiment $\mathcal{B}_1$

```
1: for j ← 1 to μ do
2:     R_u ← {0,1}^n
3:     for i ← 1 to q_max do
4:         u_{2i-1}^j ←$ R_u, R_u ← R_u \ {u_{2i-1}^j}
5:         u_{2i}^j ←$ R_u, R_u ← R_u \ {u_{2i}^j}
6:         r_{2i-1}^j ← Tr_m(u_{2i-1}^j), r_{2i}^j ← Tr_m(u_{2i}^j)
7:         y_i^j ← r_{2i-1}^j ⊕ r_{2i}^j
8:     Z^j ← (y_1^j, ··· , y_{q_max}^j)
9: return (Z^1, ..., Z^μ)
```

Experiment $\mathcal{C}_0$

```
1: for j ← 1 to μ do
2:     R_u ← {0,1}^n
3:     for i ← 1 to q_max do
4:         y_i^j ←$ {0,1}^m
5:         T_i^j(y_i^j) ← {(u,v) : u,v ∈ R_u, u ≠ v, Tr_m(u ⊕ v) = y_i^j}
6:         if |T_i^j(y_i^j)| > 0 then
7:             (u_{2i-1}^j, u_{2i}^j) ←$ T_i^j(y_i^j)
8:         else
9:             (u_{2i-1}^j, u_{2i}^j) ← (⊥, ⊥)
10:        R_u ← R_u \ {u_{2i-1}^j, u_{2i}^j}
11:        r_{2i-1}^j ← Tr_m(u_{2i-1}^j), r_{2i}^j ← Tr_m(u_{2i}^j)
12:        z_i^j ← (r_{2i-1}^j, y_i^j)
13:    Z^j ← (z_1^j, ··· , z_{q_max}^j)
14: return (Z^1, ..., Z^μ)
```

Experiment $\mathcal{C}_1$

```
1: for j ← 1 to μ do
2:     R_u ← {0,1}^n
3:     for i ← 1 to q_max do
4:         u_{2i-1}^j ←$ R_u, R_u ← R_u \ {u_{2i-1}^j}
5:         u_{2i}^j ←$ R_u, R_u ← R_u \ {u_{2i}^j}
6:         r_{2i-1}^j ← Tr_m(u_{2i-1}^j), r_{2i}^j ← Tr_m(u_{2i}^j)
7:         y_i^j ← r_{2i-1}^j ⊕ r_{2i}^j
8:         z_i^j ← (r_{2i-1}^j, y_i^j)
9:     Z^j ← (z_1^j, ··· , z_{q_max}^j)
10: return (Z^1, ··· , Z^μ)
```

The main purpose of the algorithm is to transform the distinguishing game between $\mathcal{S}_0$ and $\mathcal{S}_1$ into the game between $\mathcal{C}_0$ and $\mathcal{C}_1$ (see equation (2)) in order to evaluate the distinguishing advantage using the chi-squared method. The game between $\mathcal{C}_0$ and $\mathcal{C}_1$ has two major differences from the game between $\mathcal{S}_0$ and $\mathcal{S}_1$:

1. $\mathcal{C}_0$ and $\mathcal{C}_1$ take no input, which can be seen as a reduction from an adaptive adversary to a non-adaptive adversary and this reduction makes it easy to apply the chi-squared method.
2. The outputs of $\mathcal{C}_0$ and $\mathcal{C}_1$ have additional information, namely r^j_{2i-1}.

Note that $\mathcal{B}_0$ and $\mathcal{B}_1$ are intermediate games that yield equation (2).

For Experiment $\mathcal{C}_0$ in Algorithm 1, the following lemma holds.

Lemma 1. *For any $q_{\max} \leq 2^{n-3}$, Experiment $\mathcal{C}_0$ in Algorithm 1 never returns $(\perp, \perp)$.*

Proof. We suppose any $j \in [\mu]$ and omit j for simplicity. If $i = 1$, it is trivial that $|\mathcal{T}_i(y_i)| > 0$ since $|\mathcal{T}_i(y_i)| = 2^n(2^{n-m} - 1)$ for $y_i = \mathbf{0}$ and $|\mathcal{T}_i(y_i)| = 2^{2n-m}$ for $y_i \neq \mathbf{0}$. For $2 \leq i \leq q_{\max}$, we have $|\mathcal{R}_u| = 2^n - 2(i-1)$ and therefore $|\mathcal{T}_i(y_i)| \geq 2^{2n-m} - (4i-3)2^{n-m} > 0$ since $i \leq q_{\max} \leq 2^{n-3}$ by our assumption. □

Let $\mathcal{S}_0$ be a random oracle with $\mathsf{Func}(n-1, m)$ and $\mathcal{S}_1$ be a random oracle with $\mathsf{SaT1}$. It is obvious that transcripts for $\mathcal{S}_0$ (or $\mathcal{S}_1$) has same probability distribution with the output of $\mathcal{B}_0$ (or $\mathcal{B}_1$). Secondly, statistical distance between $\mathcal{C}_0$ and $\mathcal{C}_1$ is larger than statistical distance between $\mathcal{B}_0$ and $\mathcal{B}_1$ since the outputs of $\mathcal{C}_0$ (or $\mathcal{C}_1$) contains the outputs of $\mathcal{B}_0$ (or $\mathcal{B}_1$), respectively. The two facts make following inequality to be held.

$$\|\mathsf{p}^q_{\mathcal{S}_0}(\cdot) - \mathsf{p}^q_{\mathcal{S}_1}(\cdot)\| = \|\mathsf{p}^q_{\mathcal{B}_0}(\cdot) - \mathsf{p}^q_{\mathcal{B}_1}(\cdot)\| \leq \|\mathsf{p}^q_{\mathcal{C}_0}(\cdot) - \mathsf{p}^q_{\mathcal{C}_1}(\cdot)\|. \tag{2}$$

By (2) and Lemma 2, we can prove Theorem 1.

Lemma 2. *For any $q_{\max} \leq 2^{n-3}$, let $\mathcal{C}_0$ and $\mathcal{C}_1$ be the experiments described in Algorithm 1. Then we have*

$$\|\mathsf{p}^q_{\mathcal{C}_0}(\cdot) - \mathsf{p}^q_{\mathcal{C}_1}(\cdot)\| \leq \left(\frac{20\mu q^3_{\max}}{2^{4n-m}} + \frac{21\mu q_{\max}}{2^{2n-m}}\right)^{\frac{1}{2}}.$$

4.1 Proof of Lemma 2

Let $q = \mu q_{\max}$. For $i \in [q]$ where $i = (j-1)q_{\max} + k$ such that $j \in [\mu]$ and $k \in [q_{\max}]$, the response of the i-th query is seen as $z_i = z^j_k$. Then, we can easily check that the support of $\mathsf{p}^{i-1}_{\mathcal{C}_1}(\cdot)$ is contained in the support of $\mathsf{p}^{i-1}_{\mathcal{C}_0}(\cdot)$ for $i = 1, \ldots, q$, allowing us to use the chi-squared method.

Let $\Omega = \{0,1\}^m \times \{0,1\}^m$. For fixed $i \in \{1,\ldots,q\}$ and $\mathbf{z} \in \Omega^{i-1}$ such $\mathsf{p}_{\mathcal{C}_1}^{i-1}(\mathbf{z}) > 0$, we will compute

$$\chi^2(\mathbf{z}) = \sum_{\substack{z\in\Omega \text{ such that} \\ \mathsf{p}_{\mathcal{C}_0,i}^{\mathbf{z}}(z)>0}} \frac{\left(\mathsf{p}_{\mathcal{C}_1,i}^{\mathbf{z}}(z) - \mathsf{p}_{\mathcal{C}_0,i}^{\mathbf{z}}(z)\right)^2}{\mathsf{p}_{\mathcal{C}_0,i}^{\mathbf{z}}(z)}$$

$$= \sum_{\substack{z\in\Omega \text{ such that} \\ \mathsf{p}_{\mathcal{C}_0,i}^{\mathbf{z}}(z)>0}} \mathsf{p}_{\mathcal{C}_0,i}^{\mathbf{z}}(z)\left(1 - \frac{\mathsf{p}_{\mathcal{C}_1,i}^{\mathbf{z}}(z)}{\mathsf{p}_{\mathcal{C}_0,i}^{\mathbf{z}}(z)}\right)^2$$

Firstly, note that $\mathbf{z} = (z_1,\ldots,z_{i-1})$ and $z_l = (r_{2l-1}, y_l)$ for $l = 1,\ldots,i-1$. Let $\hat{\Omega} = \{0,1\}^n \times \{0,1\}^n$, $h_l = (u_{2l-1}, y'_l) \in \hat{\Omega}$ and $\mathbf{h} = (h_1,\ldots,h_{i-1})$ for $l = 1,\ldots,i-1$. Note that $\mathbf{h}$ includes $\mathbf{z}$. Let $H_{\mathcal{C}_1,i}$ be the random variable over $\hat{\Omega}$ that follows the distribution of the internal values (u, y') in $\mathcal{C}_1$ interacting the i-th query by $\mathcal{A}$. Let

$$\mathbf{H}_{\mathcal{C}_1}^{i-1} \stackrel{\text{def}}{=} (H_{\mathcal{C}_1,1},\ldots,H_{\mathcal{C}_1,i-1})$$

for $\mathbf{h} \in \hat{\Omega}^{i-1}$. For a fixed $\mathbf{z} = ((r_1,y_1),(r_3,y_2),\ldots,(r_{2i-3},y_{i-1}))$, we denote $\mathbf{h} \vdash \mathbf{z}$ if and only if $h_l = (u_{2l-1}, y'_l)$ satisfies $\mathsf{Tr}_m(u_{2l-1}) = r_{2l-1}$ and $\mathsf{Tr}_m(y'_l) = y_l$ for all $l = 1,\ldots,i-1$, where $\mathbf{h} = (h_1,h_2,\ldots,h_{i-1})$. Then one has

$$\begin{aligned}
\underset{\mathbf{z}}{\mathbf{Ex}}\left[\chi^2(\mathbf{z})\right] &= \sum_{\mathbf{z}\in\Omega^{i-1}} \mathsf{p}_{\mathcal{C}_1}^{i}(\mathbf{z})\cdot\chi^2(\mathbf{z}) \\
&= \sum_{\mathbf{z}\in\Omega^{i-1}} \sum_{\substack{\mathbf{h}\in\hat{\Omega}^{i-1} \text{ such} \\ \text{that } \mathbf{h}\vdash\mathbf{z}}} \mathsf{p}_{\mathcal{C}_1}^{i}(\mathbf{z})\cdot\Pr\left[\mathbf{H}_{\mathcal{C}_1}^{i-1} = \mathbf{h} \mid \mathbf{Z}_{\mathcal{C}_1}^{i-1} = \mathbf{z}\right]\cdot\chi^2(\mathbf{z}) \\
&= \sum_{\mathbf{h}\in\hat{\Omega}^{i-1}} \Pr\left[\mathbf{H}_{\mathcal{C}_1}^{i-1} = \mathbf{h}\right]\cdot\chi^2(\mathbf{z}) \\
&= \underset{\mathbf{h}}{\mathbf{Ex}}\left[\chi^2(\mathbf{z})\right]
\end{aligned} \tag{3}$$

where the last expectation is taken over the distribution $\mathbf{H}_{\mathcal{C}_1}^{i-1}$. Furthermore, let $i = (j-1)q_{\max} + k$ such that $j \in [\mu]$ and $k \in [q_{\max}]$. For $\alpha \in \{0,1\}^m$, we define $U_k^j(\alpha)$ as the number of elements α in $(r_l^j)_{l=1,\ldots,2k-2}$. In other words,

$$U_k^j(\alpha) = \left|\{l \in [2k-2] \mid \alpha = r_l^j\}\right|.$$

Also, for $y \in \{0,1\}^m$, let $T_k^j(y) = \left|\mathcal{T}_k^j(y)\right|$. Note that, for any $j' \in [j-1]$, z_i is independent with $\mathbf{Z}^{j'}$. Therefore, we see that, for $y = \mathbf{0}$,

$$\mathsf{p}_{\mathcal{C}_0,i}^{\mathbf{z}}(r,\mathbf{0}) = \frac{(2^{n-m} - U_k^j(r))(2^{n-m} - U_k^j(r) - 1)}{2^m T_k^j(\mathbf{0})},$$

$$\mathsf{p}_{\mathcal{C}_1,i}^{\mathbf{z}}(r,\mathbf{0}) = \frac{(2^{n-m} - U_k^j(r))(2^{n-m} - U_k^j(r) - 1)}{(2^n - 2k + 2)(2^n - 2k + 1)},$$

and otherwise ($y \neq \mathbf{0}$),

$$\mathsf{p}^{\mathbf{z}}_{C_0,i}(r,y) = \frac{(2^{n-m} - U^j_k(r))(2^{n-m} - U^j_k(r \oplus y))}{2^m T^j_k(y)},$$

$$\mathsf{p}^{\mathbf{z}}_{C_1,i}(r,y) = \frac{(2^{n-m} - U^j_k(r))(2^{n-m} - U^j_k(r \oplus y))}{(2^n - 2k+2)(2^n - 2k+1)}.$$

For any $y \in \{0,1\}^m$,

$$\begin{aligned} T^j_k(y) &\geq \sum_{\alpha \in \{0,1\}^m} (2^{n-m} - U^j_k(\alpha))(2^{n-m} - U^j_k(\alpha \oplus y) - 1) \\ &\geq 2^{2n-m} - (4k-3)2^{n-m}. \end{aligned}$$

Let

$$G^j_k(y) \stackrel{\text{def}}{=} \left(\frac{(2^n - 2k+2)_2}{2^m} - T^j_k(y) \right)^2.$$

Then we have,

$$\begin{aligned} \chi^2(\mathbf{z}) = & \sum_{\substack{z=(r,y)\in\Omega \text{ such that} \\ \mathsf{p}^{\mathbf{z}}_{C_0,i}(z)>0 \text{ and } y\neq\mathbf{0}}} \frac{(2^{n-m} - U^j_k(r))(2^{n-m} - U^j_k(r \oplus y))}{2^m T^j_k(y)} \left(1 - \frac{2^m T^j_k(y)}{(2^n-2k+2)_2}\right)^2 \\ & + \sum_{\substack{z=(r,\mathbf{0})\in\Omega \text{ such} \\ \text{that } \mathsf{p}^{\mathbf{z}}_{C_0,i}(z)>0}} \frac{(2^{n-m} - U^j_k(r))(2^{n-m} - U^j_k(r) - 1)}{2^m T^j_k(\mathbf{0})} \left(1 - \frac{2^m T^j_k(\mathbf{0})}{(2^n-2k+2)_2}\right)^2 \\ \leq & \sum_{\substack{(r,y)\in\Omega \text{ such} \\ \text{that } \mathsf{p}^{\mathbf{z}}_{C_0,i}(r,y)>0}} \frac{2^{2n-2m}\left((2^n-2k+2)_2 - 2^m T^j_k(y)\right)^2}{2^m T^j_k(y)\left((2^n-2k+2)_2\right)^2} \\ \leq & \sum_{y\in\{0,1\}^m} \frac{7G^j_k(y)}{2^{4n-m}}. \end{aligned} \tag{4}$$

since $k \leq q_{\max} \leq 2^{n-3}$. We claim the following lemma.

Lemma 3. *For any $y \neq \mathbf{0}$, one has*

$$\mathop{\mathbf{Ex}}_{\mathbf{h}}\left[G^j_k(y)\right] \leq \frac{8(k-1)^2}{2^m} + 3 \cdot 2^{2n-2m},$$

$$\mathop{\mathbf{Ex}}_{\mathbf{h}}\left[G^j_k(\mathbf{0})\right] \leq 8(k-1)^2 + 3 \cdot 2^{2n}.$$

The proof of Lemma 3 is deferred to Sect. 7. From (4) and Lemma 3, it follows that

$$\begin{aligned} \mathop{\mathbf{Ex}}_{\mathbf{h}}\left[\chi^2(\mathbf{z})\right] &\leq \frac{7}{2^{4n-m}} \mathop{\mathbf{Ex}}_{\mathbf{h}}\left[\left(\sum_{y\in\{0,1\}^m\setminus\mathbf{0}} G^j_k(y)\right) + G^j_k(\mathbf{0})\right] \\ &\leq \frac{112(k-1)^2}{2^{4n-m}} + \frac{42}{2^{2n-m}} \end{aligned}$$

and finally, we have

$$\begin{aligned}\|\mathsf{p}^q_{\mathcal{C}_0}(\cdot) - \mathsf{p}^q_{\mathcal{C}_1}(\cdot)\| &\le \left(\frac{1}{2}\sum_{i=1}^{q}\mathbf{Ex}\left[\chi^2(\mathbf{z})\right]\right)^{\frac{1}{2}} \\ &\le \left(\frac{1}{2}\sum_{j=1}^{\mu}\sum_{k=1}^{q_{\max}}\mathbf{Ex}\left[\chi^2(\mathbf{z})\right]\right)^{\frac{1}{2}} \\ &\le \left(\frac{1}{2}\sum_{j=1}^{\mu}\sum_{k=1}^{q_{\max}}\frac{112(k-1)^2}{2^{4n-m}} + \frac{42}{2^{2n-m}}\right)^{\frac{1}{2}} \\ &\le \left(\frac{20\mu q_{\max}^3}{2^{4n-m}} + \frac{21\mu q_{\max}}{2^{2n-m}}\right)^{\frac{1}{2}}.\end{aligned}$$

5 Proof of Theorem 2

Similarly to Sect. 4, we define random experiments. See Algorithm 2. For Experiment $\mathcal{C}_0$ in Algorithm 2, the following lemma holds.

Lemma 4. *For any $q_{\max} \le 2^{n-2}$, Experiment $\mathcal{C}_0$ in Algorithm 2 never returns $(\perp, \perp)$.*

Proof. We suppose any $j \in [\mu]$ and omit y for simplicity. If $i = 1$, it is trivial that $|\mathcal{T}_i(y_i)| = 2^{2n-m} > 0$. For $2 \le i \le q_{\max}$, we have $|\mathcal{R}^U| = |\mathcal{R}^V| = 2^n - (i-1)$ and therefore $|\mathcal{T}_i(y_i)| \ge 2^{2n-m} - 2(i-1)2^{n-m} > 0$ since $i \le q_{\max} \le 2^{n-2}$ by our assumption. □

Let $\mathcal{S}_0$ be a random oracle with $\mathsf{Func}(n, m)$ and $\mathcal{S}_1$ be a random oracle with $\mathsf{SaT2}$. Similarly to the reasoning of (2), one has

$$\|\mathsf{p}^q_{\mathcal{S}_0}(\cdot) - \mathsf{p}^q_{\mathcal{S}_1}(\cdot)\| = \|\mathsf{p}^q_{\mathcal{B}_0}(\cdot) - \mathsf{p}^q_{\mathcal{B}_1}(\cdot)\| \le \|\mathsf{p}^q_{\mathcal{C}_0}(\cdot) - \mathsf{p}^q_{\mathcal{C}_1}(\cdot)\|. \quad (5)$$

By (5) and Lemma 5, we can prove Theorem 2.

Lemma 5. *For any $q_{\max} \le 2^{n-2}$, let $\mathcal{C}_0$ and $\mathcal{C}_1$ be the experiments described in Algorithm 2. Then we have*

$$\|\mathsf{p}^q_{\mathcal{C}_0}(\cdot) - \mathsf{p}^q_{\mathcal{C}_1}(\cdot)\| \le \left(\frac{2\mu q_{\max}^3}{2^{4n-m}}\right)^{\frac{1}{2}}.$$

Algorithm 2. Experiments for $\mathsf{SaT2}$

Experiment $\mathcal{B}_0$

1: **for** $j \leftarrow 1$ to μ **do**
2: **for** $i \leftarrow 1$ to $q_{\max}$ **do**
3: $y_i^j \leftarrow_\$ \{0,1\}^m$
4: $\mathbf{Z}^j \leftarrow (y_1^j, \ldots, y_{q_{\max}}^j)$
5: **return** $(\mathbf{Z}^1, \ldots, \mathbf{Z}^\mu)$

Experiment $\mathcal{B}_1$

1: **for** $j \leftarrow 1$ to μ **do**
2: $\mathcal{R}_u, \mathcal{R}_v \leftarrow \{0,1\}^n$
3: **for** $i \leftarrow 1$ to $q_{\max}$ **do**
4: $u_i^j \leftarrow_\$ \mathcal{R}_u$, $\mathcal{R}_u \leftarrow \mathcal{R}_u \setminus \{u_i^j\}$
5: $v_i^j \leftarrow_\$ \mathcal{R}_v$, $\mathcal{R}_v \leftarrow \mathcal{R}_v \setminus \{v_i^j\}$
6: $r_i^j \leftarrow \mathsf{Tr}_m(u_i^j)$, $s_i^j \leftarrow \mathsf{Tr}_m(v_i^j)$
7: $y_i^j \leftarrow r_i^j \oplus s_i^j$
8: $\mathbf{Z}^j \leftarrow (y_1^j, \ldots, y_{q_{\max}}^j)$
9: **return** $(\mathbf{Z}^1, \ldots, \mathbf{Z}^\mu)$

Experiment $\mathcal{C}_0$

1: **for** $j \leftarrow 1$ to μ **do**
2: $\mathcal{R}_u, \mathcal{R}_v \leftarrow \{0,1\}^n$
3: **for** $i \leftarrow 1$ to $q_{\max}$ **do**
4: $y_i^j \leftarrow_\$ \{0,1\}^m$
5: $\mathcal{T}_i^j(y_i^j) \leftarrow \{(u,v) : u \in \mathcal{R}_u, v \in \mathcal{R}_v, \mathsf{Tr}_m(u \oplus v) = y_i^j\}$
6: **if** $|\mathcal{T}_i^j(y_i^j)| > 0$ **then**
7: $(u_i^j, v_i^j) \leftarrow_\$ \mathcal{T}_i^j(y_i^j)$
8: **else**
9: $(u_i^j, v_i^j) \leftarrow (\perp, \perp)$
10: $\mathcal{R}_u \leftarrow \mathcal{R}_u \setminus \{u_i^j\}$, $\mathcal{R}_v \leftarrow \mathcal{R}_v \setminus \{v_i^j\}$
11: $r_i^j \leftarrow \mathsf{Tr}_m(u_i^j)$, $s_i^j \leftarrow \mathsf{Tr}_m(v_i^j)$
12: $z_i^j \leftarrow (r_i^j, y_i^j)$
13: $\mathbf{Z}^j \leftarrow (z_1^j, \ldots, z_{q_{\max}}^j)$
14: **return** $(\mathbf{Z}^1, \ldots, \mathbf{Z}^\mu)$

Experiment $\mathcal{C}_1$

1: **for** $j \leftarrow 1$ to μ **do**
2: $\mathcal{R}_u, \mathcal{R}_v \leftarrow \{0,1\}^n$
3: **for** $i \leftarrow 1$ to $q_{\max}$ **do**
4: $u_i^j \leftarrow_\$ \mathcal{R}_u$, $\mathcal{R}_u \leftarrow \mathcal{R}_u \setminus \{u_i^j\}$
5: $v_i^j \leftarrow_\$ \mathcal{R}_v$, $\mathcal{R}_v \leftarrow \mathcal{R}_v \setminus \{v_i^j\}$
6: $r_i^j \leftarrow \mathsf{Tr}_m(u_i^j)$, $s_i^j \leftarrow \mathsf{Tr}_m(v_i^j)$
7: $y_i^j \leftarrow r_i^j \oplus s_i^j$
8: $z_i^j \leftarrow (r_i^j, y_i^j)$
9: $\mathbf{Z}^j \leftarrow (z_1^j, \ldots, z_{q_{\max}}^j)$
10: **return** $(\mathbf{Z}^1, \ldots, \mathbf{Z}^\mu)$

5.1 Proof of Lemma 5

Let $q = \mu q_{\max}$. For $i \in [q]$, where $i = (j-1)q_{\max} + k$ such that $j \in [\mu]$ and $k \in [q_{\max}]$, the response of the i-th query is seen as $z_i = z_k^j$. Then, we can easily check that the support of $\mathsf{p}_{\mathcal{C}_1}^{i-1}(\cdot)$ is contained in the support of $\mathsf{p}_{\mathcal{C}_0}^{i-1}(\cdot)$ for $i = 1, \ldots, q$, allowing us to use the chi-squared method. Let $\Omega = \{0,1\}^m \times \{0,1\}^m$. For fixed $i \in \{1, \ldots, q\}$ and $\mathbf{z} \in \Omega^{i-1}$ such $\mathsf{p}_{\mathcal{C}_1}^{i-1}(\mathbf{z}) > 0$, we will compute

$$\chi^2(\mathbf{z}) = \sum_{\substack{z \in \Omega \text{ such that} \\ \mathsf{p}_{\mathcal{C}_0,i}^{\mathbf{z}}(z) > 0}} \frac{\left(\mathsf{p}_{\mathcal{C}_1,i}^{\mathbf{z}}(z) - \mathsf{p}_{\mathcal{C}_0,i}^{\mathbf{z}}(z)\right)^2}{\mathsf{p}_{\mathcal{C}_0,i}^{\mathbf{z}}(z)}$$
$$= \sum_{\substack{z \in \Omega \text{ such that} \\ \mathsf{p}_{\mathcal{C}_0,i}^{\mathbf{z}}(z) > 0}} \mathsf{p}_{\mathcal{C}_0,i}^{\mathbf{z}}(z) \left(1 - \frac{\mathsf{p}_{\mathcal{C}_1,i}^{\mathbf{z}}(z)}{\mathsf{p}_{\mathcal{C}_0,i}^{\mathbf{z}}(z)}\right)^2$$

Firstly, note that $\mathbf{z} = (z_1, \ldots, z_{i-1})$ and $z_l = (r_l, y_l)$ for $l = 1, \ldots, i-1$. Let $\hat{\Omega} = \{0,1\}^n \times \{0,1\}^n$, $h_l = (u_l, y_l') \in \hat{\Omega}$ and $\mathbf{h} = (h_1, \ldots, h_{i-1})$ for $l = 1, \ldots, i-1$. Let $H_{\mathcal{C}_1,i}$ be the random variable over $\hat{\Omega}$ that follows the distribution of the internal values (u, y') in $\mathcal{C}_1$ interacting the i-th query by $\mathcal{A}$. Let

$$\mathbf{H}_{\mathcal{C}_1}^{i-1} \stackrel{\text{def}}{=} (H_{\mathcal{C}_1,1}, \ldots, H_{\mathcal{C}_1,i-1})$$

for $\mathbf{h} \in \hat{\Omega}^{i-1}$. Similarly to (3), one has

$$\mathop{\mathbf{Ex}}_{\mathbf{z}}\left[\chi^2(\mathbf{z})\right] = \mathop{\mathbf{Ex}}_{\mathbf{h}}\left[\chi^2(\mathbf{z})\right]$$

where the last expectation is taken over the distribution $\mathbf{H}_{\mathcal{C}_1}^{i-1}$. Furthermore, let $i = (j-1)q_{\max} + k$ such that $j \in [\mu]$ and $k \in [q_{\max}]$. For $\alpha \in \{0,1\}^m$, we define $U_k^j(\alpha)$ and $V_k^j(\alpha)$ be the number of elements α in $(r_l^j)_{l=1,\ldots,k-1}$ and $(s_l^j)_{l=1,\ldots,k-1}$, respectively. In other words,

$$U_k^j(\alpha) = \left|\{l \in [k-1] \mid \alpha = r_l^j\}\right|,$$
$$V_k^j(\alpha) = \left|\{l \in [k-1] \mid \alpha = s_l^j\}\right|.$$

Also, for $y \in \{0,1\}^m$, let $T_k^j(y) = \left|\mathcal{T}_k^j(y)\right|$. Note that, for any $j' \in [j-1]$, z_i is independent with $\mathbf{Z}^{j'}$. Therefore, we see that

$$\mathsf{p}_{\mathcal{C}_0,i}^{\mathbf{z}}(r, y) = \frac{(2^{n-m} - U_k^j(r))(2^{n-m} - V_k^j(r \oplus y))}{2^m T_k^j(y)},$$
$$\mathsf{p}_{\mathcal{C}_1,i}^{\mathbf{z}}(r, y) = \frac{(2^{n-m} - U_k^j(r))(2^{n-m} - V_k^j(r \oplus y))}{(2^n - k + 1)^2},$$

and

$$\begin{aligned}
T_k^j(y) &= \sum_{\alpha \in \{0,1\}^m} (2^{n-m} - U_k^j(\alpha))(2^{n-m} - V_k^j(\alpha \oplus y)) \\
&= 2^{2n-m} - 2(k-1)2^{n-m} + \sum_{\alpha \in \{0,1\}^m} U_k^j(\alpha) V_k^j(\alpha \oplus y) \\
&\geq 2^{2n-m} - 2(k-1)2^{n-m}.
\end{aligned}$$

Therefore,

$$\begin{aligned}
\chi^2(\mathbf{z}) &= \sum_{\substack{z=(r,y)\in\Omega \text{ such} \\ \text{that } \mathsf{p}^{\mathbf{z}}_{C_0,i}(z)>0}} \frac{(2^{n-m} - U_k^j(r))(2^{n-m} - V_k^j(r \oplus y))}{2^m T_k^j(y)} \left(1 - \frac{2^m T_k^j(y)}{(2^n - k + 1)^2}\right)^2 \\
&\leq \sum_{\substack{(r,y)\in\Omega \text{ such} \\ \text{that } \mathsf{p}^{\mathbf{z}}_{C_0,i}(r,y)>0}} \frac{2^{2n-2m}\left((2^n - k + 1)^2 - 2^m T_k^j(y)\right)^2}{2^m T_k^j(y)(2^n - k + 1)^4} \\
&\leq \sum_{\substack{(r,y)\in\Omega \text{ such} \\ \text{that } \mathsf{p}^{\mathbf{z}}_{C_0,i}(r,y)>0}} \frac{7\left((2^n - k + 1)^2 - 2^m T_k^j(y)\right)^2}{2^{4n+2m}} \\
&\leq \sum_{y\in\{0,1\}^m} \frac{7}{2^{4n-m}} \left(\frac{(2^n - k + 1)^2}{2^m} - T_k^j(y)\right)^2. \qquad (6)
\end{aligned}$$

since $k \leq q_{\max} \leq 2^{n-2}$. We claim the following lemma.

Lemma 6. *One has*

$$\begin{aligned}
\mathop{\mathbf{Ex}}_{\mathbf{h}}\left[T_k^j(y)\right] &= \frac{(2^n - k + 1)^2}{2^m}, \\
\mathop{\mathbf{Var}}_{\mathbf{h}}\left[T_k^j(y)\right] &\leq \frac{(k-1)^2}{2^m}.
\end{aligned}$$

The proof of Lemma 6 is given in the full version. From (6) and Lemma 6, it follows that

$$\begin{aligned}
\mathop{\mathbf{Ex}}_{\mathbf{h}}\left[\chi^2(\mathbf{z})\right] &\leq \mathop{\mathbf{Ex}}_{\mathbf{h}}\left[\sum_{y\in\{0,1\}^m} \frac{7}{2^{4n-m}} \left(\frac{(2^n - k + 1)^2}{2^m} - T_k^j(y)\right)^2\right] \\
&\leq \frac{7}{2^{4n-m}} \sum_{y\in\{0,1\}^m} \mathop{\mathbf{Var}}_{\mathbf{h}}\left[T_k^j(y)\right] \\
&\leq \frac{7(k-1)^2}{2^{4n-m}}
\end{aligned}$$

and finally, we have

$$\begin{aligned}\|\mathsf{p}^q_{\mathcal{C}_0}(\cdot) - \mathsf{p}^q_{\mathcal{C}_1}(\cdot)\| &\le \left(\frac{1}{2}\sum_{i=1}^{q} \mathbf{Ex}\left[\chi^2(\mathbf{z})\right]\right)^{\frac{1}{2}} \\ &\le \left(\frac{1}{2}\sum_{j=1}^{\mu}\sum_{k=1}^{q_{\max}} \mathbf{Ex}\left[\chi^2(\mathbf{z})\right]\right)^{\frac{1}{2}} \\ &\le \left(\frac{1}{2}\sum_{j=1}^{\mu}\sum_{k=1}^{q_{\max}} \frac{7(k-1)^2}{2^{4n-m}}\right)^{\frac{1}{2}} \\ &\le \left(\frac{2\mu q_{\max}^3}{2^{4n-m}}\right)^{\frac{1}{2}}.\end{aligned}$$

6 Multi-user PRF Security of SoP3-2

In this section, we prove the security of SoP3-2. Bhattacharya and Nandi [6] proved mu-prf advantage of SoP3-1 is upper bounded by

$$\frac{20\sqrt{\mu q_{\max}}}{2^n}$$

for all $q_{\max} \le 2^n/12$. However, to the best of our knowledge, the security of SoP3-2 has not been analyzed. Let

$$\begin{aligned}\mathsf{SoP3\text{-}2}[\mathsf{P}_1, \mathsf{P}_2, \mathsf{P}_3] : \{0,1\}^n &\longrightarrow \{0,1\}^n \\ x &\longmapsto \mathsf{P}_1(x) \oplus \mathsf{P}_2(x) \oplus \mathsf{P}_3(x)\end{aligned}$$

where P_1, P_2 and P_3 are three independent random permutations from $\mathsf{Perm}(n)$. The mu-prf security of SoP3-2 is represented by the following theorem.

Theorem 3. *Let n, μ, and $q_{\max}$ be positive integers such that $q_{\max} \le 2^{n-2}$. Then one has*

$$\mathbf{Adv}^{\mathsf{mu\text{-}prf}}_{\mathsf{SoP3\text{-}2}}(\mu, q_{\max}) \le \left(\frac{3\mu q_{\max}^4}{2^{5n}}\right)^{\frac{1}{2}}.$$

One can consider SoP3-2 based on an n-bit block cipher $\mathsf{E} : \mathcal{K} \times \{0,1\}^n \to \{0,1\}^n$ with key space $\mathcal{K}$, which is defined as

$$\mathsf{SoP3\text{-}2}[\mathsf{E}](K_1, K_2, K_3, x) = \mathsf{E}_{K_1}(x) \oplus \mathsf{E}_{K_2}(x) \oplus \mathsf{E}_{K_3}(x).$$

Up to the mu-prp security of E, one can derive the multi-user security of SoP3-2[E].

$$\mathbf{Adv}^{\mathsf{mu\text{-}prf}}_{\mathsf{SoP3\text{-}2[E]}}(\mu, q_{\max}, t) \le \mathbf{Adv}^{\mathsf{mu\text{-}prp}}_{\mathsf{E}}(3\mu, q_{\max}, t') + \left(\frac{3\mu q_{\max}^4}{2^{5n}}\right)^{\frac{1}{2}}.$$

where $t' \approx t + 3\mu q_{\max}$.

6.1 Proof of Theorem 3

Similarly to Sect. 4, we define random experiments. See Algorithm 3. For Experiment $\mathcal{C}_0$ in Algorithm 3, the following lemma holds.

Lemma 7. *For any $q_{\max} \leq 2^{n-2}$, Experiment $\mathcal{C}_0$ in Algorithm 3 never returns $(\bot, \bot, \bot)$.*

Proof. We suppose any $j \in [\mu]$ and omit y for simplicity. If $i = 1$, it is trivial that $|\mathcal{T}_i(y_i)| = 2^{2n} > 0$. For $2 \leq i \leq q_{\max}$, we have $|\mathcal{R}_U| = |\mathcal{R}_V| = |\mathcal{R}_W| = 2^n - (i-1)$ and therefore $|\mathcal{T}_i(y_i)| \geq 2^{2n} - 3(i-1) \cdot 2^n > 0$ since $i \leq q_{\max} \leq 2^{n-2}$ by our assumption. □

Let $\mathcal{S}_0$ be a random oracle with $\mathsf{Func}(n, n)$ and $\mathcal{S}_1$ be a random oracle with SoP3-2. Similarly to the reasoning of (2), one has

$$\|\mathsf{p}^q_{\mathcal{S}_0}(\cdot) - \mathsf{p}^q_{\mathcal{S}_1}(\cdot)\| = \|\mathsf{p}^q_{\mathcal{B}_0}(\cdot) - \mathsf{p}^q_{\mathcal{B}_1}(\cdot)\| \leq \|\mathsf{p}^q_{\mathcal{C}_0}(\cdot) - \mathsf{p}^q_{\mathcal{C}_1}(\cdot)\|. \quad (7)$$

By (7) and Lemma 8, we can prove Theorem 3.

Lemma 8. *For any $q_{\max} \leq 2^{n-2}$, let $\mathcal{C}_0$ and $\mathcal{C}_1$ be the experiments described in Algorithm 3. Then we have*

$$\|\mathsf{p}^q_{\mathcal{C}_0}(\cdot) - \mathsf{p}^q_{\mathcal{C}_1}(\cdot)\| \leq \left(\frac{3\mu q^4_{\max}}{2^{5n}}\right)^{\frac{1}{2}}.$$

6.2 Proof of Lemma 8

Let $q = \mu q_{\max}$. For $i \in [q]$ where $i = (j-1)q_{\max} + k$ such that $j \in [\mu]$ and $k \in [q_{\max}]$, the response of the i-th query is seen as $z_i = z^j_k$. We can easily check that the support of $\mathsf{p}^{i-1}_{\mathcal{C}_1}(\cdot)$ is contained in the support of $\mathsf{p}^{i-1}_{\mathcal{C}_0}(\cdot)$ for $i = 1, \ldots, q$, allowing us to use the chi-squared method. Let $\Omega = \{0,1\}^n \times \{0,1\}^n \times \{0,1\}^n$.

For a fixed $i \in \{1, \ldots, q\}$, let $i \in [q]$ where $i = (j-1)q_{\max} + k$ such that $j \in [\mu]$ and $k \in [q_{\max}]$. Fix $\mathbf{z} \in \Omega^{i-1}$ such that $\mathsf{p}^{i-1}_{\mathcal{C}_1}(\mathbf{z}) > 0$. Then, we will compute

$$\chi^2(\mathbf{z}) = \sum_{\substack{z=(u,v,y)\in\Omega \text{ such} \\ \text{that } \mathsf{p}^{\mathbf{z}}_{\mathcal{C}_0,i}(z)>0}} \frac{\left(\mathsf{p}^{\mathbf{z}}_{\mathcal{C}_1,i}(z) - \mathsf{p}^{\mathbf{z}}_{\mathcal{C}_0,i}(z)\right)^2}{\mathsf{p}^{\mathbf{z}}_{\mathcal{C}_0,i}(z)}$$

$$= \sum_{\substack{z=(u,v,y)\in\Omega \text{ such} \\ \text{that } \mathsf{p}^{\mathbf{z}}_{\mathcal{C}_0,i}(z)>0}} \mathsf{p}^{\mathbf{z}}_{\mathcal{C}_0,i}(z)\left(1 - \frac{\mathsf{p}^{\mathbf{z}}_{\mathcal{C}_1,i}(z)}{\mathsf{p}^{\mathbf{z}}_{\mathcal{C}_0,i}(z)}\right)^2$$

Algorithm 3. Experiments for SoP3-2

Experiment $\mathcal{B}_0$

1: **for** $j \leftarrow 1$ to μ **do**
2:     **for** $i \leftarrow 1$ to $q_{\max}$ **do**
3:         $y_i^j \leftarrow_\$ \{0,1\}^n$
4:     $\mathbf{Z}^j \leftarrow (y_1^j, \ldots, y_{q_{\max}}^j)$
5: **return** $(\mathbf{Z}^1, \ldots, \mathbf{Z}^\mu)$

Experiment $\mathcal{B}_1$

1: **for** $j \leftarrow 1$ to μ **do**
2:     $\mathcal{R}_u, \mathcal{R}_v, \mathcal{R}_w \leftarrow \{0,1\}^n$
3:     **for** $i \leftarrow 1$ to $q_{\max}$ **do**
4:         $u_i^j \leftarrow_\$ \mathcal{R}_u$, $\mathcal{R}_u \leftarrow \mathcal{R}_u \setminus \{u_i^j\}$
5:         $v_i^j \leftarrow_\$ \mathcal{R}_v$, $\mathcal{R}_v \leftarrow \mathcal{R}_v \setminus \{v_i^j\}$
6:         $w_i^j \leftarrow_\$ \mathcal{R}_w$, $\mathcal{R}_w \leftarrow \mathcal{R}_w \setminus \{w_i^j\}$
7:         $y_i^j \leftarrow u_i^j \oplus v_i^j \oplus w_i^j$
8:     $\mathbf{Z}^j \leftarrow (y_1^j, \ldots, y_{q_{\max}}^j)$
9: **return** $(\mathbf{Z}^1, \ldots, \mathbf{Z}^\mu)$

Experiment $\mathcal{C}_0$

1: **for** $j \leftarrow 1$ to μ **do**
2:     $\mathcal{R}_u, \mathcal{R}_v, \mathcal{R}_w \leftarrow \{0,1\}^n$
3:     **for** $i \leftarrow 1$ to $q_{\max}$ **do**
4:         $y_i^j \leftarrow_\$ \{0,1\}^n$
5:         $\mathcal{T}_i^j(y_i^j) \leftarrow \{(u,v,w) : u \in \mathcal{R}_u, v \in \mathcal{R}_v, w \in \mathcal{R}_w, u \oplus v \oplus w = y_i^j\}$
6:         **if** $\left|\mathcal{T}_i^j(y_i^j)\right| > 0$ **then**
7:             $(u_i^j, v_i^j, w_i^j) \leftarrow_\$ \mathcal{T}_i^j(y_i^j)$
8:         **else**
9:             $(u_i^j, v_i^j, w_i^j) \leftarrow (\perp, \perp, \perp)$
10:        $\mathcal{R}_u \leftarrow \mathcal{R}_u \setminus \{u_i^j\}$, $\mathcal{R}_v \leftarrow \mathcal{R}_v \setminus \{v_i^j\}$, $\mathcal{R}_w \leftarrow \mathcal{R}_w \setminus \{w_i^j\}$
11:        $z_i^j \leftarrow (u_i^j, v_i^j, y_i^j)$
12:    $\mathbf{Z}^j \leftarrow (z_1^j, \ldots, z_{q_{\max}}^j)$
13: **return** $(\mathbf{Z}^1, \ldots, \mathbf{Z}^\mu)$

Experiment $\mathcal{C}_1$

1: **for** $j \leftarrow 1$ to μ **do**
2:     $\mathcal{R}_u, \mathcal{R}_v, \mathcal{R}_w \leftarrow \{0,1\}^n$
3:     **for** $i \leftarrow 1$ to $q_{\max}$ **do**
4:         $u_i^j \leftarrow_\$ \mathcal{R}_u$, $\mathcal{R}_u \leftarrow \mathcal{R}_u \setminus \{u_i^j\}$
5:         $v_i^j \leftarrow_\$ \mathcal{R}_v$, $\mathcal{R}_v \leftarrow \mathcal{R}_v \setminus \{v_i^j\}$
6:         $w_i^j \leftarrow_\$ \mathcal{R}_w$, $\mathcal{R}_w \leftarrow \mathcal{R}_w \setminus \{w_i^j\}$
7:         $z_i^j \leftarrow (u_i^j, v_i^j, u_i^j \oplus v_i^j \oplus w_i^j)$
8:     $\mathbf{Z}^j \leftarrow (z_1^j, \ldots, z_{q_{\max}}^j)$
9: **return** $(\mathbf{Z}^1, \ldots, \mathbf{Z}^\mu)$

For $y \in \{0,1\}^n$, let $T_k^j(y) = \left|\mathcal{T}_k^j(y)\right|$. From the proof of Lemma 7, we have

$$T_k^j(y) \geq 2^{2n} - 3(k-1)2^n.$$

Moreover, we see that

$$\mathsf{p}^{\mathbf{z}}_{\mathcal{C}_0,i}(u,v,y) = \frac{1}{2^n T_k^j(y)},$$
$$\mathsf{p}^{\mathbf{z}}_{\mathcal{C}_1,i}(u,v,y) = \frac{1}{(2^n-k+1)^3}.$$

Therefore,

$$\begin{aligned}
\chi^2(\mathbf{z}) &= \sum_{\substack{z=(u,v,y)\in\Omega \text{ such} \\ \text{that } \mathsf{p}^{\mathbf{z}}_{\mathcal{C}_0,i}(z)>0}} \frac{1}{2^m T_k^j(y)}\left(1-\frac{2^n T_k^j(y)}{(2^n-k+1)^3}\right)^2 \\
&\leq \sum_{\substack{(u,v,y)\in\Omega \text{ such} \\ \text{that } \mathsf{p}^{\mathbf{z}}_{\mathcal{C}_0,i}(u,v,y)>0}} \frac{\left((2^n-k+1)^3 - 2^n T_k^j(y)\right)^2}{2^n T_k^j(y)(2^n-k+1)S^6} \\
&\leq \sum_{\substack{(u,v,y)\in\Omega \text{ such} \\ \text{that } \mathsf{p}^{\mathbf{z}}_{\mathcal{C}_0,i}(u,v,y)>0}} \frac{23\left((2^n-k+1)^3 - 2^n T_k^j(y)\right)^2}{2^{9n}} \\
&\leq \frac{23}{2^{5n}} \sum_{y\in\{0,1\}^n} \left(\frac{(2^n-k+1)^3}{2^n} - T_k^j(y)\right)^2. \qquad (8)
\end{aligned}$$

since $k \leq q_{\max} \leq 2^{n-2}$. We claim the following lemma.

Lemma 9. *One has*

$$\mathop{\mathbf{Ex}}_{\mathbf{z}}\left[T_k^j(y)\right] = \frac{(2^n-k+1)^3}{2^n},$$
$$\mathop{\mathbf{Var}}_{\mathbf{z}}\left[T_k^j(y)\right] \leq \frac{(k-1)^3}{2^n}.$$

The proof of Lemma 9 is given in the full version. From (8) and Lemma 9, it follows that

$$\begin{aligned}
\mathop{\mathbf{Ex}}_{\mathbf{z}}\left[\chi^2(\mathbf{z})\right] &\leq \frac{23}{2^{5n}} \mathop{\mathbf{Ex}}_{\mathbf{z}}\left[\sum_{y\in\{0,1\}^n}\left(\frac{(2^n-k+1)^3}{2^n} - T_k^j(y)\right)^2\right] \\
&\leq \frac{23}{2^{5n}} \sum_{y\in\{0,1\}^n} \mathop{\mathbf{Var}}_{\mathbf{z}}\left[T_k^j(y)\right] \\
&\leq \frac{23(k-1)^3}{2^{5n}}
\end{aligned}$$

and finally, we have

$$\begin{aligned}\|\mathsf{p}_{\mathcal{C}_0}^q(\cdot) - \mathsf{p}_{\mathcal{C}_1}^q(\cdot)\| &\le \left(\frac{1}{2}\sum_{i=1}^{q} \mathbf{Ex}\left[\chi^2(\mathbf{z})\right]\right)^{\frac{1}{2}} \\ &\le \left(\frac{1}{2}\sum_{j=1}^{\mu}\sum_{k=1}^{q_{\max}} \mathbf{Ex}\left[\chi^2(\mathbf{z})\right]\right)^{\frac{1}{2}} \\ &\le \left(\frac{1}{2}\sum_{j=1}^{\mu}\sum_{k=1}^{q_{\max}} \frac{23(k-1)^3}{2^{5n}}\right)^{\frac{1}{2}} \\ &\le \left(\frac{3\mu q_{\max}^4}{2^{5n}}\right)^{\frac{1}{2}}.\end{aligned}$$

7 Proof of Lemma 3

First, suppose $y \neq \mathbf{0}$. Let $\Psi = \{0,1\}^m \times \{0,1\}^{n-m} \times \{0,1\}^{n-m}$ and fix j, k, $\mathbf{h}$ and y. Let I_ψ where $\psi = (\alpha, \beta, \gamma) \in \Psi$ be an indicator variable

$$I_\psi = 1 \Leftrightarrow (\alpha \parallel \beta), (\alpha \oplus y \parallel \gamma) \in \{0,1\}^n \setminus \{u_l^j\}_{l \in [2k-2]}.$$

Observe that

$$T_k^j(y) = \sum_{\psi \in \Psi} I_\psi$$

and

$$\mathop{\mathbf{Ex}}_{\mathbf{h}}\left[I_\psi\right] = \frac{(2^n - 2k + 2)(2^n - 2k + 1)}{2^n(2^n - 1)}.$$

Thus, we have

$$\begin{aligned}\mathop{\mathbf{Ex}}_{\mathbf{h}}\left[T_k^j(y)\right] &= \sum_{\psi \in \Psi} \frac{(2^n - 2k + 2)(2^n - 2k + 1)}{2^n(2^n - 1)} \\ &= \frac{2^n(2^n - 2k + 2)(2^n - 2k + 1)}{2^m(2^n - 1)}.\end{aligned} \tag{9}$$

Now, we compute the following expectation

$$\mathop{\mathbf{Ex}}_{\mathbf{h}}\left[\left(T_k^j(y)\right)^2\right] = \mathop{\mathbf{Ex}}_{\mathbf{h}}\left[\left(\sum_{\psi \in \Psi} I_\psi\right)^2\right] = \mathop{\mathbf{Ex}}_{\mathbf{h}}\left[\sum_{(\psi, \psi') \in \Psi^2} I_\psi I_{\psi'}\right].$$

For $\psi = (\alpha, \beta, \gamma)$ and $\psi' = (\alpha', \beta', \gamma')$, let r be the size of the following set

$$\{\alpha \parallel \beta, \alpha' \parallel \beta', (\alpha \oplus y) \parallel \gamma, (\alpha' \oplus y) \parallel \gamma'\}.$$

We see that, for $r = 2, \ldots, 4$,

$$\mathop{\mathbf{Ex}}_{\mathbf{h}}[I_\psi I_{\psi'}] = \frac{(2^n - 2k + 2)_r}{(2^n)_r}.$$

For a fixed $\psi \in \Psi$, we have

$$\begin{aligned}
|\{\psi' \in \Psi \mid r = 2\}| &= 2, \\
|\{\psi' \in \Psi \mid r = 3\}| &= 2^{n-m+2} - 4, \\
|\{\psi' \in \Psi \mid r = 4\}| &= 2^{2n-m} - 2^{n-m+2} + 2.
\end{aligned}$$

It follows that

$$\begin{aligned}
\sum_{\substack{\psi' \in \Psi, \\ r=2}} \mathop{\mathbf{Ex}}_{\mathbf{h}}[I_\psi I_{\psi'}] &= 2\frac{(2^n - 2k + 2)_2}{(2^n)_2}, \\
\sum_{\substack{\psi' \in \Psi, \\ r=3}} \mathop{\mathbf{Ex}}_{\mathbf{h}}[I_\psi I_{\psi'}] &= (2^{n-m+2} - 4)\left(1 - \frac{2k-2}{2^n - 2}\right)\frac{(2^n - 2k + 2)_2}{(2^n)_2}, \\
\sum_{\substack{\psi' \in \Psi, \\ r=4}} \mathop{\mathbf{Ex}}_{\mathbf{h}}[I_\psi I_{\psi'}] &= (2^{2n-m} - 2^{n-m+2} + 2)\left(1 - \frac{2k-2}{2^n - 2}\right) \\
&\quad \times \left(1 - \frac{2k-2}{2^n - 3}\right)\frac{(2^n - 2k + 2)_2}{(2^n)_2}.
\end{aligned}$$

As $\mathop{\mathbf{Ex}}_{\mathbf{h}}\left[\sum_{(\psi,\psi') \in \Psi^2} I_\psi I_{\psi'}\right] = \sum_{(\psi,\psi') \in \Psi^2} \mathop{\mathbf{Ex}}_{\mathbf{h}}[I_\psi I_{\psi'}] = \sum_{\psi \in \Psi} \sum_{\psi' \in \Psi} \mathop{\mathbf{Ex}}_{\mathbf{h}}[I_\psi I_{\psi'}]$ and the sum is divided into three cases according to the value of r, the sum of the expectations is given as

$$\begin{aligned}
\mathop{\mathbf{Ex}}_{\mathbf{h}}\left[\sum_{(\psi,\psi') \in \Psi^2} I_\psi I_{\psi'}\right] = 2^{2n-m} \Bigg(&\sum_{\substack{\psi' \in \Psi, \\ r=2}} \mathop{\mathbf{Ex}}_{\mathbf{h}}[I_\psi I_{\psi'}] + \sum_{\substack{\psi' \in \Psi, \\ r=3}} \mathop{\mathbf{Ex}}_{\mathbf{h}}[I_\psi I_{\psi'}] \\
&+ \sum_{\substack{\psi' \in \Psi, \\ r=4}} \mathop{\mathbf{Ex}}_{\mathbf{h}}[I_\psi I_{\psi'}] \Bigg). \qquad (10)
\end{aligned}$$

Therefore, by (10), we have

$$\begin{aligned}
\mathop{\mathbf{Ex}}_{\mathbf{h}}\left[\sum_{(\psi,\psi') \in \Psi^2} I_\psi I_{\psi'}\right] = \frac{(2^n - 2k + 2)_2}{2^n - 1} \Bigg(&2^{3n-2m} - (2^{2n-2m+1} + 2^{n-2m})(2k - 2) \\
&+ 2^{n-2m}(2k-2)^2 \\
&+ (2^{2n-2m} - 6 \cdot 2^{n-2m} + 2^{n-m+1})\frac{(2k-2)(2k-3)}{(2^n - 2)(2^n - 3)} \Bigg)
\end{aligned}$$

and

$$\mathop{\mathbf{Ex}}_{\mathbf{h}}\left[\frac{(2^n-2k+2)(2^n-2k+1)}{2^m}\cdot T_k^j(y)\right]=\frac{2^n(2^n-2k+2)^2(2^n-2k+1)^2}{2^{2m}(2^n-1)}.$$

Hence, for $y \neq \mathbf{0}$, it follows that

$$\begin{aligned}\mathop{\mathbf{Ex}}_{\mathbf{h}}\left[G_k^j(y)\right]&=\mathop{\mathbf{Ex}}_{\mathbf{h}}\left[\left(\frac{(2^n-2k+2)(2^n-2k+1)}{2^m}-T_k^j(y)\right)^2\right]\\&=\frac{(2^n-2k+2)_2}{2^n-1}(A_y+B_y)\end{aligned}\tag{11}$$

where

$$\begin{aligned}A_y&=2^{3n-2m}-(2^{2n-2m+1}+2^{n-2m})(2k-2)+2^{n-2m}(2k-2)^2\\&\quad+(2^{2n-2m}-6\cdot 2^{n-2m}+2^{n-m+1})\frac{(2k-2)(2k-3)}{(2^n-2)(2^n-3)}\end{aligned}$$

and

$$\begin{aligned}B_y&=-\frac{2^{n+1}(2^n-2k+2)(2^n-2k+1)}{2^{2m}}+\frac{(2^n-1)(2^n-2k+2)(2^n-2k+1)}{2^{2m}}\\&=-2^{3n-2m}+4k\cdot 2^{2n-2m}-4\cdot 2^{2n-2m}+4k\cdot 2^{n-2m}-3\cdot 2^{n-2m}\\&\quad-(2^{n-2m}+2^{-2m})(4k^2-6k+2).\end{aligned}$$

Therefore, we have

$$\begin{aligned}A_y+B_y&=3\cdot 2^{n-2m}-2^{n-2m+1}-2^{-2m+2}(k-1)\\&\quad+(2^{n-m+1}-2^{n-2m}-6\cdot 2^{-2m})\frac{(2k-2)(2k-3)}{(2^n-2)(2^n-3)}\\&\le\frac{8(k-1)^2}{2^{n+m}}+3\cdot 2^{n-2m}.\end{aligned}\tag{12}$$

By (11) and (12), conclude that

$$\mathop{\mathbf{Ex}}_{\mathbf{h}}\left[G_k^j(y)\right]\le\frac{8(k-1)^2}{2^m}+3\cdot 2^{2n-2m}.\tag{13}$$

On the other hand, suppose $y=\mathbf{0}$. Note that $I_\psi=0$ if $\beta=\gamma$. So, for $\psi=(\alpha,\beta,\gamma)\in\Psi$ such that $\beta\neq\gamma$, we have

$$\mathop{\mathbf{Ex}}_{\mathbf{h}}\left[I_\psi\right]=\frac{(2^n-2k+2)(2^n-2k+1)}{2^n(2^n-1)}.$$

Thus, we have

$$\begin{aligned}\mathop{\mathbf{Ex}}_{\mathbf{h}}\left[T_k^j(\mathbf{0})\right]&=\sum_{\psi\in\Psi}\frac{(2^n-2k+2)(2^n-2k+1)}{2^n(2^n-1)}\\&=\frac{(2^{n-m}-1)(2^n-2k+2)(2^n-2k+1)}{2^n-1}.\end{aligned}\tag{14}$$

Now, we compute the following expectation

$$\mathop{\mathbf{Ex}}_{\mathbf{h}}\left[\left(T_k^j(\mathbf{0})\right)^2\right] = \mathop{\mathbf{Ex}}_{\mathbf{h}}\left[\left(\sum_{\psi\in\Psi} I_\psi\right)^2\right] = \mathop{\mathbf{Ex}}_{\mathbf{h}}\left[\sum_{(\psi,\psi')\in\Psi^2} I_\psi I_{\psi'}\right].$$

For $\psi = (\alpha, \beta, \gamma)$ and $\psi' = (\alpha', \beta', \gamma')$, let r be the size of following set

$$\{\alpha \parallel \beta, \alpha' \parallel \beta', \alpha \parallel \gamma, \alpha' \parallel \gamma'\}.$$

We see that, for $r = 2, \ldots, 4$,

$$\mathop{\mathbf{Ex}}_{\mathbf{h}}\left[I_\psi I_{\psi'}\right] = \frac{(2^n - 2k + 2)_r}{(2^n)_r}.$$

For a fixed $\psi \in \Psi$, we have

$$\begin{aligned}
|\{\psi' \in \Psi \mid r = 2\}| &= 2,\\
|\{\psi' \in \Psi \mid r = 3\}| &= 2^{n-m+2} - 8,\\
|\{\psi' \in \Psi \mid r = 4\}| &= 2^{2n-m} - 2^{n-m+2} - 2^n + 6.
\end{aligned}$$

It follows that

$$\begin{aligned}
\sum_{\substack{\psi'\in\Psi,\\ r=2}} \mathop{\mathbf{Ex}}_{\mathbf{h}}\left[I_\psi I_{\psi'}\right] &= 2\frac{(2^n - 2k + 2)_2}{(2^n)_2},\\
\sum_{\substack{\psi'\in\Psi,\\ r=3}} \mathop{\mathbf{Ex}}_{\mathbf{h}}\left[I_\psi I_{\psi'}\right] &= (2^{n-m+2} - 8)\left(1 - \frac{2k-2}{2^n-2}\right)\frac{(2^n - 2k + 2)_2}{(2^n)_2},\\
\sum_{\substack{\psi'\in\Psi,\\ r=4}} \mathop{\mathbf{Ex}}_{\mathbf{h}}\left[I_\psi I_{\psi'}\right] &= (2^{2n-m} - 2^{n-m+2} - 2^n + 6)\left(1 - \frac{2k-2}{2^n-2}\right)\\
&\quad \times \left(1 - \frac{2k-2}{2^n-3}\right)\frac{(2^n - 2k + 2)_2}{(2^n)_2}.
\end{aligned}$$

Similarly to (10), we have

$$\begin{aligned}
\mathop{\mathbf{Ex}}_{\mathbf{h}}\left[\sum_{(\psi,\psi')\in\Psi^2} I_\psi I_{\psi'}\right] &= \frac{(2^{n-m} - 1)(2^n - 2k + 2)_2}{2^n - 1}\Bigg(2^{2n-m} - 2^n\\
&\quad - (2^{n-m+1} + 2^{-m} - 2)(2k - 2) + 2^{-m}(2k - 2)^2\\
&\quad + (2^{n-m} - 2^n + 6 - 6 \cdot 2^{-m})\frac{(2k-2)(2k-3)}{(2^n-2)(2^n-3)}\Bigg)
\end{aligned}$$

Also, we have

$$\mathop{\mathbf{Ex}}_{\mathbf{h}}\left[\frac{(2^n - 2k + 2)(2^n - 2k + 1)}{2^m} \cdot T_k^j(\mathbf{0})\right] = \frac{(2^{n-m} - 1)\left((2^n - 2k + 2)_2\right)^2}{2^m(2^n - 1)}.$$

So, for $y = \mathbf{0}$, we have

$$\mathop{\mathbf{Ex}}_{\mathbf{h}}\left[G_k^j(\mathbf{0})\right] = \mathop{\mathbf{Ex}}_{\mathbf{h}}\left[\left(\frac{(2^n-2k+2)_2}{2^m} - T_k^j(\mathbf{0})\right)^2\right] = \frac{(2^n-2k+2)_2}{2^n-1}(A_{\mathbf{0}}+B_{\mathbf{0}}) \quad (15)$$

where

$$\begin{aligned}A_{\mathbf{0}} &= (2^{n-m}-1)\bigg(2^{2n-m} - 2^n - (2^{n-m+1}+2^{-m}-2)(2k-2) + 2^{-m}(2k-2)^2 \\ &\quad + (2^{n-m}-2^n+6-6\cdot 2^{-m})\frac{(2k-2)(2k-3)}{(2^n-2)(2^n-3)}\bigg) \\ &= 2^{3n-2m} - 2^{2n-m+1} + 2^n + (2^{n-2m}-2^{-m})(2k-2)^2 \\ &\quad - (2^{2n-2m+1} - 2^{n-m+2} + 2^{n-2m} - 2^{-m} + 2)(2k-2) \\ &\quad + (2^{n-m}-1)(2^{n-m}-2^n+6-6\cdot 2^{-m})\frac{(2k-2)(2k-3)}{(2^n-2)(2^n-3)}\end{aligned}$$

and

$$\begin{aligned}B_{\mathbf{0}} &= -\frac{(2^{n+1}-2^{m+1})(2^n-2k+2)_2}{2^{2m}} + \frac{(2^n-1)(2^n-2k+2)_2}{2^{2m}} \\ &= -\frac{(2^n-2^{m+1}+1)(2^n-2k+2)_2}{2^{2m}} \\ &= -2^{3n-2m} + 4k\cdot 2^{2n-2m} - 4\cdot 2^{2n-2m} + 2^{2n-m+1} - 4k\cdot 2^{n-m+1} + 6\cdot 2^{n-m} \\ &\quad + 4k\cdot 2^{n-2m} - 3\cdot 2^{n-2m} - (2^{n-2m} - 2^{-m+1} + 2^{-2m})(2k-2)(2k-1).\end{aligned}$$

Therefore, we have

$$\begin{aligned}A_{\mathbf{0}}+B_{\mathbf{0}} &= 2^n - 2^{n-m+1} + 2^{n-2m} - 4\left(1-\frac{1}{2^m}\right)^2(k-1) \\ &\quad + \left(1-\frac{1}{2^m}\right)(2^n+2^{n-m}-6+6\cdot 2^{-m})\frac{(2k-2)(2k-3)}{(2^n-2)(2^n-3)} \\ &\le \frac{8(k-1)^2}{2^n} + 3\cdot 2^n. \end{aligned} \quad (16)$$

By (15) and (16), conclude that

$$\mathop{\mathbf{Ex}}_{\mathbf{h}}\left[G_k^j(\mathbf{0})\right] = 8(k-1)^2 + 3\cdot 2^{2n}. \quad (17)$$

By (13) and (17), the proof completes.

References

1. Bellare, M., Impagliazzo, R.: A tool for obtaining tighter security analyses of pseudorandom function based constructions, with applications to prp to prf conversion. Cryptology ePrint Archive, Paper 1999/024 (1999). https://eprint.iacr.org/1999/024

2. Bellare, M., Kilian, J., Rogaway, P.: The security of cipher block chaining. In: Desmedt, Y.G. (ed.) CRYPTO 1994. LNCS, vol. 839, pp. 341–358. Springer, Heidelberg (1994). https://doi.org/10.1007/3-540-48658-5_32
3. Bellare, M., Krovetz, T., Rogaway, P.: Luby-Rackoff backwards: increasing security by making block ciphers non-invertible. In: Nyberg, K. (ed.) EUROCRYPT 1998. LNCS, vol. 1403, pp. 266–280. Springer, Heidelberg (1998). https://doi.org/10.1007/BFb0054132
4. Bellare, M., Rogaway, P.: The security of triple encryption and a framework for code-based game-playing proofs. In: Vaudenay, S. (ed.) EUROCRYPT 2006. LNCS, vol. 4004, pp. 409–426. Springer, Heidelberg (2006). https://doi.org/10.1007/11761679_25
5. Bhattacharya, S., Nandi, M.: Full indifferentiable security of the xor of two or more random permutations using the χ^2 Method. In: Nielsen, J.B., Rijmen, V. (eds.) EUROCRYPT 2018. LNCS, vol. 10820, pp. 387–412. Springer, Cham (2018). https://doi.org/10.1007/978-3-319-78381-9_15
6. Bhattacharya, S., Nandi, M.: Luby-Rackoff backwards with more users and more security. In: Tibouchi, M., Wang, H. (eds.) ASIACRYPT 2021. LNCS, vol. 13092, pp. 345–375. Springer, Cham (2021). https://doi.org/10.1007/978-3-030-92078-4_12
7. Bose, P., Hoang, V.T., Tessaro, S.: Revisiting AES-GCM-SIV: multi-user security, faster key derivation, and better bounds. In: Nielsen, J.B., Rijmen, V. (eds.) EUROCRYPT 2018. LNCS, vol. 10820, pp. 468–499. Springer, Cham (2018). https://doi.org/10.1007/978-3-319-78381-9_18
8. Chen, Y.L., Lambooij, E., Mennink, B.: How to build pseudorandom functions from public random permutations. In: Boldyreva, A., Micciancio, D. (eds.) CRYPTO 2019. LNCS, vol. 11692, pp. 266–293. Springer, Cham (2019). https://doi.org/10.1007/978-3-030-26948-7_10
9. Choi, W., Lee, B., Lee, J.: Indifferentiability of truncated random permutations. In: Galbraith, S.D., Moriai, S. (eds.) ASIACRYPT 2019. LNCS, vol. 11921, pp. 175–195. Springer, Cham (2019). https://doi.org/10.1007/978-3-030-34578-5_7
10. Choi, W., Lee, B., Lee, J., Lee, Y.: Toward a fully secure authenticated encryption scheme from a pseudorandom permutation. In: Tibouchi, M., Wang, H. (eds.) ASIACRYPT 2021. LNCS, vol. 13092, pp. 407–434. Springer, Cham (2021). https://doi.org/10.1007/978-3-030-92078-4_14
11. Cogliati, B., Lampe, R., Patarin, J.: The indistinguishability of the XOR of k permutations. In: Cid, C., Rechberger, C. (eds.) FSE 2014. LNCS, vol. 8540, pp. 285–302. Springer, Heidelberg (2015). https://doi.org/10.1007/978-3-662-46706-0_15
12. Cogliati, B., Seurin, Y.: EWCDM: an efficient, beyond-birthday secure, nonce-misuse resistant MAC. In: Robshaw, M., Katz, J. (eds.) CRYPTO 2016. LNCS, vol. 9814, pp. 121–149. Springer, Heidelberg (2016). https://doi.org/10.1007/978-3-662-53018-4_5
13. Cogliati, B., Seurin, Y.: Analysis of the single-permutation encrypted Davies-Meyer construction. Des. Codes Cryptogr. **86**(12), 2703–2723 (2018)
14. Dai, W., Hoang, V.T., Tessaro, S.: Information-theoretic indistinguishability via the chi-squared method. In: Katz, J., Shacham, H. (eds.) CRYPTO 2017. LNCS, vol. 10403, pp. 497–523. Springer, Cham (2017). https://doi.org/10.1007/978-3-319-63697-9_17

15. Dutta, A., Nandi, M., Talnikar, S.: Beyond birthday bound secure MAC in faulty nonce model. In: Ishai, Y., Rijmen, V. (eds.) EUROCRYPT 2019. LNCS, vol. 11476, pp. 437–466. Springer, Cham (2019). https://doi.org/10.1007/978-3-030-17653-2_15
16. Gilboa, S., Gueron, S., Morris, B.: How many queries are needed to distinguish a truncated random permutation from a random function? J. Cryptol. **31**(1), 162–171 (2018)
17. Gueron, S., Langley, A., Lindell, Y.: AES-GCM-SIV: specification and Analysis. IACR Cryptology ePrint Archive, Report 2017/168 (2017)
18. Gueron, S., Lindell, Y.: GCM-SIV: full nonce misuse-resistant authenticated encryption at under one cycle per byte. In: Proceedings of the 22nd ACM SIGSAC Conference on Computer and Communications Security, pp. 109–119 (2015)
19. Gunsing, A., Mennink, B.: The summation-truncation hybrid: reusing discarded bits for free. In: Micciancio, D., Ristenpart, T. (eds.) CRYPTO 2020. LNCS, vol. 12170, pp. 187–217. Springer, Cham (2020). https://doi.org/10.1007/978-3-030-56784-2_7
20. Hall, C., Wagner, D., Kelsey, J., Schneier, B.: Building PRFs from PRPs. In: Krawczyk, H. (ed.) CRYPTO 1998. LNCS, vol. 1462, pp. 370–389. Springer, Heidelberg (1998). https://doi.org/10.1007/BFb0055742
21. Hoang, V.T., Tessaro, S.: Key-alternating ciphers and key-length extension: exact bounds and multi-user security. In: Robshaw, M., Katz, J. (eds.) CRYPTO 2016. LNCS, vol. 9814, pp. 3–32. Springer, Heidelberg (2016). https://doi.org/10.1007/978-3-662-53018-4_1
22. Hoang, V.T., Tessaro, S.: The multi-user security of double encryption. In: Coron, J.-S., Nielsen, J.B. (eds.) EUROCRYPT 2017. LNCS, vol. 10211, pp. 381–411. Springer, Cham (2017). https://doi.org/10.1007/978-3-319-56614-6_13
23. Lee, J.: Indifferentiability of the sum of random permutations toward optimal security. IEEE Trans. Inf. Theory **63**(6), 4050–4054 (2017)
24. Lucks, S.: The sum of PRPs is a secure PRF. In: Preneel, B. (ed.) EUROCRYPT 2000. LNCS, vol. 1807, pp. 470–484. Springer, Heidelberg (2000). https://doi.org/10.1007/3-540-45539-6_34
25. Mennink, B.: Linking stam's bounds with generalized truncation. In: Matsui, M. (ed.) CT-RSA 2019. LNCS, vol. 11405, pp. 313–329. Springer, Cham (2019). https://doi.org/10.1007/978-3-030-12612-4_16
26. Mennink, B., Neves, S.: Encrypted davies-meyer and its dual: towards optimal security using mirror theory. In: Katz, J., Shacham, H. (eds.) CRYPTO 2017. LNCS, vol. 10403, pp. 556–583. Springer, Cham (2017). https://doi.org/10.1007/978-3-319-63697-9_19
27. Mennink, B., Preneel, B.: On the XOR of multiple random permutations. In: Malkin, T., Kolesnikov, V., Lewko, A. B., Polychronakis, M. (eds.) ACNS 2015, pp. 619–634 (2015)
28. Mouha, N., Luykx, A.: Multi-key security: the even-mansour construction revisited. In: Gennaro, R., Robshaw, M. (eds.) CRYPTO 2015. LNCS, vol. 9215, pp. 209–223. Springer, Heidelberg (2015). https://doi.org/10.1007/978-3-662-47989-6_10
29. Nandi, M.: Mind the composition: birthday bound attacks on EWCDMD and SoKAC21. In: Canteaut, A., Ishai, Y. (eds.) EUROCRYPT 2020. LNCS, vol. 12105, pp. 203–220. Springer, Cham (2020). https://doi.org/10.1007/978-3-030-45721-1_8
30. Patarin, J.: A proof of security in $O(2^n)$ for the Xor of Two Random Permutations. In: Safavi-Naini, R. (ed.) ICITS 2008. LNCS, vol. 5155, pp. 232–248. Springer, Heidelberg (2008). https://doi.org/10.1007/978-3-540-85093-9_22

31. Patarin, J.: Introduction to Mirror Theory: Analysis of Systems of Linear Equalities and Linear Non Equalities for Cryptography. IACR Cryptology ePrint Archive, Report 2010/287 (2010)
32. Stam, A.: Distance between sampling with and without replacement. Statistica Neerlandica **32**(2), 81–91 (1978)
33. Tessaro, S.: Optimally secure block ciphers from ideal primitives. In: Iwata, T., Cheon, J.H. (eds.) ASIACRYPT 2015. LNCS, vol. 9453, pp. 437–462. Springer, Heidelberg (2015). https://doi.org/10.1007/978-3-662-48800-3_18

Correction to: Flashproofs: Efficient Zero-Knowledge Arguments of Range and Polynomial Evaluation with Transparent Setup

Nan Wang and Sid Chi-Kin Chau

Correction to:
Chapter "Flashproofs: Efficient Zero-Knowledge Arguments of Range and Polynomial Evaluation with Transparent Setup" in: S. Agrawal and D. Lin (Eds.): *Advances in Cryptology – ASIACRYPT 2022*, LNCS 13792, https://doi.org/10.1007/978-3-031-22966-4_8

The original version of this paper contains errors in table 2. This has been updated.

The updated original version of this chapter can be found at
https://doi.org/10.1007/978-3-031-22966-4_8

S. Agrawal and D. Lin (Eds.): ASIACRYPT 2022, LNCS 13792, p. C1, 2023.
https://doi.org/10.1007/978-3-031-22966-4_24

Author Index

Printed in the United States
by Baker & Taylor Publisher Services